W9-AWP-488

PHILOSOPHY
OF
LAW

SECOND EDITION

edited by

Joel Feinberg

and

Hyman Gross

WADSWORTH PUBLISHING COMPANY

BELMONT, CALIFORNIA

A Division of Wadsworth, Inc.

© 1980 by Wadsworth, Inc.
Copyright © 1975 by Dickenson Publishing Company, Inc.
All rights reserved. No part of this book may be reproduced,
stored in a retrieval system, or transcribed, in any form or
by any means—electronic, mechanical, photocopying, recording,
or otherwise—without the prior written permission of the publisher.

Printed in the United States of America

2 3 4 5 6 7 8 9 10 — 84 83 82 81

Library of Congress Cataloging in Publication Data
Main entry under title:

Philosophy of law.

   Includes bibliographies.
   1. Law—Philosophy.   I. Feinberg, Joel, 1926-
II. Gross, Hyman.
K226.P47 1980   340'.1   80-12482
ISBN 0-534-00835-6

CONTENTS

PART 3 JUSTICE

PART 4 RESPONSIBILITY

PART 5 PUNISHMENT

PREFACE

There is currently a widespread and truly philosophical perplexity about law that is occasioned by the events of the day and by the legal proceedings to which they give rise. Increasing numbers of students have been attracted to courses in philosophy of law and social philosophy offered by philosophy departments, and law students, constantly challenged by the theoretical dimensions of law school subjects, are prompted more than ever to enroll in jurisprudence courses. These students often are disappointed by what seems to them an excessively abstract approach. Portentous terms such as "Law," "Morality," and "Justice," are manipulated like counters in an uncertain game, and hoary figures from the past are marched by, each with his or her distinctive dogmatic pronouncement and his or her own curious technical vocabulary. No wonder traditional jurisprudence often seems among the driest and most remote of academic subjects.

We have tried in this volume to relate the traditional themes of legal philosophy to the live concerns of modern society in a way that invigorates one and illuminates the other. The volume begins with essays by classic and contemporary figures on the essential nature of law, and on the relation of law to morality or other sources of principle outside the legal system. No attempt is made to give contending doctrines equal time, or even to give them all a day in court. We have passed over much excellent material that might have been included, though this is sure to cause some displeasure in an area of jurisprudential concern that is so marked by doctrinal partisanship. Our endeavor is not to represent all important points of view, nor to represent any in a truly comprehensive way, but instead to offer a series of selections that raise sharply the most important issues. Many of these philosophical issues debated in the first part recur later in the book where authors take up specific problems about liberty, justice, responsibility, and punishment.

Opinions in sixteen court cases, together with two literary inventions and one newspaper story, serve to illuminate more abstract discussion and to test the adequacy of principles developed in them. These materials cover such problems as the law in conflict with itself during successive regimes in a single country, how to determine the hitherto unknown scope of a manufacturer's liability, obscene public displays, compulsory medical treatment, the right to privacy, equality between the sexes, Good Samaritans and officious intermeddlers (and how to tell them apart), "slayers' bounties" (and how to prevent them), criminal insanity, and capital punishment. Our aim here is not to supplement the essays with further discussion but to make clear the concreteness and immediacy of matters of philosophical interest in a way that will stimulate further discussion of them.

This second edition contains many new features. The selection from Aquinas has been enlarged by the inclusion of some sections previously omitted. Part One, "Law," also now includes an essay in the important tradition of American legal realism, the chapter on "The Law" from John Chipman Gray's *The Nature and Sources of the Law*. The subsection on "Law and Morality" has the complete text of the late Lon Fuller's rejoinder to Hart's essay on positivism, as well as a brief selection from Gustav Radbruch (in an original new translation by Stanley Paulson). Radbruch is the German writer whose work partly occasioned the Hart-Fuller debate. The subsection on "The Obligation to Obey the Law" now contains the two currently most influential works on the morality of civil disobedience, by M. B. E. Smith and John Rawls; and also Ronald Dworkin's article (formerly in Part Two) on the closely related topic of the rights and duties of state officials in response to civil disobedience. Many readers have requested that we include in this edition an article on legal reasoning; and in response we have added H. L. A. Hart's encyclopedia article, probably the best brief survey of the problems of legal reasoning.

Part Two now contains a completely new subsection on the important subject of "Rights," which contains three articles (including indispensable material from Wesley Hohfeld).

Part Three, "Justice," adds David Hume's historically important chapter "Of Justice" to J. S. Mill's defense of utilitarianism, and in addition Nicholas Rescher's clear and ingenious statement of the difficulties in the utilitarian account of distributive justice. That section of the book has also been updated by the addition of Robert Nozick's much discussed criticism of the "principle of fairness," and by selections from the opinions in the landmark *Bakke* case.

Part Five, "Punishment," has been much improved by the addition of Jeffrie Murphy's "Marxism and Retribution," Andrew von Hirsch's "Desert" (from his *Doing Justice*), Ferdinand Schoeman's "Incapacitating the Dangerous," and the recent precedent-setting capital punishment cases, *Gregg* v. *Georgia* (1976) and *Coker* v. *Georgia* (1977). The selection from Jeremy Bentham has been augmented by the addition of two more chapters from his *Introduction to the Principles of Morals and Legislation,* for greater coherence.

We have benefited from the advice of many professors who used the first edition; and we especially wish to thank Kurt Baier, Robert P. Churchill, F. Patrick Hubbard, Bruce Miller, Jeffrie G. Murphy, Jerome Neu, Stanley Paulson, Don Scheid, and the numerous others who were kind enough to list their preferences on our questionnaire. We are also grateful to Kay Clark, Melissa Feinberg, Ann S. Hickman, and Suzanne A. Thurston for their cheerful and efficient help in typing, assembling, and duplicating the manuscript.

Joel Feinberg
Hyman Gross

PART 1 LAW

The question "What is law?" seems at first glance hardly to deserve a philosopher's attention. Ask a lawyer about the law: if he or she is unable to give an answer on the spot, such a professional knows where to look it up, or at least where to get the ingredients for a reliable opinion. Statutes, judicial opinions, administrative regulations, constitutional provisions are all official pronouncements of law. When these texts leave the matter ambiguous, a lawyer knows the appropriate techniques to resolve the ambiguity, and in aid of that consults scholarly works of interpretation and other sources of authoritative opinion. The question "What is law?" then seems simply a request for a general definition that covers all those, and only those, items of official pronouncement that lawyers finally treat as law. It is true that even the best dictionary may leave us unsatisfied, for something more informative than a mere guide for word use is wanted. Still, at first sight nothing in the question appears to need the fine grinding of the philosopher's mill, and we conclude that we are adequately acquainted with the notion of something as familiar as law, only details remaining to be filled in.

Our simple belief is shattered not only by philosophical reflection but also by the common experience of those who use and are subject to the law. Professor H. L. A. Hart, whose work now dominates Anglo-American legal philosophy, has described this illusion of understanding in this way. "The same predicament was expressed by some famous words of St. Augustine about the notion of time. 'What then is time? If no one asks me I know: if I wish to explain it to one that asks I know not.' It is in this way that even skilled lawyers have felt that, though they know the law, there is much about law and its relations to other things that they cannot explain and do not fully understand. Like a man who can get from one point to another in a familiar town but cannot explain or show others how to do it, those who press for a definition need a map exhibiting clearly the relationships dimly felt to exist between the law they know and other things."[1]

1. *The Concept of Law* (1961), pp. 13-14.

What then are the further questions left unanswered by simple definitions, and what is their importance? In theories of law, three different interpretations have been given to the question "What is law?" These different versions of the question are not always clearly distinguished, but an analogy may serve to clarify the difference.

Suppose the question were "What is a postage stamp?" One interpretation would call for a statement of *what counts as* a postage stamp, or, putting it another way, *what deserves to be called* a postage stamp. The answer would distinguish postage stamps from, and relate them to, revenue stamps, Christmas seals, postage meter imprints, postal privilege franks, and postage due stamps. A second way of viewing the question is as a request for information about *what is properly given effect* as a postage stamp. What counts as a postage stamp is not at issue, but it is recognized that a seriously torn or blemished stamp will not be treated as valid for postage, nor will a counterfeit stamp, one withdrawn from use, or a foreign stamp; and so *criteria of validity* are sought. Finally, a third way of interpreting the question stresses *the nature* of postage, requiring an explanation of the postal system of which stamps are a part and a description of the role of stamps in it. Turning to the far weightier question about law, we notice first that law is the ultimate social resource of civilized people when claims are in conflict. There are many other standards to which people may and often do turn in regulating their affairs, but when these fail, standards bearing the authority of the state are the last resort. It is important, therefore, for the citizen as well as for the judge weighing his or her claim to be able to tell exactly what is law, so that the force of law is not given to lawlike things of other sorts, such as standards of customary practice, moral precepts, by-laws and private regulations.

Once items that are properly called laws are distinguished from other lawlike pronouncements how do we distinguish those that are valid from those that are not? Invalid licenses, arguments, coupons, and orders are not properly given effect, and neither are invalid laws (though it is important to note that in all these cases invalidity does not affect the *kind* of thing it is). What then in general supports the claim that a law may not be given effect? Suppose it is regularly disobeyed and unenforced? Suppose it is hideously unjust? Suppose it is the product of a political regime that is clearly illegitimate? Suppose there are no means for enforcing or changing the law? Here the issue is whether moral, social, or political standards of validity that are (in the first instance, at least) outside the law must be met if a law is to be valid.

A third range of questions concerns the nature of law, and particularly its relation to morality. At every turn lawyers, judges, legislators, and citizens grapple with moral questions: What is fair, who is to blame, what rights does one have, what is wrong with doing that? To make sure the law reflects the lives we live as moral creatures, we need to understand the relation between our law and our morals. In addition, another aspect of the nature of law raises questions about its formal properties: Are laws rules or standards of some other sort? And just what difference is there between what is included as an item of law and other expressions of the same form that are not part of the law?

THE NATURE AND VALIDITY OF LAW

It is a truism that no question in legal philosophy is far removed from any other, and the reader will find that these closely related matters are not treated in isolation from one another. This is exemplified by the selection from the work of Thomas

Aquinas, the first reading in this part. His unifying doctrine is one of natural law. Law, in this view, is universal because it springs from reason possessed by all people, and it is this natural law that shapes the positive law that we ordinarily speak of as "the law." Positive law stands in contrast both to natural law and to divine law, and the relations among the three in the ordering of human life are explained by Aquinas. In this connection the question of special importance is whether (and in what way) human law is derived from natural law. Positive law determined by natural law is for the common good, and it is binding upon the conscience of the human race because it is just. Aquinas's concept of law, then, is of an ideal to be found in laws. It is absent when unjust exercise of power produces laws in name only, and for the most part these need not be obeyed. Aquinas's views on law and morality may surprise those who think of objections to legislating morality as a modern movement. Only moral wrongs that are socially significant as harms to others properly concern the law, according to Aquinas. His idea of conscientious objection to unjust laws and his approval of a qualified civil disobedience will also seem surprising to those who think such views are of recent origin.

Several critical questions might usefully be kept in mind while reading this selection. Is there an adequate distinction drawn between what characterizes good law and what characterizes any law whether good or bad? Is there sufficient appreciation of the difference in what appears to be just to equally rational persons whose interests or circumstances are different? Is reason really disinterested, so that everyone using reason will have the same view of what the law ought to be? Is it possible that a great many perfectly good laws make no appeal at all to conscience, but are recommended by sheer expediency? Is there an adequate criterion for determining the legitimacy of human laws, particularly when the political authority that promulgates them lacks the consent of those who are governed by such laws?

A word about form may help those who are reading Aquinas for the first time. The method is dialectical, with the issue posed in the form of a question at the start (there are fifteen such questions comprising this selection); then objections that make the matter problematic are presented, many of these based on pronouncements of noted authorities. Next, Aquinas gives a general statement of his own position on the question (beginning always with a supporting statement from a church authority); and finally, there are the specific replies of Aquinas to each of the objections previously presented. The authorities cited are mostly religious, though "the Philosopher" (Aristotle) and "the jurists" (from the Code of Justinian) are secular.

The very brief excerpt from a work of Sir Ernest Barker, *Traditions of Civility,* presents concisely the "natural law" conception of law and contrasts it sharply with the view of those who reject natural law. The author also reminds us of the power of these jurisprudential ideas in political history, and particularly of their influence on the American Revolution. The contrast he presents continues to be reflected in the very different notions of constitutional principles found in the British and in the American legal systems.

John Austin's *The Province of Jurisprudence Determined* was published in England in 1832 and has long been regarded in the Anglo-American tradition as the leading work in opposition to natural law theory. It is exceedingly careful work of great range and refinement, the portions reprinted here setting forth only the essentials of Austin's views about the nature of law. Positive law is what Austin seeks to define, and this he does by distinguishing *laws properly so called* from other lawlike utterances and other things called laws. *Laws properly so called* turn out to be *commands* requiring conduct, and some, called positive law, issue from a sovereign to members of an *independent political society* over which sovereignty is exercised. *Commands* entail a purpose and a power to impose sanctions upon those who disobey; a *sovereign* is a determinate human superior (that is, one who can compel others to obey) who is not in a habit of obedience to such a superior and who also receives habitual obedience; and an *independent political society* is one in which the bulk of the society habitually obeys a sovereign.

Austin's theory of law has surely called forth more abundant and more eminent criticism than any other. The reader will likely wonder whether Austin's analysis is not too much influenced by his own legal system and form of government. Can, for example, the features of a federal system like that of the United States be comfortably accommodated in Austin's model? And there are other kinds of troubling questions. Is the power-dependent notion of a command adequate, or would the authority-dependent notion of a rule prove more illuminating, since it allows subtler analysis of law in terms more complex than threats of force? Has Austin taken penal laws to be the prototype for all laws, thereby distorting the features of other kinds of laws and exaggerating the role of sanctions in their operation? Are the rules that govern the validity of laws to be taken as commands by the sovereign to himself or herself; and, if so, does that account do justice to claims of invalidity that are advanced in modern legal systems? Austin's account of judge-made law is one of acquiescence by the sovereign in what a minister has decided. That seems plausible enough with reference to the case being decided. But looking at the way judicial opinions are used subsequently in legal arguments as a source of law, can they really be said to be commands of the sovereign "though not by its express declaration?" Does Austin's account of sovereignty distinguish *legitimate* exercise of political power through legislation from *effective* legislative exercise of political power, presumably only the former qualifying as law?

In the United States and the Scandinavian countries especially, the focus of jurisprudential interest has been on the courts. The authoritative interpretation of whatever sources of law a legal system provides is ultimately a job for judges. Even more important, it is the judicial utterance about legal rights and duties that represents the state of the law at any time and tells those with contending views just what the law is. Saying that the law is whatever the courts say it is has a sobering effect and tends to undermine the comfortable belief that at any time the law is fixed and certain, waiting only to be brought out of the shadows by judges skilled in the arts of judicial revelation.

Instead, those who have come to be known as the legal realists see judges making law according to the craft conventions of their legal system, by using what are recognized as sources of law in that system, but also admitting as ingredients (not always consciously) such things as prevailing moral notions, current social attitudes, commonsense ideas, and even their own personal prejudices. In America the names of Karl Llewellyn and Jerome Frank are most notably associated with the realist conception of law. John Chipman Gray's *The Nature and Sources of the Law* is an earlier work that develops this point of view with admirable balance and clarity, and the selection from that book presents a case that merits very serious consideration.

Gray first examines three conceptions of law that in essence cast judges merely in the role of mouthpieces to give the law its expression. The first of these is found in Austin's theory where law is the sovereign's commands. Gray rejects this as a very misleading way of viewing the ultimate power that the state admittedly has in determining what judges may find the law to be, for in fact, judges enjoy a very large discretion, and it seems exceedingly odd to imagine that in exercising it they are somehow obeying a command. The second conception, represented by the nineteenth century German jurist Friedrich Karl von Savigny, views courts as giving voice to what previously existed in the "common consciousness of the people." Gray rejects this as contrary to the evidence provided by popular opinion on questions of law that are presented to courts when judges exercise their discretionary powers. Their answers cannot be said to reflect what the ordinary man thinks, and even more telling is the fact that not infrequently the answers are in conflict with ordinary views. In the third conception of law that Gray finds unacceptable, the source of law in judicial decisions is not clearly identified when there are novel questions presented, but it is thought nevertheless that judges are finding the law and not inventing it. There is then a belief in ideal law waiting to be declared by a court when a suitable case provides the opportunity, and Gray argues that it is unwillingness to countenance what appears to be the unsavory practice of lawmaking after the fact that sustains this belief. This conception of law appears unsatisfactory, according to Gray, when one considers how questions of law really are decided; and also when one compares decisions in jurisdictions whose ideal law would presumably be the same and finds these decisions very much at odds with one another.

In a statement that merits very careful consideration, Gray suggests that "the function of a judge is not mainly to declare the law, but to maintain the peace by deciding controversies." Do we then have the purported injustice of *ex post facto* laws in novel cases? Are we then really at the mercy of the courts when we expect the best decision on principle in such a case? Are the insights in the three theories that Gray rejects given greater importance when the role of the judge is viewed in this way? Controversies are decided by invoking general rules and do serve as law for the future. But is this sort of decision necessary "to maintain the peace"? If so, why?

LAW AND MORALITY

Controversy about the nature and validity of law most often revolves around the question of what relationship morality has to law. Those who are spoken of as positivists tend to view a legal system as having its own criteria for valid laws, and so tend to regard moral judgments of laws as important in deciding what the law should be, yet not relevant in deciding what the law is. The work now generally regarded as the most important modern statement of the positivist position in the Anglo-American tradition is H. L. A. Hart's book *The Concept of Law,* published in 1961. It is in no sense a narrow defense of a partisan tradition in legal theory, but rather undertakes a broad reexamination of the fundamental questions of jurisprudence, clarifying them and securing their importance. Perhaps more than any other book in the field this one deserves to be read in its entirety, and for that reason no attempt has been made to provide excerpts here. But an article by Hart entitled "Positivism and the Separation of Law and Morals" was published three years before his book, and it is included here for the light it casts on many issues presented in some of the other selections.

Professor Lon L. Fuller, in his article "Positivism and Fidelity to Law—A Reply to Professor Hart," presents a view in opposition to Professor Hart's on a number of important issues. Together the two articles have become a classic debate in the modern literature of legal philosophy on the role of moral considerations in rendering judgments about what the law is. The main points in controversy emerge with clarity and force. What is the relation between the law that is and the law that ought to be? Of what significance are attitudes toward the concept of law, particularly the attitude toward law as an ideal which can compel fidelity? Must definitions of law in some way reflect morally worthy ideals? Upon what social or political facts does the very existence of law depend, and in what way does this bind law to morality? Is there an indispensable minimum moral foundation for any legal system determined by certain universal features of the human condition and by principles of procedure that cannot be systematically ignored?

In section IV of his article, Professor Hart considers the positivist's dilemma when confronted with the need to recognize as law the odious edicts of a morally depraved regime. Professor Fuller in section V of his reply presses the case for the dependency of law upon moral constraints by further examining what passes for law under such a regime. He cites the cases of grudge informers. In his widely regarded book, *The Morality of Law,* published in 1964, Professor Fuller elaborates the important themes in the present article and includes in that book "The Problem of the Grudge Informer" that appears as the next selection in this volume. In seeking a solution, it is helpful first to separate the major issues that present themselves. Is it a question of whether the laws of the previous regime were valid? Whether all valid laws furnish a defense to those who acted under them? Whether criminal laws that are enacted after the crime are never to be applied retroactively? Whether prosecution or some other measure under public authority represents the better policy to be pursued now by the government?

THE OBLIGATION TO OBEY THE LAW

When there are laws that permit officials or citizens to do what is morally wrong, law and morality come into conflict. When the law requires things that are morally wrong, or when it prohibits what is morally right, the conflict becomes a struggle rooted in the conscience of the community. At stake in this struggle is a presumed obligation to obey the law that normally influences law-abiding members of society to choose among different courses of conduct only those that are in accordance with the law. These occasions of moral crisis when law and morality are sharply at odds serve to remind us of a question that is always with us. What is the nature of our obligation to obey the law at any time, and what limits are there to this obligation? The answer calls for good and sufficient reasons for such an obligation to exist, and for further good and sufficient reasons for the suspension of such an obligation under certain special circumstances.

Almost everyone who has written on the subject is willing to concede (at the very least) that there is a *prima facie* obligation to obey the law, for one then admits only that there is an obligation to obey the law unless there is something objectionable about it. In "Is There a *Prima Facie* Obligation to Obey the Law?" Professor M. B. E. Smith questions the existence of even a *prima facie* obligation. Perhaps so, he says, but it has yet to be shown to exist; and the arguments that appear to support such a *prima facie* obligation do not, he argues, furnish the needed support. He first makes clear just what the relevant *prima facie* obligation is, for the terms *prima facie* and *obligation* both lend themselves to some confusion. He then examines the arguments usually advanced, which are of three varieties. Sometimes it is argued that because of the benefits received from government, there is a *prima facie* obligation to obey its laws. At other times it is argued that an implicit consent or promise by members of society creates such a *prima facie* obligation. And finally, there are arguments from the utility of laws or from the general good that law normally promotes. Through critical examination of these arguments, Smith undermines the usual assumption of the existence of at least a *prima facie* obligation; and thereby he adds a considerable measure of profundity to scepticism about the existence of a full-fledged obligation to obey the law.

In *A Theory of Justice,* John Rawls sketches a theory of civil disobedience for what he calls "a nearly just society, one that is well-ordered for the most part but in which some serious violations of justice nevertheless do occur." He first makes clear what he means by civil disobedience, distinguishing it from conscientious refusal and from acts hostile to the constituted public order. It is nonviolent but unlawful, a form of conscientious public protest that is meant to bring about "a change in the law or policies of the government." Professor Rawls' underlying concern is with the duties and obligations of the good citizen in what we think of as a modern liberal democratic society, and civil disobedience turns out to be justifiable as an altogether expedient way of appealing in an urgent and dramatic fashion to the conscience of the majority when some serious injustice weighs upon the conscience of others in the community.

Rawls introduces a number of conditions that must be met, among them the infringement of "the principle of equal liberty," or "blatant violations of . . . the principle of fair equality of opportunity." The first of these grounds of justifiable civil disobedience comprehends laws and acts of government that violate "liberty of conscience and freedom of thought, liberty of the person, and equal political rights"—what Rawls conceives as "the liberties of equal citizenship" in chapter IV of his book. The second restriction makes reference to a fundamental principle of justice (discussed in chapter II) that requires positions of responsibility and authority to be equally accessible to all members of society. But Rawls does not view purported trangressions of "the difference principle" (also developed in chapter II of his book) as grounds for civil disobedience, since it is normally too uncertain whether particular laws and policies tend to promote or to alleviate inequalities in the distribution of property and other benefits of life.

The warrant for civil disobedience that Professor Rawls presents seems well-suited to ease the discomforts of the law-abiding citizen whose deep convictions are offended by unjust measures and who wishes to protest with the special drama that accompanies violation of law. But there are questions to be put to advocates of this view. Why must civil disobedience be an act of conscience? And why must it be a political act? Suppose a member of the community perceives some serious injustice but accepts it with an air of resignation as only one among many countervailing injustices that on balance leave the world quite imperfect but tolerable enough. Why should he not be free to join in acts of civil disobedience with his politically militant friends out of sociability or simply because he finds the activity a rather exciting diversion from what is normally a rather dull existence? Why should it matter what his motives or state of mind are so long as he behaves in an appropriately restrained way in circumstances that make it likely that the conscience of the majority will be moved against the prevailing injustice by what he and others are doing?

Another problem is this: in the account Rawls gives it would seem that civil disobedience is justifiable as a matter of expediency in a nearly just society. But prevailing attitudes among the majority may well be unsympathetic to unlawful conduct engaged in only to draw attention to what is said to be the exceedingly unjust character of some unrelated law. Law and order may be the formula insisted on by most people in the community, with attempts to change the law limited to lawful means only. Civil disobedience would then seem to have very little chance of success and its uselessness would then count heavily against it when it is to be justified as a measure of expediency. In such a social atmosphere civil disobedience may be a less practical remedy for the good citizen to adopt, but do we really wish to conclude that it is a less justifiable measure of opposition to injustice?

Finally, we might well want to know more about those occasions when civil disobedience is justifiable, and particularly when it is "that in one's sincere and considered opinion the conditions of free cooperation are being violated." It seems a good bet that rarely, if ever, can we count on those who contemplate civil disobedience to examine carefully their opinions in the light of fundamental principles of social justice. But if there is not such an examination, and hence quite understandably the majority view the unlawful acts only as a dramatic expression of dissenting views, does civil disobedience then play a role that can be justified along the lines Rawls suggests?

It is usually the moral position of the good citizen that occupies writers on civil disobedience and conscientious refusal. For a morally sound society, the position of the good official is no less important. In his essay "On Not Prosecuting Civil Disobedience," Ronald Dworkin presents a subtle and complicated argument in support of very great official restraint in prosecuting those who violate the law when its moral footings are unsure. Though the problems that occupy the center of the stage were posed by the Vietnam War, the dilemmas Professor Dworkin deals with are general in character and recur constantly when the deep moral commitments of the community come into conflict with laws that seem to a democratic majority a desirable and perhaps even urgent measure of social regulation. In considering Dworkin's arguments, it seems a good idea to distinguish the different sorts of violations of law that might have moral backing, and to weigh the claims of principle and of expediency on both sides to test the position of the official who feels constrained one way or the other in deciding whether to prosecute. In doing this it may well appear that the term civil disobedience comprehends many different sorts of violations of law whose moral diversity must be taken into account if there are to be sound judgments about prosecution in each case.

LAW AND THE JUDICIAL DECISION

Several selections that have already been discussed draw attention to the fact that courts are most often the legal institution of greatest interest to those who want to know what law is. Within the legal system, whenever there is a question about what the law is, it is judges who give the official answer; and in the course of deciding what the law is, judges say things that become sources of law for the future when what they say is later interpreted and applied by other judges in other cases. In reaching his or her decision, a judge turns to sources of law such as legislation and decisions in previous cases. But judicial decision is hardly ever an enterprise in which rules of law dictate a decision to which the judge merely attaches authority by his or her pronouncement of it. Reasoned argument that requires judicial choice among competing grounds of decision is the essence of the judicial process. This suggests a considerable latitude of discretion that judges enjoy, as well as characteristic modes of reasoning to be followed in reaching a proper judicial decision. The discretion is limited by the provisions of legislation and other clear statements of the law; and the judge's discretion is not as great as that of the legislator who (except for the constitutional limitations upon him or her that judges announce) is untrammeled by prior judicial decision. But when the judge exercises discretion it is to decide what the law is and to give it effect, not simply to decide what the law will be. Great power this is, and it must be exercised in a responsible way. Legislators who abuse their power are subject to retribution through the political process, while judges are kept insulated from political retaliation. It is especially important, therefore, that judicial decisions be defensible under the standards and according to the modes of reasoning that are deemed fitting in the legal system.

In the selection titled "Problems of Legal Reasoning," Professor H. L. A. Hart canvasses the main issues of judicial reasoning that have become embroiled in jurisprudential controversy. One such issue is the character of judicial logic and the role it plays in the process of reaching a decision. The character, origin, and function of rules in the process of decision is another matter that has generated controversy. Still another concerns the role of precedent: when does it "bind" subsequent decision; how can clear cases be distinguished from hard cases; what makes clear cases clear; to what extent does precedent allow for judicial discretion? The question of acceptable modes of interpreting legislation presents yet another difficulty in giving account of judicial reasoning. In reading Professor Hart's illuminating exposition, it is well to bear in mind the threefold distinction regarding theories of judicial reasoning which he presents in the course of the article. The account of judicial reasoning that is relevant here is not an account of the usual processes or habits of thought by which judges reach their decisions. Nor is it an account of how judges should ideally reach their decisions. Rather it is an account of how decisions are justified, of the standards judges are bound to respect (and normally do) when they justify their decisions. It would seem that much needless cynicism, which understandably results from discovery of irrational influences in actual procedures of decision, could be avoided by observing this distinction, as could the needless disappointed expectation of those who look in vain for logical rigor. The right sort of theory of judicial reasoning provides us with sound principles to guide the exercise of judicial authority and also with critical tools to expose bad decisions and thus nullify their effect on the law.

The judicial decision is currently the most widely debated topic in the philosophy of law. The major problems are the extent to which judges do make law, the extent to which they should, and what the proper way is for them to decide novel questions of law. Those who have read the Hart-Fuller debate and especially the selection by Gray will already have some acquaintance with much of the terrain. The selection by Ronald Dworkin entitled "The Model of Rules" brings the main features sharply into focus. Initially Dworkin argues against the "realist" view (which he ironically styles "nominalist") denying that the questions of what law *is* are answered by descriptions of what courts in fact *do* in exercising their power. He then subjects to critical analysis the theory of law which Professor Hart presented in *The Concept of Law*. The burden of his opposition to Hart as the exemplar of positivism is that rules are only one variety of standard to be invoked by a judge in deciding legal issues. There are other standards, the most important of which are principles and policies, and those other standards are not extralegal, but are law as much as rules are. Furthermore, there is no master rule, no matter how complex, which determines their validity as law. The arguments are subtle, thorough, and complex, and they have set the stage for a continuing debate of this topic.

Professor Dworkin makes use of two cases—*Riggs v. Palmer* and *Henningsen v. Bloomfield Motors, Inc.*—to illustrate how standards other than rules function as law. Excerpts from the opinions in those cases are included here to allow the reader to decide himself about the character of what the court provides as support for its decision. It is useful to distinguish the different kinds of standards as they appear in the opinions; to consider whether the judge is bound or has discretion in using them, and in what sense they are binding or discretionary; and also to consider the origins of whatever authority they have. Furthermore, it is worthwhile to consider how Dworkin might deal with the dissenting opinion in *Riggs*.

H.G.

THOMAS AQUINAS

Concerning the Nature of Law*

WHETHER LAW IS SOMETHING PERTAINING TO REASON?

Objection 1. It would seem that law is not something pertaining to reason. For the Apostle says (*Rom.* vii. *23*): *I see another law in my members,* etc. But nothing pertaining to reason is in the members, since the reason does not make use of a bodily organ. Therefore law is not something pertaining to reason.

Obj. 2. Further, in the reason there is nothing else but power, habit and act. But law is not the power itself of reason. In like manner, neither is it a habit of reason, because the habits of reason are the intellectual virtues, of which we have spoken above. Nor again is it an act of reason, because then law would cease when the act of reason ceases, for instance, while we are asleep. Therefore law is nothing pertaining to reason.

Obj. 3. Further, the law moves those who are subject to it to act rightly. But it belongs properly to the will to move to act, as is evident from what has been said above. Therefore law pertains, not to the reason, but to the will, according to the words of the Jurist: *Whatsoever pleaseth the sovereign has the force of law.*

On the contrary, It belongs to the law to command and to forbid. But it belongs to reason to command, as was stated above. Therefore law is something pertaining to reason.

I answer that, Law is a rule and measure of acts, whereby man is induced to act or is restrained from acting; for *lex* [*law*] is derived from *ligare* [*to bind*], because it binds one to act. Now the rule and measure of human acts is the reason, which is the first principle of human acts, as is evident from what has been stated above. For it belongs to the reason to direct to the end, which

is the first principle in all matters of action, according to the Philosopher. Now that which is the principle in any genus is the rule and measure of that genus: for instance, unity in the genus of numbers, and the first movement in the genus of movements. Consequently, it follows that law is something pertaining to reason.

Reply Obj. 1. Since law is a kind of rule and measure, it may be in something in two ways. First, as in that which measures and rules; and since this is proper to reason, it follows that, in this way, law is in the reason alone.—Secondly, as in that which is measured and ruled. In this way, law is in all those things that are inclined to something because of some law; so that any inclination arising from a law may be called a law, not essentially, but by participation as it were. And thus the inclination of the members to concupiscence is called *the law of the members.*

Reply Obj. 2. Just as, in external action, we may consider the work and the work done, for instance, the work of building and the house built, so in the acts of reason, we may consider the act itself of reason, *i.e.,* to understand and to reason, and something produced by this act. With regard to the speculative reason, this is first of all the definition; secondly, the proposition; thirdly, the syllogism or argument. And since the practical reason also makes use of the syllogism in operable matters, as we have stated above and as the Philosopher teaches, hence we find in the practical reason something that holds the same position in regard to operations as, in the speculative reason, the proposition holds in regard to conclusions. Such universal propositions of the practical reason that are directed to operations have the nature of law. And these propositions are sometimes under our actual consideration, while sometimes they are retained in the reason by means of a habit.

Reply Obj. 3. Reason has its power of moving from the will, as was stated above; for it is due to the fact that one wills the end, that the reason issues its commands as regards things ordained to

*From *Summa Theologica, The Basic Writings of Saint Thomas Aquinas* ed. Anton C. Pegis (New York: Random House, Inc., 1945), Vol.II, pp. 742–53, 773–80, 784–85, 791–95. Copyright © 1945 Random House, Inc. Reprinted by permission of the publisher and The Very Rev. Prior Provincial O.P., St. Dominic's Priory, London. Footnotes appearing in the original of this edition are omitted.

the end. But in order that the volition of what is commanded may have the nature of law, it needs to be in accord with some rule of reason. And in this sense is to be understood the saying that the will of the sovereign has the force of law; or otherwise the sovereign's will would savor of lawlessness rather than of law.

WHETHER LAW IS ALWAYS DIRECTED TO THE COMMON GOOD?

Objection 1. It would seem that law is not always directed to the common good as to its end. For it belongs to law to command and to forbid. But commands are directed to certain individual goods. Therefore the end of law is not always the common good.

Obj. 2. Further, law directs man in his actions. But human actions are concerned with particular matters. Therefore law is directed to some particular good.

Obj. 3. Further, Isidore says: *If law is based on reason, whatever is based on reason will be a law.* But reason is the foundation not only of what is ordained to the common good, but also of that which is directed to private good. Therefore law is not directed only to the good of all, but also to the private good of an individual.

On the contrary, Isidore says that *laws are enacted for no private profit but for the common benefit of the citizens.*

I answer that, As we have stated above, law belongs to that which is a principle of human acts, because it is their rule and measure. Now as reason is a principle of human acts, so in reason itself there is something which is the principle in respect of all the rest. Hence to this principle chiefly and mainly law must needs be referred. Now the first principle in practical matters, which are the object of the practical reason, is the last end: and the last end of human life is happiness or beatitude, as we have stated above. Consequently, law must needs concern itself mainly with the order that is in beatitude. Moreover, since every part is ordained to the whole as the imperfect to the perfect, and since one man is a part of the perfect community, law must needs concern itself properly with the order directed to universal happiness. Therefore the Philospher, in the above definition of legal matters mentions both happiness and the body politic, since he says that we call these legal matters *just which are adapted to produce and preserve happiness and its parts for the body politic.* For the state is a perfect community, as he says in *Politics* i.

Now, in every genus, that which belongs to it chiefly is the principle of the others, and the others belong to that genus according to some order towards that thing. Thus fire, which is chief among hot things, is the cause of heat in mixed bodies, and these are said to be hot in so far as they have a share of fire. Consequently, since law is chiefly ordained to the common good, any other precept in regard to some individual work must needs be devoid of the nature of a law, save in so far as it regards the common good. Therefore every law is ordained to the common good.

Reply Obj. 1. A command denotes the application of a law to matters regulated by law. Now the order to the common good, at which law aims, is applicable to particular ends. And in this way commands are given even concerning particular matters.

Reply Obj. 2. Actions are indeed concerned with particular matters, but those particular matters are referable to the common good, not as to a common genus or species, but as to a common final cause, according as the common good is said to be the common end.

Reply Obj. 3. Just as nothing stands firm with regard to the speculative reason except that which is traced back to the first indemonstrable principles, so nothing stands firm with regard to the practical reason, unless it be directed to the last end which is the common good. Now whatever stands to reason in this sense has the nature of a law.

WHETHER THE REASON OF ANY MAN IS COMPETENT TO MAKE LAWS?

Objection 1. It would seem that the reason of any man is competent to make laws. For the Apostle says (Rom ii. 14) that *when the Gentiles, who have not the law, do by nature those things that are of the law, ... they are a law to themselves.* Now he says this of all in general. Therefore anyone can make a law for himself.

Obj. 2. Further, as the Philosopher says, *the intention of the lawgiver is to lead men to virtue.* But every man can lead another to virtue. Therefore the reason of any man is competent to make laws.

Obj. 3. Further, just as the sovereign of a state governs the state, so every father of a family governs his household. But the sovereign of a state can make laws for the state. Therefore every father of a family can make laws for his household.

On the contrary, Isidore says, and the *Decretals* repeat: *A law is an ordinance of the people, whereby something is sanctioned by the Elders together with the Commonalty.* Therefore not everyone can make laws.

I answer that, A law, properly speaking regards first and foremost the order to the common good. Now to order anything to the common good belongs either to the whole people, or to someone who is the viceregent of the whole people. Hence the making of a law belongs either to the whole people or to a public personage who has care of the whole people; for in all other matters the directing of anything to the end concerns him to whom the end belongs.

Reply Obj. 1. As we stated above, a law is in a person not only as in one that rules, but also, by participation, as in one that is ruled. In the latter way, each one is a law to himself, in so far as he shares the direction that he receives from one who rules him. Hence the same text goes on: *Who show the work of the law written in their hearts* (Rom. ii. 15).

Reply Obj. 2. A private person cannot lead another to virtue efficaciously; for he can only advise, and if his advice be not taken, it has not coercive power, such as the law should have, in order to prove an efficacious inducement to virtue, as the Philosopher says. But this coercive power is vested in the whole people or in some public personage, to whom it belongs to inflict penalties, as we shall state further on. Therefore the framing of laws belongs to him alone.

Reply Obj. 3. As one man is a part of the household, so a household is a part of the state; and the state is a perfect community, according to *Politics* i. Therefore, just as the good of one man is not the last end, but is ordained to the common good, so too the good of one household is ordained to the good of a single state, which is a perfect community. Consequently, he that governs a family can indeed make certain commands of ordinances, but not such as to have properly the nature of law.

WHETHER PROMULGATION IS ESSENTIAL TO LAW?

Objection 1. It would seem that promulgation is not essential to law. For the natural law, above all, has the character of law. But the natural law needs no promulgation. Therefore it is not essential to law that it be promulgated.

Obj. 2. Further, it belongs properly to law to bind one to do or not to do something. But the obligation of fulfilling a law touches not only those in whose presence it is promulgated, but

also others. Therefore promulgation is not essential to law.

Obj. 3. Further, the binding force of law extends even to the future, since *laws are binding in matters of the future,* as the jurists say. But promulgation concerns those who are present. Therefore it is not essential to law.

On the contrary, It is laid down in the *Decretals* that *laws are established when they are promulgated.*

I answer that, As was stated above, a law is imposed on others as a rule and measure. Now a rule or measure is imposed by being applied to those who are to be ruled and measured by it. Therefore, in order that a law obtain the binding force which is proper to a law, it must needs be applied to the men who have to be ruled by it. But such application is made by its being made known to them by promulgation. Therefore promulgation is necessary for law to obtain its force.

Thus, from the four preceding articles, the definition of law may be gathered. Law is nothing else than an ordinance of reason for the common good, promulgated by him who has the care of the community.

Reply Obj. 1. The natural law is promulgated by the very fact that God instilled it into man's mind so as to be known by him naturally.

Reply Obj. 2. Those who are not present when a law is promulgated are bound to observe the law, in so far as it is made known or can be made known to them by others, after it has been promulgated.

Reply Obj. 3. The promulgation that takes place in the present extends to future time by reason of the durability of written characters, by which means it is continually promulgated. Hence Isidore says that *lex* [*law*] *is derived from legere* [*to read*] *because it is written.*

ON THE VARIOUS KINDS OF LAW

WHETHER THERE IS AN ETERNAL LAW?

Objection I. It would seem that there is no eternal law. For every law is imposed on someone. But there was not someone from eternity on whom a law could be imposed, since God alone was from eternity. Therefore no law is eternal.

Obj. 2. Further, promulgation is essential to law. But promulgation could not be from eternity, because there was no one to whom it could be promulgated from eternity. Therefore no law can be eternal.

Obj. 3. Further, law implies order to an end. But nothing ordained to an end is eternal, for the last end alone is eternal. Therefore no law is eternal.

On the contrary, Augustine says: *That law which is the supreme Reason cannot be understood to be otherwise than unchangeable and eternal.*

I answer that, As we have stated above, law is nothing else but a dictate of practical reason emanating from the ruler who governs a perfect community. Now it is evident, granted that the world is ruled by divine providence, as was stated in the First Part, that the whole community of the universe is governed by the divine reason. Therefore the very notion of the government of things in God, the ruler of the universe, has the nature of a law. And since the divine reason's conception of things is not subject to time, but is eternal, according to *Prov.* viii. 23, therefore it is that this kind of law must be called eternal.

Reply Obj. I. Those things that do not exist in themselves exist in God, inasmuch as they are known and preordained by Him, according to *Rom.* iv. 17: *Who calls those things that are not, as those that are.* Accordingly, the eternal concept of the divine law bears the character of an eternal law in so far as it is ordained by God to the government of things foreknown by Him.

Reply Obj. 2. Promulgation is made by word of mouth or in writing, and in both ways the eternal law is promulgated, because both the divine Word and the writing of the Book of Life are eternal. But the promulgation cannot be from eternity on the part of the creature that hears or reads.

Reply Obj. 3. Law implies order to the end actively, namely, in so far as it directs certain things to the end; but not passively,—that is to say, the law itself is not ordained to the end, except accidentally, in a governor whose end is extrinsic to him, and to which end his law must needs be ordained. But the end of the divine government is God Himself, and His law is not something other than Himself. Therefore the eternal law is not ordained to another end.

WHETHER THERE IS IN US A NATURAL LAW?

Objection I. It would seem that there is no natural law in us. For man is governed sufficiently by the external law, since Augustine says that *the eternal law is that by which it is right that all things should be most orderly.* But nature does not abound in superfluities as neither does she fail

in necessaries. Therefore man has no natural law.

Obj. 2. Further, by the law man is directed, in his acts, to the end, as was stated above. But the directing of human acts to their end is not a function of nature, as is the case in irrational creatures, which act for an end solely by their natural appetite; whereas man acts for an end by his reason and will. Therefore man has no natural law.

Obj. 3. Further, the more a man is free, the less is he under the law. But man is freer than all the animals because of his free choice, with which he is endowed in distinction from all other animals. Since, therefore, other animals are not subject to a natural law, neither is man subject to a natural law.

On the contrary, The *Gloss* on *Rom* ii. 14 (*When the Gentiles, who have not the law, do by nature those things that are of the law*) comments as follows: *Although they have no written law, yet they have the natural law, whereby each one knows, and is conscious of, what is good and what is evil.*

I answer that, As we have stated above, law, being a rule and measure, can be in a person in two ways: in one way, as in him that rules and measures; in another way, as in that which is ruled and measured, since a thing is ruled and measured in so far as it partakes of the rule or measure. Therefore, since all things subject to divine providence are ruled and measured by the eternal law, as was stated above, it is evident that all things partake in some way in the eternal law, in so far as, namely, from its being imprinted on them, they derive their respective inclinations to their proper acts and ends. Now among all others, the rational creature is subject to divine providence in a more excellent way, in so far as it itself partakes of a share of providence, by being provident both for itself and for others. Therefore it has a share of the eternal reason, whereby it has a natural inclination to its proper act and end; and this participation of the eternal law in the rational creature is called the natural law. Hence the Psalmist, after saying (*Ps.* iv. 6): *Offer up the sacrifice of justice,* as though someone asked what the works of justice are, adds: *Many say, Who showeth us good things?* in answer to which question he says: *The light of Thy countenance, O Lord, is signed upon us.* He thus implies that the light of natural reason, whereby we discern what is good and what is evil, which is the function of the natural law, is nothing else than an imprint on us of the divine light. It is therefore evident that the natural law is nothing else than the rational creature's participation of the eternal law.

Reply Obj. I. This argument would hold if the natural law were something different from the eternal law; whereas it is nothing but a participation thereof, as we have stated above.

Reply Obj. 2. Every act of reason and will in us is based on that which is according to nature, as was stated above. For every act of reasoning is based on principles that are known naturally, and every act of appetite in respect of the means is derived from the natural appetite in respect of the last end. Accordingly, the first direction of our acts to their end must needs be through the natural law.

Reply Obj. 3. Even irrational animals partake in their own way of the eternal reason, just as the rational creature does. But because the rational creature partakes thereof in an intellectual and rational manner, therefore the participation of the eternal law in the rational creature is properly called a law, since a law is something pertaining to reason, as was stated above. Irrational creatures, however, do not partake thereof in a rational manner, and therefore there is no participation of the eternal law in them, except by way of likeness.

WHETHER THERE IS A HUMAN LAW?

Objection I. It would seem that there is not a human law. For the natural law is a participation of the eternal law, as was stated above. Now through the eternal law *all things are most orderly,* as Augustine states. Therefore the natural law suffices for the ordering of all human affairs. Consequently there is no need for a human law.

Obj. 2. Further, law has the character of a measure, as was stated above. But human reason is not a measure of things, but *vice versa,* as is stated in *Metaph.* x. Therefore no law can emanate from the human reason.

Obj. 3. Further, a measure should be most certain, as is stated in *Metaph.* x. But the dictates of the human reason in matters of conduct are uncertain, according to *Wis.* ix. 14: *The thoughts of mortal men are fearful, and our counsels uncertain.* Therefore no law can emanate from the human reason.

On the contrary, Augustine distinguishes two kinds of law, the one eternal, the other temporal, which he calls human.

I answer that, As we have stated above, a law is a dictate of the practical reason. Now it is to be observed that the same procedure takes place

in the practical and in the speculative reason, for each proceeds from principles to conclusions, as was stated above. Accordingly, we conclude that, just as in the speculative reason, from naturally known indemonstrable principles we draw the conclusions of the various sciences, the knowledge of which is not imparted to us by nature, but acquired by the efforts of reason, so too it is that from the precepts of the natural law, as from common and indemonstrable principles, the human reason needs to proceed to the more particular determination of certain matters. These particular determinations, devised by human reason, are called human laws, provided that the other essential conditions of law be observed, as was stated above. Therefore Tully says in his *Rhetoric* that *justice has its source in nature; thence certain things came into custom by reason of their utility; afterwards these things which emanated from nature, and were approved by custom, were sanctioned by fear and reverence for the law.*

Reply Obj. I. The human reason cannot have a full participation of the dictate of the divine reason, but according to its own mode, and imperfectly. Consequently, just as on the part of the speculative reason, by a natural participation of divine wisdom, there is in us the knowledge of certain common principles, but not a proper knowledge of each single truth, such as that contained in the divine wisdom, so, too, on the part of the practical reason, man has a natural participation of the eternal law, according to certain common principles, but not as regards the particular determinations of individual cases, which are, however, contained in the eternal law. Hence the need for human reason to proceed further to sanction them by law.

Reply Obj. 2. Human reason is not, of itself, the rule of things. But the principles impressed on it by nature are the general rules and measures of all things relating to human conduct, of which the natural reason is the rule and measure, although it is not the measure of things that are from nature.

Reply Obj. 3. The practical reason is concerned with operable matters, which are singular and contingent, but not with necessary things, with which the speculative reason is concerned. Therefore human laws cannot have that inerrancy that belongs to the demonstrated conclusions of the sciences. Nor is it necessary for every measure to be altogether unerring and certain, but according as it is possible in its own particular genus.

WHETHER THERE WAS ANY NEED FOR A DIVINE LAW?

Objection I. It would seem that there was no need for a divine law. For, as was stated above, the natural law is a participation in us of the eternal law. But the eternal law is the divine law, as was stated above. Therefore there is no need for a divine law in addition to the natural law and to human laws derived therefrom.

Obj. 2. Further, it is written (*Ecclus.* xv. 14) that *God left man in the hand of his own counsel.* Now counsel is an act of reason, as was stated above. Therefore man was left to the direction of his reason. But a dictate of human reason is a human law, as was stated above. Therefore there is no need for man to be governed also by divine law.

Obj. 3. Further, human nature is more self-sufficing than irrational creatures. But irrational creatures have no divine law besides the natural inclination impressed on them. Much less, therefore, should the rational creature have a divine law in addition to the natural law.

On the contrary, David prayed God to set His law before him, saying (*Ps.* cxviii. 33): *Set before me for a law the way of Thy justifications, O Lord.*

I answer that, Besides the natural and the human law it was necessary for the directing of human conduct to have a divine law. And this for four reasons. First, because it is by law that man is directed how to perform his proper acts in view of his last end. Now if man were ordained to no other end than that which is proportionate to his natural ability, there would be no need for man to have any further direction, on the part of his reason, in addition to the natural law and humanly devised law which is derived from it. But since man is ordained to an end of eternal happiness which exceeds man's natural ability, as we have stated above, therefore it was necessary that, in addition to the natural and the human law, man should be directed to his end by a law given by God.

Secondly, because, by reason of the uncertainty of human judgment, especially on contingent and particular matters, different people form different judgments on human acts; whence also different and contrary laws result. In order, therefore, that man may know without any doubt what he ought to do and what he ought to avoid, it was necessary for man to be directed in his proper acts by a law given by God, for it is certain that such a law cannot err.

Thirdly, because man can make laws in those matters of which he is competent to judge. But man is not competent to judge of interior movements, that are hidden, but only of exterior acts which are observable; and yet for the perfection of virtue it is necessary for man to conduct himself rightly in both kinds of acts. Consequently, human law could not sufficiently curb and direct interior acts, and it was necessary for this purpose that a divine law should supervene.

Fourthly, because, as Augustine says, human law cannot punish or forbid all evil deeds, since, while aiming at doing away with all evils, it would do away with many good things, and would hinder the advance of the common good, which is necessary for human living. In order, therefore, that no evil might remain unforbidden and unpunished, it was necessary for the divine law to supervene, whereby all sins are forbidden.

And these four causes are touched upon in *Ps.* cxviii. 8, where it is said: *The law of the Lord is unspotted, i.e.,* allowing no foulness of sin; *converting souls,* because it directs not only exterior, but also interior, acts; *the testimony of the Lord is faithful,* because of the certainty of what is true and right; *giving wisdom to little ones,* by directing man to an end supernatural and divine.

Reply Obj. I. By the natural law the eternal law is participated proportionately to the capacity of human nature. But to his supernatural end man needs to be directed in a yet higher way. Hence the additional law given by God, whereby man shares more perfectly in the eternal law.

Reply Obj. 2. Counsel is a kind of inquiry, and hence must proceed from some principles. Nor is it enough for it to proceed from principles imparted by nature, which are the precepts of the natural law, for the reasons given above; but there is need for certain additional principles, namely, the precepts of the divine law.

Reply Obj. 3. Irrational creatures are not ordained to an end higher than that which is proportionate to their natural powers. Consequently the comparison fails . . .

THE NATURAL LAW

WHETHER THE NATURAL LAW CONTAINS SEVERAL PRECEPTS, OR ONLY ONE?

Objection I. It would seem that the natural law contains not several precepts, but only one. For law is a kind of precept, as was stated above. If therefore there were many precepts of the natural law, it would follow that there are also many natural laws.

Obj. 2. Further, the natural law is consequent upon human nature. But human nature, as a whole, is one, though, as to its parts, it is manifold. Therefore, either there is but one precept of the law of nature because of the unity of nature as a whole, or there are many by reason of the number of parts of human nature. The result would be that even things relating to the inclination of the concupiscible power would belong to the natural law.

Obj. 3. Further, law is something pertaining to reason, as was stated above. Now reason is but one in man. Therefore there is only one precept of the natural law.

On the contrary, The precepts of the natural law in man stand in relation to operable matters as first principles do to matters of demonstration. But there are several first indemonstrable principles. Therefore there are also several precepts of the natural law.

I answer that, As was stated above, the precepts of the natural law are to the practical reason what the first principles of demonstrations are to the speculative reason, because both are self-evident principles. Now a thing is said to be self-evident in two ways: first, in itself; secondly, in relation to us. Any proposition is said to be self-evident in itself, if its predicate is contained in the notion of the subject; even though it may happen that to one who does not know the definition of the subject, such a proposition is not self-evident. For instance, this proposition, *Man is a rational being,* is, in its very nature, self-evident, since he who says *man,* says *a rational being*; and yet to one who does not know what a man is, this proposition is not self-evident. Hence it is that, as Boethius says, certain axioms or propositions are universally self-evident to all; and such are the propositions whose terms are known to all, as, *Every whole is greater than its part,* and, *Things equal to one and the same are equal to one another.* But some propositions are self-evident only to the wise, who understand the meaning of the terms of such propositions. Thus to one who understands that an angel is not a body, it is self-evident that an angel is not circumscriptively in a place. But this is not evident to the unlearned, for they cannot grasp it.

Now a certain order is to be found in those things that are apprehended by men. For that which first falls under apprehension is *being,* the understanding of which is included in all things whatsoever a man apprehends. Therefore the first indemonstrable principle is that *the same thing cannot be affirmed and denied at the same time,* which is based on the notion of *being* and *not-being*: and on this principle all others are based, as is stated in *Metaph.* iv. Now as *being* is the first thing that falls under the apprehension absolutely, so *good* is the first thing that falls under apprehension of the practical reason, which is directed to action (since every agent acts for an end, which has the nature of good). Consequently, the first principle in the practical reason is one founded on the nature of good, viz., that *good is that which all things seek after.* Hence this is the first precept of law, that *good is to be done and promoted, and evil is to be avoided.* All other precepts of the natural law are based upon this; so that all the things which the practical reason naturally apprehends as man's good belong to the precepts of the natural law under the form of things to be done or avoided.

Since, however, good has the nature of an end, and evil, the nature of the contrary, hence it is that all those things to which man has a natural inclination are naturally apprehended by reason as being good, and consequently as objects of pursuit, and their contraries as evil, and objects of avoidance. Therefore, the order of the precepts of the natural law is according to the order of natural inclinations. For there is in man, first of all, an inclination to good in accordance with the nature which he has in common with all substances, inasmuch, namely, as every substance seeks the preservation of its own being, according to its nature; and by reason of this inclination, whatever is a means of preserving human life and of warding off its obstacles, belongs to the natural law. Secondly, there is in man an inclination to things that pertain to him more specially, according to that nature which he has in common with other animals; and in virtue of this inclination, those things are said to belong to the natural law *which nature has taught to all animals,* such as sexual intercourse, the education of offspring and so forth. Thirdly, there is in man an inclination to good according to the nature of his reason, which nature is proper to him. Thus man has a natural inclination to know the truth about God, and to live in society; and in this respect, whatever pertains to this inclination belongs to the natural law: *e.g.,* to shun ignorance, to avoid offending those among whom one has to live, and other such things regarding the above inclination.

Reply Obj. I. All these precepts of the law of nature have the character of one natural law, inasmuch as they flow from one first precept.

Reply Obj. 2. All the inclinations of any parts whatsoever of human nature, *e.g.,* of the concupiscible and irascible parts, in so far as they are ruled by reason, belong to the natural law, and are reduced to one first precept, as was stated above. And thus the precepts of the natural law are many in themselves, but they are based on one common foundation.

Reply Obj. 3. Although reason is one in itself, yet it directs all things regarding man; so that whatever can be ruled by reason is contained under the law of reason.

WHETHER ALL THE ACTS OF THE VIRTUES ARE PRESCRIBED BY THE NATURAL LAW?

Objection I. It would seem that not all the acts of the virtues are prescribed by the natural law. For, as was stated above, it is of the nature of law that it be ordained to the common good. But some acts of the virtues are ordained to the private good of the individual, as is evident especially in regard to acts of temperance. Therefore, not all the acts of the virtues are the subject of natural laws.

Obj. 2. Further, every sin is opposed to some virtuous act. If therefore all the acts of the virtues are prescribed by the natural law, it seems to follow that all sins are against nature; whereas this applies to certain special sins.

Obj. 3. Further, those things which are according to nature are common to all. But the acts of the virtues are not common to all, since a thing is virtuous in one, and vicious in another. Therefore, not all the acts of the virtues are prescribed by the natural law.

On the contrary, Damascene says that *virtures are natural.* Therefore virtuous acts also are subject to the natural law.

I answer that, We may speak of virtuous acts in two ways: first, in so far as they are virtuous; secondly, as such and such acts considered in their proper species. If, then, we are speaking of the acts of the virtues in so far as they are virtuous, thus all virtuous acts belong to the natural law. For it has been stated that to the natural law belongs everything to which man is inclined according to his nature. Now each thing is inclined naturally to an operation that is suitable to it according to its form: *e.g.,* fire is inclined to give heat. Therefore, since the rational soul is the proper form of man, there is in every man a natural inclination to act according to reason; and this is to act according to virtue. Consequently, considered thus, all the acts of the virtues are prescribed by the natural law, since each one's reason naturally dictates to him to act virtuously. But if we speak of virtuous acts, considered in themselves, *i.e.,* in their proper species, thus not all virtuous acts are prescribed by the natural law. For many things are done virtuously, to which nature does not primarily incline, but which, through the inquiry of reason, have been found by men to be conducive to well-living.

Reply Obj. I. Temperance is about the natural concupiscences of food, drink and sexual matters, which are indeed ordained to the common good of nature, just as other matters of law are ordained to the moral common good.

Reply Obj. 2. By human nature we may mean either that which is proper to man, and in this sense all sins, as being against reason, are also against nature, as Damascene states; or we may mean that nature which is common to man and other animals, and in this sense, certain special sins are said to be against nature: *e.g.,* contrary to sexual intercourse, which is natural to all animals, is unisexual lust, which has received the special name of the unnatural crime.

Reply Obj. 3. This argument considers acts in themselves. For it is owing to the various conditions of men that certain acts are virtuous for some, as being proportioned and becoming to them, while they are vicious for others, as not being proportioned to them.

WHETHER THE NATURAL LAW IS THE SAME IN ALL MEN?

Objection 1. It would seem that the natural law is not the same in all. For it is stated in the *Decretals* that *the natural law is that which is contained in the Law and the Gospel.* But this is not common to all men, because, as it is written (*Rom. x.* 16), *all do not obey the Gospel.* Therefore the natural law is not the same in all men.

Obj. 2. Further, *Things which are according to the law are said to be just,* as is stated in *Ethics* v. But it is stated in the same book that nothing is so just for all as not to be subject to change in regard to some men. Therefore even the natural law is not the same in all men.

Obj. 3. Further, as was stated above, to the natural law belongs everything to which a man is inclined according to his nature. Now different men are naturally inclined to different things,—

some to the desire of pleasures, other to the desire of honors, and other men to other things. Therefore, there is not one natural law for all.

On the contrary, Isidore says: *The natural law is common to all nations.*

I answer that, As we have stated above, to the natural law belong those things to which a man is inclined naturally; and among these it is proper to man to be inclined to act according to reason. Now it belongs to the reason to proceed from what is common to what is proper, as is stated in *Physics i.* The speculative reason, however, is differently situated, in this matter, from the practical reason. For, since the speculative reason is concerned chiefly with necessary things, which cannot be otherwise than they are, its proper conclusions, like the universal principles, contain the truth without fail. The practical reason, on the other hand, is concerned with contingent matters, which is the domain of human actions; and, consequently, although there is necessity in the common principles, the more we descend towards the particular, the more frequently we encounter defects. Accordingly, then, in speculative matters truth is the same in all men, both as to principles and as to conclusions; although the truth is not known to all as regards the conclusions, but only as regards the principles which are called *common notions.* But in matters of action, truth or practical rectitude is not the same for all as to what is particular, but only as to the common principles; and where there is the same rectitude in relation to particulars, it is not equally known to all.

It is therefore evident that, as regards the common principles whether of speculative or of practical reason, truth or rectitude is the same for all, and is equally known by all. But as to the proper conclusions of the speculative reason, the truth is the same for all, but it is not equally known to all. Thus, it is true for all that the three angles of a triangle are together equal to two right angles, although it is not known to all. But as to the proper conclusions of the practical reason, neither is the truth or rectitude the same for all, nor where it is the same, is it equally known by all. Thus, it is right and true for all to act according to reason, and from this principle it follows, as a proper conclusion, that goods entrusted to another should be restored to their owner. Now this is true for the majority of cases. But it may happen in a particular case that it would be injurious, and therefore unreasonable, to restore goods held in trust; for instance, if they are claimed for the purpose of fighting against one's country. And this principle will be found to fail the more, according as we descend further towards the particular, for example, if one were to say that goods held in trust should be restored with such and such a guarantee, or in such and such a way; because the greater the number of conditions added, the greater the number of ways in which the principle may fail, so that it be not right to restore or not to restore.

Consequently, we must say that the natural law, as to the first common principles, is the same for all, both as to rectitude and as to knowledge. But as to certain more particular aspects, which are conclusions, as it were, of those common principles, it is the same for all in the majority of cases, both as to rectitude and as to knowledge; and yet in some few cases, it may fail, both as to rectitude, by reason of certain obstacles (just as natures subject to generation and corruption fail in some few cases because of some obstacle), and as to knowledge, since in some the reason is perverted by passion, or evil habit, or an evil disposition of nature. Thus at one time theft, although it is expressly contrary to the natural law, was not considered wrong among the Germans, as Julius Caesar relates.

Reply Obj. 1. The meaning of the sentence quoted is not that whatever is contained in the Law and the Gospel belongs to the natural law, since they contain many things that are above nature; but that whatever belongs to the natural law is fully contained in them. Therefore Gratian, after saying that *the natural law is what is contained in the Law and the Gospel,* adds at once, by way of example, *by which everyone is commanded to do to others as he would be done by.*

Reply Obj. 2. The saying of the Philosopher is to be understood of things that are naturally just, not as common principles, but as conclusions drawn from them, having rectitude in the majority of cases, but failing in a few.

Reply Obj. 3. Just as in man reason rules and commands the other powers, so all the natural inclinations belonging to the other powers must needs be directed according to reason. Therefore it is universally right for all men that all their inclinations should be directed according to reason.

WHETHER THE NATURAL LAW CAN BE CHANGED?

Objection I. It would seem that the natural law can be changed. For on *Ecclus.* xvii. 9 (*He gave* them instructions, and the law of life) the *Gloss* says: *He wished the law of the letter to be written, in order to correct the law of nature.* But that which is corrected is changed. Therefore the natural law can be changed.

Obj. 2. Further, the slaying of the innocent, adultery and theft are against the natural law. But we find these things changed by God: as when God commanded Abraham to slay his innocent son (*Gen.* xxii. 2); and when He ordered the Jews to borrow and purloin the vessels of the Egyptians (*Exod.* xii. 35); and when He commanded Osee to take to himself *a wife of fornications* (*Osee* i. 2). Therefore the natural law can be changed.

Obj. 3. Further, Isidore says that *the possession of all things in common, and universal freedom, are matters of natural law.* But these things are seen to be changed by human laws. Therefore it seems that the natural law is subject to change.

On the contrary, It is said in the *Decretals: The natural law dates from the creation of the rational creature. It does not vary according to time, but remains unchangeable.*

I answer that, A change in the natural law may be understood in two ways. First, by way of addition. In this sense, nothing hinders the natural law from being changed, since many things for the benefit of human life have been added over and above the natural law, both by the divine law and by human laws.

Secondly, a change in the natural law may be understood by way of subtraction, so that what previously was according to the natural law, ceases to be so. In this sense, the natural law is altogether unchangeable in its first principles. But in its secondary principles, which, as we have said, are certain detailed proximate conclusions drawn from the first principles, the natural law is not changed so that what it prescribes be not right in most cases. But it may be changed in some particular cases of rare occurrence, through some special causes hindering the observance of such precepts, as was stated above.

Reply Obj. I. The written law is said to be given for the correction of the natural law, either because it supplies what was wanting to the natural law, or because the natural law was so perverted in the hearts of some men, as to certain matters, that they esteemed those things good which are naturally evil; which perversion stood in need of correction.

Reply Obj. 2. All men alike, both guilty and innocent, die the death of nature; which death of nature is inflicted by the power of God because of original sin, according to *I Kings* ii. 6: *The Lord killeth and maketh alive.* Consequently, by the command of God, death can be inflicted on any man, guilty or innocent, with any injustice whatever.—In like manner, adultery is intercourse with another's wife; who is allotted to him by the law emanating from God. Consequently intercourse with any woman, by the command of God, is neither adultery nor fornication.—The same applies to theft, which is the taking of another's property. For whatever is taken by the command of God, to Whom all things belong, is not taken against the will of its owner, whereas it is in this that theft consists.—Nor is it only in human things that whatever is commanded by God is right; but also in natural things, whatever is done by God is, in some way, natural, as was stated in the First Part.

Reply Obj. 3. A thing is said to belong to the natural law in two ways. First, because nature inclines thereto: *e.g.,* that one should not do harm to another. Secondly, because nature did not bring with it the contrary. Thus, we might say that for man to be naked is of the natural law, because nature did not give him clothes, but art invented them. In this sense, *the possession of all things in common and universal freedom* are said to be of the natural law, because, namely, the distinction of possessions and slavery were not brought in by nature, but devised by human reason for the benefit of human life. Accordingly, the law of nature was not changed in this respect, except by addition ...

HUMAN LAW

WHETHER EVERY HUMAN LAW IS DERIVED FROM THE NATURAL LAW?

Objection I. It would seem that not every human law is derived from the natural law. For the Philosopher says that *the legal just is that which originally was a matter of indifference.*[11] But those things which arise from the natural law are not matters of indifference. Therefore the enactments of human laws are not all derived from the natural law.

Obj. 2. Further, positive law is divided against natural law, as is stated by Isidore and the Philosopher. But those things which flow as conclusions from the common principles of the natural law belong to the natural law, as was stated above. Therefore that which is established by human law is not derived from the natural law.

Obj. 3. Further, the law of nature is the same for all, since the Philosopher says that *the natural just is that which is equally valid everywhere.* If therefore human laws were derived from the natural law, it would follow that they too are the same for all; which is clearly false.

Obj. 4. Further, it is possible to give a reason for things which are derived from the natural law. But *it is not possible to give the reason for all the legal enactments of the lawgivers,* as the Jurist says. Therefore not all human laws are derived from the natural law.

On the contrary, Tully says: *Things which emanated from nature, and were approved by custom, were sanctioned by fear and reverence for the laws.*

I answer that, As Augustine says, *that which is not just seems to be no law at all.* Hence the force of a law depends on the extent of its justice. Now in human affairs a thing is said to be just from being right, according to the rule of reason. But the first rule of reason is the law of nature, as is clear from what has been stated above. Consequently, every human law has just so much of the nature of law as it is derived from the law of nature. But if in any point it departs from the law of nature, it is no longer a law but a perversion of law.

But it must be noted that something may be derived from the natural law in two ways: first, as a conclusion from principles; secondly, by way of a determination of certain common notions. The first way is like to that by which, in the sciences, demonstrated conclusions are drawn from the principles; while the second is likened to that whereby, in the arts, common forms are determined to some particular. Thus, the craftsman needs to determine the common form of a house to the shape of this or that particular house. Some things are therefore derived from the common principles of the natural law by way of conclusions: *e.g.,* that *one must not kill* may be derived as a conclusion from the principle that *one should do harm to no man;* while some are derived therefrom by way of determination: *e.g.,* the law of nature has it that the evil-doer should be punished, but that he be punished in this or that way is a determination of the law of nature.

Accordingly, both modes of derivation are found in the human law. But those things which are derived in the first way are contained in human law, not as emanating therefrom exclusively, but as having some force from the natural law also. But those things which are derived in the second way have no other force than that of hu-

man law.

Reply Obj. 1. The Philosopher is speaking of those enactments which are by way of determination or specification of the precepts of the natural law.

Reply Obj. 2. This argument holds for those things that are derived from the natural law by way of conclusion.

Reply Obj. 3. The common principles of the natural law cannot be applied to all men in the same way because of the great variety of human affairs; and hence arises the diversity of positive laws among various people.

Reply Obj. 4. These words of the Jurist are to be understood as referring to the decisions of rulers in determining particular points of the natural law; and to these determinations the judgment of expert and prudent men is related as to its principles, in so far, namely, as they see at once what is the best thing to decide. Hence the Philosopher says that, in such matters, *we ought to pay as much attention to the undemonstrated sayings and opinions of persons who surpass us in experience, age and prudence, as to their demonstrations . . .*

WHETHER IT BELONGS TO HUMAN LAW TO REPRESS ALL VICES?

Objection 1. It would seem that it belongs to human law to repress all vices. For Isidore says that *laws were made in order that, in fear thereof, man's audacity might be held in check.* But it would not be held in check sufficiently unless all evils were repressed by law. Therefore human law should repress all evils.

Obj. 2. Further, the intention of the lawgiver is to make the citizens virtuous. But a man cannot be virtuous unless he forbear from all kinds of vice. Therefore it belongs to human law to repress all vices.

Obj. 3. Further, human law is derived from the natural law, as was stated above. But all vices are contrary to the law of nature. Therefore human law should repress all vices.

On the contrary, We read in *DeLibero Arbitrio,* i: *It seems to me that the law which is written for the governing of the people rightly permits these things, and that divine providence punishes them. But divine providence punishes nothing but vices. Therefore human law rightly allows some vices, by not repressing them.*

I answer that, As we stated above, law is framed as a rule or measure of human acts. Now a measure should be homogeneous with that which it measures, as is stated in *Metaph.* x, since different things are measured by different measures. Therefore laws imposed on men should also be in keeping with their condition, for, as Isidore says, law should be *possible both according to nature, and according to the customs of the country.* Now the ability or facility of action is due to an interior habit or disposition, since the same thing is not possible to one who has not a virtuous habit, as is possible to one who has. Thus the same thing is not possible to a child as to a full-grown man, and for which reason the law for children is not the same as for adults, since many things are permitted to children, which in an adult are punished by law or at any rate are open to blame. In like manner, many things are permissible to men not perfect in virtue, which would be intolerable in a virtuous man.

Now human law is framed for the multitude of human beings, the majority of whom are not perfect in virtue. Therefore human laws do not forbid all vices, from which the virtuous abstain, but only the more grievous vices, from which it is possible for the majority to abstain; and chiefly those that are injurious to others, without the prohibition of which human society could not be maintained. Thus human law prohibits murder, theft and the like.

Reply Obj. 1. Audacity seems to refer to the assailing of others. Consequently, it belongs to those sins chiefly whereby one's neighbor is injured. These sins are forbidden by human law, as was stated.

Reply Obj. 2. The purpose of human law is to lead men to virtue, not suddenly, but gradually. Therefore it does not lay upon the multitude of imperfect men the burdens of those who are already virtuous, to wit, that they should abstain from all evil. Otherwise these imperfect ones, being unable to bear such precepts, would break out into yet greater evils. As it is written (*Prov.* xxx. 33): *He that violently bloweth his nose, bringeth out blood;* again (*Matt.* ix. 17): if *new wine, that is,* precepts of a perfect life, is *put into old bottles,* that is, into imperfect men, *the bottles break, and the wine runneth out,* that is, the precepts are despised, and those men, from contempt, break out into evils worse still.

Reply Obj. 3. The natural law is a participation in us of the eternal law, while human law falls short of the eternal law. For Augustine says: *The law which is framed for the government of states allows and leaves unpunished many things that are punished by divine providence. Nor, if this law*

does not attempt to do everything, is this a reason why it should be blamed for what it does. Therefore, human law likewise does not prohibit … everything that is forbidden by the natural law.

WHETHER HUMAN LAW BINDS A MAN IN CONSCIENCE?

Objection 1. It would seem that human law does not bind a man in conscience. For an inferior power cannot impose its law on the judgment of a higher power. But the power of man, which frames human law, is beneath the divine power. Therefore human law cannot impose its precept on a divine judgment, such as is the judgment of conscience.

Obj. 2. Further, the judgment of conscience depends chiefly on the commandments of God. But sometimes God's commandments are made void by human laws, according to *Matt.* xv. 6: *You have made void the commandment of God for your tradition.* Therefore human law does not bind a man in conscience.

Obj. 3. Further, human laws often bring loss of character and injury on man, according to *Isa.* x. 1, 2: *Woe to them that make wicked laws, and when they write, write injustice; to oppress the poor in judgment, and do violence to the cause of the humble of My people.* But it is lawful for anyone to avoid oppression and violence. Therefore human laws do not bind man in conscience.

On the contrary, It is written (*I Pet.* ii. 19): *This is thanksworthy, if for conscience … a man endure sorrows, suffering wrongfullly.*

I answer that, Laws framed by man are either just or unjust. If they be just, they have the power of binding in conscience from the eternal law whence they are derived, according to *Prov.* viii. 15: *By Me kings reign, and lawgivers decree just things.* Now laws are said to be just, both from the end (when, namely, they are ordained to the common good), from their author (that is to say, when the law that is made does not exceed the power of the lawgiver), and from their form (when, namely, burdens are laid on the subjects according to an equality of proportion and with a view to the common good). For, since one man is a part of the community, each man, in all that he is and has, belongs to the community; just as a part, in all that it is belongs to the whole. So, too, nature inflicts a loss on the part in order to save the whole; so that for this reason such laws as these, which impose proportionate burdens, are just and binding in conscience, and are legal laws.

On the other hand, laws may be unjust in two ways: first, by being contrary to human good, through being opposed to the things mentioned above:—either in respect of the ends, as when as authority imposes on his subjects burdensome laws, conducive, not to the common good, but rather to his own cupidity or vainglory; or in respect of the author, as when a man makes a law that goes beyond the power committed to him; or in respect of the form, as when burdens are imposed unequally on the community, although with a view to the common good. Such are acts of violence rather than laws, because, as Augustine says, *a law that is not just seems to be no law at all.* Therefore, such laws do not bind in conscience, except perhaps in order to avoid scandal or disturbance, for which cause a man should even yield his right, according to *Matt.* v. 40, 41: *If a man . . . take away thy coat, let go thy cloak also unto him; and whosoever will force thee one mile, go with him other two.*

Secondly, laws may be unjust through being opposed to the divine good. Such are the laws of tyrants inducing to idolatry, or to anything else contrary to the divine law. Laws of this kind must in no way be observed, because, as is stated in *Acts* v. 29, *we ought to obey God rather than men.*

Reply Obj. 1. As the Apostle says (*Rom.* xiii. 1, 2), all human power is from God . . . *therefore he that resisteth the power,* in matters that are within its scope, *resisteth the ordinance of God;* so that he becomes guilty in conscience.

Reply Obj. 2. This argument is true of laws that are contrary to the commandments of God, which is beyond the scope of [human] power. Therefore in such matters human law should not be obeyed.

Reply Obj. 3. This argument is true of a law that inflicts an unjust burden on its subjects. Furthermore, the power that man holds from God does not extend to this. Hence neither in such matters is man bound to obey the law, provided he avoid giving scandal or inflicting a more grievous injury. . . .

ERNEST BARKER

Natural Law and English Positivism*

There were two ways in which the theory of natural law affected American thought and action. The first way was that of destruction. It served as a charge of powder which blasted the connection with Great Britain and cleared the way for the Declaration of Independence. The second way was that of construction. It served as a foundation for the building of new constitutions in the independent colonies from 1776 onwards, and for the addition to those constitutions (or rather to some of them) of an entrance-hall or façade called a declaration of rights. The idea of nature can be revolutionary; but it can also promote and support evolution. It worked in both ways in the American colonies. First it made revolution; and then, when that was done, it fostered evolution. In order to understand its accomplishment, we must pause to consider its principles and to examine its potentialities.

We may begin by noting (for it is a fact of crucial importance) that the English thinkers and lawyers of the eighteenth century have little regard for natural law and natural rights. Indeed, it may be said that natural law is generally repugnant to the genius of English legal thought, generally busied with a "common law" which, however common, is still peculiar, and anyhow is sufficiently actual, sufficiently practical, sufficiently definite, to suit the English temper. To Burke any speech of natural law and natural rights is metaphysics, and not politics. To Blackstone—though he is inconsistent, writing in one way when he theorises on the nature of laws in general, and in another when he comments on the laws of England—the law of nature is not a concern of English courts, and may therefore be treated, for their purposes, as nonexistent. To Bentham, when he wrote the *Fragment on Government* in 1776, the law of nature was "nothing but a

phrase": its natural tendency was "to impel a man, by the force of conscience, to rise up in arms against any law whatever that he happens not to like"; and a far better clue—indeed "the only clue to guide a man through these straits"—was the principle of utility.

The general view of the English thinkers of the period may be resumed in two propositions. In the first place, law is a body of rules which is recognised and enforced in courts of law; and it is simply that body of rules. Since the courts of law recognise and enforce both the judge-made law of tradition and the statute law enacted by parliament, law is these two things, and only these two things. Since, again, the judge-made law of tradition may be regarded as an *opus perfectum* (so, at any rate, Blackstone seems to think), and since law now grows only or mainly by the addition of the statutes enacted by parliament—since, in a word, it is parliament only which now gives new rules to the judges, either by amending the law of the past, both judge-made and parliament-made, or by enacting fresh law *de novo*—parliament must be acknowledged as "the sovereign legislative", maker and author supreme of all law, an uncontrollable authority acting by its own motion, "as essential to the body politic" (so a member of parliament declared) "as the Deity to religion." Such is the gist and sweep of the first of the two propositions. The second proposition is similar, and may be said to be consequential. It is a proposition affirming that constitutional law is not in any way different in kind from the rest of the law, but is merely a part of the general law. It is simply that part of the general law which, as Paley says, "regulates the form of the legislative." Being part of the general law, it is subject, like all other law, to the control of the sovereign legislature—which thus regulates itself and determines its own form. You cannot therefore distinguish between constitutional law and ordinary law, or say that the one is made and amended by one process and the other by another. In origin, and in kind, the two are simply

*From *Traditions of Civility* by Sir Ernest Barker (London: Cambridge University Press, 1948), pp. 310–12. Reprinted by permission of the publisher.

identical; and they are under the same control. You cannot say that a law is unconstitutional; if it is a law—that is to say, if it is made by parliament—it is necessarily constitutional. In a word, the legal is also the constitutional: "the terms *constitutional* and *unconstitutional,*" as Paley writes, "mean the legal and illegal."

In the light of these two propositions we may now turn to natural law, and note how it differs from English law in regard to both. The origin of the idea of natural law may be ascribed to an old and indefeasible movement of the human mind (we may trace it already in the *Antigone* of Sophocles) which impels it towards the notion of an eternal and immutable justice; a justice which human authority expresses, or ought to express— but does not make; a justice which human authority may fail to express—and must pay the penalty for failing to express by the diminution, or even the forfeiture, of its power to command. This justice is conceived as being the higher or ultimate law, proceeding from the nature of the universe from the Being of God and the reason of man. It follows that law—in the sense of the law of the last resort—is somehow above lawmaking. It follows that lawmakers, after all, are somehow under and subject to law.

JOHN AUSTIN

A Positivist Conception of Law*

LECTURE I

The matter of jurisprudence is positive law: law, simply and strictly so called: or law set by political superiors to political inferiors. But positive law (or law, simply and strictly so called) is often confounded with objects to which it is related by *resemblance,* and with objects to which it is related in the way of *analogy:* with objects which are *also* signified, *properly* and *improperly,* by the large and vague expression *law.* To obviate the difficulties springing from that confusion, I begin my projected Course with determining the province of jurisprudence, or with distinguishing the matter of jurisprudence from those various related objects: trying to define the subject of which I intend to treat, before I endeavour to analyse its numerous and complicated parts.

A law, in the most general and comprehensive acceptation in which the term, in its literal meaning, is employed, may be said to be a rule laid down for the guidance of an intelligent being by an intelligent being having power over him. Under this definition are concluded, and without impropriety, several species. It is necessary to define accurately the line of demarcation which separates these species from one another, as much mistiness and intricacy has been infused into the science of jurisprudence by their being confounded or not clearly distinguished. In the comprehensive sense above indicated, or in the largest meaning which it has, without extension by metaphor or analogy, the term *law* embraces the following objects:—Laws set by God to his human creatures, and laws set by men to men.

The whole or a portion of the laws set by God to men is frequently styled the law of nature, or natural law: being, in truth, the only natural law of which it is possible to speak without a metaphor, or without a blending of objects which ought to be distinguished broadly. But, rejecting the appellation Law of Nature as ambiguous and

misleading, I name those laws or rules, as considered collectively or in a mass, the *Divine law,* or the *law of God.*

Laws set by men to men are of two leading or principal classes: classes which are often blended, although they differ extremely; and which, for that reason, should be severed precisely, and opposed distinctly and conspicuously.

Of the laws or rules set by men to men, some are established by *political* superiors, sovereign and subject: by persons exercising supreme and subordinate *government,* in independent nations, or independent political societies. The aggregate of the rules thus established, or some aggregate forming a portion of that aggregate, is the appropriate matter of jurisprudence, general or particular. To the aggregate of the rules thus established, or to some aggregate forming a portion of that aggregate, the term *law,* as used simply and strictly, is exclusively applied. But, as contradistinguished to *natural* law, or to the law of *nature* (meaning, by those expressions, the law of God), the aggregate of the rules, established by political superiors, is frequently styled *positive* law, or law existing *by position.* As contradistinguished to the rules which I style *positive morality,* and on which I shall touch immediately, the aggregate of the rules, established by political superiors, may also be marked commodiously with the name of *positive law.* For the sake, then, of getting a name brief and distinctive at once, and agreeable to frequent usage, I style that aggregate of rules, or any portion of that aggregate, *positive law:* though rules, which are *not* established by political superiors are also *positive,* or exist *by position,* if they be rules or laws, in the proper signification of the term.

Though *some* of the laws or rules, which are set by men to men, are established by political superiors, *others* are *not* established by political superiors, or are *not* established by political superiors, in that capacity or character.

Closely analogous to human laws of this second class, are a set of objects frequently but *im-*

*From *The Province of Jurisprudence Determined,* Selections from Lectures I and VI. First published in 1832.

properly termed *laws,* being rules set and enforced by *mere opinion,* that is, by the opinions or sentiments held or felt by an indeterminate body of men in regard to human conduct. Instances of such a use of the term *law* are the expressions—'The law of honour'; 'The law set by fashion'; and rules of this species constitute much of what is usually termed 'International law.'

The aggregate of human laws properly so called belonging to the second of the classes above mentioned, with the aggregate of objects *improperly* but by *close analogy* termed laws, I place together in a common class, and denote them by the term *positive morality.* The name *morality* severs them from *positive law,* while the epithet *positive* disjoins them from the *law of God.* And to the end of obviating confusion, it is necessary or expedient that they *should* be disjoined from the latter by that distinguishing epithet. For the name *morality* (or *morals*), when standing unqualified or alone, denotes indifferently either of the following objects: namely, positive morality *as it is,* or without regard to its merits; and positive morality *as it would be,* if it conformed to the law of God, and were, therefore, deserving of *approbation.*

Besides the various sorts of rules which are included in the literal acceptation of the term law, and those which are by a close and striking analogy, though improperly, termed laws, there are numerous applications of the term law, which rest upon a slender analogy and are merely metaphorical or figurative. Such is the case when we talk of *laws* observed by the lower animals; of *laws* regulating the growth or decay of vegetables; of *laws* determining the movements of inanimate bodies or masses. For where *intelligence* is not, or where it is too bounded to take the name of *reason,* and, therefore, is too bounded to conceive the purpose of a law, there is not the *will* which law can work on, or which duty can incite or restrain. Yet through these misapplications of a *name,* flagrant as the metaphor is, has the field of jurisprudence and morals been deluged with muddy speculation.

Having suggested the *purpose* of my attempt to determine the province of jurisprudence: to distinguish positive law, the appropriate matter of jurisprudence, from the various objects to which it is related by resemblance, and to which it is related, nearly or remotely, by a strong or slender analogy: I shall now state the essentials of *a law* or *rule* (taken with the largest signification which

can be given to the term *properly*).

Every *law* or *rule* (taken with the largest signification which can be given to the term *properly*) is a *command.* Or, rather, laws or rules, properly so called, are a *species* of commands.

Now, since the term *command* comprises the term *law,* the first is the simpler as well as the larger of the two. But, simple as it is, it admits of explanation. And, since it is the *key* to the sciences of jurisprudence and morals, its meaning should be analysed with precision.

Accordingly, I shall endeavour, in the first instance, to analyse the meaning of *'command':* an analysis which I fear, will task the patience of my hearers, but which they will bear with cheerfulness, or, at least, with resignation, if they consider the difficulty of performing it. The elements of a science are precisely the parts of it which are explained least easily. Terms that are the largest, and, therefore, the simplest of a series, are without equivalent expressions into which we can resolve them *concisely.* And when we endeavour to *define* them, or to translate them into terms which we suppose are better understood, we are forced upon awkward and tedious circumlocutions.

If you express or intimate a wish that I shall do or forbear from some act, and if you will visit me with an evil in case I comply not with your wish, the *expression* or *intimation* of your wish is a *command.* A command is distinguished from other significations of desire, not by the style in which the desire is signified, but by the power and the purpose of the party commanding to inflict an evil or pain in case the desire be disregarded. If you cannot or will not harm me in case I comply not with your wish, the expression of your wish is not a command, although you utter your wish in imperative phrase. If you are able and willing to harm me in case I comply not with your wish, the expression of your wish amounts to a command, although you are prompted by a spirit of courtesy to utter it in the shape of a request. *'Preces* erant, sed *quibus contradici non posset.'* Such is the language of Tacitus, when speaking of a petition by the soldiery to a son and lieutenant of Vespasian.

A command, then, is a signification of desire. But a command is distinguished from other significations of desire by this peculiarity: that the party to whom it is directed is liable to evil from the other, in case he comply not with the desire.

Being liable to evil from you if I comply not with a wish which you signify, I am *bound* or *obliged* by your command, or I lie under a *duty* to obey it. If, in spite of that evil in prospect, I comply not with the wish which you signify, I am said to disobey your command, or to violate the duty which it imposes.

Command and duty are, therefore, correlative terms: the meaning denoted by each being implied or supposed by the other. Or (changing the expression) wherever a duty lies, a command has been signified; and whenever a command is signified, a duty is imposed.

Concisely expressed, the meaning of the correlative expressions is this: He who will inflict an evil in case his desire be disregarded, utters a command by expressing or intimating his desire. He who is liable to the evil in case he disregard the desire, is bound or obliged by the command.

The evil which will probably be incurred in case a command be disobeyed or (to use an equivalent expression) in case a duty be broken, is frequently called a *sanction,* or an *enforcement of obedience.* Or (varying the phrase) the command or the duty is said to be *sanctioned* or *enforced* by the chance of incurring the evil.

Considered as thus abstracted from the command and the duty which it enforces, the evil to be incurred by disobedience is frequently styled a *punishment.* But, as punishments, strictly so called, are only a *class* of sanctions, the term is too narrow to express the meaning adequately.

I observe that Dr. Paley, in his analysis of the term *obligation,* lays much stress upon the *violence* of the motive to compliance. In so far as I can gather a meaning from his loose and inconsistent statement, his meaning appears to be this: that unless the motive to compliance be *violent* or *intense,* the expression or intimation of a wish is not a *command,* nor does the party to whom it is directed lie under a *duty* to regard it.

If he means, by a *violent* motive, a motive operating with certainty, his proposition is manifestly false. The greater the evil to be incurred in case the wish be disregarded, and the greater the chance of incurring it on that same event, the greater, no doubt, is the *chance* that the wish will *not* be disregarded. But no conceivable motive will *certainly* determine to compliance, or no conceivable motive will render obedience inevitable. If Paley's proposition be true, in the sense which I have now ascribed to it, commands and duties are simply impossible. Or, reducing his proposition to absurdity by a consequence as manifestly false, commands and duties are possible, but are never disobeyed or broken.

If he means by a *violent* motive, an evil which inspires fear, his meaning is simply this: that the party bound by a command is bound by the prospect of an evil. For that which is not feared is not apprehended as an evil: or (changing the shape of the expression) is not an evil in prospect.

The truth is, that the magnitude of the eventual evil, and the magnitude of the chance of incurring it, are foreign to the matter in question. The greater the eventual evil, and the greater the chance of incurring it, the greater is the efficacy of the command, and the greater is the strength of the obligation: Or (substituting expressions exactly equivalent), the greater is the *chance* that the command will be obeyed, and that the duty will not be broken. But where there is the smallest chance of incurring the smallest evil, the expression of a wish amounts to a command, and, therefore, imposes a duty. The sanction, if you will, is feeble or insufficient; but still there *is* a sanction, and, therefore, a duty and a command.

By some celebrated writers (by Locke, Bentham, and, I think, Paley), the term *sanction,* or *enforcement of obedience,* is applied to conditional good as well as to conditional evil: to reward as to punishment. But, with all my habitual veneration for the names of Locke and Bentham, I think that this extension of the term is pregnant with confusion and perplexity.

Rewards are, indisputably, *motives* to comply with the wishes of others. But to talk of commands and duties as *sanctioned* or *enforced* by rewards, or to talk of rewards as *obliging* or *constraining* to obedience, is surely a wide departure from the established meaning of the terms.

If *you* expressed a desire that *I* should render a service, and if you proffered a reward as the motive or inducement to render it, *you* would scarcely be said to *command* the service, nor should *I,* in ordinary language, be *obliged* to render it. In ordinary language, *you* would *promise* me a reward, on condition of my rendering the service, whilst *I* might be *incited* or *persuaded* to render it by the hope of obtaining the reward.

Again: If a law hold out a *reward* as an inducement to do some act, an eventual *right* is conferred, and not an *obligation* imposed, upon those who shall act accordingly: The *imperative* part of the law being addressed or directed to the party whom it requires to *render* the reward.

In short, I am determined or inclined to comply with the wish of another, by the fear of disadvantage or evil. I am also determined or inclined to comply with the wish of another, by the hope of advantage or good. But it is only by the chance of incurring *evil,* that I am *bound* or *obliged* to compliance. It is only by conditional *evil,* that duties are *sanctioned* or *enforced.* It is the power and the purpose of inflicting eventual *evil,* and *not* the power and the purpose of imparting eventual *good,* which gives to the expression of a wish the name of a *command.*

If we put *reward* into the import of the term *sanction,* we must engage in a toilsome struggle with the current of ordinary speech; and shall often slide unconsciously, notwithstanding our efforts to the contrary, into the narrower and customary meaning.

It appears, then, from what has been premised, that the ideas or notions comprehended by the term *command* are the following. 1. A wish or desire conceived by a rational being, that another rational being shall do or forbear. 2. An evil to proceed from the former, and to be incurred by the latter, in case the latter comply not with the wish. 3. An expression or intimation of the wish by words or other signs.

It also appears from what has been premised, that *command, duty,* and *sanction* are inseparably connected terms: that each embraces the same ideas as the others, though each denotes those ideas in a peculiar order or series.

'A wish conceived by one, and expressed or intimated to another, with an evil to be inflicted and incurred in case the wish be disregarded,' are signified directly and indirectly by each of the three expressions. Each is the name of the same complex notion.

But when I am talking *directly* of the expression or intimation of the wish, I employ the term *command:* The expression or intimation of the wish being presented *prominently* to my hearer; whilst the evil to be incurred, with the chance of incurring it, are kept (if I may so express myself) in the background of my picture.

When I am talking *directly* of the chance of incurring the evil, or (changing the expression) of the liability or obnoxiousness to the evil, I employ the term *duty,* or the term *obligation:* The liability or obnoxiousness to the evil being put foremost, and the rest of the complex notion being signified implicitly.

When I am talking *immediately* of the evil itself, I employ the term *sanction,* or a term of the like import: The evil to be incurred being signified directly; whilst the obnoxiousness to that evil, with the expression or intimation of the wish, are

indicated indirectly or obliquely.

To those who are familiar with the language of logicians (language unrivalled for brevity, distinctness, and precision), I can express my meaning accurately in a breath:—Each of the three terms *signifies* the same notion; but each *denotes* a different part of that notion, and *connotes* the residue.

Commands are of two species. Some are *laws* or *rules.* The others have not acquired an appropriate name, nor does language afford an expression which will mark them briefly and precisely. I must, therefore, note them as well as I can by the ambiguous and inexpressive name of '*occasional* or *particular* commands'.

The term *laws* or *rules* being not unfrequently applied to occasional or particular commands, it is hardly possible to describe a line of separation which shall consist in every respect with established forms of speech. But the distinction between laws and particular commands may, I think, be stated in the following manner.

By every command, the party to whom it is directed is obliged to do or to forbear.

Now where it obliges *generally* to acts or forbearances of a *class,* a command is a law or rule. But where it obliges to a *specific* act or forbearance, or to acts or forbearances which it determines *specifically* or *individually,* a command is occasional or particular. In other words, a class or description of acts is determined by a law or rule, and acts of that class or description are enjoined or forbidden generally. But where a command is occasional or particular, the act or acts, which the command enjoins or forbids, are assigned or determined by their specific or individual natures as well as by the class or description to which they belong.

The statement which I have given in abstract expressions I will now endeavour to illustrate by apt examples.

If you command your servant to go on a given errand, or *not* to leave your house on a given evening, or to rise at such an hour on such a morning, or to rise at that hour during the next week or month, the command is occasional or particular. For the act or acts enjoined or forbidden are specially determined or assigned.

But if you command him *simply* to rise at that hour, or to rise at that hour *always,* or to rise at that hour *till further orders,* it may be said, with propriety, that you lay down a *rule* for the guidance of your servant's conduct. For no specific act is assigned by the command, but the command obliges him generally to acts of a determined class.

If a regiment be ordered to attack or defend a post, or to quell a riot, or to march from their present quarters, the command is occasional or particular. But an order to exercise daily till further orders shall be given would be called a *general* order, and *might* be called a *rule*.

If Parliament prohibited simply the exportation of corn, either for a given period or indefinitely, it would establish a law or rule: a *kind* or *sort* of acts being determined by the command, and acts of that kind or sort being *generally* forbidden. But an order issued by Parliament to meet an impending scarcity, and stopping the exportation of corn *then shipped and in port,* would not be a law or rule, though issued by the sovereign legislature. The order regarding exclusively a specified quantity of corn, the negative acts or forbearances, enjoined by the command, would be determined specifically or individually by the determinate nature of their subject.

As issued by a sovereign legislature, and as wearing the form of a law, the order which I have now imagined would probably be *called* a law. And hence the difficulty of drawing a distinct boundary between laws and occasional commands.

Again: An act which is not an offence, according to the existing law, moves the sovereign to displeasure: and, though the authors of the act are legally innocent or unoffending, the sovereign commands that they shall be punished. As enjoining a specific punishment in that specific case, and as not enjoining generally acts or forbearances of a class, the order uttered by the sovereign is not a law or rule.

Whether such an order would be *called* a law, seems to depend upon circumstances which are purely immaterial: immaterial, that is, with reference to the present purpose, though material with reference to others. If made by a sovereign assembly deliberately, and with the forms of legislation, it would probably be called a law. If uttered by an absolute monarch, without deliberation or ceremony, it would scarcely be confounded with acts of legislation, and would be styled an arbitrary command. Yet, on either of these suppositions, its nature would be the same. It would not be a law or rule, but an occasional or particular command of the sovereign One or Number.

To conclude with an example which best illustrates the distinction, and which shows the importance of the distinction most conspicuously,

judicial commands are commonly occasional or particular, although the commands which they are calculated to enforce are commonly laws or rules.

For instance, the lawgiver commands that thieves shall be hanged. A specific theft and a specified thief being given, the judge commands that the thief shall be hanged, agreeably to the command of the lawgiver.

Now the lawgiver determines a class or description of acts; prohibits acts of the class generally and indefinitely; and commands, with the like generality, that punishment shall follow transgression. The command of the lawgiver is, therefore, a law or rule. But the command of the judge is occasional or particular. For he orders a specific punishment, as the consequence of a specific offence.

According to the line of separation which I have now attempted to describe, a law and a particular command are distinguished thus:—Acts or forbearances of a *class* are enjoined *generally* by the former. Acts *determined specifically* are enjoined or forbidden by the latter.

A different line of separation has been drawn by Blackstone and others. According to Blackstone and others, a law and a particular command are distinguished in the following manner: —A law obliges *generally* the members of the given community, or a law obliges *generally* persons of a given class. A particular command obliges a *single* person, or persons whom it determines *individually*.

That laws and particular commands are not to be distinguished thus, will appear on a moment's reflection.

For, *first*, commands which oblige generally the members of the given community, or commands which oblige generally persons of given classes, are not always laws or rules.

Thus, in the case already supposed; that in which the sovereign commands that all corn actually shipped for exportation be stopped and detained; the command is obligatory upon the whole community, but as it obliges them only to a set of acts individually assigned, it is not a law. Again, suppose the sovereign to issue an order, enforced by penalties, for a general mourning, on occasion of a public calamity. Now, though it is addressed to the community at large, the order is scarcely a rule, in the usual acceptation of the term. For, though it obliges generally the members of the entire community, it obliges to acts which it assigns specifically, instead of obliging generally to acts or forbearances of a class. If the sovereign commanded that *black* should be the dress of his subjects, his command would amount to a law. But if he commanded them to wear it on a specified occasion, his command would be merely particular.

And, *secondly,* a command which obliges exclusively persons individually determined, may amount, notwithstanding, to a law or a rule.

For example, A father may set a *rule* to his child or children: a guardian, to his ward: a master, to his slave or servant. And certain of God's *laws* were as binding on the first man, as they are binding at this hour on the millions who have sprung from his loins.

Most, indeed, of the laws which are established by political superiors, or most of the laws which are simply and strictly so called, oblige generally the members of the political community, or oblige generally persons of a class. To frame a system of duties for every individual of the community, were simply impossible: and if it were possible, it were utterly useless. Most of the laws established by political superiors are, therefore, *general* in a twofold manner: as enjoining or forbidding generally acts of kinds or sorts; and as binding the whole community, or, at least, whole classes of its members.

But if we suppose that Parliament creates and grants an office, and that Parliament binds the grantee to services of a given description, we suppose a law established by political superiors, and yet exclusively binding a specified or determinate person.

Laws established by political superiors, and exclusively binding specified or determinate persons, are styled, in the language of the Roman jurists, *privilegia.* Though that, indeed, is a name which will hardly denote them distinctly: for, like most of the leading terms in actual systems of law, it is not the name of a definite class of objects, but a heap of heterogeneous objects.[1]

It appears, from what has been premised, that a law, properly so called, may be defined in the following manner.

A law is a command which obliges a person or persons.

But, as contradistinguished or opposed to an occasional or particular command, a law is a command which obliges a person or persons, and obliges *generally* to acts or forbearances of a class.

In language more popular but less distinct and precise, a law is a command which obliges a person or persons to a *course* of conduct.

Laws and other commands are said to proceed from *superiors,* and to bind or oblige *inferiors.* I will, therefore, analyse the meaning of those correlative expressions; and will try to strip them of a certain mystery, by which that simple meaning appears to be obscured.

Superiority is often synonymous with *precedence* or *excellence.* We talk of superiors in rank; of superiors in wealth; of superiors in virtue: comparing certain persons with certain other persons; and meaning that the former precede or excel the latter in rank, in wealth, or in virtue.

But, taken with the meaning wherein I here understand it, the term *superiority* signifies *might:* the power of affecting others with evil or pain, and of forcing them, through fear of that evil, to fashion their conduct to one's wishes.

For example, God is emphatically the *superior* of Man. For his power of affecting us with pain, and of forcing us to comply with his will, is unbounded and resistless.

To a limited extent, the sovereign One or Number is the superior of the subject or citizen: the master, of the slave or servant: the father, of the child.

In short, whoever can *oblige* another to comply with his wishes, is the *superior* of that other, so far as the ability reaches: The party who is obnoxious to the impending evil, being, to that same extent, the *inferior.*

The might or superiority of God, is simple or absolute. But in all or most cases of human superiority, the relation of superior and inferior, and the relation of inferior and superior, are reciprocal. Or (changing the expression) the party who is the superior as viewed from one aspect, is the inferior as viewed from another.

For example, To an indefinite, though limited extent, the monarch is the superior of the governed: his power being commonly sufficient to enforce compliance with his will. But the governed, collectively or in mass, are also the superior of the monarch: who is checked in the abuse of his might by his fear of exciting their anger; and of rousing to active resistance the might which slumbers in the multitude.

A member of a sovereign assembly is the superior of the judge: the judge being bound by the law which proceeds from that sovereign body. But, in his character of citizen or subject, he is the inferior of the judge: the judge being the minister of the law, and armed with the power of enforcing it.

It appears, then, that the term *superiority* (like the terms *duty* and *sanction*) is implied by the term *command*. For superiority is the power of enforcing compliance with a wish: and the expression or intimation of a wish, with the power and the purpose of enforcing it, are the constituent elements of a command.

'That *laws* emanate from *superiors*' is, therefore, an identical proposition. For the meaning which it affects to impart is contained in its subject.

If I mark the peculiar source of a given law, or if I mark the peculiar source of laws of a given class, it is possible that I am saying something which may instruct the hearer. But to affirm of laws universally 'that they flow from *superiors*', or to affirm of laws universally 'that *inferiors* are bound to obey them,' is the merest tautology and trifling.

Like most of the leading terms in the sciences of jurisprudence and morals, the term *laws* is extremely ambiguous. Taken with the largest signification which can be given to the term properly, *laws* are a species of *commands*. But the term is improperly applied to various objects which have nothing of the imperative character: to objects which are *not* commands; and which, therefore, are *not* laws, properly so called.

Accordingly, the proposition 'that laws are commands' must be taken with limitations. Or, rather, we must distinguish the various meanings of the term *laws;* and must restrict the proposition to that class of objects which is embraced by the largest signification that can be given to the term properly.

I have already indicated, and shall hereafter more fully describe, the objects improperly termed laws, which are *not* within the province of jurisprudence (being either rules enforced by opinion and closely analogous to laws properly so called, or being laws so called by a metaphorical application of the term merely). There are other objects improperly termed laws (not being commands) which yet may properly be included within the province of jurisprudence. These I shall endeavour to particularise:—

1. Acts on the part of legislatures to *explain* positive law, can scarcely be called laws, in the proper signification of the term. Working no change in the actual duties of the governed, but simply declaring what those duties *are,* they

properly are acts of *interpretation* by legislative authority. Or, to borrow an expression from the writers on the Roman Law, they are acts of *authentic* interpretation.

But, this notwithstanding, they are frequently styled laws; *declaratory* laws, or declaratory statutes. They must, therefore, be noted as forming an exception to the proposition 'that laws are a species of commands.'

It often, indeed, happens (as I shall show in the proper place), that laws declaratory in name are imperative in effect: Legislative, like judicial interpretation, being frequently deceptive; and establishing new law, under guise of expounding the old.

2. Laws to repeal laws, and to release from existing duties, must also be excepted from the proposition 'that laws are a species of commands.' In so far as they release from duties imposed by existing laws, they are not commands, but revocations of commands. They authorize or permit the parties, to whom the repeal extends, to do or to forbear from acts which they were commanded to forbear from or to do. And, considered with regard to *this,* their immediate or direct purpose, they are often named *permissive laws,* or, more briefly and more properly, *permissions.*

Remotely and indirectly, indeed, permissive laws are often or always imperative. For the parties released from duties are restored to liberties or rights: and duties answering those rights are, therefore, created or revived.

But this is a matter which I shall examine with exactness, when I analyse the expressions 'legal right', 'permission by the sovereign or state', and 'civil or political liberty'.

3. Imperfect laws, or laws of imperfect obligation, must also be excepted from the proposition 'that laws are a species of commands'.

An imperfect law (with the sense wherein the term is used by the Roman jurists) is a law which wants a sanction, and which, therefore, is not binding. A law declaring that certain acts are crimes, but annexing no punishment to the commission of acts of the class, is the simplest and most obvious example.

Though the author of an imperfect law signifies a desire, he manifests no purpose of enforcing compliance with the desire. But where there is not a purpose of enforcing compliance with the desire, the expression of a desire is not a command. Consequently, an imperfect law is not so properly a law, as counsel, or exhortation, addressed by a superior to inferiors.

Examples of imperfect laws are cited by the Roman jurists. But with us in England, laws professedly imperative are always (I believe) perfect or obligatory. Where the English legislature affects to command, the English tribunals not unreasonably presume that the legislature exacts obedience. And, if no specific sanction be annexed to a given law, a sanction is supplied by the courts of justice, agreeably to a general maxim which obtains in cases of the kind.

The imperfect laws, of which I am now speaking, are laws which are imperfect, in the sense of *the Roman jurists:* that is to say, laws which speak the desires of political superiors, but which their authors (by oversight or design) have not provided with sanctions. Many of the writers on *morals,* and on the so called *law of nature,* have annexed a different meaning to the term *imperfect.* Speaking of imperfect obligations, they commonly mean duties which are *not legal:* duties imposed by commands of God, or duties imposed by positive morality, as contradistinguished to duties imposed by positive law. An imperfect obligation, in the sense of the Roman jurists, is exactly equivalent to no obligation at all. For the term *imperfect* denotes simply, that the law wants the sanction appropriate to laws of the kind. An imperfect obligation, in the other meaning of the expression, is a religious or a moral obligation. The term *imperfect* does not denote that the law imposing the duty wants the appropriate sanction. It denotes that the law imposing the duty is *not* a law established by a political superior: that it wants that *perfect,* or that surer or more cogent sanction, which is imparted by the sovereign or state.

I believe that I have now reviewed all the classes of objects, to which the term *laws* is improperly applied. The laws (improperly so called) which I have here lastly enumerated, are (I think) the only laws which are not commands, and which yet may be properly included within the province of jurisprudence. But though these, with the so called laws set by opinion and the objects metaphorically termed laws, are the only laws which *really* are not commands, there are certain laws (properly so called) which may *seem* not imperative. Accordingly, I will subjoin a few remarks upon laws of this dubious character.

1. There are laws, it may be said, which *merely* create *rights:* And, seeing that every command imposes a *duty,* laws of this nature are not imperative.

But, as I have intimated already, and shall show completely hereafter, there are no laws *merely* creating *rights.* There are laws, it is true, which *merely* create *duties:* duties not correlating with correlating rights, and which, therefore may be styled *absolute.* But every law, really conferring a right, imposes expressly or tacitly a *relative* duty, or a duty correlating with the right. If it specify the remedy to be given, in case the right shall be infringed, it imposes the relative duty expressly. If the remedy to be given be not specified, it refers tacitly to pre-existing law, and clothes the right which it purports to create with a remedy provided by that law. Every law, really conferring a right, is, therefore, imperative: as imperative, as if its only purpose were the creation of a duty, or as if the relative duty, which it inevitably imposes, were merely absolute.

The meanings of the term *right,* are various and perplexed; taken with its proper meaning, it comprises ideas which are numerous and complicated; and the searching and extensive analysis, which the term, therefore, requires, would occupy more room than could be given to it in the present lecture. It is not, however, necessary, that the analysis should be performed here. I purpose, in my earlier lectures, to determine the province of jurisprudence; or to distinguish the laws established by political superiors, from the various laws, proper and improper, with which they are frequently confounded. And this I may accomplish exactly enough, without a nice inquiry into the import of the term *right.*

2. According to an opinion which I must notice *incidentally* here, though the subject to which it relates will be treated *directly* hereafter, *customary laws* must be excepted from the proposition 'that laws are a species of command.'

By many of the admirers of customary laws (and, especially, of their German admirers), they are thought to oblige legally (independently of the sovereign or state), *because* the citizens or subjects have observed or kept them. Agreeably to this opinion, they are not the *creatures* of the sovereign or state, although the sovereign or state may abolish them at pleasure. Agreeably to this opinion, they are positive law (or law, strictly so called), inasmuch as they are enforced by the courts of justice: But, that notwithstanding, they exist as *positive law* by the spontaneous adoption of the governed, and not by position or establishment on the part of political superiors. Consequently, customary laws, considered as positive law, are not commands. And, consequently, customary laws, considered as positive law, are not laws or rules properly so called.

An opinion less mysterious, but somewhat allied to this, is not uncommonly held by the adverse party: by the party which is strongly opposed to customary law; and to all law made judicially, or in the way of judicial legislation. According to the latter opinion, all judge-made law, or all judge-made law established by *subject* judges, is purely the creature of the judges by whom it is established immediately. To impute it to the sovereign legislature, or to suppose that it speaks the will of the sovereign legislature, is one of the foolish or knavish *fictions* with which lawyers, in every age and nation, have perplexed and darkened the simplest and clearest truths.

I think it will appear, on a moment's reflection, that each of these opinions is groundless: that customary law is *imperative,* in the proper signification of the term; and that all judge-made law is the creature of the sovereign or state.

At its origin, a custom is a rule of conduct which the governed observe spontaneously, or not in pursuance of a law set by a political superior. The custom is transmuted into positive law, when it is adopted as such by the courts of justice, and when the judicial decisions fashioned upon it are enforced by the power of the state. But before it is adopted by the courts, and clothed with the legal sanction, it is merely a rule of positive morality: a rule generally observed by the citizens or subjects; but deriving the only force, which it can be said to possess, from the general disapprobation falling on those who transgress it.

Now when judges transmute a custom into a legal rule (or make a legal rule not suggested by a custom), the legal rule which they establish is established by the sovereign legislature. A subordinate or subject judge is merely a minister. The portion of the sovereign power which lies at his disposition is merely delegated. The rules which he makes derive their legal force from authority given by the state: an authority which the state may confer expressly, but which it commonly imparts in the way of acquiescence. For, since the state may reverse the rules which he makes, and yet permits him to enforce them by the power of the political community, its sovereign will 'that his rules shall obtain as law' is clearly evinced by its conduct, though not by its express declaration.

The admirers of customary law love to trick out their idol with mysterious and imposing attributes. But to those who can see the difference between positive law and morality, there is nothing of mystery about it. Considered as rules of positive morality, customary laws arise from the consent of the governed, and not from the position or establishment of political superiors. But, considered as moral rules turned into positive laws, customary laws are established by the state: established by the state directly, when the customs are promulgated in its statutes; established by the state circuitously, when the customs are adopted by its tribunals.

The opinion of the party which abhors judge-made laws, springs from their inadequate conception of the nature of commands.

Like other significations of desire, a command is express or tacit. If the desire be signified by *words* (written or spoken), the command is express. If the desire be signified by conduct (or by any signs of desire which are *not* words), the command is tacit.

Now when customs are turned into legal rules by decisions of subject judges, the legal rules which emerge from the customs are *tacit* commands of the sovereign legislature. The state, which is able to abolish, permits its ministers to enforce them: and it, therefore, signifies its pleasure, by that its voluntary acquiescence, 'that they shall serve as a law to the governed.'

My present purpose is merely this: to prove that the positive law styled *customary* (and all positive law made judicially) is established by the state directly or circuitously, and, therefore, is *imperative.* I am far from disputing, that law made judicially (or in the way of improper legislation) and law made by statute (or in the properly legislative manner) are distinguished by weighty differences. I shall inquire, in future lectures, what those differences are; and why subject judges, who are properly ministers of the law, have commonly shared with the sovereign in the business of making it.

I assume, then, that the only laws which are not imperative, and which belong to the subject-matter of jurisprudence, are the following:—1. Declaratory laws, or laws explaining the import of existing positive law. 2. Laws abrogating or repealing existing positive law. 3. Imperfect laws, or laws of imperfect obligation (with the sense wherein the expression is used by the Roman jurists).

But the space occupied in the science by these improper laws is comparatively narrow and insignificant. Accordingly, although I shall take them into account so often as I refer to them directly, I shall throw them out of account on other occasions. Or (changing the expression) I shall limit the term *law* to laws which are imperative, unless I extend it expressly to laws which are not.

LECTURE VI

. . . The superiority which is styled sovereignty, and the independent political society which sovereignty implies, is distinguished from other superiority, and from other society, by the following marks or characters:—1. The *bulk* of the given society are in a *habit* of obedience or submission to a *determinate* and *common* superior: let that common superior be a certain individual person or a certain body or aggregate of individual persons. 2. That certain individual, or that certain body of individuals, is *not* in a habit of obedience to a determinate human superior. Laws (improperly so called) which opinion sets or imposes, may permanently affect the conduct of that certain individual or body. To express or tacit commands of other determinate parties, that certain individual or body may yield occasional submission. But there is no determinate person, or determinate aggregate of persons, to whose commands, express or tacit, that certain individual or body renders habitual obedience.

Or the notions of sovereignty and independent political society may be expressed concisely thus. —If a *determinate* human superior, *not* in a habit of obedience to a like superior, receive *habitual* obedience from the *bulk* of a given society, that determinate superior is sovereign in that society, and the society (including the superior) is a society political and independent.

To that determinate superior, the other members of the society are *subject:* or on that determinate superior, to other members of the society are *dependent.* The position of its other members towards that determinate superior, is *a state of subjection,* or *a state of dependence.* The mutual relation which subsists between that superior and them, may be styled *the relation of sovereign and subject,* or *the relation of sovereignty and subjection.*

Hence it follows, that it is only through an ellipsis, or an abridged form of expression, that the *society* is styled *independent.* The party truly independent (independent, that is to say, of a determinate human superior), is not the society, but the sovereign portion of the society: that certain member of the society, or that certain body of its members, to whose commands, expressed or intimated, the generality or bulk of its members render habitual obedience. Upon that certain person, or certain body of persons, the other members of the society are *dependent:* or to that certain person, or certain body of persons, the other

members of the society are *subject.* By 'an independent political society,' or 'an independent and sovereign nation,' we mean a political society consisting of a sovereign and subjects, as opposed to a political society which is merely subordinate: that is to say, which is merely a limb or member of another political society, and which therefore consists entirely of persons in a state of subjection.

In order that a given society may form a society political and independent, the two distinguishing marks which I have mentioned above must unite. The *generality* of the given society must be in the *habit* of obedience to a *determinate* and *common* superior: whilst that determinate persons, or determinate body of persons must *not* be habitually obedient to a determinate person or body. It is the union of that positive, with this negative mark, which renders that given society (including that certain superior) a society political and independent.

To show that the union of those marks renders a given society a society political and independent, I call your attention to the following positions and examples.

1. In order that a given society may form a society political, the generality or bulk of its members must be in a *habit* of obedience to a determinate and common superior.

In case the generality of its members obey a determinate superior, but the obedience be rare or transient and not habitual or permanent, the relation of sovereignty and subjection is not created thereby between that certain superior and the members of that given society. In other words, that determinate superior and the members of that given society do not become thereby an independent political society. Whether that given society be political and independent or not, it is not an independent political society whereof that certain superior is the sovereign portion.

For example: In 1815 the allied armies occupied France; and so long as the allied armies occupied France, the commands of the allied sovereigns were obeyed by the French government, and, through the French government, by the French people generally. But since the commands and the obedience were comparatively rare and transient, they were not sufficient to constitute the relation of sovereignty and subjection between the allied sovereigns and the members of the invaded nation. In spite of those commands, and in spite of that obedience, the French government was sovereign or independent. Or in spite of those commands, and in spite of that obedience, the French government and its subjects were an independent political society whereof the allied sovereigns were not the sovereign portion.

Now if the French nation, before the obedience to those sovereigns, had been an independent society in a state of nature or anarchy, it would not have been changed by the obedience into a society political. And it would not have been changed by the obedience into a society political, because the obedience was not habitual. For, inasmuch as the obedience was not habitual, it was not changed by the obedience from a society political and independent, into a society political but subordinate. —A given society, therefore, is not a society political, unless the generality of its members be in a *habit* of obedience to a determinate and common superior.

Again: A feeble state holds its independence precariously, or at the will of the powerful states to whose aggressions it is obnoxious. And since it is obnoxious to their aggressions, it and the bulk of its subjects render obedience to commands which they occasionally express or intimate. Such, for instance, is the position of the Saxon government and its subjects in respect of the conspiring sovereigns who form the Holy Alliance. But since the commands and the obedience are comparatively few and rare, they are not sufficient to constitute the relation of sovereignty and subjection between the powerful states and the feeble state with its subjects. In spite of those commands, and in spite of that obedience, the feeble state is sovereign or independent. Or in spite of those commands, and in spite of that obedience, the feeble state and its subjects are an independent political society whereof the powerful states are not the sovereign portion. Although the powerful states are permanently *superior,* and although the feeble state is permanently *inferior,* there is neither a *habit* of command on the part of the former, nor a *habit* of obedience on the part of the latter. Although the latter is unable to defend and maintain its independence, the latter is independent of the former in fact or practice.

From the example now adduced, as from the example adduced before, we may draw the following inference: that a given society is not a society political, unless the generality of its members be in a *habit* of obedience to a determinate and common superior.—By the obedience to the powerful states, the feeble state and its subjects are not changed from an independent, into a sub-

ordinate political society. And they are not changed by the obedience into a subordinate political society, because the obedience is not habitual. Consequently, if they were a natural society (setting that obedience aside), they would not be changed by that obedience into a society political.

2. In order that a given society may form a society political, habitual obedience must be rendered, by the *generality* or *bulk* of its members, to a determinate and *common* superior. In other words, habitual obedience must be rendered, by the *generality* or *bulk* of its members, to *one and the same* determinate person, or determinate body of persons.

Unless habitual obedience be rendered by the *bulk* of its members, and be rendered by the bulk of its members to *one and the same* superior, the given society is either in a state of nature, or is split into two or more independent political societies.

For example: In case a given society be torn by intestine war, and in case the conflicting parties be nearly balanced, the given society is in one of the two positions which I have now supposed.— As there is no common superior to which the bulk of its members render habitual obedience, it is not a political society single or undivided.—If the bulk of each of the parties be in a habit of obedience to its head, the given society is broken into two or more societies, which, perhaps, may be styled independent political societies.—If the bulk of each of the parties be not in that habit of obedience, the given society is simply or absolutely in a state of nature or anarchy. It is either resolved or broken into its individual elements, or into numerous societies of an extremely limited size: of a size so extremely limited, that they could hardly be styled societies independent and *political.* For, as I shall show hereafter, a given independent society would hardly be styled *political,* in case it fell short of a *number* which cannot be fixed with precision, but which may be called considerable, or not extremely minute.

3. In order that a given society may form a society political, the generality or bulk of its members must habitually obey a superior *determinate* as well as common.

On this position I shall not insist here. For I have shown sufficiently in my fifth lecture, that no indeterminate party can command expressly or tacitly, or can receive obedience or submission: that no indeterminate body is capable of corporate conduct, or is capable, as a body, of positive or negative deportment.

4. It appears from what has preceded, that, in order that a given society may form a society political, the bulk of its members must be in a habit of obedience to a certain and common superior. But, in order that the given society may form a society political and independent, that certain superior must *not* be habitually obedient to a determinate human superior.

The given society may form a society political and independent, although that certain superior be habitually affected by laws which opinion sets or imposes. The given society may form a society political and independent, although that certain superior render occasional submission to commands of determinate parties. But the society is not independent, although it may be political, in case that certain superior habitually obey the commands of a certain person or body.

Let us suppose, for example, that a viceroy obeys habitually the author of his delegated powers. And, to render the example complete, let us suppose that the viceroy receives habitual obedience from the generality or bulk of the persons who inhabit his province.—Now though he commands habitually within the limits of his province, and receives habitual obedience from the generality or bulk of its inhabitants, the viceroy is not sovereign within the limits of his province, nor are he and its inhabitants an independent political society. The viceroy, and (through the viceroy) the generality or bulk of its inhabitants, are habitually obedient or submissive to the sovereign of a larger society. He and the inhabitants of his province are therefore in a state of subjection to the sovereign of that larger society. He and the inhabitants of his province are a society political but subordinate, or form a political society which is merely a limb of another.

NOTES

1. Where a *privilegium* merely imposes a duty, it exclusively obliges a determinate person or persons. But where a *privilegium* confers a right, and the right conferred *avails against the world at large,* the law is *privilegium* as viewed from a certain aspect, but is also *a general law* as viewed from another aspect. In respect of the right conferred, the law exclusively regards a determinate person, and, therefore, is *privilegium.* In respect of the duty imposed, and corresponding to the right conferred, the law regards generally the members of the entire community.

This I shall explain particularly at a subsequent point of my Course, when I consider the peculiar nature of so-called *privilegia,* or of so-called *private laws.*

JOHN CHIPMAN GRAY

A Realist Conception of Law*

DEFINITION OF THE LAW

The Law of the State or of any organized body of men is composed of the rules which the courts, that is, the judicial organs of that body, lay down for the determination of legal rights and duties. The difference in this matter between contending schools of Jurisprudence arises largely from not distinguishing between the Law and the Sources of the Law. On the one hand, to affirm the existence of *nicht positivisches Recht,* that is, of Law which the courts do not follow, is declared to be an absurdity; and on the other hand, it is declared to be an absurdity to say that the Law of a great nation means the opinions of half-a-dozen old gentlemen, some of them, conceivably, of very limited intelligence.

The truth is, each party is looking at but one side of the shield. If those half-a-dozen old gentlemen form the highest judicial tribunal of a country, then no rule or principle which they refuse to follow is Law in that country. However desirable, for instance, it may be that a man should be obliged to make gifts which he has promised to make, yet if the courts of a country will not compel him to keep his promise, it is not the Law of that country that promises to make a gift are binding. On the other hand, those six men seek the rules which they follow not in their own whims, but they derive them from sources often of the most general and permanent character, to which they are directed, by the organized body to which they belong, to apply themselves. I believe the definition of Law that I have given to be correct; but let us consider some other definitions of the Law which have prevailed and which still prevail.

Of the many definitions of the Law which have been given at various times and places, some are absolutely meaningless, and in others a spark of truth is distorted by a mist of rhetoric. But there are three theories which have commended themselves to accurate thinkers, which have had and which still have great acceptance, and which deserve examination. In all of them it is denied that the courts are the real authors of the Law, and it is contended that they are merely the mouthpieces which give it expression.

LAW AS THE COMMAND OF THE SOVEREIGN

The *first* of these theories is that Law is made up of the commands of the sovereign. This is Austin's view. "Every Positive Law," he says, "obtaining in any community, is a creature of the Sovereign or State; having been established immediately by the monarch or supreme body, as exercising legislative or judicial functions; or having been established immediately by a subject individual or body, as exercising rights or powers of direct or judicial legislation, which the monarch or supreme body has expressly or tacitly conferred."[1]

In a sense, this is true; the State can restrain its courts from following this or that rule; but it often leaves them free to follow what they think right; and it is certainly a forced expression to say that one commands things to be done, because he has power (which he does not exercise) to forbid their being done.

Mr. A. B., who wants a house, employs an architect, Mr. Y. Z., to build it for him. Mr. Y. Z. puts up a staircase in a certain way; in such a case, nine times out of ten, he puts it up in that way, because he always puts up staircases in that way, or because the books on construction say they ought to be so put up, or because his professional brethren put up their staircases in that fashion, or because he thinks to put it up so would be a good building, or in good taste, or because it costs him less trouble than to put it up in some other way; he seldom thinks whether Mr. A. B. would like it in that way or not; and probably Mr. A. B. never thinks whether it could have been put up in any other fashion. Here it certainly seems

*From *The Nature and Sources of Law,* by John Chipman Gray, New and revised edition copyright 1921 by Roland Gray (New York: Macmillan Co., 1921), pp. 84–112.

strained to speak, as Austin would do, of the staircase as being the "creature" of Mr. A. B.; and yet Mr. A. B. need not have had his staircase put up in that way, and indeed need never have had any staircase or any house at all.

When an agent, servant, or official does acts as to which he has received no express orders from his principal, he may aim, or may be expected to aim, *directly* at the satisfaction of the principal, or he may not. Take an instance of the first,—a cook, in roasting meat or boiling eggs, has, or at any rate the ideal cook is expected to have, *directly* in view the wishes and tastes of her master. On the other hand, when a great painter is employed to cover a church wall with a picture, he is not expected to keep constantly in mind what will please the wardens and vestry; they are not to be in all his thoughts; if they are men of ordinary sense, they will not wish to be; he is to seek his inspiration elsewhere, and the picture when done is not the "creature" of the wardens and vestry; whereas, if the painter had adopted an opposite course, and had bent his whole energies to divining what he thought would please them best, he would have been their "tool," and the picture might not unfairly be described as their creature.

Now it is clear into which of these classes a judge falls. Where he has not received direct commands from the State, he does not consider, he is not expected to consider, *directly* what would please the State; his thoughts are directed to the questions—What have other judges held? What does Ulpian or Lord Coke say about the matter? What decision does *elegantia juris* or sound morals require?

It is often said by hedonistic moralists that, while happiness is the end of human life, it is best attained by not aiming directly at it; so it may be the end of a court, as of any other organ of a body, to carry out the wishes of that body, but it best reaches that object by not directly considering those wishes.

Austin's statement that the Law is entirely made up of commands directly or indirectly imposed by the State is correct, therefore, only on the theory that everything which the State does not forbid its judges to do, and which they in fact do, the State commands, although the judges are not animated by a direct desire to carry out the State's wishes, but by entirely different ones.

"A LAW" AND "THE LAW"

In this connection, the meaning of "Law," when preceded by the indefinite, is to be distinguished from that which it bears when preceded by the definite, article. Austin, indeed, defines the Law as being the aggregate of the rules established by political superiors;[2] and Bentham says, "*Law,* or *the Law,* taken indefinitely, is an abstract and collective term; which, when it means anything, can mean neither more nor less than the sum total of a number of individual laws taken together."[3] But this is not, I think, the ordinary meaning given to "the Law." *A* law ordinarily means a statute passed by the legislature of a State. "*The* Law" is the whole system of rules applied by the courts. The resemblance of the terms suggests the inference that the body of rules applied by the courts is composed wholly of the commands of the State; but to erect this suggestion into a demonstration, and say:—The system administered by the courts is "the Law," "the Law" consists of nothing but an aggregate of single laws, and all single laws are commands of the State,—is not justifiable.

It is to Sir Henry Maine that we owe the distinct pointing out that Austin's theory "is founded on a mere artifice of speech, and that it assumes courts of justice to act in a way and from motives of which they are quite unconscious. . . . Let it be understood that it is quite possible to make the theory fit in with such cases, but the process is a mere straining of language. It is carried on by taking words and propositions altogether out of the sphere of the ideas habitually associated with them."[4]

Austin's theory was a natural reaction against the views which he found in possession of the field. Law had been defined as "the art of what is good and equitable"; "that which reason in such sort defines to be good that it must be done"; "the abstract expression of the general will existing in and for itself"; "the organic whole of the external conditions of the intellectual life."[5] If Austin went too far in considering the Law as always proceeding from the State, he conferred a great benefit on Jurisprudence by bringing out clearly that the Law is at the mercy of the State.

LAW IN THE CONSCIOUSNESS OF THE PEOPLE

The *second* theory on the nature of Law is that the courts, in deciding cases, are, in truth, applying what has previously existed in the common consciousness of the people. Savigny is the ablest expounder of this theory. At the beginning of the *System des heutigen römischen Rechts,* he has set it forth thus: "It is in the common consciousness of the people that the positive law lives, and hence we have to call it *Volksrecht*.... It is the *Volksgeist*, living and working in all the individuals in common, which begets the positive law, so that for the consciousness of each individual there is, not by chance but necessarily, one and the same law.... The form, in which the Law lives in the common consciousness of the people, is not that of abstract rule, but the living intuition of the institute of the Law in its organic connection.... When I say that the exercise of the *Volksrecht* in single cases must be considered as a means to become acquainted with it, an indirect acquaintance must be understood, necessary for those who look at it from the outside, without being themselves members of the community in which the *Volksrecht* has arisen and leads its continuous life. For the members of the community, no such inference from single cases of exercise is necessary, since their knowledge of it is direct and based on intuition."[6]

Savigny is careful to discriminate between the common consciousness of the people and custom: "The foundation of the Law," he says, "has its existence, its reality, in the common consciousness of the people. This existence is invisible. How can we become acquainted with it? We become acquainted with it as it manifests itself in external acts, as it appears in practice, manners, and custom: by the uniformity of a continuous and continuing mode of action, we recognize that the belief of the people is its common root, and not mere chance. Thus, custom is the sign of positive law, not its foundation."[7]

OPINIONS OF JURISTS

Savigny is confronted by a difficulty of the same kind as confronted Austin. The great bulk of the Law as it exists in any community is unknown to its rulers, and it is only by aid of the doctrine that what the sovereign permits he commands, that the Law can be considered as emanating from him; but equally, the great bulk of the Law is unknown to the people; how, then, can it be the product of their "common consciousness"? How can it be that of which they "feel the necessity as law"?

Take a simple instance, one out of thousands. By the law of Massachusetts, a contract by letter is not complete until the answer of acceptance is received.[8] By the law of New York, it is complete when the answer is mailed. Is the common consciousness of the people of Massachusetts different on this point from that of the people of New York? Do the people of Massachusetts feel the necessity of one thing as law, and the people of New York feel the necessity of the precise opposite? In truth, not one in a hundred of the people of either State has the dimmest notion on the matter. If one of them has a notion, it is as likely as not to be contrary to the law of his State.

Savigny meets the difficulty thus: "The Law, originally the common property of the collected people, in consequence of the ramifying relations of real life, is so developed in its details that it can no more be mastered by the people generally. Then a separate class of legal experts is formed which, itself an element of the people, represents the community in this domain of thought. In the special consciousness of this class, the Law is only a continuation and peculiar development of the *Volksrecht*. The last leads, henceforth, a double life. In its fundamental principles it continues to live in the common consciousness of the people; the exact determination and the application to details is the special calling of the class of jurisconsults."[9]

But the notion that the opinions of the jurisconsults are the developed opinions of the people is groundless. In the countries of the English Common Law, where the judges are the jurists whose opinions go to make up the Law, there would be less absurdity in considering them as expressing the opinions of the people; but on the Continent of Europe, in Germany for instance, it is difficult to think of the unofficial and undeterminate class of jurists, past and present, from whose writings so great a part of the Law has been derived, as expressing the opinions of the people. In their reasonings, it is not the opinions of the people of their respective countries, Prussia, or Schwartzburg-Sonderhausen, which guide their judgment. They may bow to the authority of statutes, but in the domain of Law which lies outside of statute, the notions on Law, if they exist and are discoverable, which they are mostly not, of the persons among whom they live, are the last things which they take into account. What they look to are the opinions of foreign lawyers, of Papinian, of Accursius, of Cujacius, or at the *elegantia juris*, or at "juristic necessity."[10]

The jurists set forth the opinions of the people no more and no less than any other specially educated or trained class in a community set forth the opinions of that community, each in its own sphere. They in no other way set forth the *Volksgeist* in the domain of Law than educated physicians set forth the *Volksgeist* in the matter of medicine. It might be very desirable that the conceptions of the *Volksgeist* should be those of the most skilful of the community, but however desirable this might be, it is not the case. The *Volksgeist* carries a piece of sulphur in its waistcoat pocket to keep off rheumatism, and thinks that butchers cannot sit on juries.

Not only is popular opinion apart from professional opinion in Law as in other matters, but it has been at times positively hostile. Those who hold that jurists are the mouthpieces of the popular convictions in matters of law have never been able to deal satisfactorily with the reception of the Roman law in Germany, for that Law was brought in not only without the wishes, but against the wishes, of the great mass of the people.

JUDGES AS DISCOVERERS OF THE LAW

A *third* theory of the Law remains to consider. That theory is to this effect: The rules followed by the courts in deciding questions are not the expression of the State's commands, nor are they the expression of the common consciousness of the people, but, although what the judges rule is the Law, it is putting the cart before the horse to say that the Law is what the judges rule. The Law, indeed, is identical with the rules laid down by the judges, but those rules are laid down by the judges because they are the law, they are not the Law because they are laid down by the judges; or, as the late Mr. James C. Carter puts it, the judges are the discoverers, not the creators, of the Law. And this is the way that judges themselves are apt to speak of their functions.

ONLY WHAT THE JUDGES LAY DOWN IS LAW

This theory concedes that the rules laid down by the judges correctly state the Law, but it denies that it is Law because they state it. Before considering the denial, let us look a moment at the concession. It is a proposition with which I think most Common-Law lawyers would agree. But we ought to be sure that our ideas are not colored by the theories or practice of the particular system of law with which we are familiar. In the Common Law, it is now generally recognized that the judges have had a main part in erecting the Law; that, as it now stands, it is largely based on the opinions of past generations of judges; but in the Civil Law, as we shall see hereafter, this has been true to a very limited extent. In other words, judicial precedents have been the chief material

for building up the Common Law, but this has been far otherwise in the systems of the Continent of Europe. But granting all that is said by the Continental writers on the lack of influence of judicial precedents in their countries to be true, yet, although a past decision may not be a source of Law, a present decision is certainly an expression of what the Law now is. The courts of France to-day may, on the question whether a blank indorsement of a bill of exchange passes title, care little or nothing for the opinions formerly expressed by French judges on the point, but, nevertheless, the opinion of those courts to-day upon the question is the expression of the present Law of France, for it is in accordance with such opinion that the State will compel the inhabitants of France to regulate their conduct. To say that any doctrine which the courts of a country refuse to adopt is Law in that country, is to set up the idol of *nicht positivisches Recht,* and, therefore, it is true, in the Civil as well as in the Common Law, that the rules laid down by the courts of a country state the present Law correctly.

The great gain in its fundamental conceptions which Jurisprudence made during the last century was the recognition of the truth that the Law of a State or other organized body is not an ideal, but something which actually exists. It is not that which is in accordance with religion, or nature, or morality; it is not that which ought to be, but that which is. To fix this definitely in the Jurisprudence of the Common Law, is the feat that Austin accomplished. He may have been wrong in treating the Law of the State as being the command of the sovereign, but he was right in teaching that the rules for conduct laid down by the persons acting as judicial organs of the State are the Law of the State, and that no rules not so laid down are the Law of the State.

The Germans have been singularly inappreciative of Bentham and Austin, and, as so often happens, the arrival at a sound result has been greatly hampered by nomenclature. Ethics is, in Continental thought, divided into two parts, one dealing with matters which can be enforced by external compulsion, and the other with those which cannot. The former of these is called *Rechtslehre.* According to Kant, Moral philosophy *(Metaphysik der Sitten)* is divisible into two parts: (1) the metaphysical principles of Jurisprudence *(Rechtslehre),* and (2) the metaphysical principles of ethics *(Tugendlehre).* [11] Jurisprudence has for its subject-matter the aggregate of all the laws which it is possible to promulgate by external legislation.[12] All duties are either duties of justice *(Rechtspflict)* or duties of virtue *(Tugendpflicht)*. The former are such as *admit* of external legislation; the latter are those for which such legislation is not possible[13]. *Rechtslehre,* that is, deals not only with the rules which the State has actually imposed upon conduct, but also with all conduct which can be *potentially subjected* to such rules; and this has tended to obscure the distinction between the rules which have actually been laid down from those which might have been laid down. But of late years, the Germans, in their own way, have been coming round to Austin's view; and now the abler ones are abjuring all *"nicht positivisches Recht."*[14]

QUESTIONS NOT PREVIOUSLY DECIDED

To come, then, to the question whether the judges discover preëxisting Law, or whether the body of rules that they lay down is not the expression of preëxisting Law, but the Law itself. Let us take a concrete instance: On many matters which have come in question in various jurisdictions, there is no doctrine received *semper, ubique, et ab omnibus.* For instance, Henry Pitt has built a reservoir on his land, and has filled it with water; and, without any negligence on his part, either in the care or construction of his reservoir, it bursts, and the water, pouring forth, floods and damages the land of Pitt's neighbor, Thomas Underhill. Has Underhill a right to recover compensation from Pitt? In England, in the leading case of *Rylands* v. *Fletcher,*[15] it was held that he could recover, and this decision has been followed in some of the United States—for instance, in Massachusetts; but in others, as, I believe, in New Jersey, the contrary is held.[16]

Now, suppose that Pitt's reservoir is in one of the newer States, say Utah, and suppose, further, that the question has never arisen there before; that there is no statute, no decision, no custom on the subject; the court has to decide the case somehow; suppose it should follow *Rylands* v. *Fletcher* and should rule that in such cases the party injured can recover. The State, then, through its judicial organ, backed by the executive power of the State, would be recognizing the rights of persons injured by such accidents, and, therefore, the doctrine of *Rylands* V. *Fletcher* would be undoubtedly the present Law in Utah.

Suppose, again, that a similar state of facts arises in the adjoining State of Nevada, and that there also the question is presented for the first

time, and that there is no statute, decision, or custom on the point; the Nevada court has to decide the case somehow; suppose it should decline to follow *Rylands* v. *Fletcher,* and should rule that in such cases the party injured is without remedy. Here the State of Nevada would refuse to recognize any right in the injured party and, therefore, it would unquestionably be the present Law in Nevada that persons injured by such an accident would have no right to compensation.

Let us now assume that the conditions and habits of life are the same in these two adjoining States; that being so, these contradictory doctrines cannot both conform to an ideal rule of Law, and let us, therefore, assume that an all-wise and all-good intelligence, considering the question, would think that one of these doctrines was right and the other wrong, according to the true standard of morality, whatever that may be. It matters not, for the purposes of the discussion, which of the two doctrines it is, but let us suppose that the intelligence aforesaid would approve *Rylands* v. *Fletcher;* that is, it would think the Law as established in Nevada by the decision of its court did not conform to the eternal principles of right.

The fact that the ideal theory of Law disapproved the Law as established in Nevada would not affect the present existence of that Law. However wrong intellectually or morally it might be, it would be the Law of that State to-day. But what was the Law in Nevada a week before a rule for decision of such questions was adopted by the courts of that State? Three views seem possible: *first,* that the Law was then ideally right, and contrary to the rule now declared and practised on; *second,* that the Law was then the same as is now declared practised; *third,* that there was then no Law on the matter.

The first theory seems untenable on any notion of discovery. A discoverer is a discoverer of that which is,—not of that which is not. The result of such a theory would be that when Underhill received the injury and brought his suit, he had an interest which would be protected by the State, and that it now turns out that he did not have it, —a contradiction in terms.

NO LAW PREVIOUS TO DECISION

We have thus to choose between the theory that the Law was at that time what it now is, and the theory that there was then no law at all on the subject. The latter is certainly the view of reason and common sense alike. There was, at the time in question, *ex hypothesi,* no statute, no precedent, no custom on the subject; of the inhabitants of the State not one out of a hundred had an opinion on the matter or had ever thought of it; of the few, if any, to whom the question had ever occurred, the opinions were, as likely as not, conflicting. To say that on this subject there was really Law existing in Nevada, seems only to show how strong a root legal fictions can strike into our mental processes.

When the element of long time is introduced, the absurdity of the view of Law preëxistent to its declaration is obvious. What was the Law in the time of Richard Coeur de Lion on the liability of a telegraph company to the persons to whom a message was sent? It may be said that though the Law can preëxist its declaration, it is conceded that the Law with regard to a natural force cannot exist before the discovery of the force. Let us take, then, a transaction which might have occurred in the eleventh century: A sale of chattels, a sending to the vendee, his insolvency, and an order by the vendor to the carrier not to deliver. What was the Law on stoppage *in transitu* in the time of William the Conqueror?

The difficulty of believing in preëxisting Law is still greater when there is a change in the decision of the courts. In Massachusetts it was held in 1849, by the Supreme Judicial Court, that if a man hired a horse in Boston on a Sunday to drive to Nahant, and drove instead to Nantasket, the keeper of the livery stable had no right to sue him in trover for the conversion of the horse. But in 1871 this decision was overruled, and the right was given to the stable-keeper.[17] Now, did stable-keepers have such rights, say, in 1845? If they did, then the court in 1849 did not discover the Law. If they did not, then the court in 1871 did not discover the Law.

COURTS MAKE *EX POST FACTO* LAW

And this brings us to the reason why courts and jurists have so struggled to maintain the preëxistence of the Law, why the common run of writers speak of the judges as merely stating the Law, and why Mr. Carter, in an advance towards the truth, says of the judges that they are discoverers of the Law. That reason is the unwillingness to recognize the fact that the courts, with the consent of the State, have been constantly in the practice of applying, in the decision of controversies, rules which were not in existence and were, therefore, not knowable by the parties when the causes of controversy occurred. It is the unwill-

ingness to face the certain fact that courts are constantly making *ex post facto* Law.[18]

The unwillingness is natural, particularly on the part of the courts, who do not desire to call attention to the fact that they are exercising a power which bears so unpopular a name, but it is not reasonable. Practically in its application to actual affairs, for most of the laity, the Law, except for a few crude notions of the equity involved in some of its general principles, is all *ex post facto.* When a man marries, or enters into a partnership, or buys a piece of land, or engages in any other transaction, he has the vaguest possible idea of the Law governing the situation, and with our complicated system of Jurisprudence, it is impossible it should be otherwise. If he delayed to make a contract or do an act until he understood exactly all the legal consequences it involved, the contract would never be made or the act done. Now the Law of which a man has no knowledge is the same to him as if it did not exist.

Again, the function of a judge is not mainly to declare the Law, but to maintain the peace by deciding controversies. Suppose a question comes up which has never been decided,—and such questions are more frequent than persons not lawyers generally suppose,—the judge must decide the case somehow; he will properly wish to decide it not on whim, but on principle, and he lays down some rule which meets acceptance with the courts, and future cases are decided in the same way. That rule is the Law, and yet the rights and duties of the parties were not known and were not knowable by them. That is the way parties are treated and have to be treated by the courts; it is solemn juggling to say that the Law, undiscovered and undiscoverable, and which is finally determined in opposite ways in two communities separated only by an artificial boundary, has existed in both communities from all eternity. I shall recur to this matter when we come to consider the topic of Judicial Precedents.

LAW AND THE NATURAL SCIENCES

It may be said that there are reasons, based on the highest welfare of the human race, why the Law should be so or otherwise, and that it is one of the functions and duties of a judge to investigate those reasons; that he is an investigator as much as, in his sphere, was Sir Isaac Newton; that he may make mistakes, just as Newton did; and yet that truth is largely discovered by his means. But the difference between the judges and Sir Isaac is that a mistake by Sir Isaac in calculating the orbit of the earth would not send it spinning round the sun with an increased velocity; his answer to the problem would be simply wrong; while if the judges, in investigating the reasons on which the Law should be based, come to a wrong result, and give forth a rule which is discordant with the eternal verities, it is none the less Law. The planet can safely neglect Sir Isaac Newton, but the inhabitants thereof have got to obey the assumed pernicious and immoral rules which the courts are laying down, or they will be handed over to the sheriff.

DECISIONS AS CONCLUSIVE EVIDENCE OF THE LAW

It is possible to state the facts in the terms of discovery by use of a device familiar enough in the Common Law. We may say that the rule has always existed, and that the opinions and consequent action of the judges are only conclusive evidence that such is the rule; but this is merely a form of words to hide the truth. Conclusive evidence is not evidence at all; it is something which takes the place of evidence and of the thing to be proved, as well. When we say that men are conclusively presumed to know the Criminal Law, we mean that men are to be punished for certain acts without regard to whether they know them to be against the Law or not; when we say that the registration of a deed is conclusive evidence against all the world, we mean that all the world are [sic] bound by a registered deed whether they know or not of its existence.

Rules of conduct laid down and applied by the courts of a country are coterminous with the Law of that country, and as the first change, so does the latter along with them. Bishop Hoadly has said: "Whoever hath an *absolute authority* to *interpret* any written or spoken laws, it is *he* who is truly the *Law-giver* to all intents and purposes, and not the person who first wrote or spoke them";[19] *a fortiori*, whoever hath an absolute authority not only to interpret the Law, but to say what the Law is, is truly the Law-giver. *Entia non multiplicanda.* There seems to be nothing gained by seeking to discover the sources, purposes, and relations of a mysterious entity called "The Law," and then to say this Law is exactly expressed in the rules by which the courts decide cases. It is better to consider directly the sources, purposes, and relations of the rules themselves, and to call the rules "The Law."

There is a feeling that makes one hesitate to accept the theory that the rules followed by the courts constitute the Law, in that it seems to be approaching the Law from the clinical or therapeutic side; that it is as if one were to define medicine as the science of the rules by which physicians diagnose and treat diseases; but the difference lies in this, that the physicians have not received from the ruler of the world any commission to decide what diseases are, to kill or to cure according to their opinion whether a sickness is mortal; whereas, this is exactly what the judges do with regard to the cases brought before them. If the judges of a country decide that it is Law that a man whose reservoir bursts must pay the damage, Law it is; but all the doctors in town may declare that a man has the yellow fever, and yet he may have only the German measles. If when a board of physicians pronounced that Titius had the colic, *ipso facto* Titius did have the colic, then I conceive the suggested definition of medicine would be unobjectionable.

To sum up. The State exists for the protection and forwarding of human interests, mainly through the medium of rights and duties. If every member of the State knew perfectly his own rights and duties, and the rights and duties of everybody else, the State would need no judicial organs; administrative organs would suffice. But there is no such universal knowledge. To determine, in actual life, what are the rights and duties of the State and of its citizens, the State needs and establishes judicial organs, the judges. To determine rights and duties, the judges settle what facts exist, and also lay down rules according to which they decide legal consequences from facts. Theses rules are the Law.[20]

LAW DISTINGUISHED FROM OTHER RULES FOR CONDUCT

There are one or two other matters connected with the Law which remain for consideration: *First,* The rules which constitute the Law of a community are distinguished from the other rules by which members of the community govern their conduct by the fact that the former are the rules laid down by the courts of the community in accordance with which they make their decrees. Very often these rules are overridden in the mind of a member of a community by other rules, of supposed morality, for instance, or of fashion, as where a man aids a runaway slave, or fights a duel. And again, when the conduct prescribed by the rules of Law is followed, the fact that those rules are laid down by the courts is not always, nor generally, the chief or predominant motive in the minds of those who follow them. The motive that restrains Titius from killing Balbus, or deters John Doe from taking Richard Roe's handkerchief out of his pocket, is not primarily that the one fears being hanged or the other fears being sent to jail; it is some other reason, religious, moral, social, sentimental, or aesthetic, which moves him. There is generally no occasion for the courts to apply their rules, but the fact that the courts will apply them, if necessary, makes them the Law.

Further, when persons do not voluntarily act in accordance with the rules laid down by the courts, but are compelled thereto by force, the force is often applied, not in consequence of a judicial order, but by the persons directly interested in having the rules followed or by some administrative officer not acting under judicial authority,—as when Stiles expels Batkins as a trespasser from his domestic castle, or policeman X. arrests Watkins for being drunk and disorderly. But in all such cases, the rules are Law, because, in the ultimate resort, the judges will apply them in protecting Stiles and the policeman against any violent acts or any prosecution in the courts by the intrusive Batkins or the vagabond Watkins.

THE LAW NOT ALWAYS OBEYED

Second. Suppose, however, that the bulk of the community habitually act contrary to certain rules laid down by the courts,—will you call such rules Law? The question is the same when asked with regard to those rules which the judges lay down in compliance with statutes passed by the legislative organ of the State, as in regard to those which they frame of their own motion. Suppose the Legislature enacts a statute which is so odious to the inhabitants of the State that the bulk of the community disobey it from the start, and yet the judges declare that it has been duly and constitutionally enacted. In countries where statutes can be abrogated by disuse . . . the courts may, after a space of time, declare that such a statute is no longer to be considered binding, but we are here considering a case where the courts lay down a rule in accordance with the statute. Is such a rule Law? I submit that it is most in accordance with usage, and most convenient in practice, to consider the declaration of the courts following the action of the Legislature as being "the Law." If there is a statute recognized by the courts forbidding the sale of wine, and yet wine is sold publicly

and with impunity, it seems best to say, not that the Law allows the sale of wine, but that the Law against the sale of wine is disregarded. And it must be the same, as I have said, whether the declaration of the court is founded on a statute or is derived from any of the other sources of the Law.

In certain of these cases, an unnecessary difficulty arises from misunderstanding what the Law is. Let us take such a case as I have suggested: Suppose that in one of the United States there is a statute providing that whoever sells wine shall be punished by fine or imprisonment, and suppose, further, that the statute is so hated that juries will not convict. This statute, being followed by the courts, is an element of the Law in the State, but it is not the whole of the Law. It is also doubtless Law in the State that no one shall be punished for crime except after being found guilty by a jury. The whole Law must be taken together. We say the Law is that a man selling wine shall be punished, but in truth the Law is, that a man selling wine *and convicted thereof by a jury,* shall be .punished. If there has been no conviction by a jury, one of the elements which the Law declares necessary for the infliction of the punishment does not exist. In old statutes this essential element is often expressed, *e. g.* St. 14 Eliz. *c.* 3: "If any person or persons" shall counterfeit coin, "the offenders therein, being convict according to the laws of this realm of such offenses, shall be imprisoned," etc.

THE LAW CONSISTS OF RULES MADE BY THE STATE

Third. To say that the Law of an organized body is composed of the rules *acted on* by its courts would be too broad. It is only the rules which the courts lay down of their own motion, or which they follow as being prescribed for them by the body of which they are the courts, that, according to the ordinary usage of language, can be called the Law of that body.

Take, for instance, the courts of a political society. They have constantly, in the causes brought before them, to apply general rules of conduct which are yet not laws. Thus, A. and B. may enter into an agreement by which A., for a consideration, expressly or impliedly promises to obey the commands of B. on certain matters; those commands may take the form of general rules; and the existence and validity of such a rule may be brought in question in a court of law. In most cases where the legal relation of master and servant is established there are such general rules. Gladys, who has hired Norah for a housemaid, dismisses her for misconduct; Norah sues for her wages; the alleged misconduct is the not wearing of a cap; the existence of a rule requiring the wearing of a cap, its legality and scope, may all have to be determined by the court, yet Gladys's household ordinance is not the Law of the land.

It may be said that such rules are made by agreement of the parties, and are given by them to the court as rules by which, in controversies between them, it is to decide. But such rules do not always spring from contract. In many communities, the relations between master and slave have formed an important topic in the Law; and at the present day, in all countries, a father has authority to make rules on many subjects for his children, *e. g.* that they are to live in such a place, or are to go to bed at a certain hour. But these rules are no part of the Law, as commonly understood, though they can conceivably come before a court, and the court must pass in its decision upon their existence and validity.

A class of these rules forming no part of the Law of a country, and yet daily discussed and applied by its courts, are the by-laws of corporations. It would seem as if Austin[21] counted the by-laws of corporations as part of the Law of the land existing as Law by the express or tacit authority of the supreme legislature. He makes them a part of the Law in the same manner in which he brings judicial precedents under that head. He considers both by-laws and judicial precedents to be commands of the sovereign, by virtue of the doctrine that what the sovereign permits he commands.

But there seems to be no distinction between the valid regulations of a corporation and the valid regulations of a *paterfamilias*. I should suppose Austin would hardly make these last part of the Law of the land. To do so would amount to saying that all commands not directed to particular acts which the State allows to be made and enforced by any reward or punishment are part of the Law of the land,—a nomenclature, to say the least, very inconvenient, and a wide departure from usage, both popular and professional.

LAWS OF BODIES OTHER THAN THE STATE

It should be borne in mind that rules, although not the Law of the State, may yet be the Law of another organized body. Thus, the by-laws of a private corporation may be part of the Law of the organized body which that corporation is, and yet not be part of the Law of the land. So the rules by which Titius governs his children are no part of the Law of Titius's State, but they may all the same be part of the Law of Titius's family.

Such organizations may be the creatures of the State, as insurance or other business corporations; or they may be independent of the State, as the Roman Catholic Church; or even hostile to it, as a Nihilist club; but that is immaterial on the question whether such an organization has its own Law. It is true that an interest which a member of a club, for instance, may have that another member of the club itself should do or forbear, may be protected by the State by virtue of some rule which the courts of the State follow,—say, with regard to contracts generally,—or may be denied protection by the State by virtue of some rule which the courts of the State follow,—say, with regard to gambling,—but apart from its relations with the State, if any organized body of men has persons or bodies appointed to decide questions, then that body has judges or courts, and if those judges or courts in their determinations follow general rules, then the body has Law and the members of the body may have rights under that Law. Thus, the Roman Catholic Church has courts and a Law, and by virtue of its power in inflicting excommunication and other spiritual censures, it gives rights to itself and its members.[22]

GENERAL ADMINISTRATIVE RULES ARE LAWS

Fourth. One question more presents itself: Are all the general rules for conduct made by the administrative organs of a political (or other) organization to be called "laws"? Or is there a class of such rules to which the name of "laws" is to be denied?

We must bear in mind the distinction to which I have referred between *a* law and *the* Law, as those terms are generally employed. *A* law is a formal general command of the State or other organized body; *the* Law is the body of rules which the courts of that body apply in deciding cases. So there are really two questions: First, is a general order of an administrative organ of an organized body *a* law of that body? Secondly, is such an order a source of *the* Law of that body?

Such an order certainly seems to be a command of the organized body and, therefore, *a* law of that body. To take cases like those which Mr. Frederic Harrison suggests as showing that there are rules of the State which are not laws; a regulation by the proper authority (or, indeed, by the supreme legislature) that all recruits for the army shall be five feet six inches high, or a direction in the infantry tactics that the goose step shall be twenty-eight inches, or an order by the commandant of a fort that a sentry shall always be posted before a certain cellar.[23] Are such regulations, directions, and orders laws? They are unquestionably commands with sanctions; they are of a general and permanent character; they are formally issued by a person empowered by the State to issue them and they are issued on behalf of and for the supposed advantage of the State. They seem to be as much laws of the State as statutes passed by its legislative organ.

Are these regulations and orders sources of the Law? It is hard to imagine any of them which may not be brought before a court for application and whose ultimate sanction is not that the courts will apply to them. Let us take one of Mr. Harrison's instances,—a regulation from the British War Office that no recruit shall be enlisted who is not five feet six inches high. Suppose a recruiting officer musters in a man who is five feet five inches only in height, and pays him the King's shilling; afterwards the officer is sued by the Government for being short in his accounts; among other items he claims to be allowed the shilling paid to the undersized recruit. The court has to consider and apply this regulation and, whatever its effect may be, that effect will be given to it by the court exactly as effect will be given to a statute providing that murderers shall be hanged, or that last wills must have two witnesses.

It is, therefore, on the best consideration I can give the subject, impossible to say that any general rule of conduct laid down by an administrative organ of a political (or other) organized body, and applied, if necessary, by its courts, is not a source of Law.

NOTES

1. *2 Jur.* (4th ed.) 550, 551.
2. *Ibid.,* 89.
3. 1 Benth. *Works,* 148.
4. Maine, *Early Hist. of Inst.* 364, 365.
5. Celsus; Hooker; Hegel; Krause. See Holland, *Jur.* (11th ed.) 20.
6. 1 Savigny, *Heut. röm. Recht,* § 7, pp. 14, 16; § 12, p. 38.
7. *Heut. röm. Recht, § 12, p. 35.*
8. This used to be the law in Massachusetts. I am not so sure that it is now (See 1 Williston, *Contracts,* § 81.)
9. 1 *Heut. röm. Recht,* § 14, p. 45.
10. See an article by Roscoe Pound, in 31 *Harvard Law Rev.* 1047.

11. Kant, *Rechtslehre (Philosophy of Law),* Preface, at beginning. Hastie's trans., p. 43.
12. *Ibid.,* Introduction to Jurisprudence, A. What is Jurisprudence?, at beginning. Hastie trans., p. 43.
13. *Ibid.,* Introduction to Moral Philosophy, III. Hastie trans., p. 24. See John W. Salmon in 11 *Law Quarterly Rev.,* 121, 140, on the law of nature. See also Willoughby, *Nature of the State,* 113, note.
14. See Bergbohm, *Jurisprudenz et Rechtsphilosophie, passim.*
15. L. R. 3 H. L. 330.
16. *Wilson* v. *New Bedford,* 108 Mass. 261; *Marshall* v. *Welwood,* 38 N. J. Law, 339.
17. *Gregg* v. *Wyman,* 4 Cush. 322; *Hall* v. *Corcoran,* 107 Mass. 251.
18. Technically the term *"ex post facto Law"* is confined with us to statutes creating crimes or punishments. I use the term here in its broader sense of retroactive Law.
19. Benjamin Hoadly, Bishop of Bangor, sermon preached before the King, 1717, p. 12.
20. The Law has sometimes been said to be the rules which the courts will follow. See O. W. Holmes's article in 10 *Harvard Law Rev.* 457, *Collected Legal Papers,* 167, and his opinion in *American Banana Co.* v. *United Fruit Co.,* 213 U. S. 347, 356. When this form of expression is used, we must not say in reference to a case like our hypothetical quarrel between Mr. Pitt and Mr. Underhill (preceding) that there was then no law on the subject in Nevada, but we must say that it was not then known what the Law *would* be.
21. *2 Jur.* c. 28 (4th ed.), p. 538.
22. The peculiar history of the Church of England, the compromise between temporal and spiritual interests which was affected at the Reformation, and the fundamental differences among its members as to the grounds on which its frame of government rests, make it difficult to say whether that frame, in the opinion of its judges, has its foundation in the revealed will of God or in Acts of Parliament. The range of opinion within it extends from those dwellers in an ecclesiastical Tooley Street, who regard themselves as the remnant from which all other Christian bodies, Greek, Roman, and Protestant, are parted by schism, to that keeper of the King's conscience who said to a delegation of Presbyterians, "Gentlemen, I am against you and for the Established Church. Not that I like the Established Church a bit better than any other church, but because it *is* established. And whenever you get your damned religion established, I'll be for that too." (Lord Thurlow. See Campbell's *Lives of the Chancellors,* 5th ed., Vol. 7, p. 319.) Sir Robert Phillimore and Lord Westbury were both judges in the English Church, but it is likely that they hold very different theories as to the grounds on which the hierarchy of that Church is based. But it is not easy to believe that a religious organization, whose highest court is the Judicial Committee of His Majesty's Privy Council, was ever revealed directly or impliedly from Heaven; and the true doctrine would seem to be that the English Church owes its constitution to the State, and that although in the opinion of many of its members, it would be sinful in the State to give it any other constitution, yet the judges of the Church must look to Law of the land, the King's Ecclesiastical Law, to determine the nature of the organization whose judges they are, and that so long as the Church is established, it is practically impossible that it should be otherwise. The report of the Hampden Case (11 Queen's Bench Reports, 483 (1948), and full report by R. Jebb, will be found instructive on this point.
23. 30 *Fortnightly Rev.,* 690; *Jurisprudence and the Conflict of Laws,* p. 49.

H. L. A. HART

Positivism and the Separation of Law and Morals*

In this article I shall discuss and attempt to defend a view which Mr. Justice Holmes, among others, held and for which he and they have been much criticized. But I wish first to say why I think that Holmes, whatever the vicissitudes of his American reputation may be, will always remain for Englishmen a heroic figure in jurisprudence. This will be so because he magically combined two qualities: One of them is imaginative power, which English legal thinking has often lacked; the other is clarity, which English legal thinking usually possesses. The English lawyer who turns to read Holmes is made to see that what he had taken to be settled and stable is really always on the move. To make this discovery with Holmes is to be with a guide whose words may leave you unconvinced, sometimes even repelled, but never mystified. Like our own Austin, with whom Holmes shared many ideals and thoughts, Holmes was sometimes clearly wrong; but again like Austin, when this was so he was always wrong clearly. This surely is a sovereign virtue in jurisprudence. Clarity I know is said not to be enough; this may be true, but there are still questions in jurisprudence where the issues are confused because they are discussed in a style which Holmes would have spurned for its obscurity. Perhaps this is inevitable: Jurisprudence trembles so uncertainly on the margin of many subjects that there will always be need for someone, in Bentham's phrase, "to pluck the mask of Mystery" from its face.[1] This is true, to a preeminent degree, of the subject of this article. Contemporary voices tell us we must recognize something obscured by the legal "positivists" whose day is now over: that there is a "point of intersection between law and morals,"[2] or that what *is* and what *ought* to be are somehow indissolubly fused or inseparable,[3] though the positivists denied it. What do these phrases mean? Or rather which of the many things that they *could* mean, *do* they mean? Which of them do "positivists" deny and why is it wrong to do so?

I.

I shall present the subject as part of the history of an idea. At the close of the eighteenth century and the beginning of the nineteenth the most earnest thinkers in England about legal and social problems and the architects of great reforms were the great utilitarians. Two of them, Bentham and Austin, constantly insisted on the need to distinguish, firmly and with the maximum of clarity, law as it is from law as it ought to be. This theme haunts their work, and they condemned the natural-law thinkers precisely because they had blurred this apparently simple but vital distinction. By contrast, at the present time in this country and to a lesser extent in England, this separation between law and morals is held to be superficial and wrong. Some critics have thought that it blinds men to the true nature of law and its roots in social life.[4] Others have thought it not only intellectually misleading but corrupting in practice, at its worst apt to weaken resistance to state tyranny or absolutism,[5] and at its best apt to bring law into disrespect. The nonpejorative name "legal positivism," like most terms which are used as missiles in intellectual battles, has come to stand for a baffling multitude of different sins. One of them is the sin, real or alleged, of insisting, as Austin and Bentham did, on the separation of law as it is and law as it ought to be.

How then has this reversal of the wheel come about? What are the theoretical errors in this distinction? Have the practical consequences of stressing the distinction as Bentham and Austin did been bad? Should we now reject it or keep it? In considering these questions we should recall the social philosophy which went along with the utilitarians' insistence on this distinction. They stood firmly but on their own utilitarian ground for all the principles of liberalism in law and government. No one has ever combined, with such

*From 71 *Harvard Law Review* 593 (1958). Copyright © 1958 by The Harvard Law Review Association. Reprinted by permission of the author and the publisher.

even-minded sanity as the utilitarians, the passion for reform with respect for law together with a due recognition of the need to control the abuse of power even when power is in the hands of reformers. One by one in Bentham's works you can identify the elements of the *Rechtstaat* and all the principles for the defense of which the terminology of natural law has in our day been revived. Here are liberty of speech, and of press, the right of association,[6] the need that laws should be published and made widely known before they are enforced,[7] the need to control administrative agencies,[8] the insistence that there should be no criminal liability without fault,[9] and the importance of the principle of legality, *nulla poena sine lege.*[10] Some, I know, find the political and moral insight of the utilitarians a very simple one, but we should not mistake this simplicity for superficiality nor forget how favorably their simplicities compare with the profundities of other thinkers. Take only one example: Bentham on slavery. He says the question at issue is not whether those who are held as slaves can reason, but simply whether they suffer.[11] Does this not compare well with the discussion of the question in terms of whether or not there are some men whom Nature has fitted only to be the living instruments of others? We owe it to Bentham more than anyone else that we have stopped discussing this and similar questions of social policy in that form.

So Bentham and Austin were not dry analysts fiddling with verbal distinctions while cities burned, but were the vanguard of a movement which laboured with passionate intensity and much success to bring about a better society and better laws. Why then did they insist on the separation of law as it is and law as it ought to be? What did they mean? Let us first see what they said. Austin formulated the doctrine:

The existence of law is one thing; its merit or demerit is another. Whether it be or be not is one enquiry; whether it be or be not conformable to an assumed standard, is a different enquiry. A law, which actually exists, is a law, though we happen to dislike it, or though it vary from the text, by which we regulate our approbation and disapprobation. This truth, when formally announced as an abstract proposition, is so simple and glaring that it seems idle to insist upon it. But simple and glaring as it is, when enunciated in abstract expressions the enumeration of the instances in which it has been forgotten would fill a volume.

Sir William Blackstone, for example, says in his

"Commentaries," that the laws of God are superior in obligation to all other laws; that no human laws should be suffered to contradict them; that human laws are of no validity if contrary to them; and that all valid laws derive their force from that Divine original.

Now, he *may* mean that all human laws ought to conform to the Divine laws. If this be his meaning, I assent to it without hesitation. . . . Perhaps, again, he means that human lawgivers are themselves obliged by the Divine laws to fashion the laws which they impose by that ultimate standard, because if they do not, God will punish them. To this also I entirely assent. . . .

But the meaning of this passage of Blackstone, if it has a meaning, seems rather to be this: that no human law which conflicts with the Divine law is obligatory or binding; in other words, that no human law which conflicts with the Divine law *is a law.* . . .[12]

Austin's protest against blurring the distinction between what law is and what it ought to be is quite general: it is a mistake, whatever our standard of what ought to be, whatever "the text by which we regulate our approbation or disapprobation." His examples, however, are always a confusion between law as it is and law as morality would require it to be. For him, it must be remembered, the fundamental principles of morality were God's commands, to which utility was an "index": besides this there was the actual accepted morality of a social group or "positive" morality.

Bentham insisted on this distinction without characterizing morality by reference to God but only, of course, by reference to the principles of utility. Both thinkers' prime reason for this insistence was to enable men to see steadily the precise issues posed by the existence of morally bad laws, and to understand the specific character of the authority of a legal order. Bentham's general recipe for life under the government of laws was simple: it was *"to obey punctually; to censure freely."*[13] But Bentham was especially aware, as an anxious spectator of the French revolution, that this was not enough: the time might come in any society when the law's commands were so evil that the question of resistance had to be faced, and it was then essential that the issues at stake at this point should neither be oversimplified nor obscured.[14] Yet, this was precisely what the confusion between law and morals had done and Bentham found that the confusion had spread symmetrically in two different directions. On the one hand Bentham had in mind the anarchist who argues thus: "This ought not to be the law, therefore it is not and I am free not merely to censure but to disregard it." On the other hand he thought of the reactionary who argues: "This is the law, therefore it is what it ought to be," and thus stifles criticism at its birth. Both errors, Bentham thought, were to be found in Blackstone: there was his incautious statement that human laws were invalid if contrary to the law of God,[15] and "that spirit of obsequious *quietism* that seems constitutional in our Author" which "will scarce ever let him recognise a difference" between what is and what ought to be.[16] This indeed was for Bentham the occupational disease of lawyers: "[I]n the eyes of lawyers—not to speak of their dupes—that is to say, as yet, the generality of non-lawyers—the *is* and *ought to be* ... were one and indivisible."[17] There are therefore two dangers between which insistence on this distinction will help us to steer: the danger that law and its authority may be dissolved in man's conceptions of what law ought to be and the danger that the existing law may supplant morality as a final test of conduct and so escape criticism.

In view of later criticisms it is also important to distinguish several things that the utilitarians did not mean by insisting on their separation of law and morals. They certainly accepted many of the things that might be called "the intersection of law and morals." First, they never denied that, as a matter of historical fact, the development of legal systems had been powerfully influenced by moral opinion, and, conversely, that moral standards had been profoundly influenced by law, so that the content of many legal rules mirrored moral rules or principles. It is not in fact always easy to trace this historical causal connection, but Bentham was certainly ready to admit its existence; so too Austin spoke of the "frequent coincidence"[18] of positive law and morality and attributed the confusion of what law is with what law ought to be to this very fact.

Secondly, neither Bentham nor his followers denied that by explicit legal provisions moral principles might at different points be brought into a legal system and form part of its rules, or that courts might be legally bound to decide in accordance with what they thought just or best. Bentham indeed recognized, as Austin did not, that even the supreme legislative power might be subjected to legal restraints by a constitution[19] and would not have denied that moral principles, like those of the Fifth Amendment, might form the content of such legal constitutional restraints. Austin differed in thinking that restraints on the supreme legislative power could not have the force of law, but would remain merely political or moral checks;[20] but of course he would have recognized that a statute, for example, might confer a delegated legislative power and restrict the area of its exercise by reference to moral principles.

What both Bentham and Austin were anxious to assert were the following two simple things: first, in the absence of an expressed constitutional or legal provision, it could not follow from the mere fact that a rule violated standards of morality that it was not a rule of law; and, conversely, it could not follow from the mere fact that a rule was morally desirable that it was a rule of law.

The history of this simple doctrine in the nineteenth century is too long and too intricate to trace here. Let me summarize it by saying that after it was propounded to the world by Austin it dominated English jurisprudence and constitutes part of the framework of most of those curiously English and perhaps unsatisfactory productions—the omnibus surveys of the whole field of jurisprudence. A succession of these were published after a full text of Austin's lectures finally appeared in 1863. In each of them the utilitarian separation of law and morals is treated as something that enables lawyers to attain a new clarity. Austin was said by one of his English successors, Amos, "to have delivered the law from the dead body of morality that still clung to it";[21] and even Maine, who was critical of Austin at many points, did not question this part of his doctrine. In the United States men like N. St. John Green,[22] Gray, and Holmes considered that insistence on this distinction had enabled the understanding of law as a means of social control to get off to a fruitful new start; they welcomed it both as self-evident and as illuminating—as a revealing tautology. This distinction is, of course, one of the main themes of Holmes' most famous essay "The Path of the Law,"[23] but the place it had in the estimation of these American writers is best seen in what Gray wrote at the turn of the century in *The Nature and Sources of the Law.* He said:

The great gain in its fundamental conceptions which Jurisprudence made during the last century was the recognition of the truth that the Law of a State ... is not an ideal, but something which actually exists. ... [I]t is not that which ought to be, but that which is. To fix this definitely in the Jurisprudence of the Common Law, is the feat that Austin accomplished.[24]

II.

So much for the doctrine in the heyday of its success. Let us turn now to some of the criticisms. Undoubtedly, when Bentham and Austin insisted on the distinction between law as it is and as it ought to be, they had in mind *particular* laws the meanings of which were clear and so not in dispute, and they were concerned to argue that such laws, even if morally outrageous, were still laws. It is, however, necessary, in considering the criticisms which later developed, to consider more than those criticisms which were directed to this particular point if we are to get at the root of the dissatisfaction felt; we must also take account of the objection that, even if what the utilitarians said on this particular point were true, their insistence on it, in a terminology suggesting a general cleavage between what is and ought to be law, obscured the fact that at other points there is an essential point of contact between the two. So in what follows I shall consider not only criticisms of the particular point which the utilitarians had in mind, but also the claim that an essential connection between law and morals emerges if we examine how laws, the meanings of which are in dispute, are interpreted and applied in concrete cases; and that this connection emerges again if we widen our point of view and ask, not whether every particular rule of law must satisfy a moral minimum in order to be a law, but whether a system of rules which altogether failed to do this could be a legal system.

There is, however, one major initial complexity by which criticism has been much confused. We must remember that the utilitarians combined with their insistence on the separation of law and morals two other equally famous but distinct doctrines. One was the important truth that a purely analytical study of legal concepts, a study of the meaning of the distinctive vocabulary of the law, was as vital to our understanding of the nature of law as historical or sociological studies, though of course it could not supplant them. The other doctrine was the famous imperative theory of law— that law is essentially a command.

These three doctrines constitute the utilitarian tradition in jurisprudence; yet they are distinct doctrines. It is possible to endorse the separation between law and morals and to value analytical inquiries into the meaning of legal concepts and yet think it wrong to conceive of law as essentially a command. One source of great confusion in the criticism of the separation of law and morals was the belief that the falsity of any one of these three

doctrines in the utilitarian tradition showed the other two to be false; what was worse was the failure to see that there were three quite separate doctrines in this tradition. The indiscriminate use of the label "positivism" to designate ambiguously each one of these three separate doctrines (together with some others which the utilitarians never professed) has perhaps confused the issue more than any other single factor.[25] Some of the early American critics of the Austinian doctrine were, however, admirably clear on just this matter. Gray, for example, added at the end of the tribute to Austin, which I have already quoted, the words, "He may have been wrong in treating the Law of the State as being the command of the sovereign"[26] and he touched shrewdly on many points where the command theory is defective. But other critics have been less clearheaded and have thought that the inadequacies of the command theory which gradually came to light were sufficient to demonstrate the falsity of the separation of law and morals.

This was a mistake, but a natural one. To see how natural it was we must look a little more closely at the command idea. The famous theory that law is a command was a part of a wider and more ambitious claim. Austin said that the notion of a command was "the *key* to the sciences of jurisprudence and morals,"[27] and contemporary attempts to elucidate moral judgments in terms of "imperative" or "prescriptive" utterances echo this ambitious claim. But the command theory, viewed as an effort to identify even the quintessence of law, let along the quintessence of morals, seems breathtaking in its simplicity and quite inadequate. There is much, even in the simplest legal system, that is distorted if presented as a command. Yet the utilitarians thought that the essence of a legal system could be conveyed if the notion of a command were supplemented by that of a habit of obedience. The simple scheme was this: What is a command? It is simply an expression by one person of the desire that another person should do or abstain from some action, accompanied by a threat of punishment which is likely to follow disobedience. Commands are laws if two conditions are satisfied: First, they must be general; second, they must be commanded by what (as both Bentham and Austin claimed) exists in every political society whatever its constitutional form, namely, a person or a group of persons who are in receipt of habitual obedience from most of the society but pay no such obedience to others. These persons are its sovereign. Thus law is the command of the uncommanded commanders of society—the creation of the legally untrammelled will of the sovereign who is by definition outside the law.

It is easy to see that this account of a legal system is threadbare. One can also see why it might seem that its inadequacy is due to the omission of some essential connection with morality. The situation which the simple trilogy of command, sanction, and sovereign avails to describe, if you take these notions at all precisely, is like that of a gunman saying to his victim, "Give me your money or your life." The only difference is that in the case of a legal system the gunman says it to a large number of people who are accustomed to the racket and habitually surrender to it. Law surely is not the gunman situation writ large, and legal order is surely not to be thus simply identified with compulsion.

This scheme, despite the points of obvious analogy between a statute and a command, omits some of the most characteristic elements of law. Let me cite a few. It is wrong to think of a legislature (and a fortiori an electorate) with a changing membership, as a group of persons habitually obeyed: this simple idea is suited only to a monarch sufficiently long-lived for a "habit" to grow up. Even if we waive this point, nothing which legislators do makes law unless they comply with fundamental accepted rules specifying the essential lawmaking procedures. This is true even in a system having a simple unitary constitution like the British. These fundamental accepted rules specifying what the legislature must do to legislate are not commands habitually obeyed, nor can they be expressed as habits of obedience to persons. They lie at the root of a legal system, and what is most missing in the utilitarian scheme is an analysis of what it is for a social group and its officials to accept such rules. This notion, not that of a command as Austin claimed, is the "key to the science of jurisprudence," or at least one of the keys.

Again, Austin, in the case of a democracy, looked past the legislators to the electorate as "the sovereign" (or in England as part of it). He thought that in the United States the mass of the electors to the state and federal legislatures were the sovereign whose commands, given by their "agents" in the legislatures, were law. But on this footing the whole notion of the sovereign outside the law being "habitually obeyed" by the "bulk" of the population must go: for in this case the "bulk" obeys the bulk, that is, it obeys itself.

Plainly the general acceptance of the authority of a lawmaking procedure, irrespective of the changing individuals who operate it from time to time, can be only distorted by an analysis in terms of mass habitual obedience to certain persons who are by definition outside the law, just as the cognate but much simpler phenomenon of the general social acceptance of a rule, say of taking off the hat when entering a church, would be distorted if represented as habitual obedience by the mass to specific persons.

Other critics dimly sensed a further and more important defect in the command theory, yet blurred the edge of an important criticism by assuming that the defect was due to the failure to insist upon some important connection between law and morals. This more radical defect is as follows. The picture that the command theory draws of life under law is essentially a simple relationship of the commander to the commanded, of superior to inferior, of top to bottom; the relationship is vertical between the commanders or authors of the law conceived of as essentially outside the law and those who are commanded and subject to the law. In this picture no place, or only an accidental or subordinate place, is afforded for a distinction between types of legal rules which are in fact radically different. Some laws require men to act in certain ways or to abstain from acting whether they wish to or not. The criminal law consists largely of rules of this sort: like commands they are simply "obeyed" or "disobeyed." But other legal rules are presented to society in quite different ways and have quite different functions. They provide facilities more or less elaborate for individuals to create structures of rights and duties for the conduct of life within the coercive framework of the law. Such are the rules enabling individuals to make contracts, wills, and trusts, and generally to mould their legal relations with others. Such rules, unlike the criminal law, are not factors designed to obstruct wishes and choices of an antisocial sort. On the contrary, these rules provide facilities for the realization of wishes and choices. They do not say (like commands) "do this whether you wish it or not," but rather "if you wish to do this, here is the way to do it." Under these rules we exercise powers, make claims, and assert rights. These phrases mark off characteristic features of laws that confer rights and powers; they are laws which are, so to speak, put at the disposition of individuals in a way in which the criminal law is not. Much ingenuity has gone into the task of "reducing" laws of this second sort to some complex variant of laws of the first sort. The effort to show that laws conferring rights are "really" only conditional stipulations of sanctions to be exacted from the person ultimately under a legal duty characterizes much of Kelsen's work.[28] Yet to urge this is really just to exhibit dogmatic determination to suppress one aspect of the legal system in order to maintain the theory that the stipulation of a sanction, like Austin's command, represents the quintessence of law. One might as well urge that the rules of baseball were "really" only complex conditional directions to the scorer and that this showed their real or "essential" nature.

One of the first jurists in England to break with the Austinian tradition, Salmond, complained that the analysis in terms of commands left the notion of a right unprovided with a place.[29] But he confused the point. He argued first, and correctly, that if laws are merely commands it is inexplicable that we should have come to speak of legal rights and powers as conferred or arising under them, but then wrongly concluded that the rules of a legal system must necessarily be connected with moral rules or principles of justice and that only on this footing could the phenomenon of legal rights be explained. Otherwise, Salmond thought, we would have to say that a mere "verbal coincidence" connects the concepts of legal and moral right. Similarly, continental critics of the utilitarians, always alive to the complexity of the notion of a subjective right, insisted that the command theory gave it no place. Hägerström insisted that if laws were merely commands the notion of an individual's right was really inexplicable, for commands are, as he said, something which we either obey or we do not obey; they do not confer rights.[30] But he, too, concluded that moral, or, as he put it, commonsense, notions of justice must therefore be necessarily involved in the analysis of any legal structure elaborate enough to confer rights.[31]

Yet, surely these arguments are confused. Rules that confer rights, though distinct from commands, need not be moral rules or coincide with them. Rights, after all, exist under the rules of ceremonies, games, and in many other spheres regulated by rules which are irrelevant to the question of justice or what the law ought to be. Nor need rules which confer rights be just or morally good rules. The rights of a master over his slaves show us that. "Their merit or demerit," as Austin termed it, depends on how rights are distributed in society and over whom or what they are exercised. These critics indeed revealed the inadequacy of the simple notions of command and habit for the analysis of law; at many points it is apparent that the social acceptance of a rule or standard of authority (even if it is motivated only by fear or superstition or rests on inertia) must be brought into the analysis and cannot itself be reduced to the two simple terms. Yet nothing in this showed the utilitarian insistence on the distinction between the existence of law and its "merits" to be wrong.

III.

I now turn to a distinctively American criticism of the separation of the law that is from the law that ought to be. It emerged from the critical study of the judicial process with which American jurisprudence has been on the whole so beneficially occupied. The most skeptical of these critics—the loosely named "Realists" of the 1930s—perhaps too naïvely accepted the conceptual framework of the natural sciences as adequate for the characterization of law and for the analysis of rule-guided action of which a living system of law at least partly consists. But they opened men's eyes to what actually goes on when courts decide cases, and the contrast they drew between the actual facts of judicial decision and the traditional terminology for describing it as if it were a wholly logical operation was usually illuminating; for in spite of some exaggeration the "Realists" made us acutely conscious of one cardinal feature of human language and human thought, emphasis on which is vital not only for the understanding of law but in areas of philosophy far beyond the confines of jurisprudence. The insight of this school may be presented in the following example. A legal rule forbids you to take a vehicle into the public park. Plainly this forbids an automobile, but what about bicycles, roller skates, toy automobiles? What about airplanes? Are these, as we say, to be called "vehicles" for the purpose of the rule or not? If we are to communicate with each other at all, and if, as in the most elementary form of law, we are to express our intentions that a certain type of behavior be regulated by rules, then the general words we use—like "vehicle" in the case I consider—must have some standard instance in which no doubts are felt about its application. There must be a core of settled meaning, but there will be, as well, a penumbra of debatable cases in which words are neither obviously applicable nor obviously ruled out. These cases will each have some features in common with the standard case; they will lack others or be accompanied by features not present in the standard case. Human invention and natural processes continually throw up such variants on the familiar, and if we are to say that these ranges of facts do or do not fall under existing rules, then the classifier must make a decision which is not dictated to him, for the facts and phenomena to which we fit our words and apply our rules are as it were *dumb*. The toy automobile cannot speak up and say, "I am a vehicle for the purpose of this legal rule," nor can the roller skates chorus, "We are not a vehicle." Fact situations do not await us neatly labeled, creased, and folded, nor is their legal classification written on them to be simply read off by the judge. Instead, in applying legal rules, someone must take the responsibility of deciding that words do or do not cover some case in hand with all the practical consequences involved in this decision.

We may call the problems which arise outside the hard core of standard instances or settled meaning "problems of the penumbra"; they are always with us whether in relation to such trivial things as the regulation of the use of the public park or in relation to the multidimensional generalities of a constitution. If a penumbra of uncertainty must surround all legal rules, then their application to specific cases in the penumbral area cannot be a matter of logical deduction, and so deductive reasoning, which for generations has been cherished as the very perfection of human reasoning, cannot serve as a model for what judges, or indeed anyone, should do in bringing particular cases under general rules. In this area men cannot live by deduction alone. And it follows that if legal arguments and legal decisions of penumbral questions are to be rational, their rationality must lie in something other than a logical relation to premises. So if it is rational or "sound" to argue and to decide that for the purposes of this rule an airplane is not a vehicle, this argument must be sound or rational without being logically conclusive. What is it then that makes such decisions correct or at least better than alternative decisions? Again, it seems true to say that the criterion which makes a decision sound in such cases is some concept of what the law ought to be; it is easy to slide from that into saying that it must be a moral judgment about what law ought to be. So here we touch upon a point of necessary "intersection between law and morals" which demonstrates the falsity

or, at any rate, the misleading character of the utilitarians' emphatic insistence on the separation of law as it is and ought to be. Surely, Bentham and Austin could only have written as they did because they misunderstood or neglected this aspect of the judicial process, because they ignored the problems of the penumbra.

The misconception of the judicial process which ignores the problems of the penumbra and which views the process as consisting preeminently in deductive reasoning is often stigmatized as the error of "formalism" or "literalism." My question now is, how and to what extent does the demonstration of this error show the utilitarian distinction to be wrong or misleading? Here there are many issues which have been confused, but I can only disentangle some. The charge of formalism has been leveled both at the "positivist" legal theorist and at the courts, but of course it must be a very different charge in each case. Leveled at the legal theorist, the charge means that he has made a theoretical mistake about the character of legal decision; he has thought of the reasoning involved as consisting in deduction from premises in which the judges' practical choices or decision play no part. It would be easy to show that Austin was guiltless of this error; only an entire misconception of what analytical jurisprudence is and why he thought it important has led to the view that he, or any other analyst, believed that the law was a closed logical system in which judges deduced their decisions from premises.[32] On the contrary, he was very much alive to the character of language, to its vagueness or open character;[33] he thought that in the penumbral situation judges must necessarily legislate,[34] and, in accents that sometimes recall those of the late Judge Jerome Frank, he berated the common-law judges for legislating feebly and timidly and for blindly relying on real or fancied analogies with past cases instead of adapting their decisions to the growing needs of society as revealed by the moral standard of utility.[35] The villains of this piece, responsible for the conception of the judge as an automaton, are not the utilitarian thinkers. The responsibility, if it is to be laid at the door of any theorist, is with thinkers like Blackstone and, at an earlier stage, Montesquieu. The root of this evil is preoccupation with the separation of powers and Blackstone's "childish fiction" (as Austin termed it) that judges only "find," never "make," law.

But we are concerned with "formalism" as a vice not of jurists but of judges. What precisely is it for a judge to commit this error, to be a "formalist," "automatic," a "slot machine"? Curiously enough the literature which is full of the denunciation of these vices never makes this clear in concrete terms; instead we have only descriptions which cannot mean what they appear to say: it is said that in the formalist error courts make an excessive use of logic, take a thing to "a dryly logical extreme,"[36] or make an excessive use of analytical methods. But just how in being a formalist does a judge make an excessive use of logic? It is clear that the essence of his error is to give some general term an interpretation which is blind to social values and consequences (or which is in some other way stupid or perhaps merely disliked by critics). But logic does not prescribe interpretation of terms; it dictates neither the stupid nor intelligent interpretation of any expression. Logic only tells you hypothetically that *if* you give a certain term a certain interpretation then a certain conclusion follows. Logic is silent on how to classify particulars—and this is the heart of a judicial decision. So this reference to logic and to logical extremes is a misnomer for something else, which must be this. A judge has to apply a rule to a concrete case—perhaps the rule that one may not take a stolen "vehicle" across state lines, and in this case an airplane has been taken.[37] He either does not see or pretends not to see that the general terms of this rule are susceptible of different interpretations and that he has a choice left open uncontrolled by linguistic conventions. He ignores, or is blind to, the fact that he is in the area of the penumbra and is not dealing with a standard case. Instead of choosing in the light of social aims, the judge fixes the meaning in a different way. He either takes the meaning that the word most obviously suggests in its ordinary nonlegal context to ordinary men, or one which the word has been given in some other legal context, or, still worse, he thinks of a standard case and then arbitrarily identifies certain features in it—for example, in the case of a vehicle, (1) normally used on land, (2) capable of carrying a human person, (3) capable of being self-propelled—and treats these three as always necessary and always sufficient conditions for the use in all contexts of the word "vehicle," irrespective of the social consequences of giving it this interpretation. This choice, not "logic," would force the judge to include a toy motor car (if electrically propelled) and to exclude bicycles and the airplane. In all this there is possibly great stupidity but no more "logic," and no less, than in cases in which the interpretation given to a

general term and the consequent application of some general rule to a particular case is consciously controlled by some identified social aim.

Decisions made in a fashion as blind as this would scarcely deserve the name of decisions; we might as well toss a penny in applying a rule of law. But it is at least doubtful whether any judicial decisions (even in England) have been quite as automatic as this. Rather either the interpretations stigmatized as automatic have resulted from the conviction that it is fairer in a criminal statute to take a meaning which would jump to the mind of the ordinary man at the cost even of defeating other values, and this itself is a social policy (though possibly a bad one); or much more frequently, what is stigmatized as "mechanical" and "automatic" is a determined choice made indeed in the light of a social aim but of a conservative social aim. Certainly many of the Supreme Court decisions at the turn of the century which have been so stigmatized[38] represent clear choices in the penumbral area to give effect to a policy of a conservative type. This is peculiarly true of Mr. Justice Peckham's opinions defining the spheres of police power and due process.[39]

But how does the wrongness of deciding cases in an automatic and mechanical way and the rightness of deciding cases by reference to social purposes show that the utilitarian insistence on the distinction between what the law is and what it ought to be is wrong? I take it that no one who wished to use these vices of formalism as proof that the distinction between what is and what ought to be is mistaken would deny that the decisions stigmatized as automatic are law; nor would he deny that the system in which such automatic decisions are made is a legal system. Surely he would say that they are law, but they are bad law, they ought not to be law. But this would be to use the distinction, not to refute it; and of course both Bentham and Austin used it to attack judges for failing to decide penumbral cases in accordance with the growing needs of society.

Clearly, if the demonstration of the errors of formalism is to show the utilitarian distinction to be wrong, the point must be drastically restated. The point must be not merely that a judicial decision to be rational must be made in the light of some conception of what ought to be, but that the aims, the social policies and purposes to which judges should appeal if their decisions are to be rational, are themselves to be considered as part of the law in some suitably wide sense of "law" which is held to be more illuminating than that used by the utilitarians. This restatement of the point would have the following consequence: Instead of saying that the recurrence of penumbral questions shows us that legal rules are essentially incomplete, and that, when they fail to determine decisions, judges must legislate and so exercise a creative choice between alternatives, we shall say that the social policies which guide the judges' choice are in a sense there for them to discover; the judges are only "drawing out" of the rule what, if it is properly understood, is "latent" within it. To call this judicial legislation is to obscure some essential continuity between the clear cases of the rule's application and the penumbral decisions. I shall question later whether this way of talking is salutory, but I wish at this time to point out something obvious, but likely, if not stated, to tangle the issues. It does not follow that, because the opposite of a decision reached blindly in the formalist or literalist manner is a decision intelligently reached by reference to some conception of what ought to be, we have a junction of law and morals. We must, I think, beware of thinking in a too simple-minded fashion about the word "ought." This is not because there is no distinction to be made between law as it is and ought to be. Far from it. It is because the distinction should be between what is and what from many different points of view ought to be. The word "ought" merely reflects the presence of some standard of criticism; one of these standards is a moral standard but not all standards are moral. We say to our neighbour, "You ought not to lie," and that may certainly be a moral judgment, but we should remember that the baffled poisoner may say, "I ought to have given her a second dose." The point here is that intelligent decisions which we oppose to mechanical or formal decisions are not necessarily identical with decisions defensible on moral grounds. We may say of many a decision: "Yes, that is right; that is as it ought to be," and we may mean only that some accepted purpose or policy has been thereby advanced; we may not mean to endorse the moral propriety of the policy or the decision. So the contrast between the mechanical decision and the intelligent one can be reproduced inside a system dedicated to the pursuit of the most evil aims. It does not exist as a contrast to be found only in legal systems which, like our own, widely recognize principles of justice and moral claims of individuals.

An example may make this point plainer. With us the task of sentencing in criminal cases is the one that seems most obviously to demand from the judge the exercise of moral judgment. Here the factors to be weighed seem clearly to be moral factors: society must not be exposed to wanton attack; too much misery must not be inflicted on either the victim or his dependents; efforts must be made to enable him to lead a better life and regain a position in the society whose laws he has violated. To a judge striking the balance among these claims, with all the discretion and perplexities involved, his task seems as plain an example of the exercise of moral judgment as could be; and it seems to be the polar opposite of some mechanical application of a tariff of penalties fixing a sentence careless of the moral claims which in our system have to be weighed. So here intelligent and rational decision is guided however uncertainly by moral aims. But we have only to vary the example to see that this need not necessarily be so and surely, if it need not necessarily be so, the utilitarian point remains unshaken. Under the Nazi regime men were sentenced by courts for criticism of the regime. Here the choice of sentence might be guided exclusively by consideration of what was needed to maintain the state's tyranny effectively. What sentence would both terrorize the public at large and keep the friends and family of the prisoner in suspense so that both hope and fear would cooperate as factors making for subservience? The prisoner of such a system would be regarded simply as an object to be used in pursuit of these aims. Yet, in contrast with a mechanical decision, decision on these grounds would be intelligent and purposive, and from one point of view the decision would be as it ought to be. Of course, I am not unaware that a whole philosophical tradition has sought to demonstrate the fact that we cannot correctly call decisions or behavior truly rational unless they are in conformity with moral aims and principles. But the example I have used seems to me to serve at least as a warning that we cannot use the errors of formalism as something which per se demonstrates the falsity of the utilitarian insistence on the distinction between law as it is and law as *morally* it ought to be.

We can now return to the main point. It is true that the intelligent decision of penumbral questions is one made not mechanically but in the light of aims, purposes, and policies, though not necessarily in the light of anything we would call moral principles, is it wise to express this important fact by saying that the firm utilitarian distinction between what the law is and what it ought to be should be dropped? Perhaps the claim that it is wise cannot be theoretically refuted for it is, in effect, an *invitation* to revise our conception of what a legal rule is. We are invited to include in the "rule" the various aims and policies in the light of which its penumbral cases are decided on the ground that these aims have, because of their importance, as much right to be called law as the core of legal rules whose meaning is settled. But though an invitation cannot be refuted, it may be refused and I would proffer two reasons for refusing this invitation. First, everything we have learned about the judicial process can be expressed in other less mysterious ways. We can say laws are incurably incomplete and we must decide the penumbral cases rationally by reference to social aims. I think Holmes, who had such a vivid appreciation of the fact that "general propositions do not decide concrete cases," would have put it that way. Second, to insist on the utilitarian distinction is to emphasize that the hard core of settled meaning is law in some centrally important sense and that even if there are borderlines, there must first be lines. If this were not so the notion of rules controlling courts' decisions would be senseless as some of the "Realists" —in their most extreme moods, and, I think, on bad grounds—claimed.[40]

By contrast, to soften the distinction, to assert mysteriously that there is some fused identity between law as it is and as it ought to be, is to suggest that all legal questions are fundamentally like those of the penumbra. It is to assert that there is no central element of actual law to be seen in the core of central meaning which rules have, that there is nothing in the nature of a legal rule inconsistent with *all* questions being open to reconsideration in the light of social policy. Of course, it is good to be occupied with the penumbra. Its problems are rightly the daily diet of the law schools. But to be occupied with the penumbra is one thing, to be preoccupied with it another. And preoccupation with the penumbra is, if I may say so, as rich a source of confusion in the American legal tradition as formalism in the English. Of course we might abandon the notion that rules have authority; we might cease to attach force or even meaning to an argument that a case falls clearly within a rule and the scope of a precedent. We might call all such reasoning "automatic" or "mechanical," which is already the routine invective of the courts. But until we decide that this *is* what we want; we should not encourage it by obliterating the utilitarian distinction.

IV.

The third criticism of the separation of law and morals is of a very different character; it certainly is less an intellectual argument against the utilitarian distinction than a passionate appeal supported not by detailed reasoning but by reminders of a terrible experience. For it consists of the testimony of those who have descended into Hell, and, like Ulysses or Dante, brought back a message for human beings. Only in this case the Hell was not beneath or beyond earth, but on it; it was a Hell created on earth by men for other men.

This appeal comes from those German thinkers who lived through the Nazi regime and reflected upon its evil manifestations in the legal system. One of these thinkers, Gustav Radbruch, had himself shared the "positivist" doctrine until the Nazi tyranny, but he was converted by this experience and so his appeal to other men to discard the doctrine of the separation of law and morals has the special poignancy of a recantation. What is important about this criticism is that it really does confront the particular point which Bentham and Austin had in mind in urging the separation of law as it is and as it ought to be. These German thinkers put their insistence on the need to join together what the utilitarians separated just where this separation was of most importance in the eyes of the utilitarians; for they were concerned with the problem posed by the existence of morally evil laws.

Before his conversion Radbruch held that resistance to law was a matter for the personal conscience, to be thought out by the individual as a moral problem, and the validity of a law could not be disproved by showing that the effect of compliance with the law would be more evil than the effect of disobedience. Austin, it may be recalled, was emphatic in condemning those who said that if human laws conflicted with the fundamental principles of morality then they cease to be laws, as talking "stark nonsense."

The most pernicious laws, and therefore those which are most opposed to the will of God, have been and are continually enforced as laws by judicial tribunals. Suppose an act innocuous, or positively beneficial, be prohibited by the sovereign under the penalty of death; if I commit this act, I shall be tried and condemned, and if I object to the sentence, that it is contrary to the law of God . . . the court of justice will demonstrate the inconclusiveness of my reasoning by hanging me up, in pursuance of the law of which I have impugned the validity. An exception, demurrer, or plea, founded on the law of God was never heard in a Court of Justice, from the creation of the world down to the present moment.[41]

These are strong, indeed brutal words, but we must remember that they went along—in the case of Austin and, of course, Bentham—with the conviction that if laws reached a certain degree of iniquity then there would be a plain moral obligation to resist them and to withhold obedience. We shall see, when we consider the alternatives, that this simple presentation of the human dilemma which may arise has much to be said for it.

Radbruch, however, had concluded from the ease with which the Nazi regime had exploited subservience to mere law—or expressed, as he thought, in the "positivist" slogan "law as law" *(Gesetz als Gesetz)*—and from the failure of the German legal profession to protest against the enormities which they were required to perpetrate in the name of law, that "positivism" (meaning here the insistence on the separation of law as it is from law as it ought to be) had powerfully contributed to the horrors. His considered reflections led him to the doctrine that the fundamental principles of humanitarian morality were part of the very concept of *Recht* or Legality and that no positive enactment or statute, however clearly it was expressed and however clearly it conformed with the formal criteria of validity of a given legal system, could be valid if it contravened basic principles of morality. This doctrine can be appreciated fully only if the nuances imported by the German word *Recht* are grasped. But it is clear that the doctrine meant that every lawyer and judge should denounce statutes that transgressed the fundamental principles not as merely immoral or wrong but as having no legal character, and enactments which on this ground lack the quality of law should not be taken into account in working out the legal position of any given individual in particular circumstances. The striking recantation of his previous doctrine is unfortunately omitted from the translation of his works, but it should be read by all who wish to think afresh on the question of the interconnection of law and morals.[42]

It is impossible to read without sympathy Radbruch's passionate demand that the German legal conscience should be open to the demands of morality and his complaint that this has been too little the case in the German tradition. On the other hand there is an extraordinary naïveté in the view that insensitiveness to the demands of morality and subservience to state power in a people like the Germans should have arisen from the belief that law might be law though it failed to conform with the minimum requirements of morality. Rather this terrible history prompts inquiry into why emphasis on the slogan "law is law," and the distinction between law and morals, acquired a sinister character in Germany, but elsewhere, as with the utilitarians themselves, went along with the most enlightened liberal attitudes. But something more disturbing than naïveté is latent in Radbruch's whole presentation of the issues to which the existence of morally iniquitous laws give rise. It is not, I think, uncharitable to say that we can see in his argument that he has only half digested the spiritual message of liberalism which he is seeking to convey to the legal profession. For everything that he says is really dependent upon an enormous overvaluation of the importance of the bare fact that a rule may be said to be a valid rule of law, as if this, once declared, was conclusive of the final moral question: "Ought this rule of law to be obeyed?" Surely the truly liberal answer to any sinister use of the slogan "law is law" or of the distinction between law and morals is, "Very well, but that does not conclude the question. Law is not morality; do not let it supplant morality."

However, we are not left to a mere academic discussion in order to evaluate the plea which Radbruch made for the revision of the distinction between law and morals. After the war Radbruch's conception of law as containing in itself the essential moral principle of humanitarianism was applied in practice by German courts in certain cases in which local war criminals, spies, and informers under the Nazi regime were punished. The special importance of these cases is that the persons accused of these crimes claimed that what they had done was not illegal under the laws of the regime in force at the time these actions were performed. This plea was met with the reply that the laws upon which they relied were invalid as contravening the fundamental principles of morality. Let me cite briefly one of these cases.[43]

In 1944 a woman, wishing to be rid of her husband, denounced him to the authorities for insulting remarks he had made about Hitler while home on leave from the German army. The wife was under no legal duty to report his acts, though what he had said was apparently in violation of statutes making it illegal to make statements detrimental to the government of the Third Reich or to impair by any means the military defense of the

German people. The husband was arrested and sentenced to death, apparently pursuant to these statutes, though he was not executed but was sent to the front. In 1949 the wife was prosecuted in a West German court for an offense which we would describe as illegally depriving a person of his freedom *(rechtswidrige Freiheitsberaubung)*. This was punishable as a crime under the German Criminal Code of 1871 which had remained in force continuously since its enactment. The wife pleaded that her husband's imprisonment was pursuant to the Nazi statutes and hence that she had committed no crime. The court of appeal to which the case ultimately came held that the wife was guilty of procuring the deprivation of her husband's liberty by denouncing him to the German courts, even though he had been sentenced by a court for having violated a statute, since, to quote the words of the court, the statute "was contrary to the sound conscience and sense of justice of all decent human beings." This reasoning was followed in many cases which have been hailed as a triumph of the doctrines of natural law and as signaling the overthrow of positivism. The unqualified satisfaction with this result seems to me to be hysteria. Many of us might applaud the objective—that of punishing a woman for an outrageously immoral act—but this was secured only by declaring a statute established since 1934 not to have the force of law, and at least the wisdom of this course must be doubted. There were, of course, two other choices. One was to let the woman go unpunished; one can sympathize with and endorse the view that this might have been a bad thing to do. The other was to face the fact that if the woman were to be punished it must be pursuant to the introduction of a frankly retrospective law and with a full consciousness of what was sacrificed in securing her punishment in this way. Odious as retrospective criminal legislation and punishment may be, to have pursued it openly in this case would at least have had the merits of candour. It would have made plain that in punishing the woman a choice had to be made between two evils, that of leaving her unpunished and that of sacrificing a very precious principle of morality endorsed by most legal systems. Surely if we have learned anything from the history of morals it is that the thing to do with a moral quandary is not to hide it. Like nettles, the occasions when life forces us to choose between the lesser of two evils must be grasped with the consciousness that they are what they are. The vice of this use of the principle that, at certain limiting points, what is

utterly immoral cannot be law or lawful is that it will serve to cloak the true nature of the problems with which we are faced and will encourage the romantic optimism that all the values we cherish ultimately will fit into a single system, that no one of them has to be sacrificed or compromised to accommodate another.

> "All Discord Harmony not understood
> All Partial Evil Universal Good"

This is surely untrue and there is an insincerity in any formulation of our problem which allows us to describe the treatment of the dilemma as if it were the disposition of the ordinary case.

It may seem perhaps to make too much of forms, even perhaps of words, to emphasize one way of disposing of this difficult case as compared with another which might have led, so far as the woman was concerned, to exactly the same result. Why should we dramatize the difference between them? We might punish the woman under a new retrospective law and declare overtly that we were doing something inconsistent with our principles as the lesser of two evils; or we might allow the case to pass as one in which we do not point out precisely where we sacrifice such a principle. But candour is not just one among many minor virtues of the administration of law, just as it is not merely a minor virtue of morality. For if we adopt Radbruch's view, and with him the German courts make our protest against evil law in the form of an assertion that certain rules cannot be law because of their moral iniquity, we confuse one of the most powerful, because it is the simplest, forms of moral criticism. If with the utilitarians we speak plainly, we say that laws may be law but too evil to be obeyed. This is a moral condemnation which everyone can understand and it makes an immediate and obvious claim to moral attention. If, on the other hand, we formulate our objection as an assertion that these evil things are not law, here is an assertion which many people do not believe, and if they are disposed to consider it at all, it would seem to raise a whole host of philosophical issues before it can be accepted. So perhaps the most important single lesson to be learned from this form of the denial of the utilitarian distinction is the one that the utilitarians were most concerned to teach: when we have the ample resources of plain speech we must not present the moral criticism of institutions as propositions of a disputable philosophy.

V.

I have endeavored to show that, in spite of all that has been learned and experienced since the utilitarians wrote, and in spite of the defects of other parts of their doctrine, their protest against the confusion of what is and what ought to be law has a moral as well as an intellectual value. Yet it may well be said that, though this distinction is valid and important if applied to any particular law of a system, it is at least misleading if we attempt to apply it to "law," that is, to the notion of a legal system, and that if we insist, as I have, on the narrower truth (or truism), we obscure a wider (or deeper) truth. After all, it may be urged, we have learned that there are many things which are untrue of laws taken separately, but which are true and important in a legal system considered as a whole. For example, the connection between law and sanctions and between the existence of law and its "efficacy" must be understood in this more general way. It is surely not arguable (without some desperate extension of the word "sanction" or artificial narrowing of the word "law") that every law in a municipal legal system must have a sanction, yet it is at least plausible to argue that a legal system must, to be a legal system, provide sanctions for certain of its rules. So too, a rule of law may be said to exist though enforced or obeyed in only a minority of cases, but this could not be said of a legal system as a whole. Perhaps the differences with respect to laws taken separately and a legal system as a whole are also true of the connection between moral (or some other) conceptions of what law ought to be and law in this wider sense.

This line of argument, found (at least in embryo form) in Austin, where he draws attention to the fact that every developed legal system contains certain fundamental notions which are "necessary" and "bottomed in the common nature of man,"[44] is worth pursuing—up to a point—and I shall say briefly why and how far this is so.

We must avoid, if we can, the arid wastes of inappropriate definition, for, in relation to a concept as many-sided and vague as that of a legal system, disputes about the "essential" character, or necessity to the whole, of any single element soon begin to look like disputes about whether chess could be "chess" if played without pawns. There is a wish, which may be understandable, to cut straight through the question whether a legal system, to be a legal system, must measure up to some moral or other standard with simple statements of fact: for example, that no system which utterly failed in this respect has ever existed or could endure; that the normally fulfilled assumption that a legal system aims at some form of justice colours the whole way in which we interpret specific rules in particular cases, and if this normally fulfilled assumption were not fulfilled no one would have any reason to obey except fear (and probably not that) and still less, of course, any moral obligation to obey. The connection between law and moral standards and principles of justice is therefore as little arbitrary and as "necessary" as the connection between law and sanctions, and the pursuit of the question whether this necessity is logical (part of the "meaning" of law) or merely factual or causal can safely be left as an innocent pastime for philosophers.

Yet in two respects I should wish to go further (even though this involves the use of a philosophical fantasy) and show what could intelligibly be meant by the claim that certain provisions in a legal system are "necessary." The world in which we live, and we who live in it, may one day change in many different ways; and if this change were radical enough not only would certain statements of fact now true be false and vice versa, but whole ways of thinking and talking which constitute our present conceptual apparatus, through which we see the world and each other, would lapse. We have only to consider how the whole of our social, moral, and legal life, as we understand it now, depends on the contingent fact that though our bodies do change in shape, size, and other physical properties they do not do this so drastically nor with such quicksilver rapidity and irregularity that we cannot identify each other as the same persistent individual over considerable spans of time. Though this is but a contingent fact which may one day be different, on it at present rest huge structures of our thought and principles of action and social life. Similarly, consider the following possiblity (not because it is more than a possibility but because it reveals why we think certain things necessary in a legal system and what we mean by this): suppose that men were to become invulnerable to attack by each other, were clad perhaps like giant land crabs with an impenetrable carapace, and could extract the food they needed from the air by some internal chemical process. In such circumstances (the details of which can be left to science fiction) rules forbidding the free use of violence and rules constituting the minimum form of property—with its rights and duties sufficient to enable food to grow and be retained until eaten—would not have the necessary nonarbitrary status which they have for us, constituted as we are in a world like ours. At present, and until such radical changes supervene, such rules are so fundamental that if a legal system did not have them there would be no point in having any other rules at all. Such rules overlap with basic moral principles vetoing murder, violence, and theft; and so we can add to the factual statement that all legal systems in fact coincide with morality at such vital points, the statement that this is, in this sense, necessarily so. And why not call it a "natural" necessity?

Of course even this much depends on the fact that in asking what content a legal system must have we take this question to be worth asking only if we who consider it cherish the humble aim of survival in close proximity to our fellows. Natural-law theory, however, in all its protean guises, attempts to push the argument much further and to assert that human beings are equally devoted to and united in their conception of aims (the pursuit of knowledge, justice to their fellow men) other than that of survival, and these dictate a further necessary content to a legal system (over and above my humble minimum) without which it would be pointless. Of course we must be careful not to exaggerate the differences among human beings, but it seems to me that above this minimum the purposes men have for living in society are too conflicting and varying to make possible much extension of the argument that some fuller overlap of legal rules and moral standards is "necessary" in this sense.

Another aspect of the matter deserves attention. If we attach to a legal system the minimum meaning that it must consist of general rules—general both in the sense that they refer to courses of action, not single actions, and to multiplicities of men, not single individuals—this meaning connotes the principle of treating like cases alike, though the criteria of when cases are alike will be, so far, only the general elements specified in the rules. It is, however, true that *one* essential element of the concept of justice is the principle of treating like cases alike. This is justice in the administration of the law, not justice of the law. So there is, in the very notion of law consisting of general rules, something which prevents us from treating it as if morally it is utterly neutral, without any necessary contact with moral principles. Natural procedural justice consists therefore of those principles of objectivity and impartiality in the administration of the law which implement just this aspect of law and which are designed to ensure that rules are applied only to what are genuinely cases of the rule or at least to minimize the risks of inequalities in this sense.

These two reasons (or excuses) for talking of a certain overlap between legal and moral standards as necessary and natural, of course, should not satisfy anyone who is really disturbed by the utilitarian or "positivist" insistence that law and morality are distinct. This is so because a legal system that satisfied these minimum requirements might apply, with the most pedantic impartiality as between the persons affected, laws which were hideously oppressive, and might deny to a vast rightless slave population the minimum benefits of protection from violence and theft. The stink of such societies is, after all, still in our nostrils and to argue that they have (or had) no legal system would only involve the repetition of the argument. Only if the rules failed to provide these essential benefits and protection for anyone —even for a slave-owning group—would the minimum be unsatisfied and the system sink to the status of a set of meaningless taboos. Of course no one denied those benefits would have any reason to obey except fear and would have every moral reason to revolt.

VI.

I should be less than candid if I did not, in conclusion, consider something which, I suspect, most troubles those who react strongly against "legal positivism." Emphasis on the distinction between law as it is and law as it ought to be may be taken to depend upon and to entail what are called "subjectivist" and "relativist" or "noncognitive" theories concerning the very nature of moral judgments, moral distinctions, or "values." Of course the utilitarians themselves (as distinct from later positivists like Kelsen) did not countenance any such theories, however unsatisfactory their moral philosophy may appear to us now. Austin thought ultimate moral principles were the commands of God, known to us by revelation or through the "index" of utility, and Bentham thought they were verifiable propositions about utility. Nonetheless I think (though I cannot prove) that insistence upon the distinction between law as it is and ought to be has been, under the general head of "positivism," confused with a moral theory according to which statements of what is the case ("statements of fact") belong to a category or type radically different from statements of what ought to be ("value statements"). It may therefore be well to dispel this source of confusion.

There are many contemporary variants of this type of moral theory: according to some, judgments of what ought to be, or ought to be done, either are or include as essential elements expression of "feeling," "emotion," or "attitudes" or "subjective preferences"; in others such judgments both express feelings or emotions or attitudes and enjoin others to share them. In other variants such judgments indicate that a particular case falls under a general principle or policy of action which the speaker has "chosen" or to which he is "committed" and which is itself not a recognition of what is the case but analogous to a general "imperative" or command addressed to all including the speaker himself. Common to all these variants is the insistence that judgments of what ought to be done, because they contain such "non-cognitive" elements, cannot be argued for or established by rational methods as statements of fact can be, and cannot be shown to follow from any statement of fact but only from other judgments of what ought to be done in conjunction with some statement of fact. We cannot, on such a theory, demonstrate, for example, that an action was wrong, ought not to have been done, merely by showing that it consisted of the deliberate infliction of pain solely for the gratification of the agent. We only show it to be wrong if we add to those verifiable "cognitive" statements of fact a general principle not itself verifiable or "cognitive" that the infliction of pain in such circumstances is wrong, ought not to be done. Together with this general distinction between statements of what is and what ought to be go sharp parallel distinctions between statements about means and statements of moral ends. We can rationally discover and debate what are appropriate means to given ends, but ends are not rationally discoverable or debatable; they are "fiats of the will," expression of "emotions," "preferences," or "attitudes."

Against all such views (which are of course far subtler than this crude survey can convey) others urge that all these sharp distinctions between is and ought, fact and value, means and ends, cognitive and noncognitive, are wrong. In acknowledging ultimate ends or moral values we are recognizing something as much imposed upon us by the character of the world in which we live, as little a matter of choice, attitude, feeling, emotion

as the truth of factual judgments about what is the case. The characteristic moral argument is not one in which the parties are reduced to expressing or kindling feelings or emotions or issuing exhortations or commands to each other but one by which parties come to acknowledge after closer examination and reflection that an initially disputed case falls within the ambit of a vaguely apprehended principle (itself no more "subjective," no more a "fiat of our will" than any other principle of classification) and this has as much title to be called "cognitive" or "rational" as any other initially disputed classification of particulars.

Let us now suppose that we accept this rejection of "noncognitive" theories of morality and this denial of the drastic distinction in type between statements of what is and what ought to be, and that moral judgments are as rationally defensible as any other kind of judgments. What would follow from this as to the nature of the connection between law as it is and law as it ought to be? Surely, from this alone, nothing. Laws, however morally iniquitous, would still (so far as this point is concerned) be laws. The only difference which the acceptance of this view of the nature of moral judgments would make would be that the moral iniquity of such laws would be something that could be demonstrated; it would surely follow merely from a statement of what the rule required to be done that the rule was morally wrong and so ought not to be law or conversely that it was morally desirable and ought to be law. But the demonstration of this would not show the rule not to be (or to be) law. Proof that the principles by which we evaluate or condemn laws are rationally discoverable, and not mere "fiats of the will," leaves untouched the fact that there are laws which may have any degree of iniquity or stupidity and still be laws. And conversely there are rules that have every moral qualification to be laws and yet are not laws.

Surely something further or more specific must be said if disproof of "noncognitivism" or kindred theories in ethics is to be relevant to the distinction between law as it is and law as it ought to be, and to lead to the abandonment at some point or some softening of this distinction. No one has done more than Professor Lon Fuller of the Harvard Law School in his various writings to make clear such a line of argument and I will end by criticising what I take to be its central point. It is a point which again emerges when we consider not those legal rules or parts of legal rules the meanings of which are clear and excite no debate but the interpretation of rules in concrete cases where doubts are initially felt and argument develops about their meaning. In no legal system is the scope of legal rules restricted to the range of concrete instances which were present or are believed to have been present in the minds of legislators; this indeed is one of the important differences between a legal rule and a command. Yet, when rules are recognized as applying to instances beyond any that legislators did or could have considered, their extension to such new cases often presents itself not as a deliberate choice or fiat on the part of those who so interpret the rule. It appears neither as a decision to give the rule a new or extended meaning nor as a guess as to what legislators, dead perhaps in the eighteenth century, would have said had they been alive in the twentieth century. Rather, the inclusion of the new case under the rule takes its place as a natural elaboration of the rule, as something implementing a "purpose" which it seems natural to attribute (in some sense) to the rule itself rather than to any particular person dead or alive. The utilitarian description of such interpretative extension of old rules to new cases as judicial legislation fails to do justice to this phenomenon; it gives no hint of the differences between a deliberate fiat or decision to treat the new case in the same way as past cases and a recognition (in which there is little that is deliberate or even voluntary) that inclusion of the new case under the rule will implement or articulate a continuing and identical purpose, hitherto less specifically apprehended.

Perhaps many lawyers and judges will see in this language something that precisely fits their experience; others may think it a romantic gloss on facts better stated in the utilitarian language of judicial "legislation" or in the modern American terminology of "creative choice."

To make the point clear Professor Fuller uses a nonlegal example from the philosopher Wittgenstein which is, I think, illuminating.

Someone says to me: "Show the children a game." I teach them gaming with dice and the other says "I did not mean that sort of game." Must the exclusion of the game with dice have come before his mind when he gave me the order?[45]

Something important does seem to me to be touched on in this example. Perhaps there are the following (distinguishable) points. First, we nor-

mally do interpret not only what people are trying to do but what they say in the light of assumed common human objectives so that unless the contrary were expressly indicated we would not interpret an instruction to show a young child a game as a mandate to introduce him to gambling even though in other contexts the word "game" would be naturally so interpreted. Second, very often, the speaker whose words are thus interpreted might say: "Yes, that's what I mean [or "that's what I meant all along"] though I never thought of it until you put this particular case to me." Third, when we thus recognize, perhaps after argument or consultation with others, a particular case not specifically envisaged beforehand as falling within the ambit of some vaguely expressed instruction, we may find this experience falsified by description of it as a mere decision on our part so to treat the particular case, and that we can only describe this faithfully as coming to realize and to articulate what we "really" want or our "true purpose"—phrases which Professor Fuller uses later in the same article.[46]

I am sure that many philosophical discussions of the character of moral argument would benefit from attention to cases of the sort instanced by Professor Fuller. Such attention would help to provide a corrective to the view that there is a sharp separation between "ends" and "means" and that in debating "ends" we can only work on each other nonrationally, and that rational argument is reserved for dicussion of "means." But I think the relevance of his point to the issue whether it is correct or wise to insist on the distinction between law as it is and law as it ought to be is very small indeed. Its net effect is that in interpreting legal rules there are some cases which we find after reflection to be so natural an elaboration or articulation of the rule that to think of and refer to this as "legislation," "making law," or a "fiat" on our part would be misleading. So, the argument must be, it would be misleading to distinguish in such cases between what the rule is and what it ought to be—at least in some sense of ought. We think it ought to include the new case and come to see after reflection that it really does. But even if this way of presenting a recognizable experience as an example of a fusion between is and is admitted, two caveats must be borne in mind. The first is that "ought" in this case need have nothing to do with morals for the reasons explained already in section III: there may be just the same sense that a new case will implement and articulate the purpose of a rule in interpreting the rules of a game or some hideously immoral code of oppression whose immorality is appreciated by those called in to interpret it. They too can see what the "spirit" of the game they are playing requires in previously unenvisaged cases. More important is this: After all is said and done we must remember how rare in the law is the phenomenon held to justify this way of talking, how exceptional is this feeling that one way of deciding a case is imposed upon us as the only natural or rational elaboration of some rule. Surely it cannot be doubted that, for most cases of interpretation, the language of choice between alternatives, "judicial legislation" or even "fiat" (though not arbitrary fiat), better conveys the realities of the situation. Within the framework of relatively well-settled law there jostle too many alternatives too nearly equal in attraction between which judge and lawyer must uncertainly pick their way to make appropriate here language which may well describe those experiences which we have in interpreting our own or others' principles of conduct, intention, or wishes, when we are not conscious of exercising a deliberate choice, but rather of recognizing something awaiting recognition. To use in the description of the interpretation of laws the suggested terminology of a fusion of inability to separate what is law and ought to be will serve (like earlier stories that judges only find, never make, law) only to conceal the facts, that here if anywhere we live among uncertainties between which we have to choose, and that the existing law imposes only limits on our choice and not the choice itself.

NOTES

1. Bentham, *A Fragment on Government,* in 1 Works 221, 235 (Bowring ed. 1859) (preface, 41st para.).
2. D'Entrèves, Natural Law 116 (2d ed. 1952).
3. Fuller, The Law in Quest of Itself 12 (1940); Brecht, *The Myth of Is and Ought,* 54 Harv. L. Rev. 811 (1941); Fuller, *Human Purpose and Natural Law,* 53 J. Philos 697 (1953).
4. See Friedmann, Legal Theory 154, 294–95 (3d ed. 1953). Friedmann also says of Austin that "by his sharp distinction between the science of legislation and the science of law," he "inaugurated an era of legal positivism and self-sufficiency which enabled the rising national State to assert its authority undisturbed by juristic doubts." *Id.* at 416. Yet, "the existence of a highly organised State which claimed sovereignty and unconditional obedience of the citizen" is said to be "the political condition which makes analytical positivism possible." *Id.* at 163. There is therefore some difficulty in determining which, in this account, is to be hen and which egg (analytical positivism or political condition). Apart from this,

there seems to be little evidence that any national State rising in or after 1832 (when the *Province of Jurisprudence Determined* was first published) was enabled to assert its authority by Austin's work or "the era of legal positivism" which he "inaugurated."
5. See Radbruch, *Die Erneuerung des Rechts,* 2 Die Wandlung 8 (Germany 1947); Radbruch, *Gesetzliches Unrecht und Übergesetzliches Recht,* 1 Süddeutsche Juristen-Zeitung 105 (Germany 1946) (reprinted in Radbruch, Rechtsphilosophie 347 (4th ed. 1950). Radbruch's views are discussed at pp. 617–21 *infra.*
6. Bentham, *A Fragment on Government,* in 1 Works 221, 230 (Bowring ed. 1859) (preface, 16th para.); Bentham, *Principles of Penal Law,* in 1 Works 365, 574–75, 576–78 (Bowring ed. 1859) (pt. III, c. XXI, 8th para., 12th para.).
7. Bentham, *Of Promulgation of the Laws,* in 1 Works 155 (Bowring ed. 1859); Bentham, *Principles of the Civil Code,* in 1 Works 297, 323 (Bowring ed. 1859) (pt. I, c. XVII, 2d para.); Bentham, *A Fragment on Government,* in 1 Works 221, 233 n.[m] (Bowring ed. 1859) (preface, 35th para.).
8. Bentham, *Principles of Penal Law,* in 1 Works 365, 576 (Bowring ed. 1859) (pt. III, c. XXI, 10th para., 11th para.).
9. Bentham, *Principles of Morals and Legislation,* in 1 Works I, 84 (Bowring ed. 1859) (c. XIII).
10. Bentham, *Anarchical Fallacies,* in 2 Works 489, 511–12 (Bowring ed. 1859) (art. VIII); Bentham, *Principles of Morals and Legislation,* in 1 Works 1, 144 (Bowring ed. 1859) (c. XIX, 11th para.).
11. *Id.* at 142 n.§ (c. XIX, 4th para. n.§).
12. Austin, The Province of Jurisprudence Determined 184–85 (Library of Ideas ed. 1954).
13. Bentham, *A Fragment on Government,* in 1 Works 221, 230 (Bowring ed. 1859) (preface, 16th para.).
14. See Bentham, *Principles of Legislation,* in The Theory of Legislation 1, 65 n.* (Ogden ed. 1931) (c. XII, 2d para. n.*).
Here we touch upon the most difficult of questions. If the law is not what it ought to be; if it openly combats the principle of utility; ought we to obey it? Ought we to violate it? Ought we to remain neuter between the law which commands an evil, and morality which forbids it?
See also Bentham, *A Fragment on Government,* in 1 Works 221, 287–88 (Bowring ed. 1859) (c. IV, 20th–25th paras.).
15. 1 Blackstone, Commentaries *41. Bentham criticized "this dangerous maxim," saying "the natural tendency of such a doctrine is to impel a man, by the force of conscience, to rise up in arms against any law whatever that he happens not to like." Bentham, *A Fragment on Government,* in 1 Works 221, 287 (Bowring ed. 1859) (c. IV, 19th para.). See also *Bentham, A Comment on the Commentaries* 49 (1928) (c. III). For an expression of a fear lest anarchy result from such a doctrine, combined with a recognition that resistance may be justified on grounds of utility, See Austin, *op. cit. supra* note 12, at 186.
16. Bentham, *A Fragment on Government,* in 1 Works 221, 294 (Bowring ed. 1859) (c. V, 10th para.).
17. Bentham, *A Commentary on Humphreys' Real Property Code,* in 5 Works 389 (Bowring ed. 1843).
18. Austin, *op. cit. supra* note 12, at 162.
19. Bentham, *A Fragment on Government,* in 1 Works 221, 289–90 (Bowring ed. 1859) (c. IV, 33d–34th paras.).
20. See Austin, *op. cit. supra* note 12, at 231.
21. Amos, The Science of Law 4 (5th ed. 1881). See also Markby, Elements of Law 4–5 (5th ed. 1896):
Austin, by establishing the distinction between positive law and morals, not only laid the foundation for a science of law, but cleared the conception of law . . . of a number of perni-

cious consequences to which . . . it had been supposed to lead. Positive laws, as Austin has shown, must be legally binding, and yet a law may be unjust. . . . He has admitted that law itself may be immoral, in which case it may be our moral duty to disobey it. . . .
Cf. Holland, Jurisprudence 1–20 (1880).

22.   See Green, Book Review, 6 Am. L. Rev. 57, 61 (1871) (reprinted in Green, Essays and Notes on the Law of Tort and Crime 31, 35 (1933)).

23.   10 Harv. L. Rev. 457 (1897).

24.   Gray, The Nature and Sources of the Law 94 (1st ed. 1909) (§ 213).

25.   It may help to identify five (there may be more) meanings of "positivism" bandied about in contemporary jurisprudence:
(1) the contention that laws are commands of human beings, see pp. 602–06 *infra,*
(2) the contention that there is no necessary connection between law and morals or law as it is and ought to be, see pp. 594–600 *supra,*
(3) the contention that the analysis (or study of the meaning of legal concepts is (a) worth pursuing and (b) to be distinguished from historical inquiries into the causes or origins of laws, from sociological inquiries into the relation of law and other social phenomena, and from the criticism or appraisal of law whether in terms of morals, social aims, "functions," or otherwise, see pp. 608–10 *infra,*
(4) the contention that a legal system is a "closed logical system" in which correct legal decisions can be deduced by logical means from predetermined legal rules without reference to social aims, policies, moral standards, see pp. 608–10 *infra,* and
(5) the contention that moral judgments cannot be established or defended, as statements of facts can, by rational argument, evidence, or proof ("noncognitivism" in ethics), see pp. 624–26 *infra.*
Bentham and Austin held the views described in (1), (2), and (3) but not those in (4) and (5). Opinion (4) is often ascribed to analytical jurists, see pp. 608–10 *infra,* but I know of no "analyst" who held this view.

26.   Gray, The Nature and Sources of the Law 94–95 (2d ed. 1921).

27.   Austin, *op. cit. supra* note 12, at 13.

28.   See, *e.g.,* Kelsen, General Theory of Law and State 58–61, 143–44 (1945). According to Kelsen, all laws, not only those conferring rights and powers, are reducible to such "primary norms" conditionally stipulating sanctions.

29.   Salmond, The First Principles of Jurisprudence 97–98 (1893). He protested against "the creed of what is termed the English school of jurisprudence," because it "attempted to deprive the idea of law of that ethical significance which is one of its most essential elements." *Id.* at 9, 10.

30.   Hägerström, Inquiries Into the Nature of Law and Morals 217 (Olivecrona ed. 1953): "[T]he whole theory of the subjective rights of private individuals . . . is incompatible with the imperative theory." See also *id.* at 221:
The description of them [claims to legal protection] as rights is wholly derived from the idea that the law which is concerned with them is a true expression of rights and duties in the sense in which the popular notion of justice understands these terms.

31.   *Id.* at 218.

32.   This misunderstanding of analytical jurisprudence is to be found in, among others, Stone, The Province and Function of Law 141 (1950):
In short, rejecting the implied assumption that all propositions of all parts of the law must be logically consistent with

each other and proceed on a single set of definitions . . . he [Cardozo, J.,] denied that the law is actually what the analytical jurist, *for his limited purposes,* assumes it to be.
See also *id.* at 49, 52, 138, 140; Friedmann, Legal Theory 209 (3d ed. 1953). This misunderstanding seems to depend on the unexamined and false belief that analytical studies of the meaning of legal terms would be impossible or absurd if, to reach sound decisions in particular cases, more than a capacity for formal logical reasoning from unambiguous and clear predetermined premises is required.

33.   See the discussion of vagueness and uncertainty in law, in Austin, *op. cit. supra* note 12, at 202–05, 207, in which Austin recognized that, in consequence of this vagueness, often only "fallible tests" can be provided for determining whether particular cases fall under general expressions.

34.   See Austin, *op. cit. supra* note 12, at 191: "I cannot understand how any person who has considered the subject can suppose that society could possibly have gone on if judges had not legislated. . . ." As a corrective to the belief that the analytical jurist must take a "slot machine" or "mechanical" view of the judicial process it is worth noting the following observations made by Austin:
(1) Whenever law has to be applied, the " 'competition of opposite analogies' " may arise, for the case "may resemble in some of its points" cases to which the rule has been applied in the past and in other points "cases from which the application of the law has been withheld." 2 Austin, Lectures on Jurisprudence 633 (5th ed. 1885).
(2) Judges have commonly decided cases and so derived new rules by "building" on a variety of grounds including sometimes (in Austin's opinion too rarely) their views of what law ought to be. Most commonly they have derived law from preexisting law by "consequence founded on analogy," *i.e.,* they have made a new rule "in *consequence* of the existence of a similar rule applying to subjects which are *analogous.* . . ." 2 *id.* at 638–39.
(3) "[I]f every rule in a system of law were perfectly definite or precise," these difficulties incident to the application of law would not arise. "But the ideal completeness and correctness I now have imagined is not attainable in fact. . . . though the system had been built and ordered with matchless solicitude and skill." 2 *id.* at 997–98. Of course he thought that much could and should be done by codification to eliminate uncertainty. See 2 *id.* at 662–81.

35.   2 *id.* at 641:
Nothing, indeed, can be more natural, than that legislators, direct or judicial (especially if they be narrow-minded, timid and unskillful), should lean as much as they can on the examples set by their predecessors.
See also 2 *id.* at 647:
But it is much to be regretted that Judges of capacity, experience and weight, have not seized every opportunity of introducing a new rule (a rule beneficial for the future). . . . This is the reproach I should be inclined to make against Lord Eldon. . . . [T]he Judges of the Common Law Courts would not do what they ought to have done, namely to model their rules of law and of procedure to the growing exigencies of society, instead of stupidly and sulkily adhering to the old and barbarous usages.

36.   Hynes v. New York Cent. R.R., 231 N.Y. 229, 235, 131 N.E. 898, 900 (1921); see Pound, Interpretations of Legal History 123 (2d ed. 1930); Stone, *op. cit. supra* note 32, at 140–41.

37.   See McBoyle v. United States, 283 U.S. 25 (1931).

38.   See, *e.g.,* Pound, *Mechanical Jurisprudence,* 8 Colum. L. Rev. 605, 615–16 (1908).

39.   See, *e.g.,* Lochner v. New York, 198 U.S. 45 (1905).

Justice Peckham's opinion that there were no reasonable grounds for interfering with the right of free contract by determining the hours of labour in the occupation of a baker may indeed be a wrongheaded piece of conservatism but there is nothing automatic or mechanical about it.

40.   One recantation of this extreme position is worth mention in the present context. In the first edition of *The Bramble Bush*, Professor Llewellyn committed himself wholeheartedly to the view that "what these officials do about disputes is, to my mind, the law itself" and that "*rules* . . . are important so far as they help you . . . predict what judges will do. . . . That is all their importance, except as pretty playthings." Llewellyn, The Bramble Bush 3, 5 (1st ed. 1930). In the second edition he said that these were "unhappy words when not more fully developed, and they are plainly at best a very partial statement of the whole truth. . . . [O]ne office of law is to control officials in some part, and to guide them even . . . where no thoroughgoing control is possible, or is desired. . . . [T]he words fail to take proper account . . . of the office of the institution of law as an instrument of conscious shaping. . . ." Llewellyn, The Bramble Bush 9 (2d ed. 1951).

41.   Austin, the Province of Jurisprudence Determined 185 (Library of Ideas ed. 1954).

42.   See Radbruch, *Gesetzliches Unrecht und Übergesetzliches Recht,* 1 Süddeutsche Juristen-Zeitung 105 (Germany 1946) (reprinted in Radbruch, Rechts-philosophie 347 (4th ed. 1950)). I have used the translation of part of this essay and of Radbruch, *Die Erneuerung des Rechts,* 2 Die Wandlung 8 (Germany 1947), prepared by Professor Lon Fuller of the Harvard Law School as a mimeographed supplement to the readings in jurisprudence used in his course at Harvard.

43.   Judgment of July 27, 1949, Oberlandesgericht, Bamberg, 5 Süddeutsche Juristen-Zeitung 207 (Germany 1950), 64 Harv. L. Rev. 1005 (1951); See Freidmann, Legal Theory 457 (3d ed. 1953).

44.   Austin, *Uses of the Study of Jurisprudence,* in The Province of Jurisprudence Determined 365, 373, 367–69 (Library of Ideas ed. 1954).

45.   Fuller, *Human Purpose and Natural Law,* 53 J. Philos. 697, 700 (1956).

46   *Id.* at 701, 702.

LON L. FULLER

Positivism and Fidelity to Law—A Reply to Professor Hart*

Professor Hart has made an enduring contribution to the literature of legal philosophy. I doubt if the issues he discusses will ever again assume quite the form they had before being touched by his analytical powers. His argument is no mere restatement of Bentham, Austin, Gray, and Holmes. Their views receive in his exposition a new depth that are uniquely his own.

I must confess that when I first encountered the thoughts of Professor Hart's essay, his argument seemed to me to suffer from a deep inner contradiction. On the one hand, he rejects emphatically any confusion of "what is" with "what ought to be." He will tolerate no "merger" of law and conceptions of what law ought to be, but at the most an antiseptic "intersection." Intelligible communication on any subject, he seems to imply, becomes impossible if we leave it uncertain whether we are talking about "what is" or "what ought to be." Yet it was precisely this uncertainty about Professor Hart's own argument which made it difficult for me at first to follow the thread of his thought. At times he seemed to be saying that the distinction between law and morality is something that exists, and will continue to exist, however we may talk about it. It expresses a reality which, whether we like it or not, we must accept if we are to avoid talking nonsense. At other times, he seemed to be warning us that the reality of the distinction is itself in danger and that if we do not mend our ways of thinking and talking we may lose a "precious moral ideal," that of fidelity to law. It is not clear, in other words, whether in Professor Hart's own thinking the distinction between law and morality simply "is," or is something that "ought to be" and that we should join with him in helping to create and maintain.

These were the perplexities I had about Professor Hart's argument when I first encountered it. But on reflection I am sure any criticism of his essay as being self-contradictory would be both unfair and unprofitable. There is no reason why the argument for a strict separation of law and morality cannot be rested on the double ground that this separation serves both intellectual clarity and moral integrity. If there are certain difficulties in bringing these two lines of reasoning into proper relation to one another, these difficulties affect also the position of those who reject the views of Austin, Gray, and Holmes. For those of us who find the "positivist" position unacceptable do ourselves rest our argument on the double ground that its intellectual clarity is specious and that its effects are, or may be, harmful. On the one hand, we assert that Austin's definition of law, for example, violates the reality it purports to describe. Being false in fact, it cannot serve effectively what Kelsen calls "an interest of cognition." On the other hand, we assert that under some conditions the same conception of law may become dangerous, since in human affairs what men mistakenly accept as real tends, by the very act of their acceptance, to become real.

It is a cardinal virtue of Professor Hart's argument that for the first time it opens the way for a truly profitable exchange of views between those whose differences center on the distinction between law and morality. Hitherto there has been no real real joinder of issue between the opposing camps. On the one side, we encounter a series of definitional fiats. A rule of law is—that is to say, it really and simply and always is—the command of a sovereign, a rule laid down by a judge, a prediction of the future incidence of state force, a pattern of official behavior, etc. When we ask what purpose these definitions serve, we receive the answer, "Why, no purpose, except to describe accurately the social reality that corresponds to the word 'law.' " When we reply, "But

*From 71 *Harvard Law Review* 630 (1958). Copyright © 1958 by The Harvard Law Review Association. Reprinted by permission of the publisher.

it doesn't look like that to me," the answer comes back, "Well, it does to me." There the matter has to rest.

This state of affairs has been most unsatisfactory for those of us who are convinced that "positivistic" theories have had a distorting effect on the aims of legal philosophy. Our dissatisfaction arose not merely from the impasse we confronted, but because this impasse seemed to us so unnecessary. All that was needed to surmount it was an acknowledgment on the other side that its definitions of "what law really is" are not mere images of some datum of experience, but direction posts for the application of human energies. Since this acknowledgment was not forthcoming, the impasse and its frustrations continued. There is indeed no frustration greater than to be confronted by a theory which purports merely to describe, when it not only plainly prescribes, but owes its special prescriptive powers precisely to the fact that it disclaims prescriptive intentions. Into this murky debate, some shafts of light did occasionally break through, as in Kelsen's casual admission, apparently never repeated, that his whole system might well rest on an emotional preference for the ideal of order over that of justice.[1] But I have to confess that in general the dispute that has been conducted during the last twenty years has not been very profitable.

Now, with Professor Hart's paper, the discussion takes a new and promising turn. It is now explicitly acknowledged on both sides that one of the chief issues is how we can best define and serve the ideal of fidelity to law. Law, as something deserving loyalty, must represent a human achievement; it cannot be a simple fiat of power or a repetitive pattern discernible in the behavior of state officials. The respect we owe to human laws must surely be something different from the respect we accord to the law of gravitation. If laws, even bad laws, have a claim to our respect, then law must represent some general direction of human effort that we can understand and describe, and that we can approve in principle even at the moment when it seems to us to miss its mark.

If, as I believe, it is a cardinal virtue of Professor Hart's argument that it brings into the dispute the issue of fidelity to law, its chief defect, if I may say so, lies in a failure to perceive and accept the implications that this enlargement of the frame of argument necessarily entails. This defect seems to me more or less to permeate the whole essay, but it comes most prominently to the fore in his discussion of Gustav Radbruch and the Nazi regime.[2] Without any inquiry into the actual workings of whatever remained of a legal system under the Nazis, Professor Hart assumes that something must have persisted that still deserved the name of law in a sense that would make meaningful the ideal of fidelity to law. Not that the Professor Hart believes the Nazis' laws should have been obeyed. Rather he considers that a decision to disobey them presented not a mere question of prudence or courage, but a genuine moral dilemma in which the ideal of fidelity to law had to be sacrificed in favor of more fundamental goals. I should have thought it unwise to pass such a judgment without first inquiring with more particularity what "law" itself meant under the Nazi regime.

I shall present later my reasons for thinking that Professor Hart is profoundly mistaken in his estimate of the Nazi situation and that he gravely misinterprets the thought of Professor Radbruch. But first I shall turn to some preliminary definitional problems in which what I regard as the central defect in Professor Hart's thesis seems immediately apparent.

I. THE DEFINITION OF LAW

Throughout his essay Professor Hart aligns himself with a general position which he associates with the names of Bentham, Austin, Gray, and Holmes. He recognizes, of course, that the conceptions of these men as to "what law is" vary considerably, but this diversity he apparently considers irrelevant in his defense of their general school of thought.

If the only issue were that of stipulating a meaning for the word "law" that would be conducive to intellectual clarity, there might be much justification for treating all of these men as working in the same direction. Austin, for example, defines law as the command of the highest legislative power, called the sovereign. For Gray, on the other hand, law consists in the rules laid down by judges. A statute is, for Gray, not a law, but only a source of law, which becomes law only after it has been interpreted and applied by a court. Now if our only object were to obtain that clarity which comes from making our definitions explicit and then adhering strictly to those definitions, one could argue plausibly that either conception of the meaning of "law" will do. Both conceptions appear to avoid a confusion of morals and law, and both writers let the reader know what meaning they propose to attribute to the word "law."

The matter assumes a very different aspect, however, if our interest lies in the ideal of fidelity to law, for then it may become a matter of capital importance what position is assigned to the judiciary in the general frame of government. Confirmation for this observation may be found in the slight rumbling of constitutional crisis to be heard in this country today. During the past year readers of newspapers have been writing to their editors urging solemnly, and even apparently with sincerity, that we should abolish the Supreme Court as a first step toward a restoration of the rule of law. It is unlikely that this remedy for our governmental ills derives from any deep study of Austin or Gray, but surely those who propose it could hardly be expected to view with indifference the divergent definitions of law offered by those two jurists. If it be said that it is a perversion of Gray's meaning to extract from his writings any moral for present controversies about the role of the Supreme Court, then it seems to me there is equal reason for treating what he wrote as irrelevant to the issue of fidelity of law generally.

Another difference of opinion among the writers defended by Professor Hart concerns Bentham and Austin and their views on constitutional limitations on the power of the sovereign. Bentham considered that a constitution might preclude the highest legislative power from issuing certain kinds of laws. For Austin, on the other hand, any legal limit on the highest lawmaking power was an absurdity and an impossibility. What guide to conscience would be offered by these two writers in a crisis that might some day arise out of the provision of our constitution to the effect that the amending power can never be used to deprive any state without its consent of its equal representation in the Senate?[3] Surely it is not only in the affairs of everyday life that we need clarity about the obligation of fidelity to law, but most particularly and urgently in times of trouble. If all the positivist school has to offer in such times is the observation that, however you may choose to define law, it is always something different from morals, its teachings are not of much use to us.

I suggest, then, that Professor Hart's thesis as it now stands is essentially incomplete and that before he can attain the goals he seeks he will have to concern himself more closely with a definition of law that will make meaningful the obligation of fidelity to law.

II. THE DEFINITION OF MORALITY

It is characteristic of those sharing the point of view of Professor Hart that their primary concern is to preserve the integrity of the concept of law. Accordingly, they have generally sought a precise definition of law, but have not been at pains to state just what it is they mean to exclude by their definitions. They are like men building a wall for the defense of a village, who must know what it is they wish to protect, but who need not, and indeed cannot, know what invading forces those walls may have to turn back.

When Austin and Gray distinguish law from morality, the word "morality" stands indiscriminately for almost every conceivable standard by which human conduct may be judged that is not itself law. The inner voice of conscience, notions of right and wrong based on religious belief, common conceptions of decency and fair play, culturally conditioned prejudices—all of these are grouped together under the heading of "morality" and are excluded from the domain of law. For the most part Professor Hart follows in the tradition of his predecessors. When he speaks of morality he seems generally to have in mind all sorts of extra-legal notions about "what ought to be," regardless of their sources, pretensions, or intrinsic worth. This is particularly apparent in his treatment of the problem of interpretation, where uncodified notions of what ought to be are viewed as affecting only the penumbra of law, leaving its hard core untouched.

Toward the end of the essay, however, Professor Hart's argument takes a turn that seems to depart from the prevailing tenor of his thought. This consists in reminding us that there is such a thing as an immoral morality and that there are many standards of "what ought to be" that can hardly be called moral.[4] Let us grant, he says, that the judge may properly and inevitably legislate in the penumbra of a legal enactment, and that this legislation (in default of any other standard) must be guided by the judge's notions of what ought to be. Still, this would be true even in a society devoted to the most evil ends, where the judge would supply the insufficiencies of the statute with the iniquity that seemed to him most apt for the occasion. Let us also grant, says Professor Hart toward the end of his essay, that there is at times even something that looks like discovery in the judicial process, when a judge by restating a principle seems to bring more clearly to light what was really sought from the beginning. Again, he reminds us, this could happen in a society devoted to the highest refinements of sin, where the implicit demands of an evil rule might be a matter for discovery when the rule was applied to a situation not consciously considered when it was formulated.

I take it that this is to be a warning addressed to those who wish "to infuse more morality into the law." Professor Hart is reminding them that if their program is adopted the morality that actually gets infused may not be to their liking. If this is his point it is certainly a valid one, though one wishes it had been made more explicitly, for it raises much the most fundamental issue of his whole argument. Since the point is made obliquely, and I may have misinterpreted it, in commenting I shall have to content myself with a few summary observations and questions.

First, Professor Hart seems to assume that evil aims may have as much coherence and inner logic as good ones. I, for one, refuse to accept that assumption. I realize that I am here raising, or perhaps dodging, questions that lead into the most difficult problems of the epistemology of ethics. Even if I were competent to undertake an excursus in that direction, this is not the place for it. I shall have to rest on the assertion of a belief that may seem naïve, namely, that coherence and goodness have more affinity than coherence and evil. Accepting this belief, I also believe that when men are compelled to explain and justify their decisions, the effect will generally be to pull those decisions toward goodness, by whatever standards of ultimate goodness there are. Accepting these beliefs, I find a considerable incongruity in any conception that envisages a possible future in which the common law would "work itself pure from case to case" toward a more perfect realization of iniquity.

Second, if there is a serious danger in our society that a weakening of the partition between law and morality would permit an infusion of "immoral morality," the question remains, what is the most effective protection against this danger? I cannot myself believe it is to be found in the positivist position espoused by Austin, Gray, Holmes, and Hart. For those writers seem to me to falsify the problem into a specious simplicity which leaves untouched the difficult issues where real dangers lie.

Third, let us suppose a judge bent on realizing through his decisions an objective that most ordinary citizens would regard as mistaken or evil. Would such a judge be likely to suspend the letter of the statute by openly invoking a "higher law"? Or would he be more likely to take refuge behind the maxim that "law is law" and explain his decision in such a way that it would appear to be demanded by the law itself?

Fourth, neither Professor Hart nor I belong to anything that could be said in a significant sense to be a "minority group" in our respective countries. This has its advantages and disadvantages to one aspiring to a philosophic view of law and government. But suppose we were both transported to a country where our beliefs were anathemas, and where we, in turn, regarded the prevailing morality as thoroughly evil. No doubt in this situation we would have reason to fear that the law might be covertly manipulated to our disadvantage; I doubt if either of us would be apprehensive that its injunctions would be set aside by an appeal to a morality higher than law. If we felt that the law itself was our safest refuge, would it not be because even in the most perverted regimes there is a certain hesitancy about writing cruelties, intolerances, and inhumanities into law? And is it not clear that this hesitancy itself derives, not from a separation of law and morals, but precisely from an identification of law with those demands of morality that are the most urgent and the most obviously justifiable, which no man need be ashamed to profess?

Fifth, over great areas where the judicial process functions, the danger of an infusion of immoral, or at least unwelcome, morality does not, I suggest, present a real issue. Here the danger is precisely the opposite. For example, in the field of commercial law the British courts in recent years have, if I may say so, fallen into a "law-is-law" formalism that constitutes a kind of belated counterrevolution against all that was accomplished by Mansfield.[5] The matter has reached a stage approaching crisis as commercial cases are increasingly being taken to arbitration. The chief reason for this development is that arbitrators are willing to take into account the needs of commerce and ordinary standards of commercial fairness. I realize that Professor Hart repudiates "formalism," but I shall try to show later why I think his theory necessarily leads in that direction.[6]

Sixth, in the thinking of many there is one question that predominates in any discussion of the relation of law and morals, to the point of coloring everything that is said or heard on the subject. I refer to the kind of question raised by the Pope's pronouncement concerning the duty of Catholic judges in divorce actions.[7] This pronouncement does indeed raise grave issues. But it does not present a problem of the relation between law, on the one hand, and, on the other, generally shared views of right conduct that have grown spontaneously through experience and discussion. The issue is rather that of a conflict between two pronouncements, both of which claim to be authoritative; if you will, it is one kind of law against another. When this kind of issue is taken as the key to the whole problem of law and morality, the discussion is so denatured and distorted that profitable exchange becomes impossible. In mentioning this last aspect of the dispute about "positivism," I do not mean to intimate that Professor Hart's own discussion is dominated by any *arriére-pensée;* I know it is not. At the same time I am quite sure that I have indicated accurately the issue that will be uppermost in the minds of many as they read his essay.

In resting content with these scant remarks, I do not want to seem to simplify the problem in a direction opposite to that taken by Professor Hart. The questions raised by "immoral morality" deserve a more careful exploration than either Professor Hart or I have offered in these pages.

III. THE MORAL FOUNDATIONS OF A LEGAL ORDER

Professor Hart emphatically rejects "the command theory of law," according to which law is simply a command backed by a force sufficient to make it effective. He observes that such a command can be given by a man with a loaded gun, and "law surely is not the gunman situation writ large."[8] There is no need to dwell here on the inadequacies of the command theory, since Professor Hart has already revealed its defects more clearly and succinctly than I could. His conclusion is that the foundation of a legal system is not coercive power, but certain "fundamental accepted rules specifying the essential lawmaking procedures."[9]

When I reached this point in his essay, I felt certain that Professor Hart was about to acknowledge an important qualification on his thesis. I confidently expected that he would go on to say something like this: I have insisted throughout on the importance of keeping sharp the distinction between law and morality. The question may now be raised, therefore, as to the nature of these fundamental rules that furnish the framework within which the making of law takes place.

On the one hand, they seem to be rules, not of law, but of morality. They derive their efficacy from a general acceptance, which in turn rests ultimately on a perception that they are right and necessary. They can hardly be said to be law in the sense of an authoritative pronouncement, since their function is to state when a pronouncement is authoritative. On the other hand, in the daily functioning of the legal system they are often treated and applied much as ordinary rules of law are. Here, then, we must confess there is something that can be called a "merger" of law and morality, and to which the term "intersection" is scarcely appropriate.

Instead of pursuing some such course of thought, to my surprise I found Professor Hart leaving completely untouched the nature of the fundamental rules that make law itself possible, and turning his attention instead to what he considers a confusion of thought on the part of the critics of positivism. Leaving out of account his discussion of analytical jurisprudence, his argument runs something as follows: Two views are associated with the names of Bentham and Austin. One is the command theory of law, the other is an insistence on the separation of law and morality. Critics of these writers came in time to perceive—"dimly," Professor Hart says—that the command theory is untenable. By a loose association of ideas they wrongly supposed that in advancing reasons for rejecting the command theory they had also refuted the view that law and morality must be sharply separated. This was a "natural mistake," but plainly a mistake just the same.

I do not think any mistake is committed in believing that Bentham and Austin's error in formulating improperly and too simply the problem of the relation of law and morals was part of a larger error that led to the command theory of law. I think the connection between these two errors can be made clear if we ask ourselves what would have happened to Austin's system of thought if he had abandoned the command theory.

One who reads Austin's Lectures V and VI[10] cannot help being impressed by the way he hangs doggedly to the command theory, in spite of the fact that every pull of his own keen mind was toward abandoning it. In the case of a sovereign monarch, law is what the monarch commands. But what shall we say of the "laws" of succession which tell who the "lawful" monarch it? It is of the essence of a command that it be addressed by a superior to an inferior, yet in the case of a "sovereign many," say, a parliament, the sovereign seems to command itself since a member of parliament may be convicted under a law he himself drafted and voted for. The sovereign must be unlimited in legal power, for who could adjudicate the legal bounds of a supreme lawmaking power? Yet a "sovereign many" must accept the limitation of rules before it can make law at all. Such a body can gain the power to issue commands only by acting in a "corporate capacity"; this it can do only by proceeding "agreeably to the modes and forms" established and accepted for the making of law. Judges exercise a power delegated to them by the supreme lawmaking power, and are commissioned to carry out its "direct or circuitous commands." Yet in a federal system it is the courts which must resolve conflicts of competence between the federation and its components.

All of these problems Austin sees with varying degrees of explicitness, and he struggles mightily with them. Over and over again he teeters on the edge of an abandonment of the command theory in favor of what Professor Hart has described as a view that discerns the foundations of a legal order in "certain fundamental accepted rules specifying the essential lawmaking procedures." Yet he never takes the plunge. He does not take it because he had a sure insight that it would forfeit the black-and-white distinction between law and morality that was the whole object of his Lectures—indeed, one may say, the enduring object of a dedicated life. For if law is made possible by "fundamental accepted rules"—which for Austin must be rules, not of law, but of positive morality—what are we to say of the rules that the lawmaking power enacts to regulate its own lawmaking? We have election laws, laws allocating legislative representation to specific geographic areas, rules of parliamentary procedure, rules for the qualification of voters, and many other laws and rules of similar nature. These do not remain fixed, and all of them shape in varying degrees the lawmaking process. Yet how are we to distinguish between those basic rules that owe their validity to acceptance, and those which are properly rules of law, valid even when men generally consider them to be evil or ill-advised? In other words, how are we to define the words "fundamental" and "essential" in Professor Hart's own formulation: "certain fundamental accepted rules specifying the essential lawmaking procedure"? The solution for this problem in Kelsen's the-

ory is instructive. Kelsen does in fact take the plunge over which Austin hesitated too long. Kelsen realizes that before we can distinguish between what is law and what is not, there must be an acceptance of some basic procedure by which law is made. In any legal system there must be some fundamental rule that points unambiguously to the source from which laws must come in order to be laws. This rule Kelsen called "the basic norm." In his own words,

The basic norm is not valid because it has been created in a certain way, but its validity is assumed by virtue of its content. It is valid, then, like a norm of natural law. . . . The idea of a pure positive law, like that of natural law, has its limitations.[11]

It will be noted that Kelsen speaks, not as Professor Hart does, of "fundamental rules" that regulate the making of law, but of a single rule or norm. Of course, there is no such single rule in any modern society. The notion of the basic norm is admittedly a symbol, not a fact. It is a symbol that embodies the positivist quest for some clear and unambiguous test of law, for some clean, sharp line that will divide the rules which owe their validity to acceptance and intrinsic appeal. The difficulties Austin avoided by sticking with the command theory, Kelsen avoids by a fiction which simplifies reality into a form that can be absorbed by positivism.

A full exploration of all the problems that result when we recognize that law becomes possible only by virtue of rules that are not law, would require drawing into consideration the effect of the presence or absence of a written constitution. Such a constitution in some ways simplifies the problems I have been discussing, and in some ways complicates them. In so far as a written constitution defines basic lawmaking procedure, it may remove the perplexities that arise when a parliament in effect defines itself. At the same time, a legislature operating under a written constitution may enact statutes that profoundly affect the lawmaking procedure and its predictable outcome. If these statutes are drafted with sufficient cunning, they may remain within the frame of the constitution and yet undermine the institutions it was intended to establish. If the "court–packing" proposal of the thirties does not illustrate this danger unequivocally, it at least suggests that the fear of it is not fanciful. No written constitution can be self-executing. To be effective it requires not merely the respectful deference we show for ordinary legal enactments, but that willing convergence of effort we give to moral principles in which we have an active belief. One may properly work to amend a constitution, but so long as it remains unamended one must work with it, not against it or around it. All this amounts to saying that to be effective a written constitution must be accepted, at least provisionally, not just as law, but as good law.

What have these considerations to do with the ideal of fidelity to law? I think they have a great deal to do with it, and that they reveal the essential incapacity of the positivistic view to serve that ideal effectively. For I believe that a realization of this ideal is something for which we must plan, and that is precisely what positivism refuses to do.

Let me illustrate what I mean by planning for a realization of the ideal of fidelity to law. Suppose we are drafting a written constitution for a country just emerging from a period of violence and disorder in which any thread of legal continuity with previous governments has been broken. Obviously such a constitution cannot lift itself unaided into legality; it cannot be law simply because it says it is. We should keep in mind that the efficacy of our work will depend upon general acceptance and that to make this acceptance secure there must be a general belief that the constitution itself is necessary, right, and good. The provisions of the constitution should, therefore, be kept simple and understandable, not only in language, but also in purpose. Preambles and other explanations of what is being sought, which would be objectionable in an ordinary statute, may find an appropriate place in our constitution. We should think of our constitution as establishing a basic procedural framework for future governmental action in the enactment and administration of laws. Substantive limitations on the power of government should be kept to a minimum and should generally be confined to those for which a need can be generally appreciated. In so far as possible, substantive aims should be achieved procedurally, on the principle that if men are compelled to act in the right way, they will generally do the right things.

These considerations seem to have been widely ignored in the constitutions that have come into existence since World War II. Not uncommonly these constitutions incorporate a host of economic and political measures of the type one would ordinarily associate with statutory law. It is hardly likely that these measures have been written into the constitution because they represent aims that are generally shared. One suspects that the reason for their inclusion is precisely the opposite, namely, a fear that they would not be able to survive the vicissitudes of an ordinary exercise of parliamentary power. Thus, the divisions of opinion that are a normal accompaniment of lawmaking are written into the document that makes law itself possible. This is obviously a procedure that contains serious dangers for a future realization of the ideal of fidelity to law.

I have ventured these remarks on the making of constitutions not because I think they can claim any special profundity, but because I wished to illustrate what I mean by planning the conditions that will make it possible to realize the ideal of fidelity to law. Even within the limits of my modest purpose, what I have said may be clearly wrong. If so, it would not be for me to say whether I am also wrong clearly. I will, however, venture to assert that if I am wrong, I am wrong significantly. What disturbs me about the school of legal positivism is that it not only refuses to deal with problems of the sort I have just discussed, but bans them on principle from the province of legal philosophy. In its concern to assign the right labels to the things men do, this school seems to lose all interest in asking whether men are doing the right things.

IV. THE MORALITY OF LAW ITSELF

Most of the issues raised by Professor Hart's essay can be restated in terms of the distinction between order and good order. Law may be said to represent order *simpliciter.* Good order is law that corresponds to the demands of justice, or morality, or men's notions of what ought to be. This rephrasing of the issue is useful in bringing to light the ambitious nature of Professor Hart's undertaking, for surely we would all agree that it is no easy thing to distinguish order from good order. When it is said, for example, that law simply represents that public order which obtains under all governments—democratic, Fascist, or Communist [12]—the order intended is certainly not that of a morgue or cemetery. We must mean a functioning order, and such an order has to be at least good enough to be considered as functioning by some standard or other. A reminder that workable order usually requires some play in the joints, and therefore cannot be too orderly, is enough to suggest some of the complexities that would be involved in any attempt to draw a sharp distinction between order and good order.

For the time being, however, let us suppose we can in fact clearly separate the concept of order from that of good order. Even in this unreal and abstract form the notion of order itself contains what may be called a moral element. Let me illustrate this "morality of order" in its crudest and most elementary form. Let us suppose an absolute monarch, whose word is the only law known to his subjects. We may further suppose him to be utterly selfish and to seek in his relations with his subjects solely his own advantage. This monarch from time to time issues commands, promising rewards for compliance and threatening punishment for disobedience. He is, however, a dissolute and forgetful fellow, who never makes the slightest attempt to ascertain who have in fact followed his directions and who have not. As a result he habitually punishes loyalty and rewards disobedience. It is apparent that this monarch will never achieve even his own selfish aims until he is ready to accept that minimum self-restraint that will create a meaningful connection between his words and his actions.

Let us now suppose that our monarch undergoes a change of heart and begins to pay some attention to what he said yesterday when, today, he has occasion to distribute bounty or to order the chopping off of heads. Under the strain of this new responsibility, however, our monarch relaxes his attention in other directions and becomes hopelessly slothful in the phrasing of his commands. His orders become so ambiguous and are uttered in so inaudible a tone that his subjects never have any clear idea what he wants them to do. Here, again, it is apparent that if our monarch for his own selfish advantage wants to create in his realm anything like a system of law he will have to pull himself together and assume still another responsibility. Law, considered merely as order, contains, then, its own implicit morality. This morality of order must be respected if we are to create anything that can be called law, even bad law. Law by itself is powerless to bring this morality into existence. Until our monarch is really ready to face the responsibilities of his position, it will do no good for him to issue still another futile command, this time self-addressed and threatening himself with punishment if he does not mend his ways.

There is a twofold sense in which it is true that law cannot be built on law. First of all, the authority to make law must be supported by moral attitudes that accord to it the competency it claims. Here we are dealing with a morality external to law, which makes law possible. But this alone is not enough. We may stipulate that in our monarchy the accepted "basic norm" designates the monarch himself as the only possible source of law. We still cannot have law until our monarch is ready to accept the internal morality of law itself.

In the life of a nation these external and internal moralities of law reciprocally influence one another; a deterioration of the one will almost inevitably produce a deterioration in the other. So closely related are they that when the anthropologist Lowie speaks of "the generally accepted ethical postulates underlying our ... legal institutions as their ultimate sanction and guaranteeing their smooth functioning,"[13] he may be presumed to have both of them in mind.

What I have called "the internal morality of law" seems to be almost completely neglected by Professor Hart. He does make brief mention of "justice in the administration of the law," which consists in the like treatment of like cases, by whatever elevated or perverted standards the word "like" may be defined.[14] But he quickly dismisses this aspect of law as having no special relevance to his main enterprise.

In this I believe he is profoundly mistaken. It is his neglect to analyze the demands of a morality of order that leads him throughout his essay to treat law as a datum projecting itself into human striving. When we realize that order itself is something that must be worked for, it becomes apparent that the existence of a legal system, even a bad or evil legal system, is always a matter of degree. When we recognize this simple fact of everyday legal experience, it becomes impossible to dismiss the problems presented by the Nazi regime with a simple assertion: "Under the Nazis there was law, even if it was bad law." We have instead to inquire how much of a legal system survived the general debasement and perversion of all forms of social order that occurred under the Nazi rule, and what moral implications this mutilated system had for the conscientious citizen forced to live under it.

It is not necessary, however, to dwell on such moral upheavals as the Nazi regime to see how completely incapable the positivistic philosophy is of serving the one high moral ideal it professes, that of fidelity to law. Its default in serving this ideal actually becomes most apparent, I believe, in the everyday problems that confront those who are earnestly desirous of meeting the moral demands of a legal order, but who have responsible functions to discharge in the very order toward which loyalty is due.

Let us suppose the case of a trial judge who has had an extensive experience in commercial matters and before whom a great many commercial disputes are tried. As a subordinate in a judicial hierarchy, our judge has of course the duty to follow the law laid down by his supreme court. Our imaginary Scrutton has the misfortune, however, to live under a supreme court which he considers woefully ignorant of the ways and needs of commerce. To his mind, many of this court's decisions in the field of commercial law simply do not make sense. If a conscientious judge caught in this dilemma were to turn to the positivistic philosophy what succor could he expect? It will certainly do no good to remind him that he has an obligation of fidelity to law. He is aware of this already and painfully so, since it is the source of his predicament. Nor will it help to say that if he legislates, it must be "interstitially," or that his contributions must be "confined from molar to molecular motions."[15] This mode of statement may be congenial to those who like to think of law, not as a purposive thing, but as an expression of the dimensions and directions of state power. But I cannot believe that the essentially trite idea behind this advice can be lifted by literary eloquence to the point where it will offer any real help to our judge; for one thing, it may be impossible for him to know whether his supreme court would regard any particular contribution of his as being wide or narrow.

Nor is it likely that a distinction between core and penumbra would be helpful. The predicament of our judge may well derive, not from particular precedents, but from a mistaken conception of the nature of commerce which extends over many decisions and penetrates them in varying degrees. So far as his problem arises from the use of particular words, he may well find that the supreme court often uses the ordinary terms of commerce in senses foreign to actual business dealings. If he interprets those words as a business executive or accountant would, he may well reduce the precedents he is bound to apply to a logical shambles. On the other hand, he may find great difficulty in discerning the exact sense in which the supreme court used those words, since in his mind that sense is itself the product of a confusion.

Is it not clear that it is precisely positivism's insistence on a rigid separation of law as it is from law as it ought to be that renders the positivistic philosophy incapable of aiding our judge? Is it not also clear that our judge can never achieve a satisfactory resolution of his dilemma unless he views his duty of fidelity to law in a context which also embraces his responsibility for making law what it ought to be?

The case I have supposed may seem extreme, but the problem it suggests pervades our whole legal system. If the divergence of views between our judge and his supreme court were less drastic, it would be more difficult to present his predicament graphically, but the perplexity of his position might actually increase. Perplexities of this sort are a normal accompaniment of the discharge of any adjudicative function; they perhaps reach their most poignant intensity in the field of administrative law.

One can imagine a case—surely not likely in Professor Hart's country or mine—where a judge might hold profound moral convictions that were exactly the opposite of those held, with equal attachment, by his supreme court. He might also be convinced that the precedents he was bound to apply were the direct product of a morality he considered abhorrent. If such a judge did not find the solution for his dilemma in surrendering his office, he might well be driven to a wooden and literal application of precedents which he could not otherwise apply because he was incapable of understanding the philosophy that animated them. But I doubt that a judge in this situation would need the help of legal positivism to find these melancholy escapes from his predicament. Nor do I think that such a predicament is likely to arise within a nation where both law and good law are regarded as collaborative human achievements in need of constant renewal, and where lawyers are still at least as interested in asking "What is good law?" as they are in asking "What is law?"

V. THE PROBLEM OF RESTORING RESPECT FOR LAW AND JUSTICE AFTER THE COLLAPSE OF A REGIME THAT RESPECTED NEITHER

After the collapse of the Nazi regime the German courts were faced with a truly frightful predicament. It was impossible for them to declare the whole dictatorship illegal or to treat as void every decision and legal enactment that had emanated from Hitler's government. Intolerable dislocations would have resulted from any such wholesale outlawing of all that occurred over a span of twelve years. On the other hand, it was equally impossible to carry forward into the new government the effects of every Nazi perversity that had been committed in the name of law; any such course would have tainted an indefinite future with the poisons of Nazism.

This predicament—which was, indeed, a pervasive one, affecting all branches of law—came to a dramatic head in a series of cases involving informers who had taken advantage of the Nazi terror to get rid of personal enemies or unwanted spouses. If all Nazi statutes and judicial decisions were indiscriminately "law," then these despicable creatures were guiltless, since they had turned their victims over to processes which the Nazis themselves knew by the name of law. Yet it was intolerable, especially for the surviving relatives and friends of the victims, that these people should go about unpunished, while the objects of their spite were dead, or were just being released after years of imprisonment, or, more painful still, simply remained unaccounted for.

The urgency of this situation does not by any means escape Professor Hart. Indeed, he is moved to recommend an expedient that is surely not lacking itself in a certain air of desperation. He suggests that a retroactive criminal statute would have been the least objectionable solution to the problem. This statute would have punished the informer, and branded him as a criminal, for an act which Professor Hart regards as having been perfectly legal when he committed it.[16]

On the other hand, Professor Hart condemns without qualification those judicial decisions in which the courts themselves undertook to declare void certain of the Nazi statutes under which the informer's victims had been convicted. One cannot help raising at this point the question whether the issue as presented by Professor Hart himself is truly that of fidelity to law. Surely it would be a necessary implication of a retroactive criminal statute against informers that, for purposes of that statute at least, the Nazi laws as applied to the informers or their victims were to be regarded as void. With this turn the question seems no longer to be whether what was once law can now be declared not to have been law, but rather who should do the dirty work, the courts or the legislature.

But, as Professor Hart himself suggests, the issues at stake are much too serious to risk losing them in a semantic tangle. Even if the whole question were one of words, we should remind ourselves that we are in an area where words have a powerful effect on human attitudes. I should

like, therefore, to undertake a defense of the German courts, and to advance reasons why, in my opinion, their decisions do not represent the abandonment of legal principle that Professor Hart sees in them. In order to understand the background of those decisions we shall have to move a little closer, within smelling distance of the witches' caldron, than we have been brought so far by Professor Hart. We shall have also to consider an aspect of the problem ignored in his essay, namely, the degree to which the Nazis observed what I have called the inner morality of law itself.

Throughout his discussion Professor Hart seems to assume that the only difference between Nazi law and, say, English law is that the Nazis used their laws to achieve ends that are odious to an Englishman. This assumption is, I think, seriously mistaken, and Professor Hart's acceptance of it seems to me to render his discussion unresponsive to the problem it purports to address.

Throughout their period of control the Nazis took generous advantage of a device not wholly unknown to American legislatures, the retroactive statute curing past legal irregularities. The most dramatic use of the curative powers of such a statute occurred on July 3,1934, after the "Roehm purge." When this intraparty shooting affair was over and more than seventy Nazis had been —one can hardly avoid saying—"rubbed out," Hitler returned to Berlin and procured from his cabinet a law ratifying and confirming the measures taken between June 30, and July 1, 1934, without mentioning the names of those who were now considered to have been lawfully executed.[17] Some time later Hitler declared that during the Roehm purge "the supreme court of the German people ... consisted of myself,"[18] surely not an overstatement of the capacity in which he acted if one takes seriously the enactment conferring retroactive legality on "the measures taken."

Now in England and America it would never occur to anyone to say that "it is in the nature of law that it cannot be retroactive," although, of course, constitutional inhibitions may prohibit certain kinds of retroactivity. We would say it is normal for a law to operate prospectively, and that it may be arguable that it ought never operate otherwise, but there would be a certain occult unpersuasiveness in any assertion that retroactivity violates the very nature of law itself. Yet we have only to imagine a country in which all laws are retroactive in order to see that retroactivity presents a real problem for the internal morality of law. If we suppose an absolute monarch who allows his realm to exist in a constant state of anarchy, we would hardly say that he could create a regime of law simply by enacting a curative statute conferring legality on everything that had happened up to its date and by announcing an intention to enact similar statutes every six months in the future.

A general increase in the resort to statutes curative of past legal irregularities represents a deterioration in that form of legal morality without which law itself cannot exist. The threat of such statutes hangs over the whole legal system, and robs every law on the books of some of its significance. And surely a general threat of this sort is implied when a government is willing to use such a statute to transform into lawful execution what was simple murder when it happened.

During the Nazi regime there were repeated rumors of "secret laws." In the article criticized by Professor Hart, Radbruch mentions a report that the wholesale killings in concentration camps were made "lawful" by a secret enactment.[19] Now surely there can be no greater legal monstrosity than a secret statute. Would anyone seriously recommend that following the war the German courts should have searched for unpublished laws among the files left by Hitler's government so that citizens' rights could be determined by a reference to these laws?

The extent of the legislator's obligation to make his laws known to his subjects is, of course, a problem of legal morality that has been under active discussion at least since the Secession of the Plebs. There is probably no modern state that has not been plagued by this problem in one form or another. It is most likely to arise in modern societies with respect to unpublished administrative directions. Often these are regarded in quite good faith by those who issue them as affecting only matters of internal organization. But since the procedures followed by an administrative agency, even in its "internal" actions, may seriously affect the rights and interests of the citizen, these unpublished, or "secret," regulations are often a subject for complaint.

But as with retroactivity, what in most societies is kept under control by the tacit restraints of legal decency broke out in monstrous form under Hitler. Indeed, so loose was the whole Nazi morality of law that it is not easy to know just what should be regarded as an unpublished or secret law. Since unpublished instructions to those administering the law could destroy the letter of any published law by imposing on it an outrageous interpretation, there was a sense in which the meaning of every law was "secret." Even a verbal order from Hitler that a thousand prisoners in concentration camps be put to death was at once an administrative direction and a validation of everything done under it as being "lawful."

But the most important affronts to the morality of law by Hitler's government took no such subtle forms as those exemplified in the bizarre outcroppings I have just discussed. In the first place, when legal forms became inconvenient, it was always possible for the Nazis to bypass them entirely and "to act through the party in the streets." There was no one who dared bring them to account for whatever outrages might thus be committed. In the second place, the Nazi-dominated courts were always ready to disregard any statute, even those enacted by the Nazis themselves, if this suited their convenience or if they feared that a lawyer-like interpretation might incur displeasure "above."

This complete willingness of the Nazis to disregard even their own enactments was an important factor leading Radbruch to take the position he did in the articles so severely criticized by Professor Hart. I do not believe that any fair appraisal of the action of the postwar German courts is possible unless we take this factor into account, as Professor Hart fails completely to do.

These remarks may seem inconclusive in their generality and to rest more on assertion than evidentiary fact. Let us turn at once, then, to the actual case discussed by Professor Hart.[20]

In 1944 a German soldier paid a short visit to his wife while under travel orders on a reassignment. During the single day he was home, he conveyed privately to his wife something of his opinion of the Hitler government. He expressed disapproval of (*sich abfßllig geäussert über*) Hitler and other leading personalities of the Nazi party. He also said it was too bad Hitler had not met his end in the assassination attempt that had occurred on July 20th of that year. Shortly after his departure, his wife, who during his long absence on military duty "had turned to other men" and who wished to get rid of him reported his remarks to the local leader of the Nazi party, observing that "a man who would say a thing like that does not deserve to live." The result was a trial of the husband by a military tribunal and a sentence of death. After a short period of imprisonment, instead of being executed, he was sent to the front again. After the collapse of the Nazi regime, the wife was brought to trial for having procured the imprisonment of her husband. Her defense rested on the ground that her husband's statements to her about Hitler and the Nazis constituted a crime under the laws then in force. Accordingly, when she informed on her husband she was simply bringing a criminal to justice.

This defense rested on two statutes, one passed in 1934, the other in 1938. Let us first consider the second of these enactments, which was part of a more comprehensive legislation creating a whole series of special wartime criminal offenses. I reproduce below a translation of the only pertinent section:

The following persons are guilty of destroying the national power of resistance and shall be punished by death: Whoever publicly solicits or incites a refusal to fulfill the obligations of service in the armed forces of Germany, or in armed forces allied with Germany, or who otherwise publicly seeks to injure or destroy the will of the German people or an allied people to assert themselves stalwartly against their enemies.[21]

It is almost inconceivable that a court of present-day Germany would hold the husband's remarks to his wife, who was barred from military duty by her sex, to be a violation of the final catch-all provision of this statute, particularly when it is recalled that the test reproduced above was part of a more comprehensive enactment dealing with such things as harboring deserters, escaping military duty by self-inflicted injuries, and the like. The question arises, then, as to the extent to which the interpretive principles applied by the courts of Hitler's government should be accepted in determining whether the husband's remarks were indeed unlawful.

This question becomes acute when we note that the act applies only to *public* acts or utterances, whereas the husband's remarks were in the privacy of his own home. Now it appears that the Nazi courts (and it should be noted we are dealing with a special military court) quite generally disregarded this limitation and extended the act to all utterances, private or public.[22] Is Professor Hart prepared to say that the legal meaning of this statute is to be determined in the light of this apparently uniform principle of judicial interpretation?

Let us turn now to the other statute upon which Professor Hart relies in assuming that the husband's utterance was unlawful. This is the act of 1934, the relevant portions of which are translated below:

(1) Whoever publicly makes spiteful or provocative statements directed against, or statements which disclose a base disposition toward, the leading personalities of the nation or of the National Socialist German Workers' Party, or toward measures taken or institutions established by them, and of such a nature as to undermine the people's confidence in their political leadership, shall be punished by imprisonment.

(2) Malicious utterances not made in public shall be treated in the same manner as public utterances when the person making them realized or should have realized they would reach the public.

(3) Prosecution for such utterances shall be only on the order of the National Minister of Justice; in case the utterance was directed against a leading personality of the National Socialist German Workers' Party, the Minister of Justice shall order prosecution only with the advice and consent of the Representative of the Leader.

(4) The National Minister of Justice shall, with the advice and consent of the Representative of the Leader, determine who shall belong to the class of leading personalities for purposes of Section 1 above.[23]

Extended comment on this legislative monstrosity is scarcely called for, overlarded and undermined as it is by uncontrolled administrative discretion. We may note only: first, that it offers no justification whatever for the death penalty actually imposed on the husband, though never carried out; second, that if the wife's act in informing on her husband made his remarks "public," there is no such thing as a private utterance under this statute. I should like to ask the reader whether he can actually share Professor Hart's indignation that, in the perplexities of the postwar reconstruction, the German courts saw fit to declare this thing not a law. Can it be argued seriously that it would have been more beseeming to the judicial process if the postwar courts had undertaken a study of "the interpretative principles" in force during Hitler's rule and had then solemnly applied those "principles" to ascertain the meaning of this statute? On the other hand, would the courts really have been showing respect for Nazi law if they had construed the Nazi statutes by their own, quite different, standards of interpretation? Professor Hart castigates the German courts and Radbruch, not so much for what they believed had to be done, but because they failed to see that they were confronted by a moral dilemma of a sort that would have been immediately apparent to Bentham and Austin. By the simple dodge of saying, "When a statute is sufficiently evil it ceases to be law," they ran away from the problem they should have faced.

This criticism is, I believe, without justification. So far as the courts are concerned, matters certainly would not have been helped if, instead of saying, "This is now law," they had said, "This is law but it is so evil we will refuse to apply it." Surely moral confusion reaches its height when a court refuses to apply something it admits to be law, and Professor Hart does not recommend any such "facing of the true issue" by the courts themselves. He would have preferred a retroactive statute. Curiously, this was also the preference of Radbruch.[24] But unlike Professor Hart, the German courts and Gustav Radbruch were living participants in a situation of drastic emergency. The informer problem was a pressing one, and if legal institutions were to be rehabilitated in Germany it would not do to allow the people to begin taking the law into their own hands, as might have occurred while the courts were waiting for a statute.

As for Gustav Radbruch, it is, I believe, wholly unjust to say that he did not know he was faced with a moral dilemma. His postwar writings repeatedly stress the antinomies confronted in the effort to rebuild decent and orderly government in Germany. As for the ideal of fidelity to law, I shall let Radbruch's own words state his position:

We must not conceal from ourselves—especially not in the light of our experiences during the twelve-year dictatorship—what frightful dangers for the rule of law can be contained in the notion of "statutory lawlessness" and in refusing the quality of law to duly enacted statutes.[25]

The situation is not that legal positivism enables a man to know when he faces a difficult problem of choice, while Radbruch's beliefs deceive him into thinking there is no problem to face. The real issue dividing Professors Hart and Radbruch is: How shall we state the problem? What is the nature of the dilemma in which we are caught?

I hope I am not being unjust to Professor Hart when I say that I can find no way of describing the dilemma as he sees it but to use some such words as the following: On the one hand, we have an amoral datum called law, which has the peculiar quality of creating a moral duty to obey it. On the other hand, we have a moral duty to do what we think is right and decent. When we are confronted by a statute we believe to be thoroughly evil, we have to choose between those two duties.

If this is the positivist position, then I have no hesitancy in rejecting it. The "dilemma" it states has the verbal formulation of a problem, but the problem it states makes no sense. It is like saying I have to choose between giving food to a starving man and being mimsy with the borogoves. I do not think it is unfair to the positivistic philosophy to say that it never gives any coherent meaning to the moral obligation of fidelity to law. This obligation seems to be conceived as sui generis, wholly unrelated to any of the ordinary, extralegal ends of human life. The fundamental postulate of positivism—that law must be strictly severed from morality—seems to deny the possibility of any bridge between the obligation to obey law and other moral obligations. No mediating principle can measure their respective demands on conscience, for they exist in wholly separate worlds.

While I would not subscribe to all of Radbruch's postwar views—especially those relating to "higher law"—I think he saw, much more clearly than does Professor Hart, the true nature of the dilemma confronted by Germany in seeking to rebuild her shattered legal institutions. Germany had to restore both respect for law and respect for justice. Though neither of these could be restored without the other, painful antinomies were encountered in attempting to restore both at once, as Radbruch saw all too clearly. Essentially Radbruch saw the dilemma as that of meeting the demands of order, on the one hand, and those of good order, on the other. Of course no pat formula can be derived from this phrasing of the problem. But, unlike legal positivism, it does not present us with opposing demands that have no living contact with one another, that simply shout their contradictions across a vacuum. As we seek order, we can meaningfully remind ourselves that order itself will do us no good unless it is good for something. As we seek to make our order good, we can remind ourselves that justice itself is impossible without order, and that we must not lose order itself in the attempt to make it good.

VI. THE MORAL IMPLICATIONS OF LEGAL POSITIVISM

We now reach the question whether there is any ground for Gustav Radbruch's belief that a general acceptance of the positivistic philosophy in pre-Nazi Germany made smoother the route to dictatorship. Understandably, Professor Hart regards this as the most outrageous of all charges against positivism.

Here indeed we enter upon a hazardous area of controversy, where ugly words and ugly charges have become commonplace. During the last half century in this country no issue of legal philosophy has caused more spilling of ink and adrenalin than the assertion that there are "totalitarian" implications in the views of Oliver Wendell Holmes, Jr. Even the most cautiously phrased criticisms of that grand old figure from the age of Darwin, Huxley, and Haeckel seem to stir the reader's mind with the memory of past acerbities.[26] It does no good to suggest that perhaps Holmes did not perceive all the implications of his own philosophy, for this is merely to substitute one insult for another. Nor does it help much to recall the dictum of one of the closest companions of Holmes' youth—surely no imperceptive observer—that Holmes was "composed of at least two and a half different people rolled into one, and the way he keeps them together in one tight skin, without quarreling any more than they do, is remarkable."[27]

In the venturing upon these roughest of all jurisprudential waters, one is not reassured to see even so moderate a man as Professor Hart indulging in some pretty broad strokes of the oar. Radbruch disclosed "an extraordinary naïveté" in assessing the temper of his own profession in Germany and in supposing that its adherence to positivism helped the Nazis to power.[28] His judgment on this and other matters shows that he had "only half–digested the spiritual message of liberalism he mistakenly thought he was conveying to his countrymen.[29] A state of "hysteria"[30] is revealed by those who see a wholesome reorientation of German legal thinking in such judicial decisions as were rendered in the informer cases.

Let us put aside at least the blunter tools of invective and address ourselves as calmly as we can to the question whether legal positivism, as practiced and preached in Germany, had, or could have had, any causal connection with Hitler's ascent to power. It should be recalled that in the seventy-five years before the Nazi regime the positivistic philosophy had achieved in Germany a standing such as it enjoyed in no other country. Austin praised a German scholar for bringing international law within the clarity-producing restraints of positivism.[31] Gray reported with pleasure that the "abler" German jurists of his time

were "abjuring all 'nicht positivisches Recht,'" and cited Bergbohm as an example.[32] This is an illuminating example, for Bergbohm was a scholar whose ambition was to make German positivism live up to its own pretensions. He was distressed to encounter vestigial traces of natural-law thinking in writings claiming to be positivistic. In particular, he was disturbed by the frequent recurrence of such notions as that law owes its efficacy to a perceived moral need for order, or that it is in the nature of man that he requires a legal order, etc. Bergbohm announced a program, never realized, to drive from positivistic thinking these last miasmas from the swamp of natural law.[33] German jurists generally tended to regard the Anglo-American common law as a messy and unprincipled conglomerate of law and morals.[34] Positivism was the only theory of law that could claim to be "scientific" in an Age of Science. Dissenters from this view were characterized by positivists with that epithet modern man fears above all others: "naïve." The result was that it could be reported by 1927 that "to be found guilty of adherence to natural law theories is a kind of social disgrace."[35]

To this background we must add the observation that the Germans seem never to have achieved that curious ability possessed by the British, and to some extent by the Americans, of holding their logic on short leash. When a German defines law, he means his definition to be taken seriously. If a German writer had hit upon the slogan of American legal realism, "Law is simply the behavior patterns of judges and other state officials," he would not have regarded this as an interesting little conversation-starter. He would have believed it and acted on it.

German legal positivism not only banned from legal science any consideration of the moral ends of law, but it was also indifferent to what I have called the inner morality of law itself. The German lawyer was therefore peculiarly prepared to accept as "law" anything that called itself by that name, was printed at government expense, and seemed to come "von oben herab."

In the light of these considerations I cannot see either absurdity or perversity in the suggestion that the attitudes prevailing in the German legal profession were helpful to the Nazis. Hitler did not come to power by a violent revolution. He was Chancellor before he became the Leader. The exploitation of legal forms started cautiously and became bolder as power was consolidated. The first attacks on the established order were on ramparts which, if they were manned by anyone, were manned by lawyers and judges. These ramparts fell almost without a struggle.

Professor Hart and others have been understandably distressed by references to a "higher law" in some of the decisions concerning informers and in Radbruch's postwar writings. I suggest that if German jurisprudence had concerned itself more with the inner morality of law, it would not have been necessary to invoke any notion of this sort in declaring void the more outrageous Nazi statutes.

To me there is nothing shocking in saying that a dictatorship which clothes itself with a tinsel of legal form can so far depart from the morality of order, from the inner morality of law itself, that it ceases to be a legal system. When a system calling itself law is predicated upon a general disregard by judges of the terms of the laws they purport to enforce, when this system habitually cures its legal irregularities, even the grossest, by retroactive statutes, when it has only to resort to forays of terror in the streets, which no one dares challenge, in order to escape even those scant restraints imposed by the pretence of legality—when all these things have become true of a dictatorship, it is not hard for me, at least, to deny to it the name of law.

I believe that the invalidity of the statutes involved in the informer cases could have been grounded on considerations such as I have just outlined. But if you were raised with a generation that said "law is law" and meant it, you may feel the only way you can escape one law is to set another off against it, and this perforce must be a "higher law." Hence these notions of "higher law," which are a justifiable cause for alarm, may themselves be a belated fruit of German legal positivism.

It should be remarked at this point that it is chiefly in Roman Catholic writings that the theory of natural law is considered, not simply as a search for those principles that will enable men to live together successfully, but as a quest for something that can be called "a higher law." This identification of natural law with a law that is above human laws seems in fact to be demanded by any doctrine that asserts the possibility of an authoritative pronouncement of the demands of natural law. In those areas affected by such pronouncements as have so far been issued, the conflict between Roman Catholic doctrine and opposing views seems to me to be a conflict between two forms of positivism. Fortunately, over

most of the area with which lawyers are concerned, no such pronouncements exist. In these areas I think those of us who are not adherents of its faith can be grateful to the Catholic Church for having kept alive the rationalistic tradition in ethics.

I do not assert that the solution I have suggested for the informer cases would not have entailed its own difficulties, particularly the familiar one of knowing where to stop. But I think it demonstrable that the most serious deterioration in legal morality under Hitler took place in branches of the law like those involved in the informer cases; no comparable deterioration was to be observed in the ordinary branches of private law. It was in those areas where the ends of law were most odious by ordinary standards of decency that the morality of law itself was most flagrantly disregarded. In other words, where one would have been most tempted to say, "This is so evil it cannot be a law," one could usually have said instead, "This thing is the product of a system so oblivious to the morality of law that it is not entitled to be called a law." I think there is something more than accident here, for the overlapping suggests that legal morality cannot live when it is severed from a striving toward justice and decency.

But as an actual solution for the informer cases, I, like Professors Hart and Radbruch, would have preferred a retroactive statute. My reason for this preference is not that this is the most nearly lawful way of making unlawful what was once law. Rather I would see such a statute as a way of symbolizing a sharp break with the past, as a means of isolating a kind of cleanup operation from the normal functioning of the judicial process. By this isolation it would become possible for the judiciary to return more rapidly to a condition in which the demands of legal morality could be given proper respect. In other words, it would make it possible to plan more effectively to regain for the ideal of fidelity to law its normal meaning.

VII. THE PROBLEM OF INTERPRETATION: THE CORE AND THE PENUMBRA

It is essential that we be just as clear as we can be about the meaning of Professor Hart's doctrine of "the core and the penumbra,"[36] because I believe the casual reader is likely to misinterpret what he has to say. Such a reader is apt to suppose that Professor Hart is merely describing something that is a matter of everyday experience for the lawyer, namely, that in the interpretation of legal rules it is typically the case (though not universally so) that there are some situations which will seem to fall rather clearly within the rule, while others will be more doubtful. Professor Hart's thesis takes no such jejune form. His extended discussion of the core and the penumbra is not just a complicated way of recognizing that some cases are hard, while others are easy. Instead, on the basis of a theory about language meaning generally, he is proposing a theory of judicial interpretation which is, I believe, wholly novel. Certainly it has never been put forward in so uncompromising a form before.

As I understand Professor Hart's thesis (if we add some tacit assumptions implied by it, as well as some qualifications he would no doubt wish his readers to supply) a full statement would run something as follows: The task of interpretation is commonly that of determining the meaning of the individual words of a legal rule, like "vehicle" in a rule excluding vehicles from a park. More particularly, the task of interpretation is to determine the range of reference of such a word, or the aggregate of things to which it points. Communication is possible only because words have a "standard instance," or a "core of meaning" that remains relatively constant, whatever the context in which the word may appear. Except in unusual circumstances, it will always be proper to regard a word like "vehicle" as embracing its "standard instance," that is, that aggregate of things it would include in all ordinary contexts, within or without the law. This meaning the word will have in any legal rule, whatever its purpose. In applying the word to its "standard instance," no creative role is assumed by the judge. He is simply applying the law "as it is."

In addition to a constant core, however, words also have a penumbra of meaning which, unlike the core, will vary from context to context. When the object in question (say, a tricycle) falls within this penumbral area, the judge is forced to assume a more creative role. He must now undertake, for the first time, an interpretation of the rule in the light of its purpose or aim. Having in mind what was sought by the regulation concerning parks, ought it to be considered as barring tricycles? When questions of this sort are decided there is at least an "intersection" of "is" and "ought," since the judge, in deciding what the rule "is," does so in the light of his notions of what "it ought to be" in order to carry out its purpose.

If I have properly interpreted Professor Hart's theory as it affects the "hard core," then I think it is quite untenable. The most obvious defect of his theory lies in its assumption that problems of interpretation typically turn on the meaning of individual words. Surely no judge applying a rule of the common law ever followed any such procedure as that described (and, I take it, prescribed) by Professor Hart; indeed, we do not normally even think of his problem as being one of "interpretation." Even in the case of statutes, we commonly have to assign meaning, not to a single word, but to a sentence, a paragraph, or a whole page or more of text. Surely a paragraph does not have a "standard instance" that remains constant whatever the context in which it appears. If a statute seems to have a kind of "core meaning" that we can apply without a too precise inquiry into its exact purpose, this is because we can see that, however one might formulate the precise objective of the statute, *this* case would still come within it.

Even in situations where our interpretive difficulties seem to head up in a single word, Professor Hart's analysis seems to me to give no real account of what does or should happen. In his illustration of the "vehicle," although he tells us this word has a core of meaning that in all contexts defines unequivocally a range of objects embraced by it, he never tells us what these objects might be. If the rule excluding vehicles from parks seems easy to apply in some cases, I submit this is because we can see clearly enough what the rule "is aiming at in general" so that we know there is no need to worry about the difference between Fords and Cadillacs. If in some cases we seem to be able to apply the rule without asking what its purpose is, this is not because we can treat a directive arrangement as if it had no purpose. It is rather because, for example, whether the rule be intended to preserve quiet in the park, or to save carefree strollers from injury, we know, "without thinking," that a noisy automobile must be excluded.

What would Professor Hart say if some local patriots wanted to mount on a pedestal in the park a truck used in World War II, while other citizens, regarding the proposed memorial as an eyesore, support their stand by the "no vehicle" rule? Does this truck, in perfect working order, fall within the core or the penumbra?

Professor Hart seems to assert that unless words have "standard instances" that remain constant regardless of context, effective communication would break down and it would become impossible to construct a system of "rules which have authority."[37] If in every context words took on a unique meaning, peculiar to that context, the whole process of interpretation would become so uncertain and subjective that the ideal of a rule of law would lose its meaning. In other words, Professor Hart seems to be saying that unless we are prepared to accept his analysis of interpretation, we must surrender all hope of giving an effective meaning to the ideal of fidelity to law. This presents a very dark prospect indeed, if one believes, as I do, that we cannot accept his theory of interpretation. I do not take so gloomy a view of the future of the ideal of fidelity to law.

An illustration will help to test, not only Professor Hart's theory of the core and the penumbra, but its relevance to the ideal of fidelity to law as well. Let us suppose that in leafing through the statutes, we come upon the following enactment: "It shall be a misdemeanor, punishable by a fine of five dollars, to sleep in any railway station." We have no trouble in perceiving the general nature of the target toward which this state is aimed. Indeed, we are likely at once to call to mind the picture of a disheveled tramp, spread out in an ungainly fashion on one of the benches of the station, keeping weary passengers on their feet and filling their ears with raucous and alcoholic snores. This vision may fairly be said to represent the "obvious instance" contemplated by the statute, though certainly it is far from being the "standard instance" of the physiological state called "sleep."

Now let us see how this example bears on the ideal of fidelity to law. Suppose I am a judge, and that two men are brought before me for violating this statute. The first is a passenger who was waiting at 3 A.M. for a delayed train. When he was arrested he was sitting upright in an orderly fashion, but was heard by the arresting officer to be gently snoring. The second is a man who had brought a blanket and pillow to the station and had obviously settled himself down for the night. He was arrested, however, before he had a chance to go to sleep. Which of these cases presents the "standard instance" of the word "sleep"? If I disregard that question, and decide to fine the second man and set free the first, have I violated a duty of fidelity to law? Have I violated that duty if I interpret the word "sleep" as used in this statute to mean something like "to spread oneself out on a bench or floor to spend the night, or as if to spend the night"?

Testing another aspect of Professor Hart's theory, is it really ever possible to interpret a word in a statute without knowing the aim of the statute? Suppose we encounter the following incomplete sentence: "All improvements must be promptly reported to . . ." Professor Hart's theory seems to assert that even if we have only this fragment before us we can safely construe the word "improvement" to apply to its "standard instance," though we would have to know the rest of the sentence before we could deal intelligently with "problems of the penumbra." Yet surely in the truncated sentence I have quoted, the word "improvement" is almost as devoid of meaning as the symbol "X."

The word "improvement" will immediately take on meaning if we fill out the sentence with the words, "the head nurse," or, "the Town Planning Authority," though the two meanings that come to mind are radically dissimilar. It can hardly be said that these two meanings represent some kind of penumbral accretion to the word's "standard instance." And one wonders, parenthetically, how helpful the theory of the core and the penumbra would be in deciding whether, when the report is to be made to the planning authorities, the word "improvement" includes an unmortgageable monstrosity of a house that lowers the market value of the land on which it is built.

It will be instructive, I think, to consider the effect of other ways of filling out the sentence. Suppose we add to, "All improvements must be promptly reported to . . ." the words, "the Dean of the Graduate Division." Here we no longer seem, as we once did, to be groping in the dark; rather, we seem now to be reaching into an empty box. We achieve a little better orientation if the final clause reads, "to the Principal of the School," and we feel completely at ease if it becomes, "to the Chairman of the Committee on Relations with the Parents of Children in the Primary Division."

It should be noted that in deciding what the word "improvement" means in all these cases, we do not proceed simply by placing the word in some general context, such as hospital practice, town planning, or education. If this were so, the "improvement" in the last instance might just as well be that of the teacher as that of the pupil. Rather, we ask ourselves, What can this rule be for? What evil does it seek to avert? What good is it intended to promote? When it is "the head nurse" who receives the report, we are apt to find ourselves asking, "Is there, perhaps, a shortage of hospital space, so that patients who improve sufficiently are sent home or are assigned to a ward where they will receive less attention?" If "Principal" offers more orientation than "Dean of the Graduate Division," this must be because we know something about the differences between primary education and education on the postgraduate university level. We must have some minimum acquaintance with the ways in which these two educational enterprises are conducted, and with the problems encountered in both of them, before any distinction between "Principal" and "Dean of the Graduate Division" would affect our interepretation of "improvement." We must, in other words, be sufficiently capable of putting ourselves in the position of those who drafted the rule to know what they thought "ought to be." It is in the light of this "ought" that we must decide what the rule "is."

Turning now to the phenomenon Professor Hart calls "preoccupation with the penumbra," we have to ask ourselves what is actually contributed to the process of interpretation by the common practice of supposing various "borderline" situations. Professor Hart seems to say, "Why, nothing at all, unless we are working with problems of the penumbra." If this is what he means, I find his view a puzzling one, for it still leaves unexplained why, under this theory, if one is dealing with a penumbral problem, it could be useful to think about other penumbral problems.

Throughout his whole discussion of interpretation, Professor Hart seems to assume that it is a kind of cataloguing procedure. A judge faced with a novel situation is like a library clerk who has to decide where to shelve a new book. There are easy cases: the *Bible* belongs under Religion, *The Wealth of Nations* under Economics, etc. Then there are hard cases, when the librarian has to exercise a kind of creative choice, as in deciding whether *Das Kapital* belongs under Politics or Economics, *Gulliver's Travels* under Fantasy or Philosophy. But whether the decision where to shelve is easy or hard, once it is made all the librarian has to do is to put the book away. And so it is with judges, Professor Hart seems to say, in all essential particulars. Surely the judicial process is something more than a cataloguing procedure. The judge does not discharge his responsibility when he pins an apt diagnostic label on the case. He has to do something about it, to treat it, if you will. It is this larger responsibility which explains why interpretative problems

almost never turn on a single word, and also why lawyers for generations have found the putting of imaginary borderline cases useful, not only "on the penumbra," but in order to know where the penumbra begins.

These points can be made clear, I believe, by drawing again on our example of the statutory fragment which reads, "All improvements must be promptly reported to. . . ." Whatever the concluding phrase may be, the judge has not solved his problems simply by deciding what kind of improvement is meant. Almost all of the words in the sentence may require interpretation, but most obviously this is so of "promptly" and "reported." What kind of "report" is contemplated: a written note, a call at the office, entry in a hospital record? How specific must it be? Will it be enough to say "a lot better," or "a big house with a bay window"?

Now it should be apparent to any lawyer that in interpreting words like "improvement," "prompt," and "report," no real help is obtained by asking how some extralegal "standard instance" would define these words. But, much more important, when these words are all parts of a single structure of thought, they are in interaction with one another during the process of interpretation. "What is an 'improvement'? Well, it must be something that can be made the subject of a report. So, for purposes of this statute 'improvement" really means 'reportable improvement.' What kind of 'report' must be made? Well, that depends upon the sort of 'improvement' about which information is desired and the reasons for desiring the information."

When we look beyond individual words to the statute as a whole, it becomes apparent how the putting of hypothetical cases assists the interpretative process generally. By pulling our minds first in one direction, then in another, these cases help us to understand the fabric of thought before us. This fabric is something we seek to discern, so that we may know truly what it is, but it is also something that we inevitably help to create as we strive (in accordance with our obligation of fidelity to law) to make the statute a coherent, workable whole.

I should have considered all these remarks much too trite to put down here if they did not seem to be demanded in an answer to the theory of interpretation proposed by Professor Hart, a theory by which he puts such store that he implies we cannot have fidelity to law in any meaningful sense unless we are prepared to accept it.

Can it be possible that the positivistic philosophy demands that we abandon a view of interpretation which sees as its central concern, not words, but purpose and structure? If so, then the stakes in this battle of schools are indeed high.

I am puzzled by the novelty Professor Hart attributes to the lessons I once tried to draw from Wittgenstein's example about teaching a game to children.[38] I was simply trying to show the role reflection plays in deciding what ought to be done. I was trying to make such simple points as that decisions about what ought to be done are improved by reflection, by an exchange of views with others sharing the same problems, and by imagining various situations that might be presented. I was assuming that all of these innocent and familiar measures might serve to sharpen our perception of what we were trying to do, and that the product of the whole process might be, not merely a more apt choice of means for the end sought, but a clarification of the end itself. I had thought that a famous judge of the English bench had something like this in mind when he spoke of the common law as working "itself pure."[39] If this view of the judicial process is no longer entertained in the country of its origin, I can only say that, whatever the vicissitudes of Lord Mansfield's British reputation may be, he will always remain for us in this country a heroic figure of jurisprudence.

I have stressed here the deficiencies of Professor Hart's theory as that theory affects judicial interpretation. I believe, however, that its defects go deeper and result ultimately from a mistaken theory about the meaning of language generally. Professor Hart seems to subscribe to what may be called "the pointer theory of meaning,"[40] a theory which ignores or minimizes the effect on the meaning of words of the speaker's purpose and the structure of language. Characteristically, this school of thought embraces the notion of "common usage." The reason is, of course, that it is only with the aid of this notion that it can seem to attain the inert datum of meaning it seeks, a meaning isolated from the effects of purpose and structure.

It would not do to attempt here an extended excursus into linguistic theory. I shall have to content myself with remarking that the theory of meaning implied in Professor Hart's essay seems to me to have been rejected by three men who stand at the very head of modern developments in logical analysis: Wittgenstein, Russell, and Whitehead. Wittgenstein's posthumous *Philo-sophical Investigations* constitutes a sort of running commentary on the way words shift and transform their meanings as they move from context to context. Russell repudiates the cult of "common usage," and asks what "instance" of the word "word" itself can be given that does not imply some specific intention in the use of it.[41] Whitehead explains the appeal that "the deceptive identity of the repeated word" has for modern philosophers; only by assuming some linguistic constant (such as the "core of meaning") can validity be claimed for procedures of logic which of necessity move the word from one context to another.[42]

VIII. THE MORAL AND EMOTIONAL FOUNDATIONS OF POSITIVISM

If we ignore the specific theories of law associated with the positivistic philosophy, I believe we can say that the dominant tone of positivism is set by a fear of a purposive interpretation of law and legal institutions, or at least by a fear that such an interpretation may be pushed too far. I think one can find confirmatory traces of this fear in all of those classified as "positivists" by Professor Hart, with the outstanding exception of Bentham, who is in all things a case apart and who was worlds removed from anything that could be called *ethical* positivism.

Now the belief that many of us hold, that this fear of purpose takes a morbid turn in positivism, should not mislead us into thinking that the fear is wholly without justification, or that it reflects no significant problem in the organization of society.

Fidelity to law *can* become impossible if we do not accept the broader responsibilities (themselves purposive, as all responsibilities are and must be) that go with a purposive interpretation of law. One can imagine a course of reasoning that might run as follows: This statute says absinthe shall not be sold. What is its purpose? To promote health. Now, as everyone knows, absinthe is a sound, wholesome, and beneficial beverage. Therefore, interpreting the statute in the light of its purpose, I construe it to direct a general sale and consumption of that most healthful of beverages, absinthe.

If the risk of this sort of thing is implicit in a purposive interpretation, what measures can we take to eliminate it, or to reduce it to bearable proportions? One is tempted to say. "Why, just use ordinary common sense." But this would be an evasion, and would amount to saying that although we know the answer, we cannot say what it is. To give a better answer, I fear I shall have to depart from those high standards of clarity Professor Hart so rightly prizes and so generally exemplifies. I shall have to say that the answer lies in the concept of *structure*. A statute or a rule of common law has, either explicitly, or by virtue of its relation with other rules, something that may be called a structural integrity. This is what we have in mind when we speak of "the intent of the statute," though we know it is men who have intentions and not words on paper. Within the limits of that structure, fidelity to law not only permits but demands a creative role from the judge, but beyond that structure it does not permit him to go. Of course, the structure of which I speak presents its own "problems of the penumbra." But the penumbra in this case surrounds something real, somthing that has a meaning and integrity of its own. It is not a purposeless collocation of words that gets its meaning on loan from lay usage.

It is one of the great virtues of Professor Hart's essay that it makes explicit positivism's concern for the ideal of fidelity to law. Yet I believe, though I cannot prove, that the basic reason why positivism fears a purposive interpretation is not that it may lead to anarchy, but that it may push us too far in the opposite direction. It sees in a purposive interpretation, carried too far, a threat to human freedom and human dignity.

Let me illustrate what I mean by supposing that I am a man without religious beliefs living in a community of ardent Protestant Christian faith. A statute in this community makes it unlawful for me to play golf on Sunday. I find this statute an annoyance and accept its restraints reluctantly. But the annoyance I feel is not greatly different from that I might experience if, though it were lawful to play on Sunday, a power failure prevented me from taking the streetcar I would normally use in reaching the course. In the vernacular, "it is just one of those things."

What a different complexion the whole matter assumes if a statute compels me to attend church, or, worse still, to kneel and recite prayers! Here I may feel a direct affront to my integrity as a human being. Yet the purpose of both statutes may well be to increase church attendance. The difference may even seem to be that the first statute seeks its end slyly and by indirection, the second, honestly and openly. Yet surely this is a case in which indirection has its virtues and honesty its heavy price in human dignity.

Now I believe that positivism fears that a too explicit and uninhibited interpretation in terms of purpose may well push the first kind of statute in the direction of the second. If this is a basic concern underlying the positivistic philosophy, that philosophy is dealing with a real problem, however inept its response to the problem may seem to be. For this problem of the impressed purpose is a crucial one in our society. One thinks of the obligation to bargain "in good faith" imposed by the National Labor Relations Act.[43] One recalls the remark that to punish a criminal is less of an affront to his dignity than to reform and improve him. The statutory preamble comes to mind: the increasing use made of it, its legislative wisdom, the significance that should be accorded to it in judicial interpretation. The flag salute cases[44] will, of course, occur to everyone. I myself recall the splendid analysis by Professor von Hippel of the things that were fundamentally wrong about Nazism, and his conclusion that the grossest of all Nazi perversities was that of coercing acts, like the putting out of flags and saying, "Heil Hitler!" that have meaning only when done voluntarily, or, more accurately, have a meaning when coerced that is wholly parasitic on an association of them with past voluntary expressions.[45]

Questions of this sort are undoubtedly becoming more acute as the state assumes a more active role with respect to economic activity. No significant economic activity can be organized exclusively by "don'ts." By its nature economic production requires a co-operative effort. In the economic field there is special reason, therefore, to fear that "This you may not do" will be transformed into "This you must do—but willingly." As we all know, the most tempting opportunity for effecting this transformation is presented by what is called in administrative practice "the prehearing conference," in which the negative threat of a statute's sanctions may be used by its administrators to induce what they regard, in all good conscience, as "the proper attitude."

I look forward to the day when legal philosophy can address itself earnestly to issues of this sort, and not simply exploit them to score points in favor of a position already taken. Professor Hart's essay seems to me to open the way for such a discussion, for it eliminates from the positivistic philosophy a pretense that has hitherto obscured every issue touched by it. I mean, of course, the pretense of the ethical neutrality of positivism. That is why I can say in all sincerity that, despite my almost paragraph-by-paragraph disagreement with the views expressed in his essay, I believe Professor Hart has made an enduring contribution to legal philosophy.

NOTES

1. Kelsen, *Die Idee des Naturrechtes,* 7 ZEITSCHRIFT FÜR ÖFFENTLICHES RECHT 221, 248 (Austria 1927).

2. Hart, *Positivism and the Separation of Law and Morals,* 71 HARV. L. REV. 593, 615–21 (1958).

3. U. S. CONSTITUTION art. V.

4. Hart, *supra* note 2, at 624.

5. For an outstanding example, see G. Scammell and Nephew, Ltd. v. Custom, [1941] A.C.251 (1940). I personally would be inclined to put under the same head Victoria Laundry, Ltd. v. Newman Industries, Ltd., [1949] 2 K.B. 528 (C.A.).

6. See Hart, *supra* note 2, at 608–12.

7. See N.Y. Times, Nov. 8, 1949, p. 1, col. 4 (late city ed.) (report of a speech made on November 7, 1949 to the Central Committee of the Union of Catholic Italian Lawers).

8. Hart, *supra* note 2, at 603.

9. *Ibid.*

10. I AUSTIN, LECTURES ON JURISPRUDENCE 167–341 (5th ed. 1885).

11. KELSEN, GENERAL THEORY OF LAW AND STATE 401 (3d ed. 1949).

12. *E.g.,* Friedmann, *The Planned State and the Rule of Law,* 22 AUSTR. L. J. 162, 207 (1948).

13. LOWIE, THE ORIGIN OF THE STATE 113 (1927).

14. Hart, *supra* note 2, at 623–24.

15. Southern Pacific Co. v. Jensen, 244 U.S. 205, 221 (1917) (Holmes J., dissenting), paraphrasing Storti v. Commonwealth, 178 Mass. 549, 554, 60 N.E. 210, 211 (1901) (Holmes, C.J.) in which it was held that a statute providing for electrocution as a means of inflicting the punishment of death was not cruel or unusual punishment within the Massachusetts Declaration of Rights, MASS. CONST. pt. First, art. XXVI, simply because it accomplished its object by molecular, rather than molar, motions.

16. See Hart, *supra* note 2, at 619–20.

17. N.Y. Times, July 4, 1934, p. 3, col. 3 (late city ed.).

18. See N.Y. Times, July 14, 1934, p.5, col. 2 (late city ed.).

19. Radbruch, *Die Erneuerung des Rechts,* 2 DIE WANDLUNG 8, 9 (Germany 1947). A useful discussion of the Nazi practice with reference to the publicity given laws will be found in Giese, *Verkündung und Gesetzeskraft,* 76 ARCHIV DES ÖFFENTLICHEN RECHTS 464, 471–72 (Germany 1951). I rely on this article for the remarks that follow in the text.

20. Judgment of July 27, 1949, Oberlandesgericht, Bamberg, 5 SÜDDEUTSCHE JURISTEN-ZEITUNG 207 (Germany 1950), 64 HARV. L. REV. 1005 (1951).

21. The passage translated is § 5 of a statute creating a Kriegssonderstrafrecht. Law of Aug. 17, 1938, [1939] 2 REICHSGESETZBLATT pt. 1, at 1456. The translation is mine.

22. See 5 SÜDDEUTSCHE JURISTEN-ZEITUNG 207, 210 (Germany 1950).

23. The translated passage is article II of A Law Against Malicious Attacks on the State and the Party and for the Protection of the Party Uniform, Law of Dec. 20, 1934, [1934] 1 REICHSGESETZBLATT 1269. The translation is mine.

24. See Radbruch, *Die Erneuerung des Rechts,* 2 DEI WANDLUNG 8, 10 (Germany 1947).

25. Radbruch, *Gesetzliches Unrecht und Übergesetzliches Recht,* 1 SÜDDEUTSCHE JURISTEN-ZEITUNG 105, 107 (Germany 1946) (reprinted in RADBRUCH, RECHTSPHILOSOPHIE

347, 354 (4th ed. 1950)). The translation is mine.

26. See, *e.g.,* Howe, *The Positivism of Mr. Justice Holmes,* 64 HARV. L. REV. 529 (1951).

27. See 1 PERRY, THE THOUGHT AND CHARACTER OF WILLIAM JAMES 297 (1935) (quoting a letter written by William James in 1869).

28. Hart, *supra* note 2, at 617–18.

29. *Id.* at 618.

30. *Id.* at 619.

31. 1 AUSTIN, LECTURES ON JURISPRUDENCE 173 (5th ed. 1885) (Lecture V).

32. GRAY, THE NATURE AND SOURCES OF THE LAW 96 (2d ed.1921).

33. 1 BERGBOHM, JURISPRUDENZ UND RECHTSPHILOSOPHIE 355–552 (1892).

34. See, *e.g.* Heller, *Die Krisis der Staatslehre,* 55 ARCHIV FÜR SOZIALWISSENSCHAFT UND SOZIALPOLITIK 289, 309 (Germany 1926).

35. Voegelin, *Kesen's Pure Theory of Law,* 42 POL. SCI. Q. 268, 269 (1927).

36. Hart, *supra* note 2, at 606–08.

37. See *id.* at 607.

38. Fuller, *Human Purpose and Natural Law,* 53 J. PHILOS. 697, 700 (1956).

39. Omychund v. Barker, 1 Atk. 21, 33, 26 Eng. Rep. 15, 22–23 (Ch. 1744) (argument of Solicitor-General Murray, later Lord Mansfield): "All occasions do not arise at once; . . . a statute very seldom can take in all cases, therefore the common law, *that works itself pure* by rules drawn from the fountain of justice, is for this reason superior to an act of Parliament."

40. I am speaking of the linguistic theory that seems to be implied in the essay under discussion here. In Professor Hart's brilliant inaugural address, *Definition and Theory in Jurisprudence,* 70, L.Q. REV. 37 (1954), the most important point made is that terms like "rule," "right," and "legal person" cannot be defined by pointing to correspondent things or actions in the external world, but can only be understood in terms of the function performed by them in the larger system, just as one cannot understand the umpire's ruling, "You're out!" without having at least a general familiarity with the rules of baseball. Even in the analysis presented in the inaugural address, however, Professor Hart seems to think that the dependence of meaning on function and context is a peculiarity of formal and explicit systems, like those of a game or a legal system. He seems not to recognize that what he has to say about explicit systems is also true of the countless informal and overlapping systems that run through language as a whole. These implicit systematic or structural elements in language often enable us to understand at once the meaning of a word used in a wholly novel sense, as in the statement, "Experts regard the English Channel as the most difficult swim in the world." In the essay now being discussed, Professor Hart seems nowhere to recognize that a rule or statute has a structural or systematic quality that reflects itself in some measure into the meaning of every principal term in it.

41. RUSSELL, *The Cult of "Common Usage,"* in PORTRAITS FROM MEMORY AND OTHER ESSAYS 166, 170–71 (1956).

42. WHITEHEAD, *Analysis of Meaning,* in ESSAYS IN SCIENCE AND PHILOSOPHY 122, 127 (1947).

43. § 8 (d), added by 61 Stat. 142 (1947), 29 U.S.C. § 158 (d) (1952): see NLRA §§ 8(a) (5), (b) (3), as amended, 61 Stat. 141 (1947), 29 U.S.C. §§ 158 (a) (5), (b) (3) (1952).

44. Minersville School Dist. v. Gobitis, 310 U.S. 586 (1940), *overruled,* West Virginia State Bd. of Educ. v. Barnette, 319 U.S. 624 (1943).

45. VON HIPPEL DIE NATIONALSOZIALISTISCHE HERRSCHAFISORDNUNG ALS WARNUNG UND LHERE 6–7 (1946).

GUSTAV RADBRUCH

Five Minutes of Legal Philosophy

FIRST MINUTE

"An order is an order," the soldier is told. "A law is a law," says the jurist. The soldier, however, is required neither by duty nor by law to obey an order that he knows to have been issued with a felony or misdemeanor in mind, while the jurists, since the last of the natural law theorists among them disappeared a hundred years ago, have recognized no such exceptions to the validity of a law or to the requirement of obedience by those subject to it. A law is valid because it is a law, and it is a law if in the general run of cases it has the power to prevail.

This view of the nature of a law and of its validity (we call it the positivistic theory) has rendered the jurist as well as the people defenseless against laws, however arbitrary, cruel, or criminal they may be. In the end, the positivistic theory equates the law with power; there is law only where there is power.

SECOND MINUTE

There have been attempts to supplement or replace this tenet with another: Law is what benefits the people.

That is, arbitrariness, breach of contract, and illegality, provided only that they benefit the people, are law. Practically speaking, that means that every whim and caprice of the despot, punishment without laws or judgment, lawless killing of the sick—whatever the state authorities deem to be of benefit to the people—is law. That *can* mean that the private benefit of those in power is regarded as a public benefit. The equating of the law with supposed or ostensible benefits to the people thus transformed a *Rechtsstaat* into a state of lawlessness.

* "Fünf Minuten Rechtsphilosophie," translated by Stanley L. Paulson, first appeared in the Rhein-Neckar-Zeitung, September 12, 1945, and was reprinted in the 8th edition of Gustav Radbruch's *Rechtsphilosophie,* edited by Erik Wolf and Hans-Peter Schneider (Stuttgart: K. F. Koehler Verlag, 1973), pp. 327-29. The translation is printed with the kind permission of the K. F. Koehler Verlag.

No, this tenet should not be read as: Whatever benefits the people is law. Rather, it is the other way around: Only what is law benefits the people.

THIRD MINUTE

Law is the will to justice, and justice means: To judge without regard to the person, to treat everyone according to the same standard.

If one applauds the assassination of political opponents and orders the murder of those of another race while meting out the most cruel, degrading punishments for the same acts committed against those of one's own persuasion, that is neither justice nor law.

If laws consciously deny the will to justice, if, for example, they grant and deny human rights arbitrarily, then these laws lack validity, the people owe them no obedience, and even the jurists must find the courage to deny their legal character.

FOURTH MINUTE

Surely public benefit, along with justice, is an end of the law. Surely laws as such, even bad laws, have value nonetheless—the value of safeguarding the law against doubt. And surely, owing to human imperfection, the three values of the law—public benefit, legal certainty, and justice—cannot always be united harmoniously in laws. It remains, then, only to consider whether validity is to be granted to bad, detrimental, or unjust laws for the sake of legal certainty or whether it is to be denied them because they are unjust or socially detrimental. One thing, however, must be indelibly impressed on the consciousness of the people and the jurists: there *can* be laws that are so unjust, so socially detrimental that their validity, indeed their very character as laws, must be denied.

FIFTH MINUTE

There are, therefore, principles of law that are stronger than any statute, so that a law conflicting with these principles is devoid of validity. One calls these principles the natural law or the law of reason. To be sure, their details remain somewhat doubtful, but the work of centuries has established a solid core of them and they have come to enjoy such a far-reaching consensus in the declarations of human and civil rights that only the deliberate skeptic can still entertain doubts about some of them.

In religious language the same thoughts have been recorded in two biblical passages. On the one hand it is written that you are to obey the authorities who have power over you. But then on the other, it is also written that you are to obey God before man—and this is not simply a pious wish, but a valid proposition of law. The tension between these two directives cannot, however, be relieved by appealing to a third—say, to the maxim: Render unto Caesar the things that are Caesar's and unto God the things that are God's. For this directive too, leaves the boundary in doubt. Rather, it leaves the solution to the voice of God, which speaks to the conscience of the individual only in the exceptional case.

LON L. FULLER

The Problem of the Grudge Informer*

By a narrow margin you have been elected Minister of Justice of your country, a nation of some twenty million inhabitants. At the outset of your term of office you are confronted by a serious problem that will be described below. But first the background of this problem must be presented.

For many decades your country enjoyed a peaceful, constitutional and democratic government. However, some time ago it came upon bad times. Normal relations were disrupted by a deepening economic depression and by an increasing antagonism among various factional groups, formed along economic, political, and religious lines. The proverbial man on horseback appeared in the form of the Headman of a political party or society that called itself the Purple Shirts.

In a national election attended by much disorder the Headman was elected President of the Republic and his party obtained a majority of the seats in the General Assembly. The success of the party at the polls was partly brought about by a campaign of reckless promises and ingenious falsifications, and partly by the physical intimidation of night-riding Purple Shirts who frightened many people away from the polls who would have voted against the party.

When the Purple Shirts arrived in power they took no steps to repeal the ancient Constitution or any of its provisions. They also left intact the Civil and Criminal Codes and the Code of Procedure. No official action was taken to dismiss any government official or to remove any judge from the bench. Elections continued to be held at intervals and ballots were counted with apparent honesty. Nevertheless, the country lived under a reign of terror.

Judges who rendered decisions contrary to the wishes of the party were beaten and murdered.

The accepted meaning of the Criminal Code was perverted to place political opponents in jail. Secret statutes were passed, the contents of which were known only to the upper levels of the party hierarchy. Retroactive statutes were enacted which made acts criminal that were legally innocent when committed. No attention was paid by the government to the restraints of the Constitution, of antecedent laws, or even of its own laws. All opposing political parties were disbanded. Thousands of political opponents were put to death, either methodically in prisons or in sporadic night forays of terror. A general amnesty was declared in favor of persons under sentence for acts "committed in defending the fatherland against subversion." Under this amnesty a general liberation of all prisoners who were members of the Purple Shirt party was effected. No one not a member of the party was released under the amnesty.

The Purple Shirts as a matter of deliberate policy preserved an element of flexibility in their operations by acting at times through the party "in the streets," and by acting at other times through the apparatus of the state which they controlled. Choice between the two methods of proceeding was purely a matter of expediency. For example, when the inner circle of the party decided to ruin all the former Socialist-Republicans (whose party put up a last-ditch resistance to the new regime), a dispute arose as to the best way of confiscating their property. One faction, perhaps still influenced by prerevolutionary conceptions, wanted to accomplish this by a statute declaring their goods forfeited for criminal acts. Another wanted to do it by compelling the owners to deed their property over at the point of a bayonet. This group argued against the proposed statute on the ground that it would attract unfavorable comment abroad. The Headman decided in favor of direct action through the party to be followed by a secret statute ratifying the party's action and confirming the titles obtained by threats of physical violence.

*From *The Morality of Law,* Revised Edition, by Lon L. Fuller (New Haven: Yale University Press, 1969), pp. 245–53. Reprinted by permission of the author and the publisher.

The Purple Shirts have now been overthrown and a democratic and constitutional government restored. Some difficult problems have, however, been left behind by the deposed regime. These you and your associates in the new government must find some way of solving. One of these problems is that of the "grudge informer."

During the Purple Shirt regime a great many people worked off grudges by reporting their enemies to the party or to the government authorities. The activities reported were such things as the private expression of views critical of the government, listening to foreign radio broadcasts, associating with known wreckers and hooligans, hoarding more than the permitted amount of dried eggs, failing to report a loss of identification papers within five days, etcetera. As things then stood with the administration of justice, any of these acts, if proved, could lead to a sentence of death. In some cases this sentence was authorized by "emergency" statutes; in others it was imposed without statutory warrant, though by judges duly appointed to their offices.

After the overthrow of the Purple Shirts, a strong public demand grew up that these grudge informers be punished. The interim government, which preceded that with which you are associated, temporized on this matter. Meanwhile it has become a burning issue and a decision concerning it can no longer be postponed. Accordingly, your first act as Minister of Justice has been to address yourself to it. You have asked your five Deputies to give thought to the matter and to bring their recommendations to conference. At the conference the five Deputies speak in turn as follows:

FIRST DEPUTY. "It is perfectly clear to me that we can do nothing about these so-called grudge informers. The acts they reported were unlawful according to the rules of the government then in actual control of the nation's affairs. The sentences imposed on their victims were rendered in accordance with principles of law then obtaining. These principles differed from those familar to us in ways that we consider detestable. Nevertheless they were then the law of the land. One of the principal differences between that law and our own lies in the much wider discretion it accorded to the judge in criminal matters. This rule and its consequences are as much entitled to respect by us as the reform which the Purple Shirts introduced into the law of wills, whereby only two witnesses were required instead of three. It is im-

material that the rule granting the judge a more or less uncontrolled discretion in criminal cases was never formally enacted but was a matter of tacit acceptance. Exactly the same thing can be said of the opposite rule which we accept that restricts the judge's discretion narrowly. The difference between ourselves and the Purple Shirts is not that theirs was an unlawful government—a contradiction in terms—but lies rather in the field of ideology. No one has a greater abhorrence than I for Purple Shirtism. Yet the fundamental difference between our philosophy and theirs is that we permit and tolerate differences in viewpoint, while they attempted to impose their monolithic code on everyone. Our whole system of government assumes that law is a flexible thing, capable of expressing and effectuating many different aims. The cardinal point of our creed is that when an objective has been duly incorporated into a law or judicial decree it must be provisionally accepted even by those that hate it, who must await their chance at the polls, or in another litigation, to secure a legal recognition for their own aims. The Purple Shirts, on the other hand, simply disregarded laws that incorporated objectives of which they did not approve, not even considering it worth the effort involved to repeal them. If we now seek to unscramble the acts of the Purple Shirt regime, declaring this judgment invalid, that statute void, this sentence excessive, we shall be doing exactly the thing we most condemn in them. I recognize that it will take courage to carry through with the program I recommend and we shall have to resist strong pressures to public opinion. We shall also have to be prepared to prevent the people from taking the law into their own hands. In the long run, however, I believe the course I recommend is the only one that will insure the triumph of the conceptions of law and government in which we believe."

SECOND DEPUTY. "Curiously, I arrive at the same conclusion as my colleague, by an exactly opposite route. To me it seems absurd to call the Purple Shirt regime a lawful government. A legal system does not exist simply because policemen continue to patrol the streets and wear uniforms or because a constitution and code are left on the shelf unrepealed. A legal system presupposes laws that are known, or can be known, by those subject to them. It presupposes some uniformity of action and that like cases will be given like treatment. It presupposes the absence of some lawless power, like the Purple Shirt Party, standing above the government and able at any time to interfere with the administration of justice whenever it does not function according to the whims of that power. All of these presuppositions enter into the very conception of an order of law and have nothing to do with political and economic ideologies. In my opinion law in any ordinary sense of the word ceased to exist when the Purple Shirts came to power. During their regime we had, in effect, an interregnum in the rule of law. Instead of a government of laws we had a war of all against all conducted behind barred doors, in dark alleyways, in palace intrigues, and prison-yard conspiracies. The acts of these so-called grudge informers were just one phase of that war. For us to condemn these acts as criminal would involve as much incongruity as if we were to attempt to apply juristic conceptions to the struggle for existence that goes on in the jungle or beneath the surface of the sea. We must put this whole dark, lawless chapter of our history behind us like a bad dream. If we stir among its hatreds, we shall bring upon ourselves something of its evil spirit and risk infection from its miasmas. I therefore say with my colleague, let bygones be bygones. Let us do nothing about the so-called grudge informers. What they did do was neither lawful nor contrary to law, for they lived, not under a regime of law, but under one of anarchy and terror."

THIRD DEPUTY. "I have a profound suspicion of any kind of reasoning that proceeds by an 'either-or' alternative. I do not think we need to assume either, on the one hand, that in some manner the whole of the Purple Shirt regime was outside the realm of law, or, on the other, that all of its doings are entitled to full credence as the acts of a lawful government. My two colleagues have unwittingly delivered powerful arguments against these extreme assumptions by demonstrating that both of them lead to the same absurd conclusion, a conclusion that is ethically and politically impossible. If one reflects about the matter without emotion it becomes clear that we did not have during the Purple Shirt regime a 'war of all against all.' Under the surface much of what we call normal human life went on—marriages were contracted, goods were sold, wills were drafted and executed. This life was attended by the usual dislocations—automobile accidents, bankruptcies, unwitnessed wills, defamatory misprints in the newspapers. Much of this normal life and most of these equally normal dislocations of it were unaffected by the Purple Shirt ideology. The legal questions that arose in this area were handled by the courts much as they had been formerly and much as they are being handled today. It would invite an intolerable chaos if we were to declare everything that happened under the Purple Shirts to be without legal basis. On the other hand, we certainly cannot say that the murders committed in the streets by members of the party acting under orders from the Headman were lawful simply because the party had achieved control of the government and its chief had become President of the Republic. If we must condemn the criminal acts of the party and its members, it would seem absurd to uphold every act which happened to be canalized through the apparatus of a government that had become, in effect, the alter ego of the Purple Shirt Party. We must therefore, in this situation, as in most human affairs, discriminate. Where the Purple Shirt philosophy intruded itself and perverted the administration of justice from its normal aims and uses, there we must interfere. Among these perversions of justice I would count, for example, the case of a man who was in love with another man's wife and brought about the death of the husband by informing against him for a wholly trivial offense, that is, for not reporting a loss of his identification papers within five days. This informer was a murderer under the Criminal Code which was in effect at the time of his act and which the Purple Shirts had not repealed. He encompassed the death of one who stood in the way of his illicit passions and utilized the courts for the realization of his murderous intent. He knew that the courts were themselves the pliant instruments of whatever policy the Purple Shirts might for the moment consider expedient. There are other cases that are equally clear. I admit that there are also some that are less clear. We shall be embarrassed, for example, by the cases of mere busybodies who reported to the authorities everything that looked suspect. Some of these persons acted not from desire to get rid of those they accused, but with a desire to curry favor with the party, to divert suspicions (perhaps ill-found) raised against themselves, or through sheer officiousness. I don't know how these cases should be handled, and make no recommendation with regard to them. But the fact that these troublesome cases exist should not deter us from acting at once in the cases that are clear, of which there are far too many to permit us to disregard them."

FOURTH DEPUTY. "Like my colleague I too distrust 'either-or' reasoning, but I think we need to reflect more than he has about where we are headed. This proposal to pick and choose among the acts of this deposed regime is thoroughly objectionable. It is, in fact, Purple Shirtism itself, pure and simple. We like this law, so let us enforce it. We like this judgment, let it stand. This law we don't like, therefore it never was a law at all. This governmental act we disapprove, let it be deemed a nullity. If we proceed this way, we take toward the laws and acts of the Purple Shirt government precisely the unprincipled attitude they took toward the laws and acts of the government they supplanted. We shall have chaos, with every judge and every prosecuting attorney a law unto himself. Instead of ending the abuses of the Purple Shirt regime, my colleague's proposal would perpetuate them. There is only one way of dealing with this problem that is compatible with our philosophy of law and government and that is to deal with it by duly enacted law, I mean, by a special statute directed toward it. Let us study this whole problem of the grudge informer, get all the relevant facts, and draft a comprehensive law dealing with it. We shall not then be twisting old laws to purposes for which they were never intended. We shall furthermore provide penalties appropriate to the offense and not treat every informer as a murderer simply because the one he informed against was ultimately executed. I admit that we shall encounter some difficult problems of draftsmanship. Among other things, we shall have to assign a definite legal meaning to 'grudge' and that will not be easy. We should not be deterred by these difficulties, however, from adopting the only course that will lead us out of a condition of lawless, personal rule."

FIFTH DEPUTY. "I find a considerable irony in the last proposal. It speaks of putting a definite end to the abuses of the Purple Shirtism, yet it proposes to do this by resorting to one of the most hated devices of the Purple Shirt regime, the ex post facto criminal statute. My colleague dreads the confusion that will result if we attempt without a statute to undo and redress 'wrong' acts of the departed order, while we uphold and enforce its 'right' acts. Yet he seems not to realize that his proposed statute is a wholly specious cure for this uncertainty. It is easy to make a plausible argument for an undrafted statute; we all agree it would be nice to have things down in black and white on paper. But just what would this statute provide? One of my colleagues speaks of someone who had failed for five days to report a loss of his indentification papers. My colleague implies that the judicial sentence imposed for that offense, namely death, was so utterly disproportionate as to be clearly wrong. But we must remember that at that time the underground movement against the Purple Shirts was mounting in intensity and that the Purple Shirts were being harassed constantly by people with false identification papers. From their point of view they had a real problem, and the only objection we can make to their solution of it (other than the fact that we didn't want them to solve it) was that they acted with somewhat more rigor than the occasion seemed to demand. How will my colleague deal with this case in his statute, and with all of its cousins and second cousins? Will he deny the existence of any need for law and order under the Purple Shirt regime? I will not go further into the difficulties involved in drafting this proposed statute, since they are evident enough to anyone who reflects. I shall instead turn to my own solution. It has been said on very respectable authority that the main purpose of the criminal law is to give an outlet to the human instinct for revenge. There are times, and I believe this is one of them, when we should allow that instinct to express itself directly without the intervention of forms of law. This matter of the grudge informers is already in process of straightening itself out. One reads almost every day that a former lackey of the Purple Shirt regime has met his just reward in some unguarded spot. The people are quietly handling this thing in their own way and if we leave them alone, and instruct our public prosecutors to do the same, there will soon be no problem left for us to solve. There will be some disorders, of course, and a few innocent heads will be broken. But our government and our legal system will not be involved in the affair and we shall not find ourselves hopelessly bogged down in an attempt to unscramble all the deeds and misdeeds of the Purple Shirts."

As Minister of Justice, which of these recommendations would you adopt?

THE OBLIGATION TO OBEY THE LAW

M. B. E. SMITH

Is There a Prima Facie Obligation to Obey the Law?

It isn't a question of whether it was legal or illegal. That isn't enough. The question is, what is morally wrong.
—Richard Nixon, "Checkers Speech" 1952.

Many political philosophers have thought it obvious that there is a prima facie obligation to obey the law; and so, in discussing this obligation, they have thought their task to be more that of explaining its basis than of arguing for its existence. John Rawls has, for example, written:

I shall assume, as requiring no argument, that there is, at least in a society such as ours, a moral obligation to obey the law, although it may, of course, be overridden in certain cases by other more stringent obligations.[1]

As against this, I suggest that it is not at all obvious that there is such an obligation, that this is something that must be shown, rather than so blithely assumed. Indeed, were he uninfluenced by conventional wisdom, a reflective man might on first considering the question be inclined to deny any such obligation: As H. A. Prichard once remarked, "the mere receipt of an order backed by force seems, if anything, to give rise to the duty of resisting, rather than obeying."[2]

I shall argue that, although those subject to a government often have a prima facie obligation to obey particular laws (e.g., when disobedience has seriously untoward consequences or involves an act that is *mala in se*), they have no prima facie obligation to obey all its laws. I do not hope to prove this contention beyond a reasonable doubt. My goal is rather the more modest one of showing that it is a reasonable position to maintain by first criticizing arguments that purport to establish the obligation and then presenting some positive argument against it.

First, however, I must explain how I use the phrase "prima facie obligation." I shall say that a person S has a prima facie obligation to do an act X if, and only if, there is a moral reason for

S to do X which is such that, unless he has a moral reason not to do X at least as strong as his reason to do X, S's failure to do X is wrong.[3] In this discussion it will also be convenient to distinguish two kinds of prima facie obligation via the difference between the two kinds of statement which ascribe them. A specific statement asserts that some particular person has a prima facie obligation to perform some particular act. In contrast, a generic statement (e.g., "Parents have a prima facie obligation to care for their infant children") asserts that everyone who meets a certain description has a prima facie obligation to perform a certain kind of act whenever he has an opportunity to do so. I shall therefore say that a person S has a *specific* prima facie obligation to do X if, and only if, the specific statement "S has a prima facie obligation to do X" is true; and that he has a *generic* prima facie obligation to do X if, and only if, S meets some description D and the generic statement "Those who are D have a prima facie obligation to do X" is true.[4]

Now, the question of whether there is a prima facie obligation to obey the law is clearly about a generic obligation. Everyone, even the anarchist, would agree that in many circumstances individuals have specific prima facie obligations to obey specific laws. Since it is clear that there is in most circumstances a specific prima facie obligation to refrain from murder, rape, or breach of contract, it is plain that in these circumstances each of us has a specific prima facie obligation not to violate laws which prohibit these acts. Again, disobeying the law often has seriously untoward consequences; and, when this is so, virtually everyone would agree that there is a specific prima facie obligation to obey. Therefore, the interesting question about our obligation vis-á-vis the law is not "Do individual citizens ever have specific prima facie obligations to obey particular laws?," but rather "Is the moral relation of any government to its citizens such that they have a prima facie obligation to do certain things merely because they are legally required to do so?" This is, of course, equivalent to asking "Is there a generic

Reprinted by permission of the author, and of The Yale Law Journal and Fred B. Rothman & Company from *The Yale Law Journal*, vol. 82, pp. 950-976.

prima facie obligation to obey the law?" Hereafter, when I use the phrase "the prima facie obligation to obey the law" I shall be referring to a generic obligation.

One final point in clarification: As used here, the phrase "prima facie" bears a different meaning than it does when used in legal writing. In legal materials, the phrase frequently refers to evidence sufficiently persuasive so as to require rebuttal. Hence, were a lawyer to ask "Is there a prima facie obligation to obey the law?," a reasonable interpretation of his question might be "May a reasonable man take mere illegality to be sufficient evidence that an act is morally wrong, so long as there is no specific evidence tending to show it is right?" Let us call this the "lawyer's question." Now, the question of primary concern in this inquiry is "Is there any society in which mere illegality is a moral reason for an act's being wrong?" The difference between these questions is that, were there a prima facie obligation to obey the law in the lawyer's sense, mere illegality would, in the absence of specific evidence to the contrary, be evidence of wrongdoing, but it would not necessarily be relevant to a determination of whether lawbreaking is wrong where there is reason to think such conduct justified or even absolutely obligatory. In contrast, if there is a prima facie obligation to obey the law in the sense in which I am using the phrase, the mere illegality of an act is always relevant to the determination of its moral character, despite whatever other reasons are present.[5] Hence, there may be a prima facie obligation to obey the law in the lawyer's sense and yet be no such obligation in the sense of the phrase used here. Near the end of this article I shall return briefly to the lawyer's question; for the present, I raise it only that it may not be confused with the question I wish to examine.

I

The arguments I shall examine fall into three groups: First, those which rest on the benefits each individual receives from government; second, those relying on implicit consent or promise; third, those which appeal to utility or the general good. I shall consider each group in turn.

Of those in the first group, I shall begin with the argument from gratitude. Although they differ greatly in the amount of benefits they provide, virtually all governments do confer substantial benefits on their subjects. Now, it is often claimed that, when a person accepts benefits from another, he thereby incurs a debt of gratitude

towards his benefactor. Thus, if it be maintained that obedience to the law is the best way of showing gratitude towards one's government, it may with some plausibility be concluded that each person who has received benefits from his government has a prima facie obligation to obey the law.

On reflection, however, this argument is unconvincing. First, it may reasonably be doubted whether most citizens have an obligation to act gratefully towards their government. Ordinarily, if someone confers benefits on me without any consideration of whether I want them, and if he does this in order to advance some purpose other than promotion of my particular welfare, I have no obligation to be grateful towards him. Yet the most important benefits of government are not accepted by its citizens, but are rather enjoyed regardless of whether they are wanted. Moreover, a government typically confers these benefits, not to advance the interests of particular citizens, but rather as a consequence of advancing some purpose of its own. At times, its motives are wholly admirable, as when it seeks to promote the general welfare; at others, they are less so, as when it seeks to stay in power by catering to the demands of some powerful faction. But, such motives are irrelevant: Whenever government forces benefits on me for reasons other than my particular welfare, I clearly am under no obligation to be grateful to it.

Second, even assuming *arguendo* that each citizen has an obligation to be grateful to his government, the argument still falters. It is perhaps true that cheerful and willing obedience is the best way to show one's gratitude towards government, in that it makes his gratitude unmistakable. But, when a person owes a debt of gratitude towards another, he does not necessarily acquire a prima facie obligation to display his gratitude in the most convincing manner: A person with demanding, domineering parents might best display his gratitude towards them by catering to their every whim, but he surely has no prima facie obligation to do so. Without undertaking a lengthy case-by-case examination, one cannot delimit the prima facie obligation of acting gratefully, for its existence and extent depends on such factors as the nature of the benefits received, the manner in which they are conferred, the motives of the benefactor, and so forth. But, even without such an examination, it is clear that the mere fact that a person has conferred on me even the most momentous benefits does not establish his right to dictate all of my behavior; nor does it establish that I always have an obligation to consider his wishes when I am deciding what I shall do. If, then, we have a prima facie obligation to act gratefully towards government, we undoubtedly have an obligation to promote its interests when this does not involve great sacrifice on our part and to respect some of its wishes concerning that part of our behavior which does not directly affect its interests. But, our having this obligation to be grateful surely does not establish that we have a prima facie obligation to obey the law.

A more interesting argument from the benefits individuals receive from government is the argument from fair play. It differs from the argument from gratitude in contending that the prima facie obligation to obey the law is owed, not to one's government but rather to one's fellow citizens. Versions of this argument have been offered by H. L. A. Hart and John Rawls.

According to Hart, the mere existence of cooperative enterprise gives rise to a certain prima facie obligation. He argues that:

when a number of persons conduct any joint enterprise according to rules and thus restrict their liberty, those who have submitted to these restrictions when required have a right to a similar submission from those who have benefitted by their submission. The rules may provide that officials should have authority to enforce obedience and make further rules, and this will create a structure of legal rights and duties, but the moral obligation to obey the rules in such circumstances is *due* to the cooperating members of the society, and they have the correlative moral right to obedience.[6]

Rawl's account of this obligation in his essay, *Legal Obligation and the Duty of Fair Play,*[7] is rather more complex. Unlike Hart, he sets certain requirements on the kinds of cooperative enterprises that give rise to the obligation: First, that success of the enterprise depends on near-universal obedience to its rules, but not on universal cooperation; second, that obedience to its rules involves some sacrifice, in that obeying the rules restricts one's liberty; and finally, that the enterprise conform to the principles of justice.[8] Rawls also offers an explanation of the obligation: He argues, that, if a person benefits from participating in such an enterprise and if he intends to continue receiving its benefits, he acts unfairly when he refuses to obey its rules. With Hart, however, Rawls claims that this obligation is owed not to the enterprise itself, nor to its officials, but rather to those members whose obedience has made the benefits possible. Hart and Rawls also agree that this obligation of fair play— "fair play" is Rawls' term—is a fundamental obligation, not derived from utility or from mutual promise or consent.[9] Finally, both Hart and Rawls conceive of legal systems, at least those in democratic societies, as complex practices of the kind which give rise to the obligation of fair play; and they conclude that those who benefit from such legal systems have a prima facie obligation to obey their laws.

These arguments deserve great respect. Hart and Rawls appear to have isolated a kind of prima facie obligation overlooked by other philosophers and have thereby made a significant contribution to moral theory. However, the significance of their discovery to jurisprudence is less clear. Although Hart and Rawls have discovered the obligation of fair play, they do not properly appreciate its limits. Once these limits are understood, it is clear that the prima facie obligation to obey the law cannot be derived from the duty of fair play.

The obligation of fair play seems to arise most clearly within small, voluntary cooperative enterprises. Let us suppose that a number of persons have gone off into the wilderness to carve out a new society, and that they have adopted certain rules to govern their communal life. Their enterprise meets Rawls' requirements on success, sacrifice, and justice. We can now examine the moral situation of the members of that community in a number of circumstances, taking seriously Hart's insistence that cooperating members have a right to the obedience of others and Rawls' explanation of this right and its correlative obligation on grounds of fairness.

Let us take two members of the community, *A* and *B. B,* we may suppose, has never disobeyed the rules, and *A* has benefitted from *B*'s previous submission. Has *B* a right to *A*'s obedience? It would seem necessary to know the consequences of *A*'s obedience. If, in obeying the rules, *A* will confer on *B* a benefit roughly equal to those he has received from *B*, it would be plainly unfair for *A* to withhold it from *B*; and so, in this instance, *B*'s right to *A*'s obedience is clear. Similarly, if, in disobeying the rule, *A* will harm the community, *B*'s right to *A*'s obedience is again clear. This is because in harming the community *A* will harm *B* indirectly, by threatening the existence or efficient functioning of an institution on which *B*'s vital interests depend. Since *A* has benefitted from *B*'s previous submission to the rules, it is unfair for *A* to do something which will lessen B's chances of receiving like benefits in the future. However, if A's compliance with some particular rule does not benefit B and if his disobedience will not harm the community, it is difficult to see how fairness to B could dictate that A must comply. Surely, the fact that A has benefitted from B's submission does not give B the right to insist that A obey when B's interests are unaffected. A may in this situation have an obligation to obey, perhaps because he has promised or because his disobedience would be unfair to some other member; but, if he does disobey, he has surely not been unfair to B.

We may generalize from these examples. Considerations of fairness apparently do show that, when cooperation is perfect and when each member has benefitted from the submission of every other, each member of an enterprise has a prima facie obligation to obey its rules when obedience benefits some other member or when disobedience harms the enterprise. For, if in either circumstance a member disobeys, he is unfair to at least one other member and is perhaps unfair to them all. However, if a member disobeys when his obedience would have benefitted no other member and when his disobedience does no harm, his moral situation is surely different. If his disobedience is then unfair, it must be unfair to the group but not to any particular member. But this, I take it, is impossible: Although the moral properties of a group are not always a simple function of the moral properties of its members, it is evident that one cannot be unfair to a group without being unfair to any of its members. It would seem, then, that even when cooperation is perfect, considerations of fairness do not establish that members of a cooperative enterprise have a simple obligation to obey all of its rules, but have rather the more complex obligation to obey when obedience benefits some other member or when disobedience harms the enterprise. This does not, it is worth noting, reduce the obligation of fair play to a kind of utilitarian obligation, for it may well be that fair play will dictate in certain circumstances that a man obey when disobedience would have better consequences. My point is merely that the obligation of fair play governs a man's actions only when some benefit or harm turns on whether he obeys. Surely, this is as it should be, for questions of fairness typically arise from situations in which burdens or benefits are distributed or in which some harm is done.

The obligation of fair play is therefore much more complex than Hart or Rawls seem to have imagined. Indeed, the obligation is even more complex than the above discussion suggests, for the assumption of perfect cooperation is obviously unrealistic. When that assumption is abandoned, the effect of previous disobedience considered, and the inevitable disparity among the various members' sacrifice in obeying the rules taken into account, the scope of the obligation is still further limited; we shall then find that it requires different things of different members, depending on their previous pattern of compliance and the amount of sacrifice they have made.[10] These complications need not detain us, however, for they do not affect the fact that fairness requires obedience only in situations where noncompliance would withhold benefits from someone or harm the enterprise. Now it must be conceded that all of this makes little difference when we confine our attention to small, voluntary, cooperative enterprises. Virtually any disobedience may be expected to harm such enterprises to some extent, by diminishing the confidence of other members in its probable success and therefore reducing their incentive to work diligently towards it. Moreover, since they are typically governed by a relatively small number of rules, none of which ordinarily require behavior that is useless to other members, we may expect that when a member disobeys he will probably withhold a benefit from some other member and that he has in the past benefitted significantly from that member's obedience. We may therefore expect that virtually every time the rules of a small, voluntary enterprise call on a member to obey he will have a specific prima facie obligation to do so because of his obligation of fair play.

In the case of legal systems, however, the complexity of the obligation makes a great deal of difference. Although their success may depend on the "habit of obedience" of a majority of their subjects, all legal systems are designed to cope with a substantial amount of disobedience.[11] Hence, individual acts of disobedience to the law only rarely have an untoward effect on legal systems. What is more, because laws must necessarily be designed to cover large numbers of cases, obedience to the law often benefits no one. Perhaps the best illustration is obedience of the traffic code: Very often I benefit no one when I stop at a red light or observe the speed limit. Finally, virtually every legal system contains a number of pointless or even positively harmful laws, obedience to which either benefits no one or, worse still, causes harm. Laws prohibiting homosexual activity or the dissemination of birth control information are surely in this category. Hence, even if legal systems are the kind of cooperative enterprise that gives rise to the obligation of fair play, in a great many instances that obligation will not require that we obey specific laws. If, then, there is a generic prima facie obligation to obey the laws of any legal system, it cannot rest on the obligation of fair play. The plausibility of supposing that it does depends on an unwarranted extrapolation from what is largely true of our obligations within small, cooperative enterprises to what must always be true of our obligations within legal systems.

In his recent book, Rawls has abandoned the argument from fair play as proof that the entire citizenry of even just governments has a prima facie obligation to obey the law. He now distinguishes between obligations (*e.g.*, to be fair or to keep promises) and natural duties (*e.g.*, to avoid injury to others). Obligations, according to Rawls, are incurred only by one's voluntary acts, whereas this is not true of natural duties.[12] In his book, he retains the obligation of fair play (now "fairness"); but he now thinks that this obligation applies only to those citizens of just governments who hold office or who have advanced their interests through the government. He excludes the bulk of the citizenry from having a prima facie obligation to obey the law on the ground that, for most persons, receiving benefits from government is nothing they do voluntarily, but is rather something that merely happens to them.[13] He does not, however, take this to imply that most citizens of a reasonably just government are morally free to disobey the law: He maintains that everyone who is treated by such a government with reasonable justice has a natural duty to obey all laws that are not grossly unjust, on the ground that everyone has a natural duty to uphold and to comply with just institutions.[14]

It is tempting to criticize Rawls' present position in much the same way that I criticized his earlier one. One might argue that, while it is true that officeholders and those who have profited by invoking the rules of a just government must in fairness comply with its laws when disobedience will result in harm to that government or when it withholds a benefit from some person who has a right to it, it is simply false that fairness dictates obedience when disobedience does no harm or withholds no benefit. One might further argue that the utility of a just government is such that one has a prima facie duty to obey when disobedi-

ence is harmful to it, but that, so long as disobedience does no harm, the government's character is irrelevant to the question of whether one has a prima facie obligation to obey. These criticisms would, I think, show that if we are to base our normative ethics on an appeal to intuitively reasonable principles of duty and obligation, Rawls' present position is no more satisfying than is his earlier one. However, although certainly relevant to an assessment of Rawls' present position, these arguments cannot be regarded as decisive, for in his book Rawls does not rely on a bare appeal to moral intuition. He does not disregard the evidence of intuition, and he is glad to enlist its aid when he can; but, in putting forward particular principles of duty and obligation, he is more concerned with showing that they follow from his general theory of justice. Hence, to refute Rawls' present position, one would have to set out his elaborate theory and then show either that it is mistaken or that the particular claims he makes on its basis do not follow from it. Such a task is beyond the scope of this article; and I shall therefore be content to observe that Rawls' present position lacks intuitive support and, hence, that it rests solely on a controversial ethical theory and a complicated argument based upon it, neither of which have as yet emerged unscathed from the fire of critical scrutiny. His view deserves great respect and demands extended discussion, but it is not one which we must now accept, on pain of being unreasonable.

II

The second group of arguments are those from implicit consent or promise. Recognizing that among the clearest cases of prima facie obligation are those in which a person voluntarily assumes the obligation, some philosophers have attempted to found the citizen's obligation to obey the law upon his consent or promise to do so. There is, of course, a substantial difficulty in any such attempt, *viz.*, the brute fact that many persons have never so agreed. To accommodate this fact, some philosophers have invoked the concept of implicit promise or consent. In the *Second Treatise,* Locke argued that mere residence in a country, whether for an hour or a lifetime, constitutes implicit consent to its law.[15] Plato[16] and W. D. Ross[17] made the similar argument that residence in a country, and appeal to the protection of its laws constitutes an implicit promise to obey.

Nevertheless, it is clear that residence and use of the protection of the law do not constitute any usual kind of promise to obey its laws. The phrases "implicit consent" and "implicit promise" are somewhat difficult to understand, for they are not commonly used; nor do Locke, Plato, or Ross define them. Still, a natural way of understanding them is to assume that they refer to acts which differ from explicit consent or promise only in that, in the latter cases, the person has said "I consent . . ." or "I promise . . .," whereas in the former, he has not uttered such words but has rather performed some act which counts as giving consent or making a promise. Now, as recent investigation in the philosophy of language has shown, certain speech acts are performed only when someone utters certain words (or performs some other conventional act) with the intention that others will take what he did as being an instance of the particular act in question.[18] And it is certain that, in their ordinary usage, "consenting" and "promising" refer to speech acts of this kind. If I say to someone, "I promise to give you fifty dollars," but it is clear from the context that I do not intend that others will take my utterance as a promise, no one would consider me as having promised. Bringing this observation to bear on the present argument, it is perhaps possible that some people reside in a country and appeal to the protection of its laws with the intention that others will take their residence and appeal as consent to the laws or as a promise to obey; but this is surely true only of a very small number, consisting entirely of those enamoured with social contract theory.[19]

It may be argued, however, that my criticism rests on an unduly narrow reading of the words "consent" and "promise." Hence, it may be supposed that, if I am to refute the implicit consent or promise arguments, I must show that there is no other sense of the words "consent" or "promise" in which it is true that citizens, merely by living in a state and going about their usual business, thereby consent or promise to obey the law. This objection is difficult to meet, for I know of no way to show that there is no sense of either word that is suitable for contractarian purposes. However, I can show that two recent attempts, by John Plamenatz and Alan Gewirth, to refurbish the implicit consent argument along this line have been unsuccessful.[20] I shall not quarrel with their analyses of "consent," though I am suspicious of them; rather, I shall argue that given their definitions of "consent" the fact that a man consents to government does not establish that he has a prima facie obligation to obey the law.

Plamenatz claims that there are two kinds of consent. The first, which is common-garden variety consent, he terms "direct." He concedes that few citizens directly consent to their government.[21] He suggests, however, that there is another kind of consent, which he calls "indirect," and that, in democratic societies, consent in this sense is widespread and establishes a prima facie obligation to obey the law. Indirect consent occurs whenever a person freely votes or abstains from voting.[22] Voting establishes a prima facie obligation of obedience because:

> Even if you dislike the system and wish to change it, you put yourself by your vote under a *prima facie* obligation to obey whatever government comes legally to power. . . . For the purpose of an election is to give authority to the people who win it and, if you vote knowing what you are doing and without being compelled to do it, you voluntarily take part in a process which gives authority to these people.[23]

Plamenatz does not explain why abstention results in a prima facie obligation, but perhaps his idea is that, if a person abstains, he in effect acknowledges the authority of whoever happens to win.

The key premise then in the argument is that "the purpose of an election is to give authority to the people who win it," and it is clear that Plamenatz believes that this implies that elections do give authority to their winners. In assessing the truth of these contentions, it is, of course, vital to know what Plamenatz means by "authority." Unfortunately, he does not enlighten us, and we must therefore speculate as to his meaning. To begin, the word "authority," when used without qualification, is often held to mean the same as "legitimate authority." Since prima facie obligation is the weakest kind of obligation, part of what we mean when we ascribe authority to some government is that those subject to it have at least a prima facie obligation to obey. However, if this is what Plamenatz means by "authority," his argument simply begs the question: For, in order to be justified in asserting that the purpose of an election is to confer authority and that elections succeed in doing this, he must first show that everyone subject to an elected government has a prima facie obligation to obey its law, both those eligible to vote and those ineligible.

It is possible, however, that Plamenatz is using "authority" in some weaker sense, one that does not entail that everyone subject to it has a prima facie obligation to obey. If this is so, his premises will perhaps pass, but he must then show that those who are eligible to take part in conferring authority have a prima facie obligation to obey it. However, it is difficult to see how this can be done. First, as Plamenatz recognizes, voting is not necessarily consenting in the "direct" or usual sense, and merely being eligible to vote is even more clearly not consenting. Hence, the alleged prima facie obligation to obey it. However, it is difficult to see how this can be done. First, as Plamenatz recognizes, voting is not necessarily consenting in the "direct" or usual sense, and merely being eligible to vote is even more clearly not consenting. Hence, the alleged prima facie obligation of obedience incurred by those eligible to vote is not in consequence of their direct consent. Second, Plamenatz cannot appeal to "common moral sentiment" to bolster his argument: This is because if we really believed that those eligible to vote have a prima facie obligation to obey, an obligation not incurred by the ineligible, we should then believe that the eligible have a stronger obligation than those who are ineligible. But, as far as I can tell, we do not ordinarily think that this is true. Finally, Plamenatz cannot rely on a purely conceptual argument to make his point. It is by no means an analytic truth that those subject to elected governments have a prima facie obligation to obey the law.[24] The radical who says, "The present government of the United States was freely elected, but because it exploits people its citizens have no obligation to obey it," has perhaps said something false, but he has not contradicted himself. Plamenatz's argument is therefore either question-begging or inconclusive, depending on what he means by "authority."

Gewirth's argument is similar to Plamenatz's in that he also holds that a person's vote establishes his prima facie obligation of obedience. He argues that men consent to government when "certain institutional arrangements exist in the community as a whole," including "the maintenance of a method which leaves open to every sane, noncriminal adult the opportunity to discuss, criticize, and vote for or against the government."[25] He holds that the existence of such consent "justifies" government and establishes the subject's prima facie obligation to obey because:

The method of consent combines and safeguards the joint values of freedom and order as no other method does. It provides a choice in the power of government which protects the rights of the electorate more effectively than does any other method. It does more justice to man's potential rationality than does any other method, for it gives all men the opportunity to participate in a reasoned discussion of the problem of society and to make their discussion effective in terms of political control.[26]

As it stands, Gewirth's argument is incomplete. He makes certain claims about the benefits of government by consent which are open to reasonable doubt. Some communists, for example, would hold that Gewirth's method of consent has led to exploitation, and that human rights and freedom are better protected by the rule of the party. This aside, Gewirth's argument still needs strengthening. The fact that certain benefits are given only by government with a method of consent establishes only that such a government is better than one which lacks such a method. But, to show that one government is better than another, or even to show that it is the best possible government, does not prove that its subjects have a prima facie obligation to obey its laws: There is a prior question, which remains to be settled, as to whether there can be a prima facie obligation to obey any government. Gewirth does not carry the argument farther in his discussion of "consent," but earlier in his paper he hints as to how he would meet this objection. He argues that "government as such" is justified, or made legitimate, by its being necessary to avoid certain evils.[27] Indeed, although he does not explicitly so state, he seems to think that utilitarian considerations demonstrate that there is a prima facie obligation to obey any government that protects its subjects from these evils, but that there is an additional prima facie obligation to obey a government with a method of consent because of the more extensive benefits it offers. In the next section, I shall discuss whether a direct appeal to utility can establish a prima facie obligation to obey the law.

III

I shall consider three utilitarian arguments: the first appealing to a weak form of act-utilitarianism, the second and third to rule-utilitarian theories. To my knowledge, the first argument has never been explicitly advanced. It is nevertheless worth considering, both because it possesses a certain plausibility and because it has often been hinted at when philosophers, lawyers, and political theorists have attempted to derive an obligation to obey the law from the premise that government is necessary to protect society from great evil. The argument runs as follows:

There is obviously a prima facie obligation to perform acts which have good consequences. Now, government is absolutely necessary for securing the general good: The alternative is the state of nature in which everyone is miserable, in which life is "solitary, poor, nasty, brutish and short." But, no government can long stand in the face of widespread disobedience, and government can therefore promote the general good only so long as its laws are obeyed. Therefore, obedience to the law supports the continued existence of government and, hence, always has good consequences. From that it follows that there is a prima facie obligation to obey the law.

On even brief scrutiny, however, this argument quickly disintegrates. The first thing to be noticed is that its principle of prima facie obligation is ambiguous. It may be interpreted as postulating either (a) an obligation to perform those acts which have any good consequences, or (b) an obligation to perform optimific acts (*i.e.,* those whose consequences are better than their alternatives). Now, (a) and (b) are in fact very different principles. The former is obviously absurd. It implies, for example, that I have a prima facie obligation to kill whomever I meet, since this would have the good consequence of helping to reduce overpopulation. Thus, the only weak act-utilitarian principle with any plausibility is (b). But, regardless of whether (b) is acceptable—and some philosophers would not accept it[28]—the conclusion that there is a prima facie obligation to obey the law, cannot be derived from it, inasmuch as there are obvious and familiar cases in which breach of a particular law has better consequences than obedience. The only conclusion to be derived from (b) is that there is a specific prima facie obligation to obey the law whenever obedience is optimific. But no generic prima facie obligation to obey can be derived from weak act-utilitarianism.[29]

The second utilitarian argument appeals not to the untoward consequences of individual disobedience, but rather to those of general disobedience. Perhaps the most common challenge to those who defend certain instances of civil disobedience is "What would happen if everyone disobeyed the law?" One of the arguments implicit in this question is the generalization argument, which may be expanded as follows:

No one can have a right to do something unless every-

one has a right to do it. Similarly, an act cannot be morally indifferent unless it would be morally indifferent if everyone did it. But, everyone's breaking the law is not a matter of moral indifference; for no government can survive in such a circumstance and, as we have already agreed, government is necessary for securing and maintaining the general good. Hence, since the consequences of general disobedience would be disastrous, each person subject to law has a prima facie obligation to obey it.

In assessing this argument, we must first recognize that the generalization argument is a moral criterion to be applied with care, as virtually everyone who has discussed it has recognized.[30] If we simply note that if everyone committed a certain act there would be disastrous consequences and thereupon conclude that there is a prima facie obligation not to commit acts of that kind, we will be saddled with absurdities. We will have to maintain, for example, that there is a prima facie obligation not to eat dinner at five o'clock, for if everyone did so, certain essential services could not be maintained. And, for similar reasons, we will have to maintain that there is a prima facie obligation not to produce food. Now, those who believe that the generalization argument is valid argue that such absurdities arise when the criterion is applied to acts which are either too generally described or described in terms of morally irrelevant features. They would argue that the generalization argument appears to go awry when applied to these examples because the description "producing food" is too general to give the argument purchase and because the temporal specification in "eating dinner at five o'clock" is morally irrelevant.[31]

However, such a restriction on the generalization argument is fatal to its use in proving a prima facie obligation to obey the law. This is because a person who denies any such obligation is surely entitled to protest that the description "breaking the law" is overly general, on the ground that it refers to acts of radically different moral import.[32] Breaking the law perhaps always has some bad consequences; but sometimes the good done by it balances the bad or even outweighs it. And, once we take these differences in consequences into account, we find that utilitarian generalization, like weak act-utilitarianism, can only establish a specific prima facie obligation to obey the law when obedience is optimific. Were everyone to break the law when obedience is optimific, the consequences would undoubtedly be disastrous; but it is by no means clear that it would be disastrous if everyone broke the law when obedience is not optimific. Since no one knows, with respect to any society, how often obedience is not optimific, no one can be certain as to the consequences of everyone acting in this way. Indeed, for all we know, if everyone broke the law when obedience was not optimific the good done by separate acts of law-breaking might more than compensate for any public disorder which might result. In sum, even if the generalization argument is regarded as an acceptable principle of prima facie obligation, the most it demonstrates is that there is a specific prima facie obligation to obey the law whenever the consequences of obedience are optimific.

Some readers—especially those unfamiliar with the recent literature on utilitarianism[33]—may suspect that this last argument involves sleight of hand. They may object:

In your discussion of the generalization argument, you argued that we have no way of knowing the consequences if everyone disobeyed when obedience was not optimific. But, your argument rests on the premise that the act-utilitarian formula can be perfectly applied, whereas this is in fact impossible: The consequences of many acts are difficult or impossible to foretell; and so, were we all to attempt to be act-utilitarians, we would either make horrendous mistakes or be paralyzed into inaction. In constructing a rule-utilitarian theory of prima facie obligations, we should therefore concentrate not on the consequences of everyone following certain rules, but rather on the consequences of everyone trying to follow them. And it seems reasonable to believe that, in such a theory, the rule "Obey the law" would receive utilitarian blessing.

As it stands, this objection is overdrawn. My argument does not presuppose that persons can generally succeed in applying the act-utilitarian formula: I merely speculated on the consequences of everyone behaving in a certain way; and I made no assumption as to what made them act that way. Moreover, the objection severely overestimates the difficulty in being a confirmed act-utilitarian. Still, the objection makes one substantial point that deserves further attention. Rule-utilitarian theories which focus on the consequences of everyone accepting (although not always following) a certain set of rules do differ markedly from the generalization argument; and so the question remains as to whether such a theory could establish a prima facie obligation to obey the law. I shall therefore discuss whether the most carefully developed such theory, that given by R. B. Brandt,[34] does just this.

In Brandt's theory, one's obligations are (within certain limits) relative to his society and are determined by the set of rules whose acceptance in that society would have better consequences than would acceptance of any other set.[35] According to this theory, then, there can be a generic prima facie obligation to obey the law within a given society if, and only if, general acceptance of the rule "Obey the law," as a rule of prima facie obligation, would have better consequences than were no rule accepted with respect to obeying the law, as well as better consequences than were some alternative rule accepted (e.g., "Obey the law when obedience to the law is optimific," or "Obey the law so long as it is just"). Now, to many it may seem obvious that the ideal set of rules for any society will contain the rule "Obey the law," on the ground that, were its members not generally convinced of at least a prima facie obligation to obey, disobedience would be widespread, resulting in a great many crimes against person and property. But, there are two reasons to doubt such a gloomy forecast. First, we must surely suppose that in this hypothetical society the laws are still backed by sanctions, thereby giving its members a strong incentive to obey its laws. Second, we must also assume that the members of that society accept other moral rules (e.g., "Do not harm others," "Keep promises," "Tell the truth") which will give them a moral incentive to obey the law in most circumstances. It is, in short, a mistake to believe that unless people are convinced that they have a generic prima facie obligation to obey the law, they cannot be convinced that in most circumstances they have a specific prima facie obligation to obey particular laws. We may therefore expect that, even though members of our hypothetical society do not accept a moral rule about obedience to the law per se, they will still feel a prima facie obligation to act in accordance with the law, save when disobedience does no harm. There is, then, no reason to think that an orgy of lawbreaking would ensue were no rule about obedience to the law generally recognized; nor, I think, is there any good reason to believe that acceptance of the rule "Obey the law" would in any society have better consequences than recognition of some alternative rule. In sum, Brandt's theory requires that we be able to determine the truth-value of a large number of counter-factual propositions about what would happen were entire societies persuaded of the truth of certain moral rules. But, even if we assume—and it is hardly clear that we should [36]—that we can reliably determine the truth-value of such counterfactuals through "common sense" and our knowledge of human nature, Brandt's form of rule utilitarianism gives no support for the proof of a prima facie obligation to obey the law.

IV

In the foregoing discussion, I have played the skeptic, contending that no argument has as yet succeeded in establishing a prima facie obligation to obey the law. I want now to examine this supposed obligation directly. I shall assume *arguendo* that such an obligation exists in order to inquire as to how it compares in moral weight with other prima facie obligations. As we shall see, this question is relevant to whether we should hold that such an obligation exists.

To discuss this question, I must, of course, first specify some test for determining the weight of a prima facie obligation. It will be recalled that I defined "prima facie obligation" in terms of wrongdoing: To say that a person S has a prima facie obligation to do an act X is to say that S has a moral reason to do X which is such that, unless he has a reason not to do X that is at least as strong, S's failure to do X is wrong. Now, we are accustomed, in our reflective moral practice, to distinguish degrees of wrongdoing. And so, by appealing to this notion, we can formulate two principles that may reasonably be held to govern the weight of prima facie obligations: First, that a prima facie obligation is a serious one if, and only if, an act which violates that obligation and fulfils no other is seriously wrong; and, second, that a prima facie obligation is a serious one if, and only if, violation of it will make considerably worse an act which on other grounds is already wrong.[37] These principles, which constitute tests for determining an obligation's weight, are closely related, and application of either to a given prima facie obligation is a sufficient measure; but I shall apply both to the presumed prima facie obligation to obey the law in order to make my argument more persuasive.

First, however, we should convince ourselves of the reliability of these tests by applying them to some clear cases. I suppose it will be granted that we all have a prima facie obligation not to kill (except perhaps in self-defense), and that this obligation is most weighty. Our first test corroborates this, for, if a person kills another when he is not defending himself and if he has no specific

prima facie obligation to kill that person, his act is seriously wrong. By contrast, our prima facie obligation to observe rules of etiquette—if indeed there is any such obligation—is clearly trifling. This is borne out by our test, for if I belch audibly in the company of those who think such behavior rude, my wrongdoing is at most trivial. The same results are obtained under our second test. If I attempt to extort money from someone my act is much worse if I kill one of his children and threaten the rest than if I merely threatened them all; and so the obligation not to kill again counts as substantial. Similarly, the prima facie obligation to observe the rules of etiquette is again trivial, for if I am rude during the extortion my act is hardly worse than it would have been had I been polite.

By neither of these tests, however, does the prima facie obligation to obey the law count as substantial. As for the first test, let us assume that while driving home at two o'clock in the morning I run a stop sign. There is no danger, for I can see clearly that there was no one approaching the intersection, nor is there any impressionable youth nearby to be inspired to a life of crime by my flouting of the traffic code. Finally, we may assume that I nevertheless had no specific prima facie obligation to run the stop sign. If, then, my prima facie obligation to obey the law is of substantial moral weight, my action must have been a fairly serious instance of wrongdoing. But clearly it was not. If it was wrong at all—and to me this seems dubious—it was at most a mere peccadillo. As for the second test, we may observe that acts which are otherwise wrong are not made more so—if they are made worse at all—by being illegal.[38] If I defraud someone my act is hardly worse morally by being illegal than it would have been were it protected by some legal loophole. Thus, if there is a prima facie obligation to obey the law, it is at most of trifling weight.

This being so, I suggest that considerations of simplicity indicate that we should ignore the supposed prima facie obligation to obey the law and refuse to count an act wrong merely because it violates some law. There is certainly nothing to be lost by doing this, for we shall not thereby recommend or tolerate any conduct that is seriously wrong, nor shall we fail to recommend any course of action that is seriously obligatory. Yet, there is much to be gained, for in refusing to let trivialities occupy our attention, we shall not be diverted from the important questions to be asked about illegal conduct, *viz.*, "What kind of act was it?," "What were its consequences?," "Did the agent intend its consequences?," and so forth. Morality is, after all, a serious business; and we are surely right not to squander our moral attention and concern on matters of little moral significance.

To illustrate what can be gained, let us consider briefly the issue of civil disobedience. Most philosophers who have written on the subject have argued that, at least in democratic societies, there is always a strong moral reason to obey the law. They have therefore held that civil disobedience is a tactic to be employed only when all legal means of changing an unjust law have failed, and that the person who engages in it must willingly accept punishment as a mark of respect for the law and recognition of the seriousness of lawbreaking. However, once we abandon the notion that civil disobedience is morally significant per se, we shall judge it in the same way we judge most other kinds of acts, that is, on the basis of their character and consequences. Indeed, we can then treat civil disobedience just as we regard many other species of illegal conduct. If breaking the law involves an act which is *mala in se* or if it has untoward consequences, we are ordinarily prepared to condemn it and to think that the malefactor ought to accept punishment. But if lawbreaking does not involve an act that is *mala in se* and if it has no harmful consequences, we do not ordinarily condemn it, nor do we think that its perpetrator must accept punishment, unless evading punishment itself has untoward consequences. If we adopt this view of civil disobedience, we shall have done much to escape the air of mystery that hovers about most discussions of it.

Of course, this is not to say it will be easy to determine when civil disobedience is justified. Some have maintained that the civil disobedience of the last decade has led to increasing violation of laws which safeguard people and property.[39] If this is true, each instance of disobedience which has contributed to this condition has a share in the evil of the result. Others maintain that such disobedience has had wholly good consequences, that it has helped to remedy existing injustice.[40] Still others think its consequences are mixed. Which position is correct is difficult to determine. I myself am inclined to believe that, although the consequences have been mixed, the good far outweigh the bad; but I would be hard pressed to prove it. What is clear, however, is that either abandoning or retaining the supposed prima facie

obligation to obey the law will not help settle these questions about consequences. But, if we do abandon it, we shall then at least be able to focus on these questions without having to worry about a prima facie obligation of trivial weight that must nevertheless somehow be taken into account. Finally, if we abandon the prima facie obligation to obey the law, we shall perhaps look more closely at the character of acts performed in the course of civil disobedience, and this may, in turn, lead to fruitful moral speculation. For example, we shall be able to distinguish between acts which cannot conceivably violate the obligation of fair play (*e.g.*, burning one's draft card) and acts which may do so (*e.g.*, tax refusal or evasion of military service). This is turn may provide an incentive to reflect further on the obligation of fair play, to ask, for example, whether Rawls is right in his present contention that a person can incur the obligation of fair play only so long as his acceptance of the benefits of a cooperative enterprise is wholly voluntary.

V

It is now time to take stock. I initially suggested that it is by no means obvious that there is any prima facie obligation to obey the law. In the foregoing, I have rejected a number of arguments that purport to establish its existence. The only plausible argument I have not rejected is the one of Rawls that purports to prove that there is a natural duty to obey the laws of reasonably just governments. However, I did note that his position lacks intuitive support and rests on a controversial ethical theory which has not yet withstood the test of critical scrutiny. Finally, I have shown that even if such an obligation is assumed, it is of trivial weight and that there are substantial advantages in ignoring it. I suggest that all of this makes it reasonable to maintain that there is in no society a prima facie obligation to obey the law.

Before I conclude my discussion, however, I want to tie up one loose thread. Near the beginning of my argument I distinguished the question to be discussed from that which I called the lawyer's question, "May a reasonable man take mere illegality to be sufficient evidence that an act is morally wrong, so long as he lacks specific evidence that tends to show that it is right?" Since I have raised the question, I believe that, for the sake of completeness, I should consider it, if only briefly. To begin, it seems very doubtful that there is, in the lawyer's sense, a prima facie obligation to obey the law. It is undoubtedly true that most instances of lawbreaking are wrong, but it is also true that many are not: This is because there are, as Lord Devlin once remarked, "many fussy regulations whose breach it would be pedantic to call immoral," and because some breaches of even non-fussy regulations are justified. Now, unless—as in a court of law—there is some pressing need to reach a finding, the mere fact that most As are also B does not, in the absence of evidence that a particular A is not B, warrant an inference that the A in question is also a B: In order for this inference to be reasonable, one must know that virtually all As are Bs. Since, then, it rarely happens that there is a pressing need to reach a moral finding, and since to know merely that an act is illegal is not to know very much of moral significance about it, it seems clear that, if his only information about an act was that it was illegal, a reasonable man would withhold judgment until he learned more about it. Indeed, this is not only what the fictitious reasonable man would do, it is what we should expect the ordinary person to do. Suppose we were to ask a large number of people: "Jones has broken a law; but I won't tell you whether what he did is a serious crime or merely violation of a parking regulation, nor whether he had good reason for his actions. Would you, merely on the strength of what I have just told you, be willing to say that what he did was morally wrong?" I have conducted only an informal poll; but, on its basis, I would wager that the great majority would answer "I can't yet say—you must tell me more about what Jones did."

More importantly, it appears to make little difference what answer we give to the lawyer's question. While an affirmative answer establishes a rule of inference that an illegal act is wrong in the absence of specific information tending to show it to be right, it is a rule that would in fact virtually never be applied in any reasonable determination of whether an illegal act is wrong. If, on the one hand, we have specific information about an illegal act which tends to show it to be right, then the rule is irrelevant to our determination of the act's moral character. Should we be inclined, in this instance, to hold the act wrong we must have specific information which tends to show this; and it is clear that our conclusions about its moral character must be based on this specific information, and not on the supposed reasonableness of holding illegal conduct wrong in the absence of specific information tending to show it is right. On the other hand, if we have specific information tending to show that an illegal act is wrong and no information tending to show it is right, the rule is applicable but otiose: Since we

have ample specific reason to condemn the act, the rule is superfluous to our judgment. It would seem, then, that the rule is relevant only when we have no specific information about the illegal conduct's rightness or wrongness; and this, I suggest, is something that virtually never occurs. When we are prompted to make a moral judgment about an illegal act, we virtually always know something of its character or at least its consequences; and it is these that we consider important in determining the rightness or wrongness of lawbreaking. In short, it seems to make little difference what answer we give to the lawyer's question; I raise it here only that it may hereafter be ignored.

In conclusion, it is, I think, important to recognize that there is nothing startling in what I am recommending, nothing that in any way outrages common sense. Even the most conscientious men at times violate trivial and pointless laws for some slight gain in convenience and, when they do so, they do not feel shame or remorse. Similarly, when they observe other men behaving in a like fashion, they do not think of passing moral censure. For most people, violation of the law becomes a matter for moral concern only when it involves an act which is believed to be wrong on grounds apart from its illegality. Hence, anyone who believes that the purpose of normative ethics is to organize and clarify our reflective moral practice should be skeptical of any argument purporting to show that there is a prima facie obligation to obey the law. It is necessary to state this point with care: I am not contending that reflective and conscientious citizens would, if asked, deny that there is a prima facie obligation to obey the law. Indeed, I am willing to concede that many more would affirm its existence then deny it. But, this is in no way inconsistent with my present point. We often find that reflective people will accept general statements which are belied by their actual linguistic practice. That they also accept moral generalizations that are belied by their actual reflective moral practice should occasion no suprise.

This last point may, however, be challenged on the ground that it implies that there is in our reflective moral practice no distinction between raw power and legitimate authority. As I noted above, the concept of legitimate authority is often analyzed in terms of the right to command, where "right" is used in the strict sense as implying some correlative obligation of obedience. Given this definition, if it is true that the principle

"There is a prima facie obligation to obey the law" is not observed in our reflective moral practice, it follows that we do not really distinguish between governments which possess legitimate authority (*e.g.,* that of the United States) and those which do not (*e.g.,* the Nazi occupation government of France). And this, it may justly be held, is absurd. What I take this argument to show, however, is not that the principle is enshrined in our reflective morality, but rather that what we ordinarily mean when we ascribe legitimate authority to some government is not captured by the usual analysis of "legitimate authority." It is a mistake to believe that, unless we employ the concept of authority as it is usually analyzed, we cannot satisfactorily distinguish between the moral relation of the government of the United States vis-á-vis Americans and the moral relation of the Nazi occupation government vis-á-vis Frenchmen. One way of doing this, for example, is to define "legitimate authority" in terms of "the right to command and to enforce obedience," where "right" is used in the sense of "what is morally permissible." Thus, according to this analysis of the notion, the government of the United States counts as having legitimate authority over its subjects because within certain limits there is nothing wrong in its issuing commands to them and enforcing their obedience, whereas the Nazi occupation government lacked such authority because its issuing commands to Frenchmen was morally impermissible. It is not my intention to proffer this as an adequate analysis of the notion of legitimate authority or to suggest that it captures what we ordinarily mean when we ascribe such authority to some government. These are difficult matters, and I do not wish to address myself to them here. My point is rather that the questions "What governments enjoy legitimate authority?" and "Have the citizens of any government a prima facie obligation to obey the law?" both can be, and should be, kept separate.

NOTES

1. Rawls, *Legal Obligation and the Duty of Fair Play,* in LAW AND PHILOSOPHY 3 (S. Hook, ed., 1964).
2. H. A. PRICHARD, *Green's Principles of Political Obligation,* in MORAL OBLIGATION 54 (1949).
3. The distinction between prima facie and absolute obligation was first made by W. D. Ross in THE RIGHT AND THE GOOD, ch. 2 (1930). My account of prima facie obligation differs somewhat from Ross'; but I believe it adequately captures current philosophical usage. As for absolute obligation, I shall not often speak of it; but when I do, what I shall mean by "*S* has an absolute obligation to do *X*" is that "*S*'s failure to do *X* is wrong."
4. My motive for distinguishing generic and specific prima facie obligations is simply convenience, and not because I think it provides a perspicuous way of classifying prima facie obligations. As a classification it is obviously defective: The two kinds of obligation overlap, since in a trivial sense every specific obligation can be construed as a generic one; and there are some prima facie obligations (*e.g.,* the obligation to keep one's promise), that fit neither definition.
5. An example may help to make the point clear. If I promise that I will meet someone at a certain time, I have a prima facie obligation to keep my promise. Now, were this merely a prima facie obligation in the lawyer's sense, without evidence to the contrary the fact that I promised would be sufficient to hold that a breach of my promise was wrong, yet it would not be evidence of wrongdoing were there reason to believe the breach was justified or even obligatory. But, in fact, this is not what we think of promising. We think that if someone promises to do a thing there is a strong moral reason for him to do it and that, although this reason may sometimes be opposed by stronger reasons to the contrary, its weight does not disappear. In such cases, my promise is yet relevant to what I am absolutely obligated to do, although it is not always determinative. But, even when this reason is outweighed, it still discloses its existence by imposing fresh prima facie obligations (*e.g.,* to tell the person I promised why I broke it). Hence, there is a prima facie obligation to keep one's promise in the sense in which I here use the phrase.
6. Hart, *"Are There Any Natural Rights?,"* 64 PHIL. REV. 185 (1955). I must note that Hart does not use the phrase "prima facie obligation," maintaining that his argument establishes an obligation *sans phrase* to comply with the rules of cooperative enterprises. However, since his use of "obligation" seems much the same as my use of "prima facie obligation," I shall ignore his terminological scruples.
7. Rawls, *supra* note 1. The same argument appears although in less detail, in Rawls, *Justice as Fairness,* 67 PHIL. REV. 164 (1958), and Rawls, *"The Justification of Civil Disobedience,"* in CIVIL DISOBEDIENCE: THEORY AND PRACTICE (H. A. Bedau, ed., 1969).
8. Rawls, *"Legal Obligation and the Duty of Fair Play,"* in LAW AND PHILOSOPHY 10 (S. Hook, ed., 1964). According to Rawls, the principles of justice are "that everyone have an equal right to the most extensive liberty compatible with a like liberty for all; . . . *and* that inequalities are arbitrary unless it is reasonable to expect that they will work out for everyone's advantage and provided that the positions and offices to which they attached or from which they may be gained are open to all." *Id.* at 11.
9. *Id.* at 13; Hart, *supra* note 6, at 185.
10. Those intrigued by the mention of these additional factors may be interested to know that, when imperfect cooperation is taken into account, it can be shown that considerations of fairness establish no more than: (1) that a member *A* of a cooperative enterprise has a prima facie obligation to obey when his obedience will benefit some other member *B* from whose submission *A* has previously benefitted and it is not the case that *B* has withheld from *A* more significant benefits than *A* withholds from *B*; and (2) that *A* has a prima facie obligation to obey when his disobedience harms the enterprise and there is some other member *B* from whose submission *A* has previously benefitted and *B* has by his disobedience harmed the enterprise less than the harm which would be done by *A*'s disobedience.

As for the effect of disparity in sacrifice, it was only recently suggested to me that this factor must be taken into account, and I have not yet attempted to determine its effects precisely.

A moment's reflection discloses, however, that this additional factor would make the obligation still more complex. Were anyone to attempt a precise specification of the citizen's obligations vis-á-vis the laws of his government, he would have to master these complexities; but my task is not so ambitious.

11.   Indeed, it seems strange that Rawls should have attempted to base the prima facie obligation to obey the law on fair play, since he maintains that this latter obligation is incurred within cooperative enterprises that depend on near-universal cooperation. Rawls, *"Legal Obligation and the Duty of Fair Play,"* in LAW AND PHILOSOPHY 10 (S. Hook, ed., 1964).

12.   J. RAWLS, A THEORY OF JUSTICE 108 (1971).

13.   *Id.* at 336, 344.

14.   *Id.* at 334-37, 350-62.

15.   J. LOCKE, TWO TREATISES OF GOVERNMENT Bk. II, ¶119 (1690).

16.   1 PLATO, DIALOGUES 435 (B. Jowett transl. 1892).

17.   Ross, *supra* note 3, at 27.

18.   *Cf.* Strawson, *"Intention and Convention in Speech Acts,"* 73 PHIL. REV. 439, 448-49, 457-59 (1964).

19.   A similar argument could also be made utilizing the analysis of promising in J. Searle, SPEECH ACTS: AN ESSAY IN THE PHILOSOPHY OF LANGUAGE 60 (1969).

20.   Another recent tacit consent theory is found in J. TUSSMAN, OBLIGATION AND THE BODY POLITIC (1960). I shall not discuss this theory, however, because it has already received adequate criticism in Pitkin, *"Obligation and Consent I,"* 59 Am. Pol. Sci. Rev. 990 (1965). Nor shall I discuss Pitkin's own "hypothetical consent" theory that obedience is owed to those governments to which one ought to consent, because in her discussion of how political obligation is justified she does not appeal to the concept of hypothetical consent. She takes the problem of justifying political obligation to be the question "Why am I ever obligated to obey even legitimate authority?" She gives the question short shrift, however, replying that it is simply part of the meaning of the phrase "legitimate authority" that those subject to legitimate authority have a prima facie obligation to obey it. *See* Pitkin, *Obligation and Consent II,* 60 AM POL. SCI. REV. 39, 45-49 (1966).

21.   J. PLAMENATZ, MAN AND SOCIETY 228, 238-39 (1963).

22.   *Id.* at 349-40.

23.   *Id.*

24.   A defender of Plamenatz, John Jenkins, appears to hold that something like this is an analytic truth, maintaining that: if a person supposes that he has no obligation to a successful candidate because that candidate happens not to be the person for whom he cast his vote, then there is an excellent case for saying that the man has failed to understand the nature of the electoral process. Jenkins, *"Political Consent"* 20 PHIL. Q. 61 (1970).

This seems a silly claim. Many who voted for George McGovern believe themselves to be under no obligation to Richard Nixon. Some are highly educated and close observers of the political scene. Were such a person to explain his belief that he is not obligated to Nixon solely on the ground that he did not vote for him, we might think him mistaken or wish that he had chosen a better reason, but we should have no reason at all to think that he fails to understand "the nature of the electoral process."

25.   Earlier in his discussion Gewirth distinguishes three senses of "consent": an "occurrence" sense, a "dispositional" sense, and an "opportunity" sense. *Id.* at 131. It is only the last that will concern us here, since he admits that the prima facie obligation to obey the law cannot be shown by relying on the occurrence or the dispositional senses. Gewirth, *"Political Justice,"* in Social Justice 138 (R. Brandt, ed., 1962).

26.   *Id.* at 139.

27.   *Id.* at 135.

28.   For example, some philosophers would hold that there is a prima facie obligation to refrain from acts which have undesirable consequences, but not that there is an obligation to perform the one act which has the best consequences. *See, e.g.,* M. G. SINGER, GENERALIZATION IN ETHICS, ch. 7 (1961).

29.   For purposes of clarification, I should emphasize that I am here concerned with act-utilitarianism as a theory of prima facie, not absolute, obligation. There is no incongruity here. The consequences of acts count as having great moral significance on virtually every moral theory; and so, one need not be a strict act-utilitarian in order to maintain the principle that there is a prima facie obligation to act optimifically. Indeed, for a strict act-utilitarian such as Bentham, it is pointless to worry about whether there is a prima facie obligation to obey the law: He would hold that there is an absolute obligation to obey the law when, and only when, obedience is optimific, and would there end the discussion. At most, an act-utilitarian would hold that the rule "Obey the law" is a useful rule of thumb, to be followed only when the consequences of obedience or disobedience are difficult to discern.

30.   Singer, *supra* note 28, at ch. 4.

31.   I have borrowed these cases and this strategy for handling them from Singer. *Id.* at 71-83.

32.   According to Singer, a mark of a description's being overly general is that the generalization argument is "invertible" with respect to it, *i.e.,* the consequences of everyone's doing the act (given that description) is disastrous and the consequences of everyone's failing to do it is also disastrous. *Id.* at 76-77. It is relevant to note that the generalization argument is plainly invertible with respect to the description "breaking the law." Sometimes breaking the law is the only way to avoid a great evil; and so, if everyone were always to obey the law, such evils could never be avoided.

33.   That the generalization argument and weak act-utilitarianism offer the same advice on the topic of obedience to the law should surprise no one familiar with D. LYONS, FORMS AND LIMITS OF UTILITARIANISM (1965). Lyons there shows that act-utilitarianism and the generalization argument are extensionally equivalent. There is, it should be noted, a substantial difference between Lyons' argument for equivalence and the argument I have here offered. Lyons argues for equivalence on a priori grounds, whereas I have relied on the empirical impossibility of determining the consequences of everyone disobeying the law when obedience is not optimific.

34.   Brandt. *Toward a Credible Utilitarianism,* in MORALITY AND THE LANGUAGE OF CONDUCT 107 (H. N. Castenada & G. Nakhnikian, eds., 1963). In the following I shall not be attacking a position Brandt holds, but only an argument that might be offered on the basis of his theory. In fact, in *Utility and the Obligation to Obey the Law,* in LAW AND PHILOSOPHY 43, 47-49 (S. Hook, ed., 1964) Brandt expresses doubt as to whether there is such an obligation.

35.   According to Brandt's theory, there is an absolute obligation to perform an act if it

conforms with that learnable set of rules the recognition of which as morally binding—roughly at the time of the act—by everyone in the society of the agent, except for the retention by individuals of already formed and decided moral convictions, would maximize intrinsic value.

Brandt, *"Toward a Credible Utilitarianism,"* in Morality and The Language of Conduct 107, 139 (H. N. Castenada & G. Nakhnikian, eds., 1963). He distinguishes three levels of rules, the first stating prima facie obligations and the latter two dealing with cases in which lower-level rules conflict. At evey level, however, those in the favored set of rules are those whose recognition would have the best consequences, *i.e.,* consequences better than were any alternative rule accepted, as well as better than were no such rule accepted. *Id.* at 118-19.

36. As an illustration of the difficulty, Brandt suggests that the first-level rule "Keep your promises" is neither the one that we accept nor the rule about promising that would maximize utility. *Id.* at 131-32. I think he is right to say that it is not the rule we accept, but how does he know that some more complex rule maximizes utility?

37. The second principle may be thought objectionable on the ground that it trivializes obviously weighty prima facie obligations. It may perhaps be held that, were a man to kill a thousand persons, his act would not have been much worse had he killed but one more. The principle therefore seems to imply that the prima facie obligation not to kill that one person is trivial. The objection is plausible, but misguided. Surely there is a substantial moral difference between killing a thousand persons and killing a thousand-and-one—exactly the difference between killing one person and killing none. To deny this is to imply that the thousand-and-first person's life has little moral significance. At first glance, however, we may be inclined to take the difference to be trivial, because both acts are so monstrous that we should rarely see any point in distinguishing between them. That this objection might be raised against the principle was pointed out to me by Anne Bowen.

38. I have taken this point from 1 W. Blackstone, Commentaries 54: Neither do divine or natural *duties* (such as, for instance, the worship of God, the maintenance of children, and the like) receive any stronger sanction from being also declared to be duties by the law of the land. The case is the same as to crimes and misdemeanors, that are forbidden by the superior laws, and therefore styled *mala in se,* such as murder, theft, and perjury; which contract no additional turpitude from being declared unlawful by the inferior legislature.

39. C. Whittaker, *"First Lecture-"* in Law, Order and Civil Disobedience (1967).

40. *See* H. Zinn, Disobedience and Democracy (1968).

JOHN RAWLS

Civil Disobedience

THE DEFINITION OF CIVIL DISOBEDIENCE

I now wish to illustrate the content of the principles of natural duty and obligation by sketching a theory of civil disobedience. As I have already indicated, this theory is designed only for the special case of a nearly just society, one that is well-ordered for the most part but in which some serious violations of justice nevertheless do occur. Since I assume that a state of near justice requires a democratic regime, the theory concerns the role and the appropriateness of civil disobedience to legitimately established democratic authority. It does not apply to the other forms of government nor, except incidentally, to other kinds of dissent or resistance. I shall not discuss this mode of protest, along with militant action and resistance, as a tactic for transforming or even overturning an unjust and corrupt system. There is no difficulty about such action in this case. If any means to this end are justified, then surely nonviolent opposition is justified. The problem of civil disobedience, as I shall interpret it, arises only within a more or less just democratic state for those citizens who recognize and accept the legitimacy of the constitution. The difficulty is one of a conflict of duties. At what point does the duty to comply with laws enacted by a legislative majority (or with executive acts supported by such a majority) cease to be binding in view of the right to defend one's liberties and the duty to oppose injustice? This question involves the nature and limits of majority rule. For this reason the problem of civil disobedience is a crucial test case for any theory of the moral basis of democracy.

A constitutional theory of civil disobedience has three parts. First, it defines this kind of dissent and separates it from other forms of opposition to democratic authority. These range from legal demonstrations and infractions of law designed to raise test cases before the courts to mili-

tant action and organized resistance. A theory specifies the place of civil disobedience in this spectrum of possibilities. Next, it sets out the grounds of civil disobedience and the conditions under which such action is justified in a (more or less) just democratic regime. And finally, a theory should explain the role of civil disobedience within a constitutional system and account for the appropriateness of this mode of protest within a free society.

Before I take up these matters, a word of caution. We should not expect too much of a theory of civil disobedience, even one framed for special circumstances. Precise principles that straightway decide actual cases are clearly out of the question. Instead, a useful theory defines a perspective within which the problem of civil disobedience can be approached; it identifies the relevant considerations and helps us to assign them their correct weights in the more important instances. If a theory about these matters appears to us, on reflection, to have cleared our vision and to have made our considered judgments more coherent, then it has been worthwhile. The theory has done what, for the present, one may reasonably expect it to do: namely, to narrow the disparity between the conscientious convictions of those who accept the basic principles of a democratic society.

I shall begin by defining civil disobedience as a public, nonviolent, conscientious yet political act contrary to law usually done with the aim of bringing about a change in the law or policies of the government.[1] By acting in this way one addresses the sense of justice of the majority of the community and declares that in one's considered opinion the principles of social cooperation among free and equal men are not being respected. A preliminary gloss on this definition is that it does not require that the civilly disobedient act breach the same law that is being protested.[2] It allows for what some have called indirect as well as direct civil disobedience. And this a definition should do, as there are sometimes strong reasons for not infringing on the law or policy held to be unjust. Instead, one may disobey traffic ordinances or laws of trespass as a way of presenting one's case. Thus, if the government enacts a vague and harsh statute against treason, it would not be appropriate to commit treason as a way of objecting to it, and in any event, the penalty might be far more than one should reasonably be ready to accept. In other cases there is no way to violate the government's policy directly, as when it concerns foreign affairs, or affects another part of the country. A second gloss is that the civilly disobedient act is indeed thought to be contrary to law, at least in the sense that those engaged in it are not simply presenting a test case for a constitutional decision; they are prepared to oppose the statute even if it should be upheld. To be sure, in a constitutional regime, the courts may finally side with the dissenters and declare the law or policy objected to unconstitutional. It often happens, then, that there is some uncertainty as to whether the dissenters' action will be held illegal or not. But this is merely a complicating element. Those who use civil disobedience to protest unjust laws are not prepared to desist should the courts eventually disagree with them, however pleased they might have been with the opposite decision.

It should also be noted that civil disobedience is a political act not only in the sense that it is addressed to the majority that holds political power, but also because it is an act guided and justified by political principles, that is, by the principles of justice which regulate the constitution and social institutions generally. In justifying civil disobedience one does not appeal to principles of personal morality or to religious doctrines, though these may coincide with and support one's claims; and it goes without saying that civil disobedience cannot be grounded solely on group or self-interest. Instead one invokes the commonly shared conception of justice that underlies the political order. It is assumed that in a reasonably just democratic regime there is a public conception of justice by reference to which citizens regulate their political affairs and interpret the constitution. The persistent and deliberate violation of the basic principles of this conception over any extended period of time, especially the infringement of the fundamental equal liberties, invites either submission or resistance. By engaging in civil disobedience a minority forces the majority to consider whether it wishes to have its actions construed in this way, or whether, in view of the common sense of justice, it wishes to acknowledge the legitimate claims of the minority.

A further point is that civil disobedience is a public act. Not only is it addressed to public principles, it is done in public. It is engaged in openly with fair notice; it is not covert or secretive. One may compare it to public speech, and being a form of address, an expression of profound and conscientious political conviction, it takes place in the public forum. For this reason, among others, civil disobedience is nonviolent. It tries to avoid the use of violence, especially against persons, not from the abhorrence of the use of force in principle, but because it is a final expression of one's case. To engage in violent acts likely to injure and to hurt is incompatible with civil disobedience as a mode of address. Indeed, any interference with the civil liberties of others tends to obscure the civilly disobedient quality of one's act. Sometimes if the appeal fails in its purpose, forceful resistance may later be entertained. Yet civil disobedience is giving voice to conscientious and deeply held convictions; while it may warn and admonish, it is not itself a threat.

Civil disobedience is nonviolent for another reason. It expresses disobedience to law within the limits of fidelity to law, although it is at the outer edge thereof.[3] The law is broken, but fidelity to law is expressed by the public and nonviolent nature of the act, by the willingness to accept the legal consequences of one's conduct.[4] This fidelity to law helps to establish to the majority that the act is indeed politically conscientious and sincere, and that it is intended to address the public's sense of justice. To be completely open and nonviolent is to give bond of one's sincerity, for it is not easy to convince another that one's acts are conscientious, or even to be sure of this before oneself. No doubt it is possible to imagine a legal system in which conscientious belief that the law is unjust is accepted as a defense for noncompliance. Men of great honesty with full confidence in one another might make such a system work. But as things are, such a scheme would presumably be unstable even in a state of near justice. We must pay a certain price to convince others that our actions have, in our carefully considered view, a sufficient moral basis in the political convictions of the community.

Civil disobedience has been defined so that it falls between legal protest and the raising of test cases on the one side, and conscientious refusal and the various forms of resistance on the other. In this range of possibilities it stands for that form of dissent at the boundary of fidelity to law. Civil disobedience, so understood, is clearly distinct from militant action and obstruction; it is far removed from organized forcible resistance. The militant, for example, is much more deeply opposed to the existing political system. He does not accept it as one which is nearly just or reasonably so; he believes either that it departs widely from its professed principles or that it pursues a mistaken conception of justice altogether. While his action is conscientious in its own terms, he does not appeal to the sense of justice of the majority (or those having effective political power), since he thinks that their sense of justice is erroneous, or else without effect. Instead, he seeks by well-framed militant acts of disruption and resistance, and the like, to attack the prevalent view of justice or to force a movement in the desired direction. Thus the militant may try to evade the penalty, since he is not prepared to accept the legal consequences of his violation of the law; this would not only be to play into the hands of forces that he believes cannot be trusted, but also to express a recognition of the legitimacy of the constitution to which he is opposed. In this sense militant action is not within the bounds of fidelity to law, but represents a more profound opposition to the legal order. The basic structure is thought to be so unjust or else to depart so widely from its own professed ideals that one must try to prepare the way for radical or even revolutionary change. And this is to be done by trying to arouse the public to an awareness of the fundamental reforms that need to be made. Now in certain circumstances militant action and other kinds of resistance are surely justified. I shall not, however, consider these cases. As I have said, my aim here is the limited one of defining a concept of civil disobedience and understanding its role in a nearly just constitutional regime.

THE DEFINITION OF CONSCIENTIOUS REFUSAL

Although I have distinguished civil disobedience from conscientious refusal, I have yet to explain the latter notion. This will now be done. It must be recognized, however, that to separate these two ideas is to give a narrower definition to civil disobedience than is traditional; for it is customary to think of civil disobedience in a broader sense as any noncompliance with law for conscientious reasons, at least when it is not covert and does not involve the use of force. Thoreau's essay is characteristic, if not definitive, of the tradi-

tional meaning.[5] The usefulness of the narrower sense will, I believe, be clear once the definition of conscientious refusal is examined.

Conscientious refusal is noncompliance with a more or less direct legal injunction or administrative order. It is refusal since an order is addressed to us and, given the nature of the situation, whether we accede to it is known to the authorities. Typical examples are the refusal of the early Christians to perform certain acts of piety prescribed by the pagan state, and the refusal of the Jehovah's Witnesses to salute the flag. Other examples are the unwillingness of a pacifist to serve in the armed forces, or of a soldier to obey an order that he thinks is manifestly contrary to the moral law as it applies to war. Or again, in Thoreau's case, the refusal to pay a tax on the grounds that to do so would make him an agent of grave injustice to another. One's action is assumed to be known to the authorities, however much one might wish, in some cases, to conceal it. Where it can be covert, one might speak of conscientious evasion rather than conscientious refusal. Covert infractions of a fugitive slave law are instances of conscientious evasion.[6]

There are several contrasts between conscientious refusal (or evasion) and civil disobedience. First of all, conscientious refusal is not a form of address appealing to the sense of justice of the majority. To be sure, such acts are not generally secretive or covert, as concealment is often impossible anyway. One simply refuses on conscientious grounds to obey a command or to comply with a legal injunction. One does not invoke the convictions of the community, and in this sense conscientious refusal is not an act in the public forum. Those ready to withhold obedience recognize that there may be no basis for mutual understanding; they do not seek out occasions for disobedience as a way to state their cause. Rather, they bide their time hoping that the necessity to disobey will not arise. They are less optimistic than those undertaking civil disobedience and they may entertain no expectation of changing laws or policies. The situation may allow no time for them to make their case, or again there may not be any chance that the majority will be receptive to their claims.

Conscientious refusal is not necessarily based on political principles; it may be founded on religious or other principles at variance with the constitutional order. Civil disobedience is an appeal to a commonly shared conception of justice, whereas conscientious refusal may have other grounds. For example, assuming that the early Christians would not justify their refusal to comply with the religious customs of the Empire by reasons of justice but simply as being contrary to their religious convictions, their argument would not be political; nor, with similar qualifications, are the views of a pacifist, assuming that wars of self-defense at least are recognized by the conception of justice that underlies a constitutional regime. Conscientious refusal may, however, be grounded on political principles. One may decline to go along with a law thinking that it is so unjust that complying with it is simply out of the question. This would be the case if, say, the law were to enjoin our being the agent of enslaving another, or to require us to submit to a similar fate. These are patent violations of recognized political principles.

It is a difficult matter to find the right course when some men appeal to religious principles in refusing to do actions which, it seems, are required by principles of political justice. Does the pacifist possess an immunity from military service in a just war, assuming that there are such wars? Or is the state permitted to impose certain hardships for noncompliance? There is a temptation to say that the law must always respect the dictates of conscience, but this cannot be right. As we have seen in the case of the intolerant, the legal order must regulate men's pursuit of their religious interests so as to realize the principle of equal liberty; and it may certainly forbid religious practices such as human sacrifice, to take an extreme case. Neither religiosity nor conscientiousness suffices to protect this practice. A theory of justice must work out from its own point of view how to treat those who dissent from it. The aim of a well-ordered society, or one in a state of near justice, is to preserve and strengthen the institutions of justice. If a religion is denied its full expression, it is presumably because it is in violation of the equal liberties of others. In general, the degree of tolerance accorded opposing moral conceptions depends upon the extent to which they can be allowed an equal place within a just system of liberty.

If pacifism is to be treated with respect and not merely tolerated, the explanation must be that it accords reasonably well with the principles of justice, the main exception arising from its attitude toward engaging in a just war (assuming here that in some situations wars of self-defense are justified). The political principles recognized by the community have a certain affinity with the doctrine the pacifist professes. There is a common abhorrence of war and the use of force, and a belief in the equal status of men as moral persons. And given the tendency of nations, particularly great powers, to engage in war unjustifiably and to set in motion the apparatus of the state to suppress dissent, the respect accorded to pacifism serves the purpose of alerting citizens to the wrongs that governments are prone to commit in their name. Even though his views are not altogether sound, the warnings and protests that a pacifist is disposed to express may have the result that on balance the principles of justice are more rather than less secure. Pacifism as a natural departure from the correct doctrine conceivably compensates for the weakness of men in living up to their professions.

It should be noted that there is, of course, in actual situations no sharp distinction between civil disobedience and conscientious refusal. Moreover the same action (or sequence of actions) may have strong elements of both. While there are clear cases of each, the contrast between them is intended as a way of elucidating the interpretation of civil disobedience and its role in a democratic society. Given the nature of this way of acting as a special kind of political appeal, it is not usually justified until other steps have been taken within the legal framework. By contrast this requirement often fails in the obvious cases of legitimate conscientious refusal. In a free society no one may be compelled, as the early Christians were, to perform religious acts in violation of equal liberty, nor must a soldier comply with inherently evil commands while awaiting an appeal to higher authority. These remarks lead up to the question of justification.

THE JUSTIFICATION OF CIVIL DISOBEDIENCE

With these various distinctions in mind, I shall consider the circumstances under which civil disobedience is justified. For simplicity I shall limit the discussion to domestic institutions and so to injustices internal to a given society. The somewhat narrow nature of this restriction will be mitigated a bit by taking up the contrasting problem of conscientious refusal in connection with the moral law as it applies to war. I shall begin by setting out what seem to be reasonable conditions for engaging in civil disobedience, and then later connect these conditions more systematically with the place of civil disobedience in a state of near justice. Of course, the conditions enumerated should be taken as presumptions; no doubt there will be situations when they do not hold, and other arguments could be given for civil disobedience.

The first point concerns the kinds of wrongs that are appropriate objects of civil disobedience. Now if one views such disobedience as a political act addressed to the sense of justice of the community, then it seems reasonable, other things equal, to limit it to instances of substantial and clear injustice, and preferably to those which obstruct the path to removing other injustices. For this reason there is a presumption in favor of restricting civil disobedience to serious infringements of the first principle of justice, the principle of equal liberty, and to blatant violations of the second part of the second principle, the principle of fair equality of opportunity. Of course, it is not always easy to tell whether these principles are satisfied. Still, if we think of them as guaranteeing the basic liberties, it is often clear that these freedoms are not being honored. After all, they impose certain strict requirements that must be visibly expressed in institutions. Thus when certain minorities are denied the right to vote or to hold office, or to own property and to move from place to place, or when certain religious groups are repressed and others denied various opportunities, these injustices may be obvious to all. They are publicly incorporated into the recognized practice, if not the letter, of social arrangements. The establishment of these wrongs does not presuppose an informed examination of institutional effects.

By contrast infractions of the difference principle are more difficult to ascertain. There is usually a wide range of conflicting yet rational opinion as to whether this principle is satisfied. The reason for this is that it applies primarily to economic and social institutions and policies. A choice among these depends upon theoretical and speculative beliefs as well as upon a wealth of statistical and other information, all of this seasoned with shrewd judgment and plain hunch. In view of the complexities of these questions, it is difficult to check the influence of self-interest and prejudice; and even if we can do this in our own case, it is another matter to convince others of our good faith. Thus unless tax laws, for example, are clearly designed to attack or to abridge a basic equal liberty, they should not normally be protested by civil disobedience. The appeal to the public's conception of justice is not sufficiently clear. The resolution of these issues is best left to the political process provided that the requisite equal liberties are secure. In this case a reasonable compromise can presumably be reached. The violation of the principle of equal liberty is, then, the more appropriate object of civil disobedience. This principle defines the common status of equal citizenship in a constitutional regime and lies at the basis of the political order. When it is fully honored the presumption is that other injustices, while possibly persistent and significant, will not get out of hand.

A further condition for civil disobedience is the following. We may suppose that the normal appeals to the political majority have already been made in good faith and that they have failed. The legal means of redress have proved of no avail. Thus, for example, the existing political parties have shown themselves indifferent to the claims of the minority or have proved unwilling to accommodate them. Attempts to have the laws repealed have been ignored and legal protests and demonstrations have had no success. Since civil disobedience is a last resort, we should be sure that it is necessary. Note that it has not been said, however, that legal means have been exhausted. At any rate, further normal appeals can be repeated; free speech is always possible. But if past actions have shown the majority immovable or apathetic, further attempts may reasonably be thought fruitless, and a second condition for justified civil disobedience is met. This condition is, however, a presumption. Some cases may be so extreme that there may be no duty to use first only legal means of political opposition. If, for example, the legislature were to enact some outrageous violation of equal liberty, say by forbidding the religion of a weak and defenseless minority, we surely could not expect that sect to oppose the law by normal political procedures. Indeed, even civil disobedience might be much too mild, the majority having already convicted itself of wantonly unjust and overtly hostile aims.

The third and last condition I shall discuss can be rather complicated. It arises from the fact that while the two preceding conditions are often sufficient to justify civil disobedience, this is not always the case. In certain circumstances the natural duty of justice may require a certain restraint. We can see this as follows. If a certain minority is justified in engaging in civil disobedience, then any other minority in relevantly similar circumstances is likewise justified. Using the two previous conditions as the criteria of relevantly similar circumstances, we can say that, other things equal, two minorities are similarly justified in resorting to civil disobedience if they have suffered for the same length of time from the same degree of injustice and if their equally sincere and normal political appeals have likewise been to no avail. It is conceivable, however, even if it is unlikely, that there should be many groups with an equally sound case (in the sense just defined) for being civilly disobedient; but that, if they were all to act in this way, serious disorder would follow which might well undermine the efficacy of the just constitution. I assume here that there is a limit on the extent to which civil disobedience can be engaged in without leading to a breakdown in the respect for law and the constitution, thereby setting in motion consequences unfortunate for all. There is also an upper bound on the ability of the public forum to handle such forms of dissent; the appeal that civilly disobedient groups wish to make can be distorted and their intention to appeal to the sense of justice of the majority lost sight of. For one or both of these reasons, the effectiveness of civil disobedience as a form of protest declines beyond a certain point; and those contemplating it must consider these constraints.

The ideal solution from a theoretical point of view calls for a cooperative political alliance of the minorities to regulate the overall level of dissent. For consider the nature of the situation: there are many groups each equally entitled to engage in civil disobedience. Moreover they all wish to exercise this right, equally strong in each case; but if they all do so, lasting injury may result to the just constitution to which they each recognize a natural duty of justice. Now when there are many equally strong claims which if taken together exceed what can be granted, some fair plan should be adopted so that all are equitably considered. In simple cases of claims to goods that are indivisible and fixed in number, some rotation or lottery scheme may be the fair solution when the number of equally valid claims is too great.[7] But this sort of device is completely unrealistic here. What seems called for is a political understanding among the minorities suffering from injustice. They can meet their duty to democratic institutions by coordinating their actions so that while each has an opportunity to exercise its right, the limits on the degree of civil disobedience are not exceeded. To be sure, an alliance of this sort is difficult to arrange; but with perceptive leadership, it does not appear impossible.

Certainly the situation envisaged is a special one, and it is quite possible that these sorts of considerations will not be a bar to justified civil disobedience. There are not likely to be many groups similarly entitled to engage in this form of dissent while at the same time recognizing a duty to a just constitution. One should note, however, that an injured minority is tempted to believe its claims as strong as those of any other; and therefore even if the reasons that different groups have for engaging in civil disobedience are not equally compelling, it is often wise to presume that their claims are indistinguishable. Adopting this maxim, the circumstance imagined seems more likely to happen. This kind of case is also instructive in showing that the exercise of the right to dissent, like the exercise of rights generally, is sometimes limited by others having the very same right. Everyone's exercising this right would have deleterious consequences for all, and some equitable plan is called for.

Suppose that in the light of the three conditions, one has a right to appeal one's case by civil disobedience. The injustice one protests is a clear violation of the liberties of equal citizenship, or of equality of opportunity, this violation having been more or less deliberate over an extended period of time in the face of normal political opposition, and any complications raised by the question of fairness are met. These conditions are not exhaustive; some allowance still has to be made for the possibility of injury to third parties, to the innocent, so to speak. But I assume that they cover the main points. There is still, of course, the question whether it is wise or prudent to exercise this right. Having established the right, one is now free, as one is not before, to let these matters decide the issue. We may be acting within our rights but nevertheless unwisely if our conduct only serves to provoke the harsh retaliation of the majority. To be sure, in a state of near justice, vindictive repression of legitimate dissent is unlikely, but it is important that the action be properly designed to make an effective appeal to the wider community. Since civil disobedience is a mode of address taking place in the public forum, care must be taken to see that it is understood. Thus the exercise of the right to civil disobedience should, like any other right, be rationally framed to advance one's ends or the ends of those one wishes to assist. The theory of justice has nothing specific to say about these practical considerations. In any event questions of strategy and tactics depend upon the circumstances of each case. But the theory of justice should say at what point these matters are properly raised.

Now in this account of the justification of civil disobedience I have not mentioned the principle of fairness. The natural duty of justice is the primary basis of our political ties to a constitutional regime. As we noted before ... only the more favored members of society are likely to have a clear political obligation as opposed to a political duty. They are better situated to win public office and find it easier to take advantage of the political system. And having done so, they have acquired an obligation owed to citizens generally to uphold the just constitution. But members of subjected minorities, say, who have a strong case for civil disobedience will not generally have a political obligation of this sort. This does not mean, however, that the principle of fairness will not give rise to important obligations in their case.[8] For not only do many of the requirements of private life derive from this principle, but it comes into force when persons or groups come together for common political purposes. Just as we acquire obligations to others with whom we have joined in various private associations, those who engage in political action assume obligatory ties to one another. Thus while the political obligation of dissenters to citizens generally is problematical, bonds of loyalty and fidelity still develop between them as they seek to advance their cause. In general, free association under a just constitution gives rise to obligations provided that the ends of the group are legitimate and its arrangements fair. This is as true of political as it is of other associations. These obligations are of immense significance and they constrain in many ways what individuals can do. But they are distinct from an obligation to comply with a just constitution. My discussion of civil disobedience is in terms of the duty of justice alone; a fuller view would note the place of these other requirements.

THE JUSTIFICATION OF CONSCIENTIOUS REFUSAL

In examining the justification of civil disobedience I assumed for simplicity that the laws and policies protested concerned domestic affairs. It is natural to ask how the theory of political duty applies to foreign policy. Now in order to do this it is necessary to extend the theory of justice to the law of nations. I shall try to indicate how this can be done. To fix ideas I shall consider briefly the justification of conscientious refusal to engage in certain acts of war, or to serve in the armed forces. I assume that this refusal is based upon political and not upon religious or other principles; that is, the principles cited by way of justification are those of the conception of justice underlying the constitution. Our problem, then, is to relate the just political principles regulating the conduct of states to the contract doctrine and to explain the moral basis of the law of nations from this point of view.

Let us assume that we have already derived the principles of justice as these apply to societies as units and to the basic structure. Imagine also that the various principles of natural duty and of obligation that apply to individuals have been adopted. Thus the persons in the original position have agreed to the principles of right as these apply to their own society and to themselves as members of it. Now at this point one may extend the interpretation of the original position and think of the parties as representatives of different nations who must choose together the fundamental principles to adjudicate conflicting claims among states. Following out the conception of the initial situation, I assume that these representatives are deprived of various kinds of information. While they know that they represent different nations each living under the normal circumstances of human life, they know nothing about the particular circumstances of their own society, its power and strength in comparison with other nations, nor do they know their place in their own society. Once again the contracting parties, in this case representatives of states, are allowed only enough knowledge to make a rational choice to protect their interests but not so much that the more fortunate among them can take advantage of their special situation. This original position is fair between nations; it nullifies the contingencies and biases of historical fate. Justice between states is determined by the principles that would be chosen in the original position so interpreted. These principles are political principles, for they govern public policies toward other nations.

I can give only an indication of the principles that would be acknowledged. But, in any case, there would be no surprises, since the principles chosen would, I think, be familar ones.[9] The basic principle of the law of nations is a principle of equality. Independent peoples organized as states have certain fundamental equal rights. This principle is analogous to the equal rights of citizens in a constitutional regime. One consequence of this equality of nations is the principle of self-determination, the right of a people to settle its own affairs without the intervention of foreign powers. Another consequence is the right of self-defense against attack, including the right to form defensive alliances to protect this right. A further principle is that treaties are to be kept, provided they are consistent with the other principles governing the relations of states. Thus treaties for self-defense, suitably interpreted, would be binding, but agreements to cooperate in an unjustified attack are void *ab initio*.

These principles define when a nation has a just cause in war or, in the traditional phrase, its *jus ad bellum*. But there are also principles regulating the means that a nation may use to wage war, its *jus in bello*. [10] Even in a just war certain forms of violence are strictly inadmissible; and where a country's right to war is questionable and uncertain, the constraints on the means it can use are all the more severe. Acts permissible in a war of legitimate self-defense, when these are necessary, may be flatly excluded in a more doubtful situation. The aim of war is a just peace, and therefore the means employed must not destroy the possibility of peace or encourage a contempt for human life that puts the safety of ourselves and of mankind in jeopardy. The conduct of war is to be constrained and adjusted to this end. The representatives of states would recognize that their national interest, as seen from the original position, is best served by acknowledging these limits on the means of war. This is because the national interest of a just state is defined by the principles of justice that have already been acknowledged. Therefore such a nation will aim above all to maintain and to preserve its just institutions and the conditions that make them possible. It is not moved by the desire for world power or national glory; nor does it wage war for purposes of economic gain or the acquisition of territory. These ends are contrary to the conception of justice that defines a society's legitimate interest, however prevalent they have been in the actual conduct of states. Granting these presumptions, then, it seems reasonable to suppose that the traditional prohibitions incorporating the natural duties that protect human life would be chosen.

Now if conscientious refusal in time of war appeals to these principles, it is founded upon a political conception, and not necessarily upon religious or other notions. While this form of denial may not be a political act, since it does not take place in the public forum, it is based upon the same theory of justice that underlies the constitution and guides its interpretation. Moreover, the legal order itself presumably recognizes in the form of treaties the validity of at least some of these principles of the law of nations. Therefore if a soldier is ordered to engage in certain illicit acts of war, he may refuse if he reasonably and conscientiously believes that the principles applying to the conduct of war are plainly violated. He can maintain that, all things considered, his natural duty not to be made the agent of grave injustice and evil to another outweighs his duty to obey. I cannot discuss here what constitutes a manifest violation of these principles. It must suffice to note that certain clear cases are perfectly familiar. The essential point is that the justification cites political principles that can be accounted for by the contract doctrine. The theory of justice can be developed, I believe, to cover this case.

A somewhat different question is whether one should join the armed forces at all during some particular war. The answer is likely to depend upon the aim of the war as well as upon its conduct. In order to make the situation definite, let us suppose that conscription is in force and that the individual has to consider whether to comply with his legal duty to enter military service. Now I shall assume that since conscription is a drastic interference with the basic liberties of equal citizenship, it cannot be justified by any needs less compelling than those of national security. [11] In a well-ordered society (or in one nearly just) these needs are determined by the end of preserving just institutions. Conscription is permissible only if it is demanded for the defense of liberty itself, including here not only the liberties of the citizens of the society in question, but also those of persons in other societies as well. Therefore if a conscript army is less likely to be an instrument of unjustified foreign adventures, it may be justified on this basis alone despite the fact that conscription infringes upon the equal liberties of citizens. But in any case, the priority of liberty (assuming serial order to obtain) requires that conscription be used only as the security of liberty necessitates. Viewed from the standpoint of the legislature (the appropriate stage for this question), the mechanism of the draft can be defended only on this ground. Citizens agree to this arrangement as a fair way of sharing in the burdens of national defense. To be sure, the hazards that any particular individual must face are in part the result of accident and historical happenstance. But in a well-ordered society anyway, these evils arise externally, that is, from unjustified attacks from the outside. It is impossible for just institutions to eliminate these hardships entirely. The most that they can do is to try to make sure that the risks of suffering from these imposed misfortunes are more or less evenly shared by all members of society over the course of their life, and that there is no avoidable class bias in selecting those who are called for duty.

Imagine, then, a democratic society in which conscription exists. A person may conscientiously refuse to comply with his duty to enter the armed forces during a particular war on the ground that the aims of the conflict are unjust. It may be that the objective sought by war is economic advantage or national power. The basic liberty of citizens cannot be interfered with to achieve these ends. And, of course, it is unjust and contrary to the law of nations to attack the liberty of other societies for these reasons. Therefore a just cause for war does not exist, and this may be sufficiently evident that a citizen is justified in refusing to discharge his legal duty. Both the law of nations and the principles of justice for his own society uphold him in this claim. There is sometimes a further ground for refusal based not on the aim of the war but upon its conduct. A citizen may maintain that once it is clear that the moral law of war is being regularly violated, he has a right to decline military service on the ground that he is entitled to insure that he honors his natural duty. Once he is in the armed forces, and in a situation where he finds himself ordered to do acts contrary to the moral law of war, he may not be able to resist the demand to obey. Actually, if the aims of the conflict are sufficiently dubious and the likelihood of receiving flagrantly unjust commands is sufficiently great, one may have a duty and not only a right to refuse. Indeed, the conduct and aims of states in waging war, especially large and powerful ones, are in some circumstances so likely to be unjust that one is forced to conclude that in the foreseeable future one must abjure military service altogether. So understood a form of contingent pacifism may be a perfectly reasonable position: the possibility of a just war is conceded but not under present circumstances.[12]

What is needed, then, is not a general pacifism but a discriminating conscientious refusal to engage in war in certain circumstances. States have not been loath to recognize pacifism and to grant it a special status. The refusal to take part in all war under any conditions is an unworldly view bound to remain a sectarian doctrine. It no more challenges the state's authority than the celibacy of priests challenges the sanctity of marriage.[13] By exempting pacifists from its prescriptions the state may even seem to display a certain magnanimity. But conscientious refusal based upon the principles of justice between peoples as they apply to particular conflicts is another matter. For such refusal is an affront to the government's pretensions, and when it becomes widespread, the continuation of an unjust war may prove impossible. Given the often predatory aims of state power, and the tendency of men to defer to their government's decision to wage war, a general willingness to resist the state's claims is all the more necessary.

THE ROLE OF CIVIL DISOBEDIENCE

The third aim of a theory of civil disobedience is to explain its role within a constitutional system and to account for its connection with a democratic polity. As always, I assume that the society in question is one that is nearly just; and this implies that it has some form of democratic government, although serious injustices may nevertheless exist. In such a society I assume that the principles of justice are for the most part publicly recognized as the fundamental terms of willing cooperation among free and equal persons. By engaging in civil disobedience one intends, then, to address the sense of justice of the majority and to serve fair notice that in one's sincere and considered opinion the conditions of free cooperation are being violated. We are appealing to others to reconsider, to put themselves in our position, and to recognize that they cannot expect us to acquiesce indefinitely in the terms they impose upon us.

Now the force of this appeal depends upon the democratic conception of society as a system of cooperation among equal persons. If one thinks of society in another way, this form of protest may be out of place. For example, if the basic law is thought to reflect the order of nature and if the sovereign is held to govern by divine right as God's chosen lieutenant, then his subjects have only the right of suppliants. They can plead their cause but they cannot disobey should their appeal be denied. To do this would be to rebel against the final legitimate moral (and not simply legal) authority. This is not to say that the sovereign cannot be in error but only that the situation is not one for his subjects to correct. But once society is interpreted as a scheme of cooperation among equals, those injured by serious injustice need not submit. Indeed, civil disobedience (and conscientious refusal as well) is one of the stabilizing devices of a constitutional system, although by definition an illegal one. Along with such things as free and regular elections and an independent judiciary empowered to interpret the constitution (not necessarily written), civil disobedience used with due restraint and sound judgment helps to maintain and strengthen just institutions. By resisting injustice within the limits of fidelity to law, it serves to inhibit departures from justice and to correct them when they occur. A general disposition to engage in justified civil disobedience introduces stability into a well-ordered society, or one that is nearly just.

It is necessary to look at this doctrine from the standpoint of the persons in the original position. There are two related problems which they must consider. The first is that, having chosen principles for individuals, they must work out guidelines for assessing the strength of the natural duties and obligations, and, in particular, the strength of the duty to comply with a just constitution and one of its basic procedures, that of majority rule. The second problem is that of finding reasonable principles for dealing with unjust situations, or with circumstances in which the compliance with just principles is only partial. Now it seems that given the assumptions characterizing a nearly just society, the parties would agree to the presumptions (previously discussed) that specify when civil disobedience is justified. They would acknowledge these criteria as spelling out when this form of dissent is appropriate. Doing this would indicate the weight of the natural duty of justice in one important special case. It would also tend to enhance the realization of justice throughout the society by strengthening men's self-esteem as well as their respect for one another. As the contract doctrine emphasizes, the principles of justice are the principles of willing cooperation among equals. To deny justice to another is either to refuse to recognize him as an equal (one in regard to whom we are prepared to constrain our actions by principles that we would choose in a situation of equality that is fair), or to manifest a willingness to exploit the contingencies of natural fortune and happenstance for our own advantage. In either case deliberate injustice invites submission or resistance. Submission

arouses the contempt of those who perpetuate injustice and confirms their intention, whereas resistance cuts the ties of community. If after a decent period of time to allow for reasonable political appeals in the normal way, citizens were to dissent by civil disobedience when infractions of the basic liberties occurred, these liberties would, it seems, be more rather than less secure. For these reasons, then, the parties would adopt the conditions defining justified civil disobedience as a way of setting up, within the limits of fidelity to law, a final device to maintain the stability of a just constitution. Although this mode of action is strictly speaking contrary to law, it is nevertheless a morally correct way of maintaining a constitutional regime.

In a fuller account the same kind of explanation could presumably be given for the justifying conditions of conscientious refusal (again assuming the context of a nearly just state). I shall not, however, discuss these conditions here. I should like to emphasize instead that the constitutional theory of civil disobedience rests solely upon a conception of justice. Even the features of publicity and nonviolence are explained on this basis. And the same is true of the account of conscientious refusal, although it requires a further elaboration of the contract doctrine. At no point has a reference been made to other than political principles; religious or pacifist conceptions are not essential. While those engaging in civil disobedience have often been moved by convictions of this kind. there is no necessary connection between them and civil disobedience. For this form of political action can be understood as a way of addressing the sense of justice of the community, an invocation of the recognized principles of cooperation among equals. Being an appeal to the moral basis of civic life, it is a political and not a religious act. It relies upon common sense principles of justice that men can require one another to follow and not upon the affirmations of religious faith and love which they cannot demand that everyone accept. I do not mean, of course, that nonpolitical conceptions have no validity. They may, in fact, confirm our judgment and support our acting in ways known on other grounds to be just. Nevertheless, it is not these principles but the principles of justice, the fundamental terms of social cooperation between free and equal persons, that underlie the constitution. Civil disobedience as defined does not require a sectarian foundation but is derived from the public conception of justice that characterizes a democratic society. So understood a conception of civil disobedience is part of the theory of free government.

One distinction between medieval and modern constitutionalism is that in the former the supremacy of law was not secured by established institutional controls. The check to the ruler who in his judgments and edicts opposed the sense of justice of the community was limited for the most part to the right of resistance by the whole society, or any part. Even this right seems not to have been interpreted as a corporate act; an unjust king was simply put aside.[14] Thus the Middle Ages lacked the basic ideas of modern constitutional government, the idea of the sovereign people who have final authority and the institutionalizing of this authority by means of elections and parliaments— and other constitutional forms. Now in much the same way that the modern conception of constitutional government builds upon the medieval, the theory of civil disobedience supplements the purely legal conception of constitutional democracy. It attempts to formulate the grounds upon which legitimate democratic authority may be dissented from in ways that while admittedly contrary to law nevertheless express a fidelity to law and appeal to the fundamental political principles of a democratic regime. Thus to the legal forms of constitutionalism one may adjoin certain modes of illegal protest that do not violate the aims of a democratic constitution in view of the principles by which such dissent is guided. I have tried to show how these principles can be accounted for by the contract doctrine.

Some may object to this theory of civil disobedience that it is unrealistic. It presupposes that the majority has a sense of justice, and one might reply that moral sentiments are not a significant political force. What moves men are various interests, the desires for power, prestige, wealth, and the like. Although they are clever at producing moral arguments to support their claims, between one situation and another their opinions do not fit into a coherent conception of justice. Rather their views at any given time are occasional pieces calculated to advance certain interests. Unquestionably there is much truth in this contention, and in some societies it is more true than in others. But the essential question is the relative strength of the tendencies that oppose the sense of justice and whether the latter is ever strong enough so that it can be invoked to some significant effect.

A few comments may make the account presented more plausible. First of all, I have assumed throughout that we have to do with a nearly just society. This implies that there exists a constitutional regime and a publicly recognized conception of justice. Of course, in any particular situation certain individuals and groups may be tempted to violate its principles but the collective sentiment in their behalf has considerable strength when properly addressed. These principles are affirmed as the necessary terms of cooperation between free and equal persons. If those who perpetrate injustice can be clearly identified and isolated from the larger community, the convictions of the greater part of society may be of sufficient weight. Or if the contending parties are roughly equal, the sentiment of justice of those not engaged can be the deciding factor. In any case, should circumstances of this kind not obtain, the wisdom of civil disobedience is highly problematic. For unless one can appeal to the sense of justice of the larger society, the majority may simply be aroused to more repressive measures if the calculation of advantages points in this direction. Courts should take into account the civilly disobedient nature of the protester's act, and the fact that it is justifiable (or may seem so) by the political principles underlying the constitution, and on these grounds reduce and in some cases suspend the legal sanction.[15] Yet quite the opposite may happen when the necessary background is lacking. We have to recognize then that justifiable civil disobedience is normally a reasonable and effective form of dissent only in a society regulated to some considerable degree by a sense of justice.

There may be some misapprehension about the manner in which the sense of justice is said to work. One may think that this sentiment expresses itself in sincere professions of principle and in actions requiring a considerable degree of self-sacrifice. But this supposition asks too much. A community's sense of justice is more likely to be revealed in the fact that the majority cannot bring itself to take the steps necessary to suppress the minority and to punish acts of civil disobedience as the law allows. Ruthless tactics that might be contemplated in other societies are not entertained as real alternatives. Thus the sense of justice affects, in ways we are often unaware of, our interpretation of political life, our perception of the possible courses of action, our will to resist the justified protests of others, and so on. In spite of its superior power, the majority may abandon its position and acquiesce in the proposals of the dissenters; its desire to give justice weakens its capacity to defend its unjust advantages. The sentiment of justice will be seen as a more vital political force once the subtle forms in which it exerts its influence are recognized, and in particular its role in rendering certain social positions indefensible.

In these remarks I have assumed that in a nearly just society there is a public acceptance of the same principles of justice. Fortunately this assumption is stronger than necessary. There can, in fact, be considerable differences in citizens' conceptions of justice provided that these conceptions lead to similar political judgments. And this is possible, since different premises can yield the same conclusion. In this case there exists what we may refer to as overlapping rather than strict consensus. In general, the overlapping of professed conceptions of justice suffices for civil disobedience to be a reasonable and prudent form of political dissent. Of course, this overlapping need not be perfect; it is enough that a condition of reciprocity is satisfied. Both sides must believe that however much their conceptions of justice differ, their views support the same judgment in the situation at hand, and would do so even should their respective positions be interchanged. Eventually, though, there comes a point beyond which the requisite agreement in judgment breaks down and society splits into more or less distinct parts that hold diverse opinions on fundamental political questions. In this case of strictly partitioned consensus, the basis for civil disobedience no longer obtains. For example, suppose those who do not believe in toleration, and who would not tolerate others had they the power, wish to protest their lesser liberty by appealing to the sense of justice of the majority which holds the principle of equal liberty. While those who accept this principle should, as we have seen, tolerate the intolerant as far as the safety of free institutions permits, they are likely to resent being reminded of this duty by the intolerant who would, if positions were switched, establish their own dominion. The majority is bound to feel that their allegiance to equal liberty is being exploited by others for unjust ends. This situation illustrates once again the fact that a common sense of justice is a great collective asset which requires the cooperation of many to maintain. The intolerant can be viewed as free-riders, as persons who seek the advantages of just institutions while not doing their share to uphold them. Although those who acknowledge the principles of justice should always be guided by them, in a fragmented society as well as in one moved by group egoisms, the conditions for civil disobedi-

ence do not exist. Still, it is not necessary to have strict consensus, for often a degree of overlapping consensus allows the reciprocity condition to be fulfilled.

There are, to be sure, definite risks in the resort to civil disobedience. One reason for constitutional forms and their judicial interpretation is to establish a public reading of the political conception of justice and an explanation of the application of its principles to social questions. Up to a certain point it is better that the law and its interpretation be settled than that it be settled rightly. Therefore it may be protested that the preceding account does not determine who is to say when circumstances are such as to justify civil disobedience. It invites anarchy by encouraging everyone to decide for himself, and to abandon the public rendering of political principles. The reply to this is that each person must indeed make his own decision. Even though men normally seek advice and counsel, and accept the injunctions of those in authority when these seem reasonable to them, they are always accountable for their deeds. We cannot divest ourselves of our responsibility and transfer the burden of blame to others. This is true of any theory of political duty and obligation that is compatible with the principles of a democratic constitution. The citizen is autonomous yet he is held responsible for what he does . . . If we ordinarily think that we should comply with the law, this is because our political principles normally lead to this conclusion. Certainly in a state of near justice there is a presumption in favor of compliance in the absence of strong reasons to the contrary. The many free and reasoned decisions of individuals fit together into an orderly political regime.

But while each person must decide for himself whether the circumstances justify civil disobedience, it does not follow that one is to decide as one pleases. It is not by looking to our personal interests, or to our political allegiances narrowly construed, that we should make up our minds. To act autonomously and responsibly a citizen must look to the political principles that underlie and guide the interpretation of the constitution. He must try to assess how these principles should be applied in the existing circumstances. If he comes to the conclusion after due consideration that civil disobedience is justified and conducts himself accordingly, he acts conscientiously. And though he may be mistaken, he has not done as he pleased. The theory of political duty and obligation enables us to draw these distinctions.

There are parallels with the common understandings and conclusions reached in the sciences. Here, too, everyone is autonomous yet responsible. We are to assess theories and hypotheses in the light of the evidence by publicly recognized principles. It is true that there are authoritative works, but these sum up the consensus of many persons each deciding for himself. The absence of a final authority to decide, and so of an official interpretation that all must accept, does not lead to confusion, but is rather a condition of theoretical advance. Equals accepting and applying reasonable principles need have no established superior. To the question, who is to decide? The answer is: all are to decide, everyone taking counsel with himself, and with reasonableness, comity, and good fortune, it often works out well enough.

In a democratic society, then, it is recognized that each citizen is responsible for his interpretation of the principles of justice and for his conduct in the light of them. There can be no legal or socially approved rendering of these principles that we are always morally bound to accept, not even when it is given by a supreme court or legislature. Indeed each constitutional agency, the legislature, the executive, and the court, puts forward its interpretation of the constitution and the political ideals that inform it.[16] Although the court may have the last say in settling any particular case, it is not immune from powerful political influences that may force a revision of its reading of the constitution. The court presents its doctrine by reason and argument; its conception of the constitution must, if it is to endure, persuade the major part of the citizens of its soundness. The final court of appeal is not the court, nor the executive or the legislature, but the electorate as a whole. The civilly disobedient appeal in a special way to this body. There is no danger of anarchy so long as there is a sufficient working agreement in citizens' conceptions of justice and the conditions for resorting to civil disobedience are respected. That men can achieve such an understanding and honor these limits when the basic political liberties are maintained is an assumption implicit in a democratic polity. There is no way to avoid entirely the danger of divisive strife, any more than one can rule out the possibility of profound scientific controversy. Yet if justified civil disobedience seems to threaten civic concord, the responsibility falls not upon those who protest but upon those whose abuse of authority and power justifies such opposition. For to employ the coercive apparatus of the state in order to maintain manifestly unjust institutions is itself a form of illegitimate force that men in due course have a right to resist.

NOTES

1.   Here I follow H. A. Bedau's definition of civil disobedience. See his "On Civil Disobedience," *Journal of Philosophy,* vol. 58 (1961), p. 653–661. It should be noted that this definition is narrower that the meaning suggested by Thoreau's essay, as I note in the next section. A statement of a similar view is found in Martin Luther King's "Letter from Birmingham City Jail" (1963), reprinted in H. A. Bedau, ed., *Civil Disobedience* (New York: Pegasus, 1969), pp. 72–89. The theory of civil disobedience in the text tries to set this sort of conception into a wider framework. Some recent writers have also defined civil disobedience more broadly. For example, Howard Zinn, *Disobedience and Democracy* (New York: Random House, 1968), pp. 119f., defines it as "the deliberate, discriminate violation of law for a vital social purpose." I am concerned with a more restricted notion. I do not at all mean to say that only this form of dissent is ever justified in a democratic state.

2.   This and the following gloss are from Marshall Cohen, "Civil Disobedience in a Constitutional Democracy," *The Massachusetts Review,* vol. 10 (1969), pp. 224–226, 218–221, respectively.

3.   For a fuller discussion of this point, see Charles Fried, "Moral Causation," *Harvard Law Review,* vol. 77 (1964), pp. 1268f. For clarification below of the notion of militant action, I am indebted to Gerald Loev.

4.   Those who define civil disobedience more broadly might not accept this description. See for example, Zinn, *Disobedience and Democracy,* pp. 27–31, 39, 119f. Moreover, he denies that civil disobedience need be nonviolent. Certainly one does not accept the punishment as right, that is as deserved for an unjustified act. Rather one is willing to undergo the legal consequences for the sake of fidelity to law, which is a different matter. There is room for latitude here in that the definition allows that the charge may be contested in court, should this prove appropriate. But there comes a point beyond which dissent ceases to be civil disobedience as defined here.

5.   See Henry David Thoreau, "Civil Disobedience" (1848) reprinted in H. A. Bedau, ed., *Civil Disobedience,* pp. 27–48. For a critical discussion, see Bedau's remarks, pp. 15–26.

6.   For these distinctions I am indebted to Burton Drebin.

7.   For a discussion of the conditions when some fair arrangement is called for, see Kurt Baier, *The Moral Point of View* (Ithaca, N.Y.: Cornell University Press, 1958), pp. 207–213; and David Lyons, *Forms and Limits of Utilitarianism* (Oxford: The Clarendon Press, 1965), pp. 160–176. Lyons gives an example of a fair rotation scheme and he also observes that (waiving costs of setting them up) such fair procedures may be reasonably efficient. See pp. 169–171. I accept the conclusions of his account, including his contention that the notion of fairness cannot be explained by assimilating it to utility, p. 176f. The earlier discussion by C. D. Broad, "On the Function of False Hypotheses in Ethics," *International Journal of Ethics,* vol. 26 (1916), esp. pp. 385–390, should also be noted here.

8.   For a discussion of these obligations, see Michael Walzer, *Obligations: Essays on Disobedience, War, and Citizenship* (Cambridge: Harvard University Press, 1970), chap. III.

9.   See J. L. Brierly, *The law of Nations,* 6th ed. (Oxford: The Clarendon Press, 1963), especially chapters IV–V. This work contains all that we need here.

10.   For a recent discussion, see Paul Ramsey, *War and the Christian Conscience* (Durham, N.C.: The Duke University Press, 1961); and also R. B. Potter, *War and Moral Discourse* (Richmond, Va.: John Knox Press, 1969). The latter contains a useful bibliographical essay, pp. 87–123.

11.   I am indebted to R. G. Albritton for clarification on this and other matters in this paragraph.

12.   See *Nuclear Weapons and Christian Conscience,* ed., Walter Stein (London: The Merlin Press, 1965), for a presentation of this sort of doctrine in connection with nuclear war.

13.   I borrow this point from Walzer, *Obligations,* p. 127.

14.   See J. H. Franklin, ed., *Constitutionalism and Resistance in the Sixteenth Century* (New York: Pegasus, 1969), in the introduction, pp. 11–15.

15.   For a general discussion, see Ronald Dworkin, "On Not Prosecuting Civil Disobedience," *The New York Review of Books,* June 6, 1968. (This volume, next selection.)

16.   For a presentation of this view, to which I am indebted, see A. M. Bickel, *The Least Dangerous Branch* (New York: Bobbs-Merrill, 1962), especially chapters V and VI.

RONALD M. DWORKIN

On Not Prosecuting Civil Disobedience*

How should the government deal with those who disobey the draft laws out of conscience? Many people think the answer is obvious: the government must prosecute the dissenters, and if they are convicted it must punish them. Some people reach this conclusion easily, because they hold the mindless view that conscientious disobedience is the same as lawlessness. They think that the dissenters are anarchists who must be punished before their corruption spreads. Many lawyers and intellectuals come to the same conclusion, however, on what looks like a more sophisticated argument. They recognize that disobedience to law may be *morally* justified, but they insist that it cannot be *legally* justified, and they think that it follows from this truism that the law must be enforced. Erwin Griswold, the Solicitor General of the United States, and the former dean of the Harvard Law School, appears to have adopted this view in a recent statement. "[It] is of the essence of law," he said, "that it is equally applied to all, that it binds all alike, irrespective of personal motive. For this reason, one who contemplates civil disobedience out of moral conviction should not be surprised and must not be bitter if a criminal conviction ensues. And he must accept the fact that organized society cannot endure on any other basis."

The New York Times applauded that statement. A thousand faculty members of several universities had signed a *Times* advertisement calling on the Justice Department to quash the indictments of the Rev. William Sloane Coffin, Dr. Benjamin Spock, Marcus Raskin, Mitchell Goodman, and Michael Ferber, for conspiring to counsel various draft offenses. The *Times* said that the request to quash the indictments "confused moral rights with legal responsibilities."

But the argument that, because the government believes a man has committed a crime, it must prosecute him is much weaker than it seems. Society "cannot endure" if it tolerates all disobedience; it does not follow, however, nor is there evidence, that it will collapse if it tolerates some. In the United States prosecutors have discretion whether to enforce criminal laws in particular cases. A prosecutor may properly decide not to press charges if the lawbreaker is young, or inexperienced, or the sole support of a family, or is repentant, or turns state's evidence, or if the law is unpopular or unworkable or generally disobeyed, or if the courts are clogged with more important cases, or for dozens of other reasons. This discretion is not license—we expect prosecutors to have good reasons for exercising it—but there are, at least *prima facie,* some good reasons for not prosecuting those who disobey the draft laws out of conscience. One is the obvious reason that they act out of better motives than those who break the law out of greed or a desire to subvert government. Another is the practical reason that our society suffers a loss if it punishes a group that includes—as a group of draft dissenters does—some of its most thoughtful and loyal citizens. Jailing such men solidifies their alienation from society, and alienates many like them who are deterred by the threat.

Those who think that conscientious draft offenders should always be punished must show that these are not good reasons for exercising discretion, or they must find contrary reasons that outweigh them. What arguments might they produce? There are practical reasons for enforcing the draft laws, and I shall consider some of these later. But Dean Griswold and those who agree with him seem to rely on a fundamental moral argument that it would be unfair, not merely impractical, to let the dissenters go unpunished. They think it would be unfair, I gather, because society could not function if everyone disobeyed laws he disapproved of or found disadvantageous. If the government tolerates those few who will not "play the game," it allows them to secure the benefits of everyone else's deference to

*Reprinted from *New York Review of Books,* June 6, 1968. Copyright © 1968, NYREV, Inc. Reprinted by permission of the author and the publisher.

law, without shouldering the burdens, such as the burden of the draft.

This argument is a serious one. It cannot be answered simply by saying that the dissenters would allow everyone else the privilege of disobeying a law he believed immoral. In fact, few draft dissenters would accept a changed society in which sincere segregationists were free to break civil rights laws they hated. The majority want no such change, in any event, because they think that society would be worse off for it; until they are shown this is wrong, they will expect their officials to punish anyone who assumes a privilege which they, for the general benefit, do not assume.

There is, however, a flaw in the argument. The reasoning contains a hidden assumption that makes it almost entirely irrelevant to the draft cases, and indeed to any serious case of civil disobedience in the United States. The argument assumes that the dissenters know that they are breaking a valid law, and that the privilege they assert is the privilege to do that. Of course, almost everyone who discusses civil disobedience recognizes that in America a law may be invalid because it is unconstitutional. But the critics handle this complexity by arguing on separate hypotheses: If the law is invalid, then no crime is committed, and society may not punish. If the law is valid, then a crime has been committed, and society must punish. This reasoning hides the crucial fact that the validity of the law may be doubtful. The officials and judges may believe that the law is valid, the dissenters may disagree, and both sides may have plausible arguments for their positions. If so, then the issues are different from what they would be if the law were clearly valid or clearly invalid, and the argument of fairness, designed for these alternatives, is irrelevant.

Doubtful law is by no means special or exotic in cases of civil disobedience. On the contrary. In the United States, at least, almost any law which a significant number of people would be tempted to disobey on moral grounds would be doubtful —if not clearly invalid—on constitutional grounds as well. The Constitution makes our conventional political morality relevant to the question of validity; any statute that appears to compromise that morality raises constitutional questions, and if the compromise is serious, the constitutional doubts are serious also.

The connection between moral and legal issues is especially clear in the current draft cases. Dissent has largely been based on the following

moral objections: (a) The United States is using immoral weapons and tactics in Vietnam. (b) The war has never been endorsed by deliberate, considered, and open vote of the peoples' representatives. (c) The United States has no interest at stake in Vietnam remotely strong enough to justify forcing a segment of its citizens to risk death there. (d) If an army is to be raised to fight that war, it is immoral to raise it by a draft that defers or exempts college students, and thus discriminates against the economically underprivileged. (c) The draft exempts those who object to all wars on religious grounds, but not those who object to particular wars on moral grounds; there is no relevant difference between these positions, and so the draft, by making the distinction, implies that the second group is less worthy of the nation's respect than the first. (f) The law that makes it a crime to counsel draft resistance stifles those who oppose the war, because it is morally impossible to argue that the war is profoundly immoral, without encouraging and assisting those who refuse to fight it.

Lawyers will recognize that these moral positions, if we accept them, provide the basis for the following constitutional arguments: (a) The Constitution makes treaties part of the law of the land, and the United States is a party to international conventions and covenants that make illegal the acts of war the dissenters charge the nation with committing. (b) The Constitution provides that Congress must declare war; the legal issue of whether our action in Vietnam is a "war" and whether the Tonkin Bay Resolution was a "declaration" is the heart of the moral issue of whether the government has made a deliberate and open decision. (c) Both the due process clause of the Fifth and Fourteenth Amendments and the equal protection clause of the Fourteenth Amendment condemn special burdens placed on a selected class of citizens when the burden or the classification is not reasonable; the burden is unreasonable when it patently does not serve the public interest, or when it is vastly disproportionate to the interest served. If our military action in Vietnam is frivolous or perverse, as the dissenters claim, then the burden we place on men of draft age is unreasonable and unconstitutional. (d) In any event, the discrimination in favor of college students denies to the poor the equal protection of the law that is guaranteed by the Constitution. (e) If there is no pertinent difference between religious objection to all wars, and moral objection to some wars, then the classification the draft makes is arbitrary and unreasonable, and uncon stitutional on that ground. The "establishment of religion" clause of the First Amendment forbids governmental pressure in favor of organized religion; if the draft's distinction coerces men in this direction, it is invalid on that count also. (f) The First Amendment also condemns invasions of freedom of speech. If the draft law's prohibition on counseling does inhibit expression of a range of views on the war, it abridges free speech.

The principal counterargument, supporting the view that the courts ought not to hold the draft unconstitutional, also involves moral issues. Under the so-called "political question" doctrine, the courts deny their own jurisdiction to pass on matters—such as foreign or military policy—whose resolution is best assigned to other branches of the government. The Boston court trying the Coffin, Spock case has already declared, on the basis of this doctrine, that it will not hear arguments about the legality of the war. But the Supreme Court has shown itself (in the reapportionment cases, for example) reluctant to refuse jurisdiction when it believed that the gravest issues of political morality were at stake and that no remedy was available through the political process. If the dissenters are right, and the war and the draft are state crimes of profound injustice to a group of citizens, then the argument that the courts must refuse jurisdiction is considerably weakened.

We cannot conclude from these arguments that the draft (or any part of it) is unconstitutional. If the Supreme Court is called upon to rule on the question, it will probably reject some of them, and refuse to consider the others on grounds that they are political. The majority of lawyers would probably agree with this result. But the arguments of unconstitutionality are at least plausible, and a reasonable and competent lawyer might well think that they present a stronger case, on balance, than the counterarguments. If he does, he will consider that the draft is not constitutional, and there will be no way of proving that he is wrong.

Therefore we cannot assume, in judging what to do with the draft dissenters, that they are asserting a privilege to disobey valid laws. We cannot decide that fairness demands their punishment until we try to answer the further question: What should a citizen do when the law is unclear, and when he thinks it allows what others think it does not? I do not mean to ask, of course, what it is *legally* proper for him to do, or

what his *legal* rights are—that would be begging the question, because it depends upon whether he is right or they are right. I mean to ask what his proper course is as a citizen, what in other words, we would consider to be "playing the game." That is a crucial question, because it cannot be wrong not to punish him if he is acting as, given his opinions, we think he should.[1]

There is no obvious answer on which most citizens would readily agree, and that is itself significant. If we examine our legal institutions and practices, however, we shall discover some relevant underlying principles and policies. I shall set out three possible answers to the question, and then try to show which of these best fits our practices and expectations. The three possibilities I want to consider are these:

(1) If the law is doubtful, and it is therefore unclear whether it permits someone to do what he wants, he should assume the worst, and act on the assumption that it does not. He should obey the executive authorities who command him, even though he thinks they are wrong, while using the political process, if he can, to change the law.

(2) If the law is doubtful, he may follow his own judgment, that is, he may do what he wants if he believes that the case that the law permits this is stronger than the case that it does not. But he may follow his own judgment only until an authoritative institution, like a court, decides the other way in a case involving him or someone else. Once an institutional decision has been reached, he must abide by that decision, even though he thinks that it was wrong. (There are, in theory, many subdivisions of this second possibility. We may say that the individual's choice is foreclosed by the contrary decision of any court, including the lowest court in the system if the case is not appealed. Or we may require a decision of some particular court or institution. I shall discuss this second possibility in its most liberal form, namely that the individual may properly follow his own judgment until a contrary decision of the highest court competent to pass on the issue, which, in the case of the draft, is the United States Supreme Court.)

(3) If the law is doubtful, he may follow his own judgment, even after a contrary decision by the highest competent court. Of course, he must take the contrary decision of any court into account in making his judgment of what the law requires. Otherwise the judgment would not be an honest or reasonable one, because the doctrine

of precedent, which is an established part of our legal system, has the effect of allowing the decision of the courts to *change* the law. Suppose, for example, that a taxpayer believes that he is not required to pay tax on certain forms of income. If the Supreme Court decides to the contrary, he should, taking into account the practice of according great weight to the decisions of the Supreme Court on tax matters, decide that the Court's decision has itself tipped the balance, and that the law now requires him to pay the tax.

Someone might think that this qualification erases the difference between the third and the second models, but it does not. The doctrine of precedent gives different weights to the decisions of different courts, and greatest weight to the decisions of the Supreme Court, but it does not make the decision of any court conclusive. Sometimes, even after a contrary Supreme Court decision, an individual may still reasonably believe that the law is on his side; such cases are rare, but they are most likely in disputes over constitutional law when civil disobedience is involved. The Court has shown itself more likely to overrule its past decisions if these have limited important personal or political rights, and it is just these decisions that a dissenter might want to challenge.

We cannot assume, in other words, that the Constitution is always what the Supreme Court says it is. Oliver Wendell Holmes, for example, did not follow such a rule in his famous dissent in the *Gitlow* case. A few years before, in *Abrams,* he had lost his battle to persuade the court that the First Amendment protected an anarchist who had been urging general strikes against the government. A similar issue was presented in *Gitlow,* and Holmes once again dissented. "It is true," he said, "that in my opinion this criterion was departed from in [Abrams] but the convictions that I expressed in that case are too deep for it to be possible for me as yet to believe that it . . . settled the law." Holmes voted for acquitting Gitlow, on the ground that what Gitlow had done was no crime, even though the Supreme Court had recently held that it was.

Here then are three possible models for the behavior of dissenters who disagree with the executive authorities when the law is doubtful. Which of them best fits our legal and social practices?

I think it plain that we do not follow the first of these models, that is, that we do not expect citizens to assume the worst. If no court has decided the issue, and a man thinks, on balance, that the law is on his side, most of our lawyers and critics think it perfectly proper for him to follow his own judgment. Even when many disapprove of what he does—such as peddling pornography—they do not think he must desist just because its legality is subject to doubt.

It is worth pausing a moment to consider what society would lose if it did follow the first model or, to put the matter the other way, what society gains when people follow their own judgment in cases like this. When the law is uncertain, in the sense that lawyers can reasonably disagree on what a court ought to decide, the reason usually is that different legal principles and policies have collided, and it is unclear how best to accommodate these conflicting principles and policies.

Our practice, in which different parties are encouraged to pursue their own understanding, provides a means of testing relevant hypotheses. If the question is whether a particular rule would have certain undesirable consequences, or whether these consequences would have limited or broad ramifications, then, before the issue is decided, it is useful to know what does in fact take place when some people proceed on that rule. (Much anti-trust and business regulation law has developed through this kind of testing.) If the question is whether and to what degree a particular solution would offend principles of justice or fair play deeply respected by the community, it is useful, again, to experiment by testing the community's response. The extent of community indifference to anticontraception laws, for example, would never have become established had not some organizations deliberately flouted those laws in Connecticut.

If the first model were followed, we would lose the advantages of these tests. The law would suffer, particularly if this model were applied to constitutional issues. When the validity of a criminal statute is in doubt, the statute will almost always strike some people as being unfair or unjust, because it will infringe some principle of liberty or justice or fairness which they take to be built into the Constitution. If our practice were that whenever a law is doubtful on these grounds, one must act as if it were valid, then the chief vehicle we have for challenging the law on moral grounds would be lost, and over time the law we obeyed would certainly become less fair and just, and the liberty of our citizens would certainly be diminished.

We would lose almost as much if we used a variation of the first model, that a citizen must assume the worst unless he can anticipate that the courts will agree with his view of the law. If everyone deferred to his guess of what the courts would do, society and its law would be poorer. Our assumption in rejecting the first model was that the record a citizen makes in following his own judgment, together with the arguments he makes supporting that judgment when he has the opportunity, are helpful in creating the best judicial decision possible. This remains true even when, at the time the citizen acts, the odds are against his success in court. We must remember, too, that the value of the citizen's example is not exhausted once the decision has been made. Our practices require that the decision be criticized, by the legal profession and the law schools, and the record of dissent may be invaluable here.

Of course a man must consider what the courts will do when he decides whether it would be *prudent* to follow his own judgment. He may have to face jail, bankruptcy, or opprobrium if he does. But it is essential that we separate the calculation of prudence from the question of what, as a good citizen, he may properly do. We are investigating how society ought to treat him when its courts believe that he judged wrong; therefore we must ask what he is justified in doing when his judgment differs from others. We beg the question if we assume that what he may properly do depends on his guess as to how society will treat him.

We must also reject the second model, that if the law is unclear a citizen may properly follow his own judgment until the highest court has ruled that he is wrong. This fails to take into account the fact that any court, including the Supreme Court, may overrule itself. In 1940 the Court decided that a West Virginia law requiring students to salute the Flag was constitutional. In 1943 it reversed itself, and decided that such a statute was unconstitutional after all. What was the duty, as citizens, of those people who in 1941 and 1942 objected to saluting the Flag on grounds of conscience, and thought that the Court's 1940 decision was wrong? We can hardly say that their duty was to follow the first decision. They believed that saluting the Flag was unconscionable, and they believed, reasonably, that no valid law required them to do so. The Supreme Court later decided that in this they were right. The Court did not simply hold that after the second decision failing to salute would not be a crime; it held (as in a case like this it almost always would) that it was no crime after the first decision either.

Some will say that the flag-salute dissenters should have obeyed the Court's first decision, while they worked in the legislatures to have the law repealed, and tried in the courts to find some way to challenge the law again without actually violating it. That would be, perhaps, a plausible recommendation if conscience were not involved, because it would then be arguable that the gain in orderly procedure was worth the personal sacrifice of patience. But conscience was involved, and if the dissenters had obeyed the law while biding their time, they would have suffered the irreparable injury of having done what their conscience forbade them to do. It is one thing to say that an individual must sometimes violate his conscience when he knows that the law commands him to do it. It is quite another to say that he must violate his conscience even when he reasonably believes that the law does not require it, because it would inconvenience his fellow citizens if he took the most direct, and perhaps the only, method of attempting to show that he is right and they are wrong.

Since a court may overrule itself, the same reasons we listed for rejecting the first model count against the second as well. If we did not have the pressure of dissent, we would not have a dramatic statement of the degree to which a court decision against the dissenter is felt to be wrong, a demonstration that is surely pertinent to the question of whether it was right. We would increase the chance of being governed by rules that offend the principles we claim to serve.

These considerations force us, I think, from the second model, but some will want to substitute a variation of it. They will argue that once the Supreme Court has decided that a criminal law is valid, then citizens have a duty to abide by that decision until they have a reasonable belief, not merely that the decision is bad law, but that the Supreme Court is likely to overrule it. Under this view the West Virginia dissenters who refused to salute the flag in 1942 were acting properly, because they might reasonably have anticipated that the Court would change its mind. But if the Court were to hold the draft laws constitutional, it would be improper to continue to challenge these laws, because there would be no great likelihood that the Court would soon change its mind. This suggestion must also be rejected, however. For once we say that a citizen may properly follow his own judgment of the law, in spite of his judgment that the courts will probably find against him, there is no plausible reason why he should act differently because a contrary decision is already on the books.

Thus the third model, or something close to it, seems to be the fairest statement of a man's social duty in our community. A citizen's allegiance is to the law, not to any particular person's view of what the law is, and he does not behave improperly or unfairly so long as he proceeds on his own considered and reasonable view of what the law requires. Let me repeat (because it is crucial) that this is not the same as saying that an individual may disregard what the courts have said. The doctrine of precedent lies near the core of our legal system, and no one can make a reasonable effort to follow the law unless he grants the courts the general power to alter it by their decisions. But if the issue is one touching fundamental personal or political rights, and it is arguable that the Supreme Court has made a mistake, a man is within his social rights in refusing to accept that decision as conclusive.

One large question remains before we can apply these observations to the problem of draft resistance. I have been talking about the case of a man who believes that the law is not what other people think, or what the courts have held. This description may fit some of those who disobey the draft laws out of conscience, but it does not fit most of them. Most of the dissenters are not lawyers or political philosophers; they believe that the laws on the books are immoral, and inconsistent with their country's legal ideals, but they have not considered the question of whether they may be invalid as well. Of what relevance to their situation, then, is the proposition that one may properly follow one's own view of the law?

To answer this, I shall have to return to the point I made earlier. The Constitution, through the due process clause, the equal protection clause, the First Amendment, and the other provisions I mentioned, injects an extraordinary amount of our political morality into the issue of whether a law is valid. The statement that most draft dissenters are unaware that the law is invalid therefore needs qualification. They hold beliefs that, if true, strongly support the view that the law is on their side; the fact that they have not reached that further conclusion can be traced, in at least most cases, to their lack of legal sophistication. If we believe that when the law is doubtful people who follow their own judgment of the law may be acting properly, it would seem wrong not to extend that view to those dissenters whose judgments come to the same thing. No part of the case that I made for the third model would entitle

us to distinguish them from their more knowledgeable colleagues.

We can draw several tentative conclusions from the argument so far: When the law is uncertain, in the sense that a plausible case can be made on both sides, then a citizen who follows his own judgment is not behaving unfairly. Our practices permit and encourage him to follow his own judgment in such cases. For that reason, our government has a special responsibility to try to protect him, and soften his predicament, whenever it can do so without great damage to other policies. It does not follow that the government can guarantee him immunity—it cannot adopt the rule that it will prosecute no one who acts out of conscience, or convict no one who reasonably disagrees with the courts. That would paralyze the government's ability to carry out its policies; it would, moreover, throw away the most important benefit of following the third model. If the state never prosecuted, then the courts could not act on the experience and the arguments the dissent has generated. But it does follow from the government's responsibility that when the practical reasons for prosecuting are relatively weak in a particular case, or can be met in other ways, the path of fairness may lie in tolerance. The popular view that the law is the law and must always be enforced refuses to distinguish the man who acts on his own judgment of a doubtful law, and thus behaves as our practices provide, from the common criminal. I know of no reason, short of moral blindness, for not drawing a distinction in principle between the two cases.

I anticipate a philosophical objection to these conclusions: that I am treating law as a "brooding omnipresence in the sky." I have spoken of people making judgments about what the law requires, even in cases in which the law is unclear and undemonstrable. I have spoken of cases in which a man might think that the law requires one thing, even though the Supreme Court has said that it requires another, and even when it was not likely that the Supreme Court would soon change its mind. It will therefore be charged with the view that there is always a "right answer" to a legal problem to be found in natural law or locked up in some transcendental strongbox.

The strongbox theory of law is, of course, nonsense. When I say that people hold views on the law when the law is doubtful, and that these views are not merely predictions of what the courts will hold, I intend no such metaphysics. I mean only to summarize as accurately as I can many of the practices that are part of our legal process.

Lawyers and judges make statements of legal right and duty, even when they know these are not demonstrable, and support them with arguments even when they know that these arguments will not appeal to everyone. They make these arguments to one another in the professional journals, in the classroom, and in the courts. They respond to these arguments, when others make them, by judging them good or bad or mediocre. In so doing they assume that some arguments for a given doubtful position are better than others. They also assume that the case on one side of a doubtful proposition may be stronger than the case on the other, which is what I take a claim of law in a doubtful case to mean. They distinguish, without too much difficulty, these arguments from predictions of what the courts will decide.

These practices are poorly represented by the theory that judgments of law on doubtful issues are nonsense, or are merely predictions of what the courts will do. Those who hold such theories cannot deny the fact of these practices; perhaps these theorists mean that the practices are not sensible, because they are based on suppositions that do not hold, or for some other reason. But this makes their objection mysterious, because they never specify what they take the purposes underlying these practices to be; and unless these goals are specified, one cannot decide whether the practices are sensible. I understand these underlying purposes to be those I described earlier: the development and testing of the law through experimentation by citizens and through the adversary process.

Our legal system pursues these goals by inviting citizens to decide the strengths and weaknesses of legal arguments for themselves, or through their own counsel, and to act on these judgments, although that permission is qualified by the limited threat that they may suffer if the courts do not agree. Success in this strategy depends on whether there is sufficient agreement within the community on what counts as a good or bad argument, so that, although different people will reach different judgments, these differences will be neither so profound nor so frequent as to make the system unworkable, or dangerous for those who act by their own lights. I believe there is sufficient agreement on the criteria of the argument to avoid these traps, although one of the main tasks of legal philosophy is to exhibit and clarify these criteria. In any event, the practices I have described have not yet been shown to be misguided; they therefore must count in determining whether it is just and fair to be lenient to those who break what others think is the law.

I have said that the government has a special responsibility to those who act on a reasonable judgment that a law is invalid. It should make accommodation for them as far as possible, when this is consistent with other policies. It may be difficult to decide what the government ought to do, in the name of that responsibility, in particular cases. The decision will be a matter of balance, and flat rules will not help. Still, some principles can be set out.

I shall start with the prosecutor's decision whether to press charges. He must balance both his responsibility to be lenient and the risk that convictions will rend the society, against the damage to the law's policy that may follow if he leaves the dissenters alone. In making his calculation he must consider not only the extent to which others will be harmed, but also how the law evaluates that harm; and he must therefore make the following distinction. Every rule of law is supported, and presumably justified, by a set of policies it is supposed to advance and principles it is supposed to respect. Some rules (the laws prohibiting murder and theft, for example) are supported by the proposition that the individuals protected have a moral right to be free from the harm proscribed. Other rules (the more technical anti-trust rules, for example) are not supported by any supposition of an underlying right; their support comes chiefly from the alleged utility of the economic and social policies they promote. These may be supplemented with moral principles (like the view that it is a harsh business practice to undercut a weak competitor's prices) but these fall short of recognizing a moral right against the harm in question.

The point of the distinction here is this: The judgment that someone has a moral right to be free from certain injuries is a very strong form of moral judgment, because a moral right, once acknowledged, outweighs competing claims of utility or virtue. When a law rests on such a judgment, that is a powerful argument against tolerating violations which inflict those injuries—for example, violations that involve personal injury or the destruction of property. The prosecutor may respect the dissenter's view that the law is invalid, but unless he agrees, he must honor the law's judgment that others have an overriding claim of right.

It may be controversial, of course, whether a law rests on the assumption of a right. One must study the background and administration of the law, and reflect on whether any social practices of right and obligation support it. We may take one example in which the judgment is relatively easy. There are many sincere and ardent segregationists who believe that the civil rights laws and decisions are unconstitutional, because they compromise principles of local government and of freedom of association. This is an arguable, though not a persuasive, view. But the constitutional provisions that support these laws clearly embody the view that Negroes, as individuals, have a right not to be segregated. They do not rest simply on the judgment that national policies are best pursued by preventing their segregation. If we take no action against the man who blocks the school house door, therefore, we violate the rights, confirmed by law, of the schoolgirl he blocks. The responsibility of leniency cannot go this far.

The schoolgirl's position is different, however, from that of the draftee who may be called up sooner or given a more dangerous post if draft offenders are not punished. The draft laws do not reflect a judgment that a man has a social or moral right to be drafted only after certain other men or groups have been called. The draft classifications, and the order-of-call according to age within classifications, are arranged for social and administrative convenience. They also reflect considerations of fairness, like the proposition that a mother who has lost one of two sons in war ought not to be made to risk losing the other. But they presuppose no fixed rights. The draft boards are given considerable discretion in the classification process, and the army, of course, has almost complete discretion in assigning dangerous posts. If the prosecutor tolerates draft offenders, he makes small shifts in the law's calculations of fairness and utility. These may cause disadvantage to others in the pool of draftees but that is a different matter from contradicting their social or moral rights.

It is wrong therefore to analyze draft cases and segregation cases in the same way, as many critics do when considering whether tolerance is justified. I do not mean that fairness to others is irrelevant in draft cases; it must be taken into account, and balanced against fairness to dissenters and the long-term benefit to society. But it does not play the commanding role here that it does in segregation cases, and in other cases when rights are at stake.

Where, then, does the balance of fairness and utility lie in the case of those who counsel draft resistance? If these men had encouraged violence or otherwise trespassed on the rights of others, then there would be a strong case for prosecution. But in the absence of such actions, the balance of fairness and utility seems to me to lie the other way, and I therefore think that the decision to prosecute Coffin, Spock, Raskin, Goodman, and Ferber was wrong. It may be argued that if those who counsel draft resistance are free from prosecution, the number who resist induction will increase; but it will not, I think, increase much beyond the number of those who would resist on any event.

If I am wrong, and there is much greater resistance, then a sense of this residual discontent is of importance to policy makers, and it ought not to be hidden under a ban on speech. Conscience is deeply involved—it is hard to believe that many who counsel resistance do so on any other grounds. The case is strong that the laws making counseling a crime are unconstitutional; even those who do not find the case persuasive will admit that its arguments have substance. The harm to potential draftees, both those who may be persuaded to resist and those who may be called earlier because others have been persuaded, is remote and speculative.

The cases of men who refuse induction when drafted are more complicated. The crucial question is whether a failure to prosecute will lead to wholesale refusals to serve. It may not—there are social pressures, including the threat of career disadvantages, that would force many young Americans to serve if drafted, even if they knew they would not go to jail if they refused. If the number would not much increase, then the state should leave the dissenters alone, and I see no great harm in delaying any prosecution until the effect of that policy becomes clearer. If the number of those who refuse induction turns out to be large, this would argue for prosecution. But it would also make the problem academic, because if there were sufficient dissent to bring us to that pass, it would be most difficult to pursue the war in any event, except under a near-totalitarian regime.

There may seem to be a paradox in these conclusions. I argued earlier that when the law is unclear citizens have the right to follow their own judgment, partly on the grounds that this practice helps to shape issues for adjudication; now I propose a course that eliminates or postpones adjudication. But the contradiction is only apparent. It does not follow from the fact that our practice facilitates adjudication, and renders it more useful in developing the law, that a trial should follow whenever citizens do act by their own lights. The question arises in each case whether the issues are ripe for adjudication, and whether adjudication would settle these issues in a manner that would decrease the chance of, or remove the grounds for, further dissent.

In the draft cases, the answer to both these questions is negative: There is much ambivalence about the war just now, and uncertainty and ignorance about the scope of the moral issues involved in the draft. It is far from the best time for a court to pass on these issues, and tolerating dissent for a time is one way of allowing the debate to continue until it has produced something clearer. Moreover, it is plain that an adjudication of the constitutional issues now will not settle the law. Those who have doubts whether the draft is constitutional will have the same doubts even if the Supreme Court says that it is. This is one of those cases, touching fundamental rights, in which our practices of precedent will encourage these doubts. Certainly this will be so if, as seems likely, the Supreme Court appeals to the political question doctrine, and refuses to pass on the more serious constitutional issues.

Even if the prosecutor does not act, however, the underlying problem will be only temporarily relieved. So long as the law appears to make acts of dissent criminal, a man of conscience will face danger. What can Congress, which shares the responsibility of leniency, do to lessen this danger?

Congress can review the laws in question to see how much accommodation can be given the dissenters. Every program a legislature adopts is a mixture of policies and restraining principles. We accept loss of efficiency in crime detection and urban renewal, for example, so that we can respect the rights of accused criminals and compensate property owners for their damages. Congress may properly defer to its responsibility toward the dissenters by adjusting or compromising other policies. The relevant questions are these: What means can be found for allowing the greatest possible tolerance of conscientious dissent while minimizing its impact on policy? How strong is the government's responsibility for leniency in this case—how deeply is conscience involved, and how strong is the case that the law is invalid after all? How important is the policy in question—is interference with that policy too great a price to pay? These questions are no doubt too simple, but they suggest the heart of the choices that must be made.

For the same reasons that those who counsel resistance should not be prosecuted, I think that the law that makes this a crime should be repealed. The case is strong that this law abridges free speech. It certainly coerces conscience, and it probably serves no beneficial effect. If counseling would persuade only a few to resist who otherwise would not, the value of the restraint is small; if counseling would persuade many, that should be known.

The issues are more complex, again, in the case of draft resistance itself. Those who believe that the war in Vietnam is itself a grotesque blunder will favor any change in the law that makes peace more likely. But if we take the position of those who think the war is necessary, then we must admit that a policy that continues the draft but wholly exempts dissenters would be unwise. Two less drastic alternatives might be considered, however: a volunteer army, and an expanded conscientious objector category that includes those who find this war immoral. There is much to be said against both proposals, but once the requirement of respect for dissent is recognized, the balance of principle may be tipped in their favor.

So the case for not prosecuting conscientious draft offenders, and for changing the laws in their favor, is a strong one. It would be unrealistic to expect this policy to prevail, however, for political pressures now oppose it. Relatively few of those who have refused induction have been indicted so far, but the pace of prosecution is quickening, and many more indictments are expected if the resistance many college seniors have pledged does in fact develop. The Coffin, Spock trial continues, although when the present steps toward peace negotiation were announced, many lawyers had hoped it would be dropped or delayed. There is no sign of any movement to amend the draft laws in the way I have suggested.

We must consider, therefore, what the courts can and should now do. A court might, of course, uphold the arguments that the draft laws are in some way unconstitutional, in general or as applied to the defendants in the case at hand. Or it may acquit the defendants because the facts necessary for conviction are not proved. I shall not argue the constitutional issues, or the facts of any particular case. I want instead to suggest that a court ought not to convict, at least in some circumstances, even if it sustains the statutes and finds the facts as charged. The Supreme Court has not ruled on the chief arguments that the present draft is unconstitutional, nor has it held that these arguments raise political questions that are not relevant to its jurisdiction. If the alleged violations take place before the Supreme Court has decided these issues, and the case reaches that Court, there are strong reasons why the Court should acquit even if it does then sustain the draft. It ought to acquit on the ground that before its decision the validity of the draft was doubtful, and it is unfair to punish men for disobeying a doubtful law.

There would be precedent for a decision along these lines. The Court has several times reversed criminal convictions, on due process grounds, because the law in question was too vague. (It has overturned convictions, for example, under laws that made it a crime to charge "unreasonable prices" or to be a member of a "gang.") Conviction under a vague criminal law offends the moral and political ideals of due process in two ways. First, it places a citizen in the unfair position of either acting at his peril or accepting a more stringent restriction on his life than the legislature may have authorized: As I argued earlier, it is not acceptable, as a model of social behavior, that in such cases he ought to assume the worst. Second, it gives power to the prosecutor and the courts to make criminal law, by opting for one or the other possible interpretations after the event. This would be a delegation of authority by the legislature that is inconsistent with our scheme of separation of powers.

Conviction under a criminal law whose terms are not vague, but whose constitutional validity is doubtful, offends due process in the first of these ways. It forces a citizen to assume the worst, or

act at his peril. It offends due process in something like the second way as well. Most citizens would be deterred by a doubtful statute if they were to risk jail by violating it. Congress, and not the courts, would then be the effective voice in deciding the constitutionality of criminal enactments, and this also violates the separation of powers.

If acts of dissent continue to occur after the Supreme Court has ruled that the laws are valid, or that the political question doctrine applies, then acquittal on the grounds I have described is no longer appropriate. The Court's decision will not have finally settled the law, for the reasons given earlier, but the Court will have done all that can be done to settle it. The courts may still exercise their sentencing discretion, however, and impose minimal or suspended sentences as a mark of respect for the dissenters' position.

Some lawyers will be shocked by my general conclusion that we have a responsibility toward those who disobey the draft laws out of conscience, and that we may be required not to prosecute them, but rather to change our laws or adjust our sentencing procedures to accommodate them. The simple Draconian propositions, that crime must be punished, and that he who misjudges the law must take the consequences, have an extraordinary hold on the professional as well as the popular imagination. But the rule of law is more complex and more intelligent than that and it is important that it survive.

NOTES

1. I do not mean to imply that the government should always punish a man who deliberately breaks a law he knows is valid. There may be reasons of fairness or practicality, like those I listed in the third paragraph, for not prosecuting such men. But cases like the draft cases present special arguments for tolerance; I want to concentrate on these arguments and therefore have isolated these cases.

LAW AND THE JUDICIAL DECISION

H. L. A. HART

Problems of Legal Reasoning*

Since the early twentieth century, the critical study of the forms of reasoning by which courts decide cases has been a principal concern of writers on jurisprudence, especially in America. From this study there has emerged a great variety of theories regarding the actual or proper place in the process of adjudication of what has been termed, often ambiguously, "logic." Most of these theories are skeptical and are designed to show that despite appearances, deductive and inductive reasoning play only a subordinate role. Contrasts are drawn between "logic" and "experience" (as in Holmes's famous dictum that "the life of the law has not been logic; it has been experience") or between "deductivism" or "formalism" on the one hand and "creative choice" or "intuitions of fitness" on the other. In general, such theories tend to insist that the latter members of these contrasted sets of expressions more adequately characterize the process of legal adjudication, despite its appearance of logical method and form. According to some variants of these theories, although logic in the sense of deductive and inductive reasoning plays little part, there are other processes of legal reasoning or rational criteria which courts do and should follow in deciding cases. According to more extreme variants, the decisions of courts are essentially arbitrary.

LEGISLATION AND PRECEDENT

In Anglo-American jurisprudence the character of legal reasoning has been discussed chiefly with reference to the use of the courts of two "sources" of law: (1) the general rules made by legislative bodies (or by other rule-making agencies to which legislative powers have been delegated) and (2) particular precedents or past decisions of courts which are treated as material from which legal rules may be extracted al-

though, unlike legislative rules, there is no authoritative or uniquely correct formulation of the rules so extracted. Conventional accounts of the reasoning involved in the application of legislative rules to particular cases have often pictured it as exclusively a matter of deductive inference. The court's decision is represented as the conclusion of a syllogism in which the major premise consists of the rule and the minor premise consists of the statement of the facts which are agreed or established in the case. Similarly, conventional accounts of the use of precedents by courts speak of the courts' extraction of a rule from past cases as inductive reasoning and the application of that rule to the case in hand as deductive reasoning.

In their attack on these conventional accounts of judicial reasoning, skeptical writers have revealed much that is of great importance both to the understanding and to the criticism of methods of legal adjudication. There are undoubtedly crucially important phases in the use of legal rules and precedents to decide cases which do not consist merely of logical operations and which have long been obscured by the traditional terminology adopted both by the courts themselves in deciding cases and by jurists in describing the activities of courts. Unfortunately, the general claim that logic has little or no part to play in the judicial process is, in spite of its simple and monolithic appearance, both obscure and ambiguous; it embraces a number of different and sometimes conflicting contentions which must be separately investigated. The most important of these issues are identified and discussed below. There are, however, two preliminary issues of peculiar concern to philosophers and logicians which demand attention in any serious attempt to characterize the forms of legal reasonings.

DEDUCTIVE REASONING

It has been contended that the application of legal rules to particular cases cannot be regarded as a syllogism or any other kind of deductive inference, on the grounds that neither general

*Reprinted with permission of the author and of the publisher from the *Encyclopedia of Philosophy.* Paul Edwards, Editor in Chief. Volume 6, Pages 268–72. Copyright © 1967 by Crowell Collier and Macmillan, Inc.

legal rules nor particular statements of law (such as those ascribing rights or duties to individuals) can be characterized as either true or false and thus cannot be logically related either among themselves or to statements of fact; hence, they cannot figure as premises or conclusions of a deductive argument. This view depends on a restrictive definition, in terms of truth and falsehood, of the notion of a valid deductive inference and of logical relations such as consistency and contradiction. This would exclude from the scope of deductive inference not only legal rules or statements of law but also commands and many other sentential forms which are commonly regarded as susceptible of logical relations and as constituents of valid deductive arguments. Although considerable technical complexities are involved, several more general definitions of the idea of valid deductive inference that render the notion applicable to inferences the constituents of which are not characterized as either true or false have now been worked out by logicians. In what follows, as in most of contemporary jurisprudential literature, the general acceptability of this more generalized definition of valid inference is assumed.

INDUCTIVE REASONING

Considerable obscurity surrounds the claim made by more conventional jurisprudential writers that inductive reasoning is involved in the judicial use of precedents. Reference to induction is usually made in this connection to point a contrast with the allegedly deductive reasoning involved in the application of legislative rules to particular cases. "Instead of starting with a general rule the judge must turn to the relevant cases, discover the general rule implicit in them. . . . The outstanding difference between the two methods is the source of the major premise—the deductive method assumes it whereas the inductive sets out to discover it from particular instances" (G. W. Paton, *A Textbook of Jurisprudence,* 2d ed., Oxford, 1951, pp. 171–172).

It is of course true that courts constantly refer to past cases both to discover rules and to justify their acceptance of them as valid. The past cases are said to be "authority" for the rules "extracted" from them. Plainly, one necessary condition must be satisfied if past cases are in this way to justify logically the acceptance of a rule: the past case must be an instance of the rule in the sense that the decision in the case could be deduced from a statement of the rule together with

a statement of the facts of the case. The reasoning insofar as the satisfaction of this necessary condition is concerned is in fact an inverse application of deductive reasoning. But this condition is, of course, only one necessary condition and not a sufficient condition of the court's acceptance of a rule on the basis of past cases, since for any given precedent there are logically an indefinite number of alternative general rules which can satisfy the condition. The selection, therefore, of one rule from among these alternatives as the rule for which the precedent is taken to be authority must depend on the use of other criteria limiting the choice, and these other criteria are not matters of logic but substantive matters which may vary from system to system or from time to time in the same system. Thus, some theories of the judicial use of precedent insist that the rule for which a precedent is authority must be indicated either explicitly or implicitly by the court through its choice of facts to be treated as "material" to a case. Other theories insist that the rule for which a precedent is authority is the rule which a later court considering the precedent would select from the logically possible alternatives after weighing the usual moral and social factors.

Although many legal writers still speak of the extraction of general rules from precedents, some would claim that the reasoning involved in their use of precedents is essentially reasoning from case to case "by example": A court decides the present case in the same way as a past case if the latter "sufficiently" resembles the former in "relevant" respects, and thus makes use of the past case as a precedent without first extracting from it and formulating any general rule. Nevertheless, the more conventional accounts, according to which courts use past cases to discover and justify their acceptance of general rules, are sufficiently widespread and plausible to make the use of the term "induction" in this connection worth discussing.

The use of "induction" to refer to the inverse application of deduction involved in finding that a past case is the instance of a general rule may be misleading: it suggests stronger analogies than exist with the modes of probabilistic inference used in the sciences when general propositions of fact or statements about unobserved particulars are inferred from or regarded as confirmed by observed particulars. "Induction" may also invite confusion with the form of deductive inference known as perfect induction, or with real or alleged methods of discovering generalizations sometimes referred to as intuitive induction.

It is however, true that the inverse application of deduction involved in the use of precedents is also an important part of scientific procedure, where it is known as hypothetic inference or hypotheticodeductive reasoning. Hence, there are certain interesting analogies between the interplay of observation and theory involved in the progressive refining of a scientific hypothesis to avoid its falsification by contrary instances and the way in which a court may refine a general rule both to make it consistent with a wide range of different cases and to avoid a formulation which would have unjust or undesirable consequences.

Notwithstanding these analogies, the crucial difference remains between the search for general propositions of fact rendered probable by confirming instances but still falsifiable by future experience, and rules to be used in the decision of cases. An empirical science of the judicial process is of course possible: it would consist of factual generalization about the decisions of courts and might be an important predictive tool. However, it is important to distinguish the general propositions of such an empirical science from the rules formulated and used by courts.

DESCRIPTIVE AND PRESCRIPTIVE THEORIES

The claim that logic plays only a subordinate part in the decision of cases is sometimes intended as a corrective to misleading descriptions of the judicial process, but sometimes it is intended as a criticism of the methods used by courts, which are stigmatized as "excessively logical," "formal," "mechanical," or "automatic." Descriptions of the methods actually used by courts must be distinguished from prescriptions of alternative methods and must be separately assessed. It is, however, notable that in many discussions of legal reasoning these two are often confused, perhaps because the effort to correct conventional misdescriptions of the judicial process and the effort to correct the process itself have been inspired by the realization of the same important but often neglected fact: the relative indeterminacy of legal rules and precedents. This indeterminacy springs from the fact that it is impossible in framing general rules to anticipate and provide for every possible combination of circumstances which the future may bring. For any rule, however precisely formulated, there will always be some factual situations in which the question whether the situations fall within the

scope of the general classificatory terms of the rule cannot be settled by appeal to linguistic rules or conventions or to canons of statutory interpretation, or even by reference to the manifest or assumed purposes of the legislature. In such cases the rules may be found either vague or ambiguous. A similar indeterminacy may arise when two rules apply to a given factual situation and also where rules are expressly framed in such unspecific terms as "reasonable" or "material." Such cases can be resolved only by methods whose rationality cannot lie in the logical relations of conclusions to premises. Similarly, because precedents can logically be subsumed under an indefinite number of general rules, the identification of *the* rule for which a precedent is an authority cannot be settled by an appeal to logic.

These criticisms of traditional descriptions of the judicial process are in general well taken. It is true that both jurists and judges, particularly in jurisdictions in which the separation of powers is respected, have frequently suppressed or minimized the indeterminancy of legal rules or precedents when giving an account of the use of them in the process of decision. On the other hand, another complaint often made by the same writers, that there is an excess of logic or formalism in the judicial process, is less easy to understand and to substantiate. What the critics intend to stigmatize by these terms is the failure of courts, when applying legal rules or precedents, to take advantage of the relative indeterminacy of the rules or precedents to give effect to social aims, policies, and values. Courts, according to these critics, instead of exploiting the fact that the meaning of a statutory rule is indeterminate at certain points, have taken the meaning to be determinate simply because in some different legal context similar wording has been interpreted in a certain way or because a given interpretation is the "ordinary" meaning of the words used.

This failure to recognize the indeterminacy of legal rule (often wrongly ascribed to analytical jurisprudence and stigmatized as conceptualism) has sometimes been defended on the ground that it maximizes certainty and the predictability of decisions. It has also sometimes been welcomed as furthering an ideal of a legal system in which there are a minimum number of independent rules and categories of classification.

The vice of such methods of applying rules is that their adoption prejudges what is to be done in ranges of different cases whose composition cannot be exhaustively known beforehand: rigid classification and divisions are set up which ignore differences and similarities of social and moral importance. This is the burden of the complaint that there is an excessive use of logic in the judicial process. But the expression "an excessive use of logic" is unhappy, for when social values and distinctions of importance are ignored in the interpretation of legal rules and the classification of particulars, the decision reached is not more logical than decisions which give due recognition to these factors: logic does not determine the interpretation of words or the scope of classifications. What is true is that in a system in which such rigid modes of interpretation are common, there will be more occasions when a judge can treat himself as confronted with a rule whose meaning has been predetermined.

METHODS OF DISCOVERY AND STANDARDS OF APPRAISAL

In considering both descriptive and prescriptive theories of judicial reasoning, it is important to distinguish (1) assertions made concerning the usual processes or habits of thought by which judges actually reach their decisions, (2) recommendations concerning the processes to be followed, and (3) the standards by which judicial decisions are to be appraised. The first of these concerns matters of descriptive psychology, and to the extent that assertions in this field go beyond the descriptions of examined instances, they are empirical generalizations or laws of psychology; the second concerns the art or craft of legal judgment, and generalizations in this field are principles of judicial technology; the third relates to the assessment or justification of decisions.

These distinctions are important because it has sometimes been argued that since judges frequently arrive at decisions without going through any process of calculation or inference in which legal rules or precedents figure, the claim that deduction from legal rules plays any part in decision is mistaken. This argument is confused, for in general the issue is not one regarding the manner in which judges do, or should, come to their decisions; rather, it concerns the standards they respect in justifying decisions, however reached. The presence or absence of logic in the appraisal of decisions may be a reality whether the decisions are reached by calculation or by an intuitive leap.

CLEAR CASES AND INDETERMINATE RULES

When the various issues identified above are distinguished, two sets of questions emerge. The first of these concerns the decisions of courts in "clear" cases where no doubts are felt about the meaning and applicability of a single legal rule, and the second concerns decisions where the indeterminacy of the relevant legal rules and precedents is acknowledged.

CLEAR CASES

Even where courts acknowledge that an antecedent legal rule uniquely determines a particular result, some theorists have claimed that this cannot be the case, that courts always "have a choice," and that assertions to the contrary can only be ex post facto rationalizations. Often this skepticism springs from the confusion of the questions of methods of discovery with standards of appraisal noted above. Sometimes, however, it is supported by references to the facts that even if courts fail to apply a clearly applicable rule using a determinate result, this is not a punishable offense, and that the decision given is still authoritative and, if made by a supreme tribunal, final. Hence, it is argued that although courts may show a certain degree of regularity in decision, they are never bound to do so: they always are free to decide otherwise than they do. These last arguments rest on a confusion of finality with infallibility in decisions and on a disputable interpretation of the notion of "being bound" to respect legal rules.

Yet skepticism of this character, however unacceptable, does serve to emphasize that it is a matter of some difficulty to give any exhaustive account of what makes a "clear case" clear or makes a general rule obviously and uniquely applicable to a particular case. Rules cannot claim their own instances, and fact situations do not await the judge neatly labeled with the rule applicable to them. Rules cannot provide for their own application, and even in the clearest case a human being must apply them. The clear cases are those in which there is general agreement that they fall within the scope of a rule, and it is tempting to ascribe such agreements simply to the fact that there are necessarily such agreements in the use of the shared conventions of language. But this would be an oversimplification because it does not allow for the special conventions of the legal use of words, which may diverge from their common use, or for the way in which the meanings of words may be clearly controlled by reference to the purpose of a statutory enactment which itself may be either explicitly stated or generally agreed. A full exploration of these questions is the subject matter of the study of the interpretation of statute.

INDETERMINATE RULES

The decisions of cases which cannot be exhibited as deductions from determinate legal rules have often been described as arbitrary. Although much empirical study of the judicial process remains to be done, it is obvious that this description and the dichotomy of logical deduction and arbitrary decision, if taken as exhaustive, is misleading. Judges do not generally, when legal rules fail to determine a unique result, intrude their personal preferences or blindly choose among alternatives; and when words like "choice" and "discretion," or phrases such as "creative activity" and "interstitial legislation" are used to describe decisions, these do not mean that courts do decide arbitrarily without elaborating reasons for their decisions—and still less that any legal system authorizes decisions of this kind.

It is of crucial importance that cases for decision do not arise in a vacuum but in the course of the operation of a working body of rules, an operation in which a multiplicity of diverse considerations are continuously recognized as good reasons for a decision. These include a wide variety of individual and social interests, social and political aims, and standards of morality and justice; and they may be formulated in general terms as principles, policies, and standards. In some cases only one such consideration may be relevant, and it may determine decision as unambiguously as a determinate legal rule. But in many cases this is not so, and judges marshal in support of their decisions a plurality of such considerations which they regard as jointly sufficient to support their decision, although each separately would not be. Frequently these considerations conflict, and courts are forced to balance or weigh them and to determine priorities among them. The same considerations (and the same need for weighing them when they conflict) enter into the use of precedents when courts must choose between alternative rules which can be extracted from them, or when courts consider whether a present case sufficiently resembles a past case in relevant respects.

Perhaps most modern writers would agree up to this point with this account of judicial decision where legal rules are indeterminate, but beyond this point there is a divergence. Some theorists claim that notwithstanding the heterogeneous and often conflicting character of the factors which are relevant to decision, it is still meaningful to speak of a decision as *the* uniquely correct decision in any case and of the duty of the judge to discover it. They would claim that a judicial choice or preference does not become rational because it is deferred until after the judge has considered the factors that weigh for and against it.

Other theorists would repudiate the idea that in such cases there is always a decision which is uniquely correct, although they of course agree that many decisions can be clearly ruled out as incorrect. They would claim that all that courts do and can do at the end of the process of coolly and impartially considering the relevant considerations is to choose one alternative which they find the most strongly supported, and that it is perfectly proper for them to concede that another equally skilled and impartial judge might choose the other alternative. The theoretical issues are not different from those which arise at many points in the philosophical discussions of moral argument. It may well be that terms like "choice," "discretion," and "judicial legislation" fail to do justice to the phenomenology of considered decision: its felt involuntary or even inevitable character which often marks the termination of deliberation on conflicting considerations. Very often the decision to include a new case in the scope of a rule or to exclude it is guided by the sense that this is the "natural" continuation of a line of decisions or carries out the "spirit" of a rule. It is also true that if there were not also considerable agreement in judgment among lawyers who approach decisions in these ways, we should not attach significance and value to them or think of such decisions as reached through a rational process. Yet however it may be in moral argument, in the law it seems difficult to substantiate the claim that a judge confronted with a set of conflicting considerations must always assume that there is a single uniquely correct resolution of the conflict and attempt to demonstrate that he has discovered it.

RULES OF EVIDENCE

Courts receive and evaluate testimony of witnesses, infer statements of fact from other statements, and accept some statements as probable or more probable than others or as "beyond reasonable doubt." When it is said that in these activities special modes of legal reasoning are exhibited and that legal proof is different from ordinary proof, reference is usually intended to the exclusionary rules of the law of evidence (which frequently require courts, in determining questions of fact, to disregard matters which are logically relevant), or to various presumptions which assign greater or lesser weight to logically relevant considerations than ordinary standards of reasoning do.

The most famous examples of exclusionary rules are those against "hearsay," which (subject to certain exceptions) make inadmissible, as evidence of the facts stated, reports tendered by a witness, however credible, of statements made by another person. Another example is the rule that when a person is charged with a crime, evidence of his past convictions and disposition to commit similar crimes is not admissible as evidence to show that he committed the crime charged. An example of a rule which may give certain facts greater or less probative weight than ordinary standards do is the presumption that unless the contrary is proved beyond reasonable doubt, a child born to a woman during wedlock is the child of both parties to the marriage.

The application of such rules and their exceptions gives rise to results which may seem paradoxical, even though they are justifiable in terms of the many different social needs which the courts must satisfy in adjudicating cases. Thus, one consequence of the well-known exception to the hearsay rule that a report of a statement is admissible as evidence of a fact stated if it is made against the interest of the person who stated it, is that a court may find that a man committed adultery with a particular woman but be unable to draw the conclusion that she committed adultery with him. A logician might express the resolution of the paradox by saying that from the fact that p entails q it does not follow that "it is legally proved that p" entails "it is legally proved that q".

Apart from such paradoxes, the application of the rules of evidence involves the drawing of distinctions of considerable philosophical importance. Thus, although in general the law excludes reports of statements as evidence of the facts stated, it may admit such reports for other purposes, and in fact draws a distinction between statements of fact and what J. L. Austin called performatory utterances. Hence, if the issue is whether a given person made a promise or placed a bet, reports that he uttered words which in the context amounted to a promise or a bet are admissible. So, too, reports of a person's statement of his contemporary mental states or sensations are admissible, and some theorists justify this on the ground that such first-person statements are to be assimilated to behavior manifesting the mental state or sensation in question.

RONALD M. DWORKIN

The Model of Rules*

EMBARRASSING QUESTIONS

Lawyers lean heavily on the connected concepts of legal right and legal obligation. We say that someone has a legal right or duty, and we take that statement as a sound basis for making claims and demands, and for criticizing the acts of public officials. But our understanding of these concepts is remarkably fragile, and we fall into trouble when we try to say what legal rights and obligations are. We say glibly that whether someone has a legal obligation is determined by applying "the law" to the particular facts of this case, but this is not a helpful answer, because we have the same difficulties with the concept of law.

We are used to summing up our troubles in the classic questions of jurisprudence: What is "the law"? When two sides disagree, as often happens, about a proposition "of law," what are they disagreeing about, and how shall we decide which side is right? Why do we call what "the law" says a matter of legal "obligation"? Is "obligation" here just a term of art, meaning only "what the law says"? Or does legal obligation have something to do with moral obligation? Can we say that we have, in principle at least, the same reasons for meeting our legal obligations that we have for meeting our moral obligations?

These are not puzzles for the cupboard, to be taken down on rainy days for fun. They are sources of continuing embarrassment, and they nag at our attention. They embarrass us in dealing with particular problems that we must solve, one way or another. Suppose a novel right-of-privacy case comes to court, and there is no statute or precedent either granting or denying the particular right of anonymity claimed by the plaintiff. What role in the court's decision should be played by the fact that most people in the community think that private individuals are "morally" entitled to that particular privacy? Suppose the Supreme Court orders some prisoner

freed because the police used procedures that the Court now says are constitutionally forbidden, although the Court's earlier decisions upheld these procedures. Must the Court, to be consistent, free all other prisoners previously convicted through these same procedures?[1] Conceptual puzzles about "the law" and "legal obligation" become acute when a court is confronted with a problem like this.

These eruptions signal a chronic disease. Day in and day out we send people to jail, or take money away from them, or make them do things they do not want to do, under coercion of force, and we justify all of this by speaking of such persons as having broken the law or having failed to meet their legal obligations, or having interfered with other people's legal rights. Even in clear cases (a bank robber or a willful breach of contract), when we are confident that someone had a legal obligation and broke it, we are not able to give a satisfactory account of what that means, or why that entitles the state to punish or coerce him. We may feel confident that what we are doing is proper, but until we can identify the principles we are following we cannot be sure that they are sufficient, or whether we are applying them consistently. In less clear cases, when the issue of whether an obligation has been broken is for some reason controversial, the pitch of these nagging questions rises, and our responsibility to find answers deepens.

Certain lawyers (we may call them "nominalists") urge that we solve these problems by ignoring them. In their view the concepts of "legal obligation" and "the law" are myths, invented and sustained by lawyers for a dismal mix of conscious and subconscious motives. The puzzles we find in these concepts are merely symptoms that they are myths. They are unsolvable because unreal, and our concern with them is just one feature of our enslavement. We would do better to flush away the puzzles and the concepts altogether, and pursue our important social objectives without this excess baggage.

*From 35 *University of Chicago Law Review* 14 (1967). Reprinted by permission of the author and the publisher.

This is a tempting suggestion, but it has fatal drawbacks. Before we can decide that our concepts of law and of legal obligation are myths, we must decide what they are. We must be able to state, at least roughly, what it is we all believe that is wrong. But the nerve of our problem is that we have great difficulty in doing just that. Indeed, when we ask what law is and what legal obligations are, we are asking for a theory of how we use these concepts and of the conceptual commitments our use entails. We cannot conclude, before we have such a general theory, that our practices are stupid or superstitious.

Of course, the nominalists think they know how the rest of us use these concepts. They think that when we speak of "the law," we mean a set of timeless rules stocked in some conceptual warehouse awaiting discovery by judges, and that when we speak of legal obligation we mean the invisible chains these mysterious rules somehow drape around us. The theory that there are such rules and chains they call "mechanical jurisprudence," and they are right in ridiculing its practitioners. Their difficulty, however, lies in finding practitioners to ridicule. So far they have had little luck in caging and exhibiting mechanical jurisprudents (all specimens captured—even Blackstone and Joseph Beale—have had to be released after careful reading of their texts).

In any event, it is clear that most lawyers have nothing like this in mind when they speak of the law and of legal obligation. A superficial examination of our practices is enough to show this, for we speak of laws changing and evolving, and of legal obligation sometimes being problematical. In these and other ways we show that we are not addicted to mechanical jurisprudence.

Nevertheless, we do use the concepts of law and legal obligation, and we do suppose that society's warrant to punish and coerce is written in that currency. It may be that when the details of this practice are laid bare, the concepts we do use will be shown to be as silly and as thick with illusion as those the nominalists invented. If so, then we shall have to find other ways to describe what we do, and either provide other justifications or change our practices. But until we have discovered this and made these adjustments, we cannot accept the nominalists' premature invitation to turn our backs on the problems our present concepts provide.

Of course the suggestion that we stop talking about "the law" and "legal obligation" is mostly bluff. These concepts are too deeply cemented into the structure of our political practices—they cannot be given up like cigarettes or hats. Some of the nominalists have half-admitted this and said that the myths they condemn should be thought of as Platonic myths and retained to seduce the masses into order. This is perhaps not so cynical a suggestion as it seems; perhaps it is a covert hedging of a dubious bet.

If we boil away the bluff, the nominalist attack reduces to an attack on mechanical jurisprudence. Through the lines of the attack, and in spite of the heroic calls for the death of law, the nominalists themselves have offered an analysis of how the terms "law" and "legal obligation" should be used which is not very different from that of more classical philosophers. Nominalists present their analysis as a model of how legal institutions (particularly courts) "really operate." But their model differs mainly in emphasis from the theory first made popular by the nineteenth century philosopher John Austin, and now accepted in one form or another by most working and academic lawyers who hold views on jurisprudence. I shall call this theory, with some historical looseness, "positivism." I want to examine the soundness of positivism, particularly in the powerful form that Professor H. L. A. Hart of Oxford has given to it. I choose to focus on his position, not only because of its clarity and elegance, but because here, as almost everywhere else in legal philosophy, constructive thought must start with a consideration of his views.

POSITIVISM

Positivism has a few central and organizing propositions as its skeleton, and though not every philosopher who is called a positivist would subscribe to these in the way I present them, they do define the general position I want to examine. These key tenets may be stated as follows:

(a) The law of a community is a set of special rules used by the community directly or indirectly for the purpose of determining which behavior will be punished or coerced by the public power. These special rules can be identified and distinguished by specific criteria, by tests having to do not with their content but with their *pedigree* or the manner in which they were adopted or developed. These tests of pedigree can be used to distinguish valid legal rules from spurious legal rules (rules which lawyers and litigants wrongly argue are rules of law) and also from other sorts of social rules (generally lumped together as "moral rules") that the community follows but does not enforce through public power.

(b) The set of these valid legal rules is exhaustive of "the law," so that if someone's case is not clearly covered by such a rule (because there is none that seems appropriate, or those that seem appropriate are vague, or for some other reason) then that case cannot be decided by "applying the law." It must be decided by some official, like a judge, "exercising his discretion," which means reaching beyond the law for some other sort of standard to guide him in manufacturing a fresh legal rule or supplementing an old one.

(c) To say that someone has a "legal obligation" is to say that his case falls under a valid legal rule that requires him to do or to forbear from doing something. (To say he has a legal right, or has a legal power of some sort, or a legal privilege or immunity, is to assert, in a shorthand way, that others have actual or hypothetical legal obligations to act or not to act in certain ways touching him.) In the absence of such a valid legal rule there is no legal obligation; it follows that when the judge decides an issue by exercising his discretion, he is not enforcing a legal obligation as to that issue.

This is only the skeleton of positivism. The flesh is arranged differently by different positivists, and some even tinker with the bones. Different versions differ chiefly in their description of the fundamental test of pedigree a rule must meet to count as a rule of law.

Austin, for example, framed his version of the fundamental test as a series of interlocking definitions and distinctions.[2] He defined having an obligation as lying under a rule, a rule as a general command, and a command as an expression of desire that others behave in a particular way, backed by the power and will to enforce that expression in the event of disobedience. He distinguished classes of rules (legal, moral or religious) according to which person or group is the author of the general command the rule represents. In each political community, he thought, one will find a sovereign—a person or a determinate group whom the rest obey habitually, but who is not in the habit of obeying anyone else. The legal rules of a community are the general commands its sovereign has deployed. Austin's definition of legal obligation followed from this definition of law. One has a legal obligation, he thought, if one is among the addressees of some general order of the sovereign, and is in danger of suffering a sanction unless he obeys that order.

Of course, the sovereign cannot provide for all contingencies through any scheme of orders, and some of his orders will inevitably be vague or have furry edges. Therefore (according to Austin) the sovereign grants those who enforce the law (judges) discretion to make fresh orders when novel or troublesome cases are presented. The judges then make new rules or adapt old rules, and the sovereign either overturns their creations, or tacitly confirms them by failing to do so.

Austin's model is quite beautiful in its simplicity. It asserts the first tenet of positivism, that the law is a set of rules specially selected to govern public order, and offers a simple factual test— what has the sovereign commanded?— as the sole criterion for identifying those special rules. In time, however, those who studied and tried to apply Austin's model found it too simple. Many objections were raised, among which were two that seemed fundamental. First, Austin's key assumption that in each community a determinate group or institution can be found, which is in ultimate control of all other groups, seemed not to hold in a complex society. Political control in a modern nation is pluralistic and shifting, a matter of more or less, of compromise and cooperation and alliance, so that it is often impossible to say that any person or group has that dramatic control necessary to qualify as an Austinian sovereign. One wants to say, in the United States for example, that the "people" are sovereign. But this means almost nothing, and in itself provides no test for determining what the "people" have commanded, or distinguishing their legal from their social or moral commands.

Second, critics began to realize that Austin's analysis fails entirely to account for, even to recognize, certain striking facts about the attitudes we take toward "the law." We make an important distinction between law and even the general orders of a gangster. We feel that the law's strictures—and its sanctions—are different in that they are obligatory in a way that the outlaw's commands are not. Austin's analysis has no place for any such distinction, because it defines an obligation as subjection to the threat of force, and so founds the authority of law entirely on the sovereign's ability and will to harm those who disobey. Perhaps the distinction we make is illusory—perhaps our feelings of some special authority attaching to the law is based on religious hangover or another sort of mass self-deception. But Austin does not demonstrate this, and we are entitled to insist that an analysis of our concept of law either acknowledge and explain our attitudes, or show why they are mistaken.

H. L. A. Hart's version of positivism is more complex than Austin's, in two ways. First, he recognizes, as Austin did not, the rules are of different logical kinds (Hart distinguishes two kinds, which he calls "primary" and "secondary" rules). Second, he rejects Austin's theory that a rule is a kind of command, and substitutes a more elaborate general analysis of what rules are. We must pause over each of these points, and then note how they merge in Hart's concept of law.

Hart's distinction between primary and secondary rules is of great importance.[3] Primary rules are those that grant rights or impose obligations upon members of the community. The rules of the criminal law that forbid us to rob, murder or drive too fast are good examples of primary rules. Secondary rules are those that stipulate how, and by whom, such primary rules may be formed, recognized, modified or extinguished. The rules that stipulate how Congress is composed, and how it enacts legislation, are examples of secondary rules. Rules about forming contracts and executing wills are also secondary rules because they stipulate how very particular rules governing particular legal obligations (that is, the terms of a contract or the provisions of a will) come into existence and are changed.

His general analysis of rules is also of great importance.[4] Austin had said that every rule is a general command, and that a person is obligated under a rule if he is liable to be hurt should he disobey it. Hart points out that this obliterates the distinction between being *obliged* to do something and being *obligated* to do it. If one is bound by a rule he is obligated, not merely obliged, to do what it provides, and therefore being bound by a rule must be different from being subject to an injury if one disobeys an order. A rule differs from an order, among other ways, by being *normative,* by setting a standard of behavior that has a call on its subject beyond the threat that may enforce it. A rule can never be binding just because some person with physical power wants it to be so. He must have *authority* to issue the rule or it is no rule, and such authority can only come from another rule which is already binding on those to whom he speaks. That is the difference between a valid law and the orders of a gunman.

So Hart offers a general theory of rules that does not make their authority depend upon the physical power of their authors. If we examine the way different rules come into being, he tells us, and attend to the distinction between primary

and secondary rules, we see that there are two possible sources of a rule's authority.[5]

(a) A rule may become binding upon a group of people because that group through its practices *accepts* the rule as a standard for its conduct. It is not enough that the group simply conforms to a pattern of behavior: even though most Englishmen may go to the movies on Saturday evening, they have not accepted a rule requiring that they do so. A practice constitutes the acceptance of a rule only when those who follow the practice regard the rule as binding, and recognize the rule as a reason or justification for their own behavior and as a reason for criticizing the behavior of others who do not obey it.

(b) A rule may also become binding in quite a different way, namely by being enacted in conformity with some *secondary* rule that stipulates that rules so enacted shall be binding. If the constitution of a club stipulates, for example, that by-laws may be adopted by a majority of the members, then particular by-laws so voted are binding upon all the members, not because of any practice of acceptance of these particular by-laws, but because the constitution says so. We use the concept of *validity* in this connection: rules binding because they have been created in a manner stipulated by some secondary rule are called "valid" rules. Thus we can record Hart's fundamental distinction this way: a rule may be binding (a) because it is accepted or (b) because it is valid.

Hart's concept of law is a construction of these various distinctions.[6] Primitive communities have only primary rules, and these are binding entirely because of practices of acceptance. Such communities cannot be said to have "law," because there is no way to distinguish a set of legal rules from amongst other social rules, as the first tenet of positivism requires. But when a particular community has developed a fundamental secondary rule that stipulates how legal rules are to be identified, the idea of a distinct set of legal rules, and thus of law, is born.

Hart calls such a fundamental secondary rule a "rule of recognition." The rule of recognition of a given community may be relatively simple ("What the king enacts is law") or it may be very complex (the United States Constitution, with all its difficulties of interpretation, may be considered a single rule of recognition). The demonstration that a particular rule is valid may therefore require tracing a complicated chain of validity back from that particular rule ultimately to the fundamental rule. Thus a parking ordinance of the city of New Haven is valid because it is adopted by a city council, pursuant to the procedures and within the competence specified by the municipal law adopted by the state of Connecticut, in conformity with the procedures and within the competence specified by the constitution of the state of Connecticut, which was in turn adopted consistently with the requirements of the United States Constitution.

Of course, a rule of recognition cannot itself be valid, because by hypothesis it is ultimate, and so cannot meet tests stipulated by a more fundamental rule. The rule of recognition is the sole rule in a legal system whose binding force depends upon its acceptance. If we wish to know what rule of recognition a particular community has adopted or follows, we must observe how its citizens, and particularly its officials, behave. We must observe what ultimate arguments they accept as showing the validity of a particular rule, and what ultimate arguments they use to criticize other officials or institutions. We can apply no mechanical test, but there is no danger of our confusing the rule of recognition of a community with its rules of morality. The rule of recognition is identified by the fact that its province is the operation of the governmental apparatus of legislatures, courts, agencies, policemen, and the rest.

In this way Hart rescues the fundamentals of positivism from Austin's mistakes. Hart agrees with Austin that valid rules of law may be created through the acts of officials and public institutions. But Austin thought that the authority of these institutions lay only in their monopoly of power. Hart finds their authority in the background of constitutional standards against which they act, constitutional standards that have been accepted, in the form of a fundamental rule of recognition, by the community which they govern. This background legitimates the decisions of government and gives them the cast and call of obligation that the naked commands of Austin's sovereign lacked. Hart's theory differs from Austin's also, in recognizing that different communities use different ultimate tests of law, and that some allow other means of creating law than the deliberate act of a legislative institution. Hart mentions "long customary practice" and "the relation [of a rule] to judicial decisions" as other criteria that are often used, though generally along with and subordinate to the test of legislation.

So Hart's version of positivism is more complex than Austin's, and his test for valid rules of law is more sophisticated. In one respect, however, the two models are very similar. Hart, like Austin, recognizes that legal rules have furry edges (he speaks of them as having "open texture") and, again like Austin, he accounts for troublesome cases by saying that judges have had exercise discretion to decide these cases by fresh legislation.[7] (I shall later try to show why one who thinks of law as a special set of rules is almost inevitably drawn to account for difficult cases in terms of someone's exercise of discretion.)

RULES, PRINCIPLES, AND POLICIES

I want to make a general attack on positivism, and I shall use H. L. A. Hart's version as a target, when a particular target is needed. My strategy will be organized around the fact that when lawyers reason or dispute about legal rights and obligations, particularly in those hard cases when our problems with these concepts seem most acute, they make use of standards that do not function as rules, but operate differently as principles, policies, and other sorts of standards. Positivism, I shall argue, is a model of and for a system of rules, and its central notion of a single fundamental test for law forces us to miss the important roles of these standards that are not rules.

I just spoke of "principles, policies, and other sorts of standards." Most often I shall use the term "principle" generically, to refer to the whole set of these standards other than rules; occasionally, however, I shall be more precise, and distinguish between principles and policies. Although nothing in the present argument will turn on the distinction, I should state how I draw it. I call a "policy" that kind of standard that sets out a goal to be reached, generally an improvement in some economic, political, or social feature of the community (though some goals are negative, in that they stipulate that some present feature is to be protected from adverse change). I call a "principle" a standard that is to be observed, not because it will advance or secure an economic, political, or social situation deemed desirable, but because it is a requirement of justice or fairness or some other dimension of morality. Thus the standard that automobile accidents are to be decreased is a policy, and the standard that no man may profit by his own wrong a principle. The distinction can be collapsed by construing a principle as stating a social goal (that is, the goal of a society in which no man profits by his own wrong), or by construing a policy as stating a principle (that is, the principle that the goal the policy embraces is a worthy one) or by adopting the utilitarian thesis that principles of justice are disguised statements of goals (securing the greatest happiness of the greatest number). In some contexts the distinction has uses which are lost if it is thus collapsed.[8]

My immediate purpose, however, is to distinguish principles in the generic sense from rules, and I shall start by collecting some examples of the former. The examples I offer are chosen haphazardly; almost any case in a law school casebook would provide examples that would serve as well. In 1889 a New York court, in the famous case of *Riggs v. Palmer,*[9] had to decide whether an heir named in the will of his grandfather could inherit under that will, even though he had murdered his grandfather to do so. The court began its reasoning with this admission: "It is quite true that statutes regulating the making, proof and effect of wills, and the devolution of property, if literally construed, and if their force and effect can in no way and under no circumstances be controlled or modified, give this property to the murderer."[10] But the court continued to note that "all laws as well as all contracts may be controlled in their operation and effect by general, fundamental maxims of the common law. No one shall be permitted to profit by his own fraud, or to take advantage of his own wrong, or to found any claim upon his own iniquity, or to acquire property by his own crime."[11] The murderer did not receive his inheritance.

In 1960, a New Jersey court was faced, in *Henningsen v. Bloomfield Motors, Inc.,*[12] with the important question of whether (or how much) an automobile manufacturer may limit his liability in case the automobile is defective. Henningsen had bought a car, and signed a contract which said that the manufacturer's liability for defects was limited to "making good" defective parts—"this warranty being expressly in lieu of all other warranties, obligations or liabilities." Henningsen argued that, at least in the circumstances of his case, the manufacturer ought not to be protected by this limitation, and ought to be liable for the medical and other expenses of persons injured in a crash. He was not able to point to any statute, or to any established rule of law, that prevented the manufacturer from standing on the contract. The court nevertheless agreed with Henningsen. At various points in the court's argument the following appeals to standards are made: (a) "[W]e must keep in mind the general principal that, in the absence of fraud, one who does not choose to read a contract before signing it cannot later relieve himself of its burdens."[13] (b) "In applying that principle, the basic tenet of freedom of competent parties to contract is a factor of importance."[14] (c) "Freedom of contract is not such an immutable doctrine as to admit of no qualification in the area in which we are concerned."[15] (d) "In a society such as ours where the automobile is a common and necessary adjunct of daily life, and where its use is so fraught with danger to the driver, passengers and the public, the manufacturer is under a special obligation in connection with the construction, promotion and sale of his cars. Consequently, the courts must examine purchase agreements closely to see if consumer and public interests are treated fairly."[16] (e) " '[I]s there any principle which is more familiar or more firmly embedded in the history of Anglo-American law than the basic doctrine that the courts will not permit themselves to be used as instruments of inequity and injustice?' "[17] (f) " 'More specifically, the courts generally refuse to lend themselves to the enforcement of a "bargain" in which one party has unjustly taken advantage of the economic necessities of other. . . .' "[18]

The standards set out in these quotations are not the sort we think of as legal rules. They seem very different from propositions like "The maximum legal speed on the turnpike is sixty miles an hour" or "A will is invalid unless signed by three witnesses." They are different because they are legal principles rather than legal rules.

The difference between legal principles and legal rules is a logical distinction. Both sets of standards point to particular decisions about legal obligation in particular circumstances, but they differ in the character of the direction they give. Rules are applicable in an all-or-nothing fashion. If the facts a rule stipulates are given, then either the rule is valid, in which case the answer it supplies must be accepted, or it is not, in which case it contributes nothing to the decision.

This all-or-nothing is seen most plainly if we look at the way rules operate, not in law, but in some enterprise they dominate—a game, for example. In baseball a rule provides that if the batter has had three strikes, he is out. An official cannot consistently acknowledge that this is an accurate statement of a baseball rule, and decide that a batter who has had three strikes is not out. Of course, a rule may have exceptions (the batter who has taken three strikes is not out if the catcher drops the third strike.) However, an accurate statement of the rule would take this exception into account, and any that did not would be incomplete. If the list of exceptions is very large, it would be too clumsy to repeat them each time the rule is cited; there is, however, no reason in theory why they could not all be added on, and the more that are, the more accurate is the statement of the rule.

If we take baseball rules as a model, we find that rules of law, like the rule that a will is invalid unless signed by three witnesses, fit the model well. If the requirement of three witnesses is a valid legal rule, then it cannot be that a will has been signed by only two witnesses and is valid. The rule might have exceptions, but if it does then it is inaccurate and incomplete to state the rule so simply, without enumerating the exceptions. In theory, at least, the exceptions could all be listed, and the more of them that are, the more complete is the statement of the rule.

But this is not the way the sample principles in the quotations operate. Even those which look most like rules do not set out legal consequences that follow automatically when the conditions provided are met. We say that our law respects the principle that no man may profit from his own wrong, but we do not mean that the law never permits a man to profit from wrongs he commits. In fact, people often profit, perfectly legally, from their legal wrongs. The most notorious case is adverse possession—if I trespass on your land long enough, some day I will gain a right to cross your land whenever I please. There are many less dramatic examples. If a man leaves one job, breaking a contract, to take a much higher paying job, he may have to pay damages to his first employer, but he is usually entitled to keep his new salary. If a man jumps bail and crosses state lines to make a brilliant investment in another state, he may be sent back to jail, but he will keep his profits.

We do not treat these—and countless other counter-instances that can easily be imagined—as showing that the principle about profiting from one's wrongs is not a principle of our legal system, or that it is incomplete and needs qualifying exceptions. We do not treat counter-instances as exceptions (at least not exceptions in the way in which a catcher's dropping the third strike is an exception) because we could not hope to capture these counter-instances simply by a more extended statement of the principle. They are not, even in theory, subject to enumeration, because we would have to include not only these cases

(like adverse possession) in which some institution has already provided that profit can be gained through a wrong, but also those numberless imaginary cases in which we know in advance that the principle would not hold. Listing some of these might sharpen our sense of the principle's weight (I shall mention that dimension in a moment), but it would not make for a more accurate or complete statement of the principle.

A principle like "No man may profit from his own wrong" does not even purport to set out conditions that make its application necessary. Rather, it states a reason that argues in one direction, but does not necessitate a particular decision. If a man has or is about to receive something, as a direct result of something illegal he did to get it, then that is a reason which the law will take into account in deciding whether he should keep it. There may be other principles or policies arguing in the other direction—a policy of securing title, for example, or a principle limiting punishment to what the legislature has stipulated. If so, our principle may not prevail, but that does not mean that it is not a principle of our legal system, because in the next case, when these contravening considerations are absent or less weighty, the principle may be decisive. All that is meant, when we say that a particular principle is a principle of our law, is that the principle is one which officials must take into account, if it is relevant, as a consideration inclining in one direction or another.

The logical distinction between rules and principles appears more clearly when we consider principles that do not even look like rules. Consider the proposition, set out under "(d)" in the excerpts from the *Henningsen* opinion, that "the manufacturer is under a special obligation in connection with the construction, promotion and sale of his cars." This does not even purport to define the specific duties such a special obligation entails, or to tell us what rights automobile consumers acquire as a result. It merely states—and this is an essential link in the *Henningsen* argument—that automobile manufacturers must be held to higher standards than other manufacturers, and are less entitled to rely on the competing principle of freedom of contract. It does not mean that they may never rely on that principle, or that courts may rewrite automobile purchase contracts at will; it means only that if a particular clause seems unfair or burdensome, courts have less reason to enforce the clause than if it were for the purchase of neckties. The "special obligation" counts in favor, but does not in itself necessitate, a decision refusing to enforce the terms of an automobile purchase contract.

This first difference between rules and principles entails another. Principles have a dimension that rules do not—the dimension of weight or importance. When principles intersect (the policy of protecting automobile consumers intersecting with principles of freedom of contract, for example), one who must resolve the conflict has to take into account the relative weight of each. This cannot be, of course, an exact measurement, and the judgment that a particular principle or policy is more important than another will often be a controversial one. Nevertheless, it is an integral part of the concept of a principle that it has this dimension, that it makes sense to ask how important or how weighty it is.

Rules do not have this dimension. We can speak of rules as being *functionally* important or unimportant (the baseball rule that three strikes are out is more important than the rule that runners may advance on a balk, because the game would be much more changed with the first rule altered than the second). In this sense, one legal rule may be more important than another because it has a greater or more important role in regulating behavior. But we cannot say that one rule is more important than another within the system of rules, so that when two rules conflict one supersedes the other by virtue of its greater weight. If two rules conflict, one of them cannot be a valid rule. The decision as to which is valid, and which must be abandoned or recast, must be made by appealing to considerations beyond the rules themselves. A legal system might regulate such conflicts by other rules, which prefer the rule enacted by the higher authority, or the rule enacted later, or the more specific rule, or something of that sort. A legal system may also prefer the rule supported by the more important principles. (Our own legal system uses both of these techniques.)

It is not always clear from the form of a standard whether it is a rule or a principle. "A will is invalid unless signed by three witnesses" is not very different in form from "A man may not profit from his own wrong," but one who knows something of American laws knows that he must take the first as stating a rule and the second as stating a principle. In many cases the distinction is difficult to make—it may not have been settled how the standard should operate, and this issue may itself be a focus of controversy. The First Amendment to the United States Constitution contains the provision that Congress shall not abridge freedom of speech. Is this a rule, so that if a particular law does abridge freedom of speech, it follows that it is unconstitutional? Those who claim that the first amendment is "an absolute" say that it must be taken in this way, that is, as a rule. Or does it merely state a principle, so that when an abridgement of speech is discovered, it is unconstitutional unless the context presents some other policy or principle which in the circumstances is weighty enough to permit the abridgement? That is the position of those who argue for what is called the "clear and present danger" test or some other form of "balancing."

Sometimes a rule and a principle can play much the same role, and the difference between them is almost a matter of form alone. The first section of the Sherman Act states that every contract in restraint of trade shall be void. The Supreme Court had to make the decision whether this provision should be treated as a rule in its own terms (striking down every contract "which restrains trade," which almost any contract does) or as a principle, providing a reason for striking down a contract in the absence of effective contrary policies. The Court construed the provision as a rule, but treated that rule as containing the word "unreasonable," and as prohibiting only "unreasonable" restraints of trade.[19] This allowed the provision to function logically as a rule (whenever a court finds that the restraint is "unreasonable" it is bound to hold the contract invalid) and substantially as a principle (a court must take into account a variety of other principles and policies in determining whether a particular restraint in particular economic circumstances is "unreasonable").

Words like "reasonable," "negligent," "unjust," and "significant" often perform just this function. Each of these terms makes the application of the rule which contains it depend to some extent upon principles or policies lying beyond the rule, and in this way makes that rule itself more like a principle. But they do not quite turn the rule into a principle, because even the least confining of these terms restricts the *kind* of other principles and policies on which the rule depends. If we are bound by a rule that says that "unreasonable" contracts are void, or that grossly "unfair" contracts will not be enforced, much more judgment is required than if the quoted terms were omitted. But suppose a case in which some consideration of policy or principle suggests that a contract should be enforced even though its restraint is not reasonable, or even though it is grossly unfair. Enforcing these contracts would be forbidden by our rules, and thus permitted only if these rules were abandoned or modified. If we were dealing, however, not with a rule but with a policy against enforcing unreasonable contracts, or a principle that unfair contracts ought not to be enforced, the contracts could be enforced without alteration of the law.

PRINCIPLES AND THE CONCEPT OF LAW

Once we identify legal principles as separate sorts of standards, different from legal rules, we are suddenly aware of them all around us. Law teachers teach them, lawbooks cite them, legal historians celebrate them. But they seem most energetically at work, carrying most weight, in difficult lawsuits like *Riggs and Henningsen*. In cases like these principles play an essential part in arguments supporting judgments about particular legal rights and obligations. After the case is decided, we may say that the case stands for a particular rule (that is, the rule that one who murders is not eligible to take under the will of his victim). But the rule does not exist before the case is decided; the court cites principles as its justification for adopting and applying a new rule. In *Riggs,* the court cited the principle that no man may profit from his own wrong as a background standard against which to read the statute of wills and in this way justified a new interpretation of that statute. In *Henningsen,* the court cited a variety of intersecting principles and policies as authority for a new rule respecting manufacturer's liability for automobile defects.

An analysis of the concept of legal obligation must therefore account for the important role of principles in reaching particular decisions of law. There are two very different tacks we might take.

(a) We might treat legal principles the way we treat legal rules and say that some principles are binding as law and must be taken into account by judges and lawyers who make decisions of legal obligation. If we took this tack, we should say that in the United States, at least, the "law" includes principles as well as rules.

(b) We might, on the other hand, deny that principles can be binding the way some rules are.

We would say, instead, that in cases like *Riggs* or *Henningsen* the judge reaches beyond the rules that he is bound to apply (reaches, that is, beyond the "law") for extralegal principles he is free to follow if he wishes.

One might think that there is not much difference between these two lines of attack, that it is only a verbal question of how one wants to use the word "law." But that is a mistake, because the choice between these two accounts has the greatest consequences for an analysis of legal obligation. It is a choice between two *concepts* of a legal principle, a choice we can clarify by comparing it to a choice we might make between two concepts of a legal rule. We sometimes say of someone that he "makes it a rule" to do something, when we mean that he has chosen to follow a certain practice. We might say that someone has made it a rule, for example, to run a mile before breakfast because he wants to be healthy and believes in a regimen. We do not mean, when we say this, that he is *bound* by the rule that he must run a mile before breakfast, or even that he regards it as binding upon him. Accepting a rule as binding is something different from making it a rule to do something. If we use Hart's example again, there is a difference between saying that Englishmen make it a rule to see a movie once a week, and saying that the English have a rule that one must see a movie once a week. The second implies that if an Englishman does not follow the rule, he is subject to criticism or censure, but the first does not. The first does not exclude the possibility of a *sort* of criticism—we can say that one who does not see movies is neglecting his education—but we do not suggest that he is doing something wrong *just* in not following the rule.[20]

If we think of the judges of a community as a group, we could describe the rules of law they follow in these two different ways. We could say, for instance, that in a certain state the judges make it a rule not to enforce wills unless there are three witnesses. This would not imply that the rare judge who enforces such a rule is doing anything wrong just for that reason. On the other hand we can say that in that state a rule of law requires judges not to enforce such wills; this does imply that a judge who enforces them is doing something wrong. Hart, Austin and other positivists, of course, would insist on this latter account of legal rules; they would not at all be satisfied with the "make it a rule" account. It is not a verbal question of which account is right. It is a question of which describes the social situation more accurately. Other important issues turn on which description we accept. If judges simply "make it a rule" not to enforce certain contracts, for example, then we cannot say, before the decision, that anyone is "entitled" to that result, and that proposition cannot enter into any justification we might offer for the decision.

The two lines of attack on principles parallel these two accounts of rules. The first tack treats principles as binding upon judges, so that they are wrong not to apply the principles when they are pertinent. The second tack treats principles as summaries of what most judges "make it a principle" to do when forced to go beyond the standards that bind them. The choice between these approaches will affect, perhaps even determine, the answer we can give to the question whether the judge in a hard case like *Riggs* or *Henningsen* is attempting to enforce preexisting legal rights and obligations. If we take the first tack, we are still free to argue that because such judges are applying binding legal standards they are enforcing legal rights and obligations. But if we take the second, we are out of court on that issue, and we must acknowledge that the murderer's family in *Riggs* and the manufacturer in *Henningsen* were deprived of their property by an act of judicial discretion applied *ex post facto.* This may not shock many readers—the notion of judicial discretion has percolated through the legal community—but it does illustrate one of the most nettlesome of the puzzles that drive philosophers to worry about legal obligation. If taking property away in cases like these cannot be justified by appealing to an established obligation, yet another justification must be found, and nothing satisfactory has yet been supplied.

In my skeleton diagram of positivism, previously set out, I listed the doctrine of judicial discretion as the second tenet. Positivists hold that when a case is not covered by a clear rule, a judge must exercise his discretion to decide that case by what amounts to a fresh piece of legislation. There may be an important connection between this doctrine and the question of which of the two approaches to legal principles we must take. We shall therefore want to ask whether the doctrine is correct, and whether it implies the second approach, as it seems on its face to do. En route to these issues, however, we shall have to polish our understanding of the concept of discretion. I shall try to show how certain confusions about that concept, and in particular a failure to discriminate different senses in which it is used, account for the popularity of the doctrine of discretion. I

shall argue that in the sense in which the doctrine does have a bearing on our treatment of principles, it is entirely unsupported by the arguments the positivists use to defend it.

DISCRETION

The concept of discretion was lifted by the positivists from ordinary language, and to understand it we must put it back *in habitat* for a moment. What does it mean, in ordinary life, to say that someone "has discretion"? The first thing to notice is that the concept is out of place in all but very special contexts. For example, you would not say that I either do or do not have discretion to choose a house for my family. It is not true that I have "no discretion" in making that choice, and yet it would be almost equally misleading to say that I do have discretion. The concept of discretion is at home in only one sort of context: when someone is in general charged with making decisions subject to standards set by a particular authority. It makes sense to speak of the discretion of a sergeant who is subject to orders of superiors, or the discretion of a sports official or contest judge who is governed by a rule book or the terms of the contest. Discretion, like the hole in a doughnut, does not exist except as an area left open by a surrounding belt of restriction. It is therefore a relative concept. It always makes sense to ask, "Discretion under which standards?" or "Discretion as to which authority?" Generally the context will make the answer to this plain, but in some cases the official may have discretion from one standpoint though not from another.

Like almost all terms, the precise meaning of "discretion" is affected by features of the context. The term is always colored by the background of understood information against which it is used. Although the shadings are many, it will be helpful for us to recognize some gross distinctions.

Sometimes we use "discretion" in a weak sense, simply to say that for some reason the standards an official must apply cannot be applied mechanically but demand the use of judgment. We use this weak sense when the context does not already make that clear, when the background our audience assumes does not contain that piece of information. Thus we might say, "The sergeant's orders left him a great deal of discretion," to those who do not know what the sergeant's orders were or who do not know something that made those orders vague or hard to carry out. It would make perfect sense to add, by way of amplification, that the lieutenant had ordered the sergeant to take his five most experienced men on patrol but that it was hard to determine which were the most experienced.

Sometimes we use the term in a different weak sense, to say only that some official has final authority to make a decision and cannot be reviewed and reversed by any other official. We speak this way when the official is part of a hierarchy of officials structured so that some have higher authority but in which the patterns of authority are different for different classes of decision. Thus we might say that in baseball certain decisions, like the decision whether the ball or the runner reached second base first, are left to the discretion of the second base umpire, if we mean that on this issue the head umpire has no power to substitute his own judgment if he disagrees.

I call both of these senses weak to distinguish them from a stronger sense. We use "discretion" sometimes not merely to say that an official must use judgment in applying the standards set him by authority, or that no one will review that exercise of judgment, but to say that on some issue he is simply not bound by standards set by the authority in question. In this sense we say that a sergeant has discretion who has been told to pick any five men for patrol he chooses or that a judge in a dog show has discretion to judge airedales before boxers if the rules do not stipulate an order of events. We use this sense not to comment on the vagueness or difficulty of the standards, or on who has the final word in applying them, but on their range and the decisions they purport to control. If the sergeant is told to take the five most experienced men, he does not have discretion in this strong sense because that order purports to govern his decision. The boxing referee who must decide which fighter has been the more aggressive does not have discretion, in the strong sense, for the same reason.[21]

If anyone said that the sergeant or the referee had discretion in these cases, we should have to understand him, if the context permitted, as using the term in one of the weak senses. Suppose, for example, the lieutenant ordered the sergeant to select the five men he deemed most experienced, and then added that the sergeant had discretion to choose them. Or the rules provided that the referee should award the round to the more aggressive fighter, with discretion in selecting him. We should have to understand these statements in the second weak sense, as speaking to the question of review of the decision. The first weak sense —that the decisions take judgment—would be otiose, and the third, strong sense is excluded by the statements themselves.

We must avoid one tempting confusion. The strong sense of discretion is not tantamount to license, and does not exclude criticism. Almost any situation in which a person acts (including those in which there is no question of decision under special authority, and so no question of discretion) makes relevant certain standards of rationality, fairness and effectiveness. We criticize each other's acts in terms of these standards, and there is no reason not to do so when the acts are within the center rather than beyond the perimeter of the doughnut of special authority. So we can say that the sergeant who was given discretion (in the strong sense) to pick a patrol did so stupidly or maliciously or carelessly, or that the judge who had discretion in the order of viewing dogs made a mistake because he took boxers first although there were only three airedales and many more boxers. An official's discretion means not that he is free to decide without recourse to standards of sense and fairness, but only that his decision is not controlled by a standard furnished by the particular authority we have in mind when we raise the question of discretion. Of course this latter sort of freedom is important; that is why we have the strong sense of discretion. Someone who has discretion in this third sense can be criticized, but not for being disobedient, as in the case of the soldier. He can be said to have made a mistake, but not to have deprived a participant of a decision to which he was entitled, as in the case of a sports official or contest judge.

We may now return, with these observations in hand, to the positivists' doctrine of judicial discretion. That doctrine argues that if a case is not controlled by an established rule, the judge must decide it by exercising discretion. We want to examine this doctrine and to test its bearing on our treatment of principles; but first we must ask in which sense of discretion we are to understand it.

Some nominalists argue that judges always have discretion, even when a clear rule is in point, because judges are ultimately the final arbiters of the law. This doctrine of discretion uses the second weak sense of that term, because it makes the point that no higher authority reviews the decisions of the highest court. It therefore has no bearing on the issue of how we account for principles, any more than it bears on how we account for rules.

The positivists do not mean their doctrine this way, because they say that a judge has no discretion when a clear and established rule is available. If we attend to the positivists' arguments for the doctrine, we may suspect that they use discretion in the first weak sense to mean only that judges must sometimes exercise judgment in applying legal standards. Their arguments call attention to the fact that some rules of law are vague (Professor Hart, for example, says that all rules of law have "open texture"), and that some cases arise (like *Henningsen*) in which no established rule seems to be suitable. They emphasize that judges must sometimes agonize over points of law, and that two equally trained and intelligent judges will often disagree.

These points are easily made; they are commonplace to anyone who has any familiarity with law. Indeed, that is the difficulty with assuming that positivists mean to use "discretion" in this weak sense. The proposition that, when no clear rule is available discretion in the sense of judgment must be used, is a tautology. It has no bearing, moreover, on the problem of how to account for legal principles. It is perfectly consistent to say that the judge in *Riggs,* for example, had to use judgment, and that he was bound to follow the principle that no man may profit from his own wrong. The positivists speak as if their doctrine of judicial discretion is an insight rather than a tautology, and as if it does have a bearing on the treatment of principles. Hart, for example, says that when the judge's discretion is in play, we can no longer speak of his being bound by standards, but must speak rather of what standards he "characteristically uses."[22] Hart thinks that when judges have discretion, the principles they cite must be treated on our second approach, as what courts "make it a principle" to do.

It therefore seems that positivists, at least sometimes, take their doctrine in the third, strong sense of discretion. In that sense it does bear on the treatment of principles; indeed, in that sense it is nothing less than a restatement of our second approach. It is the same thing to say that when a judge runs out of rules he has discretion, in the sense that he is not bound by any standards from the authority of law, as to say that the legal standards judges cite other than rules are not binding on them.

So we must examine the doctrine of judicial discretion in the strong sense. (I shall henceforth use the term "discretion" in that sense.) Do the principles judges cite in cases like *Riggs* or *Henningsen* control their decisions, as the sergeant's orders to take the most experienced men or the referee's duty to choose the more aggressive fighter control the decisions of these officials? What arguments could a positivist supply to show that they do not?

(1) A positivist might argue that principles cannot be binding or obligatory. That would be a mistake. It is always a question, of course, whether any particular principle is *in fact* binding upon some legal official. But there is nothing in the logical character of a principle that renders it incapable of binding him. Suppose that the judge in *Henningsen* had failed to take any account of the principle that automobile manufacturers have a special obligation to their consumers, or the principle that the courts seek to protect those whose bargaining position is weak, but had simply decided for the defendant by citing the principle of freedom of contract without more. His critics would not have been content to point out that he had not taken account of considerations that other judges have been attending to for some time. Most would have said that it was his duty to take the measure of these principles and that the plaintiff was entitled to have him do so. We mean no more, when we say that a *rule* is binding upon a judge, than that he must follow it if it applies, and that if he does not he will on that account have made a mistake.

It will not do to say that in a case like *Henningsen* the court is only "morally" obligated to take particular principles into account, or that it is "institutionally" obligated, or obligated as a matter of judicial "craft," or something of that sort. The question will still remain why this type of obligation (whatever we call it) is different from the obligation that rules impose upon judges, and why it entitles us to say that principles and policies are not part of the law but are merely extralegal standards "courts characteristically use."

(2) A positivist might argue that even though some principles are binding, in the sense that the judge must take them into account, they cannot determine a particular result. This is a harder argument to assess because it is not clear what it means for a standard to "determine" a result. Perhaps it means that the standard *dictates* the result whenever it applies so that nothing else counts. If so, then it is certainly true that individual principles do not determine results, but that

is only another way of saying that principles are not rules. Only rules dictate results, come what may. When a contrary result has been reached, the rule has been abandoned or changed. Principles do not work that way; they incline a decision one way, though not conclusively, and they survive intact when they do not prevail. This seems no reason for concluding that judges who must reckon with principles have discretion because a set of principles *can* dictate a result. If a judge believes that principles he is bound to recognize point in one direction and that principles pointing in the other direction, if any, are not of equal weight, then he must decide accordingly, just as he must follow what he believes to be a binding rule. He may, of course, be wrong in his assessment of the principles, but he may also be wrong in his judgment that the rule is binding. The sergeant and the referee, we might add, are often in the same boat. No one factor dictates which soldiers are the most experienced or which fighter the more aggressive. These officials must make judgments of the relative weights of these various factors; they do not on that account have discretion.

(3) A positivist might argue that principles cannot count as law because their authority, and even more so their weight, are congenitally *controversial*. It is true that generally we cannot *demonstrate* the authority or weight of a particular principle as we can sometimes demonstrate the validity of a rule by locating it in an act of Congress or in the opinion of an authoritative court. Instead, we make a case for a principle, and for its weight, by appealing to an amalgam of practice and other principles in which the implications of legislative and judicial history figure along with appeals to community practices and understandings. There is no litmus paper for testing the soundness of such a case—it is a matter of judgment, and reasonable men may disagree. But again this does not distinguish the judge from other officials who do not have discretion. The sergeant has no litmus paper for experience, the referee none for aggressiveness. Neither of these has discretion, because he is bound to reach an understanding, controversial or not, of what his orders or the rules require, and to act on that understanding. That is the judge's duty as well.

Of course, if the positivists are right in another of the doctrines—the theory that in each legal system there is an ultimate *test* for binding law like Professor Hart's rule of recognition—it follows that principles are not binding law. But the incompatibility of principles with the positivists' theory can hardly be taken as an argument that principles must be treated any particular way. That begs the question; we are interested in the status of principles because we want to evaluate the positivists' model. The positivist cannot defend his theory of a rule of recognition by fiat; if principles are not amenable to a test he must show some other reason why they cannot count as law. Since principles seem to play a role in arguments about legal obligation (witness, again *Riggs* and *Henningsen*), a model that provides for that role has some initial advantage over one that excludes it, and the latter cannot properly be inveighed in its own support.

These are the most obvious of the arguments a positivist might use for the doctrine of discretion in the strong sense, and for the second approach to principles. I shall mention one strong counter-argument against that doctrine and in favor of the first approach. Unless at least some principles are acknowledged to be binding upon judges, requiring them as a set to reach particular decisions, then no rules, or very few rules, can be said to be binding upon them either.

In most American jurisdictions, and now in England also, the higher courts not infrequently reject established rules. Common law rules—those developed by earlier court decisions—are sometimes overruled directly, and sometimes radically altered by further development. Statutory rules are subjected to interpretation and reinterpretation, sometimes even when the result is not to carry out what is called the "legislative intent."[23] If courts had discretion to change established rules, then these rules would of course not be binding upon them, and so would not be law on the positivists' model. The positivist must therefore argue that there are standards, themselves binding upon judges, that determine when a judge may overrule or alter an established rule, and when he may not.

When, then, is a judge permitted to change an existing rule of law? Principles figure in the answer in two ways. First, it is necessary, though not sufficient, that the judge find that the change would advance some policy or serve some principle, which policy or principle thus justifies the change. In *Riggs* the change (a new interpretation of the statute of wills) was justified by the principle that no man should profit from his own wrong; in *Henningsen* certain rules about automobile manufacturer's liability were altered on the basis of the principles and policies I quoted from the opinion of the court.

But not any principle will do to justify a change, or no rule would ever be safe. There must be some principles that count and others that do not, and there must be some principles that count for more than others. It could not depend on the judge's own preferences amongst a sea of respectable extralegal standards, any one in principle eligible, because if that were the case we could not say that any rules were binding. We could always imagine a judge whose preferences amongst extralegal standards were such as would justify a shift or radical reinterpretation of even the most entrenched rule.

Second, any judge who proposes to change existing doctrine must take account of some important standards that argue against departures from established doctrine, and these standards are also for the most part principles. They include the doctrine of "legislative supremacy," a set of principles and policies that require the courts to pay a qualified deference to the acts of the legislature. They also include the doctrine of precedent, another set of principles and policies reflecting the equities and efficiencies of consistency. The doctrines of legislative supremacy and precedent incline toward the *status quo,* each within its sphere, but they do not command it. Judges are not free, however, to pick and choose amongst the principles and policies that make up these doctrines—if they were, again, no rule could be said to be binding.

Consider, therefore, what someone implies who says that a particular rule is binding. He may imply that the rule is affirmatively supported by principles the court is not free to disregard, and which are collectively more weighty than other principles that argue for a change. If not, he implies that any change would be condemned by a combination of conservative principles of legislative supremacy and precedent that the court is free to ignore. Very often, he will imply both, for the conservative principles, being principles and not rules, are usually not powerful enough to save a common law rule or an aging statute that is entirely unsupported by substantive principles the court is bound to respect. Either of these implications, of course, treats a body of principles and policies as law in the sense that rules are; it treats them as standards binding upon the officials of a community, controlling their decisions of legal right and obligation.

We are left with this issue. If the positivists' theory of judicial discretion is either trivial because it uses "discretion" in a weak sense, or

unsupported because the various arguments we can supply in its defense fall short, why have so many careful and intelligent lawyers embraced it? We can have no confidence in our treatment of that theory unless we can deal with that question. It is not enough to note (although perhaps it contributes to the explanation) that "discretion" has different senses that may be confused. We do not confuse these senses when we are not thinking about law.

Part of the explanation, at least, lies in a lawyer's natural tendency to associate laws and rules, and to think of "the law" as a collection or system of rules. Roscoe Pound, who diagnosed this tendency long ago, thought that English-speaking lawyers were tricked into it by the fact that English uses the same word, changing only the article, for "a law" and "the law."[24] (Other languages, on the contrary, use two words: "loi" and "droit," for example, and "Gesetz" and "Recht.") This may have had its effect, with the English speaking positivists, because the expression "a law" certainly does suggest a rule. But the principal reason for associating law with rules runs deeper, and lies, I think, in the fact that legal education has for a long time consisted of teaching and examining those established rules that form the cutting edge of law.

In any event, if a lawyer thinks of law as a system of rules, and yet recognizes, as he must, that judges change old rules and introduce new ones, he will come naturally to the theory of judicial discretion in the strong sense. In those other systems of rules with which he has experience (like games), the rules are the only special authority that govern official decisions, so that if an umpire could change a rule, he would have discretion as to the subject matter of that rule. Any principles umpires might mention when changing the rules would represent only their "characteristic" preferences. Positivists treat law like baseball revised in this way.

There is another, more subtle consequence of this initial assumption that law is a system of rules. When the positivists do attend to principles and policies, they treat them as rules *manque.* They assume that *if* they are standards of law they must be rules, and so they read them as standards that are trying to be rules. When a positivist hears someone argue that legal principles are part of the law, he understands this to be an argument for what he calls the "higher law" theory, that these principles are the rules of a law above the law.[25] He refutes this theory by pointing out that these "rules" are sometimes followed and sometimes not, that for every "rule" like "no man shall profit from his own wrong" there is another competing "rule" like "the law favors security of title," and that there is no way to test the validity of "rules" like these. He concludes that these principles and policies are not valid rules of a law above the law, which is true, because they are not rules at all. He also concludes that they are extralegal standards which each judge selects according to his own lights in the exercise of his discretion, which is false. It is as if a zoologist had proved that fish are not mammals, and then concluded that they are really only plants.

THE RULE OF RECOGNITION

This discussion was provoked by our two competing accounts of legal principles. We have been exploring the second account, which the positivists seem to adopt through their doctrine of judicial discretion, and we have discovered grave difficulties. It is time to return to the fork in the road. What if we adopt the first approach? What would the consequences of this be for the skeletal structure of positivism? Of course we should have to drop the second tenet, the doctrine of judicial discretion (or, in the alternative, to make plain that the doctrine is to be read merely to say that judges must often exercise judgment). Would we also have to abandon or modify the first tenet, the proposition that law is distinguished by tests of the sort that can be set out in a master rule like Professor Hart's rule of recognition? If principles of the *Riggs* and *Henningsen* sort are to count as law, and we are nevertheless to preserve the notion of a master rule for law, then we must be able to deploy some test that all (and only) the principles that do count as law meet. Let us begin with the test Hart suggests for identifying valid *rules* of law, to see whether these can be made to work for principles as well.

Most rules of law, according to Hart, are valid because some competent institution enacted them. Some were created by a legislature, in the form of statutory enactments. Others were created by judges who formulated them to decide particular cases, and thus established them as precedents for the future. But this test of pedigree will not work for the *Riggs* and *Henningsen* principles. The origin of these as legal principles lies not in a particular decision of some legislature or court, but in a sense of appropriateness developed in the profession and the public over time. Their continued power depends upon this sense of appropriateness being sustained. If it no longer seemed unfair to allow people to profit by their wrongs, or fair to place special burdens upon oligopolies that manufacture potentially dangerous machines, these principles would no longer play much of a role in new cases, even if they had never been overruled or repealed. (Indeed, it hardly makes sense to speak of principles like these as being "overruled" or "repealed." When they decline they are eroded, not torpedoed.)

True, if we were challenged to back up our claim that some principle is a principle of law, we would mention any prior cases in which that principle was cited, or figured in the argument. We would also mention any statute that seemed to exemplify that principle (even better if the principle was cited in the preamble of the statute, or in the committee reports or other legislative documents that accompanied it). Unless we could find some such institutional support, we would probably fail to make out our case, and the more support we found, the more weight we could claim for the principle.

Yet we could not devise any formula for testing how much and what kind of institutional support is necessary to make a principle a legal principle, still less to fix its weight at a particular order of magnitude. We argue for a particular principle by grappling with a whole set of shifting, developing and interacting standards (themselves principles rather than rules) about institutional responsibility, statutory interpretation, the persuasive force of various sorts of precedent, the relation of all these to contemporary moral practices, and hosts of other such standards. We could not bolt all of these together into a single "rule," even a complex one, and if we could the result would bear little relation to Hart's picture of a rule of recognition, which is the picture of a fairly stable master rule specifying "some feature or features possession of which by a suggested rule is taken as a conclusive affirmative indicating that it is a rule. . . ."[26]

Moreover, the techniques we apply in arguing for another principle do not stand (as Hart's rule of recognition is designed to) on an entirely different level from the principles they support. Hart's sharp distinction between acceptance and validity does not hold. If we are arguing for the principle that a man should not profit from his own wrong, we could cite the acts of courts and legislatures that exemplify it, but this speaks as much to the principle's acceptance as its validity. (It seems odd to speak of a principle as being valid at all, perhaps because validity is an all-or-nothing concept, appropriate for rules, but inconsistent with a principle's dimension of weight.) If we are asked (as we might well be) to defend the particular doctrine of precedent, or the particular technique of statutory interpretation, that we used in this argument, we should certainly cite the practice of others in using that doctrine or technique. But we should also cite other general principles that we believe support that practice, and this introduces a note of validity into the chord of acceptance. We might argue, for example, that the use we make of earlier cases and statutes is supported by a particular analysis of the point of practice of legislation or the doctrine of precedent, or by the principles of democratic theory, or by a particular position on the proper division of authority between national and local institutions, or something else of that sort. Nor is this path of support a one-way street leading to some ultimate principle resting on acceptance alone. Our principles of legislation, precedent, democracy, or federalism might be challenged too; and if they were we should argue for them, not only in terms of practice, but in terms of each other and in terms of the implications of trends of judicial and legislative decisions, even though this last would involve appealing to those same doctrines of interpretation we justified through the principles we are now trying to support. At this level of abstraction, in other words, principles rather hang together than link together.

So even though principles draw support from the official acts of legal institutions, they do not have a simple or direct enough connection with these acts to frame that connection in terms of criteria specified by some ultimate master rule of recognition. Is there any other route by which principles might be brought under such a rule?

Hart does say that a master rule might designate as law not only rules enacted by particular legal institutions, but rules established by *custom* as well. He has in mind a problem that bothered other positivists, including Austin. Many of our most ancient legal rules were never explicitly created by a legislature or a court. When they made their first appearance in legal opinions and texts, they were treated as already being part of the law because they represented the customary practice of the community, or some specialized part of it, like the business community. (The examples ordinarily given are rules of mercantile practice, like the rules governing what rights arise under a standard form of commercial paper.)[27] Since Austin thought that all law was the command of a determinate sovereign, he held that

these customary practices were not law until the courts (as agents of the sovereign) recognized them, and that the courts were indulging in a fiction in pretending otherwise. But that seemed arbitrary. If everyone thought custom might in itself be law, the fact that Austin's theory said otherwise was not persuasive.

Hart reversed Austin on this point. The master rule, he says, might stipulate that some custom counts as law even before the courts recognize it. But he does not face the difficulty this raises for this general theory, because he does not attempt to set out the criteria a master rule might use for this purpose. It cannot use, as its only criterion, the provision that the community regard the practice as *morally* binding, for this would not distinguish legal customary rules from moral customary rules, and of course not all of the community's long-standing customary moral obligations are enforced at law. If, on the other hand, the test is whether the community regards the customary practice as *legally* binding, the whole point of the master rule is undercut, at least for this class of legal rules. The master rule, says Hart, marks the transformation from a primitive society to one with law, because it provides a test for determining social rules of law other than by measuring their acceptance. But if the master rule says merely that whatever other rules the community accepts as legally binding are legally binding, then it provides no such test at all, beyond the test we should use were there no master rule. The master rule becomes (for these cases) a nonrule of recognition; we might as well say that every primitive society has a secondary rule of recognition, namely the rule that whatever is accepted as binding is binding. Hart himself, in discussing international law, ridicules the idea that such a rule could be a rule of recognition, by describing the proposed rule as "an empty repetition of the mere fact that the society concerned . . . observes certain standards of conduct as obligatory rules."[28]

Hart's treatment of custom amounts, indeed, to a confession that there are at least some rules of law that are not binding because they are valid under standards laid down by a master rule but are binding—like the master rule—because they are accepted as binding by the community. This chips at the neat pyramidal architecture we admired in Hart's theory: we can no longer say that only the master rule is binding because of its acceptance, all other rules being valid under its terms.

This is perhaps only a chip, because the customary rules Hart has in mind are no longer a very significant part of the law. But it does suggest that Hart would be reluctant to widen the damage by bringing under the head of "custom" all those crucial principles and policies we have been discussing. If he were to call these part of the law and yet admit that the only test of their force lies in the degree to which they are accepted as law by the community or some part thereof, he would very sharply reduce that area of the law over which his master rule held any dominion. It is not just that all the principles and policies would escape its sway, though that would be bad enough. Once these principles and policies are accepted as law, and thus as standards judges must follow in determining legal obligations, it would follow that *rules* like those announced for the first time in *Riggs* and *Henningsen* owe their force at least in part to the authority of principles and policies, and so not entirely to the master rule of recognition.

So we cannot adapt Hart's version of positivism by modifying his rule of recognition to embrace principles. No tests of pedigree, relating principles to acts of legislation, can be formulated, nor can his concept of customary law, itself an exception to the first tenet of positivism, be made to serve without abandoning that tenet altogether. One more possibility must be considered, however. If no rule of recognition can provide a test for identifying principles, why not say that principles are ultimate, and *form* the rule of recognition of our law? The answer to the general question "What is valid law in an American jurisdiction?" would then require us to state all the principles (as well as ultimate constitutional rules) in force in that jurisdiction at the time, together with appropriate assignments of weight. A positivist might then regard the complete set of these standards as the rule of recognition of the jurisdiction. This solution has the attraction of paradox, but of course it is an unconditional surrender. If we simply designate our rule of recognition by the phrase "the complete set of principles in force," we achieve only the tautology that law is law. If, instead, we tried actually to list all the principles in force we would fail. They are controversial, their weight is all important, they are numberless, and they shift and change so fast that the start of our list would be obsolete before we reached the middle. Even if we succeeded, we would not have a key for law because there would be nothing left for our key to unlock.

I conclude that if we treat principles as law we must reject the positivists' first tenet, that the law of a community is distinguished from other social standards by some test in the form of a master rule. We have already decided that we must then abandon the second tenet—the doctrine of judicial discretion—or clarify it into triviality. What of the third tenet, the positivists' theory of legal obligation?

This theory holds that a legal obligation exists when (and only when) an established rule of law imposes such an obligation. It follows from this that in a hard case—when no such established rule can be found—there is no legal obligation until the judge creates a new rule for the future. The judge may apply that new rule to the parties in the case, but this is *ex post facto* legislation, not the enforcement of an existing obligation.

The positivists' doctrine of discretion (in the strong sense) required this view of legal obligation, because if a judge has discretion there can be no legal right or obligation—no entitlement—that he must enforce. Once we abandon that doctrine, however, and treat principles as law, we raise the possibility that a legal obligation might be imposed by a constellation of principles as well as by an established rule. We might want to say that a legal obligation exists whenever the case supporting such an obligation, in terms of binding legal principles of different sorts, is stronger than the case against it.

Of course, many questions would have to be answered before we could accept that view of legal obligation. If there is no rule of recognition, no test for law in that sense, how do we decide which principles are to count, and how much, in making such a case? How do we decide whether one case is better than another? If legal obligation rests on an undemonstrable judgment of that sort, how can it provide a justification for a judicial decision that one party had a legal obligation? Does this view of obligation square with the way lawyers, judges and laymen speak, and is it consistent with our attitudes about moral obligation? Does this analysis help us to deal with the classical jurisprudential puzzles about the nature of law?

These questions must be faced, but even the questions promise more than positivism provides. Positivism, on its own thesis, stops short of just those puzzling, hard cases that send us to look for theories of law. When we reach these cases, the positivist remits us to a doctrine of discretion that leads nowhere and tells nothing. His picture of law as a system of rules has exercised a tenacious hold on our imagination, perhaps through its very simplicity. If we shake ourselves loose from this model of rules, we may be able to build a model truer to the complexity and sophistication of our own practices.

NOTES

1. *See* Linkletter v. Walker, 381 U.S. 618 (1965).
2. J. Austin, The Province of Jurisprudence Determined (1832).
3. *See* H. L. A. Hart, The Concept of Law 89–96 (1961).
4. *Id.* at 79–88.
5. *Id.* at 97–107.
6. *Id. passim,* particularly ch. VI.
7. *Id.* ch. VII.
8. *See* Dworkin, *Wasserstrom: The Judicial Decision,* 75 Ethics 47 (1964), reprinted as *Does Law Have a Function?,* 74 Yale L. J. 640 (1965).
9. 115 N.Y. 506, 22 N.E. 188 *1889); [p. 155 this volume.]
10. *Id.* at 509, 22 N.E. at 189; [p. 155 this volume.]
11. *Id.* at 511, 22 N.E. at 190. [p. 156 this volume.]
12. 32 N.J. 358, 161 A.2d 69 (1960).[p. 159 this volume.]
13. *Id.* at 386, 161 A.2d at 84. [p. 159 this volume.]
14. *Id.*
15. *Id.* at 388, 161 A.2d at 86. [p. 160 this volume.]
16. *Id.* at 387, 161 A.2d at 85. [p. 160 this volume.]
17. *Id.* at 389, 161 A.2d at 86 (quoting Frankfurter, J., in United States v. Bethlehem Steel, 315 U.S. 289, 326 (1942). [p. 160 this volume.]
18. *Id.* [p. 161 this volume.]

19. Standard Oil v. United States, 221 U.S. 1, 60 (1911); United States v. American Tobacco Co., 221 U.S. 106, 180 (1911).
20. The distinction is in substance the same as that made by Rawls, *Two Concepts of Rules,* 64 Philosophical Rev. 3 (1955).
21. I have not spoken of that jurisprudential favorite, "limited" discretion, because that concept presents no special difficulties if we remember the relativity of discretion. Suppose the sergeant is told to choose from "amongst" experienced men, or to "take experience into account." We might say either that he has (limited) discretion in picking his patrol, or (full) discretion to either pick amongst experienced men or decide what else to take into account.
22. H. L. A. Hart, The Concept of Law 144 (1961).
23. *See* Wellington & Albert, *Statutory Interpretation and the Political Process: A Comment on Sinclair v. Atkinson,* 72 Yale L. J. 1547 (1963).
24. R. Pound, An Introduction to the Philosophy of Law 56 (rev. ed. 1954).
25. *See, e.g.,* Dickinson, *The Law Behind Law* (pts. 1 & 2), 29 Colum. L. Rev. 112, 254 (1929).
26. H. L. A. Hart, The Concept of Law 92 (1961).
27. *See* Note, *Custom and Trade Usage: Its Application to Commercial Dealings and the Common Law,* 55 Colum. L. Rev. 1192 (1955), and materials cited therein at 1193 n.1. As that note makes plain, the actual practices of courts in recognizing trade customs follow the pattern of applying a set of general principles and policies rather than a test that could be captured as part of a rule of recognition.
28. H. L. A. Hart, The Concept of Law 230 (1961).

RIGGS v. PALMER

New York Court of Appeals, 1889*

Earl, J. On the 13th day of August, 1880, Francis B. Palmer made his last will and testament, in which he gave small legacies to his two daughters, Mrs. Riggs and Mrs. Preston, the plaintiffs in this action, and the remainder of his estate to his grandson, the defendant Elmer E. Palmer, subject to the support of Susan Palmer, his mother, with a gift over to the two daughters, subject to the support of Mrs. Palmer in case Elmer should survive him and die under age, unmarried, and without any issue. The testator, at the date of his will, owned a farm, and considerable personal property. He was a widower, and thereafter, in March, 1882, he was married to Mrs. Bresee, with whom, before his marriage, he entered into an antenuptial contract, in which it was agreed that in lieu of dower and all other claims upon his estate in case she survived him she should have her support upon his farm during her life, and such support was expressly charged upon the farm. At the date of the will, and subsequently to the death of the testator, Elmer lived with him as a member of his family, and at his death was 16 years old. He knew of the provisions made in his favor in the will, and, that he might prevent his grandfather from revoking such provisions, which he had manifested some intention to do, and to obtain the speedy enjoyment and immediate possession of his property, he willfully murdered him by poisoning him. He now claims the property, and the sole question for our determination is, can he have it?

The defendants say that the testator is dead; that his will was made in due form, and has been admitted to probate; and that therefore it must have effect according to the letter of the law. It is quite true that statutes regulating the making, proof, and effects of wills and the devolution of property if literally construed, and if their force and effect can in no way and under no circumstances be controlled or modified, give this property to the murderer. The purpose of those statutes was to enable testators to dispose of their estates to the objects of their bounty at death, and to carry into effect their final wishes legally expressed; and in consid-

ering and giving effect to them this purpose must be kept in view. It was the intention of the law-makers that the donees in a will should have the property given to them. But it never could have been their intention that a donee who murdered the testator to make the will operative should have any benefit under it. If such a case had been present to their minds, and it had been supposed necessary to make some provision of law to meet it, it cannot be doubted that they would have provided for it. It is a familiar canon of construction that a thing which is within the intention of the makers of a statute is as much within the statute as if it were within the letter; and a thing which is within the letter of the statute is not within the statute unless it be within the intention of the makers. The writers of laws do not always express their intention perfectly, but either exceed it or fall short of it, so that judges are to collect it from probable or rational conjectures only, and this is called "rational interpretation;" and Rutherford, in his Institutes, (page 420,) says: "Where we make use of rational interpretation, sometimes we restrain the meaning of the writer so as to take in less, and sometimes we extend or enlarge his meaning so as to take in more, than his words express." Such a construction ought to be put upon a statute as will best answer the intention which the makers had in view, for *qui haret in litera, h£ret in cortice.* In Bac. Abr. "Statutes," 1, 5; Puff. Law Nat. bk. 5, c. 12; Ruth. Inst. 422, 427, and in Smith's Commentaries, 814, many cases are mentioned where it was held that matters embraced in the general words of statutes nevertheless were not within the statutes, because it could not have been the intention of the law-makers that they should be included. They were taken out of the statutes by an equitable construction; and it is said in Bacon: "By an equitable construction a case not within the letter of a statute is sometimes holden to be within the meaning, because it is within the mischief for which a remedy is provided. The reason for such construction is that the law-makers could not set down every case in express terms. In order to form a right judgment whether a case be within the equity of a statute, it is a good way to suppose the law-maker present, and that you have asked him this question: Did you intend to compre-

*22 N.E. 188 (1889). A portion of the court's opinion has been omitted here.

hend this case? Then you must give yourself such answer as you imagine he, being an upright and reasonable man, would have given. If this be that he did mean to comprehend it, you may safely hold the case to be within the equity of the statute; for while you do no more than he would have done, you do not act contrary to the statute, but in conformity thereto." 9 Bac. Abr. 248. In some cases the letter of a legislative act is restrained by an equitable construction; in others, it is enlarged; in others, the construction is contrary to the letter. The equitable construction which restrains the letter of a statute is defined by Aristotle as frequently quoted in this manner: *Æquitas est correctio legis generaliter latæ qua parte deficit.* If the lawmakers could, as to this case, be consulted, would they say that they intended by their general language that the property of a testator or of an ancestor should pass to one who had taken his life for the express purpose of getting his property? In 1 Bl. Comm. 91, the learned author, speaking of the construction of statutes, says: "If there arise out of them collaterally any absurd consequences manifestly contradictory to common reason, they are with regard to those collateral consequences void. * * * Where some collateral matter arises out of the general words, and happens to be unreasonable, there the judges are in decency to conclude that this consequence was not foreseen by the parliament, and therefore they are at liberty to expound the statute by equity, and only *quoad hoc* disregard it;" and he gives as an illustration, if an act of parliament gives a man power to try all causes that arise within his manor of Dale, yet, if a cause should arise in which he himself is party, the act is construed not to extend to that, because it is unreasonable that any man should determine his own quarrel. There was a statute in Bologna that whoever drew blood in the streets should be severely punished, and yet it was held not to apply to the case of a barber who opened a vein in the street. It is commanded in the decalogue that no work shall be done upon the Sabbath, and yet giving the command a rational interpretation founded upon its design the Infallible Judge held that it did not prohibit works of necessity, charity, or benevolence on that day.

What could be more unreasonable than to suppose that it was the legislative intention in the general laws passed for the orderly, peaceable, and just devolution of property that they should have operation in favor of one who murdered his ancestor that he might speedily come into the possession of his estate? Such an intention is inconceivable. We need not, therefore, be much troubled by the general language contained in the laws. Besides, all laws, as well as all contracts, may be controlled in their operation and effect by general, fundamental maxims of the common law. No one shall be permitted to profit by his own fraud, or to take advantage of his own wrong, or to found any claim upon his own iniquity, or to acquire property by his own crime. These maxims are dictated by public policy, have their foundation in universal law administered in all civilized countries, and have nowhere been superseded by statutes. They were applied in the decision of the case of Insurance Co. v. Armstrong, 117 U.S. 599, 6 Sup. Ct. Rep. 877. There it was held that the person who procured a policy upon the life of another, payable at his death, and then murdered the assured to make the policy payable, could not recover thereon. Mr. Justice FIELD, writing the opinion, said: "Independently of any proof of the motives of Hunter in obtaining the policy, and even assuming that they were just and proper, he forfeited all rights under it when, to secure its immediate payment, he murdered the assured. It would be a reproach to the jurisprudence of the country if one could recover insurance money payable on the death of a party whose life he had feloniously taken. As well might he recover insurance money upon a building that he had willfully fired." These maxims, without any statute giving them force or operation, frequently control the effect and nullify the language of wills. A will procured by fraud and deception, like any other instrument, may be decreed void, and set aside; and so a particular portion of a will may be excluded from probate, or held inoperative, if induced by the fraud or undue influence of the person in whose favor it is. Allen v. McPherson, 1 H. L. Cas. 191; Harrison's Appeal, 48 Conn. 202. So a will may contain provisions which are immoral, irreligious, or against public policy, and they will be held void.

Here there was no certainty that this murderer would survive the testator, or that the testator would not change his will, and there was no certainty that he would get this property if nature was allowed to take its course. He therefore murdered the testator expressly to vest himself with an estate. Under such circumstances, what law, human or divine, will allow him to take the estate and enjoy the fruits of his crime? The will spoke and became operative at the death of the testator. He caused that death, and thus by his crime made it speak and have operation. Shall it speak and operate in his favor? If he had met the testator, and taken his property by force, he would have had no title to it. Shall he acquire title by murdering him? If he had gone to the testator's house, and by force compelled him, or by fraud or undue influence had induced him, to will him his property, the law would not allow him to hold it. But can he give effect and operation to a will by murder, and yet take the property? To answer these questions in the affirmative it seems to me would be a reproach to the jurisprudence of our state, and an offense against public policy. Under the civil law, evolved from the general principles of natural law and justice by many generations of jurisconsults, philosophers, and statesmen, one cannot take property by inheritance or will from an ancestor or benefactor whom he has murdered. Dom, Civil Law, pt. 2, bk. 1, tit. 1, § 3; Code Nap. § 727; Mack Rom. Law, 530, 550. In the Civil Code of Lower Canada the provisions on the subject in the Code Napoleon have been substantially copied. But, so far as I can find, in no country where the common law prevails has it been deemed important to enact a law to provide for such a case. Our revisers and law-makers were familiar with the civil law, and they did not deem it important to incorporate into our statutes its provisions upon his subject. This is not a *casus omissus.* It was evidently supposed that the maxims of the common law were sufficient to regulate such a case, and that a specific enactment for that purpose was not needed. For the same reasons the defendant Palmer cannot take any of this property as heir. Just before the murder he was not an heir, and it was not certain that he ever would be. He might have died before his grandfather, or might have been disinherited by him. He made himself an heir by the murder, and he seeks to take property as the fruit of his crime. What has before been said as to him as legatee applies to him with equal force as an heir. He cannot vest himself with title by crime. My view of this case does not inflict upon Elmer any greater or other punishment for his crime than the law specifies. It takes from him no property, but simply holds that he shall not acquire property by his crime, and thus be rewarded for its commission.

Our attention is called to Owens v. Owens, 100 N.C. 240, 6 S.E. Rep. 794, as a case quite like this. There a wife had been convicted of being an accessory before the fact to the murder of her husband, and it was held that she was nevertheless entitled to dower. I am unwilling to assent to the doctrine of that case. The status provide dower for a wife who has the misfortune to survive her husband, and thus lose his support and protection. It is clear beyond their purpose to make provision for a wife who by her own crime makes herself a widow, and willfully and intentionally deprives herself of the support and protection of her husband. As she might have died before him, and "though" never have been his widow, she cannot by her crime vest herself with an estate. The principle which lies at the bottom of the maxim *volenti non fit injuria* should be applied to such a case, and a widow should not, for the purpose of acquiring, as such, property rights, be permitted to allege a widowhood which she has wickedly and intentionally created.

Gray, J. (dissenting). The appellants' argument for a reversal of the judgment, which dismissed their complaint, is that the respondent unlawfully prevented a revocation of the existing will, or a new will from being made, by his crime; and that he terminated the enjoyment by the testator of his property, and effected his own succession to it, by the same crime. They say that to permit the respondent to take the property willed to him would be to permit him to take advantage of his own wrong. To sustain their position that the appellants' counsel has submitted an able and elaborate brief, and, if I believed that the decision of the question could be effected by considerations of an equitable nature, I should not hesitate to assent to views which commend themselves to the conscience. But the matter does not lie within the domain of conscience. We are bound by the rigid rules of law, which have been established by the legislature, and within the limits of which the determination of this question is confined. The question we are dealing with is whether a testamentary disposition can be altered, or a will revoked, after the testator's death, through an appeal to the courts, when the legislature has by its enactments prescribed exactly when and how wills may be made, altered, and revoked, and apparently, as it seems to me, when they have been fully complied with, has left no room for the exercise of an equitable jurisdiction by courts over such matters. Modern jurisprudence, in recognizing the right of the individual, under more or less restrictions, to dispose of his property after his death, subjects it to legislative control, both as to extent and as to mode of exercise. Complete freedom of testamentary disposition of one's property has not been and is not the universal rule, as we see from the provisions of the Napoleonic Code, from the systems of jurisprudence in countries which are modeled upon the Roman law, and from the the statutes of many of our states. To the statutory restraints which are imposed upon the disposition of one's property by will are added strict and systematic statutory rules for the execution, alteration, and revocation of the will, which must be, at least substantially, if not exactly, followed to insure validity and performance. The reason for the establishment of such rules, we may naturally assume, consists in the purpose to create those safeguards about these grave and important acts which experience has demonstrated to be the wisest and surest. That freedom which is permitted to be exercised in the testamentary disposition of one's estate by the laws of the state is subject to its being exercised in conformity with the regulations of the statutes. The capacity and the power of the individual to dispose of his property after death, and the mode by which that power can be exercised, are matters of which the legislature has assumed the entire control, and has undertaken to regulate with comprehensive particularity . . .

I cannot find any support for the argument that the respondent's succession to the property should be avoided because of his criminal act, when the laws are silent. Public policy does not demand it; for the demands of public policy are satisfied by the proper execution of the laws and the punishment of the crime. There has been no convention between the testator and his legatee. The appellants' argument practically amounts to this: that, as the legatee has been guilty of a crime, by the commission of which he is placed in a position to sooner receive the benefits of the testamentary provision, his rights to the property should be forfeited, and he should be divested of his estate. To allow their argument to prevail would involve the diversion by the court of the testator's estate into the hands of persons whom, possibly enough, for all we know, the testator might not have chosen or desired as its recipients. Practically the court is asked to make another will for the testator. The laws do not warrant this judicial action, and mere presumption would not be strong enough to sustain it. But, more than this, to concede the appellants' views would involve the imposition of an additional punishment or penalty upon the respondent. What power or warrant have the courts to add to the respondent's penalties by depriving him of property? The law has punished him for his crime, and we may not say that it was an insufficient punishment. In the trial and punishment of the respondent the law has vindicated itself for the outrage which he committed, and further judicial utterance upon the subject of punishment or deprivation of rights is barred. We may not, in the language of the court in People v. Thornton, 25 Hun, 456, "enhance the pains, penalties, and forfeitures provided by law for the punishment of crime." The judgment should be affirmed, with costs.

HENNINGSEN v. BLOOMFIELD MOTORS, INC.

Supreme Court of New Jersey, 1960*

Action by automobile buyer's wife and buyer himself against manufacturer and dealer to recover damages on account of injuries sustained by wife while she was driving allegedly defective automobile shortly after its purchase. The trial court entered judgment in favor of buyer and wife and manufacturer and dealer appealed and matter was certified by Supreme Court prior to consideration in Appellate Division. The Supreme Court, Francis. J., held that where purchase order for new automobile contained therein an express warranty by which manufacturer warranted vehicle free from defects in material or workmanship and warranty further stated that it was expressly in lieu of all other warranties express or implied, and such warranty was the uniform warranty of the Automobile Manufacturers Association to which all major automobile manufacturers belonged, under circumstances, manufacturer's attempted disclaimer of an implied warranty of merchantability and of the obligations arising therefrom was so inimical to public good as to compel an adjudication of its invalidity.

. . . Judicial notice may be taken of the fact that automobile manufacturers, including Chrysler Corporation, undertake large scale advertising programs over television, radio, in newspapers, magazines and all media of communication in order to persuade the public to buy their products. As has been observed above, a number of jurisdictions, conscious of modern marketing practices, have declared that when a manufacturer engages in advertising in order to bring his goods and their quality to the attention of the public and thus to create consumer demand, the representations made constitute an express warranty running directly to a buyer who purchases in reliance thereon. The fact that the sale is consummated with an independent dealer does not obviate that warranty. Mannsz v. Macwhyte

Co., supra; Bahlman v. Hudson Motor Car Co., supra; Rogers v. Toni Home Permanent Co., supra; Meyer v. Packard Cleveland Motor Co., 106 Ohio St. 328, 140 N.E. 118, 28 A.L.R. 986 (1922); Baxter v. Ford Motor Co., supra; 1 Williston, Sales, supra § 244a.

In view of the cases in various jurisdictions suggesting the conclusion which we have now reached with respect to the implied warranty of merchantability, it becomes apparent that manufacturers who enter into promotional activities to stimulate consumer buying may incur warranty obligations of either or both the express or implied character. These developments in the law inevitably suggest the inference that the form of express warranty made part of the Henningsen purchase contract was devised for general use in the automobile industry as a possible means of avoiding the consequences of the growing judicial acceptance of the thesis that the described express or implied warranties run directly to the consumer.

In the light of these matters, what effect should be given to the express warranty in question which seeks to limit the manufacturer's liability to replacement of defective parts, and which disclaims all other warranties, express or implied? In assessing its significance we must keep in mind the general principle that, in the absence of fraud, one who does not choose to read a contract before signing it, cannot later relieve himself of its burdens. Fivey v. Pennsylvania R. R. Co., 67 N.J.L. 627, 52 A. 472, (E.& A.1902). And in applying that principle, the basic tenet of freedom of competent parties to contract is a factor of importance. But in the framework of modern commercial life and business practices, such rules cannot be applied on a strict, doctrinal basis. The conflicting interests of the buyer and seller must be evaluated realistically and justly, giving due weight to the social policy evinced by the Uniform Sales Act, the progressive decisions of the courts engaged in administering it, the mass production methods of manufacture and distribution to the public, and the bargaining position occupied by the ordinary consumer in such an economy. This history of the law shows that legal doctrines, as first expounded, often

*161 A. 2d 69 (1960). The first paragraph printed here is a summary of the facts which appeared in the report of the case. It is not a part of the court's opinion. The excerpt from the opinion reprinted here is only a small portion of the whole opinion.

prove to be inadequate under the impact of later experience. In such case, the need for justice has stimulated the necessary qualifications or adjustments. Perkins v. Endicott Johnson Corporation, 128 F.2d 208, 217 (2 Cir. 1942), affirmed 317 U.S. 501, 63 S.Ct. 339, 87 L.Ed. 424 (1943); Greenberg v. Lorenz, supra.

In these times, an automobile is almost as much a servant of convenience for the ordinary person as a household utensil. For a multitude of other persons it is a necessity. Crowded highways and filled parking lots are a commonplace of our existence. There is no need to look any farther than the daily newspaper to be convinced that when an automobile is defective, it has great potentiality for harm.

No one spoke more graphically on this subject than Justice Cardozo in the landmark case of MacPherson v. Buick Motor Co., 217 N.Y. 382, 111 N.E. 1050, 1053, L.R.A.1916F, 696 (Ct.App.1916):

"Beyond all question, the nature of an automobile gives warning of probable danger if its construction is defective. This automobile was designed to go 50 miles per hour. Unless its wheels were sound and strong, injury was almost certain. It was as much a thing of danger as a defective engine for a railroad. * * * The dealer was indeed the one person of whom it might be said with some approach to certainty that by him the car would not be used. * * * Precedents drawn from the days of travel by stagecoach do not fit the conditions of travel to-day. The principle that the danger must be imminent does not change, but the things subject to the principle do change. They are whatever the needs of life in a developing civilization require them to be."

In the 44 years that have intervened since that utterance, the average car has been constructed for almost double the speed mentioned; 60 miles per hour is permitted on our parkways. The number of automobiles in use has multiplied many times and the hazard to the user and the public has increased proportionately. The Legislature has intervened in the public interest, not only to regulate the manner of operation on the highway but also to require periodic inspection of motor vehicles and to impose a duty on manufacturers to adopt certain safety devices and methods in their construction. R.S. 39:3–43 et seq., N.J.S.A. It is apparent that the public has an interest not only in the safe manufacture of automobiles, but also, as shown by the Sales Act, in protecting the rights and remedies of purchasers, so far as it can be accomplished consistently with our system of free enterprise. In a society such as ours, where the automobile is a common and necessary adjunct of daily life, and where its use is so fraught with danger to the driver, passengers and the public, the manufacturer is under a special obligation in connection with the construction, promotion and sale of his cars. Consequently, the courts must examine

purchase agreements closely to see if consumer and public interests are treated fairly.

What influence should these circumstances have on the restrictive effect of Chrysler's express warranty in the framework of the purchase contract? As we have said, warranties originated in the law to safeguard the buyer and not to limit the liability of the seller or manufacturer. It seems obvious in this instance that the motive was to avoid the warranty obligations which are normally incidental to such sales. The language gave little and withdrew much. In return for the delusive remedy of replacement of defective parts at the factory, the buyer is said to have accepted the exclusion of the maker's liability for personal injuries arising from agreed to the elimination of any other express or implied warranty. An instinctively felt sense of justice cries out against such a sharp bargain. But does the doctrine that a person is bound by his signed agreement in the absence of fraud, stand in the way of any relief?

In the modern consideration of problems such as this, Corbin suggests that practically all judges are "chancellors" and cannot fail to be influenced by any equitable doctrines that are available. And he opines that "there is sufficient flexibility in the concepts of fraud, duress, misrepresentation and undue influence, not to mention differences in economic bargaining power" to enable the courts to avoid enforcement of unconscionable provisions in long printed standardized contracts. 1 Corbin on Contracts (1950) § 128, p. 188. Freedom of contract is not such an immutable doctrine as to admit of no qualification in the area in which we are concerned. As Chief Justice Hughes said in his dissent in Morehead v. People of State of New York ex rel. Tipaldo, 298 U.S. 587, 627, 56 S.Ct. 918, 930, 80 L.Ed. 1347, 1364 (1936):

"We have had frequent occasion to consider the limitations on liberty of contract. While it is highly important to preserve that liberty from arbitrary and capricious interference, it is also necessary to prevent its abuse, as otherwise it could be used to override all public interests and thus in the end destroy the very freedom of opportunity which it is designed to safeguard."

That sentiment was echoed by Justice Frankfurter in his dissent in United States v. Bethlehem Steel Corp., 315 U.S. 289, 326, 62 S.Ct. 581, 599, 86 L.Ed. 855, 876 (1942):

"It is said that familiar principles would be outraged if Bethlehem were denied recovery on these contracts. But is there any principle which is more familiar or more firmly embedded in the history of anglo-American law than the basic doctrine that the courts will not permit themselves to be used as instruments of inequity and injustice? Does any principle in our law have more universal application than the doctrine that courts will not enforce transactions in which the relative positions of the parties are such that one has unconscionably taken advantage of the necessities of the other?

"These principles are not foreign to the law of contracts. Fraud and physical duress are not the only grounds upon which courts refuse to enforce contracts. The law is not so primitive that it sanctions every injustice except brute force and downright fraud. More specifically, the courts generally refuse to lend themselves to the enforcement of a 'bargain' in which one party has unjustly taken advantage of the economic necessities of the other. * * * *"

The traditional contract is the result of free bargaining of parties who are brought together by the play of the market, and who meet each other on a footing of approximate economic equality. In such a society there is no danger that freedom of contract will be a threat to the social order as a whole. But in present-day commercial life the standardized mass contract has appeared. It is used primarily by enterprises with strong bargaining power and position. "The weaker party, in need of the goods or services, is frequently not in a position to shop around for better terms, either because the author of the standard contract has a monopoly (natural or artifical) or because all competitors use the same clauses. His contractual intention is but a subjection more or less voluntary to terms dictated by the stronger party, terms whose consequences are often understood in a vague way, if at all." Kessler, "Contracts of Adhesion—Some Thoughts About Freedom of Contract," 43 Colum.L.Rev. 629, 632 (1943); Ehrenzweig, "Adhesion Contracts in the Conflict of Laws," 53 Colum.L.Rev. 1072, 1075, 1089 (1953). Such standardized contracts have been described as those in which one predominant party will dictate its law to an undetermined multiple rather than to an individual. They are said to resemble a law rather than a meeting of the minds. Siegelman v. Cunard White Star, 221 F.2d 189, 206 (2 Cir. 1955).

Suggestions for Further Reading

Ames, J. B., "Law and Morals," 22 *Harv. L. Rev.* 97 (1908).

Bedau, Hugo, ed., *Civil Disobedience: Theory and Practice* (1969).

Benditt, Theodore, *Law as Rule and Principle* (1978).

Bentham, Jeremy, *An Introduction to the Principles of Morals and Legislation,* (ed. H. L. A. Hart. 1970).

Cairns, Huntington,. *Legal Philosophy from Plato to Hegel* (1949).

Care, N. S. and T. K. Trelogan, eds., *Issues in Law and Morality* (1973).

Cardozo, Benjamin N., *The Nature of the Judicial Process* (1921).

Carrio, G., *Legal Principles and Legal Positivism* (1971).

Christie, G. C., "The Model of Principles" 1968 *Duke L. J.* 649.

Cogley, J., et. al, *Natural Law and Modern Society* (1962).

Cohen, Carl, *Conscience, Tactics, and the Law* (1971).

Cohen, Marshall, "Liberalism and Disobedience," *Philosophy and Public Affairs,* Vol. 1 (1972).

Daube, David, *Civil Disobedience in Antiquity* (1972).

Davis, Kenneth C., *Discretionary Justice* (1969).

d'Entreves, A. P., *Natural Law* (1951).

Dworkin, Ronald M., "Social Rules and Legal Theory" 81 *Yale L.J.* (1972).

Dworkin, Ronald M., *Taking Rights Seriously* (1977).

Feinberg, Joel, "Civil Disobedience in the Modern World," *Humanities in Society,* Vol 2. (1979).

Finnis, J. M., "Revolutions and Continuity of Law," in *Oxford Essays in Jurisprudence,* 2nd series, ed by A. W. B. Simpson (1973).

Fortas, Abe, *Concerning Dissent and Civil Disobedience* (1968).

Frank, Jerome, *Courts on Trial* (1949).

Frank, Jerome, *Law and the Modern Mind* (1930).

Friedmann, Wolfgang, *Legal Theory,* 4th ed. (1960).

Friedrich, C. J., *The Philosophy of Law in Historical Perspective,* 2nd ed. (1963).

Fuller, Lon L., *Anatomy of Law* (1968).

Gierke, O. F., *Natural Law and The Theory of Society,* trans. E. Barker (1934).

Golding, Martin P., *Philosophy of Law* (1974).

Goodhart, Arthur L., *English Law and the Moral Law* (1953).

Gross, Hyman, "Standards as Law," 1968/69 *Annual Survey of American Law* 575.

Guest, A. G., "Logic in the Law" in *Oxford Essays in Jurisprudence,* ed. A. G. Guest, (1961).

Hägerström, A., *Inquiries into the Nature of Law and Morals,* Trans. Broad, C. D. Stockholm (1953).

Hall, Robert, *The Morality of Civil Disobedience* (1971).

Hart, H. L. A., *The Concept of Law* (1961).

Hoebel, E. Adamson, *The Law of Primitive Man* (1954).

Holmes, Oliver, W., Jr., "The Path of the Law" 10 *Harv. L. Rev.* 457 (1897).

Hook, Sidney, ed., *Law and Philosophy,* Parts II and III (1964).

Hughes, Graham, "Civil Disobedience and the Political Question Doctrine" 43 *N.Y.U. L. Rev.* 1 (1968).

Hughes, Graham, "Rules, Policy and Decision Making" 77 *Yale L. J.* 411 (1968).

Hughes, Graham, *The Conscience of the Courts: Law and Morals in American Life* (1975), Chap. 3.

Jones, Harry W., "Law and Morality in the Perspective of Legal Realism," 61 *Col. L. Rev.* 799 (1961).

Kadish, M. R. and S. H. Kadish, *Discretion to Disobey: A Study of Lawful Departures from Legal Rules* (1973).

Kantorowicz, Hermann, *The Definition of Law* (1958).

Kaufman, Arnold S. and Oppenheim, Felix E., "Democracy and Disorder, A Symposium" in *Society, Revolution and Reform,* eds. R. H. Grimm and A. F. MacKay (1971).

Kelsen, Hans *General Theory of Law and State,* Trans. A. Wedberg (1949).

Leiser, Burton M., *Custom, Law and Morality* (1969).

Levi, Edward H., *An Introduction to Legal Reasoning* (1948).

Llewellyn, K. N., *The Bramble Bush* (1930).

Llewellyn, K. N., *Jurisprudence: Realism in Theory and Practice* (1962).

Llewellyn, K. N., *The Common Law Tradition: Deciding Appeals* (1960).

MacCormick, Neil, "Law as Institutional Fact," 90 *Law Quarterly Review* 102 (1974).

MacCormick, Neil *Legal Reasoning and Legal Theory* (1978).

Maine, Henry S., *Lectures on the Early History of Institutions,* 7th ed. (1897).

Meiklejohn, Alexander, *Political Freedom: The Constitutional Powers of the People* (1965).

Morris, Herbert, "Verbal Disputes and the Legal Philosophy of John Austin," 7 *U.C.L.A. L. Rev.* 27 (1960).

Olivecrona, Karl, *Law as Facts* (1939).

Pennock, J. R. and J. W. Chapman, eds. Nomos XII: *Political and Legal Obligation* (1970).

Perry, Thomas D., *Moral Reasoning and Truth: An Essay in Philosophy and Jurisprudence* (1976).

Pound, Roscoe, *An Introduction to the Philosophy of Law* (1922).

Raz, Joseph, *The Concept of a Legal System* (1970).

Raz, Joseph, "Legal Principles and the Limits of Law" 81 *Yale L.J.* (1972).

Raz, Joseph, *Practical Reason and Norms* (1975).

Raz, Joseph, *The Authority of Law: Essays on Law and Morality* (1979).

Richards, David A. J., *The Moral Criticism of Law* (1977).

Ross, Alf, *On Law and Justice* (1958).

Salmond, John, *Jurisprudence,* 12th ed. ed. P. J. Fitzgerald, London (1966).

Sartorius, Rolf, "Social Policy and Judicial Legislation," *American Philosophical Quarterly,* Vol. 8 (1971), pp. 151–70.

Sartorius, Rolf, *Individual Conduct and Social Norms* (1975).

Selznick, Philip, "Sociology and Natural Law," *Natural Law Forum,* Vol. 6 (1961), 84–104.

Simmons, A. John, *Moral Principles and Political Obligations* (1979).

Singer, Peter, *Democracy and Disobedience* (1973).

Stumpf, Samuel E., *Morality and the Law* (1965).

Summers, Robert S., "Professor H. L. A. Hart's Concept of Law," *Duke L.J.* 629.

Symposium: Jurisprudence, 11 *Georgia Law Review* (1977). Fourteen important articles on the nature of law and legal reasoning, including Ronald M. Dworkin's reply to seven critics.

Symposium: Philosophy of Law, 18 *William and Mary Law Review* (1975). Six important articles on the nature of law and legal reasoning.

Tapper, C., "A Note on Principles," 1971 *Modern L. Rev.* 628 (1971).

Walzer, Michael, *Obligations: Essays on Disobedience, War, and Citizenship* (1970).

Wasserstrom, Richard A., "The Obligation to Obey the Law," 10 *U.C.L.A. Law Review* 780 (1963).

Williams, Glanville, "The Controversy Concerning the Word 'Law'," in *Philosophy, Politics, and Society* (ed. P. Laslett, 1956).

Wolff, Robert Paul, *In Defense of Anarchism* (1970).

Wollheim, Richard, "The Nature of Law," *Political Studies,* Vol. 2. (1954).

Woozley, A. D., "Socrates on Disobeying the Law," in *The Philosophy of Socrates,* ed. Gregory Vlastos (1971).

Zinn, Howard, *Disobedience and Democracy* (1968).

PART 2 LIBERTY

For what purposes can the state rightly interfere with the liberty of individual citizens to do as they please? This central question of political theory becomes a vital question in legal philosophy too in virtue of the fact that in democracies, at least, the legal system is the primary means by which restraints on liberty are imposed. Certain kinds of conduct are directly prohibited by criminal statutes which threaten punishment, typically fines or imprisonment, for noncompliance. Other kinds of undesirable behavior are controlled by regulatory devices which employ the criminal law only indirectly, as a kind of "sanction of last resort."[1] Citizens must be licensed, for example, to drive automobiles or to practice medicine, a requirement that permits the state to regulate these dangerous activities carefully and to withdraw licenses from those who fail to perform to reasonable standards. Withdrawal of license is itself an administrative penalty diminishing the liberty of those subjected to it, but it is not a criminal penalty. The criminal sanction is reserved as a backup threat to prevent persons from driving or practicing medicine without a license. Similarly, "cease and desist" orders and other injunctions restrict the liberty of those to whom they are addressed without any recourse to the criminal law, which comes into play only to prevent or to punish disobedience. Still another form of administrative or noncriminal restriction of liberty is the civil commitment procedure by which mentally disturbed persons judged dangerous to others or incompetent to govern themselves are compelled to reside in hospitals or other nonpenal institutions. For some classes of harmful conduct—for example, defamatory statements, invasions of privacy, and certain kinds of trespass and nuisance —the civil law seems better suited than the criminal law to provide threatened parties with protection. Our liberty to tell damaging lies about our neighbors, to prevent them from enjoying their property, or to tap their telephone lines, is restricted by their legal power to bring a civil suit against us which can culminate in a judgment directing us to pay compensatory or punitive damages to them. Again, the criminal law is not involved except as a backup sanction to enforce court orders.

Most writers agree that restrictions of individual liberty, whether by direct criminal prohibition or by some other legal instrumentality, always need some special justification. That is to say that other things being equal, it is always preferable that individuals be left free to make their own choices and that undesirable conduct be discouraged by such noncoercive measures as education, exhortation, taxation (of undesirable conduct) or provision of positive incentives such as economic subsidies or rewards (for alternatives to undesirable conduct). It is not easy to state the grounds of this presumption in favor of liberty. Various philosophers, in making the presumptive case for liberty, have argued that absence of coercion is a necessary (though certainly not a sufficient) condition for individual self-realization and social progress, and for such specific goods as individual spontaneity, social diversity, and the full flowering of various moral and intellectual virtues. In any case, most of us are fully convinced that our own personal liberty is a precious thing, and consistency inclines us to suppose that it is equally precious, and equally worth respecting, in others.

The value of liberty, however, is easily overstated. Liberty may be precious but it is by no means the only thing of value. Contentment and happiness, while difficult in the absence of freedom, are not impossible. Moreover, one can have perfect political liberty and yet be alienated and discontented, which also shows that no matter how intimately they may be related, freedom and contentment are distinct values not reducible one to the other. Similarly, a given society may enjoy political liberty while yet permitting large-scale social injustice, a possibility which indicates that liberty and justice are distinct social values. Failure to appreciate these distinctions has led hasty thinkers to make certain familiar errors in their discussions of liberty. Some have argued that any liberty that conflicts with contentment or with justice is not "true liberty" but rather some beguiling counterfeit. It is more accurate to say that liberty is but one value among many, that it is vitally important but not sufficient, that it can conflict with other values, and even that in some circumstances it may not be worth its price as measured against other values.

Other writers have argued that political liberty in the absence of certain specific powers and opportunities is not "true liberty" at all, but a sham and a deceit. If an invalid confined to his bed were to scoff at a legal system that grants him freedom of movement, we should no doubt reply to him that our politically guaranteed liberty to move about at will is a genuine liberty and a geniune good, even though it may be worthless to a paralyzed person. What the invalid's plight shows is that health and mobility are also important and independent goods, not that political liberty is a sham. Similarly, the political radical in a capitalist bourgeois society might deny that he has true liberty of speech on the ground that he does not have fair access to the communications media which are dominated by wealthy corporations. Again, this shows that his freedom of expression is not worth as much as a wealthier person's, and that economic power is also an important good, not that he is not "really" at liberty to speak his mind. His complaint shows us that it is possible to praise liberty too much, but if he claims further that he would be no worse off if his political opinions were criminally proscribed, he is either disingenuous or naively under-appreciative of liberty's actual value.

It must be acknowledged, however, that a given person's lack of power or opportunity—his or her poverty, ignorance, or poor health—may be the *indirect result* of a structure of coercive laws. To make a crude and obvious hypothetical example, racial laws on the South African model might explicitly prohibit blacks from engaging in certain remunerative occupations. As a result blacks would be poorer than other citizens, and perhaps undernourished and undereducated as well. In that case there would be a very real point in describing a given black's lack of power or opportunity to make his views heard and considered as a diminished liberty. Political liberty is best understood as the absence of political coercion (typically, the absence of criminal prohibitions and other coercive legal instrumentalities), and not simply as *de facto* ability or opportunity. But where a law preventing a class of citizens from doing *X* leads indirectly to an absence of ability or opportunity for members of that class to do *Y*, there is a clear reason to describe the latter as a negation of the *liberty* to do *Y*.

FREEDOM OF EXPRESSION

Under what conditions, and for what reasons, can the presumption in favor of political liberty be overridden? This is not merely an abstract question addressed to philosophers, but an unavoidable practical question to be faced by every democratic legislator. In effect, it is a question about the limits beyond which restrictive lawmaking is morally illegitimate. John Stuart Mill, the first essayist presented in this part, gives the classic liberal answer to the question. Restriction of the liberty of one citizen, he argues, can be justified only to prevent harm to others. We can refer to Mill's position as the "harm to others principle," or more succinctly, the "harm principle." Several things should be noted about this principle at the outset. First, Mill means by "harm" not only direct personal injury such as broken bones or the loss of money, but also more diffuse social harms such as air pollution or the impairment of public institutions. Second, the principle does not propose a sufficient condition for the restriction of liberty, because some harms to others are too slight to outbalance the very real harm or danger involved in the restriction of liberty. Thus, in close cases, legislators must balance the value of the interests to be restricted by proposed coercive legislation *and* the collateral costs of enforcing any coercive law on the one hand against the value of the interests to be protected by the proposed legislation on the other. It is only when the probable harms prevented by the statute are greater than those that it will cause that the legislation is justified. Finally, the harm principle should be interpreted as a claim about *reasons:* Only one *kind* of consideration is ever morally relevant to the justification of coercion, namely, that it is necessary to prevent harm to others. It is never a relevant reason that the conduct to be restricted is merely offensive (as opposed to harmful) or even that it is intrinsically immoral, nor is it relevant that coercion is necessary to prevent a person from harming himself or herself (as opposed to others).

No one would disagree that prevention of harm to others is always *a* relevant reason for coercion, but many disagree with Mill's contention that it is the *only* relevant consideration. Thus, no one will seriously suggest that laws against battery, larceny, and homicide are unjustified, but many maintain that the state is also justified, at least in some circumstances, in prohibiting (1) "immoralities" even when they harm no one but their perpetrators (the principle of legal moralism), (2) actions that hurt or endanger the actor himself or herself (the principle of legal paternalism), or (3) conduct that is offensive though not harmful to others (the offense principle). These rival doctrines cannot easily be proved or refuted in the abstract. Rather, they are best judged by how faithfully they reflect, and how systematically they organize, our considered judgments in particular cases; for such principles, after all, purport to be explicit renderings of the axioms to which we are committed by the most confident judgments we make in everyday discourse about problems of liberty. The main areas of controversy in which such problems arise are those concerning unorthodox expressions of opinion, "morals offenses" in the criminal law (especially when committed in private by solitary individuals or among consenting adults), pornography and obscenity (when offered or displayed to the public or to nonconsenting individuals), activities that are harmful or dangerous to those who voluntarily engage in them, voluntary suicide and euthanasia, otherwise harmless invasions of the privacy of others, and conscientious acts of civil disobedience. The cautious theorist will begin with Mill's harm principle as an account of at least one set of reasons that is always relevant in such controversies, and then apply it to the various problem areas to determine the extent, if any, to which it must be supplemented to provide solutions that are both plausible and consistent. In particular, we must decide, in each area, whether we need have recourse to the offense principle, legal moralism, or legal paternalism.

Under most of the problem area headings, there is still another kind of controversy to be settled, namely, whether even the unsupplemented harm principle can justify *too much* coercion, and whether, therefore, doing justice to our considered judgments requires also a doctrine of *natural rights* limiting the applicability of the harm principle (or for that matter of any of the other liberty-limiting principles that might apply at all). This kind of question arises most prominently perhaps in the area of free expression of opinion. There is no doubt that expressions of opinion, in speech or writing, do often cause vast amounts of harm. Politicians sometimes advocate policies that would lead to disastrous consequences if adopted, and scientists sometimes defend theories that are false and detrimental to scientific progress. If we apply the harm principle in a straightforward unqualified way by prohibiting all particular expressions which seem on the best evidence likely to cause more harm than good, we might very well justify widespread invasions of what we should naturally take to be a moral right of free speech. Quite clearly, if he or she is to avoid this embarrassing consequence, the partisan of the harm principle will have to propose subtle refinements and mediating norms for the application of this principle, weighing such matters as the balancing of rival interests and social costs, and the measurements of probabilities, dangers, and risks.

Mill especially wished to avoid such embarrassment since he placed an extremely high value on free expression. As a utilitarian he wished to forego all benefit in argument from the notion of a natural right, yet he insisted that, short of the usual legal boundaries of libel, slander, incitement, and fraud, *all* restrictions on the expression of opinion are illegitimate, whether in morals, politics, religion, or whatever. His strategy was to establish an extra strong presumption in favor of freedom of expression, even beyond the standing presumption in favor of liberty generally. An individual's own interest in freedom of expression, in the first place, is an especially vital one. Human beings are essentially opinion-forming and communicating animals, and to squelch a person in the expression of his opinion is to hurt him "where he lives." Moreover, each individual is in a way wronged by restrictions on the expressions of all the others, for to keep an individual in ignorance of all but officially sanctioned opinions is to violate his or her autonomy as a rational being who, as another author has said is "sovereign in deciding what to believe and in weighing competing reasons for action."[2] Moreover, it diminishes him as a rational thinker and decider, impairs his dignity, weakens his "moral and intellectual muscles," and so, in a subtle but real way, *harms* him. Mill gives most emphasis, however, to the powerful *social* interest in free expression. Unless all opinions are given a free airing, he argues, we can never be confident that we have the truth about anything, having heard only one side of the case. A political community that deprives itself of important sources of truth is like a ship with a defective rudder, sure to flounder sooner or later on some rocky shore. That legally unhindered open debate of public issues is necessary to the pursuit of truth is a point of lasting importance never made more impressively than by Mill, but to regard the absence of legally enforced orthodoxy as sufficient guarantee of the triumph of truth would be extremely naive. Even Mill, in fact, is subject to some criticism for underemphasizing the importance of equal access to the public media for the effective operation of a "free marketplace of ideas." To tell an impecunious radical who aims to influence public policy that he enjoys political freedom of expression may be very much like congratulating a pauper on his legal right to buy a Cadillac. Free expression does not really fit Mill's description as a means of promoting knowledge and truth unless there are people about, powerful people, to listen.

In the second essay in this section, Joel Feinberg considers further how the harm principle must be qualified if it is to guarantee free expression of opinion in a morally satisfactory way. He examines first the relatively noncontroversial limits on free speech imposed by Anglo-American law: civil liability for defamatory utterances and for nondefamatory statements that reveal information which is properly private, criminal liability for irresponsible statements that cause panics or riots, laws against incitements to crime and (more controversially) sedition. They are considered in part because each raises its own questions of interest for the philosophy of law, and in part because each provides a challenge for the harm principle to provide a rationale for sensible restrictions on liberty that will not at the same time justify restrictions on free speech unacceptable to Mill and other liberals. Feinberg then attempts to provide a philosophical rationale for Justice Holmes's "clear and present danger" test, and then concludes with comments on the inevitable "balancing of interests" so central to the harm principle approach to problems of liberty.

For over a decade beginning in the mid 1950s, a committee of the American Law Institute (an elite group of lawyers, judges, and law professors) worked on a massive rewriting of the criminal law. Their goal was to produce a model penal code that might influence legislatures to rewrite the codes then in effect in most of the fifty states. The main "reporters" for this project, and the authors of the numerous tentative drafts, were Herbert Wechsler of the Columbia University Law School and Louis B. Schwartz of the University of Pennsylvania Law School. In his article included here, Professor Schwartz turns his attention to a class of crimes in our codes that are very difficult to justify by the unsupplemented harm principle. These so-called "offenses against morality" include not only tabooed sexual behavior, but also a somewhat puzzling miscellany of nonsexual conduct including mistreatment of corpses and desecration of the flag. The offense principle provides a rationale for judging some of these as crimes (for example, "open lewdness") even when they cause no one any injury, but other morals offenses (for example, homosexual relations between consenting adults in private) can be defended only by recourse to the principle of legal moralism, which maintains that the law may properly be used to enforce the prevailing morality as such, even in the absence of harm or offense.

The Model Penal Code recommendations about morals offenses are the work of a group of enlightened "would-be lawmakers" who are very much opposed to legal moralism but unwilling, if only on grounds of political realism, to urge extremely radical departures from the past ways of the law. Sexual behavior that is immoral by conventional standards should not be made criminal, according to the code, unless it involves violence or exploitation of children and other incompetents; and the traditional crimes of fornication, adultery, and sodomy are to be wiped from the books. In the absence of harm to others, Schwartz and his colleagues insist, the sexual behavior of individuals is no one else's business. "Open lewdness," on the other hand, like other "flagrant affronts" to the sensibilities of others, is another matter. Not only conventionally "immoral" sexual acts but even perfectly "normal" ones can be criminally proscribed if done in *public,* not because public sex acts harm anyone, but because they cause *offense* (quite another thing) to the unwilling observer. Thus the Model Penal Code, while rejecting legal moralism, seems to endorse the offense principle.

This combination of principles seems to have rather clear implications in respect to obscenity control. Freely consenting adults, one would think, would be given the unfettered liberty to read or witness anything they choose, provided only that they do not display offensive materials in public or impose them on unsuspecting passersby or on children. The Model Penal Code, however, while approximating this position, prefers a more "oblique approach." The code would ban not only public exhibitions but also advertising and sale of materials "whose predominant appeal is to prurient interest." The target of this restriction, Schwartz assures us, is not "the sin of obscenity" but rather a kind of unfair business practice: "Just as merchants may be prohibited from selling their wares by appeal to the public's weakness for gambling, so they may be restrained from purveying books, movies, or other commercial exhibition by exploiting the well-nigh universal weakness for a look behind the curtain of modesty." This commercial approach to the problem of obscenity apparently influenced the Supreme Court in the famous case that sent Ralph Ginzburg to prison. With the benefit of hindsight, one can wonder whether the Model Penal Code's "oblique approach" is not simply a less direct way of accomplishing what legal moralism would do forthrightly. Is not the legal judgment that prurient interest in sex is a moral "weakness" itself a way of enveloping the conventional morality in the law?

A different aspect of the problem of obscenity was dramatically illustrated in the United States Supreme Court case of *Cohen v. California* in 1971. This case raised issues that connect the themes of the articles by Schwartz and Feinberg. Cohen was convicted by a Los Angeles municipal court for lingering in the corridors of a public building while wearing a jacket emblazoned with the words "Fuck the Draft." In his appeal to the Supreme Court of California and later to the United States Supreme Court, Cohen claimed that his right to free speech guaranteed by the First and Fourteenth Amendments had been violated, whereas the California authorities argued that they had properly applied against him a valid statute forbidding "willfully . . . offensive conduct." Now there are two ways in which a written or spoken statement can be offensive: It can express an opinion that some auditors might find offensive or it can express an opinion in language that is itself offensive independently of the "substantive message it conveys." Neither the United States Constitution nor the libertarian principles of free expression of opinion espoused by Mill and Feinberg would permit legal interference with free speech to prevent the expression of an "offensive opinion." However, restrictions on obscene, scurrilous, and incitive words, quite apart from their role in the expression of unpopular opinions, might well be justified by the offense principle, and indeed by the Constitution itself insofar as it tacitly employs the offense principle to mark out a class of exceptions to the free speech guarantee. Justice Harlan, however, rejected this approach to the case. The free expression of opinion protected by the Constitution, he argued, extends not merely to the proposition declared by a statement, but also to the speaker's (or writer's) emotions, or the intensity of his attitudes—in the case at hand "the depths of his feelings against the Vietnam War and the draft." Harlan's distinction points to an important function of what are ordinarily called obscene words. "Unseemly epithets" can shock and jolt, and in virtue of their very character as socially unacceptable, give expression to intense feelings more accurately than any other words in the language.

Unlike the authors preceding him in this section, Irving Kristol is primarily concerned not with expressions of opinion or attitude, but rather with expression in works of drama and literature and their counterfeits. Moreover, he gives a spirited defense of a kind of censorship which he claims to be quite consistent with a generally liberal attitude toward state coercion. His explicit target is the prevailing liberal view that consenting adults should be permitted to see or read anything they please and that censorship and prior restraint are justified only to protect children and unwilling witnesses. Censorship, he argues, is required for at least two additional kinds of reasons: (1) to protect the general quality of life, indeed our civilized institutions themselves (an appeal to the harm principle); and (2) to exclude practices that "brutalize and debase our citizenry" (an appeal to a kind of "moral paternalism," the need to protect even adults from moral corruption). One of the more difficult challenges Kristol poses for the liberal view he is attacking consists of an embarrassing hypothetical example. Suppose an enterprising promoter sought to stage gladiatorial contests like those of Ancient Rome in Yankee Stadium, in which well-paid gladiators fought to the death to the roars of large crowds. How could he be prevented from doing this on liberal grounds? Presumably the spectacle would be restricted to consenting adults so that interference would not be necessary to protect children and offended witnesses. The gladiators too would be consenting adults, fully prepared to shoulder enormous risks to life and limb, supposedly for the sake of money. (We can imagine that, with closed circuit TV, the promoter could offer the winning gladiator some twenty million dollars.) To interfere with the liberty of the gladiators to make agreements with promoters on the ground that the rewards they seek are not worth the risks they *voluntarily* assume would be to invoke the principle of legal paternalism, which is anathema to liberals who follow Mill. Kristol himself is not so much interested in protecting his hypothetical gladiators from death or physical harm as he is in defending the audience from a kind of moral harm, or harm to character.

SELF-DETERMINATION

The dilemma of paternalism is vividly exemplified in the New Jersey case of *Kennedy Memorial Hospital v. Heston* (1971). In his opinion reprinted here, Chief Justice Weintraub of the New Jersey Supreme Court decided in the affirmative the question whether an adult may be forced to submit against her will and against her religious convictions to a blood transfusion deemed by competent medical authority to be necessary not merely to her health but to her very life. The paternalism issue is not quite as clear in this instance as it might be since the patient was unconscious at the time the decision to proceed with the transfusion had to be made, so that it was her mother whose legal consent was solicited. Like her mother, however, the patient was a member of the Jehovah's Witnesses sect and presumably would have refused to permit the transfusion had she been conscious, and the court therefore addressed itself also to the legal consequences of her hypothetical refusal. There is no legal right to choose to die, the unanimous court concluded, suggesting that a failure to give the transfusion would be, in effect, to aid and abet an act of suicide by omission.

Under the English common law, suicide was a felony, and, unlike the law in most other American states it remains so in New Jersey, where all common law crimes are still punishable "if not otherwise provided for by act of the legislature."[3] Among the other legal consequences of the criminalization of suicide, the following were prominent: Property of the felon was forfeited to the Crown and thus denied to his heirs; life insurance was rendered void; attempted suicide was also a crime, often punished by imprisonment; all citizens had the right and duty to prevent commission of the crime by others when attempted in their presence; successful counseling of suicide, and knowing assistance in another's suicide were both murder; accidental killing of another in an attempt on one's own life was manslaughter (at least). Legal consent to one's own killing by another has always been impossible under Anglo-American law, hence even the merciful extinction of a dying patient's life in order to relieve his suffering *at his request* has been and still is a crime, usually murder. Thus, "under the present law, voluntary euthanasia [mercy killing] would, except in certain narrow circumstances, be regarded as suicide in the patient who consents and murder in the doctor who administers."[4] No doubt, some rationales of these laws are moralistic and others paternalistic, but they all agree that even when no other parties will be harmed, there can be no liberty to extinguish one's own, or another's life, even where death is ardently desired.

In a broader analysis of paternalism, Gerald Dworkin considers in a comprehensive and systematic way the question of whether paternalistic statutes (defined roughly as those interfering with a person's liberty "for his own good") are ever justified. He treats Mill's absolutistic position with respect, but points out how widespread paternalistic restrictions are, and how drastic their total elimination would be. Laws requiring hunters to wear red caps and motorcyclists to wear helmets, and those requiring medical prescriptions for certain therapeutic drugs, for example, seem innocuous to most of us. All the more so do laws actually protecting children and incompetents from their own folly, and laws which persons could regard as "social insurance" against any future decision of their own that would be not only dangerous but irreversible. Dworkin then attempts to find criteria that can be used to separate unjustified paternalistic restrictions from those he thinks any rational man would welcome.

PRIVACY

The relation of liberty to privacy is often obscured by subtle differences of sense and nuance in various applications of those abstract words. Privacy is often contrasted with liberty, or cited (as in Feinberg's article) as one of the moral limits to free activity. In this sense, one person's privacy is a limit to *another* person's liberty. Privacy so described is what is common to a set of claims citizens have not only against one another but also against policemen and other agents of the state. In other contexts privacy is spoken of as itself a kind of liberty—a liberty to be left alone, to enjoy one's solitude, not to be intruded upon or even known about in certain respects. Expressed in this way, privacy is a negative sort of freedom, a freedom (indeed, a right) *not* to be treated in certain ways. Thus one person's right to privacy characteristically conflicts with more active liberties of movement and surveillance by others. So conceived, privacy is not one of the "liberties" normally ascribed to the state. Some state officials and agencies, to be sure, enjoy immunities and privileges of nondisclosure, but these forms of protected secrecy characteristically have as their rationales the need to enhance efficient functioning, not the need to protect privacy. Only persons have private thoughts, inner lives, and unknown histories that in virtue of their intimate character essentially merit protection from unwanted scrutiny; and the state, as such, is not a genuine person.

The notion of privacy first entered American law in the law of torts where it served to protect a miscellany[5] of personal interests against invasions by private individuals or groups by authorizing law suits for damages. Yet in an implicit way, the idea of a private realm into which the state cannot legitimately penetrate, a domain which is simply not the state's proper business, is both ancient and ubiquitous. In the fictitious "Invitation to Dinner Case" included in this section, all of the legal requirements for an action for breach of contract appear to have been met, yet it is questionable whether such an action should be entertained. A dinner party, the judge might well be expected to say, is a householder's private affair and no proper concern of the courts. Here in a civil contest is the suggestion, normally made only with regard to criminal prohibitions, that public authority has no business interfering in private affairs.

The idea of privacy made its major entry into American constitutional law through the celebrated case of *Griswold v. Connecticut,* decided by the United States Supreme Court in 1965. The opinions in that case raise a variety of genuinely philosophical issues, and might well have been included with equal relevance in any of the first three sections of this anthology. The decision overturned a Connecticut statute making the use of contraceptives by "any person" a criminal offense. That statute was unconstitutional, Mr. Justice Douglas wrote, because it violated a right of marital privacy, "older than the Bill of Rights," but included in the "penumbra" of the First, Fourth, Fifth, Eighth, Ninth, and Fourteenth Amendments. A "penumbra" of a right is a set of further rights not specifically guaranteed in so many words but properly inferrable from the primary right either as necessary means for its fulfillment or as implied by it in certain factual circumstances not necessarily foreseen by those who formulated it.

Still, the Constitution does not specifically spell out a right of marital privacy, and the dissenters on the Court (Justices Stewart and Black) were suspicious of the technique of finding anything a judge thinks just and reasonable in the penumbra of a specific guarantee. Justice Goldberg in his concurring opinion had rested his case for a constitutional right of marital privacy on the Ninth Amendment's reference to fundamental rights "retained by the people," and Justices Harlan and White in their concurring opinions (not reprinted here) derived the unconstitutionality of the anticontraception statute from its capriciousness, irrationality, and offensiveness to a "sense of fairness and justice." A careful reader of Part One of this book will recognize here the overtones of the natural law tradition, whereas in Justice Black's skeptical stricture on the "catchwords" of "natural justice," in his dissenting opinion, there is the powerful echo of the tradition of legal positivism.

What is this privacy which, in some cultures at least, is held so dear, and which is so easily confused with the privileges of property, the residue of shame, or the essence of personal autonomy, among other things? By sorting out various separable elements, Hyman Gross makes a strong start on a philosophical analysis of the concept. A central theme in his account is that the loss of privacy is a loss of *control* over information about and impressions of oneself. Gross then proceeds to illuminate the connections between this aspect of privacy and self-determination, self-respect, and moral responsibility— connections that help explain the high value put on privacy, both by citizens and (now) by the law.

RIGHTS

Discussions of liberty can hardly avoid using the terminology of rights, and indeed the concepts of "liberty" and "right" are so intimately intertwined that clarification of either without understanding of the other is next to impossible. Where one can speak of a liberty to do, to be, or to possess something, one might also speak of a right to do, be, or possess that thing, except that the right, in most usage, is a stronger kind of liberty, an open option that is guaranteed, or reenforced, by a corresponding duty imposed on other parties not to interfere or else to provide necessary means. A liberty and a right to a given X, then, are different ways of having an open option with respect to that X. Sometimes, however, we speak of liberty as itself something people have a right to, in which case we mean not merely that certain basic options *ought* to be left open for them, but rather that the state is *bound* by moral principle to keep those options open for them by imposing legal duties both on itself and on others not to interfere.

The most basic philosophical questions about rights are those calling for analysis or clarification of the concept of a right. These in turn can be divided into two types. What we might call (with tongue in cheek) "varsity analysis" (as opposed to "intramural analysis") is the attempt to analyze the moral-legal concept of a right in terms of an altogether different—nonmoral and nonlegal—kind. If varsity analysis is possible at all, then "right" (and similar moral and legal terms) can be defined in terms, say, of "powers," "interests," "wants," or "needs," in which case rights-talk can be reduced to talk of some other kind, and perhaps seen in principle to be properly the province of one (or all) of the social sciences. The social sciences, after all, are the disciplines that investigate patterns of power, as well as human wants and needs. If questions about rights are really only very indirect ways of asking questions about objects of empirical investigation, then it is to these disciplines that we must eventually turn for answers; and much of jurisprudence is really a branch of the social sciences, as is much of ethics. (Similarly if "right" could be analyzed somehow, without remainder, into statements about God's will, then much of ethics and jurisprudence would be a branch of theology.)

The aim of "varsity analysis," then, is to produce *reductive definitions* of such legal terms as "right," analyses that reduce those concepts to some more basic nonlegal components. What we can call "intramural analysis," on the other hand, usually (but not necessarily) begins with scepticism about the possibility of reductive definitions of the normative terms of jurisprudence, but attempts the more modest task of stating logical relations among these terms themselves. Its aim, in short, is to provide nonreductive interdefinitions of normative legal terms such as "right," "duty," "immunity," "liability," and so on. Intramural analysis traces the patterns of logical interrelationship and reducibility among these legal terms themselves, rather than between legal and extra-legal terms.

H. L. A. Hart's Oxford inaugural lecture on "Definition and Theory in Jurisprudence" is an essay both about and in varsity analysis. On the one hand, he criticizes his predecessors for making certain characteristic and recurrent errors in their attempts to define such terms as "right," and concludes that reductive definitions in the traditional sense are impossible. On the other hand, he argues that much can be done anyway to clarify the concept of a legal right without misguided efforts to reduce it to something that it is not. Hart's "method of elucidation" is to examine not the single word "right" but rather typical whole sentences such as "*X* has a right," and to specify the conditions under which such sentences are true, and also to describe the distinctive sorts of jobs such statements are used to perform within a legal system.

The alternative method that Hart rejects begins with the misleading question "What is a right?," which looks at first sight very much like a request for a genus and difference definition—"a right is a so-and-so (genus) that differs from other so-and-sos in virtue of its such-and-such (specific difference)."

Hart argues that attempts to fill in the blanks have led in the past to a "familiar triad" of kinds of theories, all of which make the mistake of assuming that, if a word has meaning, then it must *stand for* something—something in this case not obvious to our inspection and too subtle, no doubt, for the dictionary makers. The first kind of theory claims that a right stands for some "unexpected variant of the familiar—a complex fact where we expected something . . . simple, a future fact where we expected something present, a psychological fact where we expected something external." Thus Spinoza, Hobbes, and Austin defined rights in terms of complexes of powers; Holmes in terms of predictions of future court decisions; others in terms of felt wants or needs. The second kind of theory in "the familiar triad" maintains that a right "stands for" nothing real, but rather for a kind of "legal fiction." A. Hägerstrom, for example, says that rights "have their roots in traditional ideas of mystical forces or bonds." The third familiar kind of theory holds that a right stands for something real enough, but something invisible, intangible, inaudible.

Similar triads of theories appear in ethical theory where "ethical naturalists" hold that ethical terms stand for complex natural facts, "ethical intuitionists" hold that they stand for "non-natural," irreducibly ethical facts, and "noncognitivists" hold that they don't stand for anything at all. Hart's own theory about the analysis of rights is similar in some ways to noncognitivism in ethics. He denies that the term "right" stands for anything, but holds that it is a constituent part of larger units of legal discourse that do have truth value, and whose meaning can be elucidated by a statement of their truth conditions and their characteristic uses or functions in a legal system.

By far the most ingenious and influential work of "intramural conceptual analysis" in jurisprudence is *Fundamental Legal Conceptions* by the former Yale University law professor, Wesley Hohfeld, first published in 1919. Hohfeld surveyed all of the various sorts of "jural relations" that can hold between two persons (e.g., "master-servant," "principal-agent," "husband-wife") and found that they could be reduced to four different kinds of underlying normative relationships, the basic building blocks out of which all jural relations can be constructed. Each of these basic relations is sometimes described by the word "right," so it might be maintained that "right" as used in the law is a highly ambiguous term referring to any one of a cluster of four distinct relations, but Hohfeld thinks that this apparent ambiguity is largely the product of careless usage, and that only one of the four kinds of rights can claim the title of "right in the strict sense." A right in this sense (sometimes called a "claim" or "claim right") is logically correlated with the duties of one or more other people. If Jones owes one thousand dollars to Smith, then he has a duty to pay the money to Smith, which is simply Smith's right to that money seen from another vantage point. Smith's right and Jones's duty are equivalent ways of describing one "jural relation" that holds between them. Smith has a legally enforcible claim against Jones, corresponding to Jones's legal duty to Smith.

Sometimes, however, we use the word "right" (somewhat loosely, Hohfeld would say) to refer to a *privilege* or a *liberty* of a person that is not correlated with the duties of any one else. To say that Smith has a privilege to X, or is at liberty to X, is to say that he has *no duty not* to X. That in turn implies nothing whatever about any other person's duties toward Smith in respect to X. Normally Smith has a duty not to strike Jones with his fist, but if Jones attacks Smith and strikes him first, then the legal situation changes and Smith no longer has a duty to refrain from punching Jones, which is to say that he has the legal privilege of striking back or (equivalently) that he is at liberty to strike back. That statement implies nothing about Jones's duties to Smith, but it does entail that Jones no longer has a claim on Smith's forbearance. Thus the statement of Smith's liberty ("no duty not . . . ") does entail the negative statement that Jones has "no right" that Smith not hit him.

The third basic jural relation is that connected with the idea of a legal *power* (also loosely called a "right"). Smith has a legal power with respect to Jones insofar as he has the ability to bring into existence, by his own voluntary behavior, new legal relations involving Jones, or to alter or extinguish existing relations. Thus if Smith strikes Jones, he creates the privilege in Jones, which otherwise would not exist, of striking Smith. If Jones has made Smith an offer, then Smith has the power of creating a claim-duty contractual relation with Jones by accepting. If he accepts, then Jones will have a duty, which he would not otherwise have, of doing his side of the bargain. The correlative to Smith's power, in these examples, is Jones's *liability* to changes in his legal position. The fourth basic relation is that associated with the idea of an *immunity* (also sometimes loosely called a "right"). Smith has an immunity with respect to Jones just insofar as his legal relations are not subject to alteration by Jones. In some states Mrs. Smith can change Mr. Smith's legal status simply by filing for a "no-fault" divorce, but Jones lacks this power of Mrs. Smith; no voluntary act of his can have the immediate legal effect of making Smith divorced. Jones is under a legal disability in this respect, which is the *correlative* to Smith's immunity.

Hohfeld then can sum up the basic jural relations in the following manner. Smith's claim-right against Jones is correlated with Jones's duty to Smith. The opposite of such a claim-right is a "no-right." Smith's privilege or liberty to act in a certain way toward Jones is correlated with Jones's "no-right" against Smith. The opposite of such a liberty is a duty. Smith's legal power over Jones is correlated with Jones's liability in respect to Smith. The opposite of such a power is a disability. Finally, Smith's immunity in some respect to Jones is correlated with Jones's disability in that respect toward Smith. The opposite of such an immunity is a liability. The system is worked out with perfect symmetry and great elegance.

Unlike the first two writers, Joel Feinberg takes as his subject the generic notion of a right, that which is common to legal and moral rights. He restricts his inquiry to what Hohfeld calls "rights in the strict sense," but not only to the legal species of these. In a sense he undertakes a "varsity analysis," even though he admits from the start that an enlightening reductive definition is impossible. He admits that his own definition of a right as a valid claim is, strictly speaking, circular; since one would have to know what a right is in order to understand what is meant by a "claim," as well as the other way round. Nevertheless, he insists that even a circular definition can have some utility when it provides an equivalent expression for the term to be defined that is more easily manipulated to good purpose or that is more suggestive or productive of insight.

In this case, the term "claim" lends itself more readily to an examination of the whole complex activity of claiming, which is at the heart of our understanding of what rights are all about. An examination of the role and function of claiming in human life is especially important to any account of why rights are such valuable things to have, since the disposition to make claims is an essential basis of personal dignity, self-respect, and respect for others.

Feinberg's account of these matters is an effort to answer widespread scepticism about the value of rights voiced by those who ask what we would lose if we had no rights but had everything else we wanted. In particular he considers an imaginary world called Nowheresville I where everyone does his duty regularly but no one has any conception of personal rights. Nowheresville I is not as bad as many another possible world that we can imagine, but Feinberg argues that it will be severely deficient in the sort of dignity and respect that requires acknowledgment of rights. In a postscript, however, he corrects his emphasis. An examination of another imaginary world, Nowheresville II, reveals that while awareness of rights may be necessary to a morally adequate life it is by no means sufficient. The residents of that unattractive place always do their duties and always insist on their rights, and thus achieve the ugly righteousness of the scribes and pharisees.

NOTES

1. The phrase is Herbert Packer's. See his *The Limits of the Criminal Sanction* (Stanford, Calif.: Stanford University Press, 1968), pp. 253–56.

2. The quoted phrase is from Thomas Scanlon, "A Theory of Free Expression," *Philosophy and Public Affairs*, Vol. I (1972), p. 215. This essay is somewhat difficult, but very strongly recommended nevertheless.

3. See Glanville Williams, *The Sanctity of Life and the Criminal Law* (New York: Alfred A. Knopf, 1968), p. 289.

4. *Ibid.*, p. 318.

5. Cf. Prosser on *Torts* 2nd ed. (St. Paul, Minn.: West Publishing Co., 1955), chap. 20.

FREEDOM OF EXPRESSION

JOHN STUART MILL

On Liberty*

The object of this Essay is to assert one very simple principle, as entitled to govern absolutely the dealings of society with the individual in the way of compulsion and control, whether the means used be physical force in the form of legal penalties, or the moral coercion of public opinion. That principle is, that the sole end for which mankind are warranted, individually or collectively, in interfering with the liberty of action of any of their number, is self-protection. That the only purpose for which power can be rightfully exercised over any member of a civilized community, against his will, is to prevent harm to others. His own good, either physical or moral, is not a sufficient warrant. He cannot rightfully be compelled to do or forbear because it will be better for him to do so, because it will make him happier, because, in the opinions of others, to do so would be wise, or even right. There are good reasons for remonstrating with him, or reasoning with him, or persuading him, or entreating him, but not for compelling him, or visiting him with any evil, in case he do otherwise. To justify that, the conduct from which it is desired to deter him must be calculated to produce evil to some one else. The only part of the conduct of any one, for which he is amenable to society, is that which concerns others. In the part which merely concerns himself, his independence is, of right, absolute. Over himself, over his own body and mind, the individual is sovereign.

It is, perhaps, hardly necessary to say that this doctrine is meant to apply only to human beings in the maturity of their faculties. We are not speaking of children, or of young persons below the age which the law may fix as that of manhood or womanhood. Those who are still in a state to require being taken care of by others, must be protected against their own actions as well as against external injury. For the same reason, we may leave out of consideration those backward states of society in which the race itself may be considered as in its nonage. The early difficulties in the way of spontaneous progress are so great, that there is seldom any choice of means for overcoming them; and a ruler full of the spirit of improvement is warranted in the use of any expedients that will attain an end, perhaps otherwise unattainable. Despotism is a legitimate mode of government in dealing with barbarians, provided the end be their improvement, and the means justified by actually effecting that end. Liberty, as a principle, has no application to any state of things anterior to the time when mankind have become capable of being improved by free and equal discussion. Until then, there is nothing for them but implicit obedience to an Akbar or a Charlemagne, if they are so fortunate as to find one. But as soon as mankind have attained the capacity of being guided to their own improvement by conviction or persuasion (a period long since reached in all nations with whom we need here concern ourselves), compulsion, either in the direct form or in that of pains and penalties for non-compliance, is no longer admissible as a means to their own good, and justifiable only for the security of others.

It is proper to state that I forego any advantage which could be derived to my argument from the idea of abstract right, as a thing independent of utility. I regard utility as the ultimate appeal on all ethical questions; but it must be utility in the largest sense, grounded on the permanent interests of man as a progressive being. Those interests, I contend, authorize the subjection of individual spontaneity to external control, only in respect to those actions of each, which concern the interest of other people. If any one does an act hurtful to others, there is a *primâ facie* case for punishing him, by law, or, where legal penalties are not safely applicable, by general disapprobation. There are also many positive acts for the benefit of others, which he may rightfully be compelled to perform; such as, to give evidence in a court of justice; to bear his fair share in the com-

*From *On Liberty,* Excerpts from Chapters I and II, and all of Chapter IV. First published in 1859.

mon defence, or in any other joint work necessary to the interest of the society of which he enjoys the protection; and to perform certain acts of individual beneficence, such as saving a fellow creature's life, or interposing to protect the defenceless against ill-usage, things which whenever it is obviously a man's duty to do, he may rightfully be made responsible to society for not doing. A person may cause evil to others not only by his actions but by his inaction, and in either case he is justly accountable to them for the injury. The latter case, it is true, requires a much more cautious exercise of compulsion than the former. To make any one answerable for doing evil to others, is the rule; to make him answerable for not preventing evil, is, comparatively speaking, the exception. Yet there are many cases clear enough and grave enough to justify that exception. In all things which regard the external relations of the individual, he is *de jure* amenable to those whose interests are concerned, and if need be, to society as their protector. There are often good reasons for not holding him to the responsibility; but these reasons must arise from the special expediencies of the case: either because it is a kind of case in which he is on the whole likely to act better, when left to his own discretion, than when controlled in any way in which society have it in their power to control him; or because the attempt to exercise control would produce other evils, greater than those which it would prevent. When such reasons as these preclude the enforcement of responsibility, the conscience of the agent himself should step into the vacant judgment-seat, and protect those interests of others which have no external protection; judging himself all the more rigidly, because the case does not admit of his being made accountable to the judgment of his fellow-creatures.

But there is a sphere of action in which society, as distinguished from the individual, has, if any, only an indirect interest; comprehending all that portion of a person's life and conduct which affects only himself, or, if it also affects others, only with their free, voluntary, and undeceived consent and participation. When I say only himself, I mean directly, and in the first instance: for whatever affects himself, may affect others *through* himself; and the objection which may be grounded on this contingency, will receive consideration in the sequel. This, then, is the appropriate region of human liberty. It comprises, first, the inward domain of consciousness; demanding liberty of conscience, in the most comprehensive sense; liberty of thought and feeling; absolute freedom of opinion and sentiment on all subjects, practical or speculative, scientific, moral, or theological. The liberty of expressing and publishing opinions may seem to fall under a different principle, since it belongs to that part of the conduct of an individual which concerns other people; but, being almost of as much importance as the liberty of thought itself, and resting in great part on the same reasons, is practically inseparable from it. Secondly, the principle requires liberty of tastes and pursuits; of framing the plan of our life to suit our own character; of doing as we like, subject to such consequences as may follow; without impediment from our fellow-creatures, so long as what we do does not harm them, even though they should think our conduct foolish, perverse, or wrong. Thirdly, from this liberty of each individual, follows the liberty, within the same limits, of combination among individuals; freedom to unite, for any purpose not involving harm to others: the persons combining being supposed to be of full age, and not forced or deceived.

No society in which these liberties are not, on the whole, respected, is free, whatever may be its form of government; and none is completely free in which they do not exist absolute and unqualified. The only freedom which deserves the name, is that of pursuing our own good in our own way, so long as we do not attempt to deprive others of theirs, or impede their efforts to obtain it. Each is the proper guardian of his own health, whether bodily, or mental and spiritual. Mankind are greater gainers by suffering each other to live as seems good to themselves, than by compelling each to live as seems good to the rest . . .

We have now recognized the necessity to the mental well-being of mankind (on which all their other well-being depends) of freedom of opinion, and freedom of the expression of opinion, on four distinct grounds; which we will now briefly recapitulate.

First, if any opinion is compelled to silence, that opinion may, for aught we can certainly know, be true. To deny this is to assume our own infallibility.

Secondly, though the silenced opinion be an error, it may, and very commonly does, contain a portion of truth; and since the general or prevailing opinion on any subject is rarely or never the whole truth, it is only by the collision of adverse opinions that the remainder of the truth has any chance of being supplied.

Thirdly, even if the received opinion be not only true, but the whole truth; unless it is suffered to be, and actually is vigorously and earnestly contested, it will, by most of those who receive it, be held in the manner of a prejudice, with little comprehension or feeling of its rational grounds. And not only this, but, fourthly, the meaning of the doctrine itself will be in danger of being lost, or enfeebled, and deprived of its vital effect on the character and conduct: the dogma becoming a mere formal profession, inefficacious for good, but cumbering the ground, and preventing the growth of any real and heartfelt conviction from reason or personal experience . . .

OF THE LIMITS TO THE AUTHORITY OF SOCIETY OVER THE INDIVIDUAL

What, then, is the rightful limit to the sovereignty of the individual over himself? Where does the authority of society begin? How much of human life should be assigned to individuality, and how much to society?

Each will receive its proper share, if each has that which more particularly concerns it. To individuality should belong the part of life in which it is chiefly the individual that is interested; to society, the part which chiefly interests society.

Though society is not founded on a contract, and though no good purpose is answered by inventing a contract in order to deduce social obligations from it, every one who receives the protection of society owes a return for the benefit, and the fact of living in society renders it indispensable that each should be bound to observe a certain line of conduct towards the rest. This conduct consists, first, in not injuring the interests of one another; or rather certain interests, which, either by express legal provision or by tacit understanding, ought to be considered as rights; and secondly, in each person's bearing his share (to be fixed on some equitable principle) of the labors and sacrifices incurred for defending the society or its members from injury and molestation. These conditions society is justified in enforcing, at all costs to those who endeavor to withhold fulfillment. Nor is this all that society may do. The acts of an individual may be hurtful to others, or wanting in due consideration for their welfare, without going the length of violating any of their constituted rights. The offender may then be justly punished by opinion, though not by law. As soon as any part of a person's conduct affects prejudicially the interests of others, society has jurisdiction over it, and the question whether the general welfare will or will not be promoted by interfering with it, becomes open to discussion. But there is no room for entertain-

ing any such question when a person's conduct affects the interests of no persons besides himself, or needs not affect them unless they like (all the persons concerned being of full age, and the ordinary amount of understanding). In all such cases there should be perfect freedom, legal and social, to do the action and stand the consequences.

It would be a great misunderstanding of this doctrine, to suppose that it is one of selfish indifference, which pretends that human beings have no business with each other's conduct in life, and that they should not concern themselves about the well-doing or well-being of one another, unless their own interest is involved. Instead of any diminution, there is need of a great increase of disinterested exertion to promote the good of others. But disinterested benevolence can find other instruments to persuade people to their good, than whips and scourges, either of the literal or the metaphorical sort. I am the last person to undervalue the self-regarding virtues; they are only second in importance, if even second, to the social. It is equally the business of education to cultivate both. But even education works by conviction and persuasion as well as by compulsion, and it is by the former only that, when the period of education is past, the self-regarding virtues should be inculcated. Human beings owe to each other help to distinguish the better from the worse, and encouragement to choose the former and avoid the latter. They should be forever stimulating each other to increased exercise of their higher faculties, and increased direction of their feelings and aims towards wise instead of foolish, elevating instead of degrading, objects and contemplations. But neither one person, nor any number of persons, is warranted in saying to another human creature of ripe years, that he shall not do with his life for his own benefit what he chooses to do with it. He is the person most interested in his own well-being: the interest which any other person, except in cases of strong personal attachment, can have in it, is trifling, compared with that which he himself has; the interest which society has in him individually (except as to his conduct to others) is fractional, and altogether indirect: while, with respect to his own feelings and circumstances, the most ordinary man or woman has means of knowledge immeasurably surpassing those that can be possessed by anyone else. The interference of society to overrule his judgment and purposes in what only regards himself, must be grounded on general presumptions; which may be altogether wrong, and even if right, are as likely as not to be misapplied to individual cases, by persons no better acquainted with the circumstances of such cases than those are who look at them merely from without. In this department, therefore, of human affairs, Individuality has its proper field of action. In the conduct of human beings towards one another, it is necessary that general rules should for the most part be observed, in order that people may know what they have to expect; but in each person's own concerns, his individual spontaneity is entitled to free exercise. Considerations to aid his judgment, exhortations to strengthen his will, may be offered to him, even obtruded on him, by others; but he, himself, is the final judge. All errors which he is likely to commit against advice and warning, are far outweighed by the evil of allowing others to constrain him to what they deem his good.

I do not mean that the feelings with which a person is regarded by others, ought not to be in any way affected by his self-regarding qualities or deficiencies. This is neither possible nor desirable. If he is eminent in any of the qualities which conduce to his own good, he is, so far, a proper object of admiration. He is so much the nearer to the ideal perfection of human nature. If he is grossly deficient in those qualities, a sentiment the opposite of admiration will follow. There is a degree of folly, and a degree of what may be called (though the phrase is not unobjectionable) lowness or depravation of taste, which, though it cannot justify doing harm to the person who manifests it, renders him necessarily and properly a subject of distaste, or, in extreme cases, even of contempt: a person would not have the opposite qualities in due strength without entertaining these feelings. Though doing no wrong to anyone, a person may so act as to compel us to judge him, and feel to him, as a fool, or as a being of an inferior order: and since this judgment and feeling are a fact which he would prefer to avoid, it is doing him a service to warn him of it beforehand, as of any other disagreeable consequence to which he exposes himself. It would be well, indeed, if this good office were much more freely rendered than the common notions of politeness at present permit, and if one person could honestly point out to another that he thinks him in fault, without being considered unmannerly or presuming. We have a right, also, in various ways, to act upon our unfavorable opinion of any one, not to the oppression of his individuality, but in the exercise of ours. We are not bound, for example, to seek his society; we have a right to avoid it (though not to parade the avoidance), for

we have a right to choose the society most acceptable to us. We have a right, and it may be our duty to caution others against him, if we think his example or conversation likely to have a pernicious effect on those with whom he associates. We may give others a preference over him in optional good offices, except those which tend to his improvement. In these various modes a person may suffer very severe penalties at the hands of others, for faults which directly concern only himself; but he suffers these penalties only in so far as they are the natural, and, as it were, the spontaneous consequences of the faults themselves, not because they are purposely inflicted on him for the sake of punishment. A person who shows rashness, obstinacy, self-conceit—who cannot live within moderate means—who cannot restrain himself from hurtful indulgences—who pursues animal pleasures at the expense of those of feelings and intellect—must expect to be lowered in the opinion of others, and to have a less share of their favorable sentiments, but of this he has no right to complain, unless he has merited their favor by special excellence in his social relations, and has thus established a title to their good offices, which is not affected by his demerits towards himself.

What I contend for is, that the inconveniences which are strictly inseparable from the unfavorable judgment of others, are the only ones to which a person should ever be subjected for that portion of his conduct and character which concerns his own good, but which does not affect the interests of others in their relations with him. Acts injurious to others require a totally different treatment. Encroachment on their rights; infliction on them of any loss or damage not justified by his own rights; falsehood or duplicity in dealing with them; unfair or ungenerous use of advantages over them; even selfish abstinence from defending them against injury—these are fit objects of moral reprobation, and, in grave cases, of moral retribution and punishment. And not only these acts, but the dispositions which lead to them, are properly immoral, and fit subjects of disapprobation which may rise to abhorrence. Cruelty of disposition; malice and ill-nature; that most anti-social and odious of all passions, envy; dissimulation and insincerity; irascibility on insufficient cause, and resentment disproportioned to the provocation; the love of domineering over others; the desire to engross more than one's share of advantages (the πλεονεξία of the Greeks); the pride which derives gratification from the abasement of others; the egotism which thinks self and its concerns more important than everything else, and decides all doubtful questions in his own favor—these are moral vices, and constitute a bad and odious moral character: unlike the self-regarding faults previously mentioned, which are not properly immoralities, and to whatever pitch they may be carried, do not constitute wickedness. They may be proofs of any amount of folly, or want of personal dignity and self-respect; but they are only a subject or moral reprobation when they involve a breach of duty to others, for whose sake the individual is bound to have care for himself. What are called duties to ourselves are not socially obligatory, unless circumstances render them at the same time duties to others. The term duty to oneself, when it means anything more than prudence, means self-respect or self-development; and for none of these is any one accountable to his fellow-creatures, because for none of them is it for the good of mankind that he be held accountable to them.

The distinction between the loss of consideration which a person may rightly incur by defect of prudence or of personal dignity, and the reprobation which is due to him for an offence against the rights of others, is not a merely nominal distinction. It makes a vast difference both in our feelings and in our conduct towards him, whether he displeases us in things in which we think we have a right to control him, or in things in which we know that we have not. If he displeases us, we may express our distaste, and we may stand aloof from a person as well as from a thing that displeases us; but we shall not therefore feel called on to make his life uncomfortable. We shall reflect that he already bears, or will bear, the whole penalty of his error; if he spoils his life by mismanagement, we shall not, for that reason, desire to spoil it still further: instead of wishing to punish him, we shall rather endeavor to alleviate his punishment, by showing him how he may avoid or cure the evils his conduct tends to bring upon him. He may be to us an object of pity, perhaps of dislike, but not of anger or resentment; we shall not treat him like an enemy of society: the worst we shall think ourselves justified in doing is leaving him to himself, if we do not interfere benevolently by showing interest or concern for him. It is far otherwise if he has infringed the rules necessary for the protection of his fellow-creatures, individually or collectively. The evil consequences of his acts do not then fall on himself, but on others; and society, as the protector of all its members, must retaliate on him; must inflict pain on him for the express purpose of punishment,

and must take care that it be sufficiently severe. In the one case, he is an offender at our bar, and we are called on not only to sit in judgment on him, but, in one shape or another, to execute our own sentence: in the other case, it is not our part to inflict any suffering on him, except what may incidentally follow from our using the same liberty in the regulation of our own affairs, which we allow to him in his.

The distinction here pointed out between the part of a person's life which concerns only himself, and that which concerns others, many persons will refuse to admit. How (it may be asked) can any part of the conduct of a member of society be a matter of indifference to the other members? No person is an entirely isolated being; it is impossible for a person to do anything seriously or permanently hurtful to himself, without mischief reaching at least to his near connections, and often far beyond them. If he injures his property, he does harm to those who directly or indirectly derived support from it, and usually diminishes, by a greater or less amount, the general resources of the community. If he deteriorates his bodily or mental faculties, he not only brings evil upon all who depended on him for any portion of their happiness, but disqualifies himself for rendering the services which he owes to his fellow-creatures generally; perhaps becomes a burden on their affection or benevolence; and if such conduct were very frequent, hardly any offence that is committed would detract more from the general sum of good. Finally, if by his vices or follies a person does no direct harm to others, he is nevertheless (it may be said) injurious by his example; and ought to be compelled to control himself, for the sake of those whom the sight or knowledge of his conduct might corrupt or mislead.

And even (it will be added) if the consequences of misconduct could be confined to the vicious or thoughtless individual, ought society to abandon to their own guidance those who are manifestly unfit for it? If protection against themselves is confessedly due to children and persons under age, is not society equally bound to afford it to persons of mature years who are equally incapable of self-government? If gambling, or drunkenness, or incontinence, or idleness, or uncleanliness, are as injurious to happiness, and as great a hindrance to improvement, as many or most of the acts prohibited by law, why (it may be asked) should not law, so far as is consistent with practicability and social convenience, endeavor to repress these also? And as a supplement to the unavoidable imperfections of law, ought not opinion at least to organize a powerful police against these vices, and visit rigidly with social penalties those who are known to practise them? There is no question here (it may be said) about restricting individuality, or impeding the trial of new and original experiments in living. The only things it is sought to prevent are things which have been tried and condemned from the beginning of the world until now; things which experience has shown not to be useful or suitable to any person's individuality. There must be some length of time and amount of experience, after which a moral or prudential truth may be regarded as established: and it is merely desired to prevent generation after generation from falling over the same precipice which has been fatal to their predecessors.

I fully admit that the mischief which a person does to himself, may seriously affect, both through their sympathies and their interests, those nearly connected with him, and in a minor degree, society at large. When, by conduct of this sort, a person is led to violate a distinct and assignable obligation to any other person or persons, the case is taken out of the self-regarding class, and becomes amenable to moral disapprobation in the proper sense of the term. If, for example, a man, through intemperance or extravagance, becomes unable to pay his debts, or, having undertaken the moral responsibility of a family, becomes from the same cause incapable of supporting or educating them, he is deservedly reprobated, and might be justly punished; but it is for the breach of duty to his family or creditors, not for the extravagance. If the resources which ought to have been devoted to them, had been diverted from them for the most prudent investment, the moral culpability would have been the same. George Barnwell murdered his uncle to get money for his mistress, but if he had done it to set himself up in business, he would equally have been hanged. Again, in the frequent case of a man who causes grief to his family by addiction to bad habits, he deserves reproach for his unkindness or ingratitude; but so he may for cultivating habits not in themselves vicious, if they are painful to those with whom he passes his life, or who from personal ties are dependent on him for their comfort. Whoever fails in the consideration generally due to the interests and feelings of others, not being compelled by some more imperative duty, or justified by allowable self-preference, is a subject of moral disapprobation for that failure, but not for the cause of it, nor for the errors, merely personal to himself, which may have remotely led to it. In like manner, when a person disables himself, by conduct purely self-regarding, from the performance of some definite duty incumbent on him to the public, he is guilty of a social offence. No person ought to be punished simply for being drunk; but a soldier or a policeman should be punished for being drunk on duty. Whenever, in short, there is a definite damage, or a definite risk of damage, either to an individual or to the public, the case is taken out of the province of liberty, and placed in that of morality or law.

But with regard to the merely contingent, or, as it may be called, constructive injury which a person causes to society, by conduct which neither violates any specific duty to the public, nor occasions perceptible hurt to any assignable individual except himself; the inconvenience is one which society can afford to bear, for the sake of the greater good of human freedom. If grown persons are to be punished for not taking proper care of themselves, I would rather it were for their own sake, than under pretence of preventing them from impairing their capacity of rendering to society benefits which society does not pretend it has a right to exact. But I cannot consent to argue the point as if society had no means of bringing its weaker members up to its ordinary standard of rational conduct, except waiting till they do something irrational, and then punishing them, legally or morally, for it. Society has had absolute power over them during all the early portion of their existence: it has had the whole period of childhood and nonage in which to try whether it could make them capable of rational conduct in life. The existing generation is master both of the training and the entire circumstances of the generation to come; it cannot indeed make them perfectly wise and good, because it is itself so lamentably deficient in goodness and wisdom; and its best efforts are not always, in individual cases, its most successful ones; but it is perfectly well able to make the rising generation, as a whole, as good as, and a little better than, itself. If society lets any considerable number of its members grow up mere children, incapable of being acted on by rational consideration of distant motives, society has itself to blame for the consequences. Armed not only with all the powers of education, but with the ascendency which the authority of a received opinion always exercises over the minds who are least fitted to judge for themselves; and aided by the *natural* penalties which cannot be prevented from falling on those who incur the distaste or the contempt of those who know them; let not society pretend that it needs, besides all this, the power to issue commands and enforce obedience in the personal concerns of individuals, in which, on all principles of justice and policy, the decision ought to rest with those who are to abide the consequences. Nor is there anything which tends more to discredit and frustrate the better means of influencing conduct, than a resort to the worse. If there be among those whom it is attempted to coerce into prudence or temperance, any of the material of which vigorous and independent characters are made, they will infallibly rebel against the yoke. No such person will ever feel that others have a right to control him in his concerns, such as they have to prevent him from injuring them in theirs; and it easily comes to be considered a mark of spirit and courage to fly in the face of such usurped authority, and do with ostentation the exact opposite of what it enjoins; as in the fashion of grossness which succeeded, in the time of Charles II, to the fanatical moral intolerance of the Puritans. With respect to what is said of the necessity of protecting society from the bad example set to others by the vicious or the self-indulgent; it is true that bad example may have a pernicious effect, especially the example of doing wrong to others with impunity to the wrongdoer. But we are now speaking of conduct which, while it does no wrong to others, is supposed to do great harm to the agent himself: and I do not see how those who believe this, can think otherwise than that the example, on the whole, must be more salutary than hurtful, since, if it displays the misconduct, it displays also the painful or degrading consequences which, if the conduct is justly censured, must be supposed to be in all or most cases attendant on it.

But the strongest of all the arguments against the interference of the public with purely personal conduct, is that when it does interfere, the odds are that it interferes wrongly, and in the wrong place. On questions of social morality, of duty to others, the opinion of the public, that is, of an overruling majority, though often wrong, is likely to be still oftener right; because on such questions they are only required to judge of their own interests; of the manner in which some mode of conduct, if allowed to be practised, would affect themselves. But the opinion of a similar majority, imposed as a law on the minority, on questions of self-regarding conduct, is quite as likely to be wrong as right; for in these cases public opinion means, at the best, some people's opinion of what is good or bad for other people;

while very often it does not even mean that; the public, with the most perfect indifference, passing over the pleasure or convenience of those whose conduct they censure, and considering only their own preference. There are many who consider as an injury to themselves any conduct which they have a distaste for, and resent it as an outrage to their feelings; as a religious bigot, when charged with disregarding the religious feelings of others, has been known to retort that they disregard his feelings, by persisting in their abominable worship or creed. But there is no parity between the feeling of a person for his own opinion, and the feeling of another who is offended at his holding it; no more than between the desire of a thief to take a purse, and the desire of the right owner to keep it. And a person's taste is as much his own peculiar concern as his opinion or his purse. It is easy for any one to imagine an ideal public, which leaves the freedom and choice of individuals in all uncertain matters undisturbed, and only requires them to abstain from modes of conduct which universal experience has condemned. But where has there been seen a public which set any such limit to its censorship? or when does the public trouble itself about universal experience? In its interferences with personal conduct it is seldom thinking of anything but the enormity of acting or feeling differently from itself; and this standard of judgment, thinly disguised, is held up to mankind as the dictate of religion and philosophy, by nine tenths of all moralists and speculative writers. These teach that things are right because they are right; because we feel them to be so. They tell us to search in our own minds and hearts for laws of conduct binding on ourselves and on all others. What can the poor public do but apply these instructions, and make their own personal feelings of good and evil, if they are tolerably unanimous in them, obligatory on all the world?

The evil here pointed out is not one which exists only in theory; and it may perhaps be expected that I should specify the instances in which the public of this age and country improperly invests its own preferences with the character of moral laws. I am not writing an essay on the aberrations of existing moral feeling. That is too weighty a subject to be discussed parenthetically, and by way of illustration. Yet examples are necessary, to show that the principle I maintain is of serious and practical moment, and that I am not endeavoring to erect a barrier against imaginary evils. And it is not difficult to show, by abundant instances, that to extend the bounds of what may be called moral police, until it encroaches on the most unquestionably legitimate liberty of the individual, is one of the most universal of all human propensities.

As a first instance, consider the antipathies which men cherish on no better grounds than that persons who religious opinions are different from theirs, do not practise their religious observances, especially their religious abstinences. To cite a rather trivial example, nothing in the creed or practice of Christians does more to envenom the hatred of Mahomedans against them, than the fact of their eating pork. There are few acts which Christians and Europeans regard with more unaffected disgust, than Mussulmans regard this particular mode of satisfying hunger. It is, in the first place, an offence against their religion; but this circumstance by no means explains either the degree or the kind of their repugnance; for wine also is forbidden by their religion, and to partake of it is by all Mussulmans accounted wrong, but not disgusting. Their aversion to the flesh of the "unclean beast" is, on the contrary, of that peculiar character, resembling an instinctive antipathy, which the idea of uncleanness, when once it thoroughly sinks into the feelings, seems always to excite even in those whose personal habits are anything but scrupulously cleanly, and of which the sentiment of religious impurity, so intense in the Hindoos, is a remarkable example. Suppose now that in a people, of whom the majority were Mussulmans, that majority should insist upon not permitting pork to be eaten within the limits of the country. This would be nothing new in Mahomedan countries.* Would it be a legitimate exercise of the moral authority of public opinion? and if not, why not? The practice is really revolting to such a public. They also sincerely think that it is forbidden and abhorred by the Deity. Neither could the prohibition be censured as religious persecution. It might be religious in its origin, but it would not be persecution for religion, since nobody's religion makes it a duty to eat pork. The only tenable ground of condemnation would be, that with the

personal tastes and self-regarding concerns of individuals the public has no business to interfere.

To come somewhat nearer home: the majority of Spaniards consider it a gross impiety, offensive in the highest degree to the Supreme Being, to worship him in any other manner than the Roman Catholic; and no other public worship is lawful on Spanish soil. The people of all Southern Europe look upon a married clergy as not only irreligious, but unchaste, indecent, gross, disgusting. What do Protestants think of these perfectly sincere feelings, and of the attempt to enforce them against non-Catholics? Yet, if mankind are justified in interfering with each other's liberty in things which do not concern the interests of others, on what principle is it possible consistently to exclude these cases? or who can blame people for desiring to suppress what they regard as a scandal in the sight of God and man? No stronger case can be shown for prohibiting anything which is regarded as a personal immorality, than is made out for suppressing these practices in the eyes of those who regard them as impieties; and unless we are willing to adopt the logic of persecutors, and to say that we may persecute others because we are right, and that they must not persecute us because they are wrong, we must be aware of admitting a principle of which we should resent as a gross injustice the application to ourselves.

The preceding instances may be objected to, although unreasonably, as drawn from contingencies impossible among us: opinion, in this country, not being likely to enforce abstinence from meats, or to interfere with people for worshipping, and for either marrying or not marrying, according to their creed or inclination. The next example, however, shall be taken from an interference with liberty which we have by no means passed all danger of. Wherever the puritans have been sufficiently powerful, as in New England, and in Great Britain at the time of the Commonwealth, they have endeavored, with considerable success, to put down all public, and nearly all private, amusements: especially music, dancing, public games, or other assemblages for purposes of diversion, and the theatre. There are still in this country large bodies of persons by whose notions of morality and religion these recreations are condemned; and those persons belonging chiefly to the middle class, who are the ascendant power in the present social and political condition of the kingdom, it is by no means impossible that persons of these sentiments may at some time or other command a majority in Parliament. How will the remaining portion of

*The case of the Bombay Parsees is a curious instance in point. When this industrious and enterprising tribe, the descendants of the Persian fire-worshippers, flying from their native country before the Caliphs, arrived in Western India, they were admitted to toleration by the Hindoo sovereigns, on condition of not eating beef. When those regions afterwards fell under the dominion of Mahomedan conquerors, the Parsees obtained from them a continuance of indulgence, on condition of refraining from pork. What was at first obedience to authority became a second nature, and the Parsees to this day abstain both from beef and pork. Though not required by their religion, the double abstinence has had time to grow into a custom of their tribe; and custom, in the East, is a religion.

the community like to have the amusements that shall be permitted to them regulated by the religious and moral sentiments of the stricter Calvinists and Methodists? Would they not, with considerable peremptoriness, desire these intrusively pious members of society to mind their own business? This is precisely what should be said to every government and every public, who have the pretension that no person shall enjoy any pleasure which they think wrong. But if the principle of the pretension be admitted, no one can reasonably object to its being acted on in the sense of the majority, or other preponderating power in the country; and all persons must be ready to conform to the idea of a Christian commonwealth, as understood by the early settlers in New England, if a religious profession similar to theirs should ever succeed in regaining its lost ground, as religions supposed to be declining have so often been known to do.

To imagine other contingency, perhaps more likely to be realized than the one last mentioned. There is confessedly a strong tendency in the modern world towards a democratic constitution of society, accompanied or not by popular political institutions. It is affirmed that in the country where this tendency is most completely realized —where both society and the government are most democratic—the United States—the feeling of the majority, to whom any appearance of a more showy or costly style of living than they can hope to rival is disagreeable, operates as a tolerably effectual sumptuary law, and that in many parts of the Union it is really difficult for a person possessing a very large income, to find any mode of spending it, which will not incur popular disapprobation. Though such statements as these are doubtless much exaggerated as a representation of existing facts, the state of things they describe is not only a conceivable and possible, but a probable result of democratic feeling, combined with the notion that the public has a right to a veto on the manner in which individuals shall spend their incomes. We have only further to suppose a considerable diffusion of Socialist opinions, and it may become infamous in the eyes of the majority to possess more property than some very small amount, or any income not earned by manual labor. Opinions similar in principle to these, already prevail widely among the artisan class, and weigh oppressively on those who are amenable to the opinion chiefly of that class, namely, its own members. It is known that the bad workmen who form the majority of the operatives in many branches of industry, are decid-

edly of opinion that bad workmen ought to receive the same wages as good, and that no one ought to be allowed, through piecework or otherwise, to earn by superior skill or industry more than others can without it. And they employ a moral police, which occasionally becomes a physical one, to deter skilful workmen from receiving, and employers from giving, a larger remuneration for a more useful service. If the public have any jurisdiction over private concerns, I cannot see that these people are in fault, or that any individual's particular public can be blamed for asserting the same authority over his individual conduct, which the general public asserts over people in general.

But, without dwelling upon suppositious cases, there are, in our own day, gross usurpations upon the liberty of private life actually practised, and still greater ones threatened with some expectation of success, and opinions proposed which assert an unlimited right in the public not only to prohibit by law everything which it thinks wrong, but in order to get at what it thinks wrong, to prohibit any number of things which it admits to be innocent.

Under the name of preventing intemperance, the people of one English colony, and of nearly half the United States, have been interdicted by law from making any use whatever of fermented drinks, except for medical purposes: for prohibition of their sale is in fact, as it is intended to be, prohibition of their use. And though the impracticability of executing the law has caused its repeal in several of the States which had adopted it, including the one from which it derives its name, an attempt has notwithstanding been commenced, and is prosecuted with considerable zeal by many of the professed philanthropists, to agitate for a similar law in this country. The association, or "Alliance" as it terms itself, which has been formed for this purpose, has acquired some notoriety through the publicity given to a correspondence between its Secretary and one of the very few English public men who hold that a politician's opinions ought to be founded on principles. Lord Stanley's share in this correspondence is calculated to strengthen the hopes already built on him, by those who know how rare such qualities as are manifested in some of his public appearances, unhappily are among those who figure in political life. The organ of the Alliance, who would "deeply deplore the recognition of any principle which could be wrested to justify bigotry and persecution," undertakes to point out the "broad and impassable barrier" which divides such principles from those of the association. "All matters relating to thought, opinion, conscience, appear to me," he says, "to be without the sphere of legislation; all pertaining to social act, habit, relation, subject only to a discretionary power vested in the State itself, and not in the individual, to be within it." No mention is made of a third class, different from either of these, viz., acts and habits which are not social, but individual; although it is to this class, surely, that the act of drinking fermented liquors belongs. Selling fermented liquors, however, is trading, and trading is a social act. But the infringement complained of is not on the liberty of the seller, but on that of the buyer and consumer; since the State might just as well forbid him to drink wine, as purposely make it impossible for him to obtain it. The Secretary, however, says, "I claim, as a citizen, a right to legislate whenever my social rights are invaded by the social act of another." And now for the definition of these "social rights." "If anything invades my social rights, certainly the traffic in strong drink does. It destroys my primary right of security, by constantly creating and stimulating social disorder. It invades my right of equality, by deriving a profit from the creation of a misery, I am taxed to support. It impedes my right to free moral and intellectual development, by surrounding my path with dangers, and by weakening and demoralizing society, from which I have a right to claim mutual aid and intercourse." A theory of "social rights," the like of which probably never before found its way into distinct language—being nothing short of this—that it is the absolute social right of every individual, that every other individual shall act in every respect exactly as he ought; that whosoever fails thereof in the smallest particular, violates my social right, and entitles me to demand from the legislature the removal of the grievance. So monstrous a principle is far more dangerous than any single interference with liberty; there is no violation of liberty which it would not justify; it acknowledges no right to any freedom whatever, except perhaps to that of holding opinions in secret, without ever disclosing them: for the moment an opinion which I consider noxious, passes any one's lips, it invades all the "social rights" attributed to me by the Alliance. The doctrine ascribes to all mankind a vested interest in each other's moral, intellectual, and even physical perfection, to be defined by each claimant according to his own standard.

Another important example of illegitimate interference with the rightful liberty of the individual, not simply threatened, but long since carried into triumphant effect, is Sabbatarian legislation. Without doubt, abstinence on one day in the week, so far as the exigencies of life permit, from the usual daily occupation, though in no respect religiously binding on any except Jews, it is a highly beneficial custom. And inasmuch as this custom cannot be observed without a general consent to that effect among the industrious classes, therefore, in so far as some persons by working may impose the same necessity on others, it may be allowable and right that the law should guarantee to each, the observance by others of the custom, by suspending the greater operations of industry on a particular day. But this justification, grounded on the direct interest which others have in each individual's observance of the practice, does not apply to the self-chosen occupations in which a person may think fit to employ his leisure; nor does it hold good, in the smallest degree, for legal restrictions on amusements. It is true that the amusement of some is the day's work of others; but the pleasure, not to say the useful recreation, of many, is worth the labor of a few, provided the occupation is freely chosen, and can be freely resigned. The operatives are perfectly right in thinking that if all worked on Sunday seven days' work would have to be given for six days' wages: but so long as the great mass of employments are suspended, the small number who for the enjoyment of others must still work, obtain a proportional increase of earnings; and they are not obliged to follow those occupations, if they prefer leisure to emolument. If a further remedy is sought, it might be found in the establishment by custom of a holiday on some other day of the week for those particular classes of persons. The only ground, therefore, on which restrictions on Sunday amusements can be defended, must be that they are religiously wrong; a motive of legislation which never can be too earnestly protested again. "Deorum injuriæ Diis curæ." It remains to be proved that society or any of its officers holds a commission from on high to avenge any supposed offence to Omnipotence, which is not also a wrong to our fellow-creatures. The notion that it is one man's duty that another should be religious, was the foundation of all the religious persecutions ever perpetrated, and if admitted, would fully justify them. Though the feeling which breaks out in the repeated attempts to stop railway travelling on Sunday, in the resistance to the opening of Museums, and the like, has not the cruelty of the old persecutors, the state of mind indicated by it is fundamentally the same. It is a determination not to tolerate others in doing what is permitted by their religion, because it is not permitted by the persecutor's religion. It is a belief that God not only abominates the act of the misbeliever, but will not hold us guiltless if we leave him unmolested.

I cannot refrain from adding to these examples of the little account commonly made of human liberty, the language of downright persecution which breaks out from the press of this country, whenever it feels called on to notice the remarkable phenomenon of Mormonism. Much might be said on the unexpected and instructive fact, that an alleged new revelation, and a religion founded on it, the product of palpable imposture, not even supported by the *prestige* of extraordinary qualities in its founder, is believed by hundreds of thousands, and has been made the foundation of a society, in the age of newspapers, railways, and the electric telegraph. What here concerns us is, that this religion, like other and better religions, has its martyrs; that its prophet and founder was, for his teaching, put to death by a mob; that others of its adherents lost their lives by the same lawless violence; that they were forcibly expelled, in a body, from the country in which they first grew up; while, now that they have been chased into a solitary recess in the midst of a desert, many of this country openly declare that it would be right (only that it is not convenient) to send an expedition against them, and compel them by force to conform to the opinion of other people. The article of the Mormonite doctrine which is the chief provocative to the antipathy which thus breaks through the ordinary restraints of religious tolerance, is its sanction of polygamy; which, though permitted to Mahomedans, and Hindoos, and Chinese, seems to excite unquenchable animosity when practised by persons who speak English, and profess to be a kind of Christians. No one has a deeper disapprobation than I have of this Mormon institution; both for other reasons, and because, far from being in any way countenanced by the principle of liberty, it is a direct infraction of that principle, being a mere riveting of the chains of one half of the community, and an emancipation of the other from reciprocity of obligation towards them. Still, it must be remembered that this relation is as much voluntary on the part of the women concerned in it, and who may be deemed the sufferers by it, as is the case with any other form of the marriage institution; and however surprising this fact may appear, it has its explanation in the common ideas and customs of the world, which teaching women to think marriage the one thing needful, make it intelligible that many a woman should prefer being one of several wives, to not being a wife at all. Other countries are not asked to recognize such unions, or release any portion of their inhabitants from their own laws on the score of Mormonite opinions. But when the dissentients have conceded to the hostile sentiments of others, far more than could justly be demanded; when they have left the countries to which their doctrines were unacceptable, and established themselves in a remote corner of the earth, which they have been the first to render habitable to human beings; it is difficult to see on what principles but those of tyranny they can be prevented from living there under what laws they please, provided they commit no aggression on other nations, and allow perfect freedom of departure to those who are dissatisfied with their ways. A recent writer, in some respects of considerable merit, proposes (to use his own words) not a crusade, but a *civilizade,* against this polygamous community, to put an end to what seems to him a retrograde step in civilization. It also appears so to me, but I am not aware that any community has a right to force another to be civilized. So long as the sufferers by the bad law do not invoke assistance from other communities, I cannot admit that persons entirely unconnected with them ought to step in and require that a condition of things with which all who are directly interested appear to be satisfied, should be put and end to because it is a scandal to persons some thousands of miles distant, who have no part or concern in it. Let them send missionaries, if they please, to preach against it; and let them, by any fair means (of which silencing the teachers is not one), oppose the progress of similar doctrines among their own people. If civilization has got the better of barbarism when barbarism had the world to itself, it is too much to profess to be afraid lest barbarism, after having been fairly got under, should revive and conquer civilization. A civilization that can thus succumb to its vanquished enemy must first have become so degenerate, that neither its appointed priests and teachers, nor anybody else, has the capacity, or will take the trouble, to stand up for it. If this be so, the sooner such a civilization receives notice to quit, the better. It can only go on from bad to worse, until destroyed and regenerated (like the Western Empire) by energetic barbarians.

JOEL FEINBERG

Limits to the Free Expression of Opinion*

The purpose of this essay is to determine how the liberal principles that support free expression of opinion generally also define the limits to what the law can permit to be said. The liberal principle in question, put vaguely, is that state coercion is justified only to prevent personal or public harm. That more harm than good can be expected to come from suppression of dissenting opinions in politics and religion has been amply documented by experience and argument, but concentration on this important truth, despite its salutary practical effects, is likely to mislead us into thinking that the liberal "harm principle" is simple in its meaning and easy in its application. For that reason, this essay will only summarize (in Part I) the impressive case for total freedom of expression of opinions of certain kinds in normal contexts, and concentrate instead (in Part II) on the types of expressions *excluded* by the harm principle: defamation and "malicious truth," invasions of privacy, and expressions that cause others to do harm (those that cause panics, provoke retaliatory violence, or incite others to crime or insurrection). Part III will examine the traditional crime of "sedition," and conclude that it is not properly among the categories of expressions excluded by the harm principle. Among the other lessons that will emerge from these exercises, I hope, is that the harm principle is a largely empty formula in urgent need of supplementation by tests for determining the relative importance of conflicting interests and by measures of the degree to which interests are endangered by free expressions.

I   THE CASE FOR FREEDOM

The classic case for free expression of opinion was made by John Stuart Mill.[1] Mill's purpose in his famous chapter "Of the Liberty of Thought and Discussion" was to consider, as a beginning, just one class of actions and how his "harm principle" applied to them. The actions in question

were instances of expressing orally or in print opinions about matters of fact, and about historical, scientific, theological, philosophical, political, and moral questions. Mill's conclusion was that suppressing such expressions is always more harmful than the expressions themselves would be and therefore is never justified. But don't expressions of opinion *ever* harm others? Of course they do, and it would be silly to ascribe to Mill the absurd contrary view. Expressions of opinion harm others when they are: defamatory (libelous or slanderous), seditious, incitive to violence, malicious publications of damaging or embarrassing truths, or invasions of privacy. In fact, in classifying an expression under one of these headings, we are *ipso facto* declaring that it is harmful. Mill is not radical about this. Putting these obviously harmful expressions to one side (he is best understood as asking) is there any [further] ground for suppressing mere "opinions"? To *this* question Mill's answer is radical and absolutist: If an expression cannot be subsumed under one of these standard headings for harmfulness, then it can never be sufficiently injurious to be justifiably suppressed. Apart from direct harm to assignable persons, no other ground is ever a sufficient reason for overriding the presumption in favor of liberty. One may *never* properly suppress an expression on the grounds, for example, that it is immoral, shocking to sensibilities, annoying, heretical, unorthodox, or "dangerous," and especially not on the ground simply that it is false.

Expressions of opinion thus occupy a very privileged position, in Mill's view. That is because their suppression, he contends, is not only a private injury to the coerced party but also and inevitably a very serious harm to the public in general. The argument has two distinct branches. The first has us consider the possibility that the suppressed opinion is wholly or partially true. On this assumption, of course, repression will have the harmful social consequence of loss of truth.

The crucial contention in this wing of the argument, however, is much stronger than that. Mill

* This essay has not been previously published.

contends that there is *always* a chance, for all we can know, that the suppressed opinion is at least partially true, so that the act of repression itself necessarily involves some risk. Moreover, the risk is always an unreasonable one, never worth taking, since the risk of its alternative—permitting free expression generally—to our interest in acquiring knowledge and avoiding error, is negligible. By letting every opinion, no matter how "certainly true," be challenged, we minimize the risk of permanent commitment to falsehood. In the process, of course, we allow some falsehoods to be expressed, but since the truth is not denied its champions either, there is very little risk that the tolerated falsehood will become permanently enthroned. The balance of favorable risks then is clearly on the side of absolute freedom of expression.

This argument is especially convincing in the world of science, where no hypothesis bears its evidence on its face, and old errors are continually exposed by new and easily duplicable evidence and by more careful and refined experimental techniques. Even totalitarian regimes have learned that it is in their own interest to permit physicists and plant geneticists to go their theoretical ways unencumbered by ideological restrictions. Sometimes, to be sure, the truth of a scientific theory is so apparent that it is well worth acting on even though it strains governmental priorities to do so and requires large investment of funds; but this very confidence, Mill argued, is justified only when every interested party has had an opportunity to refute the theory. In respect at least to scientific theories, the more open to attack an opinion is, the more confident we can eventually be of its truth. That "no one has disproved it yet" is a convincing reason for accepting a theory only when everyone has been free to try.

To deny that it is possible for a given opinion to be true, Mill maintained, is to assume one's own infallibility. This is no doubt an overstatement, but what does seem clear is that to deny that a given proposition can possibly be true is to assume one's own infallibility with respect to *it*, though of course not one's infallibility generally. To say that one cannot possibly be wrong in holding a given belief is to say that one knows that one's knowledge of its truth is authentic. We claim to know infallibly when we claim to know that we know. It is also clear, I think, that we are sometimes justified in making such claims. I know that I know that $2 + 3 = 5$, that I am seated at my desk writing, and that New York is

in the United States. In the face of challenges from the relentless epistemological skeptic, I may have to admit that I don't know *how* I know these things, but it doesn't follow from that that I don't know them. It seems then that there is no risk, after all, in suppressing some opinions, namely, the denials of such truisms.

Yet what could ever be the point of forbidding persons from denying that $2 + 3 = 5$ or that New York is in the United States? There is surely no danger that general confidence in these true propositions would be undermined. There is no risk of loss of truth, I suppose, in suppressing their denials, but also no risk in allowing them free circulation. Conceding that we can know truisms infallibly, therefore, can hardly commit us to approve of the suppression of their denials, at least so long as we adhere, with Mill, exclusively to the harm principle. More importantly, there are serious risks involved in granting any mere man or group of men the power to draw the line between those opinions that are known infallibly to be true and those not so known, in order to ban expression of the former. Surely, if there is one thing that is *not* infallibly known, it is how to draw *that* line.

In any case, when we leave tautologies and truisms behind and consider only those larger questions of substance, doctrines about which have in fact been banned by rulers in the past as certainly false (for example, the shape of the earth, the cause of disease, the wisdom of certain wars or economic policies, and the morality of certain kinds of conduct) our own fallibility is amply documented by history. The sad fact is that at every previous stage of history including the recent past there have been questions of the highest importance about which nearly *everyone,* including the wisest and most powerful, has been dead wrong. The more important the doctrines, then, the greater the risk we run in forbidding expressions of disagreement.

Mill's account, in this first wing of his argument, of the public interest in the discovery and effective dissemination of truth has many important practical implications. Mill himself thought that we should seek out our ideological enemies and offer them public forums in which to present and defend their views, or failing that, hire "devil's advocates" to defend unpopular positions in schools and in popular debates. Mill's reasons for these proposals also provide the grounding for the so-called "adversary theory of politics." The argument is (in the words of Zechariah Chafee): "Truth can be sifted out from falsehood only if the government is vigorously and constantly cross-examined . . . Legal proceedings prove that an opponent makes the best cross-examiner."[2] This states the rationale of the two-party system exactly. The role of the out-party is like that of the prosecutor in a criminal trial, or plaintiff in a civil action. It is a vitally important role too. Numerous historical instances suggest that we are in grave danger when both parties agree. Witness, for example, the Vietnam debacle, which was the outcome of a twenty-year "bipartisan foreign policy." Foreign policy decisions are as difficult as they are important; hence the need for constant reexamination, probing for difficulties and soft spots, bringing to light new and relevant facts, and subjecting to doubt hitherto unquestioned first premises. Without these aids, we tend to drift quite complacently into dead ends and quagmires.[3]

The second branch of the argument has us assume that the unorthodox opinion we are tempted to suppress really is false anyway. Even in this case, Mill insists, we will all be the losers, in the end, for banning it. When people are not forced by the stimulus of dissent to rethink the grounds of their convictions, then their beliefs tend to wither and decay. The rationales of the tenets are forgotten, their vital direction and value lost, their very meaning altered, until at last they are held in the manner of dead dogmas rather than living truths.

No part of Mill's argument in *On Liberty* is more impressive than his case for totally free expression of opinion. It is especially ingenious in that it rests entirely on social advantages and foregoes all help that might come from appeals to "the inalienable right to say what one pleases whether it's good for society or not." But that very utilitarian ingenuity may be its Achilles heel; for if liberty of expression is justified only because it is socially useful, then some might think that it is justified only *when* it is socially useful. The possibility of special circumstances in which repression is still *more* useful is real enough to disturb allies of Mill who love liberty fully as much as he and would seek therefore a still more solid foundation for it. But even if the case for absolute liberty of opinion must rest ultimately on some theory of natural rights, Mill has given that case powerful utilitarian reinforcement.

II   LIMITS TO FREEDOM

Despite the impressive case for complete liberty of expression, there are obvious instances where permitting a person to speak his mind freely will cause more harm than good all around. These instances have been lumped together in various distinct legal categories whose names have come to stand for torts or crimes and to suggest, by a powerful linguistic convention, unpermitted wrongdoing. Thus, there can be no more right to defame or to incite to riot than there can be a right way, in Aristotle's example,[4] to commit adultery. Underlying these linguistic conventions, however, are a settled residue of interest weightings as well as actual and hypothetical applications of the harm principle, often filled in or mediated in various ways by principles of other kinds. The various categories of excluded expressions are worth examining not only for the light they throw on the harm principle, but also for the conceptual and normative problems each raises on its own for political theory.

1. *Defamation and "Malicious Truth."* Defamatory statements are those that damage a person's reputation by their expression to third parties in a manner that "tends to diminish the esteem in which the plaintiff is held, or to excite adverse feelings or opinions against him."[5] The primary mode of discouraging defamers in countries adhering to the common law has been the threat of civil liability to a court-enforced order to pay cash to the injured party in compensation for the harm done his reputation. In cases of especially malicious defamation, the defendant may be ordered to pay a stiff fine ("punitive damages") to the plaintiff as well. Only in the most egregious cases (and rarely even then) has criminal liability been imposed for defamation, but nevertheless the threat of civil suit as sufficient to entitle us to say that our law does not leave citizens (generally) free to defame one another. Here then is one clear limit to our freedom of expression.

Not all expressions that harm another's reputation, of course, are legally forbidden. Even when damaging defamation has been proved by the plaintiff, the defendant may yet escape liability by establishing one of two kinds of defense. He may argue that his utterance or publication was "privileged," or simply that it is *true.* The former defense is established by showing either that the defendant, in virtue of his public office or his special relation to the plaintiff, has been granted an absolute immunity from liability for defamation (for example, he spoke in a judicial or legislative proceeding, or he had the prior consent of the plaintiff), or that he had a prior immunity contingent on the reasonableness of his conduct. Examples of this category of privilege are the immunity of a person protecting himself or another by a warning that someone is of poor character, or of a drama, literary, or political critic making "fair comment" of an extremely unfavorable kind about a performance, a book, or a policy. These immunities are still other examples of public policies that protect an interest (in this case, the interest in reputation) just to the point where the protection interferes with interests deemed more important—either to the public in general or to other private individuals. These policies imply that a person's reputation is a precious thing that deserves legal protection just as his life, health, and property do, but on the other hand, a certain amount of rough handling of reputations is to be expected in courtrooms, in the heated spontaneous debates of legislative chambers, in reviews of works presented to the public for critical comment, and in the rough-and-tumble competition among eminent persons for power or public acclaim. To withhold immunities in these special contexts would be to allow nervous inhibitions to keep hard truths out of law courts to the detriment of justice, or out of legislatures to the detriment of the laws themselves; or to make critics overly cautious, to the detriment of those who rely on their judgments; or to make political commentators overly deferential to power and authority, to the detriment of reform.

There is, however, no public interest in keeping those who are not in these special contexts uninhibited when they speak or write about others. Indeed, we should all be nervous when we make unfavorable comments, perhaps not on the ground that feelings and reputations will simply be damaged (there may be both justice and social gain in such damage), but at least on the ground that the unfavorable comment may be *false*. In a way, the rationale for the defamation action at law is the opposite of Mill's case for the free expression of opinion. The great public interest in possessing the truth in science, philosophy, politics, and so on, is best served by keeping everyone uninhibited in the expression of his views; but there are areas where there is a greater interest in avoiding falsehood than in acquiring truth, and here we are best served by keeping people very nervous indeed when they are tempted to speak their minds.

Once the plaintiff has proved that the defendant has published a defamatory statement about him, the defendant may avoid liability in another way, namely, by showing that the statement in question is *true*. "Out of a tender regard for reputations," writes Professor Prosser, "the law presumes in the first instance that all defamation is false, and the defendant has the burden of pleading and proving its truth." In the large majority of American jurisdictions, truth is a "complete defense" which will relieve the defendant of liability even when he published his defamation merely out of spite, in the absence of any reasonable social purpose. One wonders why this should be. Is the public interest in "the truth" so great that it should always override a private person's interest in his own reputation? An affirmative answer, I should think, would require considerable argument.

Most of the historical rationales for the truth defense worked out in the courts and in legal treatises will not stand scrutiny. They all founder, I think, on the following kind of case. A New York girl supports her drug addiction by working as a prostitute in a seedy environment of crime and corruption. After a brief jail sentence, she decides to reform, and travels to the Far West to begin her life anew. She marries a respectable young man, becomes a leader in civic and church affairs, and raises a large and happy family. Then twenty years after her arrival in town, her neurotically jealous neighbor learns of her past, and publishes a lurid but accurate account of it for the eyes of the whole community. As a consequence, her "friends" and associates snub her; she is asked to resign her post as church leader; gossipmongers prattle ceaselessly about her; and obscene inscriptions appear on her property and in her mail. She dare not sue her neighbor for defamation since the defamatory report is wholly true. She has been wronged, but she has no legal remedy.

Applied to this case the leading rationales for the truth defense are altogether unconvincing. One argument claims that the true gravamen of the wrong in defamation is the deception practiced on the public in misrepresenting the truth, so that where there is no misrepresentation there is no injury—as if the injury to the reformed sinner is of no account. A variant of this argument holds the reformed sinner to be deserving of exposure on the ground that he (or she) in covering up his past deceives the public, thereby compounding the earlier delinquency. If this sort of "deception" is morally blameworthy, then so is every form of 'covering up the truth,' from cosmetics to window blinds! Others have argued that a delinquent plaintiff should not be allowed any standing in court because of his established bad character. A related contention is that "a person is in no position to complain of a reputation which is consistent with his actual character and behavior."[7] Both of these rationales apply well enough to the unrepentant sinner, but work nothing but injustice and suffering on the reformed person, on the plaintiff defamed in some way that does not reflect upon his character, or on the person whose "immoralities" have been wholly private and scrupulously kept from the public eye. It does not follow from the fact that a person's reputation is consistent with the truth that it is "deserved."

The most plausible kind of argument for the truth defense is that it serves some kind of overriding public interest. Some have argued that fear of eventual exposure can serve as effectively as the threat of punishment to *deter* wrongdoing. This argument justifies a kind of endless social penalty and is therefore more cruel than a system of criminal law, which usually permits a wrongdoer to wipe his slate clean. Others have claimed that exposure of character flaws and past sins protects the community by warning it of dangerous or untrustworthy persons. That argument is well put (but without endorsement) by Harper and James when they refer to ". . . the social desirability as a general matter, of leaving individuals free to warn the public of antisocial members of the community, provided only that the person furnishing the information take the risk of its being false."[8] (Blackstone went so far as to assert that the defendant who can show the truth of his defamatory remarks has rendered a public service in exposing the plaintiff and deserves the public's gratitude.)[9] This line of argument is convincing enough when restricted to public-spirited defamers and socially dangerous plaintiffs; but it lacks all plausibility when applied to the malicious and useless exposure of past misdeeds, or to nonmoral failings and "moral" flaws of a wholly private and well-concealed kind.

How precious a thing, after all, is this thing denoted by the glittering abstract noun, the "Truth"? The truth in general is a great and noble cause, a kind of public treasury more important than any particular person's feelings; but the truth about a particular person may be of no great value at all except to that person. When the personal interest in reputation outweighs the dilute public interest in truth (and there is no doubt that this is sometimes the case) then it must be protected even at some cost to our general knowledge of the truth. The truth, like any other commodity, is not so valuable that it is a bargain at *any* cost. A growing number of American states have now modified the truth defense so that it applies only when the defamatory statement has been published with good motives, or is necessary for some reasonable public purpose, or (in some cases) both. The change is welcome.

In summary, the harm principle would permit all harmless statements about others whether true or false (harmless statements by definition are not defamatory), but it would impose liability for all defamatory false statements and all seriously defamatory true statements except those that serve (or seem likely to serve) some beneficial social purpose.

2. *Invasions of Privacy.* Still other expressions are neither defamatory nor false, and yet they can unjustly wound the persons they describe all the same. These do not invade the interest in a good reputation so much as a special kind of interest in peace of mind, sometimes called a sense of dignity, sometimes the enjoyment of solitude, but most commonly termed the interest in personal privacy. As the legal "right to privacy" is now understood, it embraces a miscellany of things, protecting the right-holder not only from "physical intrusions upon his solitude" and "publicity given to his name or likeness or to private information about him" without his permission, but also from being placed "in a false light [but without defamation] in the public eye" and from the "commercial appropriation of elements of his personality."[10] (Some of these are really invasions of one's property rights through unpermitted commercial exploitation of one's name, image, personality, and so on. For that reason it has been urged that the invaded right in these cases be called "the right to publicity.") What concerns us here are statements conveying true and nondefamatory information about the plaintiff, of a very intimate and properly private kind, gathered and published without his consent, often to his shame and mortification. Business advantage and journalistic profit have become ever stronger motives for such statements, and the invention of tiny, very sensitive snooping devices has made the data easier than ever to come by.

Since the "invasion of privacy" tort has been recognized, plaintiffs have recovered damages from defendants who have shadowed them, looked into their windows, investigated their bank accounts, and tapped their telephone wires. In many of these cases, the court's judgment protected the plaintiff's interest in "being let alone," but in other cases the interest protected was not merely this, or not this at all, but rather the interest in *not being known about.* If there is a right not to be known about in some respects by anyone, then *a fortiori* there is a right not to be known about, in those respects, by nearly everyone. Privacy law has also protected the interests of those who don't want details of their lives called to the public's attention and made the subject of public wonder, amusement, discussion, analysis, or debate. Hence some plaintiffs have recovered from defendants who have published embarrassing details of their illness or physical deformity; their personal letters or unpublished notes, or inventories of their possessions; their photographs in a "good looks" popularity contest, or in a "before and after" advertisement for baldness or obesity cures, or on the labels of tomato cans; and from defendants who have published descriptions of the plaintiffs' sexual relations, hygienic habits, and other very personal matters. No life, of course, can be kept wholly private, or immune from public inspection even in some of its most personal aspects. "No one enjoys being stared at," Harper and James remind us, yet if a person "goes out on the street he [can have] no legal objection to people looking at him."[11] On the other hand, life would be hardly tolerable if there were no secrets we could keep (away from "the street"), no preserve of dignity, no guaranteed solitude.

There would probably be very little controversy over the existence of a right to privacy were it not the case that the interest in being let alone is frequently in conflict with other interests that seem at least equally deserving of protection. Even where the right is recognized by law, it is qualified by the recognition of very large classes of privileged expressions. First of all, like most other torts and crimes, the charge of invasion of privacy is completely defeated by proof that the plaintiff gave his consent to the defendant's conduct. Secondly, and more interestingly, the right of privacy can conflict with the constitutionally guaranteed freedom of the press, which, according to Prosser, "justifies the publication of news and all other matters of legitimate public interest and concern."[12] For a court to adjudicate between a paper's right to publish and an individual's right to privacy then, it must employ some standard for determining what is of legitimate public concern or, what amounts to the same thing, which news about a person is "fit to print." Such legal standards are always in the making, never finished, but the standard of "legitimate interest" has begun to take on a definite shape. American courts have decided, first of all, that "the person who intentionally puts himself in the public eye . . . has no right to complain of any publicity which reasonably bears on his activ-

ity."[13] The rationale for this judgment invokes the maxim that a person is not wronged by that to which he consents, or by that the risk of which he has freely assumed. The person who steps into the public spotlight ought to know what he is letting himself in for; hence the law presumes that he *does* know, and therefore that he is asking for it. Much the same kind of presumption lies behind the "fair comment" defense in defamation cases: The man who voluntarily publishes his own work is presumed to be inviting criticism and is therefore not entitled to complain when the criticism is adverse or harsh, providing only that it is relevant and not personally abusive. One can put oneself voluntarily into the public eye by running for or occupying public office; by becoming an actor, musician, entertainer, poet, or novelist; by inventing an interesting device or making a geographical or scientific discovery; or even by becoming wealthy. Once a person has become a public figure, he has sacrificed much of his right of privacy to the public's legitimate curiosity. Of course, one never forfeits *all* rights of privacy; even the public figure has a right to the privacy of his very most intimate affairs. (This may, however, be very small consolation to him.)

One cannot always escape the privilege of the press to invade one's privacy simply by avoiding public roles and offices, for the public spotlight can catch up with anyone. "Reluctant public characters" are nonetheless public and therefore, according to the courts, as legitimate objects of public curiosity as the voluntary public figures. Those unfortunates who attract attention unwillingly by becoming involved, even as victims, in accidents, or by being accused of crimes, or even as innocent bystanders to interesting events, have become "news," and therefore subject to the public's right to know. They maintain this unhappy status "until they have reverted to the lawful and unexciting life led by the great bulk of the community," but until then, "they are subject to the privileges which publishers have to satisfy the curiosity of the public as to their leaders, heroes, villains, and victims."[14] Again, the privilege to publish is not unlimited so that "the courts must somehow draw the distinction between conduct which outrages the common decencies and goes beyond what the public mores will tolerate, and that which the plaintiff must be expected in the circumstances to endure."[15]

When interests of quite different kinds head toward collisions, how can one determine which has the right of way? This problem, which lies behind the most puzzling questions about the grounds for liberty and coercion, tends to be concealed by broadly stated principles. The conflict between the personal interest in privacy and the public curiosity is one of the best illustrations of the problem, but it is hardly unique. In defamation cases, as we have seen, there is often a conflict between the public interest in truth and the plaintiff's interest in his own good name. In nuisance law, there is a conflict between the plaintiff's interest in the peaceful enjoyment of his land and the defendant's interest in keeping a hogpen, or a howling dog, or a small boiler factory. In suburban neighborhoods, the residents' interest in quiet often conflicts with motorcyclists' interest in cheap and speedy transportation. In buses and trains, one passenger's interest in privacy[16] can conflict with another's interest in listening to rock and roll music on a portable radio, or for that matter, with the interests of two nearby passengers in making unavoidably audible, but avoidably inane, conversation. The principle of "the more freedom the better" doesn't tell us whose freedom must give way in these competitive situations.

The invasion of privacy cases are among the very clearest examples of the inevitable clash of interests in populous modern communities. They are, moreover, examples that show that solving the problem is not just a matter of minimizing harm all around. Harm is the invasion of an interest, and invasions do differ in degree, but when interests of radically different kinds are invaded to the same degree, where is the greater harm? Perhaps we should say that some interests are more important than others in the sense that harm to them is likely to lead to greater damage to the whole economy of personal (or as the case may be, community) interests than harm to the lesser interest, just as harm to one's heart or brain will do more damage to one's bodily health than an "equal degree" of harm to less vital organs. Determining which interests are more "vital" in an analogous sense would be no easy task, but even if we could settle this matter, there would remain serious difficulties. In the first place, interests pile up and reinforce one another. My interest in peace and quiet may be more vital in my system than the motorcyclist's interests in speed, excitement, and economy are in his, but there is also the interest of the cyclists' employer in having workers efficiently transported to his factory, and the economic interest of the community in general (including me) in the flourishing of the factory owner's business; the interest of the motorcycle manufacturers in their own profits; the

interest of the police and others (perhaps including me) in providing a relatively harmless outlet for adolescent exuberance, and in not having a difficult rule to enforce. There may be nowhere near so great a buildup of reinforcing interests, personal and public, in the quietude of my neighborhood.

There is still another kind of consideration that complicates the delicate task of interest-balancing. Interests differ not only in the extent to which they are thwarted, in their importance or "vitality," and the degree to which they are backed up by other interests, but also in their inherent moral quality. Some interests, simply by reason of their very natures, we might think better worth protecting than others. The interest in knowing the intimate details of Brigitte Bardot's married sex life (the subject of a sensational law suit in France) is a morally repugnant peeping tom's interest. The sadist's interest in having others suffer pain is a morbid interest. The interest in divulging a celebrity's private conversations is a busybody's interest. It is probably not conducive to the public good to encourage development of the character flaws from which these interests spring, but even if there were social advantage in the individual vices, there would be a case against protecting their spawned interests, based upon their inherent unworthiness. The interests in understanding, diagnosing, and simply being apprised of newsworthy events might well outbalance a given individual's reluctance to be known about, but photographs and descriptions with no plausible appeal except to the morbid and sensational can have very little weight in the scales.

3. *Causing Panic.* Defamatory statements, "malicious truths," and statements that wrongfully invade privacy do harm to the persons they are about by conveying information or falsehood to third parties. Their publication tends to instill certain beliefs in others, and the very existence of those beliefs constitutes a harm to the person spoken or written about. Other classes of injurious expressions do harm in a rather different way, namely, by causing those who listen to them (or more rarely, those who read them) to act in violent or otherwise harmful ways. In these cases, the expressions need not be about any specifiable persons, or if they are about persons, those individuals are not necessarily the victims of the subsequent harm. When spoken words cause panic, breach the peace, or incite to crime or revolt, a variety of important interests, personal and social, will be seriously harmed. Such expres-

sions, therefore, are typically proscribed by the criminal, and not merely the civil, law.

"The most stringent protection of free speech," wrote Holmes in his most celebrated opinion, "would not protect a man in falsely shouting fire in a theatre and causing a panic."[17] In some circumstances a person can cause even more harm by *truthfully* shouting "Fire!" in a crowded theater, for the flames and smoke might reinforce the tendency of his words to cause panic, and the fire itself might block exits, leading the hysterical crowds to push and trample. But we do not, and cannot fairly, hold the excited alarm sounder criminally responsible for his warning when it was in fact true and shouted with good intentions. We can hardly demand on pain of punishment that persons pick their words carefully in emergencies, when emotions naturally run high and there is no time for judicious deliberation. A person's warning shout in such circumstances is hardly to be treated as a full-fledged voluntary act at all. Perhaps it can be condemned as negligent, but given the mitigating circumstances, such negligence hardly amounts to the gross and wanton kind that can be a basis of criminal liability. The law, then, can only punish harmful words of this class when they are spoken or written with the intention of causing the harm that in fact ensues, or when they are spoken or written in conscious disregard of a high and unreasonable risk that the harm will ensue. The practical joker in a crowded auditorium who whispers to his comrade, "Watch me start a panic," and then shouts "Fire!" could be convicted for using words intentionally to cause a panic. The prankster who is willing to risk a general panic just for the fun of alarming one particular person in the audience could fairly be convicted for the grossly reckless use of dangerous words. Indeed, his recklessness is akin to that of the motorist who drives at an excessive speed just to frighten a timorous passenger.

Suppose, however, that the theater is virtually empty, and as the lights come on at the end of the film, our perverse or dim-witted jokester shouts "Fire! Fire!" just for the sake of confusing the three or four other patrons and alarming the ushers. The ushers quickly see through the ruse and suffer only a few moments of anxiety, and the patrons walk quickly to the exits and depart. No harm to speak of has been done; nor could any have reasonably been anticipated. This example shows how very important are the surrounding circumstances of an utterance to the question of its permissibility. Given the presumptive case for liberty in general, and especially the powerful social interest in leaving persons free to use *words* as they see fit, there can be a countervailing case for suppression on the grounds of the words' dangerous tendency only when the danger in fact is great and the tendency immediate. These matters are determined not only by the particular words used, but by the objective character of the surrounding circumstances—what lawyers call "the time, place, and manner" of utterance.

The question of legal permissibility should not be confused with that of moral blameworthiness or even with civil liability. The practical joker, even in relatively harmless circumstances, is no moral paragon. But then neither are the liar, the vulgarian, the rude man, and the scandalmonger, most of whose faults are not fit subjects for penal legislation. We cannot make every instance of mendacity, rudeness, and malicious gossip criminal, but we can protect people from the serious injury that comes from fraud, battery, or defamation. Similarly, practical jokers should be blamed but not punished, unless their tricks reach the threshold of serious danger to others. On the other hand, almost all lies, bad tales, jokes, and tricks create some risk, and there is no injustice in making the perpetrator compensate (as opposed to being punished) even his unlikely victim. Thus, if a patron in the nearly empty theater described above sprains an ankle in hurrying towards an exit, there is no injustice in requiring the jokester to pay the medical expenses.

It is established in our law that when words did not in fact cause harm the speaker may nevertheless be punished for having uttered them only if there was high danger when they were spoken that serious harm would result. This condition of course could be satisfied even though the harm in fact was averted: Not everything probable becomes actual. Similarly, for a person rightly to be punished even for harm in fact caused by his words, the harm in its resultant magnitude must have been an objectively probable consequence of the spoken words in the circumstances; otherwise the speaker will be punished for an unforeseeable fluke. In either case, then, the clear and present danger that serious harm will follow a speaker's words is necessary if he is rightly to be punished.

As we have seen, punishment for the harm caused by words is proper only if the speaker caused the harm either *intentionally* or *recklessly*. Both of these "mental conditions" of guilt require the satisfaction of the clear and present danger formula, or something like it. Consider recklessness first. For there to be recklessness there must really be a substantial risk consciously and unreasonably run. A speaker is not being reckless if he utters words that have only a remote and speculative tendency to cause panics or riots.

Intentional harm-causing by words raises more complications. Suppose an evil-minded person wishes to cause a panic and believes what is false and wholly unsupported by any real evidence, namely, that his words will have that effect. Imagine that he attends a meeting of the Policemen's Benevolent Association and, at what he takes to be the strategic moment, he stands up and shrieks, "There's a mouse under my chair!" Perhaps these words would cause a panic at a meeting of Girl Scouts but it merely produces a round of contemptuous laughter here. Wanting a panic and sincerely believing that one is causing a panic by one's words, then, are not sufficient. Suppose however we complicate the story so that by some wholly unforeseeable fluke the spoken words do precipitate a panic. The story is hard to invent at this point, but let us imagine that one patrolman laughs so hard that he tips over his chair causing another to drop his pipe, starting a fire, igniting live bullets, et cetera. Now, in addition to evil desire, and conscious belief in causal efficacy, we have a third important element: The words actually do initiate a causal process resulting in the desired panic. But these conditions still are not sufficient to permit us to say that the speaker *intentionally caused* a panic. Without the antecedent objective probability that a panic would follow these words in these circumstances, we have only a bizarre but tragic coincidence.

We would say much the same thing of a superstitious lady who "attempts" to start a riot by magic means. In an inconspicuous corner of a darkened theater, she sticks pins into a doll and mutters under her breath a magic incantation designed to produce a panic. Of course this doesn't work in the way intended, but a nearsighted and neurotic passerby observes her, takes the doll to be a real baby, and screams. The hoped-for panic then really follows. The evil lady cannot be found guilty of intentionally causing a panic, even though she intended to cause one and really did cause (or at least initiate a causal process that resulted in) one. She can be condemned for having very evil motives. But if people are sufficiently ignorant and impotent, the law, applying the harm principle, allows them to be as evil as they wish.

4. *Provoking Retaliatory Violence.* Suppose a person utters words which have as their unhappy effects violence directed *at him* by his angry audience, counterviolence by his friends and protectors, and escalation into a riotous breach of the peace. This is still another way of causing harm by words. Should the speaker be punished? In almost every conceivable case, the answer should be No. There is a sense, of course, in which the speaker did not start the physical violence. He used only words, and while words can sting and infuriate, they are not instruments of violence in the same sense that fists, knives, guns, and clubs are. If the law suppresses public speech, either by withholding permits in advance or punishing afterwards, simply on the ground that the expressed views are so unpopular that some auditors can be expected to start fighting, then the law punishes some for the criminal proclivities of others. "A man does not become a criminal because someone else assaults him ...," writes Zechariah Chafee. Moreover, he continues, on any such theory, "a small number of intolerant men ... can prevent *any kind* of meeting ... A gathering which expressed the sentiment of a majority of law-abiding citizens would become illegal because a small gang of hoodlums threatened to invade the hall."[18] When violent response to speech threatens, the obvious remedy is not suppression, but rather increased police protection.

So much seems evident, but there may be some exceptions. Some words uttered in public places in the presence of many unwilling auditors may be so abusive or otherwise offensive as to be "reasonably considered a direct provocation to violence."[19] The captive auditor, after all, is not looking for trouble as he walks the public streets intent on his private errands. If he is forced to listen, as he walks past a street meeting, to speakers denouncing and ridiculing his religion, and forced to notice a banner with a large and abusive caricature of the Pope,[20] his blood might reasonably be expected to boil. Antireligious and anticlerical opinions, of course, no matter how unpopular, are entitled to the full protection of the law. Even abusive, virulent, and mocking expressions of such views are entitled to full protection if uttered to private gatherings, in private or privately reserved places. Such expressions become provocative only when made in public places to captive auditors.

What makes an expression "provocative?" Surely, if words are to be suppressed on the ground that they are provocative of violence, they must be more than merely "provoking," else all unpopular opinions will be suppressed, to the great public loss. As far as I know, the concept of provocation has received thorough legal elaboration only in the law of homicide, where provocation reduces a charge of murder to that of manslaughter, thus functioning as a kind of mitigating consideration rather than as a justification or complete excuse. In the common law, for there to be sufficient provocation to mitigate: (1) The behavior of the victim must have been so aggravating that it would have produced "such excitement and passion as would obscure the reason of an ordinary man and induce him ... to strike the blow."[21] (2) There must not have elapsed so much time between the provocation and the violence that a reasonable man's blood would have cooled. (3) But for the victim's provocation the violence would not have occurred. In short, provocation mitigates only when it in fact produces a reason-numbing rage in the attacker and is such that it could be expected to produce such a rage in any normal person in his circumstances. Nazi emblems might be expected to have this effect on a former inmate of a Nazi death camp, but the Democratic party line cannot be sufficiently provocative to excuse a violent Republican, and similarly the other way round. Indeed, in the law of homicide, *no mere words alone,* no matter how abusive or scurrilous, can be adequate provocation to justify or totally excuse killing as a response.

There would seem to be equally good reason not to consider mere words either as justifying or totally excusing nonlethal acts of violence. The "reasonable man" in a democracy must be presumed to have enough self-control to refrain from violent responses to odious words and doctrines. If he is followed, insulted, taunted, and challenged, he can get injunctive relief, or bring charges against his tormentor as a nuisance; if there is no time for this and he is backed to the wall he may be justified in using "reasonable force" in self-defense; or if he is followed to his own home, he can use the police to remove the nuisance. But if he is not personally harrassed in these ways, he can turn on his heels and leave the provocation behind, and this is what the law, perhaps, should require of him.

Only when public speech satisfies stringent tests qualifying it as "direct provocation to violence," (if that is possible at all) will the harm principle justify its suppression. But there are many possible modes of suppression, and some are far more restrictive of liberty than others. Orders to cease and desist on pain of arrest are most economical, for they permit the speaker to continue to air his views in a nonprovocative way or else retire with his audience to a less public place. Lawful removal of the provocation (as a public nuisance) may be more satisfactory than permitting violent response to it, and is infinitely preferable to punishing the speaker. Nowhere in the law where provocation is considered as a defense do the rules deem the proven provoker (the victim) a criminal himself! At best his conduct mitigates the crime of his attacker, who is the only criminal.

One final point. While it is conceivable that some public *speech* can satisfy the common law test for provocation by being so aggravating that even a reasonable man could be expected to lose control of his reason when exposed to it, this can never be true of books. One can always escape the provocation of the printed word simply by declining to read it, and where escape from provocation is that easy, no "reasonable man" will succumb to it.

5. *Incitement to Crime or Insurrection.* In the criminal law, anyone who "counsels, commands, or encourages another to commit a crime" is himself guilty of the resultant crime as an "accessory before the fact." Counseling, commanding, and encouraging, however, must consist in more than merely uttering certain words in the presence of others. Surely there must also be serious (as opposed to playful) intent and some possibility at least of the words having their desired effect. It is not possible that these conditions can be satisfied if I tell my secretary that she should overthrow the United States government, or if a speaker tells an audience of bank presidents that they should practice embezzlement whenever they can. These situations are analogous to the efforts to start a panic by magical means or to panic policemen with words about mice.

The problem of interpreting the meaning of a rule making the counseling of crime itself a crime is similar, I should think, to that raised by a statute forbidding the planting of a certain kind of plant. One does not violate such a statute if he scatters the appropriate kind of seeds on asphalt pavement or in barren desert, even with evil intent. (Again, if you are stupid enough, the law—insofar as it derives from the harm principle—can allow you to be as evil as you wish.) To violate the statute, either one would have to dig a little hole in the appropriate sort of soil, deposit the appropriate seeds, cultivate, fertilize, allow for sufficient water, protect against winds, worms, and dogs; *or* one would have to find suitable conditions ready-made, where the soil is already receptive and merely dropping the seeds will create a substantial likelihood that plants will grow and thrive. By analogy, even words of advice, if they are to count as incitements to crime, must fall on reasonably receptive ears. The harm principle provides a ready rationale for this requirement. If we permit coercive repression of nondangerous words we will confer such abundant powers on the repressive organs of the state that they are certain to be abused. Moreover, we will so inhibit persons in their employment of language as to discourage both spontaneity and serious moral discussion, thus doing a great deal of harm and virtually no good at all. (The only "gain," if it is that, to be expected from looser standards of interpretation would be that nondangerous persons with evil motives could be scooped up in the state's tighter nets and punished.)

Counseling others to crime is not the only use of speech that can be described as incitement. We must also come to terms with instigating, egging on, and inflaming others to violence. Even Mill conceded that the opinion that "corn dealers are starvers of the poor," which deserves protection when published in the press, may nevertheless "justly incur punishment when delivered orally to an excited mob assembled before the house of a corn dealer . . ."[22] The metaphor of planting seeds in receptive soil is perhaps less apt for this situation than the commonly employed "spark and tinder" analogy. Words which merely express legitimate though unpopular opinion in one context become "incendiary" when addressed to an already inflammable mob. As Chafee put it: "Smoking is all right, but not in a powder magazine."[23] Of course the man who carries a cigar into a powder magazine may not know that the cigar he is carrying is lighted, or he may not know that he has entered a powder magazine. He may plead his lack of intention afterward (if he is still alive) as a defense. Similarly, the man who speaks his opinion to what he takes to be a calm audience, or an excited audience with *different* axes all ground fine, may plead his ignorance in good faith as a defense. But "the law" (as judges are fond of saying) "presumes that a man intends the natural and probable consequences of his actions," so that a defendant who denies that he intended to cause a riot may have the burden of proving his innocent intention to the jury.

In summary, there are two points to emphasize in connection with the punishment of inflammatory incitements. First, the audience must really be tinder, that is to say not merely sullen, but angry to the point of frenzy, and so predisposed to violence. A left-wing radical should be permitted to deliver a revolutionary tirade before the ladies of the D.A.R., even if his final words are "to the barricades!", for that would be to light a match not in a powder magazine but in a Turkish steam bath. Second, no one should be punished for inciting others to violence unless he used words intentionally, or at least recklessly, with respect to that consequence. Otherwise at best a speaker will be punished for his mere negligence, and at worst he will be punished though perfectly innocent.

There is one further problem raised by the concept of incitement as a crime. It might well be asked how one person—the inciter—can be held criminally responsible for the free and deliberate actions of another person—the one who is incited by his words. This problem is common to both kinds of incitement, counseling and inflaming or egging on, but it seems especially puzzling in the case of advising and persuading; for the deliberate, thoughtful, unforced, and undeceived acceptance of the advice of another person is without question itself a voluntary act. Yet there may well be cases which are such that had not the advice been given, the crime would never have been perpetrated, so that the advisor can truly be said to have "got" the advisee to do something he might otherwise never have done. In this case, the initiative was the advisor's, and his advice was the crucial causal factor that led to the criminal act, so that it would be no abuse of usage to call it "the cause." And yet, for all of that, no one *forced* the advisee to act; he could have rejected the advice, but he didn't.

If there is the appearance of paradox in this account, or in the very idea of one person's causing another to act voluntarily, it is no doubt the result of an unduly restrictive conception of what a cause is. There are, of course, a great many ways of causing another person to behave in a given way by the use of words. If we sneak up behind him and shout "boo!" we may startle him so that he jumps and shrieks. In this case our word functioned as a cause not in virtue of its meaning or the mediation of the other person's understanding, but simply as a noise, and the person's startled reaction to this physical stimulus was as involuntary as an eye-twitch or a knee-jerk. Some philosophers would restrict the notion of causing behavior to cases of this kind, but there is no good reason for such a restriction, and a strong case can be built against it based both on its capacity to breed paradox and on common sense and usage. I can "get" an acquaintance to say "Good morning" by putting myself directly in his line of vision, smiling, and saying "Good morning" to him. If I do these things and he predictably responds in the way I intended, I can surely say that my behavior was the cause, in those circumstances, of his behavior; for my conduct is not only a circumstance but for which his action would not have occurred, it is also a circumstance which, when added to those already present, made the difference between his speaking and remaining silent. Yet I did not force him to speak; I did not deceive him; I did not trick him. Rather I exploited those of his known policies and dispositions that made him antecedently "receptive" to my words. To deny that I caused him to act voluntarily, in short, is either to confuse causation with compulsion (a venerable philosophical mistake) or to regard one person's initiative as incompatible with another person's responsibility.[24]

In any case, where one person causes another to act voluntarily either by giving him advice or information or by otherwise capitalizing on his carefully studied dispositions and policies, there is no reason why *both* persons should not be held responsible for the act if it should be criminal. It is just as if the law made it criminal to contribute to a human explosion either by being human dynamite or by being a human spark: either by being predisposed by one's character to crime or by one's passions to violence, or else by providing the words or materials which could fully be anticipated to incite the violent or criminal conduct of others. It is surely no reasonable defense of the spark to say that but for the dynamite there would have been no explosion. Nor is it any more reasonable to defend the dynamite by arguing that but for the spark it should have remained forever quiescent.

There is probably even less reason for excluding from responsibility the speaker haranguing an inflammable mob on the grounds that the individuals in the throng are free adults capable of refraining from violence in the circumstances. A mob might well be understood as a kind of fictitious collective person whose passions are much more easily manipulated and whose actions more easily maneuvered than those of individual persons. If one looks at it this way, the caused behavior of an inflamed mob may be a good deal less than fully voluntary, even though the component individuals in it, being free adults, are all acting voluntarily on their own responsibility.

III SEDITION

Causing panic, provoking violence, and inciting to crime or insurrection are all made punishable by what Chafee calls "the normal criminal law of words."[25] The relevant common law categories are riot, breach of the peace, solicitation, and incitement. All these crimes, as we have seen, require either intentionally harmful or reckless conduct, and all of them require, in addition—and for reasons partly derived from and explicable by the harm principle—that there be some objective likelihood that the relevant sort of harm will be produced by the words uttered in the circumstances. In addition to these traditional common law crimes, many governments have considered it necessary to create statutes making *sedition* a crime. It will be useful to consider the question of sedition against the background of the normal criminal law of words, for this will lead us quickly to two conclusions. The first is that sedition laws are wholly unnecessary to avert the harm they are ostensibly aimed at. The second is that if we must nevertheless put up with sedition laws, they must be applied by the courts in accordance with the same standards of objective likelihood and immediate danger that govern the application of the laws against provoking and inciting violence. Otherwise sedition statutes are likely to do far more social harm than good. Such laws when properly interpreted by enforcers and courts are at best legal redundancies. At worst they are corrosive of the values normally protected by freedom of expression.

The word "sedition," which in its oldest, prelegal sense meant simply divisiveness and strife, has never been the name of a crime in the English common law. Rather the adjective "seditious" forms part of the name of the common law crimes of "seditious words," "seditious libel," and "seditious conspiracy." Apparently the common ingredient in these offenses was so-called "seditious intent." The legal definition of "seditious intent" has changed over the centuries. In the beginning any spoken or written words which in fact had a tendency, however remote, to cause dissension or to weaken the grip of governmental authorities, and were spoken or published intentionally (with or without the further purpose of weakening the government or causing dissension) were held to manifest the requisite intent. In the fifteenth and sixteenth centuries, for example, publicly to call the king a fool, even in jest, was to risk capital punishment. There was to be less danger somewhat later for authors of *printed* words; for all books and printed papers had to be submitted in advance to the censorship (a practice denounced in Milton's eloquent *Areopagitica*), so that authors of politically dangerous words risked not punishment but only prior restraint. There is little evidence, however, that many of them felt more free as a consequence of this development.

The abandonment of the censorship in 1695 was widely hailed as a triumph for freedom of the press, but it was soon replaced by an equally repressive and far more cruel series of criminal trials for "seditious libel." Juries were permitted to decide only narrow factual questions, whereas the matter of "seditious intent" was left up to very conservative judges who knew well where their own personal interests lay. Moreover, truth was not permitted as a defense[26]—a legal restriction which in effect destroyed all right of adverse political criticism. Zechariah Chafee[27] has argued convincingly that the First Amendment to the United States Constitution was proposed and adopted by men who were consciously reacting against the common law of seditious libel, and in particular against the applications of that law in the English trials of the time. "Reform" (of sorts) came in England through Fox's Libel Act of 1792, which allowed juries to decide the question of seditious intent and permitted the truth defense if the opinions were published with good motives. (The ill-advised and short-lived American Sedition Act of 1798 was modeled after this act.) In the hysterical reaction to the French Revolution and the Napoleonic Wars, however, juries proved to be even more savage than judges, and hundreds were punished even for the mildest political unorthodoxy.

Throughout most of the nineteenth century, the prevailing definition of seditious intent in English law derived from a statute passed during the repressive heyday of the Fox Act sedition trials. Men were punished for publishing any words with:

the intention of (1) exciting disaffection, hatred, or contempt against the sovereign, or the government and constitution of the kingdom, or either house of parliament, or the administration of justice, *or* (2) exciting his majesty's subjects to attempt, otherwise than by lawful means, the alteration of any matter in church or state by law established, *or* (3) to promote feelings of ill will and hostility between different classes.[28]

In short, the three possible modes of seditious libel were defamation of the institutions or officers of the government, incitement to unlawful acts, and a use of language that tends toward the breach of the peace "between classes." The normal criminal law of words sufficiently covers the last two modes; and the civil law of defamation would apply to the first. The criminal law, as we have seen, employs a clear and present danger test for incitement and breach of peace, and does so for good reasons derived from the harm principle and the analysis of "intentional causing." For other good reasons, also derived from the harm principle, the law of defamation privileges fair comment on public officials, and gives no protection at all to institutions. So there would seem to be no further need, at least none demonstrated by the harm principle, for a criminal law of sedition.[29]

Still, many have thought that the harm principle requires sedition laws, and some still do. The issue boils down to the question of whether the normal law of words with its strict standard of immediate danger is too lax to prevent serious harms, and whether, therefore, it needs supplementing by sedition laws employing the looser standards of "bad tendency" and "presumptive intent." By the standard of bad tendency, words can be punished for their dangerous propensity "long before there is any probability that they will break out into unlawful acts";[30] and by the test of presumptive intent, it is necessary only that the defendant intended to publish his words, not that he intended further harm by them. It is clear that most authors of sedition statutes have meant them to be interpreted by the courts in accordance with the tests of bad tendency and presumptive intent (although the United States Supreme Court has in recent decades declared that such interpretations are contrary to the First Amendment of the Constitution). Part of the rationale for the older tests was that if words make a definite contribution to a situation which is on its way to being dangerous, it is folly not to punish them well before that situation reaches the threshold of actual harm. There may seem to be no harm in piling up twigs as such, but if this is done with the purpose (or even the likely outcome) of starting a fire eventually, why not stop it now before it is too late? Those who favor this argument have often employed the harm principle also to defend laws against institutional defamation. The reason why it should be unlawful to bring the Constitution or the courts (or even the *flag*) into disrepute by one's words, they argue, is not simply that such words are offensive, but rather that they tend to undermine respect and loyalty and thereby contribute to more serious harm in the long run.

The focus of the disagreement over sedition laws is the status of *advocacy*. The normal law of words quite clearly outlaws counseling, urging, or demanding (under certain conditions) that others resort to crime or engage in riots, assassinations, or insurrections. But what if a person uses language not directly to counsel or call for violence but rather (where this is different) to *advocate* it? In the wake of the Russian Revolution, many working class parties in America and Europe adopted some variant of an ideology which declared that the propertied classes derived their wealth from the systematic exploitation of the poor; capitalists controlled the major media of news and opinion as well as parliaments and legislators; the grievances of the workers therefore could not be remedied through normal political channels but required instead direct pressure through such means as general strikes, boycotts, and mass demonstrations; and that the working class would inevitably be triumphant in its struggle, expropriate the exploiters, and itself run industry. Spokesmen for this ideology were known for their flamboyant rhetoric, which invariably contained such terms as "arise," "struggle," "victory," and "revolution." Such persons were commonly charged with violations of the Federal Espionage Act during and after World War I, of state sedition laws during the 1920s, and, after World War II, of the Smith Act. Often the key charge in the indictment was "teaching or advocating" riot, assassination, or the violent overthrow of the government.

Trials of Marxists for advocacy of revolution tended to be extremely difficult and problematic partly because it was never clear whether revolution in any usual sense was something taught and approved by them, and partly because it was unclear whether the form of reference to revolution in the Marxist ideology amounted to "advocacy" of it. Marxists disagreed among themselves over the first point. Many thought that forms of group pressure well short of open violence would be sufficient to overturn the capitalists; others thought that "eventually" (when is that?), when conditions were at last ripe, a brief violent seizure of power might be necessary. Does this, in any case, amount to the advocacy of revolution? If it is criminal advocacy to teach that there are conceivable circumstances under which revolution would be justified, then almost everyone, including this author, "advocates" revolution. Suppose one holds further that the "conceivable justifying conditions" may one day become actual, or that it is even probable that they will be actual at some indeterminate future time. Is this to count as criminal advocacy?

Not according to Justice Holmes in his famous opinion in *U.S. v. Schenk.* Schenk and others had encouraged draft resistance in 1917 by mailing circulars denouncing conscription as unconstitutional and urging in very emotional prose that draft-eligible men "assert their rights." The lower court found this to be advocacy of unlawful conduct, a violation, in particular, of the Espionage Act of 1917. The Supreme Court upheld the conviction but nevertheless laid down in the words of O. W. Holmes the test which was to be applied, in a more generous spirit, in later cases: "The question in every case is whether the words ... are used in such circumstances and are of such a nature as to create a clear and present danger that they will bring about the substantive evils that Congress has a right to prevent." Since Congress has the right to raise armies, any efforts to interfere by words or action with the exercise of that right are punishable. But the clear and present danger standard brings advocacy under the same kind of test as that used for incitement in the normal law of words. One can "advocate" draft resistance over one's breakfast table to one's daughter (though perhaps not to one's son), but not to a sullen group waiting to be sworn in at the induction center.

There is, on the other hand, never any real danger in this country in permitting the open advocacy of *revolution,* except, perhaps, as Chafee puts it, "in extraordinary times of great tension." He continues:

The chances of success are so infinitesimal that the probability of any serious attempt following the utterances seems too slight to make them punishable. ... This is especially true if the speaker urges revolution at some future day, so that no immediate check is needed to save the country.[31]

Advocacy of assassination, on the other hand, is less easily tolerated. In the first place, the soil is always more receptive to that seed. It is not that potential assassins are more numerous than potential revolutionaries, although at most times that is true. Potential assassins include among their number persons who are contorted beyond reason by hate, mentally unstable persons, and unpredictable crackpots. Further, a successful assassination requires only one good shot. Since it is more likely to be tried and easier to achieve, its danger is always more "clear and present." There will be many circumstances, therefore, in which Holmes's test would permit advocacy of revolution but punish advocacy of assassination. Still in most contexts of utterance it would punish neither. It should no doubt be criminal for a prominent politician to advocate assassination of the president in a talk over national television, or in a letter to the *New York Times*,[32] but when a patron of a neighborhood tavern heatedly announces to his fellow drinkers that "the bum ought to be shot," the president's life will not be significantly endangered. There are times and places where it doesn't matter in the slightest how carelessly one chooses one's words, and others where one's choice of words can be a matter of life and death.

I shall, in conclusion, sketch a rationale for the clear and present danger test, as a kind of mediating standard for the application of the harm principle in the area of political expression. The natural challenge to the use of that test has been adumbrated above. It is true, one might concede, that the teaching of Communist ideology here and now will not create a clear and present danger of violent revolution. Every one knows that, including the Communists. Every trip, however, begins with some first steps, and that includes trips to forbidden destinations. The beginning steps are meant to increase numbers, add strength, and pick up momentum at later stages. To switch the metaphor to one used previously, the Communists are not just casting seeds on barren ground; their words are also meant to cultivate the ground and irrigate it. If the law prohibits planting a certain kind of shrub and we see people storing the forbidden seeds, garden tools, and fertilizer, and actually digging trenches for irrigation pipes, why wait until they are ready to plant the seed before stopping them? Even at these early stages of preparation, they are clearly attempting to achieve what is forbidden. So the argument goes.

The metaphor employed by the argument, however, is not very favorable to its cause. There is a world of difference between making plans and preparations for a future crime and actually launching an attempt, and this distinction has long been recognized by the ordinary criminal law. Mere preparations without actual steps in the direction of perpetration are not sufficient for the crime of attempt (though if preparation involves talking with collaborators, it may constitute the crime of conspiracy). Not even preliminary "steps" are sufficient; for "the act must reach far enough toward the accomplishment of the desired result to amount to the commencement of the consummation."[33] So the first

faltering steps of a surpassingly difficult fifty-year trip toward an illegal goal can hardly qualify as an "attempt" in either the legal or the everyday sense.

If the journey is a collective enterprise, the participants could be charged with *conspiracy* without any violation of usage. The question is whether it would be sound public policy to suppress dissenting voices in this manner so long before they reach the threshold of public danger. The argument to the contrary has been given very clear statement in our time by Zechariah Chafee. Consider what interests are involved when the state employs some coercive technique to prevent a private individual or group from expressing an opinion on some issue of public policy, or from teaching or advocating some political ideology. Chafee would have us put these various interests in the balance to determine their relative weights. In the one pan of the scale, there are the private interests of the suppressed individual or group in having their opinions heard and shared, and in winning support and eventual acceptance for them. These interests will be effectively squelched by state suppression. In the other pan is the public interest in peace and order, and the preservation of democratic institutions. These interests may be endangered to some degree by the advocacy of radical ideologies. Now if these are the only interests involved, there is no question that the public interest (which after all includes all or most private interests) sits heavier in the pan. There is, however, another public interest involved of very considerable weight. That is the public interest in the discovery and dissemination of all information that can have any bearing on public policy, and of all opinions about what public policy should be. The dangers that come from neglecting *that* interest are enormous at all times. (See Part I above.) And the more dangerous the times—the more serious the questions before the country's decision makers (and *especially* when these are questions of war and peace)—the more important it is to keep open all the possible avenues to truth and wisdom.

Only the interest in national safety can outweigh the public interest in open discussion, but *it sits in the scale only to the degree that it is actually imperiled.* From the point of view of the public interest alone, with no consideration whatever of individual rights, it would be folly to sacrifice the social benefits of free speech for the bare possibility that the public safety may be somewhat affected. The greater the certainty and imminence of danger, however, the more the interest in public safety moves on to the scale, until at the point of clear and present danger it is heavy enough to tip the scales its way.

The scales analogy, of course, is only an elaborate metaphor for the sorts of deliberations that must go on among enforcers and interpreters of the law when distinct public interests come into conflict. These clashes of interest are most likely to occur in times of excitement and stress when interest "balancing" calls for a clear eye, a sensitive scale, and a steady hand. At such times the clear and present danger rule is a difficult one to apply, but other guides to decision have invariably gone wrong, while the clear and present danger test has hardly ever been seriously tried. Perhaps that helps account, to some degree, for the sorry human record of cruelty, injustice, and war.

NOTES

1. In Chapter Two of *On Liberty,* not reprinted in this volume.
2. Zechariah Chafee, Jr., *Free Speech in the United States* (1941), p. 33.
3. This point applies especially to discussions of moral, social, political, legal, and economic questions, as well as matters of governmental policy, domestic and foreign. "Cross-examination" in science and philosophy is perhaps less important.
4. Aristotle, *Nicomachean Ethics,* Bk. II, Chap. 6, 1107 ª. "When a man commits adultery, there is no point in asking whether it was with the right woman or at the right time or in the right way, for to do anything like that is simply wrong."
5. William L. Prosser, *Handbook of the Law of Torts,* 2nd ed. (St. Paul: West Publishing Co., 1955), p. 584.
6. *Ibid.,* p. 631.
7. Fowler V. Harper and Fleming James, Jr., *The Law of Torts* (Boston: Little, Brown and Co., 1956), Vol. I, p. 416. The authors do not endorse this view.
8. *Ibid.*
9. William Blackstone, *Commentaries on the Laws of England,* Vol. III, 1765 Reprint (Boston: Beacon Press, 1962), p. 125.

10. Prosser, *op. cit.,* p. 644.
11. Harper and James, *op. cit.,* p. 680.
12. Prosser, *op. cit.,* p. 642.
13. *Loc. cit.*
14. American Law Institute, *Restatement of the Law of Torts* (St. Paul, 1934) § 867, comment c.
15. Prosser, *op. cit.,* p. 644.
16. "There are two aspects of the interest in seclusion. First, the interest in preventing others from seeing and hearing what one does and says. Second, *the interest in avoiding seeing and hearing what other people do and say....* It may be as distasteful to suffer the intrusions of a garrulous and unwelcome guest as to discover an eavesdropper or peeper." Harper and James, *op. cit.,* p. 681. (Emphasis added.)
17. Schenck v. United States, 249 U.S. 47 (1919).
18. Chafee, *op. cit.,* pp. 152, 161, 426. cf. Terminiello v. Chicago 337 U.S. 1, (1949).
19. Chafee, *op. cit.,* p. 426.
20. *Ibid.,* p. 161.
21. Toler v. State, 152 Tenn. 1, 13, 260 S.W. 134 (1923).
22. Mill, *op. cit.,* pp. 67–8.
23. Chafee, *op. cit.,* p. 397.
24. For a more detailed exposition of this view see my "Causing Voluntary Actions" in *Doing and Deserving* (Princeton, N.J.: Princeton University Press, 1970), p. 152.
25. Chafee, *op. cit.,* p. 149.
26. In the words of the great common law judge, William Murray, First Earl of Mansfield, "The Greater the Truth, the Greater the Libel," hence Robert Burns's playful lines in his poem, "The Reproof":
        "Dost not know that old Mansfield
          Who writes like the Bible,
        Says the more 'tis a truth, sir,
          The more 'tis a libel?"
27. Chafee, *op. cit.,* pp. 18–22.
28. *Ibid.,* p. 506.
29. Such things, however, as patriotic sensibilities are capable of being highly *offended* by certain kinds of language. The rationale of sedition laws, therefore, may very well derive from the "offense-principle," which warrants prohibition of offensive behavior even when it is (otherwise) harmless.
30. Chafee, *op. cit.,* p. 24.
31. *Ibid.,* p. 175.
32. In which case the newspaper too would be criminally responsible for publishing the letter.
33. Lee v. Commonwealth, 144 Va. 594, 599, 131 S.E. 212, 214 (1926) as quoted in Rollin M. Perkins, *Criminal Law* (Brooklyn Foundation Press, 1957), p. 482.

LOUIS B. SCHWARTZ

Morals Offenses and the Model Penal Code*

What are the "offenses against morals"? One thinks first of the sexual offenses, adultery, fornication, sodomy, incest, and prostitution, and then, by easy extension, of such sex-related offenses as bigamy, abortion, open lewdness, and obscenity. But if one pauses to reflect on what sets these apart from offenses "against the person," or "against property," or "against public administration," it becomes evident that sexual offenses do not involve violation of moral principles in any peculiar sense. Virtually the entire penal code expresses the community's ideas of morality, or at least of the most egregious immoralities. To steal, to kill, to swear falsely in legal proceedings —these are certainly condemned as much by moral and religious as by secular standards. It also becomes evident that not all sexual behavior commonly condemned by prevailing American penal laws can be subsumed under universal moral precepts. This is certainly the case as to laws regulating contraception and abortion. But it is also true of such relatively uncontroversial (in the Western World) "morals" offenses as bigamy and polygamy; plural marriage arrangements approved by great religions of the majority of mankind can hardly be condemned out-of-hand as "immoralities."

What truly distinguishes the offenses commonly thought of as "against morals" is not their relation to morality but the absence of ordinary justification for punishment by a nontheocratic state. The ordinary justification for secular penal controls is preservation of public order. The king's peace must not be disturbed, or, to put the matter in the language of our time, public security must be preserved. Individuals must be able to go about their lawful pursuits without fear of attack, plunder, or other harm. This is an interest that only organized law enforcement can effectively safeguard. If individuals had to protect themselves by restricting their movements to avoid dangerous persons or neighborhoods, or by restricting their investments for fear of violent dispossession, or by employing personal bodyguards and armed private police, the economy would suffer, the body politic would be rent by conflict of private armies, and men would still walk in fear.

No such results impend from the commission of "morals offenses." One has only to stroll along certain streets in Amsterdam to see that prostitution may be permitted to flourish openly without impairing personal security, economic prosperity, or indeed the general moral tone of a most respected nation of the Western World. Tangible interests are not threatened by a neighbor's rash decision to marry two wives or (to vary the case for readers who may see this as economic suicide) by a lady's decision to be supported by two husbands, assuming that the arrangement is by agreement of all parties directly involved. An obscene show, the predilection of two deviate males for each other, or the marriage of first cousins— all these leave nonparticipants perfectly free to pursue their own goals without fear or obstacle. The same can be said of certain nonsexual offenses, which I shall accordingly treat in this paper as "morals offenses": cruelty to animals, desecration of a flag or other generally venerated symbol, and mistreatment of a human corpse. What the dominant lawmaking groups appear to be seeking by means of morals legislation is not security and freedom in their own affairs but restraint of conduct by others that is regarded as offensive.

Accordingly, Professor Louis Henkin has suggested[1] that morals legislation may contravene constitutional provisions designed to protect liberty, especially the liberty to do as one pleases without legal constraints based solely on religious beliefs. There is wisdom in his warning, and it is the purpose of this article to review in the light of that warning some of the Model Penal Code[2] sections that venture into the difficult area of morals legislation. Preliminarily, I offer some

*From *Columbia Law Review,* Vol. 63, p. 669 (1963). Reprinted by permission of the author and the publisher.

general observations on the point of view that necessarily governed the American Law Institute as a group of would-be lawmakers. We were sensitive, I hope, to the supreme value of individual liberty, but aware also that neither legislatures nor courts will soon accept a radical change in the boundary between permissible social controls and constitutionally protected nonconformity.

I. CONSIDERATIONS IN APPRAISING MORALS LEGISLATION

The first proposition I would emphasize is that a statute appearing to express nothing but religious or moral ideas is often defensible on secular grounds.[3] Perhaps an unrestricted flow of obscenity *will* encourage illicit sexuality or violent assaults on women, as some proponents of the ban believe. Perhaps polygamy and polyandry as well as adultery are condemnable on Benthamite grounds. Perhaps tolerance of homosexuality *will* undermine the courage and discipline of our citizen militia, notwithstanding contrary indications drawn from the history of ancient Greece. The evidence is hopelessly inconclusive. Professor Henkin and I may believe that those who legislate morals are minding other people's business, not their own, but the great majority of people believe that morals of "bad" people do, at least in the long run, threaten the security of the "good" people. Thus, *they* believe that it is their own business they are minding. And that belief is not demonstrably false, any more than it is demonstrably true. It is hard to deny people the right to legislate on the basis of their beliefs not demonstrably erroneous, especially if these beliefs are strongly held by a very large majority. The majority cannot be expected to abandon a credo and its associated sensitivities, however irrational, in deference to a minority's skepticism.

The argument of the preceding paragraph does not mean that all laws designed to enforce morality are acceptable or constitutionally valid if enough people entertain a baseless belief in their social utility. The point is rather that recognizing irrational elements in the controversy over morals legislation, we ought to focus on other elements, about which rational debate and agreement are possible. For example, one can examine side effects of the effort to enforce morality by penal law. One can inquire whether enforcement will be so difficult that the offense will seldom be prosecuted and, therefore, risk of punishment will not in fact operate as a deterrent. One can ask whether the rare prosecutions for sexual derelictions are arbitrarily selected, or facilitate private blackmail or police discriminations more often than general compliance with legal norms. Are police forces, prosecution resources, and court time being wastefully diverted from the central insecurities of our metropolitan life—robbery, burglary, rape, assault, and governmental corruption?

A second proposition that must be considered in appraising morals legislation is that citizens may legitimately demand of the state protection of their psychological as well as their physical integrity. No one challenges this when the protection takes the form of penal laws guarding against fear caused by threat or menace. This is probably because these are regarded as incipient physical attacks. Criminal libel laws are clearly designed to protect against psychic pain;[4] so also are disorderly conduct laws insofar as they ban loud noises, offensive odors, and tumultuous behavior disturbing the peace. In fact, laws against murder, rape, arson, robbery, burglary, and other violent felonies afford not so much protection against direct attack—that can be done only by self-defense or by having a policeman on hand at the scene of the crime—as psychological security and comfort stemming from the knowledge that the probabilities of attack are lessened by the prospect of punishment and, perhaps, from the knowledge that an attacker will be condignly treated by society.

If, then, penal law frequently or typically protects us from psychic aggression, there is basis for the popular expectation that it will protect us also from blasphemy against a cherished religion, outrage to patriotic sentiments, blatant pornography, open lewdness affronting our sensibilities in the area of sexual mores, or stinging aspersions against race or nationality. Psychiatrists might tell us that the insecurities stirred by these psychic aggressions are deeper and more acute than those involved in crimes of physical violence. Physical violence is, after all, a phenomenon that occurs largely in the domain of the ego; we can rationally measure the danger and its likelihood, and our countermeasures can be proportioned to the threat. But who can measure the dark turbulences of the unconscious when sex, race, religion or patriotism (that extension of father-reverence) is the concern?

If unanimity of strongly held moral views is approached in a community, the rebel puts himself, as it were, outside the society when he arraigns himself against those views. Society owes debt to martyrs, madmen, criminals, and professors who occasionally call into question its fundamental assumptions, but the community cannot be expected to make their first protests respectable or even tolerated by law. It is entirely understandable and in a sense proper that blasphemy should have been criminal in Puritan Massachusetts, and that cow slaughter in a Hindu state, hog-raising in a theocratic Jewish or Moslem state, or abortion in a ninety-nine per cent Catholic state should be criminal. I do not mean to suggest a particular percentage test of substantial unanimity. It is rather a matter of when an ancient and unquestioned tenet has become seriously debatable in a given community. This may happen when it is discovered that a substantial, although inarticulate, segment of the population has drifted away from the old belief. It may happen when smaller numbers of articulate opinion-makers launch an open attack on the old ethic. When this kind of a beach-head has been established in the hostile country of traditional faith, then, and only then, can we expect constitutional principles to restrain the fifty-one per cent majority from suppressing the public flouting of deeply held moral views.

Some may find in all this an encouragement or approval of excessive conservatism. Societies, it seems, are by this argument morally entitled to use force to hold back the development of new ways of thought. I do not mean it so. Rather, I see this tendency to enforce old moralities as an inherent characteristic of organized societies, and I refrain from making moral judgments on group behavior that I regard as inevitable. If I must make a moral judgment, it is in favor of the individual visionaries who are willing to pay the personal cost to challenge the old moral order. There is a morality in some lawbreaking, even when we cannot condemn the law itself as immoral, for it enables conservative societies to begin the re-examination of even the most cherished principles.

Needless to say, recognizing the legitimacy of the demand for protection against psychic discomfort does not imply indiscriminate approval of laws intended to give such protection. Giving full recognition to that demand, we may still find that other considerations are the controlling ones. Can we satisfy the demand without impairing other vital interests? How can we protect religious feelings without "establishing" religion or impairing the free exercise of proselytizing faiths? How can we protect racial sensibilities without exacerbating race hatreds and erecting a government censorship of discussion?[5] How shall we prevent pain and disgust to many who are deeply offended by portrayal of sensuality without stultifying our artists and writers?

A third aspect of morals legislation that will enter into the calculations of the rational legislator is that some protection against offensive immorality may be achieved as a by-product of legislation that aims directly at something other than immorality. We may be uneasy about attempting to regulate private sexual behavior, but we will not be so hesitant in prohibiting the commercialization of vice. This is a lesser intrusion on freedom of choice in personal relations. It presents a more realistic target for police activity. And conceptually such regulation presents itself as a ban on a form of economic activity rather than a regulation of morals. It is not the least of the advantages of this approach that it preserves to some extent the communal disapproval of illicit sexuality, thus partially satisfying those who would really prefer outright regulation of morality. So also, we may be reluctant to penalize blasphemy or sacrilege, but feel compelled to penalize the mischievous or zealous blasphemer who purposely disrupts a religious meeting or procession with utterances designed to outrage the sensibilities of the group and thus provoke a riot.[6] Reasonable rules for the maintenance of public peace incidentally afford a measure of protection against offensive irreligion. Qualms about public "establishment" of religion must yield to the fact that the alternative would be to permit a kind of violent private interference with freedom to conduct religious ceremonies.

It remains to apply the foregoing analysis to selected provisions of the Model Penal Code.

II. THE MODEL PENAL CODE APPROACH

A. FLAGRANT AFFRONTS AND PENALIZATION OF PRIVATE IMMORALITY

The Model Penal Code does not penalize the sexual sins, fornication, adultery, sodomy or other illicit sexual activity not involving violence or imposition upon children, mental incompetents, wards, or other dependents. This decision to keep penal law out of the area of private sexual relations approaches Professor Henkin's suggestion that private morality be immune from secular regulation. The Comments in Tentative Draft No. 4 declared:

The Code does not attempt to use the power of the state to enforce purely moral or religious standards. We deem it inappropriate for the government to attempt to control behavior that has no substantial significance except as to the morality of the actor. Such matters are best left to religious, educational and other social influences. Apart from the question of constitutionality which might be raised against legislation avowedly commanding adherence to a particular religious or moral tenet, it must be recognized, as a practical matter, that in a heterogeneous community such as ours, different individuals and groups have widely divergent views of the seriousness of various moral derelictions.[7]

Although this passage expresses doubt as to the constitutionality of state regulation of morals, it does so in a context of "widely divergent views of the seriousness of various moral derelictions." Thus, it does not exclude the use of penal sanctions to protect a "moral consensus" against flagrant breach. The Kinsey studies and others are cited to show that sexual derelictions are widespread and that the incidence of sexual dereliction varies among social groups. The Comments proceed to discuss various secular goals that might be served by penalizing illicit sexual relations, such as promoting the stability of marriage, preventing illegitimacy and disease, or forestalling private violence against seducers. The judgment is made that there is no reliable basis for believing that penal laws substantially contribute to these goals. Punishment of private vice is rejected on this ground as well as on grounds of difficulty of enforcement and the potential for blackmail and other abuse of rarely enforced criminal statutes.[8] The discussion with regard to homosexual offenses follows a similar course.[9]

The Code does, however, penalize "open lewdness"—"any lewd act which [the actor] . . . knows is likely to be observed by others who would be affronted or alarmed."[10] The idea that "flagrant affront to commonly held notions of morality" might have to be differentiated from other sorts of immorality appeared in the first discussions of the Institute's policy on sexual offenses, in connection with a draft that would have penalized "open and notorious" illicit relations.[11] Eventually, however, the decision was against establishing a penal offense in which guilt would depend on the level of gossip to which the moral transgression gave rise. Guilt under the open lewdness section turns on the likelihood that the lewd act itself will be observed by others who would be affronted.

Since the Code accepts the propriety of penalizing behavior that affects others only in flagrantly affronting commonly held notions of morality, the question arises whether such repression of offensive immorality need be confined to acts done in public where others may observe and be outraged. People may be deeply offended upon learning of private debauchery. The Code seems ready at times to protect against this type of "psychological assault," at other times not. Section 250.10 penalizes mistreatment of a corpse "in a way that [the actor] . . . knows would outrage ordinary family sensibilities," although the actor may have taken every precaution for secrecy. Section 250.11 penalizes cruel treatment of an animal in private as well as in public. On the other hand, desecration of the national flag or other object of public veneration, an offense under section 250.9, is not committed unless others are likely to "observe or discover." And solicitation of deviate sexual relations is penalized only when the actor "loiters in or near any public place" for the purpose of such solicitation.[12] The Comments make it clear that the target of this legislation is not private immorality but a kind of public "nuisance" caused by congregation of homosexuals offensively flaunting their deviance from general norms of behavior.[13]

As I search for the principle of discrimination between the morals offenses made punishable only when committed openly and those punishable even when committed in secrecy, I find nothing but differences in the intensity of the aversion with which the different kinds of behavior are regarded. It was the intuition of the draftsman and his fellow lawmakers in the Institute that disrespectful behavior to a corpse and cruelty to animals were more intolerable affronts to ordinary feelings than disrespectful behavior to a flag. Therefore, in the former cases, but not the latter, we overcame our general reluctance to extend penal controls of immorality to private behavior that disquiets people soley because they learn that things of this sort are going on.

Other possible explanations do not satisfy me. For example, it explains nothing to say that we wish to "protect" the corpse or the mistreated dog, but not the flag itself. The legislation on its face seeks to deter mistreatment of all three. All three cases involve interests beyond, and merely represented by, the thing that is immediately "protected." It is not the mistreated dog who is the ultimate object of concern; his owner is entirely free to kill him (though not "cruelly") without interference from other dog owners. Our concern is for the feelings of other human beings, a large proportion of whom, although accustomed to the slaughter of animals for food, readily identify themselves with a tortured dog or horse and respond with great sensitivity to its sufferings. The desire to protect a corpse from degradation is not a deference to this remnant of a human being—the dead have no legal rights and no legislative lobby—but a protection of the feelings of the living. So also in the case of the flag, our concern is not for the bright bit of cloth but for what it symbolizes, a cluster of patriotic emotions. I submit that legislative tolerance for private flag desecration is explicable by the greater difficulty an ordinary man has in identifying with a country and all else that a flag symbolizes as compared with the ease in identifying with a corpse or a warm-blooded domestic animal. This is only an elaborate way of saying that he does not feel the first desecration as keenly as the others. Perhaps also, in the case of the flag, an element of tolerance is present for the right of political dissent when it goes no further than private disrespect for the symbol of authority.[14]

A penal code's treatment of private homosexual relations presents the crucial test of a legislator's views on whether a state may legimately protect people from "psychological assault" by repressing not merely overt affront to consensus morals but also the most secret violation of that moral code. As is often wise in legislative affairs, the Model Penal Code avoids a clear issue of principle. The decision against penalizing deviate sexuality is rested not merely on the idea of immunity from regulation of private morality, but on a consideration of practical difficulties and evils in attempting to use the penal law in this way.[15] The Comments note that existing laws dealing with homosexual relations are nullified in practice, except in cases of violence, corruption of children, or public solicitation. Capricious selection of a few cases for prosecution, among millions of infractions, is unfair and chiefly benefits extortioners and seekers of private vengeance. The existence of the criminal law prevents some deviates from seeking psychiatric aid. Furthermore, the pursuit of homosexuals involves policemen in degrading entrapment practices, and diverts attention and effort that could be employed more usefully against the crimes of violent aggression, fraud, and government corruption, which are the overriding concerns of our metropolitan civilization.

If state legislators are not persuaded by such arguments to repeal the laws against private deviate sexual relations among adults, the constitutional issue will ultimately have to be faced by the courts. When that time comes, one of the impor-

tant questions will be whether homosexuality is in fact the subject of a "consensus." If not, that is, if a substantial body of public opinion regards homosexuals' private activity with indifference, or if homosexuals succeed in securing recognition as a considerable minority having otherwise "respectable" status, this issue of private morality may soon be held to be beyond resolution by vote of fifty-one per cent of the legislators.[16] As to the status of homosexuality in this country, it is significant that the Supreme Court has reversed an obscenity conviction involving a magazine that was avowedly published by, for, and about homosexuals and that carried on a ceaseless campaign against the repressive laws.[17] The much smaller group of American polygamists have yet to break out of the class of idiosyncratic heretic-martyrs[18] by bidding for public approval in the same group-conscious way.

B. THE OBSCENITY PROVISIONS

The obscenity provisions of the Model Penal Code best illustrate the Code's preference for an oblique approach to morals offenses, that is, the effort to express the moral impulses of the community in a penal prohibition that is nevertheless pointed at and limited to something else than sin. In this case the target is not the "sin of obscenity," but primarily a disapproved form of economic activity—commercial exploitation of the widespread weakness for titillation by pornography. This is apparent not only from the narrow definition of "obscene" in section 251.4 of the Code, but even more from the narrow definition of the forbidden behavior; only sale, advertising, or public exhibition are forbidden, and noncommercial dissemination within a restricted circle of personal associates is expressly exempt.[19]

Section 251.4 defines obscenity as material whose "predominant appeal is to prurient interest. . . ."[20] The emphasis is on the "appeal" of the material, rather than on its "effect," an emphasis designed explicitly to reject prevailing definitions of obscenity that stress the "effect."[21] This effect is traditionally identified as a tendency to cause "sexually impure and lustful thoughts" or to "corrupt or deprave."[22] The Comments on section 251.4 take the position that repression of sexual thoughts and desires is not a practicable or legitimate legislative goal. Too many instigations to sexual desire exist in a society like ours, which approves much eroticism in literature, movies, and advertising, to suppose that any conceivable repression of pornography would substantially diminish the volume of such impulses. Moreover, "thoughts and desires not manifested in overt antisocial behavior are generally regarded as the exclusive concern of the individual and his spiritual advisors."[23] The Comments, rejecting also the test of tendency to corrupt or deprave, point out that corruption or depravity are attributes of character inappropriate for secular punishment when they do not lead to misconduct, and there is a paucity of evidence linking obscenity to misbehavior.[24]

The meretricious "appeal" of a book or picture is essentially a question of the attractiveness of the merchandise from a certain point of view: what makes it sell. Thus, the prohibition of obscenity takes on an aspect of regulation of unfair business or competitive practices. Just as merchants may be prohibited from selling their wares by appeal to the public's weakness for gambling,[25] so they may be restrained from purveying books, movies, or other commercial exhibition by exploiting the well-nigh universal weakness for a look behind the curtain of modesty. This same philosophy of obscenity control is evidenced by the Code provision outlawing advertising appeals that attempt to sell material "whether or not obscene, by representing or suggesting that it is obscene."[26] Moreover, the requirement under section 251.4 that the material go "substantially beyond customary limits of candor" serves to exclude from criminality the sorts of appeal to eroticism that, being prevalent, can hardly give a particular purveyor a commercial advantage.

It is important to recognize that material may predominantly "appeal" to prurient interest notwithstanding that ordinary adults may actually respond to the material with feelings of aversion or disgust. Section 251.4 explicitly encompasses material dealing with excretory functions as well as sex, which the customer is likely to find *both* repugnant and "shameful" and yet attractive in a morbid, compelling way. Not recognizing that material may be repellent and appealing at the same time, two distinguished commentators on the Code's obscenity provisions have criticized the "appeal" formula, asserting that "hard core pronography," concededly the main category we are trying to repress, has no appeal for "ordinary adults," who instead would be merely repelled by the material.[27] Common experience suggests the contrary. It is well known that policemen, lawyers, and judges involved in obscenity cases not infrequently regale their fellows with viewings of the criminal material. Moreover, a poll conducted by this author among his fellow law professors—"mature" and, for the present purposes, "ordinary" adults—evoked uniformly affirmative answers to the following question: "Would you look inside a book that you had been certainly informed has grossly obscene hard-core pornography if you were absolutely sure that no one else would ever learn that you had looked?" It is not an answer to this bit of amateur sociological research to say that people would look "out of curiosity." It is precisely such shameful curiosity to which "appeal" is made by the obscene, as the word "appeal" is used in section 251.4.

Lockhart and McClure, the two commentators referred to above, prefer a "variable obscenity" concept over the Institute's "constant obscenity" concept. Under the "constant obscenity" concept, material is normally judged by reference to "ordinary adults."[28] The "variable obscenity" concept always takes account of the nature of the comtemplated audience; material would be obscene if it is "primarily directed to an audience of the sexually immature for the purpose of satisfying their craving for erotic fantasy."[29] The preference for "variable obscenity" rests not only on the mistaken view that hard-core pornography does not appeal to ordinary adults, but also on the ground that this concept facilitates the accomplishment of several ancillary legislative goals, namely, exempting transactions in "obscene" materials by persons with scholarly, scientific, or other legitimate interests in the obscene and prohibiting the advertising of material "not intrinsically pornographic as if it were hard-core pornography."[30] The Code accomplishes these results by explicit exemption for justifiable transactions in the obscene and by specific prohibition of suggestive advertising.[31] This still seems to me the better way to draft a criminal statute.

The Code's exemption for justifiable dealing in obscene material provides a workable criterion of public gain in permitting defined categories of transactions. It requires no analysis of the psyche of customers to see whether they are sexually immature or given to unusual craving for erotic fantasy. It makes no impractical demand on the sophistication of policemen, magistrates, customs officers, or jurymen. The semantics of the variable obscenity concept assumes without basis that the Kinsey researchers were immune to the prurient appeal of the materials with which they worked.[32] Would it not be a safe psychiatric guess that some persons are drawn into research of this sort precisely to satisfy in a socially approved way the craving that Lockhart and McClure deplore? In any event, it seems a confusing distortion of language to say that a porno- graphic picture is not obscene as respects the blasé [sexually mature?] shopkeeper who stocks it, the policeman who confiscates it, or the Model Penal Code reporter who appraises it.

As for the prohibition against suggestive adver- tising, this is certainly handled more effectively by explicitly declaring the advertisement criminal without regard to the "obscene" character of the material advertised than by the circumlocution that an advertisement is itself to be regarded as obscene if it appeals to the cravings of the sexu- ally immature. That kind of test will prove more than a little troublesome for the advertising de- partments of some respectable literary journals.

If the gist of section 251.4 is, as suggested above, commercial exploitation of the weakness for obscenity, the question arises whether the definition of the offense should not be formulated in terms of "pandering to an interest in ob- scenity," that is, "exploiting such an interest pri- marily for pecuniary gain. . . . "[33] This proposal, made by Professor Henry Hart, a member of the Criminal Law Advisory Committee, was rejected because of the indefiniteness of "exploiting . . . primarily for pecuniary gain," and because it would clearly authorize a bookseller, for exam- ple, to procure any sort of hard-core pornography upon the unsolicited order of a customer. "Ex- ploiting . . . primarily for pecuniary gain" is not a formula apt for guiding either judicial interpre- tation or merchants' behavior. It is not clear what the prosecution would have to prove beyond sale of the objectionable item. Would advertising or an excessive profit convert sale into "exploita- tion"? Would the formula leave a bookseller free to enjoy a gradually expanding trade in obscenity so long as he kept his merchandise discreetly un- der the counter and let word-of-mouth publicize the availability of his tidbits? Despite these diffi- culties, it may well be that the Code section on obscenity has a constitutional infirmity of the sort that concerned Professor Henkin insofar as the section restricts the freedom of an adult to buy, and thus to read, whatever he pleases. This prob- lem might be met by framing an appropriate ex- emption for such transactions to be added to those now set forth in subsection (3).

The rejection of the Hart "pandering" formu- lation highlights another aspect of section 251.4, namely, its applicability to a class of completely noncommercial transactions that could not con- ceivably be regarded as "pandering." This ban on certain noncommercial disseminations results from the fact that subsection (2) forbids every

dissemination except those exempted by subsec- tion (3), and subsection (3) exempts noncommer- cial dissemination only if it is limited to "personal associates of the actor." Thus, a general distribu- tion or exhibition of obscenity is prohibited even though no one is making money from it: a zealot for sex education may not give away pamphlets at the schoolyard gates containing illustrations of people engaged in erotic practices; a rich homo- sexual may not use a billboard on Times Square to promulgate to the general populace the tech- niques and pleasures of sodomy. Plainly, this is not the economic regulation to which I have pre- viously tried to assimilate the Code's anti- obscenity regulations. But equally, it is not merely sin-control of the sort that evoked Profes- sor Henkin's constitutional doubts. Instead, the community is merely saying: "Sin, if you must, in private. Do not flaunt your immoralities where they will grieve and shock others. If we do not impose our morals upon you, neither must you impose yours upon us, undermining the restraints we seek to cultivate through family, church, and school." The interest being protected is not, di- rectly or exclusively, the souls of those who might be depraved or corrupted by the obscenity, but the right of parents to shape the moral notions of their children, and the right of the general public not to be subjected to violent psychological affront.

C. PROSTITUTION

The prostitution provisions of the Model Penal Code, like the obscenity provisions, reflect the policy of penalizing not sin but commercial ex- ploitation of a human weakness, or serious affront to public sensibilities. The salient features of sec- tion 251.2 are as follows. Sexual activity is penal- ized only when carried on as a business or for hire. The section covers any form of sexual grati- fication. "Promoters" of prostitution—that is, procurers, pimps, keepers of houses of prostitu- tion—are penalized more severely than the pros- titutes. The patron of the prostitute is subject to prosecution for a "violation" only, that is, he may be fined but not jailed, and the offense is, by defi- nition, not a "crime." Dependents of a prostitute are not declared to be criminals by virtue of the fact that they live off the proceeds of prostitution, as under many present laws, but the circumstance of being supported by a prostitute is made pre- sumptive evidence that the person supported is engaged in pimping or some other form of com- mercial exploitation of prostitution.

The main issues in the evolution of the Institute's position on prostitution were, on the one hand, whether to penalize all "promiscuous" intercourse even if not for hire or, on the other hand, whether even intercourse for hire should be immune from prosecution when it is carried on discreetly out of the public view. Those who favored extending the criminal law to promiscuous noncommercial sexuality did so on secular, not moral, grounds. They pointed to the danger that promiscuous amateurs would be carriers of venereal disease, and they argued that law enforcement against hire-prostitution would be facilitated if the law, proceeding on the basis that most promiscuity is accompanied by hire, dispensed with proof of actual hire. Others doubted the utility or propriety of the law's intervening in private sexual relations on the basis of a vague and moralistic judgment of promiscuity; and these doubts prevailed.

It was more strenuously contended that the Model Penal Code should, following the English pattern, penalize prostitution only when it manifests itself in annoying public solicitation.[34] This position was defeated principally by the argument that "call-houses" were an important cog in the financial machine of the underworld, linked to narcotics peddling and other "rackets." I find more interesting and persuasive the parallel between this problem of the discreet exploitation of sex and the suggestion in the obscenity and context that discreet sale of obscene books to patrons who request them might not constitute "pandering." Both distinctions present the difficulty of drawing an administrable line between aggressive merchandising and passive willingness to make profits by catering to a taste for spicy life or literature.

Other provisions of section 251.2 also demonstrate its basic orientation against undesirable commerce rather than sin. The grading of offenses under the section ranges from the classification of the patron's guilt as a noncriminal "violation," through the "petty misdemeanor" classification (thirty-day maximum imprisonment) for the prostitute herself, and the "misdemeanor" classification (one year maximum) for minor participation in the promotion of prostitution, to the "third degree felony" classification (five year maximum) for owning or managing a prostitution business, bringing about an association between a prostitute and a house of prostitution, or recruiting persons into prostitution. Clearly, from the point of view of the sinfulness of illicit sexual relations, the patron's guilt is equal to that of the prostitute, but it is the seller

rather than the sinful customer who is labelled a criminal. And the higher the rank in the selling organization, the graver the penalty—a significant departure from the normal assimilation of accessorial guilt to that of the principal offender. This emphasis on the businessman in sex is underscored by the fact that the higher penalties applicable to him do not depend on whether he is the instigator of the relationship; if a prostitute persuades someone to manage her illicit business or to accept her in a house of prostitution, it is he, not she, who incurs the higher penalty.

In one respect, the Code's provisions against illicit sexual activity depart from the regulation of commerce. Section 251.3 makes it a petty misdemeanor to loiter "in or near any public place for the purpose of soliciting or being solicited to engage in deviate sexual relations." This extension is explained as follows in the accompanying status note:

[T]he main objective is to suppress the open flouting of prevailing moral standards as a sort of nuisance in public thoroughfares and parks. In the case of females, suppression of professionals is likely to accomplish that objective. In the case of males, there is a greater likelihood that non-professional homosexuals will congregate and behave in a manner grossly offensive to other users of public facilities.[35]

The situation is analogous to that of noncommercial dissemination of obscenity by billboard publication or indiscriminate gratuitous distribution of pornography. In a community in which assemblages of "available" women evoke the same degree of violent resentment as assemblages of homosexuals, it would be consistent with this analysis to make public loitering to solicit illicit heterosexual relations an offense regardless of proof of "hire." On the other hand, the legislator may well decide that even in such a community it is not worth risking the possibility of arbitrary police intrusion into dance halls, taverns, corner drug stores, and similar resorts of unattached adolescents, on suspicion that some of the girls are promiscuous, though not prostitutes in the hire sense . . .

NOTES

1. See Henkin, *Morals and the Constitution: The Sin of Obscenity,* 63 Colum. L. Rev. 391 (1963), to which the present article is a companion piece. Controversy on the role of the state in the enforcement of morals has recently reached a new pitch of intensity. See Hart, *Law, Liberty, and Morality* (1963); Devlin, *The Enforcement of Morals* (1959); Devlin, *Law, Democracy, and Morality,* 110 U. Pa. L. Rev. 635

(1962). I shall not attempt to judge this debate, cf. Rostow, the Sovereign Prerogative 45–80 (1962), and I leave it to others to align the present essay with one or another of the sides. The recent controversy traverses much the same ground as was surveyed in the nineteenth century. See Mill *On Liberty* (1859); Stephen, *Liberty, Equality, Fraternity* (1873).

2. The Model Penal Code is hereinafter cited as MPC. Unless otherwise indicated, all citations are to the 1962 Official Draft.

3. See McGowan v. Maryland, 366 U.S. 420 (1961). The Supreme Court upheld the constitutionality of a law requiring business establishments to close on Sunday, on the ground that such regulation serves the secular goal of providing a common day of rest and recreation, notwithstanding that the statute proscribed profanation of "the Lord's day."

4. The Model Penal Code does not make libel a criminal offense. But this decision rests upon a judgment that the penal law is not a useful or safe instrument for repressing defamation; by no means is it suggested that the hurt experienced by one who is libelled is an inappropriate concern of government. See MPC § 250.7, comment 2 (Tent. Draft No. 13, 1961).

5. See MPC § 250.7 & comments 1–4 (Tent. Draft No. 13, 1961) ("Fomenting Group Hatred"). The section was not included in the Official Draft of 1962.

6. See MPC §§ 250.8, 250.3 & comment (Tent. Draft No. 13, 1961).

7. MPC § 207.1, comment at 207 (Tent. Draft No. 4, 1955).

8. MPC § 207.1, comment at 205–10 (Tent. Draft No. 4, 1955).

9. MPC § 207.5, comment at 278–79 (Tent. Draft NO. 4, 1955). "No harm to the secular interests of the community is involved in atypical sex practice in private between consenting adult partners. This area of private morals is the distinctive concern of spiritual authorities. . . . [T]here is the fundamental question of the protection to which every individual is entitled against state interference in his personal affairs when he is not hurting others." MPC § 207.5, comment at 277–78 (Tent. Draft No. 4, 1955).

10. MPC § 251.1; *cf.* MPC § 213.5, which penalizes exposure of the genitals for the purpose of arousing or gratifying sexual desire in circumstances likely to cause affront or alarm. This later offense carries a heavier penalty than open lewdness, "since the behavior amounts to, or at least is often taken as, threatening sexual aggression." MPC § 213.4 & 251.1, comment at 82 (Tent. Draft No. 13, 1961).

11. MPC § 207.1 & comment at 209 (Tent. Draft No. 4, 1955).

12. MPC § 251.3; see text accompanying note 35 *infra.*

13. MPC § 251.3, status note at 237.

14. Not all legislatures are so restrained. See, e.g., Pa. Stat. Ann. tit. 18, § 4211 (1945) ("publicly or privately mutilates, defaces, defiles or tramples upon, or casts contempt either by words or act upon, any such flag"). Query as to the constitutionality of this effort to repress a private expression of political disaffection.

15. MPC § 207.5, comment 278–79 (Tent. Draft No. 4, 1955).

16. *Cf.* Robinson v. California, 371 U.S. 905 (1962) (invalidating statute that penalized addiction to narcotics).

17. One, Inc. v. Oleson, 355 U.S. 371 (1958), *reversing*

241 F.2d 772 (9th Cir. 1957). On the "homosexual community" see Helmer, *New York's "Middle-class" Homosexuals,* Harper's, March 1963, p. 85 (evidencing current nonshocked attitude toward this minority group).

18. See Cleveland v. United States, 329 U.S. 14 (1946); Reynolds v. United States, 98 U.S. 145 (1878).

19. MPC § 251.4(2), (3).

20. (1) *Obscene Defined.* Material is obscene if, considered as a whole, its predominant appeal is to prurient interest, that is, a shameful or morbid interest, in nudity, sex or excretion, and if in addition it goes substantially beyond customary limits of candor in describing or representing such matters. Predominant appeal shall be judged with reference to ordinary adults unless it appears from the character of the material or the circumstances of its dissemination to be designed for children or other specially susceptible audience. . . . MPC § 251.4(1).

21. See MPC § 207.10, comment 6 at 19, 29 (Tent. Draft No. 6, 1957) (§ 207.10 was subsequently renumbered § 251.4).

22. See MPC § 207.10, comment 6 at 19 n.21, 21 (Tent. Draft No. 6, 1957).

23. MPC § 207.10, comment 6 at 20 (Tent. Draft No. 6, 1957).

24. MPC § 207.10, comment 6 at 22–28 (Tent. Draft No. 6, 1957).

25. See FTC v. R. F. Keppel & Brother, 291 U.S. 304 (1934) (sale of penny candy by device of awarding prizes to lucky purchasers of some pieces). The opinion of the Court declares that Section 5 of the Federal Trade Commission Act, proscribing unfair methods of competition, "does not authorize business men," *ibid.,* p. 313, but that the Commission may prevent exploitation of consumers by the enticement of gambling, as well as imposition upon competitors by use of a morally obnoxious selling appeal.

26. MPC § 251.4(2)(e). Equivalent provisions appear in some state laws. E.g., N.Y. Pen. Law § 1141. There is some doubt whether federal obscenity laws reach such advertising. See Manual Enterprises, Inc. v. Day, 370 U.S. 478. 491 (1962). *But see* United States v. Hornick, 229 F.2d 120, 121 (3d Cir. 1956).

27. See Lockhart & McClure, *Censorship of Obscenity: The Developing Constitutional Standards,* 45 Minn. L. Rev. 72–73 (1960).

28. The Model Penal Code employs the "variable obscenity" concept in part, since § 251.4(1) provides that "appeal" shall be judged with reference to the susceptibilities of children or other specially susceptible audience when it appears that the material is designed for or directed to such an audience.

29. Lockhart & McClure, *supra* note 27, at 79.

30. *Ibid.*

31. MPC § 251.4(2)(e), (3)(a).

32. *Cf.* United States v. 31 Photographs, 156 F. Supp. 350 (S.D.N.Y. 1957), in which, absent a statutory exemption, the court was compelled to rely on variable obscenity in order to sanction import of obscene pictures by the [Kinsey] Institute for Sex Research.

33. MPC § 207.10(1) (Tent. Draft No. 6, 1957) (alternative).

34. See Street Offenses Act, 1959, 7 & 8 Eliz. 2, c. 57.

COHEN V. CALIFORNIA

U.S. Supreme Court, 1971*

OPINION OF THE COURT

Mr. Justice Harlan delivered the opinion of the Court.

This case may seem at first blush too inconsequential to find its way into our books, but the issue it presents is of no small constitutional significance.

Appellant Paul Robert Cohen was convicted in the Los Angeles Municipal Court of violating that part of California Penal Code § 415 which prohibits "maliciously and willfully disturb[ing] the peace or quiet of any neighborhood or person . . . by . . . offensive conduct . . . "[1] He was given 30 days' imprisonment. The facts upon which his conviction rests are detailed in the opinion of the Court of Appeal of California, Second Appellate District, as follows:

"On April 26, 1968, the defendant was observed in the Los Angeles County Courthouse in the corridor outside of division 20 of the municipal court wearing a jacket bearing the words 'Fuck the Draft' which were plainly visible. There were women and children present in the corridor. The defendant was arrested. The defendant testified that he wore the jacket knowing that the words were on the jacket as a means of informing the public of the depth of his feelings against the Vietnam War and the draft.

"The defendant did not engage in, nor threaten to engage in, nor did anyone as the result of his conduct in fact commit or threaten to commit any act of violence. The defendant did not make any loud or unusual noise, nor was there any evidence that he uttered any sound prior to his arrest."*

In affirming the conviction the Court of Appeal held that "offensive conduct" means "behavior which has a tendency to provoke others to acts of violence or to in turn disturb the peace," and that the State had proved this element because, on the facts of this case, "[i]t was certainly reasonably foreseeable that such conduct might cause others to rise up to commit a violent act against the person of the defendant or attempt to forceably remove his jacket."* The California Supreme Court declined review by a divided vote. We brought

the case here, postponing the consideration of the question of our jurisdiction over this appeal to a hearing of the case on the merits.* We now reverse.

I

In order to lay hands on the precise issue which this case involves, it is useful first to canvass various matters which this record does *not* present.

The conviction quite clearly rests upon the asserted offensiveness of the *words* Cohen used to convey his message to the public. The only "conduct" which the State sought to punish is the fact of communication. Thus, we deal here with a conviction resting solely upon "speech",* not upon any separately identifiable conduct which allegedly was intended by Cohen to be perceived by others as expressive of particular views but which, on its face, does not necessarily convey any message and hence arguably could be regulated without effectively repressing Cohen's ability to express himself.* Further, the State certainly lacks power to punish Cohen for the underlying content of the message the inscription conveyed. At least so long as there is no showing of an intent to incite disobedience to or disruption of the draft, Cohen could not, consistently with the First and Fourteenth Amendments, be punished for asserting the evident position on the inutility or immorality of the draft his jacket reflected.*

Appellant's conviction, then, rests squarely upon his exercise of the "freedom of speech" protected from arbitrary governmental interference by the Constitution and can be justified, if at all, only as a valid regulation of the manner in which he exercised that freedom, not as a permissible prohibition on the substantive message it conveys. This does not end the inquiry, of course, for the First and Fourteenth Amendments have never been thought to give absolute protection to every individual to speak whenever or wherever he pleases, or to use any form of address in any circumstances that he chooses. In this vein, too, however, we think it important to note that several issues typically associated with such problems are not presented here.

In the first place, Cohen was tried under a statute applicable throughout the entire State. Any attempt to support this conviction on the ground that the statute

*408 U.S. 15 (1971). Some footnotes omitted.
*Citation omitted [Eds.]

seeks to preserve an appropriately decorous atmosphere in the courthouse where Cohen was arrested must fail in the absence of any language in the statute that would have put appellant on notice that certain kinds of otherwise permissible speech or conduct would nevertheless, under California law, not be tolerated in certain places.* No fair reading of the phrase "offensive conduct" can be said sufficiently to inform the ordinary person that distinctions between certain locations are thereby created.[2]

In the second place, as it comes to us, this case cannot be said to fall within those relatively few categories of instances where prior decisions have established the power of government to deal more comprehensively with certain forms of individual expression simply upon a showing that such a form was employed. This is not, for example, an obscenity case. Whatever else may be necessary to give rise to the States' broader power to prohibit obscene expression, such expression must be, in some significant way, erotic.* It cannot plausibly be maintained that this vulgar allusion to the Selective Service System would conjure up such psychic stimulation in anyone likely to be confronted with Cohen's crudely defaced jacket.

This Court has also held that the States are free to ban the simple use, without a demonstration of additional justifying circumstances, of so-called "fighting words," those personally abusive epithets which, when addressed to the ordinary citizen, are, as a matter of common knowledge, inherently likely to provoke violent reaction.* While the four-letter word displayed by Cohen in relation to the draft is not uncommonly employed in a personally provocative fashion, in this instance it was clearly not "directed to the person of the hearer."* No individual actually or likely to be present could reasonably have regarded the words on appellant's jacket as a direct personal insult. Nor do we have here an instance of the exercise of the State's police power to prevent a speaker from intentionally provoking a given group to hostile reaction.* There is, as noted above, no showing that anyone who saw Cohen was in fact violently aroused or that appellant intended such a result.

Finally, in arguments before this Court much has been made of the claim that Cohen's distasteful mode of expression was thrust upon unwilling or unsuspecting viewers, and that the State might therefore legitimately act as it did in order to protect the sensitive from otherwise unavoidable exposure to appellant's crude form of protest. Of course, the mere presumed presence of unwitting listeners or viewers does not serve automatically to justify curtailing all speech capable of giving offense.* While this Court has recognized that government may properly act in many situations to prohibit intrusion into the privacy of the home of unwelcome views and ideas which cannot be totally banned from the public dialogue,* we have at the same time consistently stressed that "we are often 'captives' outside the sanctuary of the home and subject to objectionable speech."* The ability of government, consonant with the Constitution, to shut off discourse solely to protect others from hearing it is, in other words, dependent upon a showing that substantial privacy interests are being invaded in an essentially intolerable manner. Any broader view of this authority would effectively empower a majority to silence dissidents simply as a matter of personal predilections.

In this regard, persons confronted with Cohen's jacket were in a quite different posture than, say, those subjected to the raucous emissions of sound trucks blaring outside their residences. Those in the Los Angeles courthouse could effectively avoid further bombardment of their sensibilities simply by averting their eyes. And, while it may be that one has a more substantial claim to a recognizable privacy interest when walking through a courthouse corridor than, for example, strolling through Central Park, surely it is nothing like the interest in being free from unwanted expression in the confines of one's own home.* Given the subtlety and complexity of the factors involved, if Cohen's "speech" was otherwise entitled to constitutional protection, we do not think the fact that some unwilling "listeners" in a public building may have been briefly exposed to it can serve to justify this breach of the peace conviction where, as here, there was no evidence that persons powerless to avoid appellant's conduct did in fact object to it, and where that portion of the statute upon which Cohen's conviction rests evinces no concern, either on its face or as construed by the California courts, with the special plight of the captive auditor, but, instead, indiscriminately sweeps within its prohibitions all "offensive conduct" that disturbs "any neighborhood or person."*

II

Against this background, the issue flushed by this case stands out in bold relief. It is whether California can excise, as "offensive conduct," one particular scurrilous epithet from the public discourse, either upon the theory of the court below that its use is inherently likely to cause violent reaction or upon a more general assertion that the States, acting as guardians of public morality, may properly remove this offensive word from the public vocabulary.

The rationale of the California court is plainly untenable. At most it reflects an "undifferentiated fear or apprehension of disturbance [which] is not enough to overcome the right to freedom of expression."* We have been shown no evidence that substantial numbers of citizens are standing ready to strike out physically at whoever may assault their sensibilities with execrations like that uttered by Cohen. There may be some persons about with such lawless and violent proclivities, but that is an insufficient base upon which to erect, consistently with constitutional values, a governmental power to force persons who wish to ventilate their dissident views into avoiding particular forms of expression. The argument amounts to little more than the self-defeating proposition that to avoid physical censorship of one who has not sought to provoke such a response by a hypothetical coterie of the violent and lawless, the States may more appropriately effectuate that censorship themselves.*

Admittedly, it is not so obvious that the First and Fourteenth Amendments must be taken to disable the States from punishing public utterance of this unseemly expletive in order to maintain what they regard as a suitable level of discourse within the body politic. We think, however, that examination and reflection will reveal the shortcomings of a contrary viewpoint.

At the outset, we cannot overemphasize that, in our judgment, most situations where the State has a justifiable interest in regulating speech will fall within one or more of the various established exceptions, discussed above but not applicable here, to the usual rule that governmental bodies may not prescribe the form or content of individual expression. Equally important to our conclusion is the constitutional backdrop against which our decision must be made. The constitutional right of free expression is powerful medicine in a society as diverse and populous as ours. It is designed and intended to remove governmental restraints from the arena of public discussion, putting the decision as to what views shall be voiced largely into the hands of each of us, in the hope that use of such freedom will ultimately produce a more capable citizenry and more perfect polity and in the belief that no other approach would comport with the premise of individual dignity and choice upon which our political system rests.*

To many, the immediate consequence of this freedom may often appear to be only verbal tumult, discord, and even offensive utterance. These are, however, within established limits, in truth necessary side effects of the broader enduring values which the process of open debate permits us to achieve. That the air may at times seem filled with verbal cacophony is, in this sense not a sign of weakness but of strength. We cannot lose sight of the fact that, in what otherwise might seem a trifling and annoying instance of individual distasteful abuse of a privilege, these fundamental societal values are truly implicated. That is why "[w]holly neutral futilities . . . come under the protection of free speech as fully as do Keats' poems or Donne's sermons," Winters v New York, (1948)* (Frankfurter, J., dissenting), and why "so long as the means are peaceful, the communication need not meet standards of acceptability," Organization for a Better Austin v Keefe, (1971).*

Against this perception of the constitutional policies involved, we discern certain more particularized considerations that peculiarly call for reversal of this conviction. First, the principle contended for by the State seems inherently boundless. How is one to distinguish this from any other offensive word? Surely the State has no right to cleanse public debate to the point where it is grammatically palatable to the most squeamish among us. Yet no readily ascertainable general principle exists for stopping short of that result were we to affirm the judgment below. For, while the particular four-letter word being litigated here is perhaps more distasteful than most others of its genre, it is nevertheless often true that one man's vulgarity is another's lyric. Indeed, we think it is largely because governmental officials cannot make principled distinctions in this area that the Constitution leaves matters of taste and style so largely to the individual.

Additionally, we cannot overlook the fact, because it is well illustrated by the episode involved here, that much linguistic expression serves a dual communicative function: it conveys not only ideas capable of relatively precise, detached explication, but otherwise inexpressible emotions as well. In fact, words are often chosen as much for their emotive as their cognitive force. We cannot sanction the view that the Constitution, while solicitous of the cognitive content of individual speech, has little or no regard for that emotive function which, practically speaking, may often be the more important element of the overall message sought to be communicated. Indeed, as Mr. Justice Frankfurter has said, "[o]ne of the prerogatives of American citizenship is the right to criticize public men and measures—and that means not only informed and responsible criticism but the freedom to speak foolishly and without moderation." Baumgartner v United States, (1944).*

Finally, and in the same vein, we cannot indulge the facile assumption that one can forbid particular words without also running a substantial risk of suppressing ideas in the process. Indeed, governments might soon seize upon the censorship of particular words as a convenient guise for banning the expression of unpopular

---

*Citation omitted [Eds.]

*Citation omitted [Eds.]

views. We have been able, as noted above, to discern little social benefit that might result from running the risk of opening the door to such grave results.

It is, in sum, our judgment that, absent a more particularized and compelling reason for its actions, the State may not, consistently with the First and Fourteenth Amendments, make the simple public display here involved of this single four-letter expletive a criminal offense. Because that is the only arguably sustainable rationale for the conviction here at issue, the judgment below must be reversed.

SEPARATE OPINION

Mr. Justice **Blackmun,** with whom The **Chief Justice** and Mr. Justice **Black** join.

I dissent, and I do so for two reasons:

1. Cohen's absurd and immature antic, in my view, was mainly conduct and little speech.* The California Court of Appeal appears so to have described it,* and I cannot characterize it otherwise. Further, the case appears to me to be well within the sphere of Chaplinsky v New Hampshire,* where Mr. Justice Murphy, a known champion of First Amendment freedoms, wrote for a unanimous bench. As a consequence, this

*Citation omitted [Eds.]

Court's agonizing First Amendment values seems misplaced and unnecessary.

2. I am not at all certain that the California Court of Appeal's construction of § 415 is now the authoritative California construction . . .

NOTES

1. The statute provides in full:
"Every person who maliciously and willfully disturbs the peace or quiet of any neighborhood or person, by loud or unusual noise, or by tumultuous or offensive conduct, or threatening, traducing, quarreling, challenging to fight, or fighting, or who, on the public streets of any unincorporated town, or upon the public highways in such unincorporated town, run any horse race, either for a wager or for amusement, or fire any gun or pistol in such unincorporated town, or use any vulgar language within the presence or hearing of women or children, in a loud and boisterous manner, is guilty of a misdemeanor, and upon conviction by any Court of competent jurisdiction shall be punished by fine not exceeding two hundred dollars, or by imprisonment in the County Jail for not more than ninety days, or by both fine and imprisonment, or either, at the discretion of the Court."

2. It is illuminating to note what transpired when Cohen entered a courtroom in the building. He removed his jacket and stood with it folded over his arm. Meanwhile, a policeman sent the presiding judge a note suggesting that Cohen be held in contempt of court. The judge declined to do so and Cohen was arrested by the officer only after he emerged from the courtroom.

IRVING KRISTOL

"Pornography, Obscenity, and the Case for Censorship"*

Being frustrated is disagreeable, but the real disasters in life begin when you get what you want. For almost a century now, a great many intelligent, well-meaning, and articulate people—of a kind generally called liberal or intellectual, or both—have argued eloquently against any kind of censorship of art and/or entertainment. And within the past ten years, the courts and the legislatures of most Western nations have found these arguments persuasive—so persuasive that hardly a man is now alive who clearly remembers what the answers to these arguments were. Today, in the United States and other democracies, censorship has to all intents and purposes ceased to exist.

Is there a sense of triumphant exhilaration in the land? Hardly. There is, on the contrary, a rapidly growing unease and disquiet. Somehow, things have not worked out as they were supposed to, and many notable civil libertarians have gone on record as saying this was not what they meant at all. They wanted a world in which "Desire Under the Elms" could be produced, or "Ulysses" published, without interference by philistine busybodies holding public office. They have got that, of course; but they have also got a world in which homosexual rape takes place on the stage, in which the public flocks during lunch hours to witness varieties of professional fornication, in which Times Square has become little more than a hideous market for the sale and distribution of printed filth that panders to all known (and some fanciful) sexual perversions.

But disagreeable as this may be, does it really matter? Might not our unease and disquiet be merely a cultural hangover—a "hangup," as they say? What reason is there to think that anyone was ever corrupted by a book?

This last question, oddly enough, is asked by the very same people who seem convinced that advertisements in magazines or displays of violence on television do indeed have the power to corrupt. It is also asked, incredibly enough and in all sincerity, by people—e.g., university professors and school teachers—whose very lives provide all the answers one could want. After all, if you believe that no one was ever corrupted by a book, you have also to believe that no one was ever improved by a book (or a play or a movie). You have to believe, in other words, that all art is morally trivial and that, consequently, all education is morally irrelevant. No one, not even a university professor, really believes that.

To be sure, it is extremely difficult, as social scientists tell us, to trace the effects of any single book (or play or movie) on an individual reader or any class of readers. But we all know, and social scientists know it too, that the ways in which we use our minds and imaginations do shape our characters and help define us as persons. That those who certainly know this are nevertheless moved to deny it merely indicates how a dogmatic resistance to the idea of censorship can—like most dogmatism—result in a mindless insistence on the absurd.

I have used these harsh terms—"dogmatism" and "mindless"—advisedly. I might also have added "hypocritical." For the plain fact is that none of us is a complete civil libertarian. We all believe that there is some point at which the public authorities ought to step in to limit the "self-expression" of an individual or a group, even where this might be seriously intended as a form of artistic expression, and even where the artistic transaction is between consenting adults. A playwright or theatrical director might, in this crazy world of ours, find someone willing to commit suicide on the stage, as called for by the script. We would not allow that—any more than we would permit scenes of real physical torture on the stage, even if the victim were a willing masochist. And I know of no one, no matter how free in spirit, who argues that we ought to permit gladiatorial contests in Yankee Stadium, similar to those once performed in the Colosseum at Rome—even if only consenting adults were involved.

*From The New York Times Magazine, March 28, 1971. Reprinted by permission of the author.

The basic point that emerges is one that Prof. Walter Berns has powerfully argued: No society can be utterly indifferent to the ways its citizens publicly entertain themselves.* Bearbaiting and cockfighting are prohibited only in part out of compassion for the suffering animals; the main reason they were abolished was because it was felt that they debased and brutalized the citizenry who flocked to witness such spectacles. And the question we face with regard to pornography and obscenity is whether, now that they have such strong legal protection from the Supreme Court, they can or will brutalize and debase our citizenry. We are, after all, not dealing with one passing incident—one book, or one play, or one movie. We are dealing with a general tendency that is suffusing our entire culture.

I say pornography *and* obscenity because, though they have different dictionary definitions and are frequently distinguishable as "artistic" genres, they are nevertheless in the end identical in effect. Pornography is not objectionable simply because it arouses sexual desire or lust or prurience in the mind of the reader or spectator; this is a silly Victorian notion. A great many nonpornographic works—including some parts of the Bible—excite sexual desire very successfully. What is distinctive about pornography is that, in the words of D. H. Lawrence, it attempts "to do dirt on [sex] . . . [It is an] insult to a vital human relationship."

In other words, pornography differs from erotic art in that its whole purpose is to treat human beings obscenely, to deprive human beings of their specifically human dimension. That is what obscenity is all about. It is light years removed from any kind of carefree sensuality—there is no continuum between Fielding's "Tom Jones" and the Marquis de Sade's "Justine." These works have quite opposite intentions. To quote Susan Sontag: "What pornographic literature does is precisely to drive a wedge between one's existence as a full human being and one's existence as a sexual being—while in ordinary life a healthy person is one who prevents such a gap from opening up." This definition occurs in an essay *defending* pornography—Miss Sontag is a candid as well as gifted critic—so the definition, which I accept, is neither tendentious nor censorious.

Along these same lines, one can point out—as C. S. Lewis pointed out some years back—that it is no accident that in the history of all literatures obscene words—the so-called "four-letter words"—have always been the vocabulary of farce or vituperation. The reason is clear—they reduce men and women to some of their mere bodily functions—they reduce man to his animal component, and such a reduction is an essential purpose of farce or vituperation.

Similarly, Lewis also suggested that it is not an accident that we have no offhand, colloquial, neutral terms—not in any Western European language at any rate—for our most private parts. The words we do use are either (a) nursery terms, (b) archaisms, (c) scientific terms or (d) a term from the gutter (that is, a demeaning term). Here I think the genius of language is telling us something important about man. It is telling us that man is an animal with a difference: he has a unique sense of privacy, and a unique capacity for shame when this privacy is violated. Our "private parts" are indeed private, and not merely because convention prescribes it. This particular convention is indigenous to the human race. In practically all primitive tribes, men and women cover their private parts; and in practically all primitive tribes, men and women do not copulate in public.

It may well be that Western society, in the latter half of the 20th century, is experiencing a drastic change in sexual mores and sexual relationships. We have had many such "sexual revolutions" in the past—and the bourgeois family and bourgeois ideas of sexual propriety were themselves established in the course of a revolution against 18th century "licentiousness"—and we shall doubtless have others in the future. It is, however, highly improbable (to put it mildly) that what we are witnessing is the Final Revolution which will make sexual relations utterly unproblematic, permit us to dispense with any kind of ordered relationships between the sexes, and allow us freely to redefine the human condition. And so long as humanity has not reached that utopia, obscenity will remain a problem.

One of the reasons it will remain a problem is that obscenity is not merely about sex, any more than science fiction is about science. Science fiction, as every student of the genre knows, is a peculiar vision of power: what it is really about is politics. And obscenity is a peculiar vision of humanity: what it is really about is ethics and metaphysics.

*This is as good a place as any to express my profound indebtedness to Walter Berns's superb essay, "Pornography vs. Democracy," in the winter, 1971, issue of The Public Interest.

Imagine a man—a well-known man, much in the public eye—in a hospital ward, dying an agonizing death. He is not in control of his bodily functions, so that his bladder and his bowels empty themselves of their own accord. His consciousness is overwhelmed and extinguished by pain, so that he cannot communicate with us, nor we with him. Now, it would be, technically, the easiest thing in the world to put a television camera in his hospital room and let the whole world witness this spectacle. We don't do it—at least we don't do it as yet—because we regard this as an *obscene* invasion of privacy. And what would make the spectacle obscene is that we would be witnessing the extinguishing of humanity in a human animal.

Incidentally, in the past our humanitarian crusaders against capital punishment understood this point very well. The abolitionist literature goes into great physical detail about what happens to a man when he is hanged or electrocuted or gassed. And their argument was—and is—that what happens is shockingly obscene, and that no civilized society should be responsible for perpetrating such obscenities, particularly since in the nature of the case there must be spectators to ascertain that this horror was indeed being perpetrated in fulfillment of the law.

Sex—like death—is an activity that is both animal and human. There are human sentiments and human ideals involved in this animal activity. But when sex is public, the viewer does not see—cannot see—the sentiments and the ideals. He can only see the animal coupling. And that is why, when men and women make love, as we say, they prefer to be alone—because it is only when you are alone that you can make love, as distinct from merely copulating in an animal and casual way. And that, too, is why those who are voyeurs, if they are not irredeemably sick, also feel ashamed at what they are witnessing. When sex is a public spectacle, a human relationship has been debased into a mere animal connection.

It is also worth noting that this making of sex into an obscenity is not a mutual and equal transaction, but is rather an act of exploitation by one of the partners—the male partner. I do not wish to get into the complicated question as to what, if any, are the essential differences—as distinct from conventional and cultural differences—between male and female. I do not claim to know the answer to that. But I do know—and I take it as a sign which has meaning—that pornography is, and always has been, a man's work; that women rarely write pornography; and that women tend to be indifferent consumers of pornography.* My own guess, by way of explanation, is that a woman's sexual experience is ordinarily more suffused with human emotion than is man's, that men are more easily satisfied with autoerotic activities, and that men can therefore more easily take a more "technocratic" view of sex and its pleasures. Perhaps this is not correct. But whatever the explanation, there can be no question that pornography is a form of "sexism," as the Women's Liberation Movement calls it, and that the instinct of Women's Lib has been unerring in perceiving that, when pornography is perpetrated, it is perpetrated against them, as part of a conspiracy to deprive them of their full humanity.

But even if all this is granted, it might be said—and doubtless will be said—that I really ought not to be unduly concerned. Free competition in the cultural marketplace—it is argued by people who have never otherwise had a kind word to say for laissez-faire—will automatically dispose of the problem. The present fad for pornography and obscenity, it will be asserted, is just that, a fad. It will spend itself in the course of time; people will get bored with it, will be able to take it or leave it alone in a casual way, in a "mature way," and, in sum, I am being unnecessarily distressed about the whole business. The New York Times, in an editorial, concludes hopefully in this vein.

"In the end . . . the insensate pursuit of the urge to shock, carried from one excess to a more abysmal one, is bound to achieve its own antidote in total boredom. When there is no lower depth to descend to, ennui will erase the problem."

I would like to be able to go along with this line of reasoning, but I cannot. I think it is false, and for two reasons, the first psychological, the second political.

The basic psychological fact about pornography and obscenity is that it appeals to and provokes a kind of sexual regression. The sexual pleasure one gets from pornography and obscenity is autoerotic and infantile; put bluntly, it is a masturbatory exercise of the imagination,

*There are, of course, a few exceptions—but of a kind that prove the rule. "L'Histoire d'O," for instance, written by a woman, is unquestionably the most *melancholy* work of pornography ever written. And its theme is precisely the dehumanization accomplished by obscenity.

when it is not masturbation pure and simple. Now, people who masturbate do not get bored with masturbation, just as sadists don't get bored with sadism, and voyeurs don't get bored with voyeurism.

In other words, infantile sexuality is not only a permanent temptation for the adolescent or even the adult—it can quite easily become a permanent, self-reinforcing neurosis. It is because of an awareness of this possibility of regression toward the infantile condition, a regression which is always open to us, that all the codes of sexual conduct ever devised by the human race take such a dim view of autoerotic activities and try to discourage autoerotic fantasies. Masturbation is indeed a perfectly natural autoerotic activity, as so many sexologists blandly assure us today. And it is precisely because it is so perfectly natural that it can be so dangerous to the mature or maturing person, if it is not controlled or sublimated in some way. That is the true meaning of Portnoy's complaint. Portnoy, you will recall, grows up to be a man who is incapable of having an adult sexual relationship with a woman; his sexuality remains fixed in an infantile mode, the prison of his autoerotic fantasies. Inevitably, Portnoy comes to think, in a perfectly *infantile* way, that it was all his mother's fault.

It is true that, in our time, some quite brilliant minds have come to the conclusion that a reversion to infantile sexuality is the ultimate mission and secret destiny of the human race. I am thinking in particular of Norman O. Brown, for whose writings I have the deepest respect. One of the reasons I respect them so deeply is that Mr. Brown is a serious thinker who is unafraid to face up to the radical consequences of his radical theories. Thus, Mr. Brown knows and says that for his kind of salvation to be achieved, humanity must annul the civilization it has created—not merely the civilization we have today, but all civilization —so as to be able to make the long descent backwards into animal innocence.

What is at stake is civilization and humanity, nothing less. The idea that "everything is permitted," as Nietzsche put it, rests on the premise of nihilism and has nihilistic implications. I will not pretend that the case against nihilism and for civilization is an easy one to make. We are here confronting the most fundamental of philosophical questions, on the deepest levels. But that is precisely my point—that the matter of pornography and obscenity is not a trivial one, and that only superficial minds can take a bland and untroubled view of it.

In this connection, I might also point out those who are primarily against censorship on liberal grounds tell us not to take pornography or obscenity seriously, while those who are for pornography and obscenity, on radical grounds, take it very seriously indeed. I believe the radicals— writers like Susan Sontag, Herbert Marcuse, Norman O. Brown, and even Jerry Rubin—are right, and the liberals are wrong. I also believe that those young radicals at Berkeley, some five years ago, who provoked a major confrontation over the public use of obscence words, showed a brilliant political instinct. Once the faculty and administration had capitulated on this issue— saying: "Oh, for God's sake, let's be adult: what difference does it make anyway?"—once they said that, they were bound to lose on every other issue. And once Mark Rudd could publicly ascribe to the president of Columbia a notoriously obscene relationship to his mother, without provoking any kind of reaction, the S.D.S. had already won the day. The occupation of Columbia's buildings merely ratified their victory. Men who show themselves unwilling to defend civilization against nihilism are not going to be either resolute or effective in defending the university against anything.

I am already touching upon a political aspect of pornography when I suggest that it is inherently and purposefully subversive of civilization and its institutions. But there is another and more specifically political aspect,when has to do with the relationship of pornography and/or obscenity to democracy, and especially to the quality of public life on which democratic government ultimately rests.

Though the phrase, "the quality of life," trips easily from so many lips these days, it tends to be one of those clichés with many trivial meanings and no large, serious one. Sometimes it merely refers to such externals as the enjoyment of cleaner air, cleaner water, cleaner streets. At other times it refers to the merely private enjoyment of music, painting or literature. Rarely does it have anything to do with the way the citizen in a democracy views himself—his obligations, his intentions, his ultimate self-definition.

Instead, what I would call the "managerial" conception of democracy is the predominant opinion among political scientists, sociologists and economists, and has, through the untiring efforts of these scholars, become the conventional journalistic opinion as well. The root idea behind this "managerial" conception is that democracy is a "political system" (as they say) which can be adequately defined in terms of—can be fully reduced to—its mechanical arrangements. Democracy is then seen as a set of rules and procedures, and *nothing but* a set of rules and procedures, whereby majority rule and minority rights are reconciled into a state of equilibrium. If everyone follows these rules and procedures, then a democracy is in working order. I think this is a fair description of the democratic idea that currently prevails in academia. One can also fairly say that it is now the liberal idea of democracy par excellence.

I cannot help but feel that there is something ridiculous about being this kind of a democrat, and I must further confess to having a sneaking sympathy for those of our young radicals who also find it ridiculous. The absurdity is the absurdity of idolatry—of taking the symbolic for the real, the means for the end. The purpose of democracy cannot possibly be the endless functioning of its own political machinery. The purpose of any political regime is to achieve some version of the good life and the good society. It is not at all difficult to imagine a perfectly functioning democracy which answers all questions except one—namely, why should anyone of intelligence and spirit care a fig for it?

There is, however, an older idea of democracy —one which was fairly common until about the beginning of this century—for which the conception of the quality of public life is absolutely crucial. This idea starts from the proposition that democracy is a form of self-government, and that if you want it to be a meritorious polity, you have to care about what kind of people govern it. Indeed, it puts the matter more strongly and declares that, if you want self-government, you are only entitled to it if that "self" is worthy of governing. There is no inherent right to self-government if it means that such government is vicious, mean, squalid and debased. Only a dogmatist and a fanatic, an idolater of democratic machinery, could approve of self-government under such conditions.

And because the desirability of self-government depends on the character of the people who govern, the older idea of democracy was very solicitous of the condition of this character. It was solicitous of the individual self, and felt an obligation to educate it into what used to be called "republican virtue." And it was solicitous of that collective self which we call public opinion and which, in a democracy, governs us collectively. Perhaps in some respects it was nervously

oversolicitous—that would not be surprising. But the main thing is that it cared, cared not merely about the machinery of democracy but about the quality of life that this machinery might generate.

And because it cared, this older idea of democracy had no problem in principle with pornography and/or obscenity. It censored them—and it did so with a perfect clarity of mind and a perfectly clear conscience. It was not about to permit people capriciously to corrupt themselves. Or, to put it more precisely: in this version of democracy, the people took some care not to let themselves be governed by the more infantile and irrational parts of themselves.

I have, it many be noticed, uttered that dreadful word, "censorship." And I am not about to back away from it. If you think pornography and/or obscenity is a serious problem, you have to be for censorship. I'll go even further and say that if you want to prevent pornography and/or obscenity from becoming a problem, you have to be for censorship. And lest there be any misunderstanding as to what I am saying, I'll put it as bluntly as possible: if you care for the quality of life in our American democracy, then you have to be for censorship.

But can a liberal be for censorship? Unless one assumes that being a liberal *must* mean being indifferent to the quality of American life, then the answer has to be: yes, a liberal can be for censorship—but he ought to favor a liberal form of censorship.

Is that a contradiction in terms? I don't think so. We have no problem in contrasting *repressive* laws governing alcohol and drugs and tobacco with laws *regulating* (that is, discouraging the sale of) alcohol and drugs and tobacco. Laws encouraging temperance are not the same thing as laws that have as their goal prohibition or abolition. We have not made the smoking of cigarettes a criminal offense. We have, however, and with good liberal conscience, prohibited cigarette advertising on television, and may yet, again with good liberal conscience, prohibit it in newspapers and magazines. The idea of restricting individual freedom, in a liberal way, is not at all unfamiliar to us.

I therefore see no reason why we should not be able to distinguish repressive censorship from liberal censorship of the written and spoken word. In Britain, until a few years ago, you could perform almost any play you wished—but certain plays, judged to be obscene, had to be performed in private theatrical clubs which were deemed to have a "serious" interest in theater. In the U.S. all of us who grew up using public libraries are familiar with the circumstances under which certain books could be circulated only to adults, while still other books had to be read in the library reading room, under the librarian's skeptical eye. In both cases, a small minority that was willing to make a serious effort to see an obscence play or read an obscene book could do so. But the impact of obscenity was circumscribed and the quality of public life was only marginally affected.*

I am not saying it is easy in practice to sustain a distinction between liberal and repressive censorship, especially in the public realm of a democracy, where popular opinion is so vulnerable to demagoguery. Moreover, an acceptable system of liberal censorship is likely to be exceedingly difficult to devise in the United States today, because our educated classes, upon whose judgment a liberal censorship must rest, are so convinced that there is no such thing as a problem of obscenity, or even that there is no such thing as obscenity at all. But, to counterbalance this, there is the further, fortunate truth that the tolerable margin for error is quite large, and single mistakes or single injustices are not all that important.

This possibility, of course, occasions much distress among artists and academics. It is a fact, one that cannot and should not be denied, that any system of censorship is bound, upon occasion, to treat unjustly a particular work of art—to find pornography where there is only gentle eroticism, to find obscenity where none really exists, or to find both where its existence ought to be tolerated because it serves a larger moral purpose. Though most works of art are not obscene, and though most obscenity has nothing to do with art, there are some few works of art that are, at least in part, pornographic and/or obscene. There are also some few works of art that are in the special category of the comic-ironic "bawdy" (Boccaccio, Rabelais). It is such works of art that are likely to suffer at the hands of the censor. That is the price one has to be prepared to pay for censorship—even liberal censorship.

But just how high is this price? If you believe, as so many artists seem to believe today, that art

is the only sacrosanct activity in our profane and vulgar world—that any man who designates himself an artist thereby acquires a sacred office—then obviously censorship is an intolerable form of sacrilege. But for those of us who do not subscribe to this religion of art, the costs of censorship do not seem so high at all.

If you look at the history of American or English literature, there is precious little damage you can point to as a consequence of the censorship that prevailed throughout most of that history. Very few works of literature—of real literary merit, I mean—ever were suppressed; and those that were, were not suppressed for long. Nor have I noticed, now that censorship of the written word has to all intents and purposes ceased in this country, that hitherto suppressed or repressed masterpieces are flooding the market. Yes, we can now read "Fanny Hill" and the Marquis de Sade. Or, to be more exact, we can now openly purchase them, since many people were able to read them even though they were publicly banned, which is as it should be under a liberal censorship. So how much have literature and the arts gained from the fact that we can all now buy them over the counter, that, indeed, we are all now encouraged to buy them over the counter? They have not gained much that I can see.

And one might also ask a question that is almost never raised: how much has literature lost from the fact that everything is now permitted? It has lost quite a bit, I should say. In a free market, Gresham's Law can work for books or theater as efficiently as it does for coinage—driving out the good, establishing the debased. The cultural market in the United States today is being preempted by dirty books, dirty movies, dirty theater. A pornographic novel has a far better chance of being published today than a nonpornographic one, and quite a few pretty good novels are not being published at all simply because they are not pornographic, and are therefore less likely to sell. Our cultural condition has not improved as a result of the new freedom. American cultural life wasn't much to brag about 20 years ago; today one feels ashamed for it.

Just one last point which I dare not leave untouched. If we start censoring pornography or obscenity, shall we not inevitably end up censoring political opinion? A lot of people seem to think this would be the case—which only shows the power of doctrinaire thinking over reality. We had censorship of pornography and obscenity for

*It is fairly predictable that some one is going to object that this point of view is "elitist"—that, under a system of liberal censorship, the rich will have privileged access to pornography and obscenity. Yes, of course they will—just as at present, the rich have privileged acess to heroin if they want it. But one would have to be an egalitarian maniac to object to this state of affairs on the grounds of equality.

150 years, until almost yesterday, and I am not aware that freedom of opinion in this country was in any way diminished as a consequence of this fact. Fortunately for those of us who are liberal, freedom is not indivisible. If it were, the case for liberalism would be indistinguishable from the case for anarchy; and they are two very different things.

But I must repeat and emphasize: What kind of laws we pass governing pornography and obscenity, what kind of censorship—or, since we are still a federal nation—what kinds of censorship we institute in our various localities may indeed be difficult matters to cope with; nevertheless the real issue is one of principle. I myself subscribe to the liberal view of the enforcement problem: I think that pornography should be illegal and available to anyone who wants it so badly as to make a pretty strenuous effort to get it. We have lived with under-the-counter pornography for centuries now, in a fairly comfortable way. But the issue of principle, of whether it should be over or under the counter, has to be settled before we can reflect on the advantages and disadvantages of alternative modes of censorship. I think the settlement we are living under now, in which obscenity and democracy are regarded as equals, is wrong; I believe it is inherently unstable; I think it will, in the long run, be incompatible with any authentic concern for the quality of life in our democracy.

JOHN F. KENNEDY MEMORIAL HOSPITAL v. HESTON

Supreme Court of New Jersey, 1971*

The opinion of the Court was delivered by WEINTRAUB, C.J.

Delores Heston, age 22 and unmarried, was severely injured in an automobile accident. She was taken to the plaintiff hospital where it was determined that she would expire unless operated upon for a ruptured spleen and that if operated upon she would expire unless whole blood was administered. Miss Heston and her parents are Jehovah's Witnesses and a tenet of their faith forbids blood transfusions. Miss Heston insists she expressed her refusal to accept blood, but the evidence indicates she was in shock on admittance to the hospital and in the judgment of the attending physicians and nurses was then or soon became disoriented and incoherent. Her mother remained adamant in her opposition to a transfusion, and signed a release of liability for the hospital and medical personnel. Miss Heston did not execute a release; presumably she could not. Her father could not be located.

Death being imminent, plaintiff on notice to the mother made application at 1:30 A.M. to a judge of the Superior Court for the appointment of a guardian for Miss Heston with directions to consent to transfusions as needed to save her life. At the hearing, the mother and her friends thought a certain doctor would pursue surgery without a transfusion, but the doctor, in response to the judge's telephone call, declined the case. The court appointed a guardian with authority to consent to blood transfusions "for the preservation of the life of Delores Heston." Surgery was performed at 4:00 A.M. the same morning. Blood was administered. Miss Heston survived.

Defendants then moved to vacate the order. Affidavits were submitted by both sides. The trial court declined to vacate the order. This appeal followed. We certified it before argument in the Appellate Division.

The controversy is moot. Miss Heston is well and no longer in plaintiff's hospital. The prospect of her return at some future day in like circumstances is too remote to warrant a declaratory judgment as between the parties. Nonetheless, the public interest warrants a resolution of the cause, and for that reason we accept the issue. (See State v. Perricone, N.J.* 1962).

In *Perricone,* we sustained an order for compulsory blood transfusion for an infant despite the objection of the parents who were Jehovah's Witnesses. In Raleigh Fitkin-Paul Morgan Memorial Hospital v. Anderson, N.J. (1964),* it appeared that both the mother, a Jehovah's Witness, and the child she was bearing would die if blood were not transfused should she hemorrhage. We held that a blood transfusion could be ordered if necessary to save the lives of the mother and the unborn child. We said:

We have no difficulty in so deciding with respect to the infant child. The more difficult question is whether an adult may be compelled to submit to such medical procedures when necessary to save his life. Here we think it is unnecessary to decide that question in broad terms because the welfare of the child and the mother are so intertwined and inseparable that it would be impracticable to attempt to distinguish between them with respect to the sundry factual patterns which may develop. The blood transfusions (including transfusions made necessary by the delivery) may be administered if necessary to save her life or the life of her child, as the physician in charge at the time may determine.

The case at hand presents the question we thus reserved in *Raleigh Fitkin-Paul Morgan Memorial Hospital.*

It seems correct to say there is no constitutional right to choose to die. Attempted suicide was a crime at common law and was held to be a crime under N.J.S.A. 2A:85–1.* It is now denounced as a disorderly persons offense. N.J.S.A. 2A:170–25.6. Ordinarily nothing would be gained by a prosecution, and hence the offense is rarely charged. Nonetheless the Constitution does not deny the State an interest in the subject. It is commonplace for the police and other citizens, often at great risk to themselves, to use force or stratagem to defeat efforts at suicide, and it could hardly be said that thus to save someone from himself violated a right of his under the Constitution subjecting the rescuer to civil or penal consequences.

Nor is constitutional right established by adding that

*Citation omitted [Eds.]

one's religious faith ordains his death. Religious beliefs are absolute, but conduct in pursuance of religious beliefs is not wholly immune from governmental restraint. Mountain Lakes Bd. of Educ. v. Maas, N.J.* (1960) (vaccination of children); Bunn v. North Carolina,* (1949) (the use of snakes in a religious ritual); Baer v. City of Bend,* Or. (1956) (fluoridation of drinking water). Of immediate interest is Reynolds v. United States,* (1878), in which it was held that Congress could punish polygamy in a territory notwithstanding that polygamy was permitted or demanded by religious tenet, and in which the Court said:

* * * Laws are made for the government of actions, and while they cannot interfere with mere religious belief and opinions, they may with practices. Suppose one believed that human sacrifices were a necessary part of religious worship, would it be seriously contended that the civil government under which he lived could not interfere to prevent a sacrifice? Or if a wife religiously believed it was her duty to burn herself upon the funeral pile of her dead husband, would it be beyond the power of the civil government to prevent her carrying her belief into practice?

Complicating the subject of suicide is the difficulty of knowing whether a decision to die is firmly held. Psychiatrists may find that beneath it all a person bent on self-destruction is hoping to be rescued, and most who are rescued do not repeat the attempt, at least not at once. Then, too, there is the question whether in any event the person was and continues to be competent (a difficult concept in this area) to choose to die. And of course there is no opportunity for a trial of these questions in advance of intervention by the State or a citizen.

Appellant suggests there is a difference between passively submitting to death and actively seeking it. The distinction may be merely verbal, as it would be if an adult sought death by starvation instead of a drug. If the State may interrupt one mode of self-destruction, it may with equal authority interfere with the other. It is arguably different when an individual, overtaken by illness, decides to let it run a fatal course. But unless the medical option itself is laden with the risk of death or of serious infirmity, the State's interest in sustaining life in such circumstances is hardly distinguishable from its interest in the case of suicide.

Here we are not dealing with deadly options. The risk of death or permanent injury because of a transfusion is not a serious factor. Indeed, Miss Heston did not resist a transfusion on that basis. Nor did she wish to die. She wanted to live, but her faith demanded that she refuse blood even at the price of her life. The question is not whether the State could punish her for refusing a transfusion. It may be granted that it would serve no State interest to deal criminally with one who resisted a transfusion on the basis of religious faith. The question is whether the State may authorize force to prevent death or may tolerate the use of force by others to that end. Indeed, the issue is not solely between the State and Miss Heston, for the controversy is also between Miss Heston and a hospital and staff who did not seek her out and upon whom the dictates of her faith will fall as a burden.

Hospitals exist to aid the sick and the injured. The medical and nursing professions are consecrated to preserving life. That is their professional creed. To them, a failure to use a simple, established procedure in the circumstances of this case would be malpractice, however the law may characterize that failure because of the patient's private convictions. A surgeon should not be asked to operate under the strain of knowing that a transfusion may not be administered even though medically required to save his patient. The hospital and its staff should not be required to decide whether the patient is or continues to be competent to make a judgment upon the subject, or whether the release tendered by the patient or a member of his family will protect them from civil responsibility. The hospital could hardly avoid the problem by compelling the removal of a dying patient, and Miss Heston's family made no effort to take her elsewhere.

When the hospital and staff are thus involuntary hosts and their interests are pitted against the belief of the patient, we think it reasonable to resolve the problem by permitting the hospital and its staff to pursue their functions according to their professional standards. The solution sides with life, the conservation of which is, we think, a matter of State interest. A prior application to a court is appropriate if time permits it, although in the nature of the emergency the only question that can be explored satisfactorily is whether death will probably ensue if medical procedures are not followed. If a court finds, as the trial court did, that death will likely follow unless a transfusion is administered, the hospital and the physician should be permitted to follow that medical procedure.

The precedents are few ... With one exception, Erickson v. Dilgard, (Sup.Ct.1962), transfusions for adults were ordered despite their religious tenets.*

Two cases reached an appellate level. In *Georgetown College,* a single judge of the Court of Appeals ordered the transfusion. Thereafter a majority of the court denied a petition for rehearing en banc, without however indicating the precise basis for that denial. One dissenting opinion approached the merits. The sole appellate decision expressly reaching the merits appears to be In re Estate of Brooks.* There a conservator was appointed to authorize the transfusion for a Jehovah's

*Citation omitted [Eds.]
*Citation omitted [Eds.]

Witness. After the transfusion, the patient and her husband sought unsuccessfully to have the order expunged. The Supreme Court of Illinois reversed. The court could find no "clear and present danger" warranting interference with the patient's religious proscription. It has been suggested that the "clear and present danger" test, appropriate with respect to free speech, is not the appropriate criterion here, and that the relevant question is whether there is a "compelling State interest" justifying the State's refusal to permit the patient to refuse vital aid.* We think the latter test is the correct one, but it cannot be said with confidence that *Brooks* would have gone the other way if the decision had been made in its light. In fact the court there did mention conceivable interests. Thus it noted that the patient did not have minor children who might become charges of the State. But the court did not expressly consider whether the State had an interest in sustaining life, a consideration which would not be apparent when the focus is upon a "clear and present danger." Nor did the court consider the sufficiency of

the interest of a hospital or its staff when the patient is thrust upon them. In fact there the applicant was the patient's regular physician who had long treated her for an ulcer, knew of her religious tenet, and had assured her that he would not administer blood. The court noted, too, a fact of uncertain force in its decision, that the application was made to the trial court without notice to the patient or her husband, although time was adequate to that end.

It is not at all clear that *Brooks* would be applied in Illinois to an emergent factual pattern in which a hospital and its staff are the involuntary custodians of an adult. In any event, for the reasons already given, we find that the interest of the hospital and its staff, as well as the State's interest in life, warranted the transfusion of blood under the circumstances of this case. The judgment is accordingly affirmed. No costs.

For affirmance: Chief Justice WEINTRAUB and Justices JACOBS, FRANCIS, PROCTOR, HALL and SCHETTINO—6.

For reversal: None.

*Citation omitted [Eds.]

GERALD DWORKIN

Paternalism*

*Neither one person, nor any number of persons, is war-
ranted in saying to another human creature of ripe
years, that he shall not do with his life for his own benefit
what he chooses to do with it. [Mill]*

*I do not want to go along with a volunteer basis. I think
a fellow should be compelled to become better and not
let him use his discretion whether he wants to get
smarter, more healthy or more honest. [General Her-
shey]*

I take as my starting point the "one very simple
principle" proclaimed by Mill *On Liberty* . . .

That principle is, that the sole end for which mankind
are warranted, individually or collectively, in interfering with the liberty of action of any of their number,
is self-protection. That the only purpose for which
power can be rightfully exercised over any member of
a civilized community, against his will, is to prevent
harm to others. He cannot rightfully be compelled to
do or forbear because it will be better for him to do so,
because it will make him happier, because, in the opinion of others, to do so would be wise, or even right.

This principle is neither "one" nor "very simple." It is at least two principles; one asserting
that self-protection or the prevention of harm to
others is sometimes a sufficient warrant and the
other claiming that the individual's own good is
never a sufficient warrant for the exercise of compulsion either by the society as a whole or by its
individual members. I assume that no one, with
the possible exception of extreme pacifists or anarchists, questions the correctness of the first half
of the principle. This essay is an examination of
the negative claim embodied in Mill's principle—
the objection to paternalistic interferences with a
man's liberty.

*From *Morality and the Law* edited by Richard A. Wasserstrom. Copyright © 1971 by Wadsworth Publishing Company, Inc., Belmont, California 94002. Reprinted by
permission of the publisher and the author.

I

By paternalism I shall understand roughly the
interference with a person's liberty of action justified by reasons referring exclusively to the welfare, good, happiness, needs, interests or values of
the person being coerced. One is always well-
advised to illustrate one's definitions by examples
but it is not easy to find "pure" examples of paternalistic interferences. For almost any piece of legislation is justified by several different kinds of
reasons and even if historically a piece of legislation can be shown to have been introduced for
purely paternalistic motives, it may be that advocates of the legislation with an antipaternalistic
outlook can find sufficient reasons justifying the
legislation without appealing to the reasons
which were originally adduced to support it.
Thus, for example, it may be that the original
legislation requiring motorcyclists to wear safety
helmets was introduced for purely paternalistic
reasons. But the Rhode Island Supreme Court
recently upheld such legislation on the grounds
that it was "not persuaded that the legislature is
powerless to prohibit individuals from pursuing a
course of conduct which could conceivably result
in their becoming public charges," thus clearly
introducing reasons of a quite different kind.
Now I regard this decision as being based on
reasoning of a very dubious nature but it illustrates the kind of problem one has in finding examples. The following is a list of the kinds of
interferences I have in mind as being paternalistic.

II

1. Laws requiring motorcyclists to wear
   safety helmets when operating their machines.
2. Laws forbidding persons from swimming
   at a public beach when lifeguards are not
   on duty.
3. Laws making suicide a criminal offense.
4. Laws making it illegal for women and children to work at certain types of jobs.

5. Laws regulating certain kinds of sexual conduct, for example, homosexuality among consenting adults in private.
6. Laws regulating the use of certain drugs which may have harmful consequences to the user but do not lead to antisocial conduct.
7. Laws requiring a license to engage in certain professions with those not receiving a license subject to fine or jail sentence if they do engage in the practice.
8. Laws compelling people to spend a specified fraction of their income on the purchase of retirement annuities (Social Security).
9. Laws forbidding various forms of gambling (often justified on the grounds that the poor are more likely to throw away their money on such activities than the rich who can afford to).
10. Laws regulating the maximum rates of interest for loans.
11. Laws against duelling.

In addition to laws which attach criminal or civil penalties to certain kinds of action there are laws, rules, regulations, decrees which make it either difficult or impossible for people to carry out their plans and which are also justified on paternalistic grounds. Examples of this are:

1. Laws regulating the types of contracts which will be upheld as valid by the courts, for example, (an example of Mill's to which I shall return) no man may make a valid contract for perpetual involuntary servitude.
2. Not allowing assumption of risk as a defense to an action based on the violation of a safety statute.
3. Not allowing as a defense to a charge of murder or assault the consent of the victim.
4. Requiring members of certain religious sects to have compulsory blood transfusions. This is made possible by not allowing the patient to have recourse to civil suits for assault and battery and by means of injunctions.
5. Civil commitment procedures when these are specifically justified on the basis of preventing the person being committed from harming himself. The D.C. Hospitalization of the Mentally Ill Act provides for involuntary hospitalization of a person who "is mentally ill, and because of that illness, is likely to injure himself or others if allowed to remain at liberty." The term injure in this context applies to unintentional as well as intentional injuries.

All of my examples are of existing restrictions on the liberty of individuals. Obviously one can think of interferences which have not yet been imposed. Thus one might ban the sale of cigarettes, or require that people wear safety belts in automobiles (as opposed to merely having them installed), enforcing this by not allowing motorist to sue for injuries even when caused by other drivers if the motorist was not wearing a seat belt at the time of the accident.

I shall not be concerned with activities which though defended on paternalistic grounds are not interferences with the liberty of persons, for example, the giving of subsidies in kind rather than in cash on the grounds that the recipients would not spend the money on the goods which they really need, or not including a $1,000 deductible provision in a basic protection automobile insurance plan on the ground that the people who would elect it could least afford it. Nor shall I be concerned with measures such as "truth-in-advertising" acts and Pure Food and Drug legislation which are often attacked as paternalistic but which should not be considered so. In these cases all that is provided—it is true by the use of compulsion—is information which it is presumed that rational persons are interested in having in order to make wise decisions. There is no interference with the liberty of the consumer unless one wants to stretch a point beyond good sense and say that his liberty to apply for a loan without knowing the true rate of interest is diminished. It is true that sometimes there is sentiment for going further than providing information, for example when laws against usurious interest are passed preventing those who might wish to contract loans at high rates of interest from doing so, and these measures may correctly be considered paternalistic.

III

Bearing these examples in mind, let me return to a characterization of paternalism. I said earlier that I meant by the term, roughly, interference with a person's liberty for his own good. But, as some of the examples show, the class of persons whose good is involved is not always identical with the class of persons whose freedom is restricted. Thus, in the case of professional licensing it is the practitioner who is directly interfered with but it is the would-be patient whose interests are presumably being served. Not allowing the consent of the victim to be a defense to certain types of crime primarily affects the would-be aggressor but it is the interests of the willing victim that we are trying to protect. Sometimes a person may fall into both classes as would be the case if we banned the manufacture and sale of cigarettes and a given manufacturer happened to be a smoker as well.

Thus we may first divide paternalistic interferences into "pure" and "impure" cases. In "pure" paternalism the class of persons whose freedom is restricted is identical with the class of persons whose benefit is intended to be promoted by such restrictions. Examples: the making of suicide a crime, requiring passengers in automobiles to wear seat belts, requiring a Christian Scientist to receive a blood transfusion. In the case of "impure" paternalism in trying to protect the welfare of a class of persons we find that the only way to do so will involve restricting the freedom of other persons besides those who are benefitted. Now it might be thought that there are no cases of "impure" paternalism since any such case could always be justified on nonpaternalistic grounds, that is, in terms of preventing harm to others. Thus we might ban cigarette manufacturers from continuing to manufacture their product on the grounds that we are preventing them from causing illness to others in the same way that we prevent other manufacturers from releasing pollutants into the atmosphere, thereby causing danger to the members of the community. The difference is, however, that in the former but not the latter case the harm is of such a nature that it could be avoided by those individuals affected if they so chose. The incurring of the harm requires, so to speak, the active cooperation of the victim. It would be mistaken theoretically and hypocritical in practice to assert that our interference in such cases is just like our interference in standard cases of protecting others from harm. At the very least someone interfered with in this way can reply that no one is complaining about his activities. It may be that impure paternalism requires arguments or reasons of a stronger kind in order to be justified, since there are persons who are losing a portion of their liberty and they do not even have the solace of having it be done "in their own interest." Of course in some sense, if paternalistic justifications are ever correct, then we are protecting others, we are preventing some from injuring others, but it is important to

see the differences between this and the standard case.

Paternalism then will always involve limitations on the liberty of some individuals in their own interest but it may also extend to interferences with the liberty of parties whose interests are not in question.

IV

Finally, by way of some more preliminary analysis, I want to distinguish paternalistic interference with liberty from a related type with which it is often confused. Consider, for example, legislation which forbids employees to work more than, say, forty hours per week. It is sometimes argued that such legislation is paternalistic for if employees desired such a restriction on their hours of work they could agree among themselves to impose it voluntarily. But because they do not the society imposes its own conception of their best interests upon them by the use of coercion. Hence this is paternalism.

Now it may be that some legislation of this nature is, in fact, paternalistically motivated. I am not denying that. All I want to point out is that there is another possible way of justifying such measures which is not paternalistic in nature. It is not paternalistic because, as Mill puts it in a similar context, such measures are "required not to overrule the judgment of individuals respecting their own interest, but to give effect to that judgment: they being unable to give effect to it except by concert, which concert again cannot be effectual unless it receives validity and sanction from the law." (*Principles of Political Economy*).

The line of reasoning here is a familiar one first found in Hobbes and developed with great sophistication by contemporary economists in the last decade or so. There are restrictions which are in the interests of a class of persons taken collectively but are such that the immediate interest of each individual is furthered by his violating the rule when others adhere to it. In such cases the individuals involved may need the use of compulsion to give effect to their collective judgment of their own interest by guaranteeing each individual compliance by the others. In these cases compulsion is not used to achieve some benefit which is not recognized to be a benefit by those concerned, but rather because it is the only feasible means of achieving some benefit which *is* recognized as such by all concerned. This way of viewing matters provides us with another characterization of paternalism in general. Paternalism might be thought of as the use of coercion to achieve a good which is not recognized as such by those persons for whom the good is intended. Again while this formulation captures the heart of the matter—it is surely what Mill is objecting to in *On Liberty*—the matter is not always quite like that. For example, when we force motorcyclists to wear helmets we are trying to promote a good—the protection of the person from injury—which is surely recognized by most of the individuals concerned. It is not that a cyclist doesn't value his bodily integrity; rather, as a supporter of such legislation would put it, he either places, perhaps irrationally, another value or good (freedom from wearing a helmet) above that of physical well-being or, perhaps, while recognizing the danger in the abstract, he either does not fully appreciate it or he underestimates the likelihood of its occurring. But now we are approaching the question of possible justifications of paternalistic measures and the rest of this essay will be devoted to that question.

V

I shall begin for dialectical purposes by discussing Mill's objections to paternalism and then go on to discuss more positive proposals.

An initial feature that strikes one is the absolute nature of Mill's prohibitions against paternalism. It is so unlike the carefully qualified admonitions of Mill and his fellow utilitarians on other moral issues. He speaks of self-protection as the *sole* end warranting coercion, of the individual's own goals as *never* being a sufficient warrant. Contrast this with his discussion of the prohibition against lying in *Utilitarianism*:

Yet that even this rule, sacred as it is, admits of possible exception, is acknowledged by all moralists, the chief of which is where the with-holding of some fact . . . would save an individual . . . from great and unmerited evil.

The same tentativeness is present when he deals with justice:

It is confessedly unjust to break faith with any one: to violate an engagement, either express or implied, or disappoint expectations raised by our own conduct, at least if we have raised these expectations knowingly and voluntarily. Like all the other obligations of justice already spoken of, this one is not regarded as absolute, but as capable of being overruled by a stronger obligation of justice on the other side.

This anomaly calls for some explanation. The structure of Mill's argument is as follows:

1. Since restraint is an evil the burden of proof is on those who propose such restraint.
2. Since the conduct which is being considered is purely self-regarding, the normal appeal to the protection of the interests of others is not available.
3. Therefore we have to consider whether reasons involving reference to the individual's own good, happiness, welfare, or interests are sufficient to overcome the burden of justification.
4. We either cannot advance the interests of the individual by compulsion, or the attempt to do so involves evils which outweigh the good done.
5. Hence the promotion of the individual's own interests does not provide a sufficient warrant for the use of compulsion.

Clearly the operative premise here is (4), and it is bolstered by claims about the status of the individual as judge and appraiser of his welfare, interests, needs, et cetera.:

With respect to his own feelings and circumstances, the most ordinary man or woman has means of knowledge immeasurably surpassing those that can be possessed by any one else.

He is the man most interested in his own well-being: the interest which any other person, except in cases of strong personal attachment, can have in it is trifling, compared to that which he himself has.

These claims are used to support the following generalizations concerning the utility of compulsion for paternalistic purposes.

The interferences of society to overrule his judgment and purposes in what only regards himself must be grounded on general presumptions; which may be altogether wrong, and even if right, are as likely as not to be missapplied to individual cases.

But the strongest of all the arguments against the interference of the public with purely personal conduct is that when it does interfere, the odds are that it interferes wrongly and in the wrong place.

All errors which the individual is likely to commit against advice and warning are far outweighed by the evil of allowing others to constrain him to what they deem his good.

Performing the utilitarian calculation by balancing the advantages and disadvantages, we find that: "Mankind are greater gainers by suffering each other to live as seems good to themselves, than by compelling each other to live as seems good to the rest." Ergo, (4).

This classical case of a utilitarian argument with all the premises spelled out is not the only line of reasoning present in Mill's discussion. There are asides, and more than asides, which look quite different and I shall deal with them later. But this is clearly the main channel of Mill's thought and it is one which has been subjected to vigorous attack from the moment it appeared— most often by fellow utilitarians. The link that they have usually seized on is, as Fitzjames Stephen put it in *Liberty, Equality, Fraternity,* the absence of proof that the "mass of adults are so well acquainted with their own interests and so much disposed to pursue them that no compulsion or restraint put upon them by any others for the purpose of promoting their interest can really promote them." Even so sympathetic a critic as H. L. A. Hart is forced to the conclusion that:

In Chapter 5 of his essay [On Liberty] Mill carried his protests against paternalism to lengths that may now appear to us as fantastic . . . No doubt if we no longer sympathise with this criticism this is due, in part, to a general decline in the belief that individuals know their own interest best.

Mill endows the average individual with "too much of the psychology of a middle-aged man whose desires are relatively fixed, not liable to be artificially stimulated by external influences; who knows what he wants and what gives him satisfaction or happiness; and who pursues these things when he can."

Now it is interesting to note that Mill himself was aware of some of the limitations on the doctrine that the individual is the best judge of his own interests. In his discussion of government intervention in general (even where the intervention does not interfere with liberty but provides alternative institutions to those of the market) after making claims which are parallel to those just discussed, for example, "People understand their own business and their own interests better, and care for them more, than the government does, or can be expected to do," he goes on to an intelligent discussion of the "very large and conspicuous exceptions" to the maxim that:

Most persons take a juster and more intelligent view of their own interest, and of the means of promoting it

than can either be prescribed to them by a general enactment of the legislature, or pointed out in the particular case by a public functionary.

Thus there are things

of which the utility does not consist in ministering to inclinations, nor in serving the daily uses of life, and the want of which is least felt where the need is greatest. This is peculiarly true of those things which are chiefly useful as tending to raise the character of human beings. The uncultivated cannot be competent judges of cultivation. Those who most need to be made wiser and better, usually desire it least, and, if they desire it, would be incapable of finding the way to it by their own lights.

. . . A second exception to the doctrine that individuals are the best judges of their own interest, is when an individual attempts to decide irrevocably now what will be best for his interest at some future and distant time. The presumption in favor of individual judgment is only legitimate, where the judgment is grounded on actual, and especially on present, personal experience; not where it is formed antecedently to experience, and not suffered to be reversed even after experience has condemned it.

The upshot of these exceptions is that Mill does not declare that there should never be government interference with the economy but rather that

. . . in every instance, the burden of making out a strong case should be thrown not on those who resist but those who recommend government interference. Letting alone, in short, should be the general practice: every departure from it, unless required by some great good, is a certain evil.

In short, we get a presumption, not an absolute prohibition. The question is why doesn't the argument against paternalism go the same way?

I suggest that the answer lies in seeing that in addition to a purely utilitarian argument Mill uses another as well. As a utilitarian, Mill has to show, in Fitzjames Stephen's words, that: "Self-protection apart, no good object can be attained by any compulsion which is not in itself a greater evil than the absence of the object which the compulsion obtains." To show this is impossible, one reason being that it isn't true. Preventing a man from selling himself into slavery (a paternalistic measure which Mill himself accepts as legitimate), or from taking heroin, or from driving a car without wearing seat belts may constitute a lesser evil than allowing him to do any of these things. A consistent utilitarian can only argue against paternalism on the grounds that it (as a matter of fact) does not maximize the good. It is always a contingent question that may be returned by the evidence. But there is also a non-contingent argument which runs through *On Liberty.* When Mill states that "there is a part of the life of every person who has come to years of discretion, within which the individuality of that person ought to reign uncontrolled either by any other person or by the public collectively," he is saying something about what it means to be a person, an autonomous agent. It is because coercing a person for his own good denies this status as an independent entity that Mill objects to it so strongly and in such absolute terms. To be able to choose is a good that is independent of the wisdom of what is chosen. A man's "mode of laying out his existence is the best, not because it is the best in itself, but because it is his own mode." It is the privilege and proper condition of a human being, arrived at the maturity of his faculties, to use and interpret experience in his own way.

As further evidence of this line of reasoning in Mill, consider the one exception to his prohibition against paternalism.

In this and most civilised countries, for example, an engagement by which a person should sell himself, or allow himself to be sold, as a slave, would be null and void; neither enforced by law nor by opinion. The ground for thus limiting his power of voluntarily disposing of his own lot in life, is apparent, and is very clearly seen in this extreme case. The reason for not interfering, unless for the sake of others, with a person's voluntary acts, is consideration for his liberty. His voluntary choice is evidence that what he so chooses is desirable, or at least endurable, to him, and his good is on the whole best provided for by allowing him to take his own means of pursuing it. But by selling himself for a slave, he abdicates his liberty; he foregoes any future use of it beyond that single act. He therefore defeats, in his own case, the very purpose which is the justification of allowing him to dispose of himself. He is no longer free; but is thenceforth in a position which has no longer the presumption in its favour, that would be afforded by his voluntarily remaining in it. The principle of freedom cannot require that he should be free not to be free. It is not freedom to be allowed to alienate his freedom.

Now leaving aside the fudging on the meaning of freedom in the last line, it is clear that part of this argument is incorrect. While it is true that *future* choices of the slave are not reasons for thinking that what he chooses then is desirable for him, what is at issue is limiting his immediate choice; and since this choice is made freely, the individual may be correct in thinking that his interests are best provided for by entering such a contract. But the main consideration for not allowing such a contract is the need to preserve the liberty of the person to make future choices. This gives us a principle—a very narrow one—by which to justify some paternalistic interferences. Paternalism is justified only to preserve a wider range of freedom for the individual in question. How far this principle could be extended, whether it can justify all the cases in which we are inclined upon reflection to think paternalistic measures justified, remains to be discussed. What I have tried to show so far is that there are two strains of argument in Mill—one a straight-forward utilitarian mode of reasoning and one which relies not on the goods which free choice leads to but on the absolute value of the choice itself. The first cannot establish any absolute prohibition but at most a presumption and indeed a fairly weak one given some fairly plausible assumptions about human psychology; the second, while a stronger line of argument, seems to me to allow on its own grounds a wider range of paternalism than might be suspected. I turn now to a consideration of these matters.

VI

We might begin looking for principles governing the acceptable use of paternalistic power in cases where it is generally agreed that it is legitimate. Even Mill intends his principles to be applicable only to mature individuals, not those in what he calls "non-age." What is it that justifies us in interfering with children? The fact that they lack some of the emotional and cognitive capacities required in order to make fully rational decisions. It is an empirical question to just what extent children have an adequate conception of their own present and future interests but there is not much doubt that there are many deficiencies. For example, it is very difficult for a child to defer gratification for any considerable period of time. Given these deficiencies and given the very real and permanent dangers that may befall the child, it becomes not only permissible but even a duty of the parent to restrict the child's freedom in various ways. There is however an important moral limitation on the exercise of such parental power which is provided by the notion of the child eventually coming to see the correctness of his parent's interventions. Parental paternalism may be thought of as a wager by the parent on the child's subsequent recognition of the wisdom of the restrictions. There is an emphasis on what could be called future-oriented consent—on what the child will come to welcome, rather than on what he does welcome.

The essence of this idea has been incorporated by idealist philosophers into various types of "real-will" theory as applied to fully adult persons. Extensions of paternalism are argued for by claiming that in various respects, chronologically mature individuals share the same deficiencies in knowledge, capacity to think rationally, and the ability to carry out decisions that children possess. Hence in interfering with such people we are in effect doing what they would do if they were fully rational. Hence we are not really opposing their will, hence we are not really interfering with their freedom. The dangers of this move have been sufficiently exposed by Berlin in his Two Concepts of Liberty. I see no gain in theoretical clarity nor in practical advantage in trying to pass over the real nature of the interferences with liberty that we impose on others. Still the basic notion of consent is important and seems to me the only acceptable way of trying to delimit an area of justified paternalism.

Let me start by considering a case where the consent is not hypothetical in nature. Under certain conditions it is rational for an individual to agree that others should force him to act in ways which, at the time of action, the individual may not see as desirable. If, for example, a man knows that he is subject to breaking his resolves when temptation is present, he may ask a friend to refuse to entertain his requests at some later stage.

A classical example is given in the Odyssey when Odysseus commands his men to tie him to the mast and refuse all future orders to be set free, because he knows the power of the Sirens to enchant men with their songs. Here we are on relatively sound ground in later refusing Odysseus' request to be set free. He may even claim to have changed his mind but, since it is *just* such changes that he wished to guard against, we are entitled to ignore them.

A process analogous to this may take place on a social rather than individual basis. An electorate may mandate its representatives to pass legislation which when it comes time to "pay the price" may be unpalatable. I may believe that a tax increase is necessary to halt inflation though

I may resent the lower pay check each month. However in both this case and that of Odysseus, the measure to be enforced is specifically requested by the party involved and at some point in time there is genuine consent and agreement on the part of those persons whose liberty is infringed. Such is not the case for the paternalistic measures we have been speaking about. What must be involved here is not consent to specific measures but rather consent to a system of government, run by elected representatives, with an understanding that they may act to safeguard our interests in certain limited ways.

I suggest that since we are all aware of our irrational propensities, deficiencies in cognitive and emotional capacities, and avoidable and unavoidable ignorance, it is rational and prudent for us to in effect take out "social insurance policies." We may argue for and against proposed paternalistic measures in terms of what fully rational individuals would accept as forms of protection. Now clearly, since the initial agreement is not about specific measures we are dealing with a more-or-less blank check and therefore there have to be carefully defined limits. What I am looking for are certain kinds of conditions which make it plausible to suppose that rational men could reach agreement to limit their liberty even when other men's interest are not affected.

Of course as in any kind of agreement schema there are great difficulties in deciding what rational individuals would or would not accept. Particularly in sensitive areas of personal liberty, there is always a danger of the dispute over agreement and rationality being a disguised version of evaluative and normative disagreement.

Let me suggest types of situations in which it seems plausible to suppose that fully rational individuals would agree to having paternalistic restrictions imposed upon them. It is reasonable to suppose that there are "goods" such as health which any person would want to have in order to pursue his own good—no matter how that good is conceived. This is an argument used in connection with compulsory education for children but it seems to me that it can be extended to other goods which have this character. Then one could agree that the attainment of such goods should be promoted even when not recognized to be such, at the moment, by the individuals concerned.

An immediate difficulty arises from the fact that men are always faced with competing goods and that there may be reasons why even a value such as health—or indeed life—may be overridden by competing values. Thus the problem with the Christian Scientist and blood transfusions. It may be more important for him to reject "impure substances" than to go on living. The difficult problem that must be faced is whether one can give sense to the notion of a person irrationally attaching weights to competing values.

Consider a person who knows the statistical data on the probability of being injured when not wearing seat belts in an automobile and knows the types and gravity of the various injuries. He also insists that the inconvenience attached to fastening the belt every time he gets in and out of the car outweighs for him the possible risks to himself. I am inclined in this case to think that such a weighing is irrational. Given his life plans, which we are assuming are those of the average person, his interests and commitments already undertaken, I think it is safe to predict that we can find inconsistencies in his calculations at some point. I am assuming that this is not a man who for some conscious or unconscious reasons is trying to injure himself nor is he a man who just likes to "live dangerously." I am assuming that he is like us in all the relevant respects but just puts an enormously high negative value on inconvenience—one which does not seem comprehensible or reasonable.

It is always possible, of course, to assimilate this person to creatures like myself. I, also, neglect to fasten my seat belt and I concede such behavior is not rational but not because I weigh the inconvenience differently from those who fasten the belts. It is just that having made (roughly) the same calculation as everybody else, I ignore it in my actions. [Note: a much better case of weakness of the will than those usually given in ethics tests.] A plausible explanation for this deplorable habit is that although I know in some intellectual sense what the probabilities and risks are I do not fully appreciate them in an emotionally genuine manner.

We have two distinct types of situation in which a man acts in a nonrational fashion. In one case he attaches incorrect weights to some of his values; in the other he neglects to act in accordance with his actual preferences and desires. Clearly there is a stronger and more persuasive argument for paternalism in the latter situation. Here we are really not—by assumption—imposing a good on another person. But why may we not extend our interference to what we might call evaluative delusions? After all, in the case of cognitive delusions we are prepared, often, to act against the expressed will of the person involved. If a man believes that when he jumps out the

window he will float upwards—Robert Nozick's example—would not we detain him, forcibly if necessary? The reply will be that this man doesn't wish to be injured and if we could convince him that he is mistaken as to the consequences of his action, he would not wish to perform the action. But part of what is involved in claiming that the man who doesn't fasten his seat-belts is attaching an incorrect weight to the inconvenience of fastening them is that if he were to be involved in an accident and severely injured he would look back and admit that the inconvenience wasn't as bad as all that. So there is a sense in which, if I could convince him of the consequences of his action, he also would not wish to continue his present course of action. Now the notion of consequences being used here is covering a lot of ground. In one case it's being used to indicate what will or can happen as a result of a course of action and in the other it's making a prediction about the future evaluation of the consequences—in the first sense—of a course of action. And whatever the difference between facts and values—whether it be hard and fast or soft and slow—we are genuinely more reluctant to consent to interferences where evaluative differences are the issue. Let me now consider another factor which comes into play in some of these situations which may make an important difference in our willingness to consent to paternalistic restrictions.

Some of the decisions we make are of such a character that they produce changes which are in one or another way irreversible. Situations are created in which it is difficult or impossible to return to anything like the initial stage at which the decision was made. In particular, some of these changes will make it impossible to continue to make reasoned choices in the future. I am thinking specifically of decisions which involve taking drugs that are physically or psychologically addictive and those which are destructive of one's mental and physical capacities.

I suggest we think of the imposition of paternalistic interferences in situations of this kind as being a kind of insurance policy which we take out against making decisions which are far-reaching, potentially dangerous and irreversible. Each of these factors is important. Clearly there are many decisions we make that are relatively irreversible. In deciding to learn to play chess, I could predict in view of my general interest in games that some portion of my free time was going to be preempted and that it would not be easy to give up the game once I acquired a certain competence. But my whole life style was not going to be jeopardized in an extreme manner. Further it might be argued that even with addictive drugs such as heroin one's normal life plans would not be seriously interfered with if an inexpensive and adequate supply were readily available. So this type of argument might have a much narrower scope than appears to be the case at first.

A second class of cases concerns decisions which are made under extreme psychological and sociological pressures. I am not thinking here of the making of the decision as being something one is pressured into—for example, a good reason for making duelling illegal is that unless this is done many people might have to manifest their courage and integrity in ways in which they would rather not do so—but rather of decisions, such as that to commit suicide, which are usually made at a point where the individual is not thinking clearly and calmly about the nature of his decision. In addition, of course, this comes under the previous heading of all-too-irrevocable decisions. Now there are practical steps which a society could take if it wanted to decrease the possibility of suicide—for example not paying social security benefits to the survivors or, as religious institutions do, not allowing persons to be buried with the same status as natural deaths. I think we may count these as interferences with the liberty of persons to attempt suicide and the question is whether they are justifiable.

Using my argument schema the question is whether rational individuals would consent to such limitations. I see no reason for them to consent to an absolute prohibition but I do think it is reasonable for them to agree to some kind of enforced waiting period. Since we are all aware of the possibility of temporary states, such as great fear of depression, that are inimical to the making of well-informed and rational decisions, it would be prudent for all of us if there were some kind of institutional arrangement whereby we were restrained from making a decision which is so irreversible. What this would be like in practice is difficult to envisage and it may be that if no practical arrangements were feasible we would have to conclude that there should be no restriction at all on this kind of action. But we might have a "cooling off" period, in much the same way that we now require couples who file for divorce to go through a waiting period. Or, more far-fetched, we might imagine a Suicide Board composed of a psychologist and another member picked by the applicant. The Board would be required to meet and talk with the person proposing to take his life, though its approval would not be required.

A third class of decisions—these classes are not supposed to be disjoint—involves dangers which are either not sufficiently understood or appreciated correctly by the persons involved. Let me illustrate, using the example of cigarette smoking, a number of possible cases.

1. A man may not know the facts—for example, smoking between one and two packs a day shortens life expectancy 6.2 years, the costs and pain of the illness caused by smoking, et cetera.
2. A man may know the facts, wish to stop smoking, but not have the requisite will-power.
3. A man may know the facts but not have them play the correct role in his calculation because, say, he discounts the danger psychologically since it is remote in time and/or inflates the attractiveness of other consequences of his decision which he regards as beneficial.

In case 1 what is called for is education, the posting of warnings, et cetera. In case 2 there is no theoretical problem. We are not imposing a good on someone who rejects it. We are simply using coercion to enable people to carry out their own goals. (Note: There obviously is a difficulty in that only a subclass of the individuals affected wish to be prevented from doing what they are doing.) In case 3 there is a sense in which we are imposing a good on someone in that given his current appraisal of the facts he doesn't wish to be restricted. But in another sense we are not imposing a good since what is being claimed—and what must be shown or at least argued for—is that an accurate accounting on his part would lead him to reject his current course of action. Now we all know that such cases exist, that we are prone to disregarding dangers that are only possibilities, that immediate pleasures are often magnified and distorted.

If in addition the dangers are severe and far-reaching, we could agree to allow the state a certain degree of power to intervene in such situations. The difficulty is in specifying in advance, even vaguely, the class of cases in which intervention will be legitimate.

A related difficulty is that of drawing a line so that it is not the case that all ultra-hazardous activities are ruled out, for example, mountain-climbing, bull-fighting, sports-car racing, et cetera. There are some risks—even very great ones —which a person is entitled to take with his life.

A good deal depends on the nature of the deprivation—for example, does it prevent the person from engaging in the activity completely or merely limit his participation—and how important to the nature of the activity is the absence of restriction when this is weighed against the role that the activity plays in the life of the person. In the case of automobile seat belts, for example, the restriction is trivial in nature, interferes not at all with the use or enjoyment of the activity, and does, I am assuming, considerably reduce a high risk of serious injury. Whereas, for example, making mountain-climbing illegal completely prevents a person from engaging in an activity which may play an important role in his life and his conception of the person he is.

In general, the easiest cases to handle are those which can be argued about in the terms which Mill thought to be so important—a concern not just for the happiness or welfare, in some broad sense, of the individual but rather a concern for the autonomy and freedom of the person. I suggest that we would be most likely to consent to paternalism in those instances in which it preserves and enhances for the individual his ability to rationally consider and carry out his own decisions.

I have suggested in this essay a number of types of situations in which it seems plausible that rational men would agree to granting the legislative powers of a society the right to impose restrictions on what Mill calls "self-regarding" conduct. However, rational men knowing something about the resources of ignorance, ill-will and stupidity available to the lawmakers of a society—a good case in point is the history of drug legislation in the United States—will be concerned to limit such intervention to a minimum. I suggest in closing two principles designed to achieve this end.

In all cases of paternalistic legislation there must be a heavy and clear burden of proof placed on the authorities to demonstrate the exact nature of the harmful effects (or beneficial consequences) to be avoided (or achieved) and the probability of their occurrence. The burden of proof here is twofold—what lawyers distinguish as the burden of going forward and the burden of persuasion. That the authorities have the burden of going forward means that it is up to them to raise the question and bring forward evidence of the evils to be avoided. Unlike the case of new drugs, where the manufacturer must produce some evidence that the drug has been tested and found not harmful, no citizen has to show with respect to self-regarding conduct that it is not harmful or promotes his best interest. In addition the nature and cogency of the evidence for the harmfulness of the course of action must be set at a high level. To paraphrase a formulation of the burden of proof for criminal proceedings—better ten men ruin themselves than one man be unjustly deprived of liberty.

Finally, I suggest a principle of the least restrictive alternative. If there is an alternative way of accomplishing the desired end without restricting liberty although it may involve great expense, inconvenience, et cetera, the society must adopt it.

PRIVACY

HENRY M. HART, JR. and ALBERT M. SACKS

The Invitation to Dinner Case*

On the way home for lunch on Friday, January 6, 1956, Mr. Patrick met Mr. David, an acquaintance of his. Mr. Patrick told Mr. David that he expected Professor Thomas for dinner and would like Mr. David to join them both for dinner and for bridge afterward. Mr. Patrick explained to Mr. David that he must be sure about coming so that there would be enough persons for bridge. Bridge, he said, was a favorite game of Professor Thomas's, and he wanted to humor the professor because he needed his help in getting a job. Mr. David asked what there would be for dinner, and Mr. Patrick promised to have planked steak, which he knew to be a favorite dish of Mr. David's. On hearing this, Mr. David promised firmly to be there at 7 P.M.

At 6:30 P.M., while Mr. David was dressing, the telephone rang. On the line was his friend, Mr. Jack, who asked him to come over for a game of poker. Mr. David agreed at once, and left soon for Jack's house, telling his wife that he was going to Patrick's.

At 9 P.M. the telephone rang in Jack's house, and a voice asked for Mr. David. Mr. David answered, fearful that it was his wife, but it was Mr. Patrick, who could hardly talk from anger. He said: "So I knew where to find you, you . . . If you do not come over to my place at once, I'll sue you in court." Mr. David hung up the phone without answering, and told the story to Jack and his friends who had a good laugh. All of them kept on playing until the early morning hours.

Mr. Patrick was as good as his word, and his lawyer filed an action against Mr. David. He claimed damages for breach of contract, including the price of a portion of planked steak specially prepared for the defendant; $2,500 compensation for not getting a job (Professor Thomas having left in dudgeon immediately after dinner); and $1,000 for mental suffering.

Mr. Patrick's lawyer claimed that there had been a legally binding contract, supported by consideration, and that the defendant had wilfully and maliciously failed to fulfill his legal and moral obligation. While acknowledging that he could find no case directly in point, he argued that the common law is elastic, and capable of developing a remedy for every wrong, especially in a case such as this where there was reliance on a promise made upon consideration, damage suffered because of malicious default, and warning to the defendant that the matter would be taken to court.

Mr. David appeared without a lawyer, telling the judge that he never thought he could be summoned to court over a social dinner invitation, and asked that the case be dismissed.

How should the judge decide?

*From *The Legal Process* by Henry M. Hart, Jr. and Albert M. Sacks (Cambridge, Mass.: Tentative Edition, 1958), pp. 477–78. Copyright © 1958 by Henry M. Hart, Jr. and Albert M. Sacks. Reprinted by permission of Albert M. Sacks. (This problem was suggested by Mr. Y. Dror, LL.M. Harvard, 1955, and a candidate for the degree of S. J. D. at the Harvard Law School during the academic year 1955–56.)

GRISWOLD v. CONNECTICUT

United States Supreme Court, 1965*

Mr. Justice Douglas delivered the opinion of the Court.

Appellant Griswold is Executive Director of the Planned Parenthood League of Connecticut. Appellant Buxton is a licensed physician and a professor at the Yale Medical School who served as Medical Director for the League at its Center in New Haven—a center open and operating from November 1 to November 10, 1961, when appellants were arrested.

They gave information, instruction, and medical advice to *married persons* as to the means of preventing conception. They examined the wife and prescribed the best contraceptive device or material for her use. Fees were usually charged, although some couples were serviced free.

The statutes whose constitutionality is involved in this appeal are §§ 53–32 and 54–196 of the General Statutes of Connecticut (1958 rev.). The former provides:

"Any person who uses any drug, medicinal article or instrument for the purpose of preventing conception shall be fined not less than fifty dollars or imprisoned not less than sixty days nor more than one year or be both fined and imprisoned."

Section 54–196 provides:

"Any person who assists, abets, counsels, causes, hires or commands another to commit any offense may be prosecuted and punished as if he were the principal offender."

The appellants were found guilty as accessories and fined $100 each, against the claim that the accessory statute as so applied violated the Fourteenth Amendment. The Appellate Division of the Circuit Court affirmed. The Supreme Court of Errors affirmed that judgment.*

We think that appellants have standing to raise the constitutional rights of the married people with whom they had a professional relationship. . . . Certainly the accessory should have standing to assert that the offense which he is charged with assisting is not, or cannot constitutionally be, a crime . . .

Coming to the merits, we are met with a wide range of questions that implicate the Due Process Clause of the Fourteenth Amendment. Overtones of some arguments suggest that *Lochner* v. *New York,* 198 U.S. 45, should be our guide. But we decline that invitation.* We do not sit as a super-legislature to determine the wisdom, need, and propriety of laws that touch economic problems, business affairs, or social conditions. This law, however, operates directly on an intimate relation of husband and wife and their physician's role in one aspect of that relation.

The association of people is not mentioned in the Constitution nor in the Bill of Rights. The right to educate a child in a school of the parents' choice—whether public or private or parochial—is also not mentioned. Nor is the right to study any particular subject or any foreign language. Yet the First Amendment has been construed to include certain of those rights.

By *Pierce* v. *Society of Sisters,* * the right to educate one's children as one chooses is made applicable to the States by the force of the First and Fourteenth Amendments. By *Meyer* v. *Nebraska,* * the same dignity is given the right to study the German language in a private school. In other words, the State may not, consistently with the spirit of the First Amendment, contract the spectrum of available knowledge. The right of freedom of speech and press includes not only the right to utter or to print, but the right to distribute, the right to receive, the right to read* and freedom of inquiry, freedom of thought, and freedom to teach*—indeed the freedom of the entire university community.* Without those peripheral rights the specific rights would be less secure . . .

In *NAACP* v. *Alabama,* 357 U.S. 449, 462, we protected the "freedom to associate and privacy in one's associations," noting that freedom of association was a peripheral First Amendment right. Disclosure of membership lists of a constitutionally valid association, we held, was invalid "as entailing the likelihood of a substantial restraint upon the exercise by petitioner's members of their right to freedom of association." *Ibid.* In other words, the First Amendment has a penumbra where privacy is protected from governmental intru-

*381 U.S. 479 (1965). Excerpts only. Footnotes renumbered.

*Citation omitted (Eds.)

sion. In like context, we have protected forms of "association" that are not political in the customary sense but pertain to the social, legal, and economic benefit of the members.* In *Schware* v. *Board of Bar Examiners,* 353 U.S. 232, we held it not permissible to bar a lawyer from practice, because he had once been a member of the Communist Party. The man's "association with that Party" was not shown to be "anything more than a political faith in a political party"* and was not action of a kind proving bad moral character.*

Those cases involved more than the "right of assembly"—a right that extends to all irrespective of their race or ideology.* The right of "association," like the right of belief,* is more than the right to attend a meeting; it includes the right to express one's attitudes or philosophics by membership in a group or by affiliation with it or by other lawful means. Association in that context is a form of expression of opinion; and while it is not expressly included in the First Amendment its existence is necessary in making the express guarantees fully meaningful.

The foregoing cases suggest that specific guarantees in the Bill of Rights have penumbras, formed by emanations from those guarantees that help give them life and substance.* Various guarantees create zones of privacy. The right of association contained in the penumbra of the First Amendment is one, as we have seen. The Third Amendment in its prohibition against the quartering of soldiers "in any house" in time of peace without the consent of the owner is another facet of that privacy. The Fourth Amendment explicitly affirms the "right of the people to be secure in their persons, houses, papers, and effects, against unreasonable searches and seizures." The Fifth Amendment in its Self-Incrimination Clause enables the citizen to create a zone of privacy which government may not force him to surrender to his detriment. The Ninth Amendment provides: "The enumeration in the Constitution, of certain rights, shall not be construed to deny or disparage others retained by the people."

The Fourth and Fifth Amendments were described in *Boyd* v. *United States,* 116 U.S. 616, 630, as protection against all governmental invasions "of the sanctity of a man's home and the privacies of life." We recently referred in *Mapp* v. *Ohio,* 367 U.S. 643, 656, to the Fourth Amendment as creating a "right to privacy, no less important than any other right carefully and particularly reserved to the people."* These cases bear witness that the right of privacy which presses for recognition here is a legitimate one.

The present case, then, concerns a relationship lying within the zone of privacy created by several fundamental constitutional guarantees. And it concerns a

law which, in forbidding the *use* of contraceptives rather than regulating their manufacture or sale, seeks to achieve its goals by means having a maximum destructive impact upon that relationship. Such a law cannot stand in light of the familiar principle, so often applied by this Court, that a "governmental purpose to control or prevent activities constitutionally subject to state regulation may not be achieved by means which sweep unnecessarily broadly and thereby invade the area of protected freedoms." *NAACP* v. *Alabama,* 377 U.S. 288, 307. Would we allow the police to search the sacred precincts of marital bedrooms for telltale signs of the use of contraceptives? The very idea is repulsive to the notions of privacy surrounding the marriage relationship.

We deal with a right of privacy older than the Bill of Rights—older than our political parties, older than our school system. Marriage is a coming together for better or for worse, hopefully enduring, and intimate to the degree of being sacred. It is an association that promotes a way of life, not causes; a harmony in living, not political faiths; a bilateral loyalty, not commercial or social projects. Yet it is an association for as noble a purpose as any involved in our prior decisions.

Reversed.

Mr. Justice Goldberg, whom The Chief Justice and Mr. Justice Brennan join, concurring ... My Brother Stewart dissents on the ground that he "can find no ... general right of privacy in the Bill of Rights, in any other part of the Constitution, or in any case ever before decided by this Court." He would require a more explicit guarantee than the one which the Court derives from several constitutional amendments. This Court, however, has never held that the Bill of Rights or the Fourteenth Amendment protects only those rights that the Constitution specifically mentions by name ...

My Brother Stewart, while characterizing the Connecticut birth control law as "an uncommonly silly law," would nevertheless let it stand on the ground that it is not for the courts to " 'substitute their social and economic beliefs for the judgment of legislative bodies, who are elected to pass laws.' " Elsewhere, I have stated that "[w]hile I quite agree with Mr. Justice Brandeis that ... 'a ... State may ... serve as a laboratory; and try novel social and economic experiments,'* I do not believe that this includes the power to experiment with the fundamental liberties of citizens...." The vice of the dissenters' views is that it would permit such experimentation by the States in the area of the fundamental personal rights of its citizens. I cannot agree that the Constitution grants such either to the States or to the Federal Government.

The logic of the dissents would sanction federal or state legislation that seems to me even more plainly

*Citation omitted [Eds.]

unconstitutional than the statute before us. Surely the Government, absent a showing of a compelling subordinating state interest, could not decree that all husbands and wives must be sterilized after two children have been born to them. Yet by their reasoning such an invasion of marital privacy would not be subject to constitutional challenge because, while it might be "silly," no provision of the Constitution specifically prevents the Government from curtailing the marital right to bear children and raise a family. While it may shock some of my Brethren that the Court today holds that the Constitution protects the right of marital privacy in my view it is far more shocking to believe that the personal liberty guaranteed by the Constitution does not include protection against such totalitarian limitation of family size, which is at complete variance with our constitutional concepts. Yet, if upon a showing of a slender basis of rationality, a law outlawing voluntary birth control by married persons is valid, then, by the same reasoning a law requiring compulsory birth control also would seem to be valid. In my view, however, both types of law would unjustifiably intrude upon rights of marital privacy which are constitutionally protected.

In a long series of cases this Court has held that where fundamental personal liberties are involved, they may not be abridged by the States simply on a showing that a regulatory statute has some rational relationship to the effectuation of a proper state purpose. "Where there is a significant encroachment upon personal liberty, the State may prevail only upon showing a subordinating interest which is compelling," *Bates* v. *Little Rock,* 361 U.S. 516, 524. The law must be shown "necessary, and not merely rationally related, to the accomplishment of a permissible state policy." *McLaughlin* v. *Florida,* 379 U.S. 184, 196.*

Although the Connecticut birth-control law obviously encroaches upon a fundamental personal liberty, the State does not show that the law serves any "subordinating [state] interest which is compelling" or that it is "necessary . . . to the accomplishment of a permissible state policy." The State, at most, argues that there is some rational relation between this statute and what is admittedly a legitimate subject of state concern—the discouraging of extra-marital relations. It says that preventing the use of birth-control devices by married persons helps prevent the indulgence by some in such extra-marital relations. The rationality of this justification is dubious, particularly in light of the admitted widespread availability to all persons in the State of Connecticut, unmarried as well as married, of birth-control devices for the prevention of disease, as distin-

guished from the prevention of conception.* But, in any event, it is clear that the state interest in safeguarding marital fidelity can be served by a more discriminately tailored statute, which does not, like the present one, sweep unnecessarily broadly, reaching far beyond the evil sought to be dealt with and intruding upon the privacy of all married couples.* Here, as elsewhere, "[p]recision of regulation must be the touchstone in an area so closely touching our most precious freedoms." *NAACP* v. *Button,* 371 U.S. 415, 438. The State of Connecticut does have statutes, the constitutionality of which is beyond doubt, which prohibit adultery and fornication.* These statutes demonstrate that means for achieving the same basic purpose of protecting marital fidelity are available to Connecticut without the need to "invade the area of protected freedoms." *NAACP* v. *Alabama, supra,* at 307.*

Finally, it should be said of the Court's holding today that it in no way interferes with a State's proper regulation of sexual promiscuity or misconduct. As my Brother Harlan so well stated in his dissenting opinion in *Poe* v. *Ullman,*

"Adultery, homosexuality and the like are sexual intimacies which the State forbids . . . but the intimacy of husband and wife is necessarily an essential and accepted feature of the institution of marriage, an institution which the State not only must allow, but which always and in every age it has fostered and protected. It is one thing when the State exerts its power either to forbid extra-marital sexuality . . . or to say who may marry, but it is quite another when, having acknowledged a marriage and the intimacies inherent in it, it undertakes to regulate by means of the criminal law the details of that intimacy."

In sum, I believe that the right of privacy in the marital relation is fundamental and basic—a personal right "retained by the people" within the meaning of the Ninth Amendment. Connecticut cannot constitutionally abridge this fundamental right, which is protected by the Fourteenth Amendment from infringement by the States. I agree with the Court that petitioners' convictions must therefore be reversed . . .

Mr. Justice Black, with whom Mr. Justice Stewart joins, dissenting.

I agree with my Brother Stewart's dissenting opinion. And like him I do not to any extent whatever base my view that this Connecticut law is constitutional on a belief that the law is wise or that its policy is a good one. In order that there may be no room at all to doubt why I vote as I do, I feel constrained to add that the law is every bit as offensive to me as it is to my Brethren of the majority and my Brothers Harlan, White and Goldberg who, reciting reasons why it is offensive to them, hold it unconstitutional. There is no single one of the graphic and eloquent strictures and criticisms fired at the policy of this Connecticut law either by the Court's opinion or by those of my concurring Brethren

*Citation omitted [Eds.]

to which I cannot subscribe—except their conclusion that the evil qualities they see in the law make it unconstitutional . . .

The Court talks about a constitutional "right of privacy" as though there is some constitutional provision or provisions forbidding any law ever to be passed which might abridge the "privacy" of individuals. But there is not. There are, of course, guarantees in certain specific constitutional provisions which are designed in part to protect privacy at certain times and places with respect to certain activities. Such, for example, is the Fourth Amendment's guarantee against "unreasonable searches and seizures." But I think it belittles that Amendment to talk about it as though it protects nothing but "privacy." To treat it that way is to give it a niggardly interpretation, not the kind of liberal reading I think any Bill of Rights provision should be given. The average man would very likely not have his feelings soothed any more by having his property seized openly than by having it seized privately and by stealth. He simply wants his property left alone. And a person can be just as much, if not more, irritated, annoyed and injured by an unceremonious public arrest by a policeman as he is by a seizure in the privacy of his office or home.

One of the most effective ways of diluting or expanding a constitutionally guaranteed right is to substitute for the crucial word or words of a constitutional guarantee another word or words, more or less flexible and more or less restricted in meaning. This fact is well illustrated by the use of the term "right of privacy" as a comprehensive substitute for the Fourth Amendment's guarantee against "unreasonable searches and seizures." "Privacy" is a broad, abstract and ambiguous concept which can easily be shrunken in meaning but which can also, on the other hand, easily be interpreted as a constitutional ban against many things other than searches and seizures. I have expressed the view many times that First Amendment freedoms, for example, have suffered from a failure of the courts to stick to the simple language of the First Amendment in construing it, instead of invoking multitudes of words substituted for those the Framers used.* For these reasons I get nowhere in this case by talk about a constitutional "right of privacy" as an emanation from one or more constitutional provisions. I like my privacy as well as the next one, but I am nevertheless compelled to admit that government has a right to invade it unless prohibited by some specific constitutional provision. For these reasons I cannot agree with the Court's judgment and the reasons it gives for holding this Connecticut law unconstitutional . . .

The due process argument which my Brothers Har-

lan and White adopt here is based, as their opinions indicate, on the premise that this Court is vested with power to invalidate all state laws that it considers to be arbitrary, capricious, unreasonable, or oppressive, or on this Court's belief that a particular state law under scrutiny has no "rational or justifying" purpose, or is offensive to a "sense of fairness and justice." If these formulas based on "natural justice," or others which mean the same thing,[1] are to prevail, they require judges to determine what is or is not constitutional on the basis of their own appraisal of what laws are unwise or unnecessary. The power to make such decisions is of course that of a legislative body. Surely it has to be admitted that no provision of the Constitution specifically gives such blanket power to courts to exercise such a supervisory veto over the wisdom and value of legislative policies and to hold unconstitutional those laws which they believe unwise or dangerous. I readily admit that no legislative body, state or national, should pass laws that can justly be given any of the invidious labels invoked as constitutional excuses to strike down state laws. But perhaps it is not too much to say that no legislative body ever does pass laws without believing that they will accomplish a sane, rational, wise and justifiable purpose. While I completely subscribe to the holding of *Marbury* v. *Madison,* and subsequent cases, that our Court has constitutional power to strike down statutes, state or federal, that violate commands of the Federal Constitution, I do not believe that we are granted power by the Due Process Clause or any other constitutional provision or provisions to measure constitutionality by our belief that legislation is arbitrary, capricious or unreasonable, or accomplishes no justifiable purpose, or is offensive to our own notions of "civilized standards of conduct."[2] Such an appraisal of the wisdom of legislation is an attribute of the power to make laws, not of the power to interpret them. The use by federal courts of such a formula or doctrine or whatnot to veto federal or state laws simply takes away from Congress and States the power to make laws based on their own judgment of fairness and wisdom and transfers that power to this Court for ultimate determination—a power which was specifically denied to federal courts by the convention that framed the Constitution. . . .

My Brother Goldberg has adopted the recent discovery[3] that the Ninth Amendment as well as the Due Process Clause can be used by this Court as authority to strike down all state legislation which this Court thinks violates "fundamental principles of liberty and justice," or is contrary to the "traditions and [collective] conscience of our people." He also states, without proof satisfactory to me, that in making decisions on this basis judges will not consider "their personal and private notions." One may ask how they can avoid considering them. Our Court certainly has no machinery with which to take a Gallup Poll.[4] And the scientific miracles of this age have not yet produced a gadget which the Court can use to determine what traditions are rooted in the "[collective] conscience of our people." Moreover, one would certainly have to look far beyond the language of the Ninth Amendment[5] to find that the Framers vested in this Court any such awesome veto powers over lawmaking, either by the States or by the Congress. Nor does anything in the history of the Amendment offer any support for such a shocking doctrine. The whole history of the adoption of the Constitution and Bill of Rights points the other way, and the very material quoted by my Brother Goldberg shows that the Ninth Amendment was intended to protect against the idea that "by enumerating particular exceptions to the grant of power" to the Federal Government, "those rights which were not singled out, were intended to be assigned into the hands of the General Government [the United States], and were consequently insecure."[6] That Amendment was passed, not to broaden the powers of this Court or any other department of "the General Government," but, as every student of history knows, to assure the people that the Constitution in all its provisions was intended to limit the Federal Government to the powers granted expressly or by necessary implication. If any broad, unlimited power to hold laws unconstitutional because they offend what this Court conceives to be the "[collective] conscience of our people" is vested in this Court by the Ninth Amendment, the Fourteenth Amendment, or any other provision of the Constitution, it was not given by the Framers, but rather has been bestowed on the Court by the Court. This fact is perhaps responsible for the peculiar phenomenon that for a period of a century and a half no serious suggestion was ever made that the Ninth Amendment, enacted to protect state powers against federal invasion, could be used as a weapon of federal power to prevent state legislatures from passing laws they consider appropriate to govern local affairs. Use of any such broad, unbounded judicial authority would make of this Court's members a day-to-day constitutional convention.

NOTES

1. A collection of the catchwords and catch phrases invoked by judges who would strike down under the Fourteenth Amendment laws which offend their notions of natural justice would fill many pages. Thus it has been said that this Court can forbid state action which "shocks the conscience," *Rochin* v. *California,* 342 U.S. 165, 172, sufficiently to "shock itself into the protective arms of the Constitution," *Irvine* v. *California,* 347 U.S. 128, 138 (concurring opinion). It has been

urged that States may not run counter to the "decencies of civilized conduct," *Rochin, supra,* at 173, or "some principle of justice so rooted in the traditions, and conscience of our people as to be ranked as fundamental," *Snyder* v. *Massachusetts,* 291 U.S. 97, 105, or to "those canons of decency and fairness which express the notions of justice of English-speaking peoples," *Malinski* v. *New York,* 324 U.S. 401, 417 (concurring opinion), or to "the community's sense of fair play and decency," *Rochin, supra,* at 173. It has been said that we must decide whether a state law is "fair, reasonable and appropriate," or is rather "an unreasonable, unnecessary and arbitrary interference with the right of the individual to his personal liberty or to enter into . . . contracts," *Lochner* v. *New York,* 198 U.S. 45, 56. States, under this philosophy, cannot act in conflict with "deeply rooted feelings of the community," *Haley* v. *Ohio,* 332 U.S. 596, 604 (separate opinion), or with "fundamental notions of fairness and justice," *id.,* 607. See also, e.g., *Wolf* v. *Colorado,* 338 U.S. 25, 27 ("rights . . . basic to our free society"); *Hebert* v. *Louisiana,* 272 U.S. 312, 316 ("fundamental principles of liberty and justice"); *Adkins* v. *Children's Hospital,* 261 U.S. 525, 561 ("arbitrary restraint of . . . liberties"); *Betts* v. *Brady,* 316 U.S. 455, 462 ("denial of fundamental fairness, shocking to the universal sense of justice"); *Poe* v. *Ullman,* 367 U.S. 497, 539 (dissenting opinion) ("intolerable and unjustifiable"). Perhaps the clearest, frankest and briefest explanation of how this due process approach works is the statement in another case handed down today that this Court is to invoke the Due Process Clause to strike down state procedures or laws which it can "not tolerate." *Linkletter* v. *Walker, post,* p. 618, at 631.

2. See Hand, The Bill of Rights (1958) 70: "[J]udges are seldom content merely to annul the particular solution before them; they do not, indeed they may not, say that taking all things into consideration, the legislators' solution is too strong for the judicial stomach. On the contrary they wrap up their veto in a protective veil of adjectives such as 'arbitrary,' 'artificial,' 'normal,' 'reasonable,' 'inherent.' 'fundamental,' or 'essential,' whose office usually, though quite innocently, is to disguise what they are doing and impute to it a derivation far more impressive than their personal preferences, which are all that in fact lie behind the decision." [Citations omitted—Eds.]

3. See Patterson, The Forgotten Ninth Amendment (1955). Mr. Patterson urges that the Ninth Amendment be used to protect unspecified "natural and inalienable rights." P. 4. The Introduction by Roscoe Pound states that "there is a marked revival of natural law ideas throughout the world. Interest in the Ninth Amendment is a symptom of that revival." P. iii.

4. Of course one cannot be oblivious to the fact that Mr. Gallup has already published the results of a poll which he says show that 46% of the people in this country believe schools should teach about birth control. Washington Post, May 21, 1965, p. 2, col. 1. I can hardly believe, however, that Brother Goldberg would view 46% of the persons polled as so overwhelming a proportion that this Court may now rely on it to declare that the Connecticut law infringes "fundamental" rights, and overrule the long-standing view of the people of Connecticut expressed through their elected representatives.

5. U.S. Const., Amend. IX, provides: "The enumeration in the Constitution, of certain rights, shall not be construed to deny or disparage others retained by the people."

6. Annuals of Congress 439.

HYMAN GROSS

Privacy and Autonomy*

[handwritten marginalia: what are / + determinants / + boundaries / of + right privacy / + what should to be]

Why is privacy desirable? When is its loss objectionable and when is it not? How much privacy is a person entitled to? These questions challenge at the threshold our concern about protection of privacy. Usually they are pursued by seeking agreement on the boundary between morbid and healthy reticence, and by attempting to determine when unwanted intrusion or notoriety is justified by something more important than privacy. Seldom is privacy considered as the condition under which there is *control* over acquaintance with one's personal affairs by the one enjoying it, and I wish here to show how consideration of privacy in this neglected aspect is helpful in answering the basic questions. First I shall attempt to make clear this part of the idea of privacy, next suggest why privacy in this aspect merits protection, then argue that some important dilemmas are less vexing when we do get clear about these things, and finally offer a cautionary remark regarding the relation of privacy and autonomy.

I

What in general is it that makes certain conduct offensive to privacy? To distinguish obnoxious from innocent interference with privacy we must first see clearly what constitutes loss of privacy at all, and then determine why loss of privacy when it does occur is sometimes objectionable and sometimes not.

Loss of privacy occurs when the limits one has set on acquaintance with his personal affairs are not respected. Almost always we mean not respected by *others,* though in unusual cases we might speak of a person not respecting his own privacy—he is such a passionate gossip, say, that he gossips even about himself and later regrets it. Limits on acquaintance may be maintained by the physical insulation of a home, office, or other private place within which things that are to be private may be confined. Or such bounds may exist by virtue of exclusionary social conventions, for example those governing a private conversation in a public place; or through restricting conventions which impose an obligation to observe such limits, as when disclosure is made in confidence. Limits operate in two ways. There are restrictions on what is known, and restrictions on who may know it. Thus, a curriculum vitae furnished to or for a prospective employer is not normally an invitation to undertake a detective investigation using the items provided as clues. Nor is there normally license to communicate to others the information submitted. In both instances there would be disregard of limitations implied by considerations of privacy, unless the existence of such limitations is unreasonable under the circumstances (the prospective employer is the CIA, or the information is furnished to an employment agency). But there is no loss of privacy when such limits as do exist are respected, no matter how ample the disclosure or how extensive its circulation. If I submit a detailed account of my life while my friend presents only the barest résumé of his, I am not giving up more of privacy than he. And if I give the information to a hundred employers, I lose no more in privacy than my friend who confides to only ten, provided those informed by each of us are equally restricted. More people know more about me, so my *risk* of losing privacy is greater and the threatened loss more serious. Because I am a less private person than my friend, I am more willing to run that risk. But until there is loss of control over what is known, and by whom, my privacy is uncompromised—though much indeed may be lost in secrecy, mystery, obscurity, and anonymity.

Privacy is lost in either of two ways. It may be given up, or it may be taken away. Abandonment of privacy (though sometimes undesired) is an inoffensive loss, while deprivation by others is an offensive loss.

*From *Nomos XIII, Privacy,* ed. by John Chapman and J. Roland Pennock (New York: Lieber-Atherton, 1971), pp. 169–182. Reprinted by permission of the publisher.

If one makes a public disclosure of personal matters or exposes himself under circumstances that do not contain elements of restriction on further communication, there is loss of control for which the person whose privacy is lost is himself responsible. Such abandonment may result from indifference, carelessness, or a positive desire to have others become acquainted. There are, however, instances in which privacy is abandoned though this was not intended. Consider indiscrete disclosures while drunk which are rued when sober. If the audience is not under some obligation (perhaps the duty of a confidant) to keep dark what was revealed, there has been a loss of privacy for which the one who suffers it is responsible. But to constitute an abandonment, the loss of privacy must result from voluntary conduct by the one losing it, and the loss must be an expectable result of such conduct. If these two conditions are not met, the person who suffers the loss cannot be said to be responsible for it. Accordingly, a forced revelation, such as an involuntary confession, is not an abandonment of privacy, because the person making it has not given up control but has had it taken from him.

Regarding the requirement of expectability, we may see its significance by contrasting the case of a person whose conversation is overheard in Grand Central Station with the plight of someone made the victim of eavesdropping in his living room. In a public place loss of control is expectable by virtue of the circumstances of communication: part of what we mean when we say a place is public is that there is not present the physical limitation upon which such control depends. But a place may be called private only when there is such limitation, so communication in it is expectably limited and the eavesdropping an offensive violation for which the victim is not himself responsible. And consider the intermediate case of eavesdropping on a conversation in a public place —a distant parabolic microphone focused on a street-corner conversation, or a bugging device planted in an airplane seat. The offensive character of such practices derives again from their disregard of expectable limitations, in this instance the force of an exclusionary social convention which applies to all except those whose immediate presence enables them to overhear.

So far there has been consideration of what constitutes loss of privacy, and when it is objectionable. But to assess claims for protection of privacy we must be clear also about *why* in general loss of privacy is objectionable. This becomes especially important when privacy and other things we value are in competition, one needing to be sacrificed to promote the other. It becomes important then to understand what good reasons there are for valuing privacy, and this is our next item of business.

II

There are two sorts of things we keep private, and with respect to each, privacy is desirable for somewhat different reasons. Concern for privacy is sometimes concern about which facts about us can become known, and to whom. This includes acquaintance with all those things which make up the person as he may become known—identity, appearance, traits of personality and character, talents, weaknesses, tastes, desires, habits, interests—in short, things which tell us who a person is and what he's like. The other kind of private matter is about our lives—what we've done, intend to do, are doing now, how we feel, what we have, what we need—and concern about privacy here is to restrict acquaintance with these matters. Together these two classes of personal matters comprise all those things which can be private. Certain items of information do indeed have aspects which fit them for either category. For example, a person's belief is something which pertains to him when viewed as characteristic of him, but pertains to the events of his life when viewed as something he has acquired, acts on, and endeavors to have others adopt.

Why is privacy of the person important? This calls mainly for consideration of what is necessary to maintain an integrated personality in a social setting. Although we are largely unaware of what influences us at the time, we are constantly concerned to control how we appear to others, and act to implement this concern in ways extremely subtle and multifarious. Models of image and behavior are noticed, imitated, adopted, so that nuances in speech, gesture, facial expression, *politesse,* and much more become a person as known on an occasion. The deep motive is to influence the reactions of others, and this is at the heart of human social accommodation. Constraints to imitation and disguise can become a pathological problem of serious proportions when concern with appearances interferes with normal functioning, but normal behavior allows, indeed requires, that we perform critically in presenting and withholding in order to effect certain appearances. If these editorial efforts are not to be wasted, we must have a large measure of control over what of us is seen and heard, when, where, and by whom. For this reason we see as offensive the candid camera which records casual behavior with the intention of later showing it as entertainment to a general audience. The victim is not at the time aware of who will see him and so does not have the opportunity to exercise appropriate critical restraint in what he says and does. Although subsequent approval for the showing eliminates grounds for objection to the publication as an offense to privacy, there remains the lingering objection to the prior disregard of limits of acquaintance which are normal to the situation and so presumably relied on by the victim at the time. The nature of the offense is further illuminated by considering its aggravation when the victim has been deliberately introduced unawares into the situation for the purpose of filming his behavior, or its still greater offensiveness if the setting is a place normally providing privacy and assumed to be private by the victim. What we have here are increasingly serious usurpations of a person's prerogative to determine how he shall appear, to whom, and on what occasion.

The same general objection applies regarding loss of privacy where there is information about our personal affairs which is obtained, accumulated, and transmitted by means beyond our control. It is, however, unlike privacy of personality in its untoward consequences. A data bank of personal information is considered objectionable, but not because it creates appearances over which we have no control. We are willing to concede that acquaintance with our reputation is in general not something we are privileged to control, and that we are not privileged to decide just what our reputation shall be. If the reputation is correct we cannot object because we do not appear as we would wish. What then are the grounds of objection to a data bank, an objection which indeed persists even if its information is correct and the inferences based on the information are sound? A good reason for objecting is that a data bank is an offense to self-determination. We are subject to being acted on by others because of conclusions about us which we do not know and whose effect we have no opportunity to counteract. There is a loss of control over reputation which is unacceptable because we no longer have the ability to try to change what is believed about us. We feel entitled to know what others believe, and why, so that we may try to change misleading impressions and on occasion show why a decision about us ought not to be based on reputation even if the reputation is justified. If our account in the data bank were made known to us and opportunity given to change its effect, we should drop most (though not all) of our objection to it. We might still fear the danger of abuse by public forces concerned more with the demands of administrative convenience than justice, but because we could make deposits and demand a statement reflecting them, we would at least no longer be in the position of having what is known and surmised about us lie beyond our control.

Two aspects of privacy have been considered separately, though situations in which privacy is violated sometimes involve both. Ordinary surveillance by shadowing, peeping, and bugging commonly consists of observation of personal behavior as well as accumulation of information. Each is objectionable for its own reasons, though in acting against the offensive practice we protect privacy in both aspects. Furthermore, privacy of personality and of personal affairs have some common ground in meriting protection, and this has to do with a person's role as a responsible moral agent.

In general we do not criticize a person for untoward occurrences which are a result of his conduct if (through no fault of his own) he lacked the ability to do otherwise. Such a person is similarly ineligible for applause for admirable things which would not have taken place but for his conduct. In both instances we claim that he is not responsible for what happened, and so should not be blamed or praised. The principle holds true regarding loss of privacy. If a person cannot control how he is made to appear (nor could he have prevented his loss of control), he is not responsible for how he appears or is thought of, and therefore cannot be criticized as displeasing or disreputable (nor extolled as the opposite). He can, of course, be condemned for conduct which is the basis of the belief about him, but that is a different matter from criticism directed solely to the fact that such a belief exists. Personal gossip (even when believed) is not treated by others as something for which the subject need answer, because its existence defies his control. Responsible appraisal of anyone whose image or reputation is a matter of concern requires that certain private items illicitly in the public domain be ignored in the assessment. A political figure may, with impunity, be known as someone who smokes, drinks, flirts, and tells dirty jokes, so long (but only so long) as this is not the public image *he* presents. The contrasting fortunes of recent political leaders remind us that not being responsible for what is believed by others can be most important. If such a man is thought in his private life to engage in discreet though illicit liaisons he is not held accountable for rumors without more. However, once he has allowed himself to be publicly exposed in a situation which is in the slightest compromising, he must answer for mere appearances. And on this same point, we might consider why a woman is never held responsible for the way she appears in the privacy of her toilette.

To appreciate the importance of this sort of disclaimer of responsibility we need only imagine a community in which it is not recognized. Each person would be accountable for himself however he might be known, and regardless of any precautionary seclusion which was undertaken in the interest of shame, good taste, or from other motives of self-regard. In such a world modesty is sacrificed to the embarrassment of unwanted acclaim, and self-criticism is replaced by the condemnation of others. It is part of the vision of Orwell's *1984*, in which observation is so thorough that it forecloses the possibility of a private sector of life under a person's exclusionary control, and so makes him answerable for everything observed without limits of time or place. Because of this we feel such a condition of life far more objectionable than a community which makes the same oppressive social demands of loyalty and conformity but with the opportunity to be free of concern about appearances in private. In a community without privacy, furthermore, there can be no editorial privilege exercised in making oneself known to others. Consider, for example, the plight in which Montaigne would find himself. He observed that "No quality embraces us purely and universally. If it did not seem crazy to talk to oneself, there is not a day when I would not be heard growling at myself: 'Confounded fool!' And yet I do not intend that to be my definition." Respect for privacy is required to safeguard our changes of mood and mind, and to promote growth of the person through self-discovery and criticism. We want to run the risk of making fools of ourselves and be free to call ourselves fools, yet not be fools in the settled opinion of the world, convicted out of our own mouths.

III

Privacy is desirable, but rights to enjoy it are not absolute. In deciding what compromises must be made some deep quandaries recur, and three of them at least seem more manageable in light of what has been said so far.

In the first place, insistence on privacy is often taken as implied admission that there is cause for shame. The assumption is that the only reason for

keeping something from others is that one is ashamed of it (although it is conceded that sometimes there is in fact no cause for shame even though the person seeking privacy thinks there is). Those who seek information and wish to disregard interests in privacy often play on this notion by claiming that the decent and the innocent have no cause for shame and so no need for privacy: "Only those who have done or wish to do something shameful demand privacy." But it is unsound to assume that demands for privacy imply such an admission. Pride, or at least wholesome self-regard, is the motive in many situations. The famous Warren and Brandeis article on privacy which appeared in the *Harvard Law Review* in 1890 was impelled in some measure, we are told, by Samuel Warren's chagrin. His daughter's wedding, a very social Boston affair, had been made available to the curious at every newsstand by the local press. Surely he was not ashamed of the wedding even though outraged by the publicity. Or consider Miss Roberson, the lovely lady whose picture was placed on a poster advertising the product of Franklin Mills with the eulogistic slogan "Flour of the family," thereby precipitating a lawsuit whose consequences included the first statutory protection of privacy in the United States. What was exploited was the lady's face, undoubtedly a source of pride.

Both these encroachments on privacy illustrate the same point. Things which people like about themselves are taken by them to belong to them in a particularly exclusive way, and so control over disclosure or publication is especially important to them. The things about himself which a person is most proud of he values most, and thus are things over which he is most interested to exercise exclusive control. It is true that shame is not infrequently the motive for privacy, for often we do seek to maintain conditions necessary to avoid criticism and punishment. But since it is not the only motive, the quest for privacy does not entail tacit confessions. Confusion arises here in part because an assault on privacy always does involve humiliation of the victim. But this is because he has been deprived of control over something personal which is given over to the control of others. In short, unwilling loss of privacy always results in the victim being shamed, not because of what others learn, but because they and not he may then determine who else shall know it and what use shall be made of it.

Defining the privilege to make public what is otherwise private is another source of persistent difficulty. There is a basic social interest in making available information about people, in exploring the personal aspects of human affairs, in stimulating and satisfying curiosity about others. The countervailing interest is in allowing people who have not offered themselves for public scrutiny to remain out of sight and out of mind. In much of the United States the law has strained with the problem of drawing a line of protection which accords respect to both interests. The result, broadly stated, has been recognition of a privilege to compromise privacy for news and other material whose primary purpose is to impart information, but to deny such privileged status to literary and other art, to entertainment, and generally to any appropriation for commercial purposes. Development of the law in New York after Miss Roberson's unsuccessful attempt to restrain public display of her picture serves as a good example. A statute was enacted prohibiting unauthorized use of the name, portrait, or picture of any living person for purposes of trade or advertising, and the legislation has been interpreted by the courts along the general lines indicated. But it is still open to speculation why a writer's portrayal of a real person as a character in a novel could qualify as violative, while the same account in biographical or historical work would not. It has not been held that history represents a more important social interest than art and so is more deserving of a privileged position in making known personal matters, or, more generally, that edification is more important than entertainment. Nor is the question ever raised, as one might expect, whether an item of news is sufficiently newsworthy to enjoy a privilege in derogation of privacy. Further, it was not held that the implied statutory criterion of intended economic benefit from the use of a personality would warrant the fundamental distinctions. Indeed, the test of economic benefit would qualify both television's public affairs programs and its dramatic shows as within the statute, and the reportage of *Life* Magazine would be as restricted as the films of De Mille or Fellini. But in each instance the former is in general free of the legal prohibition while the latter is not. What, then, is the basis of distinction? Though not articulated, a sound criterion does exist.

Unauthorized *use* of another person—whether for entertainment, artistic creation, or economic gain—is offensive. So long as we remain in charge of how we are used, we have no cause for complaint. In those cases in which a legal wrong is recognized, there has been use by others in disregard of this authority, but in those cases in which a privilege is found, there is not *use* of personality or personal affairs at all, at least not use in the sense of one person assuming control over another, which is the gist of the offense to autonomy. We do indeed suffer a loss of autonomy whenever the power to place us in free circulation is exercised by others, but we consider such loss offensive only when another person assumes the control of which we are deprived, when we are used and not merely exposed. Failure to make clear this criterion of offensiveness has misled those who wish to define the protectable area, and they conceive the problem as one of striking an optimal balance between two valuable interests, when in fact it is a matter of deciding whether the acts complained of are offensive under a quite definite standard of offensiveness. The difficult cases here have not presented a dilemma of selecting the happy medium, but rather the slippery job of determining whether the defendant had used the plaintiff or whether he had merely caused things about him to become known, albeit to the defendant's profit. The difference is between managing another person as a means to one's own ends, which is offensive, and acting merely as a vehicle of presentation (though not gratuitously) to satisfy established social needs, which is not offensive. Cases dealing with an unauthorized biography that was heavily anecdotal and of questionable accuracy, or with an entertaining article that told the true story of a former child prodigy who became an obscure eccentric, are perplexing ones because they present elements of both offensive and inoffensive publication, and a decision turns on which is predominant.

There remains another balance-striking quandary to be dismantled. It is often said that privacy as an interest must be balanced against security. Each, we think, must sacrifice something of privacy to promote the security of all, though we are willing to risk some insecurity to preserve a measure of privacy. Pressure to reduce restrictions on wiretapping and searches by police seeks to push the balance toward greater security. But the picture we are given is seriously misleading. In the first place we must notice the doubtful assumption on which the argument rests. It may be stated this way: the greater the ability to watch what is going on, or obtain evidence of what has gone on, the greater the ability to prevent crime. It is a notion congenial to those who believe that more efficient law enforcement contributes significantly to a reduction in crime. We must, however, determine if such a proposition is in fact sound, and we must see what crimes are suppressible, even in principle, before any sacrifice of privacy can be justified. There is, at least *in limine,* much to be said for the conflicting proposition that, once a generally efficient system of law enforcement exists, an increase in its efficiency does not result in a corresponding reduction in crime, but only in an increase in punishments. Apart from that point, there is an objection relating more directly to what has been said here about privacy. Security and privacy are both desirable, but measures to promote each are on different moral footing. Men ought to be secure, we say, because only in that condition can they live a good life. Privacy, however, like peace and prosperity, is itself part of what we mean by a good life, a part having to do with self-respect and self-determination. Therefore, the appropriate attitudes when we are asked to sacrifice privacy for security are first a critical one which urges alternatives that minimize or do not at all require the sacrifice, and ultimately regret for loss of a cherished resource if the sacrifice proves necessary.

IV

In speaking of privacy and autonomy, there is some danger that privacy may be conceived as autonomy. Such confusion has been signaled in legal literature by early and repeated use of the phrase "right to be let alone" as a synonym for "right of privacy." The United States Supreme Court succumbed completely in 1965 in its opinion in *Griswold v. Connecticut,* and the ensuing intellectual disorder warrants comment.

In that case legislative prohibition of the use of contraceptives was said to be a violation of a constitutional right of privacy, at least when it affected married people. The court's opinion relied heavily on an elaborate *jeu de mots,* in which different senses of the word "privacy" were punned upon, and the legal concept generally mismanaged in ways too various to recount here. In the *Griswold* situation there had been an attempt by government to regulate personal affairs, not get acquainted with them, and so there was an issue regarding autonomy and not privacy. The opinion was not illuminating on the question of what are proper bounds for the exercise of legislative power, which was the crucial matter before the court. It is precisely the issue of what rights to autonomous determination of his affairs are enjoyed by a citizen. The *Griswold* opinion not only failed to take up that question in a forthright manner, but promoted confusion about privacy in the law by unsettling the intellectual focus on it which had been developed in torts and constitutional law. If the confusion in the court's argument was inadvertent, one may sympathize with the deep conceptual difficulties which produced it, and if it was deliberately contrived, admire its ingenuity. Whatever its origin, its effect is to muddle the separate issues, which must be analyzed and argued along radically different lines when protection is sought either for privacy or for autonomy. Hopefully, further developments will make clear that while an offense to privacy is an offense to autonomy, not every curtailment of autonomy is a compromise of privacy.

H. L. A. HART

Definition and Theory in Jurisprudence*

I

In law as elsewhere, we can know and yet not understand. Shadows often obscure our knowledge which not only vary in intensity but are cast by different obstacles to light. These cannot all be removed by the same methods and till the precise character of our perplexity is determined we cannot tell what tools we shall need.

The perplexities I propose to discuss are voiced in those questions of analytical jurisprudence which are usually characterised as requests for definitions: What is law? What is a State? What is a right? What is possession? I choose this topic because it seems to me that the common mode of definition is ill-adapted to the law and has complicated its exposition; its use has, I think, led at certain points to a divorce between jurisprudence and the study of the law at work, and has helped to create the impression that there are certain fundamental concepts that the lawyer cannot hope to elucidate without entering a forbidding jungle of philosophical argument. I wish to suggest that this is not so; that legal notions however fundamental can be elucidated by methods properly adapted to their special character. Such methods were glimpsed by our predecessors but have only been fully understood and developed in our own day.

Questions such as those I have mentioned "What is a State?" "What is law?" "What is a right?" have great ambiguity. The same form of words may be used to demand a definition or the cause or the purpose or the justification or the origin of a legal or political institution. But if, in the effort to free them from this risk of confusion with other questions, we rephrase these requests for definitions as "What is the meaning of the word 'State'?", "What is the meaning of the word

'right'?", those who ask are apt to feel uneasy as if this had trivialised their question. For what they want cannot be got out of a dictionary and this transformation of their question suggests it can. This uneasiness is the expression of an instinct which deserves respect: it emphasises the fact that those who ask these questions are not asking to be taught how to use these words in the correct way. This they know and yet are still puzzled. Hence it is no answer to this type of question merely to tender examples of what are correctly called rights, laws, or corporate bodies, and to tell the questioner if he is still puzzled that he is free to abandon the public convention and use words as he pleases.[1] For the puzzle arises from the fact that though the common use of these words is known it is not understood; and it is not understood because compared with most ordinary words these legal words are in different ways anomalous. Sometimes, as with the word "law" itself, one anomaly is that the range of cases to which it is applied has a diversity which baffles the initial attempt to extract any principle behind the application, yet we have the conviction that even here there is some principle and not an arbitrary convention underlying the surface differences; so that whereas it would be patently absurd to ask for elucidation of the principle in accordance with which different men are called Tom, it is not felt absurd to ask why, within municipal law the immense variety of different types of rules are called law, nor why municipal law and international law, in spite of striking differences, are so called.

But in this and other cases, we are puzzled by a different and more troubling anomaly. The first efforts to define words like "corporation", "right", or "duty" reveal that these do not have the straightforward connection with counterparts in the world of fact which most ordinary words have and to which we appeal in our definition of ordinary words. There is nothing which simply "corresponds" to these legal words and when we try to define them we find that the expressions we

*H. L. A. Hart, "Definition and Theory in Jurisprudence," *The Law Quarterly Review,* Vol. 70 (1954), pp. 32–49. This was Professor Hart's inaugural lecture, delivered before the University of Oxford on May 30, 1953. Part IV and V have been deleted. Reprinted by permission of the author and the publisher.

tender in our definition specifying kinds of persons, things, qualities, events, and processes, material or psychological, are never precisely the equivalent of these legal words though often connected with them in some way. This is most obvious in the case of expressions for corporate bodies and is commonly put by saying that a corporation is not a series or aggregate of persons. But it is true of other legal words. Though one who has a right usually has some expectation or power the expression "a right" is not synonymous with words like "expectation" or "power" even if we add "based on law" or "guaranteed by law." And so too, though we speak of men having duties to do or abstain from certain actions the word "duty" does not stand for or describe anything as ordinary words do. It has an altogether different function which makes the stock form of definition, "a duty is a . . .," seem quite inappropriate.

These are genuine difficulties and in part account for something remarkable: that out of these innocent requests for definitions of fundamental legal notions there should have arisen vast and irreconcilable theories so that not merely whole books but whole schools of juristic thought may be characterised by the type of answer they give to questions like "What is a right?" or "What is a corporate body?" This alone, I think, suggests that something is wrong with the approach to definition; can we really not elucidate the meaning of words which every developed legal system handles smoothly and alike without assuming this incubus of theory? And the suspicion that something is amiss is confirmed by certain characteristics that many such theories have. In the first place they fall disquietingly often into a familiar triad.[2] Thus the American Realists striving to give us an answer in terms of plain fact tell us that a right is a term by which we describe the prophecies we make of the probable behaviour of courts or officials[3]; the Scandinavian jurists, after dealing the Realist theory blows that might well be thought fatal (if these matters were strictly judged), say that a right is nothing real at all but an ideal or fictitious or imaginary power,[4] and then join with their opponents to denigrate the older type of theory that a right is an "objective reality"—an invisible entity existing apart from the behaviour of men. These theories are in form similar to the three great theories of corporate personality, each of which has dealt deadly blows to the other. There too we have been told by turn that the name of a corporate body like a limited company or an organisation like the State is really just a collective name or abbreviation for some complex but still plain facts about ordinary persons, or alternatively that it is the name of a fictitious person, or that on the contrary it is the name of a real person existing with a real will and life, but not a body of its own. And this same triad of theories has haunted the jurist even when concerned with relatively minor notions. Look for example at Austin's discussion of status[5] and you will find that the choice lies for him between saying that it is a mere collective name for a set of special rights and duties, or that it is an "ideal" or "fictitious" basis for these rights and duties, or that it is an "occult quality" in the person who has the status, distinguishable both from the rights and duties and from the facts engendering them.

Secondly. Though these theories spring from the effort to define notions actually involved in the practice of a legal system they rarely throw light on the precise work they do there. They seem to the lawyer to stand apart with their head at least in the clouds; and hence it is that very often the use of such terms in a legal system is neutral between competing theories. For that use "can be reconciled with any theory, but is authority for none."

Thirdly. In many of these theories there is often an amalgam of issues that should be distinguished. It is of course clear that the assertion that corporate bodies are real persons and the counterassertion that they are fictions of the law were often not the battle cries of analytical jurists. They were ways of asserting or denying the claims of organised groups to recognition by the State. But such claims have always been confused with the baffling analytical question "What is a corporate body?" so that the classification of such theories as Fiction or Realist or Concessionist is a criss-cross between logical and political criteria. So too the American Realist theories have much to tell us of value about the judicial process and how small a part deduction from predetermined premises may play in it, but the lesson is blurred when it is presented as a matter of definition of "law" or "a right"; not only analytical jurisprudence but every sort of jurisprudence suffers by this confusion of aim.

Hence though theory is to be welcomed, the growth of theory on the back of definition is not. Theories so grown indeed represent valuable efforts to account for many puzzling things in law; and among these is the great anomaly of legal language—our inability to define its crucial words in terms of ordinary factual counterparts.[7] But here I think they largely fail because their method of attack commits them all, in spite of their mutual hostility, to a form of answer that can only distort the distinctive characteristics of legal language.

II

Long ago Bentham issued a warning that legal words demanded a special method of elucidation and he enunciated a principle that is the beginning of wisdom in this matter though it is not the end. He said we must never take these words alone, but consider whole sentences in which they play their characteristic role. We must take not the *word* "right" but the sentence "You have a right" not the *word* "State" but the sentence "He is a member or an official of the State."* His warning has largely been disregarded and jurists have continued to hammer away at single words. This may be because he hid the product of his logical insight behind technical terms of his own invention, "Archetypation," "Phraseoplerosis," and the rest; it may also be because his further suggestions were not well adapted to the peculiarities of legal language which as part of the works of "Judge & Co." was perhaps distasteful to him. But in fact the language involved in the enunciation and application of rules constitutes a special segment of human discourse with special features which lead to confusion if neglected. Of this type of discourse the law is one very complex example and sometimes to see its features we need to look away from the law to simpler cases, which in spite of many differences share these features. The economist or the scientist often uses a simple model with which to understand the complex; and this can be done for the law. So in what follows I shall use as a simple analogy the rules of a game, which at many vital points have the same puzzling logical structure as rules of law. And I shall describe four distinctive features which show, I think, the method of elucidation we should apply to the law and why the common mode of definition fails.

1. First, let us take words like "right" or "duty" or the names of corporations not alone but in examples of typical contexts where these words are at work. Consider them when used in statements made on a particular occasion by a judge or an ordinary lawyer. They will be statements such as "A has a right to be paid £10 by B." "A is under a duty to fence off his machinery." "A & Company, Ltd. have a contract with B." It is obvious that the use of these sentences silently assumes a special and very complicated setting, namely the existence of a legal

system with all that this implies by way of general obedience, the operation of the sanctions of the system, and the general likelihood that this will continue. But though this complex situation is assumed in the use of these statements of rights or duties they do not *state* that it exists. There is a parallel situation in a game. "He is out" said in the course of a game of cricket has as its proper context the playing of the game with all that *this* implies by way of general compliance by both the players and the officials of the game in the past, present, and future. Yet one who says "He is out" does not *state* that a game is being played or that the players and officials will comply with the rules. "He is out" is an expression used to appeal to rules, to make claims, or give decisions under them; it is not a statement *about* the rules to the effect that they will be enforced or acted on in a given case nor any other kind of statement *about* them. The analysis of statements of rights and duties as predictions ignores this distinction, yet it is just as erroneous to say that "A has a right" is a prediction that a court or official will treat A in a certain way as to say that "He is out" is a prediction that the umpire is likely to order the batsman off the field or the scorer to mark him out. No doubt, when someone has a legal right a corresponding prediction will normally be justified, but this should not lead us to identify two quite different forms of statement.

2. If we take "A has a right to be paid £10 by B" as an example, we can see what the distinctive function of this form of statement is. For it is clear that as well as presupposing the existence of a legal system, the use of this statement has also a special connection with a particular rule of the system. This would be made explicit if we asked "Why has A this right"? For the appropriate answer could only consist of two things: first, the statement of some rule or rules of law (say those of Contract), under which given certain facts certain legal consequences follow; and secondly, a statement that these facts were here the case. But again it is important to see that one who says that "A has a right" does not *state* the relevant rule of law; and that though, given certain facts, it is correct to say "A has a right" one who says this does not state or describe those facts. He has done something different from either of these two things: he has drawn a conclusion from the relevant but unstated rule, and from the relevant but unstated facts of the case. "A has a right" like "He is out" is therefore the tail-end of a simple legal calculation: it records a result and may be well called a conclusion of law. It is not therefore

used to predict the future as the American Realists say; it refers to the present as their opponents claim but unlike ordinary statements does not do this by describing present or continuing facts. This it is—this matter of principle—and not the existence of stray exceptions for lunatics or infants that frustrates the definition of a right in factual terms such as expectations or powers. A paralysed man watching the thief's hand close over his gold watch is properly said to have a right to retain it as against the thief, though he has neither expectation nor power in any ordinary sense of these words. This is possible just because the expression "a right" in this case does not describe or stand for any expectation, or power, or indeed anything else, but has meaning only as part of a sentence the function of which as a whole is to draw a conclusion of law from a specific kind of legal rule.

3. A third peculiarity is this: the assertion "Smith has a right to be paid £10" said by a judge in deciding the case has a different status from the utterance of it out of court, where it may be used to make a claim, or an admission and in many other ways. The judge's utterance is official, authoritative and, let us assume, final; the other is none of these things, yet in spite of these differences the sentences are of the same sort: they are both conclusions of law. We can compare this difference in spite of similarity with "He is out" said by the umpire in giving his decision and said by a player to make a claim. Now of course the unofficial utterance may have to be withdrawn in the light of a later official utterance, but this is not a sufficient reason for treating the first as a prophecy of the last, for plainly not all mistakes are mistaken predictions. Nor surely need the finality of a judge's decision either be confused with infallibility or tempt us to *define* laws in terms of what courts do, even though there are many laws which the courts must first interpret before they can apply. We can acknowledge that what the scorer says is final; yet we can still abstain from defining the notion of a score as what the scorer says. And we can admit that the umpire may be wrong in his decision, though the rules gives us no remedy if he is, and though there may be doubtful cases which he has to decide with but little help from the rules.

4. In any system, legal or not, rules may for excellent practical reasons attach identical consequences to any one of a set of very different facts. The rule of cricket attaches the same consequence to the batsman's being bowled, stumped, or caught. And the word "out" is used in giving decisions or making claims under the rule and in other verbal applications of it. It is easy to see here that no one of these different ways of being out is more essentially what the word means than the others, and that there need be nothing common to all these ways of being out other than their falling under the same rule, though there *may* be some similarity or analogy between them . . .

III

These four general characteristics of legal language explain both why definition of words like "right," "duty," and "corporation" is baffled by the absence of some counterpart to "correspond" to these words, and also why the unobvious counterparts which have been so ingeniously contrived—the future facts, the complex facts or the psychological facts—turn out not to be something in terms of which we can define these words, although to be connected with them in complex or indirect ways. The fundamental point is that the primary function of these[9] words is not to stand for or describe anything but a distinct function; this makes it vital to attend to Bentham's warning that we should not, as does the traditional method of definition, abstract words like "right" and "duty," "State," or "corporation" from the sentences in which alone their full function can be seen, and then demand of them so abstracted their genus and differentia.

Let us see what the use of this traditional method of definition presupposes and what the limits of its efficacy are, and why it may be misleading. It is of course the simplest form of definition, and also a peculiarly satisfying form because it gives us a set of words which can always be substituted for the word defined whenever it is used; it gives us a comprehensible synonym or translation for the word which puzzles us. It is peculiarly appropriate where the words have the straightforward function of standing for some kind of thing, or quality, person, process, or event, for here we are not mystified or puzzled about the general characteristics of our subject-matter, but we ask for a definition simply to locate within this familiar general kind or class some special subordinate kind or class.[10] Thus since we are not puzzled about the general notions of furniture or animal we can take a word like "chair" or "cat" and give the principle of its use by first specifying the general class to which what it is used to describe belongs, and then going on to define the specific differences that mark it off from other species of the same general kind.

And of course if we are *not* puzzled about the general notion of a corporate body but only wish to know how one species (say a college) differs from another (say a limited company) we can use this form of definition of single words perfectly well. But just because the method is appropriate at this level of inquiry, it cannot help us when our perplexities are deeper. For if our question arises, as it does with fundamental legal notions because we are puzzled about the general category to which something belongs and how some general type of expression relates to fact, and not merely about the place within that category, then until the puzzle is cleared up this form of definition is at the best unilluminating and at the worst profoundly misleading. It is unilluminating because a mode of definition designed to locate some subordinate species within some familiar category cannot elucidate the characteristics of some anomalous category; and it is misleading because it will suggest that what is in fact an anomalous category is after all some species of the familiar. Hence if applied to legal words like "right," "duty," "State," or "corporation" the common mode of definition suggests that these words like ordinary words stand for or describe some thing, person, quality, process, or event; when the difficulty of finding these becomes apparent, different contrivances varying with tastes are used to explain or explain away the anomaly. Some say the difference is that the things for which these legal words stand are real but not sensory, others that they are fictitious entities, others that these words stand for plain fact but of a complex, future, or psychological variety. So this standard mode of definition forces our familiar triad of theories into existence as a confused way of accounting for the anomalous character of legal words.

How then shall we define such words? If definition is the provision of a synonym which will not equally puzzle us these words cannot be defined. But I think there is a method of elucidation of quite general application and which we can call definition, if we wish. Bentham and others practised it, though they did not preach it. But before applying it to the highly complex legal cases, I shall illustrate it from the simple case of a game. Take the notion of a trick in a game of cards. Somebody says "What is a trick?" and you reply "I will explain: when you have a game and among its rules is one providing that when each of our players has played a card then the player who has put down the highest card scores a point, in these circumstances that player is said to have 'taken a trick'." This natural explanation has not taken the form of a definition of the single word "trick": no synonym has been offered for it. Instead we have taken a sentence in which the word "trick" plays its characteristic role and explained it first by specifying the conditions under which the whole sentence is true, and secondly by showing how it is used in drawing a conclusion from the rules in a particular case. Suppose now that after such an explanation your questioner presses on: "That is all very well, that explains 'taking a trick'; but I still want to know what the word 'trick' means just by itself. I want a definition of 'trick'; I want something which can be substituted for it whenever it is used." If we yield to this demand for a single word definition we might reply: "The trick is just a collective name for the four cards." But someone may object: "The trick is not just a name for the four cards because these four cards will not always constitute a trick. It must therefore be some entity to which the four cards belong." A third might say: "No, the trick is a fictitious entity which the players pretend exists and to which by fiction, which is part of the game, they ascribe the cards." But in so simple a case we would not tolerate these theories, fraught as they are with mystery and empty of any guidance as to the use made of the word within the game: we would stand by the original two-fold explanation; for this surely gave us all we needed when it explained the conditions under which the statement "He has taken a trick" is true and showed us how it was used in drawing a conclusion from the rules in a particular case.

If we turn back to Bentham we shall find that when his explanation of legal notions is illuminating, as it very often is, it conforms to this method though only loosely. Yet curiously what he tells us to do is something different: it is to take a word like "right" or "duty" or "State": to embody it in a sentence such as "you have a right" where it plays a characteristic role and then to find a *translation* of it into what we should call factual[11] terms. This he called the method of paraphrase—giving phrase for phrase, not word for word. Now this method is applicable to many cases and has shed much light; but it distorts many legal words like "right" or "duty" whose characteristic role is not played in statements of fact but in conclusions of law. A paraphrase of these in factual terms is not possible and when Bentham proffers such a paraphrase it turns out not to be one at all.

But more often and much to our profit he does not claim to paraphrase: but he makes a different kind of remark, in order to elucidate these words —remarks such as these: "What you have a right to have me made do, is that which I am liable according to law upon a requisition made on your behalf to be punished for not doing"[12] or "To know how to expound a right carry your eye to the act which in the circumstances in question would be a violation of that right; the law creates the right by forbidding that act."[13] These, though defective, are on the right lines. They are not paraphrases but they specify some of the conditions necessary for the truth of a sentence of the form "You have a right." Bentham shows us how these conditions include the existence of a law imposing a duty on some other person; and moreover, that it must be a law which provides that the breach of the duty shall be visited with a sanction if you or someone on your behalf so choose. This has many virtues. By refusing to identify the meaning of the word "right" with any psychological or physical fact it correctly leaves open the question whether on any given occasion a person who has a right has in fact any expectation or power; and so it leaves us free to treat men's expectations or powers as what in general men will have if there is a system of rights, and as part of what a system of rights is generally intended to secure. Some of the improvements which should be made on Bentham's efforts are obvious. Instead of characterising a right in terms of punishment many would do so in terms of the remedy. But I would prefer to show the special position of one who has a right by mentioning not the remedy but the choice which is open to one who has a right as to whether the corresponding duty shall be performed or not. For it is, I think, characteristic of those laws that confer rights (as distinguished from those that only impose obligations) that the obligation to perform the corresponding duty is made by law to depend on the choice of the individual who is said to have the right or the choice of some person authorised to act on his behalf.

I would, therefore, tender the following as an elucidation of the expression "a legal right": (1) A statement of the form "X has a right" is true if the following conditions are satisfied:

(*a*) There is in existence a legal system.

(*b*) Under a rule or rules of the system some other person Y is, in the events which have happened, obliged to do or abstain from some action.

(*c*) This obligation is made by law dependent on the choice either of C or some other person authorised to act on his behalf so that either Y is bound to do or abstain from some action only if X (or some authorised person) so chooses or alternatively only until X (or such person) chooses otherwise. (2) A statement of the form "X has a right" is used to draw a conclusion of law in a particular case which falls under such rules.[14]

NOTES

1. Professor Glanville Williams in his beneficial article on "International Law and the Controversy concerning the word Law" (*British Year Book of International Law, 1945, p. 148*) advocates this short way with those who ask whether international law is law. But the way is really too short; for the puzzle is not generated always or only by the superstitions about words or essences, or the confusion of "verbal" with factual questions which he attacks. Perplexity here arises from three factors: (i) the well-founded belief that the word "law" when used of municipal and international law is not a mere homonym; (ii) the mistaken belief (false not only of complex legal and political expressions like "law," "State," "nation," but of humbler ones like "a game") that if a word is not a mere homonym, then all the instances to which it is applied must possess either a single quality or a single set of qualities in common; (iii) an exaggeration of the difference between municipal and international law due to the failure to see that the "command" of a sovereign is only one particular form of a general feature which is no doubt logically necessary in a legal system, *viz. some* general test or criterion whereby the rules of the system are identified. Of course proper attention to these three factors will only show (by revealing the complexity of the issue and exposing some prejudices) that to call international law law in spite of its differences from municipal law is not arbitrary—just as to call patience a game is not arbitrary in spite of its differences from, say, polo. But there is no conclusive answer to give to those who are very impressed with the differences—in either case.

2. The general form of this recurrent triad may be summarily described as follows. Theories of one type tell us that a word stands for some unexpected variant of the familiar—a complex fact where we expect something unified and simple, a future fact where we expect something present, a psychological fact where we expect something external; theories of the second type tell us that a word stands for what is in some sense a fiction; theories of a third (now unfashionable) type, tell us the word stands for something different from other things just in that we cannot touch it, hear it, see it, feel it.

3. W. W. Cook, *The Logical and Legal Basis of the Conflict of Laws,* p. 30: " 'Right' 'duty' ... are not names of objects or entities which have an existence apart from the behaviour of officials but terms by means of which we describe to each other the prophecies we make as to the probable occurrence of a certain sequence of events—the behaviour of officials ... we must therefore constantly resist the tendency ... to reify rights ..."

4. Karl Olivecrona, *Law as Fact,* p. 90: "We hit the mark when we define a right as a power of some kind but this power does not exist in the real world ... it is not identical with the actual control ... exercised by the owner nor with his actual ability to set the legal machinery in motion. It is a fictitious power, an ideal or imaginary power." See also A. Hagerstrom, *Inquiries into the Nature of Law and Morals,* p. 4: * The insuperable difficulty in finding the facts which correspond to our ideas of rights forces us to suppose that there are no such facts and that we are here concerned with ideas that have nothing to do with reality." On p. 6: "Thus it is shown that the notions we question cannot be reduced to anything in reality. The reason is that they have their roots in traditional ideas of mystical forces or bonds."

5. *Jurisprudence,* 5th ed. (pp. 699-700).

6. P. W. Duff, *Personality in Roman Private Law,* p. 215.

7. See Olivecrona, *op. cit.,* pp. 88-89. "It is impossible to find any facts that correspond to the idea of a right. The right eludes every attempt to pin it down and place it among the facts of social life. Though connected with the facts . . . the right is in essence something different from all facts."

8. See *A Fragment on Government,* Chap. V, notes to section vi: § (5) "For expounding the words duty, right, title, and those other terms of the same stamp that abound so much in ethics and jurisprudence either I am much deceived or the only method by which any instruction can be conveyed is that which is here exemplified. An exposition framed after this method I would term paraphrase. § (6) A word may be said to be expounded by paraphrases when not that word alone is translated into other words but some whole sentence of which it forms part is translated into another sentence. § (7) The common method of defining—the method *per genus et differentiam* as logicians call it, will in many cases not at all answer the purpose." *Cf.* also *Works,* Vol. viii, pp. 242-53, cited in C. K. Ogden, *Bentham's Theory of Fictions,* pp. 75-104, and *The Limits of Jurisprudence Defined* (Columbia University Press), p. 317.

9. Lawyers might best understand the distinctive function of such expressions as "He has a right" and others which I discuss here, by comparing them to the *operative* words of a conveyance as distinct from the *descriptive* words of the recitals. The point of similarity is that "He has a right," like "X hereby conveys," is used to *operate with* legal rules and not to state or describe facts. Of course there are great differences: one who says "He has a right" operates with a rule by drawing a conclusion from it whereas one who uses operative words in a conveyance does something to which the rule attaches legal consequences.

10. Bentham's reason for rejecting the common method of defining legal words was that "among such abstract terms we soon come to such as have no superior genus. A definition *per genus et differentiam* when applied to these it is manifest can make no advance . . . As well in short were it to define in this manner a preposition or a conjunction . . . a *through* is a . . . a *because* is a . . . and so go on defining them." *A Fragment on Government, ubi sup.* (in the place).

11. Actually he made the more stringent requirement that the translations should be in the terms calculated to raise images of "substances" or "emotions." This was in accord with Bentham's form of empiricism, but the utility of the method of paraphrases (which is identical with the modern "definition in use") is independent of this requirement.

12. *A Fragment on Government, ubi sup*.

13. *Introduction to the Principles of Morals and Legislation,* Chap. XVI.

14. This deals only with a right in the first sense (correlative to duty) distinguished by Hohfeld. But the same form of elucidation can be used for the cases of "liberty," "power," and "immunity" and will I think show what is usually left unexplained *viz.:* why these four varieties in spite of differences are referred to as "rights." The unifying element seems to be this: in all four cases the law specifically recognises the *choice* of an individual either negatively by not impeding or obstructing it (liberty and immunity) or affirmatively by giving legal effect to it (claim and power). In the negative cases there is no law to interfere if the individual chooses to do or abstain from some action (liberty) or to retain his legal position unchanged (immunity); in the affirmative cases the law gives legal effect to the choice of an individual that some other person shall do or shall abstain from some action or that the legal position of some other person shall be altered. Of course when we say in any of these four senses that a person has a right we are not referring to any *actual* choice that he has made but either the relevant rules of law are such that *if* he chooses certain consequences follow, or there are no rules to impede his choice *if* he makes it. If there are legal rights which cannot be waived these would need special treatment.

WESLEY NEWCOMB HOHFELD

Rights and Jural Relations*

FUNDAMENTAL JURAL RELATIONS CONTRASTED WITH ONE ANOTHER

One of the greatest hindrances to the clear understanding, the incisive statement, and the true solution of legal problems frequently arises from the express or tacit assumption that all legal relations may be reduced to "rights" and "duties," and that these latter categories are therefore adequate for the purpose of analyzing even the most complex legal interests, such as trusts, options, escrows, "future" interests, corporate interests, etc. Even if the difficulty related merely to inadequacy and ambiguity of terminology, its seriousness would nevertheless be worthy of definite recognition and persistent effort toward improvement; for in any closely reasoned problem, whether legal or non-legal, chameleon-hued words are a peril both to clear thought and to lucid expression. As a matter of fact, however, the above mentioned inadequacy and ambiguity of terms unfortunately reflect, all too often, corresponding paucity and confusion as regards actual legal conceptions. That this is so may appear in some measure from the discussion to follow.

The strictly fundamental legal relations are, after all, *sui generis;* and thus it is that attempts at formal definition are always unsatisfactory, if not altogether useless. Accordingly, the most promising line of procedure seems to consist in exhibiting all of the various relations in a scheme of "opposites" and "correlatives," and then proceeding to exemplify their individual scope and application in concrete cases. An effort will be made to pursue this method:

Jural Opposites

 right
 no-right

 privilege
 duty
 power
 disability
 immunity
 liability

Jural Correlatives

 right
 duty
 privilege
 no-right
 power
 liability
 immunity
 disability

Rights and Duties. As already intimated, the term "rights" tends to be used indiscriminately to cover what in a given case may be a privilege, a power, or an immunity, rather than a right in the strictest sense; and this looseness of usage is occasionally recognized by the authorities. As said by Mr. Justice Strong in *People v. Dikeman.*[1]

The word "right" is defined by lexicographers to denote, among other things, *property, interest, power, prerogative, immunity, privilege* (Walker's Dict. word "Right"). In law it is most frequently applied to property in its restricted sense, but it is often used to designate *power, prerogative, and privilege.*

Recognition of this ambiguity is also found in the language of Mr. Justice Jackson, in *United States v. Patrick.*[2]

The words "right" or "privilege" have, of course, a variety of meanings, according to the connection or context in which they are used. Their definition, as given by standard lexicographers, includes "that which one has a *legal claim to do,*" "*legal power,*" "*authority,*" "*immunity* granted by authority," "the investiture with special or peculiar rights."

*From Wesley Newcomb Hohfeld, *Fundamental Legal Conceptions,* edited by Walter Wheeler Cook (New Haven and London: Yale University Press, 1919), pp. 35-64. Reprinted by permission of the Yale University Press. Footnotes have been edited and renumbered.

And, similarly, in the language of Mr. Justice Sneed, in *Lonas v. State.* [3]

The state, then, is forbidden from making and enforcing any law which shall abridge the *privileges* and *immunities* of citizens of the United States. It is said that the words *rights, privileges* and *immunities,* are abusively used, as if they were synonymous. The word *rights* is generic, common, embracing whatever may be lawfully claimed.

It is interesting to observe, also, that a tendency toward discrimination may be found in a number of important constitutional and statutory provisions. Just how accurate the distinctions in the mind of the draftsman may have been it is, of course, impossible to say.

Recognizing, as we must, the very broad and indiscriminate use of the term "right," what clue do we find, in ordinary legal discourse, toward limiting the word in question to a definite and appropriate meaning? That clue lies in the correlative "duty," for it is certain that even those who use the word and the conception "right" in the broadest possible way are accustomed to thinking of "duty" as the invariable correlative. As said in *Lake Shore & M. S. R. Co. v. Kurtz.* [4]

A duty or a legal obligation is that which one ought or ought not to do. "Duty" and "right" are correlative terms. When a right is invaded, a duty is violated.

In other words, if X has a right against Y that he shall stay off the former's land, the correlative (and equivalent) is that Y is under a duty toward X to stay off the place. If, as seems desirable, we should seek a synonym for the term "right" in this limited and proper meaning, perhaps the word "claim" would prove the best. The latter has the advantage of being a monosyllable. In this connection, the language of Lord Watson in *Studd v. Cool* [5] is instructive:

Any words which in a settlement of movables would be recognized by the law of Scotland as sufficient to create a right or *claim* in favor of an executor . . . must receive effect if used with reference to lands in Scotland.

Privileges and "No-Rights." As indicated in the above scheme of jural relations, a privilege is the opposite of a duty, and the correlative of a "no-right." In the example last put, whereas X has a *right* or *claim* that Y, the other man, should stay off the land, he himself has the *privilege* of entering on the land; or, in equivalent words, X does not have a duty to stay off. The privilege of entering is the negation of a duty to stay off. As indicated by this case, some caution is necessary at this point; for, always, when it is said that a given privilege is the mere negation of a *duty,* what is meant, of course, is a duty having a content or tenor precisely *opposite* to that of the privilege in question. Thus, if, for some special reason, X has contracted with Y to go on the former's own land, it is obvious that X has, as regards Y, both the privilege of entering and the *duty of entering.* The privilege is perfectly consistent with this sort of duty,—for the latter is of the *same* content or tenor as the privilege;—but it still holds good that, as regards Y, X's privilege of entering is the precise negation of a duty *to stay off.* Similarly, if A has not contracted with B to perform certain work for the latter, A's privilege of *not* doing so is the very negation of a duty of *doing* so. Here again the duty contrasted is of a content or tenor exactly opposite to that of the privilege.

Passing now to the question of "correlatives," it will be remembered, of course, that a duty is the invariable correlative of that legal relation which is most properly called a right or claim. That being so, if further evidence be needed as to the fundamental and important difference between a right (or claim) and a privilege, surely it is found in the fact that the correlative of the latter relation is a "no-right," there being no single term available to express the latter conception. Thus, the correlative of X's right that Y shall not enter on the land is Y's duty not to enter; but the correlative of X's privilege of entering himself is manifestly Y's "no-right" that X shall not enter.

In view of the considerations thus far emphasized, the importance of keeping the conception of a right (or claim) and the conception of a privilege quite distinct from each other seems evident; and, more than that, it is equally clear that there should be a separate term to represent the latter relation. No doubt, as already indicated, it is very common to use the term "right" indiscriminately, even when the relation designated is really that of privilege; and only too often this identity of terms has involved for the particular speaker or writer a confusion or blurring of ideas. Good instances of this may be found even in unexpected places. Thus Professor Holland, in his work on *Jurisprudence,* referring to a different and well-known sort of ambiguity inherent in the Latin *"Ius,"* the German *"Recht,"* the Italian *"Diritto,"* and the French *"Droit,"*—terms used to express "not only 'a right,' but also 'Law' in the abstract,"—very aptly observes:

If the expression of widely different ideas by one and the same term resulted only in the necessity for . . .

clumsy paraphrases, or obviously inaccurate paraphrases, no great harm would be done; but unfortunately the identity of terms seems irresistibly to suggest an identity between the ideas expressed by them.

Curiously enough, however, in the very chapter where this appears,—the chapter on "Rights,"—the notions of right, privilege and power seem to be blended, and that, too, although the learned author states that "the correlative of . . . legal right is legal duty," and that "these pairs of terms express . . . in each case the same state of facts viewed from opposite sides." While the whole chapter must be read in order to appreciate the seriousness of this lack of discrimination, a single passage must suffice by way of example:

If . . . the power of the State will protect him in so carrying out his wishes, and will compel such acts or forbearances on the part of other people as may be necessary in order that his wishes may be so carried out, then he has a "legal right" so to carry out his wishes.[7]

The first part of this passage suggests privileges, the middle part rights (or claims), and the last part privileges.

Similar difficulties seem to exist in Professor Gray's able and entertaining work on *The Nature and Sources of Law.* In his chapter on "Legal Rights and Duties" the distinguished author takes the position that a right always has a duty as its correlative;[8] and he seems to define the former relation substantially according to the more limited meaning of "claim." Legal privileges, powers, and immunities are *prima facie* ignored, and the impression conveyed that all legal relations can be comprehended under the conceptions "right" and "duty." But, with the greatest hesitation and deference, the suggestion may be ventured that a number of his examples seem to show the inadequacy of such mode of treatment. Thus, e.g., he says:

The eating of shrimp salad is an interest of mine, and, if I can pay for it, the law will protect that interest, and it is therefore a right of mine to eat shrimp salad which I have paid for, although I know that shrimp salad always gives me the colic.[9]

This passage seems to suggest primarily two classes of relations: *first,* the party's respective privileges, as against A, B, C, D and others in relation to eating the salad, or, correlatively, the respective "no-rights" of A, B, C, D and others that the party should not eat the salad; *second,* the party's respective rights (or claims) as against A, B, C, D and others that they should not interfere with the physical act of eating the salad, or, correlatively, the respective duties of A, B, C, D and others that they should not interfere.

These two groups of relations seem perfectly distinct; and the privileges could, in a given case, exist even though the rights mentioned did not. A, B, C and D, being the owners of the salad, might say to X: "Eat the salad, if you can; you have our license to do so, but we don't agree not to interfere with you." In such a case the privileges exist, so that if X succeeds in eating the salad, he has violated no rights of any of the parties. But it is equally clear that if A had succeeded in holding so fast to the dish that X couldn't eat the contents, no right of X would have been violated.

Perhaps the essential character and importance of the distinction can be shown by a slight variation of the facts. Suppose that X, being already the legal owner of the salad, contracts with Y that he (X) will never eat this particular food. With A, B, C, D and others no such contract has been made. One of the relations now existing between X and Y is, as a consequence, fundamentally different from the relation between X and A. As regards Y, X has no privilege of eating the salad; but as regards either A or any of the others, X has such a privilege. It is to be observed incidentally that X's right that Y should not eat the food persists even though X's own privilege of doing so has been extinguished.

On grounds already emphasized, it would seem that the line of reasoning pursued by Lord Lindley in the great case of *Quinn v. Leathem*[10] is deserving of comment:

The plaintiff had the ordinary *rights* of the British subject. He was *at liberty* to earn his living in his own way, provided he did not violate ome special law prohibiting him from so doing, and provided he did not infringe the rights of other people. This *liberty* involved *the liberty* to deal with other persons who were willing to deal with him. *This liberty* is *a right* recognized by law; its *correlative* is the general *duty* of every one not to prevent the free exercise of this *liberty* except so far as his own liberty of action may justify him in so doing. But a person's *liberty* or *right* to deal with others is nugatory unless they are at liberty to deal with him if they choose to do so. Any interference with their liberty to deal with him affects him.

A "liberty" considered as a legal relation (or "right" in the loose and generic sense of that term) must mean, if it have any definite content at all, precisely the same thing as *privilege;* and certainly that is the fair connotation of the term as used the first three times in the passage quoted. It is equally clear, as already indicated, that such a privilege or liberty to deal with others at will might very conceivably exist without any peculiar concomitant rights against "third parties" as regards certain kinds of interference. Whether there should be such concomitant rights (or claims) is ultimately a question of justice and policy; and it should be considered, as such, on its merits. The only correlative logically implied by the privileges or liberties in question are the "no-rights" of "third parties." It would therefore be a *non sequitur* to conclude from the mere existence of such liberties that "third parties" are under a *duty* not to interfere, etc. Yet in the middle of the above passage from Lord Lindley's opinion there is a sudden and question-begging shift in the use of terms. First, the "liberty" in question is transmuted into a "right"; and then, possibly under the seductive influence of the latter word, it is assumed that the "correlative" must be "the general duty of every one not to prevent," etc.

Another interesting and instructive example may be taken from Lord Bowen's oft-quoted opinion in *Mogul Steamship Co. v. McGregor.* [11]

We are presented in this case with an apparent conflict or antinomy between two rights that are equally regarded by the law—the right of the plaintiffs to be protected in the legitimate exercise of their trade, and the right of the defendants to carry on their business as seems best to them, provided they commit no wrong to others.

As the learned judge states, the conflict or antinomy is only apparent; but this fact seems to be obscured by the very indefinite and rapidly shifting meanings with which the term "right" is used in the above quoted language. Construing the passage as a whole, it seems plain enough that by "the right of the plaintiffs" in relation to the defendants a legal right or claim in the strict sense must be meant; whereas by "the right of the defendants" in relation to the plaintiffs a legal privilege must be intended. That being so, the "two rights" mentioned in the beginning of the passage, being respectively claim and privilege, could not be in conflict with each other. To the extent that the defendants have privileges the plaintiffs have no rights; and, conversely, to the extent that the plaintiffs have rights the defendants have no privileges ("no-privilege" equals duty of opposite tenor).

Thus far it has been assumed that the term "privilege" is the most appropriate and satisfac-tory to designate the mere negation of duty. Is there good warrant for this?

In Mackeldey's *Roman Law* [12] it is said:

Positive laws either contain general principles embodied in the rules of law . . . or for especial reasons they establish something that differs from those general principles. In the first case they contain a common law *(jus commune),* in the second a special law *(jus singulare s. exorbitans).* The latter is either favorable or unfavorable . . . according as it enlarges or restricts, in opposition to the common rule, the rights of those for whom it is established. The favorable special law *(jus singulare)* as also the right created by it . . . in the Roman law is termed benefit of the law *(beneficium juris)* or privilege *(privilegium)* . . .

First a special law, and then by association of ideas, a special advantage conferred by such a law. With such antecedents, it is not surprising that the English word "privilege" is not infrequently used, even at the present time, in the sense of a special or peculiar legal advantage (whether right, privilege, power or immunity) belonging either to some individual or to some particular class of persons. There are, indeed, a number of judicial opinions recognizing this as one of the meanings of the term in question. That the word has a wider signification even in ordinary non-technical usage is sufficiently indicated, however, by the fact that the term *"special* privileges" is so often used to indicate a contrast to ordinary or general privileges. More than this, the dominant specific connotation of the term as used in popular speech seems to be mere *negation of duty.* This is manifest in the terse and oft-repeated expression, "That is your privilege,"—meaning, of course, "You are under no duty to do otherwise."

Such being the case, it is not surprising to find, from a wide survey of judicial precedents, that the *dominant* technical meaning of the term is, similarly, negation of *legal duty.* There are two very common examples of this, relating respectively to "privileged communications" in the law of libel and to "privileges against self-crimination" in the law of evidence. As regards the first case, it is elementary that if a certain group of operative facts are present, a privilege exists which, without such facts, would not be recognized. It is, of course, equally clear that even though all such facts be present as last supposed, the superadded fact of malice will, in cases of so-called "conditional privilege," negative the privilege that otherwise would exist. It must be evident also, that whenever the privilege does exist, it is not special in the sense of arising from a special law, or of being conferred as a special favor on a particular individual. The same privilege would exist, by virtue of general rules, for any person whatever under similar circumstances. So, also, in the law of evidence, the privilege against self-crimination signifies the mere negation of a duty to testify,— a duty which rests upon a witness in relation to all ordinary matters; and, quite obviously, such privilege arises, if at all, only by virtue of general laws.

As already intimated, while both the conception and the term "privilege" find conspicuous exemplification under the law of libel and the law of evidence, they nevertheless have a much wider significance and utility as a matter of judicial usage. To make this clear, a few miscellaneous judicial precedents will now be noticed. In *Dowman's Case,*[13] decided in the year 1583, and reported by Coke, the court applied the term to the subject of waste:

And as to the objection which was made, that the said privilege to be without impeachment of waste can not be without deed, etc. To that it was answered and resolved, that if it was admitted that a deed in such case should be requisite, yet within question all the estates limited would be good, although it is admitted, that the clause concerning the said privilege would be void.

In the great case of *Allen v. Flood*[14] the opinion of Mr. Justice Hawkins furnishes a useful passage for the purpose now in view:

Every person has a privilege . . . in the interests of public justice to put the criminal law in motion against another whom he *bona fide,* and upon reasonable and probable cause, believes to have been guilty of a crime . . . It must not, however, be supposed that hatred and ill-will existing in the mind of a prosecutor must of necessity *destroy* the *privilege,* for it is not impossible that such hatred and ill-will may have very natural and pardonable reasons for existing.

Applying the term in relation to the subject of property, Mr. Justice Foster, of the Supreme Court of Maine, said in the case of *Pulitzer v. Livingston.*[15]

It is contrary to the policy of the law that there should be any outstanding titles, estates, or powers, by the existence, operation or exercise of which, at a period of time beyond lives in being and twenty-one years and a fraction thereafter, the complete and unfettered enjoyment of an estate, *with all the rights, privileges and powers incident to ownership,* should be qualified or impeded.

As a final example in the present connection, the language of Baron Alderson in *Hilton v. Eckerly*[16] may be noticed:

Prima facie it is the privilege of a trader in a free country, in all matters not contrary to law, to regulate his own mode of carrying them on according to his discretion and choice.

The closest synonym of legal "privilege" seems to be legal "liberty" or legal "freedom." This is sufficiently indicated by an unusually discriminating and instructive passage in Mr. Justice Cave's opinion in *Allen v. Flood.*[17]

The personal rights with which we are most familiar are: 1. Rights of reputation; 2. Rights of bodily safety and freedom; 3. Rights of property; or, in other words, rights relating to mind, body and estate, . . .

In my subsequent remarks the word "right" will, as far as possible, always be used in the above sense; and it is the more necessary to insist on this as during the argument at your Lordship's bar it was frequently used in a much wider and more indefinite sense. Thus it was said that a man has a perfect right to fire off a gun, when all that was meant, apparently, was that a man has a *freedom* or *liberty* to fire off a gun, so long as he does not violate or infringe any one's rights in doing so, which is a very different thing from a right, the violation or disturbance of which can be remedied or prevented by legal process.

While there are numerous other instances of the apt use of the term "liberty," both in judicial opinions and in conveyancing documents, it is by no means so common or definite a word as "privilege." The former term is far more likely to be used in the sense of physical or personal freedom (i.e., absence of physical restraint), as distinguished from a legal relation; and very frequently there is the connotation of *general* political liberty, as distinguished from a particular relation between two definite individuals. Besides all this, the term "privilege" has the advantage of giving us, as a variable, the adjective "privileged." Thus, it is frequently convenient to speak of a privileged act, a privileged transaction, a privileged conveyance, etc.

The term "license," sometimes used as if it were synonymous with "privilege," is not strictly appropriate. This is simply another of those innumerable cases in which the mental and physical facts are so frequently confused with the legal relation which they create. Accurately used, "license" is a generic term to indicate a group of *operative* facts required to create a particular privilege,—this being especially evident when the word is used in the common phrase "leave and license." This point is brought out by a passage from Mr. Justice Adam's opinion in *Clifford v. O'Neill.* [18]

A license is merely a *permission* to do an act which, *without such permission,* would be amount to a trespass . . . nor will the continuous enjoyment of the *privilege conferred,* for any period of time cause it to ripen into a tangible interest in the land affected.

Powers and Liabilities. As indicated in the preliminary scheme of jural relations, a legal power (as distinguished, of course, from a mental or physical power) is the opposite of legal disability, and the correlative of legal liability. But what is the intrinsic nature of a legal power as such? Is it possible to analyze the conception represented by this constantly employed and very important term of legal discourse? Too close an analysis might seem metaphysical rather than useful; so that what is here presented is intended only as an approximate explanation, sufficient for all practical purposes.

A change in a given legal relation may result (1) from some superadded fact or group of facts not under the volitional control of a human being (or human beings); or (2) from some superadded fact or groups of facts which are under the volitional control of one or more human beings. As regards the second class of cases, the person (or persons) whose volitional control is paramount may be said to have the (legal) power to effect the particular change of legal relations that is involved in the problem.

This second class of cases—powers in the technical sense—must now be further considered. The nearest synonym for any ordinary case seems to be (legal) "ability"—the latter being obviously the opposite of "inability," or "disability." The term "right," so frequently and loosely used in the present connection is an unfortunate term for the purpose,—a not unusual result being confusion of thought as well as ambiguity of expression. The term "capacity" is equally unfortunate; for, as we have already seen, when used with discrimination, this word denotes a particular group of operative facts, and not a legal relation of any kind.

Many examples of legal powers may readily be given. Thus, X, the owner of ordinary personal property "in a tangible object" has the power to extinguish his own legal interest (rights, powers, immunities, etc.) through that totality of operative facts known as abandonment; and—simultaneously and correlatively—to create in other persons privileges and powers relating to the abandoned object,—e. g., the power to acquire title to the latter by appropriating it. *Similarly,* X has the power to transfer his interest to Y,—that is to extinguish his own interest and concomitantly create in Y a new and corresponding interest. So also X has the power to create contractual obligations of various kinds. Agency cases are likewise instructive. By the use of some *metaphorical* expression such as the Latin, *qui facit per alium, facit per se** the true nature of agency relations is only too frequently obscured. The creation of an agency relation involves, *inter alia,* the grant of legal powers to the so-called agent, and the creation of correlative liabilities in the principal. That is to say, one party, P, has the power to create agency powers in another party, A,—for example, the power to convey P's property, the power to impose (so called) contractual obligations on P, the power to discharge a debt owing to P, the power to "receive" title to property so that it shall vest in P, and so forth. In passing, it may be well to observe that the term "authority," so frequently used in agency cases, is very ambiguous and slippery in its connotation. Properly employed in the present connection, the word seems to be an abstract or qualitative term corresponding to the concrete "authorization,"—the latter consisting of a particular group of operative facts taking place between the principal and the agent. All too often, however, the term in question is so used as to blend and confuse these operative facts with the powers and privileges thereby created in the agent. A careful discrimination in these particulars would, it is submitted, go far toward clearing up certain problems in the law of agency.

Essentially similar to the powers of agents are powers of appointment in relation to property interests. So, too, the powers of public officers are, intrinsically considered, comparable to those of agents,—for example, the power of a sheriff to sell property under a writ of execution. The power of a donor, in a gift *causa mortis,* to revoke the gift and divest the title of the donee is another clear example of the legal quantities now being considered; also a pledgee's statutory power of sale.

There are, on the other hand, cases where the true nature of the relations involved has not, perhaps, been so clearly recognized. Thus, in the case of a conditional sale of personalty, assuming the vendee's agreement has been fully performed ex-

*"He who acts through another acts himself." That is, the acts of a person's legal agent may be attributed to the person (the principal) himself.

cept as to the payment of the last instalment and the time for the latter has arrived, what is the interest of such vendee as regards the property? Has he, as so often assumed, merely a contractural *right* to have title passed to him by consent of the vendor, on final payment being made; or has he, irrespective of the consent of the vendor the power to divest the title of the latter and to acquire a perfect title for himself? Though the language of the cases is not always so clear as it might be, the vendee seems to have precisely that sort of power. Fundamentally considered, the typical escrow transaction in which the performance of conditions is within the volitional control of the grantee, is somewhat similar to the conditional sale of personalty; and, when reduced to its lowest terms, the problem seems easily to be solved in terms of legal powers. Once the "escrow" is formed, the grantor still has the legal title; but the grantee has an irrevocable power to divest that title by performance of certain conditions (i. e., the addition of various operative facts), and concomitantly to vest title in himself. While such power is outstanding, the grantor is, of course, subject to a correlative liability to have his title divested. Similarly, in the case of a conveyance of land in fee simple subject to condition subsequent, after the condition has been performed, the original grantor is commonly said to have a "*right* of entry." If, however, the problem is analyzed, it will be seen that, as of primary importance, the grantor has two legal quantities, (1) the privilege of entering, and (2) the power, by means of such entry, to divest the estate of the grantee. The latter's estate endures, subject to the correlative liability of being divested, until such power is actually exercised.

Passing now to the field of contracts, suppose A mails a letter to B offering to sell the former's land, Whiteacre, to the latter for ten thousand dollars, such letter being duly received. The operative facts thus far mentioned have created a power as regards B and a correlative liability as regards A. B, by dropping a letter of acceptance in the box, has the power to impose a potential or inchoate obligation *ex contractu* on A and himself; and, assuming that the land is worth fifteen thousand dollars, that particular legal quantity— the "power *plus* liability" relation between A and B—seems to be worth about five thousand dollars to B. The liability of A will continue for a reasonable time unless, in exercise of his power to do so, A previously extinguishes it by that series of operative facts known as "revocation." These last matters are usually described by saying that A's

"offer" will "continue" or "remain open" for a reasonable time, or for the definite time actually specified, unless A previously "withdraws" or "revokes" such offer. While, no doubt, in the great majority of cases no harm results from the use of such expressions, yet these forms of statement seem to represent a blending of non-legal and legal quantities which, in any problem requiring careful reasoning, should preferably be kept distinct. An offer, considered as a series of physical and mental operative facts, has spent its force and become *functus officio* as soon as such series has been completed by the "offeree's receipt." The real question is therefore as to the *legal effect,* if any, at that moment of time. If the latter consist of B's power and A's correlative liability, manifestly it is those *legal relations* that "continue" or "remain open" until modified by revocation or other operative facts. What has thus far been said concerning contracts completed by mail would seem to apply, *mutatis mutandis,* to every type of contract. Even where the parties are in the presence of each other, the offer creates a liability against the offerer, together with a correlative power in favor of the offeree. The only distinction for present purposes would be in the fact that such power and such liability would expire within a very short period of time.

Perhaps the practical justification for this method of analysis is somewhat greater in relation to the subject of options. In his able work on *Contracts,*[19] Langdell says:

If the offerer stipulates that his offer shall remain open for a specified time, the first question is whether such stipulation constitutes a binding contract ... When such a stipulation is binding, the further question arises, whether it makes the offer irrevocable. It has been a common opinion that it does, but that is clearly a mistake. ... An offer is merely one of the elements of a contract; and it is indispensable to the making of a contract that the wills of the contracting parties do, in legal contemplation, concur at the moment of making it. An offer, therefore, which the party making it has no power to revoke, is a legal impossibility. Moreover, if the stipulation should make the offer irrevocable, it would be a contract incapable of being broken; which is also a legal impossibility. The only effect, therefore, of such a stipulation is to give the offeree a claim for damages if the stipulation be broken by revoking the offer.

The foregoing reasoning ignores the fact that an ordinary offer *ipso facto* creates a legal relation —a legal power and a legal liability,—and that it is this relation (rather than the physical and mental facts constituting the offer) that "remains open." If these points be conceded, there seems no difficulty in recognizing a unilateral option agreement supported by consideration or embodied in a sealed instrument as creating in the optionee an irrevocable power to create, at any time within the period specified, a bilateral obligation as between himself and the giver of the option. Correlatively to that power, there would of course, be a liability against the option-giver which he himself would have no power to extinguish. The courts seem to have no difficulty in reaching precisely this result as a matter of substance; though their explanations are always in terms of "withdrawal of offer," and similar expressions savoring of physical and mental quantities.

In connection with the powers and liabilities created respectively by an ordinary offer and by an option, it is interesting to consider the liabilities of a person engaged in a "public calling"; for, as it seems, such a party's characteristic position is, one might almost say, intermediate between that of an ordinary contractual offerer and that of an option-giver. It has indeed been usual to assert that such a party is (generally speaking) under a present *duty* to all other parties; but this is believed to be erroneous. Thus, Professor Wyman, in his work on *Public Service Companies*,[20] says:

The duty placed upon every one exercising a public calling is primarily a *duty* to serve every man who is a member of the public. . . . It is somewhat difficult to place this exceptional duty in our legal system. . . . The truth of the matter is that the obligation resting upon one who has undertaken the performance of public duty is *sui generis*.

It is submitted that the learned writer's difficulties arise primarily from a failure to see that the innkeeper, the common carrier and others similarly "holding out" are under present *liabilities* rather than present *duties*. Correlative to those liabilities are the respective powers of the various members of the public. Thus, for example, a traveling member of the public has the legal power, by making proper application and sufficient tender, to impose a duty on the innkeeper to receive him as a guest. For breach of the duty *thus* created an action would of course lie. It would therefore seem that the innkeeper is, to some extent, like one who had given an option to every traveling member of the public. He differs as regards net legal effect, only because he can extinguish his present liabilities and the correlative powers of the traveling members of the public *by*

going out of business. Yet, on the other hand, his liabilities are more onerous than that of an ordinary contractual offerer, for he cannot extinguish his liabilities by any simple performance akin to revocation of offer.

As regards all the "legal powers" thus far considered, possibly some caution is necessary. If, for example, we consider the ordinary property owner's power of alienation, it is necessary to distinguish carefully between the *legal* power, the *physical* power to do the things necessary for the "exercise" of the legal power, and, finally, the *privilege* of doing these things—that is, if such privilege does really exist. It may or may not. Thus, if X, a landowner, has contracted with Y that the former will not alienate to Z, the acts of X necessary to exercise the power of alienating to Z are privileged as between X and every party other than Y; but, obviously, as between X and Y, the former has no privilege of doing the necessary acts; or conversely, he is under a duty to Y not to do what is necessary to exercise the power.

In view of what has already been said, very little may suffice concerning a *liability* as such. The latter, as we have seen, is the correlative of power, and the opposite of immunity (or exemption). While no doubt the term "liability" is often loosely used as a synonym for "duty," or "obligation," it is believed, from an extensive survey of judicial precedents, that the connotation already adopted as most appropriate to the word in question is fully justified. A few cases tending to indicate this will now be noticed. In *McNeer v. McNeer*,[21] Mr. Justice Magruder balanced the conceptions of power and liability as follows:

So long as she lived, however, his interest in her land lacked those *elements of property,* such as *power of disposition* and *liability to sale on* execution which had formerly given it the character of a vested estate.

In *Booth v. Commonwealth*,[22] the court had to construe a Virginia statute providing "that all free white male persons who are twenty-one years of age and not over sixty, shall be *liable* to serve as jurors, except as hereinafter provided." It is plain that this enactment imposed only a *liability* and not a *duty*. It is a liability to have a duty created. The latter would arise only when, in exercise of their powers, the parties litigant and the court officers had done what was necessary to impose a specific duty to perform the functions of a juror. The language of the court, by Moncure, J., is particularly apposite as indicating that liability is the opposite, or negative, of immunity (or exemption):

The word both expressed and implied is "liable," which has a very different meaning from "qualified" ... Its meaning is "bound" or "obliged." ... A person exempt from serving on juries is not liable to serve, and a person not liable to serve is exempt from serving. The terms seem to be convertible.

A further good example of judicial usage is to be found in *Emery v. Clough*.[23] Referring to a gift *causa mortis* and the donee's liability to have his already vested interest divested by the donor's exercise of his power of revocation, Mr. Justice Smith said:

The title to the gift *causa mortis* passed by the delivery, defeasible only in the lifetime of the donor, and his death perfects the title in the donee by terminating the donor's right or *power of defeasance*. The property passes from the donor to the donee directly ... and after his death it is *liable* to be *divested* only in favor of the donor's creditors. ... His right and power ceased with his death.

Perhaps the nearest synonym is "subjection" or "responsibility." As regards the latter word, a passage from Mr. Justice Day's opinion in *McElfresh* v. *Kirkendall* is interesting:

The words "debt' and "liability" are not synonymous, and they are not commonly so understood. As applied to the pecuniary relations of the parties, liability is a term of broader significance than debt. ... Liability is responsibility.

While the term in question has the broad generic connotation already indicated, no doubt it very frequently indicates that specific form of liability (or complex of liabilities) that is correlative to a power (or complex of powers) vested in a party litigant and the various court officers. Such was held to be the meaning of a certain California statute involved in the case of *Lattin v. Gillette*.[25] Said Mr. Justice Harrison:

The word "liability" is the condition in which an individual is placed after a breach of his contract, or a violation of any obligation resting upon him. It is defined by Bouvier to be responsibility.

Immunities and Disabilities. As already brought out, immunity is the correlative of disability ("no-power"), and the opposite, or negation, of liability. Perhaps it will also be plain, from the preliminary outline and from the discussion down to this point, that a power bears the same general contrast to an immunity that a right does to a privilege. A right is one's affirmative claim against another, and a privilege is one's freedom from the right or claim of another. Similarly, a power is one's affirmative "control" over a given legal relation as against another; whereas an immunity is one's freedom from the legal power or "control" of another as regards some legal relation.

A few examples may serve to make this clear. X, a landowner, has, as we have seen, power to alienate to Y or to any other ordinary party. On the other hand, X has also various immunities as against Y, and all other ordinary parties. For Y is under a disability (i.e., has no power) so far as shifting the legal interest either to himself or to a third party is concerned; and what is true of Y applies similarly to every one else who has not by virtue of special operative facts acquired a power to alienate X's property. If, indeed, a sheriff has been duly empowered by a writ of execution to sell X's interest, that is a very different matter: correlative to such sheriff's power would be the *liability* of X,—the very opposite of immunity (or exemption). It is elementary, too, that as against the sheriff, X might be immune or exempt in relation to certain parcels of property, and be liable as to others. Similarly, if an agent has been duly appointed by X to sell a given piece of property, then, as to the latter, X has, in relation to such agent, a liability rather than an immunity.

For over a century there has been, in this country, a great deal of important litigation involving immunities from powers of taxation. If there be any lingering misgivings as to the "practical" importance of accuracy and discrimination in legal conceptions and legal terms, perhaps some of such doubts would be dispelled by considering the numerous cases on valuable taxation exemptions coming before the United States Supreme Court. Thus, in *Phoenix Ins. Co. v. Tennessee*,[26] Mr. Justice Peckham expressed the views of the court as follows:

In granting to the De Soto Company "all the rights, privileges, and immunities" of the Bluff City Company, all words are used which could be regarded as necessary to carry the exemption from taxation possessed by the Bluff City Company; while in the next following grant, that of the charter of the plaintiff in error, the word "immunity" is omitted. Is there any meaning to be attached to that omission, and if so, what? We think some meaning is to be attached to it. The word "immunity" expresses more clearly and definitely an intention to include therein an exemption from taxation than does either of the other words. Exemption from taxation is more accurately described as an "immunity" than as a privilege, although it is not to be denied that the latter word may sometimes and under some circumstances include such exemptions.

In *Morgan v. Louisiana*[27] there is an instructive discussion from the pen of Mr. Justice Field. In holding that on a foreclosure sale of the franchise and property of a railroad corporation an immunity from taxation did not pass to the purchaser, the learned judge said:

As has been often said by this court, the whole community is interested in retaining the power of taxation undiminished.... The exemption of the property of the company from taxation, and the exemption of its officers and servants from jury and military duty, were both intended for the benefit of the company, and its benefit alone. In their personal character they are analogous to exemptions from execution of certain property of debtors, made by laws of several of the states.

So far as immunities are concerned, the two judicial discussions last quoted concern respectively problems of interpretation and problems of alienability. In many other cases difficult constitutional questions have arisen as the result of statutes impairing or extending various kinds of immunities. Litigants have, from time to time, had occasion to appeal both to the clause against impairment of the obligation of contracts and to the provision against depriving a person of property without due process of law. This has been especially true as regards exemptions from taxation and exemptions from execution.

If a word may now be permitted with respect to mere terms as such, the first thing to note is that the word "right" is overworked in the field of immunities as elsewhere. As indicated, however, by the judicial expressions already quoted, the best synonym is, of course, the term "exemption." It is instructive to note, also, that the word "impunity" has a very similar connotation. This is made evident by the interesting discriminations of Lord Chancellor Finch in *Skelton v. Skelton,*[28] a case decided in 1677:

But this I would be no means allow, that equity should enlarge the restraints of the disabilities introduced by act of parliament; and as to the granting of injunctions to stay waste, I took a distinction where tenant hath only *impunitatem,* and where he hath *jus in arboribus.* If the tenant have only a bare indemnity or *exemption* from an action (at law), if he committed waste, there it is fit he should be restrained by injuction from committing it.

In the latter part of the preceding discussion, eight conceptions of the law have been analyzed and compared in some detail, the purpose having been to exhibit not only their intrinsic meaning and scope, but also their relations to one another and the methods by which they are applied, in judicial reasoning, to the solution of concrete problems of litigation. Before concluding this branch of the discussion a general suggestion may be ventured as to the great practical importance of a clear appreciation of the distinctions and discriminations set forth. If a homely metaphor be permitted, these eight conceptions,—rights and duties, privileges and no-rights, powers and liabilities, immunities and disabilities,—seem to be what may be called "the lowest common denominators of the law." Ten fractions (1/3, 2/5, etc.) may, *superficially,* seem so different from one another as to defy comparison. If, however, they are expressed in terms of their lowest common denominators (5/15, 6/15, etc.), comparison becomes easy, and fundamental similarity may be discovered. The same thing is of course true as regards the lowest generic conceptions to which any and all "legal quantities" may be reduced.

Reverting, for example, to the subject of powers, it might be difficult at first glance to discover any essential and fundamental similarity between conditional sales of personalty, escrow transactions, option agreements, agency relations, powers of appointment, etc. But if all these relations are reduced to their lowest generic terms, the conceptions of legal power and legal liability are seen to be dominantly, though not exclusively, applicable throughout the series. By such a process it becomes possible not only to discover essential similarities and illuminating analogies in the midst of what appears superficially to be infinite and hopeless variety, but also to discern common principles of justice and policy underlying the various jural problems involved. An indirect, yet very practical, consequence is that it frequently becomes feasible, by virtue of such analysis, to use as persuasive authorities judicial precedents that might otherwise seem altogether irrelevant. If this point be valid with respect to powers, it would seem to be equally so as regards all of the other basic conceptions of the law. In short, the deeper the analysis, the greater becomes one's perception of fundamental unity and harmony in the law.

NOTES

1. (1852) 7 How. Pr., 124, 130.
2. (1893) 54 Fed. Rep., 338, 348.
3. (1871) 3 Heisk. (Tenn.), 287, 306–307.
4. (1894) 10 Ind. App., 60; 37 N.E., 303, 304.
5. (1883) 8 App. Cas., at p. 597.
6. *Elements of Jurisprudence* (10th ed.), 83.
7. *Ibid.*, 82.
8. See *Nature and Sources of Law* (1909), secs. 25, 45, 184.
9. *Nature and Sources of Law (1909) sec. 48.*
10. (1901) A.C., 495, 534.
11. (1889) 23 Q.B.D., 59.
12. (Dropsie trans.) secs. 196–197.
13. (1583) 9 Coke, 1.
14. (1898) A.C., 1, 19.
15. (1896) 89 Me., 359.
16. (1856) 6 E. & B., 47, 74.
17. (1898) A.C., 1, 29.
18. (1896) 12 App. Div., 17; 42 N.Y. Sup., 607, 609.
19. Langdell, *Summary of Contracts* (2d ed., 1880) Sec. 178.
20. Secs. 330–333.
21. (1892) 142 I11., 388, 397.
22. (1861) 16 Grat., 519, 525.
23. (1885) 63 N.H., 552.
24. (1873) 36 Ia., 224, 226.
25. (1892) 95 Cal., 317, 319.
26. (1895) 161 U.S., 174, 177.
27. (1876) 93 U.S., 217, 222.
28. (1677) 2 Swanst., 170.

JOEL FEINBERG

The Nature and Value of Rights*

1

I would like to begin by conducting a thought experiment. Try to imagine Nowheresville—a world very much like our own except that no one, or hardly any one (the qualification is not important), has *rights*. If this flaw makes Nowheresville too ugly to hold very long in contemplation, we can make it as pretty as we wish in other moral respects. We can, for example, make the human beings in it as attractive and virtuous as possible without taxing our conceptions of the limits of human nature. In particular, let the virtues of moral sensibility flourish. Fill this imagined world with as much benevolence, compassion, sympathy, and pity as it will conveniently hold without strain. Now we can imagine men helping one another from compassionate motives merely, quite as much (as) or even more than they do in our actual world from a variety of more complicated motives.

This picture, pleasant as it is in some respects, would hardly have satisfied Immanuel Kant. Benevolently motivated actions do good, Kant admitted, and therefore are better, *ceteris paribus,* than malevolently motivated actions; but no action can have supreme kind of worth—what Kant called "moral worth"—unless its whole motivating power derives from the thought that it is *required by duty.* Accordingly, let us try to make Nowheresville more appealing to Kant by introducing the idea of duty into it, and letting sufficient motive for many beneficent and honorable actions. But doesn't this bring our original thought experiment to an abortive conclusion? If duties are permitted entry into Nowheresville, are not rights necessarily smuggled in along with them?

The question is well-asked, and requires here

*From *The Journal of Value Inquiry,* Vol. 4 (1970), 243–257. Reprinted by permission of the publisher.

"Postscript, 1977" is from B. and E. Bandman, eds., *Bioethics and Human Rights: A Reader for Health Professionals* (Boston: Little, Brown, 1978), pp. 32–34, and is reprinted here by permission of Little, Brown, Inc.

a brief digression so that we might consider the so-called "doctrine of the logical correlativity of rights and duties." This is the doctrine that (i) all duties entail other people's rights and (ii) all rights entail other people's duties. Only the first part of the doctrine, the alleged entailment from duties to rights, need concern us here. Is this part of the doctrine correct? It should not be surprising that my answer is: "In a sense yes and in a sense no." Etymologically, the word "duty" is associated with actions that are *due* someone else, the payments of debts *to* creditors, the keeping of agreements with promisees, the payment of club dues, or legal fees, or tariff levies to appropriate authorities or their representatives. In this original sense of "duty," all duties are correlated with the rights of those *to* whom the duty is owed. On the other hand, there seem to be numerous classes of duties, both of a legal and non-legal kind, that are *not* logically correlated with the rights of other persons. This seems to be a consequence of the fact that the word "duty" has come to be used for *any* action understood to be *required,* whether by the rights of others, or by law, or by higher authority, or by conscience, or whatever. When the notion of requirement is in clear focus it is likely to seem the only element in the idea of duty that is essential, and the other component notion—that a duty is something *due* someone else—drops off. Thus, in this widespread but derivative usage, "duty" tends to be used for any action we feel we *must* (for whatever reason) do. It comes, in short, to be a term of moral modality merely; and it is no wonder that the first thesis of the logical correlativity doctrine often fails.

Let us then introduce duties into Nowheresville, but only in the sense of actions that are, or (are) believed to be, morally mandatory, but not in the older sense of actions that are due others and can be claimed by others as their right. Nowheresville now can have duties of the sort imposed by positive law. A legal duty is not something we are implored or advised to do merely; it is something the law, or an authority under the law, *requires* us to do whether we want to or not, under pain of penalty. When traffic lights turn red, however, there is no determinate person who can plausibly be said to claim our stopping as his due, so that the motorist owes it to *him* to stop, in the way a debtor owes it to his creditor to pay. In our own actual world, of course, we sometimes owe it to our *fellow motorists* to stop; but that kind of right-correlated duty does not exist in Nowheresville. There, motorists "owe" obedience to the Law, but they owe nothing to one another. When they collide, no matter who is at fault, no one is accountable to anyone else, and no one has any sound grievance or "right to complain."

When we leave legal contexts to consider moral obligations and other extra-legal duties, a greater variety of duties-without-correlative-rights present themselves. Duties of charity, for example, require us to contribute to one or another of a large number of eligible recipients, no one of whom can claim our contribution from us as his due. Charitable contributions are more like gratuitous services, favours, and gifts than like repayments of debts or reparations; and yet we do have duties to be charitable. Many persons, moreover, in our actual world believe that they are required by their own consciences to do more than that "duty" that *can* be demanded of them by their prospective beneficiaries. I have quoted elsewhere the citation from H. B. Acton of a character in a Malraux novel who "gave all his supply of poison to his fellow prisoners to enable them by suicide to escape the burning alive which was to be their fate and his." This man, Acton adds, "probably did not think that [the others] had more of a right to the poison than he had, though he thought it his duty to give it to them."[1] I am sure that there are many actual examples, less dramatically heroic than this fictitious one, of persons who believe, rightly or wrongly, that they *must do* something (hence the word "duty") for another person in excess of what that person can appropriately demand of him (hence the absence of "right").

Now the digression is over and we can return to Nowheresville and summarize what we have put in it thus far. We now find spontaneous benevolence in somewhat larger degree than in our actual world, and also the acknowledged existence of duties of obedience, duties of charity, and duties imposed by exacting private consciences, and also, let us suppose, a degree of conscientiousness in respect to those duties somewhat in excess of what is to be found in our actual world. I doubt that Kant would be fully satisfied with Nowheresville even now that duty and respect for law and authority have been added to it; but I feel certain that he would regard their addition at least as an improvement. I will now introduce two further moral practices into Nowheresville that will make that world very little more appealing to Kant, but will make it appear more familiar to us. These are the practices connected with the notions of *personal desert* and what I call a *sovereign monopoly of rights*.

When a person is said to deserve something good from us what is meant in part is that there would be a certain propriety in our giving that good thing to him in virtue of the kind of person he is, perhaps, or more likely, in virtue of some specific thing he has done. The propriety involved here is a much weaker kind than that which derives from our having promised him the good thing or from his having qualified for it by satisfying the well-advertised conditions of some public rule. In the latter case he could be said not merely to deserve the good thing but also to have a *right* to it, that is to be in a position to demand it as his due; and of course we will not have that sort of thing in Nowheresville. That weaker kind of propriety which is mere desert is simply a kind of *fittingness* between one party's character or action and another party's favorable response, much like that between comedy and laughter, or good performance and applause.

The following seems to be the origin of the idea of deserving good or bad treatment from others: A master or lord was under no obligation to reward his servant for especially good service; still a master might naturally feel that there would be a special fittingness in giving a gratuitous reward as a grateful response to the good service (or conversely imposing a penalty for bad service). Such an act while surely fitting and proper was entirely supererogatory. The fitting response in turn from the rewarded servant should be gratitude. If the deserved reward had not been given him he should have had no complaint, since he only *deserved* the reward, as opposed to having a *right* to it, or a ground for claiming it as his due.

The idea of desert has evolved a good bit away from its beginnings by now, but nevertheless, it seems clearly to be one of these words J. L. Austin said "never entirely forget their pasts."[2] Today servants qualify for their wages by doing their agreed upon chores, no more and no less. If their wages are not forthcoming, their contractual rights have been violated and they can make legal claim to the money that is their due. If they do less than they agreed to do, however, their employers may "dock" them, by paying them proportionately less than the agreed upon fee. This is all a matter of right. But if the servant does a splendid job, above and beyond his minimal contractual duties, the employer is under no further obligation to reward him, for this was not agreed upon, even tacitly, in advance. The additional service was all the servant's idea and done entirely on his own. Nevertheless, the morally sensitive employer may feel that it would be exceptionally appropriate for him to respond, freely on *his* own, to the servant's meritorious service, with a reward. The employee cannot demand it as his due, but he will happily accept it, with gratitude, as a fitting response to his desert.

In our age of organized labor, even this picture is now archaic; for almost every kind of exchange of service is governed by hard bargained contracts so that even bonuses can sometimes be demanded as a matter of right, and nothing is given for nothing on either side of the bargaining table. And perhaps that is a good thing; for consider an anachronistic instance of the earlier kind of practice that survives, at least as a matter of form, in the quaint old practice of "tipping." The tip was originally conceived as a reward that has to be earned by "zealous service." It is not something to be taken for granted as a standard response to *any* service. That is to say that its payment is a *"gratuity,"* not a discharge of obligation, but something given apart from, or in addition to, anything the recipient can expect as a matter of right. That is what tipping originally meant at any rate, and tips are still referred to as "gratuities" in the tax forms. But try to explain all that to a New York cab driver! If he has *earned* his gratuity, by God, he has it coming, and there had better be sufficient acknowledgement of his desert or he'll give you a piece of his mind! I'm not generally prone to defend New York cab drivers, but they do have a point here. There is the making of a paradox in the queerly unstable concept of an "earned gratuity." One can understand how "desert" in the weak sense of "propriety" or "mere fittingness" tends to generate a stronger sense in which desert is itself the ground for a claim of right.

In Nowheresville, nevertheless, we will have only the original weak kind of desert. Indeed, it will be impossible to keep this idea out if we allow such practices as teachers grading students, judges awarding prizes, and servants serving benevolent but class-conscious masters. Nowheres-

ville is a reasonably good world in many ways, and its teachers, judges, and masters will generally try to give students, contestants, and servants the grades, prizes, and rewards they deserve. For this the recipients will be grateful; but they will never think to complain, or even feel aggrieved, when expected responses to desert fail. The masters, judges, and teachers don't *have* to do good things, after all, for *anyone.* One should be happy that they *ever* treat us well, and not grumble over their occasional lapses. Their hoped for responses, after all, are *gratuities,* and there is no wrong in the omission of what is merely gratuitous. Such is the response of persons who have no concept of *rights,* even persons who are proud of their own deserts.[3]

Surely, one might ask, rights have to come in somewhere, if we are to have even moderately complex forms of social organization. Without rules that confer rights and impose obligations, how can we have ownership of property, bargains and deals, promises, and contracts, appointments and loans, marriages and partnerships? Very well, let us introduce all of these social and economic practices into Nowheresville, but *with one big twist.* With them I should like to introduce the curious notion of a "sovereign right-monopoly." You will recall that the subjects in Hobbes's *Leviathan* had no rights whatever against their sovereign. He could do as he liked with them, even gratuitously harm them, but this gave them no valid grievance against him. The sovereign, to be sure, had a certain duty to treat his subjects well, but this duty was owed not to the subjects directly, but to God, just as we might have a duty to a person to treat his property well, but of course no duty to the property itself but only to its owner. Thus, while the sovereign was quite capable of *harming* his subjects, he could commit no wrong against them that they could complain about, since they had no prior claims against his conduct. The only party *wronged* by the sovereign's mistreatment of his subjects was God, the supreme lawmaker. Thus, in repenting cruelty to his subjects, the sovereign might say to God, as David did after killing Uriah, "to Thee only have I sinned."[4]

Even in the *Leviathan*, however, ordinary people had ordinary rights *against one another.* They played roles, occupied offices, made agreements, and signed contracts. In a genuine "sovereign right-monopoly," as I shall be using that phrase, they will do all those things too, and thus incur genuine obligations toward one another; but the obligations (here is the twist) will not be owed directly *to* promisees, creditors, parents, and the like but rather to God alone, or to the members of some elite, or to a single sovereign under God. Hence, the rights correlative to the obligations that derive from these transactions are all owned by some "outside" authority.

As far as I know, no philosopher has ever suggested that even our role and contract obligations (in this, our actual world) are all owed directly to a divine intermediary; but some theologians have approached such extreme moral occasionalism. I have in mind the familiar phrase in certain widely distributed religious tracts that "it takes three to marry," which suggests that marital vows are not made between bride and groom directly but between each spouse and God, so that if one breaks his vow, the other cannot rightly complain of being wronged, since only God could have claimed performance of the marital duties as his *own* due; and hence God alone had a claim-right violated by nonperformance. If John breaks his vow to God, he might then properly repent in the words of David: "To Thee only have I sinned."

In our actual world, very few spouses conceive of their mutual obligations in this way; but their small children, at a certain stage in their moral upbringing, are likely to feel precisely this way toward *their* mutual obligations. If Billy kicks Bobby and is punished by Daddy, he may come to feel contrition for his naughtiness induced by his painful estrangement from the loved parent. He may then be happy to make amends and sincere apology to *Daddy;* but when Daddy insists that he apologize to his wronged brother, that is another story. A direct apology to Billy would be a tacit recognition of Billy's status as a right-holder against him, someone he can wrong as well as harm, and someone to whom he is directly accountable for his wrongs. This is a status Bobby will happily accord Daddy; but it would imply a respect for Billy that he does not presently feel, so he bitterly resents according it to him. On the "three-to-marry" model, the relations between each spouse and God would be like those between Bobby and Daddy; respect for the other spouse as an independent claimant would not even be necessary; and where present, of course, never sufficient.

The advocates of the "three to marry" model who conceive it either as a description of our actual institution of marriage or a recommendation of what marriage ought to be, may wish to escape this embarrassment by granting rights to spouses in capacities other than as promisees. They may wish to say, for example, that when John promises God that he will be faithful to Mary, a right is thus conferred not only on God as promisee but also on Mary herself as third-party beneficiary, just as when John contracts with an insurance company and names Mary as his intended beneficiary, she has a right to the accumulated funds after John's death, even though the insurance company made no promise to her. But this seems to be an unnecessarily cumbersome complication contributing nothing to our understanding of the marriage bond. The life insurance transaction is necessarily a three party relation, involving occupants of three distinct offices, no two of whom alone could do the whole job. The transaction, after all, is defined as the purchase by the customer (first office) from the vendor (second office) of protection for a beneficiary (third office) against the customer's untimely death. Marriage, on the other hand, in this our actual world, appears to be a binary relation between a husband and wife, and even though third parties such as children, neighbors, psychiatrists, and priests may sometimes be helpful and even causally necessary for the survival of the relation, they are not logically necessary to our *conception* of the relation, and indeed many married couples do quite well without them. Still I am not now purporting to describe our actual world, but rather trying to contrast it with a counterpart world of the imagination. In *that* world, it takes three to make almost *any* moral relation and all rights are owned by God or some sovereign under God.

There will, of course, be delegated authorities in the imaginary world, empowered to give commands to their underlings and to punish them for their disobedience. But the commands are all given in the name of the right-monopoly who in turn are the only persons to whom obligations are owed. Hence, even intermediate superiors do not have claim-rights against their subordinates but only legal *powers* to create obligations in the subordinates *to* the monopolistic right-holders, and also the legal *privilege* to impose penalties in the name of that monopoly.

2

So much for the imaginary "world without rights." If some of the moral concepts and practices I have allowed into that world do not sit well with one another, no matter. Imagine Nowheresville with all of these practices if you can, or with any harmonious subset of them, if you prefer. The important thing is not what I've let into it, but what I have kept out. The remainder of this paper will be devoted to an analysis of what precisely a world is missing when it does not contain rights and why that absence is morally important.

The most conspicuous difference, I think, between the Nowheresvillians and ourselves has something to do with the activity of *claiming*. Nowheresvillians, even when they are discriminated against invidiously, or left without the things they need, or otherwise badly treated, do not think to leap to their feet and make righteous demands against one another though they may not hesitate to resort to force and trickery to get what they want. They have no notion of rights, so they do not have a notion of what is their due; hence they do not claim before they take. The conceptual linkage between personal rights and claiming has long been noticed by legal writers and is reflected in the standard usage in which "claim-rights" are distinguished from other mere liberties, immunities, and powers, also sometimes called "rights," with which they are easily confused. When a person has a legal claim-right to *X*, it must be the case (i) that he is at liberty in respect to *X*, i.e. that he has no duty to refrain from or relinquish *X*, and also (ii) that his liberty is the ground of other people's *duties* to grant him *X* or not to interfere with him in respect to *X*. Thus, in the sense of claim-rights, it is true by definition that rights logically entail other people's duties. The paradigmatic examples of such rights are the creditor's right to be paid a debt by his debtor, and the landowner's right not to be interfered with by anyone in the exclusive occupancy of his land. The creditor's right against his debtor, for example, and the debtor's duty to his creditor, are precisely the same relation seen from two different vantage points, as inextricably linked as the two sides of the same coin.

And yet, this is not quite an accurate account of the matter, for it fails to do justice to the way claim-rights are somehow prior to, or more basic than, the duties with which they are necessarily correlated. If Nip has a claim-right against Tuck, it is because of this fact that Tuck has a duty to Nip. It is only because something from Tuck is *due* Nip (directional element) that there is something Tuck *must* do (modal element). This is a relation, moreover, in which Tuck is bound and Nip is free. Nip not only *has* a right, but he can choose whether or not to exercise it, whether to claim it, whether to register complaints upon its infringement, even whether to release Tuck from his duty, and forget the whole thing. If the personal claim-right is also backed up by criminal sanctions, however, Tuck may yet have a duty of

obedience to the law from which no one, not even Nip, may release him. He would even have such duties if he lived in Nowheresville; but duties subject to acts of claiming, duties derivative from and contingent upon the personal rights of others, are unknown and undreamed of in Nowheresville.

Many philosophical writers have simply identified rights with claims. The dictionaries tend to define "claims," in turn as "assertions of right," a dizzying piece of circularity that led one philosopher to complain, "We go in search of rights and are directed to claims, and then back again to rights in bureaucratic futility."[5] What then is the relation between a claim and a right?

As we shall see, a right *is* a kind of claim, and a claim is "an assertion of right," so that a formal definition of either notion in terms of the other will not get us very far. Thus if a "formal definition" of the usual philosophical sort is what we are after, the game is over before it has begun, and we can say that the concept of a right is a "simple, undefinable, unanalysable primitive." Here as elsewhere in philosophy this will have the effect of making the commonplace seem unnecessarily mysterious. We would be better advised, I think, not to attempt definition of either "right" or "claim," but rather to use the idea of a claim in informal elucidation of the idea of a right. This is made possible by the fact that *claiming* is an elaborate sort of rule-governed *activity*. A claim is that which is claimed, the object of the act of claiming . . . If we concentrate on the whole activity of claiming, which is public, familiar, and open to our observation, rather than on its upshot alone, we may learn more about the generic nature of rights than we could ever hope to learn from a formal definition, even if one were possible. Moreover, certain facts about rights more easily, if not solely, expressible in the language of claims and claiming are essential to a full understanding not only of what rights are, but also why they are so vitally important.

Let us begin then by distinguishing between: (i) making claim to . . . , (ii) claiming that . . . , and (iii) having a claim. One sort of thing we may be doing when we claim is to *make claim to something*. This is "to petition or seek by virtue of supposed right; to demand as due." Sometimes this is done by an acknowledged right-holder when he serves notice that he now wants turned over to him that which has already been acknowledged to be his, something borrowed, say, or improperly taken from him. This is often done by turning in a chit, a receipt, an I.O.U., a check, an insurance policy, or a deed, that is, a *title* to something currently in the possession of someone else. On other occasions, making claim is making application for titles or rights themselves, as when a mining prospector stakes a claim to mineral rights, or a householder to a tract of land in the public domain, or an inventor to his patent rights. In the one kind of case, to make claim is to exercise rights one already has by presenting title; in the other kind of case it is to apply for the title itself, by showing that one has satisfied the conditions specified by a rule for the ownership of title and therefore that one can demand it as one's due.

Generally speaking, only the person who has a title or who has qualified for it, or someone speaking in his name, can make claim to something as a matter of right. It is an important fact about rights (or claims), then, that they can be claimed only by those who have them. Anyone can claim, of course, *that* this umbrella is yours, but only you or your representative can actually claim the umbrella. If Smith owes Jones five dollars, only Jones can claim the five dollars as his own, though any bystander can *claim that* it belongs to Jones. One important difference then between *making legal claim to* and *claiming that* is that the former is a legal performance with direct legal consequences whereas the latter is often a mere piece of descriptive commentary with no legal force. Legally speaking, *making claim to* can itself make things happen. This sense of "claiming," then, might well be called "the performative sense." The legal power to claim (performatively) one's right or the things to which one has a right seems to be essential to the very notion of a right. A right to which one could not make claim (i.e. not even for recognition) would be a very "imperfect" right indeed!

Claiming that one has a right (what we can call "propositional claiming" as opposed to "performative claiming") is another sort of thing one can do with language, but it is not the sort of doing that characteristically has legal consequences. To claim that one has rights is to make an assertion that one has them, and to make it in such a manner as to demand or insist that they be recognized. In this sense of "claim" many things in addition to rights can be claimed, that is, many other kinds of proposition can be asserted in the claiming way. I can claim, for example, that you, he, or she has certain rights, or that Julius Caesar once had certan rights; or I can claim that certain statements are true, or that I have certain skills, or accomplishments, or virtually anything at all. I can claim that the earth is flat. What is essential to *claiming that* is the manner of assertion. One can assert without even caring very much whether anyone is listening, but part of the point of propositional claiming is to *make sure* people listen. When I claim to others that I know something, for example, I am not merely asserting it, but rather "obtruding my putative knowledge upon their attention, demanding that it be recognized, that appropriate notice be taken of it by those concerned ... "[6] Not every truth is properly assertable, much less claimable, in every context. To claim that something is the case in circumstances that justify no more than calm assertion is to behave like a boor. (This kind of boorishness, I might add, is probably less common in Nowheresville.) But not to claim in the appropriate circumstances that one has a right is to be spiritless or foolish. A list of "appropriate circumstances" would include occasions when one is challenged, when one's possession is denied, or seems insufficiently acknowledged or appreciated; and of course even in these circumstances, the claiming should be done only with an appropriate degree of vehemence.

Even if there are conceivable circumstances in which one would admit rights diffidently, there is no doubt that their characteristic use and that for which they are distinctively well suited, is to be claimed, demanded, affirmed, insisted upon. They are especially sturdy objects to "stand upon," a most useful sort of moral furniture. Having rights, of course, makes claiming possible; but it is claiming that gives rights their special moral significance. This feature of rights is connected in a way with the customary rhetoric about what it is to be a human being. Having rights enables us to "stand up like men," to look others in the eye, and to feel in some fundamental way the equal of anyone. To think of oneself as the holder of rights is not to be unduly but properly proud, to have that minimal self-respect that is necessary to be worthy of the love and esteem of others. Indeed, respect for persons (this is an intriguing idea) may simply be respect for their rights, so that there cannot be the one without the other; and what is called "human dignity" may simply be the recognizable capacity to assert claims. To respect a person then, or to think of him as possessed of human dignity, simply *is* to think of him as a potential maker of claims. Not all of this can be packed into a definition of "rights"; but these are *facts* about the possession of rights that argue well their supreme moral importance. More than anything else I am going to say, these facts explain what is wrong with Nowheresville.

We come now to the third interesting employment of the claiming vocabulary, that involving not the verb "to claim" but the substantive "a claim." What is it to *have a claim* and how is this related to rights? I would like to suggest that *having a claim consists in being in a position to claim, that is, to make claim to or claim that.* If this suggestion is correct it shows the primacy of the verbal over the nominative forms It links claims to a kind of activity and obviates the temptation to think of claims as *things,* on the model of coins, pencils, and other material possessions which we can carry in our hip pockets. To be sure, we often make or establish our claims by presenting titles, and these typically have the form of receipts, tickets, certificates, and other pieces of paper or parchment. The title, however, is not the same thing as the claim; rather it is the evidence that establishes the claim as valid. On this analysis, one might have a claim without ever claiming that to which one is entitled, or without even knowing that one has the claim; for one might simply be ignorant of the fact that one is in a position to claim; or one might be unwilling to exploit that position for one reason or another, including fear that the legal machinery is broken down or corrupt and will not enforce one's claim despite its validity.

Nearly all writers maintain that there is some intimate connection between having a claim and having a right. Some identify right and claim without qualification; some define "right" as justified or justifiable claim, others as recognized claim, still others as valid claim. My own preference is for the latter definition. Some writers, however, reject the identification of rights with valid claims on the ground that all claims as such are valid, so that the expression "valid claim" is redundant. These writers, therefore, would identify rights with claims *simpliciter.* But this is a very simple confusion. All claims, to be sure, are *put forward* as justified, whether they are justified in fact or not. A claim conceded even by its maker to have no validity is not a claim at all, but a mere demand. The highwayman, for example, *demands* his victim's money; but he hardly makes claim to it as rightfully his own.

But it does not follow from this sound point that it is redundant to qualify claims as justified (or as I prefer, valid) in the definition of a right; for it remains true that not all claims put forward as valid really are valid; and only the valid ones can be acknowledged as rights.

If having a valid claim is not redundant, i.e. if it is not redundant to pronounce *another's* claim valid, there must be such a thing as having a claim that is not valid. What would this be like? One might accumulate just enough evidence to argue with relevance and cogency that one has a right (or ought to be granted a right), although one's case might not be overwhelmingly conclusive. In such a case, one might have strong enough argument to be entitled to a hearing and given fair consideration. When one is in this position, it might be said that one "has a claim" that deserves to be weighed carefully. Nevertheless, the balance of reasons may turn out to militate against recognition of the claim, so that the claim, which one admittedly had, and perhaps still does, is not a valid claim or right. "Having a claim" in this sense is an expression very much like the legal phrase "having a *prima facie* case." A plaintiff establishes a *prima facie* case for the defendant's liability when he establishes grounds that will be sufficient for liability unless outweighed by reasons of a different sort that may be offered by the defendant. Similarly, in the criminal law, a grand jury returns an indictment when it thinks that the prosecution has sufficient evidence to be taken seriously and given a fair hearing, whatever countervailing reasons may eventually be offered on the other side. That initial evidence, serious but not conclusive, is also sometimes called a *prima facie* case. In a parallel "*prima facie* sense" of "claim," having a claim to X is not (yet) the same as having a right to X, but is rather having a case of at least minimal plausibility that one has a right to X, a case that does establish a right, not to X, but to a fair hearing and consideration. Claims, so conceived, differ in degree: some are stronger than others. Rights, on the other hand, do not differ in degree; no one right is more of a right than another.[7]

Another reason for not identifying rights with claims *simply* is that there is a well-established usage in international law that makes a theoretically interesting distinction between claims and rights. Statesmen are sometimes led to speak of "claims" when they are concerned with the natural needs of deprived human beings in conditions of scarcity. Young orphans *need* good upbringings, balanced diets, education, and technical training everywhere in the world; but unfortunately there are many places where these goods are in such short supply that it is impossible to provision all who need them. If we persist, nevertheless, in speaking of these needs as constituting rights and not merely claims, we are committed to the conception of a right which is an entitlement *to* some good, but not a valid claim *against* any particular individual; for in conditions of scarcity there may be no determinate individuals who can plausibly be said to have a duty to provide the missing goods to those in need. J. E. S. Fawcett therefore prefers to keep the distinction between claims and rights firmly in mind. "Claims," he writes, "are needs and demands in movement, and there is a continuous transformation, as a society advances [towards greater abundance] of economic and social claims into civil and political rights . . . and not all countries or all claims are by any means at the same stage in the process."[8] The manifesto writers on the other side who seem to identify needs, or at least basic needs, with what they call "human rights," are more properly described, I think, as urging upon the world community the moral principle that *all* basic human needs ought to be recognized as *claims* (in the customary *prima facie* sense) worthy of sympathy and serious consideration right now, even though, in many cases, they cannot yet plausibly be treated as *valid* claims, that is, as grounds of any other people's duties. This way of talking avoids the anomaly of ascribing to all human beings now, even those in pre-industrial societies, such "economic and social rights" as "periodic holidays with pay."[9]

Still for all of that, I have a certain sympathy with the manifesto writers, and I am even willing to speak of a special "manifesto sense" of "right," in which a right need not be correlated with another's duty. Natural needs are real claims if only upon hypothetical future beings not yet in existence. I accept the moral principle that to have an unfulfilled need is to have a kind of claim against the world, even if against no one in particular. A natural need for some good as such, like a natural desert, is always a reason in support of a claim to that good. A person in need, then, is always "in a position" to make a claim, even when there is no one in the corresponding position to do anything about it. Such claims, based on need alone, are "permanent possibilities of rights," the natural seed from which rights grow. When manifesto writers speak of them as if already actual rights, they are easily forgiven, for this is but a powerful way of expressing the conviction that they ought to be recognized by states here and now as potential rights and consequently as determinants of *present* aspirations and guides to *present* policies. That usage, I think, is a valid exercise of rhetorical licence.

I prefer to characterize rights as valid claims rather than justified ones, because I suspect that justification is rather too broad a qualification. "Validity," as I understand it, is justification of a peculiar and a narrow kind, namely justification within a system of rules. A man has a legal right when the official recognition of his claim (as valid) is called for by the governing rules. This definition, of course, hardly applies to moral rights, but that is not because the genus of which moral rights are a species is something other than *claims.* A man has a moral right when he has a claim the recognition of which is called for — not (necessarily) by legal rules — but by moral principles, or the principles of an enlightened conscience.

There is one final kind of attack on the generic identification of rights with claims, and it has been launched with great spirit in a recent article by H. J. McCloskey, who holds that rights are not essentially claims at all, but rather entitlements. The springboard of his argument is his insistence that rights in their essential character are always *rights to,* not *rights against:*

My right to life is not a right against anyone. It is my right and by virtue of it, it is normally permissible for me to sustain my life in the face of obstacles. It does give rise to rights against others *in the sense* that others have or may come to have duties to refrain from killing me, but it is essentially a right of mine, not an infinite list of claims, hypothetical and actual, against an infinite number of actual, potential, and as yet nonexistent human beings . . . Similarly, the right of the tennis club member to play on the club courts is a right to play, not a right against some vague group of potential or possible obstructors.[10]

The argument seems to be that since rights are essentially rights *to,* whereas claims are essentially claims *against,* rights cannot be claims, though they can be grounds for claims. The argument is doubly defective though. First of all, contrary to McCloskey, rights (at least legal claim-rights) *are* held *against* others. McCloskey admits this in the case of *in personam* rights (what he calls "special rights") but denies it in the case of *in rem* rights (which he calls "general rights"):

Special rights are sometimes against specific individuals or institutions — e.g. rights created by promises, contracts, etc . . . but these differ from . . . characteristic . . . general rights where the right is simply a right to—.[11]

As far as I can tell, the only reason McCloskey gives for denying that *in rem* rights are against others is that those against whom they would have to hold make up an enormously multitudinous and "vague" group, including hypothetical people not yet even in existence. Many others have found this a paradoxical consequence of the notion of *in rem* rights, but I see nothing troublesome in it. If a general rule gives me a right of noninterference in a certain respect against everybody, then there are literally hundreds of millions of people who have a duty toward me in that respect; and if the same general rule gives the same right to everyone else, then it imposes on me literally hundreds of millions of duties — or duties towards hundreds of millions of people. I see nothing paradoxical about this, however. The duties, after all, are negative; and I can discharge all of them at a stroke simply by minding my own business. And if all human beings make up one moral community and there are hundreds of millions of human beings, we should expect there to be hundreds of millions of moral relations holding between them.

McCloskey's other premise is even more obviously defective. There is no good reason to think that all *claims* are "essentially" *against*, rather than *to*. Indeed most of the discussion of claims above has been of claims *to*, and we have seen, the law finds it useful to recognize claims *to* (or "mere claims") that are not yet qualified to be claims *against*, or rights (except in a "manifesto sense" of "rights").

Whether we are speaking of claims or rights, however, we must notice that they seem to have two dimensions, as indicated by the prepositions "to" and "against," and it is quite natural to wonder whether either of these dimensions is somehow more fundamental or essential than the other. All rights seem to merge *entitlements to* do, have, omit, or be something with *claims against* others to act or refrain from acting in certain ways. In some statements of rights the entitlement is perfectly determinate (e.g. *to* play tennis) and the claim vague (e.g. *against* "some vague group or potential or possible obstructors"); but in other cases the object of the claim is clear and determinate (e.g. *against* one's parents), and the entitlement general and indeterminate (e.g. to be given a proper upbringing.) If we mean by "entitlement" that *to* which one has a right and by "claim" something directed at those against whom the right holds (as McCloskey apparently does), then we can say that all claim-rights necessarily involve both, though in individual cases the one element or the other may be in sharper focus.

In brief conclusion: To have a right is to have a claim against someone whose recognition as valid is called for by some set of governing rules or moral principles. To have a *claim* in turn, is to have a case meriting consideration, that is, to have reasons or grounds that put one in a position to engage in performative and propositional claiming. The activity of claiming, finally, as much as any other thing, makes for self-respect and respect for others, gives a sense to the notion of personal dignity, and distinguishes this otherwise morally flawed world from the even worse world of Nowheresville.

Postscript (1977)

I would like to take this opportunity to supplement this brief account of the role of rights in human life and to correct some of its emphases. First, it appears in several places as though *having* rights is what is necessary for self-respect, dignity, and other things of value. Actually, it is not enough to have the rights; one must know that one has the rights. In fact, the poor benighted citizens of Nowheresville do have various rights, whether they know it or not. They could not possibly know—or understand—that they have rights, however, because they do not even have the *concept* of a personal right. Such a notion has never even been dreamed of in Nowheresville. The inhabitants are consequently deficient in respect for self and others, even though, as hypothetical human beings, they have dignity in the eye of our imaginations.

Second, even knowing that one has rights and being prepared to act accordingly are not sufficient (but only necessary) for a fully human and morally satisfactory life. A person who never presses his claims or stands on his rights is servile, but the person who never waives a right, never releases others from their correlative obligations, or never does another a favor when he has a right to refuse to do so is a bloodless moral automaton. If such a person fully understands and appreciates what rights are and invokes that understanding in justification of his rigid conduct, he is a self-righteous prig as well. If he can also truly testify that he always conscientiously performs *his* duties to others and respects *their* rights, he has then achieved "the righteousness of the scribes and pharisees."

The point to emphasize here is that (with some rare exceptions mentioned below) right-holders are not always obliged to exercise their rights. To have a right typically is to have the discretion or "liberty" to exercise it or not as one chooses. This freedom is another feature of right-ownership that helps to explain why rights are so valuable. When a person has a discretionary right and fully understands the power that possession gives him, he can if he chooses make sacrifices for the sake of others, voluntarily give up what is rightfully his own, freely make gifts that he is in no way obligated to make, and forgive others for their wrongs to him by declining to demand the compensation or vengeance he may have coming or by warmly welcoming them back into his friendship or love. Imagine what life would be like without these saving graces. Consider Nowheresville II where almost everyone performs his duties to others faithfully and always insists upon his own rights against others; where debtors are never forgiven their debts, wrongdoers pardoned, gratuitous gifts conferred, or sacrifices voluntarily made, so long as it is within one's rights to refuse to do any of these things. The citizens of Nowheresville II have forgotten, if they ever knew, how to exercise rightful discretion. They have but half the concept of a right; they know how to claim but not how to release, waive, or surrender.

The point I wish to emphasize is not that the saving graces show that there is a limit to the moral importance of rights, but rather that rights are even more important—and important in other ways—than my original article suggests. Knowing that one has rights makes not only claiming (and self-respect) but also releasing (and magnanimity) possible. Without the duties that others have toward one (correlated with one's rights against them) there could be no sense in the notion of one's supererogatory conduct toward other people, for to help others when one has a right to decline is precisely what conduct "above and beyond duty" amounts to. Understanding that one has rights, of course, is not *sufficient* for one to have an admirable character, for one might yet be a mean-spirited pharisee, unwilling ever to be generous, forgiving, or sacrificing. But consciousness of one's rights is *necessary* for the supererogatory virtues, for the latter cannot even be given a sense except by contrast with the disposition always to claim one's rights. Waivers and gratuities can exist only against a background of understood rules assigning rights and duties. Forgiving debts obviously would not be possible without the prior practice of loaning and repaying with its rule-structured complexes of rights and correlative duties. Even in Nowheresville I, I suppose, one person can give a useful thing to another, but he cannot make a *gift* or *gratuity,*

since giving more than the recipient can rightly claim (a gift) presupposes that others *can* make rightful claims in some circumstances and that there is such a concept and such a practice.

One final point. Some familiar political rights appear to be exceptions to the assertion above that rights confer liberty or discretion upon their possessors who may always choose, if they wish, not to exercise them. The "right to education," for example, seems to be a kind of "mandatory right" in that children who possess it have no choice whether to go to school or not. Similarly, the legal right of schoolchildren to be vaccinated against certain contagious diseases is entirely coincident (except for the exemption on religious grounds) with their legal *duty* to be vaccinated. I suggest that when we use the language of rights in this way to refer to duties, we do so because we think that some of our duties are so beneficial that we can make *claim* against others to provide the opportunity for, and to abstain from interference with, our performance of them.

Textbooks frequently say that to have a claim-right to do X is (1) to be at liberty with respect to X and (2) for others to have a duty to one to provide or (as the case may be) not to interfere with X. When a claim-right is analyzed in this fashion, its component liberty is then said to be simply the absence of a duty *not* to X. But this characterization of a liberty, I submit, is misleading. To be at liberty to do X in ordinary speech is to have *discretion* in respect to $X,$ to be free *both* of a duty not to do X *and* of a duty to do $X.$ To be free of a duty not to do X is to have only a "half-liberty" with respect to X if one should at the same time have a duty *to do X.* Thus schoolchildren have "no duty" to stay away from school (a half-liberty with respect to school attendance), though they do have a duty to go to school. They are, therefore, deprived of the other "half-liberty" that would add up to full liberty, or the discretion to decide whether to attend school or not. Most rights to do X are full liberties to do X or not to do X as one chooses, conjoined with duties of other people not to interfere with one's choice. But so-called "mandatory rights" to do X confer only the half-liberty to do X without the other half-liberty not to do $X.$ Why then are they called "rights" at all?

The answer is that the rights in question are best understood as ordinary duties with associated half-liberties rather than ordinary claim-rights with associated full liberties, but that the performance of the duty is presumed to be so beneficial to the person whose duty it is that he can *claim* the necessary means from the state and noninterference from others as *his* due. Its character as claim is precisely what his half-liberty shares with the more usual (discretionary) rights and what warrants his use of the word "right" in demanding it.

NOTES

1. H. B. Acton, Symposium on "Rights," *Proceedings of the Aristotelian Society,* Supplementary Volume 24 (1950), pp. 107–08.
2. J. L. Austin, "A Plea for Excuses," *Proceedings of the Aristotelian Society,* Vol. 57 (1956–57).
3. For a fuller discussion of the concept of personal desert see my essay "Justice and Personal Desert" in J. Feinberg, *Doing and Deserving* (Princeton, N. J.: Princeton University Press, 1970), pp. 55–94.
4. II Sam. 11. Cited with approval by Thomas Hobbes in *The Leviathan,* Part II, Chap. 21.
5. H. B. Acton, *op. cit.*
6. G. J. Warnock, "Claims to Knowledge," *Proceedings*

of the Aristotelian Society, Supplementary Volume 36 (1962), p. 21.
7. This is the important difference between rights and mere claims. It is analogous to the difference between *evidence* of guilt (subject to degrees of cogency) and *conviction* of guilt (which is all or nothing). One can "have evidence" that is not conclusive just as one can "have a claim" that is not valid. "Prima-facieness" is built into the sense of "claim," but the notion of a "prima-facie right" makes less sense. On the latter point see A. I. Melden, *Rights and Right Conduct* (Oxford: Basil Blackwell, 1959), pp. 18–20, and Herbert Morris, "Persons and Punishment," *The Monist,* vol. 52 (1968), pp. 498–99.
8. J. E. S. Fawcett, "The International Protection of Human Rights," in *Political Theory and the Rights of Man,* ed. by D. D. Raphael (Bloomington: Indiana University Press, 1967), pp. 125 and 128.
9. As declared in Article 24 of *The Universal Declaration of Human Rights* adopted on December 10, 1948, by the General Assembly of the United Nations.
10. H. J. McCloskey, "Rights," *Philosophical Quarterly,* Vol. 15 (1965), p. 118.
11. *Loc. cit.*

Suggestions for Further Reading

American Law Institute, *Model Penal Code,* Part II, Proposed Official Draft and Comments (1962).

American Motorcycle Association v. Davids, 158 N.W. 2d 72 (Mich., 1968).

Amsterdam, Anthony, "Federal Constitutional Restrictions on the Punishment of Crimes of Status, Crimes of General Obnoxiousness, Crimes of Displeasing Police Officers and the Like," 3 *Crim. L. Bull.* 205 (1967).

Bayles, Michael D.., *Principles of Legislation: The Uses of Political Authority* (1978).

Bayles, Michael, "Comments: Offensive Conduct and the Law," in *Issues in Law and Morality,* eds. N. Care and T. Trelogan (1973), pp. 111–26.

Benn, S. I. and R. S. Peters, *Social Principles and the Democratic State* (1959).

Berlin, Isaiah, *Four Essays on Liberty* (1969).

Brecher, Edward M., *Licit and Illicit Drugs* (1972).

Chafee, Zechariah, Jr., *Free Speech in the United States* (1941).

Chafee, Zechariah, Jr., *Three Human Rights in the Constitution* (1956).

Clor, Harry M., *Obscenity and Public Morality* (1969).

Commission on Obscenity and Pornography, *Report* (1970).

Cook, W. W., "Hohfeld's Contributions to the Science of Law," editor's introduction to *Hohfeld's Fundamental Legal Conceptions* (1919).

Corbin, Arthur L., "Legal Analysis and Terminology," 29 *Yale L.J.* (1919).

Corbin, Arthur L., "Rights and Duties," 33 *Yale L.J.* 501 (1923).

Devlin, Patrick, "Encounter with Lord Devlin," *Listener,* Vol. 71 (1964), pp. 980 ff.

Devlin, Patrick, *The Enforcement of Morals* (1965).

Dorsen, Norman, ed., *The Rights of Americans,* Sections II and III (1970).

Dworkin, Ronald, "Lord Devlin and the Enforcement of Morals," 75 *Yale L.J.* 986 (1966).

Dworkin, Ronald M., *Taking Rights Seriously* (1977).

Emerson, Thomas I., *The System of Freedom of Expression* (1970).

Fahr, Samuel, "Sexual Psychopath Laws," 41 *Iowa Law R.* (1956).

Feinberg, Joel, "Duties, Rights, and Claims," *American Philosophical Quarterly,* Vol. 3 (1966).

Feinberg, Joel, "Legal Paternalism," *Canadian Journal of Philosophy,* Vol. 1 (1971), pp. 105–24.

Feinberg, Joel, " 'Harmless Immoralities' and Offensive Nuisances" in *Issues in Law and Morality,* eds. N. Care and T. Trelogan (1973), pp. 85–109.

Feinberg, Joel, *Social Philosophy* (1973) Chaps. 2–6.

Feinberg, Joel, "The Rights of Animals and Future Generations," in *Philosophy and Environmental Crisis,* ed. by William T. Blackstone (1974).

Feinberg, Joel, "Euthanasia and the Inalienable Right to Life," *Philosophy and Public Affairs,* Vol. 7 (1978).

Feinberg, Joel, " The Idea of the Obscene," Lindley Lecture, University of Kansas Press, 1979.

Flathman, Richard E., *The Practice of Rights* (1956).

Frantz, Laurent B., "The First Amendment in the Balance," 71 *Yale L.J.* 1424 (1962).

Fried, Charles, "Privacy," 77 *Yale L.J.* 475 (1968).

Friedman, Milton, *Capitalism and Freedom* (1962).

Friedrich, C. J., ed., *Nomos IV: Liberty* (1962).

Fuchs, Alan E., "Further Steps Toward a General Theory of Freedom of Expression," 18 *William and Mary Law Review* (1976).

Gert, Bernard and Culver, Charles M., "Paternalistic Behavior," *Philosophy and Public Affairs,* Vol. 6 (1976).

Ginsberg, Morris, "Law and Morals," *The British Journal of Criminology* (1964).

Gross, Hyman, "The Concept of Privacy," 42 *N.Y.U. L. Rev.* 34 (1967).

Gussfield, J., "On Legislating Morals: The Symbolic Process of Designating Deviancy," 56 *Cal. L. Rev.* 54–59 (1968).

Harnett, B. and J. Thornton, "The Truth Hurts: A Critique of a Defense to Defamation," 35 *Va. L. Rev.* 425 (1949).

Hart, Harold H., ed., *Censorship, For and Against* (1971).

Hart, H. L. A., "Immorality and Treason," *Listener,* Vol. 62 (1959), pp. 162 ff.

Hart, H. L. A., *Law, Liberty, and Morality* (1963).

Hart, H. L. A., "Social Solidarity and the Enforcement of Morality," 35 *U. Chi. L. Rev.* 1 (1967).

Hayek, Friedrich von, *The Constitution of Liberty* (1960).

Henkin, L., "Morals and the Constitution: The Sin of Obscenity," 63 *Col. L. Rev.* 391 (1963).

Hobhouse, L. T., *The Elements of Social Justice* (1922), Chap. 4.

Home Office Scottish Home Department, *Report of the Committee on Homosexual Offenses and Prostitution (Wolfenden Report)* (1963).

Hook, Sydney, ed., *Law and Philosophy,* Part I (1964).

Hospers, John, *Libertarianism* (1971).

Hughes, Graham, "Morals and the Criminal Law," 71 *Yale L.J.* 662 (1962).

Hughes, Graham, *The Conscience of the Courts: Law and Morals in American Life* (1975), Chaps. 1, 2.

In Re Lynch, 503 P. 2d 921 (1972).

Kadish, S. H., "The Crisis of Overcriminalization," 374 *Annals* 157 (1957).

Kalven, Harry, Jr., "The Metaphysics of the Law of Obscenity," in *The Supreme Court Review,* ed. P. B. Kurland, (1960).

Kamenka, E. and A. Erh-Soon Tay (eds.), *Human Rights* (1978).

Kronhausen, E. and P., *Pornography and the Law,* rev. ed., (1964).

Livermore, J. M., C. P. Malmquist, and P. E. Meehl, "On the Justification for Civil Commitment," 117 *U. Pa. L. Rev.,* 75 (1968).

Louch, A. R., "Sins and Crimes," *Philosophy,* Vol. 43 (1968), pp. 163 ff.

Lyons, David, "Rights, Claimants, and Beneficiaries," *American Philosophical Quarterly,* Vol. 6 (1969).

Lyons, David, "The Correlativity of Rights and Duties," *Nous,* Vol. 4 (1970).

Lyons, David, ed. *Rights* (1978). An excellent anthology with a useful bibliography.

McCloskey, H. J., "Mills Liberalism," *Philosophical Quarterly,* Vol. XIII (1963).

McCloskey, H. J., "Rights," *Philosophical Quarterly,* Vol. 15 (1965).

McCloskey, H. J., "Liberalism," *Philosophy,* Vol. 49 (1974).

McCloskey, H. J., "The Right to Life," *Mind,* Vol. 86 (1975).

Meerlo, J., *Suicide and Mass Suicide* (1962).

Melden, A. I., *Persons and Rights* (1978).

Mewett, A., "Morality and the Criminal Law," 14 *University of Toronto L.J.* 213 (1962).

Miller, Arthur R., *The Assault on Privacy* (1971).

Morris, Norval and Gordon Hawkins, *The Honest Politician's Guide to Crime Control,* (1969), Chapters 1 and 2.

Morrow, Frank A., "Speech, Expression, and the Constitution," *Ethics,* Vol. 85 (1975).

Murphy, Jeffrie G., "Incompetence and Paternalism," *Archives for Philosophy of Law and Social Philosophy,* Vol. 40 (1974).

Murphy, Jeffrie G., "Rights and Borderline Cases," 19 *Arizona L.R.* (1978).

Note, "Civil Commitment of Narcotic Addicts," 76 *Yale L.J.* 1160 (1967).

Nozick, Robert, *Anarchy, State, and Utopia* (1974).

Packer, Herbert, *The Limits of the Criminal Sanction* (1968).

Pennock, J. R. and J. W. Chapman, eds., *Nomos XIII: Privacy* (1971).

Pennock, J. R. and J. W. Chapman, eds., *Nomos XV: Limits of Law* (1974).

Perry, Thomas D., "A Paradigm of Philosophy: Hohfeldian Legal Rights," *American Philosophical Quarterly*, Vol. 14 (1977).

Rachels, James, "Why Privacy is Important," *Philosophy and Public Affairs*, Vol. 4 (1975).

Radin, M., "A Restatement of Hohfeld," 51 *Harvard L.R.* (1938).

Raz, Joseph, "Legal Principles and the Limits of Law," 81 *Yale L.J.* (1972).

Reisman, David, "Democracy and Defamation: Control of Group Libel," 42 *Col. L. Rev.* 751 (1942).

Richards, B. A., "Inalienable Rights: Recent Criticisms and Old Doctrine," *Philosophy and Phenomenological Research*, Vol. 29 (1969).

Roe v. Wade, 410 U.S. 113 (1973).

Rostow, Eugene, *The Sovereign Prerogative* (1962), Chap. 2.

Ryan, Alan, *The Philosophy of John Stuart Mill* (1970), Chap. XIII.

Sartorius, Rolf, "The Enforcement of Morality," 81 *Yale L.J.* 891 (1972).

Scanlon, Timothy, "A Theory of Freedom of Expression," *Philosophy and Public Affairs*, Vol. I (1972), pp. 204–26.

Scanlon, T. G., "Thomson on Privacy," *Philosophy and Public Affairs*, Vol. 4 (1975).

Schauer, Frederick, F., *The Law of Obscenity* (1976).

Simpson, A. W. B., 'The Analysis of Legal Concepts," 80 *Law Quarterly Review* 535 (1964).

Skolnick, Jerome, "Coercion to Virtue," 41 *S. Cal. L. Rev.* 588 (1968).

Specht v. Patterson, 386 U.S. 605 (1967).

State v. Lee, 51 Haw 516, 465 P. 2d 573 (1970). Motorcycle Paternalism case.

Stephen, James F., *Liberty, Equality, Fraternity* (1873).

Stone, Christopher, *Should Trees Have Standing? Toward Legal Rights for Natural Objects* (1974).

Symposium: Principles of Expression and Restriction, 40 *University of Pittsburgh Law Review* (1979). Papers by T. G. Scanlon, J. Feinberg, and G. Anistopolo, and critical commentaries.

Thomson, Judith J., "The Right to Privacy," *Philosophy and Public Affairs*, Vol. 4 (1975).

Thomson, Judith J., "Self-Defense and Rights," The Lindley Lecture, University of Kansas Press, 1977.

U.S. Department of Transportation, *Traffic Laws Commentary*, Vol. 1, No. 6 (1972): "Laws Requiring Seat Belts."

Vandeveer, Donald, "Coercive Restraint of Offensive Actions," *Philosophy and Public Affairs*, Vol. 8 (1979).

Wasserstrom, Richard A., (ed.), *Morality and the Law* (1971).

Westin, Alan F., *Privacy and Freedom* (1967).

Williams, G., *The Sanctity of Life and the Criminal Law*, (1957) Chapters 7 and 8.

Williams, G., "Authoritarian Morals and the Criminal Law," [1966] *Crim. L. Rev.* 132.

Williams, G., "The Concept of Legal Liberty" in *Essays in Legal Philosophy*, ed. by R. S. Summers (1968).

Wolff, Robert Paul, *The Poverty of Liberalism* (1968).

Wollheim, Richard, "Crime, Sin and Mr. Justice Devlin," *Encounter* (1959), pp. 34 ff.

PART 3 JUSTICE

One of the very oldest conceptions of justice, which must be close to the original seed of the modern concept, derives from pre-Socratic Greek cosmology and its picture of a morally ordered universe in which everything has its assigned place, or natural role. Justice (*dike*) consisted of everything staying in that assigned place, and not usurping the place of another, which would throw the whole system out of kilter. Elements of this early notion survive in Plato's theory of justice as a virtue both of people and of states. Social justice, according to Plato, exists when every person performs the function for which he or she is best fitted by nature (his or her own proper business) and does not infringe upon the natural role of another. A corollary of this principle is that the rulers of the state should be those best fitted by their natures to rule; hence democracy, or rule by everybody, is inherently unjust.

The reason why people live in political communities in the first place, Plato argues in *The Republic,* is that no mere individual is self-sufficient. For all of us to satisfy our needs, we must divide up our labors, with each person performing the task for which he or she is best fitted by their natural aptitudes. Instead of every person being his or her own carpenter, toolmaker, farmer, tailor, soldier, and policeman, each can work at the one thing he or she does best, while enjoying the benefits of the full-time labors of other specialists. The principle of cooperation by means of the specialization of labor explains what social organization is *for*, and why it should exist. There is justice in a society when everyone does their proper work: when square pegs are in square holes; when no talent is wasted or misused; when those who are naturally fit to rule do rule, and those who are naturally fit to obey, do obey. The sole criterion, then, for justice in assigning positions in society is *fitness for a function.* This in turn is best promoted, according to Plato, by fair educational and testing procedures that give each child, regardless of his race, or sex, or the social rank of his parents, an equal opportunity to rise to his appropriate slot in the social hierarchy.

EQUAL TREATMENT

Aristotle, in the famous discussion of the virtue of justice which leads off this section, shares Plato's view that only the best should rule and also Plato's disdain for perfect equality in the distribution of political burdens and benefits. His analysis of justice, however, is more subtle and more faithful to complexities in the concept's multifaceted employment. He acknowledges at the start that the word for justice is ambiguous, referring both to the whole of social virtue ("virtue in relation to our neighbor") and to one specific type of social virtue. The wider or generic concept Aristotle calls "universal justice"; the narrower he calls "particular justice." Unlike Plato in the *Republic,* Aristotle's chief concern is with the particular virtue that is only a part, not the whole, of social virtue. He does say of universal justice, however, that it coincides with conformity to *law.* What he apparently means by this is that the positive law of the state *should* aim at the enforcement of the social virtues (including not only "particular justice" but also benevolence, charity, fidelity, and so on), and that insofar as a given legal code does support social virtue, violation of "universal justice" will at the same time be violation of positive law.

Particular justice, as Aristotle understands it, is the same as *fairness.* The Greek word for fairness in Aristotle's time also meant *equality.* Thus, Aristotle's initial contention is that there are two concepts of justice: lawfulness and equality. Particular justice (fairness), he tells us, is of two kinds: *distributive* and *rectificatory justice.* His conviction that most fair distributions are unequal, held at a time when "just" meant or strongly suggested "equal," drove him (as Gregory Vlastos has put it) to "linguistic acrobatics."[1] Distributive justice, he argued ingeniously, does not consist in absolute equality (that is, perfectly equal shares for all those among whom something is to be distributed) but rather a proportionate equality, which is to say an equality of ratios. What justice requires, he insists, is that equal cases be treated alike (equally), and that unequal cases be treated unalike (unequally) in direct proportion to the differences (inequalities) between them, so that between any two persons the ratio between their shares $(S_1:S_2)$ should equal the ratio between their qualifying characteristics $(C_1:C_2)$.

Aristotle concedes that people disagree over which characteristics of persons should be taken into account in assessing their equality or the degree of their inequality, but all parties to these disagreements (except extreme democrats who insist upon absolute equality) employ tacitly the notion of proportionate equality. However "merit" is conceived, for example, those for whom it would be the sole criterion in awarding shares would give one person twice as large a share of some benefit as they would to any other person deemed only half as meritorious. The common object of these distributors, even when they disagree over what merit is, will be to divide shares into a ratio (2 : 1) equal to the ratio of the merits of the two persons (2 : 1). Such distributions are sometimes necessarily impressionistic (how can one person's merit be seen to be exactly one-half another's?), but when the criterion of merit is exactly definable, and the shares themselves can be measured in terms of money, the calculations can sometimes achieve a mathematical precision. Aristotle sometimes seems to have in mind, for example, "the distribution of profits between partners in proportion to what each has put into the business."[2] Such contributions ("merits" in an extended, but properly Aristotelian, sense) as capital, time and labor are readily measurable.

Since any two persons will be unequal in some respects and equal in others, Aristotle's theory of distributive justice is incomplete until he tells us which personal characteristics are *relevant* factors to be considered in the balancing of ratios. Various criteria of relevance have been proposed by writers of different schools. Some have held that *A*'s share should be to *B*'s share as *A*'s ability is to *B*'s ability, or as *A*'s moral virtue is to *B*'s, or as *A*'s labor is to *B*'s, and so on. All the above maxims could be said to specify different forms of "merit," so that a *meritarian* theorist would be one who held that the only personal characteristics relevant to a just distribution of goods are such forms of personal "merit." Aristotle was undoubtedly a meritarian in this broad sense. Meritarian social philosophers then can disagree among themselves over which forms of merit are relevant and over criteria for assessing a given form of merit, or they might hold that some forms of merit are relevant to some types of distribution, and other merits to other types. A nonmeritarian theory would be one which found exclusive relevance in personal characteristics (for example, needs) that are in no sense "merits," and of course mixed theories too are possible. Even a "democratic" or "equalitarian" theory, one which is wholly nonmeritarian, might plausibly be said to employ tacitly Aristotle's *analysis* of distributive justice as proportionate equality, while rejecting of course Aristotle's suggested criteria of relevance. Even a perfect equalitarian presumably would wish to endorse such maxims as: *A*'s share should be to *B*'s share as *A*'s needs are to *B*'s needs, or as *A*'s "infinite human worth" is to *B*'s "infinite human worth" (that is, the same). It seems likely, therefore, that all complete theories of social justice must contain maxims specifying relevant characteristics, and that all of them presuppose Aristotle's formal analysis of distributive justice as proportionate equality between shares and relevant characteristics.

Distributive justice applies to statesmen distributing honors, rewards, public property (as, for example, land in a new Athenian or Macedonian colony), public assistance to the needy, or to divisions of corporate profits or inheritances. Aristotle does not discuss the distribution of burdens such as taxation and military service, but his principle of proportionate equality presumably applies to them too. The second kind of particular justice, *rectificatory justice,* applies to private transactions or business deals in which some unfair advantage or undeserved harm has occurred and one party sues for a "remedy." (Aristotle's phrase for rectificatory justice is sometimes translated as "remedial," as well as "corrective" or "compensatory" justice). A judge then must assess the damages and order one party to make a payment to the other. These cases, Aristotle says, are of two kinds. In one type the harm to the plaintiff results from a transaction in which he voluntarily participated: buying, selling, loaning, pledging, depositing, hiring out, and the like. The law governing these cases corresponds roughly to our law of contracts. In the other type of case, the harm to the plaintiff results from a "transaction" in which he involuntarily participates as a victim from the start: fraud, theft, adultery, assault, imprisonment, or homicide. The law governing these cases, when the aim is to correct an unfairness by compensating a victim for his loss or injury, corresponds roughly to our law of torts.

Rectificatory justice, too, essentially involves the notion of equality. Its aim, Aristotle says, is to redress the "inequality" that results when one person profits unfairly at the expense of another. If *A* steals one hundred dollars from *B*, for example, he becomes one hundred dollars better off, an amount that is exactly equal to the amount by which *B* becomes worse off. The "equality" between *A* and *B* was their starting position before the "transaction," and that equality is restored by an order that requires *A* to pay to *B* exactly one hundred dollars. It is well to notice that rectificatory justice, as Aristotle understands it, does not apply to the criminal law at all. If there is a justice in punishing *A* for his peculation beyond the penalty that merely restores the *status quo ante,* that must be justice of a different kind. Retributive justice, as such, does not receive a thorough discussion in Aristotle, and does not even receive a separate rubric in his classification of the types of justice.

Neither does Aristotle's analysis of rectificatory justice appear to be an adequate guide through the complexities of the law of torts. More than the restoration of equality by a simple arithmetical formula, at any rate, is involved in all but the simplest cases in deliberations aiming at the determination of compensatory damages. Suppose *A*'s wrongful act made him $500 better off and *B* (the plaintiff) $200 worse off? What if *A*'s malevolence or spitefulness toward *B* is so great that he is willing to undergo a loss for himself in order to inflict one on *B*? Suppose, in that example, that *A*'s malicious act costs himself $500 and inflicts only a $100 loss on *B*. Or suppose, what is admittedly somewhat fanciful, that *A*'s wrongful act actually creates a $100 windfall for wholly innocent *B* while earning himself $1,000. It will tax the student reader's ingenuity (in itself a good thing) to apply Aristotle's simple formulas for "arithmetical progression" to these hypothetical cases.

Some parts of Aristotle's discussion are primarily of antiquarian interest. His sketchy account in chapter 5, for example, of "Justice in Exchange" is one of the earliest discussions on record of economic justice. Several other sections of his treatment of justice are important both for their intrinsic interest and their historical influence. Chapter 7 on "Natural and Legal Justice," for instance, is a classical source for the long and still vital tradition of natural law, and the theory of Equity in chapter 10 has had a direct effect on the development of legal institutions that is still felt. In addition to the distinctions between equity and law, there is still another important distinction that Aristotle was the first to treat with great subtlety: that between the just or unjust *quality* of an act and the just or unjust *effect* of an act on others. Injustice is always a violation of someone's rights or deserts, but such an effect can be brought about involuntarily, in which case the action that produced it cannot be unjust in itself, for normally to ascribe an unjust act to a person is to blame him or her, and involuntary acts are not blameworthy. Moreover, there are occasions, unhappily, in which a person can be fully justified in voluntarily producing an unjust effect on another; when that effect, for example, is the least evil result the actor could produce in the circumstances. *A* may be justified in violating *B*'s rights instead of *C*'s and *D*'s when there is no third alternative open to him, but that justification does not cancel the injustice done to *B*. In that case, we can say that *B* was unjustly *treated* although *A*'s act resulting in that effect was not an instance of unjust *behavior.* For an act to have an unjust quality (whatever its effects) it must be, objectively speaking, the wrong thing to do in the circumstances, unexcused and unjustified, voluntarily undertaken, and deliberately chosen by an unrushed actor who is well aware of the alternatives open to him. Other parties can be injured by unforeseeable accidents (mere mishaps), foreseeable accidents (blunders), by voluntary acts done in a fit of anger (*akrasia*), or by deliberate choice. Only in the last case is there unjust behavior, although there is blameworthiness of other kinds (negligence and hot-tempered impetuousness) in blunders and in angry violence, too.

JUSTICE AND SOCIAL UTILITY

Some of the most important contributions to the theory of justice, especially in Great Britain, have been made by writers in the utilitarian moral tradition. In the eighteenth century, David Hume argued that all rules of justice (thinking primarily of rules pertaining to contracts and property) "owe their origin and existence to that utility which results to the public from their strict and regular observance."[3] Hume admitted that there may sometimes be negative social utility in a particular observance of a rule of justice. For example, restoring a fortune to a miser or a seditious bigot is just, but socially harmful. "But however single acts of justice may be contrary either to public or private interest, 'tis certain that the *whole plan or scheme* is highly conducive, or indeed absolutely requisite to the support of society and the wellbeing of every individual."[4] Hume, in short, is a rule-utilitarian, not an act-utilitarian.

There is some doubt whether John Stuart Mill, the next essayist presented, would make conductibility to the common good the standard of right conduct applying directly to *single acts,* or make it the standard of *good rules* applying to the products of the legislature's work or to the determination of the sound rules of natural morality. The balance of reasons, however, as J. O. Urmson has shown convincingly, [5] favors the interpretation of Mill as a rule-utilitarian whose view is a further elaboration of Hume's. Mill's theory is interesting primarily for the way it accounts for the "distinguishing character of justice" and the way he *argues* that justice is derived from utility rather than being an underivative independent principle in its own right.

What distinguishes injustice from other types of wrongdoing, according to Mill, is that injustice must always be injustice *to* someone or other, the violation of the rights or deserts of some "assignable" person who is thereby entitled to feel aggrieved and righteously indignant on his own behalf. Duties of justice, therefore, are only one subclass of moral duties generally. If I fail to discharge my moral obligation to be generous, or beneficent, I do wrong, but there is no determinate person who can complain of being personally wronged by my omission, for "no one has a moral right to our generosity or beneficence." But it is clearly otherwise when I renege on a promise, a vow, or a loan; when as an authority, I treat my friends or relations more leniently or generously than others; when as a teacher, I give a low grade to an excellent student who deserves better; when as a legislator, I help create a statute that arbitrarily discriminates against a whole class of persons; or when as policeman or judge, I enforce the law irregularly or unequally among those to whom it explicitly applies. In all these cases, valid moral claims have been ignored or rejected, and the claimants have at least "a right to complain," and at most, a right to rectification, restitution, or even retribution.

That the standard of justice is independent of social utility is usually supported by an attempt to show that social utility as an ultimate moral principle would in some circumstances justify acts, rules, or practices that are patently unjust. Mill does very little to defend utilitarianism against this charge, which has been debated so thoroughly by twentieth century philosophers. Instead, he takes the offensive as a utilitarian, attacking what he calls "the alternative view of justice as independent of utility, a standard *per se,* which the mind can recognize by simple introspection of itself." The argument is simple enough. If there is an autonomous sense of justice limiting the dictates of utility and guiding us to the right moral decision where utility would lead us astray, how are we to understand "why the internal oracle is so ambiguous?" When people leave off calculating utilities to voice instead their sense of justice, there is nothing but controversy, with no rational resolution of differences possible. "In fact, justice is not some one rule, principle or maxim, but many, which do not always coincide in their dictates, and in choosing between which, one is guided either by some extraneous standard [such as social utility] or by his own personal predilections."

Mill then provides numerous persuasive examples of the conflict between plausible maxims of justice that apply to controversies over punishment, distribution of wealth, and taxation. In each instance justice seems to have "two sides to it." Mill turns from these controversies in bewilderment, concluding that each of the opposed maxims "from its own point of view is unanswerable, and any choice between them on grounds of justice must be perfectly arbitrary. Social utility alone can decide the preference."

Mill's argument is hardly decisive. A defender of "the alternative theory of justice" might well reply: The contention that justice is a principle independent of, and some-times in conflict with, utility does not imply that the dictates of justice are always perfectly clear and unambiguous, or that there is even one supreme principle of justice harmonizing all the conflicting maxims. That the method of determing justice is distinct from the method of calculating social utility does not imply that one is simple and the other difficult, or even that one has necessary priority over the other. It means simply what it says: that the one is distinct from, and irreducible to, the other.

Moreover, Mill's opponent might argue, the method of utility involves just as many complexities and difficulties as the methods of justice. One might even speak of distinct and rival "maxims" of utility. What promotes the greatest good may help the smallest number and what helps the largest number may promote the smallest net good. What creates the most happiness may entail the most blissful ignorance as by-product, and what promotes knowledge may increase despair; and yet both happiness and knowledge are presumably components of "utility." And which should the utilitarian choose when he or she must choose between irreconcilable goods of separate groups or separate individuals, or when a net gain in pleasure and knowledge is balanced against a net loss in virtue and equality, or when intense pleasure of short duration is the alternative to mild pleasure of long duration? This *tu quoque*, while also undecisive, has considerable punch.

Nicholas Rescher has mustered considerations of the above kind in a generalized argument against any utilitarian theory of distributive justice. The utilitarian principle, he concludes, is an inadequate guide to the moral appraisal of distributions of goods, because crucial "questions that arise in the application of [that] principle cannot be settled by the principle itself." Rescher's methodology is especially interesting. At every stage of the argument he has us consider highly abstract hypothetical examples of distributions of acknowledged goods among certain featureless recipients. The reader is then asked to make spontaneous judgments of the fairness or unfairness of the resultant patterns of distribution (on the simplifying assumption that the unknown recipients have equal claims to the goods). The utilitarian principle is then tested by whether or not it accords with those intuitive appraisals. If the scheme of distribution favored by utilitarianism turns out to be patently unacceptable by this test, then it follows (at least) that the reader is not a utilitarian, and the examples have served as a kind of argument to convince him or her that utilitarianism is to be rejected. More often it will be unclear which scheme is favored by utilitarianism because the utilitarian principle can be interpreted in several different and mutually inconsistent ways, and deciding on the proper interpretation will require appeal to such presumably nonutilitarian notions as "equity or fairness in accommodating claims."

JUSTICE AND FAIRNESS

Philosophers often distinguish between the fairness or unfairness of procedures and the justice or injustice of outcomes. Sometimes the labels "procedural" and "substantive" justice are used to mark the distinction, and the student should be wary of confusing these technical terms with the phrases "formal" and "material," which are used to mark the quite different distinction between the "formal" requirement that similar cases be treated similarly, and "material" interpretations of that requirement that provide for the relevance of differences. (To compound the terminological confusion, Brian Barry uses the term "equity," which as we have seen already has the Aristotelian sense of "modification of general rules to meet special situations,"[6] to refer to the basic "formal" requirement that rules should treat like cases alike).

The selection from Barry presupposes the discussion in an earlier part of his important book, *Political Argument,* in which he classifies the various contexts in which the notions of fair procedure and just outcome have application. These contexts all involve the employment of techniques for settling conflicts of wants or opinions. Barry calls these "social decision procedures," and lists the following seven types.

1. *Combat.* The issue is settled directly by force.
2. *Discussion on Merits.* The parties argue the rights and wrongs of the conflict and seek agreement by appealing to jointly accepted standards, ideals, or rules.
3. *Bargaining.* "One party offers another either some advantage or the removal of the threat of disadvantage in return for the other party's performing some specific action."[7] The rights and wrongs of the conflict, or the merits of the opposed positions, are not considered.
4. *Voting* (where more than two parties are involved).
5. *Chance* (for example, by flipping a coin or drawing straws).
6. *Contest* (for example, foot races, boxing matches) for settling the question of which contestant is "best at" some activity requiring skill.
7. *Authoritative Determination.* The issue is settled by the judgment of a party (or parties) whose authority to do so, under the governing rules, is recognized by the disputants; for example, an administrative tribunal, a judge or jury, a labor arbitrator.

A decision procedure (excepting combat, a special case) may itself be fair or unfair, and even a fair procedure may be applied fairly or unfairly in a given case. Taking each type of procedure in turn, Barry tells us what fair application consists in, and what further is required as "background fairness." In the case of authoritative determination, the application of a specified procedure can be appraised as fair or unfair in a distinctively legalistic way (Barry calls this "legal justice"), namely, by determining whether rules requiring certain decisions in cases of a specified kind have been adhered to.

Barry then asks why procedural fairness should be valued as an important thing. He advances both utilitarian and equalitarian considerations (he calls these "aggregative" and "distributive," respectively) for taking "legal justice" seriously. Similarly, in respect to procedural and background fairness, he finds their justifications in their conduciveness to "some more general consideration," namely, their tendency to produce just results. Thus Barry concludes that "the value of [procedural] fairness is subordinate to that of justice," and finds in the opposite view irrational "rule worship."

John Rawls also attaches importance to the distinction between justice (of results) and fairness (of procedures), but as his title, "Justice as Fairness" indicates, fairness is given a certain methodological priority. But that is not to say that Rawls is in serious disagreement with Barry. His essay (the germ of his monumental study, *A Theory of Justice*) is addressed to somewhat different questions. Rawls is almost exclusively concerned with the justice of political, social, and economic institutions, as opposed to the justice of individual actions, persons, or policies. "The primary subject of justice," he wrote in *A Theory of Justice,* "is the basic structure of society."[8] Those basic institutions are just, Rawls maintains, that accord with the principles of justice that would be adopted by reasonable and normally self-interested persons employing an ideally fair selection procedure. Rawls describes that procedure and derives from it two basic principles of justice. These principles, and the method of their derivation, constitute the major alternative to utilitarianism among recent general theories of justice.

Rawls places great weight upon a purported duty of fair play. It requires those who accept the benefits of a social practice to follow the rules when in turn the rules require something of them. In his highly regarded book *Anarchy, State and Utopia,* Robert Nozick challenges assumptions upon which Rawls' theory of justice rests, and among the most important of these challenges is his criticism of the asserted duty of fair play. In the first of the selections from his book presented here, Nozick first argues that not all obligations need be enforceable, and so even assuming that a principle of fairness creates an obligation to abide by rules that is binding on those who take the benefits that the rules make possible, that obligation may not be enforceable. This would mean that an obligation which was in principle a just obligation might be a source of injustice if enforced. Nozick then proceeds to question the principle of fairness itself, arguing that a person who accepted and enjoyed certain benefits might nevertheless not be obligated in turn to participate according to the rules.

DISCRIMINATION AND REVERSE DISCRIMINATION

Invidiously discriminatory treatment in the distribution of benefits (including opportunities) and burdens is the essential feature of what Aristotle called "distributive injustice." In the United States grossly discriminatory rules and practices have only recently begun to crumble, and for the first time in centuries there is hope that the ideal of equal opportunity will one day be fulfilled. To expect the effects of racial and sexual discrimination to vanish overnight with the abrogation of ancient rules, however, would be exceedingly naive. Many reformers, in fact, have been urging that the elimination of discriminatory practices is not enough, and that a kind of "reverse discrimination," especially in the allocation of educational and professional opportunities for such groups as blacks and women, is required by social justice. Louis Katzner, in his penetrating article, subjects this claim to close philosophical analysis, and concludes with a statement of four conditions which must be satisfied if reverse discrimination is to be justified. It is an interesting apparent consequence of Katzner's view that, while reverse discrimination in favor of blacks might in some circumstances be justified, reverse discrimination in favor of (all) women would likely not pass Katzner's test.

Arbitrary differences in the law's treatment of various defined classes of the population is firmly prohibited by the "equal protection" clause of the Fourteenth Amendment, and (indirectly) by the "due process" clause of the Fifth Amendment. More and more, women have been relying on these constitutional grounds to secure judicial overruling of statutes that discriminate against them. In *Reed v. Reed,* included in this section, the United States Supreme Court in a unanimous opinion written by Mr. Chief Justice Burger argues that while it is constitutionally permissible for legislation to distinguish among classes, this must be done in a "reasonable, not arbitrary" way, and "not on the basis of criteria wholly unrelated to the objective of the statute." The language becomes explicitly Aristotelian when the court declares all statutes to be unconstitutional which command "dissimilar treatment for men and women who are . . . similarly situated."

In *Frontiero v. Richardson,* a somewhat more complicated case, another statute which made gender the basis of differences in the assignment of legal rights and duties was overturned, this time on the ground that the Fifth Amendment forbids discrimination that is "so unjustifiable as to be violative of due process." The Court's opinion in *Frontiero* declares that sex is a "suspect classification," that is, one whose moral or constitutional relevance is "inherently suspect," and therefore properly "subjected to close judicial scrutiny." Sexual distinctions in the law, in other words, are *prima facie* unjust, and will be declared unconstitutional unless "close judicial scrutiny" uncovers some general causal connection between sex difference and other traits that clearly are relevant to some valid legislative purpose, (presumably) like the strengthening of national security or the protection of individual privacy. Careful notice should be given to four points about the principles applied in the *Reed* and *Frontiero* decisions.

1. Like the Aristotelian "formal principle" that relevantly like cases should be treated in like ways, the Equal Protection clause of the Fourteenth Amendment also needs supplementation by criteria of the relevance or nonarbitrariness of differences between classes of persons.

2. Sex *as such* is not a relevant or nonarbitrary difference. Thus, statutory classifications whose *whole basis* is "the sex of the individuals involved" are "inherently invidious," and proscribed by the Equal Protection clause.

3. The causal connection between sex difference and traits that *are* relevant must be *perfectly* general. It is not sufficient that *most* males have greater physical strength or greater business experience than *most* females. Only if these connections were exceptionless and necessary would a statute permit sex to be a ground, say, for job qualifications, for example combat duty in the armed forces or administration of a decedent's estate. Otherwise, as Mr. Justice Brennan put it in *Frontiero,* "statutory distinctions between the sexes [would] often have the effect of invidiously relegating the entire class of females to inferior legal status without regard to the actual capabilities of its individual members."

4. Valid legislative purposes to which discrimination between the sexes might be reasonably related do not include "mere administrative convenience," though administrative convenience in the conduct of a war, say, might be so related to national security as to justify sexual distinctions in the assignment of combat duty; and *another* constitutional protection, for example, that said to be provided by the Constitution to personal privacy, might justify sexual distinctions in the rules

permitting use of public rest rooms.

Despite the trend represented by the *Reed* and *Frontiero* decisions, most feminists are not content to rest the moral aim to equality on the Fourteenth Amendment, and have advocated instead an Equal Rights Amendment to the United States Constitution specifying that "Equality of rights under the law shall not be denied or abridged by the United States or by any State on account of sex." The proposed amendment, which would have the effect of making sex a suspect classification in line with the *Frontiero* opinion, was quickly approved by the Congress, but by June 1973, it had run into fierce resistance in many state legislatures. Seldom has a controversial public issue been so ensnared in philosophical subtleties! The new equality often would make sexual difference an invalid ground for different legal classifications, but would that necessarily lead to bisexual rest rooms, female combat troops, the invalidating of statutes creating sex crimes or of those specifying the amount of weight a woman could be required to lift on a job? Even if the answers to these and similar questions are affirmative, would that necessarily be a bad thing? Leading constitutional scholars have differed in their approaches to these partly philosophical problems, and at the time of printing, the fate of the Equal Rights Amendment is still in doubt. No current public issue better illustrates the common concerns of philosophers and lawmakers.

Among cases argued before the United States Supreme Court in this century few can have excited wider public interest than the lawsuit brought by Allan Bakke to gain admission to one of the medical schools of the University of California after having been refused a place in the entering class. The admissions scheme reserved 16 of the 100 places for "disadvantaged" minority students. Bakke was unsuccessful in his application even though he apparently would have been admitted if only he had been a member of one of the designated racial or ethnic groups. The public debate concerned broad matters of principle that in a formal setting were argued before the Court, with many important questions begging to be put through the philosopher's mill. How can the ideal of equality under the law for all citizens be reconciled with favored treatment for those who simply happen to have been born into one group rather than another? What sacrifice of the interests of some citizens may government make in order to promote a better society for all and remedy the historical injustices suffered by other citizens? How shall the offensive discrimination forbidden by the Constitution be distinguished from the dissimilar treatment that inevitably must take place when some citizens are less well-off than others and those who are in a particularly unfortunate state are the objects of governmental concern directed to improving their lot? The severely edited excerpts from the *Bakke* opinions included here provide some interesting analyses of these questions as well as some answers, though for a full appreciation of the legal issues in all their complexity all of the opinions should be read in their entirety.

1. Gregory Vlastos, "Justice and Equality," in *Social Justice,* ed., Richard B. Brandt (Englewood Cliffs, N.J.; Prentice-Hall, Inc., 1962), p. 32.

2. W. D. Ross, *Aristotle* (London: Metheun & Co., 1949), p. 210.

3. David Hume, *An Enquiry Concerning the Principles of Morals* (La Salle, Illinois: The Open Court Publishing Co., 1947), p. 20.

4. David Hume, *A Treatise of Human Nature* (Oxford: The Clarendon Press, 1888), p. 497.

5. J. O. Urmson, "The Moral Philosophy of J. S. Mill," *The Philosophical Quarterly,* Vol. 3 (1953), pp. 33–39.

6. Brian Barry, *Political Argument* (London: Routledge, Kegal Paul, 1965), p. 96.

7. *Ibid.,* p. 86.

8. John Rawls, *A Theory of Justice* (Cambridge, Mass.: Harvard University Press, 1971), p. 7.

ARISTOTLE

Justice*

JUSTICE: ITS SPHERE AND OUTER NATURE: IN WHAT SENSE IT IS A MEAN

THE JUST AS THE LAWFUL (UNIVERSAL JUSTICE) AND THE JUST AS THE FAIR AND EQUAL (PARTICULAR JUSTICE): THE FORMER CONSIDERED

1. With regard to justice and injustice we must consider (1) what kind of actions they are concerned with, (2) what sort of mean justice is, and (3) between what extremes the just act is intermediate. Our investigation shall follow the same course as the preceding discussions.

We see that all men mean by justice that kind of state of character which makes people disposed to do what is just and makes them act justly and wish for what is just; and similarly by injustice that state which makes them act unjustly and wish for what is unjust. Let us too, then, lay this down as a general basis. For the same is not true of the sciences and the faculties as of states of character. A faculty or a science which is one and the same is held to relate to contrary objects, but a state of character which is one of two contraries does *not* produce the contrary results; for example, as a result of health we do not do what is the opposite of healthy, but only what is healthy; for we say a man walks healthily, when he walks as a healthy man would.

Now often one contrary state is recognized from its contrary, and often states are recognized from the subjects that exhibit them; for (A) if good condition is known, bad condition also becomes known, and (B) good condition is known from the things that are in good condition, and they from it. If good condition is firmness of flesh, it is necessary both that bad condition should be flabbiness of flesh and that the whole-some should be that which causes firmness in flesh. And it follows for the most part that if one contrary is ambiguous the other also will be ambiguous; for example, that if 'just' is so, 'unjust' will be so too.

Now 'justice' and 'injustice' seem to be ambiguous, but because their different meanings approach near to one another the ambiguity escapes notice and is not obvious as it is, comparatively, when the meanings are far apart, for example, (for here the difference in outward form is great) as the ambiguity in the use of κλείζ for the collarbone of an animal and for that with which we lock a door. Let us take as a starting-point, then, the various meanings of 'an unjust man'. Both the lawless man and the grasping and unfair man are thought to be unjust, so that evidently both the law-abiding and the fair man will be just. The just, then, is the lawful and the fair, the unjust the unlawful and the unfair.

Since the unjust man is grasping, he must be concerned with goods—not all goods, but those with which prosperity and adversity have to do, which taken absolutely are always good, but for a particular person are not always good. Now men pray for and pursue these things; but they should not, but should pray that the things that are good absolutely may also be good for them, and should choose the things that *are* good for them. The unjust man does not always choose the greater, but also the less—in the case of things bad absolutely; but because the lesser evil is itself thought to be in a sense good, and graspingness is directed at the good, therefore he is thought to be grasping. And he is unfair; for this contains and is common to both.

Since the lawless man was seen to be unjust and the law-abiding man just, evidently all lawful acts are in a sense just acts; for the acts laid down by the legislative art are lawful, and each of these, we say, is just. Now the laws in their enactments on all subjects aim at the common advantage either of all or of the best or of those who hold power, or something of the sort; so that in one sense we

*Book V from *The Nicomachean Ethics,* translated by W. D. Ross, from *The Oxford Translation of Aristotle* edited by W. D. Ross, vol. 9 (1925). Reprinted by permission of Oxford University Press, Oxford. Some footnotes have been deleted. The remainder have been renumbered.

call those acts just that tend to produce and preserve happiness and its components for the political society. And the law bids us do both the acts of a brave man (for example, not to desert our post nor take to flight nor throw away our arms), and those of a temperate man (for example, not to commit adultery nor to gratify one's lust), and those of a good-tempered man (for example, not to strike another nor to speak evil), and similarly with regard to the other virtues and forms of wickedness, commanding some acts and forbidding others; and the rightly-framed law does this rightly, and the hastily conceived one less well.

This form of justice, then, is complete virtue, but not absolutely, but in relation to our neighbour. And therefore justice is often thought to be the greatest of virtues, and 'neither evening nor morning star' is so wonderful; and proverbially 'in justice is every virtue comprehended'. And it is complete virtue in its fullest sense because it is the actual exercise of complete virtue. It is complete because he who possesses it can exercise his virtue not only in himself but towards his neighbour also; for many men can exercise virtue in their own affairs, but not in their relations to their neighbour. This is why the saying of Bias is thought to be true, that 'rule will show the man'; for a ruler is necessarily in relation to other men, and a member of a society. For this same reason justice, alone of the virtues, is thought to be 'another's good', because it is related to our neighbour; for it does what is advantageous to another, either a ruler or a co-partner. Now the worst man is he who exercises his wickedness both towards himself and towards his friends, and the best man is not he who exercises his virtue towards himself but he who exercises it towards another; for this is a difficult task. Justice in this sense, then, is not part of virtue but virtue entire, nor is the contrary injustice a part of vice but vice entire. What the difference is between virtue and justice in this sense is plain from what we have said; they are the same but their essence is not the same; what, as a relation to one's neighbour, is justice is, as a certain kind of state without qualification, virtue.

THE JUST AS THE FAIR AND EQUAL: DIVIDED INTO DISTRIBUTIVE AND RECTIFICATORY JUSTICE

2. But at all events what we are investigating is the justice which is a *part* of virtue; for there is a justice of this kind, as we maintain. Similarly it is with injustice in the particular sense that we are concerned.

That there is such a thing is indicated by the fact that while the man who exhibits in action the other forms of wickedness acts wrongly indeed, but not graspingly (for example, the man who throws away his shield through cowardice or speaks harshly through bad temper or fails to help a friend with money through meanness), when a man acts graspingly he often exhibits none of these vices—no, nor all together, but certainly wickedness of some kind (for we blame him) and injustice. There is, then, another kind of injustice which is a part of injustice in the wide sense, and a use of the word 'unjust' which answers to a part of what is unjust in the wide sense of 'contrary to the law'. Again, if one man commits adultery for the sake of gain and makes money by it, while another does so at the bidding of appetite though he loses money and is penalized for it, the latter would be held to be self-indulgent rather than grasping, but the former is unjust, but not self-indulgent; evidently, therefore, he is unjust by reason of his making gain by his act. Again, all other unjust acts are ascribed invariably to some particular kind of wickedness, for example, adultery to self-indulgence, the desertion of a comrade in battle to cowardice, physical violence to anger; but if a man makes gain, his action is ascribed to no form of wickedness but injustice. Evidently, therefore, there is apart from injustice in the wide sense another, 'particular', injustice which shares the name and nature of the first, because its definition falls within the same genus; for the significance of both consists in a relation to one's neighbour, but the one is concerned with honour or money or safety—or that which includes all these, if we had a single name for it—and its motive is the pleasure that arises from gain; while the other is concerned with all the objects with which the good man is concerned.

It is clear, then, that there is more than one kind of justice, and that there is one which is distinct from virtue entire; we must try to grasp its genus and differentia.

The unjust has been divided into the unlawful and the unfair, and the just into the lawful and the fair. To the unlawful answers the aforementioned sense of injustice. But since the unfair and the unlawful are not the same, but are different as a part is from its whole (for all that is unfair is unlawful, but not all that is unlawful is unfair), the unjust and injustice in the sense of the unfair are not the same as but different from the former kind, as part from whole; for injustice in this sense is a part of injustice in the wide sense, and similarly justice in the one sense of justice in the other. Therefore we must speak also about particular justice and particular injustice, and similarly about the just and the unjust. The justice, then, which answers to the whole of virtue, and the corresponding injustice, one being the exercise of virtue as a whole, and the other that of vice as a whole, towards one's neighbour, we may leave on one side. And how the meanings of 'just' and 'unjust' which answer to these are to be distinguished is evident; for practically the majority of the acts commanded by the law are those which are prescribed from the point of view of virtue taken as a whole; for the law bids us practise every virtue and forbids us to practise any vice. And the things that tend to produce virtue taken as a whole are those of the acts prescribed by the law which have been prescribed with a view to education for the common good. But with regard to the education of the individual as such, which makes him without qualification a good *man,* we must determine later whether this is the function of the political art or of another; for perhaps it is not the same to be a good man and a good citizen of any state taken at random.

Of particular justice and that which is just in the corresponding sense, (A) one kind is that which is manifested in distributions of honour or money or the other things that fall to be divided among those who have a share in the constitution (for in these it is possible for one man to have a share either unequal or equal to that of another), and (B) one is that which plays a rectifying part in transactions between man and man. Of this there are two divisions; of transactions (1) some are voluntary and (2) others involuntary—voluntary such transactions as sale, purchase, loan for consumption, pledging, loan for use, depositing, letting (they are called voluntary because the *origin* of these transactions is voluntary), while of the involuntary (*a*) some are clandestine, such as theft, adultery, poisoning, procuring, enticement of slaves, assassination, false witness, and (*b*) others are violent, such as assault, imprisonment, murder, robbery with violence, mutilation, abuse, insult.

DISTRIBUTIVE JUSTICE, IN ACCORDANCE WITH GEOMETRICAL PROPORTION

3. (A) We have shown that both the unjust man and the unjust act are unfair or unequal; now it is clear that there is also an intermediate between the two unequals involved in either case. And this is the equal; for in any kind of action in which there is a more and a less there is also what is

equal. If, then, the unjust is unequal, the just is equal, as all men suppose it to be, even apart from argument. And since the equal is intermediate, the just will be an intermediate. Now equality implies at least two things. The just, then, must be both intermediate and equal and relative (for example, for certain persons). And *qua* intermediate it must be between certain things (which are respectively greater and less); *qua* equal, it involves *two* things; *qua* just, it is for certain people. The just, therefore, involves at least four terms; for the persons for whom it is in fact just are two, and the things in which it is manifested, the objects distributed, are two. And the same equality will exist between the persons and between the things concerned; for as the latter—the things concerned—are related, so are the former; if they are not equal, they will not have what is equal, but this is the origin of quarrels and complaints—when either equals have and are awarded unequal shares, or unequals equal shares. Further, this is plain from the fact that awards should be 'according to merit'; for all men agree that what is just in distribution must be according to merit in some sense, though they do not all specify the same sort of merit, but democrats identify it with the status of freemen, supporters of oligarchy with wealth (or with noble birth), and supporters of aristocracy with excellence.

The just, then, is a species of the proportionate (proportion being not a property only of the kind of number which consists of abstract units, but of number in general). For proportion is equality of ratios, and involves four terms at least (that discrete proportion involves four terms is plain, but so does continuous proportion, for it uses one term as two and mentions it twice; for example, 'as the line A is to the line B, so is the line B to the line C'; the line B, then, has been mentioned twice, so that if the line B be assumed twice, the proportional terms will be four); and the just, too, involves at least four terms, and the ratio between one pair is the same as that between the other pair; for there is a similar distinction between the persons and between the things. As the term A, then, is to B, so will C be to D, and therefore, *alternando,* as A is to C, B will be to D. Therefore also the whole is in the same ratio to the whole;[1] and this coupling the distribution effects, and, if the terms are so combined, effects justly. The conjunction, then, of the term A with C and of B with D is what is just in distribution,[2] and this species of the just is intermediate, and the unjust is what violates the proportion; for the proportional is intermediate, and the just is proportional. (Mathematicians call this kind of proportion geometrical; for it is in geometrical proportion that it follows that the whole is to the whole as either part is to the corresponding part.) This proportion is not continuous; for we cannot get a single term standing for a person and a thing.

This, then, is what the just is—the proportional; the unjust is what violates the proportion. Hence one term becomes too great, the other too small, as indeed happens in practice; for the man who acts unjustly has too much, and the man who is unjustly treated too little, of what is good. In the case of evil the reverse is true; for the lesser evil is reckoned a good in comparison with the greater evil, since the lesser evil is rather to be chosen than the greater, and what is worthy of choice is good, and what is worthier of choice a greater good.

This, then, is one species of the just.

RECTIFICATORY JUSTICE, IN ACCORDANCE WITH ARITHMETICAL PROGRESSION

4. (B) The remaining one is the rectificatory, which arises in connexion with transactions both voluntary and involuntary. This form of the just has a different specific character from the former. For the justice which distributes common possessions is always in accordance with the kind of proportion mentioned above (for in the case also in which the distribution is made from the common funds of a partnership it will be according to the same ratio which the funds put into the business by the partners bear to one another); and the injustice opposed to this kind of justice is that which violates the proportion. But the justice in transactions between man and man is a sort of equality indeed, and the injustice a sort of inequality; not according to that kind of proportion, however, but according to arithmetical proportion. For it makes no difference whether a good man has defrauded a bad man or a bad man a good one, nor whether it is a good or a bad man that has committed adultery; the law looks only to the distinctive character of the injury, and treats the parties as equal, if one is in the wrong and the other is being wronged, and if one inflicted injury and the other has received it. Therefore, this kind of injustice being an inequality, the judge tries to equalize it; for in the case also in which one has received and the other has inflicted a wound, or one has slain and the other been slain, the suffering and the action have been un-

equally distributed; but the judge tries to equalize things by means of the penalty, taking away from the gain of the assailant. For the term 'gain' is applied generally to such cases—even if it be not a term appropriate to certain cases, for example, to the person who inflicts a wound—and 'loss' to the sufferer; at all events when the suffering has been estimated, the one is called loss and the other gain. Therefore the equal is intermediate between the greater and the less, but the gain and the loss are respectively greater and less in contrary ways; more of the good and less of the evil are gain, and the contrary is loss; intermediate between them is, as we saw, the equal, which we say is just; therefore corrective justice will be the intermediate between loss and gain. This is why, when people dispute, they take refuge in the judge; and to go to the judge is to go to justice; for the nature of the judge is to be a sort of animate justice; and they seek the judge as an intermediate, and in some states they call judges mediators, on the assumption that if they get what is intermediate they will get what is just. The just, then, is an intermediate, since the judge is so. Now the judge restores equality; it is as though there were a line divided into unequal parts, and he took away that by which the greater segment exceeds the half, and added it to the smaller segment. And when the whole has been equally divided, then they say they have 'their own'—that is, when they have got what is equal. The equal is intermediate between the greater and the lesser line according to arithmetical proportion. It is for this reason also that it is called just (δικαιον), because it is a division into two equal parts (διχα), just as if one were to call it διχαιον; and the judge (δικαστηζ) is one who bisects (διχαστηζ). For when something is subtracted from one of two equals and added to the other, the other is in excess by these two; since if what was taken from the one had not been added to the other, the latter would have been in excess by one only. It therefore exceeds the intermediate by one, and the intermediate exceeds by one that from which something was taken. By this, then, we shall recognize both what we must subtract from that which has more, and what we must add to that which has less; we must add to the latter that by which the intermediate exceeds it, and subtract from the greatest that by which it exceeds the intermediate. Let the lines AA', BB', CC' be equal to one another; from the line AA' let the segment AE have been subtracted, and to the line CC' let the segment CD[1] have been added, so that the whole line DCC' exceeds the line EA' by the segment CD and the segment CF; therefore it exceeds the line BB' by the segment CD.

sc. equal to AE.

These names, both loss and gain, have come from voluntary exchange; for to have more than one's own is called gaining, and to have less than one's original share is called losing, for example, in buying and selling and in all other matters in which the law has left people free to make their own terms; but when they get neither more nor less but just what belongs to themselves, they say that they have their own and that they neither lose nor gain.

Therefore the just is intermediate between a sort of gain and a sort of loss, to wit, those which are involuntary;[3] it consists in having an equal amount before and after the transaction.

JUSTICE IN EXCHANGE, RECIPROCITY IN ACCORDANCE WITH PROPORTION

5. Some think that *reciprocity* is without qualification just, as the Pythagoreans said; for they defined justice without qualification as reciprocity. Now 'reciprocity' fits neither distributive nor rectificatory justice—yet people *want* even the justice of Rhadamanthus to mean this:

Should a man suffer what he did, right justice would be done.

—for in many cases reciprocity and rectificatory justice are not in accord; for example, (1) if an official has inflicted a wound, he should not be wounded in return, and if someone has wounded an official, he ought not to be wounded only but punished in addition. Further (2) there is a great difference between a voluntary and an involuntary act. But in associations for exchange this sort of justice does hold men together—reciprocity in accordance with a proportion and not on the basis of precisely equal return. For it is by proportionate requital that the city holds together. Men seek to return either evil for evil—and if they cannot do so, think their position mere slavery—or good for good—and if they cannot do so there is no exchange, but it is by exchange that they hold together. This is why they give a prominent place to the temple of the Graces—to promote the requital of services; for this is characteristic of grace—we should serve in return one who has shown grace to us, and should another time take the initiative in showing it.

Now proportionate return is secured by cross-conjunction.[4] Let A be a builder, B a shoemaker, C a house, D a shoe. The builder, then, must get from the shoemaker the latter's work, and must himself give him in return his own. If, then, first there is proportionate equality of goods, and then reciprocal action takes place, the result we mention will be effected. If not, the bargain is not equal, and does not hold; for there is nothing to prevent the work of the one being better than that of the other; they must therefore be equated. (And this is true of the other arts also; for they would have been destroyed if what the patient suffered had not been just what the agent did, and of the same amount and kind.) For it is not two doctors that associate for exchange, but a doctor and a farmer, or in general people who are different and unequal; but these must be equated. This is why all things that are exchanged must be somehow comparable. It is for this end that money has been introduced, and it becomes in a sense an intermediate; for it measures all things, and therefore the excess and the defect—how many shoes are equal to a house or to a given amount of food. The number of shoes exchanged for a house [or for a given amount of food] must therefore correspond to the ratio of builder to shoemaker. For if this be not so, there will be no exchange and no intercourse: And this proportion will not be effected unless the goods are somehow equal. All goods must therefore be measured by some one thing, as we said before. Now this unit is in truth demand, which holds all things together (for if men did not need one another's goods at all, or did not need them equally, there would be either no exchange or not the same exchange); but money has become by convention a sort of representative of demand; and this is why it has the name 'money' (νόμισμα) —because it exists not by nature but by law (νόμος) and it is in our power to change it and make it useless. There will, then, be reciprocity when the terms have been equated so that as farmer is to shoemaker, the amount of the shoemaker's work is to that of the farmer's work for which it exchanges. But we must not bring them into a figure of proportion when they have already exchanged (otherwise one extreme will have both excesses), but when they still have their own goods. Thus they are equals and associates just because this equality can be effected in their case. Let A be a farmer, C food, B a shoemaker,

D his product equated to C. If it had not been possible for reciprocity to be thus effected, there would have been no association of the parties. That demand holds things together as a single unit is shown by the fact that when men do not need one another, that is, when neither needs the other or one does not need the other, they do not exchange, as we do when someone wants what one has oneself, for example, when people permit the exportation of corn in exchange for wine. This equation therefore must be established. And for the future exchange—that if we do not need a thing now we shall have it if ever we do need it —money is as it were our surety; for it must be possible for us to get what we want by bringing the money. Now the same thing happens to money itself as to goods—it is not always worth the same; yet it tends to be steadier. This is why all goods must have a price set on them for then there will always be exchange, and if so, association of man with man. Money, then, acting as a measure, makes goods commensurate and equates them; for neither would there have been association if there were not exchange, nor exchange if there were not equality, nor equality if there were not commensurability. Now in truth it is impossible that things differing so much should become commensurate, but with reference to demand they may become so sufficiently. There must, then, be a unit, and that fixed by agreement (for which reason it is called money); for it is this that makes all things commensurate, since all things are measured by money. Let A be a house, B ten minae, C a bed. A is half of B, if the house is worth five minae or equal to them; the bed, C, is a tenth of B; it is plain, then, how many beds are equal to a house, to wit, five. That exchange took place thus before there was money is plain; for it makes no difference whether it is five beds that exchange for a house, or the money value of five beds.

We have now defined the unjust and the just. These having been marked off from each other, it is plain that just action is intermediate between acting unjustly and being unjustly treated; for the one is to have too much and the other to have too little. Justice is a kind of mean, but not in the same way as the other virtues, but because it relates to an intermediate amount, while injustice relates to the extremes. And justice is that in virtue of which the just man is said to be a doer, by choice, of that which is just, and one who will distribute either between himself and another or between two others not so as to give more of what is desirable to himself and less to his neighbour

(and conversely with what is harmful), but so as to give what is equal in accordance with proportion; and similarly in distributing between two other persons. Injustice on the other hand is similarly related to the unjust, which is excess and defect, contrary to proportion, of the useful or hurtful. For which reason injustice is excess and defect, to wit, because it is productive of excess and defect—in one's own case excess of what is in its own nature useful and defect of what is hurtful, while in the case of others it is a whole like what it is in one's own case, but proportion may be violated in either direction. In the unjust act to have too little is to be unjustly treated; to have too much is to act unjustly.

Let this be taken as our account of the nature of justice and injustice, and similarly of the just and the unjust in general.

POLITICAL JUSTICE AND ANALOGOUS KINDS OF JUSTICE

6. Since acting unjustly does not necessarily imply being unjust, we must ask what sort of unjust acts imply that the doer is unjust with respect to each type of injustice, for example, a thief, an adulterer, or a brigand. Surely the answer does not turn on the difference between these types. For a man might even lie with a woman knowing who she was, but the origin of his act might be not deliberate choice but passion. He acts unjustly, then, but is not unjust; for example, a man is not a thief, yet he stole, nor an adulterer, yet he committed adultery; and similarly in all other cases.

Now we have previously stated how the reciprocal is related to the just, but we must not forget that what we are looking for is not only what is just without qualification but also political justice. This is found among men who share their life with a view to self-sufficiency, men who are free and either proportionately or arithmetically equal, so that between those who do not fulfill this condition there is no political justice but justice in a special sense and by analogy. For justice exists only between men whose mutual relations are governed by law; and law exists for men between whom there is injustice; for legal justice is the discrimination of the just and the unjust. And between men between whom injustice is done there is also unjust action (though there is not injustice between all between whom there is unjust action), and this is assigning too much to oneself of things good in themselves and too little of things evil in themselves. This is why we do not allow a *man* to rule, but *rational principle*, because a man behaves thus in his own interests and becomes a tyrant. The magistrate on the other hand is the guardian of justice, and, if of justice, then of equality also. And since he is assumed to have no more than his share, if he is just (for he does not assign to himself more of what is good in itself, unless such a share is proportional to his merits—so that it is for others that he labours, and it is for this reason that men, as we stated previously, say that justice is 'another's good'), therefore a reward must be given him, and this is honour and privilege; but those for whom such things are not enough become tyrants.

The justice of a master and that of a father are not the same as the justice of citizens, though they are like it; for there can be no injustice in the unqualified sense towards things that are one's own, but a man's chattel,[5] and his child until it reaches a certain age and sets up for itself, are as it were part of himself, and no one chooses to hurt himself (for which reason there can be no injustice towards oneself). Therefore the justice or injustice of citizens is not manifested in these relations; for it was as we saw according to law, and between people naturally subject to law, and these as we saw are people who have an equal share in ruling and being ruled. Hence justice can more truly be manifested towards a wife than towards children and chattels, for the former is household justice; but even this is different from political justice.

NATURAL AND LEGAL JUSTICE

7. Of political justice part is natural, part legal, —natural, that which everywhere has the same force and does not exist by people's thinking this or that; legal, that which is originally indifferent, but when it has been laid down is not indifferent, for example, that a prisoner's ransom shall be a mina, or that a goat and not two sheep shall be sacrificed, and again all the laws that are passed for particular cases, for example, that sacrifice shall be made in honour of Brasidas, and the provisions of decrees. Now some think that all justice is of this sort, because that which is by nature is unchangeable and has everywhere the same force (as fire burns both here and in Persia), while they see change in the things recognized as just. This, however, is not true in this unqualified way, but is true in a sense; or rather, with the gods it is perhaps not true at all, while with us there is something that is just even by nature, yet all of it is changeable; but still some is by nature, some not by nature. It is evident which sort of things, among things capable of being otherwise, is by nature; and which is not but is legal and conven-

tional, assuming that both are equally changeable. And in all other things the same distinction will apply; by nature the right hand is stronger, yet it is possible that all men should come to be ambidextrous. The things which are just by virtue of convention and expediency are like measures; for wine and corn measures are not everywhere equal, but larger in wholesale and smaller in retail markets. Similarly, the things which are just not by nature but by human enactment are not everywhere the same, since constitutions also are not the same, though there is but one which is everywhere by nature the best.

Of things just and lawful each is related as the universal to its particulars; for the things that are done are many, but of *them* each is one, since it is universal.

There is a difference between the act of injustice and what is unjust, and between the act of justice and what is just; for a thing is unjust by nature or by enactment; and this very thing, when it has been done, is an act of injustice, but before it is done is not yet that but is unjust. So, too, with an act of justice (though the general term is rather 'just action', and 'act of justice' is applied to the correction of the act of injustice).

Each of these must later be examined separately with regard to the nature and number of its species and the nature of the things with which it is concerned.

JUSTICE: ITS INNER NATURE AS INVOLVING CHOICE

THE SCALE OF DEGREES OF WRONGDOING

8. Acts just and unjust being as we have described them, a man acts unjustly or justly whenever he does such acts voluntarily; when involuntarily, he acts neither unjustly nor justly except in an incidental way; for he does things which happen to be just or unjust. Whether an act is or is not one of injustice (or of justice) is determined by its voluntariness or involuntariness; for when it is voluntary it is blamed, and at the same time is then an act of injustice; so that there will be things that are unjust but not yet acts of injustice, if voluntariness be not present as well. By the voluntary I mean, as has been said before, any of the things in a man's own power which he does with knowledge, that is, not in ignorance either of the person acted on or of the instrument used or of the end that will be attained (for example, whom he is striking, with what, and to what end), each such act being done not incidentally nor

under compulsion (for example, if A takes B's hand and therewith strikes C, B does not act voluntarily; for the act was not in his own power). The person struck may be the striker's father, and the striker may know that it is a man or one of the persons present, but not know that it is his father; a similar distinction may be made in the case of the end, and with regard to the whole action. Therefore that which is done in ignorance, or though not done in ignorance is not in the agent's power, or is done under compulsion, is involuntary (for many natural processes, even, we knowingly both perform and experience, none of which is either voluntary or involuntary; for example, growing old or dying). But in the case of unjust and just acts alike the injustice or justice may be only incidental; for a man might return a deposit unwillingly and from fear, and then he must not be said either to do what is just or to act justly, except in an incidental way. Similarly the man who under compulsion and unwillingly fails to return the deposit must be said to act unjustly, and to do what is unjust, only incidentally. Of voluntary acts we do some by choice, others not by choice; by choice those which we do after deliberation, not by choice those which we do without previous deliberation. Thus there are three kinds of injury in transactions between man and man; those done in ignorance are mistakes when the person acted on, the act, the instrument, or the end that will be attained is other than the agent supposed; the agent thought either that he was not hitting any one or that he was not hitting with this missile or not hitting this person or to this end, but a result followed other than that which he thought likely (for example, he threw not with intent to wound but only to prick), or the person hit or the missile was other than he supposed. Now when (1) the injury takes place contrary to reasonable expectation, it is *misadventure*. When (2) it is not contrary to reasonable expectation, but does not imply vice, it is a *mistake* (for a man makes a mistake when the fault originates in him, but is the victim of accident when the origin lies outside him). When (3) he acts with knowledge but not after deliberation, it is an *act of injustice*—for example, the acts due to anger or to other passions necessary or natural to man; for when men do such harmful and mistaken acts they act unjustly, and the acts are acts of injustice, but this does not imply that the doers are unjust or wicked; for the injury is not due to vice. But when (4) a man acts from choice, he is an *unjust man* and a vicious man.

Hence acts proceeding from anger are rightly judged not to be done of malice aforethought; for it is not the man who acts in anger but he who enraged him that starts the mischief. Again, the matter in dispute is not whether the thing happened or not, but its justice; for it is apparent injustice that occasions rage. For they do not dispute about the occurrence of the act—as in commercial transactions where one of the two parties *must* be vicious[6]—unless they do so owing to forgetfulness; but, agreeing about the fact, they dispute on which side justice lies (whereas a man who has deliberately injured another cannot help knowing that he has done so), so that one thinks he is being treated unjustly and the other disagrees.

But if a man harms another by choice, he acts unjustly; and *these* are the acts of injustice which imply that the doer is an unjust man, provided that the act violates proportion or equality. Similarly, a man *is just* when he acts justly by choice; but he *acts justly* if he merely acts voluntarily.

Of involuntary acts some are excusable, others not. For the mistakes which men make not only in ignorance but also from ignorance are excusable, while those which men do not from ignorance but (though they do them *in* ignorance) owing to a passion which is neither natural nor such as man is liable to, are not excusable.

Can a man be voluntarily treated unjustly? Is it the distributor or the recipient that is guilty of injustice in distribution? Justice is not so easy as it might seem, because it is not a way of acting but an inner disposition.

9. Assuming that we have sufficiently defined the suffering and doing of injustice, it may be asked (1) whether the truth is expressed in Euripides' paradoxical words:

'I slew my mother, that's my tale in brief.'
'Were you both willing, or unwilling both?'

Is it truly possible to be willingly treated unjustly, or is all suffering of injustice on the contrary involuntary, as all unjust action is voluntary? And is all suffering of injustice of the latter kind or else all of the former, or is it sometimes voluntary, sometimes involuntary? So, too, with the case of being justly treated; all just action is voluntary, so that it is reasonable that there should be a similar opposition in either case—that both being unjustly and being justly treated should be either alike voluntary or alike involuntary. But it would be thought paradoxical even in the case of being justly treated, if it were always voluntary; for some are unwillingly treated justly. (2) One might raise this question also, whether everyone who has suffered what is unjust is being unjustly treated, or on the other hand it is with suffering as with acting. In action and in passivity alike it is possible for justice to be done incidentally, and similarly (it is plain) injustice; for to do what is unjust is not the same as to act unjustly, nor to suffer what is unjust as to be treated unjustly, and similarly in the case of acting justly and being justly treated; for it is impossible to be unjustly treated if the other does not act unjustly, or justly treated unless he acts justly. Now if to act unjustly is simply to harm someone voluntarily, and 'voluntarily' means 'knowing the person acted on, the instrument, and the manner of one's acting', and the incontinent man voluntarily harms himself, not only will he voluntarily be unjustly treated but it will be possible to treat oneself unjustly. (This also is one of the questions in doubt, whether a man can treat himself unjustly.) Again, a man may voluntarily, owing to incontinence, be harmed by another who acts voluntarily, so that it would be possible to be voluntarily treated unjustly. Or is our definition incorrect; must we to 'harming another, with knowledge both of the person acted on, of the instrument, and of the manner' add 'contrary to the wish of the person acted on'? Then a man may be voluntarily harmed and voluntarily suffer what is unjust, but no one is voluntarily treated unjustly; for no one wishes to be unjustly treated, not even the incontinent man. He acts contrary to his wish; for no one *wishes* for what he does not think to be good, but the incontinent man does *do* things that he does not think he ought to do. Again, one who gives what is his own, as Homer says Glaucus gave Diomede

> Armour of gold for brazen, the price of a hundred
> beeves for nine,

is not unjustly treated; for though to give is in his power, to be unjustly treated is not, but there must be someone to treat him unjustly. It is plain, then, that being unjustly treated is not voluntary.

Of the questions we intended to discuss two still remain for discussion; (3) whether it is the man who has assigned to another more than his share that acts unjustly, or he who has the excessive share, and (4) whether it is possible to treat oneself unjustly. The questions are connected; for if the former alternative is possible and the distributor acts unjustly and not the man who has the excessive share, then if a man assigns more to another than to himself, knowingly and volun-

tarily, he treats himself unjustly; which is what modest people seem to do, since the virtuous man tends to take less than his share. Or does this statement too need qualification? For (*a*) he perhaps gets more than his share of some other good, for example, of honour or of intrinsic nobility. (*b*) The question is solved by applying the distinction we applied to unjust action, for he suffers nothing contrary to his own wish, so that he is not unjustly treated so far as this goes, but at most only suffers harm.

It is plain too that the distributor acts unjustly, but not always the man who has the excessive share; for it is not he to whom injustice is done that acts unjustly, but he to whom it appertains to do the unjust act voluntarily, that is, the person in whom lies the origin of the action, and this lies in the distributor, not in the receiver. Again, since the word 'do' is ambiguous, and there is a sense in which lifeless things, or a hand, or a servant who obeys an order, may be said to slay, he who gets an excessive share does not act unjustly, though he 'does' what is unjust.

Again, if the distributor gave his judgement in ignorance, he does not act unjustly in respect of legal justice, and his judgement is not unjust in this sense, but in a sense it *is* unjust (for legal justice and primordial justice are different); but if with the knowledge he judged unjustly, he is himself aiming at an excessive share either of gratitude or of revenge. As much, then, as if he were to share in the plunder, the man who has judged unjustly for these reasons has got too much; the fact that what he gets is different from what he distributes makes no difference, for even if he awards land with a view to sharing in the plunder he gets not land but money.

Men think that acting unjustly is in their power, and therefore that being just is easy. But it is not; to lie with one's neighbour's wife, to wound another, to deliver a bribe, is easy and in our power, but to do these things as a result of a certain state of character is neither easy nor in our power. Similarly to know what is just and what is unjust requires, men think, no great wisdom, because it is not hard to understand the matters dealt with by the laws (though these are not the things that are just, except incidentally); but how actions must be done and distributions effected in order to be just, to know *this* is a greater achievement than knowing what is good for the health; though even there, while it is easy to know that honey, wine, hellebore, cautery, and the use of the knife are so, to know how, to whom, and when these should be applied with a view to producing health, is no less an achievement than that of being a physician. Again, for this very reason[7] men think that acting unjustly is characteristic of the just man no less than of the unjust, because he would be not less but even more capable of doing each of these unjust acts, for he could lie with a woman or wound a neighbour; and the brave man could throw away his shield and turn to flight in this direction or in that. But to play the coward or to act unjustly consists not in doing these things, except incidentally, but in doing them as the result of a certain state of character, just as to practise medicine and healing consists not in applying or not applying the knife, in using or not using medicines, but in doing so in a certain way.

Just acts occur between people who participate in things good in themselves and can have too much or too little of them; for some beings (for example, presumably the gods) cannot have too much of them, and to others, those who are incurably bad, not even the smallest share in them is beneficial but all such goods are harmful, while to others they are beneficial up to a point; therefore justice is essentially something human.

EQUITY, A CORRECTIVE OF LEGAL JUSTICE

10. Our next subject is equity and the equitable and their respective relations to justice and the just. For on examination they appear to be neither absolutely the same nor generically different; and while we sometimes praise what is equitable and the equitable man, at other times, when we reason it out, it seems strange if the equitable, being something different from the just, is yet praiseworthy; for either the just or the equitable is not good, if they are different; or, if both are good, they are the same.

These, then, are pretty much the considerations that give rise to the problem about the equitable; they are all in a sense correct and not opposed to one another; for the equitable, though it is better than one kind of justice, yet is just, and it is not as being a different class of thing that it is better than the just. The same thing, then, is just and equitable, and while both are good the equitable is superior. What creates the problem is that the equitable is just, but not the legally just but a correction of legal justice. The reason is that all law is universal but about some things it is not possible to make a universal statement which shall be correct. In those cases, then, in which it is necessary to speak universally, but not possible to do so correctly, the law takes the usual case,

though it is not ignorant of the possibility of error. And it is none the less correct; for the error is not in the law nor in the legislator but in the nature of the thing, since the matter of practical affairs is of this kind from the start. When the law speaks universally, then, and a case arises on it which is not covered by the universal statement, then it is right, where the legislator fails us and has erred by over-simplicity, to correct the omission—to say what the legislator himself would have said had he been present, and would have put into his law if he had known. Hence the equitable is just, and better than one kind of justice—not better than absolute justice, but better than the error that arises from the absoluteness of the statement. And this is the nature of the equitable, a correction of law where it is defective owing to its universality. In fact this is the reason why all things are not determined by law, to wit, that about some things it is impossible to lay down a law, so that a decree is needed. For when the thing is indefinite the rule also is indefinite, like the leaden rule used in making the Lesbian moulding; the rule adapts itself to the shape of the stone and is not rigid, and so too the decree is adapted to the facts.

It is plain, then, what the equitable is, and that it is just and is better than one kind of justice. It is evident also from this who the equitable man is; the man who chooses and does such acts, and is no stickler for his rights in a bad sense but tends to take less than his share though he has the law on his side, is equitable, and this state of character is equity, which is a sort of justice and not a different state of character.

CAN A MAN TREAT HIMSELF UNJUSTLY?

11. Whether a man can treat himself unjustly or not, is evident from what has been said. For (a) one class of just acts are those acts in accordance with any virtue which are prescribed by the law, for example, the law does not expressly permit suicide, and what it does not expressly permit it forbids. Again, when a man in violation of the law harms another (otherwise than in retaliation) voluntarily, he acts unjustly, and a voluntary agent is one who knows both the person he is affecting by his action and the instrument he is using; and he who through anger voluntarily stabs himself does this contrary to the right rule of life, and this the law does not allow; therefore he is acting unjustly. But towards whom? Surely towards the state, not towards himself. For he suffers voluntarily, but no one is voluntarily treated unjustly.

This is also the reason why the state punishes; a certain loss of civil rights attaches to the man who destroys himself, on the ground that he is treating the state unjustly.

Further, (*b*) in that sense of 'acting unjustly' in which the man who 'acts unjustly' is unjust only and not bad all round, it is not possible to treat oneself unjustly (this is different from the former sense; the unjust man in one sense of the term is wicked in a particularized way just as the coward is, not in the sense of being wicked all round, so that his 'unjust act' does not manifest wickedness in general). For (i) that would imply the possibility of the same thing's having been subtracted from and added to the same thing at the same time; but this is impossible—the just and the unjust always involve more than one person. Further; (ii) unjust action is voluntary and done by choice, and *takes the initiative* (for the man who because he has suffered does the same in return is not thought to act unjustly); but if a man harms himself he suffers and does the same things *at the same time*. Further, (iii) if a man could treat himself unjustly, he could be voluntarily treated unjustly. Besides, (iv) no one acts unjustly without committing particular acts of injustice; but no one can commit adultery with his own wife or housebreaking on his own house or theft on his own property.

In general, the question 'Can a man treat himself unjustly?' is solved also by the distinction we applied to the question 'Can a man be voluntarily treated unjustly?'

(It is evident too that both are bad, being unjustly treated and acting unjustly; for the one means having less and the other having more than the intermediate amount, which plays the part here that the healthy does in the medical art, and the good condition does in the art of bodily training. But still acting unjustly is the worse, for it involves vice and is blameworthy—involves vice which is either of the complete and unqualified kind or almost so (we must admit the latter alternative, because not all voluntary unjust action implies injustice as a state of character), while being unjustly treated does not involve vice and injustice in oneself. In itself, then, being un-

justly treated is less bad, but there is nothing to prevent its being incidentally a greater evil. But theory cares nothing for this; it calls pleurisy a more serious mischief than a stumble; yet the latter may become incidentally the more serious, if the fall due to it leads to your being taken prisoner or put to death by the enemy.)

Metaphorically and in virtue of a certain resemblance there is a justice, not indeed between a man and himself, but between certain parts of him; yet not every kind of justice but that of master and servant or that of husband and wife. For these are the ratios in which the part of the soul that has a rational principle stands to the irrational part; and it is with a view to these parts that people also think a man can be unjust to himself, to wit, because these parts are liable to suffer something contrary to their respective desires; there is therefore thought to be a mutual justice between them as between ruler and ruled.

Let this be taken as our account of justice and the other, that is, the other moral, virtues.

NOTES

1. Person A + thing C to person B + thing D.
2. The problem of distributive justice is to divide the distributable honour or reward into parts which are to one another as are the merits of the persons who are to participate. If

A (first person): B (second person) :: C (first portion) : D (second portion),
then (*alternando*) A : C :: B : D,
and therefore (*componendo*) A + C : B + D :: A : B.

In other words the position established answers to the relative merits of the parties.

3. that is, for the loser.
4. The working of 'proportionate reciprocity' is not very clearly described by Aristotle, but seems to be as follows. A and B are workers in different trades, and will normally be of different degrees of 'worth'. Their products, therefore, will also have unequal worth, (though Aristotle does not expressly reduce the question to one of time) if A = nB, C (what A makes, say, in an hour) will be worth n times as much as D (what B makes in an hour). A fair exchange will then take place if A gets nD and B gets 1 C; that is if A gives what it takes him an hour to make, in exchange for what it takes B n hours to make.
5. that is, his slave.
6. The plaintiff, if he brings a false accusation; the defendant, if he denies a true one.
7. that is, that stated in 11. 4 f., that acting unjustly is in our own power.

DAVID HUME

Of Justice*

PART I

That Justice is useful to society, and consequently that *part* of its merit, at least, must arise from that consideration, it would be a superfluous undertaking to prove. That public utility is the *sole* origin of justice, and that reflections on the beneficial consequences of this virtue are the *sole* foundation of its merit; this proposition, being more curious and important, will better deserve our examination and enquiry.

Let us suppose, that nature has bestowed on the human race such profuse *abundance* of all *external* conveniencies, that, without any uncertainty in the event, without any care or industry on our part, every individual finds himself fully provided with whatever his most voracious appetites can want, or luxurious imagination wish or desire. His natural beauty, we shall suppose, surpasses all acquired ornaments: The perpetual clemency of the seasons renders useless all cloaths or covering: The raw herbage affords him the most delicious fare; the clear fountain, the richest beverage. No laborious occupation required: No tillage: No navigation. Music, poetry, and contemplation form his sole business: Conversation, mirth, and friendship his sole amusement.

It seems evident, that, in such a happy state, every other social virtue would flourish, and receive tenfold encrease; but the cautious, jealous virtue of justice would never once have been dreamed of. For what purpose make a partition of goods, where every one has already more than enough? Why give rise to property, where there cannot possibly be any injury? Why call this object *mine*, when, upon the seizing of it by another, I need but stretch out my hand to possess myself of what is equally valuable? Justice, in that case, being totally USELESS, would be an idle ceremonial, and could never possibly have place in the catalogue of virtues.

*Section III of *An Enquiry Concerning the Principles of Morals*, first published in London in 1751.

We see, even in the present necessitous condition of mankind, that, wherever any benefit is bestowed by nature in an unlimited abundance, we leave it always in common among the whole human race, and make no subdivisions of right and property. Water and air, though the most necessary of all objects, are not challenged as the property of individuals; nor can any man commit injustice by the most lavish use and enjoyment of these blessings. In fertile extensive countries, with few inhabitants, land is regarded on the same footing. And no topic is so much insisted on by those, who defend the liberty of the seas, as the unexhausted use of them in navigation. Were the advantages, procured by navigation, as inexhaustible, these reasoners had never had any adversaries to refute; nor had any claims ever been advanced of a separate, exclusive dominion over the ocean.

It may happen, in some countries, at some periods, that there be established a property in water, none in land;[1] if the latter be in greater abundance than can be used by the inhabitants, and the former be found, with difficulty, and in very small quantities.

Again; suppose, that, though the necessities of human race continue the same as at present, yet the mind is so enlarged, and so replete with friendship and generosity, that every man has the utmost tenderness for every man, and feels no more concern for his own interest than for that of his fellows: It seems evident, that the USE of justice would, in this case, be suspended by such an extensive benevolence, nor would the divisions and barriers of property and obligation have ever been thought of. Why should I bind another, by a deed or promise, to do me any good office, when I know that he is already prompted, by the strongest inclination, to seek my happiness, and would, of himself, perform the desired service; except the hurt, he thereby receives, be greater than the benefit accruing to me? in which case, he knows, that, from my innate humanity and friendship, I should be the first to oppose myself to his imprudent generosity. Why raise landmarks between my neighbour's field and mine, when my heart has made no division between our interests; but shares all his joys and sorrows with the same force and vivacity as if originally my own? Every man, upon this supposition, being a second self to another, would trust all his interests to the discretion of every man; without jealousy, without partition, without distinction. And the whole human race would form only one family; where all would lie in common, and be used freely, without regard to property; but cautiously too, with as entire regard to the necessities of each individual, as if our own interests were most intimately concerned.

In the present disposition of the human heart, it would, perhaps, be difficult to find compleat instances of such enlarged affections; but still we may observe, that the case of families approaches towards it; and the stronger the mutual benevolence is among the individuals, the nearer it approaches; till all distinction of property be, in a great measure, lost and confounded among them. Between married persons, the cement of friendship is by the laws supposed so strong as to abolish all division of possessions: and has often, in reality, the force ascribed to it. And it is observable, that, during the ardour of new enthusiasms, when every principle is inflamed into extravagance, the community of goods has frequently been attempted: and nothing but experience of its inconveniencies, from the returning or disguised selfishness of men, could make the imprudent fanatics adopt anew the ideas of justice and of separate property. So true is it, that this virtue derives its existence entirely from its necessary *use* to the intercourse and social state of mankind.

To make this truth more evident, let us reverse the foregoing suppositions; and carrying every thing to the opposite extreme, consider what would be the effect of these new situations. Suppose a society to fall into such want of all common necessaries, that the utmost frugality and industry cannot preserve the greater number from perishing, and the whole from extreme misery: It will readily, I believe, be admitted, that the strict laws of justice are suspended, in such a pressing emergence, and give place to the stronger motives of necessity and self—preservation. Is it any crime, after a shipwreck, to seize whatever means or instrument of safety one can lay hold of, without regard to former limitations of property? Or if a city besieged were perishing with hunger; can we imagine, that men will see

any means of preservation before them, and lose their lives, from a scrupulous regard to what, in other situations, would be the rules of equity and justice? The USE and TENDENCY of that virtue is to procure happiness and security, by preserving order in society: But where the society is ready to perish from extreme necessity, no greater evil can be dreaded from violence and injustice; and every man may now provide for himself by all the means, which prudence can dictate, or humanity permit. The public, even in less urgent necessities, opens granaries, without the consent of proprietors; as justly supposing, that the authority of magistracy may, consistent with equity, extend so far: But were any number of men to assemble, without the tye of laws or civil jurisdiction; would an equal partition of bread in a famine, though effected by power and even violence, be regarded as criminal or injurious?

Suppose likewise, that it should be a virtuous man's fate to fall into the society of ruffians, remote from the protection of laws and government; what conduct must he embrace in that melancholy situation? He sees such a desperate rapaciousness prevail; such a disregard to equity, such contempt of order, such stupid blindness to future consequences, as must immediately have the most tragical conclusion, and must terminate in destruction to the greater number, and in a total dissolution of society to the rest. He, mean while, can have no other expedient than to arm himself, to whomever the sword he seizes, or the buckler, may belong: To make provision of all means of defence and security: And his particular regard to justice being no longer of USE to his own safety or that of others, he must consult the dictates of self-preservation alone, without concern for those who no longer merit his care and attention.

When any man, even in political society, renders himself, by his crimes, obnoxious to the public, he is punished by the laws in his goods and person; that is, the ordinary rules of justice are, with regard to him, suspended for a moment, and it becomes equitable to inflict on him, for the *benefit* of society, what, otherwise, he could not suffer without wrong or injury.

The rage and violence of public war; what is it but a suspension of justice among the warring parties, who perceive, that this virtue is now no longer of any *use* or advantage to them? The laws of war, which then succeed to those of equity and justice, are rules calculated for the *advantage* and *utility* of that particular state, in which men are now placed. And were a civilized nation engaged with barbarians, who observed no rules even of war; the former must also suspend their observance of them, where they no longer serve to any purpose; and must render every action or encounter as bloody and pernicious as possible to the first aggressors.

Thus, the rules of equity or justice depend entirely on the particular state and condition, in which men are placed, and owe their origin and existence to that UTILITY, which results to the public from their strict and regular observance. Reverse, in any considerable circumstance, the condition of men: Produce extreme abundance or extreme necessity: Implant in the human breast perfect moderation and humanity, or perfect rapaciousness and malice: By rendering justice totally *useless,* you thereby totally destroy its essence, and suspend its obligation upon mankind.

The common situation of society is a medium amidst all these extremes. We are naturally partial to ourselves, and to our friends; but are capable of learning the advantage resulting from a more equitable conduct. Few enjoyments are given us from the open and liberal hand of nature; but by art, labour, and industry, we can extract them in great abundance. Hence the ideas of property become necessary in all civil society: Hence justice derives its usefulness to the public: And hence alone arises its merit and moral obligation.

These conclusions are so natural and obvious, that they have not escaped even the poets, in their descriptions of the felicity, attending the golden age or the reign of SATURN. The seasons, in that first period of nature, were so temperate, if we credit these agreeable fictions, that there was no necessity for men to provide themselves with cloaths and houses, as a security against the violence of heat and cold: The rivers flowed with wine and milk: The oaks yielded honey; and nature spontaneously produced her greatest delicacies. Nor were these the chief advantages of that happy age. Tempests were not alone removed from nature; but those more furious tempests were unknown to human breasts, which now cause such uproar, and engender such confusion. Avarice, ambition, cruelty, selfishness, were never heard of: Cordial affection, compassion, sympathy, were the only movements with which the mind was yet acquainted. Even the punctilious distinction of *mine* and *thine* was banished from among that happy race of mortals, and carried with it the very notion of property and obligation, justice and injustice.

This *poetical* fiction of the *golden age* is, in some respects, of a piece with the *philosophical* fiction of the *state of nature;* only that the former is represented as the most charming and most peaceable condition, which can possibly be imagined; whereas the latter is painted out as a state of mutual war and violence, attended with the most extreme necessity. On the first origin of mankind, we are told, their ignorance and savage nature were so prevalent, that they could give no mutual trust, but must each depend upon himself, and his own force or cunning for protection and security. No law was heard of: No rule of justice known: No distinction of property regarded: Power was the only measure of right; and a perpetual war of all against all was the result of men's untamed selfishness and barbarity.[2]

Whether such a condition of human nature could ever exist, or if it did, could continue so long as to merit the apellation of a *state,* may justly be doubted. Men are necessarily born in a family—society, at least; and are trained up by their parents to some rule of conduct and behaviour. But this must be admitted, that, if such a state of mutual war and violence was ever real, the suspension of all laws of justice, from their absolute inutility, is a necessary and infallible consequence.

The more we vary our views of human life, and the newer and more unusual the lights are, in which we survey it, the more shall we be convinced, that the origin here assigned for the virtue of justice is real and satisfactory.

Were there a species of creatures, intermingled with men, which, though rational, were possessed of such inferior strength, both of body and mind, that they were incapable of all resistance, and could never, upon the highest provocation, make us feel the effects of their resentment; the necessary consequence, I think, is, that we should be bound, by the law of humanity, to give gentle usage to these creatures, but should not, properly speaking, lie under any restraint of justice with regard to them, nor could they possess any right or property, exclusive of such arbitrary lords. Our intercourse with them could not be called society, which supposes a degree of equality; but absolute command on the one side, and servile obedience on the other. Whatever we covet, they must instantly resign: Our permission is the only tenure, by which they hold their possessions: Our compassion and kindness the only check, by which they curb our lawless will: And as no inconvenience ever results from the exercise of a power, so firmly established in nature, the restraints of justice and property, being totally *use-less,* would never have place in so unequal a confederacy.

This is plainly the situation of men, with regard to animals; and how far these may be said to possess reason, I leave it to others to determine. The great superiority of civilized EUROPEANS above barbarous INDIANS, tempted us to imagine ourselves on the same footing with regard to them, and made us throw off all restraints of justice, and even of humanity, in our treatment of them. In many nations, the female sex are reduced to like slavery, and are rendered incapable of all property, in opposition to their lordly masters. But though the males, when united, have, in all countries, bodily force sufficient to maintain this severe tyranny; yet such are the insinuation, address, and charms of their fair companions, that women are commonly able to break the confederacy, and share with the other sex in all the rights and privileges of society.

Were the human species so framed by nature as that each individual possessed within himself every faculty, requisite both for his own preservation and for the propagation of his kind: Were all society and intercourse cut off between man and man, by the primary intention of the supreme Creator: It seems evident, that so solitary a being would be as much incapable of justice, as of social discourse and conversation. Where mutual regards and forbearance serve to no manner of purpose, they would never direct the conduct of any reasonable man. The headlong course of the passions would be checked by no reflection on future consequences. And as each man is here supposed to love himself alone, and to depend only on himself and his own activity for safety and happiness, he would, on every occasion, to the utmost of his power, challenge the preference above every other being, to none of which he is bound by any ties, either of nature or of interest.

But suppose the conjunction of the sexes to be established in nature, a family immediately arises; and particular rules being found requisite for its subsistence, these are immediately embraced; though without comprehending the rest of mankind within their prescriptions. Suppose, that several families unite together into one society, which is totally disjoined from all others, the rules, which preserve peace and order, enlarge themselves to the utmost extent of that society; but becoming then entirely useless, lose their force when carried one step farther. But again suppose, that several distinct societies maintain a kind of intercourse for mutual convenience and advantage, the boundaries of justice still grow larger, in proportion to the largeness of men's views, and the force of their mutual connexions. History, experience, reason sufficiently instruct us in this natural progress of human sentiments, and in the gradual enlargement of our regards to justice, in proportion as we become acquainted with the extensive utility of that virtue.

PART II

If we examine the *particular* laws, by which justice is directed, and property determined; we shall still be presented with the same conclusion. The good of mankind is the only object of all these laws and regulations. Not only it is requisite, for the peace and interest of society, that men's possessions should be separated; but the rules, which we follow, in making the separation, are such as can best be contrived to serve farther the interests of society.

We shall suppose, that a creature, possessed of reason, but unacquainted with human nature, deliberates with himself what RULES of justice or property would best promote public interest, and establish peace and security among mankind: His most obvious thought would be, to assign the largest possessions to the most extensive virtue, and give every one the power of doing good, proportioned to his inclination. In a perfect theocracy, where a being, infinitely intelligent, governs by particular volitions, this rule would certainly have place, and might serve to the wisest purposes: But were mankind to execute such a law; so great is the uncertainty of merit, both from its natural obscurity, and from the self-conceit of each individual, that no determinate rule of conduct would ever result from it; and the total dissolution of society must be the immediate consequence. Fanatics may suppose, *that dominion is founded on grace,* and *that saints alone inherit the earth;* but the civil magistrate very justly puts these sublime theorists on the same footing with common robbers, and teaches them by the severest discipline, that a rule, which, in speculation, may seem the most advantageous to society, may yet be found, in practice, totally pernicious and destructive.

That there were *religious* fanatics of this kind in ENGLAND, during the civil wars, we learn from history; though it is probable, that the obvious *tendency* of these principles excited such horror in mankind, as soon obliged the dangerous enthusiasts to renounce, or at least conceal their tenets. Perhaps, the *levellers,* who claimed an equal distribution of property, were a kind of *political* fanatics, which arose from the religious species, and more openly avowed their pretensions; as carrying a more plausible appearance, of being practicable in themselves, as well as useful to human society.

It must, indeed, be confessed, that nature is so liberal to mankind, that, were all her presents equally divided among the species, and improved by art and industry, every individual would enjoy all the necessaries, and even most of the comforts of life; nor would ever be liable to any ills, but such as might accidentally arise from the sickly frame and constitution of his body. It must also be confessed, that, wherever we depart from this equality, we rob the poor of more satisfaction than we add to the rich, and that the slight gratification of a frivolous vanity, in one individual, frequently costs more than bread to many families, and even provinces. It may appear withal, that the rule of equality, as it would be highly *useful,* is not altogether *impracticable;* but has taken place, at least in an imperfect degree, in some republics; particularly that of SPARTA; where it was attended, it is said, with the most beneficial consequences. Not to mention, that the AGRARIAN laws, so frequently claimed in ROME, and carried into execution in many GREEK cities, proceeded, all of them, from a general idea of the utility of this principle.

But historians, and even common sense, may inform us, that, however specious these ideas of *perfect* equality may seem, they are really, at bottom, *impracticable;* and were they not so, would be extremely *pernicious* to human society. Render possessions ever so equal, men's different degrees of art, care, and industry will immediately break that equality. Or if you check these virtues, you reduce society to the most extreme indigence; and instead of preventing want and beggary in a few, render it unavoidable to the whole community. The most rigorous inquisition too is requisite to watch every inequality on its first appearance; and the most severe jurisdiction, to punish and redress it. But besides, that so much authority must soon degenerate into tyranny, and be exerted with great partialities; who can possibly be possessed of it, in such a situation as is here supposed? Perfect equality of possessions, destroying all subordination, weakens extremely the authority of magistracy, and must reduce all power mearly to a level, as well as property.

We may conclude, therefore, that, in order to establish laws for the regulation of property, we must be acquainted with the nature and situation of man; must reject appearances, which may be false, though specious; and must search for those rules, which are, on the whole, most *useful* and *beneficial.* Vulgar sense and slight experience are sufficient for this purpose; where men give not way to too selfish avidity, or too extensive enthusiasm.

Who sees not, for instance, that whatever is produced or improved by a man's art or industry ought, for ever, to be secured to him, in order to give encouragement to such *useful* habits and accomplishments? That the property ought also to descend to children and relations, for the same *useful* purpose? That it may be alienated by consent, in order to beget that commerce and intercourse, which is so *beneficial* to human society? And that all contracts and promises ought carefully to be fulfilled, in order to secure mutual trust and confidence, by which the general *interest* of mankind is so much promoted?

Examine the writers on the laws of nature; and you will always find, that, whatever principles they set out with, they are sure to terminate here at last, and to assign, as the ultimate reason for every rule which they establish, the convenience and necessities of mankind. A concession thus extorted, in opposition to systems, has more authority, than if it had been made in prosecution of them.

What other reason, indeed, could writers ever give, why this must be *mine* and that *yours;* since uninstructed nature, surely, never made any such distinction? The objects, which receive those appellations, are, of themselves, foreign to us; they are totally disjoined and separated from us; and nothing but the general interests of society can form the connexion.

Sometimes, the interests of society may require a rule of justice in a particular case; but may not determine any particular rule, among several, which are all equally beneficial. In that case, the slightest *analogies* are laid hold of, in order to prevent that indifference and ambiguity, which would be the source of perpetual dissention. Thus possession alone, and first possession, is supposed to convey property, where no body else has any preceding claim and pretension. Many of the reasonings of lawyers are of this analogical nature, and depend on very slight connexions of the imagination.

Does any one scruple, in extraordinary cases, to violate all regard to the private property of individuals, and sacrifice to public interest a distinction, which had been established for the sake of that interest? The safety of the people is the supreme law: All other particular laws are subordinate to it, and dependant on it: And if, in the *common* course of things, they be followed and regarded; it is only because the public safety and interest *commonly* demand so equal and impartial an administration.

Sometimes both *utility* and *analogy* fail, and leave the laws of justice in total uncertainty. Thus, it is highly requisite, that prescription or long possession should convey property; but what number of days or months or years should be sufficient for that purpose, it is impossible for reason alone to determine. *Civil laws* here supply the place of the natural *code,* and assign different terms for prescription, according to the different *utilities,* proposed by the legislator. Bills of exchange and promissory notes, by the laws of most countries, prescribe sooner than bonds, and mortgages, and contracts of a more formal nature.

In general, we may observe, that all questions of property are subordinate to authority of civil laws, which extend, restrain, modify, and alter the rules of natural justice, according to the particular *convenience* of each community. The laws have, or ought to have, a constant reference to the constitution of government, the manners, the climate, the religion, the commerce, the situation of each society. A late author[3] of genius, as well as learning, has prosecuted this subject at large, and has established, from these principles, a system of political knowledge, which abounds in ingenious and brilliant thoughts, and is not wanting in solidity.[4]

What is a man's property? Any thing, which it is lawful for him, and for him alone, to use. *But what rule have we, by which we can distinguish these objects?* Here we must have recourse to statutes, customs, precedents, analogies, and a hundred other circumstances; some of which are constant and inflexible, some variable and arbitrary. But the ultimate point, in which they all professedly terminate, is, the interest and happiness of human society. Where this enters not into consideration, nothing can appear more whimsical, unnatural, and even superstitious, than all or most of the laws of justice and of property.

Those, who ridicule vulgar superstitions, and expose the folly of particular regards to meats, days, places, postures, apparel, have an easy task; while they consider all the qualities and relations of the objects, and discover no adequate cause for that affection or antipathy, veneration or horror, which have so mighty an influence over a considerable part of mankind. A SYRIAN would have starved rather than taste pigeon; an EGYPTIAN would not have approached bacon: But if these species of food be examined by the senses of sight, smell, or taste, or scrutinized by the sciences of chymistry, medicine, or physics; no difference is ever found between them and any other species, nor can that precise circumstance be pitched on, which may afford a just foundation for the religious passion. A fowl on Thursday is lawful food; on Friday abominable: Eggs, in this house, and in this diocese, are permitted during Lent; a hundred paces farther, to eat them is a damnable sin. This earth or building, yesterday was profane; to—day, by the muttering of certain words, it has become holy and sacred. Such reflections as these, in the mouth of a philosopher, one may safely say, are too obvious to have any influence; because they must always, to every man, occur at first sight; and where they prevail not, of themselves, they are surely obstructed by education, prejudice, and passion, not by ignorance or mistake.

It may appear to a careless view, or rather a too abstracted reflection, that there enters a like superstition into all the sentiments of justice; and that, if a man expose its object, or what we call property, to the same scrutiny of sense and science, he will not, by the most accurate enquiry, find any foundation for the difference made by moral sentiment. I may lawfully nourish myself from this tree; but the fruit of another of the same species, ten paces off, it is criminal for me to touch. Had I worne this apparel an hour ago, I had merited the severest punishment; but a man, by pronouncing a few magical syllables, has now rendered it fit for my use and service. Were this house placed in the neighbouring territory, it had been immoral for me to dwell in it; but being built on this side of the river, it is subject to a different municipal law, and,[5] by its becoming mine, I incur no blame or censure. The same species of reasoning, it may be thought, which so successfully exposes superstition, is also applicable to justice; nor is it possible, in the one case more than in the other, to point out, in the object, that precise quality or circumstance, which is the foundation of the sentiment.

But there is this material difference between *superstition* and *justice,* that the former is frivolous, useless, and burdensome; the latter is absolutely requisite to the well-being of mankind and existence of society. When we abstract from this circumstance (for it is too apparent ever to be overlooked) it must be confessed, that all regards to right and property, seem entirely without foundation, as much as the grossest and most vulgar superstition. Were the interests of society nowise concerned, it is as unintelligible, why another's articulating certain sounds implying consent, should change the nature of my actions with regard to a particular object, as why the reciting of a liturgy by a priest, in a certain habit and posture, should dedicate a heap of brick and timber, and render it, thenceforth and for ever, sacred.[6]

These reflections are far from weakening the obligations of justice, or diminishing any thing from the most sacred attention to property. On the contrary, such sentiments must acquire new force from the present reasoning. For what stronger foundation can be desired or conceived for any duty, than to observe, that human society, or even human nature could not subsist, without the establishment of it; and will still arrive at greater degrees of happiness and perfection, the more inviolable the regard is, which is paid to that duty?[7]

The dilemma seems obvious: As justice evidently tends to promote public utility and to support civil society, the sentiment of justice is either derived from our reflecting on that tendency, or like hunger, thirst, and other appetites, resentment, love of life, attachment to offspring, and other passions, arises from a simple original instinct in the human breast, which nature has implanted for like salutary purposes.[8] If the latter be the case, it follows, that property, which is the object of justice, is also distinguished by a simple, original instinct, and is not ascertained by any argument or reflection. But who is there that ever heard of such an instinct? Or is this a subject, in which new discoveries can be made? We may as well attempt to discover, in the body, new senses, which had before escaped the observation of all mankind.

But farther, though it seems a very simple proposition to say, that nature, by an instinctive sentiment, distinguishes property, yet in reality we shall find, that there are required for that purpose ten thousand different instincts, and these employed about objects of the greatest intricacy and nicest discernment. For when a definition of *property* is required, that relation is found to resolve itself into any possession acquired by occupation, by industry, by prescription, by inheritance, by contract, &c. Can we think, that nature, by an original instinct, instructs us in all these methods of acquisition?

These words too, inheritance and contract, stand for ideas infinitely complicated; and to define them exactly, a hundred volumes of laws, and a thousand volumes of commentators, have not been found sufficient. Does nature, whose instincts in men are all simple, embrace such complicated and artificial objects, and create a rational creature, without trusting any thing to the operation of his reason?

But even though all this were admitted, it would not be satisfactory. Positive laws can certainly transfer property. Is it by another original instinct, that we recognize the authority of kings and senates, and mark all the boundaries of their jurisdiction? Judges too, even though their sentence be erroneous and illegal, must be allowed, for the sake of peace and order, to have decisive authority, and ultimately to determine property. Have we original, innate ideas of praetors and chancellors and juries? Who sees not, that all these institutions arise merely from the necessities of human society?

All birds of the same species, in every age and country, build their nests alike: In this we see the force of instinct. Men, in different times and places, frame their houses differently: Here we perceive the influence of reason and custom. A like inference may be drawn from comparing the instinct of generation and the institution of property.

How great soever the variety of municipal laws, it must be confessed, that their chief outlines pretty regularly concur; because the purposes, to which they tend, are every where exactly similar. In like manner, all houses have a roof and walls, windows and chimneys; though diversified in their shape, figure, and materials. The purposes of the latter, directed to the conveniencies of human life, discover not more plainly their origin from reason and reflection, than do those of the former, which point all to a like end.

I need not mention the variations, which all the rules of property receive from the finer turns and connexions of the imagination, and from the subtilties and abstractions of law—topics and reasonings. There is no possibility of reconciling this observation to the notion of original instincts.

What alone will beget a doubt concerning the theory, on which I insist, is the influence of education and acquired habits, by which we are so accustomed to blame injustice, that we are not, in every instance, conscious of any immediate reflection on the pernicious consequences of it. The views the most familiar to us are apt, for that very reason, to escape us; and what we have very frequently performed from certain motives, we are apt likewise to continue mechanically, without recalling, on every occasion, the reflections, which first determined us. The convenience, or rather necessity, which leads to justice, is so universal, and every where points so much to the same rules, that the habit takes place in all societies; and it is not without some scrutiny, that we are able to ascertain its true origin. The matter, however, is not so obscure, but that, even in common life, we have, every moment, recourse to the principle of public utility, and ask, *What must become of the world, if such practices prevail? How could society subsist under such disorders?* Were the distinction or separation of possessions entirely useless, can any one conceive, that it ever should have obtained in society?

Thus we seem, upon the whole, to have attained a knowledge of the force of that principle here insisted on, and can determine what degree of esteem or moral approbation may result from reflections on public interest and utility. The necessity of justice to the support of society is the SOLE foundation of that virtue; and since no moral excellence is more highly esteemed, we may conclude, that this circumstance of usefulness has, in general, the strongest energy, and most entire command over our sentiments. It must, therefore, be the source of a considerable part of the merit ascribed to humanity, benevolence, friendship, public spirit, and other social virtues of that stamp; as it is the SOLE source of the moral approbation paid to fidelity, justice, veracity, integrity, and those other estimable and useful qualities and principles. It is entirely agreeable to the rules of philosophy, and even of common reason; where any principle has been found to have a great force and energy in one instance, to ascribe to it a like energy in all similar instances.[9] This indeed is NEWTON's chief rule of philosophizing.[10]

NOTES

1. *Genesis*, chap. xiii. and xxi.
2. This fiction of a state of nature, as a state of war, was not first started by Mr. HOBBES, as is commonly imagined. PLATO endeavours to refute an hypothesis very like it in the 2nd, 3rd, and 4th books de republica. CICERO, on the contrary, supposes it certain and universally acknowledged . . .
3. [Editions G and K read: Of great genius as well as extensive learning,—the best system of political knowledge, that, perhaps, has ever yet been communicated to the world.]
4. The author of *L'Esprit des Loix*. This illustrious writer, however, sets out with a different theory, and supposes all right to be founded on certain *rapports* or relations; which is a system, that, in my opinion, never will be reconciled with true philosophy. Father MALEBRANCHE, as far as I can learn, was the first that started this abstract theory of morals which was afterwards adopted by *CUDWORTH, CLARKE, and others; and as it excludes all sentiment, and pretends to found every thing on reason, it has not wanted followers in this philosophic age. See Section 1, and Appendix I. With regard to justice, the virtue here treated of, the inference against this theory seems short and conclusive. Property is allowed to be

dependent on civil laws; civil laws are allowed to have no other object, but the interest of society: This therefore must be allowed to be the sole foundation of property and justice. Not to mention, that our obligation itself to obey the magistrate and his laws is founded on nothing but the interests of society.

If the ideas of justice, sometimes, do not follow the dispositions of civil law: we shall find, that these cases, instead of objections, are confirmations of the theory delivered above. Where a civil law is so perverse as to cross all the interest of society, it loses all its authority, and men judge by the ideas of natural justice, which are comformable to those interests. Sometimes also civil laws, for useful purposes, require a ceremony or form to any deed; and where that is wanting, their decrees run contrary to the usual tenour of justice; but one who takes advantage of such chicanes, is not commonly regarded as an honest man. Thus, the interests of society require, that contracts be fulfilled; and there is not a more material article either of natural or civil justice: But the omission of a trifling circumstance will often, by law, invalidate a contract, in *foro humano*, but not in *foro conscientiae*, as divines express themselves, In these cases, the magistrate is supposed only to withdraw his power of enforcing the right, not to have altered the right. Where his intention extends to the right, and is conformable to the interests of society; it never fails to alter the right; a clear proof of the origin of justice and of property, as assigned above. [*The reference to CUDWORTH was added in Edition O.]

5. [By its becoming mine: added in Edition Q.]
6. It is evident, that the will or consent alone never transfers property, nor causes the obligation of a promise (for the same reasoning extends to both) but the will must be expressed by words or signs, in order to impose a tye upon any man. The expression being once brought in as subservient to the will, soon becomes the principal part of the promise; nor will a man be less bound by his word, though he secretly give a different direction to his intention, and withhold the assent of his mind. But though the expression makes, on most occasions, the whole of the promise, yet it does not always so; and one who should make use of any expression, of which he knows not the meaning, and which he uses without any sense of the consequences, would not certainly be bound by it. Nay, though he know its meaning, yet if he use it in jest only, and with such signs as evidently show, that he has no serious intention of binding himself, he would not lie under any obligation of performance; but it is necessary, that the words be a perfect expression of the will, without any contrary signs. Nay, even this we must not carry so far as to imagine, that one, whom, by our quickness of understanding, we conjecture, from certain signs, to have an intention of deceiving us, is not bound by his expression or verbal promise, if we accept of it; but must limit this conclusion to those cases where the signs are of a different nature from those of deceit. All these contradictions are easily accounted for, if justice arise entirely from its usefulness to society; but will never be explained on any other hypothesis.

It is remarkable, that the moral decisions of the *Jesuits* and other relaxed casuists, were commonly formed in prosecution of some such subtilties of reasoning as are here pointed out, and proceed as much from the habit of scholastic refinement as from any corruption of the heart, if we may follow the authority of Mons. BAYLE. See his Dictionary, article LOYOLA. And why has the indignation of mankind risen so high against these casuists; but because every one perceived, that human society could not subsist were such practices authorized, and that morals must always be handled with a view to public interest, more than philosophical regularity? If the secret direction of the intention, said every man of sense, could invalidate a contract; where is our security? And yet a metaphysical schoolman might think, that where an intention was supposed to be requisite, if that intention really had not place, no consequence ought to follow, and no obligation be imposed. The casuistical subtilties may not be greater than the subtilties of lawyers, hinted at above; but as the former are *pernicious,* and the latter *innocent* and even *necessary,* this is the reason of the very different reception they meet with from the world.

*It is a doctrine of the church of ROME, that the priest, by a secret direction of his intention, can invalidate any sacrament. This position is derived from a strict and regular prosecution of the obvious truth, that empty words alone, without any meaning or intention in the speaker, can never be attended with any effect. If the same conclusion be not admitted in reasonings concerning civil contracts, where the affair is allowed to be of so much less consequence than the eternal salvation of thousands, it proceeds entirely from men's sense of the danger and inconvenience of the doctrine in the former case: And we may thence observe, that however positive, arrogant, and dogmatical any superstition may appear, it never can convey any thorough persuasion of the reality of its objects, or put them, in any degree, on a balance with the common incidents of life, which we learn from daily observation and experimental reasoning. [*This paragraph was added in Edition O.]

7.   [Edition G omits all between this point and the concluding paragraph of the section.]

8.   [Edition N omits the preceding sentence, and reads: If justice arose from a simple, original instinct in the human breast, without any reflection, even on those obvious interests of society, which absolutely require that virtue, it follows, &c.]

9.   [This sentence is printed as a note in Editions G to P; and they also call it the *second* rule.]

10.   Principia, lib. iii.

JOHN STUART MILL

On the Connection Between Justice and Utility*

In all ages of speculation, one of the strongest obstacles to the reception of the doctrine that Utility or Happiness is the criterion of right and wrong, has been drawn from the idea of Justice. The powerful sentiment and apparently clear perception which that word recalls, with a rapidity and certainty resembling an instinct, have seemed to the majority of thinkers to point to an inherent quality in things, to show that the Just must have an existence in nature as something absolute, generically distinct from every variety of the Expedient and, in idea, opposed to it, though (as is commonly acknowledged) never, in the long run, disjoined from it in fact.

In the case of this, as of our other moral sentiments, there is no necessary connection between the question of its origin and that of its binding force. That a feeling is bestowed on us by Nature does not necessarily legitimate all its promptings. The feeling of justice might be a peculiar instinct, and might yet require, like our other instincts, to be controlled and enlightened by a higher reason. If we have intellectual instincts leading us to judge in a particular way, as well as animal instincts that prompt us to act in a particular way, there is no necessity that the former should be more infallible in their sphere than the latter in theirs; it may as well happen that wrong judgments are occasionally suggested by those, as wrong actions by these. But though it is one thing to believe that we have natural feelings of justice and another to acknowledge them as an ultimate criterion of conduct, these two opinions are very closely connected in point of fact. Mankind are always predisposed to believe that any subjective feeling not otherwise accounted for, is a revelation of some objective reality. Our present object is to determine whether the reality to which the feeling of justice corresponds, is one which needs any such special revelation, whether the justice or injustice of an action is a thing intrinsically peculiar, and distinct from all its other qualities, or only a combination of certain of those qualities, presented under a peculiar aspect. For the purpose of this inquiry, it is practically important to consider whether the feeling itself of justice and injustice is *sui generis* like our sensations of color and taste, or a derivative feeling, formed by a combination of others. And this it is the more essential to examine, as people are in general willing enough to allow that, objectively, the dictates of Justice coincide with a part of the field of General Expediency; but inasmuch as the subjective mental feeling of Justice is different from that which commonly attaches to simple expediency and, except in the extreme cases of the latter, is far more imperative in its demands, people find it difficult to see, in Justice, only a particular kind or branch of general utility, and think that its superior binding force requires a totally different origin.

To throw light upon this question, it is necessary to attempt to ascertain what is the distinguishing character of justice or of injustice; what is the quality, or whether there is any quality, attributed in common to all modes of conduct designated as unjust (for justice, like many other moral attributes, is best defined by its opposite), and distinguishing them from such modes of conduct as are disapproved, but without having that particular epithet of disapprobation applied to them. If, in everything which men are accustomed to characterize as just or unjust, some one common attribute or collection of attributes is always present, we may judge whether this particular attribute, or combination of attributes, would be capable of gathering round it a sentiment of that peculiar character and intensity by virtue of the general laws of our emotional constitution, or whether the sentiment is inexplicable and requires to be regarded as a special provision of nature. If we find the former to be the case, we shall, in resolving this question, have resolved also the main problem; if the latter, we shall have to seek for some other mode of investigating it.

*Chapter 5 (complete) of *Utilitarianism.* First published in 1861.

To find the common attributes of a variety of objects, it is necessary to begin by surveying the objects themselves in the concrete. Let us therefore avert successively to the various modes of action, and arrangements of human affairs, which are classed, by universal or widely spread opinion, as Just or Unjust. The things well known to excite the sentiments associated with those names are of a very multifarious character. I shall pass them rapidly in review, without studying any particular arrangement.

In the first place, it is mostly considered unjust to deprive any one of his personal liberty, his property, or any other thing which belongs to him by law. Here, therefore, is one instance of the application of the terms Just and Unjust in a perfectly definite sense, namely, that it is just to respect, unjust to violate, the *legal rights* of any one. But this judgment admits of several exceptions, arising from the other forms in which the notions of justice and injustice present themselves. For example: The person who suffers the deprivation may (as the phrase is) have *forfeited* the rights which he is so deprived of; a case to which we shall return presently. But also,

Secondly, The legal rights of which he is deprived may be rights which *ought* not to have belonged to him; in other words, the law which confers on him these rights may be a bad law. When it is so, or when (which is the same thing for our purpose) it is supposed to be so, opinions will differ as to the justice or injustice of infringing it. Some maintain that no law, however bad, ought to be disobeyed by an individual citizen, that his opposition to it, if shown at all, should only be shown in endeavoring to get it altered by competent authority. This opinion (which condemns many of the most illustrious benefactors of mankind, and would often protect pernicious institutions against the only weapons which, in the state of things existing at the time, have any chance of succeeding against them) is defended, by those who hold it, on grounds of expediency, principally on that of the importance, to the common interest of mankind, of maintaining inviolate the sentiment of submission to law. Other persons, again, hold the directly contrary opinion that any law judged to be bad may blamelessly be disobeyed, even though it be not judged to be unjust, but only inexpedient, while others would confine the license of disobedience to the case of unjust laws. But, again, some say that all laws which are inexpedient are unjust, since every law imposes some restriction on the natural liberty of mankind, which restriction is an injustice, unless

legitimated by tending to their good. Among these diversities of opinion, it seems to be universally admitted that there may be unjust laws, and that law, consequently, is not the ultimate criterion of justice, but may give to one person a benefit, or impose on another an evil, which justice condemns. When, however, a law is thought to be unjust, it seems always to be regarded as being so in the same way in which a breach of law is unjust —namely, by infringing somebody's right; which, as it cannot in this case be a legal right, receives a different appellation and is called a moral right. We may say, therefore, that a second case of injustice consists in taking or withholding from any person that to which he has a *moral right*.

Thirdly, It is universally considered just that each person should obtain that (whether good or evil) which he *deserves,* and unjust, that he should obtain a good, or be made to undergo an evil, which he does not deserve. This is, perhaps, the clearest and most emphatic form in which the idea of justice is conceived by the general mind. As it involves the notion of desert, the question arises, What constitutes desert? Speaking in a general way, a person is understood to deserve good if he does right, evil, if he does wrong; and, in a more particular sense, to deserve good from those to whom he does or has done good, and evil from those to whom he does or has done evil. The precept of returning good for evil has never been regarded as a case of the fulfillment of justice, but as one in which the claims of justice are waived, in obedience to other considerations.

Fourthly, It is confessedly unjust to *break faith* with any one, to violate an engagement, either express or implied, or disappoint expectations raised by our own conduct, at least if we have raised those expectations knowingly and voluntarily. Like the other obligations of justice already spoken of, this one is not regarded as absolute, but as capable of being overruled by a stronger obligation of justice on the other side, or by such conduct on the part of the person concerned as is deemed to absolve us from our obligation to him and to constitute a *forfeiture* of the benefit which he has been led to expect.

Fifthly, It is, by universal admission, inconsistent with justice to be *partial,* to show favor or preference to one person over another in matters to which favor and preference do not properly apply. Impartiality, however, does not seem to be regarded as a duty in itself, but rather as instrumental to some other duty, for it is admitted that favor and preference are not always censurable, and indeed the cases in which they are condemned are rather the exception than the rule. A person would be more likely to be blamed than applauded for giving his family or friends no superiority in good offices over strangers, when he could do so without violating any other duty, and no one thinks it unjust to seek one person in preference to another as a friend, connection, or companion. Impartiality, where rights are concerned, is of course obligatory, but this is involved in the more general obligation of giving to every one his right. A tribunal, for example, must be impartial, because it is bound to award, without regard to any other consideration, a disputed object to the one of two parties who has the right to it. There are other cases in which impartiality means, being solely influenced by desert, as with those who, in the capacity of judges, preceptors, or parents, administer reward and punishment as such. There are cases, again, in which it means being solely influenced by consideration for the public interest, as in making a selection among candidates for a government employment. Impartiality, in short, as an obligation of justice, may be said to mean being exclusively influenced by the considerations which it is supposed ought to influence the particular case in hand, and resisting the solicitation of any motives which prompt to conduct different from what those considerations would dictate.

Nearly allied to the idea of impartiality is that of *equality*, which often enters as a component part both into the conception of justice and into the practice of it and, in the eyes of many persons, constitutes its essence. But, in this still more than in any other case, the notion of justice varies in different persons, and always conforms in its variations to their notion of utility. Each person maintains that equality is the dictate of justice, except where he thinks that expediency requires inequality. The justice of giving equal protection to the rights of all is maintained by those who support the most outrageous inequality in the rights themselves. Even in slave countries, it is theoretically admitted that the rights of the slave, such as they are, ought to be as sacred as those of the master, and that a tribunal which fails to enforce them with equal strictness is wanting in justice, while, at the same time, institutions which leave to the slave scarcely any rights to enforce are not deemed unjust, because they are not deemed inexpedient. Those who think that utility requires distinctions of rank do not consider it unjust that riches and social privileges should be unequally dispensed, but those who think this inequality inexpedient think it unjust also. Who-

ever thinks that government is necessary sees no injustice in as much inequality as is constituted by giving to the magistrate powers not granted to other people. Even among those who hold leveling doctrines, there are as many questions of justice as there are differences of opinion about expediency. Some Communists consider it unjust that the produce of the labor of the community should be shared on any other principle than that of exact equality, others think it just that those should receive most whose wants are greatest, while others hold that those who work harder, or who produce more, or whose services are more valuable to the community, may justly claim a larger quota in the division of the produce. And the sense of natural justice may be plausibly appealed to in behalf of every one of these opinions.

Among so many diverse applications of the term Justice, which yet is not regarded as ambiguous, it is a matter of some difficulty to seize the mental link which holds them together, and on which the moral sentiment adhering to the term essentially depends. Perhaps, in this embarrassment, some help may be derived from the history of the word, as indicated by its etymology.

[In most, if not all languages, the etymology of the word which corresponds to Just points distinctly to an origin connected with the ordinance of law. *Justum* is a form of *jussum*—that which has been ordered. Δικαιφν comes directly from δικη, a suit at law. *Recht,* from which came *right* and *righteous,* is synonymous with law. The courts of justice, the administration of justice, are the courts and administration of law. *La justice,* in French, is the established term for judicature. I am not committing the fallacy imputed with some show of truth to Horne Tooke, of assuming that a word must still continue to mean what it originally meant. Etymology is slight evidence of what the idea now signified is, but the very best evidence of how it sprang up.] There can, I think, be no doubt that the *idée mère,* the primitive element, in the formation of the notion of justice, was conformity to law. It constituted the entire idea among the Hebrews up to the birth of Christianity, as might be expected in the case of a people whose laws attempted to embrace all subjects on which precepts were required, and who believed those laws to be a direct emanation from the Supreme Being. But other nations, and in particular the Greeks and Romans, who knew that their laws had been made originally, and still continued to be made, by men, were not afraid to admit that those men might make bad laws, might do, by law, the same things, and from the same motives, which, if done by individuals without the sanction of law, would be called unjust. And hence the sentiment of justice came to be attached, not to all violations of law, but only to violations of such laws as *ought* to exist, including such as ought to exist, but do not, and to laws themselves, if supposed to be contrary to what ought to be law. In this manner, the idea of law and of its injunctions was still predominant in the notion of justice, even when the laws actually in force ceased to be accepted as the standard of it.

It is true that mankind consider the idea of justice and its obligations as applicable to many things which neither are, nor is it desired that they should be, regulated by law. Nobody desires that laws should interfere with the whole detail of private life, yet every one allows that, in all daily conduct, a person may and does show himself to be either just or unjust. But even here, the idea of the breach of what ought to be law still lingers in a modified shape. It would always give us pleasure, and chime in with our feelings of fitness, that acts which we deem unjust should be punished, though we do not always think it expedient that this should be done by the tribunals. We forego that gratification on account of incidental inconveniences. We should be glad to see just conduct enforced, and injustice repressed, even in the minutest details, if we were not with reason afraid of trusting the magistrate with so unlimited an amount of power over individuals. When we think that a person is bound in justice to do a thing, it is an ordinary form of language to say that he ought to be compelled to do it. We should be gratified to see the obligation enforced by anybody who had the power. If we see that its enforcement by law would be inexpedient, we lament the impossibility, we consider the impunity given to injustice as an evil, and strive to make amends for it by bringing a strong expression of our own and the public disapprobation to bear upon the offender. Thus the idea of legal constraint is still the generating idea of the notion of justice, though undergoing several transformations before that notion, as it exists in an advanced state of society, becomes complete.

The above is, I think, a true account, as far as it goes, of the origin and progressive growth of the idea of justice. But we must observe that it contains, as yet, nothing to distinguish that obligation from moral obligation in general. For the truth is that the idea of penal sanction, which is the essence of law, enters not only into the conception of injustice, but into that of any kind of wrong. We do not call anything wrong, unless we mean to imply that a person ought to be punished in some way or other for doing it, if not by law, by the opinion of his fellow-creatures, if not by opinion, by the reproaches of his own conscience. This seems the real turning point of the distinction between morality and simple expediency. It is a part of the notion of Duty in every one of its forms that a person may rightfully be compelled to fulfill it. Duty is a thing which may be *exacted* from a person, as one exacts a debt. Unless we think that it may be exacted from him, we do not call it his duty. Reasons of prudence, or the interest of other people, may militate against actually exacting it, but the person himself, it is clearly understood, would not be entitled to complain. There are other things, on the contrary, which we wish that people should do, which we like or admire them for doing, perhaps dislike or despise them for not doing, but yet admit that they are not bound to do; it is not a case of moral obligation; we do not blame them, that is, we do not think that they are proper objects of punishment. How we come by these ideas of deserving and not deserving punishment, will appear, perhaps, in the sequel; but I think there is no doubt that this distinction lies at the bottom of the notions of right and wrong, that we call any conduct wrong, or employ instead some other term of dislike or disparagement, according as we think that the person ought or ought not to be punished for it, and we say it would be right to do so and so, or merely that it would be desirable or laudable, according as we would wish to see the person whom it concerns compelled, or only persuaded and exhorted, to act in that manner.[1]

This, therefore, being the characteristic difference which marks off, not justice but morality in general, from the remaining provinces of Expediency and Worthiness, the character is still to be sought which distinguishes justice from other branches of morality. Now, it is known that ethical writers divide moral duties into two classes, denoted by the ill-chosen expressions, duties of perfect and of imperfect obligation; the latter being those in which, though the act is obligatory, the particular occasions of performing it are left to our choice, as in the case of charity or beneficence, which we are indeed bound to practice, but not towards any definite person, nor at any prescribed time. In the more precise language of philosophic jurists, duties of perfect obligation are those duties in virtue of which a correlative *right* resides in some person or persons; duties of imperfect obligation are those moral obligations which do not give birth to any right. I think it will be found that this distinction exactly coincides with that which exists between justice and the other obligations of morality. In our survey of the various popular acceptations of justice, the term appeared generally to involve the idea of personal right—a claim on the part of one or more individuals, like that which the law gives when it confers a proprietary or other legal right. Whether the injustice consists in depriving a person of a possession, or in breaking faith with him, or in treating him worse than he deserves, or worse than other people who have no greater claims, in each case the supposition implies two things—a wrong done, and some assignable person who is wronged. Injustice may also be done by treating a person better than others, but the wrong in this case is to his competitors, who are also assignable persons. It seems to me that this feature in the case—a right in some person, correlative to the moral obligation—constitutes the specific difference between justice and generosity or beneficence. Justice implies something which it is not only right to do and wrong not to do, but which some individual person can claim from us as his moral right. No one has a moral right to our generosity or beneficence, because we are not morally bound to practice those virtues towards any given individual. And it will be found, with respect to this as to every correct definition, that the instances which seem to conflict with it are those which most confirm it, for if a moralist attempts, as some have done, to make out that mankind generally, though not any given individual, have a right to all the good we can do them, he at once, by that thesis, includes generosity and beneficence within the category of justice. He is obliged to say that our utmost exertions are *due* to our fellow creatures, thus assimilating them to a debt, or that nothing less can be a sufficient *return* for what society does for us, thus classing the case as one of gratitude, both of which are acknowledged cases of justice. Wherever there is a right, the case is one of justice, and not of the virtue of beneficence, and whoever does not place the distinction between justice and morality in general where we have now placed it will be found to make no distinction between them at all, but to merge all morality in justice.

Having thus endeavored to determine the distinctive elements which enter into the composition of the idea of justice, we are ready to enter on the inquiry, whether the feeling which accompanies the idea is attached to it by a special dispensation of nature, or whether it could have grown up by any known laws out of the idea itself, and, in particular, whether it can have originated in considerations of general expediency.

I conceive that the sentiment itself does not arise from anything which would commonly or correctly be termed an idea of expediency, but that, though the sentiment does not, whatever is moral in it does.

We have seen that the two essential ingredients in the sentiment of justice are the desire to punish a person who has done harm, and the knowledge or belief that there is some definite individual or individuals to whom harm has been done.

Now, it appears to me that the desire to punish a person who has done harm to some individual is a spontaneous outgrowth from two sentiments, both in the highest degree natural, and which either are or resemble instincts—the impulse of self-defense, and the feeling of sympathy.

It is natural to resent, and to repel or retaliate, any harm done or attempted against ourselves or against those with whom we sympathize. The origin of this sentiment it is not necessary here to discuss. Whether it be an instinct or a result of intelligence, it is, we know, common to all animal nature, for every animal tries to hurt those who have hurt, or who it thinks are about to hurt, itself or its young. Human beings, on this point, only differ from other animals in two particulars: first, in being capable of sympathizing, not solely with their offspring or, like some of the more noble animals, with some superior animal who is kind to them, but with all human and even with all sentient beings; secondly, in having a more developed intelligence, which gives a wider range to the whole of their sentiments, whether self-regarding or sympathetic. By virtue of his superior intelligence, even apart from his superior range of sympathy, a human being is capable of apprehending a community of interest between himself and the human society of which he forms a part, such that any conduct which threatens the security of the society generally is threatening to his own, and calls forth his instinct (if instinct it be) of self-defense. The same superiority of intelligence, joined to the power of sympathizing with human beings generally, enables him to attach himself to the collective idea of his tribe, his country, or mankind, in such a manner that any act hurtful to them raises his instinct of sympathy, and urges him to resistance.

The sentiment of justice, in that one of its elements which consists of the desire to punish, is thus, I conceive, the natural feeling of retaliation or vengeance, rendered by intellect and sympathy applicable to those injuries—that is, to those hurts—which wound us through, or in common with, society at large. This sentiment in itself has nothing moral in it; what is moral is the exclusive subordination of it to the social sympathies, so as to wait on and obey their call. For the natural feeling would make us resent indiscriminately whatever any one does that is disagreeable to us, but, when moralized by the social feeling, it only acts in the directions conformable to the general good: just persons resenting a hurt to society, though not otherwise a hurt to themselves, and not resenting a hurt to themselves, however painful, unless it be of the kind which society has a common interest with them in the repression of.

It is no objection against this doctrine to say that, when we feel our sentiment of justice outraged, we are not thinking of society at large, or of any collective interest, but only of the individual case. It is common enough, certainly, though the reverse of commendable, to feel resentment merely because we have suffered pain, but a person whose resentment is really a moral feeling—that is, who considers whether an act is blamable before he allows himself to resent it—such a person, though he may not say expressly to himself that he is standing up for the interest of society, certainly does feel that he is asserting a rule which is for the benefit of others as well as for his own. If he is not feeling this, if he is regarding the act solely as it affects him individually—he is not consciously just, he is not concerning himself about the justice of his actions. This is admitted even by anti-utilitarian moralists. When Kant (as before remarked) propounds as the fundamental principle of morals, "So act that thy rule of conduct might be adopted as a law by all rational beings," he virtually acknowledges that the interest of mankind collectively, or at least of mankind indiscriminately, must be in the mind of the agent when conscientiously deciding on the morality of the act. Otherwise he uses words without a meaning, for that a rule even of utter selfishness could not *possibly* be adopted by all rational beings—that there is any insuperable obstacle in the nature of things to its adoption—cannot be even plausibly maintained. To give any meaning to Kant's principle, the sense put upon it must be that we ought to shape our conduct by a rule which all rational beings might adopt *with benefit to their collective interest.*

To recapitulate: The idea of justice supposes two things—a rule of conduct and a sentiment which sanctions the rule. The first must be supposed common to all mankind, and intended for

their good; the other (the sentiment) is a desire that punishment may be suffered by those who infringe the rule. There is involved, in addition, the conception of some definite person who suffers by the infringement, whose rights (to use the expression appropriated to the case) are violated by it. And the sentiment of justice appears to me to be the animal desire to repel or retaliate a hurt or damage to one's self or to those with whom one sympathizes, widened so as to include all persons, by the human capacity of enlarged sympathy, and the human conception of intelligent self-interest. From the latter elements, the feeling derives its morality; from the former, its peculiar impressiveness and energy of self-assertion.

I have throughout treated the idea of a *right* residing in the injured person, and violated by the injury, not as a separate element in the composition of the idea and sentiment, but as one of the forms in which the other two elements clothe themselves. These elements are a hurt to some assignable person or persons on the one hand, and a demand for punishment on the other. An examination of our own minds, I think, will show that these two things include all that we mean when we speak of violation of a right. When we call any thing a person's right, we mean that he has a valid claim on society to protect him in the possession of it, either by the force of law, or by that of education and opinion. If he has what we consider a sufficient claim, on whatever account, to have something guaranteed to him by society, we say that he has a right to it. If we desire to prove that anything does not belong to him by right, we think this done as soon as it is admitted that society ought not to take measures for securing it to him, but should leave him to chance or to his own exertions. Thus a person is said to have a right to what he can earn in fair professional competition, because society ought not to allow any other person to hinder him from endeavoring to earn in that manner as much as he can. But he has not a right to three hundred a year, though he may happen to be earning it, because society is not called on to provide that he shall earn that sum. On the contrary, if he owns ten thousand pounds three-per-cent stock, he *has* a right to three hundred a year, because society has come under an obligation to provide him with an income of that amount.

To have a right then is, I conceive, to have something which society ought to defend me in the possession of. If the objector goes on to ask why it ought, I can give him no other reason than general utility. If that expression does not seem to convey a sufficient feeling of the strength of the obligation, nor to account for the peculiar energy of the feeling, it is because there goes to the composition of the sentiment, not a rational only but also an animal element—the thirst for retaliation, and his thirst derives its intensity, as well as its moral justification, from the extraordinarily important and impressive kind of utility which is concerned. The interest involved is that of security, to every one's feelings, the most vital of all interests. All other earthly benefits are needed by one person, not needed by another, and many of them can, if necessary, be cheerfully foregone, or replaced by something else. But security no human being can possibly do without; on it we depend for all our immunity from evil, and for the whole value of all and every good, beyond the passing moment, since nothing but the gratification of the instant could be of any worth to us if we could be deprived of everything the next instant by whoever was momentarily stronger than ourselves. Now, this most indispensable of all necessaries, after physical nutriment, cannot be had, unless the machinery for providing it is kept unintermittedly in active play. Our notion, therefore, of the claim we have on our fellow creatures to join in making safe for us the very groundwork of our existence, gathers feelings around it so much more intense than those concerned in any of the more common cases of utility, that the difference in degree (as is often the case in psychology) becomes a real difference in kind. The claim assumes that character of absoluteness, that apparent infinity and incommensurability with all other considerations, which constitute the distinction between the feeling of right and wrong and that of ordinary expediency and inexpediency. The feelings concerned are so powerful, and we count so positively on finding a responsive feeling in others (all being alike interested), that *ought* and *should* grow into *must,* and recognized indispensability becomes a moral necessity, analogous to physical, and often not inferior to it in binding force.

If the preceding analysis, or something resembling it, be not the correct account of the notion of justice, if justice be totally independent of utility, and be a standard *per se,* which the mind can recognize by simple introspection of itself—it is hard to understand why that internal oracle is so ambiguous, and why so many things appear either just or unjust, according to the light in which they are regarded.

We are continually informed that Utility is an uncertain standard, which every different person interprets differently, and that there is no safety but in the immutable, ineffaceable, and unmistakable dictates of Justice, which carry their evidence in themselves and are independent of the fluctuations of opinion. One would suppose from this that, on questions of justice, there could be no controversy, that, if we take that for our rule, its application to any given case could leave us in as little doubt as a mathematical demonstration. So far is this from being the fact, that there is as much difference of opinion and as much discussion about what is just as about what is useful to society. Not only have different nations and individuals different notions of justice but, in the mind of one and the same individual, justice is not some one rule, principle, or maxim, but many, which do not always coincide in their dictates, and, in choosing between which, he is guided either by some extraneous standard, or by his own personal predilections.

For instance: There are some who say that it is unjust to punish any one for the sake of example to others, that punishment is just, only when intended for the good of the sufferer himself. Others maintain the extreme reverse, contending that to punish persons who have attained years of discretion, for their own benefit, is despotism and injustice, since, if the matter at issue is solely their own good, no one has a right to control their own judgment of it, but that they may justly be punished to prevent evil to others, this being the exercise of the legitimate right of self-defense. Mr. Owen, again, affirms that it is unjust to punish at all, for the criminal did not make his own character; his education, and the circumstances which surrounded him, have made him a criminal, and for these he is not responsible. All these opinions are extremely plausible, and so long as the question is argued as one of justice simply, without going down to the principles which lie under justice, and are the source of its authority, I am unable to see how any of these reasoners can be refuted. For, in truth, every one of the three builds upon rules of justice of singling out an individual, and making him a sacrifice, without his consent, for other people's benefit. The second relies on the acknowledged justice of self-defense, and the admitted injustice of forcing one person to conform to another's notions of what constitutes his good. The Owenite invokes the admitted principle that it is unjust to punish any one for what he cannot help. Each is triumphant so long as he is not compelled to take into consideration any other maxims of justice than the one he has selected but, as soon as their several maxims are brought face to face, each disputant seems to have exactly as much to say for himself as the others. No one of them can carry out his own notion of justice without trampling upon another equally binding. These are difficulties, they have always been felt to be such, and many devices have been invented to turn rather than to overcome them. As a refuge from the last of the three, men imagined what they called the "freedom of the will," fancying that they could not justify punishing a man whose will is in a thoroughly hateful state, unless it be supposed to have come into that state through no influence of anterior circumstances. To escape from the other difficulties, a favorite contrivance has been the fiction of a contract, whereby, at some unknown period all the members of society engaged to obey the laws, and consented to be punished for any disobedience to them, thereby giving to their legislators the right, which it is assumed they would not otherwise have had, of punishing them, either for their own good or for that of society. This happy thought was considered to get rid of the whole difficulty, and to legitimate the infliction of punishment, in virtue of another received maxim of justice, *volenti non fit injuria,* "That is not unjust which is done with the consent of the person who is supposed to be hurt by it." I need hardly remark that, even if the consent were not a mere fiction, this maxim is not superior in authority to the others which it is brought in to supersede. It is, on the contrary, an instructive specimen of the loose and irregular manner in which supposed principles of justice grow up. This particular one evidently came in use as a help to the coarse exigencies of courts of law, which are sometimes obliged to be content with very uncertain presumptions, on account of the greater evils which would often arise from any attempt on their part to cut finer. But even courts of law are not able to adhere consistently to the maxim, for they allow voluntary engagements to be set aside on the ground of fraud, and sometimes on that of mere mistake or misinformation.

Again: when the legitimacy of inflicting punishment is admitted, how many conflicting conceptions of justice come to light in discussing the proper apportionment of punishments to offenses! No rule on the subject recommends itself so strongly to the primitive and spontaneous sentiment of justice, as the *lex talionis,* "An eye for an eye, and a tooth for a tooth." Though this principle of the Jewish and of the Mohammedan law

has been generally abandoned in Europe as a practical maxim, there is, I suspect, in most minds, a secret hankering after it and, when retribution accidentally falls on an offender in that precise shape, the general feeling of satisfaction evinced bears witness how natural is the sentiment to which this repayment in kind is acceptable. With many, the test of justice in penal infliction is that the punishment should be proportioned to the offence; meaning that it should be exactly measured by the moral guilt of the culprit (whatever be their standard for measuring moral guilt): the consideration, what amount of punishment is necessary to deter from the offense, having nothing to do with the question of justice, in their estimation: while there are others to whom that consideration is all in all; who maintain that it is not just, at least for man, to inflict on a fellow-creature, whatever may be his offences, any amount of suffering beyond the least that will suffice to prevent him from repeating, and others from imitating, his misconduct.

To take another example from a subject already once referred to. In a co-operative industrial association, is it just or not that talent or skill should give a title to superior remuneration? On the negative side of the question it is argued, that whoever does the best he can, deserves equally well, and ought not in justice to be put in a position of inferiority for no fault of his own; that superior abilities have already advantages more than enough, in the admiration they excite, the personal influence they command, and the internal sources of satisfaction attending them, without adding to these a superior share of the world's goods; and that society is bound in justice rather to make compensation to the less favoured, for this unmerited inequality of advantages, than to aggravate it. On the contrary side it is contended, that society receives more from the more efficient labourer; that his services being more useful, society owes him a larger return for them; that a greater share of the joint result is actually his work, and not to allow his claim to it is a kind of robbery; that if he is only to receive as much as others, he can only be justly required to produce as much, and to give a smaller amount of time and exertion, proportioned to his superior efficiency. Who shall decide between these appeals to conflicting principles of justice? Justice has in this case two sides to it, which it is impossible to bring into harmony, and the two disputants have chosen opposite sides; the one looks to what it is just that the individual should receive, the other to what it is just that the community should give.

Each, from his own point of view, is unanswerable; and any choice between them, on grounds of justice, must be perfectly arbitrary. Social utility alone can decide the preference.

How many, again, and how irreconcilable, are the standards of justice to which reference is made in discussing the repartition of taxation. One opinion is that payment to the State should be in numerical proportion to pecuniary means. Others think that justice dictates what they term graduated taxation; taking a higher percentage from those who have more to spare. In point of natural justice a strong case might be made for disregarding means altogether, and taking the same absolute sum (whenever it could be got) from every one: as the subscribers to a mess, or to a club, all pay the same sum for the same privileges, whether they can all equally afford it or not. Since the protection (it might be said) of law and government is afforded to, and is equally required by all, there is no injustice in making all buy it at the same price. It is reckoned justice, not injustice, that a dealer should charge to all customers the same price for the same article, not a price varying according to their means of payment. This doctrine, as applied to taxation, finds no advocates because it conflicts so strongly with man's feelings of humanity and of social expediency: but the principle of justice which it invokes is as true and as binding as those which can be appealed to against it. Accordingly it exerts a tacit influence on the line of defence employed for other modes of assessing taxation. People feel obliged to argue that the State does more for the rich than for the poor, as a justification for its taking more from them: though this is in reality not true, for the rich would be far better able to protect themselves, in the absence of law or government, than the poor, and indeed would probably be successful in converting the poor into their slaves. Others again, so far defer to the same conception of justice, as to maintain that all should pay an equal capitation tax for the protection of their persons (these being of equal value to all), and an unequal tax for the protection of their property, which is unequal. To this others reply, that the all of one man is as valuable to him as the all of another. From these confusions there is no other mode of extrication than the utilitarian.

Is, then, the difference between the Just and the Expedient a merely imaginary distinction? Have mankind been under a delusion in thinking that justice is a more sacred thing than policy, and that the latter ought only to be listened to after the former has been satisfied? By no means. The exposition we have given of the nature and origin of the sentiment recognizes a real distinction, and no one of those who profess the most sublime contempt for the consequences of actions as an element in their morality attaches more importance to the distinction than I do. While I dispute the pretensions of any theory which sets up an imaginary standard of justice not grounded on utility, I account the justice which is grounded on utility to be the chief part, and incomparably the most sacred and binding part, of all morality. Justice is a name for certain classes of moral rules which concern the essentials of human well-being more nearly, and are therefore of more absolute obligation, than any other rules for the guidance of life, and the notion which we have found to be of the essence of the idea of justice, that of a right residing in an individual, implies and testifies to this more binding obligation.

The moral rules which forbid mankind to hurt one another (in which we must never forget to include wrongful interference with each other's freedom) are more vital to human well-being than any maxims, however important, which only point out the best mode of managing some department of human affairs. They have also the peculiarity that they are the main element in determining the whole of the social feelings of mankind. It is their observance which alone preserves peace among human beings; if obedience to them were not the rule, and disobedience the exception, every one would see in every one else an enemy, against whom he must be perpetually guarding himself. What is hardly less important, these are the precepts which mankind have the strongest and the most direct inducements for impressing upon one another. By merely giving to each other prudential instruction or exhortation, they may gain, or think they gain, nothing; in inculcating on each other the duty of positive beneficence, they have an unmistakable interest, but far less in degree: a person may possibly not need the benefits of others, but he always needs that they should not do him hurt. Thus the moralities which protect every individual from being harmed by others, either directly or by being hindered in his freedom of pursuing his own good, are at once those which he himself has most at heart, and those which he has the strongest interest in publishing and enforcing by word and deed. It is by a person's observance of these, that his fitness to exist as one of the fellowship of human beings, is tested and decided; for on that depends his being a nuisance or not to those with whom he is in contact. Now it is these moralities primarily, which compose the obligations of justice. The most marked cases of injustice, and those which give the tone to the feeling of repugnance which characterizes the sentiment, are acts of wrongful aggression, or wrongful exercise of power over some one; the next are those which consist in wrongfully withholding from him something which is his due; in both cases, inflicting on him a positive hurt, either in the form of direct suffering, or of the privation of some good which he had reasonable ground either of a physical or of a social kind, for counting upon.

The same powerful motives which command the observance of these primary moralities, enjoin the punishment of those who violate them; and as the impulses of self-defence, of defence of others, and of vengeance, are all called forth against such persons, retribution, or evil for evil, becomes closely connected with the sentiment of justice, and is universally included in the idea. Good for good is also one of the dictates of justice; and this, though its social utility is evident, and though it carries with it a natural human feeling, has not at first sight that obvious connexion with hurt or injury, which, existing in the most elementary cases of just and unjust, and is the source of the characteristic intensity of the sentiment. But the connexion, though less obvious, is not less real. He who accepts benefits, and denies a return of them when needed, inflicts a real hurt, by disappointing one of the most natural and reasonable of expectations, and one which he must at least tacitly have encouraged, otherwise the benefits would seldom have been conferred. The important rank, among human evils and wrongs, of the disappointment of expectation, is shown in the fact that it constitutes the principal criminality of two such highly immoral acts as a breach of friendship and a breach of promise. Few hurts which human beings can sustain are greater, and none wound more, than when that on which they habitually and with full assurance relied, fails them in the hour of need; and few wrongs are greater than this mere withholding of good; none excite more resentment, either in the person suffering, or in a sympathizing spectator. The principle, therefore, of giving to each what they deserve—that is, good for good, as well as evil for evil—is not only included within the idea of Justice as we have defined it, but is a proper object of that intensity of sentiment which places the Just, in human estimation, above the simply Expedient.

Most of the maxims of justice current in the world, and commonly appealed to in its transactions, are simply instrumental to carrying into effect the principles of justice which we have now spoken of. That a person is only responsible for what he has done voluntarily, or could voluntarily have avoided, that it is unjust to condemn any person unheard, that the punishment ought to be proportioned to the offense, and the like— are maxims intended to prevent the just principle of evil for evil from being perverted to the infliction of evil without that justification. The greater part of these common maxims have come into use from the practice of courts of justice, which have been naturally led to a more complete recognition and elaboration than was likely to suggest itself to others, of the rules necessary to enable them to fulfill their double function, of inflicting punishment when due, and of awarding to each person his right.

That first of judicial virtues, impartiality, is an obligation of justice, partly for the reason last mentioned, as being a necessary condition of the fulfillment of the other obligations of justice. But this is not the only source of the exalted rank, among human obligations, of those maxims of equality and impartiality, which, both in popular estimation and in that of the most enlightened, are included among the precepts of justice. In one point of view, they may be considered as corollaries from the principles already laid down. If it is a duty to do to each according to his deserts, returning good for good as well as repressing evil by evil, it necessarily follows that we should treat all equally well (when no higher duty forbids) who have deserved equally well of *us,* and that society should treat all equally well who have deserved equally well of *it*—that is, who have deserved equally well absolutely. This is the highest abstract standard of social and distributive justice, towards which all institutions, and the efforts of all virtuous citizens, should be made in the utmost possible degree to converge. But this great moral duty rests upon a still deeper foundation, being a direct emanation from the first principle of morals, and not a mere logical corollary from secondary or derivative doctrines. It is involved in the very meaning of Utility, or the Greatest-happiness Principle. That principle is a mere form of words without rational signification, unless one person's happiness, supposed equal in degree (with the proper allowance made for kind), is counted for exactly as much as another's. Those conditions being supplied, Bentham's dictum, "Everybody to count for one, nobody for more than one," might be written under the principle of utility as an explanatory commentary.[2] The equal claim of everybody to happiness, in the estimation of the moralist and the legislator, involves an equal claim to all the means of happiness, except in so far as the inevitable conditions of human life, and the general interest, in which that of every individual is included, set limits to the maxim, and those limits ought to be strictly construed. As every other maxim of justice, so this, is by no means applied or held applicable universally; on the contrary, as I have already remarked, it bends to every person's ideas of social expediency. But, in whatever case it is deemed applicable at all, it is held to be the dictate of justice. All persons are deemed to have a *right* to equality of treatment, except when some recognized social expediency requires the reverse. And hence all social inequalities, which have ceased to be considered expedient, assume the character, not of simple inexpediency but of injustice, and appear so tyrannical that people are apt to wonder how they ever could have been tolerated, forgetful that they themselves perhaps tolerate other inequalities under an equally mistaken notion of expediency, the correction of which would make that which they approve seem quite as monstrous as what they have at last learnt to condemn. The entire history of social improvement has been a series of transitions, by which one custom or institution after another, from being a supposed primary necessity of social existence, has passed into the rank of an universally stigmatized injustice and tyranny. So it has been with the distinctions of slaves and freemen, nobles and serfs, patricians and plebeians, and so it will be, and in part already is, with the aristocracies of color, race, and sex.

It appears, from what has been said, that justice is a name for certain moral requirements which, regarded collectively, stand higher in the scale of social utility, and are therefore of more paramount obligation, than any others, though particular cases may occur in which some other social duty is so important as to overrule any one of the general maxims of justice. Thus, to save a life, it may not only be allowable, but a duty, to steal, or take by force, the necessary food or medicine, or to kidnap and compel to officiate, the only qualified medical practitioner. In such cases, we do not call any thing justice which is not a virtue, we usually say, not that justice must give way to some other moral principle, but that what is just in ordinary cases is, by reason of that other principle, not just in the particular case. By this useful accommodation of language, the character of indefeasibility attributed to just is kept up, and we are saved from the necessity of maintaining that there can be laudable injustice.

The considerations which have now been adduced, resolve, I conceive, the only real difficulty in the utilitarian theory of morals. It has always been evident that all cases of justice are also cases of expediency; the difference is in the peculiar sentiment which attaches to the former, as contradistinguished from the latter. If this characteristic sentiment has been sufficiently accounted for, if there is no necessity to assume for it any peculiarity of origin, if it is simply the natural feeling of resentment, moralized by being made coextensive with the demands of social good, and if this feeling not only does but ought to exist in all the classes of cases to which the idea of justice corresponds—that idea no longer presents itself as a stumbling-block to the utilitarian ethics. Justice remains the appropriate name for certain social utilities which are vastly more important, and therefore more absolute and imperative, than any others are as a class (though not more so than others may be in particular cases), and which therefore ought to be, as well as naturally are, guarded by a sentiment not only different in degree, but also in kind, distinguished from the milder feeling which attaches to the mere idea of promoting human pleasure or convenience, at once by the more definite nature of its commands, and by the sterner character of its sanctions.

NOTES

1. See this point enforced and illustrated by Professor Bain, in an admirable chapter (entitled "The Ethical Emotions, or the Moral Sense") of the second of the two treatises composing his elaborate and profound work on the Mind.

2. This implication, in the first principle of the utilitarian scheme, of perfect impartiality between persons is regarded by Mr. Herbert Spencer (in his *Social Statics*) as a disproof of the pretensions of utility to be a sufficient guide to right, since (he says) the principle of utility presupposes the anterior principle, that everybody has an equal right to happiness. It may be more correctly described as supposing that equal amounts of happiness are equally desirable, whether felt by the same or by different persons. This, however, is not a *pre-*supposition, not a premise needful to support the principle of utility, but the very principle itself; for what is the principle of utility, if it be not that "happiness" and "desirable" are synonymous terms? If there is any anterior principle implied, it can be no other than this—that the truths of arithmetic are applicable to the valuation of happiness, as of all other measurable quantities.

[Mr. Herbert Spencer, in a private communication on the subject of the preceding note, objects to being considered an opponent of Utilitarianism, and states that he regards happiness as the ultimate end of morality, but deems that end only partially attainable by empirical generalizations from the observed results of conduct, and completely attainable only by deducing, from the laws of life and the conditions of existence, what kinds of action necessarily tend to produce happiness, and what kinds to produce unhappiness. With the exception of the word "necessarily," I have no dissent to express from this doctrine, and (omitting that word) I am not aware that any modern advocate of Utilitarianism is of a different opinion. Bentham certainly, to whom, in the *Social Statics,* Mr. Spencer particularly referred, is, least of all writers, chargeable with unwillingness to deduce the effect of actions on happiness from the laws of human nature and the universal conditions of human life. The common charge against him is of relying too exclusively upon such deductions, and declining altogether to be bound by the generalizations from specific experience which Mr. Spencer thinks that utilitarians generally confine themselves to. My own opinion (and, as I collect, Mr Spencer's) is, that in ethics, as in all other branches of scientific study, the consilience of the results of both these processes, each corroborating and verifying the other, is requisite to give to any general proposition the kind and degree of evidence which constitutes scientific proof.]

NICHOLAS RESCHER

Analysis of the Utilitarian Formula*

1. THE PRINCIPLE OF UTILITY IS A TWO-FACTOR CRITERION

Suppose that some three particular persons, Messrs *A, B,* and *C,* can be given the utility shares (a), (b), and (c), respectively, in accordance with either Scheme I or Scheme II:[1]

Share	Scheme I	Scheme II
(a)	3 units	2 units
(b)	3	2
(c)	3	6

Which scheme represents the superior mode of distribution? Scheme II yields "the greater good": it distributes ten units as compared with the nine of its rival. Scheme I yields a greater advantage in goods for "the greater number": two persons gain by its adoption and only one loses. The example brings out the fact that *the principle of utility is a two-factor criterion* ("greater good," "greater number"), and that these two factors can in given cases work against one another. There is thus nothing in the principle of utility itself to help us in making—let alone in dictating a particular outcome of—a choice between Scheme I and Scheme II. The principle unqualified is patently incomplete as an effective means for deciding between alternative distributions of a good.

Some utilitarians have, at least seemingly, gone from a two-factor to a one-factor criterion, placing their sole reliance upon "the greater good," dropping the last four words from the utilitarian formula. (Bentham himself inclined to this view in his later days,[2] reasoning, along lines shortly to be described, that the greater good *requires* greater numbers.) But despite its greater logical tidiness, the view that the eligibility of a proposed action with its consequent distribution of utility turns solely on the *total* good involved, without

any regard whatsoever to the *pattern of its distribution,* is pretty obviously unacceptable. On the other hand, it would obviously not do to place, in a burst of democratic enthusiasm, an *exclusive* reliance on "the greater number."[3] For consider the distributions:

Share	Scheme I	Scheme II
(a)	5 units	4 units
(b)	3	4
(c)	3	3
(d)	1	3
(e)	1	3

Doubtless the greater number of recipients would opt for Scheme I and would vote for its adoption as against Scheme II, but it is doubtful (to say the least) that the first mode of division is to be preferred. In such cases, even the most ardent of democratic theoreticians have ever seen fit to safeguard the interests of minorities in ways that preclude an automatic adoption of schemes of type I.[4]

One traditional objection to utilitarianism articulated along these lines is presented in the choice between a less populous world with a higher per capita average utility, and a more populous world with a lower per capita average utility, say between:

Scheme I	Scheme II
	(f)
	(e)
	(d)
(c)	(c)
(b)	(b)
(a)	(a)

A contemplation of these alternatives should force an adherent of the principle of utility to decide whether by "the greatest good" he is to mean the greatest *total* good or the greast good

*From Nicholas Rescher, *Distributive Justice: A Constructive Critique of the Utilitarian Theory of Distribution* (Indianapolis: Bobbs–Merrill, 1966), pp. 25-46. Reprinted by permission of the author and publisher.

per capita (i.e., the greatest *average* good). That proto-utilitarian William Paley wrote:

A larger portion of happiness is enjoyed amongst *ten* persons, possessing the means of healthy subsistence, than can be produced by five persons, under every advantage of power, affluence, and luxury . . .; it follows, that the quantity of happiness in a given district, although it is possible it may be increased the number of inhabitants remaining the same, is chiefly and most naturally affected by alteration of the numbers: that, consequently, the decay of population is the greatest evil that a state can suffer; and the improvement of it the object which ought, in all countries, to be aimed at, in preference to every other political purpose whatsoever.[5]

Other—and nowadays surely more common—sentiments go the other way. Thus C.D. Broad writes:

If Utilitarianism be true it would be one's duty to try to increase the numbers of a community, even though one reduced the average total happiness of the members, so long as the total happiness in the community would be in the least increased. It seems perfectly plain to me that this kind of action, so far from being a duty, would quite certainly be wrong.[6]

2. A "UTILITY FLOOR" IS NEEDED

Let us try the effect of one facile amendment of the principle of utility. One of the standard textbook objections to the principle is presented by the following variant of the previous example:

Scheme I	Scheme II
(c)	(c)
(b)	(b)
(a)	(a)

Here Scheme II not only yields "the greater good," but works to the advantage of "a greater number," since two of the three people involved are obvious beneficiaries of its adoption. But is it reasonable that we should in *all* such cases be prepared to sacrifice an "individual interest" in "the general benefit," as the principle of utility says we must do? The answer to this question cannot be other than *no!* We would surely not want to subject one individual to unspeakable suffering to give some insignificantly small benefit to many others (even an innumerable myriad of them.)[7] Actual privation offends our sense of justice in a more serious way than do mere inequities.

These considerations suggest adding to the principle of utility another qualifying clause, a "principle of catastrophe-prevention" stipulating a minimal *utility floor* for all individuals below which no one should be pressed. The principle at issue may be regarded as being more or less built in to the very conception of a genuinely "minimally acceptable" share of good. For we would not conceive of a given level in just *this* way unless we were prepared to do battle for the rule that an exalted priority should be given to reducing to the lowest feasible number the people who receive less than this share. We might thus add to the initial principle the proviso: *provided that nobody receives less of "the good" than a certain (i.e., some plausible) minimum amount.* Clearly one of the most basic elements of our concept of justice is to minimize the number of persons in a state of genuine *deprivation* regarding their share in the available pool of utility. Diminishing the number of those who simply do not have enough is a more fundamental element of the concept of justice than diminishing the gap between the "haves" and the "have-nots."[8] And although the idea of an acceptable minimum level has traditionally been stressed primarily in survival contexts, the idea has long been applied in such other connections as, for example, education.

The utilitarians of the eighteenth and early nineteenth centuries recognized and accepted this principle, and it led them to abandon, in the economic (but not the political) sphere, the egalitarianism to which they were otherwise committed:

If the Utilitarians rejected absolute equalitarianism, it was not because they considered society as naturally hierarchical, but because they thought the quantity of subsistence actually available was not sufficient to allow all the individuals actually existing to live . . . *adequately.*[9]

Apart from such qualification, the principle of utility is clearly deficient. It is perfectly conceivable that at some historical juncture an institution of slavery, for example, could conduce to the greater good of a greater number; but we shall not be prepared to let this fact count decisively on its behalf. Again, considerations of a cognate sort led to the economic doctrine that an economy must afford every participant a "living wage."[10]

3. AN EQUITY PRINCIPLE IS NEEDED

But the amendment proposed in the preceding section will not of itself suffice. For even when one inserts such a "utility floor" for the purpose of catastrophe-prevention, one does not provide for cases of the following sort. We have now to do with five people, Messrs *A, B, C, D,* and *E,* whose respective utility shares for two schemes of distribution are represented by (a), (b), (c), (d), and (e).

Scheme I   Scheme II

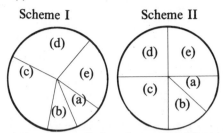

Let it be supposed that the acceptable minimal level is just exactly represented by the shares (a) and (b) on Scheme I, so that there is no question of anyone's being pressed "beneath the floor." Also the *total amounts* of utility (represented by the sizes of the two circles) may be supposed to be the same. Now the principle of utility dictates the preferability of Scheme I, since it assumes "the greater good of the greater number" of persons involved, viz., the recipients of shares (c)-(e). But even a rudimentary sensitivity to equity and justice revolts against this conclusion. For why should the hapless recipients of shares (a)-(b) be pressed to the floor in order to make the "rich" who receive (c)-(e) yet richer?

What is clearly needed, over and above the aforementioned utility floor, is some added principle of equity in the distribution of utility shares, some reference to the central tendency of utility allocations that will take equitableness into account. A reasonable (and in other contexts familiar) procedure might be *a rule of least square deviation from the average.* The adoption of such an equity principle would iron out difficulties of the type illustrated by the previous example.

Consider such a case as that of choosing between giving Messrs *A, B, C, D,* and *E* one of the following utility distributions:

Share	Scheme I	Scheme II
(a)	7 units	6 units
(b)	7	6
(c)	7	6
(d)	2	10
(e)	2	12

From the angle of *total* utility, Scheme II is superior. But Scheme I gives "the greater number" of persons (viz., 3 of them) a greater utility share than they would have in Scheme II. Also, from the standpoint of central tendency, Scheme I is

superior (the sum of the squares of deviations from the average is *30* for Scheme I but *32* for Scheme II). But, on the other hand, in adopting Scheme II in place of Scheme I, Messrs *A, B,* and *C* are each made to undergo *a trivially small sacrifice in utility in order that a substantial benefit can accrue to* D *and* E. It is clear that *if the claims of the individuals concerned are equal,* Scheme II is definitely to be preferred.[11]

Consider the alternative schemes of utility allocation in which Messrs *X, Y,* and *Z* get shares (a), (b), and (c), respectively:

Share	Scheme I	Scheme II
(a)	5 units	9 units
(b)	6	1 (=the "floor")
(c)	10	12

Note that Scheme II represents the greater good (22 units as compared with 21), and represents a greater good for a greater number (viz., Messrs *X* and *Z* are comparative beneficiaries in its adoption). But is Scheme II unqualifiedly preferable and its selection morally mandatory—regardless of who it is that is doing the selecting? (We tend to react differently if the choice of the second scheme is made by *Y* rather than by *X*.[12] The doctrinaire utilitarian has to write this difference in reaction off to foolish sentimentality.) Actually, the adoption of an equity principle of the sort under discussion would rationalize the selection of the first—patently fairer—allocation scheme. One could implement the principle by introducing the idea of an "effective average" which would discount the actual average by some function of the deviations from it (say by half of the standard deviation).[13] The concept of an effective average will be treated in greater detail in the next section.

It deserves to be stressed again at this point that we are dealing with distributions of "utility" viewed retrospectively, and not with distributions of some storable good viewed prospectively. In the distributions we are concerned with there is (by hypothesis) no question of redistribution (utility cannot be alienated or transferred, and even if it could, this would be precluded by our retroactive approach). This is important, because in ruling out redistributions we also rule out mutual agreements to reallocate in the common interest. If we were dealing with, say, money rather than utility, then consider, in this changed light, the case of a choice between giving Messrs *A, B,* and *C* shares (a), (b), and (c), respectively:

Share	Scheme I	Scheme II
(a)	3 units	10 units
(b)	3	1
(c)	3	1

Our own preference on the basis of the preceding discussion is for Scheme I (where the "effective average" is *3*). But, of course, if redistribution were possible, *A* would work out a "mutual assistance pact" with *B* and *C* to make a payoff of *3* units to each of them for going along with the adoption of Scheme II, thereby in effect bringing into the picture

Share	Scheme III
(a)	4 units
(b)	4
(c)	4

which is clearly preferable to either of the preceding schemes by *any* reasonable standard (ours not excluded). The distributor who would adopt Scheme II over against I with a view to laying the basis for a shift to III could plausibly be said to serve the interests of distributive justice. The considerations upon which our preference for I over II is based must be understood to include the ruling out of such a shift to (the nonenvisaged) alternative III.

In this way, it may be seen that the considerations of our discussion—while not in principle restricted to "utility," but applicable more generally—rest essentially on the stipulation that the set of alternative distributions under comparative evaluation be postulated as complete, without any widening of the range of alternatives by the possibility of redistribution.

4. THE CONCEPT OF AN EFFECTIVE AVERAGE

In the preceding section we introduced the concept of an effective average (EA):

$$EA = average - 1/2\ \sigma \text{ (standard deviation from the average)}$$

The role of this concept is simple: paradigmatically, it is to systematize the intuitive feeling that of the two distributions

Share	Scheme I	Scheme II
(a)	2 units	1 unit
(b)	2	1
(c)	2	3
(d)	2	3
(e)	2	3

Scheme I is superior from the angle of distributive justice to Scheme II, this being so despite the facts (1) that Scheme I yields a lesser average share (2 as contrasted with 2.2 units) and (2) that in contrasting Scheme I with Scheme II, there are two 1-unit losers as compared with three 1-unit gainers, so that Scheme II yields the greater good of a greater number. From the standpoint of our "effective average," however, the advantage lies with Scheme I (2.00 as contrasted with 1.71). The purpose of this section is to exhibit some significant features of this concept of an effective average.

The key feature of the effective average as a criterion for comparison is that it can underwrite the preferability of one distribution to another without requiring that the preferred distribution be a Pareto improvement upon its competitor. Moreover, it provides a systematic grounding for two seemingly competing intuitions as to the nature of distributive justice, viz., that in certain cases inequalities can "pay for themselves" by resulting in a situation that conduces to the general good, and, moreover, that "a lower average income, with greater equality, may make a happier society than a higher average income with less."[14] An example of the second sort of situation has just been provided. An illustration of the first sort of situation is:

Share	Scheme I	Scheme II
(a)	3 units	2.9 units
(b)	3	4
(c)	3	4
(d)	3	4
(e)		

One qualification must immediately be made. The EA is a meaningful basis of comparison, and should in fact be regarded as being defined, only when it is not too far removed from the average —say, when EA lies within 50 per cent of the actual average A. This means that we must have

$$EA \geq 1/2\ A$$

or equivalently, since EA = A – 1/2 σ (where σ = the standard deviation from the average), we must have

$$\sigma \leq A$$

that is, the standard deviation from the average is no larger than the average itself. Only under this condition should the conception of an "effective average" be applied. Thus such distributions as

Share	Scheme I	Scheme II
(a)	0 units	0 units
(b)	0	1
(c)	3	8

have no EA on this basis. In the case of very uneven distributions, when an EA is not defined, other tools must be employed. We shall not pursue the matter further here.

Compare the distributions:

Share	Scheme I	Scheme II	Scheme III	Scheme IV
(a)	2 units	0 units	x units	3 units
(b)	2	3	3	3
(c)	2	3	3	3

It is reasonably plain on the basis of intuitive considerations that Scheme I is preferable to Scheme II (since it divides the same total more equitably) and that Scheme IV is preferable to Scheme I (since everyone fares uniformly better by it). Now when $x = 0$, then III = II; and when $x = 3$, then III = IV. The question thus arises; As x is increased from 0 to 3, at what value of x does III become preferable to I? Our EA calculation yields this value as $x = 1.24$. The reader is invited to measure this result against his own intuitions, realizing that in such a matter, as elsewhere, intuition is not a precision instrument yielding exact results.

An interesting use of the concept of an effective average is its application to the analysis of income distribution data. Consider the tabulation given below, derived from two sources: (1) U. S. Bureau of the Census, *Historical Statistics of the United States* (Washington, D.C., 1960), and (2) *idem., Statistical Abstract of the United States,* 86th edn. (Washington, D.C., 1965):

Average income for families and unattached individuals in the USA (In 1,000's of 1950 dollars)

Year	Actual Average Amount	Actual Average % increase over 1929	Effective Average Amount	Effective Average % increase over 1929
1929	3.36	0	1.61	0
1941	3.66	9%	1.81	12%
1950	4.44	32%	2.33	45%
1962	5.78	72%	3.10	93%

The fact of a significant disparity in the distribution of income is revealed by the discrepancy between the actual and the effective average. On the other hand, the comparative lessening of this disparity is indicated by the significantly more rapid increase of the effective average as compared with the actual average.

Our contention is that an EA measure of this sort, when defined, appears to provide a good basis of comparison, and thus an acceptable solution of the "meshing problem" in the relative assessment of the merit of greater or lesser *amounts* versus greater or lesser *equity* in alternative distributions.

5. THE NEED FOR A SOLUTION TO THE "MESHING PROBLEM"

In the face of the considerations adduced so far, it might seem plausible to adopt the *maximin criterion* of choice, giving preference to that alternative distribution which has the largest minimum share.[15] But consider the following two distribution schemes (with, say, 1 unit as the utility "floor"):

Share	Scheme I	Scheme II
(a)	1.9 units	7 units
(b)	3.1	3
(c)	3	2
(d)	3	2
(e)	3	2
(f)	3	2
(g)	3	2

Scheme II has the greater minimum, but is, pretty obviously, not to be preferred to Scheme I.[16]

Suppose we are confronted with the choice between two alternatives schemes of utility allocation, as follows:[17]

Share	Scheme I	Scheme II
Made very happy	30 people	20 people
Made fairly happy	20	40
Made rather unhappy	45	35
Made very unhappy (i.e., pushed "below the floor")	5	5

Here, if Scheme I is adopted, the total number of happy people is decreased by 10, as compared with Scheme II, but the number of people made very happy is increased comparably. It is clear that *if the claims of the individuals are equal* we are still confronted with a possible conflict between "greater good" on the one hand and "greater number" on the other. For the orthodox utilitarian, this gap remains to be bridged—or perhaps simply faced and accepted as irresolvable at the theoretical level.

The problem was stated with model clarity by John Hospers in his ethics textbook:

The twentieth-century utilitarians ... have always interpreted the classical utilitarians as meaning that one should aim at the largest total quantity of intrinsic good, with no qualifications or additions saying that quantity of good is to be sacrificed when a more nearly equal distribution can thereby be achieved. (Why then did Bentham and Mill include the phrase "for the greatest number"? Probably to insure that every person was included in the calculations of the greatest total quantity.) Our problem, then, is this: does this classical utilitarian account of the matter (largest total quantity of good, with everybody being figured into the total) need revision in the light of the principal of equal distribution which we have said is included in our idea of justice?

Most thoughtful people, it seems, desire both ideals to be achieved: they would like to have a society in which the largest total *amount* of good is present, and if they had to choose between a society containing more good and a society containing less, they would unhesitatingly choose the first. Similarly, however, they would like to have a society in which good is, as nearly as possible, *equally distributed* (with exceptions we shall take up in the next section); and if they had to choose between a society in which good was equally distributed and one in which there were glaring inequalities, they would choose the first. The question is, what is to be done when the two ideals conflict? Are we—as the classical utilitarians would say, or at any rate as we are taking them to mean—always to select the alternative that contains the maximum total quantity of good, irrespective of its distribution? Or are we, as the supporters of justice would say, to select the alternative that contains the most nearly equal distribution of good, regardless of the amount? Or are we somehow to mediate between the two views by considering *both* principles and by believing that the right act should embody them both—the greatest total possible good that is compatible with the most nearly equal distribution thereof? It is probably fair to say that most people, once they have thought of it, would consider the third alternative—the one bringing in both principles—to be the best.[18]

This "meshing problem" of balancing the total amount of good at issue in a given putative distribution against the fairness of the distribution in cases where these two desiderata cut against one another is one which utilitarians (and non-utilitarians, for that matter) have never resolved satisfactorily. However, its analysis seems to be a pressing task for an adequate substantive theory of distributive justice. Our proposed concept of an *effective average* is offered as a tentative step toward its solution. Be this as it may, the analysis has, I believe, established one important and essentially negative result. The principle of utility cannot of itself play the part of a final arbiter in a selection among alternative distributions. The application of the principle involves choices among alternatives whose resolution requires recourse to a further and at least equally fundamental principle. As Sidgwick already clearly saw ... the principle of utility fails us in its purported role as an ultimate recourse because we cannot avoid choices among alternative modes of implementing the utilitarian principle itself, choices, therefore, of such a character that they cannot in the nature of things be settled by the principle itself.

6. THE QUESTION OF CLAIMS

Thus far we have emphasized what might be called the domestic difficulties of the principle of utility (greater good *versus* greater number). But there are also its foreign difficulties vis-á-vis the concepts of fairness and equity. These may be illustrated by contrasting the following two utility allocations:

Share	Scheme I	Scheme II
(a)	4 units	4 units
(b)	4	3
(c)	4	3
(d)	1	2

From the orthodox utilitarian standpoint, all the advantages lie with Scheme I: (i) It represents the greater *total* good (13 contrasted with 12 units) and the greater *average* good (3.25 as contrasted with 3.00 units). (ii) It represents a "greater good for a greater number" since two individuals are beneficiaries (1-unit beneficiaries) of its adoption and only one individual is the lower (1-unit loser) thereby. But on the other hand, *supposing that the individuals who are to be recipients of these four shares all have equal claims,* a very positive point of merit on the part of Scheme II must be recognized: it is significantly more equitable.[19] If one is prepared, in cases such as this, to give weight to the fairness of distributions, even when this goes against the factors operative in the principle of utility ("greater good," "greater number"), one is, in effect, abandoning this principle as the ultimate arbiter in matters of distributive justice by introducing a wholly new consideration of which the principle takes no account.

The point we are making here is certainly not new, being one of the standard objections to utilitarianism on the part of nineteenth-century critics. Herbert Spencer put the matter as follows:

"Everybody to count for one, nobody for more than one." Does this mean that, in respect of whatever is proportioned out, each is to have the same share whatever his character, whatever his conduct? Shall he if passive have as much as if active? Shall he if useless have as much as if useful? Shall he if criminal have as much as if virtuous? If the distribution is to be made without reference to the natures and deeds of the recipients, then it must be shown that a system which equalizes, as far as it can, the treatment of good and bad, will be beneficial. If the distribution is not to be indiscriminate, then the formula disappears. The something distributed must be approportioned otherwise than by equal division. There must be adjustment of amounts to deserts; and we are left in the dark as to the mode of adjustment—we have to find other guidance.[20]

In the case of an unequal group of claims, the difficulties grow more acute than ever. Here we would in general have to confront a given schedule of (legitimate) claims and a set of alternative distributions among which to effect a (rationally defensible) preferential selection. An example would be as follows:

Individuals involved	Schedule of claims	Scheme I	Scheme II	Scheme III
A	4			
B	4	5 units	8 units	1 unit
C	8	5	4	5
		6	4	10

In such a case we would (at any rate as long as the total amounts being distributed are the same) clearly prefer that distribution which has the least sum of squares-of-differences-from-the-schedule, that is Scheme I in the example. But what in the case of a tie by this criterion, as in the example:

Individuals	Claims	Scheme I	Scheme II
		Distributions	
A	2	3 units	0 units
B	3	1	4
C	4	2	2

Here we would surely prefer the intrinsically more equitable distribution, that is, the one with the larger effective average—i.e., Scheme I.

The standpoint at which we have thus arrived supports the charge of shortcomings that we had earlier found it necessary to make against the utilitarian standard for assessing distributions. The principle is involved in an internal fission which leads to the need for further choices in its application in certain cases. These choices, being choices that arise in the *application of* the utilitarian principle, cannot be settled by the principle itself. They require an outside appeal—to such concepts as equity or fairness in accommodating claims—and in this way point to the fact that the utilitarian standard must be viewed as representing one factor among others. It simply will not do to regard the principle of utility as an ultimate and complete basis for a theory of distributive justice. Furthermore, we have found the direction in which one must look to find those necessary further factors of distributive justice, namely, considerations of equity in the accommodation of claims.[21] The focus of attention must thus shift to this matter of claims.

NOTES

1. We are to think of the indicated shares *not* as representing marginal utility increments added to an otherwise fixed initial amount, but as the *total resultant* utility distribution after whatever distributing mechanism may be supposed operative has done its work.

2. Compare F. Y. Edgeworth, *Mathematical Psychics,* pp. 117-118. Edgeworth strongly endorses the alteration, remarking: "The principle of greatest happiness may have gained its popularity, but lost its meaning, by the addition 'of the greatest number.' "

3. We wholly ignore the ambiguity that is singled out by the question "Greater number of *what?*" i.e., do we have an anthropocentric form of utilitarianism, where only humans (perhaps better, *intelligent creatures*) count, or a universalistic form, where other sentient beings are also included?

4. It is important to qualify by safeguards of this sort the *census* technique by which D. Braybrooke and C. E. Lindblom seek to replace the classic utilitarian *calculus* in their recent book, *A Strategy of Decision* (New York: The Free Press of Glencoe, 1963).

5. William Paley, *The Principles of Moral and Political Philosophy* (7th edn., London: Baldwin & Co., 1790), Vol. II, Book VI, ch. 2, pp. 346-347. Bentham, Godwin, and most early utilitarians side with Paley here. See E. Halévy, *The Growth of Philosophic Radicalism,* tr. Mary Morris, pp. 218-221. Compare also Henry Sidgwick, *The Methods of Ethics,* pp. 415-416.

6. C. D. Broad, *Five Types of Ethical Theory* (London: Routledge & Kegan Paul, 1930), p. 250.

7. A somewhat out-of-the-way example of this line of reasoning is provided by the argument of some modern theologians that creation as a whole is not worthwhile if it has the consequence of eternal damnation for some creatures.

8. "There is a bottom level of instrumental good (money, or in this instance, food) below which equality is useless because it is equality in nothingness, or something so near to nothingness that it would be of no use to any of the recipients. No good would be achieved by requiring equality under such conditions. On the one hand, a person who said, 'I know we'll all starve, but we must share equally anyway' would really be running the equality principle into the ground! Precisely the

same thing has been alleged of a socialistic economy: though it provides near-equality, the incentive is so low and, human nature being what it is, the system is inevitably so inefficient that after a while there will not be much left to divide equally: we shall have what has been called a state of 'splendidly equalized destitution.' *If* it could be shown that an economy characterized by equal distribution produced this result, such an economy would be almost as useless to its members as the situation of ten men on the ice floe sharing substarvation rations." John Hospers, *Human Conduct* (New York: Harcourt, Brace & World, 1961), p. 428. (This and the following excerpts from John Hospers, *Human Conduct,* are reprinted with the permission of the publisher.) On the conception of a utility floor, see also B. de Jouvenel, *The Ethics of Redistribution,* pp. 23-24 and 85-88.

9.   E. Halévy, *The Growth of Philosophic Radicalism,* tr. Mary Morris, p. 502.

10.   For a detailed historical and ethical treatment of the living-wage concept, see John A. Ryan, *A Living Wage* (New York: Macmillan, 1906; 2nd edn., 1920).

11.   The point that we may prefer the distribution of a lesser total with greater equality is developed with force and clarity in John Hospers, *Human Conduct,* pp. 428-429. It is, of course, based on a fundamental commitment diametrically opposed to the hard-nosed maximize-the-total-and-distribution-be-damned line of utilitarianism espoused by F. Y. Edgeworth, who held that J. S. Mill "darkens the subject (as many critics seem to have felt), by imposing a condition of equality of distribution" (*Mathematical Psychics,* p. 118).

12.   Compare W. D. Ross, *Foundations of Ethics,* pp. 72, 75.

13.   This formula would yield an effective average of 5.9 for Scheme I and of 5.8 for Scheme II.

14.   R. H. Tawney, *Equality* (4th edn., London: Allen & Unwin, 1952), p. 129. The concept of an effective average thus serves (but more effectively) the same equalizing purpose that is served by the idea of a (utility) *ceiling,* in analogy with that of a *floor,* introduced by B. de Jouvenel. See his *The Ethics of Redistribution,* pp. 23-28, 86-87.

15.   This is not a version but a revision of utilitarianism. Its sole advocate known to me is (apparently) Marcus G.

Singer. See pp. 202-203 of his *Generalization in Ethics* (New York: Alfred A. Knopf, 1961).

16.   An analogous counterexample will serve against the *minimax criterion* that minimizes the maximum. A somewhat greater (but still finite) amount of ingenuity is needed to provide a counterexample to the maximin-cum-minimax combination of these two principles.

17.   I adapt this example from A. C. Ewing, "Political Differences," *The Philosophical Quarterly,* XIII (1963), 333-343 (see p. 338). Note that the numbers here represent numbers of people, and not utility units as in preceding charts.

18.   John Hospers, *Human Conduct,* p. 426. Note that any such defect in the utilitarian principle of distribution affects the rule-version just as much as the act-version of the theory.

19.   For Scheme I, the sum of the squares of the deviations from the average is 6.75. For Scheme II this factor only amounts to 2. The "effective average" for Scheme I is 2.60 contrasted with 2.65 for Scheme II. As a matter of incidental interest, it is worth noting that if this same general pattern of the distribution at issue is extended to involve a greater number of other people, the type-I distribution becomes preferable. For example, contrast:

Share	Scheme I	Scheme II
(a)	4 units	4 units
(b)	4	3
(c)	4	3
(d)	4	3
(e)	4	3
(f)	1	2

Now Scheme I is preferable to II since its *effective average* is the larger (2.9 as against 2.7).

20.   Herbert Spencer, *The Data of Ethics* (New York: D. Appleton & Co., 1879), sec. 84.

21.   When Saint Paul wrote "Masters, give unto your servants that which is just and equal" (Colossians 4:1), the "equal" at issue is not to be construed as "equal to what all the others get" but as "equal to his deserts."

BRIAN BARRY

Justice and Fairness*

PROCEDURAL FAIRNESS, BACKGROUND FAIRNESS AND LEGAL JUSTICE

PROCEDURAL FAIRNESS

To say that a procedure is being fairly operated is to say that the formalities which define the procedure have been correctly adhered to. A fair race, for example, is one in which the competitors start together (nobody 'jumps the gun'), do not elbow one another or take short cuts, and in which the first person past the line and not disqualified is recognized as the winner; a fair fight is one in which the contestants are not allowed to get away with fouls; and so on. Fairness in the operation of the authoritative determination procedure has more or less content according to the detail with which the procedure is specified in any given case. A 'fair trial', for example, must satisfy elaborate procedural safeguards, whereas a 'fair administrative decision' need mean only that the official taking it was impartial or 'fair minded'.[1] In terms of formalities an administrative tribunal or an official inquiry occupy an intermediate position.[2] The fair application of a chance procedure requires the procedure to be genuinely random (a true die, for example) so as to give everyone a 'fair chance'. A 'fair election' rules out ballot stuffing, double voting, miscounts, etc.

This leaves the first three procedures. 'Fair war' has no use (though 'just war' has): 'All's fair in love and war.' The explanation is that war does not specify rules to be followed before what is happening can be called 'war'; indeed, it is the negation of orderly procedures.[3] War in its fullest sense is an attempt to impose one's will on another by violence; as soon as conventions come in (if you capture place *A* or man *B* you win) an element of contest enters in. Winning becomes not merely *being in a position* to impose your will but *being allowed* to impose your will in virtue of

having satisfied a certain standard.[4] A duel is a contest just as a boxing match is, because if it settles, say, who gets the lady, it does so by convention: 'Let the best man win.'[5]

The notion of 'fair discussion on merits' also has no obvious use, again because there are no prescribed formalities to be observed; nor has 'fair bargaining' in general any use, since if threats are included it is simply the verbal counterpart to combat. Under more restricted conditions, however, considerations of procedural fairness can be invoked. Thus, in a context where threats are supposed to be ruled out it is 'unfair' to make threats. More subtly, in a context which is supposed to be one of 'perfect competition' it is unfair for a rich company to sell below cost in order to drive out its competitors. 'Fair trade', the traditional name for all restrictive practices aimed at protecting the inefficient producer and retailer, in theory usually means this, while in practice it normally degenerates into an attempt to guarantee 'cost plus' all around.[6] It is also used in connection with the closely similar proposal of tariffs against foreign 'dumping', which again generally comes to mean 'effective foreign competition'.

BACKGROUND FAIRNESS

While still concentrating on the way the procedure works, some evaluations in terms of 'fairness' dig a little deeper and ask whether the background conditions are satisfactory. Some examples should make the notion of 'background conditions' clear. Procedural fairness rules out one boxer having a piece of lead inside his gloves, but background fairness would also rule out any undue disparity in the weight of the boxers; similarly background fairness would rule out sailing boats or cars of different sizes being raced against one another unless suitably handicapped. In a court case the fact that one side's counsel showed far greater forensic skill than the other's would be grounds for complaint under the rubric of background fairness but not procedural fairness.

*From *Political Argument* by Brian Barry (London: Routledge & Kegan Paul, 1965), pp. 97–106. Reprinted by permission of the author and the publisher.

Background fairness in voting might be thought to require that the opportunities available to those supporting the different sides should be equal, or roughly proportional to their strength among the voters. On these grounds one might well object to the two-to-one superiority in resources of Republicans and Conservatives or to de Gaulle's use of the government monopoly in radio and television to further his referenda. Chance has no room for background fairness alongside procedural fairness, nor, except in a loose sense, has bargaining. Exactly why this is will be examined in Section 3 when I consider the justification of evaluations in terms of procedural and background fairness.

LEGAL JUSTICE

Procedural fairness and background fairness are concerned respectively with whether the prescribed formalities have been observed and whether the initial position of the parties was right. There is a third type of evaluation which is based on the working of procedures: legal or (more generally) rule-based justice.

Henry Sidgwick noted that one of the clearest and most frequent uses of 'justice' is in a legal context: A verdict is just when it is a correct application of the relevant rule of law. He also noted that it is not the *only* use of 'justice' because we can for example say (Hobbes notwithstanding) that a law is itself unjust.[7] The restriction to legal rules does not correspond to any difference in terms or evaluations; if the rules of the club allow expulsion for cheating and I am expelled without having cheated this is unjust in exactly the same way as a punishment inflicted by a court can be unjust. I shall therefore use the same term 'legal justice' whether the rule in question is a rule of law or not.[8]

The criterion of legal justice can be employed only where a decision is reached in the light of some rule(s), held by those taking the decision to give the answer in cases of that kind. It can therefore be used only in conjunction with the authoritative determination procedure. There may also perhaps be a marginal application to contest: a bad interpretation of the rules could at a pinch be called unjust; but it is more natural to say that it was unfair. This is closely bound up with a point made in the previous chapter: a referee does not determine the result of a football match in the same way as a judge determines the result of a trial. A bad decision by the referee only gives an 'unfair advantage' to one side; the other side may still win. When I try to think of a referee's decision for which I should feel 'unjust' to be the appropriate epithet, I immediately light on something like sending a man off the field or recommending his suspension, which are of course examples of a direct effect on the player rather than (or at least in addition to) an indirect effect on the result of the game.[9]

JUSTIFICATIONS

LEGAL JUSTICE

So far I have simply presented procedural and background fairness and legal justice. It must now be asked why the honorific names of 'fair' and 'just' should be applied to the correct carrying out of procedures and the correct application of rules. Unless one is a 'rule worshipper' one must presumably ask for a justification of these procedural considerations in terms of conduciveness to some more general consideration, either aggregative or distributive.[10]

I shall begin by advancing three reasons of this more general kind for taking legal justice seriously. One argument is that any consistent application of a rule creates a primitive variety of equity—like cases being treated alike—though this is a rather weak sort of distributive principle because the basis of 'likeness' is stipulated by the rule and it may be outrageous. Another argument is that if known rules are applied, everyone can if he chooses avoid the consequences of infringing them; this applies to any rule, good or bad, unless it prescribes penalties for something nobody can do anything about (such as being a Jew or a Negro) or for past voluntary actions done before the rule was promulgated (such as having joined the Communist Party in the nineteen thirties). Both distributive and aggregative justifications underlie this second argument. Reasoning on aggregative premises one may say that following rules of the required kind prevents insecurity (the knock on the door in the early morning) and allows punishment to be deterrent rather than a dead loss of total want-satisfaction. On distributive premises one may say that if the required kinds of rule are followed then at least nobody will suffer for something he could not have helped doing, and this is at least a *part* of the criteria for 'desert'.

Finally, legal justice tends to reduce the incidence of unfulfilled expectations. The principle that unfulfilled expectations should be avoided if possible can itself be justified on both aggregative and distributive grounds, and then applies to legal justice as a special case.[11] The aggregative argument, for what it is worth, was elaborately worked out by Bentham in his analysis of the competing (utilitarian) claims of security and equality.

. . . 'the *advantage of gaining* cannot be compared with the *evil of losing.*' This proposition is itself deduced from two others. On the one hand every man naturally expects to preserve what he has; the feeling of expectation is natural to man and is founded on the ordinary course of events, since, taking the whole sum of men, acquired wealth is not only preserved but even increased. All loss is therefore unexpected, and gives rise to deception, which is a pain—the pain of frustrated expectation. On the other hand the deduction (or addition) of a portion of wealth will produce in the sum of happiness of each individual a deduction (or an addition) more or less great according to the portion deducted and the remaining or original proportion.[12]

The distributive argument is of more limited import and refers specifically to cases where people have invested money, changed jobs, moved house, et cetera, in the belief that the state of affairs which induced them to do so would continue indefinitely. If they have, then it is wrong for this state of affairs to be suddenly changed.[13]

When a legislature passes a law, not for any temporary purposes, nor limited as to the time of its operation, and which therefore may be reasonably expected to be permanent,—and persons, confiding in its permanency, embark their capital, bestow their labour, or shape the course of their life, so that their only hope of success is founded on the existence of the law,—the rights which they have acquired in the reliance upon its continuance are termed *'vested rights;'* and persons in this situation are considered as having a moral claim on the legislature for the maintenance of the law, or at least for the allowance of a sufficient time to withdraw their investments, and to take the measures necessary for guarding against the loss consequent on so large a change.[14]

PROCEDURAL AND BACKGROUND FAIRNESS

Now take procedural and background fairness. What, first of all, is the relation between a fair trial and a just verdict? The answer seems to me to be the empirical one that fair trials tend to produce just verdicts more often than unfair trials and that the more respects in which a trial is fair the more likely it is to eventuate in a just verdict.[15] The value of fairness is thus a subordinate to that of justice: Fair procedures and back-ground conditions are to be valued for their tendency to produce (rule-based) justice. Procedural fairness provides the minimum conditions while background fairness constitutes a refinement.[16]

Now consider contest. Again the criteria of fairness are empirically related to a tendency for fair contests to produce the 'right' results; and it is even clearer than before that the criteria for fairness are drawn with this requirement in mind. In Section 2 and again above, I have used the expression 'the right result', and this bears the same relation to the contest procedure as 'rule-based justice' does to 'rule-based authoritative determination'. But whereas one can define 'justice' as 'conformity with the rule', one cannot give a general characterization of 'the right result' except as 'a result which is an accurate index of the quality which the contest was supposed to be testing'.

Procedural fairness (conformity with the procedural rules) is always more likely than not to produce the 'right results'—whatever they may be—because it merely specifies that everyone does the same thing. Whatever it is that the race is supposed to be testing, it is hard to see how its reliability would be improved if some competitors got away with jumping the gun, except in the perverse case where the race is a blind and the real test is in gun-jumping ability.

The criteria of background fairness, on the other hand, vary according to the 'right result'. If all that is being tested is ability to knock out an opponent, there is no need for any limits on disparity of size between boxers; but if the boxing match is supposed to be a test of skill, 'background fairness' must be brought in to specify the maximum disparity beyond which skill is secondary in determining the result to brute force. Again, if an examination is supposed to be testing *effort,* a different method of marking will be required from that necessary to test *ability.*

As with rule-based authoritative determination, the main justification for procedural and background fairness lies in its tendency to produce certain results. If these results are good then fairness, as a means to them, is also good; if not, not. The results of contest are to match rewards and deprivations (perhaps only immaterial ones such as prestige and chagrin) to performance, and for this to be desirable the scale of rewards and deprivations must be such that when it is adhered to they are appropriate to the performances. 'Equality of opportunity' (the honorific name for background and procedural fairness) is not very important if the achievements which are rewarded are base or trifling.[17] However, as before, we can suggest that there are certain virtues in procedural and background fairness in a contest regardless of the result to which the contest is directed. These are, as before, the minimal equity of like cases being treated alike (even though 'likeness' may be defined in any way) and the fact that contestants at least know what they are supposed to be trying to do. It must be allowed that these general considerations seem to be a good deal weaker than those raised in connection with rule-based authoritative determination.

The link between justifying procedural and background fairness and justifying the use of the procedure itself comes out even more clearly if we look at voting. If we suppose that the object of the voting procedure is to ascertain the opinions of the voters then plainly the formal requirements are a necessary condition of this. If in addition we say that the object is to secure their informed opinions we have to introduce the background conditions as well. If these objects are good then the means to them are good.

I have now covered the three procedures of whose operation both procedural and background fairness can be predicated. Of the rest, chance, I remarked, is liable to procedural fairness (or unfairness) only. This follows from the rather peculiar fact that there is no end in view when a chance procedure is employed beyond settling something on a random basis.[18] Since the end is identified with the actual mechanical procedure there is no room for background fairness. Indeed, procedural and substantive fairness are merged since the distributive value *is* the randomness.

I also suggested that bargaining is in the reverse position. It cannot be procedurally fair (or unfair) but at least in a loose sense background fairness (or unfairness) can sometimes be attributed to it. Indeed, I may add that the same can sometimes be said of combat. This odd state of affairs arises whenever something which those taking part in it define to themselves as combat is at the same time being evaluated by a third party as if it were a contest. This observer, but not the combatants, may then speak of fairness—but only loosely and perhaps one might even say improperly.[19]

So far I have dealt with justifications for fairness taking one procedure at a time; but are there general reasons for following a prescribed form which applies to *any* form? I can suggest two. One is the argument (offered by Rawls) from 'fair play'.[20] This is essentially a distributive argu-ment, which runs as follows: If you have accepted benefits arising from a certain practice then (unless you have given notice to the contrary) it is only fair that you should continue to adhere to it even when in some specific case it would suit you better not to. The other is an aggregative argument to the effect that the more a society is divided on substantive values, the more precious as a means of preserving social peace is any agreement that can be reached on procedure. The connection between liberalism and an emphasis on 'due process' is not fortuitous. Procedures cannot be justified by the results they produce because a result which one approves of another disapproves; the adherence to procedures is justified instead by saying that everyone agrees on them and this is the only thing on which everyone does agree. Whether these considerations are sufficiently universal or compelling to account for the importance which is often attached to a meticulous adherence to prescribed forms I shall not guess. Perhaps there is an element of 'rule worship' which can be supported by neither aggregative nor distributive principles; but the rationality of general adherence to prescribed forms is high on almost any principles.

NOTES

1.   'Impartiality as an obligation of justice may be said to mean being exclusively influenced by considerations which it is supposed ought to influence the particular case in hand, and resisting the solicitation of any motives which prompt to conduct different from what these considerations would dictate.' J. S. Mill, *Utilitarianism,* Chapter V.

2.   See the Franks Report (Cmnd 218, 1957), *passim.*

3.   It is quite correct for the old saw to include 'love' in the same category, at least if it is taken to mean 'attaining the object of sexual desire'. There are no rules, no formal requirements, to satisfy before you can get your girl (or your man); you may have all the virtues but if you don't happen to have appeal you don't win.

4.   I am not saying that war, still less combat in general, cannot be limited in its means (or in its ends) but that there cannot, by my definitions, be a conventional connection between achieving a certain feat and winning; the only connection can be that the other side in fact gives up. A strike or a lockout, for example, can be limited in means (no shooting, no sabotage) and ends (a rise of 5 per cent or a reduction of 5 per cent). But it is still combat and not contest because each is aiming directly at changing the attitude of the other, not at some separate standard of achievement which is then taken as settling the dispute. A contest would occur if the trade union and the employer agreed in advance that whichever side was the first to cost the other a million pounds should get its demand fulfilled.

5.   A duel *à l'outrance* of course removes the loser not conventionally but necessarily; but the removal is still in the course of an activity with formal rules. If we have a duel fixed for tomorrow it would still be 'unfair' for me to shoot you in the back today as you walk along the street.

6. E.g., the 'Codes of Fair Practice' produced under the NRA, in the New Deal.

7. H. Sidgwick, *The Methods of Ethics,* Book III, Chapter V.

8. Sidgwick indeed extended the term 'legal justice' to cover promises and similar social obligations.

9. The *result* of a match may be unjust in that it does not reflect the relative merits of the teams, but this is a different use of 'unjust' bound up with desert. An unjust result in this sense may be due equally to a bad decision or an unlucky gust of wind.

10. See J. J. C. Smart, *An Outline of a System of Utilitarian Ethics* (Melbourne, 1961). Smart's 'utilitarianism' appears to be *entirely* made up of a rejection of 'rule worship'. Not only is the position he defends not (necessarily) hedonistic; it is not even aggregative. This—formerly, I should have thought, the sole distinguishing mark of nonhedonistic utilitarianism—is abandoned when Smart admits that different utilitarians may disagree on distributive questions.

11. Sidgwick, in *The Methods of Ethics* suggests that the avoiding of unfulfilled expectations constitutes most of the Common Sense idea of 'justice' but (at least nowadays) 'justice' does not seem to be used so widely. There still seems to be agreement that there *is* a value in not frustrating expectations, however. Consider the contrasting attitudes of many people to death duties on one hand and a capital levy on the other. (I am referring to the opinions of those who are naïve enough to believe that death duties, as currently operated in the UK, are effective in reducing fortunes.)

12. In Halévy, *The Growth of Philosophical Radicalism* (Beacon, 1955), p. 40. Note that the second argument would sometimes *favour* redistribution. Take £10 from a man with £1,000 and give it to one with £100. You decrease the happiness of the former by 1 per cent, but increase the happiness of the latter by 10 per cent. The argument in any case rests on a peculiar assumption about the marginal utility of money —far more questionable than the simple diminishing marginal utility idea.

13. Sidgwick's claim that 'just' is used to refer to fulfilling expectations would be more plausible if restricted to cases which fall under this argument.

14. Sir George Cornewall Lewis, *Remarks on the Use and Abuse of Some Political Terms* (London, 1832), p. 25.

15. When I say that this is a matter of fact I do not mean that the dovetailing of fair procedures and just results is an accident, for the criteria of a fair trial are selected with an eye on this dovetailing. What I am denying is any analytic connection between the two such that a just verdict entails a fair trial or a fair trial entails a just verdict: there can be fair trials which still produce unjust verdicts.

16. Indeed, it is quite plausible to suggest that background fairness is only relevant to trials inasfar as they partake of contest, by their use of the adversary system which thus places a premium on equally matched counsel. Courts do not *have* to be so organized. See Sybille Bedford, *The Faces of Justice* (London, 1961).

17. Compare 'equality before the law', the honorific name for procedural fairness in connection with rule-based authoritative determination: 'Equality before the law' does not guarantee that outrageous actions are not rewarded and good ones punished. It should hardly need saying that neither form of procedural 'equality' has anything to do with substantial equality though the possibility of confusion is convenient for those who prefer the rhetoric to the reality of equality. (See, e.g., C. A. R. Crosland, *The Future of Socialism* (London, 1956)). Plato in *The Republic* and Michael Young in *The Rise of the Meritocracy* (Penguin Books, 1961) have both given us pictures of extremely hierarchical societies based on 'equality of opportunity'.

18. An apparent exception would be the use of a random device in the belief that God will arrange for a substantively good result; but then the arrangement is not (in the eyes of the people operating it) to be regarded as invoking a *chance* mechanism.

19. This point is pursued in the context of J. K. Galbraith's 'concept of countervailing power'.

20. John Rawls, 'Justice as Fairness', *Philosophical Review,* LXVII (1958). (See the next selection in this part.)

JOHN RAWLS

Justice as Fairness*

I

It might seem at first sight that the concepts of justice and fairness are the same, and that there is no reason to distinguish them, or to say that one is more fundamental than the other. I think that this impression is mistaken. In this paper I wish to show that the fundamental idea in the concept of justice is fairness; and I wish to offer an analysis of the concept of justice from this point of view. To bring out the force of this claim, and the analysis based upon it, I shall then argue that it is this aspect of justice for which utilitarianism, in its classical form, is unable to account, but which is expressed, even if misleadingly, by the idea of the social contract.

To start with I shall develop a particular conception of justice by stating and commenting upon two principles which specify it, and by considering the circumstances and conditions under which they may be thought to arise. The principles defining this conception, and the conception itself, are, of course, familiar. It may be possible, however, by using the notion of fairness as a framework, to assemble and to look at them in a new way. Before stating this conception, however, the following preliminary matters should be kept in mind.

Throughout I consider justice only as a virtue of social institutions, or what I shall call practices.[1] The principles of justice are regarded as formulating restrictions as to how practices may define positions and offices, and assign thereto powers and liabilities, rights, and duties. Justice as a virtue of particular actions or of persons I do not take up at all. It is important to distinguish these various subjects of justice, since the meaning of the concept varies according to whether it is applied to practices, particular actions, or persons. These meanings are, indeed, connected, but they are not identical. I shall confine my discussion to the sense of justice as applied to practices, since this sense is the basic one. Once it is understood, the other senses should go quite easily.

Justice is to be understood in its customary sense as representing but *one* of the many virtues of social institutions, for these may be antiquated, inefficient, degrading, or any number of other things, without being unjust. Justice is not to be confused with an all-inclusive vision of a good society; it is only one part of any such conception. It is important, for example, to distinguish that sense of equality which is an aspect of the concept of justice from that sense of equality which belongs to a more comprehensive social ideal. There may well be inequalities which one concedes are just, or at least not unjust, but which, nevertheless, one wishes, on other grounds, to do away with. I shall focus attention, then, on the usual sense of justice in which it is essentially the elimination of arbitrary distinctions and the establishment, within the structure of a practice, of a proper balance between competing claims.

Finally, there is no need to consider the principles discussed below as *the* principles of justice. For the moment it is sufficient that they are typical of a family of principles normally associated with the concept of justice. The way in which the principles of this family resemble one another, as shown by the background against which they may be thought to arise, will be made clear by the whole of the subsequent argument.

II

The conception of justice which I want to develop may be stated in the form of two principles as follows: First, each person participating in a practice, or affected by it, has an equal right to the most extensive liberty compatible with a like liberty for all; and second, inequalities are arbitrary unless it is reasonable to expect that they will work out for everyone's advantage, and provided

*From *The Philosophical Review*, Vol. 67 (1958), pp. 164–94. Reprinted by permission of the author and the publisher. An abbreviated version of this paper (less than one-half the length) was presented in a symposium with the same title at the American Philosophical Association, Eastern Division, December 28, 1957, and appeared in the *Journal of Philosophy*, LIV, 653–662. Footnotes have been renumbered.

the positions and offices to which they attach, or from which they may be gained, are open to all. These principles express justice as a complex of three ideas: liberty, equality, and reward for services contributing to the common good.[2]

The term "person" is to be construed variously depending on the circumstances. On some occasions it will mean human individuals, but in others it may refer to nations, provinces, business firms, churches, teams, and so on. The principles of justice apply in all these instances, although there is a certain logical priority to the case of human individuals. As I shall use the term "person," it will be ambiguous in the manner indicated.

The first principle holds, of course, only if other things are equal: That is, while there must always be a justification for departing from the initial position of equal liberty (which is defined by the pattern of rights and duties, powers and liabilities, established by a practice), and the burden of proof is placed on him who would depart from it, nevertheless, there can be, and often there is, a justification for doing so. Now, that similar particular cases, as defined by a practice, should be treated similarly as they arise, is part of the very concept of a practice; it is involved in the notion of an activity in accordance with rules.[3] The first principle expresses an analogous conception, but as applied to the structure of practices themselves. It holds, for example, that there is a presumption against the distinctions and classifications made by legal systems and other practices to the extent that they infringe on the original and equal liberty of the persons participating in them. The second principle defines how this presumption may be rebutted.

It might be argued at this point that justice requires only an equal liberty. If, however, a greater liberty were possible for all without loss or conflict, then it would be irrational to settle on a lesser liberty. There is no reason for circumscribing rights unless their exercise would be incompatible, or would render the practice defining them less effective. Therefore no serious distortion of the concept of justice is likely to follow from including within it the concept of the greatest equal liberty.

The second principle defines what sorts of inequalities are permissible; it specifies how the presumption laid down by the first principle may be put aside. Now by inequalities it is best to understand not *any* differences between offices and positions, but differences in the benefits and burdens attached to them either directly or indirectly, such as prestige and wealth, or liability to taxation and compulsory services. Players in a game do not protest against there being different positions, such as batter, pitcher, catcher, and the like, nor to there being various privileges and powers as specified by the rules; nor do the citizens of a country object to there being the different offices of government such as president, senator, governor, judge, and so on, each with its special rights and duties. It is not differences of this kind that are normally thought of as inequalities, but differences in the resulting distribution established by a practice, or made possible by it, of the things men strive to attain or avoid. Thus they may complain about the pattern of honors and rewards set up by a practice (for example, the privileges and salaries of government officials) or they may object to the distribution of power and wealth which results from the various ways in which men avail themselves of the opportunities allowed by it (for example, the concentration of wealth which may develop in a free price system allowing large entrepreneurial or speculative gains).

It should be noted that the second principle holds that an inequality is allowed only if there is reason to believe that the practice with the inequality, or resulting in it, will work for the advantage of *every* party engaging in it. Here it is important to stress that *every* party must gain from the inequality. Since the principle applies to practices, it implies that the representative man in every office or position defined by a practice, when he views it as a going concern, must find it reasonable to prefer his condition and prospects with the inequality to what they would be under the practice without it. The principle excludes, therefore, the justification of inequalities on the grounds that the disadvantages of those in one position are outweighed by the greater advantages of those in another position. This rather simple restriction is the main modification I wish to make in the utilitarian principle as usually understood. When coupled with the notion of a practice, it is a restriction of consequence[4], and one which some utilitarians, for example, Hume and Mill, have used in their discussions of justice without realizing apparently its significance, or at least without calling attention to it.[5] Why it is a significant modification of principle, changing one's conception of justice entirely, the whole of my argument will show.

Further, it is also necessary that the various offices to which special benefits or burdens attach are open to all. It may be, for example, to the common advantage, as just defined, to attach special benefits to certain offices. Perhaps by doing so the requisite talent can be attracted to them and encouraged to give its best efforts. But any offices having special benefits must be won in a fair competition in which contestants are judged on their merits. If some offices were not open, those excluded would normally be justified in feeling unjustly treated, even if they benefited from the greater efforts of those who were allowed to compete for them. Now if one can assume that offices are open, it is necessary only to consider the design of practices themselves and how they jointly, as a system, work together. It will be a mistake to focus attention on the varying relative positions of particular persons, who may be known to us by their proper names, and to require that each such change, as a once for all transaction viewed in isolation, must be in itself just. It is the system of practices which is to be judged, and judged from a general point of view: Unless one is prepared to criticize it from the standpoint of a representative man holding some particular office, one has no complaint against it.

III

Given these principles one might try to derive them from a priori principles of reason, or claim that they were known by intuition. These are familiar enough steps and, at least in the case of the first principle, might be made with some success. Usually, however, such arguments, made at this point, are unconvincing. They are not likely to lead to an understanding of the basis of the principles of justice, not at least as principles of justice. I wish, therefore, to look at the principles in a different way.

Imagine a society of persons amongst whom a certain system of practices is *already* well established. Now suppose that by and large they are mutually self-interested; their allegiance to their established practices is normally founded on the prospect of self-advantage. One need not assume that, in all senses of the term "person," the persons in this society are mutually self-interested. If the characterization as mutually self-interested applies when the line of division is the family, it may still be true that members of families are bound by ties of sentiment and affection and willingly acknowledge duties in contradiction to self-interest. Mutual self-interestedness in the relations between families, nations, churches, and the like, is commonly associated with intense loyalty and devotion on the part of individual members. Therefore, one can form a more realistic

conception of this society if one thinks of it as consisting of mutually self-interested families, or some other association. Further, it is not necessary to suppose that these persons are mutually self-interested under all circumstances, but only in the usual situations in which they participate in their common practices.

Now suppose also that these persons are rational: they know their own interests more or less accurately; they are capable to tracing out the likely consequences of adopting one practice rather than another; they are capable of adhering to a course of action once they have decided upon it; they can resist present temptations and the enticements of immediate gain; and the bare knowledge or perception of the difference between their condition and that of others is not, within certain limits and in itself, a source of great dissatisfaction. Only the last point adds anything to the usual definition of rationality. This definition should allow, I think, for the idea that a rational man would not be greatly downcast from knowing, or seeing, that others are in a better position than himself, unless he thought their being so was the result of injustice, or the consequence of letting chance work itself out for no useful common purpose, and so on. So if these persons strike us as unpleasantly egoistic, they are at least free in some degree from the fault of envy.[6]

Finally, assume that these persons have roughly similar needs and interests, or needs and interests in various ways complementary, so that fruitful cooperation amongst them is possible; and suppose that they are sufficiently equal in power and ability to guarantee that in normal circumstances none is able to dominate the others. This condition (as well as the others) may seem excessively vague; but in view of the conception of justice to which the argument leads, there seems no reason for making it more exact here.

Since these persons are conceived as engaging in their common practices, which are already established, there is no question of our supposing them to come together to deliberate as to how they will set these practices up for the first time. Yet we can imagine that from time to time they discuss with one another whether any of them has a legitimate complaint against their established institutions. Such discussions are perfectly natural in any normal society. Now suppose that they have settled on doing this in the following way. They first try to arrive at the principles by which complaints, and so practices themselves, are to be judged. Their procedure for this is to let each person propose the principles upon which he wishes his complaints to be tried with the understanding that, if acknowledged, the complaints of others will be similarly tried, and that no complaints will be heard at all until everyone is roughly to one mind as to how complaints are to be judged. They each understand further that the principles proposed and acknowledged on this occasion are binding on future occasions. Thus each will be wary of proposing a principle which would give him a peculiar advantage, in his present circumstances, supposing it to be accepted. Each person knows that he will be bound by it in future circumstances the peculiarities of which cannot be known, and which might well be such that the principle is then to his disadvantage. The idea is that everyone should be required to make *in advance* a firm commitment, which others also may reasonably be expected to make, and that no one be given the opportunity to tailor the canons of a legitimate complaint to fit his own special condition, and then to discard them when they no longer suit his purpose. Hence each person will propose principles of a general kind which will, to a large degree, gain their sense from the various applications to be made of them, the particular circumstances of which being as yet unknown. These principles will express the conditions in accordance with which each is the least unwilling to have his interests limited in the design of practices, given the competing interests of the others, on the supposition that the interests of others will be limited likewise. The restrictions which would so arise might be thought of as those a person would keep in mind if he were designing a practice in which his enemy were to assign him his place.

The two main parts of his conjectural account have a definite significance. The character and respective situations of the parties reflect the typical circumstances in which questions of justice arise. The procedure whereby principles are proposed and acknowledged represents constraints, analogous to those of having a morality, whereby rational and mutually self-interested persons are brought to act reasonably. Thus the first part reflects the fact that questions of justice arise when conflicting claims are made upon the design of a practice and where it is taken for granted that each person will insist, as far as possible, on what he considers his rights. It is typical of cases of justice to involve persons who are pressing on one another their claims, between which a fair balance or equilibrium must be

found. On the other hand, as expressed by the second part, having a morality must at least imply the acknowledgment of principles as impartially applying to one's own conduct as well as to another's, and moreover principles which may constitute a constraint, or limitation, upon the pursuit of one's own interests. There are, of course, other aspects of having a morality: The acknowledgment of moral principles must show itself in accepting a reference to them as reasons for limiting one's claims, in acknowledging the burden of providing a special explanation, or excuse, when one acts contrary to them, or else in showing shame and remorse and a desire to make amends, and so on. It is sufficient to remark here that having a morality is analogous to having made a firm commitment in advance; for one must acknowledge the principles of morality even when to one's disadvantage.[7] A man whose moral judgments always coincided with his interests could be suspected of having no morality at all.

Thus the two parts of the foregoing account are intended to mirror the kinds of circumstances in which questions of justice arise and the constraints which having a morality would impose upon persons so situated. In this way one can see how the acceptance of the principles of justice might come about, for given all these conditions as described, it would be natural if the two principles of justice were to be acknowledged. Since there is no way of anyone to win special advantages for himself, each might consider it reasonable to acknowledge equality as an initial principle. There is, however, no reason why they should regard this position as final; for if there are inequalities which satisfy the second principle, the immediate gain which equality would allow can be considered as intelligently invested in view of its future return. If, as is quite likely, these inequalities work as incentives to draw out better efforts, the members of this society may look upon them as concessions to human nature: they, like us, may think that people ideally should want to serve one another. But as they are mutually self-interested, their acceptance of these inequalities is merely the acceptance of the relations in which they actually stand, and a recognition of the motives which lead them to engage in their common practices. *They* have no title to complain of one another. And so provided that the conditions of the principle are met, there is no reason why they should not allow such inequalities. Indeed, it would be short-sighted of them to do so, and could result, in most cases, only from their being dejected by the bare knowledge, or perception, that others are better situated. Each person will, however, insist on an advantage to himself, and so on a common advantage, for none is willing to sacrifice anything for the others.

These remarks are not offered as a proof that persons so conceived and circumstanced would settle on the two principles, but only to show that these principles could have such a background, and so can be viewed as those principles which mutually self-interested and rational persons, when similarly situated and required to make in advance a firm commitment, could acknowledge as restrictions governing the assignment of rights and duties in their common practices, and thereby accept as limiting their rights against one another. The principles of justice may, then, be regarded as those principles which arise when the constraints of having a morality are imposed upon parties in the typical circumstances of justice.

IV

These ideas are, of course, connected with a familiar way of thinking about justice which goes back at least to the Greek Sophists, and which regards the acceptance of the principles of justice as a compromise between persons of roughly equal power who would enforce their will on each other if they could, but who, in view of the equality of forces amongst them and for the sake of their own peace and security, acknowledge certain forms of conduct insofar as prudence seems to require. Justice is thought of as a pact between rational egoists the stability of which is dependent on a balance of power and a similarity of circumstances.[8] While the previous account is connected with this tradition, and with its most recent variant, the theory of games,[9] it differs from it in several important respects which, to forestall misinterpretations, I will set out here.

First, I wish to use the previous conjectural account of the background of justice as a way of analyzing the concept. I do not want, therefore, to be interpreted as assuming a general theory of human motivation: When I suppose that the parties are mutually self-interested, and are not willing to have their (substantial) interests sacrificed to others, I am referring to their conduct and motives as they are taken for granted in cases where questions of justice ordinarily arise. Justice is the virtue of practices where there are assumed to be competing interests and conflicting claims, and where it is supposed that persons will press their rights on each other. That persons are mu-

tually self-interested in certain situations and for certain purposes is what gives rise to the question of justice in practices covering those circumstances. Amongst an association of saints, if such a community could really exist, the disputes about justice could hardly occur; for they would all work selflessly together for one end, the glory of God as defined by their common religion, and reference to this end would settle every question of right. The justice of practices does not come up until there are several different parties (whether we think of these as individuals, associations, or nations and so on, is irrelevant) who do press their claims on one another, and who do regard themselves as representatives of interests which deserve to be considered. Thus the previous account involves no general theory of human motivation. Its intent is simply to incorporate into the conception of justice the relations of men to one another which set the stage for questions of justice. It makes no difference how wide or general these relations are, as this matter does not bear on the analysis of the concept.

Again, in contrast to the various conceptions of the social contract, the several parties do not establish any particular society or practice; they do not convenant to obey a particular sovereign body or to accept a given constitution.[10] Nor do they, as in the theory of games (in certain respects a marvelously sophisticated development of this tradition), decide on individual strategies adjusted to their respective circumstances in the game. What the parties do is to *jointly* acknowledge certain *principles* of appraisal relating to their common *practices* either as already established or merely proposed. They accede to standards of judgment, not to a given practice; they do not make any specific agreement, or bargain, or adopt a particular strategy. The subject of their acknowledgment is, therefore, very general indeed; it is simply the acknowledgment of certain principles of judgment, fulfilling certain general conditions, to be used in criticizing the arrangement of their common affairs. The relations of mutual self-interest [among] the parties who are similarly circumstanced mirror the conditions under which questions of justice arise, and the procedure by which the principles of judgment are proposed and acknowledged reflects the constraints of having a morality. Each aspect, then, of preceding hypothetical account serves the purpose of bringing out a feature of the notion of justice. One could, if one liked, view the principles of justice as the "solution" of this highest order "game" of adopting, subject to the procedure described, principles of argument for all coming particular "games" whose peculiarities one can in no way foresee. But this comparison, while no doubt helpful, must not obscure the fact that this highest order "game" is of a special sort.[11] Its significance is that its various pieces represent aspects of the concept of justice.

Finally, I do not, of course, conceive the several parties as necessarily coming together to establish their common practices for the first time. Some institutions may, indeed, be set up *de novo;* but I have framed the preceding account so that it will apply when the full complement of social institutions already exists and represents the result of a long period of development. Nor is the account in any way fictitious. In any society where people reflect on their institutions they will have an idea of what principles of justice would be acknowledged under the conditions described, and there will be occasions when the questions of justice are actually discussed in this way. Therefore if their practices do not accord with these principles, this will affect the quality of their social relations. For in this case there will be some recognized situations wherein the parties are mutually aware that one of them is being forced to accept what the other would concede is injust. The foregoing analysis may then be thought of as representing the actual quality of relations [among] persons as defined by practices accepted as just. In such practices the parties will acknowledge the principles on which it is constructed, and the general recognition of this fact shows itself in the absence of resentment and in the sense of being justly treated. Thus one common objection to the theory of the social contract, its apparently historical and fictitious character, is avoided.

V

That the principles of justice may be regarded as arising in the manner described illustrates an important fact about them. Not only does it bring out the idea that justice is a primitive moral notion in that it arises once the concept of morality is imposed on mutually self-interested agents similarly circumstanced, but it emphasizes that, fundamental to justice, is the concept of fairness which relates to right dealing between persons who are cooperating with or competing against one another, as when one speaks of fair games, fair competition, and fair bargains. The question of fairness arises when free persons, who have no authority over one another, are engaging in a joint activity and amongst themselves settling acknowledging the rules which define it and which determine the respective shares in its benefits and burdens. A practice will strike the parties as fair if none feels that, by participating in it, they or any of the others are taken advantage of, or forced to give in to claims, which they do not regard as legitimate. This implies that each has a conception of legitimate claims which he thinks it reasonable for others as well as himself to acknowledge. If one thinks of the principles of justice as arising in the manner described, then they do define this sort of conception. A practice is just or fair, then, when it satisfies the principles which those who participate in it could propose to one another for mutual acceptance under the aforementioned circumstances. Persons engaged in a just, or fair, practice can face one another openly and support their respective positions, should they appear questionable, by reference to principles which it is reasonable to expect each to accept.

It is this notion of the possibility of mutual acknowledgment of principles by free persons who have no authority over one another which makes the concept of fairness fundamental to justice. Only if such acknowledgment is possible can there be true community between persons in their common practices; otherwise their relations will appear to them as founded to some extent on force. If, in ordinary speech, fairness applies more particularly to practices in which there is a choice whether to engage or not (for example, in games, business competition), and justice to practices in which there is no choice (for example, in slavery), the element of necessity does not render the conception of mutual acknowledgment inapplicable, although it may make it much more urgent to change unjust than unfair institutions. For one activity in which one can always engage is that of proposing and acknowledging principles to one another supposing each to be similarly circumstanced; and to judge practices by the principles so arrived at is to apply the standard of fairness to them.

Now if the participants in a practice accept its rules as fair, and so have no complaint to lodge against it, there arises a prima facie duty (and a corresponding prima facie right) of the parties to each other to act in accordance with the practice when it falls upon them to comply. When any number of persons engage in a practice, or conduct a joint undertaking according to rules, and thus restrict their liberty, those who have submitted to these restrictions when required have the right to a similar acquiescence on the part of those who have benefited by their submission. These conditions will obtain if a practice is correctly acknowledged to be fair, for in this case all who participate in it will benefit from it. The rights and duties so arising are special rights and duties in that they depend on previous actions voluntarily undertaken, in this case on the parties having engaged in a common practice and knowingly accepted its benefits.[12] It is not, however, an obligation which presupposes a deliberate performative act in the sense of a promise, or contract, and the like.[13] An unfortunate mistake of proponents of the idea of the social contract was to suppose that political obligation does require some such act, or at least to use language which suggests it. It is sufficient that one has knowingly participated in and accepted the benefits of a practice acknowledged to be fair. This prima facie obligation may, of course, be overridden: It may happen, when it comes one's turn to follow a rule, that other considerations will justify not doing so. But one cannot, in general, be released from this obligation by denying the justice of the practice only when it falls on one to obey. If a person rejects a practice, he should, so far as possible, declare his intention in advance, and avoid participating in it or enjoying its benefits.

This duty I have called that of fair play, but it should be admitted that to refer to it in this way is, perhaps, to extend the ordinary notion of fairness. Usually acting unfairly is not so much the breaking of any particular rule, even if the infraction is difficult to detect (cheating), but taking advantage of loopholes or ambiguities in rules, availing oneself of unexpected or special circumstances which make it impossible to enforce them, insisting that rules be enforced to one's advantage when they should be suspended, and more generally, acting contrary to the intention of a practice. It is for this reason that one speaks of the sense of fair play: Acting fairly requires more than simply being able to follow rules; what is fair must often be felt, or perceived, one wants to say. It is not, however, an unnatural extension of the duty of fair play to have it include the obligation which participants who have knowingly accepted the benefits of their common practice owe to each other to act in accordance with it when their performance falls due; for it is usually considered unfair if someone accepts the benefits of a practice but refuses to do his part in maintaining it. Thus one might say of the tax-dodger that he violates the duty of fair play: He accepts the benefits of government but will not do his part in releasing resources to it; and members of labor unions often say that fellow workers who refuse to join are being unfair: They refer to them as "free riders," as persons who enjoy what are the supposed benefits of unionism, higher wages, shorter hours, job security, and the like, but who refuse to share in its burdens in the form of paying dues, and so on.

The duty of fair play stands beside other prima facie duties such as fidelity and gratitude as a basic moral notion; yet it is not to be confused with them.[14] These duties are all clearly distinct, as would be obvious from their definitions. As with any moral duty, that of fair play implies a constraint on self-interest in particular cases; on occasion it enjoins conduct which a rational egoist strictly defined would not decide upon. So while justice does not require of anyone that he sacrifice his interests in that *general position* and procedure whereby the principles of justice are proposed and acknowledged, it may happen that in particular situations, arising in the context of engaging in a practice, the duty of fair play will often cross his interests in the sense that he will be required to forego particular advantages which the peculiarities of his circumstances might permit him to take. There is, of course, nothing surprising in this. It is simply the consequence of the firm commitment which the parties may be supposed to have made, or which they would make, in the general position, together with the fact that they have participated in and accepted the benefits of a practice which they regard as fair.

Now the acknowledgment of this constraint in particular cases, which is manifested in acting fairly or wishing to make amends, feeling ashamed, and the like, when one has evaded it, is one of the forms of conduct by which participants in a common practice exhibit their recognition of each other as persons with similar interests and capacities. In the same way that, failing a special explanation, the criterion for the recognition of suffering is helping one who suffers, acknowledging the duty of fair play is a necessary part of the criterion of recognizing another as a person with similar interests and feelings as oneself.[15] A person who never under any circumstances showed a wish to help others in pain would show, at the same time, that he did not recognize that they were in pain; nor could he have any feelings of affection or friendship for anyone; for having these feelings implies, failing special circumstances, that he comes to their aid when they are suffering. Recognition that another is a person in pain shows itself in sympathetic action; this primitive natural response of compassion is one of those responses upon which the various forms of moral conduct are built.

Similarly, the acceptance of the duty of fair play by participants in a common practice is a reflection in each person of the recognition of the aspirations and interests of the others to be realized by their joint activity. Failing a special explanation, their acceptance of it is a necessary part of the criterion for their recognizing one another as persons with similar interests and capacities, as the conception of their relations in the general position supposes them to be. Otherwise they would show no recognition of one another as persons with similar capacities and interests, and indeed, in some cases perhaps hypothetical, they would not recognize one another as persons at all, but as complicated objects involved in a complicated activity. To recognize another as a person one must respond to him and act towards him in certain ways; and these ways are intimately connected with the various prima facie duties. Acknowledging these duties in *some* degree, and so having the elements of morality, is not a matter of choice, or of intuiting moral qualities, or a matter of the expression of feelings or attitudes (the three interpretations between which philosophical opinion frequently oscillates); it is simply the possession of one of the forms of conduct in which the recognition of others as persons is manifested.

These remarks are unhappily obscure. Their main purpose here, however, is to forestall, together with the remarks in section IV, the misinterpretation that, on the view presented, the acceptance of justice and the acknowledgment of the duty of fair play depends in every day life solely on their being a *de facto* balance of forces between the parties. It would indeed be foolish to underestimate the importance of such a balance in securing justice; but it is not the only basis thereof. The recognition of one another as persons with similar interests and capacities engaged in a common practice must, failing a special explanation, show itself in the acceptance of the principles of justice and the acknowledgment of the duty of fair play.

The conception at which we have arrived, then, is that the principles of justice may be thought of as arising once the constraints of having a morality are imposed upon rational and mutually self-interested parties who are related and situated in a special way. A practice is just if it is in accordance with the principles which all who participate in it might reasonably be expected to propose or to acknowledge before one another

when they are similarly circumstanced and required to make a firm commitment in advance without knowledge of what will be their peculiar condition, and thus when it meets standards which the parties could accept as fair should occasion arise for them to debate its merits. Regarding the participants themselves, once persons knowingly engage in a practice which they acknowledge to be fair and accept the benefits of doing so, they are bound by the duty of fair play to follow the rules when it comes their turn to do so, and this implies a limitation on their pursuit of self-interest in particular cases.

Now one consequence of this conception is that, where it applies, there is no moral value in the satisfaction of a claim incompatible with it. Such a claim violates the conditions of reciprocity and community amongst persons, and he who presses it, not being willing to acknowledge it when pressed by another, has no grounds for complaint when it is denied; whereas he against whom it is pressed can complain. As it cannot be mutually acknowledged it is a resort to coercion; granting the claim is possible only if one party can compel acceptance of what the other will not admit. But it makes no sense to concede claims the denial of which cannot be complained of in preference to claims the denial of which can be objected to. Thus in deciding on the justice of a practice it is not enough to ascertain that it answers to wants and interests in the fullest and most effective manner. For if any of these conflict with justice, they should not be counted, as their satisfaction is no reason at all for having a practice. It would be irrelevant to say, even if true, that it resulted in the greatest satisfaction of desire. In tallying up the merits of a practice one must toss out the satisfaction of interests the claims of which are incompatible with the principles of justice.

VI

The discussion so far has been excessively abstract. While this is perhaps unavoidable, I should now like to bring out some of the features of the conception of justice as fairness by comparing it with the conception of justice in classical utilitarianism as represented by Bentham and Sidgwick, and its counterpart in welfare economics. This conception assimilates justice to benevolence and the latter in turn to the most efficient design of institutions to promote the general welfare. Justice is a kind of efficiency.[16]

Now it is said occasionally that this form of utilitarianism puts no restrictions on what might be a just assignment of rights and duties in that there might be circumstances which, on utilitarian grounds, would justify institutions highly offensive to our ordinary sense of justice. But the classical utilitarian conception is not totally unprepared for this objection. Beginning with the notion that the general happiness can be represented by a social utility function consisting of a sum of individual utility functions with identical weights (this being the meaning of the maxim that each counts for one and no more than one),[17] it is commonly assumed that the utility functions of individuals are similar in all essential respects. Differences [among] individuals are ascribed to accidents of education and upbringing, and they should not be taken into account. This assumption, coupled with that of diminishing marginal utility, results in a prima facie case for equality, for example, of equality in the distribution of income during any given period of time, laying aside indirect effects on the future. But even if utilitarianism is interpreted as having such restrictions built into the utility function, and even if it is supposed that these restrictions have in practice much the same result as the application of the principles of justice (and appear, perhaps, to be ways of expressing these principles in the language of mathematics and psychology), the fundamental idea is very different from the conception of justice as fairness. For one thing, that the principles of justice should be accepted is interpreted as the contingent result of a higher order administrative decision. The form of this decision is regarded as being similar to that of an entrepreneur deciding how much to produce of this or that commodity in view of its marginal revenue, or to that of someone distributing goods to needy persons according to the relative urgency of their wants. The choice between practices is thought of as being made on the basis of the allocation of benefits and burdens to individuals (these being measured by the present capitalized value of their utility over the full period of the practice's existence), which results from the distribution of rights and duties established by a practice.

Moreover, the individuals receiving these benefits are not conceived as being related in any way: They represent so many different directions in which limited resources may be allocated. The value of assigning resources to one direction rather than another depends solely on the preferences and interests of individuals as individuals. The satisfaction of desire has its value irrespective of the moral relations between persons, say as members of a joint undertaking, of the claims which, in the name of these interests, they are prepared to make on one another;[18] and it is this value which is to be taken into account by the (ideal) legislator who is conceived as adjusting the rules of the system from the center so as to maximize the value of the social utility function.

It is thought that the principles of justice will not be violated by a legal system so conceived provided these executive decisions are correctly made. In this fact the principles of justice are said to have their derivation and explanation; they simply express the most important general features of social institutions in which the administrative problem is solved in the best way. These principles have, indeed, a special urgency because, given the facts of human nature, so much depends on them; and this explains the peculiar quality of the moral feelings associated with justice.[19] This assimilation of justice to a higher order executive decision, certainly a striking conception, is central classical utilitarianism; and it also brings out its profound individualism, in one sense of this ambiguous word. It regards persons as so many *separate* directions in which benefits and burdens may be assigned; and the value of the satisfaction or dissatisfaction of desire is not thought to depend in any way on the moral relations in which individuals stand, or on the kinds of claims which they are willing, in the pursuit of their interests, to press on each other.

VII

Many social decisions are, of course, of an administrative nature. Certainly this is so when it is a matter of social utility in what one may call its ordinary sense: that is, when it is a question of the efficient design of social institutions for the use of common means to achieve common ends. In this case either the benefits and burdens may be assumed to be impartially distributed, or the question of distribution is misplaced, as in the instance of maintaining public order and security or national defense. But as an interpretation of the basis of the principles of justice, classical utilitarianism is mistaken. It *permits* one to argue, for example, that slavery is unjust on the grounds that the advantages to the slaveholder as slaveholder do not counterbalance the disadvantages to the slave and to society at large burdened by a comparatively inefficient system of labor. Now the conception of justice as fairness, when applied to the practice of slavery with its offices of slaveholder and slave, would not allow one to consider the advantages of the slaveholder in the first place. As that office is not in accordance with principles which could be mutually acknowledged, the gains accruing to the slaveholder, assuming them to exist, cannot be counted as in *any* way mitigating the injustice of the practice. The question whether these gains outweigh the disadvantages to the slave and to society cannot arise, since in considering the justice of slavery these gains have no weight at all which requires that they be overridden. Where the conception of justice as fairness applies, slavery is *always* unjust.

I am not, of course, suggesting the absurdity that the classical utilitarians approved of slavery. I am only rejecting a type of argument which their view allows them to use in support of their disapproval of it. The conception of justice as derivative from efficiency implies that judging the justice of a practice is always, in principle at least, a matter of weighing up advantages and disadvantages, each having an intrinsic value or disvalue as the satisfaction of interests, irrespective of whether or not these interests necessarily involve acquiescence in principles which could not be mutually acknowledged. Utilitarianism cannot account for the fact that slavery is always unjust, nor for the fact that it would be recognized as irrelevant in defeating the accusation of injustice for one person to say to another, engaged with him in a common practice and debating its merits, that nevertheless it allowed of the greatest satisfaction of desire. The charge of injustice cannot be rebutted in this way. If justice were derivative from a higher order executive efficiency, this would not be so.

But now, even if it is taken as established that, so far as the ordinary conception of justice goes, slavery is always unjust (that is, slavery by definition violates commonly recognized principles of justice), the classical utilitarian would surely reply that these principles, as other moral principles subordinate to that of utility, are only generally correct. It is simply for the most part true that slavery is less efficient than other institutions; and while common sense may define the concept of justice so that slavery is unjust, nevertheless, where slavery would lead to the greatest satisfaction of desire, it is not wrong. Indeed, it is then right, and for the very same reason that justice, as ordinarily understood, is usually right. If, as ordinarily understood, slavery is always unjust, to this extent the utilitarian conception of justice might be admitted to differ from that of common moral opinion. Still the utilitarian would want to hold that, as a matter of moral principle, his view is correct in giving no special

weight to considerations of justice beyond that allowed for by the general presumption of effectiveness. And this, he claims, is as it should be. The everyday opinion is morally in error, although, indeed, it is a useful error, since it protects rules of generally high utility.

The question, then relates not simply to the analysis of the concept of justice as common sense defines it, but the analysis of it in the wider sense as to how much weight considerations of justice, as defined, are to have when laid against other kinds of moral considerations. Here again I wish to argue that reasons of justice have a *special* weight for which only the conception of justice as fairness can account. Moreover, it belongs to the concept of justice that they do have this special weight. While Mill recognized that this was so, he thought that it could be accounted for by the special urgency of the moral feelings which naturally support principles of such high utility. But it is a mistake to resort to the urgency of feeling; as with the appeal to intuition, it manifests a failure to pursue the question far enough. The special weight of considerations of justice can be explained from the conception of justice as fairness. It is only necessary to elaborate a bit what has already been said as follows.

If one examines the circumstances in which a certain tolerance of slavery is justified, or perhaps better, excused, it turns out that these are of a rather special sort. Perhaps slavery exists as an inheritance from the past and it proves necessary to dismantle it piece by piece; at times slavery may conceivably be an advance on previous institutions. Now while there may be some excuse for slavery in special conditions, it is never an excuse for it that it is sufficiently advantageous to the slaveholder to outweigh the disadvantages to the slave and to society. A person who argues in this way is not perhaps making a wildly irrelevant remark; but he is guilty of a moral fallacy. There is disorder in his conception of the ranking of moral principles. For the slaveholder, by his own admission, has no moral title to the advantages which he receives as a slaveholder. He is no more prepared than the slave to acknowledge the principle upon which is founded the respective positions in which they both stand. Since slavery does not accord with principles which they could mutually acknowledge, they each may be supposed to agree that it is unjust: it grants claims which it ought not to grant and in doing so denies claims which it ought not to deny. Amongst persons in a general position who are debating the form of their common practices, it cannot, therefore, be offered as a reason for a practice that, in conceding these very claims that ought to be denied, it nevertheless meets existing interests more effectively. By their very nature the satisfaction of these claims is without weight and cannot enter into any tabulation of advantages and disadvantages.

Furthermore, it follows from the concept of morality that, to the extent that the slaveholder recognizes his position vis-à-vis the slave to be unjust, he would not choose to press his claims. His not wanting to receive his special advantages is one of the ways in which he shows that he thinks slavery is unjust. It would be fallacious for the legislator to suppose, then, that it is a ground for having a practice that it brings advantages greater than disadvantages, if those for whom the practice is designed, and to whom the advantages flow, acknowledge that they have no moral title to them and do not wish to receive them.

For these reasons the principles of justice have a special weight; and with respect to the principle of the greatest satisfaction of desire, as cited in the general position amongst those discussing the merits of their common practices, the principles of justice have an absolute weight. In this sense they are not contingent; and this is why their force is greater than can be accounted for by the general presumption (assuming that there is one) of the effectiveness, in the utilitarian sense, of practices which in fact satisfy them.

If one wants to continue using the concepts of classical utilitarianism, one will have to say, to meet this criticism, that at least the individual or social utility functions must be so defined that no value is given to the satisfaction of interests the representative claims of which violate the principles of justice. In this way it is no doubt possible to include these principles within the form of the utilitarian conception; but to do so is, of course, to change its inspiration altogether as a moral conception. For it is to incorporate within it principles which cannot be understood on the basis of a higher order executive decision aiming at the greatest satisfaction of desire.

It is worth remarking, perhaps, that this criticism of utilitarianism does not depend on whether or not the two assumptions, that of individuals having similar utility functions and that of diminishing marginal utility, are interpreted as psychological propositions to be supported or refuted by experience, or as moral and political principles expressed in a somewhat technical language. There are, certainly, several advantages in taking them in the latter fashion.[20] For one thing,

one might say that this is what Bentham and others really meant by them, as least as shown by how they were used in arguments for social reform. More importantly, one could hold that the best way to defend the classical utilitarian view is to interpret these assumptions as moral and political principles. It is doubtful whether, taken as psychological propositions, they are true of men in general as we know them under normal conditions. On the other hand, utilitarians would not have wanted to propose them merely as practical working principles of legislation, or as expedient maxims to guide reform, given the egalitarian sentiments of modern society.[21] When pressed they might well have invoked the idea of a more or less equal capacity of men in relevant respects if given an equal chance in a just society. But if the argument above regarding slavery is correct, then granting these assumptions as moral and political principles makes no difference. To view individuals as equally fruitful lines for the allocation of benefits, even as a matter of moral principle, still leaves the mistaken notion that the satisfaction of desire has value in itself irrespective of the relations between persons as members of a common practice, and irrespective of the claims upon one another which the satisfaction of interests represents. To see the error of this idea one must give up the conception of justice as an executive decision altogether and refer to the notion of justice as fairness: that participants in a common practice be regarded as having an original and equal liberty and that their common practices be considered unjust unless they accord with principles which persons so circumstanced and related could freely acknowledge before one another, and so could accept as fair. Once the emphasis is put upon the concept of the mutual recognition of principles by participants in a common practice the rules of which are to define their several relations and give form to their claims on one another, then it is clear that the granting of a claim the principle of which could not be acknowledged by each in the general position (that is, in the position in which the parties propose and acknowledge principles before one another) is not a reason for adopting a practice. Viewed in this way, the background of the claim is seen to exclude it from consideration; that it can represent a value in itself arises from the conception of individuals as separate lines for the assignment of benefits, as isolated persons who stand as claimants on an administrative or benevolent largesse. Occasionally persons do so stand to one another; but this is not the general case, nor, more importantly, is it the case when it is a matter of the justice of practices themselves in which participants stand in various relations to be appraised in accordance with standards which they may be expected to acknowledge before one another. Thus however mistaken the notion of the social contract may be as history, and however far it may overreach itself as a general theory of social and political obligation, it does express, suitably interpreted, an essential part of the concept of justice.[22]

VIII

By way of conclusion I should like to make two remarks: first, the original modification of the utilitarian principle (that it require of practices that the offices and positions defined by them be equal unless it is reasonable to suppose that the representative man in *every* office would find the inequality to his advantage), slight as it may appear at first sight, actually has a different conception of justice standing behind it. I have tried to show how this is so by developing the concept of justice as fairness and by indicating how this notion involves the mutual acceptance, from a general position, of the principles on which a practice is founded, and how this in turn requires the exclusion from consideration of claims violating the principles of justice. Thus the slight alteration of principle reveals another family of notions, another way of looking at the concept of justice.

Second, I should like to remark also that I have been dealing with the *concept* of justice. I have tried to set out the kinds of principles upon which judgments concerning the justice of practices may be said to stand. The analysis will be successful to the degree that it expresses the principles involved in these judgments when made by competent persons upon deliberation and reflection.[23] Now every people may be supposed to have the concept of justice, since in the life of every society there must be at least some relations in which the parties consider themselves to be circumstanced and related as the concept of justice as fairness requires. Societies will differ from one another not in having or in failing to have this notion but in the range of cases to which they apply it and in the emphasis which they give to it as compared with other moral concepts.

A firm grasp of the concept of justice itself is necessary if these variations, and the reasons for them, are to be understood. No study of the development of moral ideas and of the differences between them is more sound than the analysis of the fundamental moral concepts upon which it

must depend. I have tried, therefore, to give an analysis of the concept of justice which should apply generally, however large a part the concept may have in a given morality, and which can be used in explaining the course of men's thoughts about justice and its relations to other moral concepts. How it is to be used for this purpose is a large topic which I cannot, of course, take up here. I mention it only to emphasize that I have been dealing with the concept of justice itself and to indicate what use I consider such an analysis to have.

NOTES

1. I use the word "practice" throughout as a sort of technical term meaning any form of activity specified by a system of rules which defines offices, roles, moves, penalties, defenses, and so on, and which gives the activity its structure. As examples one may think of games and rituals, trials and parliaments, markets and systems of property. I have attempted a partial analysis of the notion of a practice in a paper "Two Concepts of Rules," *Philosophical Review,* LXIV (1955), 3–32.

2. These principles are, of course, well known in one form or another and appear in many analyses of justice even where the writers differ widely on other matters. Thus if the principle of equal liberty is commonly associated with Kant (see *The Philosophy of Law,* tr. by W. Hastie, Edinburgh, 1887, pp. 56 f.), it may be claimed that it can also be found in J. S. Mill's *On Liberty* and elsewhere, and in many other liberal writers. Recently H. L. A. Hart has argued for something like it in his paper "Are There Any Natural Rights?" *Philosophical Review,* LXIV (1955), 175–191. The injustice of inequalities which are not won in return for a contribution to the common advantage is, of course, widespread in political writings of all sorts. The conception of justice here discussed is distinctive, if at all, only in selecting these two principles in this form; but for another similar analysis, see the discussion by W. D. Lamont, *The Principles of Moral Judgment* (Oxford, 1946), ch. v.

3. This point was made by Sidgwick, *Methods of Ethics,* 6th ed. (London, 1901), Bk. III, ch. v, sec. 1. It has recently been emphasized by Sir Isaiah Berlin in a symposium, "Equality," *Proceedings of the Aristotelian Society,* n.s. LVI (1955–56), 305 f.

4. In the paper referred to above, footnote 1, I have tried to show the importance of taking practices as the proper subject of the utilitarian principle. The criticisms of so-called "restricted utilitarianism" by J. J. C. Smart, "Extreme and Restricted Utilitarianism," *Philosophical Quarterly,* VI (1956), 344–354, and by H. J. McCloskey, "An Examination of Restricted Utilitarianism," *Philosophical Review,* LXVI (1957), 466–485, do not affect my argument. These papers are concerned with the very general proposition, which is attributed (with what justice I shall not consider) to S. E. Toulmin and P. H. Nowell-Smith (and in the case of the latter paper, also, apparently, to me); namely, the proposition that particular moral actions are justified by appealing to moral rules, and moral rules in turn by reference to utility. But clearly I meant to defend no such view. My discussion of the concept of rules as maxims is an explicit rejection of it. What I did argue was that, in the *logically special* case of practices (although actually quite a common case) where the rules have special features and are not moral rules at all but legal rules

or rules of games and the like (except, perhaps, in the case of promises), there is a peculiar force to the distinction between justifying particular actions and justifying the system of rules themselves. Even then I claimed only that restricting the utilitarian principle to practices as defined strengthened it. I did not argue for the position that this amendment alone is sufficient for a complete defense of utilitarianism as a general theory of morals. In this paper I take up the question as to how the utilitarian principle itself must be modified, but here, too, the subject of inquiry is not all of morality at once, but a limited topic, the concept of justice.

5. It might seem as if J. S. Mill, in paragraph 36 of Chapter v of *Utilitarianism,* expressed the utilitarian principle in this modified form, but in the remaining two paragraphs of the chapter, and elsewhere, he would appear not to grasp the significance of the change. Hume often emphasizes that *every* man must benefit. For example, in discussing the utility of general rules, he holds that they are requisite to the "well-being of every individual"; from a stable system of property "every individual person must find himself a gainer in balancing the account. . . . " "Every member of society is sensible of this interest; everyone expresses this sense to his fellows along with the resolution he has taken of squaring his actions by it, on the conditions that others will do the same." *A Treatise of Human Nature,* Bk. III, Pt. II, Section II, paragraph 22.

6. It is not possible to discuss here this addition to the usual conception of rationality. If it seems peculiar, it may be worth remarking that it is analogous to the modification of the utilitarian principle which the argument as a whole is designed to explain and justify. In the same way that the satisfaction of interests, the representative claims of which violate the principles of justice, is not a reason for having a practice (see sec. VII), unfounded envy, within limits, need not to be taken into account.

7. The idea that accepting a principle as a moral principle implies that one generally acts on it, failing a special explanation, has been stressed by R. M. Hare, *The Language of Morals* (Oxford, 1952). His formulation of it needs to be modified, however, along the lines suggested by P. L. Gardiner, "On Assenting to a Moral Principle," *Proceedings of the Aristotelian Society,* n.s. LV (1955), 23–44. See also C. K. Grant, "Akrasia and the Criteria of Assent to Practical Principles," *Mind,* LXV (1956), 400–407, where the complexity of the criteria for assent is discussed.

8. Perhaps the best known statement of this conception is that given by Glaucon at the beginning of Book II of Plato's *Republic.* Presumably it was, in various forms, a common view among the Sophists; but that Plato gives a fair representation of it is doubtful. See K. R. Popper, *The Open Society and Its Enemies,* rev. ed. (Princeton, 1950), pp. 112–118. Certainly Plato usually attributes to it a quality of manic egoism which one feels must be an exaggeration; on the other hand, see the Melian Debate in Thucydides, *The Peloponnesian War,* Book V, ch. vii, although it is impossible to say to what extent the views expressed there reveal any current philosophical opinion. Also in this tradition are the remarks of Epicurus on justice in *Principal Doctrines,* XXXI–XXXVIII. In modern times elements of the conception appear in a more sophisticated form in Hobbes's *The Leviathan* and in Hume's *A Treatise of Human Nature,* Book III, Pt. II, as well as in the writings of the school of natural law such as Pufendorf's *De jure naturae et gentium.* Hobbes and Hume are especially instructive. For Hobbe's argument see Howard Warrender's *The Political Philosophy of Hobbes* (Oxford, 1957). W. J. Baumol's *Welfare Economics and the Theory of the State* (London, 1952), is valuable in showing the wide applicability of Hobbes's fundamental idea (interpreting his

natural law as principles of prudence), although in this book it is traced back only to Hume's *Treatise.*

9. See J. von Neumann and O. Morgenstern, *The Theory of Games and Economic Behavior,* 2nd ed. (Princeton, 1947). For a comprehensive and not too technical discussion of the developments since, see R. Duncan Luce and Howard Raiffa, *Games and Decisions: Introduction and Critical Survey* (New York, 1957). Chs. vi and xiv discuss the developments most obviously related to the analysis of justice.

10. For a general survey see J. W. Gough, *The Social Contract,* 2nd ed. (Oxford, 1957), and Otto von Gierke, *The Development of Political Theory,* tr. by B. Freyd (London, 1939), Pt. II, ch. II.

11. The difficulty one gets into by a mechanical application of the theory of games to moral philosophy can be brought out by considering among several possible examples, R. B. Braithwaite's study, *Theory of Games as a Tool for the Moral Philosopher* (Cambridge, 1955). On the analysis there given, it turns out that the fair division of playing time between Matthew and Luke depends on their preferences, and these in turn are connected with the instruments they wish to play. Since Matthew has a threat advantage over Luke, arising purely from the fact that Matthew, the trumpeter, prefers both of them playing at once to neither of them playing, whereas Luke, the pianist, prefers silence to cacophony, Matthew is allotted 26 evenings of play to Luke's 17. If the situation were reversed, the threat advantage would be with Luke. See pp. 36 f. But now we have only to suppose that Matthew is a jazz enthusiast who plays the drums, and Luke a violinist who plays sonatas, in which case it will be fair, on this analysis, for Matthew to play whenever and as often as he likes, assuming, of course, as it is plausible to assume, that he does not care whether Luke plays or not. Certainly something has gone wrong. To each according to his threat advantage is hardly the principle of fairness. What is lacking is the concept of morality, and it must be brought into the conjectural account in some way or other. In the text this is done by the form of the procedure whereby principles are proposed and acknowledged (section III). If one starts directly with the particular case as known, and if one accepts as given and definitive the preferences and relative positions of the parties, whatever they are, it is impossible to give an analysis of the moral concept of fairness. Braithwaite's use of the theory of games, insofar as it is intended to analyze the concept of fairness, is, I think, mistaken. This is not, of course, to criticize in any way the theory of games as a mathematical theory, to which Braithwaite's book certainly contributes, nor as an analysis of how rational (and amoral) egoists might behave (and so as an analysis of how people sometimes actually do behave). But it is to say that if the theory of games is to be used to analyze moral concepts, its formal structure must be interpreted in a special and general manner as indicated in the text. Once we do this, though, we are in touch again with a much older tradition.

12. For the definition of this prima facie duty, and the idea that it is a special duty, I am indebted to H. L. A. Hart. See his paper "Are There Any Natural Rights?" *Philosophical Review,* LXIV (1955), 185 f.

13. The sense of "performative" here is to be derived from J. L. Austin's paper in the symposium, "Other Minds," *Proceedings of the Aristotelian Society,* Supplementary Volume (1946), pp. 170–174.

14. This, however, commonly happens. Hobbes, for example, when invoking the notion of a "tacit covenant," appeals not to the natural law that promises should be kept but to his fourth law of nature, that of gratitude. On Hobbes's shift from fidelity to gratitude, see Warrender, *Political Philos-*

ophy of Hobbes (footnote 8), pp. 51–52, 233–237. While it is not a serious criticism of Hobbes, it would have improved his argument had he appealed to the duty of fair play. On his premises he is perfectly entitled to do so. Similarly Sidgwick thought that a principle of justice, such as every man ought to receive adequate requital for his labor, is like gratitude universalized. See *Methods of Ethics,* Bk. III, ch. v, Sec. 5. There is a gap in the stock of moral concepts used by philosophers into which the concept of the duty of fair play fits quite naturally.

15.   I am using the concept of criterion here in what I take to be Wittgenstein's sense. See *Philosophical Investigations,* (Oxford, 1953); and Norman Malcolm's review, "Wittgenstein's *Philosophical Investigations,*" *Philosophical Review,* LXIII (1954), 543–547. That the response of compassion, under appropriate circumstances, is part of the criterion for whether or not a person understands what "pain" means, is, I think, in the *Philosophical Investigations.* The view in the text is simply an extension of this idea. I cannot, however, attempt to justify it here. Similar thoughts are to be found, I think, in Max Scheler, *The Nature of Sympathy,* tr. by Peter Heath (New Haven, 1954). His way of writing is often so obscure that I cannot be certain.

16.   While this assimilation is implicit in Bentham's and Sidgwick's moral theory, explicit statements of it as applied to justice are relatively rare. One clear instance in *The Principles of Morals and Legislation* occurs in ch. x, footnote 2 to section XL: ". . . justice, in the only sense in which it has a meaning, is an imaginary personage, feigned for the convenience of discourse, whose dictates are the dictates of utility, applied to certain particular cases. Justice, then, is nothing more than an imaginary instrument, employed to forward on certain occasions, and by certain means, the purposes of benevolence. The dictates of justice are nothing more than a part of the dictates of benevolence, which, on certain occasions, are applied to certain subjects. . . ." Likewise in *The Limits of Jurisprudence Defined,* ed. by C. W. Everett (New York, 1945), p. 117 f., Bentham criticizes Grotius for denying that justice derives from utility; and in *The Theory of Legislation,* ed. by C. K. Ogden (London, 1931), p. 3, he says that he uses the words "just" and "unjust" along with other words "simply as collective terms including the ideas of certain pains or pleasures." That Sidgwick's conception of justice is similar to Bentham's is admittedly not evident from his discussion of justice in Book III, ch. v of *Methods of Ethics.* But it follows, I think, from the moral theory he accepts. Hence C. D. Broad's criticism of Sidgwick in the matter of distributive justice in *Five Types of Ethical Theory* (London, 1930), pp. 249–253, do not rest on a misinterpretation.

17.   This maxim is attributed to Bentham by J. S. Mill in *Utilitarianism,* ch. v, paragraph 36. I have not found it in Bentham's writings, nor seen such a reference. Similarly James Bonar, *Philosophy and Political Economy* (London, 1893), p. 234 n. But it accords perfectly with Bentham's ideas. See the hitherto unpublished manuscript in David Baumgardt, *Bentham and the Ethics of Today* (Princeton, 1952), Appendix IV. For example, "the total value of the stock of pleasure belonging to the whole community is to be obtained by multiplying the number expressing the value of it as respecting any one person, by the number expressing the multitude of such individuals" (p. 556).

18.   An idea essential to the classical utilitarian conception of justice. Bentham is firm in his statement of it: "It is only upon that principle [the principle of asceticism], and not from the principle of utility, that the most abominable pleasure which the vilest of malefactors ever reaped from his crime would be reprobated, if it stood alone. The case is, that it never does stand alone; but is necessarily followed by such a quan-

tity of pain (or, what comes to the same thing, such a chance for a certain quantity of pain) that the pleasure in comparison of it, is as nothing: and this is the true and sole, but perfectly sufficient, reason for making it a ground for punishment" (*The Principles of Morals and Legislation,* ch. II, sec. iv. See also ch. x, sec. x, footnote I). The same point is made in *The Limits of Jurisprudence Defined,* pp. 115 f. Although much recent welfare economics, as found in such important works as I. M. D. Little, *A Critique of Welfare Economics,* 2nd ed. (Oxford, 1957) and K. J. Arrow, *Social Choice and Individual Values* (New York, 1951), dispenses with the idea of cardinal utility, and uses instead the theory of ordinal utility as stated by J. R. Hicks, *Value and Capital,* 2nd ed. (Oxford, 1946), Pt. I, it assumes with utilitarianism that individual preferences have value as such, and so accepts the idea being criticized here. I hasten to add, however, that this is no objection to it as a means of analyzing economic policy, and for that purpose it may, indeed, be a necessary simplifying assumption. Nevertheless it is an assumption which cannot be made insofar as one is trying to analyze moral concepts, especially the concept of justice, as economists would, I think, agree. Justice is usually regarded as a separate and distinct part of any comprehensive criterion of economic policy. See, for example, Tibor Scitovsky, *Welfare and Competition* (London, 1952), pp. 59–69, and Little, *Critique of Welfare Economics* (this footnote), ch. VII.

19.   See J. S. Mill's argument in *Utilitarianism,* ch. v, pars. 16–25.

20.   See D. G. Ritchie, *Natural Rights* (London, 1894), pp. 95 ff., 249 ff. Lionel Robbins has insisted on this point on several occasions. See *An Essay on the Nature and Significance of Economic Science,* 2nd ed. (London, 1935), pp. 134–43, "Interpersonal Comparisons of Utility: A Comment," *Economic Journal,* XLVIII (1938), 635–41, and more recently, "Robertson on Utility and Scope," *Economica,* n.s. XX (1953), 108 f.

21.   As Sir Henry Maine suggested Bentham may have regarded them. See *The Early History of Institutions* (London, 1875), pp. 398 ff.

22.   Thus Kant was not far wrong when he interpreted the original contract merely as an "Idea of Reason"; yet he still thought of it as a *general* criterion of right and as providing a general theory of political obligation. See the second part of the essay, "On the Saying 'That may be right in theory but has no value in practice'" (1793), in *Kant's Principles of Politics,* tr. by W. Hastie (Edinburgh, 1891). I have drawn on the contractarian tradition not for a general theory of political obligation but to clarify the concept of justice.

23.   For a further discussion of the idea expressed here, see my paper, "Outline of a Decision Procedure for Ethics," in the *Philosophical Review,* LX (1951), 177–197. For an analysis, similar in many respects but using the notion of the ideal observer instead of that of the considered judgment of a competent person, see Roderick Firth, "Ethical Absolutism and the Ideal Observer," *Philosophy and Phenomenological Research,* XII (1952), 317–345. While the similarities between these two discussions are more important than the differences, an analysis based on the notion of a considered judgment of a competent person, as it is based on a kind of judgment, may prove more helpful in understanding the features of moral judgment than an analysis based on the notion of an ideal observer, although this remains to be shown. A man who rejects the conditions imposed on a considered judgment of a competent person could no longer profess to *judge* at all. This seems more fundamental than his rejecting the conditions of observation, for these do not seem to apply, in an ordinary sense, to making a moral judgment.

ROBERT NOZICK

The Principle of Fairness*

A principle suggested by Herbert Hart, which (following John Rawls) we shall call the *principle of fairness,* would be of service here if it were adequate. This principle holds that when a number of persons engage in a just, mutually advantageous, cooperative venture according to rules and thus restrain their liberty in ways necessary to yield advantages for all, those who have submitted to these restrictions have a right to similar acquiescence on the part of those who have benefited from their submission.[1] Acceptance of benefits (even when this is not a giving of express or tacit undertaking to cooperate) is enough, according to this principle, to bind one. If one adds to the principle of fairness the claim that the others to whom the obligations are owed or their agents may *enforce* the obligations arising under this principle (including the obligation to limit one's actions), then groups of people in a state of nature who agree to a procedure to pick those to engage in certain acts will have legitimate rights to prohibit "free riders." Such a right may be crucial to the viability of such agreements. We should scrutinize such a powerful right very carefully, especially as it seems to make *unanimous* consent to coercive government in a state of nature *unnecessary!* Yet a further reason to examine it is its plausibility as a counterexample to my claim that no new rights "emerge" at the group level, that individuals in combination cannot create new rights which are not the sum of preexisting ones. A right to enforce others' obligation to limit their conduct in specified ways might stem from some special feature of the obligation or might be thought to follow from some general principle that all obligations owed to others may be enforced. In the absence of argument for the special enforcement—justifying nature of the obligation supposedly arising under the principle of fairness, I shall consider first the principle of the enforceability of all obligations and then turn to the adequacy of the principle of fairness itself. If either of these principles is rejected, the right to enforce the cooperation of others in these situations totters. I shall argue that *both* of these principles must be rejected.

Herbert Hart's argument for the existence of a natural right[2] depends upon particularizing the principle of the enforceability of all obligations: someone's being under a special obligation to you to do *A* (which might have arisen, for example, by their promising to you that they would do *A*) gives you, not only the right that they do *A,* but also the right to force them to do *A*. Only against a background in which people may not force you to do *A* or other actions you may promise to do can we understand, says Hart, the *point* and purpose of special obligations. Since special obligations do have a point and purpose, Hart continues, there is a natural right not to be forced to do something unless certain specified conditions pertain; this natural right is built into the background against which special obligations exist.

This well-known argument of Hart's is puzzling. I may release someone from an obligation not to force me to do *A*. ("I now release you from the obligation not to force me to do *A*. You now are free to force me to do *A*.") Yet so releasing them does *not* create in me an obligation to them to do *A*. Since Hart supposes that my being under an obligation to someone to do *A* gives him (entails that he has) the right to force me to do *A*, and since we have seen the converse does not hold, we may consider that component of being under an obligation to someone to do something over and above his having the right to force you to do it. (May we suppose there is this distinguishable component without facing the charge of "logical atomism"?) An alternative view which rejects Hart's inclusion of the right to force in the notion of being owed an obligation might hold that this additional component is the *whole* of the content of being obligated to someone to do something. If I don't do it, then (all things being equal) I'm doing something wrong; control over the situation is in his hands; he has the power to release me from the obligation unless he's promised to someone else that he won't, and so on. Perhaps all this looks too *ephemeral* without the additional presence of rights of enforcement. Yet rights of enforcement are themselves merely *rights;* that is, permissions to do something and obligations on others not to interfere. True, one has the right to enforce these further obligations, but it is not clear that including *rights* of enforcing really shores up the whole structure if one assumes it to be insubstantial to begin with. Perhaps one must merely take the moral realm seriously and think one component amounts to something even without a connection to enforcement. (Of course, this is not to say that this component *never* is connected with enforcement!) On this view, we can explain the point of obligations without bringing in rights of enforcement and hence without supposing a general background of obligation not to force from which this stands out. (Of course, even though Hart's argument does not demonstrate the existence of such an obligation not to force, it may exist nevertheless.)

Apart from these general considerations against the principle of the enforceability of all special obligations, puzzle cases can be produced. For example, if I promise to you that I will not murder someone, this does not *give* you the right to force me not to, for you already have this right, though it does create a particular obligation *to you.* Or, if I cautiously insist that you first promise to me that you won't force me to do *A* before I will make my promise to you to do *A*, and I do receive this promise from you first, it would be implausible to say that in promising I give you the right to force me to do *A*. (Though consider the situation which results if I am so foolish as to release you unilaterally from your promise to me.)

If there were cogency to Hart's claim that only against a background of required nonforcing can we understand the point of special rights, then there would seem to be equal cogency to the claim that only against a background of *permitted* forcing can we understand the point of *general* rights. For according to Hart, a person has a general right to do *A* if and only if for all persons *P* and *Q*, *Q* may not interfere with *P*'s doing *A* or force him not to do *A*, unless *P* has acted to give *Q* a special right to do this. But not every act can be substituted for "*A*"; people have general

rights to do only particular types of action. So, one might argue, if there is to be a point to having general rights, to having rights to do a particular type of act *A*, to other's being under an obligation not to force you not to do *A*, then it must be against a contrasting background, in which there is *no* obligation on people to refrain from forcing you to do, or not to do, things, that is, against a background in which, for actions generally, people do *not* have a general right to do them. If Hart can argue to a presumption against forcing from there being a point to particular rights, then it seems he can equally well argue to the absence of such a presumption from there being a point to general rights.[3]

An argument for an enforceable obligation has two stages: the first leads to the existence of the obligation, and the second, to its enforceability. Having disposed of the second stage (at least insofar as it is supposed generally to follow from the first), let us turn to the supposed obligation to cooperate in the joint decisions of others to limit their activities. The principle of fairness, as we stated it following Hart and Rawls, is objectionable and unacceptable. Suppose some of the people in your neighborhood (there are 364 other adults) have found a public address system and decide to institute a system of public entertainment. They post a list of names, one for each day, yours among them. On his assigned day (one can easily switch days) a person is to run the public address system, play records over it, give news bulletins, tell amusing stories he has heard, and so on. After 138 days on which each person has done his part, your day arrives. Are you obligated to take your turn? You *have* benefited from it, occasionally opening your window to listen, enjoying some music or chuckling at someone's funny story. The other people *have* put themselves out. But must you answer the call when it is your turn to do so? As it stands, surely not. Though you benefit from the arrangement, you may know all along that 364 days of entertainment supplied by others will not be worth your giving up *one* day. You would rather not have any of it and not give up a day than have it all and spend one of your days at it. Given these preferences, how can it be that you are required to participate when your scheduled time comes? It would be nice to have philosophy readings on the radio to which one could tune in at any time, perhaps late at night when tired. But it may not be nice enough for you to want to give up one whole day of your own as a reader on the program. Whatever you want, can others create an obligation for you to do so by going ahead and starting the program themselves? In this case you can choose to forego the benefit by not turning on the radio; in other cases the benefits may be unavoidable. If each day a different person on your street sweeps the entire street, must you do so when your time comes? Even if you don't care that much about a clean street? Must you imagine dirt as you traverse the street, so as not to benefit as a free rider? Must you refrain from turning on the radio to hear the philosophy readings? Must you mow your front lawn as often as your neighbors mow theirs?

At the very least one wants to build into the principle of fairness the condition that the benefits to a person from the actions of the others are greater than the costs to him of doing his share. How are we to imagine this? Is the condition satisfied if you do enjoy the daily broadcasts over the PA system in your neighborhood but would prefer a day off hiking, rather than hearing these broadcasts all year? For you to be obligated to give up your day to broadcast mustn't it be true, at least, that there is nothing you could do with a day (with that day, with the increment in any other day by shifting some activities to that day) which you would prefer to hearing broadcasts for the year? If the only way to get the broadcasts was to spend the day participating in the arrangement, in order for the condition that the benefits outweigh the costs to be satisfied, you would have to be willing to spend it on the broadcasts rather than to gain *any* other available thing.

If the principle of fairness were modified so as to contain this very strong condition, it still would be objectionable. The benefits might only barely be worth the costs to you of doing your share, yet others might benefit from *this* institution much more than you do; they all treasure listening to the public broadcasts. As the person least benefited by the practice, are you obligated to do an equal amount for it? Or perhaps you would prefer that all cooperated in *another* venture, limiting their conduct and making sacrifices for *it.* It is true, *given* that they are not following your plan (and thus limiting what other options are available to you), that the benefits of their venture *are* worth to you the costs of your cooperation. However, you do not wish to cooperate, as part of your plan to focus their attention on your alternative proposal which they have ignored or not given, in your view at least, its proper due. (You want them, for example, to read the Talmud on the radio instead of the philosophy they are reading.) By lending the institution (their institution) the support of your cooperating in it, you will only make it harder to change or alter.[4]

On the face of it, enforcing the principle of fairness is objectionable. You may not decide to give me something, for example a book, and then grab money from me to pay for it, even if I have nothing better to spend the money on. You have, if anything, even less reason to demand payment if your activity that gives me the book also benefits you; suppose that your best way of getting exercise is by throwing books into people's houses, or that some other activity of yours thrusts books into people's houses as an unavoidable side effect. Nor are things changed if your inability to collect money or payments for the books which unavoidably spill over into others' houses makes it inadvisable or too expensive for you to carry on the activity with this side effect. One cannot, whatever one's purposes, just act so as to give people benefits and then demand (or seize) payment. Nor can a group of persons do this. If you may not charge and collect for benefits you bestow without prior agreement, you certainly may not do so for benefits whose bestowal costs you nothing, and most certainly people need not repay you for costless-to-provide benefits which yet *others* provided them. So the fact that we partially are "social products" in that we benefit from current patterns and forms created by the multitudinous actions of a long string of long–forgotten people, forms which include institutions, ways of doing things, and language (whose social nature may involve our current use depending upon Wittgensteinian matching of the speech of others), does not create in us a general floating debt which the current society can collect and use as it will.

Perhaps a modified principle of fairness can be stated which would be free from these and similar difficulties. What seems certain is that any such principle, if possible, would be so complex and involuted that one could not combine it with a special principle legitimating *enforcement* within a state of nature of the obligations that have arisen under it. Hence, even if the principle could be formulated so that it was no longer open to objection, it would not serve to obviate the need for other persons' *consenting* to cooperate and limit their own activities.

NOTES

1. Herbert Hart, "Are There Any Natural Rights?" *Philosophical Review,* 1955; John Rawls, *A Theory of Justice* (Cambridge, Mass.: Harvard University Press, 1971), sect. 18. My statement of the principle stays close to Rawls. The argument Rawls offers for this principle constitutes an argument

only for the narrower principle of fidelity (bona fide promises are to be kept). Though if there were no way to avoid "can't get started" difficulties about the principle of fidelity (p. 349) other than by appealing to the principle of fairness, it *would* be an argument for the principle of fairness.

2. Hart, "Are There Any Natural Rights?"

3. I have formulated my remarks in terms of the admittedly vague notion of there being a "point" to certain kinds of rights because this, I think, gives Hart's argument its most plausible construction.

4. I have skirted making the institution one that you didn't get a fair say in setting up or deciding its nature, for here Rawls would object that it doesn't satisfy his two principles of justice. Though Rawls does not require that every microinstitution satisfy his two principles of justice, but only the basic structure of the society, he seems to hold that a microinstitution must satisfy these two principles if it is to give rise to obligations under the principle of fairness.

DISCRIMINATION AND REVERSE DISCRIMINATION
LOUIS KATZNER

Is the Favoring of Women and Blacks in Employment and Educational Opportunities Justified?*

There is presently a call to favor blacks and women in employment and educational opportunities because in the past many of them have been discriminated against in these areas. The basic concern of this paper is whether or not reverse discrimination in this sense is justified. Given that, as will be shown, all acts of reverse discrimination involve prejudgment, it is appropriate to scrutinize first the notion of discrimination itself. Next, the idea of reverse discrimination will be explicated by distinguishing among several different forms that it may take; and from this explication the set of conditions under which a bias of redress is justified will emerge. Finally, the situation of blacks and women in the United States will be examined to see what conclusions can be drawn concerning the justification of reverse discrimination for these two classes.

I. DISCRIMINATION

There are certain things that are relevant to the way people should be treated and certain things that are not. The size of one's chest is relevant to the size shirt he should have, but it has nothing to do with the size his shoes should be. The rate of one's metabolism is pertinent to the amount of food she should be served, but not to the color of the napkin she is given. People should be treated on the basis of their attributes and merits that are relevant to the circumstances. When they are, those who are similar are treated similarly and those who are dissimilar are treated differently. Although these distinctions do involve treating people differently (those with larger chests get larger shirts than those with smaller chests), it does not involve discrimination. For discrimination means treating people differently when they are similar in the relevant respects or treating them similarly when they are different in the relevant respects.

It follows that to determine what constitutes discrimination in vocational and educational op-

*This essay has not been published elsewhere.

portunities, we must first determine what qualities are relevant to a career and the capacity to learn. People today generally seem to accept the principle of meritocracy—that is, that an individual's potential for success, which is a combination of his native and/or developed ability and the amount of effort he can be expected to put forth, is the sole criterion that should be used in hiring and college admissions practices. It may be that until recently many people did not accept this view, and it may be that there are some even today who do not accept it. Nevertheless, this is one of the basic principles of the "American Dream"; it is the foundation of the civil service system; it is a principle to which even the most ardent racists and sexists at least give lipservice; and it is the principle that most people seem to have in mind when they speak of the problem of discrimination in hiring and college admissions practices. And because it is generally agreed that people with the same potential should be treated similarly in employment and college admissions, and that those with more potential should receive preference over those with less, the discussion begins with this assumption.

II. REVERSE DISCRIMINATION

With the notion of discrimination clarified, it is now possible to see what is involved in the idea of reverse discrimination. Reverse discrimination is much more than a call to eliminate bias; it is a call to offset the effects of past acts of bias by skewing opportunity in the opposite direction. This paper will consider only the claims that blacks, women, et cetera, have been discriminated against in the past (that is, they have been treated as if they have less potential than they actually do); and that the only way to offset their subsequent disadvantages is to discriminate now in their favor (that is, to treat them as if they have more potential than they actually do).

It follows that those who are currently calling for the revision of admission standards at our colleges because they do not accurately reflect a student's chances of success there are not calling for reverse discrimination. They are merely saying that we should find a way of determining precisely who is qualified (that is, who has the potential) to go to college, and then admit the most qualified. On the other hand, those who are calling for us to admit students whom they allow are less qualified than others who are denied admission, and to provide these less qualified students with special tutorial help, are calling for reverse discrimination.

This example clearly illustrates the basic problem that any justification of reverse discrimination must come to grips with—viz., that every act of reverse discrimination is itself discriminatory. For every less qualified person who is admitted to a college, or hired for a job, there is a more qualified person who is being discriminated against, and who has a right to complain. Hence the justification of reverse discrimination must involve not only a justification of *discriminating for* those who are benefiting from it, it must also involve a justification of discriminating *against* those at whose expense the reverse discrimination is being practiced.

III. JUSTIFICATION OF REVERSE DISCRIMINATION: DIRECT

There are at least two significantly different kinds of situations in which reverse discrimination can be called for. On the one hand, a person might argue that he should be favored because he was arbitrarily passed over at some time in the past. Thus, for example, a Chicano might maintain that since he was denied a job for which he was the most qualified candidate simply because of his race, he should now be given one for which he is not the most qualified candidate, simply because he was discriminated against in the past. On the other hand, one might argue that he should be given preference because his ancestors (parents, grandparents, great–grandparents, et cetera) were discriminated against. In this case, the Chicano would claim that he should be given a job for which he is not the most qualified applicant because his ancestors were denied jobs for which they were the most qualified.

In the former case, that of rectifying bias against an individual by unduly favoring him, there are several interesting points that can be made. First of all, the case for reverse discrimination of this type is strongest when the person to be passed over in the reverse discrimination is the same one who benefited from the initial discriminatory act. Suppose, for example, that when it comes time to appoint the vice-president of a company, the best qualified applicant (that is, the one who has the most potential) is passed over because of his race, and a less qualified applicant is given the job. Suppose that the following year the job of president in the same firm becomes open. At this point, the vice-president, because of the training he had as second in command, is the most qualified applicant for the job. It could be argued, however, that the presidency should go to the person who was passed over for the vice-presidency. For he should have been the vice-president, and if he had been he would probably now be the best-equipped applicant for the top post; it is only because he was passed over that the current vice-president is now the most qualified candidate. In other words, since the current vice-president got ahead at his expense, it is warranted for him to move up at the vice-president's expense. In this way the wrong that was done him will be righted.

There are two main problems with this argument. First of all, certainly to be considered is how well the individual who benefited from the initial act of discrimination exploited his break. If he used this opportunity to work up to his capacity, this would seem to be a good reason for not passing him over for the presidency. If, on the other hand, although performing very adequately as vice-president, he was not working up to the limits of his capacity, then perhaps the job of president should be given to the man who was passed over in the first place—even though the vice-president's experience in his job leads one to think that he is the one most qualified to handle the difficult tasks of the presidency. In other words, how much a person has made of the benefit he has received from an act of discrimination seems to be relevant to the question of whether or not he should be discriminated against so that the victim of that discrimination may now be benefited.

Secondly, there are so few cases of this kind that even if reverse discrimination is justified in such cases, this would not show very much. In most instances of reverse discrimination, the redress is at the expense of someone who did not benefit from the initial act of discrimination rather than someone who did.

One species of this form of reverse discrimination is that in which the victim of the proposed act of reverse discrimination has not benefited from *any* acts of discrimination. In such a case, what is in effect happening is that the burden of discrimination is being transferred from one individual who does not deserve it to another individual who does not deserve it. There is no sense in which "the score is being evened," as in the case above. Because there is no reason for saying that one of the individuals deserves to be penalized by prejudice while the other one does not, it is difficult to see how this kind of reverse discrimination can be justified.

The only argument that comes to mind as a justification for this species of reverse discrimination is the following: The burdens of discrimination should be shared rather than placed on a few. It is better that the liabilities of discrimination be passed from person to person than that they remain the handicap only of those who have been disfavored. It follows that if we find someone who has been discriminated against, we are warranted in rectifying that injustice by an act of reverse discrimination, as long as the victim of the reverse discrimination has not himself been discriminated against in the past.

But this is not a very persuasive argument. For one thing, the claim that discrimination should be shared does not seem a very compelling reason for discriminating against a totally innocent bystander. Secondly, even if this is viewed as a forceful reason, the image of society that emerges is a horrifying one. The moment someone is discriminated against, he seeks out someone who has not been unfairly barred, and asks for reverse discrimination against this person to rectify the wrong he has suffered. Such a procedure would seem to entrench rather than eliminate discrimination, and would produce an incredibly unstable society.

Another species of this form of reverse discrimination is that in which the victim of the proposed reverse bias has benefited from a previous unfair decision, although it is not the particular act that is being rectified. In other words, he did not get ahead at the expense of the individual to whom we are trying to "make things up" by reverse discrimination, but he has benefited from bias against other individuals. In such a case, there is a sense, admittedly extended, in which a score is being evened.

Now it appears that such cases are more like those in which the victim of the proposed act of reverse discrimination benefited from the initial instance of discrimination than those in which he is a completely innocent bystander, and hence in such cases reverse discrimination can be justified. Of course it would be preferable if we could find the beneficiary of the original act of discrimina-

tion—but very often this just is not possible. And we must make sure that the reverse discrimination is proportionate to both the liability suffered by the proposed beneficiary and the advantage previously gained by the proposed victim—a very difficult task indeed. But there does not seem to be any reason for saying that reverse discrimination can only be visited upon those who benefited from the particular discriminatory act that is being rectified. It seems more reasonable to say that reverse discrimination can be visited upon those who benefited from either the particular instance of discrimination being rectified or from roughly similar acts.

Although the conclusions drawn from this discussion of the various species of one form of reverse discrimination do not seem conclusive, this discussion has brought to light three conditions which are necessary for the justification of reverse discrimination: First, there must have been an act of discrimination that is being rectified. Second, the initial act of discrimination must have in some way handicapped its victim, for if he has not been handicapped or set back in some way, then there is nothing to "make up to him" through reverse discrimination. And third, the victim of the proposed reverse discrimination must have benefited from an act of discrimination (either the one that is being rectified or a similar one); otherwise it is unacceptable to say that he should now be disfavored.

IV. JUSTIFICATION OF REVERSE DISCRIMINATION: INDIRECT

Not all of the claims that are made for reverse discrimination, however, assume that the individual involved has himself been the victim of bias. In many cases what is being claimed is that an individual is entitled to benefit from a rectifying bias because his ancestors (parents, grandparents, great grandparents, et cetera) were unfairly denied opportunity. Keeping in mind the three conditions necessary for reverse discrimination that we have just developed, this form of reverse discrimination will be examined.

In a society in which wealth could not be accumulated or, even if it could, it did not give one access to a better education and/or job, and a good education did not give one access to a better job and/or greater wealth, it would be hard to see how educational and/or economic discrimination against one's ancestors could be a handicap. That is, if education was not a key to economic success, then the educational discrimination one's ancestors suffered could not handicap one in the search for a job. If wealth did not buy better teachers and better schools, then the fact that one's ancestors have been handicapped economically could not be a reason for his being educationally disadvantaged. If wealth could not start a business, buy into a business, or give one direct access to a good job, then the economic shackling one's ancestors endured could in no way handicap her in the economic realm. But if wealth and education do these things, as in our society they clearly do, and if because of discrimination some people were not allowed to accumulate the wealth that their talents normally would bring, then it is quite clear that their offspring are handicapped by the discrimination they have suffered.

It is important to note that this point in no way turns on the controversy that is currently raging over the relationship between IQ and race. For it is not being claimed that unless there is complete equality there is discrimination. The members of a suppressed group may be above, below, or equal to the other members of society with regard to potential. All that is being claimed is that to the extent that the members of a group have been denied a fair chance to do work commensurate with their capacities, and to the extent that this has handicapped subsequent members of that group, reverse discrimination may be justified to offset this handicap.

But, as we have already seen, for reverse discrimination to be justified, not only must the victims of discrimination be handicapped by the discrimination, those who will suffer from its reversal must have benefited from the original injustice. In this particular case, it may be that they are the children of the beneficiaries of discrimination who have passed these advantages on to them. Or it may be that they benefit in facing reduced competition for schooling and jobs, and hence they are able to get into a better school and land a better job than they would if those suffering the effects of discrimination were not handicapped. Or they may have benefited from discrimination in some other way. But the proposed victims of reverse discrimination must be the beneficiaries of previous discrimination.

In addition to all of this, however, it seems that there is one more condition that must be met for reverse discrimination to be justified. Assuming that if we eliminated all discrimination immediately, the people who have suffered from it could compete on an equal basis with all other members of society, then reverse discrimination would not be justified. This of course is trivially true if it is only being claimed that if the elimination of all discrimination entails the eradication of all the handicaps it creates, then only the elimination of discrimination (and not reverse discrimination) is justified. But the claim involves much more than this. What is being argued is that even if the immediate elimination of all discrimination does not allow all suppressed people to compete equally with other members of society, as long as it allows equal opportunity to all children born subsequent to the end of discrimination, then reverse discrimination is not justified—*not even for those who have been handicapped by discrimination.* In other words, reverse discrimination will not prevent its debilitating effects from being passed on to generations yet unborn.

The justification of this claim is a straightforward utilitarian one (it cannot be a justification in terms of justice since what is being countenanced is blatant injustice). The social cost of implementing a policy of reverse discrimination is very high. The problems in determining who are the victims of discrimination and how great their handicaps, and who are the beneficiaries of discrimination and how great their benefits, as well as the problems in both developing and administering policies that will lead to a proper rectification of discrimination, are not merely enormously complex, they are enormously costly to solve. Moreover, the benefits of ending all discrimination are very great. Not only will many people be hired for jobs and admitted to colleges otherwise barred to them because of discrimination, but many people who have themselves been handicapped by discrimination will take great satisfaction in the knowledge that their offspring will not be held back as they have. This, of course, in no way eliminates the injustice involved in allowing acts of reverse discrimination to go unrectified. All it shows is that given the tremendous cost of implementing a comprehensive program of reverse discrimination, and given the tremendous benefits that would accrue simply from the elimination of all discrimination, it is reasonable to claim that reverse discrimination is justified only if the elimination of discrimination will not prevent its debilitating effects from being passed on to generations yet unborn.

Thus there is a fourth condition that must be added to the list of conditions that are necessary for the justification of reverse discrimination. Moreover, the addition of this condition renders the list jointly sufficient for the justification of reverse discrimination. Thus, reverse discrimination is justified if, and only if, the following conditions are met:

1. There must have been an initial act of discrimination that the reverse discrimination is going to rectify.
2. The beneficiary of the proposed act of reverse discrimination must have been handicapped by the initial act—either directly, if he was the victim of the initial discrimination, or indirectly, if he is the offspring of a victim (and inherited the handicap).
3. The victim of the proposed act of reverse discrimination must have benefited from an act of discrimination—the one that is being rectified or a similar one—and either directly, if he was the beneficiary of an initial act of discrimination or indirectly, if he is the offspring of a beneficiary (and inherited the benefit).
4. It must be the case that even if all discrimination were ended immediately, the debilitating effects of discrimination would be passed on to generations yet unborn.

V. REVERSE DISCRIMINATION FAVORING WOMEN AND BLACKS

A partial answer, at least, to the question of whether or not reverse discrimination is justified in the case of women and blacks is now possible. Let us begin with blacks.

It seems clear that the situation of many blacks in this country meets the four conditions shown to be individually necessary and jointly sufficient for the justification of reverse discrimination. First, there can be no doubt that many blacks have been the victims of educational and vocational discrimination. Second, given the relationships existing between wealth, education, and vocation, there can be no doubt that the discrimination that blacks have met with has handicapped both themselves and their offspring. Third, it also seems clear that within our economic framework, if blacks had not been discriminated against, there are many whites (those who got an education or a job at the expense of a more qualified black or in competition with the handicapped offspring of disadvantaged blacks) who would be in far less advantageous educational and vocational situations than they currently are —that is, there are people who have benefited from discrimination. And finally, again given the relationships existing among wealth, education, and vocation, even if all discrimination against

blacks were to cease immediately, many black children born subsequent to this time would not be able to compete for educational and vocational opportunities on the same basis that they would had there been no bias against their ancestors.

Of course this in no way shows that reverse discrimination for all blacks is justified. After all, there are some blacks who have not let themselves be handicapped by discrimination. There are also undoubtedly some whites who have not benefited from the discrimination against blacks. And finally, there are many whites who have endured discrimination in the same way blacks have. In other words, so far it has only been shown that all those who have been discriminated against in a way that meets the conditions established are entitled to reverse discrimination and that some blacks have been discriminated against in this way.

To move from this claim to the conclusion that blacks as a class are entitled to reverse discrimination, several additional things must be shown. First, it must be demonstrated that it is unfeasible to handle reverse discrimination on a case by case basis (for example, it might be argued that such a procedure would be far too costly). Second, it must be proven that the overwhelming percentage of blacks have been victimized by discrimination—that is, the number of blacks who would benefit from reverse discrimination, but who do not deserve to, must be very small. And finally, it must be shown that the overwhelming majority of the potential victims of bias of redress have benefited from the acts of discrimination (or similar acts) that are being rectified—that is, it must be that the number of whites who will suffer the effects of reverse discrimination, without deserving to, must also be very small. If these conditions are met, then although there will be some unwarranted discrimination resulting from the reverse discrimination in favor of blacks (that is, some blacks benefiting who were not victimized and some whites suffering who were not benefited), such cases will be kept to a bare minimum, and hence the basic result will be the offsetting of the handicaps with which blacks have unwarrantedly been saddled.

When it comes to the case of (white) women, however, the situation is quite different. There is little doubt that many women have been denied opportunity, and thus handicapped while many men have benefited from this discrimination (although I believe that discrimination has been far less pervasive in the case of women than it has been for blacks). But women generally do not constitute the kind of class in which the handicaps of discrimination are passed on to one's offspring. This is because, unlike blacks, they are not an isolated social group. Most women are reared in families in which the gains a father makes, even if the mother is limited by society's prejudice, work to the advantage of *all* offspring. (White) women have attended white schools and colleges and, even if they have been discriminated against, their children have attended these same schools and colleges. If all discrimination were ended tomorrow, there would be no external problem at all for most women in competing, commensurate with their potential, with the male population.

Two important things follow from this. First, it is illegitimate for most women to claim that they should be favored because their mothers were disfavored. Second, and most importantly, if all discrimination against women were ended immediately, in most cases none of its debilitating effects would be transmitted to the generations of women yet unborn; hence, for most women, the fourth condition necessary for the justification of reverse discrimination is not satisfied. Thus, reverse discrimination for women as a class cannot be justified, although there are undoubtedly some cases in which, for a particular woman, it can.

One must be careful, however, not to interpret this judgment too broadly. For one thing, the conclusion that reverse discrimination is not warranted for women as a class is contingent upon the immediate elimination of all discrimination. Hence it does not apply if discrimination against women continues. In other words, the conclusion does not show that reverse discrimination for women as a class is unjustified in the face of continuing bias against them. Under these circumstances, reverse discrimination may or may not be justified.

Secondly, as reverse discrimination has been described here, it involves offsetting the impact of a particular kind of discrimination (that is, in educational and job opportunities) by another instance of the same kind of discrimination (that is, preferential treatment in education and job opportunities). All our argument shows is that this is unwarranted for women as a class. One might, however, want to argue in favor of discriminating for women as a class in the area of education and jobs, not to offset previous discrimination in this area, but rather to counter the debilitating effects that institutionalized sexism has had on the female psyche. That is, one might argue that because our society has conditioned women to desire subservient roles (for example, that of a nurse rather than doctor, secretary rather than executive, housewife rather than breadwinner, and so on), even if all forms of discrimination were eliminated tomorrow, very few (or at least not enough) women would take advantage of the opportunities open to them. Hence we need (reverse) discrimination as a means of placing women in visible positions of success, so that other women will have models to emulate and will strive for success in these areas. Now although it is not clear whether or not such a program can legitimately be labelled "reverse discrimination," the important point is that this paper has not been addressed to this kind of problem, and hence has not shown that it is illegitimate to give preferential treatment to women (or blacks) for this reason.

REED v. REED ADMINISTRATOR

U.S. Supreme Court, 1971*

Mr. Chief Justice Burger delivered the opinion of the Court.

Richard Lynn Reed, a minor, died intestate in Ada County, Idaho, on March 29, 1967. His adoptive parents, who had separated sometime prior to his death, are the parties to this appeal. Approximately seven months after Richard's death, his mother, appellant Sally Reed, filed a petition in the Probate Court of Ada County, seeking appointment as administratrix of her son's estate.[1] Prior to the date set for a hearing on the mother's petition, appellee Cecil Reed, the father of the decedent, filed a competing petition seeking to have himself appointed administrator of the son's estate. The probate court held a joint hearing on the two petitions and thereafter ordered that letters of administration be issued to appellee Cecil Reed upon his taking the oath and filing the bond required by law. The court treated §§ 15–312 and 15–314 of the Idaho Code as the controlling statutes and read those sections as compelling a preference for Cecil Reed because he was a male.

Section 15–312[2] designates the persons who are entitled to administer the estate of one who dies intestate. In making these designations, that section lists 11 classes of persons who are so entitled and provides, in substance, that the order in which those classes are listed in the section shall be determinative of the relative rights of competing applicants for letters of administration. One of the 11 classes so enumerated is "[t]he father or mother" of the person dying intestate. Under this section, then, appellant and appellee, being members of the same entitlement class, would seem to have been equally entitled to administer their son's estate. Section 15–314 provides, however, that

"[o]f several persons claiming and equally entitled [under § 15–312] to administer, males must be preferred to females, and relatives of the whole to those of the half blood."

In issuing its order, the probate court implicitly recognized the equality of entitlement of the two applicants under § 15–312 and noted that neither of the applicants was under any legal disability; the court ruled, however, that appellee, being a male, was to be preferred to the female appellant "by reason of Section 15–314 of the Idaho Code." In stating this conclusion, the probate judge gave no indication that he had attempted to determine the relative capabilities of the competing applicants to perform the functions incident to the administration of an estate. It seems clear the probate judge considered himself bound by statute to give preference to the male candidate over the female, each being otherwise "equally entitled."

Sally Reed appealed from the probate court order, and her appeal was treated by the District Court of the Fourth Judicial District of Idaho as a constitutional attack on § 15–314. In dealing with the attack, that court held that the challenged section violated the Equal Protection Clause of the Fourteenth Amendment[3] and was, therefore, void; the matter was ordered "returned to the Probate Court for its determination of which of the two parties" was better qualified to administer the estate.

This order was never carried out, however, for Cecil Reed took a further appeal to the Idaho Supreme Court, which reversed the District Court and reinstated the original order naming the father administrator of the estate. In reaching this result, the Idaho Supreme Court first dealt with the governing statutory law and held that under § 15–312 "a father and mother are 'equally entitled' to letters of administration," but the preference given to males by § 15–314 is "mandatory" and leaves no room for the exercise of a probate court's discretion in the appointment of administrators. Having thus definitively and authoritatively interpreted the statutory provisions involved, the Idaho Supreme Court then proceeded to examine, and reject, Sally Reed's contention that § 15–314 violates the Equal Protection Clause by giving a mandatory preference to males over females, without regard to their individual qualifications as potential estate administrators.

Sally Reed thereupon appealed for review by this Court . . ., and we noted probable jurisdiction.* Having examined the record and considered the briefs and oral arguments of the parties, we have concluded that the

---

*Citation omitted [Eds.]

arbitrary preference established in favor of males by § 15–314 of the Idaho Code cannot stand in the face of the Fourteenth Amendment's command that no State deny the equal protection of the laws to any person within its jurisdiction.[4]

Idaho does not, of course, deny letters of administration to women altogether. Indeed, under § 15–312, a woman whose spouse dies intestate has a preference over a son, father, brother, or any other male relative of the decedent. Moreover, we can judicially notice that in this country, presumably due to the greater longevity of women, a large proportion of estates, both intestate and under wills of decedents, are administered by surviving widows.

Section 15–314 is restricted in its operation to those situations where competing applications for letters of administration have been filed by both male and female members of the same entitlement class established by § 15–312. In such situations, § 15–314 provides that different treatment be accorded to the applicants on the basis of their sex; it thus establishes a classification subject to scrutiny under the Equal Protection Clause.

In applying that clause, this Court has consistently recognized that the Fourteenth Amendment does not deny to States the power to treat different classes of persons in different ways. The Equal Protection Clause of that amendment does, however, deny to States the power to legislate that different treatment be accorded to persons placed by a statute into different classes on the basis of criteria wholly unrelated to the objective of that statute. A classification "must be reasonable, not arbitrary, and must rest upon some ground of difference having a fair and substantial relation to the object of the legislation, so that all persons similarly circumstanced shall be treated alike." *Royster Guano Co.* v. *Virginia,* 253 U.S. 412, 415 (1920). The question presented by this case, then, is whether a difference in the sex of competing applicants for letters of administration bears a rational relationship to a state objective that is sought to be advanced by the operation of §§ 15–312 and 15–314.

In upholding the latter section, the Idaho Supreme Court concluded that its objective was to eliminate one area of controversy when two or more persons, equally entitled under § 15–312, seek letters of administration and thereby present the probate court "with the issue of which one should be named." The court also concluded that where such persons are not of the same sex, the elimination of females from consideration "is neither an illogical nor arbitrary method devised by the legislature to resolve an issue that would otherwise require a hearing as to the relative merits . . . of the two or more petitioning relatives. . . ."*

Clearly the objective of reducing the workload on probate courts by eliminating one class of contests is not without some legitimacy. The crucial question, however, is whether § 15–314 advances that objective in a manner consistent with the command of the Equal Protection Clause. We hold that it does not. To give a mandatory preference to members of either sex over members of the other, merely to accomplish the elimination of hearings on the merits, is to make the very kind of arbitrary legislative choice forbidden by the Equal Protection Clause of the Fourteenth Amendment; and whatever may be said as to the positive values of avoiding intrafamily controversy, the choice in this context may not lawfully be mandated solely on the basis of sex.

We note finally that if § 15–314 is viewed merely as a modifying appendage to § 15–312 and as aimed at the same objective, its constitutionality is not thereby saved. The objective of § 15–312 clearly is to establish degrees of entitlement of various classes of persons in accordance with their varying degrees and kinds of relationship to the intestate. Regardless of their sex, persons within any one of the enumerated classes of that section are similarly situated with respect to that objective. By providing dissimilar treatment for men and women who are thus similarly situated, the challenged section violates the Equal Protection Clause.

The judgment of the Idaho Supreme Court is reversed and the case remanded for further proceedings not inconsistent with this opinion.

Reversed and remanded.

NOTES

1. In her petition, Sally Reed alleged that her son's estate, consisting of a few items of personal property and a small savings account, had an aggregate value of less than $1,000.

2. Section 15–312 provides as follows:

"Administration of the estate of a person dying intestate must be granted to some one or more of the persons hereinafter mentioned, and they are respectively entitled thereto in the following order:

"1. The surviving husband or wife or some competent person whom he or she may request to have appointed.

"2. The children.

"3. The father or mother.

"4. The brothers.

"5. The sisters.

"6. The grandchildren.

"7. The next of kin entitled to share in the distribution of the estate.

"8. Any of the kindred.

"9. The public administrator.

"10. The creditors of such person at the time of death.

"11. Any person legally competent.

"If the decedent was a member of a partnership at the time of his decease, the surviving partner must in no case be appointed administrator of his estate."

3. The court also held that the statute violated Art. I, § 1, of the Idaho Constitution.

*Citation omitted [Eds.]

4. We note that § 15–312, set out in n. 2, *supra,* appears to give a superior entitlement to brothers of an intestate (class 4) than is given to sisters (class 5). The parties now before the Court are not affected by the operation of § 15–312 in this respect, however, and appellant has made no challenge to that section.

We further note that on March 12, 1971, the Idaho Legislature adopted the Uniform Probate Code, effective July 1, 1972. Idaho Laws 1971, c. 111, p. 233. On that date, §§ 15–312 and 15–314 of the present code will, then, be effectively repealed, and there is in the new legislation no mandatory preference for males over females as administrators of estates.

FRONTIERO v. RICHARDSON

U. S. Supreme Court, 1973*

Mr. Justice Brennan announced the judgment of the Court and an opinion in which Mr. Justice Douglas, Mr. Justice White, and Mr. Justice Marshall join.

The question before us concerns the right of a female member of the uniformed services to claim her spouse as a "dependent" for the purposes of obtaining increased quarters allowances and medical and dental benefits under 37 U. S. C. §§ 401, 403, and 10 U. S. C. §§ 1072, 1076, on an equal footing with male members. Under these statutes, a serviceman may claim his wife as a "dependent" without regard to whether she is in fact dependent upon him for any part of her support. A servicewoman, on the other hand, may not claim her husband as a "dependent" under these programs unless he is in fact dependent upon her for over one-half of his support. Thus, the question for decision is whether this difference in treatment constitutes an unconstitutional discrimination against servicewomen in violation of the Due Process Clause of the Fifth Amendment. A three-judge District Court for the Middle District of Alabama, one judge dissenting, rejected this contention and sustained the constitutionality of the provisions of the statutes making this distinction.* We reverse.

I

In an effort to attract career personnel through reenlistment, Congress established a scheme for the provision of fringe benefits to members of the uniformed services on a competitive basis with business and industry. Thus, under 37 U. S. C. § 403, a member of the uniformed services with dependents is entitled to an increased "basic allowance for quarters" and, under 10 U. S. C. § 1076, a member's dependents are provided comprehensive medical and dental care.

Appellant Sharron Frontiero, a lieutenant in the United States Air Force, sought increased quarters allowances, and housing and medical benefits for her husband, appellant Joseph Frontiero, on the ground that he was her "dependent." Although such benefits would automatically have been granted with respect to

the wife of a male member of the uniformed services, appellant's application was denied because she failed to demonstrate that her husband was dependent on her for more than one-half of his support.[1] Appellants then commenced this suit, contending that, by making this distinction, the statutes unreasonably discriminate on the basis of sex in violation of the Due Process Clause of the Fifth Amendment.[2] In essence, appellants asserted that the discriminatory impact of the statutes is two-fold: first, as a procedural matter, a female member is required to demonstrate her spouse's dependency, while no such burden is imposed upon male members; and second, as a substantive matter, a male member who does not provide more than one-half of his wife's support receives benefits, while a similarly situated female member is denied such benefits. Appellants therefore sought a permanent injunction against the continued enforcement of these statutes and an order directing the appellees to provide Lieutenant Frontiero with the same housing and medical benefits that a similarly situated male member would receive.

Although the legislative history of these statutes sheds virtually no light on the purposes underlying the differential treatment accorded male and female members, a majority of the three-judge District Court surmised that Congress might reasonably have concluded that, since the husband in our society is generally the "breadwinner" in the family—and the wife typically the "dependent" partner—"it would be more economical to require married female members claiming husbands to prove actual dependency than to extend the presumption of dependency to such members."* Indeed, given the fact that approximately 99% of all members of the uniformed services are male, the District Court speculated that such differential treatment might conceivably lead to a "considerable saving of administrative expense and manpower."

II

At the outset, appellants contend that classifications based upon sex, like classifications based upon race, alienage, and national origin, are inherently suspect and must therefore be subjected to close judicial scrutiny. We agree and, indeed, find at least implicit sup-

*93 S. Ct. 1764 (1973). Some footnotes omitted, and the remainder renumbered.

port for such an approach in our unanimous decision only last Term in *Reed* v. *Reed,* 404 U. S. 71 (1971).

In *Reed,* the Court considered the constitutionality of an Idaho statute providing that, when two individuals are otherwise equally entitled to appointment as administrator of an estate, the male applicant must be preferred to the female. Appellant, the mother of the deceased, and appellee, the father, filed competing petitions for appointment as administrator of their son's estate. Since the parties, as parents of the deceased, were members of the same entitlement class, the statutory preference was invoked and the father's petition was therefore granted. Appellant claimed that this statute, by giving a mandatory preference to males over females without regard to their individual qualifications, violated the Equal Protection Clause of the Fourteenth Amendment.

The Court noted that the Idaho statute "provides that different treatment be accorded to the applicants on the basis of their sex; it thus establishes a classification subject to scrutiny under the Equal Protection Clause." Under "traditional" equal protection analysis, a legislative classification must be sustained unless it is "patently arbitrary" and bears no rational relationship to a legitimate governmental interest.*

In an effort to meet this standard, appellee contended that the statutory scheme was a reasonable measure designed to reduce the workload on probate courts by eliminating one class of contests. Moreover, appellee argued that the mandatory preference for male applicants was in itself reasonable since "men [are] as a rule more conversant with business affairs than . . . women." Indeed, appellee maintained that "it is a matter of common knowledge that women still are not engaged in politics, the professions, business or industry to the extent that men are." And the Idaho Supreme Court, in upholding the constitutionality of this statute, suggested that the Idaho Legislature might reasonably have "concluded that in general men are better qualified to act as an administrator than are women." [*Reed* v. *Reed*]

Despite these contentions, however, the Court held the statutory preference for male applicants unconstitutional. In reaching this result, the Court implicitly rejected appellee's apparently rational explanation of the statutory scheme, and concluded that, by ignoring the individual qualifications of particular applicants, the challenged statute provided "dissimilar treatment for men and women who are . . . similarly situated." *Reed* v. *Reed, supra,* at 77. The Court therefore held that, even though the State's interest in achieving administrative efficiency "is not without some legitimacy," "[t]o give a mandatory preference to members

of either sex over members of the other, merely to accomplish the elimination of hearings on the merits, is to make the very kind of arbitrary legislative choice forbidden by the [Constitution]. . . ." *Id.,* at 76. This departure from "traditional" rational basis analysis with respect to sex-based classifications is clearly justified.

There can be no doubt that our Nation has had a long and unfortunate history of sex discrimination.[3] Traditionally, such discrimination was rationalized by an attitude of "romantic paternalism" which, in practical effect, put women not on a pedestal, but in a cage. Indeed, this paternalistic attitude became so firmly rooted in our national consciousness that, exactly 100 years ago, a distinguished member of this Court was able to proclaim:

"Man is, or should be, woman's protector and defender. The natural and proper timidity and delicacy which belongs to the female sex evidently unfits it for many of the occupations of civil life. The constitution of the family organization, which is founded in the divine ordinance, as well as in the nature of things, indicates the domestic sphere as that which properly belongs to the domain and functions of womanhood. The harmony, not to say identity, of interests and views which belong, or should belong, to the family institution is repugnant to the ideas of a woman adopting a distinct and independent career from that of her husband. . . .

". . . The paramount destiny and mission of woman are to fulfil the noble and benign offices of wife and mother. This is the law of the Creator." *Bradwell* v. *Illinois,* 83 U. S. [16 Wall.] 130, 141 (1873) (Bradley, J., concurring).

As a result of notions such as these, our statute books gradually became laden with gross, stereotypical distinctions between the sexes and, indeed, throughout much of the 19th century, the position of women in our society was, in many respects, comparable to that of blacks under the pre-Civil War slave codes. Neither slaves nor women could hold office, serve on juries, or bring suit in their own names, and married women traditionally were denied the legal capacity to hold or convey property or to serve as legal guardians of their own children. See generally, L. Kantowitz, Women and the Law: The Unfinished Revolution 5–6 (1969); G. Myrdal, An American Dilemma 1073 (2d ed. 1962). And although blacks were guaranteed the right to vote in 1870, women were denied even that right—which is itself "preservative of other basic civil and political rights"[14]—until adoption of the Nineteenth Amendment half a century later.

It is true, of course, that the position of women in America has improved markedly in recent decades.[5] Nevertheless, it can hardly be doubted that, in part because of the high visibility of the sex characteristic, women still face pervasive, although at times more subtle, discrimination in our educational institutions, on the job market and, perhaps most conspicuously, in the political arena.[6] See generally, K. Amundsen, The

*Citations omitted [Eds.]

Silenced Majority: Women and American Democracy (1971).

Moreover, since sex, like race and national origin, is an immutable characteristic determined solely by the accident of birth, the imposition of special disabilities upon the members of a particular sex because of their sex would seem to violate "the basic concept of our system that legal burdens should bear some relationship to individual responsibility...." *Weber* v. *Aetna Casualty & Surety Co.,* 406 U. S. 164, 175 (1972). And what differentiates sex from such nonsuspect statutes as intelligence or physical disability, and aligns it with the recognized suspect criteria, is that the sex characteristic frequently bears no relation to ability to perform or contribute to society. As a result, statutory distinctions between the sexes often have the effect of invidiously relegating the entire class of females to inferior legal status without regard to the actual capabilities of its individual members.

We might also note that, over the past decade, Congress has itself manifested an increasing sensitivity to sex-based classifications. In Tit. VII of the Civil Rights Act of 1964, for example, Congress expressly declared that no employer, labor union, or other organization subject to the provisions of the Act shall discriminate against any individual on the basis of "race, color, religion, *sex,* or national origin." Similarly, the Equal Pay Act of 1963 provides that no employer covered by the Act "shall discriminate ... between employees on the basis of *sex.*" And §1 of the Equal Rights Amendment, passed by Congress on March 22, 1972, and submitted to the legislatures of the States for ratification, declares that "[e]quality of rights under the law shall not be denied or abridged by the United States or by any State on account of sex." Thus, Congress has itself concluded that classifications based upon sex are inherently invidious, and this conclusion of a coequal branch of Government is not without significance to the question presently under consideration.*

With these considerations in mind, we can only conclude that classifications based upon sex, like classifications based upon race, alienage, or national origin, are inherently suspect, and must therefore be subjected to strict judicial scrutiny. Applying the analysis mandated by that stricter standard of review, it is clear that the statutory scheme now before us is constitutionally invalid.

III

The sole basis of the classification established in the challenged statutes is the sex of the individuals involved. Thus, under 37 U. S. C. §§ 401, 403, and 10 U. S. C. §§ 2072, 2076, a female member of the uniformed services seeking to obtain housing and medical benefits for her spouse must prove his dependency in fact, whereas no such burden is imposed upon male members. In addition, the statutes operate so as to deny benefits to a female member, such as appellant Sharron Frontiero, who provides less than one-half of her spouse's support, while at the same time granting such benefits to a male member who likewise provides less than one-half of his spouse's support. Thus, to this extent at least, it may fairly be said that these statutes command "dissimilar treatment for men and women who are ... similarly situated." *Reed* v. *Reed, supra,* at 77.

Moreover, the Government concedes that the differential treatment accorded men and women under these statutes serves no purpose other than mere "administrative convenience." In essence, the Government maintains that, as an empirical matter, wives in our society frequently are dependent upon their husbands, while husbands rarely are dependent upon their wives. Thus, the Government argues that Congress might reasonably have concluded that it would be both cheaper and easier simply conclusively to presume that wives of male members are financially dependent upon their husbands, while burdening female members with the task of establishing dependency in fact.[7]

The Government offers no concrete evidence, however, tending to support its view that such differential treatment in fact saves the Government any money. In order to satisfy the demands of strict judicial scrutiny, the Government must demonstrate, for example, that it is actually cheaper to grant increased benefits with respect to *all* male members, than it is to determine which male members are in fact entitled to such benefits and to grant increased benefits only to those members whose wives actually meet the dependency requirement. Here, however, there is substantial evidence that, if put to the test, many of the wives of male members would fail to qualify for benefits. And in light of the fact that the dependency determination with respect to the husbands of female members is presently made solely on the basis of affidavits, rather than through the more costly hearing process, the Government's explanation of the statutory scheme is, to say the least, questionable.

In any case, our prior decisions make clear that, although efficacious administration of governmental programs is not without some importance, "the Constitution recognizes higher values than speed and efficiency."* And when we enter the realm of "strict judicial scrutiny," there can be no doubt that "administrative convenience" is not a shibboleth, the mere recitation of which dictates constitutionality.* On the contrary, any statutory scheme which draws a sharp line between the sexes, *solely* for the purpose of achieving administrative convenience, necessarily commands "dissimilar treatment for men and women who are . . . similarly situated," and therefore involves the "very kind of arbitrary legislative choice forbidden by the [Constitution]. . . ." *Reed* v. *Reed, supra,* at 77, 76. We therefore conclude that, by according differential treatment to male and female members of the uniformed services for the sole purpose of achieving administrative convenience, the challenged statutes violate the Due Process Clause of the Fifth Amendment insofar as they require a female member to prove the dependency of her husband.

Reversed.

Mr. Justice Stewart concurs in the judgment, agreeing that the statutes before us work an invidious discrimination in violation of the Constitution. *Reed* v. *Reed,* 404 U. S. 71.

Mr. Justice Rehnquist dissents for the reasons stated by Judge Rives in his opinion for the District Court, *Frontiero* v. *Laird,* 341 F. Supp. 201 (1972).

Mr. Justice Powell, with whom The Chief Justice and Mr. Justice Blackmun join, concurring in the judgment.

I agree that the challenged statutes constitute an unconstitutional discrimination against service women in violation of the Due Process Clause of the Fifth Amendment, but I cannot join the opinion of Mr. Justice Brennan, which would hold that all classifications based upon sex, "like classifications based upon race, alienage, and national origin," are "inherently suspect and must therefore be subjected to close judicial scrutiny." It is unnecessary for the Court in this case to characterize sex as a suspect classification, with all of the far-reaching implications of such a holding. *Reed* v. *Reed,* 404 U. S. 71 (1971), which abundantly supports our decision today, did not add sex to the narrowly limited group of classifications which are inherently suspect. In my view, we can and should decide this case on the authority of *Reed* and reserve for the future any expansion of its rationale.

There is another, and I find compelling, reason for deferring a general categorizing of sex classifications as invoking the strictest test of judicial scrutiny. The Equal Rights Amendment, which if adopted will resolve the substance of this precise question, has been approved by the Congress and submitted for ratification by the States. If this Amendment is duly adopted, it will represent the will of the people accomplished in the manner prescribed by the Constitution. By acting prematurely and unnecessarily, as I view it, the Court has assumed a decisional responsibility at the very time when state legislatures, functioning within the traditional democratic process, are debating the proposed Amendment. It seems to me that this reaching out to preempt by judicial action a major political decision which is currently in process of resolution does not reflect appropriate respect for duly prescribed legislative processes.

There are times when this Court, under our system, cannot avoid a constitutional decision on issues which normally should be resolved by the elected representatives of the people. But democratic institutions are weakened, and confidence in the restraint of the Court is impaired, when we appear unnecessarily to decide sensitive issues of broad social and political importance at the very time they are under consideration within the prescribed constitutional processes.

NOTES

1. Appellant Joseph Frontiero is a full-time student at Huntingdon College in Montgomery, Alabama. According to the agreed stipulation of facts, his living expenses, including his share of the household expenses, total approximately $354 per month. Since he receives $205 per month in veterans' benefits, it is clear that he is not dependent upon appellant Sharron Frontiero for more than one-half of his support.

2. "[W]hile the Fifth Amendment contains no equal protection clause, it does forbid discrimination that is 'so unjustifiable as to be violative of due process.'" *Schneider* v. *Rusk,* 377 U. S. 163, 168 (1964).

3. Indeed, the position of women in this country at its inception is reflected in the view expressed by Thomas Jefferson that women should be neither seen nor heard in society's decisionmaking councils. See M. Gruberg, Women in American Politics 4 (1968). See also A. de Tocqueville, Democracy in America, pt. 2 (Reeves tr. 1840), in World's Classic Series 400 (Galaxy ed. 1947).

4. *Reynolds* v. *Sims,* 377 U. S. 533, 562 (1964).

5. See generally, The President's Task Force on Women's Rights and Responsibilities, A Matter of Simple Justice (1970); L. Kantowitz, Women and the Law: The Unfinished Revolution (1969); A. Montague, Man's Most Dangerous Myth (4th ed. 1964); The President's Commission on the Status of Women, American Women (1963).

6. It is true, of course, that when viewed in the abstract, women do not constitute a small and powerless minority. Nevertheless, in part because of past discrimination, women are vastly underrepresented in this Nation's decisionmaking councils. There has never been a female President, nor a female member of this Court. Not a single woman presently sits in the United States Senate, and only 14 women hold seats in the House of Representatives. And, as appellants point out, this underrepresentation is present throughout all levels of our State and Federal Government. See Joint Reply Brief of Appellants and American Civil Liberties Union (*Amicus Curiae*) 9.

7. It should be noted that these statutes are not in any sense designed to rectify the effects of past discrimination against women. On the contrary, these statutes seize upon a group—women—who have historically suffered discrimination in employment, and rely on the effects of this past discrimination as a justification for heaping on additional economic disadvantages.

REGENTS OF THE UNIVERSITY OF CALIFORNIA, PETITIONER V. ALLAN BAKKE

United States Supreme Court, 1978*

SN

White male whose application to state medical school was rejected brought action challenging legality of the school's special admissions program under which 16 of the 100 positions in the class were reserved for "disadvantaged" minority students. School cross-claimed for declaratory judgment that its program was legal. The trial court declared the program illegal but refused to order the school to admit the applicant. The California Supreme Court, 18 Cal.3d 34, 132 Cal.Rpter. 680, 553 P.2d 1152, affirmed the finding that the program was illegal and ordered the student admitted and the school sought certiorari. The Supreme Court, Mr. Justice Powell, held that: (1) the special admissions program was illegal, but (2) race may be one of a number of factors considered by school in passing on applications, and (3) since the school could not show that the white applicant would not have been admitted even in the absence of the special admissions program, the applicant was entitled to be admitted.

Affirmed in part and reversed in part.

Mr. Justice Brennan, Mr. Justice White, Mr. Justice Marshall and Mr. Justice Blackmun filed an opinion concurring in the judgment in part and dissenting.

Mr. Justice White filed a separate opinion.

Mr. Justice Marshall filed a separate opinion.

Mr. Justice Blackmun filed a separate opinion.

Mr. Justice Stevens concurred in the judgment in part and dissented in part and filed an opinion in which Mr. Chief Justice Burger, Mr. Justice Stewart and Mr. Justice Rehnquist joined.

The following summary of the case, prepared by the Reporter of Decisions, precedes the opinions of the Justices (*Eds.*)

The Medical School of the University of California at Davis (hereinafter Davis) had two admissions programs for the entering class of 100 students—the regular admissions program and the special admissions program. Under the regular procedure, candidates whose overall undergraduate grade point averages fell below 2.5 on a scale of 4.0 were summarily rejected. About one out of six applicants was then given an interview, following which he was rated on a scale of 1 to 100 by each of the committee members (five in 1973 and six in 1974), his rating being based on the interviewers' summaries, his overall grade point average, his science courses grade point average, and his Medical College Admissions Test (MCAT) scores, letters of recommendation, extracurricular activities, and other biographical data, all of which resulted in a total "benchmark score." The full admissions committee then made offers of admission on the basis of their review of the applicant's file and his score, considering and acting upon applications as they were received. The committee chairman was responsible for placing names on the waiting list and had discretion to include persons with "special skills." A separate committee, a majority of whom were members of minority groups, operated the special admissions program. The 1973 and 1974 application forms, respectively, asked candidates whether they wished to be considered as "economically and/or educationally disadvantaged" applicants and members of a "minority group" (blacks, Chicanos, Asians, American Indians). If an applicant of a minority group was found to be "Disadvantaged," he would be rated in a manner similar to the one employed by the general admissions committee. Special candidates, however, did not have to meet the 2.5 grade point cut-off and were not ranked against candidates in the general admissions process. About one-fifth of the special applicants were invited for interviews in 1973 and 1974, following which they were given benchmark scores, and the top choices were then given to the general admissions committee, which could reject special candidates for failure to meet course requirements or other specific deficiencies. The special committee continued to recommend candidates until 16 special admission selections had been made. During a four-year period 63 minority students were admitted to Davis under the special program and 44 under the general program. No disadvantaged whites were admitted under the special program, though many applied. Respondent, a white male, applied to Davis in 1973 and 1974, in both years being considered only under the general admissions program. Though he had a 468 out of 500 score in 1973, he was rejected since no general applicants with scores less than 470 were being accepted after respondent's application, which was filed late in the year, had been processed and completed. At that time four special admissions slots were still unfilled. In 1974 respondent applied early, and though he had a total score of 549 out of 600, he was again rejected. In neither year was his name placed on the discretionary waiting list. In both years special applicants were admitted with significantly lower scores than respondent's. After his second rejection, respondent filed this action in state court for mandatory injunctive and declaratory relief to compel his admission to Davis, alleging that the special admissions program operated to exclude him on the basis of his race in violation of the Equal Protection Clause of the Fourteenth Amendment, a provision of the California Constitution, and § 601 of Title VI of the Civil Rights Act of 1964, which provides, *inter alia,* that no person shall on the ground of race or color be excluded from participating in any program receiving federal financial assistance. Petitioner cross-claimed for a declaration that its special admissions program was lawful. The trial court found that the special program operated as a racial quota, because minority applicants in that program were rated only against one another, and 16 places in the class of 100 were reserved for them. Declaring that petitioner could not take race into account in making admissions decision, the program was held to violate the Federal and State Constitutions and Title VI. Respondent's admission was not ordered, however, for lack of proof that he would have been admitted but for the special program. The California Supreme Court, applying a strict-scrutiny standard, concluded that the special admissions program was not the least intrusive means of achieving the goals of the admittedly compelling state interests of integrating the medi-

cal profession and increasing the number of doctors willing to serve minority patients. Without passing on the state constitutional or federal statutory grounds the court held that petitioner's special admissions program violated the Equal Protection Clause. Since petitioner could not satisfy its burden of demonstrating that respondent, absent the special program, would not have been admitted, the court ordered his admission to Davis.

Held: The judgment below is affirmed insofar as it orders respondent's admission to Davis and invalidates petitioner's special admissions program, but is reversed insofar as it prohibits petitioner from taking race into account as a factor in its future admissions decisions.

18 Cal.3d 34, 132 Cal.Rptr. 680, 553 P.2d 1152, affirmed in part and reversed in part.

Mr. Justice POWELL concluded:

1. Title VI proscribes only those racial classifications that would violate the Equal Protection Clause if employed by a State or its agencies ...

2. Racial and ethnic classifications of any sort are inherently suspect and call for the most exacting judicial scrutiny. While the goal of achieving a diverse student body is sufficiently compelling to justify consideration of race in admissions decisions under some circumstances, petitioner's special admissions program, which forecloses consideration to persons like respondent, is unnecessary to the achievement of this compelling goal and therefore invalid under the Equal Protection Clause ...

3. Since petitioner could not satisfy its burden of proving that respondent would not have been admitted even if there had been no special admissions program, he must be admitted ...

Mr. Justice BRENNAN, Mr. Justice WHITE, Mr. Justice MARSHALL, and Mr. Justice BLACKMUN concluded:

1. Title VI proscribes only those racial classifications that would violate the Equal Protection Clause if employed by a State or its agencies ...

2. Racial classifications call for strict judicial scrutiny. Nonetheless, the purpose of overcoming substantial, chronic minority underrepresentation in the medical profession is sufficiently important to justify petitioner's remedial use of race. Thus, the judgment below must be reversed in that it prohibits race from being used as a factor in university admissions ...

Mr. Justice STEVENS, joined by THE CHIEF JUSTICE, Mr. Justice STEWART, and Mr. Justice REHNQUIST, being of the view that whether race can ever be a factor in an admissions policy is not an issue here; that Title VI applies; and that respondent was excluded from Davis in violation of Title VI, concurs in the Court's judgment insofar as it affirms the judgment of the court below ordering respondent admitted to Davis. . . .

The following excerpts are from the opinion of Mr. Justice POWELL, who announced the Judgment of the Court. (*Eds.*)

The guarantees of the Fourteenth Amendment extend to persons. Its language is explicit: "No state shall . . . deny to any person within its jurisdiction the equal protection of the laws." It is settled beyond question that the "rights created by the first section of the Fourteenth Amendment are, by its terms, guaranteed to the individual. The rights established are personal rights." . . . The guarantee of equal protection cannot mean one thing when applied to one individual and something else when applied to a person of another color. If both are not accorded the same protection, then it is not equal.

. . . Nevertheless, petitioner argues that the court below erred in applying strict scrutiny to the special admissions programs because white males, such as respondent, are not a "discrete and insular minority" requiring extraordinary protection from the majoritarian political process . . . This rationale, however, has never been invoked in our decisions as a prerequisite to subjecting racial or ethnic distinctions to strict scrutiny. Nor has this Court held that discreteness and insularity constitute necessary preconditions to a holding that a particular classification is invidious . . . These characteristics may be relevant in deciding whether or not to add new types of classifications to the list of "suspect" categories or whether a particular classification survives close scrutiny.

Racial and ethnic classifications, however, are subject to stringent examination without regard to these additional characteristics. We declared as much in the first cases explicitly to recognize racial distinctions as suspect:

"Distinctions between citizens solely because of their ancestry are by their very nature odious to a free people whose institutions are founded upon the doctrine of equality." *Hirabayashi,* 320 U.S., at 100, 63 S.Ct., at 1385.

" . . . [A]ll legal restrictions which curtail the rights of a single racial group are immediately suspect. That is not to say that all such restrictions are unconstitutional. It is to say that courts must subject them to the most rigid scrutiny." *Korematsu,* 323 U.S., at 216, 65 S.Ct., at 194.

The Court has never questioned the validity of those pronouncements. Racial and ethnic distinctions of any sort are inherently suspect and thus call for the most exacting judicial examination.

Over the past 30 years, this Court has embarked upon the crucial mission of interpreting the Equal Protection Clause with the view of assuring to all persons "the protection of equal laws" . . . in a Nation confronting a legacy of slavery and racial discrimination . . . Because the landmark decisions in this area arose in response to the continued exclusion of Negroes from the mainstream of American society, they could be characterized as involving discrimination by the "majority" white race against the Negro Minority. But they need not be read as depending upon that characterization for their results. It suffices to say that "[o]ver the years, this Court consistently repudiated '[d]istinctions between citizens solely because of their ancestry' as being 'odious to a free people whose institutions are founded upon the doctrine of equality.' " *Loving v. Virginia,* 388 U.S. 1, 11. 87. S.Ct. 1817, 1823, 18 L.Ed2d 1010 (1967), quoting *Hirabayashi.* 320 U.S., at 100, 63 S.Ct., at 1385.

Petitioner urges us to adopt for the first time a more restrictive view of the Equal Protection Clause and hold that discrimination against members of the white "majority" cannot be suspect if its purpose can be characterized as "benign."[1] The clock of our liberties, however, cannot be turned back to 1868 . . . It is far too late to argue that the guarantee of equal protection to *all* persons permits the recognition of special wards entitled to a degree of protection greater than that accorded others.[2] "The Fourteenth Amendment is not directed solely against discrimination due to a 'two-class theory'—that is, based upon differences between 'white' and Negro." . . .

Once the artificial line of a "two-class theory" of the Fourteenth Amendment is put aside, the difficulties entailed in varying the level of judicial review according to a perceived "preferred" status of a particular racial or ethnic minority are intractable. The concepts of "majority" and "minority" necessarily reflect temporary arrangements and political judgments. As observed above, the white "majority" itself is composed of various minority groups, most of which can lay claim to a history of prior discrimination at the hands of the state and private individuals. Not all of these groups can receive preferential treatment and corresponding judicial tolerance of distinctions drawn in terms of race and nationality, for then the only "majority" left would be a new minority of White Anglo-Saxon Protestants. There is no principled basis for deciding which groups would merit "heightened judicial solicitude" and which would not.[3] Courts would be asked to evaluate the extent of the prejudice and consequent harm suffered by various minority groups. Those whose societal injury is thought to exceed some arbitrary level of tolerability then would be entitled to preferential classifications at the expense of individuals belonging to other groups. Those classifications would be free from exacting judicial scrutiny. As these preferences began to have their desired effect, and the consequences of past discrimination were undone, new judicial rankings would be necessary. The kind of variable sociological and political analysis necessary to produce such rankings simply does not lie within the judicial competence—even if they otherwise were politically feasible and socially desirable.

Moreover, there are serious problems of justice connected with the idea of preference itself. First, it may not always be clear that a so-called preference is in fact benign. Courts may be asked to validate burdens imposed upon individual members of particular groups in order to advance the group's general interest ... Nothing in the Constitution supports the notion that individuals may be asked to suffer otherwise impermissible burdens in order to enhance the societal standing of their ethnic groups. Second, preferential programs may only reinforce common stereotypes holding that certain groups are unable to achieve success without special protection based on a factor having no relationship to individual worth ... Third, there is a measure of inequity in forcing innocent persons in respondent's position to bear the burdens of redressing grievances not of their making.

By hitching the meaning of the Equal Protection Clause to these transitory considerations, we would be holding, as a constitutional principle, that judicial scrutiny of classifications touching on racial and ethnic background may vary with the ebb and flow of political forces. Disparate constitutional tolerance of such classifications well may serve to exacerbate racial and ethnic antagonisms rather than alleviate them ... Also, the mutability of a constitutional principle, based upon shifting political and social judgments, undermines the chances for consistent application of the Constitution from one generation to the next, a critical feature of its coherent interpretation ... In expounding the Constitution, the Court's role is to discern "principles sufficiently absolute to give them roots throughout the community and continuity over significant periods of time, and to lift them above the level of the pragmatic political judgments of a particular time and place." A. Cox, The Role of the Supreme Court in American Government 114 (1976).

If it is the individual who is entitled to judicial protection against classifications based upon his racial or ethnic background because such distinctions impinge upon personal rights, rather than the individual only because of his membership in a particular group, then constitutional standards may be applied consistently. Political judgments regarding the necessity for the particular classification may be weighed in the constitutional balance ... but the standard of justification will remain constant. This is as it should be, since those political judgments are the product of rough compromise struck by contending groups within the democratic process. When they touch upon an individual's race or ethnic background, he is entitled to a judicial determination that the burden he is asked to bear on that basis is precisely tailored to serve a compelling governmental interest. The Constitution guarantees that right to every person regardless of his background ...

Petitioner contends that on several occasions this Court has approved preferential classifications without applying the most exacting scrutiny. Most of the cases upon which petitioner relies are drawn from three areas: School desegregation, employment discrimination, and sex discrimination. Each of the cases cited presented a situation materially different from the facts of this case.

The school desegregation cases are inapposite. Each involved remedies for clearly determined constitutional violations ... Racial classifications thus were designed as remedies for the vindication of constitutional entitlement. Moreover, the scope of the remedies was not permitted to exceed the extent of the violations. ... Here, there was no judicial determination of constitutional violation as a predicate for the formulation of a remedial classification.

The employment discrimination cases also do not advance petitioner's cause. For example, in *Franks v. Bowman Transportation Co.,* 424 U.S. 747, 96 S.Ct. 1251, 47 L.Ed.2d 444 (1975), we approved a retroactive award of seniority to a class of Negro truck drivers who had been the victims of discrimination—not just by society at large, but by the respondent in that case. While this relief imposed some burdens on other employees, it was held necessary " 'to make [the victims] whole for injuries suffered on account of unlawful employment discrimination.' " ... The courts of appeals have fashioned various types of racial preferences as remedies for constitutional or statutory violations resulting in identified, race-based injuries to individuals held entitled to the preference.... Such preferences also have been upheld where a legislative or administrative body charged with the responsibility made determinations of past discrimination by the industries affected, and fashioned remedies deemed appropriate to rectify the discrimination.

But we have never approved preferential classifications in the absence of proven constitutional or statutory violations.

Nor is petitioner's view as to the applicable standard supported by the fact that gender-based classifications are not subjected to this level of scrutiny.... Gender-based distinctions are less likely to create the analytical and practical problems present in preferential programs premised on racial or ethnic criteria. With respect to gender there are only two possible classifications. The incidence of the burdens imposed by preferential classifications is clear. There are no rival groups who can claim that they, too, are entitled to preferential treatment. Classwide questions as to the group suffering previous injury and groups which fairly can be burdened are relatively manageable for reviewing courts.... The resolution of these same questions in the context of racial and ethnic preferences presents far more complex and intractable problems than gender-based classifications. More importantly, the perception of racial classifications as inherently odious stems from a lengthy and tragic history that gender-based classifications do not share. In sum, the Court has never viewed such classification as inherently suspect or as comparable to racial or ethnic classifications for the purpose of equal-protection analysis.

Petitioner also cites *Lau v. Nichols,* 414 U.S. 563, 94 S.Ct. 786, 39 L.Ed.2d 1 (1974), in support of the proposition that discrimination favoring racial or ethnic minorities has received judicial approval without the exacting inquiry ordinarily accorded "suspect" classifications. In *Lau,* we held that the failure of the San Francisco school system to provide remedial English instruction for some 1,800 students of oriental ancestry who spoke no English amounted to a violation of Title VI of the Civil Rights Act of 1964, 42 U.S.C. § 2000d, and the regulations promulgated thereun-

der. Those regulations required remedial instructions where inability to understand English excluded children of foreign ancestry from participation in educational programs.... Because we found that the students in *Lau* were denied "a meaningful opportunity to participate in the educational program," ... we remanded for the fashioning of a remedial order.

Lau provides little support for petitioner's argument. The decision rested solely on the statute, which had been construed by the responsible administrative agency to reach educational practices "which have the effect of subjecting individuals to discrimination." We stated: "Under these state-imposed standards there is no equality of treatment merely by providing students with the same facilities, textbooks, teachers and curriculum; for students who do not understand English are effectively foreclosed from any meaningful education." ... Moreover, the "preference" approved did not result in the denial of the relevant benefit—"meaningful participation in the educational program"—to anyone else. No other student was deprived by that preference of the ability to participate in San Francisco's school system, and the applicable regulations required similar assistance for all students who suffered similar linguistic deficiencies. ...

In a similar vein, petitioner contends that our recent decision in *United Jewish Organizations v. Carey,* 430 U.S. 144, 97 S.Ct. 996, 51 L.Ed.2d 229 (1977), indicates a willingness to approve racial classifications designed to benefit certain minorities, without denominating the classifications as "suspect." The State of New York had redrawn its reapportionment plan to meet objections of the Department of Justice under § 5 of the Voting Rights Act of 1965, 42 U.S.C. § 1973c. Specifically, voting districts were redrawn to enhance the electoral power of certain "nonwhite" voters found to have been the victims of unlawful "dilution" under the original reapportionment plan. *United Jewish Organizations,* like *Lau,* properly is viewed as a case in which the remedy for an administrative finding of discrimination encompassed measures to improve the previously disadvantaged group's ability to participate, without excluding individuals belonging to any other group from enjoyment of the relevant opportunity— meaningful participation in the electoral process.

In this case, unlike *Lau* and *United Jewish Organization,* there has been no determination by the legislature or a responsible administrative agency that the University engaged in a discriminatory practice requiring remedial efforts. Moreover, the operation of petitioner's special admissions program is quite different from the remedial measures approved in those cases. It prefers the designated minority groups at the expense of other individuals who are totally foreclosed from competition for the 16 special admissions seats in every medical school class. Because of that foreclosure, some individuals are excluded from enjoyment of a state-provided benefit—admission to the medical school—they otherwise would receive. When a classification denies an individual opportunities or benefits enjoyed by others solely because of his race or ethnic background, it must be regarded as suspect. . . .

IV

We have held that in "order to justify the use of a suspect classification, a State must show that its purpose or interest is both constitutionally permissible and substantial, and that its use of the classification is 'necessary . . . to the accomplishment' of its purpose or the safeguarding of its interest." . . . The special admissions program purports to serve the purposes of: (i) "reducing the historic deficit of traditionally disfavored minorities in medical schools and the medical profession," Brief for Petitioner 32; (ii) countering the effects of societal discrimination;[4] (iii) increasing the number of physicians who will practice in communities currently underserved; and (iv) obtaining the educational benefits that flow from an ethnically diverse student body. It is necessary to decide which, if any, of these purposes is substantial enough to support the use of a suspect classification.

A

. . . If petitioner's purpose is to assure within its student body some specified percentage of a particular group merely because of its race or ethnic origin, such a preferential purpose must be rejected not as insubstantial but as facially invalid. Preferring members of any one group for no reason other than race or ethnic origin is discrimination for its own sake. This the Constitution forbids. . . .

B

The State certainly has a legitimate and substantial interest in ameliorating, or eliminating where feasible, the disabling effects of identified discrimination. The line of school desegregation cases, commencing with Brown, attests to the importance of this state goal and the commitment of the judiciary to affirm all lawful means towards its attainment. In the school cases, the States were required by court order to redress the wrongs worked by specific instances of racial discrimination. That goal was far more focused than the remedying of the effects of "societal discrimination," an amorphous concept of injury that may be ageless in its reach into the past.

. . . We have never approved a classification that aids persons perceived as members of relatively victimized groups at the expense of other innocent individuals in the absence of judicial, legislative, or administrative findings of constitutional or statutory violations. . . . After such findings have been made, the governmental interest in prefering members of the injured groups at the expense of others is substantial, since the legal rights of the victims must be vindicated. In such a case, the extent of the injury and the consequent remedy will have been judicially, legislatively, or administratively defined. Also, the remedial action usually remains subject to continuing oversight to assure that it will work the least harm possible to other innocent persons competing for the benefit. Without such findings of constitutional or statutory violations, it cannot be said that the government has any greater interest in helping one individual than in refraining from harming another. Thus, the government has no compelling justification for inflicting such harm.

Petitioner does not purport to have made, and is in no position to make, such findings. Its broad mission is education, not the formulation of any legislative policy or the adjudication of particular claims of illegality. For reasons similar to those stated in Part III of this opinion, isolated segments of our vast governmental structures are not competent to make those decisions, at least in the absence of legislative mandates and legislatively determined criteria.[5] . . . Before relying upon these sorts of findings in establishing a racial classification, a governmental body must have the authority and capability to establish, in the record, that the classification is responsive to identified discrimination. . . .

. . . Hence, the purpose of helping certain groups whom the faculty of the Davis Medical School perceived as victims of "societal discrimination" does not justify a classification that imposes disadvantages upon persons like respondent, who bear no responsibility for whatever harm the beneficiaries of the special admissions program are thought to have suffered. To hold otherwise would be to convert a remedy heretofore reserved for violations of legal rights into a privilege that all institutions throughout the Nation could grant at their pleasure to whatever groups are perceived as victims of societal discrimination. That is a step we have never approved. . . .

C

Petitioner identifies, as another purpose of its program, improving the delivery of health care services to communities currently underserved. It may be assumed that in some situations a State's interest in facilitating the health care of its citizens is sufficiently compelling to support the use of a suspect classification. But there is virtually no evidence in the record indicating that petitioner's special admissions program is either needed or geared to promote that goal.[6] The court below addressed this failure of proof:

"The University concedes it cannot assure that minority doctors who entered under the program, all of whom express an interest in participating in a disadvantaged community, will actually do so. It may be correct to assume that some of them will carry out this intention, and that it is more likely they will practice in minority communities than the average white doctor. . . . Nevertheless, there are more precise and reliable ways to identify applicants who are genuinely interested in the medical problems of minorities than by race. An applicant of whatever race who has demonstrated his concern for disadvantaged minorities in the past and who declares that practice in such a community is his primary professional goal would be more likely to contribute to alleviation of the medical shortage than one who is chosen entirely on the basis of race and disadvantage. In short, there is [sic] no empirical data to demonstrate that any one race is more selflessly socially oriented or by contract that another is more selfishly acquisitive." . . .

Petitioner simply has not carried its burden of demonstrating that it must prefer members of particular ethnic groups over all other individuals in order to promote better health care delivery to deprived citizens. Indeed, petitioner has not shown that its preferential classification is likely to have any significant effect on the problem.[7]

D

. . . The fourth goal asserted by petitioner is the attainment of a diverse student body. This clearly is a constitutionally permissible goal for an institution of higher education. Academic freedom, though not a specifically enumerated constitu-

tional right, long has been viewed as a special concern of the First Amendment. The freedom of a university to make its own judgments as to education includes the selection of its student body. Mr. Justice Frankfurter summarized the "four essential freedoms" that comprise academic freedom:

" '. . . It is the business of a university to provide that atmosphere which is most conductive to speculation, experiment and creation. It is an atmosphere in which there prevail "the four essential freedoms" of a university—to determine for itself on academic grounds who may teach, what may be taught, how it shall be taught, and who may be admitted to study.' " *Sweezy v. New Hampshire,* 354 U.S. 234, 263, 77 S.Ct. 1203, 1218, 1 L.Ed.2d 1311 (1957) (Frankfurter, J., concurring).

Our national commitment to the safeguarding of these freedoms within university communities was emphasized in *Keyishian v. Board of Regents,* 385 U.S. 589, 603, 87 S.Ct. 675, 683, 17 LEd.2d 629 (1967):

"Our Nation is deeply committed to safeguarding academic freedom which is of transcendent value to all of us and not merely to the teachers concerned. That freedom is therefore a special concern of the First Amendment. . . . The Nation's future depends upon leaders trained through wide exposure to that robust exchange of ideas which discovers truth 'out of a multitude of tongues, rather than through any kind of authoritative selection.' *United States v. Associated Press,* D.C., 52 F.Supp. 362, 372."

The atmosphere of "speculation, experiment and creation"—so essential to the quality of higher education—is widely believed to be promoted by a diverse student body.[8] As the Court noted in *Keyishian,* it is not too much to say that the "nation's future depends upon leaders trained through wide exposure" to the ideas and mores of students as diverse as this Nation of many peoples.

Thus, in arguing that its universities must be accorded the right to select those students who will contribute the most to the "robust exchange of ideas," petitioner invokes a countervailing constitutional interest, that of the First Amendment. In this light, petitioner must be viewed as seeking to achieve a goal that is of paramount importance in the fulfillment of its mission.

It may be argued that there is greater force to these views at the undergraduate level than in a medical school where the training is centered primarily on professional competency. But even at the graduate level, our tradition and experience lend support to the view that the contribution of diversity is substantial. In *Sweatt v. Painter,* 339 U.S. 629, 634, 70 S.Ct. 848, 850, 94 L.Ed. 1114 (1950), the Court made a similar point with specific reference to legal education:

"The law school, the proving ground for legal learning and practice, cannot be effective in isolation from the individuals and institutions with which the law interacts. Few students and no one who has practiced law would choose to study in an academic vacuum, removed from the interplay of ideas and the exchange of views with which the law is concerned."

Physicians serve a heterogenous population. An otherwise qualified medical student with a particular background—whether it be ethnic, geographic, culturally advantaged or disadvantaged—may bring to a professional school of medicine experiences, outlooks and ideas that enrich the training of its student body and better equip its graduates to render with understanding their vital service to humanity.

Ethnic diversity, however, is only one element in a range of factors a university properly may consider in attaining the goal of a heterogeneous student body. Although a university must have wide discretion in making the sensitive judgments as to who should be admitted, constitutional limitations protecting individual rights may not be disregarded. Respondent urges—and the courts below have held—that petitioner's dual admissions program is a racial classification that impermissibly infringes his rights under the Fourteenth Amendment. As the interest of diversity is compelling in the context of a university's admissions program, the question remains whether the program's racial classification is necessary to promote this interest. . . .

V

A

It may be assumed that the reservation of a specified number of seats in each class for individuals from the preferred ethnic groups would contribute to the attainment of considerable ethnic diversity in the student body. But petitioner's argument that this is the only effective means of serving the interest of diversity is seriously flawed. In a most fundamental sense the argument misconceives the nature of the state interest that would justify consideration of race or ethnic background. It is not an interest in simple ethnic diversity, in which a specified percentage of the student body is in effect guaranteed to be members of selected ethnic groups, with the remaining percentage an undifferentiated aggregation of students. The diversity that furthers a compelling state interest encompasses a far broader array of qualifications and characteristics of which racial or ethnic origin is but a single though important element. Petitioner's special admissions program, focused *solely* on ethnic diversity, would hinder rather than further attainment of genuine diversity.

Nor would the state interest in genuine diversity be served by expanding petitioner's two-track system into a multitrack program with a prescribed number of seats set aside for each identifiable category of applicants. Indeed, it is inconceivable that a university would thus pursue the logic of petitioner's two-track program to the illogical end of insulating each category of applicants with certain desired qualifications from competition with all other applicants.

. . . The experience of other university admissions programs, which take race into account in achieving the educational diversity valued by the First Amendment, demonstrates that the assignment of a fixed number of places to a minority group is not a necessary means toward that end. An illuminating example is found in the Harvard College program:

"In recent years Harvard College has expanded the concept of diversity to include students from disadvantaged economic, racial and ethnic groups. Harvard College now recruits not only Californians or Louisianans but also blacks and Chicanos and other minority students.

.   .   .   .   .

"In practice, this new definition of diversity has meant that race has been a factor in some admission decisions. When the Committee on Admissions reviews the large middle group of applicants who are 'admissible' and deemed capable of doing good work in their courses, the race of an applicant may tip the balance in his favor just as geographic origin or a life spent on a farm may tip the balance in other candidates' cases. A farm boy from Idaho can bring something to Harvard College that a Bostonian cannot offer. Similarly, a black student can usually bring something that a white person cannot offer." See Appendix hereto.

.   .   .   .   .

"In Harvard college admissions the Committee has not set target-quotas for the number of blacks, or of musicians, football players, physicists or Californians to be admitted in a given year. . . . But that awareness [of the necessity of including more than a token number of black students] does not mean that the Committee sets the minimum number of blacks or of people from west of the Mississippi who are to be admitted. It means only that in choosing among thousands of applicants who are not only 'admissible' academically but have other strong qualities, the Committee, with a number of criteria in mind, pays some attention to distribution among many types and categories of students." Brief for Columbia University, Harvard University, Stanford University, and the University of Pennsylvania, as *Amici Curiae,* App. 2, 3.

In such an admissions program, race or ethnic background may be deemed a "plus" in a particular applicant's file, yet it does not insulate the individual from comparison with all other candidates for the available seats. The file of a particular black applicant may be examined for his potential contribution to diversity without the factor of race being decisive when compared, for example, with that of an applicant identified as an Italian-American if the latter is thought to exhibit qualities more likely to promote beneficial educational pluralism. Such qualities could include exceptional personal talents, unique work or service experience, leadership potential, maturity, demonstrated compassion, a history of overcoming disadvantage, ability to communicate with the poor, or other qualifications deemed important. In short, an admissions program operated in this way is flexible enough to consider all pertinent elements of diversity in light of the particular qualifications of each applicant, and to place them on the same footing for consideration, although not necessarily according them the same weight. Indeed, the weight attributed to a particular quality may vary from year to year depending upon the "mix" both of the student body and the applicants for the incoming class.

. . . This kind of program treats each applicant as an individual in the admissions process. The applicant who loses out on the last available seat to another candidate receiving a "plus" on the basis of ethnic background will not have been foreclosed from all consideration for that seat simply because he was not the right color or had the wrong surname. It would mean only that his combined qualifications, which may have included similar nonobjective factors, did not outweigh those of the other applicant. His qualifications would have been weighed fairly and competitively, and he would have no basis to complain of unequal treatment under the Fourteenth Amendment.

It has been suggested that an admissions program which considers race only as one factor is simply a subtle and more sophisticated—but no less effective—means of according racial preference than the Davis program. A facial intent to discriminate, however, is evident in petitioner's preference program and not denied in this case. No such facial infirmity exists in an admissions program where race or ethnic background is simply one element—to be weighed fairly against other elements—in the selection process. "A boundary line," as Mr. Justice Frankfurter remarked in another connection, "is none the worse for being narrow." . . . And a Court would not assume that a university, professing to employ a facially nondiscriminatory admissions policy, would operate it as a cover for the functional equivalent of a quota system. In short, good faith would be presumed in the absence of a showing to the contrary in the manner permitted by our cases.[9]

B

In summary, it is evident that the Davis special admission program involves the use of an explicit racial classification never before countenanced by this Court. It tells applicants who are not Negro, Asian, or "Chicano" that they are totally excluded from a specific percentage of the seats in an entering class. No matter how strong their qualifications, quantitative and extra-curricular, including their own potential for contribution to educational diversity, they are never afforded the chance to compete with applicants from the preferred groups for the special admission seats. At the same time, the preferred applicants have the opportunity to compete for every seat in the class.

The fatal flaw in petitioner's preferential program is its disregard of individual rights as guaranteed by the Fourteenth Amendment. Such rights are not absolute. But when a State's distribution of benefits or imposition of burdens hinges on the color of a person's skin or ancestry, that individual is entitled to a demonstration that the challenged classification is necessary to promote a substantial state interest. Petitioner has failed to carry this burden. For this reason, that portion of the California court's judgment holding petitioner's special admissions program invalid under the Fourteenth Amendment must be affirmed.

C

In enjoining petitioner from ever considering the race of any applicant, however, the courts below failed to recognize that the State has a substantial interest that legitimately may be served by a properly devised admissions program involving the competitive consideration of race and ethnic origin. For this reason, so much of the California court's judgment as enjoins petitioner from any consideration of the race of any applicant must be reversed.

VI

With respect to respondent's entitlement to an injunction directing his admission to the Medical School, petitioner has conceded that it could not carry its burden of proving that, but for the existence of its unlawful special admissions program, respondent still would not have been admitted. Hence, respondent is entitled to the injunction, and that portion of the judgment must be affirmed.

APPENDIX

Harvard College Admissions Program[10]

For the past 30 years Harvard College has received each year applications for admission that greatly exceed the number of places in the freshman class. The number of applicants who are deemed to be not "qualified" is comparatively small. The vast majority of applicants demonstrate through test scores, high school records and teachers' recommendations that they have the academic ability to do adequate work at Harvard, and perhaps to do it with distinction. Faced with the dilemma of choosing among a large number of "qualified" candidates, the Committee on Admissions could use the single criterion of scholarly excellence and attempt to determine who among the candidates were likely to perform best academically. But for the past 30 years the Committee on Admissions has never adopted this approach. The belief has been that if scholarly excellence were the sole or even predominant criterion, Harvard College would lose a great deal of its vitality and intellectual excellence and that the quality of the educational experience offered to all students would suffer. Final Report of W. J. Bender, Chairman of the Admission and Scholarship Committee and Dean of Admissions and Financial Aid, pp. 20 *et seq.* (Cambridge, 1960). Consequently, after selecting those students whose intellectual potential will seem extraordinary to the faculty—perhaps 150 or so out of an entering class of over 1,100—the Committee seeks—

variety in making its choices. This has seemed important . . . in part because it adds a critical ingredient to the effectiveness of the educational experience [in Harvard College] . . . *The effectiveness of our students' educational experience has seemed to the Committee to be affected as importantly by a wide variety of interests, talents, backgrounds and career goals as it is by a fine faculty and our libraries, laboratories and housing arrangements.* (Dean of Admissions Fred L. Glimp, Final Report to the Faculty of Arts and Sciences, 65 Official Register of Harvard University No. 25, 93, 104–105 (1968) (emphasis supplied).

The belief that diversity adds an essential ingredient to the educational process has long been a tenet of Harvard College admissions. Fifteen or twenty years ago, however, diversity meant students from California, New York, and Massachusetts; city dwellers and farm boys; violinists, painters and football players; biologists, historians and classicists; potential stockbrokers, academics and politicians. The result was that very few ethnic or racial minorities attended Harvard College. In recent years Harvard College has expanded the concept of diversity to include students from disadvantaged economic, racial and ethnic groups. Harvard College now recruits not only Californians or Louisianans but also blacks and Chicanos and other minority students. Contemporary conditions in the United States mean that if Harvard College is to continue to offer a first-rate education to its students, minority representation in the undergraduate body cannot be ignored by the Committee on Admissions.

In practice, this new definition of diversity has meant that race has been a factor in some admission decisions. When the Committee on Admissions reviews the large middle group of applicants who are "admissible" and deemed capable of doing good work in their courses, the race of an applicant may tip the balance in his favor just as geographic origin or a life spent on a farm may tip the balance in other candidates' cases. A farm boy from Idaho can bring something to Harvard College that a Bostonian cannot offer. Similarly, a black student can usually bring something that a white person cannot offer. The quality of the educational experience of all the students in Harvard College depends in part on these differences in the background and outlook that students bring with them.

In Harvard College admissions the Committee has not set target-quotas for the number of blacks, or of musicians, football players, physicists or Californians to be admitted in a given year. At the same time the Committee is aware that if Harvard College is to provide a truly heterogeneous environment that reflects the rich diversity of the United States, it cannot be provided without some attention to numbers. It would not make sense, for example, to have 10 or 20 students out of 1,100 whose homes are west of the Mississippi. Comparably, 10 or 20 black students could not begin to bring to their classmates and to each other the variety of points of view, backgrounds and experiences of blacks in the United States. Their small numbers might also create a sense of isolation among the black students themselves and thus make it more difficult for them to develop and achieve their potential. Consequently, when making its decisions, the Committee on Admissions is aware that there is some relationship between numbers and achieving the benefits to be derived from a diverse student body, and between numbers and providing a reasonable environment for those students admitted. But that awareness does not mean that the Committee sets a minimum number of blacks or of people from west of the Mississippi who are to be admitted. It means only that in choosing among thousands of applicants who are not only "admissible" academically but have other strong qualities, the Committee, with a number of criteria in mind, pays some attention to distribution among many types and categories of students.

The further refinements sometimes required help to illustrate the kind of significance attached to race. The Admissions Committee, with only a few places left to fill, might find itself forced to choose between A, the child of a successful black physician in an academic community with promise of superior academic performance, and B, a black who grew up in an inner-city ghetto of semi-literate parents whose academic achievement was lower but who had demonstrated energy and leadership as well as an apparently abiding interest in black power. If a good number of black students much like A but few like B had already been admitted, the Committee might prefer B; and vice versa. If C, a white student with extraordinary artistic talent, were also seeking one of the remaining places, his unique quality might give him an edge over both A and B. Thus, the critical criteria are often individual qualities or experience not dependent upon race but sometimes associated with it.

The following excerpts are from the opinion of Mr. Justice BRENNAN, Mr. Justice WHITE, Mr. Justice MARSHALL, and Mr. Justice BLACKMUN, concurring in the judgment in part and dissenting. (*Eds.*)

... We conclude, therefore, that racial classifications are not *per se* invalid under the Fourteenth Amendment. Accordingly, we turn to the problem of articulating what our role should be in reviewing state action that expressly classifies by race.

Respondent argues that racial classifications are always suspect and, consequently, that this Court should weigh the importance of the objectives served by Davis' special admissions program to see if they are compelling. In addition, he asserts that this Court must inquire whether, in its judgment, there are alternatives to racial classifications which would suit Davis' purposes. Petitioner, on the other hand, states that our proper role is simply to accept petitioner's determination that the racial classifications used by its program are reasonably related to what it tells us are its benign purposes. We reject petitioner's view, but, because our prior cases are in many respects inapposite to that before us now, we find it necessary to define with precision the meaning of that inexact term, "strict scrutiny."

... Unquestionably we have held that a government practice or statute which restricts "fundamental rights" or which contains "suspect classifications" is to be subjected to "strict scrutiny" and can be justified only if it furthers a compelling government purpose and, even then, only if no less restrictive alternative is available.... But no fundamental right is involved here.... Nor do whites as a class have any of the "traditional indicia of suspectness: the class is not saddled with such disabilities, or subjected to such a history of purposeful unequal treatment, or relegated to such a position of political powerlessness as to command extraordinary protection from the majoritarian political process." ...

Moreover, if the University's representations are credited, this is not a case where racial classifications are "irrelevant and therefore prohibited." ... Nor has anyone suggested that the University's purposes contravene the cardinal principle that racial classifications that stigmatize—because they put the weight of government behind racial hatred and separatism—are invalid without more....

On the other hand, the fact that this case does not fit neatly into our prior analytic framework for race cases does not mean that it should be analyzed by applying the very loose rational-basis standard of review that is the very least that is always applied in equal protection cases. " '[T]he mere recitation of a benign, compensatory purpose is not an automatic shield which protects against any inquiry into the actual purposes underlying a statutory scheme.' " ... Instead, a number of considerations—developed in gender discrimination cases but which carry even more force when applied to racial classifications—lead us to conclude that racial classifications designed to further remedial purposes " 'must serve important governmental objectives and must be substantially related to achievement of those objectives.' "[11] ...

First, race, like "gender-based classifications too often [has] been inexcusably utilized to stereotype and stigmatize politically powerless segments of society." ... While a carefully tailored statute designed to remedy past discrimination could avoid these vices, ... we nonetheless have recognized that the line between honest and thoughtful appraisal of the effects of past discrimination and paternalistic sterotyping is not so clear and that a statute based on the latter is patently capable of stigmatizing all women with a badge of inferiority.... State programs designed ostensibly to ameliorate the effects of past racial discrimination obviously create the same hazard of stigma, since they may promote racial separatism and reinforce the views of those who believe that members of racial minorities are inherently incapable of succeeding on their own....

Second, race, like gender and illegitimacy, ... is an immutable characteristic which its possessors are powerless to escape or set aside. While a classification is not *per se* invalid because it divides classes on the basis of an immutable characteristic, ... it is nevertheless true that such divisions are contrary to our deep belief that "legal burdens should bear some relationship to individual responsibility or wrongdoing," ... and that advancement sanctioned, sponsored, or approved by the State should ideally be based on individual merit or achievement, or at the least on factors within the control of an individual.

Because this principle is so deeply rooted it might be supposed that it would be considered in the legislative process and weighed against the benefits of programs preferring individuals because of their race. But this is not necessarily so: The "natural consequence of our governing process [may well be] that the most 'discrete and insular' of whites ... will be called upon to bear the immediate, direct costs of benign discrimina-

tion." ... Moreover, it is clear from our cases that there are limits beyond which majorities may not go when they classify on the basis of immutable characteristics.... Thus, even if the concern for individualism is weighed by the political process, that weighing cannot waive the personal rights of individuals under the Fourteenth Amendment....

In sum, because of the significant risk that racial classifications established for ostensibly benign purposes can be misused, causing effects not unlike those created by invidious classifications, it is inappropriate to inquire only whether there is any conceivable basis that might sustain such a classification. Instead, to justify such a classification an important and articulated purpose for its use must be shown. In addition, any statute must be stricken that stigmatizes any group or that singles out those least well represented in the political process to bear the brunt of a benign program. Thus our review under the Fourteenth Amendment should be strict—not " 'strict' in theory and fatal in fact," because it is stigma that causes fatality—but strict and searching nonetheless.

Properly construed, therefore, our prior cases unequivocally show that a state government may adopt race-conscious programs if the purpose of such programs is to remove the disparate racial impact its actions might otherwise have and if there is reason to believe that the disparate impact is itself the product of past discrimination, whether its own or that of society at large. There is no question that Davis' program is valid under this test.

Certainly, on the basis of the undisputed factual submissions before this Court, Davis had a sound basis for believing that the problem of underrepresentation of minorities was substantial and chronic and that the problem was attributable to handicaps imposed on minority applicants by past and present racial discrimination. Until at least 1973, the practice of medicine in this country was, in fact, if not in law, largely the prerogative of whites. In 1950, for example, while Negroes comprised 10% of the total population, Negro physicians constituted only 2.2% of the total number of physicians. The overwhelming majority of these, moreover, were educated in two predominantly Negro medical schools, Howard and Meharry. By 1970, the gap between the proportion of Negroes in medicine and their proportion in the population had widened: The number of Negroes employed in medicine remained frozen at 2.2% while the Negro population had increased to 11.1%. The number of Negro admittees to predominantly white medical schools, moreover, had declined in absolute numbers during the years 1955 to 1964. Odegaard 19.

Moreover, Davis had very good reason to believe that the national pattern of underrepresentation of minorities in medicine would be perpetuated if it retained a single admissions standard. For example, the entering classes in 1968 and 1969, the years in which such a standard was used, included only one Chicano and two Negroes out of 100 admittees. Nor is there any relief from this pattern of underrepresentation in the statistics for the regular admissions program in later years.

Davis clearly could conclude that the serious and persistent underrepresentation of minorities in medicine depicted by these statistics is the result of handicaps under which minority applicants labor as a consequence of a background of deliberate, purposeful discrimination against minorities in education and in society generally, as well as in the medical profession. From the inception of our national life, Negroes have been subjected to unique legal disabilities impairing access to equal educational opportunity. Under slavery, penal sanctions were imposed upon anyone attempting to educate Negroes. After enactment of the Fourteenth Amendment the States continued to deny Negroes equal educational opportunity, enforcing a strict policy of segregation that itself stamped Negroes as inferior, *Brown* . . . which relegated minorities to inferior educational institutions, and which denied them intercourse in the mainstream of professional life necessary to advancement. . . . Segregation was not limited to public facilities, moreover, but was enforced by criminal penalties against private action as well. Thus, as late as 1908, this Court enforced a state criminal conviction against a private college for teaching Negroes together with whites. . . .

Green v. County School Board . . . gave explicit recognition to the fact that the habit of discrimination and the cultural tradition of race, prejudice cultivated by centuries of legal slavery and segregation were not immediately dissipated when *Brown I* . . . announced the constitutional principle that equal educational opportunity and participation in all aspects of American life could not be denied on the basis of race. Rather, massive official and private resistance prevented, and to a lesser extent still prevents, attainment of equal opportunity in education at all levels and in the professions. The generation of minority students applying to Davis Medical School since it opened in 1968—most of whom were born before or about the time *Brown I* was decided—clearly have been victims of this discrimination. Judicial decrees recognizing discrimination in public education in California testify to the fact of widespread discrimination suffered by California-born minority applicants; many minority group members living in California, moreover, were born and reared in school districts in southern States segregated by law. Since separation of school children by race "generates a feeling of inferiority as to their status in the community that may affect their hearts and minds in a way unlikely ever to be undone," . . . the conclusion is inescapable that applicants to medical school must be few indeed who endured the effects of *de jure* segregation, the resistance to *Brown I,* or the equally debilitating pervasive private discrimination fostered by our long history of official discrimination, . . . and yet come to the starting line with an education equal to whites.

Moreover, we need not rest solely on our own conclusion that Davis had sound reason to believe that the effects of past discrimination were handicapping minority applicants to the Medical School, because the Department of Health, Education, and Welfare, the expert agency charged by Congress with promulgating regulations enforcing Title VI of the Civil Rights Act of 1964, . . . has also reached the conclusion that race may be taken into account in situations where a failure to do so would limit participation by minorities in federally funded programs, and regulations promulgated by the department expressly contemplate that appropriate race-conscious programs may be adopted by universities to remedy unequal access to university programs caused by their own or by past societal discrimination. . . . It cannot be questioned that, in the absence of the special admissions program, access of minority students to the Medical School would be severely limited and, accordingly, race-conscious admissions would be deemed an appropriate response under these federal regulations. Moreover, the Department's regulatory policy is not one that has gone unnoticed by Congress. . . . Indeed, although an amendment to an appropriations bill was introduced just last year that would have prevented the Secretary of Health, Education, and Welfare from mandating race-conscious programs in university admissions, proponents of this measure, significantly, did not question the validity of voluntary implementation of race-conscious admissions criteria. . . . In these circumstances, the conclusion implicit in the regulations

—that the lingering effects of past discrimination continue to make race-conscious remedial programs appropriate means for ensuring equal educational opportunity in universities—deserves considerable judicial deference. . . .

The second prong of our test—whether the Davis program stigmatizes any discrete group or individual and whether race is reasonably used in light of the program's objectives—is clearly satisfied by the Davis program.

It is not even claimed that Davis's program in any way operates to stigmatize or single out any discrete and insular, or even any identifiable, non-minority group. Nor will harm comparable to that imposed upon racial minorities by exclusion or separation on grounds of race be the likely result of the program. It does not, for example, establish an exclusive preserve for minority students apart from and exclusive of whites. Rather, its purpose is to overcome the effects of segregation by bringing the races together. True, whites are excluded from participation in the special admissions program, but this fact only operates to reduce the number of whites to be admitted in the regular admissions program in order to permit admission of a reasonable percentage—less than their proportion of the California population—of otherwise underrepresented qualified minority applicants.[12]

Nor was Bakke in any sense stamped as inferior by the Medical School's rejection of him. Indeed, it is conceded by all that he satisfied those criteria regarded by the School as generally relevant to academic performance better than most of the minority members who were admitted. Moreover, there is absolutely no basis for concluding that Bakke's rejection as a result of Davis' use of racial preference will affect him throughout his life in the same way as the segregation of the Negro school children in *Brown I* would have affected them. Unlike discrimination against racial minorities, the use of racial preferences for remedial purposes does not inflict a pervasive injury upon individual whites in the sense that wherever they go or whatever they do there is a significant likelihood that they will be treated as second-class citizens because of their color. This distinction does not mean that the exclusion of a white resulting from the preferential use of race is not sufficiently serious to require justification; but it does mean that the injury inflicted by such a policy is not distinguishable from disadvantages caused by a wide range of government actions, none of which has ever been thought impermissible for that reason alone.

In addition, there is simply no evidence that the Davis program discriminates intentionally or unintentionally against any minority group which it purports to benefit. The program does not establish a quota in the invidious sense of a ceiling on the number of minority applicants to be admitted. Nor can the program reasonably be regarded as stigmatizing the program's beneficiaries or their race as inferior. The Davis program does not simply advance less qualified applicants; rather, it compensates applicants, whom it is uncontested are fully qualified to study medicine, for educational disadvantage which it was reasonable to conclude was a product of state-fostered discrimination. Once admitted, these students must satisfy the same degree requirements as regularly admitted students; they are taught by the same faculty in the same classes; and their performance is evaluated by the same standards by which regularly admitted students are judged. Under these circumstances, their performance and degrees must be regarded equally with the regularly admitted students with whom they compete for standing. Since minority graduates cannot justifiably be regarded as less well qualified than nonminority graduates by virtue of the special admissions program, there is no reasonable basis to conclude that minority graduates at schools using such programs would be stigmatized as inferior by the existence of such programs.

We disagree with the lower courts' conclusion that the Davis program's use of race was unreasonable in light of its objectives. First, as petitioner argues, there are no practical means by which it could achieve its ends in the foreseeable future without the use of race-conscious measures. With respect to any factor (such as poverty or family educational background) that may be used as a substitute for race as an indicator of past discrimination, whites greatly outnumber racial minorities simply because whites make up a far larger percentage of the total population and therefore far outnumber minorities in absolute terms at every socioeconomic level. For example, of a class of recent medical school applicants from families with less than $10,000 income, at least 71% were white. Of all 1970 families headed by a person *not* a high school graduate which included related children under 18, 80% were white and 20% were racial minorities. Moreover, while race is positively correlated with differences in GPA and MCAT scores, economic disadvantage is not. Thus, it appears that economically disadvantaged whites do not score less well than economically advantaged whites, while economically advantaged blacks score less well than do disadvantaged whites. These statistics graphically illustrate that the University's purpose to integrate its classes by compensating for past discrimination could not be achieved by a general preference for the economically disadvantaged or the children of parents of limited education unless such groups were to make up the entire class.

Second, the Davis admissions program does not simply equate minority status with disadvantage. Rather, Davis considers on an individual basis each applicant's personal history to determine whether he or she has likely been disadvantaged by racial discrimination. The record makes clear that only minority applicants likely to have been isolated from the mainstream of American life are considered in the special program; other minority applicants are eligible only through the regular admissions program. True, the procedure by which disadvantage is detected is informal, but we have never insisted that educators conduct their affairs through adjudicatory proceedings, and such insistence here is misplaced. A case-by-case inquiry into the extent to which each individual applicant has been affected, either directly or indirectly, by racial discrimination, would seem to be, as a practical matter, virtually impossible, despite the fact that there are excellent reasons for concluding that such effects generally exist. When individual measurement is impossible or extremely impractical, there is nothing to prevent a State from using categorical means to achieve its ends, at least where the category is closely related to the goal. . . . And it is clear from our cases that specific proof that a person has been victimized by discrimination is not a necessary predicate to offering him relief where the probability of victimization is great . . .

Finally, Davis' special admissions program cannot be said to violate the Constitution simply because it has set aside a predetermined number of places for qualified minority applicants rather than using minority status as a positive factor to be considered in evaluating the applications of disadvantaged minority applicants. For purposes of constitutional adjudication, there is no difference between the two approaches. In any admissions program which accords special consideration to disadvantaged racial minorities, a determination of the degree of preference to be given is unavoidable, and any given preference that results in the exclusion of a white candidate is no more or less constitutionally acceptable than a program such as that at Davis. Furthermore,

the extent of the preference inevitably depends on how many minority applicants the particular school is seeking to admit in any particular year so long as the number of qualified minority applicants exceeds that number. There is no sensible, and certainly no constitutional, distinction between, for example, adding a set number of points to the admissions rating of disadvantaged minority applicants as an expression of the preference with the expectation that this will result in the admission of an approximately determined number of qualified minority applicants and setting a fixed number of places for such applicants as was done here.[13]

The "Harvard" program, . . . as those employing it readily concede, openly and successfully employs a racial criterion for the purpose of ensuring that some of the scarce places in institutions of higher education are allocated to disadvantaged minority students. That the Harvard approach does not also make public the extent of the preference and the precise workings of the system while the Davis program employs a specific, openly stated number, does not condemn the latter plan for purposes of Fourteenth Amendment adjudication. It may be that the Harvard plan is more acceptable to the public than is the Davis "quota." If it is, any State, including California, is free to adopt it in preference to a less acceptable alternative, just as it is generally free, as far as the Constitution is concerned, to abjure granting any racial preferences in its admissions program. But there is no basis for preferring a particular preference program simply because in achieving the same goals that the Davis Medical School is pursuing, it proceeds in a manner that is not immediately apparent to the public.

Accordingly, we would reverse the judgment of the Supreme Court of California holding the Medical School's special admissions program unconstitutional and directing respondent's admission, as well as that portion of the judgment enjoining the Medical School from according any consideration to race in the admissions process. . . .

NOTES

1. In the view of Mr. Justice BRENNAN, Mr. Justice WHITE, Mr. Justice MARSHALL, and Mr. Justice BLACKMUN, the pliable notion of "stigma" is the crucial element in analyzing racial classifications. See, *e. g., post,* at 2785. The Equal Protection Clause is not framed in terms of "stigma." Certainly the word has no clearly defined constitutional meaning. It reflects a subjective judgment that is standardless. *All* state-imposed classifications that rearrange burdens and benefits on the basis of race are likely to be

viewed with deep resentment by the individuals burdened. The denial to innocent persons of equal rights and opportunities may outrage those so deprived and therefore may be perceived as invidious. These individuals are likely to find little comfort in the notion that the deprivation they are asked to endure is merely the price of membership in the dominant majority and that its imposition is inspired by the supposedly benign purpose of aiding others. One should not lightly dismiss the inherent unfairness of, and the perception of mistreatment that accompanies, a system of allocating benefits and privileges on the basis of skin color and ethnic origin. Moreover Mr. Justice BRENNAN, Mr. Justice WHITE, Mr. Justice MARSHALL, and Mr. Justice BLACKMUN offer no principle for deciding whether preferential classifications reflect a benign remedial purpose or a malevolent stigmatic classification, since they are willing in this case to accept mere *post hoc* declarations by an isolated state entity—a medical school faculty—unadorned by particularized findings of past discrimination, to establish such a remedial purpose.

2. Professor Bickel noted the self-contradiction of that view:

"The lesson of the great decisions of the Supreme Court and the lesson of contemporary history have been the same for at least a generation: discrimination on the basis of race is illegal, immoral, unconstitutional, inherently wrong, and destructive of democratic society. Now this is to be unlearned and we are told that this is not a matter of fundamental principle but only a matter of whose ox is gored. Those for whom racial equality was demanded are to be more equal than others. Having found support in the Constitution for equality, they now claim support for inequality under the same Constitution." A. Bickel, The Morality of Consent 133 (1975).

3. As I am in agreement with the view that race may be taken into account as a factor in an admissions program, I agree with my Brothers BRENNAN, WHITE, MARSHALL, and BLACKMUN that the portion of the judgment that would proscribe all consideration of race must be reversed.... But I disagree with much that is said in their opinion.

They would require as a justification for a program such as petitioner's, only two findings: (i) that there has been some form of discrimination against the preferred minority groups "by society at large," ... (it being conceded that petitioner had no history of discrimination), and (ii) that "there is reason to believe" that the disparate impact sought to be rectified by the program is the "product" of such discrimination:

"If it was reasonable to conclude—as we hold that it was—that the failure of minorities to qualify for admission at Davis under regular procedures was due principally to the effects of past discrimination, then there is a reasonable likelihood that, but for pervasive racial discrimination, respondent would have failed to qualify for admission even in the absence of Davis' special admission program." *Post,* at 2787.

The breadth of this hypothesis is unprecedented in our constitutional system. The first step is easily taken. No one denies the regrettable fact that there has been societal discrimination in this country against various racial and ethnic groups. The second step, however, involves a speculative leap: but for this discrimination by society at large, Bakke "would have failed to qualify for admission" because Negro applicants—nothing is said about Asians, cf., *e.g., post,* at 2791 n. 57—would have made better scores. Not one word in the record supports this conclusion, and the plurality offers no standard for courts to use in applying such a presumption of causation to other racial or ethnic classifications. This failure is a grave one, since if it may be concluded *on this record* that each of the minority groups preferred by the petitioner's spe-

cial program is entitled to the benefit of the presumption, it would seem difficult to determine that any of the dozens of minority groups that have suffered "societal discrimination" cannot also claim it, in any area of social intercourse. See Part IV-B, *infra.*

4. A number of distinct sub-goals have been advanced as falling under the rubric of "compensation for past discrimination." For example, it is said that preferences for Negro applicants may compensate for harm done them personally, or serve to place then at economic levels they might have attained but for discrimination against their forebears. Greenawalt, *supra,* n. 1, at 581–586. Another view of the "compensation" goal is that it serves as a form of reparation by the "majority" to a victimized group as a whole. B. Bittker, The Case for Black Reparations (1973). That justification for racial or ethnic preference has been subjected to much criticism. *E. g.,* Greenawalt, *supra,* at 581; Posner, *supra,* n. 25, at 16–17, and n. 33. Finally, it has been argued that ethnic preferences "compensate" the group by providing examples of success whom other members of the group will emulate, thereby advancing the group's interest and society's interest in encouraging new generations to overcome the barriers and frustrations of the past. Redish, *supra,* n. 25, at 391. For purposes of analysis these sub-goals need not be considered separately.

Racial classifications in admissions conceivably could serve a fifth purpose, one which petitioner does not articulate: fair appraisal of each individual's academic promise in the light of some cultural bias in grading or testing procedures. To the extent that race and ethnic background were considered only to the extent of curing established inaccuracies in predicting academic performance, it might be argued that there is no "preference" at all. Nothing in this record, however, suggests either that any of the quantitative factors considered by the Medical School were culturally biased or that petitioner's special admissions program was formulated to correct for any such biases. Furthermore, if race or ethnic background were used solely to arrive at an unbiased prediction of academic success, the reservation of fixed numbers of seats would be inexplicable.

5. For example, the University is unable to explain its selection of only the three favored groups—Negroes, Mexican-Americans, and Asians—for preferential treatment. The inclusion of the last group is especially curious in light of the substantial numbers of Asians admitted through the regular admissions process....

6. The only evidence in the record with respect to such underservice is a newspaper article. Record 473.

7. It is not clear that petitioner's two-track system, even if adopted throughout the country, would substantially increase representation of blacks in the medical profession. That is the finding of a recent study by Sleeth & Mishell, Black Under-Representation in United States Medical Schools, New England J. of Med. 1146 (Nov. 24, 1977). Those authors maintain that the cause of black under-representation lies in the small size of the national pool of qualified black applicants. In their view, this problem is traceable to the poor premedical experiences of black undergraduates, and can be remedied effectively only by developing remedial programs for black students before they enter college.

8. The president of Princeton University has described some of the benefits derived from a diverse student body:

"... [A] great deal of learning occurs informally. It occurs through interactions among students of both sexes; of different races, religions, and backgrounds; who come from cities and rural areas, from various states and countries; who have a wide variety of interests and perspectives; and who are able, directly or indirectly, to learn from their differences and to stimulate one another to reexamine even their most deeply held assumptions about themselves and their world. As a wise graduate of ours once observed in commenting on this aspect of the educational process, 'People do not learn very much when they are surrounded only by the likes of themselves.'. . .

"In the nature of things, it is hard to know how, and when, and even if, this informal 'learning through diversity' actually occurs. It does not occur for everyone. For many, however, the unplanned, casual encounters with roommates, fellow sufferers in an organic chemistry class, student workers in the library, teammates on a basketball squad, or other participants in class affairs or student government can be subtle and yet powerful sources of improved understanding and personal growth." Bowen, Admissions and the Relevance of Race, Princeton Alumni Weekly 7, 9 (Sept. 26, 1977).

9. Universities, like the prosecutor in *Swain*, may make individualized decisions, in which ethnic background plays a part, under a presumption of legality and legitimate educational purpose. So long as the university proceeds on an individualized, case-by-case basis, there is no warrant for judicial interference in the academic process. If an applicant can establish that the institution does not adhere to a policy of individual comparisons, or can show that a systematic exclusion of certain groups results, the presumption of legality might be overcome, creating the necessity of proving legitimate educational purpose.

There also are strong policy reasons that correspond to the constitutional distinction between petitioner's preference program and one that assures a measure of competition among all applicants. Petitioner's program will be viewed as inherently unfair by the public generally as well as by applicants for admission to state universities. Fairness in individual competition for opportunities, especially those provided by the State, is a widely cherished American ethic. Indeed, in a broader sense, an underlying assumption of the rule of law is the worthiness of a system of justice based on fairness to the individual. As Mr. Justice Frankfurter declared in another connection, "[j]ustice must satisfy the appearance of justice." *Offut v. United States,* 348 U.S. 11, 14, 75 S.Ct. 11, 13, 99 L.Ed. 11 (1954).

10. This statement appears in the Appendix to the Brief of Columbia University, Harvard University, Stanford University, and the University of Pennsylvania, as *Amici Curiae.*

11. We disagree with our Brother POWELL's suggestion . . . that the presence of "rival groups who can claim that they, too, are entitled to preferential treatment," . . . distinguishes the gender cases or is relevant to the question of scope of judicial review of race classifications. We are not asked to determine whether groups other than those favored by the Davis program should similarly be favored. All we are asked

to do is to pronounce the constitutionality of what Davis has done.

But, were we asked to decide whether any given rival group —German-Americans for example—must constitutionally be accorded preferential treatment, we do have a "principled basis," . . . for deciding this question, one that is well-established in our cases: The Davis program expressly sets out four classes which receive preferred status . . . The program clearly distinguishes whites, but one cannot reason from this to a conclusion that German-Americans, as a national group, are singled out for invidious treatment. And even if the Davis program had a differential impact on German-Americans, they would have no constitutional claim unless they could prove that Davis intended invidiously to discriminate against German-Americans. . . . If this could not be shown, then "the principle that calls for the closest scrutiny of distinctions in laws denying fundamental rights . . . is inapplicable," . . . and the only question is whether it was rational for Davis to conclude that the groups it preferred had a greater claim to compensation than the groups it excluded. . . . Thus, claims of rival groups, although they may create thorny political problems, create relatively simple problems for the courts.

12. The constitutionality of the special admissions program is buttressed by its restriction to only 16% of the positions in the Medical School, a percentage less than that of the minority population in California, . . . and to those minority applicants deemed qualified for admission and deemed likely to contribute to the medical school and the medical profession. . . . This is consistent with the goal of putting minority applicants in the position they would have been in if not for the evil of racial discrimination. Accordingly, this case does not raise the question whether even a remedial use of race would be unconstitutional if it admitted unqualified minority applicants in preference to qualified applicants or admitted, as a result of preferential consideration, racial minorities in numbers significantly in excess of their proportional representation in the relevant population. Such programs might well be inadequately justified by the legitimate remedial objectives. Our allusion to the proportional percentage of minorities in the population of the State administering the program is not intended to establish either that figure or that population universe as a constitutional benchmark. In this case, even respondent, as we understand him, does not argue that, if the special admissions program is otherwise constitutional, the allotment of 16 places in each entering class for special admittees is unconstitutionally high.

13. The excluded white applicant, despite Mr. Justice POWELL's contention to the contrary, . . . receives no more or less "individualized consideration" under our approach than under his.

Suggestions for Further Reading

Arrow, Kenneth, *Social Choice and Individual Values,* 2nd ed. (1963).

Barry, Brian M., *The Liberal Theory of Justice,* 1973. A detailed criticism of Rawls.

Baldwin, R. W., *Social Justice* (1966).

Bayles, Michael, "Compensatory Reverse Discrimination in Hiring" in *Social Theory and Practice,* Vol. 2 (1973), pp. 301-12.

Bayles, Michael, "Reparation To Wronged Groups," *Analysis,* Vol. 33 (1973).

Bedau, Hugo A., ed., *Justice and Equality* (1971).

Benn, S. I. and R. S. Peters, *Social Principles and The Democratic State* (1958), Chaps. 5,6.

Bergler, E. and Meerloo, J. A. M., *Justice And Injustice* (1963).

Blackstone, William T., ed., *The Concept of Equality* (1969).

Bowie, Norman E., *Towards A New Theory of Distributive Justice* (1971).

Brandt, Richard B., *Ethical Theory* (1959), Chap. 16.

Brandt, Richard B., ed., *Social Justice* (1962).

Braybrooke, David, "Let Needs Diminish That Preferences May Prosper," *American Philosophical Quarterly* Monograph Series, Vol. 1 (1968).

Brown, Emerson, and Falk, Freedman, "The Equal Rights for Women Amendment," 80 *Yale L. J.* 871, (1971).

Cahn, Edmond, *The Sense of Injustice* (1949).

Cohen, Marshall; Nagel, Thomas; and Scanlon, Thomas, eds., *Equality and Preferential Treatment* (1977). A definitive anthology with essays by T. Nagel, J. J. Thomson, R. Simon, G. Sher, R. M. Dworkin, Owen Fiss, and A. H. Goldman.

Daniels, Norman, ed., *Reading Rawls* (1975).

Dworkin, Ronald M., *Taking Rights Seriously* (1977).

Feinberg, Joel, "Justice and Personal Desert" reprinted in *Doing and Deserving* (1970), pp. 55-94.

Feinberg, Joel, "Noncomparative Justice," *Philosophical Review*, Vol. LXXXIII (1974), pp. 297-338.

Feinberg, Joel, *Social Philosophy* (1973), Chap 7.

Frankel, Charles, "The New Egalitarianism And the Old," *Commentary*, Vol. 56, (Sept., 1973).

Frankena, William K., "Some Beliefs About Justice," Lindley Lecture, University of Kansas Press, 1966.

Freund, Paul A., "The Equal Rights Amendment Is Not The Way," 6 *Harv. Civ. Rights - Civ. Lib. L. Rev.* 234 (1971).

Friedrich, C. J. and J. W. Chapman, eds. *Nomos VI: Justice* (1963).

Getman, J. G., "Emerging Constitutional Principle of Sexual Equality," 1972 *Supreme Court Review* 157.

Ginsberg, Morris, *On Justice in Society* (1965).

Glazer, Nathan, *Affirmative Discrimination* (1975).

Godwin, William, *Political Justice* (1890).

Hardie, W. F., *Aristotle's Ethical Theory.* (1968). Chap. X.

Hart, H. L. A., *The Concept of Law* (1961), Chaps. 5,6.

Hobhouse, L. T., *Elements of Social Justice* (1922), Chaps. 5,6.

Honore, A. M., "Social Justice" 8 *McGill L.J.* 78, (1962).

Hughes, Graham, *The Conscience of the Courts: Law and Morals in American Life* (1975), Chap. 4.

Jencks, Christopher, *Inequality* (1972).

Kamenka, Eugene, *The Ethical Foundations of Marxism* (1962).

Katzner, Louis, "Presumptivist And Nonpresumptivist Principles of Formal Justice," *Ethics*, Vol. LXXXI (1971), pp. 253-58.

Kaufman, Walter, *Without Guilt and Justice* (1973), Chaps. 1-3.

Kelsen, Hans, *What is Justice?* (1957).

Kleinig, John, "The Concept of Desert," *American Philosophical Quarterly*, vol. 8 (1971).

Kurland, Philip B., "The Equal Rights Amendment: Some Problems of Construction," 6 *Harv. Civ. Rights - Civ. Lib. L. Rev.* 243 (1971).

Lamont, W. D., *The Problems of Moral Judgment* (1946), Chap. 5.

Lewis, Anthony, *Gideon's Trumpet* (1964).

Lucas, J. R., *The Principles of Politics* (1966), Chaps. 28-9, pp. 55-60.

Lyons, David, *The Forms and Limits of Utilitarianism* (1965), Chap. 5.

Lyons, David, "Mill's Theory of Justice," in *Law, Morality, and Society*, ed. P. M. S. Hacker and J. Raz (1977).

McCloskey, H. J., "Egalitarianism, Equality and Justice," *Australasian J. of Philosophy*, Vol. 44 (1966).

Miller, David, *Social Justice* (1976).

Nagel, Thomas, "Equal Treatment And Compensatory Discrimination," *Philosophy And Public Affairs*, Vol. 2 (1973), pp. 348-63.

Narveson, Jan, *Morality and Utility* (1967), Chaps. 6,7.

Nelson, William N., "Special Rights, General Rights, and Social Justice," *Philosophy and Public Affairs*, Vol. 3 (1974).

Note, "Are Sex-Based Classifications Constitutionally Suspect?" 66 *Northwestern U.L. Rev.* 581 (1971).

Note, "Decline and Fall of the New Equal Protection: A Polemical Approach," 58 *VA L. Rev.* 489 (1972).

Note, "Legality of Homosexual Marriage," 82 *Yale L. J.* 573 (1973).

Note, "Pregnancy Discharges in the Military: The Air Force Experience," 86 *Harv. L. Rev.* 568 (1973).

Note, "Reverse Discrimination," 41 *U. Cincinnatti L. Rev.* 250 (1972).

Nozick, Robert, *Anarchy, State and Utopia* (1974).

Olafson, Frederick A., ed., *Justice and Social Policy* (1961).

Pennock, J. R. and Chapman, J. W., eds., *Nomos IX: Equality* (1967).

Perelman, Chaim, *The Idea of Justice and the Problem of Argument* (1963).

Perelman, Chaim, *Justice* (1967).

Piaget, Jean, *The Moral Judgment of the Child* (1932).

Raphael, D. D., *Problems of Political Philosophy* (1970), Chap. 7.

Rashdall, Hastings, *Theory of Good and Evil* (1924), Vol. I, Chap. 8.

Rawls, John, *A Theory of Justice* (1972).

Rescher, Nicholas, *Distributive Justice* (1966).

Scanlon, Timothy M., Jr., "Rawl's Theory of Justice," 121 *U. PA. L. Rev.* 1020 (1973).

Sidgwick, Henry, *The Methods of Ethics,* 7th ed. (1874), Book I, Chap. V.

Symposium, "Equal Rights for Women: A Symposium on The Proposed Constitutional Amendment,." 6 *Harv. Civ. Rights-Civ. Lib. L. Rev.* 215 (1971).

Symposium: Robert Nozick's *Anarchy, State, and Utopia,* 19 *Arizona Law Review* (1977).

Tawney, R. H., *Equality* (1929).

Thomson, Judith J., "Preferential Hiring" *Philosophy and Public Affairs* Vol. 2 (1973), pp. 364-84.

Blastos, Gregory, "Justice and Equality" in R. B. Brandt (ed.), *Social Justice* (1962).

Von Wright, G. H., *The Varieties of Goodness* (1963), Chap. X.

Wasserstrom, Richard A., *The Judicial Decision,* (1961), Chap. 5, "Equity."

Williams, Bernard, "The Idea of Equality," in *Philosophy, Politics and Society,* 2nd series. ed., P. Laslett and W. G. Runciman (1962).

Wilson, John, *Equality* (1966).

Woozley, A. D., "Injustice," *American Philosophical Quarterly,* Monograph No. 7 (1973), pp. 109-22.

Young, Michael, *The Rise of the Meritocracy* (1958).

PART 4 RESPONSIBILITY

Critical judgments about what people do occupy a very large place in our daily life. Philosophers want to make sure that these judgments are valid, and so seek principles under which the judgments may in turn themselves be criticized. There are urgent practical reasons for making sure that our criticism of conduct is sound. We live our lives in a community of persons each of whom pursues his or her own interests, yet each is required to respect the interests of others in order to make possible the benefits of life in a civilized society. Since disinterested benevolence is not a regular feature of social life, people must be encouraged to avoid harming others as they seek their own ends. When harm is done, it is important that acceptable remedies be applied to undo the harm as much as possible. It is also important to take steps that will reduce the likelihood of harm being done in the future. This requires holding to account those (and only those) who properly are accountable when something untoward occurs. It is a matter of some importance also that those (and only those) who are entitled to recognition for good works receive it, so that encouragement of socially valuable activities is provided. What we need, then, are ways of criticizing conduct that are rational and fair. Theoretical work concerned with responsibility seeks to increase our understanding of our critical practices, and through better understanding to make our critical conclusions more reasonable and just.

Legal theory is nowhere more generously endowed with philosophical substance than in those parts that address questions of responsibility. It is also true that the law offers more promising material than any other human endeavor to the philosopher who seeks to develop a theory of responsibility. This happy coincidence makes the subjects sampled in this part of the volume preeminent among concerns of legal philosophy. It is the criminal law that presents the most philosophically important questions, for a just system of criminal liability requires as a foundation principles of responsibility that are just. Civil liability, and especially the law of torts, also poses many similar questions under such textbook headings as fault, negligence, causation, and strict liability. Regarding criminal liability, we want to know when punishment is warranted. Responsibility of the accused is always the first (and sometimes the only) consideration in deciding that. In considering civil liability, we want to know when a loss suffered by one person is to be made up by another; and that often (though not always) involves issues of responsibility, sometimes to the exclusion of all other questions.

THE IDEA OF RESPONSIBILITY

Even the little that has been said about responsibility so far will likely have created an impression in the reader's mind that the very subject of the discussion is not entirely clear. Just what is it that those who speak of responsibility are speaking of? H. L. A. Hart distinguishes the separate though related ideas concerning responsibility that are marked by different forms of expression and different contexts. There are four major categories, and within them a considerable number of important distinctions. As this sorting of expressions makes clear, much in critical practice and in its theory depends upon recognizing differences among expressions that on their face appear alike. This reminds us of J. L. Austin's observation that "words are our tools, and, as a minimum, we should use clean tools: we should know what we mean and what we do not, and must forearm ourselves against the traps that language sets us." Even more important, through work like Professor Hart's we become clear about the word and as a result of that learn about responsibility itself. Again Austin put the point sharply. "When we examine what we should say when, what words we should use in what situations, we are looking again not *merely* at words (or 'meanings,' whatever they may be) but also at the realities we use the words to talk about: we are using a sharpened awareness of words to sharpen our perception of, though not as final arbiter of, the phenomena." One may profitably consider here what the "final arbiter" is, with reference to responsibility as it is dealt with in Hart's analysis. If one wishes to understand what responsibility is, is there anything further that must be understood after one has exhaustively analyzed characteristic correct uses of the term? The value of Professor Hart's analysis is apparent to anyone who has experienced the confusion of responsibility and liability that permeates legal literature. Setting inappropriate requirements of responsibility for some legal liability, and imposing legal liability on some inappropriate occasions of responsibility, have both frequently resulted from just such confusion.

RESPONSIBILITY AND CAUSATION

In ordinary life or in legal proceedings, whenever we assert that a person is responsible for some harm, we may be challenged on grounds of causation. It often counts conclusively against responsibility that what was done by the accused did not cause the unhappy event for which we wish to hold him liable. Yet clear as that is, there is hardly a more difficult task for the theorist than that of spelling out principles which determine in any given case whether the act was or was not the cause of the harm. At the heart of the difficulty is understanding what we *mean* by a cause when the cause is an act. Formidable difficulties about causation arise when general accounts of the relations among events of the physical world are attempted, and these difficulties are often imported into the special cause accounting that issues of personal responsibility call for. But should they be? Causation in a theory of responsibility may be very different in important respects from causation in a theory of scientific explanation or in metaphysics. Many things which are singled out as counting for or against the causal status of one event in relation to another seem not really to matter, as it turns out, when we are talking about *acts* (as acts) and their consequences. Who can deny that in some sense an ancestor's act of reproduction was a cause of the death of the person that his descendent murdered, yet who would assert that the act of reproduction caused the death? Even more revealing, perhaps, is the fact that *doing* harm and *causing* harm are quite different notions, yet an act which is the *doing* surely is in some other more general sense a cause of the harm, every bit as much a cause as another act which is spoken of as *causing* it. This strongly suggests that there is indeed something special about conceiving acts as causes, quite unlike conceiving viruses or volcanoes as causes.

H. L. A. Hart and his Oxford colleague, A. M. Honoré, undertake to clarify causation as it bears on questions of responsibility in the law. In the first part of this selection from their book *Causation in the Law,* they consider the similarity in the concept of causation to be found in law and in morality. This can be accounted for by the common concern of both law and morality to ascertain responsibility. In this part they also point out certain differences, not in the very concept, but in the rules that are used by both law and morality to decide whether an act truly caused a harm. Considerations of legal policy require that the rules the law adopts be suited to the purposes the law must serve, and it is this that accounts for the difference. In the second and larger portion of this selection, the authors take up the master problem of when (ignoring such special restrictions) the consequences of an act can rightly be said to have been caused by it.

Three sorts of problematic cases are analyzed. All of them deal with intervening or supervening events but for which the harm would not have occurred. If what was done would not have resulted in the harm but for something subsequent which was quite usual, the subsequent event does not deprive the act of its causal status. If, however, there is an intervening voluntary act (subject to two major exceptions and certain qualifications), that deprives the earlier act of its causal status. Finally, in cases in which the harm is a result of mere coincidence of the consequence of the act and something else, the act is deprived of its causal status (though once again there is an important exception). After reading this selection, it seems appropriate to pose again and extend the question raised earlier. Is it the concept of causation one finds useful in explaining the physical world that is really germane to issues of responsibility? Have these authors been unduly influenced at any point by the problem of physical causation? And what, in any case, is it really that makes responsibility depend in part on whether one's act was the cause of the harm?

Robert E. Keeton shifts attention to risks in deciding whether or not an act caused harm. In "The Basic Rule of Legal Cause in Negligence Cases," Professor Keeton expounds a risk rule of causation which draws on the insight that causation issues in the law resolve themselves into issues about whether in acting one ought to have regard for some possible harm. The insight is not without its difficulties, however. One may wonder whether the modest claim that A is the cause of harm B has not been unduly enlarged in risk theory. It is not normally thought to be an objection to such a claim that act A was not negligent, for one who causes harm need not be at fault in doing so. Risk theory, however, seems to suggest the contrary. It suggests that when harm occurs and certain conduct caused it, the conduct is the cause of the harm because it created a risk of the harm and the harm was one that falls within the hazards of what was done. But creating a risk of the sort of harm that falls within the risks of what one is doing is (at the least) negligence. The challenge presented by risk analysis, then, is to separate its insight about risk from unwarranted implications concerning culpability.

The New York Times story reporting the tragedy of the Ault family presents a case in which the parents of the victim cannot be held liable for causing their daughter's death, even though they are the authors of the events that resulted in it. The story provides an opportunity for comparative testing of the voluntary intervention principle of Hart and Honoré, and the risk theory analysis of Keeton to see which provides the more illuminating account.

FAULT

"He is to blame" and "it is his fault" are judgments that often express the point of ascertaining responsibility. There is indeed a common emphatic sense of "he is responsible" that is equivalent to "he is to blame," and the subordinate considerations which lead to that are then obscured by an expression of the ultimate conclusion. In the nonlegal affairs of life we often want to fix blame when something bad has happened, either to fix the stigmata and apply for the remedies that social conventions warrant, or at least to set the record straight for future dealings. In legal contexts, both civil and criminal, fixing blame, while far from the whole matter, is nevertheless of the greatest importance in determining liability. In "Sua Culpa" Joel Feinberg separates and examines the different threads which compose a claim that a harm *is his fault*. The claim is first contrasted with two other fault-imputing expressions, *having a fault* and *being at fault*. One's act is at fault when the harm is one's fault; but there are two other conditions that must be satisfied. The act must be the cause of the harm; and the aspect of it that was faulty must be one of the aspects in virtue of which the act was the cause of the harm. The difficulties of the causal requirement again obtrude themselves, and the author endeavors to define the requirement in the face of them. Criteria for a cause are developed, and the reader may wish to consider what reason there is for an act to meet these criteria in order for blame to be fixed for that act. Finally, the suggestion that "his fault" can be dispensed with as a requirement for tort liability is assessed morally.

THE DILEMMA OF THE GOOD SAMARITAN

One variety of responsibility is the responsibility of those who could have and should have acted to save someone in distress but failed to do so. This suggests the more basic problem of when anyone is responsible for failing to act as a "volunteer" (as lawyers put it) or as a "Good Samaritan" (as moralists and laymen would characterize it). On one side, against responsibility, there are purported rights to mind one's own business, if one so chooses, and to avoid any risks—whether of legal liability for an unfortunate outcome, or of harm to oneself in the course of the intervention. In favor of some responsibility, it is argued that indifference to the plight of others in some situations is a willful disregard which is of such immoral proportions that the law must take notice. The argument against responsibility, no matter what, is obviously a losing one in a moral forum, for clearly there are sometimes moral duties of rescue. The issue, then, is whether moral duties ought ever to be recognized as legal duties, the breach of which is grounds for civil or even criminal liability. "Law, Morals, and Rescue" by A. M. Honoré takes up that question. There are subsidiary issues here which the author takes up first. What is required for there to be a moral duty of this sort that is recognized generally in the community? How shall we distinguish between moral duties and moral ideals? When is someone truly a "volunteer" rather than a person who has a duty which the law recognizes on other grounds? What are the limits to be imposed on officious intermeddling so that professed Good Samaritanism does not become an excuse for interference with privacy and self–determination? What claims for compensation may the rescuer assert, and against whom? All these are matters preliminary to the major question that the author then addresses: What policy reasons are there for imposing a legal duty of rescue that at bottom is only the enforcement of a moral duty?

The Good Samaritan may act to rescue someone apparently in distress so that he or she not only discharges a moral duty, but even more, acts beyond the call of duty as a moral hero. If such a person is then punished as a criminal, we might at first suspect the law has gone mad. But in fact the case of such a moral hero can be a close one, as the New York case of *People v. Young* makes clear. Included here in their entirety are the courts' opinions as well as the dissenting opinions in both the Appellate Division of the Supreme Court and then in the state's highest court, the Court of Appeals. The issues are subtle and challenging, and the reader will be well repaid if he or she pursues them. As it turned out, the defendant in this case was mistaken about the need for rescue when he saw a youth on the street being forced against his will to accompany two older men. Unknown to the defendant, the two men were detectives making an arrest. His attack upon the men in an attempt to aid the youth resulted in his being charged with criminal assault. As the opinions make clear, no outright justification is possible under New York law, since for that the defendant would have to be bound to protect the one he sought to help (which he was not); or—in a more strictly Good Samaritan vein—would have to have been attempting to prevent an offense against the youth (which was not constituted by the force employed in making a lawful arrest). It is the *mistake* which receives the greatest attention in these opinions. If it is reasonable it is an excuse that should exculpate, so runs the argument on one side. But whether that argument prevails depends on just what intent is legally necessary for the assault, for a mistake has relevance only if the law requires for liability that the thing done by mistake be done intentionally. Does the law, then, require that the accused intentionally do wrong, or only that he or she do intentionally what happens to be wrong? It seems on all sides to be agreed that the defendant here did the latter but not the former. Disagreement in the opinions is about what the law requires for liability. But those who hold that his mistake exonerates the defendant appear at times to go even further. There is some suggestion that even if the law only requires that he do intentionally what happens to be wrong, the attack is not wrong by virtue of the circumstances; the intimation is that there is a kind of subsidiary justification when a reasonable rescue is made, that it is a worthy endeavor which removes the curse of offensiveness from the otherwise offensive physical contacts. At this point a policy decision is called for, and the interest in safeguarding police from the perils of unwarranted interference is weighed against the countervailing interest of citizens being free to rescue each other from harm.

"MENTAL ELEMENT" REQUIREMENTS

Concern about justice has so far dominated the discussions of responsibility in a criminal context. It is concern that criminal liability be deserved. But there is another perspective that is radically different, one in which the criminal law appears as an instrument of crime prevention. Convictions, in this view, are for the purpose of being able to subject to remedial treatment those who bring about the socially significant harms that concern the criminal law. Whether a person is responsible or not is then irrelevant (at least when "responsible" means "to blame"). Indeed the very issue of responsibility is a hindrance to the proper functioning of the system of correction that the criminal law serves, for it allows those in need of correction to avoid it by showing that with respect to matters that are significant only for moral judgments they are innocent. Lady Barbara Wootton in the excerpts from her book *Crime and the Criminal Law* advocates such a new perspective and declares that "the concept of responsibility should be allowed to wither away." That concept is attacked in the selection on two fronts. First there is the matter of *mens rea,* a term of art in criminal law theory that lends itself all too readily to gross abuse. Literally it means "culprit" or "guilty" mind, but that tells us nothing about its proper use. Lady Wootton adopts an interpretation suggested by its literal meaning, however, so that questions of *mens rea* become "questions of motivation," and she then proceeds to criticize the requirement of *mens rea* for criminal liability as undesirable moralism that interferes with the objectives of a forward-looking criminal process. In advocating elimination of the requirement of *mens rea* (to what extent exactly is not clear), she proposes very extensive strict criminal liability. And instead of degrees of culpability according to intention which now separate the more and less serious forms of each kind of crime, she seems to believe that "the criterion of gravity" of an offense is "the amount of social damage which a crime causes."

Mental abnormality is the second front on which Lady Wootton attacks responsibility. Her discussion points out that unfortunate, even absurd results may be expected from the way existing defenses of mental abnormality are given effect, and this is especially so in view of present institutional arrangements. Several considerations do indeed argue for reform. One is that there be deprivation of liberty (in whatever form) only when either criminal liability or dangerousness of the person warrants it. Another is that those who are sick (whether criminals or not) be given the care and treatment that humanity requires. Finally, when a person is truly dangerous and without ability to control himself, whether subject to criminal liability for his conduct or not, he is not to be left free to harm others. One may recognize that reform is urgently needed since, as things now stand, these considerations are often not respected. But the elimination from proceedings of concern about whether the accused had capacity to conform his conduct to law may seem to many not only an unnecessary encroachment on justice, but an encouragement of opportunities for violation of rights that are among the most basic a person has. Indeed, the concluding sentence of this selection in which Lady Wootton speaks of "places of safety" for offenders cannot help but sound ominous in view of what has more recently come to be known as "Clockwork Orange" correctional regimes. Further discussion of these matters is to be found in selections in the third and fourth sections of Part Five of this volume.

Professor Hart in "Changing Conceptions of Responsibility" takes up the challenge Lady Wootton has presented. He scrutinizes the consequences of eliminating responsibility from the requirements for criminal conviction, particularly with reference to mental abnormality. Little need be said by way of introduction, for the issue is joined perfectly and the argument pursued with exemplary clarity and order. It does seem desirable, however, to note one point concerning Professor Hart's use here of the troublesome expression *mens rea.* It is a matter of some dispute among theorists whether there is *mens rea* in crimes of negligence, and also whether there can be *mens rea* when there is mental abnormality sufficient to exonerate. The first question is really about what conventions govern the use of a jargon term in criminal law theory. The second question, while it might also be construed that way, is better understood as an inquiry concerning certain matters of fact. As Professor Hart has made abundantly clear in other writings, in its characteristic employment the term is used to preclude excuses claiming that an act was done unintentionally, through assertions that there was *mens rea*. But many persons (though indeed not all) who are legally insane can act fully as intentionally as perfectly normal persons. The relevant abnormality of such a person would, for example, consist of psychotic notions of danger to himself/herself or psychotic misconceptions of the justifiability of the harm he or she does. It would seem then that while *mens rea* requirements are fully satisfied, there is still a mental abnormality defense available quite independently based on a lack of capacity to choose to do otherwise. In Professor Hart's discussion here, however, this distinction among excuses seems not to be observed.

In "Mental Abnormality as a Criminal Excuse," Hyman Gross has endeavored to make clear the full range of exculpatory claims that look to mental abnormality and to discover what good reasons there are in principle for recognizing them as defenses in a criminal prosecution. Particular attention is given to the defense of insanity in the various versions in which that defense has been developed, and there is an assessment of each version in the light of more general concerns about responsibility as a condition of criminal liability.

The most controversial among the varieties of insanity defense in the United States has been the so-called Durham rule. In 1954, in the case of *Durham v. United States,* the Federal Court of Appeals for the District of Columbia adopted as a new insanity defense for that jurisdiction the rule that an unlawful act that was the product of mental disease or defect does not subject the perpetrator to criminal liability. Such a defense had in essence first been recognized in 1870 in New Hampshire, and two American jurisdictions other than the District of Columbia have also adopted it. In using it, two principal difficulties arise. The more obvious one is how to tell when conduct is the "product" of the abnormal condition. This raises both conceptual issues about just what it takes to be a "product" in the relevant sense, and factual questions about whether what the accused did was or was not a product (in the relevant sense) of his abnormal state. A less obvious but even more basic question is why the product of any mental disease or defect should not be a basis of criminal liability. No hint is given about what grounds there are in considerations of legal policy, justice, humanity, or anything else that might justify an excuse each and every time mental abnormality "produces" the criminal product.

In 1972, the *Durham* rule was overruled in *United States v. Brawner.* The Court's opinion is an ambitious attempt to consider the problems of practice and theory in light of the experience of the intervening years, and to provide instructions for properly implementing the new rule of the Model Penal Code (the ALI rule). The excerpts from the Court's opinion that are included here put the recurring issues in sharp focus. The last portion of these excerpts deals with questions of how culpability may be affected by mental abnormality other than by ways recognized in an insanity defense.

H. G.

THE IDEA OF RESPONSIBILITY

H. L. A. HART

Responsibility*

A wide range of different, though connected, ideas is covered by the expressions 'responsibility', 'responsible', and 'responsible for', as these are standardly used in and out of the law. Though connections exist among these different ideas, they are often very indirect, and it seems appropriate to speak of different *senses* of these expressions. The following simple story of a drunken sea captain who lost his ship at sea can be told in the terminology of responsibility to illustrate, with stylistically horrible clarity, these differences of sense.

'As a captain of the ship, X was responsible for the safety of his passengers and crew. But on his last voyage he got drunk every night and was responsible for the loss of the ship with all aboard. It was rumoured that he was insane, but the doctors considered that he was responsible for his actions. Throughout the voyage he behaved quite irresponsibly, and various incidents in his career showed that he was not a responsible person. He always maintained that the exceptional winter storms were responsible for the loss of the ship, but in the legal proceedings brought against him he was found criminally responsible for his negligent conduct, and in separate civil proceedings he was held legally responsible for the loss of life and property. He is still alive and he is morally responsible for the deaths of many women and children.'

This welter of distinguishable senses of the word 'responsibility' and its grammatical cognates can, I think, be profitably reduced by division and classification. I shall distinguish four heads of classification to which I shall assign the following names:

(a) Role-Responsibility
(b) Causal-Responsibility

*From the *Law Quarterly Review* (1967), Vol. 83. Reprinted by permission of the Editor. This selection was reprinted as the first part of an essay entitled "Postscript: Responsibility and Retribution" in H. L. A. Hart, *Punishment and Responsibility* (New York and Oxford: Oxford University Press, 1968), pp. 211–30.

(c) Liability-Responsibility
(d) Capacity-Responsibility.

I hope that in drawing these dividing lines, and in the exposition which follows, I have avoided the arbitrary pedantries of classificatory systematics, and that my divisions pick out and clarify the main, though not all, varieties of responsibility to which reference is constantly made, explicitly or implicitly, by moralists, lawyers, historians, and ordinary men. I relegate to the notes[1] discussion of what unifies these varieties and explains the extension of the terminology of responsibility.

ROLE-RESPONSIBILITY

A sea captain is responsible for the safety of his ship, and that is his responsibility, or one of his responsibilities. A husband is responsible for the maintenance of his wife; parents for the upbringing of their children; a sentry for alerting the guard at the enemy's approach; a clerk for keeping the accounts of his firm. These examples of a person's responsibilities suggest the generalization that, whenever a person occupies a distinctive place or office in a social organization, to which specific duties are attached to provide for the welfare of others or to advance in some specific way the aims or purposes of the organization, he is properly said to be responsible for the performance of these duties, or for doing what is necessary to fulfil them. Such duties are a person's responsibilities. As a guide to this sense of responsibility this generalization is, I think, adequate, but the idea of a distinct role or place or office is, of course, a vague one, and I cannot undertake to make it very precise. Doubts about its extension to marginal cases will always arise. If two friends, out on a mountaineering expedition, agree that the one shall look after the food and the other the maps, then the one is correctly said to be responsible for the food, and the other for the maps, and I would classify this as a case of role-responsibility. Yet such fugitive or temporary assignments with specific duties would not usually be considered by sociologists, who mainly use the word, as an example of a 'role'. So 'role' in my classification is extended to include a task assigned to any person by agreement or otherwise. But it is also important to notice that not all the duties which a man has in virtue of occupying what in a quite strict sense of role is a distinct role, are thought or spoken of as 'responsibilities'. A private soldier has a duty to obey his superior officer and, if commanded by him to form fours or present arms on a given occasion, has a duty to do so. But to form fours or present arms would scarcely be said to be the private's responsibility; nor would he be said to be responsible for doing it. If on the other hand a soldier was ordered to deliver a message to H.Q. or to conduct prisoners to a base camp, he might well be said to be responsible for doing these things, and these things to be his responsibility. I think, though I confess to not being sure, that what distinguishes those duties of a role which are singled out as responsibilities is that they are duties of a relatively complex or extensive kind, defining a 'sphere of responsibility' requiring care and attention over a protracted period of time, while short-lived duties of a very simple kind, to do or not do some specific act on a particular occasion, are not termed responsibilities. Thus a soldier detailed off to keep the camp clean and tidy for the general's visit of inspection has this as his sphere of responsibility and is responsible for it. But if merely told to remove a piece of paper from the approaching general's path, this would be at most his duty.

A 'responsible person', 'behaving responsibly' (not 'irresponsibly'), require for their elucidation a reference to role-responsibility. A responsible person is one who is disposed to take his duties seriously; to think about them, and to make serious efforts to fulfil them. To behave responsibly is to behave as a man would who took his duties in this serious way. Responsibilities in this sense may be either legal or moral, or fall outside this dichotomy. Thus a man may be morally as well as legally responsible for the maintenance of his wife and children, but a host's responsibility for the comfort of his guests, and a referee's responsibility for the control of the players is neither legal nor moral, unless the word 'moral' is unilluminatingly used simply to exclude legal responsibility.

CAUSAL RESPONSIBILITY

'The long drought was responsible for the famine in India'. In many contexts, as in this one, it is possible to substitute for the expression 'was responsible for' the words 'caused' or 'produced' or some other causal expression in referring to consequences, results, or outcomes. The converse, however, is not always true. Examples of this causal sense of responsibility are legion. 'His neglect was responsible for her distress.' 'The Prime Minister's speech was responsible for the panic.' 'Disraeli was responsible for the defeat of the Government.' 'The icy condition of the road was responsible for the accident.' The past tense of the verb used in this causal sense of the expression 'responsible for' should be noticed. If it is said of a living person, who has in fact caused some disaster, that he *is* responsible for it, this is not, or not merely, an example of causal responsibility, but of what I term 'liability-responsibility'; it asserts his liability on account of the disaster, even though it is also true that he is responsible in that sense *because* he caused the disaster, and that he caused the disaster may be expressed by saying that he was responsible for it. On the other hand, if it is said of a person no longer living that he was responsible for some disaster, this may be either a simple causal statement or a statement of liability-responsibility, or both.

From the above examples it is clear that in this causal sense not only human beings but also their actions or omissions, and things, conditions, and events, may be said to be responsible for outcomes. It is perhaps true that only where an outcome is thought unfortunate or felicitous is its cause commonly spoken of as responsible for it. But this may not reflect any aspect of the meaning of the expression 'responsible for'; it may only reflect the fact that, except in such cases, it may be pointless and hence rare to pick out the causes of events. It is sometimes suggested that, though we may speak of a human being's action as responsible for some outcome in a purely causal sense, we do not speak of a person, as distinct from his actions, as responsible for an outcome, unless he is felt to deserve censure or praise. This is, I think, a mistake. History books are full of examples to the contrary. 'Disraeli was responsible for the defeat of the Government' need not carry even an implication that he was deserving of censure or praise; it may be purely a statement concerned with the contribution made by one human being to an outcome of importance, and be entirely neutral as to its moral or other merits. The contrary view depends, I think, on the failure to appreciate sufficiently the ambiguity of statements of the form 'X *was* responsible for Y' as distinct from 'X *is* responsible for Y' to which I have drawn attention above. The former expression in the case of a person no longer living may be (though it *need* not be) a statement of liability-responsibility.

LEGAL LIABILITY-RESPONSIBILITY

Though it was noted that role-responsibility might take either legal or moral form, it was not found necessary to treat these separately. But in the case of the present topic of liability-responsibility, separate treatment seems advisable. For responsibility seems to have a wider extension in relation to the law than it does in relation to morals, and it is a question to be considered whether this is due merely to the general differences between law and morality, or to some differences in the sense of responsibility involved.

When legal rules require men to act or abstain from action, one who breaks the law is usually liable, according to other legal rules, to punishment for his misdeeds, or to make compensation to persons injured thereby, and very often he is liable to both punishment and enforced compensation. He is thus liable to be 'made to pay' for what he has done in either or both of the senses which the expression 'He'll pay for it' may bear in ordinary usage. But most legal systems go much further than this. A man may be legally punished on account of what his servant has done, even if he in no way caused or instigated or even knew of the servant's action, or knew of the likelihood of his servant so acting. Liability in such circumstances is rare in modern systems of criminal law; but it is common in all systems of civil law for men to be made to pay compensation for injuries caused by others, generally their servants or employees. The law of most countries goes further still. A man may be liable to pay compensation for harm suffered by others, though neither he nor his servants have caused it. This is so, for example, in Anglo-American law when the harm is caused by dangerous things which escape from a man's possession, even if their escape is not due to any act or omission of his or his servants, or if harm is caused to a man's employees by defective machinery whose defective condition he could not have discovered.

It will be observed that the facts referred to in the last paragraph are expressed in terms of 'liability' and not 'responsibility'. In the preceding essay in this volume I ventured the general statement that to say that someone is legally responsible for something often means that under legal rules he is liable to be made either to suffer or to pay compensation in certain eventualities. But I now think that this simple account of liability-responsibility is in need of some considerable modification. Undoubtedly, expressions of the form 'he is legally responsible for Y' (where Y is some action or harm) and 'he is legally liable to be punished or to be made to pay compensation for Y' are very closely connected, and sometimes they are used as if they were identical in meaning. Thus, where one legal writer speaks of 'strict responsibility' and 'vicarious responsibility', another speaks of 'strict liability' and 'vicarious liability'; and even in the work of a single writer the expressions 'vicarious responsibility' and 'vicarious liability' are to be found used without any apparent difference in meaning, implication, or emphasis. Hence, in arguing that it was for the law to determine the mental conditions of responsibility, Fitzjames Stephen claimed that this must be so because 'the meaning of responsibility is liability to punishment'.[2]

But though the abstract expressions 'responsibility' and 'liability' are virtually equivalent in many contexts, the statement that a man is responsible for his actions, or for some act or some harm, is usually not identical in meaning with the statement that he is liable to be punished or to be made to pay compensation for the act or the harm, but is directed to a narrower and more specific issue. It is in this respect that my previous account of liability-responsibility needs qualification.

The question whether a man is or is not legally liable to be punished for some action that he has done opens up the quite general issue whether all of the various requirements for criminal liability have been satisfied, and so will include the question whether the kind of action done, whatever mental element accompanied it, was ever punishable by law. But the question whether he is or is not legally responsible for some action or some harm is usually not concerned with this general issue, but with the narrower issue whether any of a certain range of conditions (mainly, but not exclusively, psychological) are satisfied, it being assumed that all other conditions are satisfied. Because of this difference in scope between questions of liability to punishment and questions of responsibility, it would be somewhat misleading, though not unintelligible, to say of a man who had refused to rescue a baby drowning in a foot of water, that he was not, according to English law, legally responsible for leaving the baby to drown or for the baby's death, if all that is meant is that he was not liable to punishment because refusing aid to those in danger is not generally a crime in English law. Similarly, a book or article entitled 'Criminal Responsibility' would not be expected to contain the whole of the substantive criminal law determining the conditions of liability, but only to be concerned with a specialized range of topics such as mental abnormality, immaturity, *mens rea,* strict and vicarious liability, proximate cause, or other general forms of connection between acts and harm sufficient for liability. These are the specialized topics which are, in general, thought and spoken of as 'criteria' of responsibility. They may be divided into three classes: (i) mental or psychological conditions; (ii) causal or other forms of connection between act and harm; (iii) personal relationships rendering one man liable to be punished or to pay for the acts of another. Each of these three classes requires some separate discussion.

(i) *Mental or psychological criteria of responsibility.* In the criminal law the most frequent issue raised by questions of responsibility, as distinct from the wider question of liability, is whether or not an accused person satisfied some mental or psychological conditions required for liability, or whether liability was strict or absolute, so that the usual mental or psychological condition were not required. It is, however, important to notice that these psychological conditions are of two sorts, of which the first is far more closely associated with the use of the word responsibility than the second. On the one hand, the law of most countries requires that the person liable to be punished should at the time of his crime have had the capacity to understand what he is required by law to do or not to do, to deliberate and to decide what to do, and to control his conduct in the light of such decisions. Normal adults are generally assumed to have these capacities, but they may be lacking where there is mental disorder or immaturity, and the possession of these normal capacities is very often signified by the expression 'responsible for his actions'. This is the fourth sense of responsibility which I discuss below under the heading of 'Capacity-Responsibility'. On the other hand, except where responsibility is strict, the law may excuse from punishment persons of normal capacity if, on particular occasions where their outward conduct fits the definition of the crime, some element of intention or knowledge, or some other of the familiar constituents of *mens rea,* was absent, so that the particular action done was defective, though the agent had the normal capacity of understanding and control. Continental codes usually make a firm distinction between these two main types of psychological conditions: Questions concerning

general capacity are described as matters of responsibility or 'imputability', whereas questions concerning the presence or absence of knowledge or intention on particular occasions are not described as matters of 'imputability', but are referred to the topic of 'fault' (*schuld, faute, dolo,* et cetera).

English law and English legal writers do not mark quite so firmly this contrast between general capacity and the knowledge or intention accompanying a particular action; for the expression *mens rea* is now often used to cover all the variety of psychological conditions required for liability by the law, so that both the person who is excused from punishment because of lack of intention or some ordinary accident or mistake on a particular occasion and the person held not to be criminally responsible on account of immaturity or insanity are said not to have the requisite *mens rea.* Yet the distinction thus blurred by the extensive use of the expression *mens rea* between a persistent incapacity and a particular defective action is indirectly marked in terms of responsibility in most Anglo-American legal writing, in the following way. When a person is said to be not responsible for a particular act or crime, or when (as in the formulation of the M'Naghten Rules and s. 2 of the Homicide Act, 1957) he is said not to be responsible for his 'acts and omissions in doing' some action on a particular occasion, the reason for saying this is usually some mental abnormality or disorder. I have not succeeded in finding cases where a normal person, merely lacking some ordinary element of knowledge or intention on a particular occasion, is said for that reason not to be responsible for that particular action, even though he is for that reason not liable to punishment. But though there is this tendency in statements of liability-responsibility to confine the use of the expression 'responsible' and 'not responsible' to questions of mental abnormality or general incapacity, yet all the psychological conditions of liability are to be found discussed by legal writers under such headings as 'Criminal Responsibility' or 'Principles of Criminal Responsibility'. Accordingly I classify them here as criteria of responsibility. I do so with a clear conscience, since little is to be gained in clarity by a rigid division which the contemporary use of the expression *mens rea* often ignores.

The situation is, however, complicated by a further feature of English legal and non-legal usage. The phrase 'responsible for his actions' is, as I have observed, frequently used to refer to the capacity-responsibility of the normal person, and, so used, refers to one of the major criteria of liability-responsibility. It is so used in s. 2 of the Homicide Act 1957, which speaks of a person's mental 'responsibility' for his actions being *impaired,* and in the rubric to the section, which speaks of persons 'suffering from diminished responsibility'. In this sense the expression is the name or description of a psychological condition. But the expression is also used to signify liability-responsibility itself, that is, liability to punishment so far as such liability depends on psychological conditions, and is so used when the law is said to 'relieve insane persons of responsibility for their actions'. It was probably also so used in the form of verdict returned in cases of successful pleas of insanity under English law until this was altered by the Insanity Act 1964: the verdict was 'guilty but insane so as not to be responsible according to law for his actions'.

(ii) *Causal or other forms of connection with harm.* Questions of legal liability-responsibility are not limited in their scope to psychological conditions of either of the two sorts distinguished above. Such questions are also (though more frequently in the law of tort than in the criminal law) concerned with the issue whether some form of connection between a person's act and some harmful outcome is sufficient according to law to make him liable; so if a person is accused of murder the question whether he was or was not legally responsible for the death may be intended to raise the issue whether the death was too remote a consequence of his acts for them to count as its cause. If the law, as frequently in tort, is not that the defendant's action should have caused the harm, but that there be some other form of connection or relationship between the defendant and the harm, for example, that it should have been caused by some dangerous thing escaping from the defendant's land, this connection or relationship is a condition of civil responsibility for harm, and, where it holds, the defendant is said to be legally responsible for the harm. No doubt such questions of connection with harm are also frequently phrased in terms of liability.

(iii) *Relationship with the agent.* Normally in criminal law the minimum condition required for liability for punishment is that the person to be punished should himself have done what the law forbids, at least so far as outward conduct is concerned; even if liability is 'strict'; it is not enough to render him liable for punishment that someone else should have done it. This is often expressed in the terminology of responsibility (though here, too, 'liability' is frequently used instead of 're-

sponsibility') by saying that, generally, vicarious responsibility is not known to the criminal law. But there are exceptional cases; an innkeeper is liable to punishment if his servants, without his knowledge and against his orders, sell liquor on his premises after hours. In this case he is vicariously responsible for the sale, and of course, in the civil law of tort there are many situations in which a master or employer is liable to pay compensation for the torts of his servant or employee, and is said to be vicariously responsible.

It appears, therefore, that there are diverse types of criteria of legal liability-responsibility: The most prominent consist of certain mental elements, but there are also causal or other connections between a person and harm, or the presence of some relationship, such as that of master and servant, between different persons. It is natural to ask why these very diverse conditions are singled out as criteria of responsibility, and so are within the scope of questions about responsibility, as distinct from the wider question concerning liability for punishment. I think that the following somewhat Cartesian figure may explain this fact. If we conceive of a person as an embodied mind and will, we may draw a distinction between two questions concerning the conditions of liability and punishment. The first question is what general types of outer conduct *(actus reus)* or what sorts of harm are required for liability? The second question is how closely connected with such conduct or such harm must the embodied mind or will of an individual person be to render him liable to punishment? Or, as some would put it, to what extent must the embodied mind or will be the author of the conduct or the harm in order to render him liable? Is it enough that the person made the appropriate bodily movements? Or is it required that he did so when possessed of a certain capacity of control and with a certain knowledge or intention? Or that he caused the harm or stood in some other relationship to it, or to the actual doer of the deed? The legal rules, or parts of legal rules, that answer these various questions define the various forms of connection which are adequate for liability, and these constitute conditions of legal responsibility which form only a part of the total conditions of liability for punishment, which also include the definitions of the *actus reus* of the various crimes.

We may therefore summarize this long discussion of legal liability-responsibility by saying that, though in certain general contexts legal responsibility and legal liability have the same meaning, to say that a man is legally responsible for some act or harm is to state that his connection with the act or harm is sufficient according to law for liability. Because responsibility and liability are distinguishable in this way, it will make sense to say that because a person is legally responsible for some action he is liable to be punished for it.

LEGAL LIABILITY-RESPONSIBILITY AND MORAL BLAME

My previous account of legal liability-responsibility, in which I claimed that in one important sense to say that a person is legally responsible meant that he was legally liable for punishment or could be made to pay compensation, has been criticized on two scores. Since these criticisms apply equally to the above amended version of my original account, in which I distinguish the general issue of liability from the narrower issue of responsibility, I shall consider these criticisms here. The first criticism, made by Mr. A. W. B. Simpson,[3] insists on the strong connection between statements of legal responsibility and moral judgment, and claims that even lawyers tend to confine statements that a person is legally responsible for something to cases where he is considered morally blameworthy, and, where this is not so, tend to use the expression 'liability' rather than 'responsibility'. But, though moral blame and legal responsibility may be connected in some ways, it is surely not in this simple way. Against any such view not only is there the frequent use already mentioned of the expressions 'strict responsibility' and 'vicarious responsibility', which are obviously independent of moral blameworthiness, but there is the more important fact that we can, and frequently do, intelligibly debate the question whether a mentally disordered or very young person who has been held legally responsible for a crime is morally blameworthy. The coincidence of legal responsibility with moral blameworthiness may be a laudable ideal, but it is not a necessary truth nor even an accomplished fact.

The suggestion that the statement that a man is responsible generally means that he is blameworthy and not that he is liable to punishment is said to be supported by the fact that it is possible to cite, without redundancy, the fact that a person is responsible as a ground or reason for saying that he is liable to punishment. But, if the various kinds or senses of responsibility are distinguished, it is plain that there are many explanations of this last mentioned fact, which are quite independent of any essential connection between legal responsibility and moral blameworthiness. Thus cases where the statement that the man is responsible constitutes a reason for saying that he is liable to punishment may be cases of role-responsibility (the master is legally responsible for the safety of his ship, therefore he is liable to punishment if he loses it) or capacity-responsibility (he was responsible for his actions therefore he is liable to punishment for his crimes); or they may even be statements of liability-responsibility, since such statements refer to part only of the conditions of liability and may therefore be given, without redundancy, as a reason for liability to punishment. In any case this criticism may be turned against the suggestion that responsibility is to be equated with moral blameworthiness; for plainly the statement that someone is responsible may be given as part of the reason for saying that he is morally blameworthy.

LIABILITY RESPONSIBILITY FOR PARTICULAR ACTIONS

An independent objection is the following, made by Mr. George Pitcher.[4] The wide extension I have claimed for the notion of liability-responsibility permits us to say not only that a man is legally responsible in this sense for the consequences of his action, but also for his action or actions. According to Mr. Pitcher 'this is an improper way of talking', though common amongst philosophers. Mr. Pitcher is concerned primarily with moral, not legal, responsibility, but even in a moral context it is plain that there is a very well established use of the expression 'responsible for his actions' to refer to capacity-responsibility for which Mr. Pitcher makes no allowance. As far as the law is concerned, many examples may be cited from both sides of the Atlantic where a person may be said to be responsible for his actions, or for his act, or for his crime, or for his conduct. Mr. Pitcher gives, as a reason for saying that it is improper to speak of a man being responsible for his own actions, the fact that a man does not produce or cause his own actions. But this argument would prove far too much. It would rule out as improper not only the expression 'responsible for his actions', but also our saying that a man was responsible vicariously or otherwise for harmful outcomes which he had not caused, which is a perfectly well established legal usage.

None the less, there are elements of truth in Mr. Pitcher's objection. First, it seems to be the case that even where a man is said to be legally responsible for what he has done, it is rare to find this expressed by a phrase conjoining the verb of action with the expression 'responsible for'. Hence, 'he is legally responsible for killing her' is not usually found, whereas 'he is legally responsible for her death' is common, as are the expressions 'legally responsible for his act (in killing her)'; 'legally responsible for his crime'; or, as in the official formulation of the M'Naghten Rules, 'responsible for his actions or omissions in doing or being a party to the killing'. These common expressions in which a noun, not a verb, follows the phrase 'responsible for' are grammatically similar to statements of causal responsibility, and the tendency to use the same form no doubt shows how strongly the overtones of causal responsibility influence the terminology ordinarily used to make statements of liability-responsibility. There is, however, also in support of Mr. Pitcher's view, the point already cited that, even in legal writing, where a person is said to be responsible for his act or his conduct, the relevant mental element is usually the question of insanity or immaturity, so that the ground in such cases for the assertion that the person is responsible or is not responsible for his act is the presence of absence of 'responsibility for actions' in the sense of capacity-responsibility, and not merely the presence or absence of knowledge or intention in relation to the particular act.

MORAL LIABILITY-RESPONSIBILITY

How far can the account given above of legal liability-responsibility be applied *mutatis mutandis* to moral responsibility? The *mutanda* seem to be the following: 'deserving blame' or 'blameworthy' will have to be substituted for 'liable to punishment', and 'morally bound to make amends or pay compensation' for 'liable to be made to pay compensation'. Then the moral counterpart to the account given of legal liability-responsibility would be the following: To say that a person is morally responsible for something he has done or for some harmful outcome of his own or others' conduct, is to say that he is morally blameworthy, or morally obliged to make amends for the harm, so far as this depends on certain conditions. These conditions relate to the character or extent of a man's control over his own conduct, or to the causal or other connection between his action and harmful occurrences, or to his relationship with the person who actually did the harm.

In general, such an account of the meaning of 'morally responsible' seems correct, and the striking differences between legal and moral responsibility are due to substantive differences between the content of legal and moral rules and principles rather than to any variation in meaning of responsibility when conjoined with the word 'moral' rather than 'legal'. Thus, both in the legal and the moral case, the criteria of responsibility seem to be restricted to the psychological elements involved in the control of conduct, to causal or other connections between acts and harm, and to the relationships with the actual doer of misdeeds. The interesting differences between legal and moral responsibility arise from the differences in the particular criteria falling under these general heads. Thus a system of criminal law may make responsibility strict, or even absolute, not even exempting very young children or the grossly insane from punishment; or it may vicariously punish one man for what another has done, even though the former had no control of the latter; or it may punish an individual or make him compensate another for harm which he neither intended nor could have foreseen as likely to arise from his conduct. We may condemn such a legal system which extends strict or vicarious responsibility in these ways as barbarous or unjust, but there are no conceptual barriers to be overcome in speaking of such a system as a legal system, though it is certainly arguable that we should not speak of 'punishment' where liability is vicarious or strict. In the moral case, however, greater conceptual barriers exist: The hypothesis that we might hold individuals morally blameworthy for doing things which they could not have avoided doing, or for things done by others over whom they had no control, conflicts with too many of the central features of the idea of morality to be treated merely as speculation about a rare or inferior kind of moral system. It may be an exaggeration to say that there could not logically be such a morality or that blame administered according to principles of strict or vicarious responsibility, even in a minority of cases, could not logically be moral blame; none the less, admission of such a system as a morality would require a profound modification in our present concept of morality, and there is no similar requirement in the case of law.

Some of the most familiar contexts in which the expression 'responsibility' appears confirm these general parallels between legal and moral liability-responsibility. Thus in the famous question 'Is moral responsibility compatible with determinism?' the expression 'moral responsibility' is apt just because the bogey raised by determinism specifically relates to the usual criteria of responsibility; for it opens the question whether, if 'determinism' were true, the capacities of human beings to control their conduct would still exist or could be regarded as adequate to justify moral blame.

In less abstract or philosophical contexts, where there is a present question of blaming someone for some particular act, the assertion or denial that a person is morally responsible for his actions is common. But this expression is as ambiguous in the moral as in the legal case: It is most frequently used to refer to what I have termed 'capacity-responsibility', which is the most important criterion of moral liability-responsibility; but in some contexts it may also refer to moral liability-responsibility itself. Perhaps the most frequent use in moral contexts of the expression 'responsible for' is in cases where persons are said to be morally responsible for the outcomes or results of morally wrong conduct, although Mr. Pitcher's claim that men are never said in ordinary usage to be responsible for their actions is, as I have attempted to demonstrate above with counter-examples, an exaggerated claim.

CAPACITY-RESPONSIBILITY

In most contexts, as I have already stressed, the expression 'he is responsible for his actions' is used to assert that a person has certain normal capacities. These constitute the most important criteria of moral liability-responsibility, though it is characteristic of most legal systems that they have given only a partial or tardy recognition to all these capacities as general criteria of legal responsibility. The capacities in question arc those of understanding, reasoning, and control of conduct: the ability to understand what conduct legal rules or morality require, to deliberate and reach decisions concerning these requirements, and to conform to decisions when made. Because 'responsible for his actions' in this sense refers not to a legal status but to certain complex psychological characteristics of persons, a person's responsibility for his actions may intelligibly be said to be 'diminished' or 'impaired' as well as altogether absent, and persons may be said to be 'suffering from diminished responsibility' much as a wounded man may be said to be suffering from a diminished capacity to control the movements of his limbs.

No doubt the most frequent occasions for asserting or denying that a person is 'responsible for his actions' are cases where questions of blame or punishment for particular actions are in issue. But, as with other expressions used to denote criteria of responsibility, this one also may be used where no particular question of blame or punishment is in issue, and it is then used simply to describe a person's psychological condition. Hence it may be said purely by way of description of some harmless inmate of a mental institution, even though there is no present question of his misconduct, that he is a person who is not responsible for his actions. No doubt if there were no social practice of blaming and punishing people for their misdeeds, and excusing them from punishment because they lack the normal capacities of understanding and control, we should lack this shorthand description for describing their condition which we now derive from these social practices. In that case we should have to describe the condition of the inmate directly, by saying that he could not understand what people told him to do, or could not reason about it, or come to, or adhere to any decisions about his conduct.

Legal systems left to themselves may be very niggardly in their admission of the relevance of liability to legal punishment of the several capacities, possession of which are necessary to render a man morally responsible for his actions. So much is evident from the history sketched in the preceding chapter of the painfully slow emancipation of English criminal law from the narrow, cognitive criteria of responsibility formulated in the M'Naghten Rules. Though some Continental legal systems have been willing to confront squarely the question whether the accused 'lacked the ability to recognize the wrongness of his conduct and to act in accordance with that recognition.'[5] such an issue, if taken seriously, raises formidable difficulties of proof, especially before juries. For this reason I think that, instead of a close determination of such questions of capacity, the apparently coarser-grained technique of exempting persons from liability to punishment if they fall into certain recognized categories of mental disorder is likely to be increasingly used. Such exemption by general category is a technique long known to English law; for in the case of very young children it has made no attempt to determine, as a condition of liability, the question whether on account of their immaturity they could have understood what the law required and could have conformed to its requirements, or whether their responsibility on account of their immaturity was 'substantially impaired', but exempts them from liability for punishment if under a specified age. It seems likely that exemption by medical category rather than by individualized findings of absent or diminished capacity will be found more likely to lead in practice to satisfactory results, in spite of the difficulties pointed out in the last essay in the discussion of s. 60 of the Mental Health Act, 1959.

Though a legal system may fail to incorporate in its rules any psychological criteria of responsibility, and so may apply its sanction to those who are not morally blameworthy, it is none the less dependent for its efficacy on the possession by a sufficient number of those whose conduct it seeks to control of the capacities of understanding and control of conduct which constitute capacity-responsibility. For if a large proportion of those concerned could not understand what the law required them to do or could not form and keep a decision to obey, no legal system could come into existence or continue to exist. The general possession of such capacities is therefore a condition of the *efficacy* of law, even though it is not made a condition of liability to legal sanctions. The same condition of efficacy attaches to all attempts to regulate or control human conduct by forms of *communication:* such as orders, commands, the invocation of moral or other rules or principles, arguments, and advice.

'The notion of prevention through the medium of the mind assumes mental ability adequate to restraint'. This was clearly seen by Bentham and by Austin, who perhaps influenced the seventh report of the Criminal Law Commissioners of 1833 containing this sentence. But they overstressed the point; for they wrongly assumed that

this condition of efficacy must also be incorporated in legal rules as a condition of liability. This mistaken assumption is to be found not only in the explanation of the doctrine of *mens rea* given in Bentham's and Austin's works, but is explicit in the Commissioners' statement preceding the sentence quoted above that 'the object of penal law being the prevention of wrong, the principle does not extend to mere involuntary acts or even to harmful consequences the result of inevitable accident'. The case of morality is however different in precisely this respect: the possession by those to whom its injunctions are addressed of 'mental ability adequate to restraint' (capacity-responsibility) has there a double status and importance. It is not only a condition of the efficacy of morality; but a system or practice which did not regard the possession of these capacities as a necessary condition of liability, and so treated blame as appropriate even in the case of those who lacked them, would not, as morality is at present understood, be a morality.

NOTES

1. The author's discussion of this appears at pp. 264–65 of *Punishment and Responsibility* [editors].
2. *A History of The Criminal Law,* Vol. II, p. 183.
3. In a review of 'Changing Conceptions & Responsibility', in *Crim. L. R.* (1966) 124.
4. In 'Hart on Action and Responsibility', *The Philosophical Review* (1960), p. 266.
5. German Criminal Code, Art. 51.

H. L. A. HART AND
A. M. HONORÉ

Causation and Responsibility*

I. RESPONSIBILITY IN LAW AND MORALS

... In the moral judgments of ordinary life, we have occasion to blame people because they have caused harm to others, and also, if less frequently, to insist that morally they are bound to compensate those to whom they have caused harm. These are the moral analogues of more precise legal conceptions; for, in all legal systems, liability to be punished or to make compensation frequently depends on whether actions (or omissions) have caused harm. Moral blame is not of course confined to such cases of causing harm. We blame a man who cheats or lies or breaks promises, even if no one has suffered in the particular case: This has its legal counterpart in the punishment of abortive attempts to commit crimes, and of offences constituted by the unlawful possession of certain kinds of weapons, drugs, or materials, for example, for counterfeiting currency. When the occurrence of harm is an essential part of the ground for blame the connection of the person blamed with the harm may take any of the forms of causal connection we have examined. His action may have initiated a series of physical events dependent on each other and culminating in injury to persons or property, as in wounding and killing. These simple forms are the paradigms for the lawyer's talk of harm 'directly' caused. But we blame people also for harm which arises from or is the consequence of their neglect of common precautions; we do this even if harm would not have come about without the intervention of another human being deliberately exploiting the opportunities provided by neglect. The main legal analogue here is liability for 'negligence'. The wish of many lawyers to talk in this branch of the law of harm being 'within the risk' rather than 'caused by' the negligent conduct manifests appreciation of the fact that a different form of relationship is involved in saying that harm is the consequence, on the one hand, of an explosion and, on the other, of a failure to lock the door by which a thief has entered. Again, we blame people for the harm which we say is the consequence of their influence over others, either exerted by nonrational means or in one of the ways we have designated 'interpersonal transactions'. To such grounds for responsibility there correspond many important legal conceptions: The instigation of crimes ('commanding' or 'procuring') constitutes an important ground of criminal responsibility and the concepts of enticement and of inducement (by threats or misrepresentation) are an element in many civil wrongs as well as in criminal offences.

The law, however, especially in matters of compensation, goes far beyond these causal grounds for responsibility in such doctrines as the vicarious responsibility of a master for his servant's civil wrongs and that of the responsibility of an occupier of property for injuries suffered by passersby from defects of which the occupier had no knowledge and which he had no opportunity to repair. There is a recognition, perhaps diminishing, of this noncausal ground of responsibility outside the law; responsibility is sometimes admitted by one person or group of persons, even if no precaution has been neglected by them, for harm done by persons related to them in a special way, either by family ties or as members of the same social or political association. Responsibility may be simply 'placed' by moral opinion on one person for what others do. The simplest case of such vicarious moral responsibility is that of a parent for damage done by a child; its more complex (and more debatable) form is the moral responsibility of one generation of a nation to make compensation for their predecessors' wrong, such

*From *Causation in the Law* by H. L. A. Hart and A. M. Honoré (Oxford: The Oxford University Press, 1959), pp. 59–78, © 1959 Oxford University Press. Reprinted by permission of The Clarendon Press, Oxford. Footnotes have been renumbered.

as the Germans admitted in payment of compensation to Israel.

At this point it is necessary to issue a *caveat* about the meaning of the expression 'responsible' if only to avoid prejudicing a question about the character of *legal* determinations of causal connection with which we shall be much concerned in later chapters. Usually in discussion of the law and occasionally in morals, to say that someone is responsible for some harm means that in accordance with legal rules or moral principles it is at least permissible, if not mandatory, to blame or punish or exact compensation from him. In this use[1] the expression 'responsible for' does not refer to a factual connection between the person held responsible and the harm but simply to his liability under the rules to be blamed, punished, or made to pay. The expressions 'answerable for' or 'liable for' are practically synonymous with 'responsible for' in *this* use, in which there is no implication that the person held responsible actually *did* or *caused* the harm. In this sense a master is (in English law) responsible for the damage done by his servants acting within the scope of their authority and a parent (in French and German law) for that done by his children; it is in this sense that a guarantor or surety is responsible for the debts or the good behaviour of other persons. Very often, however, especially in discussion of morals, to say that someone is responsible for some harm is to assert (*inter alia*) that he *did* the harm or *caused* it though such a statement is perhaps rarely confined to this for it usually also carries with it the implication that it is at least permissible to blame or punish. This double use of the expression no doubt arises from the important fact that doing or causing harm constitutes not only the most usual but the primary type of ground for holding persons responsible in the first sense. We still speak of inanimate or natural causes such as storms, floods, germs, or the failure of electricity supply as 'responsible for' disasters; this mode of expression, now taken only to mean that they caused the disasters, no doubt originated in the belief that all that happens is the work of spirits when it is not that of men. Its survival in the modern world is perhaps some testimony to the primacy of causal connection as an element in responsibility and to the intimate connection between the two notions.

We shall consider later an apparent paradox which interprets in a different way the relationship between cause and responsibility. Much modern thought on causation in the law rests on the contention that the statement that someone has caused harm either means no more than that the harm would not have happened without ('but for') his action or where (as in normal legal usage and in all ordinary speech), it apparently means more than this, it is a disguised way of asserting the 'normative' judgment that he is responsible in the first sense, that is, that it is proper or just to blame or punish him or make him pay. On this view to say that a person caused harm is not really, though ostensibly it is, to give a *ground or reason* for holding him responsible in the first sense; for we are only in a position to say that he has caused harm when we have decided that he is responsible. Pending consideration of the theories of legal causation which exploit this point of view we shall use the expression 'responsible for' only in the first of the two ways explained, that is, without any implication as to the type of factual connection between the person held responsible and the harm; and we shall provisionally, though without prejudicing the issue, treat statements that a person caused harm as one sort of nontautologous ground or reason for saying that he is responsible in this sense.

If we may provisionally take what in ordinary life we say and do at its face value, it seems that there coexist in ordinary thought, apart from the law though mirrored in it, several different types of connection between a person's action and eventual harm which render him responsible for it; and in both law and morals the various forms of causal connection between act or omission and harm are the most obvious and least disputable reasons for holding anyone responsible. Yet, in order to understand the extent to which the causal notions of ordinary thought are used in the law, we must bear in mind the many factors which must differentiate moral from legal responsibility in spite of their partial correspondence: the law is not only not bound to follow the moral patterns of attribution of responsibility but, even when it does, it must take into account, in a way which the private moral judgment need not and does not, the general social consequences which are attached to its judgments of responsibility; for they are of a gravity quite different from those attached to moral censure. The use of the legal sanctions of imprisonment, or enforced monetary compensation against individuals, has such formidable repercussions on the general life of society that the fact that individuals have a type of connection with harm which is adequate for moral censure or claims for compensation is only *one* of the factors which the law must consider, in defining the kinds of connection between actions and harm for which it will hold individuals legally responsible. Always to follow the private moral judgment here would be far too expensive for the law: not only in the crude sense that it would entail a vast machinery of courts and officials, but in the more important sense that it would inhibit or discourage too many other valuable activities of society. To limit the *types* of harm which the law will recognize is not enough; even if the types of harm are limited it would still be too much for any society to punish or exact compensation from individuals whenever their connection with harm of such types would justify moral censure. Conversely, social needs may require that compensation should be paid and even (though less obviously) that punishment be inflicted where no such connection between the person held responsible and the harm exists.

So causing harm of a legally recognized sort or being connected with such harm in any of the ways that justify moral blame, though vitally important and perhaps basic in a legal system, is not and should not be either always necessary or always sufficient for legal responsibility. All legal systems in response either to tradition or to social needs both extend responsibility and cut it off in ways which diverge from the simpler principles of moral blame. In England a man is not guilty of murder if the victim of his attack does not die within a year and day. In New York a person who negligently starts a fire is liable to pay only for the first of several houses which it destroys. These limitations imposed by legal policy are *prima facie* distinguishable from limitations due to the frequent requirement of legal rules that responsibility be limited to harm caused by wrongdoing. Yet a whole school of thought maintains that this distinction does not exist or is not worth drawing.

Apart from this, morality can properly leave certain things vague into which a legal system must attempt to import some degree of precision. Outside the law nothing requires us, when we find the case too complex or too strange, to say whether any and, if so, which of the morally significant types of connection between a person's action and harm exists; we can simply say the case is too difficult for us to pass judgment, at least where moral condemnation of others is concerned. No doubt we evade less easily our questions about our own connection with harm, and the great novelists have often described, sometimes in language very like the lawyers, how the conscience may be still tortured by uncertainties as to the *character* of a part in the production of

harm, even when all the facts are known.[2] The fact that there is no precise system of punishments or rewards for common sense to administer, and so there are no 'forms of action' or 'pleadings' to define precise heads of responsibility for harm, means that the principles which guide common-sense attributions of responsibility give precise answers only in relatively simple types of case.

II. TRACING CONSEQUENCES

'To consequences no limit can be set': 'Every event which would not have happened if an earlier event had not happened is the consequence of that earlier event.' These two propositions are not equivalent in meaning and are not equally or in the same way at variance with ordinary thought. They have, however, both been urged sometimes in the same breath by the legal theorist[3] and the philosopher: They are indeed sometimes said by lawyers to be 'the philosophical doctrine' of causation. It is perhaps not difficult even for the layman to accept the first proposition as a truth about certain physical events; an explosion may cause a flash of light which will be propagated as far as the outer nebulae; its effects or consequences continue indefinitely. It is, however, a different matter to accept the view that whenever a man is murdered with a gun his death was the consequence of (still less an 'effect' of or 'caused by') the manufacture of the bullet. The first tells a perhaps unfamiliar tale about unfamiliar events; the second introduces an unfamiliar, though, of course, a possible way of speaking about familiar events. It is not that this unrestricted use of 'consequence' is unintelligible or never found; it is indeed used to refer to bizarre or fortuitous connections or coincidences: but the point is that the various causal notions employed for the purposes of explanation, attribution of responsibility or the assessment of contributions to the course of history carry with them implicit limits which are similar in these different employments.

It is, then, the second proposition, defining consequence in terms of 'necessary condition', with which theorists are really concerned. This proposition is the corollary of the view that, if we look into the past of any given event, there is an infinite number of events, each of which is a necessary condition of the given event and so, as much as any other, is its cause. This is the 'cone'[4] of causation, so-called because, since any event has a number of simultaneous conditions, the series fans out as we go back in time. The justification, indeed only partial, for calling this 'the philosophical doctrine' of causation is that it resembles Mill's doctrine that 'we have no right to give the name of cause to one of the conditions exclusive of the others of them'. It differs from Mill's view in taking the essence of causation to be 'necessary condition' and not 'the sum total'[5] of the sufficient conditions of an event.

Legal theorists have developed this account of cause and consequence to show what is 'factual', 'objective', or 'scientific' in these notions: this they call 'cause in fact' and it is usually stressed as a preliminary to the doctrine that any more restricted application of these terms in the law represents nothing in the facts or in the meaning of causation, but expresses fluctuating legal policy or sentiments of what is just or convenient. Moral philosophers have insisted in somewhat similar terms that the consequences of human action are 'infinite': this they have urged as an objection against the utilitarian doctrine that the rightness of a morally right action depends on whether its consequences are better than those of any alternative action in the circumstances. 'We should have to trace as far as possible the consequences not only for the persons affected directly but also for those indirectly affected and to these no limit can be set.'[6] Hence, so the argument runs, we cannot either inductively establish the utilitarian doctrine that right acts are 'optimific' or use it in particular cases to discover what is right. Yet, however vulnerable at other points utilitarianism may be as an account of moral judgment, this objection seems to rest on a mistake as to the sense of 'consequence'. The utilitarian assertion that the rightness of an action depends on its consequences is not the same as the assertion that it depends on all those later occurrences which would not have happened had the action not been done, to which indeed 'no limit can be set'. It is important to see that the issue here is not the linguistic one whether the word 'consequence' would be understood if used in this way. The point is that, though we could, we do not think in this way in tracing connections between human actions and events. Instead, whenever we are concerned with such connections, whether for the purpose of explaining a puzzling occurrence, assessing responsibility, or giving an intelligible historical narrative, we employ a set of concepts restricting in various ways what counts as a consequence. These restrictions colour *all* our thinking in causal terms; when we find them in the law we are not finding something invented by or peculiar to the law, though of course it is for the law to say when and how far

it will use them and, where they are vague, to supplement them.

No short account can be given of the limits thus placed on 'consequences' because these limits vary, intelligibly, with the variety of causal connection asserted. Thus we may be tempted by the generalization that consequences must always be something intended or foreseen or at least foreseeable with ordinary care: but counter-examples spring up from many types of context where causal statements are made. If smoking is shown to cause lung cancer, this discovery will permit us to describe past as well as future cases of cancer as the effect or consequence of smoking even though no one foresaw or had reasonable grounds to suspect this in the past. What is common and commonly appreciated and hence foreseeable certainly controls the scope of consequences in certain varieties of causal statement but not in all. Again the voluntary intervention of a second person very often constitutes the limit. If a guest sits down with a table laid with knife and fork and plunges the knife into his hostess's breast, her death is not in any context thought of as caused by, or the effect or result of the waiter's action in laying the table; nor would it be linked with this action as its consequence for any of the purposes, explanatory or attributive, for which we employ causal notions. Yet as we have seen there are many other types of case where a voluntary action or the harm it does are naturally attributed to some prior neglect of precaution as its consequence. Finally, we may think that a simple answer is already supplied by Hume and Mill's doctrine that causal connection rests on general laws asserting regular connection; yet, even in the type of case to which this important doctrine applies, reference to it alone will not solve our problem. For we often trace a causal connection between an antecedent and a consequent which themselves very rarely go together: we do this when the case can be broken down into intermediate stages, which themselves exemplify different generalizations, as when we find that the fall of a tile was the cause of someone's death, rare though this be. Here our problem reappears in the form of the question: When can generalizations be combined in this way?

We shall examine first the central type of case where the problem is of this last-mentioned form. Here the gist of the causal connection lies in the general connection with each other of the successive stages; and is not dependent on the special notions of one person providing another with reasons or exceptional opportunities for actions.

This form of causal connection may exist between actions and events, and between purely physical events, and it is in such cases that the words 'cause' and 'causing' used of the antecedent action or event have their most obvious application. It is convenient to refer to cases of the first type where the consequence is harm as cases of 'causing harm', and to refer to cases where harm is the consequence of one person providing another with reasons or opportunities for doing harm as cases of 'inducing', 'advising', or 'occasioning' harmful acts. In cases of the first type a voluntary act, or a conjunction of events amounting to a coincidence, operates as a limit in the sense that events subsequent to these are not attributed to the antecedent action or event as its consequence even though they would not have happened without it. Often such a limiting action or coincidence is thought of and described as 'intervening': and lawyers speak of them as 'superseding' or 'extraneous' causes 'breaking the chain of causation'. To see what these metaphors rest on (and in part obscure) and how such factors operate as a limit we shall consider the detail of three simple cases.

(i) A forest fire breaks out, and later investigation shows that shortly before the outbreak A had flung away a lighted cigarette into the bracken at the edge of the forest, the bracken caught fire, a light breeze got up, and fanned the flames in the direction of the forest. If, on discovering these facts, we hesitate before saying that A's action caused the forest fire this would be to consider the alternative hypothesis that in spite of appearances the fire only succeeded A's action in point of time, that the bracken flickered out harmlessly and the forest fire was caused by something else. To dispose of this it may be necessary to examine in further detail the process of events between the ignition of the bracken and the outbreak of fire in the forest and to show that these exemplified certain types of continuous change. If this is shown, there is no longer any room for doubt: A's action *was* the cause of the fire, whether he intended it or not. This seems and is the simplest of cases. Yet it is important to notice that even in applying our general knowledge to a case as simple as this, indeed in regarding it as simple, we make an implicit use of a distinction between types of factor which constitute a limit in tracing consequences and those which we regard as mere circumstances 'through' which we trace them. For the breeze which sprang up after A dropped the cigarette, and without which the fire would not have spread to the forest, was not only subsequent to his action but entirely independent of it:

It was, however, a common recurrent feature of the environment, and, as such, it is thought of not as an 'intervening' force but as merely part of the circumstances in which the cause 'operates'. The decision so to regard it is implicitly taken when we combine our knowledge of the successive stages of the process and assert the connection.

It is easy here to be misled by the natural metaphor of a causal 'chain', which may lead us to think that the causal process consists of a series of single events each of which is dependent upon (would not have occurred without) its predecessor in the 'chain' and so is dependent upon the initiating action or event. In truth in any causal process we have at each phase not single events but complex sets of conditions, and among these conditions are some which are not only subsequent to, but independent of, the initiating action or event. Some of these independent conditions such as the evening breeze in the example chosen, we classify as mere conditions in or on which the cause operates; others we speak of as 'interventions' or 'causes'. To decide how such independent elements shall be classified is also to decide how we shall combine our knowledge of the different general connections which the successive stages exemplify, and it is important to see that nothing *in* this knowledge itself can resolve this point. We may have to go to science for the relevant general knowledge before we can assert with proper confidence that A's action did cause the fire, but science, though it tells us that an air current was required, is silent on the difference between a current in the form of an evening breeze and one produced by someone who deliberately fanned the flames as they were flickering out in the bracken. Yet an air current in this form is not a 'condition' or 'mere circumstance' through which we can trace the consequence; its presence would force us to revise the assertion that A caused the fire. Conversely if science helped us to identify as a necessary factor in producing the fire some condition or element of which we had previously been totally ignorant, for example the persistence of oxygen, this would leave our original judgment undisturbed if this factor were a common or pervasive feature of the environment or of the thing in question. There is thus indeed an important sense in which it is true that the distinctions between cause and conditions is not a 'scientific' one. It is not determined by laws or generalizations concerning connections between events.

When we have assembled all our knowledge of the factors involved in the fire, the residual question which we then confront (the attributive question) may be typified as follows: Here is A's action, here is the fire. Can the fire be attributed to A's action as its consequence given that there is also this third factor (the breeze or B's intervention) without which the fire would not have happened? It is plain that, both in raising questions of this kind and in answering them, ordinary thought is powerfully influenced by the analogy between the straightforward cases of causal attribution (where the elements required for the production of harm in addition to the initiating action are all 'normal' conditions) and even simpler cases of responsibility which we do not ordinarily describe in causal language at all but by the simple transitive verbs of action. These are the cases of the direct manipulation of objects involving changes in them or their position: cases where we say 'He pushed it', 'He broke it,' 'He bent it.' The cases which we do confidently describe in causal language ('The fire was caused by his carelessness,' 'He caused a fire') are cases where no other human action or abnormal occurrence is required for the production of the effect, but only normal conditions. Such cases appear as mere long range or less direct versions or extensions of the most obvious and fundamental case of all for the attribution of responsibility: the case where we can simply say 'He did it.' Conversely in attaching importance to thus causing harm as a distinct ground of responsibility and in taking certain kinds of factor (whether human interventions or abnormal occurrences), without which the initiating action would not have led to harm, to preclude the description of the case in simple causal terms, common sense is affected by the fact that here, because of the manner in which the harm eventuates, the outcome cannot be represented as a mere extension of the initiating action; the analogy with the fundamental case for responsibility ('He did it') has broken down.

When we understand the power exerted over our ordinary thought by the conception that causing harm is a mere extension of the primary case of doing harm, the interrelated metaphors which seem natural to lawyers and laymen, in describing various aspects of causal connection, fall into place and we can discuss their factual basis. The persistent notion that some kinds of event required in addition to the initiating action for the production of harm 'break the chain of causation' is intelligible, if we remember that though such events actually complete the *explanation* of the harm (and so *make* rather than *break* the causal explanation) they do, unlike

mere normal conditions, break the *analogy* with cases of simple actions. The same analogy accounts for the description of these factors as 'new actions' (*novus actus*) or 'new causes', 'superseding', 'extraneous', 'intervening forces': and for the description of the initiating action when 'the chain of causation' is broken as 'no longer operative', 'having worn out', *functus officio*.[7] So too when the 'chain' is held not to be 'broken' the initiating action is said to be still 'potent',[8] 'continuing', 'contributing', 'operative', and the mere conditions held insufficient to break the chain are 'part of the background',[9] 'circumstances in which the cause operates',[10] 'the stage set', 'part of the history'.

(ii) A throws a lighted cigarette into the bracken which catches fire. B, just as the flames are about to flicker out, deliberately pours petrol on them. The fire spreads and burns down the forest. A's action, whether or not he intended the forest fire, was not the cause of the fire: B's was.

The voluntary intervention of a second human agent, as in this case, is a paradigm among those factors which preclude the assimilation in causal judgments of the first agent's connection with the eventual harm to the case of simple direct manipulation. Such an intervention displaces the prior action's title to be called the cause and, in the persistent metaphors found in the law, it 'reduces' the earlier action and its immediate effects to the level of 'mere circumstances' or 'part of the history.' B in this case was not an 'instrument' through which A worked or a victim of the circumstances A has created. He has, on the contrary, freely exploited the circumstances and brought about the fire without the cooperation of any further agent or any chance coincidence. Compared with this the claim of A's action to be ranked the cause of the fire fails. That this and not the moral appraisal of the two actions is the point of comparison seems clear. If A and B both intended to set the forest on fire, and this destruction is accepted as something wrong or wicked, their moral wickedness, judged by the criterion of intention, is the same. Yet the causal judgment differentiates between them. If their moral guilt is judged by the outcome, this judgment though it would differentiate between them cannot be the source of the causal judgment; for it presupposes it. The difference just is that B has caused the harm and A has not. Again, if we appraise these actions as good or bad from different points of view, this leaves the causal judgments unchanged. A may be a soldier of one side anxious to burn down the enemy's hideout: B may be an enemy soldier who has decided that his side is too iniquitous to defend. Whatever is the moral judgment passed on these actions by different speakers it would remain true that A had not caused the fire and B had.

There are, as we have said, situations in which a voluntary action would not be thought of as an intervention precluding causal connection in this way. These are the cases discussed further below where an opportunity commonly exploited for harmful actions is negligently provided, or one person intentionally provides another with a certain type of reason for wrongdoing. Except in such cases a voluntary intervention is a limit past which consequences are not traced. By contrast, actions which in any of a variety of different ways are less than fully voluntary are assimilated to the means by which or the circumstances in which the earlier action brings about the consequences. Such actions are not the outcome of an informed choice made without pressure from others, and the different ways in which human action may fall short in this respect range from defective muscular control, through lack of consciousness or knowledge, to the vaguer notions of duress and of predicaments, created by the first agent for the second, in which there is no 'fair' choice.

In considering examples of such actions and their bearing on causal judgments there are three dangers to avoid. It would be folly to think that in tracing connections through such actions instead of regarding them, like voluntary interventions, as a limit, ordinary thought has clearly separated out their nonvoluntary aspect from others by which they are often accompanied. Thus even in the crude case where A lets off a gun (intentionally or not) and startles B, so that he makes an involuntary movement of his arm which breaks a glass, the commonness of such a reaction as much as its compulsive character may influence the judgment that A's action was the cause of the damage.

Secondly we must not impute to ordinary thought all the fine discriminations that could be made and in fact are to be found in a legal system, or an equal willingness to supply answers to complex questions in causal terms. Where there is no precise system of punishment, compensation or reward to administer, ordinary men will not often have faced such questions as whether the injuries suffered by a motorist who collides with another in swerving to avoid a child are consequences attributable to the neglect of the child's parents in allowing it to wander on to the road. Such questions courts have to answer and in such cases common judgments provide only a general, though still an important indication of what are the relevant factors.

Thirdly, though very frequently nonvoluntary actions are assimilated to mere conditions or means by which the first agent brings about the consequences, the assimilation is never quite complete. This is manifested by the general avoidance of many causal locutions which are appropriate when the consequences are traced (as in the first case) through purely physical events. Thus even in the case in which the second agent's rôle is hardly an 'action' at all, for example, where A hits B, who staggers against a glass window and breaks it, we should say that A's blow made B stagger and break the glass, rather than that A's blow caused the glass to break, though in any explanatory or attributive context the case would be *summarized* by saying that A's action was the cause of the *damage* or that A had caused it.

In the last two cases where B's movements are involuntary in the sense that they are not part of any action which he chose or intended to do, their connection with A's action would be described by saying that A's blow *made* B stagger or *caused* him to stagger or that the noise of A's shot *made* him jump or *caused* him to jump. This would be true, whether A intended or expected B to react in this way or not, and the naturalness of treating A's action as the cause of the ultimate damage is due to the causal character of this part of the process involving B's action. The same is however true where B's actions are not involuntary movements but A is considered to have made or caused B to do them by less crude means. This is the case if, for example, A uses treats or exploits his authority over B to make B do something, for example, knock down a door. At least where A's threats are of serious harm, or B's act was unquestionably within A's authority to order, he too has made or forced or (in formal quasi-legal parlance) 'caused' B to act.

Outside the area of such cases, where B's will would be either said not to be involved at all, or to be overborne by A, are cases where A's act creates a predicament for B *narrowing* the area of choice so that he has either to inflict some harm on himself or others, or sacrifice some important interest or duty. Such cases resemble coercion in that A narrows the area of B's choice but differ from it in that this predicament need not be intentionally created. A sets a house on fire (intentionally or unintentionally): B to save himself has to jump from a height involving certain injury, or to save a child rushes in and is seriously burned. Here of course B's movements are not involuntary; the 'necessity' of his action is here of a different order. His action is the outcome of a choice between two evils forced on him by A's action. In such cases, when B's injuries are thought of as the consequence of the fire, the implicit judgment is made that his action was the lesser of two evils and in this sense a 'reasonable' one which he was obliged to make to avoid the greater evil. This is often paradoxically, though understandably, described by saying that here the agent 'had no choice' but to do what he did. Such judgments involve a comparison of the importance of the respective interests sacrificed and preserved, and the final assertion that A's action was the cause of the injuries rests on evaluations about which men may differ.

Finally, ground for treating some harm which would not have occurred without B's action as the consequence of A's action may be that B acted in ignorance of, or under a mistake as to some feature of, the situation created by A. Poisoning offers perhaps the simplest example of the bearing on causal judgments of actions which are less than voluntary in this Aristotelian sense. If A intending B's death deliberately poisons B's food and B, knowing this, deliberately takes the poison and dies, A has not caused B's death: if however B does not know the food to be poisoned, eats it and dies A has caused his death, even if he put the poison in unwittingly. Of course only the roughest judgments are passed in causal terms in such cases outside law courts, where fine degrees of 'appreciation' or reckless shutting of the eyes, may have to be discriminated from 'full knowledge'. Yet, rough as these are, they indicate clearly enough the controlling principles.

Though in the foregoing cases A's initiating action might often be described as 'the cause' of the ultimate harm, this linguistic fact is of subordinate importance to the fact that, for whatever purpose, explanatory, descriptive or evaluative, consequences of an action are traced, discriminations are made (except in the cases discussed later) between free voluntary interventions and less than voluntary reactions to the first action or the circumstances created by it.

(iii) The analogy with single simple actions which guides the tracing of consequences may be broken by certain kinds of conjunctions of physical events. A hits B who falls to the ground stunned and bruised by the blow; at that moment a tree crashes to the ground and kills B. A has certainly caused B's bruises but not his death: for though the fall of the tree was, like the evening breeze, in our earlier example, independent of and subsequent to the initiating action, it would be differentiated from the breeze in any description in causal terms of the connection of B's death with A's action. It is to be noticed that this is not a matter which turns on the intention with which A struck B. Even if A hit B inadvertently or accidentally his blow would still be the cause of B's bruises: he would have caused them though unintentionally. Conversely even if A had intended his blow to kill, this would have been an attempt to kill but still not the cause of B's death. On this legal and ordinary judgments would be found to agree; and most legal systems would distinguish for the purposes of punishment an attempt with a fatal upshot, issuing by such chance or anomalous events, from 'causing death' —the terms in which the offences of murder and manslaughter are usually defined.

Similarly the causal description of the case does not turn on the moral appraisal of A's action or the wish to punish it. A may be a robber and a murderer and B a saint guarding the place A hoped to plunder. Or B may be a murderer and A a hero who has forced his way into B's retreat. In both cases the causal judgment is the same. A had caused the minor injuries but not B's death, though he tried to kill him. A may indeed be praised or blamed but not for causing B's death. However intimate the connection between causation and responsibility, it does not determine causal judgments in this simple way. Nor does the causal judgment turn on a refusal to attribute grave consequences to actions which normally have less serious results. Had A's blow killed B outright and the tree, falling on his body, merely smashed his watch we should still treat the coincidental character of the fall of the tree as determining the form of causal statement. We should then recognize A's blow as the cause of B's death but not of the breaking of the watch.

The connection between A's action and B's death in the first case would naturally be described in the language of *coincidence*. 'It was a coincidence: it just happened that, at the very moment when A knocked B down, a tree crashed at the very place where he fell and killed him.' The common legal metaphor would describe the fall of the tree as an 'extraneous' cause. This, however, is dangerously misleading, as an analysis of the notion of coincidence will show. It suggests merely an event which is subsequent to and independent of some other contingency, and of course the fall of the tree has both these features in relation to A's blow. Yet in these respects the fall of the tree does not differ from the evening breeze in the earlier case where we found no difficulty in tracing causal connection. The full elucidation of the notion of a coincidence is a complex matter for, though it is very important as a limit in tracing consequences, causal questions are not the only ones to which the notion is relevant. The following are its most general characteristics. We speak of a coincidence whenever (1) the conjunction of two or more events in certain spatial or temporal relations is very unlikely by ordinary standards and (2) is for some reason significant or important, provided (3) that they occur without human contrivance and (4) are independent of each other. It is therefore a coincidence if two persons known to each other in London meet without design in Paris on their way to separate independently chosen destinations; or if two persons living in different places independently decide to write a book on the same subject. The first is a coincidence of time and place ('It just happened that we were at the same place at the same time'), and the second a coincidence of time only ('It just happened that they both decided to write on the subject at the same time').

Use of this general notion is made in the special case when the conjunction of two or more events occurs in temporal and/or spatial relationships which are significant, because, as our general knowledge of causal processes shows, this conjunction is required for the production of some given further event. In the language of Mill's idealized model, they form a necessary part of a complex set of jointly sufficient conditions. In the present case the fall of the tree just as B was struck down within its range satisfies the four criteria for a coincidence which we have enumerated. First, though neither event was of a very rare or exceptional kind, their conjunction would be rated very unlikely judged by the standards of ordinary experience. Secondly, this conjunction was causally significant for it was a necessary part of the process terminating in B's death. Thirdly, this conjunction was not consciously designed by A; had he known of the impending fall of the tree and hit B with the intention that he should fall within its range B's death would not have been the result of any coincidence. A would certainly have caused it. The common-sense principle that a contrived conjunction cannot be a coincidence is the element of truth in the legal maxim (too broadly stated even for legal purposes) that an intended consequence cannot be too 'remote'. Fourthly, each member of the conjunction in this

case was independent of the other; whereas if B had fallen against the tree with an impact sufficient to bring it down on him, this sequence of physical events, though freakish in its way, would not be a coincidence and in most contexts of ordinary life, as in the law, the course of events would be summarized by saying that in this case, unlike that of the coincidence, A's act was the cause of B's death, since each stage is the effect of the preceding stage. Thus, the blow forced the victim against the tree, the effect of this was to make the tree fall and the fall of the tree killed the victim.

One further criterion in addition to these four must be satisfied if a conjunction of events is to rank as a coincidence and as a limit when the consequences of the action are traced. This further criterion again shows the strength of the influence which the analogy with the case of the simple manipulation of things exerts over thought in causal terms. An abnormal *condition* existing at the time of a human intervention is distinguished both by ordinary thought and, with a striking consistency, by most legal systems from an abnormal event or conjunction of events subsequent to that intervention; the former, unlike the latter, are not ranked as coincidences or 'extraneous' causes when the consequences of the intervention come to be traced. Thus A innocently gives B a tap over the head of a normally quite harmless character, but because B is then suffering from some rare disease the tap has, as we say, 'fatal results'. In this case A has caused B's death though unintentionally. The scope of the principle which thus distinguishes contemporaneous abnormal conditions from subsequent events is unclear; but at least where a human being initiates some physical change in a thing, animal, or person, abnormal physical states of the object affected, existing at the time, are ranked as part of the circumstances in which the cause 'operates'. In the familiar controlling imagery these are part of 'the stage already set' before the 'intervention'.

Judgments about coincidences, though we often agree in making them, depend on two related ways on issues incapable of precise formulation. One of these is patent, the other latent but equally important. Just how unlikely must a conjunction be to rank as a coincidence, and in the light of what knowledge is likelihood to be assessed? The only answer is: 'very unlikely in the light of the knowledge available to ordinary men.' It is of course the indeterminacies of such standards, implicit in causal judgments, that make them inveterately disputable, and call for the exercise of discretion or choice by courts. The second and latent indeterminacy of these judgments depends on the fact that the things or events which they relate do not have pinned to them some uniquely correct description always to be used in assessing likelihood. It is an important pervasive feature of all our empirical judgments that there is a constant possibility of more or less specific description of any event or thing with which they are concerned. The tree might be described not simply as 'a tree' but as a 'rotten tree' or as a 'fir tree' or a 'tree sixty feet tall'. So too its fall might be described not as a 'fall' but as a fall of a specified distance at a specified velocity. The likelihood of conjunctions framed in these different terms would be differently assessed. The criteria of appropriate description like the standard of likelihood are supplied by consideration of common knowledge. Even if the scientist knew the tree to be rotten and could have predicted its fall with accuracy, this would not change the judgment that its fall at the time when B was struck down within its range was a coincidence; nor would it make the description 'rotten tree' appropriate for the assessment of the chances involved in this judgment. There are other controls over the choice of description derived from the degree of specificity of our interests in the final outcome of the causal process. We are concerned with the fall of an object sufficient to cause 'death' by impact and the precise force or direction which may account for the detail of the wounds is irrelevant here.

OPPORTUNITIES AND REASONS

Opportunities. The discrimination of voluntary interventions as a limit is no longer made when the case, owing to the commonness or appreciable risk of such harmful intervention, can be brought within the scope of the notion of providing an opportunity, known to be commonly exploited for doing harm. Here the limiting principles are different. When A leaves the house unlocked the range of consequences to be attributed to this neglect, as in any other case where precautions are omitted, depends primarily on the way in which such opportunities are commonly exploited. An alternative formulation of this idea is that a subsequent intervention would fall within the scope of consequences if the likelihood of its occurring is one of the reasons for holding A's omission to be negligent.

It is on these lines that we would distinguish between the entry of a thief and of a murderer; the opportunity provided is believed to be suffi-ciently commonly exploited by thieves to make it usual and often morally or legally obligatory not to provide it. Here, in attributing consequences to prior actions, causal judgments are directly controlled by the notion of the risk created by them. Neglect of such precautions is both unusual and reprehensible. For these reasons it would be hard to separate the two ways in which such neglect deviates from the 'norm'. Despite this, no simple identification can be made of the notion of responsibility with the causal connection which is a ground for it. This is so because the provision of an opportunity commonly taken by others is ranked as the cause of the outcome independently of the wish to praise or blame. The causal judgment may be made simply to assess a contribution to some outcome. Thus, whether we think well or ill of the use made of railways, we would still claim that the greater mobility of the population in the nineteenth century was a consequence of their introduction.

It is obvious that the question whether any given intervention is a sufficiently common exploitation of the opportunity provided to come within the risk is again a matter on which judgments may differ though they often agree. The courts, and perhaps ordinary thought also, often describe those that are sufficiently common as 'natural' consequences of the neglect. They have in these terms discriminated the entry of a thief from the entry of a man who burnt the house down, and refused to treat the destruction of the house as a 'natural' consequence of the neglect. . . .[11]

Reasons. In certain varieties of interpersonal transactions, unlike the case of coercion, the second action is quite voluntary. A may not threaten B but may bribe or advise or persuade him to do something. Here, A does not 'cause' or 'make' B do anything: the strongest words we should use are perhaps that he 'induced' or 'procured' B's act. Yet the law and moral principles alike may treat one person as responsible for the harm which another free agent has done 'in consequence' of the advice or the inducements which the first has offered. In such cases the limits concern the range of those actions done by B which are to rank as the consequence of A's words or deeds. In general this question depends on A's intentions or on the 'plan of action' he puts before B. If A advises or bribes B to break in and steal from an empty house and B does so, he acts in consequence of A's advice or bribe. If he deliberately burns down the house this would not be treated as the consequence of A's bribe or advice, legally or otherwise, though it may in some sense be true that the burning would not have taken place without the advice or bribe. Nice questions may arise, which the courts have to settle, where B diverges from the detail of the plan of action put before him by A.

NOTES

1. Cf. *O.E.D. sub tit.* Responsible: Answerable, Accountable (*to* another *for* something); liable to be called to account 'being responsible to the King for what might happen to us', 1662.

2. See the following passage from *The Golden Bowl* by Henry James. (Mrs. Assingham whose uncertain self-accusation is described here, had, on the eve of the Prince's marriage, encouraged him to resume an old friendship with Charlotte Stant. The relationship which developed came to threaten the marriage with disaster.) 'She had stood for the previous hour in a merciless glare, beaten upon, stared out of countenance, it fairly seemed to her, by intimations of her mistake. For what she was most immediately feeling was that she had in the past been active for these people to ends that were now bearing fruit and that might yet bear a greater crop. She but brooded at first in her corner of the carriage: it was like burying her exposed face, a face too helplessly exposed in the cool lap of the common indifference . . . a world mercifully unconscious and unreproachful. It wouldn't like the world she had just left know sooner or later what she had done or would know it only if the final consequence should be some quite overwhelming publicity. . . . The sense of seeing was strong in her, but she clutched at the comfort of not being sure of what she saw. Not to know what it would represent on a longer view was a help in turn to not making out that her hands were embrued; since if she had stood in the position of a producing cause she should surely be less vague about what she had produced. This, further, in its way, was a step toward reflecting that when one's connection with any matter was too indirect to be traced, it might be described also as too slight to be deplored' (*The Golden Bowl,* Book 3, chap. 3). We are much indebted to Mrs. H. M. Warnock for this quotation.

3. Lawson, *Negligence in the Civil Law,* p. 53.

4. Glanville Williams, *Joint Torts and Contributory Negligence,* p. 239.

5. Mill, Book III, chap. v, s. 2.

6. Ross, *The Right and the Good,* p. 36.

7. *Davies v. Swan Motor Co.,* [1947] 2 K.B. 291, 318.

8. *Minister of Pensions v. Chennell,* [1947] K.B. 250, 256. Lord Wright (1950), 13 *Mod. L.R.* 3.

9. *Norris v. William Moss & Son Ltd.,* [1954] 1 W.L.R. 46, 351.

10. *Minister of Pensions v. Chennell,* [1947] K.B. 250, 256.

11. *Bellows v. Worcester Storage Co.* (1937), 297 Mass 188, 7 N.E. 2d 588. ©

ROBERT E. KEETON

The Basic Rule of Legal Cause in Negligence Cases*

DIVERSE FORMULATIONS OF THE RISK RULE

STATEMENT AND ILLUSTRATION OF THREE FORMULATIONS

The defendant, proprietor of a restaurant, placed a large, unlabeled can of rat poison beside cans of flour on a shelf near a stove in a restaurant kitchen. The victim, while in the kitchen making a delivery to the restaurant, was killed by an explosion of the poison. Assume that the defendant's handling of the rat poison was negligent because of the risk that someone would be poisoned but that defendant had no reason to know of the risk that the poison would explode if left in a hot place. Is the defendant liable for the death of the victim?[1]

This question illustrates the central problem of scope of liability for negligence. The problem is commonly subdivided into issues associated with, first, the foreseeability of any kind of harm to the victim who, in fact, was harmed and, second, the foreseeability of the particular harm or kind of harm that occurred.

The predominant theme in judicial utterances on the scope of liability in negligence cases is expressed in a proposition that, for convenience, will be referred to as *the Risk Rule.* This rule, quite commonly expressed in substance both in charges to the jury and in appellate opinions, is as follows:

A negligent actor is legally responsible for that harm, and only that harm, of which *negligence* is a cause in fact.

Some explanatory comments are in order. First, this rule is addressed not only to matters uniformly classified as problems of legal cause but also to other matters sometimes classified as problems of duty. Comments directed specifically to this choice of terminology are reserved for the second and third chapters.[2]

Other explanatory comments that seem necessary at the outset are concerned with the meaning of the words "actor" and "negligence." "Actor" is used here to signify the person whose "conduct" is being judged, whether plaintiff or defendant, and whether charged with acting negligently or with negligently failing to act. "Conduct" is used in a sense that includes both "acting" and "failing to act." "Negligence," in the context of this rule, must be understood in a more precise sense than merely "the negligent actor's conduct." This statement of the Risk Rule makes no sense unless interpreted as meaning that the actor's *conduct* during the period of his negligence may be a cause of harm of which his *negligence* is not a cause. For example, in the case of the explosive rat poison, it is not enough to ask whether the defendant's conduct in placing the poison where he did was a cause of the death of the victim. We should, as well, ask whether the defendant's negligence was a cause of the death. As a means of arriving at a satisfactory answer to that question, it will be useful to consider another.

What was that aspect of the conduct of the defendant that caused it to be characterized as negligence? Placing rat poison on a shelf may or may not be negligence. The negligence here consisted of placing the poison where it was likely to be mistaken for something intended for human consumption. This description says nothing about the proximity of the shelf to heat. That circumstance is omitted because of the assumption that the defendant had no reason to know of the explosive character of the poison; in such a situation it would not have been negligent to put the poison in a place that happened to be near heat, provided it was not a place where the poison was likely to be mistaken as something intended for human consumption. Thus, the defendant's *negligence* (his placing the poison where it was likely to be mistaken for something intended for human consumption) was not a *sine qua non* of the harm. For present purposes I draw no distinction between the several expressions "but-for cause," "necessary antecedent," and "*sine qua non.*"[3] That is, I am speaking simply of the concept that it cannot be said that the harm of death from explosion would not have occurred but for defendant's placing the poison where it was likely to be mistaken for something intended for human consumption. Defendant's negligence was not in this sense a but-for cause, or a necessary antecedent, or a *sine qua non* of the death. But his conduct (placing the poison near heat) was, at least in a qualified sense, a *sine qua non*.

The qualification is concerned with the hypothetical character of the assertion. That is, the assertion that the harm would not have occurred but for the defendant's conduct is a hypothetical assertion the accuracy of which is not subject to demonstration. For example, how are we to know that, had the poison been placed elsewhere than near a hot stove, it would not have been exploded by some other source of heat that might have happened to be applied to the poison while the victim was present? Also, imbedded in the hypothetical assertion of what would not have happened are ambiguities in the meaning of "conduct" and "harm." Does "conduct" refer to placing the poison in the exact spot where it was placed? If so, might it not be said that the conduct was not a *sine qua non* since death at the same time and place might have occurred if the poison had been placed near a hot radiator rather than the stove? Does "the harm" refer merely to death of the victim, or to the time, place, and manner of death in all their detail, or to something between these extremes? In some instances, the ambiguity and hypothetical character of the assertion will present serious difficulty.[4] But, in the case of the explosive rat poison, we can readily understand and accept, in at least a rough sense, the assertion that the defendant's conduct was a *sine qua non* of the harm because there appears to have been no substantial possibility either that the harm in all its details would have occurred or that something generally resembling it would have occurred in the absence of defendant's conduct of placing the rat poison near heat. Also, no doubt, we can agree that if defendant's negligence is defined in the limited sense of that quality of his conduct consisting of his placing the poison where it was likely to be mistaken for something intended for human consumption, his negligence was not a *sine qua non*.

There is yet another difficulty, however, in the assertion that one aspect of his conduct was a cause of harm and another aspect of the same conduct, the same single action of putting down a can of poison, was not a cause of the harm. It is more normal, perhaps, to think of the conduct as indivisible and to reject the suggestion that the negligent aspect can be separated from other aspects for an inquiry into causal relation. Perhaps it will be helpful in this respect to think of negligence as the creation of unreasonable risks[5] and, rather than thinking of harm itself as the focus of the concept of risk, to think of a risk as a set of forces and conditions and circumstances that might foreseeably bring about harm.[6] No special point is made here regarding the choice among the terms "force," "condition," and "circumstance" to convey the intended idea, though the word "circumstance" seems the most congenial to the separation of aspects of a single state of affairs. Negligence, then, consists of creating a set of unduly risky forces or conditions or circumstances, and the negligence is a *sine qua non* of subsequent harm only if some force or condition or circumstance within this set is a *sine qua non*. In the case of the rat poison, the negligence consisted of creating a force or condition or circumstance of having a poisonous substance where it might be mistaken as something intended for human consumption. That circumstance was not a cause of the harm, though the coexisting circumstance of having an explosive substance near heat was a cause.

This focus upon the negligent aspect of conduct as the meaning of the unqualified word "negligence" in the statement of the Risk Rule presented above suggests a second, perhaps less ambiguous, formulation of exactly the same meaning:

A negligent actor is legally responsible for that harm, and only that harm, of which the *negligent aspect of his conduct* is a cause in fact.

In many cases it is less easy than in the case of the explosive rat poison to extract the negligent aspect from the total conduct. To meet this difficulty, still another formulation of the Risk Rule is helpful. A moment ago, we were thinking of risk with a focus upon the forces or conditions or circumstances that might produce harm. Shift the focus now to the harm that might be produced. With this focus, in order to find that the negligence (that is, the negligent aspect of the conduct) bears a causal relation to the harm, we must find that the harm that came about was one of the things that was risked. Another way of expressing the same idea is to say that the harm must be a result within the scope of at least one of the risks on the basis of which the actor is found to be negligent. Thus the Risk Rule of legal cause as stated in the first and second formulations above may be restated in a third formulation without change of meaning:

A negligent actor is legally responsible for the harm, and only the harm, that not only (1) is caused in fact by his conduct but also (2) is a result within the scope of the risks by reason of which the actor is found to be negligent.

In the case of the explosive rat poison, injury by explosion was not a result within the scope of the risks by reason of which the defendant was found to be negligent, though injury by poisoning would have been.

The third formulation of the rule is often expressed in the statement that the actor is responsible only for "results within the risk." Among those who remain constantly alert to its meaning, there is no objection to use of such a shorthand expression. But this cryptic phrase is apt to be misleading to the unsophisticated because it does not designate the point of view from which the composite of risks is defined. The concept of "risk" and the cognate concept of "probability" are founded on prediction from some selected point of view. But they do not necessarily imply any particular point of view, such as that of a reasonable man in the position of the actor. Thus, results that in the wisdom of hindsight are said to have been "probable" may yet have been beyond the scope of those risks by reason of which the actor's conduct is found to have been negligence. Also, such concepts as "risk," "probability," and "foreseeability" imply a point of view involving a degree of ignorance about the factors at work in a situation. To one who knows all, a future event is not "probable" or merely "foreseeable" but either certain to occur or certain not to occur. When we say a result was "probable" as a matter of hindsight, we are using a point of view that is neither that of a reasonable person in the actor's position nor that of an omniscient observer after the fact. It is a point of view based on foresight in the face of incomplete knowledge, but with greater knowledge or greater mental capacity than that of the actor or that of the standard man in the actor's circumstances. As used in the Risk Rule, on the other hand, "risk" implies a stan-

dard based on foresight from the point of view of the standard man in the actor's circumstances at the time of the conduct that is being judged.

As we examine the policy foundation of the Risk Rule, reasons will appear for using, in relation to problems of legal cause, this standard of foresight that is also used in determining whether the actor was negligent. But, first, we digress for further explanation of the use of three formulations of the Risk Rule.

WHY THREE FORMULATIONS?

The first formulation of the Risk Rule tracks language found in many jury charges today, as well as in appellate opinions, though supplemented usually by elaborations upon the theme and occasionally by qualifications. The third formulation tracks the rationale of exponents of what has come to be known as the risk theory of legal cause, and of Professor Seavey in particular.[7] Professors Harper and James also recommended an inquiry in terms generally consistent with the rationale expressed in the third formulation,[8] though they appear less happy than Professor Seavey with adherence to the limitation on scope of liability implicit in accepting this as the basic rule of legal cause. They also observed that in essence this is the same inquiry as the question whether there is causal relation "between *that aspect of the defendant's conduct which is wrongful* and the injury."[9] Thus, the second formulation offered here is supported by their analysis. This formulation is offered as a transitional bond between the first and the third, in the belief that the intended substance of these different expressions is the same. Candor requires disclosure that Professor Seavey dislikes both the first and the second formulations because of a concern, as I understand him, that they are more likely to mislead than to clarify. His disfavor is firm, though expressed in the warmhearted spirit that has characterized his rigorous intellectual assaults upon the ideas of generations of students, colleagues, and judges. At the risk of suffering an intermeddler's unhappy fate, I persist in offering the second formulation and in marshaling the three together in the hope of improving relations between adherents of two ways of thought that I believe to be compatibly directed toward the same goal.

THE RISK RULE AS A RULE OF CAUSATION

Perhaps a secondary benefit of this focus on three formulations of one rule is to expose rather persuasive evidence that the Risk Rule is indeed a rule of causation in a cause-in-fact sense. There are various deviations from the Risk Rule—some toward greater liability, some toward less—that are founded in notions beyond causation. But the predominant theme represented by the Risk Rule is a theme of causation. It concerns cause-in-fact relation between the negligent aspect of the conduct and the harm.

This conclusion is supported by only a few of the multitude of authors on legal cause—among them Professor Carpenter,[10] and, more recently, Professors Harper and James.[11] Even these three appear not willing to carry the separation of aspects of the conduct as far as is suggested here. The following passage from Harper and James is relevant:

But there are cases where causal relation exists between defendant's fault and the injury, yet where liability will not be imposed. Thus in Gorris v. Scott, L.R. 9 Ex. 125 (1874), defendants' wrongful failure to have pens for cattle on shipboard was the cause in fact of their being washed overboard in a heavy sea. There was no liability, however, since the statutory requirement was designed to protect the cattle only from perils from contagious disease, a hazard which was not encountered and from which their loss did not result. See Carpenter, Workable Rules for Determining Proximate Cause, 20 Calif. L. Rev. 396, 408 (1932).[12]

The claim of negligence in *Gorris* v. *Scott* was violation of orders issued pursuant to the Contagious Diseases (Animals) Act of 1869, the violation being failure to provide battens or foot-holds for the animals and failure to provide pens not larger than 9 by 15 feet each. Under the analysis suggested in this chapter, the negligent aspect of the conduct was not the circumstance that absence of such pens and foot-holds placed the cattle in position to be washed overboard. No doubt, reluctance to declare that there is no causal connection between the negligent aspect of the conduct and the result in these circumstances arises from the difficulty of imagining facts in which compliance with the required safeguards against disease would not also protect the cattle against being washed overboard. The case is thus unlike that of the speeding automobile that strikes a child who could not have been avoided by a driver proceeding at a reasonable speed; in that situation, speed causes the automobile to be at the scene at the critical time, but we can imagine the defendant's starting sooner and arriving in time to strike the child though he drives at a

reasonable speed throughout the journey. Perhaps the converse point of view is also relevant, however. That is, perhaps we should consider not only whether situations can be imagined in which the required safeguard would have been ineffectual to prevent the particular kind of harm of which plaintiff is complaining but also whether situations can be imagined in which despite absence of the required safeguards the plaintiff would have been fully protected against this kind of harm. This is not to say that a required safeguard is intended to be an exclusive safeguard against the dangers to which it is directed. But this point of view does suggest that, when we treat one circumstance (that absence of pens placed the cattle in position to be washed overboard) as an aspect of the conduct separate from another circumstance (that absence of pens placed the cattle in position to be subject to an increased risk of contagious disease), we are no more attempting to separate inseparable aspects of a single faulty course of conduct than in the converse situation illustrated by the case of excessive speed. Pursuing this line of thought, we may observe that it would have been possible in *Gorris* v. *Scott* to have larger pens and no footholds and yet have the cattle protected against the risk of being washed overboard. In any event, the negligence was concerned with the circumstance that absence of the required safeguards increased the risks of disease, including the risk that affected cattle would communicate the disease widely among animals not separated into small groups by use of small enclosures. It was not concerned with the circumstance that the cattle were in position to be washed overboard. Thus, there was no causal relation between the negligent aspect of the conduct and the harm.

Possibly some passages in the recent broad study of causation by a distinguished pair of English scholars, Hart and Honore, can also be fairly interpreted as supporting the assertion that the Risk Rule is concerned with causal relation between the negligent aspect of conduct and the harm of which plaintiff complains.[13] Yet, elsewhere they may be thought to be saying that foreseeability is a policy factor, that causal principles are policy neutral, and that use of foreseeability as a test for scope of liability is a departure from use of causal criteria.[14] They argue that the foreseeability test breaks down, especially in cases of what they call "ulterior" harm (e.g., harm following a foreseeable impact on an unforeseeably thin skull), and that causal criteria must be used instead.[15] Perhaps these several passages can be reconciled on the basis that Hart and Honore mean not to declare that the foreseeability test is unconcerned with causal relation between the negligent aspect of the conduct and the harm but only that in some situations, especially those of "ulterior" harm, the scope of liability is fixed by a test of causal relation between conduct and harm rather than between negligent aspect of conduct and harm. If this reading of their book is proper, then the views of Hart and Honore tend to support the assertion that the three separate formulations of the Risk Rule are in essence expressions of one idea and that this idea is concerned with cause-in-fact relation between the negligent aspect of the conduct and the harm.

To the contrary, other writers, probably a majority, have insisted that doctrines of legal cause generally, and the result-within-the-risk formulation in particular, are based on policy considerations having nothing to do with cause in fact.[16] The insight produced by a focus upon the relation between the negligent aspect of conduct and the ensuing harm is nevertheless persuasive. The persistence of courts in dealing with this problem under the rubric of causation is perhaps more than evidence of a judicial instinct for right results; perhaps it is also evidence that on occasion judicial perception surpasses that of the majority of reflective critics. This accolade to the courts is not intended to imply a preference for the first or the second formulation of the Risk Rule over the third. It does, however, express a conviction that the first and second formulations offer added illumination on the problem though the third is generally the more manageable in difficult applications. Inevitably, different formulations are likely to produce different nuances and connotations. Since all three formulations are expressions of a single theme, it will often be an aid to deliberate and rational choice to examine the implications of the Risk Rule from the several points of view of all three formulations.

THE POLICY FOUNDATION OF THE RISK RULE

SCOPE OF LIABILITY COMMENSURATE WITH THE BASIS OF LIABILITY

The policy foundation of the Risk Rule can be summarized in this way: The factors determining that the actor is liable for unintended harm caused by his conduct should also determine the scope of his liability. There is surely an interest of public policy in formulating rules that do not impose crushing liability.[17] Since the unintended consequences of one's conduct go on indefinitely, some limit of responsibility is a practical necessity. The theory of the Risk Rule is that the scope of liability should be commensurate with the basis of liability. "Prima facie at least, the reasons for creating liability should limit it."[18]

Opponents of the Risk Rule have argued that in applying the risk concept first to the issue of liability and again to the issue of scope of liability a court gives the defendant an unwarranted advantage by applying twice a restrictive test of foreseeability of harm.[19] The argument is not persuasive. In the first place, the test is expansive rather than restrictive if we start with the assumption that the burden is on the plaintiff to prove some good reason for entering a loss-shifting judgment. That is, when the test for negligence is found to have been fulfilled, liability is expanded in the sense of establishment of an obligation not previously acknowledged. Only if we make a comparison with an assumed state of broader liability, or if we start with the assumption that there is a burden on the defendant to prove nonliability, can we think of an application of the test of foreseeability of harm as restrictive rather than expansive. This is true whether it be applied to the liability issue alone, to the scope of liability issue as well, or to the combination as a unit. In the second place, separating the issues of liability and scope of liability is simply a means of organizing thought. There is no more reason for characterizing the process as a double application of a standard, either restrictive or expansive, when the issues are separated than when they are merged into one issue of liability for how much —none, all, or something between. This double-advantage argument is a conclusion derived from the premise that the scope of liability *should be* governed by a separate test. The opposing premise on which the Risk Rule is founded—the premise that the scope of liability should be limited by the factors accounting for liability—has been described as the view that there is only one question in negligence cases, not two.[20]

RELATION TO THE PRINCIPLE THAT LIABILITY IS BASED ON FAULT

The policy argument underlying use of the Risk Rule in negligence cases is a corollary of the foundation of tort law on fault. Generally one is not liable for an unintended harm caused by his nonnegligent conduct. If negligence in one respect were to make the actor liable for all unintended harms to follow, the legal consequences would be disproportionate to the fault. For example, suppose the defendant's negligence consisted of his transporting dynamite in an unmarked truck, otherwise carefully operated, and the only harm caused was injury to one who, without negligence, fainted, fell into the path of the truck, and was run down. Defendant was negligent with respect to risks of explosion but not with respect to risks of an injury of the kind that occurred. The policy judgment underlying the Risk Rule is that with respect to the kind of injury that occurred, the defendant was not at fault.

It may be argued that, as between a negligent defendant and a nonnegligent plaintiff, a loss of which defendant's conduct was a cause in fact ought to be imposed upon the defendant irrespective of whether it was a kind of loss within the risks by reason of which his conduct is characterized as negligence. But if it is relevant to take into account defendant's fault with respect to a risk different from any that would include the harm plaintiff has suffered, then would it not also be relevant to take into account his other faults as well? And would it not seem equally relevant to consider plaintiff's shortcomings? Shall we fix legal responsibility by deciding who is the better and who the worse person? An affirmative answer might involve us, and quickly too, in the morality of run-of-the-ranch TV drama, where the good guys always win.

If we reject this standard of judgment, then so long as liability is to be based on fault, should we not limit the scope of legal responsibility to those consequences with respect to which the actor was negligent—to those consequences of which the negligent aspect of his conduct was a cause? An affirmative answer implies, in relation to the hypothetical case of the transportation of explosives, that legal responsibility should be limited to damages caused by explosion or by conduct responsive to the explosion risk, rather than being extended to injuries that would have occurred even if the driver had used warning signs or had transported no explosives, while acting in other respects exactly as he did.

The policy foundation for the Risk Rule, though applicable more broadly to all problems of results outside the risk, is seen in its most persuasive context in relation to *persons outside the risk*. In this context Judge Learned Hand expressed the philosophy of the rule in an opinion that is especially illuminating on matters of legal cause. After noting that there are in tort law some instances of strict liability, he said:

But so long as it is an element of imposed liability that the wrongdoer shall in some degree disregard the sufferer's interests, it can only be an anomaly, and indeed vindictive, to make him responsible to those whose interests he has not disregarded.[21]

Perhaps this is as forcefully as one can fairly state the policy justification for the Risk Rule. Indeed, it is easy to exaggerate the weight of this argument as brought to bear upon one of those close cases about which dispute is likely. In the first place, this policy argument is essentially one of blameworthiness, resting distinctly on moral judgment. The twilight zones of disputed legal judgment are also zones of disputed moral judgment, not alone in the minds of judges, but as well in the views of the community at large.[22] Uncertainty is increased by the multiplicity of influences that bear on judgments of blameworthiness. Moreover, even aside from this element of uncertainty about which way underlying moral justifications point for a particular case in the twilight zone, the very fact that the policy is one based on a moral judgment exerts a restraint upon its influence, because we are less content today with moral justifications for our legal rules than with political, economic, and social justifications. It is characteristic of our time to be discomfited about the imposition of our moral judgments on others, especially judgments concerning individual rather than group morality.

One may disagree with the policy argument underlying the Risk Rule, or he may believe that it has been too widely influential, or he may believe that we should now move beyond the Risk Rule in sympathetic conformity with a trend away from liability based on fault and toward strict liability. But to believe that the Risk Rule is without rational policy foundation is to misunderstand, and to deny the existence of that foundation because of aversion to its moralizing quality is to misrepresent. Its force may be doubtful in a range of close cases; and, like most policy arguments, it falls short of providing a firm guide to decision in close cases. But demonstration of these uncertainties on the fringe leaves the hard core of the policy argument intact. This hard core continues to serve as the basic theme of decisions on legal cause.

NOTES

1. Cf. Larrimore v. American Nat'l Ins. Co., 184 Okla. 614, 89 P.2d 340 (1939). This hypothetical variation upon the facts of that case is chosen for the purpose of eliminating possible grounds of decision other than those to which attention is directed here.

2. The author's reference is to his discussion of the *Palgraf* case—Eds.

3. Challenges to some of the common assumptions about these expressions appear in Hart & Honore, Causation in the Law 19 n.1, 84 n.2, 103–22 (1959); and in Becht & Miller, The Test of Factual Causation in Negligence and Strict Liability Cases 13–21 (1961). See also Williams, *Causation in the Law*, 1961 Camb. L. J. 62, 63–79, for comments evoked by the Hart & Honore book.

4. See, *e.g.*, Hart & Honore, Causation in the Law 95–96 (1959); 2 Harper & James, Torts 1138 (1956). Compare Becht & Miller, The Test of Factual Causation in Negligence and Strict Liability Cases 21–25 (1961), discussing the hypothetical character of any assertion that an omission was a cause of a subsequent occurrence. Their discussion is addressed to what might be thought of as the converse of the problem referred to here. Here the issue is, Would the same thing have happened if the actor had not engaged in the conduct (whether described as an act, an omission, or a combination) alleged to be negligent? The issue they discuss is, Would the same thing have happened if the actor had done a particular thing he omitted doing? Both inquiries are hypothetical.

5. In the context of this discussion of legal cause, the plural, "risks," is chosen in preference to the more commonly used singular form as a means of avoiding the confusion that the risk within which the result falls must be such that, standing alone, it would make the conduct unreasonable. A composite of substantial, foreseeable risks is weighed against utility in judging whether the conduct is unreasonable.

6. Cf. P. Keeton, *Negligence, Duty, and Causation in Texas*, 16 Texas L. Rev. 1, 11–12 (1937). Though the idea expressed in the text above was suggested to me by the cited passage, the subsequent development in that article of the meaning of "force" (*id.* at 12–14) indicates that its author might not regard the present idea as one of the legitimate progeny of his teaching.

7. E.g., see Seavey, Cogitations on Torts 31–36 (1954); Seavey *Principles of Torts*, 56 Harv. L. Rev. 72, 90–93 (1942); Seavey, *Mr. Justice Cardozo and the Law of Torts*, 39 Colum. L. Rev. 20, 29–39; 52 Harv. L. Rev. 372, 381–91; 48 Yale L.J. 390, 399–409 (1939). For expressions of generally compatible points of view from the other side of the Atlantic, see Goodhart, *Liability and Compensation*, 76 L.O. Rev. 567 (1960) and Williams, *The Risk Principle*, 77 L.Q. Rev. 179 (1961).

8. 2 Harper & James, Torts 1138 (1956).

9. Ibid. (emphasis in original).

10. Carpenter, *Workable Rules for Determining Proximate Cause*, 20 Calif. L. Rev. 229, 231, 408–19 (1932).

11. 2 Harper & James, Torts 1138 (1956). Perhaps some degree of support for this thesis can be found in the analysis of Becht and Miller, which, for the purpose of inquiries into "factual causation," distinguishes between conduct and the "negligent segment" of it. See Becht & Miller, The Test of Causation in Negligence and Strict Liability Cases 25–28 (1961). But both the explanation of their distinction and the applications of it in their book indicate that it is a physical, rather than a qualitative, distinction. That is, a segment of conduct is an act or an omission among the many acts and omissions that make up the conduct, rather than an unreasonably risky quality of either the total conduct or some part of it. Thus, their distinction is not directed to the question whether the Risk Rule concerns cause-in-fact relation between the harm and the negligent *aspect* of conduct, as that concept is developed here. Moreover, in some situations where their thesis produces a finding of causal relation between the negligent *segment* of the conduct and the harm (and either supports liability or else explains nonliability on

the "policy" ground that the harm is not within the type against which the rule of conduct is directed), the present thesis produces a finding of no causal relation between the negligent *aspect* of the conduct and the harm. *E.g.*, they find that the negligent segment of a plaintiff's conduct in sitting on an unsafe wall was a cause of the injury he suffered when the wall was knocked down by a careless motorist whose conduct would have caused the same injuries if the wall had been safe. See *id.* at 182–84, where they criticize the view of Hart and Honore that the plaintiff's negligence in this situation was causally irrelevant. Under the thesis presented here, as under the thesis of Hart and Honore apparently, the plaintiff's negligence consisted of placing himself where he was likely to be injured by the collapse of the wall, either without an external impact or under an external impact insufficient to cause the collapse of a safe wall. This aspect of his conduct was not a *sine qua non* of the injury he suffered.

12. 2 Harper & James, Torts 1138 n. 15 (1956).

13. Hart & Honore, Causation in the Law 110–12, 192–93 (1959).

14. See, *e.g.*, *id.* at 231–38, 259, and 266.

15. See *id.* at 259.

16. E.g., Green, *The Causal Relation Issue in Negligence Law*, 60 Mich. L. Rev. 543, 576 (1962) ("the *only cause issue* is the connection between the defendant's conduct and the victim's injury"; the issue of causal relation should be unloaded of other considerations [emphasis in the original]); Prosser, Torts 252, 258, 266 (2d ed. 1955), (proximate cause "is nearly always a matter of various considerations of policy which have nothing to do with the fact of causation"; the problem of scope of liability for unforeseeable consequences "is in no way one of causation, and it does not arise until causation has been established"; the problem of intervening causes is one of policy, not causation); Restatement, Torts § 433, Reason for Changes (1948 Supp.), (Legal cause consists of two elements: 'the substantial factor' element deals with causation in fact"; the second element is concerned with whether there is a rule of law restricting "liability for harm occurring in the particular manner" at issue, and "deals with a legal policy relieving the actor of liability for harm he has, as a matter of fact, caused"; "[i]t is completely faulty analysis" to confuse "the question of policy with the question of fact"). Insistence that the result-within-the-risk problem is not one of causation is found even among advocates of the principle expressed in the several formulations of the Risk Rule. For example, Professor Goodhart declares: "But consequences cannot 'flow' from negligence. Consequences 'flow' from an act or an omission." Goodhart, *Liability for the Consequences of a "Negligent Act,"* in Cambridge Legal Essays 101, 105–6 (1926), reprinted in Goodhart, Essays in Jurisprudence and the Common Law 110, 114 (1931). See also Foster, Grant & Green, *The Risk Theory and Proximate Cause—A Comparative Study*, 32 Neb. L. Rev. 72, 79–80 (1952) (advocating the risk theory and the "relational" quality of negligence, but declaring that "proximate cause often has little if anything to do with causation in fact, except that no issue of proximate cause arises unless actual causation is present," and observing of a typical case that if defendant is held not liable "it is not because its fault was not a cause of the disaster").

17. Cf. 2 Harper & James, Torts 1132–33 (1956).

18. Seavey, *Mr. Justice Cardozo and the Law of Torts*, 39 Colum. L. Rev. 20, 34; 52 Harv. L. Rev. 372, 386; 48 Yale L. J. 390, 404 (1939).

19. E. g., Smith, *Legal Cause in Actions of Tort*, 25 Harv. L. Rev. 103, 223, 245 (1912). Cf. Green, *Foreseeability in Negligence Law*, 61 Colum. L. Rev. 1401, 1408 (1961), noting

that there are numerous devices for controlling decisions of both liability and damages, and asserting that "the foreseeability formula" need not "reach beyond the negligence issue" into the area of other limitations on scope of liability.

20.   See Pound, *Causation,* 67 Yale L. J. 1, 10 (1957), referring to Pollock's view. Pollock stated the question as one "whether the accepted test of liability for negligence in the first instance is or not also the proper measure of liability for the consequences of proved or admitted default." Pollock, *Liability for Consequences,* 38 L.Q. Rev. 165 (1922).

21.   Sinram v. Pennsylvania R.R., 61 F.2d 767, 770 (2d Cir. 1932).

22.   Cf. Morris, *Proximate Cause in Minnesota,* 34 Minn L. Rev. 185, 207 (1950).

THE AMBIGUOUS SUICIDE CASE

N.Y. Times, February 7, 1968: "Phoenix, Ariz., Feb. 6 (AP)—Linda Marie Ault killed herself, policemen said today, rather than make her dog Beauty pay for her night with a married man.

"I killed her. I killed her. It's just like I killed her myself," a detective quoted her grief-stricken father as saying.

"I handed her the gun. I didn't think she would do anything like that."

"The 21-year-old Arizona State University coed died in a hospital yesterday of a gunshot wound in the head.

"The police quoted her parents, Mr. and Mrs Joseph Ault, as giving this account:

"Linda failed to return home from a dance in Tempe Friday night. On Saturday she admitted she had spent the night with an Air Force lieutenant.

"The Aults decided on a punishment that would 'wake Linda up.' They ordered her to shoot the dog she had owned about two years.

"On Sunday, the Aults and Linda took the dog into the desert near their home. They had the girl dig a shallow grave. Then Mrs. Ault grasped the dog between her hands, and Mr. Ault gave his daughter a .22-caliber pistol and told her to shoot the dog.

"Instead, the girl put the pistol to her right temple and shot herself.

"The police said there were no charges that could be filed against the parents except possibly cruelty to animals."

FAULT

JOEL FEINBERG

Sua Culpa*

I

It is common enough for philosophers to analyze moral judgments and for philosophers—usually other philosophers—to analyze causal judgments. But statements to the effect that a given harm is some assignable person's fault, having both moral and causal components, import the complexities of judgments of the other two kinds. They are, therefore, especially challenging. Yet they are rarely considered by analytical philosophers. This neglect is to be regretted, because "his fault" judgments (as I shall call them) are important and ubiquitous in ordinary life. Historians employ them to assign blame for wars and depressions; politicians, sportswriters, and litigants use them to assign blame for losses. The disagreements they occasion are among the most common and intensely disputed in all "ethical discourse."

It may seem that most of those who quibble and quarrel about "his fault" are either children or lawyers; and even lawyers, therefore, can seem childish when they are preoccupied with the question. But investigators, editorialists, and executives must assign blame for failures and thereby judge the faults of their fellows. (Indeed, their inquiries and debates are most childish when they do *not* carefully consider fault and instead go scapegoat-hunting.) My assumption in what follows is that the faults that concern non-lawyers, both children and adults, are faults in the same sense of the word as those that concern the lawyer, that the concept of "his fault" is imported into the law from the world of everyday affairs. On the other hand, "proximate cause" (to pick just one of a thousand examples) is a technical term of law invented by lawyers to do a special

legal job and subject to continual refashioning in the interests of greater efficiency in the performance of its assigned legal task. To explain this term to a layman is precisely to explain what *lawyers* do with it; if it should ever happen that a child, or a sportswriter, or an historian should use the expression, that fact would be of no relevance to its proper analysis. But to explain the concept of "his fault," we must give an account that explains what both lawyers and laymen do with it and how it is possible for each to understand and to communicate with the other by means of it.

An equivalent way of saying that some result is a man's fault is to say that he is to *blame* for it. Precisely the same thing can also be said in the language of *responsibility*. Of course, to be responsible for something (after the fact) may also mean that one did it, or caused it, or now stands answerable, or accountable, or liable to unfavorable responses from others for it. One can be responsible for a result in all those senses without being to blame for it. One can be held liable for a result either because it is one's fault or for some quite different kind of reason; and one can be to blame for an occurrence and yet escape all liability for it. Still, when one is to blame for harm, one can properly be said to be "responsible for it *really*"; that is, there is a sense of "responsible for" that simply means "chargeable to one as one's fault." One of the commonest uses of the expression "*morally* responsible for" is for being responsible for something in this sense. (Another is for chargeability to a fault of a distinctively moral kind. Still another is for being *liable* to responses of a distinctively moral kind.)

II

The word "fault" occurs in three distinct idioms. We can say of a man that he *has a fault*, or

*From *Doing and Deserving: Essays in the Theory of Responsibility* (Princeton, N.J.: Princeton University Press, 1970), pp. 187–221. Copyright © 1970 by Princeton University Press. Reprinted by permission of the Princeton University Press.

that he is (or was) *at fault,* or that he is "to blame" for a given harm, which is to say that the harm is (or was) *his fault.* In this essay I shall be directly concerned only with the last of these idioms, except to make some necessary preliminary remarks about the other two.

TO HAVE A FAULT

A fault is a shortcoming, that is, a failure to conform to some norm or standard. Originally, perhaps, the word "fault" gave emphasis to failures through deficiency; but now any sort of failure to "measure up" is a fault, and we find no paradox in "falling short through excess." Not all defective human properties are faults. Evanescent qualities are hardly around long enough to qualify. To be a fault, a defective property must be sufficiently durable, visible, and potent to tell us something interesting about its possessor. A fault can be a durable manifestation almost constantly before the eye; but, more typically, human faults are latencies that manifest themselves only under special circumstances. Flaws of character are tendencies to act or feel in subpar ways, which, as tendencies, are *characteristic* of their possessor, that is, genuinely representative of him. Moreover, faults, like virtues, are commonly understood as comparative notions. An irascible man, for example, is not merely one who can become angry, for on that interpretation we may all be considered irascible. Rather, he is one who is more prone than most to become angry, either in the sense that he becomes angry on occasions when most men would not or in the sense that he gets angrier than most men on those occasions when most men would be angry. Equally commonly, however, we interpret a tendency-fault as a failure to satisfy not merely a statistical norm, but a norm of propriety; an irascible man has a tendency to get angry on occasions when he *ought* not to. And even when the implied norm is a statistical one, the fault predicate does more than describe neutrality. A fault word always expresses derogation.

The concept of fault has a close relation to that of harm, but it would be an overstatement to claim that all human faults create the risk of harm. David Hume was closer to the mark when he divided faults into four categories: those that cause displeasure or harm to self or others. Immediate displeasure, however, is only one of the diverse negative reactions that, quite apart from harmfulness, can be the sign of a fault. I would

also include, for example, offense, wounded feelings, disaffection, aversion, digust, shock, annoyance, and "uneasy sensations"—reactions either of the faulty self or of others. If we use the word "offensiveness" to cover the provoking of this whole class of negative responses, and if we assume that everything that is offensive to self, in this broad sense, is likely also to be offensive to others, we can summarize Hume's view by saying that it is either harmfulness or social offensiveness that makes some characteristics faults. Hume notwithstanding, there are some (though perhaps not many) faults that neither harm nor offend but simply fail to benefit, such as unimaginativeness and various minor intellectual flaws. We can modify Hume's account of the offensive faults further, perhaps in a way Hume would not have welcomed, by adding that it is not the mere *de facto* tendency of a trait to offend that renders it a fault. Normally when we attach the fault label to personal characteristics—that is, when we speak as moralists expressing our own judgments, and not merely as sociologists describing the prevailing sentiments of our communities—we are not simply predicting that the characteristics will offend; we are instead (or also) endorsing offense as an appropriate reaction to them. Most of those faults that do not harm, we think, are traits that naturally, or properly, or understandably offend (in the widest sense of "offend").

Often we speak as if a man's fault can enter into causal relations with various outcomes external to him. These assertions, when sensible, must be taken as elliptical forms of more complex statements. To say that a man's faulty disposition, his carelessness or greed, caused some harm is to say that the man's action or omission that did the causing was of the type that he characteristically does (or would do) in circumstances of the kind that in fact were present, or that the act or omission was of the sort he has a predominant tendency to do in circumstances of that kind. (He may, of course, also have a countertendency to restrain himself by an act of will, or the like.) To cite a man's character flaw as a cause of a harm, in short, is to *ascribe* the cause to an act or omission and then to *classify* that act or omission in a certain way—as characteristic of the actor. (It is just the sort of thing he *would* do, as we say.) It is also, finally, to *judge* the manifested characteristic as substandard and thereby to derogate it.

One can be *at fault* on a given occasion, however, even though one does not act in a characteristic way. Even very careful men sometimes slip up; even the most talented make mistakes; even the very calm sometimes lose their tempers. When these uncharacteristic failures cause harm, it is correct to say that a *faulty aspect* of some act or omission did the causing, but incorrect to ascribe the cause to some faulty characteristic of the actor, for that would be to imply, contrary to the hypothesis, that he is a generally careless, irascible, or inept person. This is the kind of faulty doing (as opposed to "faulty being") that could happen, as we say, to anyone; but in the long run it will be done more often to those who have serious character faults than by those who do not.

"Being at fault," even in one's perfectly voluntary and representative conduct, is in a sense partly a matter of luck. No one has complete control over what circumstances he finds himself in—whether, for example, he lives in times of war or peace, prosperity or depression, under democratic or autocratic government, in sickness or health, and so on. Consequently, a man may, by luck merely, escape those circumstances that would actualize some dreadful latency in him of which he is wholly unaware. It may even be true of *most* of us virtuous persons that we are to some small degree, at least, "lucky" in this sense. (We do not, however, normally refer to the mere absence of very bad luck as "good luck.") Not only can one *have a fault*; and "luckily" escape *being at fault* in one's actions (on analogy with the hemophiliac who never in fact gets cut); one can also have a small fault (that is, a disposition very difficult to actualize) and unluckily stumble into those very rare circumstances that can actualize it. (The latter is "bad luck" in a proper sense.) Both of these possibilities—the luckily unactualized and the unluckily actualized latencies—follow from the analysis of faults as dispositions and, if that analysis is correct, should be sufficient at least to temper anyone's self-righteousness about the faulty actions of others.

TO BE AT FAULT

When a man is "at fault" on a given occasion, the fault characterizes his action itself and not necessarily the actor, except as he was during the performance of the action. There is no necessary relation between this kind of fault and general dispositions of the actor—though, for all we know, every faultily undertaken or executed action *may* exemplify extremely complicated dispositions. When we say that a man is at fault, we usually mean only to refer to occurrent defects of acts or omissions, and only derivatively to the *actor's* flaw as the doer of the defective deed. Such judgments are at best presumptive evidence about the man's general character. An act can be faulty even when not characteristic of the actor, and the actor may be properly "to blame" for it anyway; for if the action is faulty and it is also *his* action (characteristic or not), then he must answer for it. The faultiness of an action always reflects *some* discredit upon its doer, providing the doing is voluntary.

One standard legal classification divides all ways of being at fault into three categories: intentional wrongdoing, recklessness, and negligence. The traditional legal test of intentional doing has been a disjunctive one: There is intentional wrongdoing if either one acts with a wrongful conscious objective or one knowingly produces a forbidden result even incidentally as a kind of side-effect of his effort to achieve his objective. When the occurrence of the forbidden or undesirable side-effect is not certain, but nevertheless there is a known substantial likelihood of its coming about as an incidental byproduct of one's action, its subsequent production cannot be called "intentional" or "knowing" but verges into *recklessness.* What is known in recklessness is the existence of a *risk.* When the actor knowingly runs the risk, when he is willing to gamble with his own interests or the interests of others, then, providing the risk itself is unreasonable, his act is reckless.[1]

One can hardly escape the impression that what is called "negligence" in the law is simply the miscellaneous class of faulty actions that are not intentional (done purposely or knowingly) or reckless; that in this classification of faults, once wrongful intentions and reckless quasi-intentions have been mentioned, "negligence" stands for everything else. This would leave a class of faults, however, that is *too* wide and miscellaneous. Humorlessness (to take just one example) is a kind of fault that is not intentional; yet we would hardly accuse a man of being "negligent" in failing to be amused or to show amusement at what is truly amusing. The point, I think, is that inappropriate failures to be amused are not the sorts of faults likely to cause *harm*. There is no great risk in a blank stare or a suppressed giggle. Negligence is the name of a heterogeneous class of acts and omissions that are unreasonably *dangerous.* Creation of risk is absolutely essential to the concept, and so is fault. But the fault is not merely conjoined coincidentally to the risk; rather, the fault consists in creating the risk, however unintentionally. When one knowingly creates an unreasonable risk to self or others, one is reckless; when one unknowingly but faultily creates such a risk, one is negligent.

There are a large number of ways of "unintentionally but faultily" creating an unreasonable risk. One can consciously weigh the risk but misassess it, either because of hasty or otherwise insufficient scrutiny (rashness), or through willful blindness to the magnitude of the risk, or through the conscientious exercise of inherently bad judgment. Or one can unintentionally create an unreasonable risk by failing altogether to attend either to what one is doing (the manner of execution) or to the very possibility that harmful consequences might ensue. In the former case, best called *carelessness* or *clumsiness* (in execution), one creates a risk precisely in virtue of not paying sufficient attention to what one is doing; in the latter case, which we can call *heedlessness* (in the very undertaking of the action), the risk is already there in the objective circumstances, but unperceived or mindlessly ignored.

There are still other faults that can render a given act or omission, unknown to its doer, unreasonably dangerous. Overly attentive drivers with the strongest scruples and the best intentions can drive as negligently as inattentive drivers and, indeed, a good deal more negligently than experienced drivers of strong and reliable habits who rely on those habits while daydreaming, their car being operated in effect by a kind of psychic "automatic pilot." Timidity, excitability, organic awkwardness, and slow reflexes can create unreasonable risks too, even when accompanied by attentive and conscientious advertence; and so can normal virtues like gallantry when conjoined with inexperience or poor judgment. (Imagine stopping one's car and waving a pretty pedestrian across the street right into the path of a speeding car passing on the right, unseen because momentarily in the "blind spot" of one's rear view mirror.) Almost any defect of conduct, except the likes of humorlessness, can be the *basis* of negligence, that is, the fault in virtue of which a given act or omission becomes, unknown to its actor, unreasonably dangerous. "Negligence" in the present sense is the name of a category of faulty acts. The negligence of any particular act or kind

of act in the general category is always a consequential fault, a fault supervenient upon a fault of another kind that leads to an unreasonable risk in the circumstances.

It is worth emphasizing that this analysis applies to *legal negligence* only, which is negligence in a quite special sense. In ordinary nontechnical discourse, the word "negligence" is often a rough synonym for "carelessness" and as such refers to only one of the numerous possible faults that can, in a given set of circumstances, be the faulty basis of negligent conduct in the legal sense.

III

We come now to the main business at hand: the analysis of the concept of "his fault." It should be clear at the outset that, in order for a given harm to be someone's fault, he must have been somehow "at fault" in what he did or omitted to do, and also that there must have been some sort of causal connection between his action or omission and the harm. It is equally obvious that neither of these conditions by itself can be sufficient. Thus a motorists may be at fault in driving with an expired license or in exceeding the speed limit by five miles per hour, but unless his faulty act is a cause of the collision that ensues, the accident can hardly be his fault. Fault without causally determining action, then, is not sufficient. Similarly, causation without fault is not sufficient for the caused harm to be the causer's fault. It is no logical contradiction to say that a person's action caused the harm yet the harm was not his fault.

THE TRICONDITIONAL ANALYSIS

It is natural at this point to conclude that a harm is "his fault" if and only if (1) he was at fault in acting (or omitting) and (2) his faulty act (or omission) caused the harm. This analysis, however, is incomplete, being still vulnerable to counterexamples of faulty actions causing harm that is nevertheless not the actor's fault. Suppose that *A* is unlicensed to drive an automobile but drives anyway, thereby "being at fault." The appearance of him driving in an (otherwise) faultless manner causes an edgy horse to panic and throw his rider. His faultily undertaken act caused a harm that cannot be imputed to him because the respect in which his act was faulty was causally irrelevant to the production of the harm. (When we come to give a causal explanation of the harm, we will not mention the fact that the driver had no license in his pocket. *That* is not what scared the horse.) This example suggests that a further condition is required to complete the analysis: (3) the aspect of the act that was faulty was also one of the aspects in virtue of which the act was a cause of the harm.

The third condition in the analysis is especially important when the fault in question falls under the general heading of negligence. Robert Keeton in effect devotes most of a book to commentary on a hypothetical example which illustrates this point:

The defendant, proprietor of a restaurant, placed a large unlabelled can of rat poison beside cans of flour on a shelf near a stove in a restaurant kitchen. The victim, while in the kitchen making a delivery to the restaurant, was killed by an explosion of the poison. Assume that the defendant's handling of the rat poison was negligent because of the risk that someone would be poisoned but that the defendant had no reason to know of the risk that the poison would explode if left in a hot place.[2]

The defendant's action, in Keeton's example, was faulty, and it was also the cause of the victim's death; but, on the analysis I have suggested, the death was nevertheless not his fault. The defendant's conduct was negligent because it created a risk of *poisoning,* but the harm it caused was not within the ambit of *that* risk. The risk of *explosion* was not negligently created. Hence the aspect of the act in virtue of which it was faulty was not the cause of the harm. Keeton puts the point more exactly: the harm was not "a result within the scope of the risks by reason of which the actor is found to be negligent."[3] Keeton's concern is with a theory of liability for negligence, not with an analysis of the nontechnical concept of "his fault"; but, liability aside, the analysis I have given entails that the death, in Keeton's example, was *not* the defendant's fault.

We can refer to this account as "the triconditional analysis" and to its three conditions as (in order) "the fault condition," "the causal condition" (that the act was a cause of the harm), and "the causal relevance condition" (that the faulty aspect of the act was its causal link to the harm). I shall conclude that the triconditional analysis goes a long way toward providing a correct account of the commonsense notion of "his fault"

and that its three conditions are indeed necessary to such an account even if, in the end, they must be formulated much more carefully and even supplemented by other conditions in an inevitably more complicated analysis. The remainder of this section discusses difficulties for the analysis as it stands which, I think, it can survive (at least after some tinkering, modifying, and disclaiming). One of these difficulties stems from a heterogeneous group of examples of persons who, on our analysis, would be blamed for harms that are clearly not their fault. I try to sidestep these counterexamples by affixing a restriction to the fault condition and making corresponding adjustments in the formulation of the relevance condition. The other difficulties directly concern the causal condition and the relevance condition. Both of these can involve us quickly in some fundamental philosophical problems.

RESTRICTIONS ON THE FAULT CONDITION

There are some exceptional cases (but readily accessible to the philosophical imagination) in which a person who is clearly not to blame for a given harm nevertheless is the sole person who satisfies the conditions of the tripartite analysis. These cases, therefore, constitute counterexamples to that analysis if it is taken to state not only necessary but sufficient conditions for blame. Nicholas Sturgeon has suggested an especially ingenious case:

A has made a large bet that no infractions of the law will occur at a certain place in a certain period of time; but *B,* at that place and time, opens a pack of cigarettes and fails to destroy the federal tax seal thereby breaking the law. *A,* seeing *B's* omission, is so frustrated that he suffers a fatal heart attack on the spot. (To simplify matters, we may suppose that no one has any reason to suppose *A* is endangering his health by gambling in this way.)[4]

Clearly, *A's* death is not *B's* fault. Yet (1) *B* was at fault in acting contrary to law; (2) his faulty act frustrated *A,* causing the heart attack; and (3) the aspects of *B's* act (omission) that were faulty (the illegality of his omission to destroy the tax stamps) were also among the aspects of it in virtue of which there was a causal connnection between it and the harm. A similar example is provided by John Taurek:

C is so programmed (by hypnosis, perhaps C is a clever robot, whatever) that if A lies in answering B's question, C will harm D. B asks A her age and she lies. C harms D. A's action seems to be a causal factor in the production of harm to D, and just in virtue of its faulty aspect. Yet who would hold that D's harm was A's fault?[5]

Perhaps it is possible to add further conditions to the analysis to obviate this kind of counterexample, but a more likely remedy would be to restrict the kinds of faults that can be elements of "his fault" judgments. Sometimes a man can be said to be at fault in acting (or omitting to act) precisely because his action or omission will offend or fail to benefit himself or others, or because it is a violation of faith (even a *harmless* instance of promise-breaking, such as a secret breaking of faith to a person now dead), or simply and precisely because it breaks an authoritative legal rule. Most intentional wrongdoing, on the other hand, and all recklessness and negligence are instances of being at fault for another (perhaps additional) reason—either because "they make a certain kind of harm or injury inevitable, or because they create an unreasonable risk of a certain kind of harm."[6] We can attempt to avoid counterexamples of the sort Sturgeon and Taurek suggested by tampering with the first condition (the fault condition). We can say now (of course, only tentatively and not without misgiving) that, for the purpose of this analysis, the way of being at fault required by the fault condition is to be understood as the harm-threatening way, not the nonbenefiting, offense-threatening, harmless faith-breaking, or law-violating ways. The fault condition then can be reformulated as follows (in words suggested by Sturgeon): a given harm is A's fault only if (1) A was at fault in acting or omitting to act and "the faultiness of his act or omission consisted, at least in part, in the creation of either a certainty or an unreasonable risk of harm. . . . "[7] Now the faulty smoker in Sturgeon's example and the liar in Taurek's example are no longer "at fault" in the requisite way, and the revised analysis no longer pins the blame for coincidental harms on them. To open a cigarette package in an overly fastidious fashion is not to endanger unduly the health of others; nor is lying about one's age (except in very special contexts) to threaten others with harm.

In the light of this new restriction on the fault condition, we can formulate the causal relevance condition in an alternative way, along the lines suggested by Keeton's account of harm caused by negligence. We can now say that the (harm-threatening) "faulty aspect" of an act is a cause of subsequent harm when the risk or certainty of harm in virtue of which the act was at fault was a risk or certainty of "just the sort of harm that was in fact caused,"[8] and not harm of some other sort. The resultant harm, in other words, must be within the scope of the risk (or certainty) in virtue of which the act is properly characterized as faulty. This is more than a mere explication of the original way of putting the third condition. It is a definite modification designed to rule out cases of *coincidence* where the faulty aspect of an act, even when it is of the harm-threatening sort, may be causally linked to a subsequent harm via such adventitious conditions as standing wagers and programmed robots. Under the revised formulation, the very same considerations involved in the explanation of *why* the act is faulty are also involved, essentially and sufficiently, in the explanation of *how* the harm was caused.

We have not even considered, of course, the crucial question of how reasonable risks are to be distinguished from unreasonable ones; and there are still other problems resulting from the fact that a "sort of harm" (crucial phrase) can be described in either more or less full and determinate ways. These problems, like several other closely related ones, are too complicated to be tackled here.

FAULT AND CAUSE: DEPENDENT AND INDEPENDENT DETERMINATIONS

Can we tell whether an act caused a given harm independently of knowing whether the actor was at fault in acting? The answer seems to be that we can determine the causal question independently of the fault question in some cases but not in others. Part of our problem is to explain his variation. Consider first some examples. A blaster takes every reasonable precaution, and yet by a wildly improbable fluke his explosion of dynamite sends a disjarred rock flying through the window of a distant isolated cabin. He was not at fault, but whether he was or not, we are able to say independently that his setting off the blast was the cause of the broken window. Similarly, the motorist in our earlier example, by driving (whether with or without fault is immaterial to this point) along a rarely traveled stretch of country road, caused a nervous horse to bolt. That is, it was his activity as he conducted it then and there, with its attendant noise and dust, that caused the horse to bolt; and we can know this independently of any determination of fault.

Examples provided by J. L. Mackie and William Dray, however, seem to cut the other way. Mackie[9] describes an episode in which a motorcyclist exceeded a speed limit and was chased by a policeman, also on a motorcyle, at speeds up to seventy miles per hour. An absentminded pedestrian stepped off a bus into the policeman's path and was killed instantly. The newspapers for the next few days were full of debates over the questions of whose conduct was the "real cause" of the death, debates that seemed to center on the question of whose conduct was the least *reasonable* intrusion into the normal course of events. To express an opinion at all on the causal question seemed to be to take a stand, plain and simple, about the *propriety* of pursuits by police in heavily populated areas.

Dray discusses a hypothetical debate between two historians who argue "whether it was Hitler's invasion of Poland or Chamberlain's pledge to defend it which caused the outbreak of the Second World War." The question they *must* be taken to be trying to settle, he avers, is "who was to blame." "The point," he says, "is not that we cannot hold an agent responsible for a certain happening unless his action can be said to have caused it. It is rather that, unless we are prepared to hold the agent responsible for what happened, we cannot say that his action *was* the cause."[10] Mackie comes to a similar conclusion, embracing what he calls a "curious inversion of utilitarianism," namely,that one often cannot tell whether a given harm is a causal consequence of a given act without first deciding whether the actor was *at fault* in acting the way he did.

To clarify the relations between cause and fault, it will be necessary to digress briefly and remind ourselves of certain features of causal judgments as they are made in ordinary life. That one condition is causally necessary or, in a given context, sufficient for the occurrence of a given event is normally a question simply for empirical investigation and the application of a scientific theory. Normally, however, there will be a plurality of distinguishable causal conditions (often called "causal factors") for any given event, and the aim of a causal inquiry will be to single out

one[11] of these to be denominated "the cause" of the event in question.[12] A judgment that cites one of the numerous eligible causal conditions for an event as "the cause" I call a *causal citation.* The eligibility of an event or state as a causal factor is determined empirically via the application of inductive criteria.[13] On the other hand, the citation of one of the eligible candidates as "the cause" is normally made, as we shall see, via the application of what Dray calls "pragmatic criteria." In Dray's convenient phrase, the inductive inquiry establishes the "importance of a condition to the event," whereas the causal citation indicates its "importance to the inquirer."

The point of a causal citation is to single out one of the certified causal candidates that is especially *interesting* to us, given our various practical purposes and cognitive concerns. These purposes and concerns provide a convenient way of classifying the "contexts of inquiry" in which causal citations are made. The primary division is between explanatory and nonexplanatory contexts. The occasion for an explanatory citation is one in which there is intellectual puzzlement of a quite specific kind. A suprising or unusual event has occurred which is a deviation from what is understood to be the normal course of things. A teetotaler is drunk, or an alcoholic sober; a punctual man is tardy, or a dilatory man early; it rains in the dry season, or it fails to rain in the wet season. Sometimes the breach of routine is disappointing, and we wish to know what went wrong this time. But sometimes the surprise is pleasant or, more commonly, simply stimulating to one's curiosity. We ask what caused the surprising event and expect an explanation that will cite a factor normally present but absent this time, or normally absent but present this time, that made the difference. The occasion for explanation is a breach of routine; the explanatory judgment cites another deviation from routine to correlate with it.

Very often one of the causal conditions for a given upshot is a faulty human action. Human failings tend to be more "interesting" factors than events of other kinds, even for purely explanatory purposes; but it is important to notice that this need not always be the case. Faulty human actions usually do *not* fall within the normal course of events, so that a dereliction of duty, for example, when it is a causally necessary condition for some puzzling breach of routine, being itself a departure from the normal course of things, is a prime candidate for causal citation. But when the faulty conduct of Flavius is constant and unrelieved and known to be such to Titus, it will not relieve Titus's perplexity over how a given unhappy event came about simply to cite Flavius's habitual negligence or customary dereliction of duty as "the cause." What Titus wishes to know is what new intrusive event made the difference *this* time; and it won't help *him* to mention a causal factor that has always been present even on those occasions when no unhappy result ensued.

Not all causal explanations by any means employ causal citations. Especially when we are puzzled about the "normal course of events" itself and wish explanations for standardly recurring regularities (Why do the tides come in? Why do released objects fall? Why do flowers bloom in the spring?), mere brief citations will not do. In such cases we require long stories involving the descriptions of diverse states of affairs and the invocation of various laws of nature. Similarly, not all causal citations are explanatory. Sometimes there is no gap in a person's understanding of how a given interesting event came about, and yet he may seek nevertheless to learn its "real" or "most important" cause. Nonexplanatory citations are those made for some purpose other than the desire simply to put one's curiosity to rest. Most frequently they cite the causal factor that is of a kind that is easiest to manipulate or control. Engineers and other practical men may be concerned to eliminate events of the kind that occasioned the inquiry if they are harmful or to produce more of them if they are beneficial. In either case, when they seek "the cause," they seek the causal factor that has a handle on it (in Collingwood's phrase) that they can get hold of and manipulate. Another of our practical purposes in making causal citations is to *fix the blame,* a purpose which introduces considerations not present when all the leading causal factors are things other than human actions (as they often are in agricultural, medical, or engineering inquiries). Insects, viruses, and mechanical stresses and strains are often "blamed" for harms, but the word "blame" in these uses, of course, has a metaphorical sense.

In summary, causal citations can be divided into those made from explanatory and those made from nonexplanatory standpoints, and the latter group into those made from the "engineer-ing" and those made from the "blaming" standpoints. Explanatory citations single out abnormal interferences with the normal course of events or hitherto unknown missing links in a person's understanding. They are designed simply to remove puzzlement by citing the causal factor that can shed the most light. Hence we can refer to the criterion of selection in explanatory contexts (for short) as *the lantern criterion.* Causal citations made from the "engineering standpoint" are made with a view to facilitating control over future events by citing the most efficiently and economically manipulable causal factor. The criterion for selection in engineering contexts can thus be called (for short) *the handle criterion.* The point of causal citations in purely blaming contexts is simply to pin the label of blame on the appropriate causal factor for further notice and practical use. These judgments cite a causal factor that is a human act or omission "stained" (as an ancient figure of speech would have it) with fault. The criterion in blaming contexts can be called (for short) *the stain criterion.* When we look for "the cause," then, we may be looking for the causal factor that has either a lantern, a handle, or a stain on it.

Purely blaming citations can be interpreted in two different ways. On the first model, to say that a person's act was the cause of the harm is precisely equivalent to saying that he is to blame for the harm, that is, that the harm is his fault. The causal inquiry undertaken from the purely blaming perspective, according to this view, is one and the same as the inquiry into the question of who was to blame or of whose fault it was. On this model, then, causal citation is not a condition for the fixing of blame; it is, rather, precisely the same thing. It is simply a fact of usage, which the examples of Dray and Mackie illustrate, that questions of blame often get posed and answered in wholly causal language. Historians, for example, are said by Dray often to "use expressions like 'was responsible for' [or 'was to blame for'] when they want to put into other words conclusions which they would also be prepared to frame in causal language."[14]

On the second model of interpretation, which is also sometimes *a propos,* the truth of the causal citation "His act was the cause of the harm" is only one of the *conditions* for the judgment that "The harm was his fault." Here we separate cause and fault before bringing them together again in a "his fault" judgment, insisting that the harm was his fault *only if* his action caused it. The causal inquiry, so conceived, is undertaken for the sake of the blame inquiry, but its results are established independently.

Now how do we establish a causal citation on the first model (or, what is the same thing, a "his fault" citation on the second)? Again, we have two alternatives: Either we can hold that the person (or his act) was *the cause* of the harm (meaning that he was to blame for it) only if his act was a genuine causal factor in the production of the harm; or we can require that his act be *the cause* of the harm, and not merely a "causal factor." But then we must find a way of avoiding a vitiating circularity. If we mean "the cause" as selected by *the stain criterion,* we have made a full circle; for, on this first model, our *original inquiry* is aimed at citing the cause by a stain criterion, and now we say that the achievement of this goal is a condition of itself. Clearly, if we are going to insist that his act be "the cause" as a condition of its being "the cause for purposes of fixing blame," we have to mean that it must be the cause *as determined by either the lantern or the handle criteria.* A quick examination of cases will show that this is just what we do mean.

When a man sets off a charge of dynamite and the earth shifts, dust rises, and rocks fly, the blasting is conspicuously the cause of these results by the lantern criterion (since it is the abnormal intervention) and equally clearly by the handle criterion (since it is part of the handiest causal recipe for producing results of precisely that kind). We can know, therefore, that the blasting caused the results by these commonsense criteria before we know anything at all about fault. Then we can go on to say, without circularity, that one or another of these causal criteria must be satisfied if those of the results that are harmful are to be charged to the blaster as his fault, but that further conditions of faultiness must also be satisfied.

Should we say that being "the cause" by the other commonsense criteria is *always* a necessary condition of being the cause by the stain criterion? I think this specification would prove to be artificially restrictive, for we sometimes (though perhaps not often) wish to ascribe blame whether or not the blamed action satisfies the lantern and handle criteria, and even in some instances where (allowing for the usual relativity of context) it appears not to. Suppose *A,* an impressive adult

figure, offers a cigarette to *B,* an impressionable teenager. *A* is *B's* original attractive model of a smoker and also one who deliberately seduces him into the habit. Much later, after thirty years of continuous heavy smoking, *B* begins to suffer from lung cancer. Neither the lantern nor the handle criteria in most contexts are likely to lead one to cite *A's* earlier act as the cause of *B's* cancer, for *A's* act is not conspicuously "the cause" of the harm by these criteria (as the blasting was, in the earlier example). Yet we may wish to say that *A's* seduction of *B* was the cause of his eventual cancer for purposes of fixing blame or as a mode of expressing that blame. Such a judgment may not be morally felicitous, but it can be made without committing some sort of conceptual solecism.

The best way of avoiding both circularity and artificial restriction of expression in our account of blame-fixing citations is to require not that the blamed action be citable as "the cause" (by *any* criteria), but only that it be a genuine causal factor, in the circumstances that obtained, and then to add fault and relevance conditions to the analysis. Most of the time, perhaps, being "the cause" by the lantern or handle criteria will also be required; but being a *causal factor merely* will be required always.

THE CAUSAL RELEVANCE CONDITION: IS IT ALWAYS NECESSARY?

Does the analysis of commonsense "his fault" judgments really require a causal relevance condition? Many people, I suspect, are prepared to make "his fault" judgments in particular cases even when they know that a causal relevance condition has not been satisfied; and many puzzling cases are such as to make even most of us hesitate about the matter. Consider, for example, the case of the calamitous soup-spilling at Lady Mary's formal dinner party. Sir John Stuffgut so liked his first and second bowls of soup that he demanded a third just as Lady Mary was prepared to announce with pride to the hungry and restless guests the arrival of the next course. Sir John's tone was so gruff and peremptory that Lady Mary quite lost her composure. She lifted the heavy tureen with shaking arms and, in attempting to pass it to her intemperate guest, spilled it unceremoniously in the lap of the Reverend Mr. Straightlace. Now both Sir John and Lady Mary were at fault in this episode. Sir John was thoughtless, gluttonous, and, especially, *rude* in demanding another bowl in an unsettling tone of voice. Lady Mary was (perhaps forgivably) negligent in the way she executed her action, and, besides she should have known that the tureen was too heavy for her to lift. Furthermore, both Lady Mary's faulty action and Sir John's faulty action were necessary conditions for the ensuing harm. Assuming that we must fix the blame for what happened, whose fault, should we say, was the harm?

Most of us would be inclined to single out Sir John's rudeness as "the cause" for purposes of blaming, partly because it was the most striking deviation from routine, perhaps, but mainly because, of the causal factors with stains on them, his action was the most at fault. Moreover, his action was a causal factor in the production of the harm precisely in virtue of that aspect which was faulty, namely, its unsettling rudeness, which created an unreasonable risk of upsetting the hostess, the very result that in fact ensued. Thus the causal relevance condition is satisfied in this example.

Suppose, however, that the facts had been somewhat different. Sir John, at just the wrong moment (as before), requested his third bowl, but in a quiet and gentle manner, and in a soft and mellifluous tone of voice, perfectly designed to calm its auditor. Sir John this time was not being rude, though he was still at fault in succumbing to his excessive appetites and indulging them in an unseemly public way to the inconvenience of others. In short, his primary fault in this new example was not rudeness, but plain gluttony; and (as before), but for his act which was at fault, the harm would not have occurred. Likewise (as before) the clumsiness of Lady Mary was a causal factor in the absence of which the harm would not have resulted. This case differs from the earlier one in that the causal relevance condition is not satisfied, for gluttony normally creates a risk to the glutton's own health and comfort, not to the interests of others. Unlike rudeness, it is a primary self-regarding fault. Thus that aspect of Sir John's request for more soup that was faulty was an irrelevant accompaniment of the aspects that contributed to the accident. Hence we could conclude that, although Sir John was *at fault* in what he did, the resulting harm was not *his fault.* [15]

It would be sanguine, however, to expect everybody to agree with this judgment. Mr. Straight-lace, might be altogether indisposed to let Sir John escape the blame so easily. He and others might prefer to reject the causal relevance condition out of hand as too restrictive and urge instead that the blame always be placed on the person *most at fault,* whether the fault is causally relevant or not, providing his faulty action was a genuine causal factor. This alternative would enable one to pin the blame on Sir John in both versions of the soup-spilling story. It does not commend itself to the intuitive understanding in a quiet reflective hour, however, and seems to me to have no other merit than that of letting the indignation and vindictiveness occasioned by harm have a respectable outlet in our moral judgments. If we really want to keep Sir John on the hook, *we do not have to say* that the harm was "really his fault" and thereby abuse a useful and reasonably precise concept. Rather, if we are vindictively inclined, we can say that to impose liability on a person to enforced compensation or other harsh treatment for some harm does not always require that the harm be his fault. This would be the moral equivalent of a departure from what is called "the fault principle" in the law of torts. It is an attempt to do justice to our spontaneous feelings, without confusing our concepts, and has the merits at least of openness and honesty.

Disinterested parties might reject causal relevance as a condition for being to blame in a skeptical way, offering as an alternative to it a radical contextual relativism. One might profess genuine bafflement when asked whose fault was the second soup-spilling, on the grounds that the question cannot be answered until it is known for what purpose it is asked. Is the person singled out for blame the one to be punished, forced to make compensation, expected to apologize? What is the point of narrowly pinning blame? We could, after all, simply tell the narrative as accurately as possible and decline to say whose fault, on balance, the harm was, although that evasive tactic might not be open to, say, an insurance investigator. The point, according to this skeptical theory, is that, after all the facts are in, we are still not committed by "the very logic of the everyday concept" to saying anything at all about whose fault it was. The blame-fixing decision is still logically open and will be determined in part by our practical purposes in raising the question. This skeptical theory, however, strikes me as a combined insight and *non sequitur.* The insight is that we are not *forced* to pinpoint blame unless some practical question like liability hinges on it and that is often the better part of wisdom to decline to do so when one can. But it does not follow from the fact that "his fault" judgments can sometimes be avoided that it is logically open to us to make them in any way we wish when we do make them. I hold, therefore, to the conclusion that, in fixing the blame for harm, we are restricted by our very concepts to the person(s) whose faulty act was a causal factor in the production of the harm in virtue of its causally relevant faulty aspect.

There often is room for discretion in the making of "his fault" judgments, but it comes at a different place and is subject to strict limitations. The person whose fault the harm is said to be *must* satisfy the conditions of the triconditional analysis (and perhaps others as well); but when more than one person is so qualified, the judgment-maker may sometimes choose between them on "pragmatic grounds," letting some of them off the hook. When this discretion is proper, the three conditions of our analysis must be honored as necessary, but they are no longer taken to be sufficient. Suppose one thousand persons satisfy the three conditions of our analysis in respect to harm *X,* and they acted independently (not in concert) over a period of many years. To say simply that the harm is (all) *their* fault, or part his, and part his, and part his, and so on, would be to defeat altogether the usual point of a "his fault" judgment, namely, to fix more narrowly, to single out, to focus upon. When fixings of blame become too diffuse, they can no longer perform this function. They might still, of course, be *true,* but just not very useful. It is not exactly false to say of the first soup-spilling example that it was the fault of *both* Lady Mary and Sir John; but "practical purposes" may dictate instead that we ignore minor or expectable faults and confer all the blame on the chief culprit. At any rate, if it is given that we must, for some practical purpose, single out a wrongdoer more narrowly, then we have discretion to choose among those (but only those) who satisfy the necessary conditions of the tripartite analysis.[16]

FAULT AND TORT LIABILITY

Suppose we accept the revised triconditional analysis of "his fault" but jettison the causal relevance condition as a requisite for tort *liability,* so that we can get the likes of Sir John on the hook after all, even though we admit he is not *to blame* for the harm. The prime consequence of dropping the causal relevance condition is to downgrade the role of causation as a ground for liability and to increase the importance of simply being at fault. If causal relevance is not required, it would seem that being at fault is the one centrally important necessary condition for liability, and indeed so important as to render the causal condition itself a mere dispensable formality. To upgrade the fault condition to that extent is most likely to seem reasonable when the fault is disproportionately greater than the harm it occasions. Imagine a heinously faulty act that is a necessary causal condition for a relatively minor harm. Suppose that *A,* a matricidal fiend, in the cruelest way possible sets himself to shoot his mother dead just as *B,* the lady across the street, is fondling a delicate and fragile art object. The sound of the revolver shot startles *B,* causing her to drop the art object which shatters beyond repair. Is its loss *A's* fault? Let us assume (for the sake of the argument) that the murderous act was at fault in at least two ways: (1) it created a certainty of death or severe injury to the actor's mother (the primary way it was at fault); and (2), in making a loud report, it created an unreasonable risk to (among other things) the art objects of neighbors. Thus, in virtue of (2), *A* is at fault in the manner required for his being to blame for breaking the neighbor's glass vase. His act caused the breaking and did so in virtue of its faulty aspect (2); hence it was his fault. But even if he had (thoughtfully) used a silencer on the gun, and nevertheless the very slight noise caused by his act had startled a supernervous vase-fondling neighbor, causing the dropping and breaking, we might find it proper to charge him for the damage *even though the loss was not his fault.* (The "faulty aspect" of his act—its heinousness—was causally irrelevant to that loss.) It is precisely this kind of case where common sense seems most at home without the causal relevance condition; for no question of "fairness" to the faulty one is likely to trouble us when his fault is so great.

Any number of minor harms of which his act was a necessary condition can be charged to his moral bill without disturbing us—at least so long as we remain "spontaneous" and unreflective.

It is another matter, however, when the harm is disproportionately greater than the fault, when a mere slap causes an unsuspected hemophiliac to bleed to death, or a clumsy slip on the sidewalk leads one to bump an "old soldier with an egg shell skull," causing his death. Hart and Honoré suggest that even here commonsense considerations can help justify abandonment, in some cases at least, of the causal relevance condition by mitigating its apparent harshness:

The apparent unfairness of holding a defendant liable for a loss much greater than he could foresee to some extent disappears when we consider that a defendant is often negligent without suffering punishment or having to pay compensation. I may drive at an excessive speed a hundred times before the one occasion on which my speeding causes harm. The justice of holding me liable, should the harm on that occasion turn out to be extraordinarily grave, must be judged in the light of the hundred other occasions on which, without deserving such luck, I have incurred no liability.[17]

This argument is reminiscent of the Augustinian theory of salvation. We are all sinners; therefore, no one really deserves to be saved. Hence if anyone at all is saved, it can only be through God's supererogatory grace. The others are (relatively) unlucky; but, being undeserving sinners, they can have no just complaint. All of us are negligent, goes the parallel argument; so none of us really deserves to escape liability for great harm. That majority of us who do escape are lucky, but the others who fall into liability in excess of their fault on the occasion have no just complaint, since they have accumulated enough fault on other occasions to redress the disproportion.

If justice truly requires (as the Hart-Honoré argument suggests) that blame and liability be properly apportioned to *all* a person's faults as accumulated in the long run, causal linkage to harm aside, why not go all the way in this direction and drop the "causal factor" condition altogether in the interest of Aristotelian "due proportion" and fairness? To say that we are all negligent is to say that on other occasions, at least, we have all created unreasonable risk of harms, sometimes great harms of one kind or another, to other persons. Even in circumstances where excessive harm actually results, we may have created other risks of a different kind to other individuals, risks which luckily failed to eventuate in harm. Robert Keeton foresees the consequences for the law of torts of taking all such faults seriously in the assignment of liability for particular harms:

. . . if it is relevant to take into account defendant's fault with respect to a risk different from any that would include the harm plaintiff has suffered, then would it not also be relevant to take into account his other faults as well? And would it not seem equally relevant to consider plaintiff's shortcomings? Shall we fix legal responsibility by deciding who is the better and who is the worse person? An affirmative answer might involve us, and quickly too, in the morality of run-of-the-ranch TV drama, where the good guys always win.[18]

In effect Keeton challenges those who would drop the causal relevance condition to explain why they would maintain any causal condition at all. If the existence of fault of one kind or another, on one occasion or another, is the controlling consideration, why do we not simply tally up merits and demerits and distribute our collective compensation expenses in proportion to each person's moral score?

Why not indeed? This is not an unthinkable alternative system. We could, in principle, begin with the notion of a "compensable harm" as one caused by fault. (Other harms could be paid for out of tax funds or voluntary insurance.) Then we could estimate the total cost of compensable harms throughout the country for a one-year period. We would have to acquire funds equal to that amount by assigning demerits throughout the year to persons discovered to be "at fault" in appropriate ways in their conduct. Those who fail to clear their sidewalks of ice and snow within a reasonable period after the finish of a storm would be given so many demerits per square foot of pavement. Those convicted of traffic offenses would be assigned demerits on a graduated scale corresponding to the seriousness (as compounded out of unreasonableness and dangerousness) of their offense. Then, at the end of the year, the total cost of compensable harms would be divided by the total number of assigned demerits to yield the dollar value per demerit. and each person would be fined the dollar equivalent of the sum of his demerits. These fines would all go into a central fund used to compensate all victims of faulty accidents and crimes. Such a system would impose on some persons penalties disproportionately greater than the harm they actually caused; others would pay less than the harm they caused; but as far as is practically possible, everyone would be fined in exact proportion to the unreasonable risks he created (as well as certain and deliberate harms) to others.[19]

The system just described could be called a system of "liability without *contributory* fault," since it bypasses a causation requirement. It is a system of liability based on fault simply, whether or not the fault contributes to harm. It thus differs sharply from the traditional system of liability based in part upon what is called *the fault principle,* which requires that accidental losses be borne by the party whose fault the accident was. This is liability based on "his fault" ascriptions, rather than "at fault" imputations. In contrast, the principle underlying a system of liability based on fault without causation might well be called the *retributive theory of torts.* It surely deserves this name drawn from the criminal law more than the so-called fault principle does since it bases liability *entirely* upon fault purged of all extraneous and fortuitous elements. To be sure, what is called retributivism in the criminal law[20] is a principle that would base (criminal) liability entirely on *moral* fault, and most retributivists would oppose punishing nonmoral faults, including much negligence, as ardently as they would oppose punishing the wholly faultless. A retributive principle of reparation *could* take this very moralistic form. As we have seen, legal negligence is always supervenient upon a fault of some other kind, sometimes "moral" (callousness, inconsiderateness, self-centeredness), sometimes not (timidity, excitability, awkwardness). A moralistic principle would issue demerits to negligence only when it is supervenient upon a fault judged to be a *moral* failing. In a sense, the more inclusive version of the theory is more "moralistic" still, since it treats even nonmoral failings as essentially deserving of penalty, that is, just *as if* they were moral failings. We can safely avoid these complications here.

One way to understand the retributive theory of torts is to relate it to, or derive it from, a general moral theory that bears the name of retributivism. In treating of this more general theory, it is very important to distinguish a strong from a weak version, for failure to do so has muddled discussions of retributivisms in criminal law and would very likely do the same in discussion of principles of tort liability. According to the strong version of the general retributive principle, *all* evil or, more generally still, all *fault* deserves its comeuppance; it is an end in itself, quite apart from other consequences, that all wrongdoers (or faulty doers) be made to suffer some penalty, handicap, or forfeiture as a requital

for their wrongdoing. Similarly, it is an end in itself, morally fitting and proper irrespective of other consequences, that the meritorious be rewarded with the means to happiness. Thus the best conceivable world would be that in which the virtuous (or faultless) flourish, the wicked (or, more generally, the faulty) suffer, and those in between perfect virtue and perfect wickedness enjoy happiness or suffer unhappiness in exact proportion to their virtuous and faulty conduct. Both a world in which everyone suffers regardless of moral condition and a world in which everyone flourishes regardless of moral condition would be intrinsically inferior morally to a world in which all and only the good flourish and all and only the bad suffer. If everyone without exception is a miserable sinner, then it is intrinsically better that everybody suffer than that everybody, or even anybody, be happy. There may be intrinsic goods other than the just apportionment of reward and penalty to the virtuous and the faulty respectively; but insofar as a state of affairs deviates from such apportionment, it is intrinsically defective.

Note that this way of putting retributivism makes it apply only to apportionments of a noncomparative kind, where to give to one is not necessarily to take from another and where to take from one is not necessarily to give to another. It is not, therefore, a principle of distributive justice, telling us in the abstract how all pies are to be cut up or how all necessary burdens are to be divided. Indeed, for some situations it would decree that no one get any pie, and in others that no one should suffer any burdens. It is concerned with deserving good or deserving ill, not with deserving one's fair share relative to others. To be sure, the world in which the good suffer and the evil are happy it calls a moral abomination, but not because of the conditions of the parties relative to one another, but rather because the condition of each party is the opposite of what *he* deserves, quite independently of the condition of the others. A world in which every person is equally a sinner and equally very happy would also be moral abomination, on this view, even though it involves no social inequality.

The weaker version of general retributivism, on the other hand, is essentially a comparative principle, applying to situations in which it is given that someone or other must do without, make a sacrifice, or forfeit his interest. The principle simply asserts the moral priority, *ceteris paribus,* of the innocent party. Put most pithily, it is the principle that *fault forfeits first,* if forfeit there must be. If someone must suffer, it is better, *ceteris paribus,* that it be the faulty than the meritorious. This weaker version of retributivism, which permeates the law, especially the criminal law, has strong support in common sense. It commonly governs the distribution of that special kind of benefit called "the benefit of the doubt," so that, where there is doubt, for example, about the deterrent efficacy of a particular mode of punishment for a certain class of crimes, the benefit of that doubt is given to potential victims instead of convicted criminals.

I find the weaker version of retributivism much more plausible intuitively than the stronger, though even it is limited—for example, by the values of intimacy and friendship. (If I negligently spill your coffee cup at lunch, will you insist that I pay for a new cup, or will you prefer to demonstrate how much more important my friendship is to you than the forfeiture of a dime?) The weaker principle allows us to say, if we wish, though it does not require us to say, that universal happiness, if it were possible, would be intrinsically better than happiness for the good only, with the wicked all miserable. (Indeed, what would wickedness come to if its usually negative effect on the happiness of others was universally mitigated or nullified?) The weak principle also permits but does not require us to say that, even though it is better that the faulty forfeit first where there is no alternative to *someone's* forfeiting, it is better still that some other alternative be found.

Now let us return to our tort principles. What is called the "fault principle" (or, better, the "his fault" principle) does not derive from, and indeed is not even compatible with, the strong version of general retributivism. As we have seen, the causal component of "his fault" ascriptions introduces a fortuitous element, repugnant to pure retributivism. People who are very much at fault may luckily avoid causing proportionate harm, and unlucky persons may cause harm in excess of their minor faults. In the former case, little or no harm may be a person's fault even though he is greatly at fault; hence his liability, based on "his fault," will not be the burden he deserves, and the moral universe will be out of joint. In the latter case, unhappily coexistent circumstances may step up the normal magnitude of harm resulting

from a minor fault, and again the defendant's liability will not do proper justice to his actual fault.

The tort principle that is called for by strong retributivism is that which I have called "the retributive theory of torts." Being at fault gets its proper comeuppance from this principle, whether or not it leads directly to harm; and the element of luck— except for luck in escaping detection— is largely eliminated. Hence fault suffers its due penalty, and if that is an end in itself, as strong retributivism maintains, then the retributive theory of torts is well recommended indeed. But the lack of intuitive persuasiveness of the general theory, I think, diminishes the plausibility of its offshoot in torts. Weak retributivism, which is generally more plausible, in my opinion, than its strong counterpart, does not uniquely favor either the retributive theory of torts or the "his fault" principle. Except in straightforwardly comparative contexts where the necessity of forfeiture is given, it takes no stand whatever about principles of tort liability. If *A* and *B* are involved in an accident causing a loss to *B* only, which is wholly *A's* fault, and it is given that either *A* or *B* must pay for the loss, no other source of compensation being available, then the weak principle says that *A* should be made to pay, or rather (put even more weakly in virtue of the *ceteris paribus* clause) it holds that, insofar as the loss was *A's* fault, that is a good and relevant reason why *A* should pay and, in the absence of other relevant considerations, a sufficient reason. In short, if someone has got to be hurt in this affair, let it be the wrongdoer (other things being equal). But where there is necessity that the burden of payment be restricted to the two parties involved, weak retributivism has no application and, indeed, is quite compatible with a whole range of nonfault principles.

One final point remains to be made. If we hold that we are all more or less equally sinners in respect to a certain area of conduct or a certain type of fault—if, for example, we are all as likely, more or less, to be erring defendants as wronged plaintiffs in driving accident suits—then the principle of strong retributivism itself would call for the jettisoning of the "his fault" principle in that area of activity. If fault is distributed equally, the "his fault" principle, in distributing liability *unequally* among a group, will cause a lack of correspondence between fault and penalty. On the assumption of equal distribution of fault, the use of the "his fault" principle would lead to *less* correspondence, *less* exact proportioning of penalty to fault, even than various principles of social insurance that have the effect of spreading the losses as widely as possible among a whole community of persons presumed to be equally faulty. But then these schemes of nonfault liability are supported by strong reasons of their own, principles both of justice and economy,[21] and hardly need this bit of surprising added support from the principle of strong retributivism.

NOTES

1. I intend here no more than what is in the Model Penal Code definition: "A person acts recklessly with respect to a material element of an offense when he consciously disregards a substantial and unjustifiable risk that the material element exists or will result from his conduct.... Recklessness involves conscious risk creation."

2. *Legal Cause in the Law of Torts* (Columbus: Ohio State University Press, 1963), 3. The facts in Keeton's fictitious case are closely similar to those in the actual case of *Larrimore v. American Nat. Ins. Co.,* 184 Okl. 614 (1930).

3. *Ibid.,* 10 and *passim.*

4. The example is from a very helpful letter sent to me by Professor Sturgeon after I read an earlier version of this paper at Cornell in May 1969.

5. The example is just one of many in an extremely thorough criticism of an earlier version of this paper made by Professor Taurek, who was my official commentator at the Chapel Hill Colloquium in Philosophy, Oct. 17–19, 1969.

6. Sturgeon, letter, note 4.

7. *Ibid.*

8. *Ibid.*

9. "Responsibility and Language," *Australasian Journal of Philosophy, 33* (1955), 145.

10. *Laws and Explanation in History* (London: Oxford University Press, 1957), 100.

11. In unusual cases, two or three.

12. The distinction in common sense between a "causal factor" and "the cause" corresponds roughly—very roughly—to the technical legal distinction between "cause in fact" and "proximate cause."

13. A causal factor is an earlier necessary condition in at least the weaker sense of "necessary condition," *viz.,* a member of a set of jointly sufficient conditions whose presence was necessary to the sufficiency of the set; but it need not be necessary in the stronger sense, *viz.,* a necessary element in every set of conditions that would be jointly sufficient, as oxygen is necessary to every instance of combustion. Not all prior necessary conditions, of course, are genuine causal factors. Analytic connections ("But for his having been born, the accident would not have happened") are ruled out, and so are "incidental connections" (earlier speeding bringing one to a given point just at the moment a tree falls on the road). Unlike necessary conditions connected in a merely incidental way to results, causal factors are "necessary elements in a set of conditions generally connected through intermediate stages with it." See H. L. A. Hart and A. M. Honoré, *Causation in the Law* (Oxford: Clarendon Press, 1959), 114. See also Keeton, *Legal Cause,* footnote 2, 62.

14. Dray, *Laws and Explanation in History,* footnote 10, 99–100.

15. Perhaps a better example to illustrate this condition would be the following: Sir John is not a glutton. He has requested only one bowl of soup, but it is spilled by the hostess. But Sir John is at fault in agreeing to have even one bowl passed his way, since he knows, or ought to know, that this kind of soup always gives him indigestion, insomnia, allergic reactions, and hiccups. It is not only imprudent for him to taste it; it is also inconsiderate to his wife, who is usually kept awake all night by his restlessness. When his wife is kept awake after this party, *that* is his fault; but when the hostess spills the soup (which she should not have had to pass his way in the first place), that is *not* his fault.

16. If it is given that a particular "his fault" judgment on a particular occasion must single out one or a small number to be assigned the blame, then the concept of "his fault" can perhaps be understood to limit discretion by providing two additional necessary conditions to the triconditional analysis: (4) there is no other person to whom conditions (1)–(3) apply who is substantially more at fault than the present assignee(s); and (5) there is no other person to whom conditions (1)–(3) apply whose act was a more striking deviation from routine, or of a kind patently more manipulable, or otherwise a more "direct" or "substantial" cause. In the first soup-spilling example, Lady Mary satisfies conditions (1)–(3), but certainly not condition (4) and possibly not condition (5).

17. Hart and Honoré, *Causation in The Law,* footnote 13, 243.

18. Keeton, *Legal Cause in The Law of Torts,* footnote 2, 21.

19. This is not quite true of the system as described in the text, for a man's penalty in that system is determined in part by the number of demerits others incur and the total amount of compensable harm caused, both factors over which he has no control. Thus a man who accumulates one hundred demerits in 1970 might pay a smaller fine than he does in 1971 when he accumulates only seventy five. Instead of assigning demerits, therefore, the system would have to impose penalties directly, according to a fixed and invariant retributive scale. These funds could then go into a pool to compensate victims; and if, in a given year, they prove to be insufficient, they could be supplemented, say, by tax funds instead of stepped-up fines; for, on a purely retributive theory, there is one "fitting" penalty for a given degree of fault, and that uniquely correct quantum should be independent of the fluctuations of the marketplace.

20. "Retributivism" has served as the name of the large number of distinct theories of the grounds for justifiable punishment having little in common except that they are all nonutilitarian. The theories referred to in the text are those that hold that a certain degree of pain or deprivation is *deserved* by, or matches, fits, or suits, a certain magnitude of evil, quite apart from consequences. The emphasis is on fitness or proportion; and often the theorists invoke aesthetic analogies. Cf. the definitions of A. C. Ewing in *The Morality of Punishment* (London: Kegan Paul, Trench, Trubner & Co., 1929), 13, and John Rawls, "Two Concepts of Rules," *The Philosophical Review,* 64 (1955), 4–5 G. E. Morre's "theory of organic unities" also suggests this kind of retributivism. But there are many other theories that have borne the retributive label which I do not refer to here—e.g., Hegel's theory of annulment; theories of punishment as putting the universe

back in joint, or wiping clean the criminal's slate, or paying a debt to society, or expiating a sin, or expressing social denunciation, or demonstrating to the criminal the logical consequences of the universalization of his maxim, or satisfying the natural instinct for vengeance, or preventing the criminal from prospering while his victim suffers, or restoring a moral equilibrium between the "burdens" of conformity to law as against the "benefits" of disobedience; and even the "logical truism" of A. M. Quinton (*Analysis,* 14 [1954]).

21. E.g., the *benefit principle* (of commutative justice) that accidental losses should be borne according to the degree to which people benefit from an enterprise or form of activity; the *deep pocket principle* (of distributive justice) that the burden of accidental losses should be borne by those most able to pay in direct proportion to that ability; the *spread-it-out principle* that the cost of accidental losses should be spread as widely as possible "both interpersonally and intertemporally"; the *safety* or *loss-diminution principle* that the method of distributing losses that leads to the smallest net amount of loss to be distributed is the best one.

THE DILEMMA OF THE GOOD SAMARITAN

A. M. HONORÉ

Law, Morals and Rescue*

A woman, viciously attacked, lies bleeding in the street. Fifty people pass by on the other side. A man destroys his barn to prevent a fire spreading to his neighbor's property. The neighbor refuses to compensate him. A young potholer foolishly becomes trapped below ground. A more experienced man, coming to his aid, breaks a leg. When we contemplate facts such as these, three questions seem to confront us concerning law, morals, and their interrelation. The first is about the shared morality of our society. Is there in modern industrial society, which is the only one most of us know, a shared attitude of praise or condemnation, encouragement, or dissuasion about helping those in peril? If so, two further points arise. Should the law, with its mechanisms of inducement, rewards, and compensation, be used to encourage what the shared morality treats as laudable and discourage what it reprobates? Should the law, thirdly, go further and, by the use of threats and penalties, "enforce" morality, as the saying goes? These, it seems, are the main issues. In part they concern matters which, in England at least, have lately stirred up a passionate debate.[1] Is it justifiable to use the mechanism of criminal law to "enforce" the shared morality, for instance in matters of sex? Greeks and Trojans have sallied forth and the clash of arms has rung out. Our concern, however, is with something wider and different: not sex, not only "enforcement," not only crime. I shall have a word later on, to say in criticism of the use of the word "enforce" in this context. If we pass it for the moment, it yet remains true that "enforcement" is only part of what the law can do in the Good Samaritan situation. Apart from criminal sanctions, the law can encourage or discourage compliance with the shared morality by the use of techniques drawn from tort, contract, and resti-

tution. Even "enforcement" is not confined to criminal law, because tort law, too, can be used to impose an obligation to aid others.

Our concern is not only wider but different from that of the jurists by whose brilliant and elevated jousting we have been entertained. They have debated whether some parts of the law which coincide with common morality should be scrapped. We, on the other hand, wish to know whether parts of morality, at present outside the law, should be incorporated in it. (I mean here Anglo-American law and not those systems in which this has already come about.) Some people feel that the intrusion of law into the private sphere of sex is indecent and outrageous. Others feel outraged by the failure of the law to intrude in relation to rescue and rescuers. Is the refusal to "enforce" the moral obligation to help others itself a moral offense, of which lawyers and legislators have been guilty in the English-speaking world this hundred years? Does the affront of this refusal bring the law and lawyers into disrepute? Should the law encourage or even insist on Do-Goodery? Or would this be an intrusion into yet another private sphere, not of sex, but of conscience?

Clearly we have a moral issue on our hands, and one which is concerned not with the "enforcement" of morals but with its nonenforcement. A number of writers, following Bentham[2] and Mill,[3] have advocated a legal obligation to rescue. Ames[4] and Bohlen[5] put forward an earnest plea to the same effect. But, though they mentioned, they did not closely analyze the moral issues. It is with these that I shall be principally concerned.

I THE SHARED MORALITY IN MATTERS OF RESCUE

An essential preliminary to the survey of the larger vistas of law and morals is to clear our minds about our moral views in the matter of aid to those in peril. By "our moral views" I mean the shared or common morality. Obviously this is not

*Law, Morals and Rescue," by Antony M. Honoré, from the book *The Good Samaritan and The Law,* ed. by James M. Ratcliffe (New York: Doubleday & Co., Inc., 1966), pp. 225–42, copyright © 1966 by James M. Ratcliffe. Reprinted by permission of Doubleday & Company, Inc.

the same as the statement of what people actually do in a given society—the common practice of mankind. Their actions may fall short of their moral ideals and pretensions. Nor is it the same as that which an individual may accept for himself as morally obligatory. There is a distinction between that which the individual accepts for himself and that which he regards as being of general application. A man may think he has higher ideals, a stricter sense of obligation or duty, than the ordinary run of men could well be expected to entertain. This cherished personal morality, it seems to me, is no part or ingredient of the shared morality, though it may come, in time, to spread to others and so to influence the shared morality.

The shared morality consists, rather, of those moral ideals and duties or obligations which the bulk of the community regard as applying to persons generally. But is the notion, defined, anything more than a figment? Ought we to refrain from speculating about its content until social surveys have determined whether it really exists? I think one must frankly concede that the results of properly conducted surveys would be far more authoritative than the guesses of moralists or lawyers. The survey which Messrs. Cohen, Robson, and Bates sought to ascertain the moral sense of the Nebraska community on parent-child relations[6] is, no doubt, a forerunner of what will, in time, become common practice. The shared morality of which I am speaking is not, however, quite what the Nebraska inquiry "community values" were defined as the "choices, expressed verbally, which members of the community feel the law-making authorities ought to make if confronted with alternative courses of action in specified circumstances."[7] These choices surely represent opinion as to legislation on moral issues rather than the shared morality itself. They tell us what people think legislators should do. No doubt there is a close, even a very close, connection between the two. Our view of what the law should be will be powerfully shaped by our notions of right and wrong, of what is desirable and what objectionable, but surely the two cannot without more be identified? It must *a priori* be an open question whether people who share moral ideas also think that these should be mirrored in the law. If they do, that is also a fact susceptible of and demanding confirmation by a properly conducted survey.

It remains doubtful, therefore, whether a suitable technique has yet been evolved for testing the existence and content of the shared morality of a community. Certainly the results are not yet to hand in a usable form. In the meantime, life does not stand still. Decisions must be reached with the aid of such information and intuition as we may possess. We cannot shirk the question of what shared morality says about rescues and rescuers on the excuse that one day, we hope, a truly reliable answer will be available.

It is unwise in thinking about the shared morality to treat morality as an undifferentiated mass. For instance, there is a distinction between moral ideals and moral duties.[8] This is not the same as the previous distinction between a man's personal morality and the morality which he regards as of general application. Of course, a connection exists. A person may accept as an obligation for himself what he thinks of merely as an ideal for others. Broadly speaking, moral ideals concern patterns of conduct which are admired but not exigible. Moral duties, on the other hand, concern conduct which is required but not admired. With an important exception, to which I shall come, merely to do one's duty evokes no comment. Moral duties are pitched at a point where the conformity of the ordinary man can reasonably be expected. As a corollary, while it is tolerable, if deplorable, to fall short of the highest ideals, it is not permissible to neglect one's duties.

Certain virtues, notably altruism and generosity, depend on absence of obligation. It is not altruistic to pay one's debts, or generous to support one's parents (in the latter case the duty may in Anglo-American law be merely moral, but this makes no difference). Other virtues seem to hover between the status of ideals and duties. Is this, perhaps, true of the "neighborliness" which the parable of the Good Samaritan is meant both to illustrate and to inculcate? According to Matthew[9] and Mark,[10] the precept "love your neighbor as yourself" expresses a "commandment" and presumably imposes an obligation. Luke,[11] in contrast, treats it as pointing the way to perfection or "eternal life," a moral ideal. It may be that giving aid to those in peril is sometimes an ideal, sometimes a duty. At least three situations demand separate treatment:

1 The first is the rescue undertaken by one who has professional or quasi-professional duty to undertake rescues. A fireman or life-saver is a professional rescuer. Doctors, nurses, and other members of the medical profession have a duty to save life, which, at times, demands that they should give help in an emergency. A priest must comfort the dying, a policeman must stop acts of violence. Besides these true professionals, there

are what one may call devoted amateurs; for instance, experienced mountaineers or potholers, who hold themselves out as ready to effect rescues and, I am told, often welcome the chance to display their skills. Strictly speaking, none of these are "volunteers." They are only doing what they are bound by their calling or public profession to do. A doctor is not praised for coming promptly to the scene of an accident; that is only what we expect. He would be blamed if he delayed or refused to come. But this morally neutral reaction is appropriate only when the rescuer acts without risk or serious inconvenience to himself. If the fireman, policeman, or life-saver risks life or limb to help the imperiled, he deserves and receives praise, because there is an element of self-sacrifice or even heroism in his conduct, though what he does is clearly his duty. Heroism and self-sacrifice, unlike altruism, can be evinced both by those who do their duty and those who have no duty to do.

2 The second is the rescue undertaken by one who has special ties with the person imperiled. Family links, employment, and other associative ties may generate a duty to come to the help of a class of persons more limited than those whom the professional or professed rescuer is bound to assist. It is a parent's duty to snatch his child from the path of an oncoming automobile, an employer's to rescue the workman who has been trapped in the factory machine. It may well be their duty to risk their own safety should that prove necessary. Like the professional rescuer, they can expect no encomium merely for helping, but if they risk themselves they merit commendation.

3 The third situation is that of a person not bound by his profession or by special links with the person imperiled to come to his aid. Even in this case, common opinion would, perhaps, see a limited duty to assist when this is possible without risk or grave inconvenience to the rescuer. "It is undoubtedly the moral duty," an American judge has said, "of every person to extend to others assistance when in danger, to throw, for instance, a plank or rope to the drowning man or make other efforts for his rescue, and if such efforts should be omitted by anyone when they could be made without imperilling his own life, he would, by his conduct, draw upon himself the censure and reproach of good men."[12] Common humanity, then, forges between us a link, but a weak one. The duty stops short at the brink of danger. Samaritans, it is held, must be good, but need not be moral athletes.

It is in this third situation alone, when the rescuer, bound by no professional duty or special tie to the person imperiled, exposes himself to danger, that we really call him a "volunteer." I appreciate that in Anglo-American law the notion of the "volunteer" has been at times twisted beyond recall. In order to deny the rescuer a remedy, the doctrine of voluntary assumption of risk has sometimes been extended to bar those who were merely doing their duty or responding to an appeal for help.[13] Conversely, in order to afford the rescuer a remedy, courts have at other times treated the altruist as if he were simply doing his plain duty and concluded that his action was a necessary consequence of the hazard and so of the fault of the person who created it.[14] But this is just legal fiction.

If this moral morphology is reasonably accurate, we have four types of rescuer and nonrescuer to contend with. This first is the priest or Levite who passes by on the other side. The second, in ascending order of excellence, is the man who does no more than he is bound to do, whether his duty arises from some special link with the person imperiled, or from common humanity. Third is he who, in doing his duty exposes himself to risk: possibly a hero. The fourth is the true volunteer altruistically exposing himself to danger to help those to whom he is bound by no special tie: perhaps a hero, too.

What should the law have to say to them?

II THE MYTH OF NONINTERVENTION

First, should the law encourage or discourage the rescuer, or should it remain neutral? Members of my generation remember nonintervention as the name of a policy which, during the Spanish Civil War, ensured the victory of the side which cheated most. It was called by Tallyrand a metaphysical conception, which means very much the same thing as intervention. So with the intervention of law in the sphere of morals. There is no neutrality. If the law does not encourage rescue, it is sure to discourage it. If it does not compensate, it will indirectly penalize. If the rescuer who suffers injury or incurs expense or simply expends his skill goes without compensation, the law, so far as it influences conduct at all, is discouraging rescue.

Perhaps one day sociology will devise means of discovering whether people are really influenced in what they do by the thought of legal remedies. In the meantime, it would be altogether too facile to assume that they are not. A doctor living near a dangerous crossroads is continually called to minister to the victims of the road. The injured are unconscious or, if conscious, are in no mood to contract or fill in National Health cards. Will the doctor come more readily and care for them more thoroughly if he knows he will be paid? If so, he is a man, not an angel. A mountain guide with a hungry family is called to rescue a foolish climber trapped on the north face of the Eiger. Does anyone imagine him to be indifferent to the question how his family will be kept if he is killed?

The law cannot stay out of the fight and, if it cannot, there is surely a strong case for compensating the rescuer. To do so will be in the interests of those who might be saved. The community applauds the Good Samaritan. So the law, if it encourages rescue, is helping to satisfy the interests of individuals and the wants of the community. If we think of law as being, among other things, a social service designed to maximize welfare and happiness, this is exactly what the law ought to do. One department of the law's service to society will be its moral service, which it performs by encouraging with the appropriate technical remedies whatever is morally approved and discouraging what is condemned.

Unquestionably there are limits to this function of the law. I will deal with only three. The most obvious is the limit set by oppression. If the encouragement of the shared morality and the discouragement of its breach would be a hardship to some without sufficient corresponding benefit to them or to others, the law should not endorse it. The fact that racial prejudice is approved in a given community does not mean that the courts must hold leases to Negroes in white residential areas void. But the encouragement of rescue will oppress neither rescuer nor rescued. The rescued benefits from being saved, and even if he is compelled to compensate the rescuer he will be, by and large, better off. It is true that compensation may be burdensome and I should not care to argue that civil remedies are necessarily less harsh than punishment. If an uninsured person has to pay heavy damages, he is worse off than if he were fined, for the fine, unlike the damages, is geared to his means. But this fact depends on the rules about assessment of damages in Anglo-American law, and these might be changed. It would be no hardship to suggest that the rescuer should receive compensation, if necessary, from the person imperiled, in accordance with the latter's means: *in id quod facere potest,* as the Roman formula ran.

Another limit or supposed limit may be set by the principle that virtue should be its own reward. Strictly speaking, I doubt if this applies to proposals for compensation as opposed to rewards. Still, the doctor's claim to be paid for his ministrations to the unconscious victim of a road accident may be called a claim for reward. Would it be paid? Surely the argument is obtuse. No one is compelled to claim a reward he does not want. The doctor, like the finder of lost property, can preserve immaculate his moral idealism if he wishes. No one can be compelled to be compensated.

A third limit concerns the border line between altruism and meddling. Of course we do not want our next-door neighbor to rescue the baby every time he screams or to interrupt our family quarrels. But this merely shows that the received morality draws the line at officiousness. The test of what is officious will usually be whether the intending rescuer would reasonably suppose that his help will be welcome. If the victim objects or would be expected to object, the rescuer should abstain. But this can hardly apply to those victims who are too young or too deranged to know their own interests, and one might justify the rescue of a person attempting suicide (in a jurisdiction in which suicide is not a crime) on the ground that those who attempt it often lack a settled determination in the matter.

The line will be difficult to draw exactly, but lawyers are professional line-drawers. The relevant factors are easy enough to list: the gravity of the peril, the chances of successful intervention, the attitude of the victim, and the likelihood that another better-qualified rescuer will act.

None of the three limits mentioned seems to alter the proposition that the law would be a poor thing if it did not in general encourage rescue. The means available to do this are essentially the compensation of the rescuer for expenses and injury and the rewarding of his services. It is convenient to take these separately.

1 *Injury.* No immediate difficulty is felt if the rescuer is covered by a personal accident policy or an insurance scheme connected with his employment, as would usually be true of firemen and other professional rescuers. There will still remain the question whether the insurer should be entitled to shift the loss to the person responsible for the peril. Certainly it makes for simplicity if he cannot.

When there is no insurance cover the problem is: Where should the compensation come from? Most people would be inclined to place it in the first instance on the person through whose fault the peril arose, whether the person imperiled or another. In order to justify making the person imperiled liable when he had been at fault, Bohlen argued that the basis of liability was the tendency of the defendant's conduct to cause the rescuer to take the risk involved in the attempted rescue.[15] If "cause" is to be taken seriously, this suggests that the rescuer who acts under a sense of obligation would recover for his injury, while the pure altruist would not, because the latter's act is a fresh cause. Yet altruism is not less but more worthy of the law's encouragement than the conscientious performance of one's duty. If in *Carnea v. Buyea*[16] the plaintiff who snatched the defendant from the path of the runaway automobile had been unrelated to the defendant, could that reasonably have been a ground for denying him recovery? Surely the remedy should not be confined to cases where the peril "causes" the rescue, but should extend to those in which it merely prompts the rescuer.

Other writers and courts rely on foreseeability as the ground of liabiliy. This, too, is open to objection. Suppose an intrepid but foolhardy explorer is stranded in an area where rescue is atrociously difficult and rescuers scarce. By the heroism of a James Bond he is saved. Surely the fact that rescue could not be foreseen makes no difference to Bond's claim for compensation? Is not the real basis of liability the twofold fact that the person imperiled has created a risk from which he wishes to be saved (whether he thinks rescue likely or not) and that his peril has prompted another to come to his aid (whether it has "caused" him to do so or not).

I have been dealing with the rationale of the imperiled person's duty to compensate the rescuer when the former is at fault. Legally speaking, this is the case that has evoked discussion, because it said that the person in peril owes himself no duty. When the peril is created by a third person, the objection is inapplicable. If the third person is at fault, he should be liable to compensate the rescuer for the reasons already given. If no one is at fault, it still remains a question whether compensation should be payable by either the person imperiled or the state. A remedy against the innocent person in peril can be justified either, if he is saved, on the ground that he has benefited at the rescuer's expense and should not take the benefit without paying the cost of its procurement or (whether he is saved or not) on the ground of unauthorized agency. The guiding notion of this (the Roman *negotiorum gestio* and the French *gestion d'affaire*) is that the agent, acting without the principal's authority, never-

theless does what the principal might be presumed to want done, when it is impracticable to obtain his consent. (If there is actual consent, for instance, if the person in peril calls for help, so much the easier, legally speaking, to justify giving a remedy.)[17]

Anglo-American law, in contrast with civil systems, is impregnated with the maxim, "Mind your own business," though recently there have been signs of a change. If we outflank the maxim by asserting that, to a limited extent, the peril of one is the business of all, it seems fair to make the person imperiled, though free from fault, indemnify the rescuer albeit only so far as his means reasonably permit.

None of the headings so far mentioned may afford an adequate remedy to the rescuer. In that case a state compensation scheme might well fill the gap. If the state is to compensate the victims of crimes of violence, as is now done in England,[18] why not compensate the equal heroism of those who suffer injury in effecting rescues?

2 *Expenses.* In principle the same rules should apply to expenses incurred by the rescuer as to injuries received by him. Two points may be noted. One is that the expense of organizing a rescue may nowadays be enormous. Suppose the Air Force presents the lost mariner with a bill for gasoline, maintenance of aircraft, wages of crew, and so on, perhaps incurred over several days of search. The crushing liability must be mitigated by having regard for the mariner's probably slender means. The other point is that in Anglo-American law there is a traditional reluctance to grant tort actions for negligence when the loss suffered is merely pecuniary. The rescuer who incurs expense but suffers no physical injury may thus find the way barred. It seems that courts will have to extend the bounds of the tort of negligence and the law of restitution if adequate remedies are to be supplied without legislative intervention. These are already some signs that this is happening.[19]

3 *Rewards.* The moral objections to rewarding altruism, we saw, are misconceived. But is there a positive case to be made in favor of rewarding rescuers? In practice, outstanding acts of courage in effecting rescue are marked by the award of medals and decorations. Many persons saved from danger would think themselves morally bound to offer something to their rescuers. But legal claim to be paid is usually voiced only by the professional rescuer, especially the self-employed, who may spend much time and energy in this way. Take our friend the doctor who lives

near an accident black spot. It is mere fiction to say that the unconscious victim impliedly contracts to pay for treatment.[20] Two other theories are possible: one, that payment is less a true reward than compensation for loss of profitable time; the other, that the person in peril, if he could have been consulted, would have agreed to pay for the treatment because medical services are normally paid for. The second theory, unlike the first, has a narrow range, because it does not extend to a rescuer whose services are normally given free.

III A LEGAL DUTY TO AID THOSE IN PERIL?

My third question raises an issue concerning what is usually called the "enforcement" of morals. The use of this word is, I think, apt to mislead. Literally speaking, the law cannot force citizens to do anything, but only to submit to deprivation of freedom, or to having their money taken from them. Even if "enforcement" is taken, as it normally is, in an extended sense, the notion that morality is enforced by law carries with it the false implication that it is not enforced apart from law. Yet the chief agent for enforcing morality is public opinion. If the approval or disapproval of family and friends is not visited on those who conform or rebel, the conduct in question is not part of the shared morality. Few people, I imagine, would rather incur the censure of family and friends than pay a sum of damages or a fine. This should lead us to suspect that the law, when it imposes a duty to do what the shared morality already requires, is not enforcing but *reflecting, reinforcing,* and *specifying* morality.

There are strong reasons, I think, why the law should reflect, reinforce, and specify, at least that segment of the shared morality which consists in moral duties owed to others. The first is the advantage to those who stand to benefit. It is true that legal incentives probably influence no more than a tiny minority, but they certainly influence some. A driver sees the victim of a highway accident bleeding by the roadside. He knows he ought to stop, but is tempted to drive on in order to keep an assignment. The thought that there is a law requiring him to stop may pull him up short.

Even if the impact of the law is confined to a few, there is a special reason for reinforcing the duty to aid persons in peril. Peril means danger of death or serious injury or, at least, of grave damage to property. The more serious the harm to be averted, the more worthwhile it is to save

even a handful of those who would otherwise suffer irretrievable injury or death.

Secondly, there are some reasons for holding that the law ought in general to mirror moral obligations. In doing so, it ministers to an expectation entertained by the majority of citizens. The lawyer is, perhaps, so used to rules which permit men to flout their moral duties that he is at times benumbed. Promises made without consideration are not binding. A promisor can normally not be compelled to perform his promise but only to pay damage. Children need not support their parents. Samaritans need not be good. When we first learned these rules in law school, I daresay we were a little shocked, but the shock has worn off. It has not worn off the layman.

There are several elements in the sense of shock which laymen feel at the permissive state of the law in regard to moral duties. First, there is the "sense of injustice" of which Edmund Cahn has spoken.[21] If the law permits others to do with impunity that which I am tempted to do, but resist, what is the point of my resistance to temptation? The moral-breaker, like the unpunished lawbreaker, secures an unjust advantage at my expense.

A second element in the layman's sense of shock is the feeling that the law, like an overpermissive father, has set its standard too low. Just as a child loses respect for a father who allows him to back out of his promises, so the community will fail to respect the law which does likewise. It is, I imagine, another of those indubitable and unprovable commonplaces which are the very meat of jurisprudence that people's attitudes to particular laws often depend on their reverence for the law as a whole. If so, the failure of the law to reflect and reinforce moral duties undermines other, quite distinct laws. It may not be sensible for people to think of law in this way as a single, personified whole, but apparently they do.

A third element in the layman's sense of shock is the feeling that the guiding hand has failed. People to some degree expect a lead from the law, not merely threats and incentives. Rules of law which mirror moral duties have, among other things, an educative function. They formulate, in a way which, though not infallible is yet in a sense authoritative, the content of the shared morality. They specify morality by marking, with more precision than the diffused sense of the people can manage, the minimum that can be tolerated.

The law cannot make men good, but it can, in the sphere of duty at least, encourage and help them to do good. It not only can but should reinforce the sanctions of public opinion, for the reasons given, unless it would be oppressive or impractible to do so. I need say little of the practicability of imposing a duty to aid those in peril. France, Germany, and other countries have tried it out and found that it works reasonably well. But would it be oppressive? The mere fact that the majority is shocked at certain conduct does not, in my view, justify them in imposing civil or criminal liability unless there is also a balance of advantage in doing so. Difficult as it may be to strike a balance, we have in the case of rescue to add to the evils of injustice, disrespect, and want of guidance (should the law impose no duty to act) the possible benefit of those in peril if such duty is imposed. Then we must subtract the hardship of making people conform to accepted standards of neighborliness or suffer penalties. If the balance is positive, the law not merely may, but should, intervene. It has been urged that there is something peculiarly irksome in requiring people to take positive action as opposed to subjecting them to mere prohibitions. Why this should be so is a mystery. Perhaps we have a picture of Joe lounging in an armchair. It is more effort for him to get up than to stay where he is. But this is not how the law operates. Prohibitions are usually imposed because there is a strong urge or temptation to disregard them. To control the violent impulses of our nature is surely more arduous than to overcome the temptation selfishly to leave others in the lurch. Certainly there are important spheres, for instance, taxation and military service, where the law does not shrink from demanding positive action. Why should it do so in the law of rescue?

If it is argued that to require aid to be given to those in peril saps the roots of altruism by diminishing the opportunities for its exercise, the reply would be that the proposal is merely to impose a legal duty in situations where morality already sees one. Those who go beyond their moral duty will also be going beyond their legal duty. They lose no occasion for displaying altruism, merely because the law reflects a situation which *de facto* already exists.

The apparent objections to the introduction of a legal duty to rescue hardly withstand scrutiny. Perhaps the most substantial of them, in Anglo-American law, is simply tradition. Self-reliance, the outlook epitomized in the words, "Thank you, Jack, I'm all right," an irrational conviction that because law and morals do not always coincide there is some virtue in their being different,[22] all combine to frustrate the promptings of moral

sensibility. One cannot but sense in some judicial utterances a certain pride in the irrational, incalculable depravity of the law, as if this demonstrated its status as an esoteric science, inaccessible to the common run of mankind. As the Russians said of Stalin: a monster, but ours. I will quote one or two.

"The only duty arising under such circumstance [that is, when one's employee catches her hand and wrist in a mangle] is one of humanity and for a breach thereof the law does not, so far as we are informed, impose any liability."[23] Hence, there is no need to help her to free her hand. "With purely moral obligations the law does not deal. For example, the priest and the Levite who passed by on the other side were not, it is supposed, liable at law for the continued suffering of the man who fell among thieves, which they might and morally ought to have prevented or relieved."[24] In the case from which the quotation is taken, it was held to be no legal wrong for a mill owner to allow a boy of eight to meddle with dangerous machinery, in which his hand was crushed. Indeed, the boy was guilty of committing a trespass when he touched the machinery.

Two thousand years ago a Jewish lawyer demanded a definition of the term "neighbor." This makes him, I suppose, an analytical jurist. Whether the tale of the Samaritan answered his perplexities we cannot say. But he would surely have been astonished had he been informed that there were two answers to his question, one if he was asking as a lawyer, another if he was asking as a layman. To him, neighbor was neighbor and duty, duty. Perhaps this ancient lawyer's tale has a moral for law and lawyers today.

NOTES

1. P. Devlin, *The Enforcement of Morals* (Maccabaean Lecture, 1958), reprinted in *The Enforcement of Morals* (Oxford U. P., 1965); W. Friedmann in 4 *Natural Law Forum* (1964), 151; H. L. A. Hart, *Law, Liberty and Morality* (Oxford U. P., 1963); L. Henkin in 63 *Col. L. Rev.* (1969) 393; G. Hughes in 71 *Yale L. J.* (1961) 622; M. Ginsberg in 1964 *British Journal of Criminology,* 283; A. W. Mewett in 14 *Toronto L. J.* (1962) 213; E. Rostow in 1960 *Cambridge L. J.* 174 reprinted in *The Sovereign Prerogative* (Yale U. P., 1962); N. St. John-Stevas, *Life, Death and the Law* (1961); R. S. Summers in 38 *New York U. L. Rev.* (1963), 1201; B. Wootton, *Crime and the Criminal Law* (Stevens, 1963), 41.

2. J. Bentham, *Principles of Morals and Legislation,* 323 ("Who is there that in any of these cases would think punishment misapplied?").

3. J. S. Mill, *On Liberty,* Introduction ("There are also many positive acts for the benefit of others, which he may rightfully be compelled to perform . . . such as saving a fellow-creature's life").

4. J. B. Ames, *Law and Morals, supra,* pp. 1–21.

5. F. Bohlen, *The Moral Duty to Aid Others As a Basis of Liability, 56 U. Pa. L. Rev.* (1908) 215, 316.

6. J. Cohen, R. A. H. Robson, and A. Bates, *Ascertaining the Moral Sense of the Community,* 8 *Journal of Legal Education* (1955–56) 137.

7. *Ibid.*

8. E. Cahn, *The Moral Decision* (1956), 39.

9. Matthew 22:34.

10. Mark 12:28

11. Luke 10:25.

12. U.S. v, Knowles (1864) 26 Fed. Cas. 801.

13. Cutler v. United Dairies (1933) 2 K. B. 297.

14. Pollock, *Torts* (15th ed.), 370; Haynes v. Harwood (1953) 1 K.B. at 163; Morgan v. Aylen (1942)1 All E. R. 489; Baker v. Hopkins (1959) 1 W. L. R. 966.

15. F. Bohlen, *Studies in the Law of Tort,* 569 n. 33.

16. 271 App. Div. 338. 65 N.Y.S. 2d 902 (1946).

17. Brugh v. Bigelow (1944) 16 N.Y.S. 2d 902 (1946).

18. Assessed by the Criminal Injuries Compensation Board (1964).

19. Hadley Byrne v. Heller (1964) A. C. 465.

20. Cotnam v. Wisdom 83 Ark. 601, 104 S.W. 164. 119 Am. St. R. 157 (1907); Greenspan v. Slate 12 N.J. 426, 97 Atl. 2d 390 (1953).

21. E. Cahn, *The Sense of Injustice* (1949); *The Moral Decision* (1956).

22. Historicus (Sir W. Harcourt), *Some Questions of International Law* (1863), 76, cited in R. Pound, *Law and Morals* (1924), 40. The argument that there is value in moral experiments does not apply to experiments in leaving others in the lurch.

23. Allen v. Hixson 36 S.E. 810 (1900).

24. Buch v. Amory Manufacturing Co. 69 N.H. 247; 44 Atl. 809 (1897).

PEOPLE v. YOUNG

Appellate Division, New York Supreme Court, 1961*

BREITEL, Justice.

The question is whether one is criminally liable for assault in the third degree if he goes to the aid of another who he mistakenly, but reasonably, believes is being unlawfully beaten, and thereby injures one of the apparent assaulters. In truth, the seeming victim was being lawfully arrested by two police officers in plain clothes. Defendant stands convicted of such a criminal assault, for which he received a sentence of 60 days in the workhouse, the execution of such sentence being suspended.

Defendant, aged 40, regularly employed, and with a clean record except for an $8 fine in connection with a disorderly conduct charge 19 years before in Birmingham, Alabama, observed two middle-aged men beating and struggling with a youth of 18. This was at 3:40 P.M. on October 17, 1958 in front of 64 West 64th Street in Manhattan. Defendant was acquainted with none of the persons involved; but believing that the youth was being unlawfully assaulted, and this is not disputed by the other participants, defendant went to his rescue, pulling on or punching at the seeming assailants. In the ensuing affray one of the older men got his leg locked with that of defendant and when defendant fell the man's leg was broken at the kneecap. The injured man then pulled out a revolver, announced to the defendant that he was a police officer, and that defendant was under arrest. It appears that the youth in question had played some part in a street incident which resulted in the two men, who were detectives in plain clothes, seeking to arrest him for disorderly conduct. The youth had resisted, and it was in the midst of this resistance that defendant came upon the scene.

At the trial the defendant testified that he had known nothing about what had happened before he came upon the scene; that he had gone to his aid because the youth was crying and trying to pull away from the middle-aged men; and that the older men had almost pulled the trousers off the youth. The only detective who testified states, in response to a question from the court, that defendant did not know and had no way of knowing, so far as he knew, that they were police officers or that they were making an arrest.

*210 N.Y.S. 2d 358 (1961)

Two things are to be kept sharply in mind in considering the problem at hand. The first is that all that is involved here is a criminal prosecution for simple assault (Penal Law, § 244), and that the court is not concerned with the incidence of civil liability in the law of torts as a result of what happened on the street. Second, there is not here involved any question of criminal responsibility for interfering with an arrest where it is known to the actor that police officers are making an arrest, but he mistakenly believes that the arrest is unlawful.

Assault and battery is an ancient crime cognizable at the common law. It is a crime in which an essential element is intent (1 Wharton's Crim.Law and Proc. [Anderson Ed. 1957] § 329 et seq.; 1 Russell on Crime [11th Ed.] p. 724). Of course, in this state the criminal law is entirely statutory. But, because assault and battery is a "common-law" crime, the statutory provisions, as in the case of most of the common-law crimes, do not purport to define the crime with the same particularity as those crimes which have a statutory origin initially (Penal Law, § 240 et seq.). One of the consequences, therefore, is that while the provisions governing assault, contained in the Penal Law, refer to various kinds of intent, in most instances the intent is related to a supplemental intent, in addition to the unspecified general intent to commit an assault, in order to impose more serious consequences upon the actor (for example, Penal Law § 240). In some instances, of course, the intent is spelled out to distinguish the prohibited activity from what might otherwise be an innocent act or merely an accidental wrong (for example, Penal Law § 242, subds. 1 and 2).

It is in this statutory context that it was held in People v. Katz, 290 N.Y. 361, 49 N.E.2d 482, that in order to sustain a charge of assault in the second degree, based upon the infliction of grievous bodily harm, not only must there be a general intent to commit unlawful bodily harm but there must be a ['specific intent", that is, a supplemental intent to inflict grievous bodily harm. The case therefore does provide an interesting parallel analysis forwarding the idea that assault is always an intent crime even when the statute omits to provide expressly for such general intent, as is the case with regard to assault in the third degree (Penal

Law, § 244). Even Russell notes that, "It has been the general practice of the legislature to leave unexpressed some of the mental elements of crime" (op. cit., p. 74).

With respect to intent crimes, under general principles, a mistake of fact relates as a defense to an essential element of the crime, namely, to the *mens rea* (1 Wharton, op. cit., § 157; 1 Russell, op. cit., pp. 75–85). The development of the excuse of mistake is a relatively modern one and is of expanding growth (1 Bishop on Criminal Law [9th Ed.] p. 202, et seq., esp. the exhaustive and impassioned footnote which commences at p. 206 and continues through to p. 214; see, Shorter v. People, 2 N.Y. 193). But the defense was already on the march at the time of Blackstone (4 Blackstone, Comm. § 27, see esp. the footnote discussion to that section in the Jones Ed. [1916]). Russell, supra, details the tortuous development of the defense and the long road travelled between treating it as a species of involuntary conduct until it was finally recognized as a negation of criminal intent, thus ranging from the older view that criminal liability should depend upon "objective moral guilt", rather than, as in the modern thinking, upon subjective intent, that is, *mens rea.*

Mistake of fact, under our statutes, is a species of excuse rather than a matter of justification. Consequently, reliance on section 42[1] of the Penal Law which relates exclusively to justification is misplaced. Section 42 would be applicable only to justify a third party's intervention on behalf of a victim of an unlawful assault, but this does not preclude the defense of mistake which is related to subjective intent rather than to the objective ground for action. It is interesting that in tort at the common law excuse was provable under the general issue while justification must have been specially pleaded (1 Bacon, Abr. [1868] tit. Assault and Battery [C] p. 374). While the distinctions between excuse and justification are often fuzzy, and more often fudged, in the instance of section 42 its limited application is clear from its language.

It is in the homicide statutes in which the occasions for excuse or justification are made somewhat clearer (see Penal Law, §§ 1054, 1055); but the distinction is still relevant with respect to most crimes. In homicide it is made explicitly plain that the actor's state of mind, if reasonable, is material and controlling (id. § 1055, penult. par. 1). It does not seem rational that the same reasonable misapprehension of fact should excuse a killing in seeming proper defense of a third person in one's presence but that it should not excuse a lesser personal injury.

In this State there are no discoverable precedents involving mistake of fact when one intervenes on behalf of another person and the prosecution has been for assault, rather than homicide. (The absence of precedents in this state and many others may simply mean that no enforcement agency would prosecute in the situations that must have occurred.) No one would dispute, however, that a mistake of fact would provide a defense if the prosecution were for homicide. This divided approach is sometimes based on the untenable distinction that mistake of fact may negative a "specific" intent required in the degrees of homicide but is irrelevant to the general intent required in simple assault, or, on the even less likely distinction, that the only intent involved in assault is the intent to touch without consent or legal justification (omitting the qualification of unlawfulness). The last, of course, is a partial confusion of tort law with criminal law, and even then is not quite correct (Restatement, Torts, §§ 63–75).

There have been precedents elsewhere among the states (6 C.J.S. Assault and Battery § 93; Am.Dig. System: Assault and Battery [Century Ed.], § 98 [Dec. Dig.] § 68). There is a split among the cases and in the jurisdictions. Most hold that the rescuer intervenes at his own peril (for example, State v. Ronnie, 41 N.J.Super. 339, 125 A.2d 163; Commonwealth v. Hounchell, 280 Ky. 217, 132 S.W.2d 921), but others hold that he is excused if he acts under mistaken but reasonable belief that he is protecting a victim from unlawful attack (for example, Kees v. State, 44 Tex.Cr.R. 543, 72 S.W. 855; Little v. State, 61 Tex.Cr.R. 197, 135 S.W. 119; Brannin v. State, 221 Ind. 123, 46 N.E.2d 599; State v. Mounkes, 88 Kan. 193, 127 P. 637). Many of the cases which hold that the actor proceeds at his peril involve situations where the actor was present throughout, or through most, or through enough of the transaction and, therefore, was in no position to claim a mistake of fact. Others arise in rough situations in which the feud or enmity generally to the peace officer is a significant factor. Almost all apply unanalytically the rubric that the right to intervene on behalf of another is no greater than the other's right to self-defense, a phrasing of ancient but questionable lineage going back to when crime and tort were not yet divided in the common law—indeed, when the right to private redress was not easily distinguishable from the sanction for the public wrong (Russell, op. cit., p. 20, et seq.).

It would protract the discussion and be bootless to detail all the cases, or even to make further illustrative selection. In England, however, it is interesting to observe, a defendant who intervened mistakenly in a proper arrest by peace officers has been held liable, not for assault, but under a specific statute related to police officers acting in the execution of their duty, and which, the courts construed, did not require knowledge on the part of the third party in order to make him responsible (Regina v. Forbes and Webb [1865] 10 Cox C.C. 362; Rex v. Maxwell and Clinchy [1909] 73 J.P. 77, 2 C.R.App. Rep.26 C.C.A.; 1 Russell, op. cit., pp.

764–766). Of course, in this state, too, there is an express crime for interfering with a lawful arrest (Penal Law, § 242, subd. 5). It is a felony and requires a "specific" intent to resist the lawful apprehension. So that here we have rejected the policy adopted in England expressly making innocent interference with a lawful arrest a crime.

The modern view, as already noted, is not to impose criminal responsibility in connection with intent crimes for those who act with good motivation, in mistaken but reasonable misapprehension of the facts. Indeed, Prosser would not even hold such a person responsible in tort (Torts [2d Ed.] pp. 91–92). He makes the added argument that "if an honest mistake is to relieve the defendant of liability when he thinks that he must defend himself, his meritorious defense of another should receive the same consideration." (Restatement, Torts, supra, § 76, also exculpates an actor for intervention on behalf of a third person where the actor has a reasonable belief that the third person is privileged and that such intervention is necessary. Notably, the Restatement sharply limits the persons on whose behalf the actor may intervene, but this, of course, is in the area of civil liability and, as already noted, there are those who would extend the privilege.)[2]

More recently in the field of criminal law the American Law Institute in drafting a model penal code has concerned itself with the question in this case. Under section 3.05 of the Model Penal Code the use of force for the protection of others is excused if the actor behaves under a mistaken belief (Model Penal Code, Tent.Draft No. 8, May 9, 1958.)[3]

The comments by the reporters on the Model Penal Code are quite appropriate. After stating that the defense of strangers should be assimilated to the defense of oneself the following is said:

"In support of such a ruling, it may perhaps be said that the potentiality for deterring the actor from the use of force is greater where he is protecting a stranger than where he is protecting himself or a loved one, because in the former case the interest protected is of relatively less importance to him; moreover the potential incidence of mistake in estimating fault or the need for action on his part is increased where the defendant is protecting a stranger, because in such circumstances he is less likely to know which party to the quarrel is in the right. These arguments may be said to lead to the conclusion that, in order to minimize the area for error or mistake, the defendant should act at his peril when he is protecting a stranger. This emasculates the privilege of protection of much of its content, introducing a liability without fault which is indefensible in principle. The cautious potential actor who knows the law will, in the vast majority of cases, refrain from acting at all. The result may well be that an innocent person is injured without receiving assistance from bystanders. It seems far preferable, therefore, to predicate the justification upon the actor's belief, safeguarding if thought

necessary against abuse of the privilege by the imposition of a requirement of proper care in evolving the belief. Here, as elsewhere, the latter problem is dealt with by the general provision in Section 3.09." (Model Penal Code, Tent.Draft No. 8, supra, at p. 32.)[4]

Apart from history, precedents, and the language distinctions that may be found in the statutes, it stands to reason that a man should not be punished criminally for an intent crime unless he, indeed, has the intent. Where a mistake of relevant facts is involved the premises for such intent are absent. True, there are occasions in public policy and its implementation for dispensing with intent and making one responsible for one's act even without immediate or intentional fault. This is generally accomplished by statute, and generally by statute which expressly dispenses with the presence of intent. Thus, it may well be that a Legislature determine that in order to protect the police in their activities and to make it difficult to promote false defenses one may proceed against a police officer while acting in the line of duty only at one's peril, as do the English, vide supra. But this is not a part of the intent crime of assault as it existed under common law or as it exists today under the statutes.

Indeed, if the analysis were otherwise, then the conductor who mistakenly ejects a passenger for not having paid his fare would be guilty of assault, which is hardly the case (1 Bishop, op. cit., pp. 202–203). So, too, a police officer who came to the assistance of a brother police officer would be guilty of assault if it should turn out that the brother police officer was engaged in making an unlawful arrest or was embarked upon an assault of his own private motivation (cf. Reeves v. State, Tex.Cr. App., 217 S.W. 2d 19).

It is a sterile and desolate legal system that would exact punishment for an intentional assault from one like this defendant, who acted from the most commendable motives and without excessive force. Had the facts been as he thought them, he would have been a hero and not condemned as a criminal actor. The dearth of applicable precedents—as distinguished from theoretical generalizations never, or rarely, applied—in England and in most of the states demonstrates that the benevolent intervenor has not been cast as a pariah. It is no answer to say that the policeman should be called when one sees an injustice. Even in the most populous centers, policemen are not that common or that available. Also, it ignores the peremptory response to injustice that the good man has ingrained. Again, it is to be noted, in a criminal proceeding one is concerned with the act against society, not with the wrong between individuals and the right to reparation, which is the province of tort.

Accordingly, the judgment of conviction should be reversed, on the law, and the information dismissed.

Judgment of conviction reversed upon the law and the information dismissed. All concur except VALENTE and EAGER, JJ., who dissent and vote to affirm in a dissenting opinion by VALENTE, J. Order filed.

VALENTE, Justice (dissenting).

We are concerned on this appeal with a judgment convicting defendant of the crime of assault in the third degree in violation of Section 244, subd. 1, of the Penal Law. The defendant assaulted a plain-clothes police officer, while the latter was attempting to effect a lawful and proper arrest of another. We are to determine whether the defendant's ignorance of the officer's police status and his erroneous belief that the detective was a civilian committing an unjustified assault upon the other person—who was a complete stranger to the defendant—excuses the crime. The majority of the Court, in reversing the judgment of conviction, holds that defendant's mistake removes the element of intent necessary for a criminal act.

I dissent and would affirm the conviction because the intent to commit a battery was unquestionably proven; and, since there was no relationship between defendant and the person whom the police officers were arresting, defendant acted at his peril in intervening and striking the officer. Under well-established law, defendant's rights were no greater than those of the person whom he sought to protect; and since the arrest was lawful, defendant was no more privileged to assault the police officer than the person being arrested.

Under our statutes a *specific* intent is necessary for the crimes of assault in the first and second degrees (Sections 240 and 242 of the Penal Law). See People v. Katz, 290 N.Y. 361, 49 N.E. 2d 482. Generally, the assaults contemplated by those sections were known as "aggravated" assaults under the common law. (1 Wharton's Crim.Law & Prac. [Anderson Ed. 1957] § 358.) However, assault in the third degree is defined by Section 244, subd. 1, of the Penal Law as an assault and battery not such as is specified in Sections 240 and 242. No specific intent is required under Section 244. All that is required is the knowledgeable doing of the act. "It is sufficient that the defendant voluntarily intended to commit the unlawful act of touching" (1 Wharton's op. cit. § 338, p. 685).

In the instant case, had the defendant assaulted the officer with the specific intent of preventing the lawful apprehension of the other person he would have been subject to indictment under the provisions of subdivision 5 of Section 242 of the Penal Law, which constitutes such an act assault in the second degree. But the inability to prove a specific intent does not preclude the People from establishing the lesser crime of assault in the third degree which requires proof only of the general intent "to commit the unlawful act of touching",

if such exists.

There is evidently no New York law on the precise issue on this appeal. However, certain of our statutes point to the proper direction for solution of the problem. Section 42 of the Penal Law provides:

"An act, otherwise criminal, is justifiable when it is done to protect the person committing it, or another whom he is bound to protect, from inevitable and irreparable personal injury. . . ."

Similarly, Section 246, so far as here pertinent, provides:

"To use or attempt, or offer to use, force or violence upon or towards the person of another is not unlawful in the following cases:

. . . .

"3. When committed either by the party about to be injured or by another person in his aid or defense, in preventing or attempting to prevent an offense against his person, or a trespass or other unlawful interference with real or personal property in his lawful possession, if the force or violence used is not more than sufficient to prevent such offense".

These statutes represent the public policy of this State regarding the areas in which an assault will be excused or rendered "not unlawful" where one goes to the assistance of another. They include only those cases in which the other person is one whom the defendant "is bound to protect" (Sec. 42) or where the defendant is "preventing or attempting to prevent an offense against" such other person (Sec. 246). Neither statute applies to the instant case since the other person herein was one unlawfully resisting a legal arrest—and hence no offense was being committed against his person by the officer—and he was not an individual whom defendant was "bound to protect".

It has been held in other states that one who goes to the aid of a third person acts at his peril, and his rights to interfere do not exceed the rights of the person whom he seeks to protect. State v. Ronnie, 41 N.J. Super. 339, 125 A.2d 163; Griffin v. State, 229 Ala. 482, 158 So. 316; Commonwealth v. Hounchell, 280 Ky. 217, 132 S.W.2d 921; 6 C.J.S. Assault and Battery, § 93, p. 950; 1 Wharton's op. cit., § 352; 4 Am. Jur. Assault and Battery, § 54, p. 155. We need not consider to what extent that rule is modified by Section 42 of the Penal Law since there is no question here but that the person being arrested was not in any special relation to defendant so that he was a person whom defendant was "bound to protect". It follows then that there being no right on the part of the person, to whose aid defendant came, to assault the officer—the arrest being legal—defendant had no greater right or privilege to assault the officer.

The conclusion that defendant was properly convicted in this case comports with sound public policy.

It would be a dangerous precedent for courts to announce that plain-clothes police officers attempting lawful arrests over wrongful resistance are subject to violent interference by strangers ignorant of the facts, who may attack the officers with impunity so long as their ignorance forms a reasonable basis for a snap judgment of the situation unfavorable to the officers. Although the actions of such a defendant, who acts on appearances, may eliminate the specific intent required to convict him of a felony assault, it should not exculpate him from the act of aggressive assistance to a law breaker in the process of wrongfully resisting a proper arrest.

I do not detract from the majority's views regarding commendation of the acts of a good Samaritan, although it may be difficult in some cases to distinguish such activities from those of an officious intermeddler. But opposed to the encouragement of the "benevolent intervenor" is the conflicting and more compelling interest of protection of police officers. In a city like New York, where it becomes necessary to utilize the services of a great number of plain-clothes officers, the efficacy of their continuing struggle against crime should not be impaired by the possibility of interference by citizens who may be acting from commendable motives. It is more desirable—and evidently up to this point the Legislature has so deemed it—that in such cases the intervening citizen be held to act at his peril when he assaults a stranger, who unknown to him is a police officer legally performing his duty. In this conflict of interests, the balance preponderates in favor of the protection of the police rather than the misguided intervenor.

The majority points to the recommendations of the American Law Institute in drafting a Model Penal Code which makes the use of force justifiable to protect a third person when the actor believes his intervention is necessary for the protection of such third person (Model Penal Code, Tent. Draft No. 8, § 3.05 [1(c)], p. 30). Obviously these are recommendations which properly are to be addressed to a legislature and not to courts. The comments of the reporters on the Model Penal Code, from which the majority quotes, indicate (p. 31) that in the United States the view is preserved in much state legislation that force may not be used to defend others unless they stand in a special relationship to their protector. The reporters state: "The simple solution of the whole problem is to assimilate the defense of strangers to the defense of oneself, and this the present section does". If this be so, then even under the Model Penal Code, since the stranger, who is being lawfully arrested, may not assault the officers a third person coming to his defense may not do so. In any event, the Model Penal Code recognizes that the law as it now stands requires the conviction of the defendant herein. Until the Legislature acts, the courts should adhere to the well-established rules applicable in such cases. Such adherence demands the affirmance of the conviction herein.

NOTES

1.   The section reads as follows:
"§ 42. Rule when act done in defense of self or another
"An act, otherwise criminal, is justifiable when it is done to protect the person committing it, or another whom he is bound to protect, from inevitable and irreparable personal injury, and the injury could only be prevented by the act, nothing more being done than is necessary to prevent the injury."

2.   It is interesting that Dean Prosser is now the Chief Reporter for the American Law Institute in the draft of Restatement, Torts, Second. Tentative Draft No. 1 [April 5, 1957] of Restatement, Torts, Second, deletes the limitations to section 76 restricting intervention on behalf of strangers. And in the comments it is stated, "There is no modern case holding that there is no privilege to defend a stranger."

3.   The full text of subdivision 1 of section 3.05 reads as follows:
"Section 3.05. Use of Force for the Protection of Other Persons.
"(1) The use of force upon or toward the person of another is justifiable to protect a third person when:
"(a) the actor would be justified under Section 3.04 in using such force to protect himself against the injury he believes to be threatened to the person whom he seeks to protect; and
"(b) under the circumstances as the actor believes them to be, the person whom he seeks to protect would be justified in using such protective force; and
"(c) The actor believes that his intervention is necessary for the protection of such other person."

4.   Equally valuable comments may be found at p. 17 of the same draft, and at p. 140 of Tent. Draft No. 4.

PEOPLE v. YOUNG

New York Court of Appeals, 1962*

Per Curiam. Whether one, who in good faith aggressively intervenes in a struggle between another person and a police officer in civilian dress attempting to effect the lawful arrest of the third person, may be properly convicted of assault in the third degree is a question of law of first impression here.

The opinions in the court below in the absence of precedents in this State carefully expound the opposing views found in other jurisdictions. The majority in the Appellate Division have adopted the minority rule in the other States that one who intervenes in a struggle between strangers under the mistaken but reasonable belief that he is protecting another who he assumes is being unlawfully beaten is thereby exonerated from criminal liability.* The weight of authority holds with the dissenters below that one who goes to the aid of a third person does so at his peril.*

While the doctrine espoused by the majority of the court below may have support in some States, we feel that such a policy would not be conducive to an orderly society. We agree with the settled policy of law in most jurisdictions that the right of a person to defend another ordinarily should not be greater than such person's right to defend himself. Subdivision 3 of section 246 of the Penal Law does not apply as no offense was being committed on the person of the one resisting the lawful arrest. Whatever may be the public policy where the felony charged requires proof of a specific intent and the issue is justifiable homicide, it is not relevant in a prosecution for assault in the third degree where it is only necessary to show that the defendant knowingly struck a blow.

In this case there can be no doubt that the defendant intended to assault the police officer in civilian dress. The resulting assault was forceful. Hence motive or mistake of fact is of no significance as the defendant was not charged with a crime requiring such intent or knowledge. To be guilty of third degree assault "It is sufficient that the defendant voluntarily intended to commit the unlawful act of touching" (1 Wharton's Criminal Law and Procedure [1957], § 338, p. 685). Since in these circumstances the aggression was inexcusable the defendant was properly convicted.

Accordingly, the order of the Appellate Division should be reversed and the information reinstated.

Froessel, J. (dissenting). The law is clear that one may kill in defense of another when there is reasonable, though mistaken, ground for believing that the person slain is about to commit a felony or to do some great personal injury to the apparent victim (Penal Law, § 1055); yet the majority now hold, for the first time, that in the event of a simple assault under similar circumstances, the mistaken belief, no matter how reasonable, is no defense.

Briefly, the relevant facts are these: On a Friday afternoon at about 3:40, Detectives Driscoll and Murphy, not in uniform, observed an argument taking place between a motorist and one McGriff in the street in front of premises 64 West 54th Street, in midtown Manhattan. Driscoll attempted to chase McGriff out of the roadway in order to allow traffic to pass, but McGriff refused to move back; his actions caused a crowd to collect. After identifying himself to McGriff, Driscoll placed him under arrest. As McGriff resisted, defendant "came out of the crowd" from Driscoll's rear and struck Murphy about the head with his fist. In the ensuing struggle Driscoll's right kneecap was injured when defendant fell on top of him. At the station house, defendant said he had not known or thought Driscoll and Murphy were police officers.

Defendant testified that while he was proceeding on 54th Street he observed two white men, who appeared to be 45 or 50 years old, pulling on a "colored boy" (McGriff), who appeared to be a lad about 18, whom he did not know. The men had nearly pulled McGriff's pants off, and he was crying. Defendant admitted he knew nothing of what had transpired between the officers and McGriff, and made no inquiry of anyone; he just came there and pulled the officer away from McGriff.

Defendant was convicted of assault third degree. In reversing upon the law and dismissing the information,

---

*11 N. Y. S. 2d 274 (1962)
*Citations omitted [Eds.].

the Appellate Division held that one is not "criminally liable for assault in the third degree if he goes to the aid of another whom he mistakenly, but *reasonably,* believes is being unlawfully beaten, and thereby injures one of the apparent assaulters" (emphasis supplied). While in my opinion the majority below correctly stated the law, I would reverse here and remit so that the Appellate Division may pass on the question of whether or not defendant's conduct was reasonable in light of the circumstances presented at the trial (Code Crim. Pro., §§ 543-a, 543-b).

As the majority below pointed out, assault is a crime derived from the common law (*People* v. *Katz,* 290 N. Y. 361, 365). Basic to the imposition of criminal liability both at common law and under our statutory law is the existence in the one who committed the prohibited act of what has been variously termed a guilty mind, a *mens rea* or a criminal intent.*

Criminal intent requires an awareness of wrongdoing. When conduct is based upon mistake of fact reasonably entertained, there can be no such awareness and, therefore, no criminal culpability. In *People ex rel. Hegeman* v. *Corrigan* (195 N. Y. 1, 12) we stated: "it is very apparent that the innocence or criminality of the intent in a particular act generally depends on the knowledge or belief of the actor at the time. An honest and *reasonable* belief in the existence of circumstances which, if true, would make the act for which the defendant is prosecuted innocent, would be a good defense." (Emphasis supplied.)

It is undisputed that defendant did not know that Driscoll and Murphy were detectives in plain clothes engaged in lawfully apprehending an alleged disorderly person. If, therefore, defendant *reasonably* believed he was lawfully assisting another, he would not have been guilty of a crime. Subdivision 3 of section 246 of the Penal Law provides that it is not unlawful to use force "When committed either by the party about to be injured or *by another person in his aid or defense, in preventing or attempting to prevent an offense against his person,* * * * if the force or violence used is not more than sufficient to prevent such offense" (emphasis supplied). The law is thus clear that if defendant entertained an "honest and reasonable belief" (*People ex rel. Hegeman* v. *Corrigan,* 195 N. Y. 1, 12 *supra*) that the facts were as he perceived them to be, he would be exonerated from criminal liability.

By ignoring one of the most basic principles of criminal law—that crimes *mala in se* require proof of at least general criminal intent—the majority now hold that the defense of mistake of fact is "of no significance." We are not here dealing with one of "a narrow class of exceptions" (*People* v. *Katz,* 290 N. Y. 361, 365, *supra*) where the Legislature has created crimes which do not depend on *criminal* intent but which are complete on the mere intentional doing of an act *malum prohibitum.** (9 N Y 2d 51, 58; *People* v. *Werner,* 174 N. Y. 132, *supra*).

There is no need, in my opinion, to consider the law of other States, for New York policy clearly supports the view that one may act on appearances reasonably ascertained, as does New Jersey.* Our Penal Law (§ 1055), to which I have already alluded, is a statement of that policy. The same policy was expressed by this court in *People* v. *Maine* (166 N. Y. 50). There, the defendant observed his brother fighting in the street with two other men; he stepped in and stabbed to death one of the latter. The defense was justifiable homicide under the predecessor of section 1055. The court held it reversible error to admit into evidence the declarations of the defendant's brother, made before defendant happened upon the scene, which tended to show that the brother was the aggressor. We said (p. 52): "Of course the acts and conduct of the defendant must be judged solely with reference to the situation as it was when he first and afterwards saw it." Mistake of relevant fact, reasonably entertained, is thus a defense to homicide under section 1055 (*People* v. *Governale,* 193 N. Y. 581, 588), and one who kills in defense of another and proffers this defense of justification is to be judged according to the circumstances as they appeared to him.*

The mistaken belief, however, must be one which is reasonably entertained, and the question of reasonableness is for the trier of the facts.* "The question is not merely what did the accused believe, but also, what did he have the right to believe?" (*People* v. *Rodawald,* 177 N. Y. 408, 427.) Without passing on the facts of the instant case, the Appellate Division had no right to assume that defendant's conduct was reasonable, and to dismiss the information as a matter of law. Nor do we have the right to reinstate the verdict without giving the Appellate Division the opportunity to pass upon the facts (Code Crim. Pro., § 543-b).

Although the majority of our court are now purporting to fashion a policy "conducive to an orderly society", by their decision they have defeated their avowed purpose. What public interest is promoted by a principle which would deter one from coming to the aid of a fellow citizen who he has reasonable ground to apprehend is in imminent danger of personal injury at the hands of assailants? Is it reasonable to denominate, as justifiable homicide, a slaying committed under a mistaken but reasonably held belief, and deny this same defense of justification to one using less force? Logic, as well as historical background and related precedent,

*Citations omitted [Eds.].

dictates that the rule and policy expressed by our Legislature in the case of homicide, which is an assault resulting in death, should likewise be applicable to a much less serious assault not resulting in death.

I would reverse the order appealed from and remit the case to the Appellate Division pursuant to section 543-b of the Code of Criminal Procedure "for determination upon the questions of fact raised in that court."

Chief Judge Desmond and Judges Dye, Fuld, Burke and Foster concur in *Per Curiam* opinion; Judge Froessel dissents in an opinion in which Judge Van Voorhis concurs.

Order reversed, etc.

BARBARA WOOTTON

Eliminating Responsibility*

THE FUNCTION OF THE COURTS: PENAL OR PREVENTIVE?

... Proposals for the modernisation of the methods by which the criminal courts arrive at their verdicts do not, however, raise any question as to the object of the whole exercise. Much more fundamental are the issues which arise after conviction, when many a judge or magistrate must from time to time have asked himself just what it is that he is trying to achieve. Is he trying to punish the wicked, or to prevent the recurrence of forbidden acts? The former is certainly the traditional answer and is still deeply entrenched both in the legal profession and in the minds of much of the public at large; and it has lately been reasserted in uncompromising terms by a former Lord Chief Justice. At a meeting of magistrates earlier this year Lord Goddard is reported to have said that the duty of the criminal law was to punish—and that reformation of the prisoner was not the courts' business.[1] Those who take this view doubtless comfort themselves with the belief that the two objectives are nearly identical: that the punishment of the wicked is also the best way to prevent the occurrence of prohibited acts. Yet the continual failure of a mainly punitive system to diminish the volume of crime strongly suggests that such comfort is illusory; and it will indeed be a principal theme of these lectures that the choice between the punitive and the preventive[2] concept of the criminal process is a real one; and that, according as that choice is made, radical differences must follow in the courts' approach to their task. I shall, moreover, argue that in recent years a perceptible shift has occurred away from the first and towards the second of these two conceptions of the function of the criminal law; and that this movement is greatly to be welcomed and might with advantage be both more openly acknowledged and also accelerated.

*From *Crime and the Criminal Law* by Barbara Wootton (London: Sweet & Maxwell, Ltd., 1963), pp. 40–57 and 58–84. Reprinted by permission of the author and the publisher.

First, however, let us examine the implications of the traditional view. Presumably the wickedness which renders a criminal liable to punishment must be inherent either in the actions which he has committed or in the state of mind in which he has committed them. Can we then in the modern world identify a class of inherently wicked actions? Lord Devlin, who has returned more than once to this theme, holds that we still can, by drawing a sharp distinction between what he calls the criminal and the quasi-criminal law. The distinguishing mark of the latter, in his view, is that a breach of it does not mean that the offender has done anything morally wrong. "Real" crimes, on the other hand, he describes as "sins with legal definitions"; and he adds that "It is a pity that this distinction, which I believe the ordinary man readily recognises, is not acknowledged in the administration of justice." "The sense of obligation which leads the citizen to obey a law that is good in itself is," he says, "different in quality from that which leads to obedience to a regulation designed to secure a good end." Nor does his Lordship see any reason "why the quasi-criminal should be treated with any more ignominy than a man who has incurred a penalty for failing to return a library book in time."[2a] And in a personal communication he has further defined the "real" criminal law as any part of the criminal law, new or old, which the good citizen does not break without a sense of guilt.

Nevertheless this attempt to revive the lawyer's distinction between *mala in se* and *mala prohibita*—things which are bad in themselves and things which are merely prohibited—cannot, I think, succeed. In the first place the statement that a real crime is one about which the good citizen would feel guilty is surely circular. For how is the good citizen to be defined in this context unless as one who feels guilty about committing the crimes that Lord Devlin classifies as "real"? And in the second place the badness even of those actions which would most generally be regarded as *mala in se* is inherent, not in the physical acts themselves, but in the circumstances in which they are performed. Indeed it is hard to think of any examples of actions which could, in a strictly physical sense, be said to be bad in themselves. The physical act of stealing merely involves moving a piece of matter from one place to another: what gives it its immoral character is the framework of property rights in which it occurs. Only the violation of these rights transforms an inherently harmless movement into the iniquitous act of stealing. Nor can bodily assaults be unequivocally classified as *mala in se;* for actions which in other circumstances would amount to grievous bodily harm may be not only legal, but highly beneficial, when performed by competent surgeons; and there are those who see no wrong in killing in the form of judicial hanging or in war.

One is indeed tempted to suspect that actions classified as *mala in se* are really only *mala antiqua*—actions, that is to say, which have been recognised as criminal for a very long time; and that the tendency to dismiss sundry modern offences as "merely quasi-crimes" is simply a mark of not having caught up with the realities of the contemporary world. The criminal calendar is always the expression of a particular social and moral climate, and from one generation to another it is modified by two sets of influences. On the one hand ideas about what is thought to be right or wrong are themselves subject to change; and on the other hand new technical developments constantly create new opportunities for antisocial actions which the criminal code must be extended to include. To a thoroughgoing Marxist these two types of change would not, presumably, be regarded as mutually independent: to the Marxist it is technical innovations which cause moral judgments to be revised. But for present purposes it does not greatly matter whether the one is, or is not, the cause of the other. In either case the technical and the moral are distinguishable. The fact that there is nothing in the Ten Commandments about the iniquity of driving a motor vehicle under the influence of drink cannot be read as evidence that the ancient Israelites regarded this offence more leniently than the contemporary British. On the other hand the divergent attitudes of our own criminal law and that of most European countries to homosexual practices has no obvious relation to technical development, and is clearly the expression of differing moral judgments, or at the least to different conceptions of the proper relation between morality and the criminal law.

One has only to glance, too, at the maximum penalties which the law attaches to various offences to realise how profoundly attitudes change in course of time. Life imprisonment, for example, is not only the obligatory sentence for noncapital murder and the maximum permissible for manslaughter. It may also be imposed for blasphemy or for the destruction of registers of births or baptisms. Again, the crime of abducting an heiress carries a potential sentence of fourteen years, while that for the abduction of a child under fourteen years is only half as long. For administering a drug to a female with a view to carnal knowledge a maximum of two years is provided, but for damage to cattle you are liable to fourteen years' imprisonment. For using unlawful oaths the maximum is seven years, but for keeping a child in a brothel it is a mere six months. Such sentences strike us today as quite fantastic; but they cannot have seemed fantastic to those who devised them.

For the origins of the supposed dichotomy between real crimes and quasi-crimes we must undoubtedly look to theology, as Lord Devlin's use of the term "sins with legal definitions" itself implies. The links between law and religion are both strong and ancient. Indeed, as Lord Radcliffe has lately reminded us, it has taken centuries for "English judges to realise that the tenets and injunctions of the Christian religion were not part of the common law of England";[3] and even today such realisation does not seem to be complete. As recently as 1961, in the "Ladies Directory" case, the defendant Shaw, you may remember, was convicted of conspiring to corrupt public morals, as well as of offences against the Sexual Offences Act of 1956 and the Obscene Publications Act of 1959, on account of his publication of a directory in which the ladies of the town advertised their services, sometimes, it would seem, in considerable detail. In rejecting Shaw's appeal to the House of Lords on the charge of conspiracy, Lord Simonds delivered himself of the opinion that without doubt "there remains in the courts a residual power to . . . conserve not only the safety but also the moral welfare of the state"; and Lord Hodson, concurring, added that "even if Christianity be not part of the law of England, yet the common law has its roots in Christianity."[4]

In the secular climate of the present age, however, the appeal to religious doctrine is unconvincing, and unlikely to be generally acceptable. Instead we must recognise a range of actions, the badness of which is inherent not in themselves, but in the circumstances in which they are performed, and which stretches in a continuous scale from wilful murder at one end to failure to observe a no-parking rule or to return on time a library book (which someone else may be urgently wanting) at the other. (Incidentally a certain poignancy is given to Lord Devlin's choice of this last example by a subsequent newspaper report that a book borrower in Frankfurt who omitted, in spite of repeated requests, to return a book which he had borrowed two years previously was brought before a local magistrate actually— though apparently by mistake—in handcuffs.[5]) But however great the range from the heinous to the trivial, the important point is that the gradation is continuous; and in the complexities of modern society a vast range of actions, in themselves apparently morally neutral, must be regarded as in varying degrees antisocial, and therefore in their contemporary settings as no less objectionable than actions whose criminal status is of greater antiquity. The good citizen will doubtless experience different degrees of guilt according as he may have stabbed his wife, engaged in homosexual intercourse, omitted to return his library book or failed to prevent one of his employees from watering the milk sold by his firm. Technically these are all crimes; whether or not they are also sins in a purely theological matter with which the law has no concern. If the function of the criminal law is to punish the wicked, then everything which the law forbids must in the circumstances in which it is forbidden be regarded as in its appropriate measure wicked.

Although this is, I think, the inevitable conclusion of any argument which finds wickedness inherent in particular classes of action, it seems to be unpalatable to Lord Devlin and others who conceive the function of the criminal law in punitive terms. It opens the door too wide. Still the door can be closed again by resort to the alternative theory that the wickedness of an action is inherent not in the action itself, but in the state of mind of the person who performs it. To punish people merely for what they have done, it is argued, would be unjust, for the forbidden act might have been an accident for which the person who did it cannot be held to blame. Hence the requirement, to which traditionally the law attaches so much importance, that a crime is not, so to speak, a crime in the absence of *mens rea*.

Today, however, over a wide front even this requirement has in fact been abandoned. Today many, indeed almost certainly the majority, of the cases dealt with by the criminal courts are cases of strict liability in which proof of a guilty

mind is no longer necessary for conviction. A new dichotomy is thus created, and one which in this instance exists not merely in the minds of the judges but is actually enshrined in the law itself —that is to say, the dichotomy between those offences in which the guilty mind is, and those in which it is not, an essential ingredient. In large measure, no doubt, this classification coincides with Lord Devlin's division into real and quasi-crimes; but whether or not this coincidence is exact must be a question of personal judgment. To drive a car when your driving ability is impaired through drink or drugs is an offence of strict liability: It is no defence to say that you had no idea that the drink would affect you as it did, or to produce evidence that you were such a seasoned drinker that any such result was, objectively, not to be expected. These might be mitigating circumstances after conviction, but are no bar to the conviction itself. Yet some at least of those who distinguish between real and quasi-crimes would put drunken driving in the former category, even though it involves no question of *mens rea*. In the passage that I quoted earlier Lord Devlin, it will be remembered, was careful to include new as well as old offences in his category of "real" crimes; but generally speaking it is the *mala antiqua* which are held to be both *mala in se* and contingent upon *mens rea*.

Nothing has dealt so devastating a blow at the punitive conception of the criminal process as the proliferation of offences of strict liability; and the alarm has forthwith been raised. Thus Dr. J. Ll. J. Edwards has expressed the fear that there is a real danger that the "widespread practice of imposing criminal liability independent of any moral fault" will result in the criminal law being regarded with contempt. "The process of basing criminal liability upon a theory of absolute prohibition," he writes, "may well have the opposite effect to that intended and lead to a weakening of respect for the law."[6] Nor, in his view, is it an adequate answer to say that absolute liability can be tolerated because of the comparative unimportance of the offences to which it is applied and because, as a rule, only a monetary penalty is involved; for, in the first place, there are a number of important exceptions to this rule (drunken driving for example); and, secondly, as Dr. Edwards himself points out, in certain cases the penalty imposed by the court may be the least part of the punishment. A merchant's conviction for a minor trading offence may have a disastrous effect upon his business.

Such dislike of strict liability is not by any

means confined to academic lawyers. In the courts, too, various devices have been used to smuggle *mens rea* back into offences from which, on the face of it, it would appear to be excluded. To the lawyer's ingenious mind the invention of such devices naturally presents no difficulty. Criminal liability, for instance, can attach only to voluntary acts. If a driver is struck unconscious with an epileptic seizure, it can be argued that he is not responsible for any consequences because his driving thereafter is involuntary: indeed he has been said not to be driving at all. If on the other hand he falls asleep, this defence will not serve since sleep is a condition that comes on gradually, and a driver has an opportunity and a duty to stop before it overpowers him. Alternatively, recourse can be had to the circular argument that anyone who commits a forbidden act must have intended to commit it and must, therefore, have formed a guilty intention. As Lord Devlin puts it, the word "knowingly" or "wilfully" can be read into acts in which it is not present; although as his Lordship points out this subterfuge is open to the criticism that it fails to distinguish between the physical act itself and the circumstances in which this becomes a crime.[7] All that the accused may have intended was to perform an action (such as firing a gun or driving a car) which is not in itself criminal. Again, in yet other cases such as those in which it is forbidden to permit or to allow something to be done the concept of negligence can do duty as a watered down version of *mens rea:* for how can anyone be blamed for permitting something about which he could not have known?

All these devices, it cannot be too strongly emphasised, are necessitated by the need to preserve the essentially punitive function of the criminal law. For it is not, as Dr. Edwards fears, the criminal law which will be brought into contempt by the multiplication of offences of strict liability, so much as this particular conception of the law's function. If that function is conceived less in terms of punishment than as a mechanism of prevention these fears become irrelevant. Such a conception, however, apparently sticks in the throat of even the most progressive lawyers. Even Professor Hart, in his Hobhouse lecture on *Punishment and the Elimination of Responsibility,* [8] seems to be incurably obsessed with the notion of punishment, which haunts his text as well as figuring in his title. Although rejecting many traditional theories, such as that punishment should be "retributive" or "denunciatory," he nevertheless seems wholly unable to envisage a system in which sentence is not automatically equated with "punishment." Thus he writes of "values quite distinct from those of retributive punishment which the system of responsibility does maintain, and which remain of great importance even if our aims in *punishing* are the forward-looking aims of social protection"; and again "even if we *punish* men not as wicked but as nuisances..." while he makes many references to the principle that liability to punishment must depend on a voluntary act. Perhaps it requires the naïveté of an amateur to suggest that the forward-looking aims of social protection might, on occasion, have absolutely no connection with punishment.

If, however, the primary function of the courts is conceived as the prevention of forbidden acts, there is little cause to be disturbed by the multiplication of offences of strict liability. If the law says that certain things are not to be done, it is illogical to confine this prohibition to occasions on which they are done from malice aforethought; for at least the material consequences of an action, and the reasons for prohibiting it, are the same whether it is the result of sinister malicious plotting, of negligence or of sheer accident. A man is equally dead and his relatives equally bereaved whether he was stabbed or run over by a drunken motorist or by an incompetent one; and the inconvenience caused by the loss of your bicycle is unaffected by the question whether or not the youth who removed it had the intention of putting it back, if in fact he had not done so at the time of his arrest. It is true, of course, as Professor Hart has argued,[9] that the material consequences of an action by no means exhaust its effects. "If one person hits another, the person struck does not think of the other as *just* a cause of pain to him.... If the blow was light but deliberate, it has a significance for the person struck quite different from an accidental much heavier blow." To ignore this difference, he argues, is to outrage "distinctions which not only underlie morality, but pervade the whole of our social life." That these distinctions are widely appreciated and keenly felt no one would deny. Often perhaps they derive their force from a purely punitive or retributive attitude; but alternatively they may be held to be relevant to an assessment of the social damage that results from a criminal act. Just as a heavy blow does more damage than a light one, so also perhaps does a blow which involves psychological injury do more damage than one in which the hurt is purely physical.

The conclusion to which this argument leads is, I think, not that the presence or absence of the guilty mind is unimportant, but that *mens rea* has, so to speak—and this is the crux of the matter—*got into the wrong place.* Traditionally, the requirement of the guilty mind is written into the actual definition of a crime. No guilty intention, no crime, is the rule. Obviously this makes sense if the law's concern is with wickedness: where there is no guilty intention, there can be no wickedness. But it is equally obvious, on the other hand, that an action does not become innocuous merely because whoever performed it meant no harm. If the object of the criminal law is to prevent the occurrence of socially damaging actions, it would be absurd to turn a blind eye to those which were due to carelessness, negligence or even accident. The question of motivation is *in the first instance* irrelevant.

But only in the first instance. At a later stage, that is to say, after what is now known as a conviction, the presence or absence of guilty intention is all-important for its effect on the appropriate measures to be taken to prevent a recurrence of the forbidden act. The prevention of accidental deaths presents different problems from those involved in the prevention of wilful murders. The results of the actions of the careless, the mistaken, the wicked and the merely unfortunate may be indistinguishable from one another, but each case calls for a different treatment. Tradition, however, is very strong, and the notion that these differences are relevant only after the fact has been established that the accused committed the forbidden act seems still to be deeply abhorrent to the legal mind. Thus Lord Devlin, discussing the possibility that judges might have taken the line that all "unintentional" criminals might be dealt with simply by the imposition of a nominal penalty, regards this as the "negation of law." "It would,"[10] he says, "confuse the function of mercy which the judge is dispensing when imposing the penalty with the function of justice. It would have been to deny to the citizen due process of law because it would have been to say to him, in effect: 'Although we cannot think that Parliament intended you to be punished in this case because you have really done nothing wrong, come to us, ask for mercy, and we shall grant mercy.' ... In all criminal matters the citizen is entitled to the protection of the law ... and the mitigation of penalty should not be adopted as the prime method of dealing with accidental offenders."

Within its own implied terms of reference the logic is unexceptionable. If the purpose of the law is to dispense punishment tempered with mercy, then to use mercy as a consolation for unjust punishment is certainly to give a stone for bread. But these are not the implied terms of reference of strict liability. In the case of offences of strict liability the presumption is not that those who have committed forbidden actions must be punished, but that appropriate steps must be taken to prevent the occurrence of such actions.

Here, as often in other contexts also, the principles involved are admirably illustrated by the many driving offences in which conviction does not involve proof of *mens rea*. If, for instance, the criterion of gravity is the amount of social damage which a crime causes, many of these offences must be judged extremely grave. In 1961, 299 persons were convicted on charges of causing death by dangerous driving, that is to say more than five times as many as were convicted of murder (including those found guilty but insane) and 85 per cent more than the total of convictions for all other forms of homicide (namely murder, manslaughter and infanticide) put together. It is, moreover, a peculiarity of many driving offences that the offender seldom intends the actual damage which he causes. He may be to blame in that he takes a risk which he knows may result in injury to other people or to their property, but such injury is neither an inevitable nor an intended consequence of the commission of the offence: which is not true of, for example, burglary. Dangerous or careless driving ranges in a continuous series from the almost wholly accidental, through the incompetent and the negligent to the positively and grossly culpable; and it is quite exceptionally difficult in many of these cases to establish just what point along this scale any particular instance should be assigned. In consequence the gravity of any offence tends to be estimated by its consequences rather than by the state of mind of the perpetrator—which is less usual (although attempted murder or grievous bodily harm may turn into murder, if the victim dies) in the case of other crimes. In my experience it is exceptional (though not unknown) for a driving charge to be made unless an accident actually occurs, and the nature of the charge is apt to be determined by the severity of the accident. I recall, for example, a case in which a car driver knocked down an elderly man on a pedestrian crossing, and a month later the victim died in hospital after an operation, his death being, one must suppose, in spite, rather than because, of this. Thereupon the charge, which had originally been booked by the police as careless, not even dangerous, driving was upgraded to causing death by dangerous driving.

For all these reasons it is recognised that if offences in this category are to be dealt with by the criminal courts at all, this can only be on a basis of strict liability. This particular category of offences thus illustrates all too vividly the fact that in the modern world in one way or another, as much and more damage is done by negligence, or by indifference to the welfare or safety of others, as by deliberate wickedness. In technically simpler societies this is less likely to be so, for the points of exposure to the follies of others are less numerous, and the daily chances of being run over, or burnt or infected or drowned because someone has left undone something that he ought to have done are less ominous. These new complexities were never envisaged by the founders of our legal traditions, and it is hardly to be wondered at if the law itself is not yet fully adapted to them. Yet it is by no means certain that the last chapter in the long and chequered history of the concept of guilt, which is so deeply rooted in our traditions, has yet been written. Time was when inanimate objects—the rock that fell on you, the tree that attracted the lightning that killed you— were held to share the blame for the disasters in which they were instrumental; and it was properly regarded as a great step forward when the capacity to acquire a guilty mind was deemed to be one of the distinctive capacities of human beings.[11] But now, perhaps, the time has come for the concept of legal guilt to be dissolved into a wider concept of responsibility or at least accountability, in which there is room for negligence as well as purposeful wrongdoing; and for the significance of a conviction to be reinterpreted merely as evidence that a prohibited act has been committed, questions of motivation being relevant only insofar as they bear upon the probability of such acts being repeated.

I am not, of course, arguing that all crimes should immediately be transferred into the strict liability category. To do so would in some cases involve formidable problems of definition—as, for instance, in that of larceny. But I do suggest that the contemporary extension of strict liability is not the nightmare that it is often made out to be, that it does not promise the decline and fall of the criminal law, and that it is, on the contrary, a sensible and indeed inevitable measure of adaptation to the requirements of the modern world; and above all I suggest that its supposedly nightmarish quality disappears once it is accepted that the primary objective of the criminal courts is preventive rather than punitive. Certainly we need to pay heed to Mr. Nigel Walker's reminder[12] that "under our present law it is possible for a person to do great harm in circumstances which suggest that there is a risk of his repeating it, and yet to secure an acquittal." In two types of case, in both of which such harm can result, the concept of the guilty mind has become both irrelevant and obstructive. In this lecture I have been chiefly concerned with the first of these categories—that of cases of negligence. The second category—that of mental abnormality—will be the theme of that which follows.

THE PROBLEM OF THE MENTALLY ABNORMAL OFFENDER

The problem of the mentally abnormal offender raises in a particularly acute form the question of the primary function of the courts. If that function is conceived as punitive, mental abnormality must be related to guilt; for a severely subnormal offender must be less blameworthy, and ought therefore to incur a less severe punishment, than one of greater intelligence who has committed an otherwise similar crime, even though he may well be a worse risk for the future. But from the preventive standpoint it is this future risk which matters, and the important question to be asked is not: Does his abnormality mitigate or even obliterate his guilt? but, rather, is he a suitable subject for medical, in preference to any other, type of treatment? In short, the punitive and the preventive are respectively concerned the one with culpability and the other with treatability.

In keeping with its traditional obsession with the concept of guilt, English criminal law has, at least until lately, been chiefly concerned with the effect of mental disorder upon culpability. In recent years, however, the idea that an offender's mental state might also have a bearing on his treatability has begun to creep into the picture— with the result that the two concepts now lie somewhat uneasily side by side in what has become a very complex pattern.

Under the present law there are at least six distinct legal formulae under which an accused person's mental state may be put in issue in a criminal case. First, he may be found unfit to plead, in which case of course no trial takes place at all, unless and until he is thought to have sufficiently recovered. Second, on a charge of murder (and theoretically in other cases also) a defendant may be found to be insane within the terms of the M'Naughten Rules, by the illogical verdict of guilty but insane which, to be consistent with the normal use of the term guilt, ought to be revised to read—as it once did—"not guilty on the ground of insanity." Third, a person accused of murder can plead diminished responsibility under section 2 of the Homicide Act, in which case, if this defence succeeds, a verdict of manslaughter will be substituted for one of murder.

Up to this point it is, I think, indisputable that it is the relation between the accused's mental state and his culpability or punishability which is in issue. Obviously a man who cannot be tried cannot be punished. Again, one who is insane may have to be deprived of his liberty in the interests of the public safety, but, since an insane person is not held to be blameworthy in the same way as one who is in full possession of his faculties, the institution to which he is committed must be of a medical not a penal character; and for the same reason, he must not be hanged if found guilty on a capital charge. So also under the Homicide Act a defence of diminished responsibility opens the door to milder punishments than the sentences of death and life imprisonment which automatically follow the respective verdicts of capital and noncapital murder; and the fact that diminished responsibility is conceived in terms of reduced culpability, and not as indicative of the need for medical treatment, is further illustrated by the fact that in less than half the cases in which this defence has succeeded since the courts have had power to make hospital orders under the Mental Health Act, have such orders actually been made.[13] In the great majority of all the successful cases under section 2 of the Homicide Act a sentence of imprisonment has been imposed, the duration of this ranging from life to a matter of not more than a few months. Moreover, the Court of Criminal Appeal has indicated[14] approval of such sentences on the ground that a verdict of manslaughter based on diminished responsibility implies that a "residue of responsibility" rests on the accused person and that this "residue of criminal intent" may be such as to deserve punishment—a judgment which surely presents a sentencing judge with a problem of nice mathematical calculation as to the appropriate measure of punishment.

Under the Mental Health Act of 1959, however, the notion of reduced culpability begins to be complicated by the alternative criterion of treatability. Section 60 of that Act provides the fourth and fifth of my six formulae. Under the first subsection of this section, an offender who is convicted at a higher court (or at a magistrates' court if his offence is one which carries liability to imprisonment) may be compulsorily detained in hospital, or made subject to a guardianship order, if the court is satisfied, on the evidence of two doctors (one of whom must have special experience in the diagnosis or treatment of mental disorders) that this is in all the circumstances the most appropriate way of dealing with him. In the making of such orders emphasis is clearly on the future, not on the past: The governing consideration is not whether the offender deserves to be punished, but whether in fact medical treatment is likely to succeed. No sooner have we said this, however, than the old concept of culpability rears its head again. For a hospital order made by a higher court may be accompanied by a restriction order of either specified or indefinite duration, during the currency of which the patient may only be discharged on the order of the Home Secretary; and a magistrates' court also, although it has no similar power itself to make a restriction order, may commit an offender to sessions to be dealt with, if it is of the opinion that, having regard to the nature of the offence, the antecedents of the offender and the risk of his committing further offences if set at liberty, a hospital order should be accompanied by a restriction order.

The restriction order is thus professedly designed as a protection to the public; but a punitive element also, I think, still lingers in it. For if the sole object was the protection of the public against the premature discharge of a mentally disordered dangerous offender, it could hardly be argued that the court's prediction of the safe moment for release, perhaps years ahead, is likely to be more reliable than the judgment at the appropriate time of the hospital authorities who will have had the patient continuously under their surveillance.[15] If their purpose is purely protective all orders ought surely to be of indefinite duration, and the fact that this is not so suggests that they are still tainted with the tariff notion of sentencing—that is to say, with the idea that a given offence "rates" a certain period of loss of liberty. Certainly, on any other interpretation, the judges who have imposed restriction orders on offenders to run for ten or more years must credit themselves with truly remarkable powers of medical prognosis. In fairness, however, it should be said that the practice of imposing indefinite rather than fixed term orders now seems to be growing.

So, too, with the fifth of my formulae, which is to be found in a later subsection of section 60 of the same Act. Under this, an offender who is charged before a magistrates' court with an offence for which he could be imprisoned, may be made the subject of a hospital or guardianship order *without being convicted,* provided that the court is satisfied that he did the act or made the omission of which he is accused. This power, however (which is itself an extended version of section 24 of the Criminal Justice Act, 1948, and has indeed a longer statutory history), may only be exercised if the accused is diagnosed as suffering from either mental illness or severe subnormality. It is not available in the case of persons suffering from either of the two other forms of mental disorder recognised by the Act, namely psychopathy, or simple, as distinct from severe, subnormality. And why not? One can only presume that the reason for this restriction is the fear that in cases in which only moderate mental disorder is diagnosed, or in which the diagnosis is particularly difficult and a mistake might easily be made, an offender might escape the punishment that he deserved. Even though no hospital or guardianship order can be made unless the court is of opinion that this is the "most suitable" method of disposing of the case, safeguards against the risk that this method might be used for the offender who really deserved to be punished are still written into the law.

One curious ambiguity in this provision, however, deserves notice at this stage. Before a hospital order is made, the court must be satisfied that the accused "did the act, or made the omission with which he is charged." Yet what, one may ask, is the meaning, in this context, of "the act"? Except in the case of crimes of absolute liability, a criminal charge does not relate to a purely physical action. It relates to a physical action accompanied by a guilty mind or malicious intention. If then a person is so mentally disordered as to be incapable of forming such an intention, is he not strictly incapable of performing the act with which he is charged? The point seems to have been raised when the 1948 Criminal Justice Bill was in Committee in the House of Commons, but it was not pursued.[16] Such an interpretation would, of course, make nonsense of the section, and one must presume, therefore, that the words "the act" must be construed to refer solely to the prohibited physical action, irrespective of the actor's state of mind. But in that case the effect of this subsection would seem to be to transfer every type of crime, in the case of persons of severely disordered mentality, to the category of offences of absolute liability. In practice little use appears to be made of this provision (and in my experience few magistrates are aware of its existence);

but there would seem to be an important principle here, potentially capable, as I hope to suggest later, of wider application.

The last of my six formulae, which, however, antedates all the others, stands in a category by itself. It is to be found in section 4 of the Criminal Justice Act of 1948, under which a court may make mental treatment (residential or nonresidential) a condition of a probation order, provided that the offender's mental condition is "such as requires and as may be susceptible to treatment," but is not such as to justify his being in the language of that day certified as "of unsound mind" or "mentally defective." Such a provision represents a very wholehearted step in the direction of accepting the criterion of treatability. For, although those to whom this section may be applied must be deemed to be guilty—in the sense that they have been convicted of offences involving *mens rea*—the only question to be decided is that of their likely response to medical or other treatment. Moreover, apart from the exclusion of insanity or mental defect, no restriction is placed on the range of diagnostic categories who may be required to submit to mental treatment under this section, although as always in the case of a probation order imposed on adults, the order cannot be made without the probationer's own consent. Nor is any reference anywhere made or even implied as to the effect of their mental condition upon their culpability. It is of interest, too, that, in practice, the use of these provisions has not been confined to what are often regarded as "pathological" crimes. Dr. Grünhut who made a study of cases to which the section was applied in 1953[17] found that out of a total of 636 probationers, 275 had committed offences against property, 216 sexual offences, ninety-seven offences of violence (other than sexual) and forty-eight other types of offence. Some of the property crimes had, it is true, "an apparently pathological background," but no less than 48 per cent were classified as "normal" acquisitive thefts.

All these modifications in the criminal process in the case of the mentally abnormal offender thus tend (with the possible exception of the 1948 Act) to treat such abnormality as in greater or less degree exculpatory. Their purpose is not just to secure that medical treatment should be provided for any offender likely to benefit from this, but rather to guard against the risk that the mentally disordered will be unjustly punished. Their concern with treatability, where it occurs, is in effect consequential rather than primary: The question—can the doctors help him? follows, if at all, upon a negative answer to the question: Is he really to blame?

Nowhere is this more conspicuous than in section 2 of the Homicide Act; and it was indeed from a study of the operation of that section that I was led nearly four years ago to the conclusion that this was the wrong approach; that any attempt to distinguish between wickedness and mental abnormality was doomed to failure; and that the only solution for the future was to allow the concept of responsibility to "wither away" and to concentrate instead on the problem of the choice of treatment, without attempting to assess the effect of mental peculiarities on degrees of culpability. That opinion was based on a study of the files of some seventy-three cases in which a defence of diminished responsibility had been raised,[18] which were kindly made available by the Home Office. To these have since been added the records of another 126 cases, the two series together covering the five and a half years from the time that the Act came into force down to mid-September 1962.

Before I pursue the implications of the suggestion that the concept of responsibility should be allowed to wither away, it may be well to ask whether anything in this later material calls for any modification of my earlier conclusion. I do not think it does. Indeed the experience of the past three and a half years seems to have highlighted both the practical and the philosophical difficulty—or as I would prefer to say the impossibility—of assessing other people's responsibility for their actions.

Some new issues have, however, arisen in the struggle to interpret the relevant section of the Act. Much legal argument has, for example, been devoted to the effect of drink upon responsibility. The Act, as you may remember, provides that a charge of murder may result in a conviction for manslaughter if the accused was suffering from "such abnormality of mind (whether arising from a condition of arrested or retarded development of mind or any inherent causes or induced by disease or injury) as substantially impaired his responsibility for his acts." Accordingly, it has been suggested that the transient effect of drink, if sufficient to produce a toxic effect upon the brain, might amount to an "injury" within the meaning of the Act. Alternatively (in the picturesque phrase of one defence counsel) drink might "make up the deficit" necessary to convert a preexistent minor abnormality into a substantial impairment of responsibility. None of these

issues has yet been authoritatively decided. Sometimes the court has been able to wriggle out of a decision, as the Court of Criminal Appeal did when the "injury" argument was used on behalf of Di Duca,[19] on the ground that the particular offender concerned, whether drunk or sober, showed insufficient evidence of abnormality. Sometimes the opposite escape route has been available, as when the trial judge in the case of Dowdall,[20] while careful to emphasise that the section was not to be regarded as "a drunkard's charter," reminded the jury that two doctors had testified to the defendant's gross abnormality even apart from his admitted addiction to liquor. In Samuel's[21] case, on the other hand, in which the "deficit" theory was strongly argued in the absence of the jury, the judge clearly regarded it as inadmissible and made no reference to it in his summing up. But nearly two years later the Court of Criminal Appeal[22] concluded its judgment in Clarke's appeal with a statement that "the court wished to make it clear that it had not considered the effect of drink on a mind suffering from diminished responsibility. The court had not considered whether any abnormality of mind, however slight, would constitute a defence when substantially impaired by drink. That matter would have to be considered on another occasion."

After drink, insanity. A second complication has arisen in the problem of distinguishing between persons whose responsibility is merely diminished, and those who are deemed to be insane within the meaning of the M'Naughten Rules. Here there appears to be a division of opinion among the judges as to the right of the Crown to seek to establish insanity in cases in which the defence pleads only diminished responsibility. In two out of my earlier series of seventy-three cases in which this defence was raised, and in four of the later series of 126 cases, a verdict of guilty but insane was actually returned; and in at least half a dozen others in which this defence did succeed, the witnesses called by the Crown to rebut evidence of diminished responsibility sought to establish that the accused was in fact insane. Such a procedure was in keeping with the forecast of the Attorney-General in his speech on the Second Reading of the Homicide Bill.[23] "If," he said, "the defence raise any question as to the accused's mental capacity, and evidence is called to show that he is suffering from a serious abnormality of mind, then, if the evidence goes beyond a diminution of responsibility and really shows that the accused was within the M'Naughten Rules, it would be right for the judge to leave it to the jury to determine whether the accused was, to use the old phrase, 'guilty but insane,' or to return a verdict of manslaughter on the basis that, although not insane, he suffered from diminished responsibility. . . ." Nevertheless in the case of *Price* in 1962[24] the trial judge ruled that "if the Crown raises the issue of insanity and the jury find the accused guilty but insane, he cannot challenge the verdict in any higher court. . . . It seems to me," he said, "having regard to the serious consequences which would follow to a man if the Crown does succeed in raising the issue of insanity that the law cannot be, without an Act of Parliament, that a man should lose his right of appeal. In these circumstances I rule that the Crown is not entitled to invite the jury to consider the issue of insanity."

If this ruling is upheld, the result will be that the—at the best of times exceptionally difficult—distinction between insanity and diminished responsibility will be unlikely to be drawn on the merits of the case. For, except in extreme cases, the defence is always likely to prefer a plea of diminished responsibility to one of insanity, since if the latter succeeds indefinite detention necessarily follows, whereas on a conviction for manslaughter, which is the outcome of a successful defence of diminished responsibility, the court has complete discretion to pass whatever sentence it thinks fit. Persons who may be insane within the meaning of the M'Naughten Rules are therefore always likely to be tempted to plead diminished responsibility. Yet if they do, the jury will, if the analogy of the judgment in *Price's* case is followed, be precluded from hearing evidence as to their possible insanity and so arriving at an informed judgment on the issue of diminished responsibility versus insanity.

These developments can only be said to have added to the prevailing confusion. One other step has, however, been taken, which does at least aim at clarification. In the early days of the Act's operation juries were generally given little guidance as to the meaning of diminished responsibility. Judges did not ordinarily go beyond making sure that the members of the jury were familiar with the actual words of the section, which they were then expected to interpret for themselves. In 1960, however, in allowing the appeal of Patrick Byrne, the Birmingham Y.W.C.A. murderer, the Court of Criminal Appeal[25] attempted a formulation of the meaning of diminished responsibility on which judges have subsequently been able to draw in their directions to juries. In the words used by the Lord Chief Justice in this judgment "abnormality of mind" must be defined widely enough "to cover the mind's activities in all its aspects, not only the perception of physical acts and matters, and the ability to form a rational judgment as to whether an act is right or wrong, but also the ability to exercise willpower to control physical acts in accordance with that rational judgment." Furthermore, while medical evidence on this issue was said to be "no doubt of importance," it was not necessarily conclusive and might be outweighed by other material. Juries might also legitimately differ from doctors in assessing whether any impairment of responsibility could properly be regarded as "substantial"; and to guide them on this last point it was suggested that such phrases as "partial insanity" or on "the borderline of insanity" might be possible interpretations of the kind of abnormality which would substantially impair responsibility.

How far this helps may be a matter for argument. In the following year, in the case of Victor Terry, the Worthing bank murderer, Mr. Justice Stable adopted the original course of handing the jury a transcript of the (exceptionally voluminous) medical evidence instead of attempting to sum this up himself; but this procedure did not commend itself to the Court of Criminal Appeal,[26] although the court's disapproval did not go so far as to result in the condemned man's appeal being allowed or save him from being hanged. Certainly for my part I cannot think that anyone can listen to, or read, the sophisticated subtleties in which legal disputations about degrees of responsibility persistently flounder and founder without reaching the paradoxical conclusion that the harder we try to recognise the complexity of reality, the greater the unreality of the whole discussion. Indeed it is hardly surprising that in practice most of these subtleties probably pass over the heads of juries, whose conclusions appear to be reached on simpler grounds. At least two-thirds of those persons in whose cases a defence of diminished responsibility has succeeded have produced some serious evidence of previous mental instability such as a history of previous attempts at suicide, or of discharge from the Forces on psychiatric grounds, or of some trouble for which psychiatric advice has been sought, while a much higher proportion, though not medically diagnosed, are thought by relatives to be in some way peculiar. On the other hand, well under half of those in whose case a defence of diminished responsibility was not successful appear to have had any history of mental instability. It would seem that juries, clutching perhaps at straws, are disposed to take the view that a previous history of mental disturbance indicates (on the balance of probability, which is all that they have to establish) subsequent impairment of responsibility. And in the remaining cases, in which there is no such history, the concept of diminished responsibility seems to be dissolving into what is virtually the equivalent of a mitigating circumstance. Certainly in many of the more recent cases it is difficult to establish the presence of mental abnormality unless by the circular argument that anybody who commits homicide must, by definition, be unbalanced. It was surely compassion rather than evidence of mental abnormality which accounted for the success of a defence of diminished responsibility in the case of the major who found himself the father of a Mongol baby and, after reading up the subject of Mongolism in his public library, decided that the best course for everybody concerned would be to smother the child. And in the not infrequent cases in which a defence of diminished responsibility has succeeded, when homicide has resulted from such common human motives as sexual jealousy or the desire to escape from pecuniary embarrassment, it is hard not to believe that juries were moved more by the familiarity, than by the abnormality, of the offender's mental processes.

The most important development of the past few years lies, however, in the fact that the impossibility of keeping a clear line between the wicked and the weak-minded seems now to be officially admitted. In the judgment of the Court of Criminal Appeal on Byrne's appeal, from which I have already quoted, the Lord Chief Justice frankly admitted that "the step between 'he did not resist his impulse,' and 'he could not resist his impulse' " was one which was "incapable of scientific proof. *A fortiori,*" the judgment continues, "there is no scientific measurement of the degree of difficulty which an abnormal person finds in controlling his impulses. These problems which in the present state of medical knowledge are scientifically insoluble the jury can only approach in a broad commonsense way."

Apart from admiration of the optimism which expects common sense to make good the deficiencies of science, it is only necessary to add that the problem would seem to be insoluble, not merely in the present, but indeed in any, state of medical knowledge. Improved medical knowledge may certainly be expected to give better insight into the origins of mental abnormalities, and better predictions as to the probability that particular types of individuals will in fact "control their physical acts" or make "rational judgments"; but neither medical nor any other science can ever hope to prove whether a man who does not resist his impulses does not do so because he cannot or because he will not. The propositions of science are by definition subject to empirical validation; but since it is not possible to get inside another man's skin, no objective criterion which can distinguish between "he did not" and "he could not" is conceivable.

Logic, experience and the Lord Chief Justice thus all appear to lead to the same conclusion—that is to say, to the impossibility of establishing any reliable measure of responsibility in the sense of a man's ability to have acted otherwise than as he did. After all, every one of us can say with St. Paul (who, as far as I am aware, is not generally suspected of diminished responsibility) "the good that I would I do not: but the evil which I would not, that I do."

I have dealt at some length with our experience of diminished responsibility cases under the Homicide Act because taken together, the three facts, first, that under this Act questions of responsibility have to be decided before and not after conviction; second, that these questions fall to be decided by juries; and, third, that the charges involved are of the utmost gravity, have caused the relationship of responsibility to culpability to be explored with exceptional thoroughness in this particular context. But the principles involved are by no means restricted to the narrow field of charges of homicide. They have a far wider applicability, and are indeed implicit also in section 60 of the Mental Health Act. Unfortunately, up till now, and pending completion of the researches upon which I understand that Mr. Nigel Walker and his colleagues at Oxford are engaged, little is known of the working of this section. But it seems inevitable that if in any case a convicted person wished (as might well happen) to challenge the diagnosis of mental disorder which must precede the making of a hospital order, he would quickly be plunged into arguments about subnormality and psychopathy closely parallel to those which occupy so many hours of diminished responsibility trials.

At the same time the proposal that we should bypass, or disregard, the concept of responsibility is only too easily misunderstood; and I propose, therefore, to devote the remainder of this lecture to an attempt to meet some of the criticisms which have been brought against this proposal, to clarify just what it does or does not mean in the present context and to examine its likely implications.

First, it is to be observed that the term "responsibility" is here used in a restricted sense, much narrower than that which it often carries in ordinary speech. The measure of a person's responsibility for his actions is perhaps best defined in the words that I used earlier in terms of his capacity to act otherwise than as he did. A person may be described as totally irresponsible if he is wholly incapable of controlling his actions, and as being in a state of diminished responsibility if it is abnormally difficult for him to control them. Responsibility in this restricted sense is not to be confused with the sense in which a man is often said to be responsible for an action if he has in fact committed it. The questions: Who broke the window? and could the man who broke the window have prevented himself from doing so? are obviously quite distinct. To dismiss the second as unanswerable in no way diminishes the importance of finding an answer to the first. Hence the primary job of the courts in determining by whom a forbidden act has actually been committed is wholly unaffected by any proposal to disregard the question of responsibility in the narrower sense. Indeed the only problem that arises here is linguistic, inasmuch as one is accustomed to say that X was "responsible" for breaking the window when the intention is to convey no more than that he did actually break it. Another word is needed here (and I confess that I have not succeeded in finding one) to describe "responsibility" for doing an action as distinct from the capacity to refrain from doing it. "Accountable" has sometimes been suggested, but its usage in this sense is often awkward. "Instrumental" is perhaps better, though one could still wish for an adjective such perhaps as "agential" derived from the word "agent." However, all that matters is to keep firmly in mind that responsibility in the present context has nothing to do with the authorship of an act, only with the state of mind of its author.

In the second place, to discard the notion of responsibility does not mean that the mental condition of an offender ceases to have any importance, or that psychiatric considerations become irrelevant. The difference is that they become relevant, not to the question of determining the measure of his culpability, but to the choice of the treatment most likely to be effective in discouraging him from offending again; and even if these two aspects of the matter may be related, this is not to be dismissed as a distinction without a difference. The psychiatrist to whom it falls to advise as to the probable response of an offender to medical treatment no doubt has his own opinion as to the man's responsibility or capacity for self-control; and doubtless also those opinions are a factor in his judgment as to the outlook for medical treatment, or as to the probability that the offence will be repeated. But these are, and must remain, matters of opinion, "incapable," in Lord Parker's words, "of scientific proof." Opinions as to treatability, on the other hand, as well as predictions as to the likelihood of further offences can be put to the test of experience and so proved right or wrong. And by systematic observation of that experience, it is reasonable to expect that a body of knowledge will in time be built up, upon which it will be possible to draw, in the attempt to choose the most promising treatment in future cases.

Next, it must be emphasised that nothing in what has been said involves acceptance of a deterministic view of human behaviour. It is an indisputable fact of experience that human beings do respond predictably to various stimuli—whether because they choose to or because they can do no other it is not necessary to inquire. There are cases in which medical treatment works: there are cases in which it fails. Equally there are cases in which deterrent penalties appear to deter those upon whom they are imposed from committing further offences; and there are cases in which they do not. Once the criminal law is conceived as an instrument of crime prevention, it is these facts which demand attention, and from which we can learn to improve the efficiency of that instrument; and the question whether on any occasion a man could or could not have acted otherwise than as he did can be left on one side and answered either way, as may be preferred. It is no longer relevant.

Failure to appreciate this has, I think, led to conflicts between psychiatry and the law being often fought on the wrong ground. Even so radical a criminologist as Dr. Sheldon Glueck seems to see the issue as one between "those who stress the prime social need of blameworthiness and retributive punishment as the core-concept in crime and justice and those who, under the impact of psychiatric, psychoanalytic, sociological, and anthropological views insist that man's choices are the product of forces largely beyond his conscious control . . ."[27] Indeed Dr. Glueck's discussion of the relation of psychiatry to law is chiefly devoted to an analysis of the exculpatory effect of psychiatric knowledge, and to the changes that have been, or should be, made in the assessment of guilt as the result of the growth of this knowledge. In consequence much intellectual ingenuity is wasted in refining the criteria by which the wicked may be distinguished from the weak-minded. For surely to argue thus is to argue from the wrong premises: The real difference between the psychiatric and the legal approach has nothing to do with free will and determinism. It has to do with their conceptions of the objectives of the criminal process, with the question whether the aim of that process is punitive or preventive, whether what matters is to punish the wrongdoer or to set him on the road to virtue; and, in order to take a stand on that issue, neither party need be a determinist.

So much for what disregard of responsibility does not mean. What, in a more positive sense, is it likely to involve? Here, I think, one of the most important consequences must be to obscure the present rigid distinction between the penal and the medical institution. As things are, the supposedly fully responsible are consigned to the former: Only the wholly or partially irresponsible are eligible for the latter. Once it is admitted that we have no reliable criterion by which to distinguish between those two categories, strict segregation of each into a distinct set of institutions becomes absurd and impracticable. For purposes of convenience offenders for whom medical treatment is indicated will doubtless tend to be allocated to one building, and those for whom medicine has nothing to offer to another; but the formal distinction between prison and hospital will become blurred, and, one may reasonably expect, eventually obliterated altogether. Both will be simply "places of safety" in which offenders receive the treatment which experience suggests is most likely to evoke the desired response.

Does this mean that the distinction between doctors and prison officers must also become blurred? Up to a point it clearly does. At the very least it would seem that some fundamental implications for the medical profession must be involved when the doctor becomes part of the machinery of law enforcement. Not only is the normal doctor-patient relationship profoundly disturbed, but far-reaching questions also arise as to the nature of the condition which the doctor is called upon to treat. If a tendency to break the law is not in itself to be classified as a disease, which does he seek to cure—the criminality or the illness? To the medical profession these questions, which I have discussed at length elsewhere,[28] must be of primary concern. But for present purposes it may be more relevant to notice how, as so often happens in this country, changes not yet officially recognised in theory are already creeping in by the back door. Already the long-awaited institution at Grendon Underwood is administered as an integral part of the prison system; yet the régime is frankly medical. Its purpose has been described by the Prison Commission's Director of Medical Services as the investigation and treatment of mental disorder generally recognised as calling for a psychiatric approach; the investigation of the mental condition of offenders whose offences in themselves suggest mental instability; and an exploration of the problem of the treatment of the psychopath. Recommendations for admission are to come from prison medical officers, and the prison itself is under the charge of a medical superintendent with wide experience in psychiatry.[29]

Grendon Underwood is (unless one should include Broadmoor which has, of course, a much narrower scope) the first genuinely hybrid institution. Interchange between medical and penal institutions is, however, further facilitated by the power of the Home Secretary to transfer to hospital persons whom, on appropriate medical evidence, he finds to be suffering from mental disorder of a nature or degree to warrant their detention in a hospital for medical treatment. Such transfers have the same effect as does a hospital order, and they may be (and usually are) also accompanied by an order restricting discharge. It is, moreover, of some interest that transfers are sometimes made quite soon after the court has passed sentence. Out of six cases convicted under section 2 of the Homicide Act in which transfers under section 72 were effected, three were removed to hospital less than three months after sentence. Although it is, of course, always possible that the prisoner has been mentally normal at the time of his offence and had only suffered a mental breakdown later, transfer after a relatively short period does indicate at least a possibility that in the judgment of the Home Secretary some mental abnormality may have been already present either at the time of sentence or even when the crime was committed.

The courts, however, seem to be somewhat jealous of the exercise of this power, which virtually allows the Home Secretary to treat as sick persons whom they have sentenced to imprisonment and presumably regard as wicked. Indeed it seems that, if a diagnosis of mental disorder is to be made, the courts hold that it is, generally speaking, their business, and not the Home Secretary's, to make it. So at least it would appear from the judgments of the Court of Criminal Appeal in the cases of Constance Ann James[30] and Philip Morris,[31] both of whom had been found guilty of manslaughter on grounds of diminished responsibility and had been sentenced to imprisonment. In the former case, in which the evidence as to the accused's mental condition was unchallenged, the trial judge apparently had misgivings about the public safety and in particular the safety of the convicted woman's younger child whose brother she had killed. He therefore passed a sentence of three years' imprisonment, leaving it, as he said, to the appropriate authorities to make further inquiries so that the Secretary of State might, if he thought fit, transfer the prisoner to hospital under section 72 of the Mental Health Act. The appeal was allowed, on the ground that there was obviously no need for punishment, and that there were reasonable hopes that the disorder from which the woman suffered would prove curable. In the circumstances, though reluctant to interfere with the discretion of the sentencing court, the Court of Criminal Appeal substituted a hospital order accompanied by an indefinite restriction.

In Philip Morris' case, in which, however, the appellant was unsuccessful, the matter was put even more clearly. Again the trial judge had refused to make a hospital order on grounds of the public safety and, failing any vacancy in a secure hospital, had passed a sentence of life imprisonment. But on this the Court of Criminal Appeal commented as follows: "Although the discretion . . . is very wide indeed, the basic principle must be that in the ordinary case where punishment as such is not intended, and where the sole object of the sentence is that a man should receive mental treatment, and be at large as soon as he can safely be discharged, a proper exercise of the discretion demands that steps should be taken to exercise the powers under section 60 and that the matter should not be left to be dealt with by the Secretary of State under section 72."

These difficulties are, one may hope, of a transitional nature. They would certainly not arise if all sentences involving loss of liberty were indeterminate in respect of the type of institution in which the offender is to be detained: still less if rigid distinctions between medical and penal institutions were no longer maintained. The elimination of those distinctions, moreover, though unthinkable in a primary punitive system which must at all times segregate the blameworthy from the blameless, is wholly in keeping with a criminal law which is preventive rather than punitive in

intention.

In this lecture and in that which preceded it I have tried to signpost the road towards such a conception of the law, and to indicate certain landmarks which suggest that this is the road along which we are, if hesitantly, already treading. At first blush it might seem that strict liability and mental abnormality have not much in common; but both present a challenge to traditional views as to the point at which, and the purpose for which, considerations of guilty intent become relevant; and both illustrate the contemporary tendency to use the criminal law to protect the community against damage, no matter what might be the state of mind of those by whom that damage is done. In this context, perhaps, the little-noticed provisions of section 60 (2) of the Mental Health Act, with its distinction between the forbidden act and the conviction, along with the liberal implications of section 4 of the Criminal Justice Act, with its emphasis on treatability rather than culpability, are to be seen as the writing on the wall. And perhaps, too, it is significant that Dr. Glueck, notwithstanding his immediate preoccupation with definitions of responsibility, lets fall, almost as if with a sign, the forecast that some day it may be possible "to limit criminal law to matters of behavior alone," and that in his concluding lecture he foresees the "twilight of futile blameworthiness."[32] That day may be still a long way off: but at least it seems to be nearer than it was.

NOTES

1. *The Observer,* May 5, 1963.
2. I use this word throughout to describe a system the primary purpose of which is to prevent the occurrence of offences, whether committed by persons already convicted or by other people . . .
2a. Devlin, Sir Patrick (now Lord), *Law and Morals* (University of Birmingham) 1961, pp. 3, 7, 8, 9.
3. Radcliffe, Lord, *The Law and Its Compass* (Faber) 1961, p. 12.
4. *Shaw* v. *Director of Public Prosecutions* [1961] 2 W.L.R. 897.
5. *The Times,* November 11, 1961.
6. Edwards, J. Ll. J., *Mens Rea in Statutory Offences* (Macmillan) 1955, p. 247.
7. Devlin, Lord, *Samples of Law Making* (O.U.P.) 1962, pp. 71–80.
8. Hart, H. L. A., *Punishment and the Elimination of Responsibility* (Athlone Press) 1962, pp. 27, 28. Italics mine.
9. *Op. cit.,* pp. 29, 30.
10. Devlin, Lord, *Samples of Law Making* (O.U.P.) 1962, p. 73.
11. There could be an argument here, into which I do not propose to enter, as to whether this capacity is not shared by some of the higher animals.

12. Walker, N., "Queen Victoria Was Right," *New Society,* June 27, 1963.

13. House of Lords Debates, May 1, 1963, col. 174.

14. *R.* v. *James* [1961] Crim.L.R. 842.

15. One curious feature of this provision is the fact that a hospital order can apparently be made on a diagnosis of mental disorder, even if the disorder has no connection with the offence. See the Court of Criminal Appeal's judgment in the unsuccessful appeal of *R.* v. *Hatt* ([1962] Crim.L.R. 647) in which the appellant claimed that his predilection for unnecessary surgical operations had no connection with his no less fervent passion for making off with other people's cars.

16. House of Commons Standing Committee A, February 12, 1948, col. 1054.

17. Grünhut, M., *Probation and Mental Treatment* (to be published in the Library of Criminology).

18. Wootton, Barbara, "Diminished Responsibility: A Layman's View" (1960) 76 *Law Quarterly Review* 224.

19. *R.* v. *Di Duca* [1959] 43 Cr.App.R. 167.

20. Unpublished transcript.

21. Unpublished transcript.

22. *R.* v. *Clarke* [1962] Crim.L.R.836.

23. House of Commons Debates, Vol. 560 (November 15, 1956), col. 1252.

24. *R.* v. *Price* [1962] 3 All E.R. 960.

25. *R.* v. *Byrne* (1960) 44 Cr.App.R. 246.

26. *R.* v. *Terry* (1961) 45 Cr.App.R. 180.

27. Glueck, Sheldon, *Law and Psychiatry* (Tavistock Publications) 1962, p. 6.

28. Wootton, Barbara, "The Law, The Doctor and The Deviant," *British Medical Journal,* July 27, 1963.

29. Snell, H. K. (Director of Medical Services, Prison Commission), "H. M. Prison Grendon," *British Medical Journal,* September 22, 1962.

30. *R.* v. *James* [1961] Crim.L.R. 842.

31. *R.* v. *Morris* (1961) 45 Cr.App.R. 233.

32. Glueck, Sheldon, *Law and Psychiatry* (Tavistock Publications) 1962, pp. 33, 147.

H. L. A. HART

Changing Conceptions of Responsibility*

I

This lecture is concerned wholly with criminal responsibility and I have chosen to lecture on this subject here because both English and Israeli law have inherited from the past virtually the same doctrine concerning the criminal responsibility of the mentally abnormal and both have found this inheritance embarrassing. I refer of course to the M'Naghten rules of 1843. In Israel the Supreme Court has found it possible to supplement these exceedingly narrow rules by use of the doctrine incorporated in s. 11 of the Criminal Code Ordinance of 1936 that an 'exercise of will' is necessary for responsibility. This is the effect of the famous case of *Mandelbrot* v. *Attorney General*[1] and the subsequent cases which have embedded Agranat J's construction of s. 11 in Israeli law. English lawyers though they may admire this bold step, cannot use as an escape route from the confines of the M'Naghten rules the similar doctrine that for any criminal liability there must be a 'voluntary act' which many authorities have said is a fundamental requirement of English criminal law. For this doctrine has always been understood merely to exclude cases where the muscular movements are involuntary as in sleepwalking or 'automatism' or reflex action.[2] Nonetheless there have been changes in England; after a period of frozen immobility the hardened mass of our substantive criminal law is at points softening and yielding to its critics. But both the recent changes and the current criticisms of the law in this matter of criminal responsibility have taken a different direction from development in Israel and for this reason may be of some interest to Israeli lawyers.

Let me first say something quite general and very elementary about the historical background to these recent changes. In all advanced legal systems, liability to conviction for serious crimes is made dependent, not only on the offender having done those outward acts which the law forbids, but on his having done them in a certain frame of mind or with a certain will. These are the mental conditions or 'mental elements' in criminal responsibility and, in spite of much variation in detail and terminology, they are broadly similar in most legal systems. Even if you kill a man, this is not punishable as murder in most civilised jurisdictions if you do it unintentionally, accidentally or by mistake, or while suffering from certain forms of mental abnormality. Lawyers of the Anglo-American tradition use the Latin phrase *mens rea* (a guilty mind) as a comprehensive name for these necessary mental elements; and according to conventional ideas *mens rea* is a necessary element in liability to be established *before* a verdict. It is not something which is merely to be taken into consideration in determining the sentence or disposal of the convicted person, though it may also be considered for that purpose as well.

I have said that my topic in this lecture is the recent changes in England on this matter, but I shall be concerned less with changes in the law itself than with changes among critics of the law towards the whole doctrine of the mental element in responsibility. This change in critical attitude is, I believe, more important than any particular change in the detail of the doctrine of *mens rea*. I say this because for a century at least most liberal minded people have agreed in treating respect for the doctrine of *mens rea* as a hallmark of a civilised legal system. Until recently the great aim of most critics of the criminal law has been to secure that the law should take this doctrine very seriously and wholeheartedly. Critics have sought its expansion, and urged that the courts should be required always to make genuine efforts, when a person is accused of crime, to determine before convicting him whether that person actually did have the knowledge or intention or the sanity or any other mental element

*From *The Morality of the Criminal Law* by H. L. A. Hart (Jerusalem: Magnes Press, 1965). Reprinted as Chapter VIII of *Punishment and Responsibility: Essays in the Philosophy of Law* by H. L. A. Hart (New York and Oxford: Oxford University Press, 1967), pp. 186–209.

which the law, in its definition of crimes, makes a necessary condition of criminal liability. It is true that English law has often wavered on this matter and has even quite recently flirted with the idea that it cannot really afford to inquire into an individual's actual mental state before punishing him. There have always been English judges in whom a remark made in 1477 by Chief Justice Brian of the Common Pleas strikes a sympathetic chord. He said 'The thought of man is not triable; the devil alone knoweth the thought of man.'[3] So there are in English law many compromises on this matter of the relevance of a man's mind to the criminality of his deeds. Not only are there certain crimes of 'strict' liability where neither knowledge, nor negligence is required for conviction, but there are also certain doctrines of 'objective' liability such as was endorsed by the House of Lords in the much criticized case of *The Director of Public Prosecutions* v. *Smith*[4] on which Lord Denning lectured to you three years ago.[5] This doctrine enables a court to impute to an accused person knowledge or an intention which he may not really have had, but which an average man would have had. Theories have been developed in support of this doctrine of 'objective liability' of which the most famous is that expounded by the great American judge, Oliver Wendell Holmes in his book *The Common Law*. Nonetheless generations of progressive minded lawyers and liberal critics of the law have thought of the doctrine of *mens rea* as something to be cherished and extended, and against the scepticism of Chief Justice Brian they could quote the robust assertion of the nineteenth-century Lord Justice Bowen that 'the state of a man's mind is as much a fact as the state of his digestion.'[6] And they would have added that for the criminal law the former was a good deal more important than the latter.

But recently in England progressive and liberal criticism of the law has changed its direction. Though I think this change must in the end involve the whole doctrine of *mens rea,* it at present mainly concerns the criminal responsibility of mentally abnormal persons, and I can best convey its character by sketching the course taken in the criticism of the law in this matter. The main doctrine of English law until recently was of course the famous M'Naghten Rules formulated by the Judges of the House of Lords in 1843. As everybody knows, according to this doctrine, mental abnormality sufficient to constitute a defence to a criminal charge must consist of three elements: First, the accused, at the time of his act,

must have suffered from a defect of reason; secondly, this must have arisen from disease of the mind; thirdly, the result of it must have been that the accused did not know the nature of his act or that it was illegal. From the start English critics denounced these rules because their effect is to excuse from criminal responsibility only those whose mental abnormality resulted in lack of knowledge: in the eyes of these critics this amounted to a dogmatic refusal to acknowledge the fact that a man might know what he was doing and that it was wrong or illegal and yet because of his normal mental state might lack the capacity to control his action. This lack of capacity, the critics urged, must be the fundamental point in any intelligible doctrine of responsibility. The point just is that in a civilized system only those who *could have* kept the law should be punished. Why else should we bother about a man's knowledge or intention or other mental element except as throwing light on this?

Angrily and enviously, many of the critics pointed to foreign legal systems which were free of the English obsession with this single element of knowledge as the sole constituent of responsibility. As far back as 1810, the French Code simply excused those suffering from madness (démence) without specifying any particular connection between this and the particular act done. The German Code of 1871 spoke of inability or impaired ability to recognize the wrongness of conduct or to act in accordance with this recognition. It thus, correctly, according to the critics, treated as crucial to the issue of responsibility not knowledge but the capacity to conform to law. The Belgian Loi de Défence Sociale of 1930 makes no reference to knowledge or intelligence but speaks simply of a person's lack of ability as a consequence of mental abnormality to control his action. So till recently the great aim of the critics inspired by these foreign models was essentially to secure an amendment of the English doctrine of *mens rea* on this point: to supplement its purely cognitive test by a volitional one, admitting that a man might, while knowing that he was breaking the law, be unable to conform to it.

This dispute raged through the nineteenth century and was certainly marked by some curious features. In James Fitzjames Stephen's great *History of the Criminal Law*[7] the dispute is vividly presented as one between doctors and lawyers. The doctors are pictured as accusing the lawyers of claiming to decide a medical or scientific issue about responsibility by out-of-date criteria when they limited legal inquiry to the question of knowledge. The lawyers replied that the doctors, in seeking to give evidence about other matters, were attempting illicitly to thrust upon juries their views on what should excuse a man when charged with a crime: illicitly, because responsibility is a question not of science but of law. Plainly, the argument was here entrapped in the ambiguities of the word 'responsibility' about which more should have been said. But it is also remarkable that in the course of this long dispute no clear statements were made of the reason why the law should recognise any form of insanity as an excuse. The basic question as to what was at stake in the doctrine of *mens rea* was hardly faced. Is it necessary because punishment is conceived of as paying back moral evil done with some essentially retributive 'fitting' equivalent in pain? If so, what state of mind does a theory of retribution require a person punished to have had? Or is a doctrine of *mens rea* necessary because punishment is conceived as primarily a deterrent and this purpose would be frustrated or useless if persons were punished who at the time of their crime lacked certain knowledge or ability? Or is the doctrine to give effect not to a retributive theory but to principles of fairness or justice which require that a man should not be punished and so be used for the ends of others unless he had the capacity and a fair opportunity to avoid doing the thing for which he is punished? Certainly Bentham and Blackstone had something to say on these matters of fundamental principle, but they do not figure much in the century-long war which was waged by English reformers, sometimes in a fog, against the M'Naghten Rules. But what was clear in the fog was that neither party thought of calling the whole doctrine of *mens rea* in question. What was sought was merely amendments or additions to it.

Assault after assault on the M'Naghten Rules were beaten off until 1957. It cannot be said that the defenders of the doctrine used any very sharp rapiers in their defence. The good old English bludgeon which has beaten off so many reforms of English criminal law was enough. When Lord Atkin's Committee recommended in 1923 an addition to the M'Naghten Rules to cater for what it termed "irresistible impulse,' it was enough in the debate in the House of Lords[8] for judicial members to prophesy the harm to society which would inevitably flow from the amendment. Not a word was said to meet the point that the laws of many other countries already conformed to the proposal: nothing was said about the United States where a similar modification of the M'Naghten Rules providing for inability to conform to the law's requirement as well as defects in knowledge had been long accepted in several States without disastrous results. But in 1957, largely as a result of the immensely valuable examination of the whole topic by the Royal Commission on Capital Punishment[9] the law was amended, not as recommended by the Commission, but in the form of a curious compromise. This was the introduction of the idea borrowed from Scots law of a plea of diminished responsibility. S. 2 of the Homicide Act of 1957 provides that, on a murder charge, if what is most curiously called the accused's 'mental responsibility' was 'substantially' impaired by mental abnormality, he could be convicted, not of murder, but only of manslaughter, carrying a maximum sentence of imprisonment for life. This change in the law was indeed meagre since it concerned only murder; and even here it was but a halfway house, since the accused was not excused from punishment but was to be punished less than the maximum. The change does not excuse from responsibility but mitigates the penalty.

A word or two about the operation of the new plea of diminished responsibility during the last six years is necessary. The judges at first tended to treat it merely as catering for certain cases on the borderlines of the M'Naghten Rules, not as making a major change. Thus Lord Goddard refused to direct the jury that under the new plea the question of capacity to conform to law and not merely the accused's knowledge was relevant.[10] But the present Lord Chief Justice in a remarkable judgment expressly stated that this was so, and a generous interpretation was given to the section so as to include in the phrase 'abnormality of mind' the condition of the psychopath. He said that it was important to consider not only the accused's knowledge but also his ability 'to exercise will power to control physical acts in accordance with rational judgment.'[11] However, the most remarkable feature of six year's experience of this plea is made evident by the statistics: Apprehensions that it might lead to large-scale evasions of punishment have been shown to be quite baseless. For since the Homicide Act almost precisely the same percentage—about 47 per cent —of persons charged with murder escaped conviction on the ground of mental abnormality as before. What has happened is that the plea of insanity under the old M'Naghten Rules has virtually been displaced in murder cases by the new plea.[12] Though satisfactory, in that the old fears of reform have not been realized, the plea certainly has its critics and in part the general change in attitude of which I shall speak has been accelerated by it.

II

I have said that the change made by the introduction of diminished responsibility was both meagre and half-hearted. Nonetheless it marked the end of an era in the criticism of the law concerning the criminal responsibility of the mentally abnormal. From this point on criticism has largely changed its character. Instead of demanding that the court should take more seriously the task of dividing lawbreakers into two classes—those fully responsible and justly punishable because they had an unimpaired capacity to conform to the law, and those who were to be excused for lack of this—critics have come to think this a mistaken approach. Instead of seeking an expansion of the doctrine of *mens rea* they have argued that it should be eliminated and have welcomed the proliferation of offences of strict liability as a step in the right direction and a model for the future. The bolder of them have talked of the need to 'bypass' or 'dispense with' questions of responsibility and have condemned the old efforts to widen the scope of the M'Naghten Rules as waste of time or worse. Indeed, their attitude to such reforms is like that of the Communist who condemns private charity in a capitalist system because it tends to hide the radical errors of the system and thus preserve it. By far the best informed, most trenchant and influential advocate of these new ideas is Lady Wootton whose powerful work on the subject of criminal responsibility has done much to change and, in my opinion, to raise, the whole level of discussion.[13]

Hence, since 1957 a new skepticism going far beyond the old criticisms has developed. It is indeed a skepticism of the whole institution of criminal punishment so far as it contains elements which differentiate it from a system of purely forward-looking social hygiene in which our only concern, when we have an offender to deal with, is with the future and the rational aims of the prevention of further crime, the protection of society and the care and if possible the cure of the offender. For criminal punishment, as even the most progressive older critics of the M'Naghten Rules conceived of it, is *not* mere social hygiene. It differs from such a purely forward-looking system in the stress that it places on something in the past: the state of mind of the

accused as the time, not of his trial, but when he broke the law.

To many modern critics this backward-looking reference to the accused's past state of mind as a condition of his liability to compulsory measures seems a useless deflection from the proper forward-looking aims of a rational system of social control. The past they urge is over and done with, and the offender's past state of mind is only important as a diagnosis of the causes of his offence and a prognosis of what can be done now to counter these causes. Nothing in the past, according to this newer outlook, can in itself justify or be required to license what we do to the offender now; that is something to be determined exclusively by reference to the consequences to society and to him. Lady Wootton argues that if the aim of the criminal law is to be the prevention of 'socially damaging actions' not retribution for past wickedness, the conventional doctrine puts *mens rea* 'into the wrong place.'[14] *Mens rea* is on her view relevant only *after* conviction as a guide to what measures should be taken to prevent a recurrence of the forbidden act. She considers it 'illogical,' if the aim of the criminal law is prevention, to make *mens rea* part of the definition of a crime and a necessary condition of the offender's liability to compulsory measures.[15]

This way of thinking leads to a radical revision of the penal system which in crude outline and in its most extreme form is as follows: Once it has been proved in a court that a person's outward conduct fits the legal definition of some crime, this without proof or any *mens rea,* is sufficient to bring him within the scope of compulsory measures. These may be either of a penal or therapeutic kind or both; or it may be found that no measures are necessary in a particular case and the offender may be discharged. But the choice between these alternatives is not to be made by reference to the offender's past mental state—his culpability—but by consideration of what steps, in view of his present mental state and his general situation, are likely to have the best consequences for him and for society.

I have called this the extreme form of the new approach because as I have formulated it is generally applicable to all offenders alike. It is not a system reserved solely for those who could be classed as mentally abnormal. The whole doctrine of *mens rea* would on this extreme version of the theory be dropped from the law; so that the distinctions which at present we draw and think vital to draw before convicting an offender, between, for example, intentional and unintentional wrongdoing, would no longer be relevant at this stage. To show that you have struck or wounded another unintentionally or without negligence would not save you from conviction and liability to such treatment, penal or therapeutic, as the court might deem advisable on evidence of your mental state and character.

This is, as I say, the extreme form of the theory, and it is the form that Lady Wootton now advances.[16] But certainly a less extreme though more complex form is conceivable which would replace, not the whole doctrine of *mens rea,* but only that part of it which concerns the legal responsibility of the mentally abnormal. In this more moderate form of the theory, a mentally normal person would still escape conviction if he acted unintentionally or without some other requisite mental element forming part of the definition of the crime charged. The innovation would be that no form of insanity or mental abnormality would bar a conviction, and this would no longer be investigated before conviction.[17] It would be something to be investigated only after conviction to determine what measures of punishment or treatment would be most efficacious in the particular case. It is important to observe that most advocates of the elimination of responsibility have been mainly concerned with the inadequacies or absurdities of the existing law in relation to mentally abnormal offenders, and some of these advocates may have intended only the more moderate form of the theory which is limited to such offenders. But I doubt if this is at all representative, for many, including Lady Wootton, have said that no satisfactory line can be drawn between the mentally normal and abnormal offenders: There simply are no clear or reliable criteria. They insist that general definitions of mental health are too vague and too conflicting; we should be freed from all such illusory classifications to treat, in the most appropriate way from the point of view of society, all persons who have actually manifested the behaviour which is the *actus reus* of a crime.[18] The fact that harm was done unintentionally should not preclude an investigation of what steps if any are desirable to prevent a repetition. This skepticism of the possibility of drawing lines between the normal and abnormal offenders commits advocates of the elimination of responsibility to the extreme form of the theory.

Such then are the essentials of the new idea. Of course the phrase 'eliminating responsibility' does sound very alarming and when Lady Wootton's work first made it a centre of discussion the columns of *The Times* newspaper showed how fluttered legal and other dovecotes were. But part at least of the alarm was unnecessary because it arose from the ambiguities of the word 'responsibility'; and it is, I think, still important to distinguish two of the very different things this difficult word may mean. To say that someone is legally responsible for something often means only that under legal rules he is liable to be made either to suffer or to pay compensation in certain eventualities. The expression 'he'll pay for it' covers both these things. In this the primary sense of the word, though a man is normally only responsible for his own actions or the harm he has done, he may be also responsible for the actions of other persons if legal rules so provide. Indeed in this sense a baby in arms or a totally insane person might be legally responsible—again, if the rules so provide; for the word simply means liable to be made to account or pay and we might call this sense of the word 'legal accountability.' But the new idea—the programme of eliminating responsibility—is not, as some have feared, meant to eliminate legal accountability: Persons who break the law are not just to be left free. What is to be eliminated are enquiries as to whether a person who has done what the law forbids was responsible at the time he did it and responsible in this sense does not refer to the legal status of accountability. It means the capacity, so far as this is a matter of a man's mind or will, which normal people have to control their actions and conform to law. In this sense of responsibility a man's responsibility can be said to be 'impaired.' That is indeed the language of s. 2 of the Homicide Act 1957 which introduced into English law the idea of diminished responsibility: it speaks of a person's *'mental'* responsibility and in the rubric to s. 2 even of persons 'suffering from' diminished responsibility. If is of course easy to see why this second sense of responsibility (which might be called 'personal responsibility') has grown up alongside the primary idea of legal accountability. It is no doubt because the law normally, though not always, confines legal accountability to persons who are believed to have normal capacities of control.

So perhaps the new ideas are less alarming than they seem at first. They are also less new, and those who advocate them have always been able to point to earlier developments within English law which seem to foreshadow these apparently revolutionary ideas. Lady Wootton herself makes much of the fact that the doctrine of *mens rea* in the case of normal offenders has been watered down by the introduction of strict liability and she deprecates the alarm this has raised. But apart from this, the courts have often been able to deal with mentally abnormal persons accused of crime without confronting the issue of their personal responsibility at the time of their offence. There are in fact several different ways in which this question may be avoided. A man may be held on account of his mental state to be unfit to plead when brought to trial; or he may be certified insane before trial; or, except on a charge of murder, an accused person might enter a plea of guilty with the suggestion that he should be put on probation with a condition of mental treatment.[19] In fact, only a very small percentage of the mentally abnormal have been dealt with under the M'Naghten Rules, a fact which is understandable since a successful plea under those Rules means detention in Broadmoor for an indefinite period and many would rather face conviction and imprisonment and so may not raise the question of mental abnormality at all. So the old idea of treating mental abnormality as bearing on the question of the accused's responsibility and to be settled before conviction, has with few exceptions only been a reality in murder cases to which alone is the plea of diminished responsibility applicable.

But the most important departure from received ideas incorporated in the doctrine of *mens rea* is the Mental Health Act, 1959, which expands certain principles of older legislation. S. 60 of this Act provides that in any case, except where the crime is not punishable by imprisonment or the sentence is fixed by the law (and this latter exception virtually excludes only murder), the courts may, after conviction of the offender, if two doctors agree that the accused falls into any of four specified categories of mental disorder, order his detention for medical treatment instead of passing a penal sentence, though it requires evidence that such detention is warranted. The four categories of mental disorder are very wide and include even psychopathic disorder in spite of the general lack of clear or agreed criteria of this condition. The courts are told by the statute that in exercising their choice between penal or medical measures to have regard to the nature of the offence and the character and antecedents of the offender. These powers have come to be widely used[20] and are available even in cases where a murder charge has been reduced to manslaughter on a plea of provocation or diminished responsibility.

Advocates of the programme of eliminating re-

sponsibility welcome the powers given by the Mental Health Act to substitute compulsory treatment for punishment, but necessarily they view it as a compromise falling short of what is required, and we shall understand their own views better if we see why they think so. It falls short in four respects. First the power given to courts to order compulsory treatment instead of punishment is discretionary, and even if the appropriate medical evidence is forthcoming the courts may still administer conventional punishment if they choose. The judges *may* still think in terms of responsibility, and it is plain that they occasionally do so in these cases. Thus in the majority of cases of conviction for manslaughter following on a successful plea of diminished responsibility, the courts have imposed sentences of imprisonment notwithstanding their powers under s. 60 of the Mental Health Act, and the Lord Chief Justice has said that in such cases the prisoner may on the facts be shown to have *some* responsibility for which he must be punished.[21] Secondly, the law itself still preserves a conception of penal methods, such as imprisonment, coloured by the idea that it is a payment for past wickedness and not just an alternative to medical treatment; for though the courts may order medical treatment or punish, they cannot combine these. This of course is a refusal to think, as the new critics demand we should think,[22] of punitive and medical measures as merely different forms of social hygiene to be used according to a prognosis of their effects on the convicted person. Thirdly, as it stands at present, the scheme presupposes that a satisfactory distinction can be drawn on the basis of its four categories of mental disorder between those who are mentally abnormal and those who are not. But the more radical reformers are not merely sceptical about the adequacy of the criteria which distinguish, for example, the psychopath from the normal offender: They would contend that there may exist propensities to certain types of socially harmful behaviour in people who are in other ways not abnormal and that a rational system should attend to these cases.

But fourthly, and this is most important, the scheme is vitiated for these critics because the courts' powers are only exercisable after the conviction of an offender and, for this conviction, proof of *mens rea* at the time of his offence is still required: The question of the accused's mental abnormality may still be raised before conviction as a defence if the accused so wishes. So the Mental Health Act does not 'bypass' the whole question of responsibility: It does not eliminate the doctrine of *mens rea*. It expands the courts' discretion in dealing with a convicted person, enabling them to choose between penal and therapeutic measures and making this choice in practice largely independent of the offender's state of mind at the time of his offence. Its great merit is that the mentally abnormal offender who would before have submitted to a sentence of imprisonment rather than raise a plea of insanity under the M'Naghten Rules (because success would mean indeterminate detention in Broadmorr) may now be encouraged to bring forward his mental condition after conviction, in the hope of obtaining a hospital order rather than a sentence of imprisonment.

The question which now awaits our consideration is the merits of the claim that we should proceed from such a system as we now have under the Mental Health Act to one in which the criminal courts were freed altogether from the doctrine of *mens rea* and could proceed to the use of either penal or medical measures at discretion simply on proof that the accused had done the outward acts of a crime. Prisons and hospitals under such a scheme will alike 'be simply "places of safety" in which offenders receive the treatment which experience suggests is most likely to evoke the desired response.'[23]

The case for adopting these new ideas in their entirety has been supposed by arguments of varying kinds and quality, and it is very necessary to sift the wheat from the chaff. The weakest of the arguments is perhaps the one most frequently heard, namely, that our concern with personal responsibility incorporated in the doctrine of *mens rea* only makes sense if we subscribe to a retributive theory of punishment according to which punishment is used and justified as an 'appropriate' or 'fitting' return for past wickedness and not merely as a preventive of antisocial conduct. This, as I have argued elsewhere,[24] is a philosophical confusion and Lady Wootton falls a victim to it because she makes too crude a dichotomy between 'punishment' and 'prevention.' She does not even mention a moral outlook on punishment which is surely very common, very simple and, except perhaps for the determinist, perfectly defensible. This is the view that out of considerations of fairness or justice to individuals we should restrict even punishment designed as a 'preventive' to those who had a normal capacity and a fair opportunity to obey. This is still an intelligible ideal of justice to the individuals whom we punish even if we punish them to pro-

tect society from the harm that crime does and not to pay back the harm that they have done. And it remains intelligible even if in securing this form of fairness to those whom we punish we secure a lesser measure of conformity to law than a system of total strict liability which repudiated the doctrine of *mens rea*.

But of course it is certainly arguable that, at present, in certain cases, in the application of the doctrine of *mens rea,* we recognize this principle of justice in a way which plays too high a price in terms of social security. For there are indeed cases where the application of *mens rea* operates in surprising and possibly dangerous ways. A man may cause very great harm, may even kill another person, and under the present law neither be punished for it nor subjected to any compulsory medical treatment or supervision. This happened, for example, in February 1961 when a United States Air Force sergeant,[25] after a drunken party, killed a girl, according to his own story, in his sleep. He was tried for murder but the jury were not persuaded by the prosecution, on whom the legal burden of proof rests, that the sergeant's story was false and he was accordingly acquitted and discharged altogether. It is worth observing that in recent years in cases of dangerous driving where the accused claims that he suffered from 'automatism' or a sudden lapse of consciousness, the courts have striven very hard to narrow the scope of this defence because of the obvious social dangers of an acquittal of such persons, unaccompanied by any order for compulsory treatment. They have produced a most complex body of law distinguishing between 'sane' and 'insane' automatism each with their special burdens of proof.[26] No doubt such dangerous cases are not very numerous and the risk of their occurrence is one which many people might prefer to run rather than introduce a new system dispensing altogether with proof of *mens rea*. In any case something less extreme than the new system might deal with such cases; for the courts could be given powers in the case of such physically harmful offences to order, notwithstanding an acquittal, any kind of medical treatment or supervision that seemed appropriate.

But the most important arguments in favour of the more radical system in which proof of the outward act alone is enough to make the accused liable to compulsory measures of treatment or punishment, comes from those who, like Lady Wootton, have closely scrutinized the actual working of the old plea of insanity and the plea of diminished responsibility introduced in 1957 by the Homicide Act into cases of homicide. The latter treats mental abnormality as an aspect of *mens rea* and forces the courts before the verdict to decide the question whether the accused's 'mental responsibility,' that is, his capacity to control his actions was 'substantially impaired' at the time of his offence when he killed another person. The conclusion drawn by Lady Wootton from her impressive and detailed study of all the cases (199 in number) in which this plea was raised down to mid-September of 1962, is that this question which is thus forced upon the courts should be discarded as unanswerable. Here indeed she echoes the cry, often in earlier years thundered from the Bench, that it is impossible to distinguish between an irresistable impulse and an impulse which was merely not resisted by the accused.

But here too if we are to form a balanced view we must distinguish between dubious philosophical contentions and some very good sense. The philosophical arguments (which I will not discuss here in detail) pitch the case altogether too high: They are supposed to show that the question whether a man could have acted differently is *in principle unanswerable* and not merely that in Law Courts we do not usually have clear enough evidence to answer it. Lady Wootton says that a man's responsibility or capacity to resist temptation is something 'buried in [his] consciousness, into which no human being can enter,'[27] known if at all only to him and to God: it is not something which other men may never know; and since 'it is not possible to get inside another man's skin'[28] it is not something of which they can ever form even a reasonable estimate as a matter of probability. Yet strangely enough she does not take the same view of the question which arises under the M'Naghten Rules whether a man knew what he was doing or that it was illegal, although a man's knowledge is surely as much, or as little, locked in his breast as his capacity for self control. Questions about the latter indeed may often be more difficult to answer than questions about a man's knowledge; yet in favourable circumstances if we know a man well and can trust what he says about his efforts or struggles to control himself we may have as good ground for saying 'Well he just could not do it though he tried' as we have for saying 'He didn't know that the pistol was loaded.' And we sometimes may have good general evidence that in certain conditions, for example infancy or a clinically definable state, such as depression after childbirth, human beings are unable or less able than the normal adult to master certain impulses. We are not forced by the facts to say of a child or mental defective, who has struggled vainly with tears, merely 'he usually cries when that happens.' We say—and why not? —'he could not stop himself crying though he tried as hard as he could.'

It must however be concealed that such clear cases are very untypical of those that face the Courts where an accused person is often fighting for his life or freedom. Lady Wootton's best arguments are certainly independent of her more debatable philosophical points about our ability to know what is locked in another's mind or breast. Her central point is that the evidence put before Courts on the question whether the accused lacked the capacity to conform to the law, or whether it was substantially impaired, at the best only shows the *propensity* of the accused to commit crimes of certain sorts. From this, she claims, it is a fallacy to infer that he could not have done otherwise than commit the crime of which he is accused. She calls this fallacious argument 'circular': We infer the accused's lack of capacity to control his actions from his propensity to commit crimes and then both explain this propensity and excuse his crimes by his lack of capacity. Lady Wootton's critics have challenged this view of the medical and other evidence on which the courts act in these cases.[29] They would admit that it is at any rate in part through studying a man's crimes that we may discern his incapacity to control his actions. Nonetheless the evidence for this conclusion is not merely the bare fact that he committed these crimes repeatedly, but the manner and the circumstances and the psychological state in which he did this. Secondly in forming any conclusion about a man's ability to control his action much more than his repeated crimes are taken into account. Antisocial behaviour is not just used to explain and excuse itself, even in the case of the psychopath, the definition of whose disorder presents great problems. I think there is much in these criticisms. Nonetheless the forensic debate before judge and jury of the question whether a mentally disordered person could have controlled his action or whether his capacity to do this was or was not 'substantially impaired' seems to me very often very unreal. The evidence tendered is not only often conflicting, but seems to relate to the specific issue of the accused's power or capacity for control on a specific past occasion only very remotely. I can scarcely believe that on this, the supposed issue, anything coherent penetrates to the minds of the jury after they have heard the difficult expert evidence and heard the judge's warning that these matters are 'incapable of scientific proof.'[30] And I sympathize with the judges in their difficult task of instructing juries on this plea. In Israel there are no juries to be instructed and the judges themselves must confront these same difficulties in deciding in accordance with the principle of the *Mandelbrot* case whether or not the action of a mentally abnormal person who knew what he was doing occurred 'independently of the exercise of his will.'

Because of these difficulties I would prefer to the present law the scheme which I have termed the 'moderate' form of the new doctrine. Under this scheme *mens rea* would continue to be a necessary condition of liability to be investigated and settled before conviction except so far as it relates to mental abnormality. The innovation would be that an accused person would no longer be able to adduce any form of mental abnormality as a bar to conviction. The question of his mental abnormality would under this scheme be investigated only after conviction and would be primarily concerned with his present rather than his past mental state. His past mental state at the time of his crime would only be relevant so far as it provided ancillary evidence of the nature of his abnormality and indicated the appropriate treatment. This position could perhaps be fairly easily reached by eliminating the pleas of insanity and diminished responsibility and extending the provisions of the Mental Health Act, 1959 to all offences including murder. But I would further provide that, in cases where the appropriate direct evidence of mental disorder was forthcoming, the courts should no longer be permitted to think in terms of responsibility and mete out penal sentences instead of compulsory medical treatment. Yet even this moderate reform certainly raises some difficult questions requiring careful consideration.[31]

Many I think would wish to go further than this 'moderate' scheme and would join Lady Wootton in a demand for the elimination of the whole doctrine of *mens rea* or at least in the hope that it will 'wither away.' My reasons for not joining them consist of misgivings on three principal points. The first concerns individual freedom. In a system in which proof of *mens rea* is no longer a necessary condition for conviction, the occasions for official interferences with our lives and for compulsion will be vastly increased. Take, for example, the notion of a criminal assault. If the doctrine of *mens rea* were swept away, every blow, even if it was apparent to a policeman that it was purely accidental or merely careless and therefore not, according to the present law, a criminal assault, would be a matter for investigation under the new scheme, since the possibilities of a curable or treatable condition would have to be investigated and the condition if serious treated by medical or penal methods. No doubt under the new dispensation, as at present, prosecuting authorities would use their common sense; but very considerable discretionary powers would have to be entrusted to them to sift from the mass the cases worth investigation as possible candidates for therapeutic or penal treatment. No one could view this kind of expansion of police powers with equanimity, for with it will come great uncertainty for the individual: Official interferences with his life will be more frequent but he will be less able to predict their incidence if any accidental or careless blow may be an occasion for them.

My second misgiving concerns the idea to which Lady Wootton attaches great importance: that what we now call punishment (imprisonment and the like) and compulsory medical treatment should be regarded just as alternative forms of social hygiene to be used according to the best estimate of their future effects and no judgment of responsibility should be required before we apply to a convicted person those measures, such as imprisonment, which we now think of as penal. Lady Wootton thinks this will present no difficulty as long as we take a firm hold of the idea that the purpose and justification of the criminal law is to prevent crime and not to pay back criminals for their wickedness. But I do not think objections to detaching the use of penal methods from judgments of responsibility can be disposed of so easily. Though Lady Wootton looks forward to the day when the 'formal distinction' between hospitals and prisons will have disappeared, she does not suggest that we should give up the use of measures such as imprisonment. She contemplates that 'those for whom medicine has nothing to offer'[32] may be sentenced to 'places of safety' to receive 'the treatment which experience suggests is most likely to evoke the desired responses,' and though it will only be for the purpose of convenience that their 'places of safety' will be separate from those for whom medicine has something to offer, she certainly accepts the idea that imprisonment may be used for its deterrent effect on the person sentenced to it.

This vision of the future evokes from me two different responses: One is a moral objection and the other a sociological or criminological doubt.

The moral objection is this: If we imprison a man who has broken the law in order to deter him and by his example others, we are using him for the benefit of society, and for many people, including myself, this is a step which requires to be justified by (*inter alia*) the demonstration that the person so treated could have helped doing what he did. The individual according to this outlook, which is surely neither esoteric nor confused, has a right not to be used in this way unless he could have avoided doing what he did. Lady Wootton would perhaps dismiss this outlook as a disguised form of a retributive conception of punishment. But it is in fact independent of it as I have attempted to show: for though we must seek a moral licence for punishing a man in his voluntary conduct in breaking the law, the punishment we are then licensed to use may still be directed solely to preventing future crimes on his part or on others' and not to 'retribution.'

To this moral objection it may be replied that it depends wholly on the assumption that imprisonment for deterrent purposes will, under the new scheme, continue to be regarded by people generally as radically distinct from medical treatment and still requiring justification in terms of responsibility. It may be said that this assumption should not be made; for the operation of the system itself will in time cause this distinction to fade, and conviction by a court, followed by a sentence of imprisonment, will in time be assimilated to such experiences as a compulsory medical inspection followed by detention in an isolation hospital. But here my sociological or criminological doubts begin. Surely there are two features which, at present, are among those distinguishing punishment from medical treatment and will have to be stripped away before this assimilation can take place, and the moral objection silenced. One of these is that, unlike medical treatment, we use deterrent punishment to deter not only the individual punished but others by the example of his punishment and the severity of the sentence may be adjusted accordingly. Lady Wootton is very skeptical of the whole notion that we can deter in this way potential offenders and therefore she may be prepared to forego this aspect of punishment altogether. But can we on the present available evidence safely adopt this course for all crime? The second feature distinguishing punishment from treatment is that unlike a medical inspection followed by detention in hospital, conviction by a court followed by a sentence of imprisonment is a public act expressing the odium, if not the hostility, of society for those who break the law. As long as these features attach to conviction and a sentence of imprisonment, the moral objection to their use on those who could not have helped doing what they did will remain. On the other hand, if they cease to attach, will not the law have lost an important element in its authority and deterrent force—as important perhaps for some convicted persons as the deterrent force of the actual measures which it administers.

My third misgiving is this. According to Lady Wootton's argument it is a mistake, indeed 'illogical,' to introduce a reference to *mens rea* into the definition of an offence. But it seems that a code of criminal law which omitted any reference in the definition of its offences to mental elements could not possibly be satisfactory. For there are some socially harmful activities which are now and should always be treated as criminal offences which can only be identified by reference to intention or some other mental element. Consider the idea of an attempt to commit a crime. It is obviously desirable that persons who attempt to kill or injure or steal, even if they fail, should be brought before courts for punishment or treatment; yet what distinguishes an attempt which fails from an innocent activity is just the fact that it is a step taken with the intention of bringing about some harmful consequence.

I do not consider my misgivings on these three points as necessarily insuperable objections to the programme of eliminating responsibility. For the first of them rests on a judgment of the value of individual liberty as compared with an increase in social security from harmful activities, and with this comparative judgment others may disagree. The second misgiving in part involves a belief about the dependence of the efficacy of the criminal law on the publicity and odium at present attached to conviction and sentence and on deterrence by example; psychological and sociological researches may one day show that this belief is false. The third objection may perhaps be surmounted by some ingenuity or compromise, since there are many important offences to which it does not apply. Nonetheless I am certain that the questions I have raised here should worry advocates of the elimination of responsibility more than they do; and until they have been satisfactorily answered I do not think we should move the whole way into this part of the Brave New World.

NOTES

1. (1956) 10 P.D. 281.
2. See Edwards, 'Automatism and Criminal Responsibil-

ity' 21 M. L. R. (1958), p. 375, and Acts of Will and Responsibility. Chap. IV, *supra*. The doctrine as now formulated descends from Austin, *Lectures in Jurisprudence,* Lectures XVIII and XIX.

3. *Year Book,* 17 Pasch Ed. IV. f. 1. pl. 2.

4. (1961) A. C. 290.

5. Denning, *Responsibility before the Law,* Jerusalem, 1961.

6. *Edgington* v. *Fitzmaurice* (1885), 29 Ch. D. 459.

7. Chap. XIX, Vol. II, 'On the Relation of Madness to Crime.'

8. 57 H. L. Deb. 443–76 (1924), 'if this Bill were passed very grave results would follow' (Lord Sumner, p. 459). 'What a door is being opened!' (Lord Hewart, p. 467). 'This would be a very dangerous change to make' (Lord Cave, p. 475).

9. Cmd. 8932 (1953).

10. *R.* v. *Spriggs* (1958), 1 Q. B. 270.

11. *R.* v. *Byrne* (1960), 44 Cr. App. Rep. 246.

12. For the statistics see *Murder: Home Office Research Unit Report,* H.M.S.O. 1961, Table 7, p. 10.

13. See her *Social Science and Social Pathology* (1959) esp. Chapter VIII on 'Mental Disorder and the Problem of Moral and Criminal Responsibility;' 'Diminished Responsibility: A Layman's View' 76 L.Q.R. (1960), p. 224; *Crime and the Criminal Law* (1963).

14. See *Crime and the Criminal Law,* p. 52. But she does not consider explicitly whether, even if the aim of the criminal law is to prevent crime, there are not moral objections to applying its sanctions even as preventives to those who lacked the capacity to conform to the Law. See *infra,* pp. 207–8.

15. Op. cit., p. 51.

16. In *Crime and the Criminal Law* she makes it clear that the elimination or 'withering away' of *mens rea* as a condition of liability is to apply to all its elements not merely to its provisions for mental abnormality. Hence strict liability is welcomed as the model for the future (op. cit., pp. 46–57).

17. Save as indicated *infra* p. 205, n. 31.

18. See Wootton, op. cit., p. 51.

19. In 1962 the number of persons over 17 treated in these ways were respectively 36 (unfit to plead), 5 (insane before trial), and 836 (probation with mental treatment). See *Criminal Statistics* 1962.

20. In 1962 hospital orders under this section were made in respect of 1187 convicted persons (*Criminal Statistics* 1962).

21. *R.* v. *Morris* (1961) 45 Cr. App. Rep. 185.

22. See Wootton, op. cit., pp. 79–80.

23. Wootton, op. cit., pp. 79–80.

24. 'Punishment and the Elimination of Responsibility,' Chap. VII, *supra.*

25. *The Times,* 18 February 1961 (Staff Sergeant Boshears).

26. See *Bratty* v. *Atta. Gen. For Northern Ireland* (1961), 3 All E.R., 523 and Cross, 'Reflections on Bratty's Case' 78 *L.Q.R.* (1962), p. 236.

27. See 'Diminished Responsibility: A Layman's view' 76 *L.Q.R.* (1960), p. 232.

28. See *Crime and the Criminal Law,* p. 74.

29. See N. Walker, 'M'Naghten's Ghost,' *The Listener,* 29 Aug. 1963, p. 303.

30. Per Parker C. J. in *R.* v. *Byrne* (1960) 44 Cr. App. 246 at 258.

31. Of these difficult questions the following seem the most important.

(1) If the post-conviction inquiry into the convicted person's mental abnormality is to focus on his present state, what should a court do with an offender (a) who suffered some mental disorder at the time of his crime but has since recovered? (b) who was 'normal' at the time of the crime but at the time of his conviction suffers from mental disorder?

(2) The Mental Health Act does not by its terms require the court to be satisfied before making a hospital order that there was any causal connection between the accused's disorder and his offence, but only provides that the court in the exercise of its discretion shall have regard to the nature of the offence. Would this still be satisfactory if the courts were bound to make a hospital order if the medical evidence of abnormality is forthcoming?

(3) The various elements of *mens rea* (knowledge, intention, and the minimum control of muscular movements required for an act) may be absent either in a person otherwise normal or may be absent because of some mental disorder (compare the distinctions now drawn between 'sane' and 'insane' automatism). (See *supra,* p. 202). Presumably it would be desirable that in the latter case there should not be an acquittal; but to identify such cases where there were grounds for suspecting mental abnormality, some investigation of mental abnormality would be necessary before the verdict.

32. Op. cit., p. 79–80 ('places of safety' are in quotation marks in her text).

HYMAN GROSS

Mental Abnormality as a Criminal Excuse*

I

A person's mental condition at the time he engages in criminal conduct may relieve him from criminal liability. When this is the case, we say that he is not criminally liable because he was not a responsible person at the time of the offense. To say that one was not responsible in this sense is to assert the most personal of all excuses. What interests us is not something about the performance but something about the actor. The actor is said not to have had available those personal resources that are necessary to qualify him as accountable for his conduct. Since he is not accountable he cannot be faulted for his conduct and so enjoys exemption from judgments of culpability.

Mental abnormality of a sort relevant to excusing exists, then, when mental resources necessary for accountability are lacking. There are four varieties of relevant abnormality: One is mental illness that, formerly in medical literature and still in legal literature, would be characterized as a *disease* of the mind, by virtue of a sufficiently definite pathology and sufficiently pronounced morbidity. Intoxication, whatever its source, is another variety. Mental defectiveness is a third sort of relevant abnormality, encompassing cases of serious deficiency mainly in intelligence but including deficiency of any mental capacity necessary to control behavior. Finally, there is a variety of abnormality that may be conveniently referred to as automatism, which includes behavioral phenomena diverse in origin but which all are instances of a gross separation of consciousness and action such as exists during hypnosis, somnambulism, and epileptic seizures.

Relevant impairments of mental capacity may have an origin which is extrapsychic or intrapsychic. Drugs, alcohol, hypnotic suggestion, a blow on the head, emotional shock, an extra chromo-

some, or a brain tumor are all ways in which incapacitation may be produced by external interventions upon normal mental functioning. It is clear that a person may himself be responsible for some of these interventions by doing something to himself or allowing others to. When this is the case, he is deemed responsible for the resulting condition he is in, though not otherwise. Still, one's being responsible for his condition does not always entail being criminally liable for what he does while in that condition. If he suffers mental incapacitation sufficient for him not to be responsible, he is then treated as one who is not, regardless of his having been a responsible person with reference to putting himself in that condition. A person may ultimately cause himself to suffer sieges of delirium tremens by the gradual effects of his own alcoholic indulgence. Yet he is entitled to be treated as not responsible regarding acts done during those sieges no less than a person whose delusions have an origin utterly beyond his control. But if a person while responsible does things to put himself in a state of incapacitation in which harmful conduct is expectable—he intoxicates himself to a dangerous degree—he may be liable for that when the harm occurs or, even without it occurring, when he engages in conduct that threatens the harm. The reason is that incapacitating himself while still a responsible person is itself a dangerous act, and so may be regarded as culpable. Other examples would be persons who willingly submit to drugs or hypnosis under circumstances portending harm, or who place themselves in dangerous situations knowing they are epileptics or sleepwalkers prone to violence. Culpability in such cases properly extends only to conduct that produces the loss of capacity and not the further conduct that is engaged in while the person is not responsible. One person may kill another quite deliberately under delusions produced by drugs taken quite deliberately, yet culpability is not for deliberate killing because the accused is not responsible at all for his homicidal conduct but only for the act of taking the drugs.

---

*This essay appears in a slightly altered version at pages 293–316 of *A Theory of Criminal Justice,* by Hyman Gross (Oxford University Press, 1979).

Not without some awkwardness in principle, the lesser culpability is usually reflected in the criminal law by liability for homicide of a lesser degree.

When mental impairment is intrapsychic in origin, the excuse based on it is received more charily. The same debilitation which would easily pass muster for an excuse if externally induced is regarded with skepticism when its origin is not palpably outside the mind of the actor. Initial suspicion is indeed warranted because of increased opportunity for deception. But even after genuineness of the psychopathology is established, there is often lingering skepticism regarding its significance for judgments of responsibility. This skepticism is justified to the extent that it reflects sound opinion that the actor was quite capable of doing otherwise in spite of his illness. But it is not justified when it reflects the belief that a person is in some measure responsible for his mental illness since its origins are within him and, unlike the case of mental abnormalities having identifiable physical causes, it pertains to him in an especially intimate way because of its purely psychic character. Holding a person responsible for his mental illness is in general even more unjust than holding him responsible for his physical illness. Such medical knowledge as we have bearing on the etiology of serious mental illness makes it quite clear that in most cases the sick person could not reasonably be expected to do such things as would probably have prevented the onset of his illness, while in the case of physical illness effective precautions often might quite easily have been taken.

II

It is not any mental abnormality that excuses. Even when the abnormality is of a kind that is relevant to responsibility, certain conditions of incapacitation must be met if there is to be an excuse. In the criminal law these conditions have been formulated as rules which govern the insanity defense. These rules look mainly to mental illness and defectiveness, but the conditions for excusing under them have a rationale which extends to mental abnormality of whatever variety. Four basic versions of this defense have developed in the criminal law and, as shall be shown, the conditions required by each are less dissimilar from those required by the others than would appear from the terms used in formulating each. The first version, which dominates among Anglo-American jurisdictions, turns out to be too meager. The second of these versions (which in some form is now the law in a third of the American jurisdictions and under the Model Penal Code) represents the most satisfactory statement. The third and fourth versions, though lending themselves to suitably restrictive interpretation, as they stand offer too great opportunity for unwarranted excuses and in fact are the versions most often preferred by those advocating unsound excuses. First, each version will be briefly scanned and then good reasons will be distinguished from bad among excuses of this sort. The concern here is only with why a person is not responsible, and so the very difficult medical questions having to do with exactly what states of abnormality leave a person in a condition in which he is not responsible will remain unexplored. Only the more basic question of what it means not to be responsible is taken up here. But without answers to that, one does not know what exculpatory significance, if any, to attach ultimately to the medical facts.

The first version of the insanity defense is represented by the M'Naghten rules. Stated in their original terms, these rules provide that a person has a defense of insanity if he did not know the nature and quality of the act he was doing, or did not know that it was wrong, because laboring under a defect of reason from disease of the mind. There was in the original M'Naghten rules a further proviso that, even if not so afflicted, a person would have a defense if at the time of his act he was suffering from an insane delusion about something such that if—but only if—it were in fact the case, it would furnish a defense. This part of the M'Naghten rules has been generally disregarded because of the limitation it places on delusions which may excuse, though as we shall see the right reason for ignoring the rule on these grounds has not been generally apprehended. There has been a continuing need for a rule extending the defense generally to all those who have insane delusions about the circumstances under which they act, and this requirement has encouraged strained applications of the remainder of the M'Naghten doctrine to cover such cases.

Despite variations in language and differences in fine points of interpretation, the gist of the M'Naghten formula has remained unchanged in the many jurisdictions that have adopted it since its introduction in England well over a century ago. Serious incapacitation may make it impossible for the actor to be sufficiently aware of what he is doing so that he could choose to do otherwise. It may deprive him of appreciation of the harmfulness of his conduct, or of appreciation of the harm itself, so that a normal disposition to restrain harmful conduct is not aroused. It may deprive him of the ability to comprehend the circumstances in which he acts and so make it impossible for him to choose not to do what under the circumstances is not justifiable. It may make him incapable of knowing that the law prohibits what he does, when only the fact of legal prohibition is a reason for not doing it. In any of these cases, because of a failure of personal resources he cannot help what he does.

The second version of the insanity defense consists of some form of M'Naghten to which is added an excuse based on grossly deficient inhibitory capacity. This additional part is usually referred to as the irresistible impulse rule, though any suggestion that the act need be impulsive to qualify would be seriously misleading. Under this provision, if the accused was incapable of restraining himself from doing what he knew he was doing and knew he ought not to be doing, he may invoke as an excuse his inability to exercise self-control.

The gravamen of this excuse is again the actor's helplessness in being unable to avoid doing or causing harm. The excuse is even stronger than the claim of compulsion that is asserted when one has been forced to do something harmful. Instead of succumbing to pressures which one is nevertheless able to resist, the person without significant capacity for inhibition is simply unable to resist. The excuse is sometimes misconceived, however, so that it is the untoward urge rather than the inhibitory failure which receives primary attention. This distorts the rationale of the excuse. We do not excuse because the actor wanted very desperately to do what he did. By itself powerful determination to do harm is not grounds for exemption from judgments of culpability. On the contrary, it is grounds for a judgment of greater culpability.

The third version of the insanity defense makes mental disease or defect, *when it produces criminal conduct,* the basis of an excuse for that conduct. This version has been adopted in four American jurisdictions (though recently discarded in the one that gave it the name by which it is best known), enjoys considerable psychiatric advocacy, and is generally referred to as the Durham rule. It relies heavily in practice on the same rationale of excuse as the previous version, but offers opportunities for the troublesome departures that will be discussed shortly.

A final version is constituted by those criminal insanity provisions in which mental derangement or deficiency at the time of the act is itself an excuse. The actor need only be seriously defective or not in possession of his faculties in order for his conduct in such a state to be excusable. Unlike the previous version, the relation between the abnormality and the criminal conduct is not of concern here so long as the two are contemporaneous. This version has in somewhat primitive forms preceded M'Naghten in the commom law and now appears in the criminal law of some civil law jurisdictions. It enjoys strong support among those of the medical profession who are interested in these forensic matters and is probably even more congenial to psychiatric views of the insanity defense than is the Durham version. As with Durham there is heavy reliance in practice on the same rationale of excuse that support M'Naghten and irresistible impulse; but again, as with Durham, opportunities for excusing on other grounds are made possible, and these call for careful investigation.

III

The preceding discussion has shown what grounds the law has recognized for an excuse of mental abnormality when the excuse is presented in its most dramatic form as the insanity defense. Many of those who favor the third or fourth version of the insanity defense think it a good defense simply that a person was mentally ill at the time of his criminal act, or that his criminal conduct was a result of the mental illness he suffered at the time. There are three important arguments here, one grounded in moral considerations regarding avoidance of cruelty, and the other two in exculpatory considerations thought to apply to sick persons.

The first contention is that it is wrong to punish a person *when he is sick.* It is generally regarded as inhumane to neglect the suffering of those who are in a debilitated condition and even more inhumane to inflict further suffering on them. It would therefore be barbarous if the criminal law not only withheld comfort and cure from the sick who are subject to its processes but imposed upon such persons a penal regime. Directed to present concerns, this principle of humane treatment clearly requires that a person mentally abnormal at the time of his crime not be subjected to punitive treatment while he continues to be in such a state, but that instead he receive medical treatment.

The principle of humane treatment is unquestionably sound and must be given full effect at all times. It does not, however, confer a cloak of immunity on persons who are sick when committing a crime. Conduct may be culpable even though the actor had chicken pox, pneumonia or multiple sclerosis. It may be culpable when the disorder is mental rather than physical. When a sick person's conduct is culpable, he is to be treated for his illness so long as it lasts by those in whose hands he is placed by virtue of liability for such culpable conduct. But liability for culpable conduct is not avoided by the mere fact of sickness. It is also true that even determination of liability to punishment must be postponed if the continuing illness of the accused makes impossible the proceedings necessary for a just determination of liability, and that those having custody of him must during this time abide by the imperatives of humane treatment. But again there is nothing in this to entitle the accused to exemption from liability.

A second argument derives from general requirements for culpability. It is wrong to punish someone *for being sick*. The reason is that in being sick a person has not done anything blameworthy. Since merely falling ill does not constitute culpable conduct, it may not be punished. (A person might indeed be rightly blamed for making himself sick, or allowing himself to become or to be made sick, and we might well decide that such conduct then deserves punishment when it was understood that the well-being of others depended upon the fitness of the one who became sick. In such a case there is culpability because the accused could have acted to prevent his illness.)

But insofar as a person is being punished for his conduct and not for his disorder, the requirement of culpability is not transgressed. Nevertheless, it is sometimes claimed that when a mentally disordered person is punished for his conduct, he is being punished for his disorder since the conduct is a symptom of it. Such claims are especially prominent in arguments advocating extension of a mental abnormality defense to those persons, often characterized as psychopaths or sociopaths, whose dedication to wrongdoing is especially strong and free of internal conflicts. This claim rests on a misunderstanding of what it means to be punished for something. A person may be punished for a criminal act and that act may in various other perspectives be viewed quite accurately as a symptom of his illness, or indeed of society's illness, as an act of dedicated self-sacrifice, or as an act to advance a socially worthwhile cause. Still in all these cases we are punishing him only for his culpable conduct. We may punish in spite of causes, motives, or intentions, so long as they do not furnish an excuse or other reason for not punishing.

The third argument is that it is wrong to punish someone for what he does *as a result of being mentally sick*. Unlike the previous argument, the position here is not that it is wrong to punish someone for the illness evidenced by criminal conduct, but rather that it is wrong to punish someone for his conduct when it is *produced* by the disorder. The criminal conduct is not viewed as part of a pattern of behavior such that if one so behaves one must by that very fact be judged to be abnormal. Rather the conduct is viewed as determined by the abnormality in the sense that but for the abnormality there would have been no warrant for expecting such conduct.

Treating the fact that conduct resulted from mental abnormality as a reason to excuse the conduct leaves us with no principle on which to rest the excuse. Exculpation by way of justification would indeed be warranted by a principle that what is morbidly determined is not wrong, but there are no good reasons for recognizing as a justifying principle the proposition that condemnation ought to be restricted to healthy determinations to act harmfully. It is true that a person's mental abnormality, if it is to excuse his criminal conduct, must in some significant way be related to that conduct as its cause. This may be put in an even stronger form by saying that we ought to excuse when, but only when, conduct is the "product" of abnormality in the sense that the abnormality is a sufficient condition for the conduct. In that case, but only in that case, the accused was unable to do otherwise because of the abnormality and so is entitled to be excused. It is not true that we ought to excuse simply because the wrong thing that was done would likely not have been done but for the abnormality. Otherwise we should have to excuse anyone who acted from some untoward tendency attributable to a mental abnormality whenever it is unlikely that he would have done the act if he were normal, even in cases where he was quite as capable of acting otherwise as is a normal person subject to the same tendency. This would mean that a bank employee ought to be excused when he embezzles money only because of powerful unconscious wishes to be caught which he could effectively have chosen not to succumb to, although another employee who embezzles only because tempted by healthy fantasies of a life of leisure ought not to be excused.

There is a fourth argument for not punishing wrongdoers who suffered from mental abnormality that in effect requires for an excuse too much rather than too little. It has eminent philosophical credentials and is to be found in the best legal circles as well. The argument derives from general considerations bearing on justification of punishment.

It is pointed out that prescribing punishment for what the insane do is futile since the threat of punishment can have no deterrent effect on such persons. Anyone, therefore, who considers the practice of punishment to be justified by its deterrent effect must hold punishment of the insane to be unjustified and, in fact, a purposeless infliction of suffering. It has been argued in reply that punishment of the insane may still have a deterrent effect on sane persons since it deprives them of hope of escaping punishment by successfully advancing fraudulent claims of having been insane at the time of their offense. That answer is good only to the extent that crimes are committed after decisions to commit them which include deliberation on possible legal tactics to avoid conviction. But since most crimes are committed without decisions of this sort, the deterrent effect of a threat of punishment that makes no allowance for insanity is in any event largely otiose.

There are, however, other answers to the "no deterrence" objection to punishing the insane that do not require belief in such fictitious deliberations by would-be criminals.

If it is being suggested that nondeterrability has been the rationale for the insanity defense in the law as it has developed, we may ask why the law does not refuse by the same rationale to punish those who were genuinely and blamelessly ignorant of the law they broke. Such persons were in a position indistinguishable from the insane with respect to the futility of prospective punishment, and so to punish them is equally a purposeless infliction of suffering. Yet, as we know, in the law as it stands such innocent ignorance does not excuse, and this inconsistency must raise doubts about this rationale for the insanity defense.

But there is a more cogent objection than one based on inconsistency. It is not the case that all, or perhaps even most, insane persons are incapable of being deterred by threat of punishment. Under the prevailing Anglo-American insanity defense, the M'Naghten rules, there is an excuse if the accused by virtue of a defect of reason from disease of the mind did not know he was doing what was wrong. The Model Penal Code similarly establishes as a defense a person's lack of substantial capacity to appreciate the criminality of his conduct (which means more than mere

knowledge that it is criminally prohibited) as a result of mental disease or defect. There are many persons who fit these specifications in being unable to appreciate that what they do is wrong and in fact think it for some reason justified, yet are aware and in awe of the threat of punishment quite as much as normal persons. In some of the most notable cases of the insanity defense, the defendant committed murder under the delusion that he was carrying out a divine command, or was giving his due to a man believed to be very wicked, or was killing someone who was bent on harming him. Less dramatic but far more frequent are the family and sex intrigue homicides where the killing was done in a suitably extreme abnormal mental state—usually spoken of as temporary insanity—in which the accused was likewise at the time convinced that he was justified. There is no reason to believe that in general their abnormality rendered the accused in these insanity cases incapable of being deterred by the threat of punishment, though of course like many normal defendants they were not in fact deterred by it. There is, further, every reason to believe that certain abnormal persons who would be entitled to exoneration on grounds of insanity were in fact deterred, just as normal persons would be because the law has made the conduct they contemplated punishable. If these things were not so, the insanity defense could consist simply in establishing the one point that by reason of mental abnormality the accused could not at the time of his crime be deterred by the threat of punishment. In fact what distinguishes the sane from the insane under criminal law standards is the inability of the insane to appreciate the *culpability*, not the punishability, of their conduct. Because of their abnormality the insane cannot at the time apprehend what justifies condemnation of their conduct. Even though amenable to threats of punishment, they lack a resource of appreciation that is necessary if one is to have a reason apart from avoidance of punishment for not doing what the law prohibits. Punishing such persons is indeed a useless infliction of suffering, for it can not serve to uphold the standards that the criminal law exists to preserve.

There is one other argument against mental abnormality defenses that should be noted here. Again it is an argument that by implication requires too much rather than too little for excuse. Many persons who are mentally ill and have committed crimes are dangerous, yet the very abnormality that is evidence of his being dangerous serves to shield the accused from liability. Those who see confinement of dangerous persons as a principal purpose of the criminal law are particularly distressed by this, for in effect just those who are thought to be most properly the concern of the criminal law are allowed to escape its restraints.

The answer to this argument is that not all restraint by the state need be based on criminal liability. If a person is dangerous because of mental abnormality, he may be prevented from doing harm by noncriminal commitment regardless of whether his conduct provided a basis for criminal liability. It is true that persons usually are not found to be a menace for purposes of commitment unless they have done something which would at least provide the substance of a criminal charge. But it is still dangerousness of the person and not criminality of his conduct that warrants deprivation of liberty. Since determinations of dangerousness and determinations of criminal liability are independent matters, a defense of insanity to a criminal charge does not weigh against the accused's subsequent liability to commitment because he is dangerous. Conversely, elimination or postponement of the question of insanity when determining liability would result in branding as criminals persons, whether dangerous or not, who are not to blame for what they did.

IV

The rationale of excusing for mental abnormality may be summarized in this way. Certain forms of mental incapacity deprive a person of ability to act other than the way he does because resources for an effective choice are lacking. When a person lacks capacity to tell what he is doing, whether it is offensive, or what is likely to happen; or lacks capacity to appreciate its harmful significance, or to restrain himself, he is in such a condition. It is apparent that a person incapacitated in any of these ways lacks a resource necessary for control and so necessary for culpable conduct. It is for this reason that an excuse of mental abnormality preempts the field of excuse and makes excuses going directly to culpability inappropriate. There is no point in being concerned about whether something was intentional, when whether it is intentional or not the actor was not a responsible agent. And conversely, when there is a complement of those personal resources that are necessary for responsible conduct, there is a duty to draw upon such resources to avoid harmful conduct. It follows that when a normal person claims he did not at the time appreciate the significance of sticking a knife into another person—his mind

was elsewhere—he offers a different kind of excuse than the mentally abnormal man who makes the same claim. The normal man can only expect by showing less culpability to blunt an accusation of conduct of a higher degree of culpability—he didn't harm the victim knowingly, but only negligently through absent-mindedness in failing to pay attention to the dangers of what he was occupied in doing. But the man who establishes that his failure of appreciation was due to a lack of necessary mental resources exempts himself from any judgment of culpability.

The distinction and connections between lack of responsibility and mere lack of culpability are important with regard to several difficulties surrounding the insanity defense.

We have already mentioned the usually discarded third part of the original M'Naghten rule. It provided that even if the accused person who suffered a defect of reason from disease of the mind could know the nature and quality of his act, and even if he could know that what he was doing was wrong, he still might have a defense if at the time of his act he suffered from a delusion such that had it been a correct belief it would have afforded a defense. This part of the rule has been dropped, but not in order to exclude insanity defenses based on delusion; in fact, delusion cases have always been recognized as paradigms of criminal insanity and are allowed in all M'Naghten rule jurisdictions by strained interpretations of the other parts. It is the limitation upon the kinds of delusion which are acceptable that has been found objectionable. The usual argument is that the limitation leads to absurd results. For example, in accordance with conventional legal rules that preclude criminal jurisdiction for crimes of foreign nationals committed in foreign countries, a homicide defendant in England who in a delusion at the time of his crime believed himself to be Bluebeard reenacting one of his murders in France would have a good defense. But a homicide defendant also in England who in his similar delusion believed himself to be Jack the Ripper would not. Even when the rule has been confined to delusions which bear on exculpatory claims (typically provocation and self-defense), as undoubtedly it was intended to be by its original proponents, criticism has not abated though the reason for rejecting the rule is less clear.

It seems, in fact, that the original rule was a sound one based on the premises concerning the facts of mental abnormality which the M'Naghten judges accepted, but that these premises are incorrect. The mistake from which the rule proceeded has been characterized as the doctrine of partial insanity. It holds that a person whose insanity consists merely in delusions is still capable of choosing to act in conformity with the law that governed the situation as he perceived it. He therefore is to be held accountable for not acting in conformity with law as it would apply to the situation he perceived, though by virtue of his inability to perceive the situation correctly he could not be held accountable for breaking the law with respect to the situation as it actually was. However, according to better medical knowledge, the fact of the matter is that such persons in the grip of their delusions are normally so severely incapacitated that they cannot even choose to act otherwise. We therefore cannot hold them responsible when they act as their delusion dictates and so must consider them ineligible for blame. Questions about matters of culpability (usually matters of justification) which the original rule raises are for this reason superfluous.

A second problem concerns what is meant by "wrong" under the terms of the M'Naghten rule. If the accused, because of a defect of reason from disease of the mind, did not know that what he was doing was wrong he has a defense on grounds of insanity. The question which has persistently troubled courts both in England and the United States is whether the failure of knowledge required is of legal or of moral wrong. Does a psychotic person who knows murder is a crime but believes he may nevertheless commit it because divinely commanded have a defense? What about a mental defective who knows he is not supposed to hurt other people but cannot even comprehend what a criminal law is? The Model Penal Code speaks of the accused's lack of capacity to appreciate the criminality of his conduct, but the difficulty remains, for appreciating the criminality of conduct is not the equivalent of knowing that it has been made a crime. Indeed the final draft of the Code provision offers "wrongfulness" as an optional substitute for "criminality".

The difficulty is removed by recognizing that what is crucial is capacity to know, rather than knowledge; and that it is a capacity to know something that is necessary for culpability. In a just legal system conduct ought not to be treated as legally culpable unless reasonable opportunity exists to become aware of its legal interdiction. Such opportunity for awareness has significance only if there also is ability to take advantage of it.

That in turn depends on ability to appreciate the untowardness of conduct, ability to be aware of the range of normal concerns of the law, as well as the ability to become acquainted with the law itself. If there is disabling incapacity with respect to any of these necessary conditions the person incapacitated is not responsible, for to that degree he lacks ability to take advantage of the opportunity to become aware of criminal liabilities and so his conduct cannot be deemed culpable. It turns out, then, that it is misleading to ask whether legal or moral wrong is meant. The question to be answered is whether the accused was deprived of any abilities that are necessary to take advantage of the opportunity of becoming aware of criminal liability.

Another difficulty concerns the irresistible impulse defense. There has been great hesitation in legal circles in admitting as an excuse an inability to exercise self-restraint. It challenges common sense appreciation of behavior to assert that a person possessed of all the abilities necessary to control what he is doing, nevertheless does not have the self-control to choose effectively not to do it. The excuse is therefore often construed as a direct denial of culpability analogous to external compulsion—he didn't mean to do that, he was forced to—rather than as a denial of responsibility by virtue of incapacity. The excuse so construed is then rejected as being too easy a way out for persons who either have not chosen to resist with sufficient determination powerful untoward urges or have failed to take precaution against succumbing to the urge and are therefore no less culpable than persons who lose their temper and, while in the grip of their rage, commit crimes.

But this excuse of no responsibility becomes plausible as understanding of human pathology advances, and it becomes increasingly clear that there are serious mental abnormalities which consist in inability either by repression or precaution to inhibit acting on certain urges. The claim of irresistible impulse is then no longer construed as one simply of not having effectively chosen to do otherwise, but rather more, as not having the personal resources that are necessary to choose effectively.

V

A stark separation according to mental abnormality of those who are responsible from those who are not seems at times unsatisfactory. We are bound to recognize that sometimes there is not sheer incapacity with regard to elements of control, yet there is deviation from normal capacities great enough to make desirable a limitation on accountability. Accordingly, there has developed in the law a doctrine of diminished (or partial) responsibility which, though still only little and narrowly accepted, offers a path for receiving into the law continuing insights respecting varieties of limited impairment bearing on control of conduct. The most notable legal recognition so far has been in the English Homicide Act of 1957, which reduces what otherwise would be murder to culpable homicide when the accused suffered from such abnormality of mind as "substantially impaired his mental responsibility" for his acts. The rationale for diminished responsibility is simple. If a person who is incapacitated is ineligible for blame, a person who is seriously impaired though not incapacitated is eligible to be blamed only within limits. While not utterly bereft of resources required for accountability, his resources of control are dimished to a point where full faulting according to the tenor of the conduct is inappropriate. But for reasons previously given, it would be a serious mistake to construe the defense of diminished responsibility as a declaration that the somewhat sick, simply because they are sick, ought not to be held to a liability as great as that of the healthy person. Indeed, perfectly healthy persons who have perfectly natural reactions that put them in an abnormal emotional state may rightly claim diminished responsibility. Typically, this is the case when a person acts under the influence of extreme anger or fear because provoked or threatened.

Mental abnormality may affect culpability in a more direct way, however, and some confusion about this has arisen in discussions of diminished responsibility. By virtue of his abnormality, a person may be unable to act in a way that is criminally culpable, or at least not as culpable as the conduct charged. Or, though capable of such conduct, he may simply not have been acting in the way charged but rather was acting in some other way dictated by his abnormal processes. In either case he may lodge an exculpatory claim that his conduct is different than alleged with respect to elements bearing on culpability, and he would rely on the evidence of his mental abnormality to establish this. Such an exculpatory claim in essence is no different from the sort that is appropriate when a normal person has not acted culpably, but the kind of argument which supports the claim is different. Instead of evidence indicating simply that the accused was engaged in a somewhat different enterprise than alleged, the evidence indicates that by virtue of his abnormal mental condition at the time, the accused could not or simply did not engage in the enterprise alleged. Two exculpatory claims are made in this way. Both of them have as their point what in the language of traditional criminal law theory would be called a lack of *mens rea*.

Suppose a prisoner attacks a guard with a knife and inflicts serious wounds. The prisoner is charged with first degree assault, an element of which is intent to cause serious physical injury. It is claimed on his behalf that he was at the time suffering severe paranoid anxieties which led him to misinterpret a routine warning as a sign that he was about to be attacked by the guard, and that he slashed at the guard only to fend off what he believed to be imminent blows. Evidence of his abnormal state would tend to show that he did not have the specific intent to cause serious physical injury. This would mean that while admittedly he exercised control in conducting an assault, he did not exercise control with regard to those features of it that produced the serious injury. The act done, therefore, was something less culpable than the act charged. The same would hold true for a person accused of burglary, which requires an intent to commit a felony, and who at the time of breaking and entering a home was in such a mental condition as to be incapable of having any definite further purpose.

The other challenge to culpability by way of abnormality does not concern the purpose which informs the act, but rather the earlier stages of planning the accomplishment of objectives and attending to the course of conduct while it is in progress. Such operational design and supervision as is referred to by "malice aforethought," "premeditation," "deliberation," "willfully," and "knowingly" may be beyond the accused's capacities or may simply be nonexistent by virtue of his abnormality. Powerful effects of intoxication or of lingering mental illness may render a person unable or unconcerned to form the plan or to remain in control of its execution, and so one is required to conclude that his homicidal attack was not designed with reference to the death of his victim. The Model Penal Code extends this variety of abnormality defense to all cases where evidence of mental disease or defect is relevant to the question of whether the accused had a required state of mind at the time of the crime, so that even recklessness or negligence may be disproved by evidence of appropriate abnormality.

In both of these "criminal intent" challenges based on mental abnormality, it is not responsibility that properly is said to be diminished. Culpability is what is really claimed to be diminished, and diminished to a point where the conduct is less culpable than is required for the offense charged.

VI

The excuse of insanity has presented far greater difficulties than any other for the criminal process. The main reason is that the point of the proceedings is lost sight of and confusion arises in deciding who may appropriately answer the very different kinds of questions involved, and also in deciding what the consequences of accepting or rejecting the excuse ought to be.

Much of the controversy in which medical and legal views of the insanity defense appear to be at odds results from a failure to appreciate that the law must ultimately be concerned not with who is sick but with whose conduct is excusable. Deciding that issue requires several subsidiary decisions that fall peculiarly within either medical or legal competence. There must, in the first place, be standards which set forth generally the nature of the incapacities that render a person not responsible. It is these standards that constitute the rules of the insanity defense, and deciding upon them is the responsibility of those with legislative and judicial authority who must make the law. It bears emphasis that what is called for here is not some general description of relevant clinical abnormalities in language lawyers are used to. What is required is a statement of the kinds of mental failures (due to mental illness or defectiveness) that entitle us to conclude for purposes of criminal liability that the accused could not help doing what he did. Once there are such standards of mental abnormality, proceedings to judge the abnormalities of a particular defendant with reference to such standards are possible. Then it is the opinion of medical experts which must first be looked to in order to determine the nature of the defendant's debilitation and the extent to which it affects capacities necessary for responsible conduct. Such expert opinion may be critically examined by lawyers, as indeed any expert opinion may be in a legal proceeding to determine a disputed issue. But that is not a means of substituting an inexpert for an expert opinion, but only a way of ensuring that its acceptance is ultimately based on reason rather than authority. There is finally a decision of vast discretion that is normally made by the jury. It is a conclusion about whether, according to the expert account of the mental condition that is finally accepted, there is debilitation sufficient to excuse according to the legal standards. Asking psychiatrists for expert opinions about whether such standards of incapacity are met is asking them to perform a role which is not within their special professional competence. But the job to be done in making the ultimate determination does require specialized skill in sifting among psychiatric opinions to arrive at a sound appreciation of the defendant's mental condition with reference to those features that are significant for judgments of responsibility. The paramount procedural problem of the insanity defense is to combine this specialist's appreciation with the layman's considered views about when choices to act are no longer meaningful or even possible. There is for this reason a great deal to recommend in principle suggestions, such as H. L. A. Hart's, that we adopt an "apparently coarser grained technique of exempting persons from liability to punishment if they fall into certain recognized categories of mental disorder", on the model of exemption from liability for persons under a specified age. But the establishment of a comprehensive scheme of clear categories seems at the present state of medical art a remote prospect.

Another sort of misapprehension deflects concern from responsibility to other matters, at the cost of both justice and humaneness in the administration of the criminal law. It is assumed that determining the accused to be responsible and so liable to have his conduct judged culpable is a warrant for treating him punitively rather than therapeutically. But in fact, it is said, many persons who meet legal standards for responsible conduct are nevertheless quite sick and sending them to a prison rather than a hospital is uncivilized. It is urged that the mentally ill ought therefore not to be treated as criminally responsible.

The mistake here is in giving priority to existing institutional arrangements and then attempting to have rules of liability which are humane in their effect under those arrangements. A rational and morally concerned society designs its institutions to treat in a humane way those who are liable according to just principles of liability. When a person who is liable according to proper standards of responsibility and culpability is also sick, principles of humane treatment, which are in no way inferior moral considerations, require that he be treated as sick. To the extent that inappropriate treatment may at present be expected under existing institutional arrangements and regimes, that is cause for reform of institutional arrangements and regimes, not of the rules of criminal liability.

DURHAM v. UNITED STATES

U.S. Court of Appeals, D.C. Cir., 1954*

BAZELON, Circuit Judge.

Monte Durham was convicted of housebreaking,[1] by the District Court sitting without a jury. The only defense asserted at the trial was that Durham was of unsound mind at the time of the offense. We are now urged to reverse the conviction (1) because the trial court did not correctly apply existing rules governing the burden of proof on the defense of insanity, and (2) because existing tests of criminal responsibility are obsolete and should be superseded.[2]

I.

Durham has a long history of imprisonment and hospitalization. In 1945, at the age of 17, he was discharged from the Navy after a psychiatric examination had shown that he suffered "from a profound personality disorder which renders him unfit for Naval service." In 1947 he pleaded guilty to violating the National Motor Theft Act[3] and was placed on probation for one to three years. He attempted suicide, was taken to Gallinger Hospital for observation, and was transferred to St. Elizabeths Hospital, from which he was discharged after two months. In January of 1948, as a result of a conviction in the District of Columbia Municipal Court for passing bad checks, the District Court revoked his probation and he commenced service of his Motor Theft sentence. His conduct within the first few days in jail led to a lunacy inquiry in the Municipal Court where a jury found him to be of unsound mind. Upon commitment to St. Elizabeths, he was diagnosed as suffering from "psychosis with psychopathic personality." After 15 months of treatment, he was discharged in July 1949 as "recovered" and was returned to jail to serve the balance of his sentence. In June 1950 he was conditionally released. He violated the conditions by leaving the District. When he learned of a warrant for his arrest as a parole violator, he fled to the "South and Midwest obtaining money by passing a number of bad checks." After he was found and returned to the District, the Parole Board referred him to the District Court for a lunacy inquisition, wherein a jury again found him to be of unsound mind. He was

readmitted to St. Elizabeths in February 1951. This time the diagnosis was "without mental disorder, psychopathic personality." He was discharged for the third time in May 1951. The housebreaking which is the subject of the present appeal took place two months later, on July 13, 1951.

According to his mother and the psychiatrist who examined him in September 1951, he suffered from hallucinations immediately after his May 1951 discharge from St. Elizabeths. Following the present indictment, in October 1951, he was adjudged of unsound mind in proceedings under § 4244 of Title 18 U.S.C., upon the affidavits of two psychiatrists that he suffered from "psychosis with psychopathic personality." He was committed to St. Elizabeths for the fourth time and given subshock insulin therapy. This commitment lasted 16 months—until February 1953—when he was released to the custody of the District Jail on the certificate of Dr. Silk, Acting Superintendent of St. Elizabeths, that he was "mentally competent to stand trial and. . . . able to consult with counsel to properly assist in his own defense."

He was thereupon brought before the court on the charge involved here. The prosecutor told the court:

"So I take this attitude, in view of the fact that he has been over there [St. Elizabeths] a couple of times and these cases that were charged against him were dropped, I don't think I should take the responsibility of dropping these cases against him; then Saint Elizabeths would let him out on the street, and if that man committed a murder next week then it is my responsibility. So we decided to go to trial on one case, that is the case where we found him right in the house, and let him bring in the defense, if he wants to, of unsound mind at the time the crime was committed, and then Your Honor will find him on that, and in your decision send him back to Saint Elizabeths Hospital, and then if they let him out on the street it is their responsibility."

Shortly thereafter, when the question arose whether Durham could be considered competent to stand trial merely on the basis of Dr. Silk's ex parte statement, the court said to defense counsel:

"I am going to ask you this, Mr. Ahern: I have taken the position that if once a person has been found of unsound mind after a lunacy hearing, an ex parte certificate of the superin-

*214 F. 2d 862 (1954). Excerpts only. The footnotes are numbered here as in the original.

tendent of Saint Elizabeths is not sufficient to set aside that finding and I have held another lunacy hearing. That has been my custom. However, if you want to waive that you may do it, if you admit that he is now of sound mind."

The court accepted counsel's waiver on behalf of Durham, although it had been informed by the prosecutor that a letter from Durham claimed need of further hospitalization, and by defense counsel that ". . . . the defendant does say that even today he thinks he does need hospitalization; he told me that this morning."[4] Upon being so informed, the court said, "Of course, if I hold he is not mentally competent to stand trial I send him back to Saint Elizabeths Hospital and they will send him back again in two or three months."[5] In this atmosphere Durham's trial commenced.

II.

. . . It has been ably argued by counsel for Durham that the existing tests in the District of Columbia for determining criminal responsibility, that is, the so-called right-wrong test supplemented by the irresistible impulse test, are not satisfactory criteria for determining criminal responsibility. We are urged to adopt a different test to be applied on the retrial of this case. This contention has behind it nearly a century of agitation for reform.

A. The right-wrong test, approved in this jurisdiction in 1882,[13] was the exclusive test of criminal responsibility in the District of Columbia until 1929 when we approved the irresistible impulse test as a supplemetary test in Smith v. United States.[14] The right-wrong test has its roots in England. There, by the first quarter of the eighteenth century, an accused escaped punishment if he could not distinguish "good and evil," that is, if he "doth not know what he is doing, no more than. . . . a wild beast."[15] Later in the same century, the "wild beast" test was abandoned and "right and wrong" was substituted for "good and evil."[16] And toward the middle of the nineteenth century, the House of Lords in the famous M'Naghten case[17] restated what had become the accepted "right-wrong" test[18] in a form which has since been followed, not only in England[19] but in most American jurisdictions,[20] as an exclusive test of criminal responsibility:

✓ ". . . . the jurors ought to be told in all cases that every man is to be presumed to be sane, and to possess a sufficient degree of reason to be responsible for his crimes, until the contrary be proved to their satisfaction; and that, to establish a defence on the ground of insanity, it must be clearly proved that, at the time of the committing of the act, the party accused was labouring under such a defect of reason, from disease of the mind, as not to know the nature and quality of the act he was doing, or, if he did know it, that he did not know he was doing what was wrong."[21]

As early as 1838, Isaac Ray, one of the founders of the American Psychiatric Association, in his now classic Medical Jurisprudence of Insanity, called knowledge of right and wrong a "fallacious" test of criminal responsibility.[22] This view has long since been substantiated by enormous developments in knowledge of mental life.[23] In 1928 Mr. Justice Cardozo said to the New York Academy of Medicine: "Everyone concedes that the present [legal] definition of insanity has little relation to the truths of mental life."[24]

Medico-legal writers in large numbers,[25] The Report of the Royal Commission on Capital Punishment 1949–1953,[26] and The Preliminary Report by the Committee on Forensic Psychiatry of the Group for the Advancement of Psychiatry[27] present convincing evidence that the right-and-wrong test is "based on an entirely obsolete and misleading conception of the nature of insanity."[28] The science of psychiatry now recognizes that a man is an integrated personality and that reason, which is only one element in that personality, is not the sole determinant of his conduct. The right-wrong test, which considers knowledge or reason alone, is therefore an inadequate guide to mental responsibility for criminal behavior. As Professor Sheldon Glueck of the Harvard Law School points out in discussing the right-wrong tests, which he calls the knowledge tests:

"It is evident that the knowledge tests unscientifically abstract out of the mental make-up but one phase or element of mental life, the cognitive, which, in this era of dynamic psychology, is beginning to be regarded as not the most important factor in conduct and its disorders. In brief, these tests proceed upon the following questionable assumptions of an outworn era in psychiatry: (1) that lack of knowledge of the 'nature or quality' of an act (assuming the meaning of such terms to be clear), or incapacity to know right from wrong, is the sole or even the most important symptom of mental disorder; (2) that such knowledge is the sole instigator and guide of conduct, or at least the most important element therein, and consequently should be the sole criterion of responsibility when insanity is involved; and (3) that the capacity of knowing right from wrong can be completely intact and functioning perfectly even though a defendant is otherwise demonstrably of disordered mind."[29]

Nine years ago we said:
"The modern science of psychology. . . . does not conceive that there is a separate little man in the top of one's head called reason whose function it is to guide another unruly little man called instinct, emotion, or impulse in the way he should go."[30]

By its misleading emphasis on the cognitive, the right-wrong test requires court and jury to rely upon what is, scientifically speaking, inadequate, and most often, invalid[31] and irrelevant testimony in determining criminal responsibility.[32]

The✓fundamental objection to the right-wrong test,

however, is not that criminal irresponsibility is made to rest upon an inadequate, invalid or indeterminable symptom or manifestation, but that it is made to rest upon *any* particular symptom.[33] In attempting to define insanity in terms of a symptom, the courts have assumed an impossible role,[34] not merely one for which they have no special competence.[35] As the Royal Commission emphasizes, it is dangerous "to abstract particular mental faculties, and to lay it down that unless these particular faculties are destroyed or gravely impaired, an accused person, whatever the nature of his mental disease, must be held to be criminally responsible. . . ."[36] In this field of law as in others, the fact finder should be free to consider all information advanced by relevant scientific disciplines.[37]

Despite demands in the name of scientific advances, this court refused to alter the right-wrong test at the turn of the century.[38] But in 1929, we considered in response to "the cry of scientific experts" and added the irresistible impulse test as a supplementary test for determining criminal responsibility. Without "hesitation" we declared, in Smith v. United States, "it to be the law of this District that, in cases where insanity is interposed as a defense, and the facts are sufficient to call for the application of the rule of irresistible impulse, the jury should be so charged."[39] We said:

"... The modern doctrine is that the degree of insanity which will relieve the accused of the consequences of a criminal act must be such as to create in his mind an uncontrollable impulse to commit the offense charged. This impulse must be such as to override the reason and judgment and obliterate the sense of right and wrong to the extent that the accused is deprived of the power to choose between right and wrong. The mere ability to distinguish right from wrong is no longer the correct test either in civil or criminal cases, where the defense of insanity is interposed. The accepted rule in this day and age, with the great advancement in medical science as an enlightening influence on this subject, is that the accused must be capable, not only of distinguishing between right and wrong, but that he was not impelled to do the act by an irresistible impulse, which means before it will justify a verdict of acquittal that his reasoning powers were so far dethroned by his diseased mental condition as to deprive him of the will power to resist the insane impulse to perpetrate the deed, though knowing it to be wrong."[40]

As we have already indicated, this has since been the test in the District.

Although the Smith case did not abandon the right-wrong test, it did liberate the fact finder from exclusive reliance upon that discredited criterion by allowing the jury to inquire also whether the accused suffered from an undefined "diseased mental condition [which] deprive[d] him of the will power to resist the insane impulse. . . ."[41] The term "irresistible impulse," however, carries the misleading implication that "diseased mental condition[s]" produce only sudden, momentary or spontaneous inclinations to commit unlawful acts.[42] As the Royal Commission found:

"... In many cases ... this is not true at all. The sufferer from [melancholia, for example] experiences a change of mood which alters the whole of his existence. He may believe, for instance, that a future of such degradation and misery awaits both him and his family that death for all is a less dreadful alternative. Even the thought that the acts he contemplates are murder and suicide pales into insignificance in contrast with what he otherwise expects. The criminal act, in such circumstances, may be the reverse of impulsive. It may be coolly and carefully prepared; yet it is still the act of a madman. This is merely an illustration; similar states of mind are likely to lie behind the criminal act when murders are committed by persons suffering from schizophrenia or paranoid psychoses due to disease of the brain.

We find that as an exclusive criterion the right-wrong test is inadequate in that (a) it does not take sufficient account of psychic realities and scientific knowledge, and (b) it is based upon one symptom and so cannot validly be applied in all circumstances. We find that the "irresistible impulse" test is also inadequate in that it gives no recognition to mental illness characterized by brooding and reflection and so relegates acts caused by such illness to the application of the inadequate right-wrong test. We conclude that a broader test should be adopted.[44]

In the District of Columbia, the formulation of tests of criminal responsibility is entrusted to the courts[45] and, in adopting a new test, we invoke our inherent power to make the change prospectively.[46]

The rule we now hold must be applied on the retrial of this case and in future cases is not unlike that followed by the New Hampshire court since 1870.[47] It is simply that an accused is not criminally responsible if his unlawful act was the product of mental disease or mental defect.[48]

We use "disease" in the sense of a condition which is considered capable of either improving or deteriorating. We use "defect" in the sense of a condition which is not considered capable of either improving or deteriorating and which may be either congenital, or the result of injury, or the residual effect of a physical or mental disease.

Whenever there is "some evidence" that the accused suffered from a diseased or defective mental condition at the time the unlawful act was committed, the trial court must provide the jury with guides for determining whether the accused can be held criminally responsible. We do not, and indeed could not, formulate an instruction which would be either appropriate or binding in all cases. But under the rule now announced, any instruction should in some way convey to the jury the sense and substance of the following: If you the jury believe beyond a reasonable doubt that the accused was not suffering from a diseased or defective mental condition at the time he committed the criminal act charged, you may find him guilty. If you believe he was suffering from a diseased or defective mental condition when he committed the act, but believe beyond a reasonable doubt that the act was not the product of such mental abnormality, you may find him guilty. Unless you believe beyond a reasonable doubt either that he was not suffering from a diseased or defective mental condition, or that the act was not the product of such abnormality, you must find the accused not guilty by reason of insanity. Thus your task would not be completed upon finding, if you did find, that the accused suffered from a mental disease or defect. He would still be responsible for his unlawful act if there was no causal connection between such mental abnormality and the act.[49] These questions must be determined by you from the facts which you find to be fairly deducible from the testimony and the evidence in this case.[50]

The questions of fact under the test we now lay down are as capable of determination by the jury as, for example, the questions juries must determine upon a claim of total disability under a policy of insurance where the state of medical knowledge concerning the disease involved, and its effects, is obscure or in conflict. In such cases, the jury is not required to depend on arbitrarily selected "symptoms, phases or manifestations"[51] of the disease as criteria for determining the ultimate questions of fact upon which the claim depends. Similarly, upon a claim of criminal irresponsibility, the jury will not be required to rely on such symptoms as criteria for determining the ultimate question of fact upon which such claim depends. Testimony as to such "symptoms, phases or manifestations," along with other relevant evidence, will go to the jury upon the ultimate questions of fact which it alone can finally determine. Whatever the state of psychiatry, the psychiatrist will be permitted to carry out his principal court function which, as we noted in Holloway v. U.S., "is to inform the jury of the character of [the accused's] mental disease [or defect]."[52] The jury's range of inquiry will not be limited to, but may include, for example, whether an accused, who suffered from a mental disease or defect did not know the difference between right and wrong, acted under the compulsion of an irresistible impulse, or had "been deprived of or lost the power of his will. . . ."[53]

Finally, in leaving the determination of the ultimate question of fact to the jury, we permit it to perform its traditional function which, as we said in Holloway, is to apply "our inherited ideas of moral responsibility to individuals prosecuted for crime. . . ."[54] Juries will continue to make moral judgments, still operating under the fundamental precept that "Our collective conscience does not allow punishment where it cannot impose blame."[55] But in making such judgments, they will be guided by wider horizons of knowledge concerning mental life. The question will be simply whether the accused acted because of a mental disorder, and not whether he displayed particular symptoms which medical science has long recognized do not necessarily, or even typically, accompany even the most serious mental disorder.[56]

The legal and moral traditions of the western world require that those who, of their own free will and with evil intent (sometimes called *mens rea*), commit acts which violate the law, shall be criminally responsible for those acts. Our traditions also require that where such acts stem from and are the product of a mental disease or defect as those terms are used herein, moral blame shall not attach, and hence there will not be criminal responsibility.[57] The rule we state in this opinion is designed to meet these requirements.

Reversed and remanded for a new trial.

NOTES

1. D.C. Code §§ 22–1801, 22–2201 and 22–2202 (1951).
2. Because the questions raised are of general and crucial importance, we called upon the Government and counsel whom we appointed for the indigent appellant to brief and argue this case a second time. Their able presentations have been of great assistance to us. On the question of the adequacy of prevailing tests of criminal responsibility, we received further assistance from the able brief and argument of Abram Chayes, *amicus curiae* by appointment of this Court, in Stewart v. United States, 94 U.S.App. D.C.—, 214 F.2d 879.
3. 18 U.S.C. § 408 (1946). 1948 Revision, 18 U.S.C. §§ 10, 2311–2313.
4. Durham showed confusion when he testified. These are but two examples:
"Q. Do you remember writing it? A. No. Don't you forget? People get all mixed up in machines.
"Q. What kind of a machine? A. I don't know, they just get mixed up.
"Q. Are you cured now? A. No, sir.
"Q. In your opinion? A. No. sir.
"Q. What is the matter with you? A. You hear people bother you.
"Q. What? You say you hear people bothering you? A. Yes.
"Q. What kind of people? What do they bother you about? A. (No response.)"
Although we think the court erred in accepting counsel's admission that Durham was of sound mind, the matter does not require discussion since we reverse on other grounds and the principles governing this issue are fully discussed in our decision today in Gunther v. United States, 94 U.S.App.D.C. —, 215 F.2d 493.
5. The court also accepted a waiver of trial by jury when Durham indicated, in response to the court's question, that he preferred to be tried without a jury and that he waived his right to a trial by jury.
13. 1882, 12 D.C. 498, 550, 1 Mackey 498, 550. The right-wrong test was reaffirmed in United States v. Lee, 1886, 15 D.C. 489, 496, 4 Mackey 489, 496.
14. 1929, 59 App.D.C. 144, 36 F.2d 548, 70 A.L.R. 654.
15. Glueck, Mental Disorder and the Criminal Law 138–39 (1925), citing Rex v. Arnold, 16 How.St.Tr. 695, 764 (1724).

16. Id. at 142–52, citing Earl Ferrer's case, 19 How.St.Tr. 886 (1760). One writer has stated that these tests originated in England in the 13th or 14th century, when the law began to define insanity in terms of intellect for purposes of determining capacity to manage feudal estates. Comment, *Lunacy and Idiocy—The Old Law and Its Incubus,* 18 U. of Chi.L. Rev. 361 (1951).

17. 8 Eng.Rep. 718 (1843).

18. Hall, Principles of Criminal Law 480, n. 6 (1947).

19. Royal Commission on Capital Punishment 1949–1953 Report (Cmd. 8932) 79 (1953) (hereinafter cited as Royal Commission Report).

20. Weihofen, *The M'Naghten Rule in Its Present Day Setting,* Federal Probation 8 (Sept. 1953); Weihofen, Insanity as a Denense in Criminal Law 15, 64–68, 109–47 (1933); Leland v. State of Oregon, 1952, 343 U.S. 790, 800, 72 S.Ct. 1002, 96 L.Ed. 1302.
"In five States the M'Naghten Rules have been in substance re-enacted by statute." Royal Commission Report 409; see, for example, "Sec. 1120 of the [New York State] Penal Law [McK.Consol. Laws, c. 40] [which] provides that a person is not excused from liability on the grounds of insanity, idiocy or imbecility, except upon proof that at the time of the commission of the criminal act he was laboring under such a defect or reason as (1) not to know the nature and quality of the act he was doing or (2) not to know that the act was wrong." Ploscowe, *Suggested Changes in the New York Laws and Procedures Relating to the Criminally Insane and Mentally Defective Offenders,* 43 J. Crim.L., Criminology & Police Sci. 312, 314 (1952).

21. 8 Eng.Rep. 718, 722 (1843). "Today, Oregon is the only state that requires the accused, on a plea of insanity, to establish that defense beyond a reasonable doubt. Some twenty states, however, place the burden on the accused to establish his insanity by a preponderance of the evidence or some similar measure of persuasion." Leland v. State of Oregon, supra, note 20, 343 U.S. at page 798, 72 S.Ct. 1002. Since Davis v. United States, 1895, 160 U.S. 469, 484, 16 S.Ct. 353, 40 L.Ed. 499, a contrary rule of procedure has been followed in the Federal courts. For example, in compliance with Davis, we held in Tatum v. United States, supra, note 8, 88 U.S. App.D.C. 386, 389, 190 F.2d 612, 615, and text, "as soon as 'some evidence of mental disorder is introduced, . . . sanity, like any other fact, must be proved as part of the prosecution's case beyond a reasonable doubt.' "

22. Ray, Medical Jurisprudence of Insanity 47 and 34 et seq. (1st ed. 1838). "That the insane mind is not entirely deprived of this power of moral discernment, but in many subjects is perfectly rational, and displays the exercise of a sound and well balanced mind is one of those facts now so well established, that to question it would only betray the height of ignorance and presumption." Id. at 32.

23. See Zilboorg, *Legal Aspects of Psychiatry* in One Hundred Years of American Psychiatry 1844–1944, 507, 552 (1944).

24. Cardozo, What Medicine Can Do For the Law 32 (1930).

25. For a detailed bibliography on Insanity as a Defense to Crime, see 7 The Record of the Association of the Bar of the City of New York 158–62 (1952). And see. *for example,* Alexander, the Criminal, the Judge and the Public 70 et seq. (1931); Cardozo, What Medicine Can Do For the Law 28 et seq. (1930); Cleckley, the Mask of Sanity 491 et seq. (2d ed.1950); Deutsch, The Mentally Ill In America 389–417 (2d ed. 1949); Glueck, Mental Disorder and the Criminal Law (1925). Crime and Justice 96 et seq. (1936); Guttmacher & Weihofen, Psychiatry and the Law 218, 403–23 (1952); Hall,

Principles of Criminal Law 477–538 (1947); Menninger, The Human Mind 450 (1937); Hall & Menninger, *"Psychiatry and the Law"—A Dual Review,* 38 Iowa L.Rev. 687 (1953); Overholser, The Psychiatrist and the Law 41–43 (1953); Overholser & Richmond, Handbook of Psychiatry 208–15 (1947); Ploscowe, *Suggested Changes in the New York Laws and Procedures Relating to the Criminally Insane and Mentally Defective Offenders,* 43 J.Crim.L., Criminology & Police Sci. 312, 314 (1952); Ray, Medical Jurisprudence of Insanity (1st ed.1838) (4th ed.1860); Reik, *The Doc-Ray Correspondence: A Pioneer Collaboration in the Jurisprudence of Mental Disease,* 63 Yale L.J. 183 (1953); Weihofen, Insanity as a Defense in Criminal Law (1933), *The M.Naghten Rule in Its Present Day Setting,* Federal Probation 8 (Sept. 1953); Zilboorg, Mind, Medicine and Man 246–97 (1943), *Legal Aspects of Psychiatry,* American Psychiatry 1844–1944, 507 (1944).

26. Royal Commission Report 73–129.

27. The Committee on Forensic Psychiatry (whose report is hereinafter cited as Gap Report) was composed of Drs. Philip Q. Roche, Frank S. Curran, Lawrence Z. Freedman and Manfred S. Guttmacher. They were assisted in their deliberations by leading psychiatrists, jurists, law professors, and legal practitioners.

28. Royal Commission Report 80.

29. Glueck, *Psychiatry and the Criminal Law,* 12 Mental Hygiene 575, 580 (1928), as quoted in Deutsch, The Mentally Ill in America 396 (2d ed. 1949); and see, *for example,* Menninger, The Human Mind 450 (1937); Guttmacher & Weihofen, Psychiatry and the Law 403–08 (1952).

30. Holloway v. United States, 1945, 80 U.S.App.D.C. 3, 5, 148 F.2d 665, 667, certiorari denied, 1948, 334 U.S. 852, 68, S.Ct. 1507, 92 L.Ed. 1774.
More recently, the Royal Commission, after an exhaustive survey of legal, medical and lay opinion in many Western countries, including England and the United States made a similar finding. It reported: "The gravamen of the charge against the M'Naghten Rules is that they are not in harmony with modern medical science, which, as we have seen, is reluctant to devide the mind into separate compartments—the intellect, the emotions and the will—but looks at it as a whole and considers that insanity distorts and impairs the action of the mind as a whole." Royal Commission Report 113. The Commission lends vivid support to this conclusion by pointing out that "It would be impossible to apply modern methods of care and treatment in mental hospitals, and at the same time to maintain order and discipline, if the great majority of the patients, even among the grossly insane, did not know what is forbidden by the rules and that, if they break them, they are liable to forfeit some privilege. Examination of a number of guilty but insane [the nearest English equivalent of our acquittal by reason of insanity] was returned, and rightly returned, has convinced us that there are few indeed where the accused can truly be said not to have known that his act was wrong." Id. at 103.

31. See Guttmacher & Weihofen, Psychiatry and the Law 421, 422 (1952). The M'Naghten rules "constitute not only an arbitrary restriction on vital medical data, but also impose an improper onus of decision upon the expert witness. The Rules are unanswerable in that they have no consensus with established psychiatric criteria of symptomatic description save for the case of disturbed consciousness or of idiocy,. . . ." From statement by Dr. Philip Q. Roche, quited id. at 407. See also United States ex rel. Smith v. Baldi, 3 Cir., 1951, 192 F.2d 540, 567 (dissenting opinion).

32. In a very recent case, the Supreme Court of New Mexico recognized the inadequacy of the right-wrong test, and adopted what it called an "extension of the M'Naghten

Rules." Under this extension, lack of knowledge of right and wrong is not essential for acquittal "if, by reason of disease of the mind, defendant has been deprived of or lost the power of his will. . . ." State v. White, N.M., 270 P.2d 727, 730.

33. Deutsch, The Mentally Ill in America 400 (2d ed.1949); Keedy, *Irresistible Impulses as a Defense in Criminal Law,* 100 U. of Pa.L.Rev. 956, 992 (1952).

34. Professor John Whitehorn of the Johns Hopkins Medical School, who recently prepared an informal memorandum on this subject for a Commission on Legal Psychiatry appointed by the Governor of Maryland, has said: "Psychiatrists are challenged to set forth a crystal-clear statement of what constitutes insanity. It is impossible to express this adequately in words, alone, since such diagnostic judgments involve clinical skill and experience which cannot wholly be verbalized. . . . The medical profession would be baffled if asked to write into the legal code universally valid criteria for the diagnosis of the many types of psychotic illness which may seriously disturb a person's responsibility, and even if this were attempted, the diagnostic criteria would have to be rewritten from time to time, with the progress of psychiatric knowledge." Quoted in Guttmacher & Weihofen, Psychiatry and the Law 419–20 (1952).

35. ". . . . the legal profession were invading the province of medicine, and attempting to install old exploded medical theories in the place of facts established in the progress of scientific knowledge." State v. Pike, 1870, 49 N.H. 399, 438.

36. Royal Commission Report 114. And see State v. Jones, 1871, 50 N.H. 369, 392–393.

37. Keedy, *Irresistible Impulse as a Defense in Criminal Law,* 100 U. of Pa.L. Rev. 956, 992–93 (1952).

38. See, *for example,* Taylor v. United States, 1895, 7 App.D.C. 27, 41–44, where we rejected "emotional insanity" as a defense, citing with approval the following from the trial court's instruction to the jury: "Whatever may be the cry of scientific experts, the law does not recognize, but condemns the doctrine of emotional insanity—that a man may be sane up until a moment before he commits a crime, insane while he does it, and sane again soon afterwards. Such a doctrine would be dangerous in the extreme. The law does not recognize it; and a jury cannot without violating their oaths." This position was emphatically reaffirmed in Snell v. United States, 1900, 16 App.D.C. 501, 524.

39. 1929, 59 App.D.C. 144, 146, 36 F.2d 548, 550, 70 A.L.R. 654.

40. 59 App.D.C. at page 145, 36 F.2d at page 549.

41. 59 App.D.C. at page 145, 36 F.2d at page 549.

42. Impulse, as defined by Webster's New International Dictionary (2d ed.1950), is:

"1. Act of impelling, or driving onward with *sudden* force; impulsion, esp., force so communicated as to produce motion *suddenly,* or *immediately.* . . .

"2. An incitement of the mind or spirit, esp. in the form of an *abrupt* and vivid suggestion, prompting some *unpremeditated* action or leading to unforeseen knowledge or insight; a *spontaneous* inclination. . . .

3. . . . motion produced by a *sudden* or *momentary* force. . . ." [Emphasis supplied.]

43. Royal Commission Report 110; for additional comment on the irresistible impulse test, see Glueck, Crime and Justice 101–03 (1936); Guttmacher & Weihofen, Psychiatry and the Law 410–12 (1952); Hall, General Principles of Criminal Law 505–26 (1947); Keedy, *Irresistible Impulse as a Defense in Criminal Law,* 100 U. of Pa.L.Rev. 956 (1952); Wertham, The Show of Violence 14 (1949).

The New Mexico Supreme Court in recently adopting a broader criminal insanity rule, note 32, supra, observed: ". . .

insanity takes the form of the personality of the individual and, if his tendency is toward depression, his wrongful act may come at the conclusion of a period of complete lethargy, thoroughly devoid of excitement."

44. As we recently said, ". . . former common law should not be followed where changes in conditions have made it obsolete. We have never hesitated to exercise the usual judicial function of revising and enlarging the common law." Linkins v. Protestant Episcopal Cathedral Foundation, 1950, 87 U.S.App.D.C. 351, 355, 187 F.2d 357, 361, 28 A.L.R.2d 521. Cf. Funk v. United States, 1933, 290 U.S. 371, 381–382, 54 S.Ct. 212, 78 L.Ed. 369.

45. Congress, like most State legislatures, has never undertaken to define insanity in this connection, although it recognizes the fact that an accused may be acquitted by reason of insanity. See D.C. Code § 24–301 (1951). And as this court made clear in Hill v. United States, Congress has left no doubt that "common-law procedure, in all matters relating to crime . . . still continues in force here in all cases except where special provision is made by statute to the exclusion of the common-law procedure." 22 App. D.C. 395, 401 (1903), and statutes cited therein; Linkins v. Protestant Episcopal Cathedral Foundation, 87 U.S. App.D.C. at pages 354–55, 187 F.2d at pages 360–361; and see Fisher v. United States, 1946, 328 U.S. 463, 66 S.Ct. 1318, 90 L. Ed. 1382.

46. See Great Northern R. v. Sunburst Oil & Refining Co., 1932, 287 U.S. 358, 53 S. Ct. 145, 77 L.Ed. 360; National Labor Relations Board v. Guy F. Atkinson Co., 9 Cir., 1952, 195 F.2d 141, 148; Concurring opinion of Judge Frank in Aero Spark Plug Co. v. B. G. Corporation, 2 Cir., 1942, 130 F.2d 290, 298, and note 24; Warring v. Colpoys, 1941, 74 App.D.C. 303, 122 F.2d 642, 645, 136 A.L.R. 1025; Moore & Oglebay, *The Supreme Court, Stare Decisis and Law of the Case,* 21 Texas L.Rev. 514, 535 (1943); Carpenter, *Court Decisions and the Common Law,* 17 Col.L.Rev. 593, 606–07 (1917). But see von Moschzisker, *Stare Decisis in Courts of Last Resort.* 37 Harv.L.Rev. 409, 426 (1924). Our approach is similar to that of the Supreme Court of California in People v. Maughs, 1906, 149 Cal. 253, 86 P. 187, 191, where the court prospectively invalidated a previously accepted instruction, saying:

". . . we think the time has come to say that in all future cases which shall arise, and where, after this warning, this instruction shall be given, this court will hold the giving of it to be so prejudicial to the rights of a defendant, secured to him by our Constitution and laws, as to call for the reversal of any judgment which may be rendered against him."

47. State v. Pike, 1870, 49 N.H. 399.

48. Cf. State v. Jones, 1871, 50 N.H. 369, 398.

49. "There is no *a priori* reason why every person suffering from any form of mental abnormality or disease, or from any particular kind of mental disease, should be treated by the law as not answerable for any criminal offence which he may commit, and be exempted from conviction and punishment. Mental abnormalities vary infinitely in their nature and intensity and in their effects on the character and conduct of those who suffer from them. Where a person suffering from a mental abnormality commits a crime, there must always be some likelihood that the abnormality has played some part in the causation of the crime; and, generally speaking, the graver the abnormality, . . . the more probable it must be that there is a causal connection between them. But the closeness of this connection will be shown by the facts brought in evidence in individual cases and cannot be decided on the basis of any general medical principle." Royal Commission Report 99.

50. The court may always, of course, if it deems it advisable for the assistance of the jury, point out particular areas

of agreement and conflict in the expert testimony in each case, just as it ordinarily does in summing up any other testimony.

51.   State v. Jones, 1871, 50 N.H. 369, 398.

52.   1945, 80 U.S.App.D.C. 3, 5, 148 F.2d 665, 667.

53.   State v. White, see n. 32, supra.

54.   80 U.S.App.D.C. at page 5, 148 F.2d at page 667.

55.   80 U.S.App.D.C. at pages 4–5, 148 F.2d at pages 666–667.

56.   See text, supra, 214 F.2d 870–872.

57.   An accused person who is acquitted by reason of insanity is presumed to be insane, Orencia v. Overholser, 1947, 82 U.S.App.D.C. 285, 163 F.2d 763; Barry v. White, 1933, 62 App.D.C. 69, 64 F.2d 707, and may be committed for an indefinite period to a "hospital for the insane." D.C.Code § 24–301 (1951).

We think that even where there has been a specific finding that the accused was competent to stand trial and to assist in his own defense, the court would be well advised to invoke this Code provision so that the accused may be confined as long as "the public safety and . . . [his] welfare" require. Barry v. White, 62 App.D.C. at page 71, 64 F.2d at page 709.

UNITED STATES v. BRAWNER

U.S. Court of Appeals, D.C. Cir., 1972*

Leventhal, Circuit Judge:

Passing by various minor disagreements among the witnesses, the record permits us to reconstruct the events of September 8, 1967, as follows: After a morning and afternoon of wine-drinking, appellant Archie W. Brawner, Jr. and his uncle Aaron Ross, went to a party at the home of three acquaintances. During the evening, several fights broke out. In one of them, Brawner's jaw was injured when he was struck or pushed to the ground. The time of the fight was approximately 10:30 p.m. After the fight, Brawner left the party. He told Mr. Ross that some boys had jumped him. Mr. Ross testified that Brawner "looked like he was out of his mind". Other witnesses who saw him after the fight testified that Brawner's mouth was bleeding and that his speech was unclear (but the same witness added, "I heard every word he said"); that he was staggering and angry; and that he pounded on a mailbox with his fist. One witness testified that Brawner said, "[I'm] going to get my boys" and come back, and that "someone is going to die tonight."

Half an hour later, at about eleven p.m., Brawner was on his way back to the party with a gun. One witness testified that Brawner said he was going up there to kill his attackers or be killed.

Upon his arrival at the address, Brawner fired a shot into the ground and entered the building. He proceeded to the apartment where the party was in progress and fired five shots through the closed metal hallway door. Two of the shots struck Billy Ford, killing him. Brawner was arrested a few minutes later, several blocks away. The arresting officer testified that Brawner appeared normal, and did not appear to be drunk, that he spoke clearly, and had no odor of alcohol about him.

After the Government had presented the evidence of its non-expert witnesses, the trial judge ruled that there was insufficient evidence on "deliberation" to go to the jury: accordingly, a verdict of acquittal was directed on first degree murder.

The expert witnesses, called by both defense and prosecution, all agreed that Brawner was suffering

*471 F. 2d 969 (1972). Excerpts only. The footnotes are numbered here as in the original.

from an abnormality of a psychiatric or neurological nature. The medical labels were variously given as "epileptic personality disorder," "psychologic brain syndrome associated with a convulsive disorder," "personality disorder associated with epilepsy," or, more simply, "an explosive personality." There was no disagreement that the epileptic condition would be exacerbated by alcohol, leading to more frequent episodes and episodes of greater intensity, and would also be exacerbated by a physical blow to the head. The experts agreed that epilepsy *per se* is not a mental disease or defect, but a neurological disease which is often associated with a mental disease or defect. They further agreed that Brawner had a mental, as well as a neurological, disease.

Where the experts disagreed was on the part which that mental disease or defect played in the murder of Billy Ford. The position of the witnesses called by the Government is that Brawner's behavior on the night of September 8 was not consistent with an epileptic seizure, and was not suggestive of an explosive reaction in the context of a psychiatric disorder. In the words of Dr. Platkin of St. Elizabeths Hospital, "He was just mad."

The experts called by the defense maintained the contrary conclusion. Thus, Dr. Eugene Stanmeyer, a psychologist at St. Elizabeths, was asked on direct by counsel for defense, whether, assuming accused did commit the act which occurred, there was a causal relationship between the assumed act and his mental abnormality. Dr. Stanmeyer replied in the affirmative, that there was a cause and effect relationship.

Later, the prosecutor asked the Government's first expert witness Dr. Weickhardt: "Did you . . . come to any opinion concerning whether or not the crimes in this case were causally related to the mental illness which you diagnosed?" An objection to the form of the question was overruled. The witness then set forth that in his opinion there was no causal relationship between the mental disorder and the alleged offenses. Brawner claims that the trial court erred when it permitted a prosecution expert to testify in this manner. He relies on our opinion in Washington v. United States, 129 U.S.App.D.C. 29, 390 F.2d 444 (1967).

INSANITY RULE IN OTHER CIRCUITS

The American Law Institute's Model Penal Code expressed a rule which has become the dominant force in the law pertaining to the defense of insanity. The ALI rule is eclectic in spirit, partaking of the moral focus of *M'Naghten,* the practical accommodation of the "control rules" (a term more exact and less susceptible of misunderstanding than "irresistible impulse" terminology), and responsive, at the same time, to a relatively modern, forward-looking view of what is encompassed in "knowledge."

For convenience, we quote again the basic rule propounded by the ALI's Model Penal Code:

A person is not responsible for criminal conduct if at the time of such conduct as a result of mental disease or defect he lacks substantial capacity either to appreciate the criminality [wrongfulness] of his conduct or to conform his conduct to the requirements of the law.

COMMENTS CONCERNING REASON FOR ADOPTION OF ALI RULE AND SCOPE OF RULE AS ADOPTED BY THIS COURT

In the foreglimpse stating that we had determined to adopt the ALI rule we undertook to set forth comments stating our reasons, and also the adjustments and understandings defining the ALI rule as adopted by this Court. Having paused to study the rulings in the other circuits, we turn to our comments, and to our reflections following the extensive, and intensive, exposure of this court to insanity defense issues.[9]

1. NEED TO DEPART FROM "PRODUCT" FORMULATION AND UNDUE DOMINANCE BY EXPERTS.

A principal reason for our decision to depart from the *Durham* rule is the undesirable characteristic, surviving even the *McDonald* modification, of undue dominance by the experts giving testimony. The underlying problem was identified, with stress on different facets, in the *Carter, Blocker* (concurring), and *Washington* opinions. The difficulty is rooted in the circumstance that there is no generally accepted understanding, either in the jury or the community it represents, of the concept requiring that the crime be the "product" of the mental disease.

When the court used the term "product" in *Durham* it likely assumed that this was a serviceable, and indeed a natural, term for a rule defining criminal responsibility—a legal reciprocal, as it were, for the familiar term "proximate cause," used to define civil responsibility. But if concepts like "product" are, upon refinement, reasonably understood, or at least appreciated, by judges and lawyers, and perhaps philosophers, difficulties developed when it emerged that the "product"

concept did not signify a reasonably identifiable common ground that was also shared by the nonlegal experts,[10] and the laymen serving on the jury as the representatives of the community.

The doctrine of criminal responsibility is such that there can be no doubt "of the complicated nature of the decision to be made—intertwining moral, legal, and medical judgments," see King v. United States, 125 U.S.App.D.C. 318, 324, 372 F.2d 383, 389 (1967) and *Durham* and other cases cited *supra,* note 6. Hence, as *King* and other opinions have noted, jury decisions have been accorded unusual deference even when they have found responsibility in the face of a powerful record, with medical evidence uncontradicted, pointing toward exculpation.[11] The "moral" elements of the decision are not defined exclusively by religious considerations but by the totality of underlying conceptions of ethics and justice shared by the community as expressed by its jury surrogate. The essential feature of a jury "lies in the interposition between the accused and his accuser of the commonsense judgment of a group of laymen, and in the community participation and shared responsibility that results from the group's determination of guilt or innocence." Williams v. Florida, 399 U.S. 78, 100, 90 S.Ct. 1893, 1906, 26 L.Ed.2d 466 (1970).

The expert witnesses—psychiatrists and psychologists—are called to adduce relevant information concerning what may for convenience be referred to as the "medical" component of the responsibility issue. But the difficulty—as emphasized in *Washington*—is that the medical expert comes, by testimony given in terms of a non-medical construct ("product"), to express conclusions that in essence embody ethical and legal conclusions. There is indeed, irony in a situation under which the *Durham* rule, which was adopted in large part to permit experts to testify in their own terms concerning matters within their domain which the jury should know, resulted in testimony by the experts in terms not their own to reflect unexpressed judgments in a domain that is properly not theirs but the jury's. The irony is heightened when the jurymen, instructed under the esoteric "product" standard, are influenced significantly by "product" testimony of expert witnesses really reflecting ethical and legal judgments rather than a conclusion within the witnesses' particular expertise.

It is easier to identify and spotlight the irony than to eradicate the mischief. The objective of *Durham* is still sound—to put before the jury the information that is within the expert's domain, to aid the jury in making a broad and comprehensive judgment. But when the instructions and appellate decisions define the "product" inquiry as the ultimate issue, it is like stopping the tides to try to halt the emergence of this term in the language of those with a central role in the trial—the lawyers who naturally seek to present testimony that will influence the jury who will be charged under the ultimate "product" standard, and the expert witnesses who have an awareness, gained from forensic psychiatry and related disciplines, of the ultimate "product" standard that dominates the proceeding.

The experts have meaningful information to impart, not only on the existence of mental illness or not, but also on its relationship to the incident charged as an offense. In the interest of justice this valued information should be available, and should not be lost or blocked by requirements that unnaturally restrict communication between the experts and the jury. The more we have pondered the problem the more convinced we have become that the sound solution lies not in further shaping of the *Durham* "product" approach in more refined molds, but in adopting the ALI's formulation as the linchpin of our jurisprudence.

The ALI's formulation retains the core requirement of a meaningful relationship between the mental illness and the incident charged. The language in the ALI rule is sufficiently in the common ken that its use in the courtroom, or in preparation for trial, permits a reasonable three-way communication—between (a) the law-trained, judges and lawyers; (b) the experts and (c) the jurymen—without insisting on a vocabulary that is either stilted or stultified, or conducive to a testimonial mystique permitting expert dominance and encroachment on the jury's function. There is no indication in the available literature that any such untoward development has attended the reasonably widespread adoption of the ALI rule in the Federal courts and a substantial number of state courts.

2. RETENTION OF McDONALD DEFINITION OF "MENTAL DISEASE OR DEFECT."

Our ruling today includes our decision that in the ALI rule as adopted by this court the term "mental disease or defect" includes the definition of that term provided in our 1962 en banc *McDonald* opinion, as follows:

[A] mental disease or defect includes any abnormal condition of the mind which substantially affects mental or emotional processes and substantially impairs behavior controls.

McDonald v. United States, 114 U.S.App.D.C. at 124, 312 F.2d at 851.

We take this action in response to the problem, identified by amicus comments of Mr. Dempsey and the D.C. Bar Association, that the ALI's rule, lacking definition of "mental disease or defect," contains an inherent ambiguity. These comments consider this a reason

for avoiding the ALI rule. We find more merit in the suggestion of Mr. Flynn, counsel appointed to represent appellant, that the *McDonald* definition be engrafted on to the ALI rule.[12]

In our further discussion of ALI and *McDonald,* we shall sometimes refer to "mental disease" as the core concept, without specifically referring to the possibility of exculpation by reason of a non-altering "mental defect."

The *McDonald* Rule has helped accomplish the objective of securing expert testimony needed on the subject of mental illness, while guarding against the undue dominance of expert testimony or specialized labels. It has thus permitted the kind of communication without encroachment, as between experts and juries, that has prompted us to adopt the ALI rule, and hence will help us realize our objective. This advantage overrides the surface disadvantage of any clumsiness in the blending of the *McDonald* component, defining mental disease, with the rest of the ALI rule, a matter we discuss further below.

3. INTEREST OF UNIFORMITY OF JUDICIAL APPROACH AND VOCABULARY, WITH ROOM FOR VARIATIONS AND ADJUSTMENTS

Adoption of the ALI rule furthers uniformity of judicial approach—a feature eminently desirable, not as a mere glow of "togetherness," but as an appreciation of the need and value of judicial communication. In all likelihood, this court's approach under *Durham,* at least since *McDonald,* has differed from that of other courts in vocabulary more than substance. Uniformity of vocabulary has an important value, however, as is evidenced from the familiar experience of meanings that "get lost in translation." No one court can amass all the experience pertinent to the judicial administration of the insanity defense. It is helpful for courts to be able to learn from each other without any blockage due to jargon. It is an impressive virtue of the common law, that its distinctive reliance on judicial decisions to establish the corpus of the law furthers a multiparty conversation between men who have studied a problem in various places at various times.

The value of uniformity of central approach is not shattered by the circumstance that in various particulars the different circuits have inserted variations in the ALI rule. Homogeneity does not mean rigidity, and room for local variation is likely a strength, providing a basis for comparison,[13] not a weakness. Nor is the strength of essential uniformity undercut by the caution of our appointed amicus that the formulation of the ALI rule provides extremely broad flexibility.[14] Flexibility and ductility are inherent in the insanity defense, as in any judicial rule with an extensive range

—say, negligence, or proximate cause—and the ALI rule permits appropriate guidance of juries.

In prescribing a departure from *Durham* we are not unmindful of the concern that a change may generate uncertainties as to corollaries of the change.[15] While the courts adopting the ALI rule have stated variations, as we have noted, these were all, broadly, in furtherance of one or more of the inter-related goals of the insanity defense:

    (a) a broad input of pertinent facts and opinions
    (b) enhancing the information and judgment
    (c) of a jury necessarily given latitude in light of its functioning as the representative of the entire community.

We are likewise and for the same objectives defining the ALI rule as adopted by the court, with its contours and corollaries given express statement at the outset so as to minimize uncertainty. We postpone this statement to a subsequent phase of the opinion (see. 990 et seq.) in order that we may first consider other alternatives, for in some measure our adaptation may obviate or at least blunt objections voiced to the ALI rule.

4. CONSIDERATION AND REJECTION OF OTHER SUGGESTIONS

a. *Proposal to abolish insanity defense*

A number of proposals in the journals recommend that the insanity defense be abolished altogether.[16] This is advocated in the amicus brief of the National District Attorneys Association as both desirable and lawful.[17] The amicus brief of American Psychiatric Association concludes it would be desirable, with appropriate safeguards, but would require a constitutional amendment. That a constitutional amendment would be required is also the conclusion of others, generally in opposition to the proposal.[18]

This proposal has been put forward by responsible judges for consideration, with the objective of reserving psychiatric overview for the phase of the criminal process concerned with disposition of the person determined to have been the actor.[19] However, we are convinced that the proposal cannot properly be imposed by judicial fiat.

The courts have emphasized over the centuries that "free will" is the postulate of responsibility under our jurisprudence. 4 Blackstone's Commentaries 27. The concept of "belief in freedom of the human will and a consequent ability and duty of the normal individual to choose between good and evil" is a core concept that is "universal and persistent in mature systems of law." Morissette v. United States, 342 U.S. 246, 250, 72 S.Ct. 240, 243, 96 L.Ed. 288 (1952). Criminal responsibility is assessed when through "free will" a man elects to do evil. And while, as noted in *Morissette,* the legislature

has dispensed with mental element in some statutory offenses, in furtherance of a paramount need of the community, these instances mark the exception and not the rule, and only in the most limited instances has the mental element been omitted by the legislature as a requisite for an offense that was a crime at common law.

The concept of lack of "free will" is both the root of origin of the insanity defense and the line of its growth.[20] This cherished principle is not undercut by difficulties, or differences of view, as to how best to express the free will concept in the light of the expansion of medical knowledge. We do not concur in the view of the National District Attorneys Association that the insanity defense should be abandoned judicially, either because it is at too great a variance with popular conceptions of guilt[21] or fails "to show proper respect for the personality of the criminal [who] is liable to resent pathology more than punishment."[22]

These concepts may be measured along with other ingredients in a legislative re-examination of settled doctrines of criminal responsibility, root, stock and branch. Such a reassessment, one that seeks to probe and appraise the society's processes and values is for the legislative branch, assuming no constitutional bar. The judicial role is limited, in Justice Holmes's figure, to action that is molecular, with the restraint inherent in taking relatively small steps, leaving to the other branches of government whatever progress must be made with seven-league leaps. Such judicial restraint is particularly necessary when a proposal requires, as a mandatory ingredient, the kind of devotion of resources, personnel and techniques that can be accomplished only through whole-hearted legislative commitment.

To obviate any misunderstanding from our rejection of the recommendation of those proposing judicial abolition of the insanity defense, we expressly commend their emphasis on the need for improvement of dispositional resources and programs. The defense focuses on the kind of impairment that warrants exculpation, and necessarily assigns to the prison walls many men who have serious mental impairments and difficulties. The needs of society—rooted not only in humanity but in practical need for attempting to break the recidivist cycles, and halt the spread of deviant behavior—call for the provision of psychiatrists, psychologists and counselors to help men with these mental afflictions and difficulties, as part of a total effort toward a readjustment that will permit re-integration in society.

b. *Proposal for defense if mental disease impairs capacity to such an extent that the defendant cannot "justly be held responsible."*

We have also pondered the suggestion that the jury be instructed that the defendant lacks criminal responsibility if the jury finds that the defendant's mental disease impairs his capacity or controls to such an extent that he cannot "justly be held responsible."

This was the view of a British commission,[23] adapted and proposed in 1955 by Professor Wechsler, the distinguished Reporter for the ALI's Model Penal Code, and sustained by some, albeit a minority, of the members of the ALI's Council.[24] In the ALI, the contrary view prevailed because of a concern over presenting to the jury questions put primarily in the form of "justice."

The proposal is not to be condemned out of hand as a suggestion that the jury be informed of an absolute prerogative that it can only exercise by flatly disregarding the applicable rule of law. It is rather a suggestion that the jury be informed of the matters the law contemplates it will take into account in arriving at the community judgment concerning a composite of factors.[25]

However, there is a substantial concern that an instruction overtly cast in terms of "justice" cannot feasibly be restricted to the ambit of what may properly be taken into account but will splash with unconfinable and malign consequences. The Government cautions that "explicit appeals to 'justice' will result in litigation of extraneous issues and will encourage improper arguments to the jury phrased solely in terms of 'sympathy' and 'prejudice.'"

Nor is this solely a prosecutor's concern.

Mr. Flynn, counsel appointed to represent defendant, puts it that even though the jury is applying community concepts of blameworthiness "the jury should not be left at large, or asked to find out for itself what those concepts are."

The amicus submission of the Public Defender Service argues that it would be beneficial to focus the jury's attention on the moral and legal questions intertwined in the insanity defense. It expresses concern, however, over a blameworthiness instruction without more, saying (Br. 19) "it may well be that the 'average' American condemns the mentally ill."[26] It would apparently accept an approach not unlike that proposed by the ALI Reporter, under which the justice standard is coupled with a direction to consider the individual's capacity to control his behavior. Mr. Dempsey's recommendation is of like import, with some simplification.[27] But the problem remains, whether, assuming justice calls for the exculpation and treatment of the mentally ill, that is more likely to be gained from a

jury, with "average" notions of mental illness, which is explicitly set at large to convict or acquit persons with impaired mental capacity according to its concept of justice.

The brief of the D.C. Bar Association as amicus submits that with a "justly responsible" formulation the test of insanity "would be largely swallowed up by this consideration." And it observes that the function of giving to the jury the law to be applied to the facts is not only the duty of the court, see Sparf v. United States, 156 U.S. 51, 102, 15 S.Ct. 273, 39 L.Ed. 343 (1895), but is also "a bedrock right of every citizen"—and, possibly, his "only protection," citing Justice Story in United States v. Battiste, 2 Sumn. 240, 244, Fed.Cas. No. 14,545 (C.C.D.Mass. 1835).

We are impressed by the observation of Professor Abraham S. Goldstein, one of the most careful students of the problem:

[The] overly general standard may place too great a burden upon the jury. If the law provides no standard, members of the jury are placed in the difficult position of having to find a man responsible for no other reason than their personal feeling about him. Whether the psyches of individual jurors are strong enough to make that decision, or whether the "law" should put that obligation on them, is open to serious question. It is far easier for them to perform the role assigned to them by legislature and courts if they know—or are able to rationalize—that their verdicts are "required" by law.[28]

Professor Goldstein was referring to the board "justice" standard recommended by the Royal Commission. But the problems remain acute even with the modifications in the proposal of the ALI Reporter, for that still leads to "justly responsible" as the ultimate and critical term.

There may be a tug of appeal in the suggestion that law is a means to justice and the jury is an appropriate tribunal to ascertain justice. This is a simplistic syllogism that harbors the logical fallacy of equivocation, and fails to take account of the different facets and dimensions of the concept of justice. We must not be beguiled by a play on words. The thrust of a rule that in essence invites the jury to ponder the evidence on impairment of defendant's capacity and appreciation, and then do what to them seems just, is to focus on what seems "just" as to the particular individual. Under the centuries-long pull of the Judeo-Christian ethic, this is likely to suggest a call for understanding and forgiveness of those who have committed crimes against society, but plead the influence of passionate and perhaps justified grievances against that society, perhaps grievances not wholly lacking in merit. In the domain of morality and religion, the gears may be governed by the particular instance of the individual seeking salvation. The judgment of a court of law must further justice to the community, and safeguard it against undercutting and evasion from overconcern for the individual. What this reflects is not the rigidity of retributive justice—an eye for an eye—but awareness how justice in the broad may be undermined by an excess of compassion as well as passion. Justice to the community includes penalties needed to cope with disobedience by those capable of control, undergirding a social environment that broadly inhibits behavior destructive of the common good. An open society requires mutual respect and regard, and mutually reinforcing relationships among its citizens, and its ideals of justice must safeguard the vast majority who responsibly shoulder the burdens implicit in its ordered liberty. Still another aspect of justice is the requirement for rules of conduct that establish reasonable generality, neutrality and constancy. Cf. L. Fuller, The Morality of Laws 33–94 (1964). This concept is neither static nor absolute, but it would be sapped by a rule that invites an ad hoc redefinition of the "just" with each new case.

It is the sense of justice propounded by those charged with making and declaring the law—legislatures and courts—that lays down the rule that persons without substantial capacity to know or control the act shall be excused. The jury is concerned with applying the community understanding of this broad rule to particular lay and medical facts. Where the matter is unclear it naturally will call on its own sense of justice to help it determine the matter. There is wisdom in the view that a jury generally understands well enough that an instruction composed in flexible terms gives it sufficient latitude so that, without disregarding the instruction, it can provide that application of the instruction which harmonizes with its sense of justice.[29] The ALI rule generally communicates that meaning. Wade v. United States, *supra*, 426 F.2d at 70–71. This is recognized even by those who might prefer a more explicit statement of the matter.[30] It is one thing, however, to tolerate and even welcome the jury's sense of equity as a force that affects its application of instructions which state the legal rules that crystallize the requirements of justice as determined by the lawmakers of the community. It is quite another to set the jury at large, without such crystallization, to evolve its own legal rules and standards of justice. It would likely be counter-productive and contrary to the larger interest of justice to become so explicit—in an effort to hammer the point home to the very occasional jury that would otherwise be too rigid—that one puts serious strains on the normal operation of the system of criminal justice.

Taking all these considerations into account we conclude that the ALI rule as announced is not productive of injustice, and we decline to proclaim the broad "justly responsible" standard.

5. ALI RULE IS CONTEMPLATED AS IMPROVING THE PROCESS OF ADJUDICATION, NOT AS AFFECTING NUMBER OF INSANITY ACQUITTALS

Amicus Dempsey is concerned that a change by this court from *Durham-McDonald* to ALI will be taken as an indication that this court intends that the number and percentage of insanity acquittals be modified. That is not the intendment of the rule adopted today, nor do we have any basis for forecasting that effect.

a. Statistical data concerning the use of insanity in criminal trials in this jurisdiction were presented in the December 15, 1966, Report of the President's Commission on Crime in the District of Columbia.[31] These data have been up-dated in Mr. Dempsey's brief, with the aid of data helpfully supplied by the United States Attorney's office. At least since *Durham* was modified by *McDonald,* insanity acquittals have run at about 2% of all cases terminated. In the seven years subsequent to *McDonald* jury verdicts of not guilty by reason of insanity averaged only 3 per annum.[32] In trials by the court, there has been an annual average of about 38 verdicts of not guilty by reason of insanity; these typically are cases where the Government psychiatrists agreed that the crime was the product of mental illness.[33] We perceive no basis in these data for any conclusion that the number of percentage of insanity acquittals has been either excessive or inadequate.

We have no way of forecasting what will be the effect on verdicts, of juries or judges, from the reduction in influence of expert testimony on "productivity" that reflects judgments outside the domain of expertise.[34] Whatever its effect, we are confident that the rule adopted today provides a sounder relationship in terms of the giving, comprehension and application of expert testimony. Our objective is not to steer the jury's verdict but to enhance its deliberation.[35]

b. Some judges have viewed the ALI test as going beyond *Durham* in enlarging the category of persons who may win acquittals.[36] The 1966 report of the President's Crime Commission (*supra* note 15) apparently concludes that the debate over *Durham* was stilled by *McDonald,* and that *Durham-McDonald* is not significantly different in content from the ALI test. In contrast, Mr. Dempsey is concerned that a person's ability to control his behavior could be "substantially impaired" by mental condition, thus qualifying the defense under *McDonald,* while still leaving him with "substantial capacity," rendering the defense unavailable under the ALI rule. We have no way of knowing whether psychiatrists giving testimony would draw such a distinction, and moreover there would be no difference in result unless one also indulges the assumption, which is dubious, that the jury would reason that the crime may have been the "product" of the mental condition of a man even though he retained substantial capacity.

In the last analysis, however, if there is a case where there would be a difference in result—and it would seem rare—we think the underlying freedom of will conception renders it just to assign responsibility to a person, even though his controls have been impaired, if his residual controls give him "substantial capacity" both to appreciate the wrongfulness of his conduct and to conform it to the requirement of law. Whether the ALI standard is to be given a narrow or broad conception rests not on abstract analysis[37] but on the application reflecting the underlying sense of responsibility of the jury, as the community's surrogate.[38]

6. ELEMENTS OF THE ALI RULE ADOPTED BY THIS COURT

Though it provides a general uniformity, the ALI rule leaves room for variations. Thus, we have added an adjustment in the *McDonald* definition of mental disease, which we think fully compatible with both the spirit and text of the ALI rule. In the interest of good administration, we now undertake to set forth, with such precision as the subject will permit, other elements of the ALI rule as adopted by this court.

The two main components of the rule define (1) mental disease, (2) the consequences thereof that exculpate from responsibility.

a. Intermesh of components

The first component of our rule, derived from *McDonald,* defines mental disease or defect as an abnormal condition of the mind, and a condition which substantially (a) affects mental or emotional processes and (b) impairs behavioral controls. The second component, derived from the Model Penal Code, tells which defendant with a mental disease lacks criminal responsibility for particular conduct: it is the defendant who, as a result of this mental condition, at the time of such conduct, either (i) lacks substantial capacity to appreciate that his conduct is wrongful, or (ii) lacks substantial capacity to conform his conduct to the law.

The first component establishes eligibility for an instruction concerning the defense for a defendant who presents evidence that his abnormal condition of the mind has substantially impaired behavioral controls. The second component completes the instruction and defines the ultimate issue, of exculpation in terms of whether his behavioral controls were not only substantially impaired but impaired to such an extent that he lacked substantial capacity to conform his conduct to the law.[39]

b. The "result" of the mental disease

The rule contains a requirement of causality, as is clear from the term "result." Exculpation is established not by mental disease alone but only if "as a result" defendant lacks the substantial capacity required for responsibility. Presumably the mental disease of a kleptomaniac does not entail as a "result" a lack of capacity to conform to the law prohibiting rape.

c. At the time of the conduct

Under the Ali rule the issue is not whether defendant is so disoriented or void of controls that he is never able to conform to external demands, but whether he had that capacity at the time of the conduct. The question is not properly put in terms of whether he would have capacity to conform in some untypical restraining situation—as with an attendant or policeman at his elbow. The issue is whether he was able to conform in the unstructured condition of life in an open society, and whether the result of his abnormal mental condition was a lack of substantial internal controls. These matters are brought out in the ALI's comments to § 4.01 of the Model Penal Code Tentative Draft #4, p. 158:

The schizophrenic . . . is disoriented from reality; the disorientation is extreme; but it is rarely total. Most psychotics will respond to a command of someone in authority within the mental hospital; they thus have some capacity to conform to a norm. But this is very different from the capacity to conform to requirements that are not thus immediately symbolized by an attendant or policeman at the elbow. Nothing makes the inquiry into responsibility more unreal for the psychiatrist than limitation of the issue to some ultimate extreme of total incapacity, when clinical experience reveals only a graded scale with marks along the way.

d. Capacity to appreciate wrongfulness of his conduct

As to the option of terminology noted in the ALI code, we adopt the formulation that exculpates a defendant whose mental condition is such that he lacks substantial capacity to appreciate the wrongfulness of his conduct. We prefer this on pragmatic grounds to "appreciate the criminality of his conduct" since the resulting jury instruction is more like that conventionally given to and applied by the jury. While such an instruction is of course subject to the objection that it lacks complete precision, it serves the objective of calling on the jury to provide a community judgment on a combination of factors. And since the possibility of analytical differences between the two formulations is insubstantial in fact in view of the control capacity test, we are usefully guided by the pragmatic considerations pertinent to jury instructions.[40]

In adopting the ALI formulation, this court does not follow the *Currens* opinion of the Third Circuit, which puts it that the sole issue in every case is defendant's capacity to control his behavior, and that as a matter of analysis a person who lacks substantial capacity to appreciate the wrongfulness [criminality] of his conduct necessarily lacks substantial capacity to control his behavior. Like the other circuits, we resist the *Currens* lure of logic in order to make certain that the jury will give heed to the substantiality of a defense of lack of substantial capacity to appreciate wrongfulness, a point that may elude a jury instructed solely in terms of control capacity. In a particular case, however, defendant may have reason to request omission of the phrase pertaining to lack of capacity to appreciate wrongfulness, if that particular matter is not involved on the facts, and defendant fears that a jury that does not attend rigorously to the details of the instruction may erroneously suppose that the defense is lost if defendant appreciates wrongfulness. Here again, it is not enough to rely solely on logic, when a simple change will aid jury understanding. In such a case, if defendant requests, the judge should limit the instruction to the issue involved in that case, and charge that the jury shall bring in a verdict of not guilty if as a result of mental illness defendant lacked substantial capacity to conform his conduct to the requirements of the law.

e. *Caveat paragraph*

Section 4.01 of the Model Penal Code as promulgated by ALI contains in subsection (2) what has come to be known as the "caveat paragraph":

(2) The terms "mental disease or defect" do not include an abnormality manifested only by repeated criminal or otherwise anti-social conduct.

The purpose of this provision was to exclude a defense for the so-called "psychopathic personality."[41]

There has been a split in the Federal circuits concerning this provision. Some of the courts adopting the ALI rule refer to both subsections but without separate discussion of the caveat paragraph—as in the *Chandler* and *Blake* opinions. As to the decisions considering the point, those of the Second and Third Circuits conclude the paragraph should be retained (in *Freeman* and *Currens*), while the *Smith* and *Wade* decisions, of the Sixth and Ninth Circuits, conclude it should be omitted. The Sixth Circuit's position is (404 f.2d at 727, fn.8) that there is "great dispute over the psychiatric soundness" of the caveat paragraph. The *Wade* opinion considers the matter at great length and puts forward three grounds for rejecting the caveat paragraph: (1) As a practical matter, it would be ineffectual in keeping sociopaths out of the definition of insanity; it is always possible to introduce some evidence, other than past criminal behavior, to support a plea of insanity. (2) The criminal sanction ought not be sought for criminal psychopaths—constant recidivists—because such people should be taken off the streets indefinitely, and not merely for a set term of years. (3) Its third ground is stated thus (426 f.2d at 73):

It is unclear whether [the caveat paragraph] would require that a defendant be considered legally sane if, although the only overt acts manifesting his disease or defect were "criminal or otherwise anti-social," there arises from his acts a reasonable inference of mental derangement either because of the nature of the acts or because of credible medical or other evidence.

Our own approach is influenced by the fact that our rule already includes a definition of mental disease (from *McDonald*). Under that definition, as we have pointed out, the mere existence of "a long criminal record does not excuse crime." Williams v. United States, 114 U.S.App.D.C. 135, 137, 312 F.2d 862, 864 (1962). We do not require the caveat paragraph as an insurance against exculpation of the deliberate and persistent offender.[42] Our *McDonald* rule guards against the danger of misunderstanding and injustice that might arise, say, from an expert's classification that reflects only a conception[43] defining all criminality as reflective of mental illness. There must be testimony to show both that the defendant was suffering from an abnormal condition of the mind and that it substantially affected mental or emotional processes and substantially impaired behavioral controls.

In this context, our pragmatic approach is to adopt the caveat paragraph as a rule for application by the judge, to avoid miscarriage of justice, but not for inclusion in instructions to the jury.

The judge will be aware that the criminal and antisocial conduct of a—person on the street, in the home, in the ward—is necessarily material information for assessment by the psychiatrist. On the other hand, rarely if ever would a psychiatrist base a conclusion of mental disease solely on criminal and anti-social acts. Our pragmatic solution provides for reshaping the rule for application by the court as follows: The introduction or proffer of past criminal and anti-social actions is not admissible as evidence of mental disease unless accompanied by expert testimony, supported by a showing of the concordance of a responsible segment of professional opinion, that the particular charactistics of these actions constitute convincing evidence of an underlying mental disease that substantially impairs behavioral controls.

This formulation retains the paragraph as a "caveat" rather than an inexorable rule of law. It should serve to obviate distortions of the present state of knowledge that would constitute miscarriages of justice. Yet it leaves the door open—on shouldering the "convincing evidence" burden—to accommodate our general rule to developments that may lie ahead. It is the kind of imperfect, but not unfeasible, accommodation of the abstract and pragmatic that is often found to serve the administration of justice.

We do not think it desirable to use the caveat paragraph as a basis for instructions to the jury. It would be difficult for a juryman—or anyone else—to reconcile the caveat paragraph and the basic (*McDonald*) definition of mental disease if a psychiatrist testified that he discerned from particular past criminal behavior a pattern that established defendant as suffering from an abnormal condition of the mind that substantially impaired behavioral controls. If there is no such testimony, then there would be no evidence that mere misconduct betokens mental illness, it would be impermissible for defense counsel to present such a hypothesis to the jury, and there would be very little likelihood that a jury would arrive at such a proposition on its own. On the other hand, an instruction along the lines of the caveat paragraph runs the risk of appearing to call for the rejection of testimony that is based materially, but only partially, on the history of criminal conducts.

f. *Broad presentation to the jury*

Our adoption of the ALI rule does not depart from the doctrines this court has built up over the past twenty years to assure a broad presentation to the jury concerning the condition of defendant's mind and its consequences. Thus we adhere to our rulings admitting expert testimony of psychologists,[44] as well as psychiatrists, and to our many decisions contemplating that expert testimony on this subject will be accompanied by presentation of the facts and premises underlying the opinions and conclusions of the experts,[45] and that the Government and defense may present, in Judge Blackmun's words, "all possibly relevant evidence" bearing on cognition, volition and capacity.[46] We agree with the amicus submission of the National District Attorneys Association that the law cannot "distinguish between physiological, emotional, social and cultural sources of the impairment"—assuming, of course, requisite testimony establishing exculpation under the pertinent standard—and all such causes may be both referred to by the expert and considered by the trier of fact.[47]

Breadth of input under the insanity defense is not to be confused with breadth of the doctrines establishing the defense. As the National District Attorneys Association brief points out, the latitude for salient evidence of for example, social and cultural factors pertinent to an abnormal condition of the mind significantly affecting capacity and controls, does not mean that such factors may be taken as establishing a separate defense for persons whose mental condition is such that blame can be imposed. We have rejected a broad "injustice" approach that would have opened the door to expositions of for example, cultural deprivation, unrelated to any abnormal condition of the mind.

We have recognized that "Many criminologists point out that even normal human behavior is influenced by such factors as training, environment, poverty and the like, which may limit the understanding and options of the individual." King v. United States, *supra,* 125 U.S.App.D.C.at 323, 372 F.2d at 388. Determinists may contend that every man's fate is ultimately sealed by his genes and environment, over which he has no control. Our jurisprudence, however, while not oblivious to deterministic components, ultimately rests on a premise of freedom of will. This is not to be viewed as an exercise in philosophic discourse, but as a governmental fusion of ethics and necessity, which takes into account that a system of rewards and punishments is itself part of the environment that influences and shapes human conduct. Our recognition of an insanity defense for those who lack the essential, threshold free will possessed by those in the normal range is not to be twisted, directly or indirectly, into a device for exculpation of those without an abnormal condition of the mind.

Finally, we have not accepted suggestions to adopt a rule that disentangles the insanity defense from a medical model, and announces a standard exculpating anyone whose capacity for control is insubstantial, for whatever cause or reason. There may be logic in these submissions, but we are not sufficiently certain of the nature, range and implications of the conduct involved to attempt an all-embracing unified field theory. The applicable rule can be discerned as the cases arise in regard to other conditions—somnambulism or other automatisms; blackouts due, for example, to overdose of insulin; drug addiction. Whether these somatic conditions should be governed by a rule comparable to that herein set forth for mental disease would require, at a minimum, a judicial determination, which takes medical opinion into account, finding convincing evidence of an ascertainable condition characterized by "a broad consensus that free will does not exist." Salzman v. United States, 131 U.S.App.D.C. 393, 400, 405 F.2d 358, 365 (1968) (concurring opinion of Judge Wright)

MENTAL CONDITION, THOUGH INSUFFICIENT TO EXONERATE, MAY BE RELEVANT TO SPECIFIC MENTAL ELEMENT OF CERTAIN CRIMES OR DEGREES OF CRIME.

Our decision accompanies the redefinition of when a mental condition exonerates a defendant from criminal responsibility with the doctrine that expert testimony as to a defendant's abnormal mental condition may be received and considered, as tending to show, in a responsible way, that defendant did not have the specific mental state required for a particular crime or degree of crime—even though he was aware that his act was wrongful and was able to control it, and hence was not entitled to complete exoneration.

Some of the cases following this doctrine use the term "diminished responsibility," but we prefer the example of the cases that avoid this term (for example, note 57, *infra*), for its convenience is outweighed by its confusion: Our doctrine has nothing to do with "diminishing" responsibility of a defendant because of his impaired mental condition,[52] but rather with determining whether the defendant had the mental state that must be proved as to all defendants.

Procedurally, the issue of abnormal mental condition negativing a person's intent may arise in different ways: For example, the defendant may offer evidence of mental condition not qualifying as mental disease under *McDonald*. Or he may tender evidence that qualifies under *McDonald,* yet the jury may conclude from all the evidence that defendant has knowledge and control capacity sufficient for responsibility under the ALI rule.

The issue often arises with respect to mental condition tendered as negativing the element of premeditation in a charge of first degree premeditated murder. As we noted in Austin v. United States, 127 U.S. App.D.C. 180, 382 F.2d 129 (1967), when the legislature modified the common law crime of murder so as to establish degrees, murder in the first degree was reserved for intentional homicide done deliberately and with premeditation, and homicide that is intentional but "impulsive," not done after "reflection and meditation," was made murder only in the second degree. (127 U.S.App.D.C. at 187, 382 F.2d at 135).

An offense like deliberated and premeditated murder requires a specific intent that cannot be satisfied merely by showing that defendant failed to conform to an objective standard.[53] This is plainly established by the defense of voluntary intoxication. In Hopt v. Utah, 104 U.S. 631, 634, 26 L.Ed. 873 (1881), the Court, after stating the familiar rule that voluntary intoxication is no excuse for crime, said:

[W]hen a statute establishing different degrees of murder requires deliberate premeditation in order to constitute murder in the first degree, the question of whether the accused is in such a condition of mind, by reason of drunkenness or otherwise, as to be capable of deliberate premeditation, necessarily becomes a material subject of consideration by the jury.

In Bishop v. United States, 71 App.D.C. 132, 136, 107 F.2d 297, 301 (1939), Justice Vinson noted that while voluntary intoxication per se is no defense to guilt, "the stated condition of a defendant's mind at the time of the killing ... is now a proper subject for consideration, inquiry, and determination by the jury." Thus "voluntary intoxication will not excuse murder, but it may negative the ability of the defendant" as to

premeditation, and hence effect "a reduction to second degree murder."

Enlarging on *Hopt* and *Bishop,* Judge Burger's opinion in Heideman v. United States, 104 U.S.App.D.C. 128, 131, 259 F.2d 943, 946 (1958), points out:

Drunkenness is not per se an excuse for crime, but nevertheless it may in many instances be relevant to the issue of intent. One class of cases where drunkenness may be relevant on the issue of intent is the category of crimes where specific intent is required. Robbery falls into this category, and a defendant accused of robbery is entitled to an instruction on drunkenness as bearing on intent if the evidentiary groundwork has been adequately laid.

As Judge Burger points out there must be a showing of drunkenness that does more than remove inhibitions, and is such an "incapacitating state" as to negate intent. But he also notes, citing *Hopt,* and *Bishop,* that a lesser state of drunkenness, insufficient to negate the specific intent required for robbery, may suffice to negate the premeditation required for first degree murder.

Neither logic nor justice can tolerate a jurisprudence that defines the elements of an offense as requiring a mental state such that one defendant can properly argue that his voluntary drunkenness removed his capacity to form the specific intent but another defendant is inhibited from a submission of his contention that an abnormal mental condition, for which he was in no way responsible, negated his capacity to form a particular specific intent, even though the condition did not exonerate him from all criminal responsibility.

In Fisher v. United States, 80 U.S.App.D.C. 96, 149 F.2d (1946), the court upheld the trial court's refusal to instruct the jury that on issues of premeditation and deliberation "it should consider the entire personality of the defendant, his mental, nervous, emotional and physical characteristics as developed by the evidence in the case." Justice Arnold's abbreviated opinion was evidently premised on two factors: (1) that the instruction confused the issue of insanity with the issue of deliberation; (2) that "To give an instruction like the above is to tell the jury they are at liberty to acquit one who commits a brutal crime because he has the abnormal tendencies of persons capable of such crimes." His opinion made no effort to come to terms with the *Hopt* opinion, stressed by Fisher's counsel.

Fisher went to the Supreme Court and there was affirmed, but on the limited ground of disinclination to "force" this court in a choice of legal doctrine for the District of Columbia, 328 U.S. 463, 66 S.Ct. 1318, 90 L.Ed. 1382 (1946). The Court said (at 476, 66 S.Ct. at 1325) that such a change was "more properly a subject for the exercise of legislative power or at least for the discretion of the courts of the District."

In *Stewart I,* Stewart v. United States, 94 U.S. App.D.C. 293, 214 F.2d 879 (1954) which issued only two weeks after *Durham* was announced, we said that "reconsideration of our decision in Fisher should wait until we can appraise the results [of Durham]." In Stewart v. United States, 107 U.S.App.D.C. 159, 275 F.2d 617 (1960), the court en banc again stated that more experience with *Durham* was required to evaluate *Fisher,* and the matter was appropriate for legislative consideration. That was *Stewart II.*[54]

Today we are again *en banc,* and we have the benefit of many years of experience with *Durham-McDonald.* We are changing the insanity rule, on a prospective basis, to take into account intervening scholarship and court opinions. As a corollary, we deem it appropriate to change the rule of *Fisher* on a prospective basis, and to accept the approach which the Supreme Court declined to "force" upon us in 1946, but which has been adopted by the overwhelming majority of courts that have recently faced the question. We are convinced by the analysis set forth in the recent opinions of the highest courts of California,[55] Colorado,[56] New Jersey,[57] Iowa,[58] Ohio,[59] Idaho,[60] Connecticut,[61] Nebraska,[62] New Mexico[63] and Nevada.[64] They have joined the states that spoke out before *Fisher*—New York, Rhode Island, Utah, Wisconsin and Wyoming.[65]

The pertinent reasoning was succinctly stated by the Colorado Supreme Court as follows:[66]

The question to be determined is not whether defendant was insane, but whether the homicidal act was committed with deliberation and premeditation. The evidence offered as to insanity may or may not be relevant to that issue. * * * "A claim of insanity cannot be used for the purpose of reducing a crime of murder in the first degree to murder in the second degree or from murder to manslaughter. If the perpetrator is responsible at all in this respect, he is responsible in the same degree as a sane man; and if he is not responsible at all, he is entitled to an acquittal in both degrees. However, . . . *evidence of the condition of the mind* of the accused at the time of the crime, together with the surrounding circumstances, may be introduced, not for the purpose of establishing insanity, but to prove that the situation was such that a specific intent was not entertained—that is, *to show absence of any deliberate or premeditated design."* (Emphasis in original.)

On the other side of the coin, very few jurisdictions which have recently considered this question have held to the contrary position.[67]

Intervening developments within our own jurisdiction underscore the soundness of a doctrine for consideration of abnormal mental condition on the issue of specific intent. In the *Fisher* opinion of 1946, the court was concerned lest such a doctrine "tell the jury that they are at liberty to acquit one who commits a brutal crime because he has the abnormal tendencies of persons capable of such crimes." That a man's abnormal mental condition short of legal insanity may be material as negativing premeditation and deliberation does not set him "at liberty" but reduces the degree of the criminal homicide. Our 1967 opinion in *Austin, supra,* clarifies that even "a particularly frightful and horrible murder" may not be murder in the first degree, that "many murders most brutish and bestial are committed in a consuming frenzy or heat of passion, and that these are in law only murder in the second degree."[68] Indeed the action of the trial judge in acquitting defendant of first degree murder indicates how the refinement of *Austin* has undercut the *Fish* approach. Though the defendant went back to get his gun,[69] the judge concluded that the evidence as a whole—including defendant's broken jaw, the blood streaming down his face, and his irrational pounding on the mailbox—did not establish a reasonable foundation for inferring a calculated, deliberate mind at the time of shooting. We are not called upon to consider whether that action was proper in this case; what we do take note of is the inevitable implication of *Austin.*

There has also been a material legislative development since both *Fisher* and *Stewart II.* In 1964, after extensive hearings, Congress enacted the Hospitalization of the Mentally Ill Act, which provides civil commitment for the "mentally ill" who are dangerous to themselves or others.[70] Both the terminology and the underlying conception of this statute reflected a deliberate change from the 1939 law and its use of the term "insanity," which prior to *Durham* tended to be equated to psychosis and to disorientations like delusions. The enlarged conception underlying the 1964 law has been accorded a "liberal construction"[71] for the protection of the community, going so far as to include commitment of a disturbed mental defective with behavioral reactions resulting in danger-productive behavior.[72] The law is broad enough to include not only mental illness requiring confinement in St. Elizabeths, but also conditions of mental illness calling for placement in nursing homes,[73] or, where appropriate, halfway houses or requirement of outpatient care.[74] These statutory provisions provide a shield against danger from persons with abnormal mental condition—a danger which in all likelihood bolstered, or even impelled, the draconic *Fisher* doctrine.

Further, to the extent that the 1970 law (*supra,* note 48) leads to a conviction of first degree murder when the evidence is in equipoise on the issue of insanity, there would be an additional miscarriage of justice if the evidence were not available for consideration as raising a reasonable doubt on the issue of premeditation and deliberation.

In providing for the admission and consideration of expert testimony on abnormal mental condition insufficient for complete exoneration, we insert some observations prompted by State v. Sikora, 44 N.J. 453, 210 A.2d 193 (1965), *supra,* note 57. The doctrine does not permit the receipt of psychiatric testimony based on the conception that mental disorder is only a relative concept and that the behavior of every individual is dictated by forces—ultimately, his genes and lifelong environment—that are unconscious and beyond his control. As we have already made clear, we are not embarked on enquiry that must yield to tenets of the philosophy of determinism. The law accepts free will and blameworthiness as a general premise. Expert psychiatric testimony negativing blameworthiness for a crime—whether on ground of general exoneration or lack of requisite specific intent—must rest on the premise of an exception due to abnormal mental condition.

Our rule permits the introduction of expert testimony as to abnormal condition if it is relevant to negative, or establish, the specific mental condition that is an element of the crime. The receipt of this expert testimony to negative the mental condition of specific intent requires careful administration by the trial judge. Where the proof is not offered in the first instance as evidence of exonerating mental disease or defect within the ALI rule the judge may, and ordinarily would, require counsel first to make a proffer of the proof to be adduced outside the presence of the jury. The judge will then determine whether the testimony is grounded in sufficient scientific support to warrant use in the courtroom, and whether it would aid the jury in reaching a decision on the ultimate issues.[75]

NOTES

9. Ten years ago Judge Burger said; "While the time span since 1954 is brief, our total study and collective ease consideration of the problem is equal perhaps to as much as a half century of case review of this problem in most jurisdictions." Blocker v. United States, 110 U.S.App.D.C. at 52, 288 F.2d at 864 (en banc, 1961) (concurring opinion).

10. A difference in language perception probably contributed to the development that psychiatric testimony concerning "product" causal relationship did not develop along the lines presaged by legal students of the problem. Early critiques in journals asserted that a but-for test of "product" would rarely, if ever, permit a psychiatrist to testify as to the existence of mental illness coexisting with a lack of "product" causal relationship to the crime. *See,* for example, Wechsler, The Criteria of Criminal Responsibility, 22 U.Chi.L.Rev. 367, 371 (1955); De Grazia. The Distinction of Being Mad, 22 U.Chi.L.Rev. 339, 343 (1955). Presumably, the force of this analysis was strengthened when "mental disease or defect" was defined and tightened in *McDonald.* As events have developed, however, it has become almost commonplace that psychiatrists testifying as to the presence of mental disease have nevertheless found an absence of "product" causal relation with the crime, or at least expressed substantial doubt as to such relationship. Perhaps more to the point, it has become commonplace for psychiatrists called by Government and defense to be in agreement on the mental disease aspects of

their testimony and to differ on the issue of "product" relationship. This is not intended, in any way, as a criticism of any particular testimony. There is often a genuine and difficult question as to the relationship between a particular mental disease and particular offense. What is our concern, however, is that the inherent difficulty of this core problem has been intensified, and the sources of confusion compounded, by a kind of mystique that came to surround the "product" test, and testimony cast in that language.

11. For example, Hawkins v. United States, 114 U.S. App.D.C.44, 310 F.2d 849 (1962); Isaac v. United States, 109 U.S.App.D.C. 34, 284 F.2d 168 (1960).

12. This was also the suggestion of the National District Attorneys Association subject to caveats, as the test recommended if the court did not accept its submission that the insanity defense should be abolished entirely.

13. Compare New State Ice Co. v. Liebman, 285 U.S. 262, 280, 52 S.Ct. 371, 76 L.Ed. 747 (1932) (dissenting opinion of Brandeis, J.).

14. Amicus points out that in *Freeman* the Second Circuit referred to the fact that the Third and Tenth Circuits "have employed their own language approaching the objectives of the Model Penal Code formulation," and then offered a discussion of guiding policy considerations, including Senator Dodd's espousal of an approach sending "marginal" cases to a hospital rather than prison, that, as amicus puts it, "strikes quite a different tone than, say, the analogous discussion of the Tenth Circuit in Wion."

15. See, for example, Report of President's D.C. Crime Commission at pp. 550 *ff.* A majority of the members of the Commission preferred the ALI rule, but were concerned lest departure from *Durham-McDonald* spawn confusion.

16. "[I]t may be that psychiatry and the other social and behavioral sciences cannot provide sufficient data relevant to a determination of criminal responsibility no matter what our rules of evidence are. If so, we may be forced to eliminate the insanity defense altogether, or refashion it in a way which is not tied so tightly to the medical model." Washington v. United States, 129 U.S.App.D.C. at 42, n. 33, 390 F.2d at 457 (1967).

17. It suggests that a mental condition be exculpatory solely as it negatives mens rea.

18. For example, Mr. Dempsey. To the same general effect is the position in the research memorandum from the University of Virginia Law School Research Group to Mr. Flynn, appellant's appointed counsel attached to his brief.

19. See for example, Burger, then Circuit Judge, Proceedings of the Sixth Annual Meeting of the National Conference of State Trial Judges, Chicago, Illinois, Aug. 9–11, 1963, quoted in Wion v. United States, 325 F.2d at 428, n. 10; Bazelon, Chief Judge, in Washington v. United States, 129 U.S.App.D.C. at 42, n. 33, 390 F.2d at 457 (1967); Haynesworth, Chief Judge, in en banc opinion in United States v. Chandler, 393 F.2d at 928 (1968); see also remarks of Chief Justice Weintraub (of New Jersey) in Insanity as a Defense—Panel Discussion, Annual Judicial Conference, Second Circuit, 37 F.R.D. 365, 369 (1064).

20. Davis v. United States, 160 U.S. 469, 484–485, 16 S.Ct. 353, 40 L.Ed. 499 (1895); Durham v. United States, *supra,* 94 U.S.App.D.C. at 242, 214 F.2d at 876.

21. Amicus agues that penal systems can only survive so long as they "accord substantially with the popular estimate of the enormity of guilt," citing 1 W. Lecky, History of the Rise and Influence of the Spirit of Rationalism in Europe 336–337 (1891).

22. Citing Harris, Respect for Persons in Ethics and Society 129–130 (R. DeGeorge ed. 1966).

23. In 1953 the British Royal Commission on Capital Punishment proposed: [A person is not responsible for his unlawful act if] at the time of the act the accused was suffering from disease of the mind (or mental deficiency) *to such a degree that he ought not to be held responsible.*

24. The minority, together with the Reporter for the Model Penal Code (Professor Herbert Wechsler), proposed the following test of insanity:

A person is not responsible for criminal conduct if at the time of such conduct as a result of mental disease or defect his capacity either to appreciate the criminality of his conduct or to conform his conduct to the requirements of law is *so substantially impaired that he cannot justly be held responsible.*

This proposal appears as alternative (a) to paragraph (1) of Model Penal Code § 4.01 (Tent.Draft No. 4, 1955) (emphasis added).

25. See authorities cited *supra,* note 6.

26. See, for example, Szasz, Psychiatry, Ethics and the Criminal Law, 58 Colum.L.Rev. 183, 195 (1958) "[To] have a 'psychopathic' personality is only a more elegant way of expressing moral condemnation." See also Star, "The Public's Ideas About Mental Illness" (National Opinion Research Center, 1955); H. Kalven and H. Zeisel, The American Jury 405 (1966).

27. He proposes (Br. 78) an instruction with this crucial sentence: "It is up to you to decide whether defendant had such an abnormal mental condition, and if he did whether the impairment was substantial enough, and was so related to the commission of the crime, *that he ought not be held responsible.*" (Emphasis added.).

28. A Goldstein, The Insanity Defense 81–82 (1967).

29. See H. Kalven and H. Zeisel. The American Jury (1966), passim, and particularly Chapters 5, 8, 12, 15 et seq. See also, Rifkind, Follow-up: The Jury. The Center Magazine 59, 64 (July, 1970).

30. See for example, the response of the Attorney General in Ramer v. United States, 390 F.2d 564, 575, n. 10 (9th Cir. en banc, 1968).

31. See ch. 7, section III: The Mentally Ill Offender, subsection "Experience Under the Durham Rule," at p. 534 ff of the Report, including Tables 1–10.

32. *McDonald* was decided in 1962. For fiscal years ending June 30, 1964–1970, there were 21 verdicts of not guilty by reason of insanity in trials by jury, 265 such verdicts in trials by court. These data appear in Appendix C of Mr. Dempsey's brief, as revised by submission of Sept. 21, 1971.

Mr. Dempsey provides data on all terminations for fiscal 1964–1968. The data for these five years show 7537 terminations, and 194 verdicts of not guilty by reason of insanity. The other terminations are: 3500 verdicts of guilty on plea, 1567 verdicts of guilty after trial, and 629 verdicts of not guilty.

33. These trials are discussed in the amicus submission of David Chambers, consultant, who prepared a report on the John Howard Pavilion at St. Elizabeths Hospital, submitted to the Hospital and the National Institutes of Mental Health.

Professor Chambers characterizes most insanity trials to the courts as more nearly comparable to the taking of guilty pleas—consisting of a stipulated statement of facts; a conclusory Hospital report that the crime was the product of mental illness; and brief supporting testimony from a single John Howard psychiatrist—all in a context of a "tacit or explicit understanding" that the defendant will not contest his indefinite commitment to the Hospital.

34. Any such analysis of the productivity testimony and verdicts nor only would require prodigious time and effort, but might well be inconclusive in view of the way experts testifying on the "product" issues come to diametric differ-ences in the same trial.

35. We do not share the cynical view that treats the instruction as devoid of consequence. In a study of the reactions of more than a thousand jurors to two experimental trials involving a defense of insanity, it was found that juries deliberated significantly longer when instructed under *Durham* than under *M'Naghten.* Yet this did not undercut consensus; there was no significant difference in the percentages of hung juries. R. Simon, The Jury and the Defense of Insanity 213 *ff.* (1967).

36. See the opinion of Trask, J., for six of the 13 judges on the Ninth Circuit, in Wade v. United States, 426 F.2d 64, 75, 79.

37. Mr. Dempsey is concerned lest the ALI test assigns responsibility unless capacity has been reduced "to the vagrant and trivial dimensions characteristic of the most severe afflictions of the mind," *see* Wechsler, Codification of Criminal Law in the United States: The Model Penal Code, 68 Colum.L.Rev. 1425, 1443 (1968). But the application in fact will depend in the last analysis on the jury's application of community standards to the evidence adduced.

38. Even under *McDonald* the jury has frequently brought in a verdict of guilty, when the exculpatory rules would plainly permit, or even contemplate, a verdict of not guilty by reason of insanity. King v. United States, *supra.*

39. Defendant is also exculpated if he lacks substantial capacity to appreciate the conduct is wrongful.

40. In *M'Naghten's* case, 10 Cl. & F. 200, 211, 8 Eng. Rep. 718, 722 (H.L.1843), the majority opinion of Lord Chief Justice Tindal ruled that the jury should be instructed in terms of the ability of the accused "to know that he was doing an act that was wrong." adding: "If the question were to be put as to the knowledge of the accused solely and exclusively with reference to the law of the land, it might tend to confound the jury, by inducing them to be believe that an actual knowledge of the law of the land was essential in order to lead to a conviction."

When the question arose as to whether "wrong" means moral or legal wrong, the American courts split. One group, following *M'Naghten,* held the offender sane if he knew the act was prohibited by law. A second group, following the lead of Judge Cardozo in People v. Schmidt, 216 N.Y. 324, 110 N.E. 945, 948–950 (1915) ruled that, for example, the defense was available to a defendant who knew the killing was legally wrong but thought it morally right because he was so ordered by God. The issue is discussed and authorities collected in A. Goldstein, The Insanity Defense, and notes thereto. In Sauer v. United States, 241 F.2d 640, 649 (9th Circ. 1957), Judge Barnes summed up the practicalities: "[The] practice has been to state merely the word 'wrong' and leave the decision for the jury. While not entirely condonable, such practice is explained in large measure by an awareness that the jury will eventually exercise a moral judgment as to the sanity of the accused."

This issue rarely arose under *M'Naghten,* and its substantiality was reduced if not removed by the control capacity test, since anyone under a delusion as to God's mandate would presumably lack substantial capacity to conform his conduct to the requirements of the law.

We are not informed of any case where a mental illness left a person with capacity to appreciate wrongfulness but not a capacity to appreciate criminality. If such a case ever arises, supported by credible evidence, the court can then consider its correct disposition more meaningfully, in the light of a concrete record.

41. See Comments to Fourth Draft, p. 160:

6. Paragraph (2) of section 4.01 is designed to exclude from

the concept of "mental disease or defect" the case of so-called "psychopathic personality." The reason for the exclusion is that, as the Royal Commission put it, psychopathy " is a statistical abnormality: that is to say, the psychopath differs from a normal person only quantitatively or in degree, nor qualitatively: and the diagnosis of psychopathic personality does not carry with it any explanation of the causes of the abnormality." While it may not be feasible to formulate a definition of "disease," there is much to be said for excluding a condition that is manifested only by the behavior phenomena that must, by hypothesis, be the result of disease for irresponsibility to be established. Although British psychiatrists had agreed, on the whole, that psychopathy should not be called "disease," there is considerable difference of opinion on the point in the United States. Yet it does not seem useful to contemplate the litigation of what is essentially a matter of terminology: nor is it right to have the legal result rest upon the resolution of a dispute of this kind.

42. We note that the Second Circuit adopted the caveat paragraph on the ground that

a contrary holding would reduce to absurdity a test designed to encourage full analysis of all psychiatric data and would exculpate those who knowingly and deliberately seek a life of crime. (*Freeman*, 357 F.2d at 625).

43. See, for example, D. Abrahamsen, Who Are the Guilty? 125 (1952).

44. Jenkins v. United States, 113 U.S.App.D.C. 300, 307 F.2d 637 (en banc, 1962) (assuming substantial experience in the diagnosis of disease in association with psychiatrists or neurologists).

45. For example, the opinions in *Durham, Carter, McDonald* and *Washington,* and Judge Burger's concurring opinion in *Blocker.*

46. Pope v. United States, 372 F.2d 710, 736 (8th Cir. 1967).

47. The Association points out that "the effects of poverty, historical factors and prejudice may well have an adverse effect upon an individual's mental condition."

52. Our doctrine is different from the doctrine of "partial responsibility" that permits a jury to find that a defendant's mental condition was such that he is only "partly responsible," and therefore entitled to a verdict reducing the degree of the offense. See Model Penal Code, Comments to Art. 201, app. B at 111 (Tentative Draft No. 9, 1959), quoting the English Homicide Act of 1957, 5 & 6 Eliz. 2, c. 11.

53. The term "malice" in second degree murder has been extended to include recklessness where defendant had awareness of a serious danger to life and displayed wanton disregard for human life. Lee v. United States, 72 App.D.C. 147, 150–151, 112 F.2d 46, 49–50 (1949): Austin v. United States, *supra,* 127 U.S.AppD.C. at 184, 382 F.2d at 133; United States v. Dixon, 135 U.S.App.D.C. 401, 405, 419 F.2d 288,

292 (1969) (concurring opinion).

54. There was no independent consideration in Stewart v. United States, 129 U.S.App.D.C. 303, 394 F.2d 778 (1968), which was not an en banc court, and merely cited the earlier cases.

55. People v. Nicolaus, 65 Cal.2d 866, 56 Cal.Rptr. 635, 423 P.2d 787 (1967); People v. Goedecke, 65 Cal.2d 850, 56 Cal.Rptr. 625, 423 P.2d 777 (1967); People v. Ford, 65 Cal.2d 41, 52 Cal.Rptr. 228, 416 P.2d 132 (1966); People v. Conley, 64 Cal.2d 310, 49 Cal.Rptr. 815, 411 P.2d 795, 40 Cal.Rptr. 271, 394 P.2d 959 (1964); People v. Gorshen, 51 Cal.2d 716, 336 P.2d 492 (1959); People v. Wells, 33 Cal.2d 330, 202 P.2d 53 (1949).

56. Schwickrath v. People. 159 Colo. 390, 411 P.2d 961 (1966); Gallegos v. People, 159 Colo. 379, 411 P.2d 956 (1966); Becksted v. People, 133 Colo. 72, 292 P.2d 189 (1956); Battalino v. People, 118 Colo. 587, 199 P.2d 897 (1948); Ingles v. People, 95 Colo. 518, 22 P.2d 1109 (1933).

57. State v. Di Paolo, 34 N.J. 279, 168 A.2d 401 (1961), clarified in State v. Sikora, 44 N.J. 453, 210 A.2d 193 (1965).

58. State v. Gramenz, 256 Iowa 134, 126 N.W.2d 285 (1964).

59. State v. Nichols, 3 Ohio App.2d 182, 209 N.E.2d 750 (1965).

60. State v. Clokey, 83 Idaho 322, 364 P.2d 159 (1961).

61. State v. Donahue, 141 Conn. 656, 109 A.2d 364 (1954).

62. Starkweather v. State, 167 Neb. 477, 93 N.W.2d 619 (1958).

63. State v. Padilla, 66 N.M. 289, 347 P.2d 312 (1959).

64. Fox v. State, 73 Nev. 241, 316 P.2d 924 (1957).

65. New York, People v. Moran, 249 N.Y. 179, 163 N.E. 553 (1928); Rhode Island, State v. Fenik, 45 R.I. 309, 121 A. 218 (1923); Utah, State v. Green, 78 Utah 580, 6 P.2d 177 (1931); Wisconsin, Hempton v. State, 111 Wis. 127, 86 N.W. 596 (1901) and Wyoming, State v. Pressler, 16 Wyo. 214, 92 P. 806 (1907).

66. Battalino v. People, 118 Colo. 587, 199 P.2d 897, 901 (1948).

67. State v. Janovic, 101 Ariz. 203, 417 P.2d 527 (1966); Armstead v. State. 227 Md. 73, 175 A.2d 24 (1961); State v. Flint, 142 W.Va. 509, 96 S.E.2d 677 (1957); Ezzell v. State, 88 So.2d 280 (Fla. 1956).

68. 127 U.S.App.D.C. at 189–190, 382 F.2d at 138–139.

69. *See* Belton v. United States, 127 U.S.App.D.C. 201, 203, 382 F.2d 150, 152 (1967).

70. 78 Stat. 944 (1960), 21D.C.Code § 501 et seq.

71. Millard v. Harris, 132 U.S.App. D.C. 146, 150, 406 F.2d 964, 968 (1968).

72. In re Alexander, 124 U.S.App.D.C. 352, 372 F.2d 925 (1967).

73. Lake v. Cameron, 124 U.S.App.D.C. 264, 364 F.2d 657 (1966).

75. S.Rep.No.925, 88th Cong., 2d sess., 31 (1964).

Suggestions for Further Reading

Allen, F. A., *The Borderland of Criminal Justice (1964).*

American Law Institute, *Model Penal Code,* Pt. 1, Proposed Official Draft (1962).

American Law Institute, *Restatement of the Law of Torts* (1934) and supplements (1948, 1954).

Anderson, J., "The Problem of Causality," *Australasian Jour. of Phil.* Vol. 16, (1938), pp. 127–42.

Austin, J. L., "A Plea for Excuses," *Proceedings of the Aristotelian Society* (1956–57).

Bazelon, D. L., "The Concept of Responsibility," 53 *Georgetown Law Review* (1964).

Brandt, Richard, "A Utilitarian Theory of Excuses," *Philosophical Review,* Vol. 78 (1969), pp. 337–361.

Cohen, M. R., "Moral Aspects of the Criminal Law," 49 *Yale L. J.* 987, (1940), pp. 128–129.

Comment, "Admissibility of Subjective Abnormality to Disprove Criminal Mental States," 12 *Stan. L. Rev.* (1959), pp. 588–589.

Comment Note, "Mental or Emotional Condition as Diminishing Responsibility for Crime," 22 *A.L.R.* 3d 1228 (1968).

Dershowitz, Alan M., "Psychiatry in the Legal Process: A Knife That Cuts Both Ways," 4 *Trial* 29 (1968).

Edgerton, H., "Legal Cause," 72 *U. of Pa. L. Rev.,* 211–44, 343–75 (1924).

Elkind, Jerome B., "Impossibility in Criminal Attempts: A Theorist's Headache," 54 *Virginia L. Rev.* 20 (1968).

Feinberg, Joel, "Causing Voluntary Actions," in *Doing and Deserving* (1970), pp. 152–186.

Feinberg, Joel, "Collective Responsibility," in *Doing and Deserving* (1970), pp. 222–251.

Feinberg, Joel, "Crime, Clutchability, and Individuated Treatment" in *Doing and Deserving* (1970), pp. 252–71.

Feinberg, Joel, "What Is So Special About Mental Illness?" in *Doing and Deserving* (1970), pp. 272–92.

Feldbrugge, F. J. M., "Good and Bad Samaritans, A Comparative Study of Criminal Law Provisions Concerning Failure to Rescue," 14 *Am. J. Comp. L.* 630 (1966).

Fine and Cohen, "Is Criminal Negligence a Defensible Basis for Penal Liability?" 16 *Buffalo L. Rev.* 749 (1967).

Fingarette, H., "The Concept of Mental Disease in Criminal Law Insanity Tests," 33 *U. Chi. L. Rev.* 229 (1966).

Fingarette, Herbert, *The Meaning of Criminal Insanity* (1972).

Fingarette, Herbert, "Addiction and Criminal Responsibility," 84 *Yale L.J.* 413 (1975).

Fitzgerald, P. J., "Voluntary and Involuntary Acts" in *Oxford Essays in Jurisprudence,* ed. A. G. Guest (1961).

Fletcher, George P., "Fairness and Utility in Tort Theory," 85 *Harv. L. Rev.* 537 (1972).

Fletcher, George P., "Theory of Criminal Negligence: A Comparative Analysis," 119 *U. Pa. L. Rev.* 401 (1971).

Fletcher, George P., *Rethinking Criminal Law* (1978).

Flew, Antony, *Crime or Disease?* (1973).

Friedrich, C. J., ed., Nomos III, *Responsibility* (1960).

Glover, Jonathan, *Responsibility* (1970).

Goldstein, A., *The Insanity Defense* (1967).

Goldstein, J., and Katz, J., "Abolish the 'Insanity Defense'—Why Not?" 72 *Yale L. J.* 853, (1963).

Green, L., "Are Negligence and 'Proximate' Cause Determined by the Same Test?" 1 *Texas L. Rev.* 242–60, 423–45, (1923).

Gregory, C. O., "Proximate Cause in Negligence—A Retreat from Rationalization," 6 *Univ. of Chi. L. Rev.* 36 (1938).

Griffiths, John, "Ideology in Criminal Procedure," 79 *Yale L. J.* 359 (1970).

Gross, Hyman, "Some Unacceptable Excuses," 19 *Wayne L. Rev.* 997 (1973).

Gross, Hyman, *A Theory of Criminal Justice* (1978).

Hall, J., *General Principles of Criminal Law* 2d ed. (1960).

Hall, J., "Negligent Behavior Should Be Excluded from Penal Liability," 63 *Colum. L. Rev.* 632 (1963).

Halleck, Seymour L., *Psychiatry and the Dilemmas of Crime* (1967).

Harper, F. V., "Liability Without Fault and Proximate Cause," 30 *Michigan L. Rev.,* 1001 (1932).

Hart, H. L. A., Review of *Crime and the Criminal Law* by Barbara Wooton, 74 *Yale L. J.* 1325 (1965).

Hart, H. L. A., *The Morality of the Criminal Law* (1964).

Hart, H. L. A., *Punishment and Responsibility* (1968).

Holmes, Oliver W., Jr., *The Common Law,* Lectures I, II, III (1881).

Howard, Colin, *Strict Liability* (1963).

Hughes, Graham, "Criminal Omissions," 67 *Yale L. J.* 590 (1958).

Hughes, Graham, "Attempting the Impossible" 42 *N.Y.U. L. Rev.* 1005 (1967).

James, F., Jr., "The Nature of Negligence," 3 *Utah L. Rev.,* 275 (1953).

James, F., Jr., and Perry, R. F., "Legal Cause," 60 *Yale L. J.* 761 (1954).

Kadish, S. H., "The Decline of Innocence," 26 *Camb. L. J.* 273 (1968).

Kadish, S., and Paulsen, M., *Criminal Law and Its Processes,* 3rd ed. (1975).

Keeton, R. E. and O'Connell, J., *Basic Protection for the Traffic Victim: A Blueprint for Reforming Automobile Insurance* (1966).

Kelsen, H., "Causality and Retribution," in *What is Justice?* (1957).

Kenny, Anthony, "Intention and Purpose," *Journal of Philosophy,* Vol. 63 (1966), pp. 642–651.

Kenny, A., "Intention and *Mens Rea* in Murder." in *Law, Morality, and Society,* ed. P. Hacker and J. Raz (1977).

Lewis, H. D., "Collective Responsibility," *Philosophy,* Vol. 23 (1948).

Livermore, J. M., and Meehl, P. E., "The Virtues of M'Naghten," 51 *Minn. L. Rev.* 789 (1967).

Louisell, D. W. and Hazard, G. C., "Insanity as a Defense: The Bifurcated Trial," 49 *Calif. L. Rev.* 805 (1961).

Lyons, David, "On Sanctioning Excuses," *Journal of Philosophy,* Vol. 66 (1969), pp. 646–660.

Macaulay and Other Indian Law Commissioners, *A Penal Code Prepared by the Indian Law Commissioners* (1837).

Michael, J., and Wechsler, H., eds., *Criminal Law and Its Administration* (1940).

Moreland, R., "Rationale of Criminal Negligence," 32 *Kentucky L. J.,* 1–40, 127–92, 221–61, (1943–44).

Morris, Herbert, ed., *Freedom and Responsibility* (1961).

Morris, Herbert, "Punishment for Thoughts," 49 *The Monist* 342 (1965).

Morris, Herbert, *On Guilt and Innocence* (1976).

Murphy, Jeffrie G., *Retribution, Justice, and Therapy: Essays in the Philosophy of Law* (1979).

Neu, Jerome, "Minds on Trial," Brody and Englehardt, eds., *Mental Illness and Public Policy* (1979).

Note, "Amnesia: A Case Study in the Limits of Particular Justice," 71 *Yale L. J.* 109 (1961).

Note, "Justification for the Use of Force in the Criminal Law," 13 *Stan. L. Rev.* 506 (1961).

Packer, H., "Mens Rea and the Supreme Court," (1962), *Sup. Ct. Rev.* 107.

Packer, H., *The Limits of the Criminal Sanction* (1968).

Palsgraf v. The Long Island Railroad Co., 248 N.Y. 339 (1928).

Plamenatz, J., "Responsibility, Blame and Punishment," in *Philosophy, Politics, and Society* (ed. P. Laslett and W. G. Runciman, 1967).

Prosser, W. L., *Handbook of the Law of Torts,* 2d ed. (1955).

Ratcliff, James M., ed., *The Good Samaritan and the Law* (1966).

Sayre. F. B., "Criminal Attempts," 41 *Harv. L. Rev.* 55 (1933).

Silber, J., "Being and Doing: A Study of Status Responsibility and Voluntary Responsibility," 35 *U. Chi. L. Rev.* 47 (1967).

Stone, Alan, *Mental Health and Law: A System in Transition* (N.I.M.H., 1975).

Szasz, Thomas S., *The Myth of Mental Illness* (1961).

Szasz, Thomas S., *Law, Liberty, and Psychiatry* (1962).

Wasserstrom, Richard, "H. L. A. Hart and the Doctrines of Mens Rea and Criminal Responsibility," 35 *U. Chi. L. Rev.* 92 (1967).

Wasserstrom, Richard, "Strict Liability in the Criminal Law," 12 *Stan. L. Rev.* 730 (1960).

Wechsler, H., and Michael, J., "A Rationale of the Law of Homicide," 37 *Colum. L. Rev.* 701 (1937).

Williams, G., "Absolute Liability in Traffic Offenses," (1967) *Crim. L. Rev.* 194.

Williams, G., "Causation in Homicide," (1957) *Crim. L. Rev.* 429.

Williams, G., *The Mental Element in Crime* (1965).

Wootton, Barbara, "Diminished Responsibility: A Layman's View," 76 *Law Quarterly Review* (1960).

Wootton, Barbara, *Social Science and Social Pathology,* Part II (1959).

PART 5 PUNISHMENT

Philosophical theories of punishment have always taken punishment for crime as the paradigm instance of punishment, and more often than not have proceeded to discuss criminal punishment as a problem within the general sphere of moral affairs where morally blameworthy conduct is the subject at hand. Some philosophers, as well as some theorists with a different sort of intellectual base, have approached the problems of criminal punishment in a different way, stressing the practical purposes to be served by this important social institution rather than pursuing immediately the implications of morally wrong conduct. Whichever way these problems are taken up, the first order of business is getting clear about just what sorts of measures count as criminal punishment.

WHAT IS PUNISHMENT?

The 1960 United States Supreme Court case of *Flemming v. Nestor* illustrates dramatically how important it is to have a *definition* of "punishment" as a means not only to the fruitful settlement of philosophical questions but also to the determination of the constitutional validity of certain governmental acts. The question at issue was whether or not the deprivation by the government of Mr. Nestor's social security benefits was the exercise of a "regulative" or a "punitive" sanction. If the latter, it was *ex post facto* punishment, which is unconstitutional. If the former, it was merely incidental to the regulation of an activity. It has been said, in a commentary on this case, [1] that there clearly was congressional intent to punish but that judicial confusion was caused by the fact that the sanction selected was outside the scope of the criminal law and lacked the conventional reprobative symbolism distinctive of all genuine legal punishments.

THE CLASSIC DEBATE: RETRIBUTIVISM
AGAINST UTILITARIANISM

The traditional debate among philosophers over the justification of legal punishment has been between partisans of the "retributive" and "utilitarian" theories. Neither the term "retributive" nor the term "utilitarian" has been used with perfect uniformity and precision, but by and large, those have been called utilitarians who have insisted that punishment of the guilty is at best a necessary evil justified only as a means to the prevention of evils even greater than itself. "Retributivism," on the other hand, has been the name of a large miscellany of theories united only in their opposition to the utilitarian theory. It may well best serve clarity, therefore, to define the utilitarian theory with relative precision (as above) and then define retributivism as its logical contradictory, so that the two theories are not only mutually exclusive but jointly exhaustive as well. Discussion of the various varieties of retributivism can then proceed.

Perhaps the leading form of the retributive theory is that whose major elements are caught in the following formulations:

It is an end in itself that the guilty should suffer pain . . . The primary justification of punishment is always to be found in the fact that an offense has been committed which deserves the punishment, not in any future advantage to be gained by its infliction.[2]

Punishment is justified only on the ground that wrongdoing merits punishment. It is morally fitting that a person who does wrong should suffer in proportion to his wrongdoing. That a criminal should be punished follows from his guilt, and the severity of the appropriate punishment depends on the depravity of the act. The state of affairs where a wrongdoer suffers punishment is morally better than one where he does not, and is so irrespective of consequences.[3]

Justification, according to these accounts, must look backward in time to guilt rather than forward to "advantages"; the formulations are rich in moral terminology ("merits," "morally fitting," "wrongdoing," "morally better"); there is great emphasis on *desert*. For those reasons, we might well refer to this as a "moralistic" version of the retributive theory. As such it can be contrasted with a "legalistic" version, according to which punishment is for lawbreaking, not (necessarily) for wrongdoing. Legalistic retributivism holds that the justification of punishment is always to be found in the fact that a rule has been broken for the violation of which a certain penalty is specified, whether or not the offender incurs any moral guilt. The offender, properly apprised in advance of the penalty, voluntarily assumes the risk of punishment, and when he or she receives comeuppance, he or she can have no complaint. As one recent legalistic retributivist put it,

Punishment is a corollary not of law but of lawbreaking. Legislators do not choose to punish. They hope no punishment will be needed. Their laws would succeed even if no punishment occurred. The criminal makes the essential choice: he "brings it on himself."[4]

Both moralistic and legalistic retributivism have "pure" and "impure" variants. In their pure formulations, they are totally free of utilitarian admixture. Moral or legal guilt (as the case may be) is not only a necessary condition for justified punishment, it is quite sufficient "irrespective of consequences." In the impure formulation, both guilt (moral or legal) and conducibility to good consequences are necessary for justified punishment, but neither is sufficient without the other. This mixed theory could with some propriety be called "impure utilitarianism" as well as "impure retributivism," but since we have stipulated that a retributive theory is one which is not wholly utilitarian, we are committed to the latter usage.

A complete theory of punishment will not only specify the conditions under which punishment should and should not be administered; it will also provide a general criterion for determining the amount or degree of punishment. It is not only unjust to be punished undeservedly and to be let off although meriting punishment; it is also unfair to be punished severely for a minor offense or lightly for a heinous one. What is the right amount of punishment? There is one kind of answer especially distinctive of retributivism in all of its forms: an answer in terms of fittingness or proportion. The punishment must *fit* the crime; its degree must be *proportionate* to the seriousness or moral gravity of the offense. Retributivists are often understandably vague about the practical interpretations of the key notions of fittingness, proportion, and moral gravity. Sometimes aesthetic analogies are employed (such as matching and clashing colors, or harmonious and dissonant chords). Some retributivists, including Immanuel Kant, attempt to apply the ancient principle of *lex talionis* (the law of retaliation), that the punishment should match the crime not only in the degree of harm inflicted on its victim, but also in the mode and manner of infliction: fines for larceny, physical beatings for battery, capital punishment for murder. Other retributivists, however, explicitly reject the doctrine of retaliation in kind; hence that doctrine is better treated as a logically independent thesis commonly associated with retributivism than as an essential component of the theory.

Defined as the exhaustive class of alternatives to the utilitarian theory, retributivism of course is subject to no simple summary. It will be useful to subsequent discussion, however, to summarize that popular variant of the theory which can be called *pure moralistic retributivism* as consisting (at least) of the following propositions:

1. Moral guilt is a necessary condition for justified punishment.
2. Moral guilt is a sufficient condition ("irrespective of consequences") for justified punishment.
3. The proper amount of punishment to be inflicted upon the morally guilty offender is that amount which fits, matches, or is proportionate to the moral gravity of the offense.

That it is never justified to punish a morally blameless person for his or her "offense" (thesis 1) may not be quite self-evident, but it does find strong support in moral common sense. Thesis 2, however, is likely to prove an embarrassment for the pure retributivist, for it would have him or her approve the infliction of suffering on a person (albeit a *guilty* person) even when no good to the offender, the victim, or society at large is likely to result. "How can two wrongs make a right, or two evils a good?" he or she will be asked by the utilitarian, and in this case it is the utilitarian who will claim to speak for "moral common sense." In reply, the pure retributivist is likely to concede that inflicting suffering on an offender is not "good in itself," but will also point out that single acts cannot be judged simply "in themselves" with no concern for the context in which they fit and the events preceding them which are their occasion. Personal sadness is not a "good in itself" either, and yet when it is a response to the perceived sufferings of another it has a unique appropriateness. Glee, considered "in itself," looks much more like an intrinsically good mental state, but glee does not morally fit the perception of another's pain any more than an orange shirt aesthetically fits shocking pink trousers. Similarly, it may be true (the analogy is admittedly imperfect) that "while the moral evil in the offender and the pain of the punishment are each considered separately evils, it is intrinsically good that a certain relation exist or be established between them." [5] In this way the pure retributivist, relying on moral intuitions, can deny that a deliberate imposition of suffering on a human being is either good in itself or good as a means, and yet find it justified, nevertheless, as an essential component of an intrinsically good relation. Perhaps that is to put the point too strongly. All the retributivist needs to establish is that the complex situation preceding the infliction of punishment can be made better than it otherwise would be by the addition to it of the offender's suffering.

The utilitarian is not only unconvinced by arguments of this kind, he or she is also likely to find a "suspicious connection" between philosophical retributivism and the primitive lust for vengeance. The moralistic retributivist protests that he or she eschews anger or any other passion and seeks not revenge, but justice and the satisfaction of desert. Punishment, after all, is not the only kind of treatment we bestow upon persons simply because we think they deserve it. Teachers give students the grades they have earned with no thought of "future advantage," and with eyes firmly fixed on past performance. There is no necessary jubilation at good performance or vindictive pleasure in assigning low grades. And much the same is true of the assignments of rewards, prizes, grants, compensation, civil liability, and so on. Justice requires assignment on the basis of desert alone. To be sure, there is

a great danger of revengeful and sadistic tendencies finding vent under the unconscious disguise of a righteous indignation calling for just punishment, since the evil desire for revenge, if not identical with the latter, bears a resemblance to it sufficiently close to deceive those who want an excuse. [6]

Indeed, it is commonly thought that our modern notions of retributive justice have grown out of earlier practices, like the vendetta and the law of deodand, that were through and through expressions of the urge to vengeance. [7] Still, the retributivist replies, it is unfair to *identify* a belief with one of its corruptions, or a modern practice with its historical antecedents. The latter mistake is an instance of the "genetic fallacy" which is committed whenever one confuses an account of how a thing came to be the way it is with an analysis of the thing it has become.

The third thesis of the pure moralistic retributivist has also been subject to heavy attack. Can it really be the business of the state to see to it that happiness and unhappiness are distributed among citizens in proportion to their moral deserts? Think of the practical difficulties involved in the attempt simply to apportion pain to moral guilt in a given case, with no help from utilitarian considerations. First of all, it is usually impossible to punish an offender without inflicting suffering on those who love or depend upon him and may themselves be entirely innocent, morally speaking. In that way punishing the guilty is self-defeating from the moralistic retributive point of view. It will do more to increase than to diminish the disproportion between unhappiness and desert throughout society. Secondly, the aim of apportioning pain to guilt would in some cases require punishing "trivial" moral offenses, like rudeness, as heavily as more socially harmful crimes, since there can be as much genuine wickedness in the former as the latter. Thirdly, there is the problem of accumulation. Deciding the right amount of suffering to inflict in a given case would entail an assessment of the character of the offender as manifested throughout his or her whole life (and not simply at one weak moment) and also an assessment of his or her total lifelong balance of pleasure and pain. Moreover, there are inevitably inequalities of moral guilt in the commission of the same crime by different offenders, as well as inequalities of suffering from the same punishment. Application of the pure retributive theory then would require the abandonment of fixed penalties for various crimes and the substitution of individuated penalties selected in each case by an authority to fit the offender's uniquely personal guilt and vulnerability.

The utilitarian theory of punishment holds that punishment is never good in itself, but is (like bad-tasting medicine) justified when, and only when, it is a means to such future goods as *correction* (reform) of the offender, *protection* of society against other offenses from the same offender, and *deterrence* of other would-be offenders. (The list is not exhaustive.) Giving the offender the pain he deserves because of his wickedness is either not a coherent notion, on this theory, or else not a morally respectable independent reason for punishing. In fact, the utilitarian theory arose in the eighteenth century as part of a conscious reaction to cruel and uneconomical social institutions (including prisons) that were normally defended, if at all, in righteously moralistic terms.

For purposes of clarity, the utilitarian theory of punishment should be distinguished from utilitarianism as a general moral theory. The standard of right conduct generally, according to the latter, is conducibility to good consequences. Any act at all, whether that of a private citizen, a legislator, or a judge, is morally right if and only if it is likely, on the best evidence, to do more good or less harm all around than any alternative conduct open to the actor. (The standard for judging the goodness of consequences, in turn, for Jeremy Bentham and the early utilitarians was the amount of human happiness they contained, but many later utilitarians had more complicated conceptions of intrinsic value.) All proponents of general utilitarianism, of course, are also supporters of the utilitarian theory of punishment, but there is no logical necessity that a utilitarian in respect to punishment be a general utilitarian across the board.

The utilitarian theory of punishment can be summarized in three propositions parallel to those used above to summarize pure moralistic retributivism. According to this theory:

1. Social utility (correction, prevention, deterrence, et cetera) is a necessary condition for justified punishment.
2. Social utility is a sufficient condition for justified punishment.
3. The proper amount of punishment to be inflicted upon the offender is that amount which will do the most good or the least harm to all those who will be affected by it.

The first thesis enjoys the strongest support from common sense, though not so strong as to preclude controversy. For the retributivist, as has been seen, punishing the guilty is an end in itself quite apart from any gain in social utility. The utilitarian is apt to reply that if reform of the criminal could be secured with no loss of deterrence by simply giving him or her a pill that would have that effect, then nothing would be lost by not punishing him or her, and the substitute treatment would be "sheer gain."

Thesis 2, however, is the utilitarian's greatest embarrassment. The retributivist opponent argues forcefully against it that in certain easily imaginable circumstances it would justify punishment of the (legally) innocent, a consequence which all would regard as a moral abomination. Some utilitarians deny that punishment of the innocent could *ever* be the alternative that has the best consequences in social utility, but this reply seems arbitrary and dogmatic. Other utilitarians claim that "punishment of the innocent" is a self-contradiction. The concept of punishment, they argue,[8] itself implies hard treatment imposed upon the guilty as a conscious and deliberate response to their guilt. That guilt is part of the very definition of punishment, these writers claim, is shown by the absurdity of saying "I am punishing you for something you have not done," which sounds very much like "I am curing you even though you are not sick." Since all punishment is understood to be for guilt, they conclude, they can hardly be understood to be advocating punishing without guilt. H. L. A. Hart[9] calls this move a "definitional stop," and charges that it is an "abuse of definition," and indeed it is, if put forward by a proponent of the general utilitarian theory. If the right act in all contexts is the one which is likely to have the best consequences, then conceivably the act of framing an innocent man could sometimes be right; and the question of whether such mistreatment of the innocent party could properly be called "punishment" is a mere question of words having no bearing on the utilitarian's embarrassment. If, on the other hand, the definitional stop is employed by a defender of the utilitarian theory of the justification of punishment who is not a utilitarian across the board, then it seems to be a legitimate argumentative move. Such a utilitarian is defending official infliction of hard treatment (deprivation of liberty, suffering, et cetera) on *those who are legally guilty,* a practice to which he or she refers by using the word "punishment," as justified when and only when there is probable social utility in it.

No kind of utilitarian, however, will have plausible recourse to the definitional stop in defending thesis 3 from the retributivist charge that it would, in certain easily imaginable circumstances, justify excessive and/or insufficient penalties. The appeal again is to moral common sense: It would be manifestly unfair to inflict a mere two dollar fine on a convicted murderer or life imprisonment, under a balance of terror policy, for parking offenses. In either case, the punishment imposed would violate the retributivist's thesis 3, that the punishment be proportional to the moral gravity of the offense. And yet, if these were the penalties likely to have the best effects generally, the utilitarian in the theory of punishment would be committed to their support. He or she could not argue that excessive or deficient penalites are not "really" punishments. Instead he would have to argue as does Jeremy Bentham, that the proper employment of the utilitarian method simply could not lead to penalties so far out of line with our moral intuitions as the retributivist charges.

So far vengeance has not been mentioned except in the context of charge and countercharge between theorists who have no use for it. There are writers, however, who have kind words for vengeance and give it a central role in their theories of the justification of punishment. We can call these approaches the Vindictive Theory of Punishment (to distinguish them from legalistic and moralistic forms of retributivism) and then subsume its leading varieties under either the utilitarian or the retributive rubrics. Vindictive theories are of three different kinds: (1)The *escape-valve version,* commonly associated with the names of James Fitzjames Stephen and Oliver Wendell Holmes, Jr., and currently in favor with some psychoanalytic writers, holds that legal punishment is an orderly outlet for aggressive feelings, which would otherwise demand satisfaction in socially disruptive ways. The prevention of private vendettas through a state monopoly on vengeance is one of the chief ways in which legal punishment has social utility. The escape-valve theory is thus easily assimilated by the utilitarian theory of punishment. (2) The *hedonistic version* of the vindictive theory finds the justification of punishment in the pleasure it gives people (particularly the victim of the crime and his or her loved ones) to see the criminal suffer for the crime. For most utilitarians, and certainly for Bentham, any kind of pleasure—even spiteful, sadistic, or vindictive pleasure, just insofar as it *is* pleasure—counts as a good in the computation of social utility, just as pain—any kind of pain—counts as an evil. (This is sufficient to discredit hedonistic utilitarianism thoroughly, according to its retributivist critics.) The hedonistic version of the vindictive theory, then, is also subsumable under the utilitarian rubric. Finally, (3) the *romantic version* of the vindictive theory, very popular among the uneducated, holds that the justification of punishment is to be found in the emotions of hate and anger it expresses, these emotions being those allegedly felt by all normal or right-thinking people. I call this theory "romantic," despite certain misleading associations of that word, because, like any theory so labeled, it holds that certain emotions and the actions they inspire are self-certifying, needing no further justification. It is therefore not a kind of utilitarian theory and must be classified as a variety of retributivism, although in its emphasis on feeling it is in marked contrast to more typical retributive theories that eschew emotion and emphasize proportion and desert.

Many anthropologists have traced vindictive feelings and judgments to an origin in the "tribal morality" which universally prevails in primitive cultures, and which presumably governed the tribal life of our own prehistoric ancestors. If an anthropologist turned his attention to our modern criminal codes, he would discover evidence that tribalism has never entirely vacated its position in the criminal law. There are some provisions for which the vindictive theory (in any of its forms) would provide a ready rationale, but for which the utilitarian and moralistic retributivist theories are hard put to discover a plausible defense. Completed crimes, for example, are punished more severely than attempted crimes that fail for accidental reasons. This should not be surprising since the more harm caused the victim, his or her loved ones, and those of the public who can identify imaginatively with them, the more anger there will be at the criminal. If the purpose of punishment is to satisfy that anger, then we should expect that those who succeed in harming will be punished more than the bunglers who fail, even if the motives and intentions of the bunglers were every bit as wicked.

The classical sources of the retributive theory, at least in the modern period, are in the writings of the great German philosophers, Immanuel Kant (1724–1804) and Georg Wilhelm Friedrich Hegel (1770–1831). Those writings in their English translations are notoriously difficult and obscure, and yet their historical influence, particularly on the development of retributivism in Great Britain and America, is undeniable. This section opens with a remarkably perspicuous interpretation of Kant, Hegel, and the classical retributive theory from the important recent book, *The Rationale of Legal Punishment,* by Edmund Pincoffs. The classical source of the utilitarian theory of punishment, and indeed of the general utilitarian ethical theory as well, is *Introduction to the Principles of Morals and Legislation* by Jeremy Bentham, first published in 1789. Bentham's prose is clear and his approach unmetaphysical, so he is quite able to speak for himself to the modern student. Bentham refers often to "the principle of utility," his supreme moral principle. He does not formally define that principle in his selection here, but it finds essential expression in his first sentence: "The general object which all laws . . . ought to have . . . is to augment the total happiness of the community . . . " Bentham proceeds to apply that principle to the determination of those actions which ought, and those which ought not, to be crimes, and to the problems of selecting penalties to go with the various crimes and the various circumstances in which crimes are committed. The selection from Bentham presents the classic utilitarian interpretation of the maxim made so much of by retributivists, that the punishment should fit the crime.

As a writer solidly in the tradition of Kantian moral philosophy, Jeffrie Murphy has little sympathy with the Benthamite approach to punishment. He is partial to retributivism as the one theory of punishment which "grows out of the moral theory—Kantianism—which seems (to him) generally correct." Only the Kantian version of retributivism, among the main philosophical theories of punishment, he points out, begins by asking by what *right* the state can deliberately inflict suffering on a citizen —even a guilty citizen—as a mere means to the good of others.

Only if the state's decision to punish the criminal is in some sense the criminal's own decision, somehow consented to, at least hypothetically, by him in advance, can the state's right to punish be reconciled with the citizen's sovereign right of self-determination, or "autonomy." In the Kantian theory, this challenge to the state is squarely met by the argument that punishment of a lawbreaker is justified when it follows from a rule that it would have been rational for him and all other citizens to adopt as a universal law in their community. When a given criminal is punished for violating such a rule he is, in a sense, only getting "what he asked for." Moreover, just punishment restores the moral equilibrium among citizens that is disturbed when one takes advantage of the obedience of the others for one's own benefit.

There is not always a clear "profit" in crime, but at the very least the criminal exploits other citizens when he or she abandons the common burden of self-restraint to achieve criminal ends, while the others, who might have achieved their own ends more effectively by similar means, nevertheless refrained from doing so. In that case they have been unfairly taken advantage of, and justice calls for some sort of "nullification" of the wrong that has been done them. In a sense then, just punishment bears a certain analogy to the "repayment of a debt" (with interest) or to the forfeiture (and then some) of a benefit unfairly gained.

Murphy endorses this account of just punishment as an ideal, but holds that it is not widely applicable in actual modern societies. Drawing on a Marxist critique of capitalistic society (though he is surely not a "Marxist philosopher"), Murphy shows that for the most part crime grows out of motives that are approved and generally encouraged by society, and that criminals typically are not members of a shared community of values whose rules distribute benefits equally, in the manner of a "gentleman's club." Thus, while Murphy remains a retributivist, he is very doubtful that most actual instances of legal punishment can qualify for a retributivist justification.

In the brief excerpt titled "Desert," from his book *Doing Justice,* Andrew von Hirsch presents an intriguing suggestion of how utilitarians and retributivists may close ranks and present a common front in justifying criminal punishment. Giving the criminal what he deserves adds to the sum of human suffering, but it is justified because it will deter other crimes, and so on balance prevents more suffering than it produces. A number of useful questions might be pursued here by the reader. What qualifications might be added to the author's statement that "Those who violate others' rights deserve punishment"? Why does "deliberately adding to the amount of human suffering" override the case for giving the criminal what he or she deserves? Even if punishment, through its deterrent effect, does "prevent more misery than it inflicts," why is that a sufficient reason for inflicting suffering on those who commit crimes?

Rewards and punishments admit of degrees, but does it follow that because people deserve to be punished for their crimes that their punishment ought to represent a just desert for the crime? In this very brief selection from his book, the author does not address that question, but the reader may wish to consider it in connection with the larger question of whether individual criminal sentences are to be justified in the same way as the general social practice we call criminal punishment.

The great impasse between the utilitarian and retributive theories described in the earlier paragraphs of this introduction was largely undisturbed by a century-and-a-half of disputation, until a rash of quite original articles in the 1950s and 1960s appeared, which seemed to many to make a genuine breakthrough. The article by Rawls, included here, was one of the more important of these articles. Their common tactic was to make more and better distinctions, for example, between definition and justification, moral and legal guilt, necessary and sufficient conditions, single acts and general practices, and to hold to these distinctions rigorously, thus permitting new and sharper questions to be formulated about punishment, so that retributivism and utilitarianism could be put forward as complementary answers to different questions, rather than conflicting answers to the same question.

J.F.

PUNISHMENT AND REHABILITATION

Earlier, in Part Four of this volume, a powerful attack was launched by Lady Barbara Wootton against the view that the liability of those who committed crimes should be liability to punishment. In her view, the criminal process should have as its purpose the prevention of further harm, and treatment rather than punishment is the way to accomplish that. In sharp contrast, Herbert Morris in "Persons and Punishment," argues that we have a right to punishment. It is a most fundamental human right— natural, inalienable, absolute—and deriving from the very right to be treated as a person. Deny this right, says Morris, and you deny all moral rights and duties. Admittedly, most of us would gladly forego enjoyment of the right, at least until the implications of our rejection are brought home to us. And we need not look far for that. The most sophisticated modern views of correctional treatment deny that punishment is the proper thing for those who have committed crimes. Instead, it is assumed that when a person does harm he manifests a symptom of a pathological condition. The appropriate course, therefore, is to correct what is wrong with him, or at least to keep him from infecting others. "The logic of sickness implies the logic of therapy," as Morris observes. Therapy differs from punishment in focusing on the present rather than the past, in seeking to confer benefit and help, and in having no concern with any debt that may be owed to society for violating its rules. Since therapy is avowedly beneficial, a therapeutic regime is bolder in inflicting necessary suffering, in determining occasions that justify administration of it, and is less concerned about niceties of procedure to determine who may be made subject to it. These differences make considerations of personal rights, and particularly those associated with liberty, less important when therapy rather than punishment is administered. But there are even more profound differences between the two ways of treating harmdoers that relate to how *persons* are to be treated. If a person is treated not as the author of his or her actions but as a mere instrument of happenings that constitute his or her actions, the person is deprived of the role as a creator, and perhaps most important, his or her role as a creator of himself or herself. The satisfactions of these personal achievements are closed to him or her. Since this person can take credit for nothing, nothing is earned, and he or she is either the fortunate beneficiary of others' favorable regard or is treated as an afflicted creature and made subject to the control of others. His or her values and will must be bent to conform to those of the therapist as represented by therapeutic standards of normality, without respect for his or her independent moral status. Finally, the regime of therapy regards as recalcitrant behavior the harmdoer's attempt to justify or explain away what he or she did, to be noted only for its pathological significance, and this again is a refusal to accord this person the respect due a human being.

Professor Morris, then, is arguing implicitly for the thesis that only harmdoing that is wrongdoing should be punished, and explicitly that there is a right which is of the very essence of personhood to punitive rather than therapeutic treatment for wrongdoing. It is well established in our jurisprudence that some harmdoers who are not wrongdoers may be subjected to involuntary restraint and regimes of therapy. Persons who are abnormal in ways that put their ability to avoid doing harm in serious doubt are legitimate candidates for such treatment. Those persons are not beneficiaries of a right to be punished for reasons that Professor Morris makes clear enough. But just how is the line to be drawn? What conditions must be satisfied to meet the test of pathology, and even when it is met, what capabilities of cure must be available to legitimate a regime of therapy? Are there special "social diseases" that individuals suffer whose symptoms a penal code catalogues in its definitions of crimes, and for which therapy is more appropriate not only because it is more expedient but also because it is more humane?

Further critical questions suggest themselves. Are there really no alternatives to punishment as ways of treating harmdoers except therapy? Perhaps for certain kinds of crimes it would be sufficient to impose a disability short of punishment. A person who embezzles money might be disqualified from occupying a fiduciary position, just as a person with defective eyesight might be disqualified from serving in the army. Such a person is neither punished nor cured by being excluded. On this model, there would be an initial presumption of qualification that is rebutted by criminal conviction. Instead of being either punished or cured, however, a person is simply deemed unqualified, at least until there is good reason to believe that his or her deficiency or abnormality no longer exists. Certainly this is not unrealistic for at least some persons who commit some crimes; and perhaps a more humane, economical, and just system for dealing with such crimes could be devised along these lines. In that case what shall we say about a right to punishment? If that right appears somewhat less universal than Professor Morris suggests, we may learn even more about it by considering why in some cases punishment still seems more appropriate than any other kind of response, including the nontherapeutic alternatives.

DETAINING THE DANGEROUS OFFENDER

Detention of a person accused but not yet convicted is widely regarded as a serious injustice even when it is predicted that the accused if left free may engage in further crimes. Once a person has been convicted, however, such concern evaporates, and there is general acceptance of sentences based on equally unreliable predictions of future conduct that are calculated to keep confined for a longer period than otherwise a person who is thought to be dangerous. Whether such preventive confinement is justifiable, even when practiced in a sophisticated way, is the question that is explored in this section. It can be argued that standards of dangerousness are vague, reliability of prediction is untested, and commitment procedures do not provide adequate safeguards for the individual whose commitment is proposed. Beyond these threshold objections to existing practice, there are even more formidable objections in principle. There is a theoretical difficulty in actual prediction—the false positive problem—that virtually ensures erroneous confinements that are unacceptable under principles of justice fundamental in our criminal jurisprudence. Even if ideal methods of prediction were possible and the hazard of false positives no longer existed, there are even more basic objections. A system of preventive confinement represents a grave threat to personal autonomy and to liberty of the citizen in his relations with the state. The consequences of a determination that a person is dangerous deprives him of the opportunity of choosing to act in ways that do not cause harm. Such a system lends itself to ready abuse by the organs of public power under the influence of unenlightened though widely accepted notions about crime and criminals, or to serve even more sinister political ends. These objections apply equally to a system that purports to confine dangerous persons before they have committed crimes and a system that deals only with those already convicted. Furthermore, preventive confinement cannot pass muster as (additional) punishment, since considerations of proportionality between an offense and the punishment imposed for it (discussed in earlier selections) preclude that. Nor can the avowed goal of "rehabilitative treatment" justify confinement of those who have been determined to be dangerous, since the availability of therapeutic programs does not cancel the objectionable deprivation of liberty. Not only do the same objections obtain, but there are then the additional objections to the unjustifiable compulsory therapy because of the suffering and deprivation which attend it.

The evil of preventive confinement is to be found in the conventional sentencing practices of judges everywhere as well as in the correctional systems of those few jurisdictions that have institutionalized such confinement. Indeed it is the largely unnoticed influence on the sentencing judge of his or her own crude notions of dangerousness that exerts the greatest power for injustice in this regard. At the present time it seems clear that the need to take risks in the interest of liberty and justice must be recognized, just as the need to take risks to preserve other things we value is recognized in other areas of social life. Perhaps the best we can hope for at this point are criteria of dangerousness that identify those about whom there can be no disagreement— criteria that need no validation as predictive devices since they derive their validity from what we already know. There are, after all, persons who are dangerous beyond any doubt, and from these clear cases we may by careful consideration derive general standards for defining the class of persons who are certainly dangerous. It is important to note that clear cases are not cases bearing features that warrant predictions with a very high degree of probability. Rather, they are cases in which there has been behavior (perhaps criminal, perhaps not) that, according to universally accepted ideas about threats of harm, unmistakably mark the person as dangerous. These criteria of danger-ousness are of the same general sort as criteria for identifying dangerous situations—not based on superstition or unsupported impressions, yet not based on selective ab-stractions and disinterested observation of consequences either. Rather, it is a resource of collective social intelligence—common sense about harm. This suggests that the very concept of a dangerous person that is developed statistically is the wrong one. For one thing, using the statistical concept we would be bound to pay attention to the wrong kind of factors to determine who is dangerous—racial, social, economic, and general psychopathological categories into which persons may be sorted. Our commonsense criteria, however, are designed to identify dangerous persons differently. Under these criteria, even the dangerous person himself is bound to acknowledge that his abnormal-ity marks him as dangerous, just as though he carried a contagious disease or was driving while intoxicated. It is always open to experiment and orderly observation to disclose that what common sense indicates to be dangerous is in fact innocuous. Indeed it is essential that common sense be constantly tested and revised in this way. But doing that works a correction among the types properly included as dangerous persons, and is not the substitution of a statistical idea of a dangerous person for a common sense one.

These well-known flaws in preventive detention proposals are for the most part severe *practical* difficulties that could in principle, if not in fact, be overcome. Ferdinand Schoeman, in a challenging new article, focuses on the question whether preventive detention would be morally legitimate if only we could give better definitions of "dan-gerous," make more accurate predictions, invent better procedural safeguards, and so on. In particular he asks whether it would be consistent to defend the practice of quarantine for persons with contagious diseases and yet reject incarceration for equally "dangerous" potential criminals. His cogently argued but disquieting conclusion is that the practices of civil preventive detention and quarantine are, morally speaking, in exactly the same boat.

CAPITAL PUNISHMENT

Among all the issues that criminal punishment raises, none has been the subject of greater public controversy than capital punishment. Only utopian views conceive a society without the need for some form of meaningful condemnation of persons who wrongfully do harm that is of serious public concern. The most dramatic form that such public response may take is now exciting great debate in the United States and else-where, as it has for several centuries throughout the civilized world. In the United States, recent Supreme Court cases questioning the constitutionality of the death penalty have produced the full range of arguments for and against capital punishment. With this in mind, selections from the opinions in three of these cases are presented here.

In 1972, the Supreme Court of the United States held that the imposition and carrying out of the death penalty in one case of murder and two of rape was unconstitu-tional because violative of the "cruel and unusual punishment" restriction of the Eighth Amendment. There was nothing special about the sentence, the proceedings, or the law under which the defendants were sentenced in these cases, and the Supreme Court's decision was based on general considerations regarding the death penalty. The selections from four of the nine separate opinions in *Furman v. Georgia* that are included here present all of the important arguments that were advanced. Two themes are sounded with special prominence, and they have appeared earlier in this volume in other contexts. One is the issue of arbitrary and even discriminatory application of the capital provisions of the law by judges and (even more) by juries. It is the unprincipled (though perhaps well-meaning) exercise of discretionary power that is objected to, and the objection is especially weighty because of the awful consequences that attend such abuse. The other theme recurring in the opinions addresses the moral sentiments of the community. If there is general disinclination in the community to invoke the death penalty, then that should count conclusively against its continued existence. There is disagreement among members of the Court only about what the sentiment of the community is.

The state of the law following *Furman* was unclear. If only arbitrariness is a fatal objection, which is what some state legislatures and proponents of congressional bills assumed, it would seem that in principle, at least, suitable remedies could be found. There are ways of specifying the extreme culpability that would set the capital crime apart, and of framing specific questions bearing on culpability for jurors to answer in determining whether the death penalty is warranted. If it were mandatory whenever warranted, that would seem to preclude arbitrariness. One suspects, however, that such a consequence would ordinarily cause jurors to shrink from following their instructions, with the result that unconstitutional arbitrariness would again exist for the occasional death sentence; or the death penalty would in effect become a dead letter on the books. Some of those concerned to preserve the death penalty have advocated a Draconian resort to simple-minded mandatory death penalties, which do not provide opportunity for all matters bearing on culpability to be considered. The preclusion of exculpatory considerations by such stark provisions would seem to introduce a new arbitrariness far worse than the old. It would indeed avoid the evil of discriminatory imposition of the death penalty of which Justice Douglas speaks, but would institute a regime of equal *injustice* by requiring its infliction on all members of a class regardless of culpability —all those who intentionally and without justification kill a police officer, for example, regardless of what reason there might have been which the law does not recognize as a defense.

The community sentiment argument seems not to have been fully appreciated in the *Furman* opinions. Certainly it is wrong to require jurors to condemn to death those they find guilty if something more than the natural distaste and regret that would ordinarily accompany the performance of such a duty is generally experienced. If revulsion normally overcomes those citizens who are asked as jurors to do their duty under the law, we may expect that only when there is a passionate hatred of the convicted person will capital punishment be imposed, and that would surely result in many irrational decisions that constitute precisely the injustice of discriminatory sentences which are objectionable on separate grounds. But an even more basic consideration is whether, according to principles of right and wrong that are universally invoked in the community, the death penalty is wrong. The answer is by no means plain on the face of things, and only extended moral argument can make it plain. Strong popular feeling of revulsion by itself counts only as evidence that the practice of killing a person for the crime he committed *may be* morally unacceptable. In spite of such feeling, it may not be morally unacceptable. Slaughter of animals for food may evoke such feelings, yet it may turn out not to be morally wrong, in which case the public revulsion is reason to carry on the activity discreetly, but not to prohibit it. Superficial evidence of possible general moral objection to capital punishment, such as polls that elicit unfavorable attitudes toward it, are only the first word and not the last. What justification there is for such attitudes is the question whose answer will tell us whether the death penalty is morally wrong.

In *Gregg v. Georgia* a measure of uncertainty about the death penalty was removed when the United States Supreme Court upheld the procedures prescribed by carefully drafted Georgia legislation. The case was one of homicide committed in the course of armed robbery, and the Court found that the dangers of arbitrary sentence of death no longer existed under the new bifurcated system providing for reaching a verdict first, then under separate instruction deciding on a recommendation for sentence with reference to specific findings of fact, and with judicial review by the State Supreme Court comparing death sentences to ensure against disproportionality. Ample portions of the opinions in the case are presented here in order to allow careful critical assessment of all the arguments on both sides, those fully developed as well as those merely hinted at.

In yet another case from the same state, *Coker v. Georgia,* the United States Supreme Court found the death penalty for rape to be a violation of the Eighth Amendment's prohibition against cruel and unusual punishment, holding that the punishment is then grossly disproportionate to the crime. The dissenting opinion of the Chief Justice is included here, and one might first wish to consider whether the opinion adheres to what it professes in the second sentence when it declares "Our task is not to give effect to our individual views on capital punishment; rather, we must determine what the constitution permits a State to do under its reserved powers." More particularly, is the Chief Justice's notion of just what the Eighth Amendment prohibits made sufficiently clear for the purposes at hand? The general question of proportionality between crime and punishment becomes an urgent matter in this case, as does the question of whether the death penalty may be used to exterminate people who commit crimes and are believed with good reason to be especially dangerous.

H.G.

NOTES

1. Joel Feinberg, *Doing and Deserving* (Princeton: Princeton University Press, 1970), pp. 106-09.
2. A. C. Ewing, *The Morality of Punishment* (London: Kegan Paul, 1929), p. 13.
3. John Rawls, "Concepts of Rules," *The Philosophical Review,* LXIV (1955), pp. 4,5.
4. J. D. Mabbott, "Punishment," *Mind,* XLVIII (1939), p. 161.
5. A. C. Ewing, *Ethics,* (New York: Macmillan, 1953), pp. 169–70.

6. Ewing, *Morality of Punishment,* p. 27.
7. See O. W. Holmes, Jr., *The Common Law* (Boston: Little, Brown, 1881) and Henry Maine, *Ancient Law.* 1861 Reprint. (Boston: Beacon Press, 1963).
8. See, for example, Anthony Quinton, "On Punishment," *Analysis,* XIV (1954), pp. 1933–42.
9. H. L. A. Hart, *Punishment and Responsibility* (New York and Oxford: Oxford University Press, 1968), pp. 5,6.

WHAT IS PUNISHMENT?

FLEMMING v. NESTOR

United States Supreme Court, 1960*

Mr. Justice HARLAN delivered the opinion of the Court.

From a decision of the District Court for the District of Columbia holding § 202(n) of the Social Security Act unconstitutional, the Secretary of Health, Education, and Welfare takes this direct appeal pursuant to 28 U.S.C. § 1252, 28 U.S. C.A. § 1252. The challenged section, set forth in full in the margin,[1] provides for the termination of old-age, survivor, and disability insurance benefits payable to, or in certain cases in respect of, an alien individual who, after September 1, 1954 (the date of enactment of the section), is deported under § 241(a) of the Immigration and Nationality Act on any one of certain grounds specified in § 202(n).

Appellee, an alien, immigrated to this country from Bulgaria in 1913, and became eligible for old-age benefits in November 1955. In July 1956 he was deported pursuant to § 241(a) (6) (C) (i) of the Immigration and Nationality Act for having been a member of the Communist Party from 1933 to 1939. This being one of the benefit-termination deportation grounds specified in § 202(n), appellee's benefits were terminated soon thereafter, and notice of the termination was given to his wife, who had remained in this country.[2]

III.

... The remaining, and most insistently pressed, constitutional objections rest upon Art. I, § 9, cl. 3, and Art. III, 3, of the Constitution, and the Sixth Amendment.[3] It is said that the termination of appellee's benefits amounts to punishing him without a judicial trial, see Wong Wing v. United States, 163 U.S. 228, 16 S.Ct. 977, 41 L.Ed. 140; that the termination of benefits constitutes the imposition of punishment by legislative act, rendering § 202(n) a bill of attainder, see United States v. Lovett, 328 U.S. 303, 66 S.Ct. 1073, 90 L.Ed. 1252; Cummings v. Missouri, 4 Wall. 277, 18 L.Ed. 356; and that the punishment exacted is imposed for past conduct not unlawful when engaged in, thereby violating the constitutional prohibition on *ex post facto* laws, see Ex parte Garland, 4 Wall. 333, 18 L.Ed. 366.[4] Essential to the success of each of these contentions is

*80 S. Ct. 1367 (1960). Excerpts only. Footnotes renumbered.

the validity of characterizing as "punishment" in the constitutional sense the termination of benefits under § 202(n).

In determining whether legislation which bases a disqualification on the happening of a certain past event imposes a punishment, the Court has sought to discern the objects on which the enactment in question was focused. Where the source of legislative concern can be thought to be the activity or status from which the individual is barred, the disqualification is not punishment even though it may bear harshly upon one affected. The contrary is the case where the statute in question is evidently aimed at the person or class of persons disqualified. In the earliest case on which appellee relies, a clergyman successfully challenged a state constitutional provision barring from that profession—and from many other professions and offices— all who would not swear that they had never manifested any sympathy or support for the cause of the Confederacy. Cummings v. Missouri, supra. The Court thus described the aims of the challenged enactment:

"The oath could not * * * have been required as a means of ascertaining whether parties were qualified or not for their respective callings or the trusts with which they were charged. *It was required in order to reach the person, not the calling.* It was exacted, not from any notion that the several acts designated indicated unfitness for the callings, but because it was thought that the several acts deserved punishment * * *." Id., 4 Wall. at page 320. (Emphasis supplied.)

Only the other day the governing inquiry was stated, in an opinion joined by four members of the Court, in these terms:

"The question in each case where unpleasant consequences are brought to bear upon an individual for prior conduct, is whether the legislative aim was to punish that individual for past activity, or whether the restriction of the individual comes about as a relevant incident to a regulation of a present situation, such as the proper qualifications for a profession." De Veau v. Braisted, 363 U.S. 144, 160, 80 S.Ct. 1146, 1155 (plurality opinion).

In Ex parte Garland, supra, where the Court struck down an oath—similar in content to that involved in Cummings—required of attorneys seeking to practice before any federal court, as also in Cummings, the finding of punitive intent drew heavily on the Court's first-hand acquaintance with the events and the mood of the then recent Civil War, and "the fierce passions which that struggle aroused." Cummings v. Missouri, supra, 4 Wall. at page 322.[5] Similarly, in United States v. Lovett, supra, where the Court invalidated, as a bill of attainder, a statute forbidding—subject to certain conditions—the further payment of the salaries of three named government employees, the determination that a punishment had been imposed rested in large measure on the specific Congressional history which the court was at pains to spell out in detail. See 328 U.S. at pages 308–312, 66 S.Ct., at pages 1075–1077. Most recently, in Trop v. Dulles, 356 U.S. 86, 78 S.Ct. 590, 2 L.Ed. 2d 630, which held unconstitutional a statute providing for the expatriation of one who had been sentenced by a courtmartial to dismissal or dishonorable discharge for wartime desertion, the majority of the Court characterized the statute as punitive. However, no single opinion commanded the support of a majority. The plurality opinion rested its determination, at least in part, on its inability to discern any alternative purpose which the statute could be thought to serve. Id., 356 U.S. at page 97, 78 S.Ct. at page 596. The concurring opinion found in the specific historical evolution of the provision in question compelling evidence of punitive intent. Id., 356 U.S. at pages 107–109, 78 S.Ct. at pages 601–602.

It is thus apparent that, though the governing criterion may be readily stated, each case has turned on its own highly particularized context. Where no persuasive showing of a purpose "to reach the person, not the calling," Cummings v. Missouri, supra, 4 Wall. at page 320, has been made, the Court has not hampered legislative regulation of activities within its sphere of concern, despite the often-severe effects such regulation has had on the persons subject to it.[6] Thus, deportation has been held to be not punishment, but an exercise of the plenary power of Congress to fix the conditions under which aliens are to be permitted to enter and remain in this country. Fong Yue Ting v. United States, 149 U.S. 698, 730, 13 S. Ct. 1016, 1028, 37 L.Ed. 905; see Galvan v. Press, 347 U.S. 522, 530–531, 74 S.Ct. 737, 742–743, 98 L.Ed. 911. Similarly, the setting by a State of qualifications for the practice of medicine, and their modification from time to time, is an incident of the State's power to protect the health and safety of its citizens, and its decision to bar from practice persons who commit or have committed a felony is taken as evidencing an intent to exercise that regulatory power, and not a purpose to add to the punishment of ex-felons. Hawker v. New York, 170 U.S. 189, 18 S.Ct. 573, 42 L.Ed. 1002. See De Veau v. Braisted, supra (regulation of crime on the waterfront

through disqualification of ex-felons from holding union office). Cf. Helvering v. Mitchell, 303 U.S. 391, 397–401, 58 S.Ct. 630, 632–634, 82 L.Ed. 917, holding that, with respect to deficiencies due to fraud, a 50 percent addition to the tax imposed was not punishment so as to prevent, upon principles of double jeopardy, its assessment against one acquitted of tax evasion.

Turning, then, to the particular statutory provision before us, appellee cannot successfully contend that the language and structure of § 202(n), or the nature of the deprivation, requires us to recognize a punitive design. Cf. Wong Wing v. United States, supra (imprisonment, at hard labor up to one year, of person found to be unlawfully in the country). Here the sanction is the mere denial of a noncontractual governmental benefit. No affirmative disability or restraint is imposed, and certainly nothing approaching the "infamous punishment" of imprisonment, as in Wong Wing, on which great reliance is mistakenly placed. Moreover, for reasons already given (363 U.S. at pages 611–612, 80 S. Ct. at pages 1372–1373), it cannot be said, as was said of the statute in Cummings v. Missouri, supra, 4 Wall. at page 319; see Dent v. West Virginia, 129 U.S. 114, 126, 9 S.Ct. 231, 235, 32 L.Ed. 623, that the disqualification of certain deportees from receipt of Social Security benefits while they are not lawfully in this country bears no rational connection to the purposes of the legislation of which it is a part, and must without more therefore be taken as evidencing a Congressional desire to punish. Appellee argues, however, that the history and scope of § 202(n) prove that no such postulated purpose can be thought to have motivated the legislature, and that they persuasively show that a punitive purpose in fact lay behind the statute. We do not agree.

We observe initially that only the clearest proof could suffice to establish the unconstitutionality of a statute on such a ground. Judicial inquiries into Congressional motives are at best a hazardous matter, and when that inquiry seeks to go behind objective manifestations it becomes a dubious affair indeed. Moreover, the presumption of constitutionality with which this enactment, like any other, comes to us forbids us lightly to choose that reading of the statute's setting which will invalidate it over that which will save it. "[I]t is not on slight implication and vague conjecture that the legislature is to be pronounced to have transcended its powers, and its acts to be considered as void." Fletcher v. Peck, 6 Cranch 87, 128, 3 L.Ed. 162.

Section 202(n) was enacted as a small part of an extensive revision of the Social Security program. The provision originated in the House of Representatives. H.R. 9366, 83d Cong., 2d Sess., § 108. The discussion in the House Committee Report, H.R.Rep. No. 1698, 83d Cong., 2d Sess., pp. 5, 25, 77, does not express the purpose of the statute. However, it does say that the termination of benefits would apply to those persons who were "deported from the United States because of illegal entry, conviction of a crime, or subversive activity * * *." Id., at 25. It was evidently the thought that such was the scope of the statute resulting from its application to deportation under the 14 named paragraphs of § 241(a) of the Immigration and Nationality Act. Id., at 77.[7]

The Senate Committee rejected the proposal, for the stated reason that it had "not had an opportunity to give sufficient study to all the possible implications of this provision, which involves termination of benefit rights under the contributory program of old-age and survivors insurance * * *." S. Rep. No. 1987, 83d Cong., 2d Sess., p. 23; see also id., at 76. However, in Conference, the proposal was restored in modified form,[8] and as modified was enacted as § 202(n). See H.R.Conf.Rep. No. 2679, 83d Cong., 2d Sess., p. 18.

[16, 17] Appellee argues that this history demonstrates that Congress was not concerned with the *fact* of a beneficiary's deportation—which it is claimed alone would justify this legislation as being pursuant to a policy relevant to regulation of the Social Security system—but that it sought to reach certain *grounds* for deportation, thus evidencing a punitive intent.[9] It is impossible to find in this meagre history the unmistakable evidence of punitive intent which, under principles already discussed, is required before a Congressional enactment of this kind may be struck down. Even were that history to be taken as evidencing Congress' concern with the grounds, rather than the fact, of deportation, we do not think that this, standing alone, would suffice to establish a punitive purpose. This would still be a far cry from the situations involved in such cases as Cummings, Wong Wing, and Garland (see 363 U.S. at page 617, 80 S.Ct. at page 1376), and from that in Lovett, supra, where the legislation was on its face aimed at particular individuals. The legislative record, however, falls short of any persuasive showing that Congress was in fact concerned alone with the grounds of deportation. To be sure Congress did not apply the termination provision to all deportees. However, it is evident that neither did it rest the operation of the statute on the occurrence of the underlying act. The fact of deportation itself remained an essential condition for loss of benefits, and even if a beneficiary were saved from deportation only through discretionary suspension by the Attorney General under § 244 of the Immigration and Nationality Act (66 Stat. 214, 8 U.S.C. § 1254, 8 U.S.C.A. § 1254), § 202(n) would not reach him.

Moreover, the grounds for deportation referred to in the Committee Report embrace to the great majority of those deported, as is evident from an examination of the four omitted grounds, summarized in the margin.[10] Inferences drawn from the omission of those grounds cannot establish, to the degree of certainty required, that Congressional concern was wholly with the acts leading to deportation, and not with the fact of deportation.[11] To hold otherwise would be to rest on the "slight implication and vague conjecture" against which Chief Justice Marshall warned. Fletcher v. Peck, supra, 6 Cranch at page 128.

The same answer must be made to arguments drawn from the failure of Congress to apply § 202(n) to beneficiaries voluntarily residing abroad. But cf. § 202(t), ante, note 5. Congress may have failed to consider such persons; or it may have thought their number too slight, or the permanence of their voluntary residence abroad too uncertain, to warrant application of the statute to them, with its attendant administrative problems of supervision and enforcement. Again, we cannot with confidence reject all those alternatives which imaginativeness can bring to mind, save that one which might require the invalidation of the statute.

Reversed.

Mr. Justice BLACK, dissenting.

IV

... The Court in part III of its opinion holds that the 1954 Act is not an *ex post facto* law or bill of attainder even though it creates a class of deportees who cannot collect their insurance benefits because they were once Communists at a time when simply being a Communist was not illegal. The Court also puts great emphasis on its belief that the Act here is not punishment. Although not believing that the particular label "punishment" is of decisive importance, I think the Act does impose punishment even in a classic sense. The basic reason for Nestor's loss of his insurance payments is that he was once a Communist. This man, now 69 years old, has been driven out of the country where he has lived for 43 years to a land where he is practically a stranger, under an Act authorizing his deportation many years after his Communist membership. Cf. Galvan v. Press, 347 U.S. 522, 532, 533, 74 S.Ct. 737, 743, 744, 98 L.Ed. 911 (dissenting opinions). Now a similar *ex post facto* law deprives him of his insurance, which, while petty and insignificant in amount to this great Government, may well be this exile's daily bread, for the same reason and in accord with the general fashion of the day—that is, to punish in every way possible anyone who ever made the mistake of being a Communist in this country or who is supposed ever to have been associated with anyone who made that mistake. See, e.g., Barenblatt v. United States, 360 U.S. 109, 79 S.Ct. 1081, 3 L.Ed.2d 1115, and Uphaus v. Wyman, 360 U.S. 72, 79 S.Ct. 1040, 3 L.Ed.2d 1090. In United States v. Lovett, 328

U.S. 303, 315–316, 66 S.Ct. 1073, 1079, 90 L.Ed. 1252, we said:

"* * * legislative acts, no matter what their form, that apply either to named individuals or to easily ascertainable members of a group in such a way as to inflict punishment on them without a judicial trial are bills of attainder prohibited by the Constitution."

Faithful observance of our holdings in that case, in Ex parte Garland, 4 Wall. 333, 18 L.Ed. 366, and in Cummings v. Missouri, 4 Wall. 277, 18 L.Ed. 356, would, in my judgment, require us to hold that the 1954 Act is a bill of attainder. It is a congressional enactment aimed at an easily ascertainable group; it is certainly punishment in any normal sense of the word to take away from any person the benefits of an insurance system into which he and his employer have paid their moneys for almost two decades; and it does all this without a trial according to due process of law. It is true that the Lovett, Cummings and Garland Court opinions were not unanimous, but they nonetheless represent positive precedents on highly important questions of individual liberty which should not be explained away with cobwebbery refinements. If the Court is going to overrule these cases in whole or in part, and adopt the views of previous dissenters, I believe it should be done clearly and forthrightly.

A basic constitutional infirmity of this Act, in my judgment, is that it is a part of a pattern of laws all of which violate the First Amendment out of fear that this country is in grave danger if it lets a handful of Communist fanatics or some other extremist group make their arguments and discuss their ideas. This fear, I think, is baseless. It reflects a lack of faith in the sturdy patriotism of our people and does not give to the world a true picture of our abiding strength. It is an unworthy fear in a country that has a Bill of Rights containing provisions for fair trials, freedom of speech, press and religion, and other specific safeguards designed to keep men free. I repeat once more that I think this Nation's greatest security lies, not in trusting to a momentary majority of this Court's view at any particular time of what is "patently arbitrary," but in wholehearted devotion to and observance of our constitutional freedoms. See Wieman v. Updegraff, 344 U.S. 183, 192, 73 S.Ct. 215, 219, 97 L.Ed. 216 (concurring opinion).

I would affirm the judgment of the District Court which held that Nestor is constitutionally entitled to collect his insurance.

Mr. Justice DOUGLAS, dissenting.

Appellee came to this country from Bulgaria in 1913 and was employed, so as to be covered by the Social Security Act, from December 1936 to January 1955—a period of 19 years. He became eligible for retirement and for Social Security benefits in November 1955 and was awarded $55.60 per month. In July 1956 he was deported for having been a member of the Communist Party from 1933 to 1939. Pursuant to a law, enacted September 1, 1954, he was thereupon denied payment of further Social Security benefits.

This 1954 law seems to me to be a classic example of a bill of attainder, which Art. I, § 9 of the Constitution prohibits Congress from enacting. A bill of attainder is a legislative act which inflicts punishment without a judicial trial. Cummings v. Missouri, 4 Wall. 277, 323, 18 L.Ed. 356.

In the old days punishment was meted out to a creditor or rival or enemy by sending him to the gallows. But as recently stated by Irving Brant,[12]

"* * * By smiting a man day after day with slanderous words, by taking away his opportunity to earn a living, you can drain the blood from his veins without even scratching his skin.

"Today's bill of attainder is broader than the classic form, and not so tall and sharp. There is mental in place of physical torture, and confiscation of tomorrow's bread and butter instead of yesterday's land and gold. What is perfectly clear is that hate, fear and prejudice play the same role today, in the destruction of human rights in America that they did in England when a frenzied mob of lords, judges, bishops and shoemakers turned the Titus Oates blacklist into a hangman's record. Hate, jealousy and spite continue to fill the legislative attainder lists just as they did in the Irish Parliament of ex-King James."

Bills of attainder, when they imposed punishment less than death, were bills of pains and penalties and equally beyond the constitutional power of Congress. Cummings v. Missouri, supra, 4 Wall. at page 323.

Punishment in the sense of a bill of attainder includes the "deprivation or suspension of political or civil rights." Cummings v. Missouri, supra, at page 322. In that case it was barring a priest from practicing his profession. In Ex parte Garland, 4 Wall. 333, 18 L.Ed. 366, it was excluding a man from practicing law in the federal courts. In United States v. Lovett, 328 U.S. 303, 66 S.Ct. 1073, 90 L.Ed. 1252, it was cutting off employees' compensation and barring them permanently from government service. Cutting off a person's livelihood by denying him accrued social benefits—part of his property interests—is no less a punishment. Here, as in the other cases cited, the penalty exacted has one of the classic purposes of punishment[13]—"to reprimand the wrongdoer, to deter others." Trop v. Dulles, 356 U.S. 86, 96, 78 S.Ct. 590, 595, 2 L.Ed.2d 630.

Social Security payments are not gratuities. They are products of a contributory system, the funds being raised by payment from employees and employers alike, or in case of self-employed persons, by the individual alone. See Social Security Board v. Nierotko, 327 U.S. 358, 364, 66 S.Ct. 637, 640, 90 L.Ed. 718. The funds are placed in the Federal Old-Age and Survivors Insurance Trust Fund, 42 U.S.C. § 401(a), 42 U.S.C.A. § 401(a); and only those who contribute to the fund are entitled to its benefits, the amount of benefits being related to the amount of contributions made. See Stark, Social Security: Its Importance to Lawyers, 43 A.B. A.J. 319, 321 (1957). As the late Senator George, long Chairman of the Senate Finance Committee and one of the authors of the Social Security system, said:

"There has developed through the years a feeling both in and out of Congress that the contributory social insurance principle fits our times—that it serves a vital need that cannot be as well served otherwise. It comports better than any substitute we have discovered with the American concept that free men want to earn their security and not ask for doles—that what is due as a matter of earned right is far better than a gratuity. * * *

"Social security is not a handout; it is not charity; it is not relief. It is an earned right based upon the contributions and earnings of the individual. As an earned right, the individual is eligible to receive his benefit in dignity and self-respect." 102 Cong.Rec. 15110.

Social Security benefits have rightly come to be regarded as basic financial protection against the hazards of old age and disability. As stated in a recent House Report:

"The old-age and survivors insurance system is the basic program which provides protection for America's families against the loss of earned income upon the retirement or death of the family provider. The program provides benefits related to earned income and such benefits are paid for by the contributions made with respect to persons working in covered occupations." H.R.Rep. No. 1189, 84th Cong., 1st Sess. 2.

Congress could provide that only people resident here could get Social Security benefits. Yet both both the House and the Senate rejected any residence requirements. See H.R.Rep. No. 1698, 83d Cong., 2d Sess. 24–25; S.Rep. No. 1987, 83d Cong., 2d Sess. 23. Congress concededly might amend the program to meet new conditions. But may it take away Social Security benefits from one person or from a group of persons for vindictive reasons? Could Congress on deporting an alien for having been a Communist confiscate his home, appropriate his savings accounts, and thus send him out of the country penniless? I think not. Any such Act would be a bill of attainder. The difference, as I see it, between that case and this is one merely of degree. Social Security benefits, made up in part of this alien's own earnings, are taken from him because he once was a Communist.

The view that § 202(n), with which we now deal,

imposes a penalty was taken by Secretary Folsom, appellant's predecessor, when opposing enlargement of the category of people to be denied benefits of Social Security, e.g., those convicted of treason and sedition. He said:

"Because the deprivation of benefits as provided in the amendment is in the nature of a penalty and based on considerations foreign to the objectives and provisions of the old-age and survivors insurance program, the amendment may well serve as a precedent for extension of similar provisions to other public programs and to other crimes which, while perhaps different in degree, are difficult to distinguish in principle.
"The present law recognizes only three narrowly limited exceptions[14] to the basic principle that benefits are paid without regard to the attitudes, opinions, behavior, or personal characteristics of the individual * * *." Hearings Senate Finance Committee on Social Security Amendments of 1955, 84th Cong., 2d Sess. 1319.

The Committee Reports, though meagre, support Secretary Folsom in that characterization of § 202(n). The House Report tersely stated that termination of the benefits would apply to those persons who were deported "because of illegal entry, conviction of a crime, or subversive activity." H.R.Rep. No. 1698, 83d Cong., 2d Sess. 25. The aim and purpose are clear—to take away from a person by legislative *fiat* property which he has accumulated because he has acted in a certain way or embraced a certain ideology. That is a modern version of the bill of attainder—as plain, as direct, as effective as those which religious passions once loosed in England and which later were employed against the Tories here.[15] I would affirm this judgment.

Mr. Justice BRENNAN, with whom THE CHIEF JUSTICE and Mr. Justice DOUGLAS join, dissenting.

When Nestor quit the Communist Party in 1939 his past membership was not a ground for his deportation. Kessler v. Strecker, 307 U.S. 22, 59 S.Ct. 694, 83 L.Ed. 1082. It was not until a year later that past membership was made a specific ground for deportation.[16] This past membership has cost Nestor dear. It brought him expulsion from the country after 43 years' residence—most of his life. Now more is exacted from him, for after he had begun to receive benefits in 1955—having worked in covered employment the required time and reached age 65—and might anticipate receiving them the rest of his life, the benefits were stopped pursuant to § 202(n) of the Amended Social Security Act.[17] His predicament is very real—an aging man deprived of the means with which to live after being separated from his family and exiled to live among strangers in a land he quit 47 years ago. The common sense of it is that he has been punished severely for his past conduct.

Even the 1950 statute deporting aliens for past membership raised serious questions in this Court whether the prohibition against *ex post facto* laws was violated.

In Galvan v. Press, 347 U.S. 522, 531, 74 S.Ct. 737, 742, 98 L.Ed. 911, we said "since the intrinsic consequences of deportation are so close to punishment for crime, it might fairly be said also that the *ex post facto* Clause, even though applicable only to punitive legislation, should be applied to deportation." However, precedents which treat deportation not as punishment, but as a permissible exercise of congressional power to enact the conditions under which aliens may come to and remain in this country, governed the decision in favor of the constitutionality of the statute.

However, the Court cannot rest a decision that § 202(n) does not impose punishment on Congress' power to regulate immigration. It escapes the common-sense conclusion that Congress has imposed punishment by finding the requisite rational nexus to a granted power in the supposed furtherance of the Social Security program "enacted pursuant to Congress' power to 'spend money in aid of the "general welfare.' " I do not understand the Court to deny that but for that connection, § 202(n) would impose punishment and not only offend the constitutional prohibition on *ex post facto* laws but also violate the constitutional guarantees against imposition of punishment without a judicial trial.

The Court's test of the constitutionality of § 202(n) is whether the legislative concern underlying the statute was to regulate "the activity or status from which the individual is barred" or whether the statute "is evidently aimed at the person or class of persons disqualified." It rejects the inference that the statute is "aimed at the person or class of persons disqualified" by relying upon the presumption of constitutionality. This presumption might be a basis for sustaining the statute if in fact there were two opposing inferences which could reasonably be drawn from the legislation, one that it imposes punishment and the other that it is purposed to further the administration of the Social Security program. The Court, however, does not limit the presumption to that use. Rather the presumption becomes a complete substitute for any supportable finding of a rational connection of § 202(n) with the Social Security program. For me it is not enough to state the test and hold that the presumption alone satisfies it. I find it necessary to examine the Act and its consequences to ascertain whether there is ground for the inference of a congressional concern with the administration of the Social Security program. Only after this inquiry would I consider the application of the presumption.

The Court seems to acknowledge that the statute bears harshly upon the individual disqualified, but states that this is permissible when a statute is enacted as a regulation of the activity. But surely the harshness of the consequences is itself a relevant consideration to the inquiry into the congressional purpose.[18] Cf. Trop v. Dulles, 356 U.S. 86, 110, (concurring opinion).

It seems to me that the statute itself shows that the sole legislative concern was with "the person or class of persons disqualified." Congress did not disqualify for benefits all beneficiaries residing abroad or even all dependents residing abroad who are aliens. If that had been the case I might agree that Congress' concern would have been with "the activity or status" and not with the "person or class of persons disqualified." The scales would then be tipped toward the conclusion that Congress desired to limit benefit payments to beneficiaries residing in the United States so that the American economy would be aided by expenditure of benefits here. Indeed a proposal along those lines was submitted to Congress in 1954, at the same time § 202(n) was proposed,[19] and it was rejected.[20]

Perhaps, the Court's conclusion that regulation of "the activity or status" was the congressional concern would be a fair appraisal of the statute if Congress had terminated the benefits of all alien beneficiaries who are deported. But that is not what Congress did. Section 202(n) applies only to aliens deported on one or more of 14 of the 18 grounds for which aliens may be deported.[21]

H.R.Rep No. 1698, 83d Cong., 2d Sess. 25, 77, cited by the Court, describes § 202(n) as including persons who were deported "because of unlawful entry, conviction of a crime, or subversive activity." The section, in addition, covers those deported for such socially condemned acts as narcotic addiction or prostitution. The common element of the 14 grounds is that the alien has been guilty of some blameworthy conduct. In other words Congress worked its will only on aliens deported for conduct displeasing to the lawmakers.

This is plainly demonstrated by the remaining four grounds of deportation, those which do not result in the cancellation of benefits.[22] Two of those four grounds cover persons who become public charges within five years after entry for reasons which predated the entry. A third ground covers the alien who fails to maintain his nonimmigrant status. The fourth ground reaches the alien who, prior to or within five years after entry, aids other aliens to enter the country illegally.

Those who are deported for becoming public charges clearly have not, by modern standards, engaged in conduct worthy of censure. The Government's suggestion that the reason for their exclusion from § 202(n) was an unarticulated feeling of Congress that it would be unfair to the "other country to deport such destitute persons without letting them retain their modicum of social security benefits" appears at best fanciful, especially since, by hypothesis, they are deportable because the conditions which lead to their becoming public charges existed prior to entry.

The exclusion from the operation of § 202(n) of aliens deported for failure to maintain nonimmigrant status rationally can be explained, in the context of the whole statute, only as evidencing that Congress considered that conduct less blameworthy. Certainly the Government's suggestion that Congress may have thought it unlikely that such persons would work sufficient time in covered employment to become eligible for Social Security benefits cannot be the reason for this exclusion. For frequently the very act which eventually results in the deportation of persons on that ground is the securing of private employment. Finally, it is impossible to reconcile the continuation of benefits to aliens who are deported for aiding other aliens to enter the country illegally, except upon the ground that Congress felt that their conduct was less reprehensible. Again the Government's suggestion that the reason might be Congress' belief that these aliens would not have worked in covered employment must be rejected. Five years after entry would be ample time within which to secure employment and qualify. Moreover the same five-year limitation applies to several of the 14 grounds of deportation for which aliens are cut off from benefits and the Government's argument would apply equally to them if that in fact was the congressional reason.

This appraisal of the distinctions drawn by Congress between various kinds of conduct impels the conclusion, beyond peradventure that the distinctions can be understood only if the purpose of Congress was to strike at "the person or class of persons disqualified." The Court inveighs against invalidating a statute on "implication and vague conjecture." Rather I think the Court has strained to sustain the statute on "implication and vague conjecture," in holding that the congressional concern was "the activity or status from which the individual is barred." Today's decision sanctions the use of the spending power not to further the legitimate objections of the Social Security program but to inflict hurt upon those who by their conduct have incurred the displeasure of Congress. The Framers ordained that even the worst of men should not be punished for their past acts or for any conduct without adherence to the procedural safeguards written into the Constitution. Today's decision is to me a regretful retreat from Lovett, Cummings and Garland.

Section 202(n) imposes punishment in violation of the prohibition against *ex post facto* laws and without a judicial trial.[23] I therefore dissent.

NOTES

1. Section 202(n) provides as follows:
"(n) (1) If any individual is (after the date of enactment of this subsection) deported under paragraph (1), (2), (4), (5), (6), (7), (10), (11), (12), (14), (15), (16), (17), or (18), of section 241 (a) of the Immigration and Nationality Act, then, notwithstanding any other provisions of this title—

"(A) no monthly benefit under this section or section 223 [42 U.S.C. § 423, relating to "disability insurance benefits"] shall be paid to such individual, on the basis of his wages and self-employment income, for any month occurring (i) after the month in which the Secretary is notified by the Attorney General that such individual has been so deported, and (ii) before the month in which such individual is thereafter lawfully admitted to the United States for permanent residence,

"(B) if no benefit could be paid to such individual (or if no benefit could be paid to him if he were alive) for any month by reason of subparagraph (A), no monthly benefit under this section shall be paid, on the basis of his wages and self-employment income, for such month to any other person who is not a citizen of the United States and is outside the United States for any part of such month, and

"(C) no lump-sum death payment shall be made on the basis of such individual's wages and self-employment income if he dies (i) in or after the month in which such notice is received, and (ii) before the month in which he is thereafter lawfully admitted to the United States for permanent residence.

"Section 203(b) and (c) of this Act shall not apply with respect to any such individual for any month for which no monthly benefit may be paid to him by reason of this paragraph.

"(2) As soon as practicable after the deportation of any individual under any of the paragraphs of section 241(a) of the Immigration and Nationality Act enumerated in paragraph (1) in this subsection, the Attorney General shall notify the Secretary of such deportation."

The provisions of § 241(a) of the Immigration and Nationality Act are summarized in notes 10, 13, post, 363 U.S. at pages 618, 620, 80 S.Ct. at pages 1376, 1378.

2. Under paragraph (1) (B) of § 202(n) (see note 1, ante), appellee's wife, because of her residence here, has remained eligible for benefits payable to her as the wife of an insured individual. See § 202(b), 53 Stat. 1364, as amended, 42 U.S.C. § 402(b), 42 U.S.C.A. § 402(b).

3. Art. I, § 9, cl. 3:
"No Bill of Attainder or *ex post facto* Law shall be passed."
Art. III, § 2, cl. 3:
"The Trial of all Crimes, except in Cases of Impeachment, shall be Jury; and such Trial shall be held in the State where the said Crimes shall have been committed * * * "
Amend. VI:
"In all criminal prosecutions, the accused shall enjoy the right to a speedy and public trial, by an impartial jury of the State and district wherein the crime shall have been committed, which district shall have been previously ascertained by law, and to be informed of the nature and cause of the accusation; to be confronted with the witnesses against him; to have compulsory process for obtaining witnesses in his favor, and to have the assistance of counsel for his defence."

4. Appellee also adds, but hardly argues, the contention that he has been deprived of his rights under the First Amendment, since the adverse consequences stemmed from "mere past membership" in the Communist Party. This contention, which is no more than a collateral attack on appellee's deportation, is not open to him.

5. See also Pierce v. Carskadon, 16 Wall. 234, 21 L.Ed. 276. A West Virginia statute providing that a nonresident who had suffered a judgment in an action commenced by attachment, but in which he had not been personally served and did not appear, could within one year petition the court for a reopening of the judgment and a trial on the merits, was

amended in 1865 so as to condition that right on the taking of an exculpatory oath that the defendant had never supported the Confederacy. On the authority of Cummings and Garland, the amendment was invalidated.

6.   As prior decisions make clear, compare Ex parte Garland, supra, with Hawker v. New York, supra, the severity of a sanction is not determinative of its character as "punishment."

7.   Paragraphs (1), (2), and (10) of § 241 (a) relate to unlawful entry, or entry not complying with certain conditions; paragraphs (6) and (7) apply to "subversive" and related activities; the remainder of the included paragraphs are concerned with convictions of designated crimes, or the commission of acts related to them, such as narcotics addiction or prostitution.

8.   For example, under the House version termination of benefits of a deportee would also have terminated benefits paid to secondary beneficiaries based on the earning records of the deportee. The Conference proposal limited this effect to secondary beneficiaries who were nonresident aliens. See note 2, ante.

9.   Appellee also relies on the juxtaposition of the proposed § 108 and certain other provisions, some of which were enacted and some of which were not. This argument is too conjectural to warrant discussion. In addition, reliance is placed on a letter written to the Senate Finance Committee by appellant's predecessor in office, opposing the enactment of what is now § 202(u) of the Act, 70 Stat. 838, 42 U.S.C. § 402(u), 42 U.S.C.A. § 402(u), on the ground that the section was "in the nature of a penalty and based on considerations foreign to the objectives" of the program. Social Security Amendments of 1955. Hearings before the Senate Committee on Finance, 84th Cong., 2d Sess., p. 1319. The Secretary went on to say that "present law recognizes only three narrowly limited exceptions [of which § 202(n) is one] to the basic principle that benefits are paid without regard to the attitudes, opinions, behavior, or personal characteristics of the individual * * *." It should be observed, however, that the Secretary did not speak of § 202(n) as a penalty, as he did of the proposed § 202(u). The latter provision is concededly penal, and applies only pursuant to a judgment of a court in a criminal case.

10.   They are: (1) persons institutionalized at public expense within five years after entry because of "mental disease, defect, or deficiency" not shown to have arisen subsequent to admission (§ 241(a) (3)); (2) persons becoming a public charge within five years after entry from causes not shown to have arisen subsequent to admission § 241(a) (8)); (3) persons admitted as nonimmigrants (see § 101(a) (15), 66 Stat. 167, 8 U.S.C. § 1101(a) (15), 8 U.S.C.A. § 1101(a) (15)) who fail to maintain, or comply with the conditions of, such status (§ 241(a) (9)); (4) persons knowingly and for gain inducing or aiding, prior to or within five years after entry, any other alien to enter or attempt to enter unlawfully (§ 241 (a) (13)).

11.   Were we to engage in speculation, it would not be difficult to conjecture that Congress may have been led to exclude these four grounds of deportation out of compassionate or de minimis considerations.

12.   Address entitled Bills of Attainder in 1787 and Today. Columbia Law Review dinner 1954, published in 1959 by the Emergency Civil Liberties Committee, under the title Congressional Investigations and Bills of Attainder.

13.   The broad sweep of the idea of punishment behind the concept of the bill of attainder was stated as follows by Irving Brant, op. cit. supra, note 1, 9–10:
"In 1794 the American people were in a state of excitement comparable to that which exists today. Supporters of the French Revolution had organized the Democratic Societies— blatantly adopting that subversive title. Then the Whisky Rebellion exploded in Western Pennsylvania. The Democratic Societies were blamed. A motion censuring the Societies was introduced in the House of Representatives.

"There, in 1794, you had the basic division in American thought—on one side the doctrine of political liberty for everybody, with collective security resting on the capacity of the people for self-government; on the other side the doctrine that the people could not be trusted and political liberty must be restrained.

"James Madison challenged this latter doctrine. The investigative power of Congress over persons, he contended, was limited to inquiry into the conduct of individuals in the public service. 'Opinions,' he said, 'are not the subjects of legislation.' Start criticizing people for abuse of their reserved rights, and the censure might extend to freedom of speech and press. What would be the effect on the people thus condemned? Said Madison:

" 'It is in vain to say that this indiscriminate censure is no punishment. * * * Is not this proposition, if voted, a bill of attainder?'

"Madison won his fight, not because he called the resolution a bill of attainder, but because it attainted too many men who were going to vote in the next election. The definition, however, was there—a bill of attainder—and the definition was given by the foremost American authority on the principles of liberty and order underlying our system of government."

14.   The three exceptions referred to were (1) § 202(n); (2) Act of September 1, 1954, 68 Stat. 1142, 5 U.S.C. §§ 2281–2288, 5 U.S.C.A. §§ 2281–2288; (3) Regulation of the Social Security Administration, 20 CFR § 403.409—denying dependent's benefits to a person found guilty of felonious homicide of the insured worker.

15.   Brandt, op cit., supra, note 1, states at p. 9:
"What were the framers aiming at when they forbade bills of attainder? They were, of course, guarding against the religious passions that disgraced Christianity in Europe. But American bills of attainder, just before 1787, were typically used by Revolutionary assemblies to rid the states of British Loyalists. By a curious coincidence, it was usually the Tory with a good farm who was sent into exile, and all too often it was somebody who wanted that farm who induced the legislature to attaint him. Patriotism could serve as a cloak for greed as easily as religion did in that Irish Parliament of James the Second.

"But consider a case in which nothing could be said against the motive. During the Revolution, Governor Patrick Henry induced the Virginia legislature to pass a bill of attainder condemning Josiah Phillips to death. He was a traitor, a murderer, a pirate and an outlaw. When ratification of the new Constitution came before the Virginia convention, Henry inveighed against it because it contained no Bill of Rights. Edmund Randolph taunted him with his sponsorship of the Phillips bill of attainder. Henry then made the blunder of defending it. The bill was warranted, he said, because Phillips was no Socrates. That shocking defense of arbitrary condemnation may have produced the small margin by which the Constitution was ratified."

16.   The Alien Registration Act, 1940, 54 Stat. 673, made membership in an organization which advocates the overthrow of the government of the United States by force or violence a ground for deportation even though the membership was terminated prior to the passage of that statute. See Harisiades v. Shaughnessy, 342 U.S. 580, 72 S.Ct. 512, 96 L. Ed. 586. Until the passage of the Internal Security Act of

1950, 64 Stat. 1006, 1008, it was necessary for the Government to prove in each case in which it sought to deport an alien because of membership in the Communist Party that that organization in fact advocated the violent overthrow of the Government. The 1950 Act expressly made deportable aliens who at the time of entry, or at any time thereafter were "members of or affiliated with * * * the Communist Party of the United States." See Galvan v. Press, 347 U.S. 522, 529, 74 S.Ct. 737, 742, 98 L.Ed. 911.

17. A comparable annuity was worth, at the time appellee's benefits were canceled, approximately $6,000. To date he has lost nearly $2,500 in benefits.

18. The Court, recognizing that Cummings v. Missouri, 4 Wall. 277, 18 L.Ed. 356, and Ex parte Garland, 4 Wall. 333, 18 L.Ed. 366, strongly favor the conclusion that § 202(n) was enacted with punitive intent, rejects the force of those precedents as drawing "heavily on the Court's firsthand acquaintance with the events and the mood of the then recent Civil War, and 'the fierce passions which that struggle aroused.' " This seems to be to say that the provision of § 202(n) which cuts off benefits from aliens deported for past Communist Party membership was not enacted in a similar atmosphere. Our judicial detachment from the realities of the national scene should not carry us so far. Our memory of the emotional climate stirred by the question of communism in the early 1950's cannot be so short.

19. See H.R.Rep. No. 1698, 83d Cong., 2d Sess. 24–25.

20. See S.Rep. No. 1987, 83d Cong., 2d Sess. 23; H.R.Conf.Rep. No. 2679, 83d Cong., 2d Sess. 4.

21. See Court's opinion, ante, note 1.

22. See the Court's opinion, ante, note 13.

23. It is unnecessary for me to reach the question whether the statute also constitutes a bill of attainder.

EDMUND L. PINCOFFS

Classical Retributivism*

I

The classification of Kant as a retributivist[1] is usually accompanied by a reference to some part of the following passage from the *Rechtslehre*, which is worth quoting at length.

Juridical punishment can never be administered merely as a means for promoting another good either with regard to the criminal himself or to civil society, but must in all cases be imposed only because the individual on whom it is inflicted *has committed a crime.* For one man ought never to be dealt with merely as a means subservient to the purpose of another, nor be mixed up with the subjects of real right. Against such treatment his inborn personality has a right to protect him, even though he may be condemned to lose his civil personality. He must first be found guilty and *punishable* before there can be any thought of drawing from his punishment any benefit for himself or his fellow-citizens. The penal law is a categorical imperative; and woe to him who creeps through the serpent-windings of utilitarianism to discover some advantage that may discharge him from the justice of punishment, or even from the due measure of it, according to the Pharisaic maxim: "It is better that *one* man should die than the whole people should perish." For if justice and righteousness perish, human life would no longer have any value in the world. . . .

But what is the mode and measure of punishment which public justice takes as its principle and standard? It is just the principle of equality, by which the pointer of the scale of justice is made to incline no more to the one side than the other. It may be rendered by saying that the undeserved evil which any one commits on another, is to be regarded as perpetrated on himself. Hence it may be said: "If you slander another, you slander yourself; if you steal from another, you steal from yourself; if you strike another, you strike yourself; if you kill another, you kill yourself." This is the Right of RETALIATION *(jus talionis);* and properly under-

stood, it is the only principle which in regulating a public court, as distinguished from mere private judgment, can definitely assign both the quality and the quantity of a just penalty. All other standards are wavering and uncertain; and on account of other considerations involved in them, they contain no principle conformable to the sentence of pure and strict justice.[2]

Obviously we could mull over this passage for a long time. What, exactly, is the distinction between the Inborn and the Civil Personality? How is the Penal Law a Categorical Imperative: by derivation from one of the five formulations in the *Grundlegung,* or as a separate formulation? But we are on the trail of the traditional retributive theory of punishment and do not want to lose ourselves in niceties. There are two main points in this passage to which we should give particular attention:

i. The only acceptable reason for punishing a man is that he has committed a crime.
ii. The only acceptable reason for punishing a man in a given manner and degree is that the punishment is "equal" to the crime for which he is punished.

These propositions, I think it will be agreed, express the main points of the first and second paragraphs respectively. Before stopping over these points, let us go on to a third. It is brought out in the following passage from the *Rechtslehre,* which is also often referred to by writers on retributivism.

Even if a civil society resolved to dissolve itself with the consent of all its members—as might be supposed in the case of a people inhabiting an island resolving to separate and scatter themselves throughout the whole world—the last murderer lying in prison ought to be executed before the resolution was carried out. This ought to be done in order that every one may realize the desert of his deeds, and that bloodguiltiness may not remain upon the people; for otherwise they will all be regarded as participators in the murder as a public violation of justice.[3]

*From *The Rationale of Legal Punishment* by Edmund L. Pincoffs (New York: Humanities Press, Inc., 1966), pp. 2–16. Reprinted by permission of the author and the publisher.

It is apparent from this passage that, so far anyway as the punishment of death for murder is concerned, the punishment awarded not only may but must be carried out. If it must be carried out "so that everyone may realize the desert of his deeds," then punishment for deeds other than murder must be carried out too. We will take it, then, that Kant holds that:

    iii. Whoever commits a crime must be punished in accordance with his desert.

Whereas (i) tells us what kind of reason we must have *if* we punish, (iii) now tells us that we must punish *whenever* there is desert of punishment. Punishment, Kant tells us elsewhere, is "The *juridical* effect or consequence of a culpable act of Demerit."[4] Any crime is a culpable act of demerit, in that it is an "*intentional* transgression—that is, an act accompanied with the consciousness that it is a transgression."[5] This is an unusually narrow definition of crime, since crime is not ordinarily limited to intentional acts of transgression, but may also include unintentional ones, such as acts done in ignorance of the law, and criminally negligent acts. However, Kant apparently leaves room for "culpable acts of demerit" outside of the category of crime. These he calls "faults," which are unintentional transgressions of duty, but "are nevertheless imputable to a person."[6] I can only suppose, though it is a difficulty in the interpretation of the *Rechtslehre,* that when Kant says that punishment must be inflicted "only because he has committed a crime," he is not including in "crime" what he would call a fault. Crime would, then, refer to any *intentional* imputable transgressions of duty; and these are what must be punished as involving ill desert. The difficulties involved in the definition of crime as the transgression of duty, as opposed to the mere violation of a legal prohibition, will be taken up later.

Taking the three propositions we have isolated as expressing the essence of the Kantian retributivistic position, we must now ask a direct and obvious question. What makes Kant hold this position? Why does he think it apparent that consequences should have *nothing to do* with the decision whether, and how, and how much to punish? There are two directions an answer to this question might follow. One would lead us into an extensive excursus on the philosophical position of Kant, the relation of this to his ethical theory, and the relation of his general theory of ethics to his philosophy of law. It would, in short, take our question as one about the consistency of Kant's position concerning the justification of punishment with the whole of the Kantian philosophy. This would involve discussion of Kant's reasons for believing that moral laws must be universal and categorical in virtue of their form alone, and divorced from any empirical content; of his attempt to make out a moral decision-procedure based upon an "empty" categorical imperative; and, above all, of the concept of freedom as a postulate of practical reason, and as the central concept of the philosophy of law. This kind of answer, however, we must forego here; for while it would have considerable interest in its own right, it would lead us astray from our purpose, which is to understand as well as we can the retributivist position, not as a part of this or that philosophical system but for its own sake. It is a position taken by philosophers with diverse philosophical systems; we want to take another direction, then, in our answer. Is there any *general* (nonspecial, nonsystematic) reason why Kant rejects consequences in the justification of punishment?

Kant believes that consequences have nothing to do with the justification of punishment partly because of his assumptions about the *direction* of justification; and these assumptions are, I believe, also to be found underlying the thought of Hegel and Bradley. Justification is not only *of* something, it is also *to* someone: it has an addressee. Now there are important confusions in Kant's and other traditional justifications of punishment turning on the question what the "punishment" *is* which is being justified. In Chapter IV, we will examine some of these. But if we are to feel the force of the retributivist position, we can no longer put off the question of the addressee of justification.

To whom is the Kantian justification of punishment directed? The question may seem a difficult one to answer, since Kant does not consider it himself as a separate issue. Indeed, it is not the kind of question likely to occur to a philosopher of Kant's formalistic leanings. A Kantian justification or rationale stands, so to speak, on its own. It is a structure which can be examined, tested, probed by any rational being. Even to speak of the addressee of justification has an uncomfortably relativistic sound, as if only persuasion of A or B or C is possible, and proof impossible. Yet, in practice, Kant does not address his proffered justification of punishment so much to any rational being (which, to put it otherwise, is to address it not at all), as to the being most affected: the criminal himself.

It is the criminal who is cautioned not to creep

through the serpent-windings of utilitarianism. It is the criminal's rights which are in question in the debate with Beccaria over capital punishment. It is the criminal we are warned not to mix up with property or things: the "subjects of Real Right." In the *Kritik der Praktischen Vernunst,* the intended direction of justification becomes especially clear.

Now the notion of punishment, as such, cannot be united with that of becoming a partaker of happiness; for although he who inflicts the punishment may at the same time have the benevolent purpose of directing this punishment to this end, yet it must be justified in itself as punishment, that is, as mere harm, so that if it stopped there, and the person punished could get no glimpse of kindness hidden behind this harshness, he must yet admit that justice was done him, and that his reward was perfectly suitable to his conduct. In every punishment, as such, there must first be justice, and this constitutes the essence of the notion. Benevolence may, indeed, be united with it, but the man who has deserved punishment has not the least reason to reckon upon this.[7]

Since this matter of the direction of justification is central in our understanding of traditional retributivism, and not generally appreciated, it will be worth our while to pause over this paragraph. Kant holds here, as he later holds in the *Rechtslehre,* that once it has been decided that a given "mode and measure" of punishment is justified, then "he who inflicts punishment" may do so in such a way as to increase the long-term happiness of the criminal. This could be accomplished, for example, by using a prison term as an opportunity for reforming the criminal. But Kant's point is that reforming the criminal has nothing to do with justifying the infliction of punishment. It is not inflicted because it will give an opportunity for reform, but because it is merited. The passage does not need my gloss; it is transparently clear. Kant wants the justification of punishment to be such that the criminal "who could get no glimpse of kindness behind this harshness" would have to admit that punishment is warranted.

Suppose we tell the criminal, "We are punishing you for your own good." This is wrong, because it is then open to him to raise the question whether he deserves punishment, and what you consider good to be. If he does not deserve punishment, we have no right to inflict it, especially in the name of some good of which the criminal may not approve. So long as we are to treat him

as rational—a being with dignity—we cannot force our judgments of good upon him. This is what makes the appeal to supposedly good consequences "wavering and uncertain." They waver because the criminal has as much right as anyone to question them. They concern ends which he may reject, and means which he might rightly regard as unsuited to the ends.

In the "Supplementary Explanations of the Principles of Right" of the *Rechtslehre,* Kant distinguishes between "punitive justice *(justitia punitiva),* in which the ground of the penalty is moral *(quia peccatum est),*" and "punitive *expediency,* the foundation of which is merely pragmatic *(ne peccetur)* as being grounded upon the experience of what operates most effectively to prevent crime." Punitive justice, says Kant, has an "entirely distinct place *(locus justi)* in the topical arrangement of the juridical conceptions." It does not seem reasonable to suppose that Kant makes this distinction merely to discard punitive expediency entirely, that he has no concern at all for the *ne peccetur.* But he does hold that there is no place for it in the justification of punishment proper: for this can only be to show the criminal that the punishment is just.

How is this to be done? The difficulty is that on the one hand the criminal must be treated as a rational being, an end in himself; but on the other hand the justification we offer him cannot be allowed to appear as the opening move in a rational discussion. It cannot turn on the criminal's acceptance of some premise which, as rational being, he has a perfect right to question. If the end in question is the well-being of society, we are assuming that the criminal will not have a different view of what that well-being consists in, and we are telling him that he should sacrifice himself *to* that end. As a rational being, he can question whether any end we propose is a good end. And we have no right to demand that he sacrifice himself to the public well-being, even supposing he agrees with us on what that consists in. No man has a duty, on Kant's view, to be benevolent.[8]

The way out of the quandary is to show the criminal that we are not inflicting the punishment on him for some questionable purpose of our own choice, but that he, as a free agent, has exercised *his* choice in such a way as to make the punishment a necessary consequence. "His own evil deed draws the punishment upon himself."[9] "The undeserved evil which anyone commits on another, is to be regarded as perpetuated on himself."[10] But may not the criminal rationally question this asserted connection between crime and punishment? Suppose he wishes to regard the punishment *not* as "drawn upon himself" by his own "evil deed?" Suppose he argues that no good purpose will be served by punishing him? But this line of thought leads into the "serpent-windings of utilitarianism," for if it is good consequences that govern, then justice goes by the board. What may not be done to him in the name of good consequences? What proportion would remain between what he has done and what he suffers?[11]

But punishment is *inflicted*. To tell the criminal that he "draws it upon himself" is all very well, only how do we justify *to ourselves* the infliction of it? Kant's answer is found early in the *Rechtslehre*.[12] There he relates punishment to crime *via* freedom. Crime consists in compulsion or constraint of some kind: a hindrance of freedom.[13] If it is wrong that freedom should be hindered, it is right to block this hindrance. But to block the constraint of freedom it is necessary to apply constraint. Punishment is a "hindering of a hindrance of freedom." Compulsion of the criminal is, then, justified only to the extent that it hinders his compulsion of another.

But how are we to understand Kant here? Punishment comes after the crime. How can it hinder the crime? The reference cannot be to the hindrance of future crime, or Kant's doctrine reduces to a variety of utilitarianism. The picture of compulsion *vs.* compulsion is clear enough, but how are we to apply it? Our answer must be somewhat speculative, since there is no direct answer to be found in the *Rechtslehre*. The answer must begin from yet another extension of the concept of a crime. For the crime cannot consist merely in an act. What is criminal is acting in accordance with a wrong maxim: a maxim which would, if made universal, destroy freedom. The adoption of the maxim is criminal. Should we regard punishment, then, as the hindrance of a wrong maxim? But how do we hinder a maxim? We show, exhibit, its wrongness by taking it at face value. If the criminal has adopted it, he is claiming that it can be universalized. But if it is universalized it warrants the same treatment of the criminal as he has accorded to his victim. So if he murders he must be executed; if he steals we must "steal from" him.[14] What we do to him he willed, in willing to adopt his maxim as universalizable. To justify the punishment to the criminal is to show him that the compulsion we use on him proceeds according to the same rule by which he acts. This is how he "draws the punishment upon himself." In punishing, we are not adopting his maxim but demonstrating its logical conse-

quences if universalized: We show the criminal *what* he has willed. This is the positive side of the Kantian rationale of punishment.

II

Hegel's version of this rationale has attracted more attention, and disagreement, in recent literature. It is the Hegelian metaphysical terminology which is in part responsible for the disagreement, and which has stood in the way of an understanding of the retributivist position. The difficulty turns around the notions of "annulment of crime," and of punishment as the "right" of the criminal. Let us consider "annulment" first.

In the *Philosophie des Rechts*[15] Hegel tells us that

Abstract right is a right to coerce, because the wrong which transgresses it is an exercise of force against the existence of my freedom in an external thing. The maintenance of this existent against the exercise of force therefore itself takes the form of an external act and an exercise of force annulling the force originally brought against it.[16]

Holmes complains that by the use of his logical apparatus, involving the negation of negations (or annulment), Hegel professes to establish what is only a mystic (though generally felt) bond between wrong and punishment.[17] Hastings Rashdall asks how any rational connection can be shown between the evil of the pain of punishment, and the twin evils of the suffering of the victim and the moral evil which "pollutes the offender's soul," unless appeal is made to the probable good consequences of punishment. The notion that the "guilt" of the offense must be, in some mysterious way, wiped out by the suffering of the offender does not seem to provide it.[18] Crime, which is an evil, is apparently to be "annulled" by the addition to it of punishment, which is another evil. How can two evils yield a good?[19]

But in fact Hegel is following the *Rechtslehre* quite closely here, and his doctrine is very near to Kant's. In the notes taken at Hegel's lectures,[20] we find Hegel quoted as follows:

If crime and its annulment . . . are treated as if they were unqualified evils, it must, of course, seem quite unreasonable to will an evil merely because "another evil is there already.". . . But it is not merely a question of an evil or of this, that, or the other good; the precise point at issue is wrong, and the righting of it. . . . The various considerations which are relevant to punishment as a phenomenon and to the bearing it has on the particular consciousness, and which concern its effects (deterrent, reformative, etcetera) on the imagination, are an essential topic for examination in their place, especially in connection with modes of punishment, but all these considerations presuppose as their foundation the fact that punishment is inherently and actually just. In discussing this matter the only important things are, first, that crime is to be annulled, not because it is the producing of an evil, but because it is the infringing of the right as right, and secondly, the question of what that positive existence is which crime possesses and which must be annulled; it is this existence which is the real evil to be removed, and the essential point is the question of where it lies. So long as the concepts here at issue are not clearly apprehended, confusion must continue to reign in the theory of punishment.[21]

While this passage is not likely to dethrone confusion, it does bring us closer to the basically Kantian heart of Hegel's theory. To "annul crime" should be read "right wrong." Crime is a wrong which consists in an "infringement of the right as right."[22] It would be unjust, says Hegel, to allow crime, which is the invasion of a right, to go unrequited. For to allow this is to admit that the crime is "valid": that is, that it is not in conflict with justice. But this is what we do want to admit, and the only way of showing this is to pay back the deed to the agent: coerce the coercer. For by intentionally violating his victim's rights, the criminal in effect claims that the rights of others are not binding on him; and this is to attack *das Recht* itself: the system of justice in which there are rights which must be respected. Punishment not only keeps the system in balance, it vindicates the system itself.

Besides talking about punishment's "annulment" of crime, Hegel has argued that it is the "right of the criminal." The obvious reaction to this is that it is a strange justification of punishment which makes it someone's right, for it is at best a strange kind of right which no one would ever want to claim! McTaggart's explanation of this facet of Hegel's theory is epitomized in the following quotation:

What, then, is Hegel's theory? It is, I think, briefly this: In sin, man rejects and defies the moral law. Punishment is pain inflicted on him because he has done this, and in order that he may, by the fact of his punishment, be forced into recognizing as valid the law which he rejected in sinning, and so repent of his sin—really

repent, and not merely be frightened out of doing it again.[23]

If McTaggart is right, then we are obviously not going to find in Hegel anything relevant to the justification of legal punishment, where the notions of sin and repentance are out of place. And this is the conclusion McTaggart of course reaches. "Hegel's view of punishment," he insists, "cannot properly be applied in jurisprudence, and . . . his chief mistake regarding it lay in supposing that it could."[24]

But though McTaggart may be right in emphasizing the theological aspect of Hegel's doctrine of punishment, he is wrong in denying it a jurisprudential aspect. In fact, Hegel is only saying what Kant emphasized: that to justify punishment to the criminal is to show him that *he* has chosen to be treated as he is being treated.

The injury (the penalty) which falls on the criminal is not merely *implicitly* just—as just, it is *eo ipso* his implicit will, an embodiment of his freedom, his right; on the contrary, it is also a right *established* within the criminal himself, that is, in his objectively embodied will, in his action. The reason for this is that his action is the action of a rational being and this implies that it is something universal and that by doing it the criminal has laid down a law which he has explicitly recognized in his action and under which in consequence he should be brought as under his right.[25]

To accept the retributivist position, then, is to accept a thesis about the burden of proof in the justification of punishment. Provided we make the punishment "equal" to the crime it is not up to us to justify it to the criminal, beyond pointing out to him that it is what he willed. It is not that he initiated a chain of events likely to result in his punishment, but that in willing the crime he willed that he himself should suffer in the same degree as his victim. But what if the criminal simply wanted to commit his crime and get away with it (break the window and run, take the funds and retire to Brazil, kill but live?) Suppose we explain to the criminal that *really* in willing to kill he willed to lose his life; and, unimpressed, he replies that *really* he wished to kill and save his skin. The retributivist answer is that to the extent that the criminal understands freedom and justice he will understand that his punishment was made inevitable by his own choice. No moral theory can hope to provide a justification of punishment which will seem such to the criminal merely as a nexus of passions and desires. The retributivist addresses him as a rational being, aware of the significance of his action. The burden of proof, the retributivist would argue, is on the theorist who would not start from this assumption. For to assume from the beginning that the criminal is not rational is to treat him, from the beginning, as merely a "harmful animal."

> What is involved in the action of the criminal is not only the concept of crime, the rational aspect present in crime as such whether the individual wills it or not, the aspect which the state has to vindicate, but also the abstract rationality of the individual's *volition*. Since that is so, punishment is regarded as containing the criminal's right and hence by being punished he is honored as a rational being. He does not receive this due of honor unless the concept and measure of his punishment are derived from his own act. Still less does he receive it if he is treated as a harmful animal who has to be made harmless, or with a view to deterring and reforming him.[26]

To address the criminal as a rational being aware of the significance of his action is to address him as a person who knows that he has not committed a "bare" act; to commit an act is to commit oneself to the universalization of the rule by which one acted. For a man to complain about the death sentence for murder is as absurd as for a man to complain that when he pushes down one tray of the scales, the other tray goes up; whereas the action, rightly considered, is of pushing down *and* up. "The criminal gives his consent already by his very act."[27] "The Eumenides sleep, but crime awakens them, and hence it is the very act of crime which vindicates itself."[28]

F. H. Bradley's contribution to the retributive theory of punishment adds heat but not much light. The central, and best-known, passage is the following:

> If there is any opinion to which the man of uncultivated morals is attached, it is the belief in the necessary connection of Punishment and guilt. Punishment is punishment, only where it is deserved. We pay the penalty because we owe it, and for no other reason; and if punishment is inflicted for any other reason whatever than because it is merited by wrong, it is a gross immorality, a crying injustice, an abominable crime, and not what it pretends to be. We may have regard for whatever considerations we please—our own convenience, the good of society, the benefit of the offender; we are fools, and worse, if we fail to do so. Having once the right to punish, we may modify the punishment according to the useful and the pleasant; but these are

external to the matter, they cannot give us a right to punish, and nothing can do that but criminal desert. This is not a subject to waste words over; if the fact of the vulgar view is not palpable to the reader, we have no hope, and no wish, to make it so.[29]

Bradley's sympathy with the "vulgar view" should be apparent.[30] And there is at least a seeming variation between the position he expresses here and that we have attributed to Kant and Hegel. For Bradley can be read here as leaving an open field for utilitarian reasoning, when the question is how and how much to punish. Ewing interprets Bradley this way, and argues at some length that Bradley is involved in an inconsistency.[31] However, it is quite possible that Bradley did not mean to allow kind and quantity of punishment to be determined by utilitarian considerations. He could mean, as Kant meant, that once punishment is awarded, then "it" (what the criminal must suffer: time in jail, for example) may be made use of for utilitarian purposes. But, it should by this time go without saying, the retributivist would then wish to insist that we not argue backward from the likelihood of attaining these good purposes to the rightness of inflicting the punishment.

Bradley's language is beyond question loose when he speaks, in the passage quoted, of our "modifying" the punishment, "having once the right to punish." But when he says that "we pay the penalty because we owe it, and for no other reason," Bradley must surely be credited with the insight that we may owe more or less according to the gravity of the crime. The popular view, he says, is "that punishment is justice; that justice implies the giving what is due."[32] And, "punishment is the complement of criminal desert; is justifiable only so far as deserved."[33] If Bradley accepts this popular view, then Ewing must be wrong in attributing to him the position that kind and degree of punishment may be determined by utilitarian considerations.[34]

III

Let us sum up traditional retributivism, as we have found it expressed in the paradigmatic passage we have examined. We have found no reason, in Hegel or Bradley, to take back or qualify importantly the *three propositions* we found central in Kant's retributivism:

  i. The only acceptable reason for punishing a man is that he has committed a crime.
  ii. The only acceptable reason for punishing a man in a given manner and degree is

that the punishment is "equal" to the crime.

iii. Whoever commits a crime must be punished in accordance with his desert.

To these propositions should be added *two underlying assumptions:*

i. An assumption about the direction of justification: to the criminal.

ii. An assumption about the nature of justification: to show the criminal that it is he who has willed what he now suffers.

Though it may have been stated in forbidding metaphysical terms, traditional retributivism cannot be dismissed as unintelligible, or absurd, or implausible.[35] There is no obvious contradiction in it; and there are no important disagreements among the philosophers we have studied over what it contends. Yet in spite of the importance of the theory, no one has yet done much more than sketch it in broad strokes. If, as I have surmised, it turns mainly on an assumption concerning the direction of justification, then this assumption should be explained and defended.

And the key concept of "desert" is intolerably vague. What does it mean to say that punishment must be proportionate to what a man *deserves?* This seems to imply, in the theory of the traditional retributivists, that there is some way of measuring desert, or at least of balancing punishment against it. How this measuring or balancing is supposed to be done, we will discuss later. What we must recognize here is that there are alternative criteria of "desert," and that it is not always clear which of these the traditional retributivist means to imply.

When we say of a man that he "deserves severe punishment" how, if at all, may we support our position by arguments? What kinds of considerations tend to show what a man does or does not deserve? There are at least two general sorts: those which tend to show that what he has done is a member of a class of actions which is especially heinous; and those which tend to show that his doing of this action was, in (or because of) the circumstances, particularly wicked. The argument that a man deserves punishment may rest on the first kind of appeal alone, or on both kinds. Retributivists who rely on the first sort of consideration alone would say that anyone who would do a certain sort of thing, no matter what the circumstances may have been, deserves punishment. Whether there are any such retributivists I do not know. Kant, because of his insistence on *intention* as a necessary condition of committing a crime, clearly wishes to bring in considerations of the second sort as well. It is not, on his view, merely *what* was done, but the intention of the agent which must be taken into account. No matter what the intention, a man cannot commit a crime deserving punishment if his deed is not a transgression. But if he does commit a transgression, he must do so intentionally to commit a crime; and all crime is deserving of punishment. The desert of the crime is a factor both of the seriousness of the transgression, considered by itself, and the degree to which the intention to transgress was present. If, for Kant, the essence of morality consists in knowingly acting from duty, the essence of immorality consists in knowingly acting against duty.

The retributivist can perhaps avoid the question of how we decide that one crime is morally more heinous than another by hewing to his position that no such decision is necessary so long as we make the punishment "equal" to the crime. To accomplish this, he might argue, it is not necessary to argue to the *relative* wickedness of crimes. But at best this leaves us with the problem how we *do* make punishments equal to crimes, a problem which will not stop plaguing retributivists. And there is the problem *which* transgressions, intentionally committed, the retributivist is to regard as crimes. Surely not every morally wrong action![36]

And how is the retributivist to fit in appeals to punitive expediency? None of our authors denies that such appeals may be made, but where and how do they tie into punitive justice? It will not do simply to say that justifying punishment to the criminal is one thing, and justifying it to society is another. Suppose we must justify in both directions at once? And who are "we" anyway—the players of which roles, at what stage of the game?[37] And has the retributivist cleared himself of the charge, sure to arise, that the theory is but a cover for a much less commendable motive than respect for justice: elegant draping for naked revenge?[38]

NOTES

1. ... since in our own time there are few defenders of retributivism, the position is most often referred to by writers who are opposed to it. This does not make for clarity. In the past few years, however, there has been an upsurge of interest, and some good articles have been written. Cf. esp. J. D. Mabbott, "Punishment," *Mind,* XLVIII (1939), pp. 152–67; C. S. Lewis, "The Humanitarian Theory of Punishment," *20th Century* (Australian), March, 1949; C. W. K. Mundle, "Punishment and Desert," *The Philosophical Quarterly,* IV (1954), pp. 216–228; A. S. Kaufman, "Anthony Quinton on Punishment," *Analysis,* October, 1959; and K. G. Armstrong, "The Retributivist Hits Back," LXX (1961), pp. 471–90.

2. *Rechtslehre*, Part Second, 49, E. Hastie translation, Edinburgh, 1887, pp. 195–7.

3. *Ibid.*, p. 198. Cf. also the passage on p. 196 beginning "What, then, is to be said of such a proposal as to keep a Criminal alive who has been condemned to death . . ."

4. *Ibid.*, Prolegomena, General Divisions of the Metaphysic of Morals, IV. (Hastie, p. 38).

5. *Ibid.*, p. 32.

6. *Ibid.*, p. 32.

7. Book I, Ch. I, Sect. VIII, Theorem IV, Remark II (T. K. Abbott translation, 5th ed., revised, London, 1898, p. 127).

8. *Rechtslehre.*

9. "Supplementary Explanation of The Principles of Right," V.

10. Cf. long quote from the *Rechtslehre*, above.

11. How can the retributivist allow utilitarian considerations even in the administration of the sentence? Are we not then opportunistically imposing our conception of good on the convicted man? How did we come by this right, which we did not have when he stood before the bar awaiting sentence? Kant would refer to the loss of his "Civil Personality;" but what rights remain with the "Inborn Personality," which is not lost? How is human dignity modified by conviction of crime?

12. Introduction to The Science of Right, General Definitions and Divisions, D. Right is Joined with the Title to Compel. (Hastie, p. 47).

13. This extends the definition of crime Kant has given earlier by specifying the nature of an imputable transgression of duty.

14. There are serious difficulties in the application of the "Principle of Equality" to the "mode and measure" of punishment. This will be considered . . .

15. I shall use this short title for the work with the formidable double title of *Naturrecht und Stattswissenschaft in Grundrisse; Grundlinien der Philosophie des Rechts (Natural Law and Political Science in Outline; Elements of The Philosophy of Right.)* References will be to the T. M. Knox translation (*Hegel's Philosophy of Right*, Oxford, 1942).

16. *Philosophie des Rechts*, Sect. 93 (Knox, p. 67).

17. O. W. Holmes, Jr., *The Common Law*, Boston, 1881, p. 42.

18. Hastings Rashdall, *The Theory of Good and Evil*, 2nd. Edn., Oxford, 1924, vol. 1, pp. 285–6.

19. G. E. Moore holds that, consistently with his doctrine of organic wholes, they might; or at least they might yield that which is less evil than the sum of the constituent evils. This indicates for him a possible vindication of the Retributive theory of punishment. (*Principia Ethica*, Cambridge, 1903, pp. 213–214).

20. Included in the Knox translation.

21. Knox translation, pp. 69–70.

22. There is an unfortunate ambiguity in the German word *Recht*, here translated as "right." The word can mean either that which is a right or that which is in accordance with the law. So when Hegel speaks of "infringing the right as right" it is not certain whether he means a right as such or the law as such, or whether, in fact, he is aware of the ambiguity. But to say that the crime infringes the law is analytic, so we will take it that Hegel uses *Recht* here to refer to that which is right. But what the criminal does is not merely to infringe a right, but "the right *(das recht)* as right," that is, to challenge by his action the whole system of rights. (On "*Recht,*" Cf. J. Austin, *The Province of Jurisprudence Determined,* London, Library of Ideas end., 1954), Note 26, pp. 285–288 esp. pp. 287–8.)

23. J. M. E. McTaggart, *Studies in The Hegelian Cosmology,* Cambridge, 1901, Ch. V, p. 133.

24. *Ibid.*, p. 145.

25. *Op. Cit.,* Sect. 100 (Hastie, p. 70.)

26. *Ibid.*, Lecture-notes on Sect. 100, Hastie, p. 71.

27. *Ibid.*, Addition to Sect. 100, Hastie, p. 246.

28. *Ibid.*, Addition to Sect. 101, Hastie, p. 247. There is something ineradicably *curious* about retributivism. We keep coming back to the metaphor of the balance scale. Why is the metaphor powerful and at the same time strange? Why do we agree so readily that "the assassination" cannot "trammel up the consequence," that "even-handed justice comments th' ingredients of our poisoned chalice to our own lips?"

29. F. H. Bradley, *Ethical Studies,* Oxford, 1952, pp. 26–7.

30. Yet it may not be amiss to note the part played by the "vulgar view" in Bradley's essay. In "The Vulgar Notion of Responsibility in Connection with the Theories of Free Will and Necessity," from which this passage is quoted, Bradley is concerned to show that neither the "Libertarian" nor the "Necessitarian" position can be accepted. Both of these "two great schools" which "divide our philosophy" "stand out of relation to vulgar morality." Bradley suggests that perhaps the truth is to be found not in either of these "two undying and opposite one-sidednesses but in a philosophy which "thinks what the vulgar believe." Cf. also the contrasting of the "ordinary consciousness" with the "philosophical" or "debauched" morality (p. 4). On p. 3 he says that by going to "vulgar morality" we "gain in integrity" what we "lose in refinement." Nevertheless, he does say (p. 4) "seeing the vulgar are after all the vulgar, we should not be at pains to agree with their superstitions."

31. A. C. Ewing, *The Morality of Punishment,* London, 1929, pp. 41–42.

32. *Op. Cit.,* p. 29.

33. *Ibid.*, p. 30.

34. *Op. Cit.,* p. 41.

35. Or, more ingeniously, "merely logical," the "elucidation of the use of a word;" answering the question, "When (logically) *can* we punish?" as opposed to the question answered by the utilitarians, "When (morally) *may* or *ought* we to punish?" (Cf. A. M. Quinton, "On Punishment," *Analysis,* June, 1954, pp. 133–142)

36. Cf. Ch. V. [of *The Rationale of Legal Punishment* eds.]

37. Distinctions to be made in Chapter III. [*id.* eds.]

38. To be discussed in the next chapter. [*id.* eds.]

JEREMY BENTHAM

The Utilitarian Theory of Punishment[*]

CASES UNMEET FOR PUNISHMENT

§ 1. GENERAL VIEW OF CASES UNMEET FOR PUNISHMENT

I. *The end of law is, to augment happiness.* The general object which all laws have, or ought to have, in common, is to augment the total happiness of the community; and therefore, in the first place, to exclude, as far as may be, everything that tends to subtract from that happiness: in other words, to exclude mischief.

II. *But punishment is an evil.* But all punishment is mischief: all punishment in itself is evil. Upon the principle of utility, if it ought at all to be admitted, it ought only to be admitted in as far as it promises to exclude some greater evil.

III. *Therefore ought not to be admitted;* It is plain, therefore, that in the following cases punishment ought not to be inflicted.

1. *Where groundless.* Where it is *groundless:* where there is no mischief for it to prevent; the act not being mischievous upon the whole.

2. *Inefficacious.* Where it must be *inefficacious:* where it cannot act so as to prevent the mischief.

3. *Unprofitable.* Where it is *unprofitable,* or too *expensive:* where the mischief it would produce would be greater than what it prevented.

4. *Or needless.* Where it is *needless:* where the mischief may be prevented, or cease of itself, without it: that is, at a cheaper rate.

§ 2. CASES IN WHICH PUNISHMENT IS GROUNDLESS

These are,

IV. 1. *Where there has never been any mischief: as in the case of consent.* Where there has never been any mischief: where no mischief has been produced to anybody by the act in question. Of this number are those in which the act was such as might, on some occasions, be mischievous or disagreeable, but the person whose interest it

concerns gave his *consent* to the performance of it. This consent, provided it be free, and fairly obtained, is the best proof that can be produced, that, to the person who gives it, no mischief, at least no immediate mischief, upon the whole, is done. For no man can be so good a judge as the man himself, what it is gives him pleasure or displeasure.

V. 2. *Where the mischief was outweighed: as in precaution against calamity, and the exercise of powers.* Where the mischief was *outweighed:* although a mischief was produced by that act, yet the same act was necessary to the production of a benefit which was of greater value than the mischief. This may be the case with any thing that is done in the way of precaution against instant calamity, as also with any thing that is done in the exercise of the several sorts of powers necessary to be established in every community, to wit, domestic, judicial, military, and supreme.

VI. 3. *—or will, for a certainty be cured by compensation.* Where there is a certainty of an adequate compensation: and that in all cases where the offence can be committed. This supposes two things: 1. That the offence is such as admits of an adequate compensation: 2. That such a compensation is sure to be forthcoming. Of these suppositions, the latter will be found to be a merely ideal one: a supposition that cannot, in the universality here given to it, be verified by fact. It cannot, therefore, in practice, be numbered amongst the grounds of absolute impunity. It may, however, be admitted as a ground for an abatement of that punishment, which other considerations, standing by themselves, would seem to dictate.

§ 3. CASES IN WHICH PUNISHMENT MUST BE INEFFICACIOUS

These are,

VII. 1. *Where the penal provision comes too late: as in,* 1. *An ex-post-facto law,* 2. *An ultra-legal sentence.* Where the penal provision is *not* established until after the act is done. Such are

[*]From *Introduction to the Principles of Morals and Legislation.* Excerpted from the 1823 edition (first published in 1789). Footnotes edited.

the cases, 1. Of an *ex-post-facto* law; where the legislator himself appoints not a punishment till after the act is done. 2. Of a sentence beyond the law; where the judge, of his own authority, appoints a punishment which the legislator had not appointed.

VIII. 2. *Or is not made known: as in a law not sufficiently promulgated.* Where the penal provision, though established is *not conveyed* to the notice of the person on whom it seems intended that it should operate. Such is the case where the law has omitted to employ any of the expedients which are necessary, to make sure that every person whatsoever, who is within the reach of the law, be apprized of all the cases whatsoever, in which (being in the station of life he is in) he can be subjected to the penalties of the law.

IX. 3. *Where the will cannot be deterred from any act: as in,* Where the penal provision, though it were conveyed to a man's notice *could produce no effect* on him, with respect to the preventing him from engaging in any act of the *sort* in question. Such is the case, 1. In extreme *infancy;* where a man has not yet attained that state or disposition of mind in which the prospect of evils so distant as those which are held forth by the law, has the effect of influencing his conduct. 2. In *insanity;* where the person, if he has attained to that disposition, has since been deprived of it through the influence of some permanent though unseen cause. 3. In *intoxication* where he has been deprived of it by the transient influence of a visible cause: such as the use of wine, opium, or other drugs, that act in this manner on the nervous system: which condition is indeed neither more nor less than a temporary insanity produced by an assignable cause.

X. 4. *Or not from the individual act in question, as in,* Where the penal provision (although, being conveyed to the party's notice, it might very well prevent his engaging in acts of the sort in question, provided he knew that it related to those acts) could not have this effect, with regard to the *individual* act he is about to engage in: to wit, because he knows not that it is of the number of those to which the penal provision relates. This may happen, 1. In the case of *unintentionality;* where he intends not to engage, and thereby knows not that he is about to engage, in the *act* in which eventually he is about to engage. 2. In the case of *unconsciousness;* where, although he may know that he is about to engage in the *act* itself, yet, from not knowing all the material *circumstances* attending it, he knows not of the *tendency* it has to produce that mischief, in

contemplation of which it has been made penal in most instances. 3. In the case of *missupposal;* where, although he may know of the tendency the act has to produce that degree of mischief, he supposes it, though mistakenly, to be attended with some circumstance, or set of circumstances, which, if it had been attended with, it would either not have been productive of that mischief, or have been productive of such a greater degree of good, as has determined the legislator in such a case not to make it penal.

XI. 5. *Or is acted on by an opposite superior force: as by,* Where, though the penal clause might exercise a full and prevailing influence, were it to act alone, yet by the *predominant* influence of some opposite cause upon the will, it must necessarily be ineffectual; because the evil which he sets himself about to undergo, in the case of his *not* engaging in the act, is so great, that the evil denounced by the penal clause, in case of his engaging in it, cannot appear greater. This may happen, 1. In the case of *physical danger;* where the evil is such as appears likely to be brought about by the unassisted powers of *nature.* 2. In the case of a *threatened mischief;* where it is such as appears likely to be brought about through the intentional and conscious agency of *man.*

XII. 6. *—or the bodily organs cannot follow its determination: as under* Where (though the penal clause may exert a full and prevailing influence over the *will* of the party) yet his *physical faculties* (owing to the predominant influence of some physical cause) are not in a condition to follow the determination of the will: insomuch that the act is absolutely *involuntary.* Such is the case of physical *compulsion* or *restraint,* by whatever means brought about; where the man's hand, for instance, is pushed against some object which his will disposes him *not* to touch; or tied down from touching some object which his will disposes him to touch.

§ 4. CASES WHERE PUNISHMENT IS UNPROFITABLE

These are,

XIII. 1. *Where, in the* sort *of case in question, the punishment would produce more evil than the offence would.* Where, on the one hand, the nature of the offence, on the other hand, that of the punishment, are, *in the ordinary state of things,* such, that when compared together, the evil of the latter will turn out to be greater than that of the former.

XIV. *Evil producible by a punishment—its four branches—viz.* Now the evil of the punishment divides itself into four branches, by which so many different sets of persons are affected. 1. The evil of *coercion* or *restraint:* or the pain which it gives a man not to be able to do the act, whatever it be, which by the apprehension of the punishment he is deterred from doing. This is felt by those by whom the law is *observed.* 2. The evil of *apprehension:* or the pain which a man, who has exposed himself to punishment, feels at the thoughts of undergoing it. This is felt by those by whom the law has been *broken,* and who feel themselves in *danger* of its being executed upon them. 3. The evil of *sufferance:* or the pain which a man feels, in virtue of punishment itself, from the time when he begins to undergo it. This is felt by those by whom the law is broken, and upon whom it comes actually to be executed. 4. The pain of sympathy, and the other *derivative* evils resulting to the persons who are in *connection* with the several classes of original sufferers just mentioned. Now of these four lots of evil, the first will be greater or less, according to the nature of the act from which the party is restrained: the second and third according to the nature of the punishment which stands annexed to that offence.

XV. *(The evil of the offence being different, according to the nature of the offence, cannot be represented here.)* On the other hand, as to the evil of the offence, this will also, of course, be greater or less, according to the nature of each offence. The proportion between the one evil and the other will therefore be different in the case of each particular offence. The cases, therefore, where punishment is unprofitable on this ground, can by no other means be discovered, than by an examination of each particular offence; which is what will be the business of the body of the work.

XVI. 2. *—or in the* individual *case in question: by reason of* Where, although in the *ordinary state* of things, the evil resulting from the punishment is not greater than the benefit which is likely to result from the force with which it operates, during the same space of time, towards the excluding the evil of the offences, yet it may have been rendered so by the influence of some *occasional circumstances.* In the number of these circumstances may be, 1. *The multitude of delinquents.* The multitude of delinquents at a particular juncture; being such as would increase, beyond the ordinary measure, the *quantum* of the second and third lots, and thereby also of a part of the fourth lot, in the evil of the punishment. 2. *The value of a delinquent's service.* The extraordinary value of the services of some one delinquent; in the case where the effect of the

punishment would be to deprive the community of the benefit of those services. 3. *The displeasure of the people.* The displeasure of the *people;* that is, of an indefinite number of the members of the *same* community, in cases where (owing to the influence of some occasional incident) they happen to conceive, that the offence or the offender ought not to be punished at all, or at least ought not to be punished in the way in question. 4. *The displeasure of foreign powers.* The displeasure of *foreign powers;* that is, of the governing body, or a considerable number of the members of some *foreign* community or communities, with which the community in question is connected.

§ 5. CASES WHERE PUNISHMENT IS NEEDLESS

These are,

XVII. 1. *Where the mischief is to be prevented at a cheaper rate; as,* Where the purpose of putting an end to the practice may be atained as effectually at a cheaper rate: by instruction, for instance, as well as by terror: by informing the understanding; as well as by exercising an immediate influence on the will. *By instruction.* This seems to be the case with respect to all those offences which consist in the disseminating pernicious principles in matters of *duty;* of whatever kind the duty be; whether political, or moral, or religious. And this, whether such principles be disseminated *under,* or even *without,* a sincere persuasion of their being beneficial. I say, even *without:* for though in such a case it is not instruction that can prevent the writer from endeavouring to inculcate his principles, yet it may the readers from adopting them: without which, his endeavouring to inculcate them will do no harm. In such a case, the sovereign will commonly have little need to take an active part: if it be the interest of *one* individual to inculcate principles that are pernicious, it will as surely be the interest of *other* individuals to expose them. But if the sovereign must needs takes a part in the controversy, the pen is the proper weapon to combat error with, not the sword.

OF THE PROPORTION BETWEEN PUNISHMENTS AND OFFENCES

I. *Recapitulation.* We have seen that the general object of all laws is to prevent mischief; that is to say, when it is worth while; but that, where there are no other means of doing this than punishment, there are four cases in which it is *not* worth while.

II. *Four objects of punishment.* When it *is* worth while, there are four subordinate designs or objects, which, in the course of his endeavours to compass, as far as may be, that one general object, a legislator, whose views are governed by the principle of utility, comes naturally to propose to himself.

III. 1. *1st Object—to prevent all offences.* His first, most extensive, and most eligible object, is to prevent, in as far as it is possible, and worth while, all sorts of offences whatsoever: in other words, so to manage, that no offence whatsoever may be committed.

IV. 2. *2d Object—to prevent the worst.* But if a man must needs commit an offence of some kind or other, the next object is to induce him to commit an offence *less* mischievous, *rather* than one *more* mischievous: in other words, to choose always the *least* mischievous, of two offences that will either of them suit his purpose.

V. 3. *3d Object—to keep down the mischief.* When a man has resolved upon a particular offence, the next object is to dispose him to do *no more* mischief than is *necessary* to his purpose: in other words, to do as little mischief as is consistent with the benefit he has in view.

V. 4. *4th Object—to act at the least expense.* The last object is, whatever the mischief be, which it is proposed to prevent, to prevent it at as *cheap* a rate as possible.

VII. *Rules of proportion between punishments and offences.* Subservient to these four objects, or purposes, must be the rules or canons by which the proportion of punishments to offences is to be governed.

VIII. Rule 1. *Outweigh the profit of the offence.* The first object, it has bccn seen, is to prevent, in as far as it is worth while, all sorts of offences; therefore,

The value of the punishment must not be less in any case than what is sufficient to outweigh that of the profit of the offence.

If it be, the offence (unless some other considerations, independent of the punishment, should intervene and operate efficaciously in the character of tutelary motives) will be sure to be committed notwithstanding: the whole lot of punishment will be thrown away: it will be altogether *inefficacious.*

IX. *The propriety of taking the strength of the temptation for a ground of abatement, no objection to this rule.* The above rule has been often objected to, on account of its seeming harshness: but this can only have happened for want of its being properly understood. The strength of the temptation, *caeteris paribus,* is as the profit of the offence: the quantum of the punishment must rise

with the profit of the offence: *caeteris paribus,* it must therefore rise with the strength of the temptation. This there is no disputing. True it is, that the stronger the temptation, the less conclusive is the indication which the act of delinquency affords of the depravity of the offender's disposition, so far then as the absence of any aggravation, arising from extraordinary depravity of disposition, may operate, or at the utmost, so far as the presence of a ground of extenuation, resulting from the innocence or beneficence of the offender's disposition, can operate, the strength of the temptation may operate in abatement of the demand for punishment. But it can never operate so far as to indicate the propriety of making the punishment ineffectual, which it is sure to be when brought below the level of the apparent profit of the offence.

The partial benevolence which should prevail for the reduction of it below this level, would counteract as well those purposes which such a motive would actually have in view, as those more extensive purposes which benevolence ought to have in view: it would be cruelty not only to the public, but to the very persons in whose behalf it pleads: in its effects, I mean, however opposite in its intention. Cruelty to the public, that is cruelty to the innocent, by suffering them, for want of an adequate protection, to lie exposed to the mischief of the offence: cruelty even to the offender himself, by punishing him to no purpose, and without the chance of compassing that beneficial end, by which alone the introduction of the evil of punishment is to be justified.

X. Rule 2. *Venture more against a great offence than a small one.* But whether a given offence shall be prevented in a given degree by a given quantity of punishment, is never any thing better than a chance; for the purchasing of which, whatever punishment is employed, is so much expended in advance. However, for the sake of giving it the better chance of outweighing the profit of the offence,

The greater the mischief of the offence, the greater is the expense, which it may be worth while to be at, in the way of punishment.

XI. Rule 3. *Cause the least of two offences to be preferred.* The next object is, to induce a man to choose always the least mischievous of two offences, therefore

Where two offences come in competition, the punishment for the greater offence must be sufficient to induce a man to prefer the less.

XII. Rule 4. *Punish for each particle of the mischief.* When a man has resolved upon a particular offence, the next object is, to induce him to do no more mischief than what is necessary for his purpose: therefore

The punishment should be adjusted in such manner to each particular offence, that for every part of the mischief there may be a motive to restrain the offender from giving birth to it.

XIII. Rule 5. *Punish in no degree without special reason.* The last object is, whatever mischief is guarded against, to guard against it at as cheap a rate as possible: therefore

The punishment ought in no case to be more than what is necessary to bring into conformity with the rules here given.

XIV. Rule 6. *Attend to circumstances influencing sensibility.* It is further to be observed, that owing to the different manners and degrees in which persons under different circumstances are affected by the same exciting cause, a punishment which is the same in name will not always either really produce, or even so much as appear to others to produce, in two different persons the same degree of pain: therefore

That the quantity actually inflicted on each individual offender may correspond to the quantity intended for similar offenders in general, the several circumstances influencing sensibility ought always to be taken into account.

XV. *Comparative view of the above rules.* Of the above rules of proportion, the four first, we may perceive, serve to mark out the limits on the side of diminution; the limits *below* which a punishment ought not to be *diminished:* the fifth, the limits on the side of increase; the limits *above* which it ought not to be *increased.* The five first are calculated to serve as guides to the legislator: the sixth is calculated, in some measure, indeed, for the same purpose; but principally for guiding the judge in his endeavours to conform, on both sides, to the intentions of the legislator.

XVI. *Into the account of the value of a punishment must be taken its deficiency in point of certainty and proximity.* Let us look back a little. The first rule, in order to render it more conveniently applicable to practice, may need perhaps to be a little more particularly unfolded. It is to be observed, then that for the sake of accuracy, it was necessary, instead of the word *quantity* to make use of the less perspicuous term *value.* For the word *quantity* will not properly include the circumstances either of certainty or proximity: circumstances which, in estimating the value of a lot of pain or pleasure, must be always be taken into the account. Now, on the one hand, a lot of punishment is a lot of pain; on the other hand, the

profit of an offence is a lot of pleasure, or what is equivalent to it. But the profit of the offence *is* commonly more *certain* than the punishment, or, what comes to the same thing, *appears* so at least to the offender. It is at any rate commonly more *immediate.* It follows, therefore, that, in order to maintain its superiority over the profit of the offence, the punishment must have its value made up in some other way, in proportion to that whereby it falls short in the two points of *certainty* and *proximity.* Now there is no other way in which it can receive any addition to its *value,* but by receiving an addition in point of *magnitude.* Wherever then the value of the punishment falls short, either in point of *certainty,* or of *proximity,* of that of the profit of the offence, it must receive a proportionable addition in point of *magnitude.*

XVII. *Also, into the account of the mischief, and profit of the offence, the mischief and profit of other offences of the same* habit. Yet farther. To make sure of giving the value of the punishment the superiority over that of the offence, it may be necessary, in some cases, to take into the account the profit not only of the *individual* offence to which the punishment is to be annexed, but also of such *other* offences of the *same sort* as the offender is likely to have already committed without detection. This random mode of calculation, severe as it is, it will be impossible to avoid having recourse to, in certain cases: in such, to wit, in which the profit is pecuniary, the chance of detection very small, and the obnoxious act of such a nature as indicates a habit: for example, in the case of frauds against the coin. If it be *not* recurred to, the practice of committing the offence will be sure to be, upon the balance of the account, a gainful practice. That being the case, the legislator will be absolutely sure of *not* being able to suppress it, and the whole punishment that is bestowed upon it will be thrown away. In a word (to keep to the same expressions we set out with) that whole quantity of punishment will be *inefficacious.*

XVIII. Rule 7. *Want of certainty must be made up in magnitude.* These things being considered, the three following rules may be laid down by way of supplement and explanation to Rule 1.

To enable the value of the punishment to outweigh that of the offence, it must be increased, in point of magnitude, in proportion as it falls short in point of certainty.

XIX. Rule 8. *(So also want of proximity.) Punishment must be further increased in point of magnitude, in proportion as it falls short in point of proximity.*

XX. Rule 9. *Where the act is conclusively indicative of a habit, such an increase must be given to the punishment as may enable it to outweigh the profit not only of the individual offence, but such other like offences as are likely to have been committed with impunity by the same offender.*

XXI. There may be a few other circumstances or considerations which may influence, in some small degree, the demand for punishment: but as the propriety of these is either not so demonstrable, or not so constant, or the application of them not so determinate, as that of the foregoing, it may be doubted whether they be worth putting on a level with the others.

XXII. Rule 10. *When a punishment, which in point of quality is particularly well calculated to answer its intention, cannot exist in less than a certain quantity, it may sometimes be of use, for sake of employing it, to stretch a little beyond that quantity which, on other accounts, would be strictly necessary.*

XXIII. Rule 11. *In particular, this may sometimes be the case, where the punishment proposed is of such a nature as to be particularly well calculated to answer the purpose of a moral lesson.*

(A punishment may be said to be calculated to answer the purpose of a moral lesson, when, by reason of the ignominy it stamps upon the offence, it is calculated to inspire the public with sentiments of aversion towards those pernicious habits and dispositions with which the offence appears to be connected; and thereby to inculcate the opposite beneficial habits and dispositions.)

XXIV. Rule 12. The tendency of the above consideration is to dictate an augmentation in the punishment: the following rule operates in the way of diminution. There are certain cases (it has been seen) in which, by the influence of accidental circumstances, punishment may be rendered unprofitable in the whole: in the same cases it may chance to be rendered unprofitable as to a part only. Accordingly,

In adjusting the quantum of punishment, the circumstances, by which all punishment may be rendered unprofitable, ought to be attended to.

XXV. Rule 13. It is to be observed, that the more various and minute any set of provisions are, the greater the chance is that any given article in them will not be borne in mind: without which, no benefit can ensue from it. Distinctions, which are more complex than what the conceptions of those whose conduct it is designed to influence can take in, will even be worse than

useless. The whole system will present a confused appearance: and thus the effect, not only of the proportions established by the articles in question, but of whatever is connected with them, will be destroyed. To draw a precise line of direction in such case seems impossible. However, by way of memento, it may be of some use to subjoin the following rule.

Among provisions designed to perfect the proportion between punishments and offences, if any occur, which, by their own particular good effects, would not make up for the harm they would do by adding to the intricacy of the Code, they should be omitted.

XXVII. It may be of use, in this place, to recapitulate the several circumstances, which, in establishing the proportion betwixt punishments and offences, are to be attended to. These seem to be as follows:

I. *On the part of the offence:*

   1. The profit of the offence;
   2. The mischief of the offence;
   3. The profit and mischief of other greater or lesser offences, of different sorts, which the offender may have to choose out of;
   4. The profit and mischief of other offences, of the same sort, which the same offender may probably have been guilty of already.

II. *On the part of the punishment:*

   5. The magnitude of the punishment: composed of its intensity and duration;
   6. The deficiency of the punishment in point of certainty;
   7. The deficiency of the punishment in point of proximity;
   8. The quality of the punishment;
   9. The accidental advantage in point of quality of a punishment, not strictly needed in point of quantity;
   10. The use of a punishment of a particular quality, in the character of a moral lesson.

III. *On the part of the offender:*

   11. The responsibility of the class of persons in a way to offend;
   12. The sensibility of each particular offender;
   13. The particular merits or useful qualities of any particular offender, in case of a punishment which might deprive the community of the benefit of them;
   14. The multitude of offenders on any particular occasion.

IV. *On the part of the public,* at any particular conjuncture:

   15. The inclinations of the people, for or against any quantity or mode of punishment. . . .

V. *On the part of the law:* that is, of the public for a continuance:

17. The necessity of making small sacrifices, in point of proportionality, for the sake of simplicity.

XXVIII. There are some, perhaps, who, at first sight, may look upon the nicety employed in the adjustment of such rules, as so much labour lost: for gross ignorance, they will say, never troubles itself about laws, and passion does not calculate. But the evil of ignorance admits of cure: and as to the proposition that passion does not calculate, this, like most of these very general and oracular propositions, is not true. When matters of such importance as pain and pleasure are at stake, and these in the highest degree (the only matters, in short, that can be of importance) who is there that does not calculate? Men calculate, some with less exactness, indeed, some with more: but all men calculate. I would not say, that even a madman does not calculate. Passion calculates, more or less, in every man: in different men, according to the warmth or coolness of their dispositions: according to the firmness or irritability of their minds: according to the nature of the motives by which they are acted upon. Happily, of all passions, that is the most given to calculation, from the excesses of which, by reason of its strength, constancy, and universality, society has most to apprehend: I mean that which corresponds to the motive of pecuniary interest: so that these niceties, if such they are to be called, have the best chance of being efficacious, where efficacy is of the most importance.

OF THE PROPERTIES TO BE GIVEN TO A LOT OF PUNISHMENT

I. It has been shown what the rules are, which ought to be observed in adjusting the proportion between the punishment and the offence. The properties to be given to a lot of punishment, in every instance, will of course be such as it stands in need of, in order to be capable of being applied, in conformity to those rules: the *quality* will be regulated by the *quantity*.

II. The first of those rules, we may remember, was, that the quantity of punishment must not be less, in any case, than what is sufficient to outweigh the profit of the offence: since, as often as it is less, the whole lot (unless by accident the deficiency should be supplied from some of the other sanctions) is thrown away: it is *inefficacious.* The fifth was, that the punishment ought in no case to be more than what is required by the several other rules: since, if it be, all that is above

that quantity is *needless.* The fourth was, that the punishment should be adjusted in such manner to each individual offence, that every part of the mischief of that offence may have a penalty (that is, a tutelary motive) to encounter it: otherwise, with respect to so much of the offence as has not a penalty to correspond to it, it is as if there were no punishment in the case. Now to none of those rules can a lot of punishment be conformable, unless, for every variation in point of quantity, in the mischief of the species of offence to which it is annexed, such lot of punishment admits of a correspondent variation. To prove this, let the profit of the offence admit of a multitude of degrees. Suppose it, then, at any one of these degrees: if the punishment be less than what is suitable to that degree, it will be *inefficacious;* it will be so much thrown away: if it be more, as far as the difference extends, it will be *needless;* it will therefore be thrown away also in that case.

The first property, therefore, that ought to be given to a lot of punishment, is that of being variable in point of quantity, in conformity to every variation which can take place in either the profit or mischief of the offence. This property might, perhaps, be termed, in a single word, *variability.*

III. A second property, intimately connected with the former, may be styled *equability.* It will avail but little, that a mode of punishment (proper in all other respects) has been established by the legislator; and that capable of being screwed up or let down to any degree that can be required; if, after all, whatever degree of it be pitched upon, that same degree shall be liable, according to circumstances, to produce a very heavy degree of pain, or a very slight one, or even none at all. In this case, as in the former, if circumstances happen one way, there will be a great deal of pain produced which will be *needless:* if the other way, there will be no pain at all applied, or none that will be *efficacious.* A punishment, when liable to this irregularity, may be styled an unequable one: when free from it, an equable one. The quantity of pain produced by the punishment will, it is true, depend in a considerable degree upon circumstances distinct from the nature of the punishment itself: upon the condition which the offender is in, with respect to the circumstances by which a man's sensibility is liable to be influenced. But the influence of these very circumstances will in many cases be reciprocally influenced by the nature of the punishment: in other words, the pain which is produced by any mode of punishment, will be the joint effect of the punishment which is applied to him, and the circumstances in which he is exposed to it. Now there are some punishments, of which the effect may be liable to undergo a greater alteration by the influence of such foreign circumstances, than the effect of other punishments is liable to undergo. So far, then, as this is the case, equability or unequability may be regarded as properties belonging to the punishment itself.

IV. An example of a mode of punishment which is apt to be unequable, is that of *banishment,* when the *locus a quo* (or place the party is banished from) is some determinate place appointed by the law, which perhaps the offender cares not whether he ever see or no. This is also the case with *pecuniary,* or *quasi-pecuniary* punishment, when it respects some particular species of property, which the offender may have been possessed of, or not, as it may happen. All these punishments may be split down into parcels, and measured out with the utmost nicety: being divisible by time, at least, if by nothing else. They are not, therefore, any of them defective in point of variability: and yet, in many cases, this defect in point of equability may make them as unfit for use as if they were.

V. The third rule of proportion was, that where two offences come in competition, the punishment for the greater offence must be sufficient to induce a man to prefer the less. Now, to be sufficient for this purpose, it must be evidently and uniformly greater: greater, not in the eyes of some men only, but of all men who are liable to be in a situation to take their choice between the two offences; that is, in effect, of all mankind. In other words, the two punishments must be perfectly *commensurable.* Hence arises a third property, which may be termed *commensurability:* to wit, with reference to other punishments.

VI. But punishments of different kinds are in very few instances uniformly greater one than another; especially when the lowest degrees of that which is ordinarily the greater, are compared with the highest degrees of that which is ordinarily the less: in other words, punishments of different kinds are in few instances uniformly commensurable. The only certain and universal means of making two lots of punishment perfectly commensurable, is by making the lesser an ingredient in the composition of the greater. This may be done in either of two ways. I. By adding to the lesser punishment another quantity of punishment of the same kind. 2. By adding to it another quantity of a different kind. The latter mode is not less certain than the former: for

though one cannot always be absolutely sure, that to the same person a given punishment will appear greater than another given punishment; yet one may be always absolutely sure, that any given punishment, so as it does but come into contemplation, will appear greater than none at all.

VII. Again: Punishment cannot act any farther than in as far as the idea of it, and of its connection with the offence, is present in the mind. The idea of it, if not present, cannot act at all; and then the punishment itself must be *inefficacious.* Now, to be present, it must be remembered, and to be remembered it must have been learnt. But of all punishments that can be imagined, there are none of which the connection with the offence is either so easily learnt, or so efficaciously remembered, as those of which the idea is already in part associated with some part of the idea of the offence: which is the case when the one and the other have some circumstance that belongs to them in common. When this is the case with a punishment and an offence, the punishment is said to bear an *analogy* to, or to be *characteristic* of, the offence. *Characteristicalness* is, therefore, a fourth property, which on this account ought to be given, whenever it can conveniently be given, to a lot of punishment.

VIII. It is obvious, that the effect of this contrivance will be the greater, as the analogy is the closer. The analogy will be the closer, the more *material* that circumstance is, which is in common. Now the most material circumstance that can belong to an offence and a punishment in common, is the hurt or damage which they produce. The closest analogy, therefore, that can subsist between an offence and the punishment annexed to it, is that which subsists between them when the hurt or damage they produce is of the same nature: in other words, that which is constituted by the circumstance of identity in point of damage. Accordingly, the mode of punishment, which of all others bears the closest analogy to the offence, is that which in the proper and exact sense of the word is termed *retaliation.* Retaliation, therefore, in the few cases in which it is practicable, and not too expensive, will have one great advantage over every other mode of punishment.

IX. Again: It is the idea only of the punishment (or, in other words, the *apparent* punishment) that really acts upon the mind; the punishment itself (the *real* punishment) acts not any farther than as giving rise to that idea. It is the apparent punishment, therefore, that does all the service, I mean in the way of example, which is the principal object. It is the real punishment that does all the mischief. Now the ordinary and obvious way of increasing the magnitude of the apparent punishment, is by increasing the magnitude of the real. The apparent magnitude, however, may to a certain degree be increased by other less expensive means: whenever, therefore, at the same time that these less expensive means would have answered that purpose, an additional real punishment is employed, this additional real punishment is *needless*. As to these less expensive means, they consist, 1. In the choice of a particular mode of punishment, a punishment of a particular quality, independent of the quantity. 2. In a particular set of *solemnities* distinct from the punishment itself, and accompanying the execution of it.

X. A mode of punishment, according as the appearance of it bears a greater proportion to the reality, may be said to be the more *exemplary*. Now as to what concerns the choice of the punishment itself, there is not any means by which a given quantity of punishment can be rendered more exemplary, than by choosing it of such a sort as shall bear an *analogy* to the offence. Hence another reason for rendering the punishment analogous to, or in other words characteristic of, the offence.

XI. Punishment, it is still to be remembered, is in itself an expense: it is in itself an evil. Accordingly the fifth rule of proportion is, not to produce more of it than what is demanded by the other rules. But this is the case as often as any particle of pain is produced, which contributes nothing to the effect proposed. Now if any mode of punishment is more apt than another to produce any such superfluous and needless pain, it may be styled *unfrugal;* if less, it may be styled *frugal. Frugality,* therefore, is a sixth property to be wished for in a mode of punishment.

XII. The perfection of frugality, in a mode of punishment, is where not only no superfluous pain is produced on the part of the person punished, but even that same operation, by which he is subjected to pain, is made to answer the purpose of producing pleasure on the part of some other person. Understand a profit or stock of pleasure of the self-regarding kind: for a pleasure of the dissocial kind is produced almost of course, on the part of all persons in whose breasts the offence has excited the sentiment of ill-will. Now this is the case with pecuniary punishment, as also with such punishments of the *quasi-pecuniary* kind as consist in the subtraction of such a species of possession as is transferable from one party to another. The pleasure, indeed, produced by such an operation, is not in general equal to the pain: it may, however, be so in particular circumstances, as where he, from whom the thing is taken, is very rich, and he, to whom it is given, very poor: and, be it what it will, it is always so much more than can be produced by any other mode of punishment.

XIII. The properties of exemplarity and frugality seem to pursue the same immediate end, though by different courses. Both are occupied in diminishing the ratio of the real suffering to the apparent: but exemplarity tends to increase the apparent; frugality to reduce the real.

XIV. Thus much concerning the properties to be given to punishments in general, to whatsoever offences they are to be applied. Those which follow are of less importance, either as referring only to certain offences in particular, or depending upon the influence of transitory and local circumstances.

In the first place, the four distinct ends into which the main and general end of punishment is divisible, may give rise to so many distinct properties, according as any particular mode of punishment appears to be more particularly adapted to the compassing of one or of another of those ends. To that of *example,* as being the principal one, a particular property has already been adapted. There remains the three inferior ones of *reformation, disablement,* and *compensation.*

XV. A seventh property, therefore, to be wished for in a mode of punishment, is that of *subserviency to reformation,* or *reforming tendency.* Now any punishment is subservient to reformation in proportion to its *quantity:* since the greater the punishment a man has experienced, the stronger is the tendency it has to create in him an aversion towards the offence which was the cause of it: and that with respect to all offences alike. But there are certain punishments which, with regard to certain offences, have a particular tendency to produce that effect by reason of their *quality:* and where this is the case, the punishments in question, as applied to the offences in question, will *pro tanto* have the advantage over all others. This influence will depend upon the nature of the motive which is the cause of the offence: the punishment most subservient to reformation will be the sort of punishment that is best calculated to invalidate the force of that motive.

XVI. Thus, in offences originating from the motive of ill-will, that punishment has the strongest reforming tendency, which is best calculated to weaken the force of the irascible affections. And more particularly, in that sort of offence which consists in an obstinate refusal, on the part of the offender, to do something which is lawfully required of him, and in which the obstinacy is in great measure kept up by his resentment against those who have an interest in forcing him to compliance, the most efficacious punishment seems to be that of confinement to spare diet.

XVII. Thus, also, in offences which owe their birth to the joint influence of indolence and pecuniary interest, that punishment seems to possess the strongest reforming tendency, which is best calculated to weaken the force of the former of those dispositions. And more particularly, in the cases of theft, embezzlement, and every species of defraudment, the mode of punishment best adapted to this purpose seems, in most cases, to be that of penal labour.

XVIII. An eighth property to be given to a lot of punishment in certain cases, is that of *efficacy with respect to disablement,* or, as it might be styled more briefly, *disabling efficacy.* This is a property which may be given in perfection to a lot of punishment; and that with much greater certainty than the property of subserviency to reformation. The inconvenience is, that this property is apt, in general, to run counter to that of frugality: there being, in most cases, no certain way of disabling a man from doing mischief, without, at the same time, disabling him, in a great measure, from doing good, either to himself or others. The mischief therefore of the offence must be so great as to demand a very considerable lot of punishment, for the purpose of example, before it can warrant the application of a punishment equal to that which is necessary for the purpose of disablement.

XIX. The punishment, of which the efficacy in this way is the greatest, is evidently that of death. In this case the efficacy of it is certain. This accordingly is the punishment peculiarly adapted to those cases in which the name of the offender, so long as he lives, may be sufficient to keep a whole nation in a flame. This will now and then be the case with competitors for the sovereignty, and leaders of the factions in civil wars: though, when applied to offences of so questionable a nature, in which the question concerning criminality turns more upon success than anything else; an infliction of this sort may seem more to savour of hostility than punishment. At the same time this punishment, it is evident, is in an eminent degree *unfrugal;* which forms one among the many objections there are against the use of it, in any but very extraordinary cases.

XX. In ordinary cases the purpose may be sufficiently answered by one or other of the various kinds of confinement and banishment: of which, imprisonment is the most strict and efficacious. For when an offence is so circumstanced that it cannot be committed but in a certain place, as is the case, for the most part, with offences against the person, all the law has to do, in order to disable the offender from committing it, is to prevent his being in that place. In any of the offences which consist in the breach or the abuse of any kind of trust, the purpose may be compassed at a still cheaper rate, merely by forfeiture of the trust: and in general, in any of those offences which can only be committed under favour of some relation in which the offender stands with reference to any person, or sets of persons, merely by forfeiture of that relation: that is, of the right of continuing to reap the advantages belonging to it. This is the case, for instance, with any of those offences which consist in an abuse of the privileges of marriage, or of the liberty of carrying on any lucrative or other occupation.

XXI. The *ninth* property is that of *subserviency to compensation.* This property of punishment, if it be *vindictive* compensation that is in view, will, with little variation, be in proportion to the quantity: if *lucrative,* it is the peculiar and characteristic property of pecuniary punishment.

XXII. In the rear of all these properties may be introduced that of *popularity;* a very fleeting and indeterminate kind of property, which may belong to a lot of punishment one moment, and be lost by it the next. By popularity is meant the property of being acceptable, or rather not unacceptable, to the bulk of the people, among whom it is proposed to be established. In strictness of speech, it should rather be called *absence of unpopularity:* for it cannot be expected, in regard to such a matter as punishment, that any species or lot of it should be positively acceptable and grateful to the people: it is sufficient, for the most part, if they have no decided aversion to the thoughts of it. Now the property of characteristicalness, above noticed, seems to go as far towards conciliating the approbation of the people to a mode of punishment, as any; insomuch that popularity may be regarded as a kind of secondary quality, depending upon that of characteristicalness.[1] The use of inserting this property in the catalogue, is chiefly to make it serve by way of memento to the legislator not to introduce, without a cogent necessity, any mode or lot of punishment, towards which he happens to perceive any violent aversion entertained by the body of the people.

XXIII. The effects of unpopularity in a mode of punishment are analogous to those of unfrugality. The unnecessary pain which denominates a punishment unfrugal, is most apt to be that which is produced on the part of the offender. A portion of superfluous pain is in like manner produced when the punishment is unpopular: but in this case it is produced on the part of persons altogether innocent, the people at large. This is already one mischief; and another is, the weakness which it is apt to introduce into the law. When the people are satisfied with the law, they voluntarily lend their assistance in the execution: when they are dissatisfied, they will naturally withhold that assistance; it is well if they do not take a positive part in raising impediments. This contributes greatly to the uncertainty of the punishment; by which, in the first instance, the frequency of the offence receives an increase. In process of time that deficiency, as usual, is apt to draw on an increase in magnitude: an addition of a certain quantity which otherwise would be *needless*.

XXIV. This property, it is to be observed, necessarily supposes, on the part of the people, some prejudice or other, which it is the business of the legislator to endeavour to correct. For if the aversion to the punishment in question were grounded on the principle of utility, the punishment would be such as, on other accounts, ought not to be employed: in which case its popularity or unpopularity would never be worth drawing into question. It is properly therefore a property not so much of the punishment as of the people: a disposition to entertain an unreasonable dislike against an object which merits their approbation. It is the sign also of another property, to wit, indolence or weakness, on the part of the legislator: in suffering the people, for the want of some instruction, which ought to be and might be given them, to quarrel with their own interest. Be this as it may, so long as any such dissatisfaction subsists, it behooves the legislator to have an eye to it, as much as if it were ever so well grounded. Every nation is liable to have its prejudices and its caprices, which it is the business of the legislator to look out for, to study, and to cure.

XXV. The eleventh and last of all the properties that seem to be requisite in a lot of punishment, is that of *remissibility*. The general presumption is, that when punishment is applied, punishment is needful: that it ought to be applied, and therefore cannot want to be *remitted*. But in

very particular, and those always very deplorable cases, it may by accident happen otherwise. It may happen that punishment shall have been inflicted, where, according to the intention of the law itself, it ought not to have been inflicted: that is, where the sufferer is innocent of the offence. At the time of the sentence passed he appeared guilty: but since then, accident has brought his innocence to light. This being the case, so much of the destined punishment as he has suffered already, there is no help for. The business is then to free him from as much as is yet to come. But *is* there any yet to come? There is very little chance of there being any, unless it be so much as consists of *chronical* punishment: such as imprisonment, banishment, penal labour, and the like. So much as consists of *acute* punishment, to wit where the penal process itself is over presently, however permanent the punishment may be in its effects, may be considered as *ir*remissible. This is the case, for example, with whipping, branding, mutilation, and capital punishment. The most perfectly irremissible of any is capital punishment. For though other punishments cannot, when they are over, be remitted, they may be compensated for; and although the unfortunate victim cannot be put into the same condition, yet possibly means may be found of putting him into as good a condition, as he would have been in if he had never suffered. This may in general be done very effectually where the punishment has been no other than pecuniary.

There is another case in which the property of remissibility may appear to be of use: this is, where, although the offender has been justly punished, yet on account of some good behaviour of his, displayed at a time subsequent to that of the commencement of the punishment, it may seem expedient to remit a part of it. But this it can scarcely be, if the proportion of the punishment is, in other respects, what it ought to be. The purpose of example is the more important object, in comparison of that of reformation. It is not very likely, that less punishment should be required for the former purpose than for the latter. For it must be rather an extraordinary case, if a punishment, which is sufficient to deter a man who has only thought of it for a few moments, should not be sufficient to deter a man who has been feeling it all the time. Whatever, then, is required for the purpose of example, must abide at all events: it is not any reformation on the part of the offender, that can warrant the remitting of any part of it: if it could, a man would have nothing to do but to reform immediately, and so free himself from the greatest part of that punishment which was deemed necessary. In order, then, to warrant the remitting of any part of a punishment upon this ground, it must first be supposed that the punishment at first appointed was more than was necessary for the purpose of example, and consequently that a part of it was *needless* upon the whole. This, indeed, is apt enough to be the case, under the imperfect systems that are as yet on foot: and therefore, during the continuance of those systems, the property of remissibility may, on this second ground likewise, as well as on the former, be deemed a useful one. But this would not be the case in any new-constructed system, in which the rules of proportion above laid down should be observed. In such a system, therefore, the utility of this property would rest solely on the former ground.

XXVI. Upon taking a survey of the various possible modes of punishment, it will appear evidently, that there is not any one of them that possesses all the above properties in perfection. To do the best that can be done in the way of punishment, it will therefore be necessary, upon most occasions, to compound them, and make them into complex lots, each consisting of a number of different modes of punishment put together: the nature and proportions of the constituent parts of each lot being different, according to the nature of the offence which it is designed to combat.

XXVII. It may not be amiss to bring together, and exhibit in one view, the eleven properties above established. They are as follows:

Two of them are concerned in establishing a proper proportion between a single offence and its punishment; viz.

1. Variability.
2. Equability.

One, in establishing a proportion, between more offences than one, and more punishments than one; viz.

3. Commensurability.

A fourth contributes to place the punishment in that situation in which alone it can be efficacious; and at the same time to be bestowing on it the two farther properties of exemplarity and popularity; viz.

4. Characteristicalness.

Two others are concerned in excluding all useless punishment; the one indirectly, by heightening the efficacy of what is useful; the other in a direct way; viz.

5. Exemplarity.
6. Frugality.

Three others contribute severally to the three inferior ends of punishment; viz.

7. Subserviency to reformation.
8. Efficacy in disabling.
9. Subserviency to compensation.

Another property tends to exclude a collateral mischief, which a particular mode of punishment is liable accidentally to produce; viz.

10. Popularity.

The remaining property tends to palliate a mischief, which all punishment, as such, is liable accidentally to produce; viz.

11. Remissibility.

The properties of commensurability, characteristicalness, exemplarity, subserviency to reformation, and efficacy in disabling, are more particularly calculated to augment the *profit* which is to be made by punishment: frugality, subserviency to compensation, popularity, and remissibility, to diminish the *expense:* variability and equability are alike subservient to both those purposes.

XXVIII. We now come to take a general survey of the system of *offences:* that is, of such *acts* to which, on account of the mischievous *consequences* they have a *natural* tendency to produce, and in the view of putting a stop to those consequences, it may be proper to annex a certain *artificial* consequence, consisting of punishment, to be inflicted on the authors of such acts, according to the principles just established.

NOTES

1. The property of characteristicalness, therefore, is useful in a mode of punishment in three different ways: 1. It renders a mode of punishment, before infliction, more easy to be borne in mind: 2. It enables it, especially after infliction, to make the stronger impression, when it is there; that is, renders it the more *exemplary:* 3. It tends to render it more acceptable to the people, that is, it renders it the more *popular.*

JEFFRIE G. MURPHY

Marxism and Retribution*

Punishment in general has been defended as a means either of ameliorating or of intimidating. Now what right have you to punish me for the amelioration or intimidation of others? And besides there is history—there is such a thing as statistics—which prove with the most complete evidence that since Cain the world has been neither intimidated nor ameliorated by punishment. Quite the contrary. From the point of view of abstract right, there is only one theory of punishment which recognizes human dignity in the abstract, and that is the theory of Kant, especially in the more rigid formula given to it by Hegel. Hegel says: "Punishment is the right of the criminal. It is an act of his own will. The violation of right has been proclaimed by the criminal as his own right. His crime is the negation of right. Punishment is the negation of this negation, and consequently an affirmation of right, solicited and forced upon the criminal by himself."

There is no doubt something specious in this formula, inasmuch as Hegel, instead of looking upon the criminal as the mere object, the slave of justice, elevates him to the position of a free and self-determined being. Looking, however, more closely into the matter, we discover that German idealism here, as in most other instances, has but given a transcendental sanction to the rules of existing society. Is it not a delusion to substitute for the individual with his real motives, with multifarious social circumstances pressing upon him, the abstraction of "free will"—one among the many qualities of man for man himself? . . . Is there not a necessity for deeply reflecting upon an alteration of the system that breeds these crimes, instead of glorifying the hangman who executes a lot of criminals to make room only for the supply of new ones?

Karl Marx, "Capital Punishment,"
New York Daily Tribune, 18 February 1853[1]

Philosophers have written at great length about the moral problems involved in punishing the innocent—particularly as these problems raise obstacles to an acceptance of the moral theory of Utilitarianism. Punishment of an innocent man in order to bring about good social consequences is, at the very least, not always clearly wrong on utilitarian principles. This being so, utilitarian principles are then to be condemned by any morality that may be called Kantian in character. For punishing an innocent man, in Kantian language, involves using that man as a mere means or instrument to some social good and is thus not to treat him as an end in himself, in accord with his dignity or worth as a person.

The Kantian position on the issue of punishing the innocent, and the many ways in which the utilitarian might try to accommodate that position, constitute extremely well-worn ground in comtemporary moral and legal philosophy.[2] I do not propose to wear the ground further by adding additional comments on the issue here. What I do want to point out, however, is something which seems to me quite obvious but which philosophical commentators on punishment have almost universally failed to see—namely, that problems of the very same kind and seriousness arise for the utilitarian theory with respect to the punishment of the guilty. For a utilitarian theory of punishment (Bentham's is a paradigm) must involve justifying punishment in terms of its social results—e.g., deterrence, incapacitation, and rehabilitation. And thus even a guilty man is, on this theory, being punished because of the instrumental value the action of punishment will have in the future. He is being used as a means to some future good—e.g., the deterrence of others. Thus those of a Kantian persuasion, who see the importance of worrying about the treatment of persons as mere means, must, it would seem, object just as strenuously to the punishment of the guilty on utilitarian grounds as to the punishment of the innocent. Indeed the former worry, in some respects, seems more serious. For a utilitarian can perhaps refine his theory in such a way that it does not commit him to the punishment of the innocent. However, if he is to approve of punishment at all, he must approve of punishing the

*From *Philosophy and Public Affairs,* vol. 2 (1973), pp. 218-243. Reprinted by permission of the author and the Princeton University Press.

guilty in at least some cases. This makes the worry about punishing the guilty formidable indeed, and it is odd that this has gone generally unnoticed.[3] It has generally been assumed that if the utilitarian theory can just avoid entailing the permissibility of punishing the innocent, then all objections of a Kantian character to the theory will have been met. This seems to me simply not to be the case.

What the utilitarian theory really cannot capture, I would suggest, is the notion of persons having rights. And it is just this notion that is central to any Kantian outlook on morality. Any Kantian can certainly agree that punishing persons (guilty or innocent) may have either good or bad or indifferent consequences and that insofar as the consequences (whether in a particular case or for an institution) are good, this is something in favor of punishment. But the Kantian will maintain that this consequential outlook, important as it may be, leaves out of consideration entirely that which is most morally crucial— namely, the question of rights. Even if punishment of a person would have good consequences, what gives us (i.e., society) the moral right to inflict it? If we have such a right, what is its origin or derivation? What social circumstances must be present for it to be applicable? What does this right to punish tell us about the status of the person to be punished—e.g., how are we to analyze his rights, the sense in which he must deserve to be punished, his obligations in the matter? It is this family of questions which any Kantian must regard as morally central and which the utilitarian cannot easily accommodate into his theory. And it is surely this aspect of Kant's and Hegel's retributivism, this seeing of rights as basic, which appeals to Marx in the quoted passage. As Marx himself puts it: "What right have you to punish me for the amelioration or intimidation of others?" And he further praises Hegel for seeing that punishment, if justified, must involve respecting the rights of the person to be punished.[4] Thus Marx, like Kant, seems prepared to draw the important distinction between (a) what it would be good to do on grounds of utility and (b) what we have a right to do. Since we do not always have the right to do what it would be good to do, this distinction is of the greatest moral importance; and missing the distinction is the Achilles heel of all forms of Utilitarianism. For consider the following example: A Jehovah's Witness needs a blood transfusion in order to live; but, because of his (we can agree absurd) religious belief that such transfusions are against God's

commands, he instructs his doctor not to give him one. Here is a case where it would seem to be good or for the best to give the transfusion and yet, at the very least, it is highly doubtful that the doctor has a right to give it. This kind of distinction is elementary, and any theory which misses it is morally degenerate.[5]

To move specifically to the topic of punishment: How exactly does retributivism (of a Kantian or Hegelian variety) respect the rights of persons? Is Marx really correct on this? I believe that he is. I believe that retributivism can be formulated in such a way that it is the only morally defensible theory of punishment. I also believe that arguments, which may be regarded as Marxist at least in spirit, can be formulated which show that social conditions as they obtain in most societies make this form of retributivism largely inapplicable within those societies. As Marx says, in those societies retributivism functions merely to provide a "transcendental sanction" for the status quo. If this is so, then the only morally defensible theory of punishment is largely inapplicable in modern societies. The consequence: modern societies largely lack the moral right to punish.[6] The upshot is that a Kantian moral theory (which in general seems to me correct) and a Marxist analysis of criminality (which, if properly qualified, also seems to me correct) produce a radical and not merely reformist attack, not merely on the scope and manner of punishment in our society but on the institution of punishment itself. Institutions of punishment constitute what Bernard Harrison has called structural injustices[7] and are, in the absence of a major social change, to be resisted by all who take human rights to be morally serious—i.e., regard them as genuine action guides and not merely as rhetorical devices which allow people to morally sanctify institutions which in fact can only be defended on grounds of social expediency.

Stating all of this is one thing and proving it, of course, is another. Whether I can ever do this is doubtful. That I cannot do it in one brief article is certain. I cannot, for example, here defend in detail my belief that a generally Kantian outlook on moral matters is correct.[8] Thus I shall content myself for the present with attempting to render at least plausible two major claims involved in the view that I have outlined thus far: (1) that a retributive theory, in spite of the bad press that it has received, is a morally credible theory of punishment—that it can be, H. L. A. Hart to the contrary,[9] a reasonable general justifying aim of punishment; and (2) that a Marxist analysis of a

THE RIGHT OF THE STATE TO PUNISH

It is strong evidence of the influence of a utilitarian outlook in moral and legal matters that discussions of punishment no longer involve a consideration of the right of anyone to inflict it. Yet in the eighteenth and nineteenth centuries, this tended to be regarded as the central aspect of the problem meriting philosophical consideration. Kant, Hegel, Bosanquet, Green—all tended to entitle their chapters on punishment along the lines explicitly used by Green: "The Right of the State to Punish."[10] This is not just a matter of terminology but reflects, I think, something of deeper philosophical substance. These theorists, unlike the utilitarian, did not view man as primarily a maximizer of personal satisfactions—a maximizer of individual utilities. They were inclined, in various ways, to adopt a different model of man—man as a free or spontaneous creator, man as autonomous. (Marx, it may be noted, is much more in line with this tradition than with the utilitarian outlook.)[11] This being so, these theorists were inclined to view punishment (a certain kind of coercion by the state) as not merely a causal contributor to pain and suffering, but rather as presenting at least a prima facie challenge to the values of autonomy and personal dignity and self-realization—the very values which, in their view, the state existed to nurture. The problem as they saw it, therefore, was that of reconciling punishment as state coercion with the value of individual autonomy. (This is an instance of the more general problem which Robert Paul Wolff has called the central problem of political philosophy—namely, how is individual moral autonomy to be reconciled with legitimate political authority?)[12] This kind of problem, which I am inclined to agree is quite basic, cannot even be formulated intelligibly from a utilitarian perspective. Thus the utilitarian cannot even see the relevance of Marx's charge: Even if punishment has wonderful social consequences, what gives anyone the right to inflict it on me?

Now one fairly typical way in which others acquire rights over us is by our own consent. If a neighbor locks up my liquor cabinet to protect me against my tendencies to drink too heavily, I might well regard this as a presumptuous interference with my own freedom, no matter how good the result intended or accomplished. He had no right to do it and indeed violated my rights in doing it. If, on the other hand, I had asked him to do this or had given my free consent to his suggestion that he do it, the same sort of objection on my part would be quite out of order. I had given him the right to do it, and he had the right to do it. In doing it, he violated no rights of mine—even if, at the time of his doing it, I did not desire or want the action to be performed. Here then we seem to have a case where my autonomy may be regarded as intact even though a desire of mine is thwarted. For there is a sense in which the thwarting of the desire can be imputed to me (my choice or decision) and not to the arbitrary intervention of another.

How does this apply to our problem? The answer, I think, is obvious. What is needed, in order to reconcile my undesired suffering of punishment at the hands of the state with my autonomy (and thus with the state's right to punish me), is a political theory which makes the state's decision to punish me in some sense my own decision. If I have willed my own punishment (consented to it, agreed to it) then—even if at the time I happen not to desire it—it can be said that my autonomy and dignity remain intact. Theories of the General Will and Social Contract theories are two such theories which attempt this reconciliation of autonomy with legitimate state authority (including the right or authority of the state to punish). Since Kant's theory happens to incorporate elements of both, it will be useful to take it for our sample.

MORAL RIGHTS AND THE RETRIBUTIVE THEORY OF PUNISHMENT

To justify government or the state is necessarily to justify at least some coercion.[13] This poses a problem for someone, like Kant, who maintains that human freedom is the ultimate or most sacred moral value. Kant's own attempt to justify the state, expressed in his doctrine of the *moral title (Befugnis),*[14] involves an argument that coercion is justified only in so far as it is used to prevent invasions against freedom. Freedom itself is the only value which can be used to limit freedom, for the appeal to any other value (e.g., utility) would undermine the ultimate status of the value of freedom. Thus Kant attempts to establish the claim that some forms of coercion (as opposed to violence) are morally permissible because, contrary to appearance, they are really consistent with rational freedom. The argument, in broad outline, goes in the following way. Coercion may keep people from doing what they desire or want to do on a particular occasion and is thus prima facie wrong. However, such coercion can be shown to be morally justified (and thus not absolutely wrong) if it can be established that the coercion is such that it could have been rationally willed even by the person whose desire is interfered with:

Accordingly, when it is said that a creditor has a right to demand from his debtor the payment of a debt, this does not mean that he can *persuade* the debtor that his own reason itself obligates him to this performance; on the contrary, to say that he has such a right means only that the use of coercion to make anyone do this is entirely compatible with everyone's freedom, *including the freedom of the debtor,* in accordance with universal laws.[15]

Like Rousseau, Kant thinks that it is only in a context governed by social practice (particularly civil government and its Rule of Law) that this can make sense. Laws may require of a person some action that he does not desire to perform. This is not a violent invasion of his freedom, however, if it can be shown that in some antecedent position of choice (what John Rawls calls "the original position"),[16] he would have been rational to adopt a Rule of Law (and thus run the risk of having some of his desires thwarted) rather than some other alternative arrangement like the classical State of Nature. This is, indeed, the only sense that Kant is able to make of classical Social Contract theories. Such theories are to be viewed, not as historical fantasies, but as ideal models of rational decision. For what these theories actually claim is that the only coercive institutions that are morally justified are those which a group of rational beings could agree to adopt in a position of having to pick social institutions to govern their relations:

The contract, which is called *contractus originarius,* or *pactum sociale* . . . need not be assumed to be a fact, indeed it is not [even possible as such. To suppose that would be like insisting] that before anyone would be bound to respect such a civic constitution, it be proved first of all from history that a people, whose rights and obligations we have entered into as their descendants, had *once upon a time* executed such an act and had left a reliable document or instrument, either orally or in writing, concerning this contract. Instead, this contract is a *mere idea* of reason which has undoubted practical reality; namely, to oblige every legislator to give us laws in such a manner that the laws *could* have originated from the united will of the entire people and to regard every subject in so far as he is a citizen as though he had consented to such [an expression of the

general] will. This is the testing stone of the rightness of every publicly-known law, for if a law were such that it was impossible for an entire people to give consent to it (as for example a law that a certain class of subjects, by inheritance, should have the privilege of the *status of lords*), then such a law is unjust. On the other hand, if there is a mere *possibility* that a people might consent to a (certain) law, then it is a duty to consider that the law is just even though at the moment the people might be in such a position or have a point of view that would result in their refusing to give their consent to it if asked.[17]

The problem of organizing a state, however hard it may seem, can be solved even for a race of devils, if only they are intelligent. The problem is: "Given a multiple of rational beings requiring universal laws for their preservation, but each of whom is secretly inclined to exempt himself from them, to establish a constitution in such a way that, although their private intentions conflict, they check each other, with the result that their public conduct is the same as if they had no such intentions."[18]

Though Kant's doctrine is superficially similar to Mill's later self–protection principle, the substance is really quite different. For though Kant in some general sense argues that coercion is justified only to prevent harm to others, he understands by "harm" only certain invasions of freedom and not simply disutility. Also, his defense of the principle is not grounded, as is Mill's, on its utility. Rather it is to be regarded as a principle of justice, by which Kant means a principle that rational beings could adopt in a situation of mutual choice:

The concept [of justice] applies only to the relationship of a will to another person's will, not to his wishes or desires (or even just his needs) which are the concern of acts of benevolence and charity. . . . In applying the concept of justice we take into consideration only the form of the relationship between the wills insofar as they are regarded as free, and whether the action of one of them can be conjoined with the freedom of the other in accordance with universal law. Justice is therefore the aggregate of those conditions under which the will of one person can be conjoined with the will of another in accordance with a universal law of freedom.[19]

How does this bear specifically on punishment? Kant, as everyone knows, defends a strong form of a retributive theory of punishment. He holds that guilt merits, and is a sufficient condition for, the infliction of punishment. And this claim has been universally condemned—particularly by utilitarians—as primitive, unenlightened and barbaric.

But why is it so condemned? Typically, the charge is that infliction of punishment on such grounds is nothing but pointless vengeance. But what is meant by the claim that the infliction is "pointless"? If "pointless" is tacitly being analyzed as "disutilitarian," then the whole question is simply being begged. You cannot refute a retributive theory merely by noting that it is a retributive theory and not a utilitarian theory. This is to confuse redescription with refutation and involves an argument whose circularity is not even complicated enough to be interesting.

Why, then, might someone claim that guilt merits punishment? Such a claim might be made for either of two very different reasons. (1) Someone (e. g., a Moral Sense theorist) might maintain that the claim is a primitive and unanalyzable proposition that is morally ultimate—that we can just intuit the "fittingness" of guilt and punishment. (2) It might be maintained that the retributivist claim is demanded by a general theory of political obligation which is more plausible than any alternative theory. Such a theory will typically provide a technical analysis of such concepts as crime and punishment and will thus not regard the retributivist claim as an indisputable primitive. It will be argued for as a kind of theorem within the system.

Kant's theory is of the second sort. He does not opt for retributivism as a bit of intuitive moral knowledge. Rather he offers a theory of punishment that is based on his general view that political obligation is to be analyzed, quasi—contractually, in terms of reciprocity. If the law is to remain just, it is important to guarantee that those who disobey it will not gain an unfair advantage over those who do obey voluntarily. It is important that no man profit from his own criminal wrongdoing, and a certain kind of "profit" (i. e., not bearing the burden of self-restraint) is intrinsic to criminal wrongdoing. Criminal punishment, then, has as its object the restoration of a proper balance between benefit and obedience. The criminal himself has no complaint, because he has rationally consented to or willed his own punishment. That is, those very rules which he has broken work, when they are obeyed by others, to his own advantage as a citizen. He would have chosen such rules for himself and others in the original position of choice. And, since he derives and voluntarily accepts benefits from their operation, he owes his own obedience as a debt to his fellow–citizens for their sacrifices in maintaining them. If he chooses not to sacrifice by exercising self-restraint and obedience, this is tantamount to his choosing to sacrifice in another way—namely, by paying the prescribed penalty:

A transgression of the public law that makes him who commits it unfit to be a citizen is called . . . a crime. . . .

What kind and what degree of punishment does public legal justice adopt as its principle and standard? None other than the principle of equality (illustrated by the pointer of the scales of justice), that is, the principle of not treating one side more favorably than the other. Accordingly, any undeserved evil that you inflict on someone else among the people is one you do to yourself. If you vilify him, you vilify yourself; if you steal from him, you steal from yourself; if you kill him, you kill yourself. . . .

To say, "I will to be punished if I murder someone" can mean nothing more than, "I submit myself along with everyone else to those laws which, if there are any criminals among the people, will naturally include penal laws."[20]

This analysis of punishment regards it as a debt owed to the law-abiding members of one's community; and, once paid, it allows reentry into the community of good citizens on equal status.

Now some of the foregoing no doubt sounds implausible or even obscurantist. Since criminals typically desire not to be punished, what can it really mean to say that they have, as rational men, really willed their own punishment? Or that, as Hegel says, they have a right to it? Perhaps a comparison of the traditional retributivist views with those of a contemporary Kantian—John Rawls—will help to make the points clearer.[21] Rawls (like Kant) does not regard the idea of the social contract as an historical fact. It is rather a model of rational decision. Respecting a man's autonomy, at least on one view, is not respecting what he now happens, however uncritically, to desire; rather it is to respect what he desires (or would desire) as a rational man. (On Rawls's view, for example, rational men are said to be unmoved by feelings of envy; and thus it is not regarded as unjust to a person or a violation of his rights, if he is placed in a situation where he will envy another's advantage or position. A rational man would object, and thus would never consent to, a practice where another might derive a benefit from a position at his expense. He would not, however, envy the position *simpliciter,* would not regard the position as itself a benefit.) Now on Kant's (and also, I think, on Rawls's) view, a man is genuinely free or autonomous only in so far as he is rational. Thus it is man's rational will that is to be respected.

Now this idea of treating people, not as they in fact say that they want to be treated, but rather in terms of how you think they would, if rational, will to be treated, has obviously dangerous (indeed fascistic) implications. Surely we want to avoid cramming indignities down the throats of people with the offhand observation that, no matter how much they scream, they are really rationally willing every bit of it. It would be particularly ironic for such arbitrary repression to come under the mask of respecting autonomy. And yet, most of us would agree, the general principle (though subject to abuse) also has important applications—for example, preventing the suicide of a person who, in a state of psychotic depression, wants to kill himself. What we need, then, to make the general view work, is a check on its arbitrary application; and a start toward providing such a check would be in the formulation of a public, objective theory of rationality and rational willing. It is just this, according to both Kant and Rawls, which the social contract theory can provide. On this theory, a man may be said to rationally will X if, and only if, X is called for by a rule that the man would necessarily have adopted in the original position of choice—i.e., in a position of coming together with others to pick rules for the regulation of their mutual affairs. This avoids arbitrariness because, according to Kant and Rawls at any rate, the question of whether such a rule would be picked in such a position is objectively determinable given certain (in their view) noncontroversial assumptions about human nature and rational calculation. Thus I can be said to will my own punishment if, in an antecedent position of choice, I and my fellows would have chosen institutions of punishment as the most rational means of dealing with those who might break the other generally beneficial social rules that had been adopted.

Let us take an analogous example: I may not, in our actual society, desire to treat a certain person fairly—e.g., I may not desire to honor a contract I have made with him because so doing would adversely affect my own self-interest. However, if I am forced to honor the contract by the state, I cannot charge (1) that the state has no right to do this, or (2) that my rights or dignity are being violated by my being coerced into doing it. Indeed, it can be said that I rationally will it since, in the original position, I would have chosen rules of justice (rather than rules of utility) and the principle, "contracts are to be honored," follows from the rules of justice.

Coercion and autonomy are thus reconciled, at least apparently. To use Marx's language, we may say (as Marx did in the quoted passage) that one virtue of the retributive theory, at least as expounded by Kant and Hegel on lines of the General Will and Social Contract theory, is that it manifests at least a formal or abstract respect for rights, dignity, and autonomy. For it at least recognizes the importance of attempting to construe state coercion in such a way that it is a product of each man's rational will. Utilitarian deterrence theory does not even satisfy this formal demand.

The question of primary interest to Marx, of course, is whether this formal respect also involves a material respect; i.e., does the theory have application in concrete fact in the actual social world in which we live? Marx is confident that it does not, and it is to this sort of consideration that I shall now pass.

ALIENATION AND PUNISHMENT

What can the philosopher learn from Marx? This question is a part of a more general question: What can philosophy learn from social science? Philosophers, it may be thought, are concerned to offer a priori theories, theories about how certain concepts are to be analyzed and their application justified. And what can the mundane facts that are the object of behavioral science have to do with exalted theories of this sort?

The answer, I think, is that philosophical theories, though not themselves empirical, often have such a character that their intelligibility depends upon certain empirical presuppositions. For example, our moral language presupposes, as Hart has argued,[22] that we are vulnerable creatures—creatures who can harm and be harmed by each other. Also, as I have argued elsewhere,[23] our moral language presupposes that we all share certain psychological characteristics—e.g., sympathy, a sense of justice, and the capacity to feel guilt, shame, regret, and remorse. If these facts were radically different (if, as Hart imagines for example, we all developed crustaceanlike exoskeletons and thus could not harm each other), the old moral language, and the moral theories which employ it, would lack application to the world in which we live. To use a crude example, moral prohibitions against killing presuppose that it is in fact possible for us to kill each other.

Now one of Marx's most important contributions to social philosophy, in my judgment, is simply his insight that philosophical theories are in peril if they are constructed in disregard of the nature of the empirical world to which they are supposed to apply.[24] A theory may be formally correct (i.e., coherent, or true for some possible world) but materially incorrect (i.e., inapplicable to the actual world in which we live). This insight, then, establishes the relevance of empirical research to philosophical theory and is a part, I think, of what Marx meant by "the union of theory and practice." Specifically relevant to the argument I want to develop are the following two related points:

(1) The theories of moral, social, political and legal philosophy presuppose certain empirical propositions about man and society. If these propositions are false, then the theory (even if coherent or formally correct) is materially defective and practically inapplicable. (For example, if persons tempted to engage in criminal conduct do not in fact tend to calculate carefully the consequences of their actions, this renders much of deterrence theory suspect.)

(2) Philosophical theories may put forth as a necessary truth that which is in fact merely an historically conditioned contingency. (For example, Hobbes argued that all men are necessarily selfish and competitive. It is possible, as many Marxists have argued, that Hobbes was really doing nothing more than elevating to the status of a necessary truth the contingent fact that the people around him in the capitalistic society in which he lived were in fact selfish and competitive.)[25]

In outline, then, I want to argue the following: that when Marx challenges the material adequacy of the retributive theory of punishment, he is suggesting (a) that it presupposes a certain view of man and society that is false and (b) that key concepts involved in the support of the theory (e.g., the concept of "rationality" in Social Contract theory) are given analyses which, though they purport to be necessary truths, are in fact mere reflections of certain historical circumstances.

In trying to develop this case, I shall draw primarily upon Willem Bonger's *Criminality and Economic Conditions* (1916), one of the few sustained Marxist analyses of crime and punishment. [26] Though I shall not have time here to qualify my support of Bonger in certain necessary ways, let me make clear that I am perfectly aware that his analysis is not the whole story. (No monolithic theory of anything so diverse as criminal behavior could be the whole story.) However, I am convinced that he has discovered part of the story. And my point is simply that insofar as

Bonger's Marxist analysis is correct, then to that same degree is the retributive theory of punishment inapplicable in modern societies. (Let me emphasize again exactly how this objection to retributivism differs from those traditionally offered. Traditionally, retributivism has been rejected because it conflicts with the moral theory of its opponent, usually a utilitarian. This is not the kind of objection I want to develop. Indeed, with Marx, I have argued that the retributive theory of punishment grows out of the moral theory—Kantianism—which seems to me generally correct. The objection I want to pursue concerns the empirical falsity of the factual presuppositions of the theory. If the empirical presuppositions of the theory are false, this does indeed render its application immoral. But the immorality consists, not in a conflict with some other moral theory, but immorality in terms of a moral theory that is at least close in spirit to the very moral theory which generates retributivism itself—i.e., a theory of justice.)[27]

To return to Bonger. Put bluntly, his theory is as follows. Criminality has two primary sources: (1) need and deprivation on the part of disadvantaged members of society, and (2) motives of greed and selfishness that are generated and reinforced in competitive capitalistic societies. Thus criminality is economically based—either directly in the case of crimes from need, or indirectly in the case of crimes growing out of motives or psychological states that are encouraged and developed in capitalistic society. In Marx's own language, such an economic system alienates men from themselves and from each other. It alienates men from themselves by creating motives and needs that are not "truly human." It alienates men from their fellows by encouraging a kind of competitiveness that forms an obstacle to the development of genuine communities to replace mere social aggregates.[28] And in Bonger's thought, the concept of community is central. He argues that moral relations and moral restraint are possible only in genuine communities characterized by bonds of sympathetic identification and mutual aid resting upon a perception of common humanity. All this he includes under the general rubric of reciprocity.[29] In the absence of reciprocity in this rich sense, moral relations among men will break down and criminality will increase.[30] Within bourgeois society, then, crimes are to be regarded as normal, and not psychopathological, acts. That is, they grow out of need, greed, indifference to others, and sometimes even a sense of indignation—all, alas, perfectly typical human motives.

To appreciate the force of Bonger's analysis, it is necessary to read his books and grasp the richness and detail of the evidence he provides for his claims. Here I can but quote a few passages at random to give the reader a tantalizing sample in the hope that he will be encouraged to read further into Bonger's own text:

The abnormal element in crime is a social, not a biological, element. With the exception of a few special cases, crime lies within the boundaries of normal psychology and physiology. . . .

We clearly see that [the egoistic tendencies of the present economic system and of its consequences] are very strong. Because of these tendencies the social instinct of man is not greatly developed; they have weakened the moral force in man which combats the inclination towards egoistic acts, and hence toward the crimes which are one form of these acts. . . . Compassion for the misfortunes of others inevitably becomes blunted, and a great part of morality consequently disappears. . . .

As a consequence of the present environment, man has become very egoistic and hence more *capable of crime,* than if the environment had developed the germs of altruism. . . .

There can be no doubt that one of the factors of criminality among the bourgeoisie is bad [moral] education. . . . The children—speaking of course in a general way—are brought up with the idea that they must succeed, no matter how; the aim of life is presented to them as getting money and shining in the world. . . .

Poverty (taken in the sense of absolute want) kills the social sentiments in man, destroys in fact all relations between men. He who is abandoned by all can no longer have any feeling for those who have left him to his fate. . . .

[Upon perception that the system tends to legalize the egoistic actions of the bourgeoisie and to penalize those of the proletariat], the oppressed resort to means which they would otherwise scorn. As we have seen above, the basis of the social feeling is reciprocity. As soon as this is trodden under foot by the ruling class the social sentiments of the oppressed become weak towards them. . . . [31]

The essence of this theory has been summed up by Austin J. Turk. "Criminal behavior," he says, "is almost entirely attributable to the combination of egoism and an environment in which opportunities are not equitably distributed."[32]

No doubt this claim will strike many as extreme and intemperate—a sample of the old-fashioned Marxist rhetoric that sophisticated intellectuals have outgrown. Those who are inclined to react in this way might consider just one sobering fact: of the 1.3 million criminal offenders handled each day by some agency of the United States correctional system, the vast majority (80 percent on some estimates) are members of the lowest 15-percent income level—that percent which is below the "poverty level" as defined by the Social Security Administration.[33] Unless one wants to embrace the belief that all these people are poor because they are bad, it might be well to reconsider Bonger's suggestion that many of them are "bad" because they are poor.[34] At any rate, let us suppose for purposes of discussion that Bonger's picture of the relation between crime and economic conditions is generally accurate. At what points will this challenge the credentials of the contractarian retributive theory as outlined above? I should like to organize my answer to this question around three basic topics:

1. *Rational Choice.* The model of rational choice found in Social Contract theory is egoistic—rational institutions are those that would be agreed to by calculating egoists ("devils" in Kant's more colorful terminology). The obvious question that would be raised by any Marxist is: Why give egoism this special status such that it is built, a priori, into the analysis of the concept of rationality? Is this not simply to regard as necessary that which may be only contingently found in the society around us? Starting from such an analysis, a certain result is inevitable—namely, a transcendental sanction for the status quo. Start with a bourgeois model of rationality and you will, of course, wind up defending a bourgeois theory of consent, a bourgeois theory of justice, and a bourgeois theory of punishment.

Though I cannot explore the point in detail here, it seems to me that this Marxist claim may cause some serious problems for Rawls's well-known theory of justice, a theory which I have already used to unpack some of the evaluative support for the retributive theory of punishment. One cannot help suspecting that there is a certain sterility in Rawls's entire project of providing a rational proof for the preferability of a certain conception of justice over all possible alternative evaluative principles, for the description which he gives of the rational contractors in the original position is such as to guarantee that they will come up with his two principles. This would be acceptable if the analysis of rationality presupposed were intuitively obvious or argued for on independent grounds. But it is not. Why, to take just one example, is a desire for wealth a rational trait whereas envy is not? One cannot help feeling that the desired result dictates the premises.[35]

2. *Justice, Benefits, and Community.* The retributive theory claims to be grounded on justice; but is it just to punish people who act out of those very motives that society encourages and reinforces? If Bonger is correct, much criminality is motivated by greed, selfishness, and indifference to one's fellows; but does not the whole society encourage motives of greed and selfishness ("making it," "getting ahead"), and does not the competitive nature of the society alienate men from each other and thereby encourage indifference—even, perhaps, what psychiatrists call psychopathy? The moral problem here is similar to one that arises with respect to some war crimes. When you have trained a man to believe that the enemy is not a genuine human person (but only a gook, or a chink), it does not seem quite fair to punish the man if, in a war situation, he kills indiscriminately. For the psychological trait you have conditioned him to have, like greed, is not one that invites fine moral and legal distinctions. There is something perverse in applying principles that presuppose a sense of community in a society which is structured to destroy genuine community.[36]

Related to this is the whole allocation of benefits in contemporary society. The retributive theory really presupposes what might be called a "gentlemen's club" picture of the relation between man and society—i.e., men are viewed as being part of a community of shared values and rules. The rules benefit all concerned and, as a kind of debt for the benefits derived, each man owes obedience to the rules. In the absence of such obedience, he deserves punishment in the sense that he owes payment of the benefits. For, as rational man, he can see that the rules benefit everyone (himself included) and that he would have selected them in the original position of choice.

Now this may not be too far off for certain kinds of criminals—e.g., business executives guilty of tax fraud. (Though even here we might regard their motives of greed to be a function of societal reinforcement.) But to think that it applies to the typical criminal, from the poorer classes, is to live in a world of social and political fantasy. Criminals typically are not members of a shared community of values with their jailers; they suffer from what Marx calls alienation. And they certainly would be hard–pressed to name the benefits for which they are supposed to owe obedience. If justice, as both Kant and Rawls suggest, is based on reciprocity, it is hard to see what these persons are supposed to reciprocate for. Bonger addresses this point in a passage quoted earlier ... : "The oppressed resort to means which they would otherwise scorn. . . . The basis of social feelings is reciprocity. As soon as this is trodden under foot by the ruling class, the social sentiments of the oppressed become weak towards them."

3. *Voluntary Acceptance.* Central to the Social Contract idea is the claim that we owe allegiance to the law because the benefits we have derived have been voluntarily accepted. This is one place where our autonomy is supposed to come in. That is, having benefited from the Rule of Law when it was possible to leave, I have in a sense consented to it and to its consequences—even my own punishment if I violate the rules. To see how silly the factual presuppositions of this account are, we can do no better than quote a famous passage from David Hume's essay "Of the Original Contract":

Can we seriously say that a poor peasant or artisan has a free choice to leave his country—when he knows no foreign language or manners, and lives from day to day by the small wages which he acquires? We may as well assert that a man, by remaining in a vessel, freely consents to the dominion of the master, though he was carried on board while asleep, and must leap into the ocean and perish the moment he leaves her.

A banal empirical observation, one may say. But it is through ignoring such banalities that philosophers generate theories which allow them to spread iniquity in the ignorant belief that they are spreading righteousness.

It does, then, seem as if there may be some truth in Marx's claim that the retributive theory, though formally correct, is materially inadequate. At root, the retributive theory fails to acknowledge that criminality is, to a large extent, a phenomenon of economic class. To acknowledge this is to challenge the empirical presupposition of the retributive theory—the presupposition that all men, including criminals, are voluntary participants in a reciprocal system of benefits and that the justice of this arrangement can be derived from some eternal and ahistorical concept of rationality.

The upshot of all this seems rather upsetting, as indeed it is. How can it be the case that everything we are ordinarily inclined to say about punishment (in terms of utility and retribution) can be quite beside the point? To anyone with ordinary language sympathies (one who is inclined to maintain that what is correct to say is a function of what we do say), this will seem madness. Marx will agree that there is madness, all right, but in his view the madness will lie in what we do say—what we say only because of our massive (and often self–deceiving and self–serving) factual ignorance or indifference to the circumstances of the social world in which we live. Just as our whole way of talking about mental phenomena hardened before we knew any neurophysiology—and this leads us astray, so Marx would argue that our whole way of talking about moral and political phenomena hardened before we knew any of the relevant empirical facts about man and society—and this, too, leads us astray. We all suffer from what might be called the *embourgeoisment* of language, and thus part of any revolution will be a linguistic or conceptual revolution. We have grown accustomed to modifying our language or conceptual structures under the impact of empirical discoveries in physics. There is no reason why discoveries in sociology, economics, or psychology could not and should not have the same effect on entrenched patterns of thought and speech. It is important to remember, as Russell remarked, that our language sometimes enshrines the metaphysics of the Stone Age.

Consider one example: a man has been convicted of armed robbery. On investigation, we learn that he is an impoverished black whose whole life has been one of frustrating alienation from the prevailing socio-economic structure—no job, no transportation if he could get a job, sub-standard education for his children, terrible housing and inadequate health care for his whole family, condescending-tardy-inadequate welfare payments, harassment by the police but no real protection by them against the dangers in his community, and near total exclusion from the political process. Learning all this, would we still want to talk—as many do—of his suffering punishment under the rubric of "paying a debt to society"? Surely not. Debt for what? I do not, of course, pretend that all criminals can be so described. But I do think that this is a closer picture of the typical criminal than the picture that is presupposed in the retributive theory—i.e., the picture of an evil person who, of his own free will, intentionally acts against those just rules of society which he knows, as a rational man, benefit everyone including himself.

But what practical help does all this offer, one may ask. How should we design our punitive practices in the society in which we now live? This is the question we want to ask, and it does not seem to help simply to say that our society is built on deception and inequity. How can Marx help us with our real practical problem? The answer, I think, is that he cannot and obviously does not desire to do so. For Marx would say that we have not focused (as all piecemeal reform fails to focus) on what is truly the real problem. And this is changing the basic social relations. Marx is the last person from whom we can expect advice on how to make our intellectual and moral peace with bourgeois society. And this is surely his attraction and his value.

What does Bonger offer? He suggests, near the end of his book, that in a properly designed society all criminality would be a problem "for the physician rather than the judge." But this surely will not do. The therapeutic state, where prisons are called hospitals and jailers are called psychiatrists, simply raises again all the old problems about the justification of coercion and its reconciliation with autonomy that we faced in worrying about punishment. The only difference is that our coercive practices are now surrounded with a benevolent rhetoric which makes it even harder to raise the important issues. Thus the move to therapy, in my judgment, is only an illusory solution—alienation remains and the problem of reconciling coercion with autonomy remains unsolved. Indeed, if the alternative is having our personalities involuntarily restructured by some state psychiatrist, we might well want to claim the "right to be punished" that Hegel spoke of.[37]

Perhaps, then, we may really be forced seriously to consider a radical proposal. If we think that institutions of punishment are necessary and desirable, and if we are morally sensitive enough to want to be sure that we have the moral right to punish before we inflict it, then we had better first make sure that we have restructured society in such a way that criminals genuinely do correspond to the only model that will render punishment permissible—i.e., make sure that they are autonomous and that they do benefit in the requisite sense. Of course, if we did this then—if Marx and Bonger are right—crime itself and the need to punish would radically decrease if not disappear entirely.

NOTES

1. In a sense, my paper may be viewed as an elaborate commentary on this one passage, excerpted from a discussion generally concerned with the efficacy of capital punishment in eliminating crime, For in this passage, Marx (to the surprise

of many I should think) expresses a certain admiration for the classical retributive theory of punishment. Also (again surprisingly) he expresses this admiration in a kind of language he normally avoids—i.e., the moral language of rights and justice. He then, of course, goes on to reject the applicability of that theory. But the question that initially perplexed me is the following: what is the explanation of Marx's ambivalence concerning the retributive theory; why is he both attracted and repelled by it? (This ambivalence is not shared, for example, by utilitarians—who feel nothing but repulsion when the retributive theory is even mentioned.) Now except for some very brief passages in *The Holy Family*, Marx himself has nothing more to say on the topic of punishment beyond what is contained in this brief *Daily Tribune* article. Thus my essay is in no sense an exercise in textual scholarship (there are not enough texts) but is rather an attempt to construct an assessment of punishment, Marxist at least in spirit, that might account for the ambivalence found in the quoted passage. My main outside help comes, not from Marx himself, but from the writings of the Marxist criminologist Willem Bonger.

2. Many of the leading articles on this topic have been reprinted in *The Philosophy of Punishment*, ed. H. B. Acton (London, 1969). Those papers not included are cited in Acton's excellent bibliography.

3. One writer who has noticed this is Richard Wasserstrom. See his "Why Punish the Guilty?" *Princeton University Magazine* 20 (1964), pp. 14–19.

4. Marx normally avoids the language of rights and justice because he regards such language to be corrupted by bourgeois ideology. However, if we think very broadly of what an appeal to rights involves—namely, a protest against unjustified coercion—there is no reason why Marx may not legitimately avail himself on occasion of this way of speaking. For there is surely at least some moral overlap between Marx's protests against exploitation and the evils of a division of labor, for example, and the claims that people have a right not be be used solely for the benefit of others and a right to self–determination.

5. I do not mean to suggest that under no conceivable circumstances would the doctor be justified in giving the transfusion even though, in one clear sense, he had no right to do it. If, for example, the Jehovah's Witness was a key man whose survival was necessary to prevent the outbreak of a destructive war, we might well regard the transfusion as on the whole justified. However, even in such a case, a morally sensitive man would have to regretfully realize that he was sacrificing an important principle. Such a realization would be impossible (because inconsistent) for a utilitarian, for his theory admits only one principle—namely, do that which on the whole maximizes utility. An occupational disease of utilitarians is a blindness to the possibility of genuine moral dilemmas—i.e., a blindness to the possibility that important moral principles can conflict in ways that are not obviously resolvable by a rational decision procedure.

6. I qualify my thesis by the word "largely" to show at this point my realization, explored in more detail later, that no single theory can account for all criminal behavior.

7. Bernard Harrison, "Violence and the Rule of Law," in *Violence,* ed. Jerome A. Shaffer (New York, 1971), pp. 139-176.

8. I have made a start toward such a defense in my "The Killing of the Innocent," forthcoming in *The Monist* 57, no. 4 (October 1973).

9. H. L. A. Hart, "Prolegomenon to the Principles of Punishment," from *Punishment and Responsibility* (Oxford, 1968), pp. 1–27.

10. Thomas Hill Green, *Lectures on the Principles of Political Obligation* (1885), (Ann Arbor, 1967), pp. 180–205.

11. For an elaboration of this point, see Steven Lukes, "Alienation and Anomie," in *Philosophy, Politics and Society* (Third Series), ed. Peter Laslett and W. G. Runciman (Oxford, 1967), pp. 134–156.

12. Robert Paul Wolff, *In Defense of Anarchism* (New York, 1970).

13. In this section, I have adapted some of my previously published material: *Kant: The Philosophy of Right* (London, 1970), pp. 109–112 and 140–144; "Three Mistakes About Retributivism," *Analysis* (April 1971): 166–169; and "Kant's Theory of Criminal Punishment," in *Proceedings of the Third International Kant Congress,* ed. Lewis White Beck (Dordrecht, 1972), pp. 434–441. I am perfectly aware that Kant's views on the issues to be considered here are often obscure and inconsistent—e.g., the analysis of "willing one's own punishment" which I shall later quote from Kant occurs in a passage the primary purpose of which is to argue that the idea of "willing one's own punishment" makes no sense! My present objective, however, is not to attempt accurate Kant scholarship. My goal is rather to build upon some remarks of Kant's which I find philosophically suggestive.

14. Immanuel Kant, *The Metaphysical Elements of Justice* (1797), trans. John Ladd (Indianapolis, 1965), pp. 35ff.

15. *Ibid.,* p. 37.

16. John Rawls, "Justice as Fairness," *The Philosophical Review* 67 (1958): 164–194; and *A Theory of Justice* (Cambridge, Mass., 1971), especially pp. 17–22.

17. Immanuel Kant, "Concerning the Common Saying: This May be True in Theory but Does Not Apply in Practice (1793)," in *The Philosophy of Kant,* ed. and trans. Carl J. Friedrich (New York, 1949), pp. 421–422.

18. Immanuel Kant, *Perpetual Peace* (1795), trans. Lewis White Beck in the Kant anthology *On History* (Indianapolis 1963), p. 112.

19. Immanuel Kant, *The Metaphysical Elements of Justice, p. 34.*

20. *Ibid.,* pp. 99, 101, and 105, in the order quoted.

21. In addition to the works on justice by Rawls previously cited, the reader should consult the following for Rawls's application of his general theory to the problem of political obligation: John Rawls, "Legal Obligation and the Duty of Fair Play," in *Law and Philosophy,* ed. Sidney Hook (New York, 1964), pp. 3–18. This has been reprinted in my anthology *Civil Disobedience and Violence* (Belmont, Cal., 1971), pp. 39–52. For a direct application of a similar theory to the problem of punishment, see Herbert Morris, "Persons and Punishment," *The Monist* 52, no. 4 (October 1968): 475–501.

22. H. L. A. Hart, *The Concept of Law* (Oxford, 1961), pp. 189–195.

23. Jeffrie G. Murphy, "Moral Death: A Kantian Essay on Psychopathy," *Ethics* 82, no. 4 (July 1972): 284–298.

24. Banal as this point may syem, it could be persuasively argued that all Enlightenment political theory (e. g., that of Hobbes, Locke and Kant) is built upon ignoring it. For example, once we have substantial empirical evidence concerning how democracies really work in fact, how sympathetic can we really be to classical theories for the justification of democracy? For more on this, see C. B. Macpherson, "The Maximization of Democracy," in *Philosophy, Politics and Society* (Third Series), ed. Peter Laslett and W. G. Runciman (Oxgord, 1967), pp. 83–103. This article is also relevant to the point raised in note 11 above.

25. This point is well developed in C. B. Macpherson, *The Political Theory of Possessive Individualism* (Oxford, 1962). In a sense, this point affects even the formal correctness of a

theory. For it demonstrates an empirical source of corruption in the analyses of the very concepts in the theory.

26. The writings of Willem Adriaan Bonger (1876–1940), a Dutch criminologist, have fallen into totally unjustified neglect in recent years. Anticipating contemporary sociological theories of crime, he was insisting that criminal behavior is in the province of normal psychology (though abnormal society) at a time when most other writers were viewing criminality as a symptom of psychopathology. His major works are: *Criminality and Economic Conditions* (Boston, 1916); *An Introduction to Criminology* (London, 1936); and *Race and Crime* (New York, 1943).

27. I say, "at least in spirit" to avoid begging the controversial question of whether Marx can be said to embrace a theory of justice. Though (as I suggested in note 4) much of Marx's own evaluative rhetoric seems to overlap more traditional appeals to rights and justice (and a total lack of sympathy with anything like Utilitarianism), it must be admitted that he also frequently ridicules at least the terms "rights" and "justice" because of their apparent entrenchment in bourgeois ethics. For an interesting discussion of this issue, see Allen W. Wood, "The Marxian Critique of Justice," *Philosophy & Public Affairs 1*, no. 3 (Spring 1972): 244–282.

28. The importance of community is also, I think, recognized in Gabriel de Tarde's notion of "social similarity" as a condition of criminal responsibility. See his *Penal Philosophy* (Boston, 1912). I have drawn on de Tarde's general account in my "Moral Death: A Kantian Essay on Psychopathy."

29. By "reciprocity" Bonger intends something which includes, but is much richer than, a notion of "fair trading or bargaining" that might initially be read into the term. He also has in mind such things as sympathetic identification with others and tendencies to provide mutual aid. Thus, for Bonger, reciprocity and egoism have a strong tendency to conflict. I mention this lest Bonger's notion of reciprocity be too quickly identified with the more restricted notion found in, for example, Kant and Rawls.

30. It is interesting how greatly Bonger's analysis differs from classical deterrence theory—e.g., that of Bentham. Bentham, who views men as machines driven by desires to attain pleasure and avoid pain, tends to regard terror as the primary restraint against crime. Bonger believes that, at least in a healthy society, moral motives would function as a major restraint against crime. When an environment that destroys moral motivation is created, even terror (as statistics tend to confirm) will not eradicate crime.

31. *Introduction to Criminology*, pp. 75–76, and *Criminality and Economic Conditions*, pp. 532, 402, 483–484, 436, and 407, in the order quoted. Bonger explicitly attacks Hobbes: "The adherents of [Hobbes's theory] have studied principally men who live under capitalism, or under civilization; their correct conclusion has been that egoism is the predominant characteristic of these men, and they have adopted the simplest explanation of the phenomenon and say that this trait is inborn." If Hobbists can cite Freud for modern support, Bonger can cite Darwin. For, as Darwin had argued in the *Descent of Man*, men would not have survived as a species if they had not initially had considerably greater social sentiments than Hobbes allows them.

32. Austin J. Turk, in the Introduction to his abridged edition of Bonger's *Criminality and Economic Conditions* (Bloomington, 1969), p. 14.

33. Statistical data on characteristics of offenders in America are drawn primarily from surveys by the Bureau of Census and the National Council on Crime and Delinquency. While there is of course wide disagreement on how such data are to be interpreted, there is no serious disagreement concerning at least the general accuracy of statistics like the one I have cited. Even government publications openly acknowledge a high correlation between crime and socio-economic disadvantages: "From arrest records, probation reports, and prison statistics a 'portrait' of the offender emerges that progressively highlights the disadvantaged character of his life. The offender at the end of the road in prison is likely to be a member of the lowest social and economic groups in the country, poorly educated and perhaps unemployed.... Material failure, then, in a culture firmly oriented toward material success, is the most common denominator of offenders" *The Challenge of Crime in a Free Society, A Report by the President's Commission on Law Enforcement and Administration of Justice,* U. S. Government Printing Office, Washington, D. C., 1967, pp. 44 and 160). The Marxist implications of this admission have not gone unnoticed by prisoners. See Samuel Jorden, "Prison Reform: In Whose Interest?" *Criminal Law Bulletin* 7, no. 9 (November 1971): 779–787.

34. There are, of course, other factors which enter into an explanation of this statistic. One of them is the fact that economically disadvantaged guilty persons are more likely to wind up arrested or in prison (and thus be reflected in this statistic) than are economically advantaged guilty persons. Thus economic conditions enter into the explanation, not just of criminal behavior, but of society's response to criminal behavior. For a general discussion on the many ways in which crime and poverty are related, see Patricia M. Wald, "Poverty and Criminal Justice," *Task Force Report: The Courts,* U. S. Government Printing Office, Washington, D. C., 1967, pp. 139–151.

35. The idea that the principles of justice could be proved as a kind of theorem (Rawls's claim in "Justice as Fairness") seems to be absent, if I understand the work correctly, in Rawls's recent *A Theory of Justice*. In this book Rawls seems to be content with something less than a decision procedure. He is no longer trying to pull his theory of justice up by its own bootstraps, but now seems concerned simply to *exhibit* a certain elaborate conception of justice in the belief that it will do a good job of systematizing and ordering most of our considered and reflective intuitions about moral matters. To this, of course, the Marxist will want to say something like the following: "The considered and reflective intuitions current in our society are a product of bourgeois culture, and thus any theory based upon them begs the question against us and in favor of the status quo." I am not sure that this charge cannot be answered, but I am sure that it deserves an answer. Someday Rawls may be remembered, to paraphrase Georg Lukács's description of Thomas Mann, as the last and greatest philosopher of bourgeois liberalism. The virtue of this description is that it perceives the limitations of his outlook in a way consistent with acknowledging his indisputable genius. (None of my remarks here, I should point out, are to be interpreted as denying that our civilization derived major moral benefits from the tradition of bourgeois liberalism. Just because the freedoms and procedures we associate with bourgeois liberalism—speech, press, assembly, due process of law, etc.—are not the only important freedoms and procedures, we are not to conclude with some witless radicals that these freedoms are not terribly important and that the victories of bourgeois revolutions are not worth preserving. My point is much more modest and noncontroversial—namely, that even bourgeois liberalism requires a critique. It is not self-justifying and, in certain very important respects, is not justified at all.)

36. Kant has some doubts about punishing bastard infanticide and dueling on similar grounds. Given the stigma that Kant's society attached to illegitimacy and the halo that the same society placed around military honor, it did not seem

totally fair to punish those whose criminality in part grew out of such approved motives. See *Metaphysical Elements of Justice,* pp. 106–107.

37.   This point is pursued in Herbert Morris, "Persons and Punishment." Bonger did not appreciate that "mental ill- ness," like criminality, may also be a phenomenon of social class. On this, see August B. Hollingshead and Frederick C. Redlich, *Social Class and Mental Illness* (New York, 1958). On the general issue of punishment versus therapy, see my *Punishment and Rehabilitation* (Belmont, Cal., 1973).

ANDREW VON HIRSCH

Desert*

In everyday thinking about punishment, the idea of desert figures prominently. Ask the person on the street why a wrongdoer should be punished, and he is likely to say that he "deserves" it. Yet the literature of penology seldom mentions the word. Instead, there is usually listed—along with the three traditional utilitarian aims of deterrence, incapacitation, and rehabilitation—a fourth aim of "retribution." We do not find "retribution" a helpful term. It has no regular use except in relation to punishment, so that one is precluded from learning about the concept from the word's use in other contexts. It also seems somewhat narrow. The Oxford English Dictionary, for example, defines retribution as "recompense for, or requital of evil done; return of evil"; this suggests a particular view of why punishment is deserved, namely that the offender should somehow be "paid back" for his wrong. Yet, as we will see presently, there are other explanations of deserved punishment which do not rely on this notion of requital-of-evil. Finally, the word is, perhaps through historical accident, burdened with pejorative associations.[1]

We prefer the term "desert." Its cognate, "to deserve," is widely used: rewards, prizes, and grades, as well as punishments, are said to be deserved or undeserved. And the word "desert" is somewhat less emotionally loaded.

To say someone "deserves" to be rewarded or punished is to refer to his *past* conduct, and assert that its merit or demerit is reason for according him pleasant or unpleasant treatment. The focus on the past is critical. That a student has written an outstanding paper is grounds for asserting that he deserves an award; but that the award will yield him or others future benefits (however desirable those might be) cannot be grounds for claiming he deserves it. The same holds for punishment: to assert that someone deserves to be

punished is to look to his past wrongdoing as reason for having him penalized. This orientation to the past distinguishes desert from the other purported aims of punishment—deterrence, incapacitation, rehabilitation—which seek to justify the criminal sanction by its prospective usefulness in preventing crime.

It is important here to distinguish between the rationale for punishing and the rationale for the underlying legal prohibitions. Concededly, the latter—the criminal law's substantive prohibitions—are forward-looking in their aim: murder is prohibited so that citizens will not kill one another. But the question is whether, once a violation has occurred, the basis for punishing the violator is still forward-looking, or is retrospective. Once a murder has taken place, is the only reason for penalizing the murderer to prevent subsequent violations by him or others? Or is there, at that point, a retrospective reason for punishing—that the murderer deserves to be punished? And if so, how is the notion of deserved punishment to be explained?

A useful place to begin is with Kant's explanation of deserved punishment, which he based on the idea of fair dealing among free individuals. To realize their own freedom, he contended, members of society have the reciprocal obligation to limit their behavior so as not to interfere with the freedom of others. When someone infringes another's rights, he gains an unfair advantage over all others in the society—since he has failed to constrain his own behavior while benefiting from other persons' forbearance from interfering with his rights. The punishment—by imposing a counterbalancing disadvantage on the violator—restores the equilibrium: after having undergone the punishment, the violator ceases to be at advantage over his non-violating fellows.[2] (This righting-of-the-balance is not a matter of preventing future crimes. Aside from any concern with prospective criminality, it is the violator's *past* crime that placed him in a position of advantage over others, and it is that advantage which the punishment would eliminate.) As Herbert Morris puts it in a recent restatement of the Kantian argument:

A person who violates the rules has something others have—the benefits of the system [of mutual non-inter-ference with others' rights]—but by renouncing what others have assumed, the burdens of self-restraint, he has acquired an unfair advantage. Matters are not even until this advantage is in some way erased. . . . Justice —that is punishing such individuals—restores the equilibrium of benefits and burdens. . . .

Kant's theory, however, accounts only for the imposition of *some* kind of deprivation on the offender to offset the "advantage" he obtained in violating others' rights. It does not explain why that deprivation should take the peculiar form of punishment. Punishment differs from other pur-posefully inflicted deprivations in the moral dis-approval it expresses: punishing someone conveys in dramatic fashion that his conduct was wrong and that he is blameworthy for having committed it.[3] Why, then, does the violator de-serve to be *punished,* instead of being made to suffer another kind of deprivation that connotes no special moral stigma?

To answer this question it becomes necessary, we think, to focus specifically on the reprobation implicit in punishment and argue that *it* is de-served. Someone who infringes the rights of oth-ers, the argument runs, does wrong and deserves blame for his conduct. It is because he deserves blame that the sanctioning authority is entitled to choose a response that expresses moral disap-proval: namely, punishment. In other words, the sanction ought not only to deprive the offender of the "advantage" obtained by his disregard of the rules (the Kantian explanation); but do so in a manner that ascribes blame (the reprobative ex-planation).[4]

This raises the question of what purpose the reprobation itself serves. Blaming persons who commit wrongful acts is, arguably, a way of reaffirming the moral values that were infringed. But to speak of reaffirming such values prompts the further question: Why should the violator be singled out for blame to achieve that end? The answer must ultimately be that the censure is itself deserved: that someone who is responsible for wrongdoing is blame*worthy* and hence may justly be blamed.

With this much preliminary explanation of the idea of deserved punishment, we turn to the main question: whether desert is necessary to justify the criminal sanction.

FROM DETERRENCE TO DESERT

We have already suggested one reason for pun-ishing: deterrence. The criminal sanction is called for to prevent certain kinds of injurious conduct. Why is it not sufficient to rely on that simple argument—and get on with deciding how punish-ment should rationally be allocated? Why bring in desert, with all its philosophical perplexities?

On utilitarian assumptions, deterrence would indeed suffice. The main utilitarian premise is (roughly) that a society is rightly ordered if its major institutions are arranged to achieve the maximum aggregate satisfaction and the mini-mum aggregate suffering. On this premise, pun-ishment would be justified if it deterred sufficiently—because, in sum, more suffering would be prevented through the resulting reduc-tion in crime than is caused by making those punished suffer. Our difficulty is, however, that we doubt the utilitarian premise: that the suffer-ing of a few persons is made good by the benefits accruing to the many. A free society, we believe, should recognize that an individual's rights—or at least his most important rights—are prima fa-cie entitled to priority over collective interests.[5] This idea has been best expressed, perhaps, by the philosopher John Rawls in the opening pages of his *Theory of Justice.* "Each person," he writes, "possesses an inviolability founded on justice that even the welfare of society as a whole cannot override . . . justice denies that the loss of freedom for some is made right by a greater good shared by others. It does not allow that the sacrifices imposed on a few are outweighed by the larger sum of advantages enjoyed by many."

Given this assumption of the primacy of the individual's fundamental rights, no utilitarian ac-count of punishment, deterrence included, can stand alone. While deterrence explains why most people benefit from the existence of punishment, the benefit to the many is not by itself a just basis for depriving the offender of his liberty and repu-tation. Some other reason, then, is needed to ex-plain the suffering inflicted on the offender: that reason is desert. The offender may justly be sub-jected to certain deprivations because he deserves it; and he deserves it because he has engaged in wrongful conduct—conduct that does or threat-ens injury and that is prohibited by law. The penalty is thus not just a means of crime preven-tion but a merited response to the actor's deed, "rectifying the balance" in the Kantian sense and expressing moral reprobation of the actor for the wrong. In other words: while deterrence accounts for why punishment is socially useful, desert is necessary to explain why that utility may justly be pursued at the offender's expense.[6]

In speaking thus of desert as necessary to the justification of punishment, we are not referring to channeling theories such as Oliver Wendell Holmes's: that ordinary citizens believe wrongdoers should suffer, and would resort to private vengeance were the law not to punish. Perhaps the restraint of vengeance is an important function of the criminal sanction, but this is another utilitarian claim: that there will be less social disruption if offenders are punished by the state rather than left to private retaliation.[7] What still must be explained is why, in thus benefiting society, it is just to deprive offenders of *their* rights by penalizing them. To answer that question, a moral claim must be made: not that the public thinks punishment is deserved and will do harm if its opinion is disregarded; but that punishment *is* deserved.

THE CONVERSE: FROM DESERT TO DETERRENCE

The route of argument just taken is the more familiar in current philosophical literature on punishment: begin with deterrence as a reason for punishing, then consider whether it must be supplemented by desert. However, the logic can be reversed: one can start by relying on the idea of desert. But again, the interdependence of the two concepts—desert and deterrence—will quickly become apparent.

Desert may be viewed as reason in itself for creating a social institution. This is evident in the case of rewards. Most societies, including our own, reward those who have done deeds of special merit. Rewards may serve utilitarian ends (e.g., as an incentive for desired conduct): but, even disregarding such utility, a case for rewarding merit can be made simply on the grounds that it is deserved. Good work and good acts ought to be acknowledged for their own sake, and rewards express that acknowledgment. A parallel argument might be made for punishment:[8] those who violate others' rights deserve to be punished, on the Kantian and reprobative grounds just discussed. A system of punishment is justified, the argument runs, simply because it is deserved.

However, there are countervailing moral considerations.[9] An important counterconsideration is the principle of not deliberately causing human suffering where it can possibly be avoided. With rewards, this principle does not stand in the way: for rewards per se do not inflict pain (other than the possible discomforts of envy). It is otherwise with punishment: while wrongdoers deserve punishment, it is necessarily painful. Arguably, the principle against inflicting suffering should, in the absence of other considerations, override the case for punishing based on wrongdoers' deserts.

It is at this point in the argument that the idea of deterrence becomes critical—for it can supply an answer to the countervailing concern about the infliction of suffering. When punishment's deterrent effect is taken into account, it may cause less misery than not punishing would. Moreover, not only might total misery be reduced, but its distribution would be more acceptable: fewer innocent persons will be victimized by crimes, while those less deserving—the victimizers—will be made to suffer instead. Deterrence thus tips the scales back in favor of the penal sanction. To state the argument schematically:

Step 1: Those who violate others' rights deserve punishment. That, of itself, constitutes a prima facie justification for maintaining a system of criminal sanctions.

Step 2: There is, however, a countervailing moral obligation of not deliberately adding to the amount of human suffering. Punishment necessarily makes those punished suffer. In the absence of additional argument, that overrides the case for punishment in step 1.

Step 3: The notion of deterrence, at this point, suggests that punishment may prevent more misery than it inflicts—thus disposing of the countervailing argument in step 2. With it out of the way, the prima facie case for punishment described in step 1—based on desert—stands again.

The case for punishing differs, then, from the case for rewards. With rewards, it is sufficient to argue that they are deserved: since rewards are not painful, there is no need to point to their collateral social usefulness to excuse the misery they cause. Punishments, likewise, are deserved; but, given the overriding concern with the infliction of pain, the notion of deterrence has to be relied upon as well.

The foregoing shows the interdependence of the twin concepts of deterrence and desert. When one seeks to justify the criminal sanction by reference to its deterrent utility, desert is called for to explain why that utility may justly be pursued at offenders' expense. When one seeks to justify punishment as deserved, deterrence is needed to deal with the countervailing concern about the suffering inflicted. The interdependence of these two concepts suggests that the criminal sanction rests, ultimately, on *both*.

NOTES

1. Thus, the 1972 edition of the Model Sentencing Act states: "sentences should not be based upon revenge and retribution." No explanation is supplied of why the idea of retribution should thus be summarily dismissed, or why it should be lumped together with revenge. The drafters of the Act assumed, apparently, that retribution is tantamount to vindictiveness toward offenders.

2. The Kantian argument presupposes that what violators are being punished for is the infringement of rules that safeguard the rights of *all* members of society including the violator's own rights. This raises a question . . . whether a desert-based justification for punishment, such as Kant's, can hold in a society whose penal system helps maintain a less-than-just social system.

3. For a fuller account of the reprobative element in punishment, we refer the reader to Joel Feinberg's essay, "The Expressive Function of Punishment," in his book *Doing and Deserving*—as well as Henry M. Hart's fine essay, "The Aims of the Criminal Law."

4. Whether a reprobative theory could be the *only* explanation of deserved punishment is more problematical. Feinberg suggests that punishment has two analytically separable aspects: (1) infliction of pains, and (2) symbolic condemnation. A reprobative theory accounts for why the offender deserves to be condemned, but, Feinberg suggests, this condemnatory function could conceivably be achieved by a dramatic public ritual—and if so, the infliction of pains remains to be accounted for. It may be that *both* the Kantian and the reprobative explanation are required; the former to explain why the offender is deserving of some kind of deprivation, and the latter to explain why it should take the form of public reprobation that is characteristic of punishment.

5. Which rights of the individual are of sufficient importance to be accorded this special priority can be a more difficult question. Is it all his rights, including, say, the right to hold and dispose of property? (The philosopher Robert Nozick has assumed so, and has constructed an argument for a minimal state on that basis.) Or should only certain "fundamental" rights be given this preferred status, leaving other individual interests, possibly including property, open to being distributed according to the utilitarian principle of the greatest good for the greatest number? (Peter Singer has made this suggestion, in a recent review of Nozick's book.)

But this problem of which rights are sufficiently important—perplexing as it may be when dealing with issues of economic justice—poses less difficulty for us. For the interests which punishment may intrude upon include the most important the individual can possibly have: his liberty. If *any* interests of the individual should be entitled to priority over collective interests, this surely should be among them.

6. The traditional objection to purely utilitarian theories of punishment has been that they justify too much: that if the prevention of crime is the sole aim, why not also punish the innocent if that will prevent crime more effectively? H. L. A. Hart has pointed out, however, that this objection can be met if one is careful to observe the distinction between the general justifying aim of punishment and the rules for its distribution. Even if a utilitarian view is espoused of why the criminal sanction should exist in the first place, Hart suggests, the rules for distributing punishments should still (in the interests of fairness) prohibit penalizing those who have committed no unlawful act. Our criticism of utilitarianism is somewhat different: we are not speaking of who should be punished (distribution) but of why anyone ever should be punished (general justification). We are suggesting that, given our assumption about the primacy of individual rights, the benefits accruing to society simply do not justify depriving anyone (even violators) of their fundamental rights: that it is essential to the very existence of the criminal sanction that the violator deserves to be punished.

7. Offenders would also suffer less, to the extent that the state's punishments are not so drastic as private vengeance would be. But the question at issue here is why offenders should be made to suffer *at all.*

8. We mention the parallel of rewards merely to illustrate the structure of the argument. Obviously, rewards differ from punishments in important respects (e.g., they are not visited compulsorily on the recipient), so that one might argue for a system of rewards on the basis of desert without being compelled to argue similarly for punishment.

9. To say someone deserves to be treated in a certain manner is to claim *a* reason for so treating him—but still allows one to conclude that he should not be treated as he deserves if there are sufficient countervailing reasons.

JOHN RAWLS

Punishment*

TWO CONCEPTS OF RULES

In this paper I want to show the importance of the distinction between justifying a practice[1] and justifying a particular action falling under it, and I want to explain the logical basis of this distinction and how it is possible to miss its significance. While the distinction has frequently been made,[2] and is now becoming commonplace, there remains the task of explaining the tendency either to overlook it altogether, or to fail to appreciate its importance.

To show the importance of the distinction I am going to defend utilitarianism against those objections which have traditionally been made against it in connection with punishment and the obligation to keep promises. I hope to show that if one uses the distinction in question then one can state utilitarianism in a way which makes it a much better explication of our considered moral judgments than these traditional objections would seem to admit.[3] Thus the importance of the distinction is shown by the way it strengthens the utilitarian view regardless of whether that view is completely defensible or not.

To explain how the significance of the distinction may be overlooked, I am going to discuss two conceptions of rules. One of these conceptions conceals the importance of distinguishing between the justification of a rule or practice and the justification of a particular action falling under it. The other conception makes it clear why this distinction must be made and what is its logical basis.

The subject of punishment, in the sense of attaching legal penalties to the violation of legal rules, has always been a troubling moral question.[4] The trouble about it has not been that people disagree as to whether or not punishment is justifiable. Most people have held that, freed from certain abuses, it is an acceptable institution.

Only a few have rejected punishment entirely, which is rather surprising when one considers all that can be said against it. The difficulty is with the justification of punishment: various arguments for it have been given by moral philosophers, but so far none of them has won any sort of general acceptance; no justification is without those who detest it. I hope to show that the use of the aforementioned distinction enables one to state the utilitarian view in a way which allows for the sound points of its critics.

For our purposes we may say that there are two justifications of punishment. What we may call the retributive view is that punishment is justified on the grounds that wrongdoing merits punishment. It is morally fitting that a person who does wrong should suffer in proportion to his wrongdoing. That a criminal should be punished follows from his guilt, and the severity of the appropriate punishment depends on the depravity of his act. The state of affairs where a wrongdoer suffers punishment is morally better than the state of affairs where he does not; and it is better irrespective of any of the consequences of punishing him.

What we may call the utilitarian view holds that on the principle that bygones are bygones and that only future consequences are material to present decisions, punishment is justifiable only by reference to the probable consequences of maintaining it as one of the devices of the social order. Wrongs committed in the past are, as such, not relevant considerations for deciding what to do. If punishment can be shown to promote effectively the interest of society it is justifiable, otherwise it is not.

I have stated these two competing views very roughly to make one feel the conflict between them: one feels the force of *both* arguments and one wonders how they can be reconciled. From my introductory remarks it is obvious that the resolution which I am going to propose is that in this case one must distinguish between justifying a practice as a system of rules to be applied and

*From "Two Concepts of Rules" by John Rawls, *The Philosophical Review,* Vol. 64 (1955), pp. 3–13. Reprinted by permission of the author and the publisher.

enforced, and justifying a particular action which falls under these rules, utilitarian arguments are appropriate with regard to questions about practices, while retributive arguments fit the application of particular rules to particular cases.

We might try to get clear about this distinction by imagining how a father might answer the question of his son. Suppose the son asks, "Why was *J* put in jail yesterday?" The father answers, "Because he robbed the bank at *B*. He was duly tried and found guilty. That's why he was put in jail yesterday." But suppose the son had asked a different question, namely, "Why do people put other people in jail?" Then the father might answer, "To protect good people from bad people" or "To stop people from doing things that would make it uneasy for all of us; for otherwise we wouldn't be able to go to bed at night and sleep in peace." There are two very different questions here. One question emphasizes the proper name: It asks why *J* was punished rather than someone else, or it asks what he was punished for. The other question asks why we have the institution of punishment: Why do people punish one another rather than, say, always forgiving one another?

Thus the father says in effect that a particular man is punished, rather than some other man, because he is guilty, and he is guilty because he broke the law (past tense). In his case the law looks back, the judge looks back, the jury looks back, and a penalty is visited upon him for something he did. That a man is to be punished, and what his punishment is to be, is settled by its being shown that he broke the law and that the law assigns that penalty for the violation of it.

On the other hand we have the institution of punishment itself, and recommend and accept various changes in it, because it is thought by the (ideal) legislator and by those to whom the law applies that, as a part of a system of law impartially applied from case to case arising under it, it will have the consequence, in the long run, of furthering the interests of society.

One can say, then, that the judge and the legislator stand in different positions and look in different directions: one to the past, the other to the future. The justification of what the judge does, *qua* judge, sounds like the retributive view; the justification of what the (ideal) legislator does, *qua* legislator, sounds like the utilitarian view. Thus both views have a point (this is as it should be since intelligent and sensitive persons have been on both sides of the argument); and one's initial confusion disappears once one sees that

these views apply to persons holding different offices with different duties, and situated differently with respect to the system of rules that make up the criminal law.[5]

One might say, however, that the utilitarian view is more fundamental since it applies to a more fundamental office, for the judge carries out the legislator's will so far as he can determine it. Once the legislator decides to have laws and to assign penalties for their violation (as things are there must be both the law and the penalty) an institution is set up which involves a retributive conception of particular cases. It is part of the concept of the criminal law as a system of rules that the application and enforcement of these rules in particular cases should be justifiable by arguments of a retributive character. The decision whether or not to use law rather than some other mechanism of social control, and the decision as to what laws to have and what penalties to assign, may be settled by utilitarian arguments; but if one decides to have laws then one has decided on something whose working in particular cases is retributive in form.[6]

The answer, then, to the confusion engendered by the two views of punishment is quite simple: One distinguishes two offices, that of the judge and that of the legislator, and one distinguishes their different stations with respect to the system of rules which make up the law; and then one notes that the different sorts of considerations which would usually be offered as reasons for what is done under the cover of these offices can be paired off with the competing justifications of punishment. One reconciles the two views by the time-honored device of making them apply to different situations.

But can it really be this simple? Well, this answer allows for the apparent intent of each side. Does a person who advocates the retributive view necessarily advocate, as an *institution*, legal machinery whose essential purpose is to set up and preserve a correspondence between moral turpitude and suffering? Surely not.[7] What retributionists have rightly insisted upon is that no man can be punished unless he is guilty, that is, unless he has broken the law. Their fundamental criticism of the utilitarian account is that, as they interpret it, it sanctions an innocent person's being punished (if one may call it that) for the benefit of society.

On the other hand, utilitarians agree that punishment is to be inflicted only for the violation of law. They regard this much as understood from the concept of punishment itself.[8] The point of the utilitarian account concerns the institution as a system of rules: utilitarianism seeks to limit its use by declaring it justifiable only if it can be shown to foster effectively the good of society. Historically it is a protest against the indiscriminate and ineffective use of the criminal law.[9] It seeks to dissuade us from assigning to penal institutions the improper, if not sacrilegious, task of matching suffering with moral turpitude. Like others, utilitarians want penal institutions designed so that, as far as humanly possible, only those who break the law run afoul of it. They hold that no official should have discretionary power to inflict penalties whenever he thinks it for the benefit of society; for on utilitarian grounds an institution granting such power could not be justified.[10]

The suggested way of reconciling the retributive and the utilitarian justifications of punishment seems to account for what both sides have wanted to say. There are, however, two further questions which arise, and I shall devote the remainder of this section to them.

First, will not a difference of opinion as to the proper criterion of just law make the proposed reconciliation unacceptable to retributionists? Will they not question whether, if the utilitarian principle is used as the criterion, it follows that those who have broken the law are guilty in a way which satisfies their demand that those punished deserve to be punished? To answer this difficulty, suppose that the rules of the criminal law are justified on utilitarian grounds (it is only for laws that meet his criterion that the utilitarian can be held responsible). Then it follows that the actions which the criminal law specifies as offenses are such that, if they were tolerated, terror and alarm would spread in society. Consequently, retributionists can only deny that those who are punished deserve to be punished if they deny that such actions are wrong. This they will not want to do.

The second question is whether utilitarianism doesn't justify too much. One pictures it as an engine of justification which, if consistently adopted, could be used to justify cruel and arbitrary institutions. Retributionists may be supposed to concede that utilitarians *intend* to reform the law and to make it more humane; that utilitarians do not *wish* to justify any such thing as punishment of the innocent; and that utilitarians may appeal to the fact that punishment presupposes guilt in the sense that by punishment one understands an institution attaching penalties to the infraction of legal rules, and therefore

that it is logically absurd to suppose that utilitarians in justifying *punishment* might also have justified punishment (if we may call it that) of the innocent. The real question, however, is whether the utilitarian, in justifying punishment, hasn't used arguments which commit him to accepting the infliction of suffering on innocent persons if it is for the good of society (whether or not one calls this punishment). More generally, isn't the utilitarian committed in principle to accepting many practices which he, as a morally sensitive person, wouldn't want to accept? Retributionists are inclined to hold that there is no way to stop the utilitarian principle from justifying too much except by adding to it a principle which distributes certain rights to individuals. Then the amended criterion is not the greatest benefit of society *simpliciter* [simply], but the greatest benefit of society subject to the constraint that no one's rights may be violated. Now while I think that the classical utilitarians proposed a criterion of this more complicated sort, I do not want to argue that point here.[11] What I want to show is that there is *another* way of preventing the utilitarian principle from justifying too much, or at least of making it much less likely to do so: namely, by stating utilitarianism in a way which accounts for the distinction between the justification of an institution and the justification of a particular action falling under it.

I begin by defining the institution of punishment as follows: a person is said to suffer punishment whenever he is legally deprived of some of the normal rights of a citizen on the ground that he has violated a rule of law, the violation having been established by trial according to the due process of law, provided that the deprivation is carried out by the recognized legal authorities of the state, that the rule of law clearly specifies both the offense and the attached penalty, that the courts construe statutes strictly, and that the statute was on the books prior to the time of the offense.[12] This definition specifies what I shall understand by punishment. The question is whether utilitarian arguments may be found to justify institutions widely different from this and such as one would find cruel and arbitrary.

This question is best answered, I think, by taking up a particular accusation. Consider the following from Carritt:

... the utilitarian must hold that we are justified in inflicting pain always and only to prevent worse pain or bring about greater happiness. This, then, is all we need to consider in so-called punishment, which must be purely preventive. But if some kind of very cruel crime becomes common, and none of the criminals can be caught, it might be highly expedient, as an example, to hang an innocent man, if a charge against him could be so framed that he were universally thought guilty; indeed this would only fail to be an ideal instance of utilitarian 'punishment' because the victim himself would not have been so likely as a real felon to commit such a crime in the future; in all other respects it would be perfectly deterrent and therefore felicific.[13]

Carritt is trying to show that there are occasions when a utilitarian argument would justify taking an action which would be generally condemned; and thus that utilitarianism justifies too much. But the failure of Carritt's argument lies in the fact that he makes no distinction between the justification of the general system of rules which constitutes penal institutions and the justification of particular applications of these rules to particular cases by the various officials whose job it is to administer them. This becomes perfectly clear when one asks who the "we" are of whom Carritt speaks. Who is this who has a sort of absolute authority on particular occasions to decide that an innocent man shall be "punished" if everyone can be convinced that he is guilty? Is this person the legislator, or the judge, or the body of private citizens, or what? It is utterly crucial to know who is to decide such matters, and by what authority, for all of this must be written into the rules of the institution. Until one knows these things one doesn't know what the institution is whose justification is being challenged; and as the utilitarian principle applies to the institution one doesn't know whether it is justifiable on utilitarian grounds or not.

Once this is understood it is clear what the countermove to Carritt's argument is. One must describe more carefully what the *institution* is which his example suggests, and then ask oneself whether or not it is likely that having this institution would be for the benefit of society in the long run. One must not content oneself with the vague thought that, when it's a question of *this* case, it would be a good thing if *somebody* did something even if an innocent person were to suffer.

Try to imagine, then, an institution (which we may call "telishment") which is such that the officials set up by it have authority to arrange a trial for the condemnation of an innocent man whenever they are of the opinion that doing so would be in the best interests of society. The discretion of officials is limited, however, by the rule that they may not condemn an innocent man to

undergo such an ordeal unless there is, at the time, a wave of offenses similar to that with which they charge him and telish him for. We may imagine that the officials having the discretionary authority are the judges of the higher courts in consultation with the chief of police, the minister of justice, and a committee of the legislature.

Once one realizes that one is involved in setting up an *institution*, one sees that the hazards are very great. For example, what check is there on the officials? How is one to tell whether or not their actions are authorized? How is one to limit the risks involved in allowing such systematic deception? How is one to avoid giving anything short of complete discretion to the authorities to telish anyone they like? In addition to these considerations, it is obvious that people will come to have a very different attitude towards their penal system when telishment is adjoined to it. They will be uncertain as to whether a convicted man has been punished or telished. They will wonder whether or not they should feel sorry for him. They will wonder whether the same fate won't at any time fall on them. If one pictures how such an institution would actually work, and the enormous risks involved in it, it seems clear that it would serve no useful purpose. A utilitarian justification for this institution is most unlikely.

It happens in general that as one drops off the defining features of punishment one ends up with an institution whose utilitarian justification is highly doubtful. One reason for this is that punishment works like a kind of price system: By altering the prices one has to pay for the performance of actions, it supplies a motive for avoiding some actions and doing others. The defining features are essential if punishment is to work in this way; so that an institution which lacks these features, for example, an institution which is set up to "punish" the innocent, is likely to have about as much point as a price system (if one may call it that) where the prices of things change at random from day to day and one learns the price of something after one has agreed to buy it.[14]

If one is careful to apply the utilitarian principle to the institution which is to authorize particular actions, then there is *less* danger of its justifying too much. Carritt's example gains plausibility by its indefiniteness and by its concentration on the particular case. His argument will only hold if it can be shown that there are utilitarian arguments which justify an institution whose publicly ascertainable offices and powers are such as to permit officials to exercise that kind of discretion in particular cases. But the requirement of having to build the arbitrary features of the particular decision into the institutional practice makes the justification much less likely to go through.

NOTES

1. I use the word "practice" throughout as a sort of technical term meaning any form of activity specified by a system of rules which defines offices, roles, moves, penalties, defenses, and so on, and which gives the activity its structure. As examples one may think of games and rituals, trials and parliaments.

2. The distinction is central to Hume's discussion of justice in *A Treatise of Human Nature,* bk. III, pt. ii, esp. secs. 2–4. It is clearly stated by John Austin in the second lecture of *Lectures on Jurisprudence* (4th ed.; London, 1873), I, 116ff. (1st ed., 1832). Also it may be argued that J. S. Mill took it for granted in *Utilitarianism;* on this point cf. J. O. Urmson, "The Interpretation of the Moral Philosophy of J. S. Mill," *Philosophical Quarterly,* vol. III (1953). In addition to the arguments given by Urmson there are several clear statements of the distinction in *A System of Logic* (8th ed.; London, 1872), bk. VI, ch. xii pars. 2, 3, 7. The distinction is fundamental to J. D. Mabbott's important paper, "Punishment," *Mind,* n.s., vol. XLVIII (April, 1939). More recently the distinction has been stated with particular emphasis by S. E. Toulmin in *The Place of Reason in Ethics* (Cambridge, 1950), see esp. ch. xi, where it plays a major part in his account of moral reasoning. Toulmin doesn't explain the basis of the distinction, nor how one might overlook its importance, as I try to in this paper, and in my review of this book (*Philosophical Review,* vol. LX [October, 1951]), as some of my criticisms show, I failed to understand the force of it. See also H. D. Aiken, "The Levels of Moral Discourse," *Ethics,* vol. LXII (1952), A. M. Quinton, "Punishment," *Analysis,* vol. XIV (June, 1954), and P. H. Nowell-Smith, *Ethics* (London, 1954), pp. 236–239, 271–273.

3. On the concept of explication see the author's paper *Philosophical Review,* vol. LX (April, 1951).

4. While this paper was being revised, Quinton's appeared; footnote 2 supra. There are several respects in which my remarks are similar to his. Yet as I consider some further questions and rely on somewhat different arguments, I have retained the discussion of punishment and promises together as two test cases for utilitarianism.

5. Note the fact that different sorts of arguments are suited to different offices. One way of taking the differences between ethical theories is to regard them as accounts of the reasons expected in different offices.

6. In this connection see Mabbott, *op. cit.,* pp. 163–164.

7. On this point see Sir David Ross, *The Right and the Good* (Oxford, 1930), pp. 57–60.

8. See Hobbes's definition of punishment in *Leviathan,* ch. xxviii; and Bentham's definition in *The Principle of Morals and Legislation,* ch. xii, par. 36, ch. xv, par. 28, and in *The Rationale of Punishment,* (London, 1830), bk. I, ch. i. They could agree with Bradley that: "Punishment is punishment only when it is deserved. We pay the penalty, because we owe it, and for no other reason; and if punishment is inflicted for any other reason whatever than because it is merited by wrong, it is a gross immorality, a crying injustice, an abominable crime, and not what it pretends to be." *Ethical Studies* (2nd ed.; Oxford, 1927), pp. 26–27. Certainly by definition it isn't what it pretends to be. The innocent can only be punished by mistake; deliberate "punishment" of the innocent necessarily involves fraud.

9. Cf. Leon Radzinowicz, *A History of English Criminal Law: The Movement for Reform 1750–1833* (London, 1948), esp. ch. xi on Bentham.

10. Bentham discusses how corresponding to a punitory provision of a criminal law there is another provision which stands to it as an antagonist and which needs a name as much as the punitory. He calls it, as one might expect, the *anaetiosostic,* and of it he says: "The punishment of guilt is the object of the former one: the preservation of innocence that of the latter." In the same connection he asserts that it is never thought fit to give the judge the option of deciding whether a thief (that is, a person whom he believes to be a thief, for the judge's belief is what the 300 tion must always turn upon) should hang or not, and so the law writes the provision: "The judge shall not cause a thief to be hanged unless he have been duly convicted and sentenced in course of law" (*The Limits of Jurisprudence Defined,* ed. C. W. Everett [New York, 1945], pp. 238–239).

11. By the classical utilitarians I understand Hobbes, Hume, Bentham, J. S. Mill, and Sidgwick.

12. All these features of punishment are mentioned by Hobbes; cf. *Leviathan,* ch. xxviii.

13. *Ethical and Political Thinking* (Oxford, 1947), p. 65.

14. The analogy with the price system suggests an answer to the question how utilitarian considerations insure that punishment is proportional to the offense. It is interesting to note that Sir David Ross, after making the distinction between justifying a penal law and justifying a particular application of it, and after stating that utilitarian considerations have a large place in determining the former, still holds back from accepting the utilitarian justification of punishment on the grounds that justice requires that punishment be proportional to the offense, and that utilitarianism is unable to account for this. Cf. *The Right and the Good,* pp. 61–62. I do not claim that utilitarianism can account for this requirement as Sir David might wish, but it happens, nevertheless, that if utilitarian considerations are followed penalties will be proportional to offenses in this sense: the order of offenses according to seriousness can be paired off with the order of penalties according to severity. Also the absolute level of penalties will be as low as possible. This follows from the assumption that people are rational (i.e., that they are able to take into account the "prices" the state puts on actions), the utilitarian rule that a penal system should provide a motive for preferring the less serious offense, and the principle that punishment as such is an evil. All this was carefully worked out by Bentham in *The Principles of Morals and Legislation,* chs. xiii–xv.

Persons and Punishment*

They acted and looked . . . at us, and around in our house, in a way that had about it the feeling—at least for me—that we were not people. In their eyesight we were just things, that was all. [Malcolm X]

We have no right to treat a man like a dog. [Governor Maddox of Georgia]

Alfredo Traps in Durrenmatt's tale discovers that he has brought off, all by himself, a murder involving considerable ingenuity. The mock prosecutor in the tale demands the death penalty "as reward for a crime that merits admiration, astonishment, and respect." Traps is deeply moved; indeed, he is exhilarated, and the whole of his life becomes more heroic, and, ironically, more precious. His defense attorney proceeds to argue that Traps was not only innocent but incapable of guilt, "a victim of the age." This defense Traps disavows with indignation and anger. He makes claim to the murder as his and demands the prescribed punishment—death.

The themes to be found in this macabre tale do not often find their way into philosophical discussions of punishment. These discussions deal with large and significant questions of whether or not we ever have the right to punish, and if we do, under what conditions, to what degree, and in what manner. There is a tradition, of course, not notable for its present vitality, that is closely linked with motifs in Durrenmatt's tale of crime and punishment. Its adherents have argued that justice requires a person be punished if he is guilty. Sometimes—though rarely—these philosophers have expressed themselves in terms of the criminal's *right to be punished*. Reaction to the claim that there is such a right has been astonishment combined, perhaps, with a touch of contempt for the perversity of the suggestion. A strange right that no one would ever wish to claim! With that flourish the subject is buried and

the right disposed of. In this paper the subject is resurrected.

My aim is to argue for four propositions concerning rights that will certainly strike some as not only false but preposterous: first, that we have a right to punishment; second, that this right derives from a fundamental human right to be treated as a person; third, that this fundamental right is a natural, inalienable, and absolute right; and, fourth, that the denial of this right implies the denial of all moral rights and duties. Showing the truth of one, let alone all, of these large and questionable claims, is a tall order. The attempt or, more properly speaking, the first steps in an attempt, follow.

1. When someone claims that there is a right to be free, we can easily imagine situations in which the right is infringed and easily imagine situations in which there is a point to asserting or claiming the right. With the right to be punished, matters are otherwise. The immediate reaction to the claim that there is such a right is puzzlement. And the reasons for this are apparent. People do not normally value pain and suffering. Punishment is associated with pain and suffering. When we think about punishment we naturally think of the strong desire most persons have to avoid it, to accept, for example, acquittal of a criminal charge with relief and eagerly, if convicted, to hope for pardon or probation. Adding, of course, to the paradoxical character of the claim of such a right is difficulty in imagining circumstances in which it would be denied one. When would one rightly demand punishment and meet with any threat of the claim being denied?

So our first task is to see when the claim of such a right would have a point. I want to approach this task by setting out two complex types of institutions both of which are designed to maintain some degree of social control. In the one a central concept is punishment for wrongdoing and in the other the central concepts are control of dangerous individuals and treatment of disease.

*Reprinted from *The Monist*, Volume 52:4 (October, 1968), LaSalle, Illinois, with the permission of the publisher and the author.

Let us first turn attention to the institutions in which punishment is involved. The institutions I describe will resemble those we ordinarily think of as institutions of punishment; they will have, however, additional features we associate with a system of just punishment.

Let us suppose that men are constituted roughly as they now are, with a rough equivalence in strength and abilities, a capacity to be injured by each other and to make judgments that such injury is undesirable, a limited strength of will, and a capacity to reason and to conform conduct to rules. Applying to the conduct of these men are a group of rules, ones I shall label 'primary', which closely resemble the core rules of our criminal law, rules that prohibit violence and deception and compliance with which provides benefits for all persons. These benefits consist in noninterference by others with what each person values, such matters as continuance of life and bodily security. The rules define a sphere for each person, then, which is immune from interference by others. Making possible this mutual benefit is the assumption by individuals of a burden. The burden consists in the exercise of self-restraint by individuals over inclinations that would, if satisfied, directly interfere or create a substantial risk of interference with others in proscribed ways. If a person fails to exercise self-restraint even though he might have and gives in to such inclinations, he renounces a burden which others have voluntarily assumed and thus gains an advantage which others, who have restrained themselves, do not possess. This system, then, is one in which the rules establish a mutuality of benefit and burden and in which the benefits of noninterference are conditional upon the assumption of burdens.

Connecting punishment with the violation of these primary rules, and making public the provision for punishment, is both reasonable and just. First, it is only reasonable that those who voluntarily comply with the rules be provided some assurance that they will not be assuming burdens which others are unprepared to assume. Their disposition to comply voluntarily will diminish as they learn that others are with impunity renouncing burdens they are assuming. Second, fairness dictates that a system in which benefits and burdens are equally distributed have a mechanism designed to prevent a maldistribution in the benefits and burdens. Thus, sanctions are attached to noncompliance with the primary rules so as to induce compliance with the primary rules among those who may be disinclined to obey. In this way

the likelihood of an unfair distribution is diminished.

Third, it is just to punish those who have violated the rules and caused the unfair distribution of benefits and burdens. A person who violates the rules has something others have—the benefits of the system—but by renouncing what others have assumed, the burdens of self-restraint, he has acquired an unfair advantage. Matters are not even until this advantage is in some way erased. Another way of putting it is that he owes something to others, for he has something that does not rightfully belong to him. Justice—that is punishing such individuals—restores the equilibrium of benefits and burdens by taking from the individual what he owes, that is, exacting the debt. It is important to see that the equilibrium may be restored in another way. Forgiveness—with its legal analogue of a pardon—while not the righting of an unfair distribution by making one pay his debt is, nevertheless, a restoring of the equilibrium by forgiving the debt. Forgiveness may be viewed, at least in some types of cases, as a gift after the fact, erasing a debt, which had the gift been given before the fact, would not have created a debt. But the practice of pardoning has to proceed sensitively, for it may endanger in a way the practice of justice does not, the maintenance of an equilibrium of benefits and burdens. If all are indiscriminately pardoned less incentive is provided individuals to restrain their inclinations, thus increasing the incidence of persons taking what they do not deserve.

There are also in this system we are considering a variety of operative principles compliance with which provides some guarantee that the system of punishment does not itself promote an unfair distribution of benefits and burdens. For one thing, provision is made for a variety of defenses, each one of which can be said to have as its object diminishing the chances of forcibly depriving a person of benefits others have if that person has not derived an unfair advantage. A person has not derived an unfair advantage if he could not have restrained himself or if it is unreasonable to expect him to behave otherwise than he did. Sometimes the rules preclude punishment of classes of persons such as children. Sometimes they provide a defense if on a particular occasion a person lacked the capacity to conform his conduct to the rules. Thus, someone who in an epileptic seizure strikes another is excused. Punishment in these cases would be punishment of the innocent, punishment of those who do not voluntarily renounce a burden others have assumed.

Punishment in such cases, then, would not equalize but rather cause an unfair distribution in benefits and burdens.

Along with principles providing defenses there are requirements that the rules be prospective and relatively clear so that persons have a fair opportunity to comply with the rules. There are, also, rules governing, among other matters, the burden of proof, who shall bear it and what it shall be, the prohibition on double jeopardy, and the privilege against self-incrimination. Justice requires conviction of the guilty, and requires their punishment, but in setting out to fulfill the demands of justice we may, of course, because we are not omniscient, cause injustice by convicting and punishing the innocent. The resolution arrived at in the system I am describing consists in weighing as the greater evil the punishment of the innocent. The primary function of the system of rules was to provide individuals with a sphere of interest immune from interference. Given this goal, it is determined to be a greater evil for society to interfere unjustifiably with an individual by depriving him of good than for the society to fail to punish those that have unjustifiably interfered.

Finally, because the primary rules are designed to benefit all and because the punishments prescribed for their violation are publicized and the defenses respected, there is some plausibility in the exaggerated claim that in choosing to do an act violative of the rules an individual has chosen to be punished. This way of putting matters brings to our attention the extent to which, when the system is as I have described it, the criminal "has brought the punishment upon himself" in contrast to those cases where it would be misleading to say "he has brought it upon himself," cases, for example, where one does not know the rules or is punished in the absence of fault.

To summarize, then: First, there is a group of rules guiding the behavior of individuals in the community which establish spheres of interest immune from interference by others: second, provision is made for what is generally regarded as a deprivation of some thing of value if the rules are violated; third, the deprivations visited upon any person are justified by that person's having violated the rules: fourth, the deprivation in this just system of punishment, is linked to rules that fairly distribute benefits and burdens and to procedures that strike some balance between not punishing the guilty and punishing the innocent, a class defined as those who have not voluntarily done acts violative of the law, in which it is evident that the evil of punishing the innocent is

regarded as greater than the nonpunishment of the guilty.

At the core of many actual legal systems one finds, of course, rules and procedures of the kind I have sketched. It is obvious, though, that any ongoing legal system differs in significant respects from what I have presented here, containing 'pockets of injustice'.

I want now to sketch an extreme version of a set of institutions of a fundamentally different kind, institutions proceeding on a conception of man which appears to be basically at odds with that operative within a system of punishment.

Rules are promulgated in this system that prohibit certain types of injuries and harms.

In this world we are now to imagine, when an individual harms another his conduct is to be regarded as a symptom of some pathological condition in the way a running nose is a symptom of a cold. Actions diverging from some conception of the normal are viewed as manifestations of a disease in the way in which we might today regard the arm and leg movements of an epileptic during a seizure. Actions conforming to what is normal are assimilated to the normal and healthy functioning of bodily organs. What a person does, then, is assimilated, on this conception, to what we believe today, or at least most of us believe today, a person undergoes. We draw a distinction between the operation of the kidney and raising an arm on request. This distinction between mere events or happenings and human actions is erased in our imagined system.[1]

There is, however, bound to be something strange in this erasing of a recognized distinction, for, as with metaphysical suggestions generally, and I take this to be one, the distinction may be reintroduced but given a different description, for example, 'happenings with X type of causes' and 'happenings with Y type of causes'. Responses of different kinds, today legitimated by our distinction between happenings and actions may be legitimated by this new manner of description. And so there may be isomorphism between a system recognizing the distinction and one erasing it. Still, when this distinction is erased certain tendencies of thought and responses might naturally arise that would tend to affect unfavorably values respected by a system of punishment.

Let us elaborate on this assimilation of conduct of a certain kind to symptoms of a disease. First, there is something abnormal in both the case of conduct, such as killing another, and a symptom of a disease such as an irregular heart beat. Second, there are causes for this abnormality in action such that once we know of them we can explain the abnormality as we now can explain the symptoms of many physical diseases. The abnormality is looked upon as a happening with a causal explanation rather than an action for which there were reasons. Third, the causes that account for the abnormality interfere with the normal functioning of the body, or, in the case of killing with what is regarded as a normal functioning of an individual. Fourth, the abnormality is in some way a part of the individual, necessarily involving his body. A well going dry might satisfy our three foregoing conditions of disease symptoms, but it is hardly a disease or the symptom of one. Finally, and most obscure, the abnormality arises in some way from within the individual. If Jones is hit with a mallet by Smith, Jones may reel about and fall on James who may be injured. But this abnormal conduct of Jones is not regarded as a symptom of disease. Smith, not Jones, is suffering from some pathological condition.

With this view of man the institutions of social control respond, not with punishment, but with either preventive detention, in case of 'carriers', or therapy in the case of those manifesting pathological symptoms. The logic of sickness implies the logic of therapy. And therapy and punishment differ widely in their implications. In bringing out some of these differences I want again to draw attention to the important fact that while the distinctions we now draw are erased in the therapy world, they may, in fact, be reintroduced but under different descriptions. To the extent they are, we really have a punishment system combined with a therapy system. I am concerned now, however, with what the implications would be were the world indeed one of therapy and not a disguised world of punishment and therapy, for I want to suggest tendencies of thought that arise when one is immersed in the ideology of disease and therapy.

First, punishment is the imposition upon a person who is believed to be at fault of something commonly believed to be a deprivation where that deprivation is justified by the person's guilty behavior. It is associated with resentment, for the guilty are those who have done what they had no right to do by failing to exercise restraint when they might have and where others have. Therapy is not a response to a person who is at fault. We respond to an individual, not because of what he has done, but because of some condition from which he is suffering. If he is no longer suffering from the condition, treatment no longer has a point. Punishment, then, focuses on the past;

therapy on the present. Therapy is normally associated with compassion for what one undergoes, not resentment for what one has illegitimately done.

Second, with therapy, unlike punishment, we do not seek to deprive the person of something acknowledged as a good, but seek rather to help and to benefit the individual who is suffering by ministering to his illness in the hope that the person can be cured. The good we attempt to do is not a reward for desert. The individual suffering has not merited by his disease the good we seek to bestow upon him but has, because he is a creature that has the capacity to feel pain, a claim upon our sympathies and help.

Third, we saw with punishment that its justification was related to maintaining and restoring a fair distribution of benefits and burdens. Infliction of the prescribed punishment carries the implication, then, that one has 'paid one's debt' to society, for the punishment is the taking from the person of something commonly recognized as valuable. It is this conception of 'a debt owed' that may permit, as I suggested earlier, under certain conditions, the nonpunishment of the guilty, for operative within a system of punishment may be a concept analogous to forgiveness, namely pardoning. Who it is that we may pardon and under what conditions—contrition with its elements of self-punishment no doubt plays a role —I shall not go into though it is clearly a matter of the greatest practical and theoretical interest. What is clear is that the conceptions of 'paying a debt' or 'having a debt forgiven' or pardoning have no place in a system of therapy.

Fourth, with punishment there is an attempt at some equivalence between the advantage gained by the wrongdoer—partly based upon the seriousness of the interest invaded, partly on the state of mind with which the wrongful act was performed—and the punishment meted out. Thus, we can understand a prohibition on 'cruel and unusual punishments' so that disproportionate pain and suffering are avoided. With therapy attempts at proportionality make no sense. It is perfectly plausible giving someone who kills a pill and treating for a lifetime within an institution one who has broken a dish and manifested accident proneness. We have the concept of 'painful treatment'. We do not have the concept of 'cruel treatment'. Because treatment is regarded as a benefit, though it may involve pain, it is natural that less restraint is exercised in bestowing it, than in inflicting punishment. Further, protests with respect to treatment are likely to be assimilated to the complaints of one whose leg must be amputated in order for him to live, and, thus, largely disregarded. To be sure, there is operative in the therapy world some conception of the "cure being worse than the disease," but if the disease is manifested in conduct harmful to others, and if being a normal operating human being is valued highly, there will naturally be considerable pressure to find the cure acceptable.

Fifth, the rules in our system of punishment governing conduct of individuals were rules violation of which involved either direct interference with others or the creation of a substantial risk of such interference. One could imagine adding to this system of primary rules other rules proscribing preparation to do acts violative of the primary rules and even rules proscribing thoughts. Objection to such suggestions would have many sources but a principal one would consist in its involving the infliction of punishment on too great a number of persons who would not, because of a change of mind, have violated the primary rules. Though we are interested in diminishing violations of the primary rules, we are not prepared to punish too many individuals who would never have violated the rules in order to achieve this aim. In a system motivated solely by a preventive and curative ideology there would be less reason to wait until symptoms manifest themselves in socially harmful conduct. It is understandable that we should wish at the earliest possible stage to arrest the development of the disease. In the punishment system, because we are dealing with deprivations, it is understandable that we should forbear from imposing them until we are quite sure of guilt. In the therapy system, dealing as it does with benefits, there is less reason for forbearance from treatment at an early stage.

Sixth, a variety of procedural safeguards we associate with punishment have less significance in a therapy system. To the degree objections to double jeopardy and self-incrimination are based on a wish to decrease the chances of the innocent being convicted and punished, a therapy system, unconcerned with this problem, would disregard such safeguards. When one is out to help people there is also little sense in urging that the burden of proof be on those providing the help. And there is less point to imposing the burden of proving that the conduct was pathological beyond a reasonable doubt. Further, a jury system which, within a system of justice, serves to make accommodations to the individual situation and to introduce a human element, would play no role or a minor one in a world where expertise is required in making determinations of disease and treatment.

In our system of punishment an attempt was made to maximize each individual's freedom of choice by first of all delimiting by rules certain spheres of conduct immune from interference by others. The punishment associated with these primary rules paid deference to an individual's free choice by connecting punishment to a freely chosen act violative of the rules, thus giving some plausibility to the claim, as we saw, that what a person received by way of punishment he himself had chosen. With the world of disease and therapy all this changes and the individual's free choice ceases to be a determinative factor in how others respond to him. All those principles of our own legal system that minimize the chances of punishment of those who have not chosen to do acts violative of the rules tend to lose their point in the therapy system, for how we respond in a therapy system to a person is not conditioned upon what he has chosen but rather on what symptoms he has manifested or may manifest and what the best therapy for the disease is that is suggested by the symptoms.

Now, it is clear I think, that were we confronted with the alternatives I have sketched, between a system of just punishment and a thoroughgoing system of treatment, a system, that is, that did not reintroduce concepts appropriate to punishment, we could see the point in claiming that a person has a right to be punished, meaning by this that a person had a right to all those institutions and practices linked to punishment. For these would provide him with, among other things, a far greater ability to predict what would happen to him on the occurrence of certain events than the therapy system. There is the inestimable value to each of us of having the responses of others to us determined over a wide range of our lives by what we choose rather than what they choose. A person has a right to institutions that respect his choices. Our punishment system does; our therapy system does not.

Apart from those aspects of our therapy model which would relate to serious limitations on personal liberty, there are clearly objections of a more profound kind to the mode of thinking I have associated with the therapy model.

First, human beings pride themselves in having capacities that animals do not. A common way, for example, of arousing shame in a child is to compare the child's conduct to that of an animal. In a system where all actions are assimilated to happenings we are assimilated to creatures—indeed, it is more extreme than this—whom we have always thought possessed of less than we. Fundamental to our practice of praise and order of attainment is that one who can do more—one who is capable of more and one who does more is more worthy of respect and admiration. And we have thought of ourselves as capable where animals are not of making, of creating, among other things, ourselves. The conception of man I have outlined would provide us with a status that today, when our conduct is assimilated to it in moral criticism, we consider properly evocative of shame.

Second, if all human conduct is viewed as something men undergo, thrown into question would be the appropriateness of that extensive range of peculiarly human satisfactions that derive from a sense of achievement. For these satisfactions we shall have to substitute those mild satisfactions attendant upon a healthy well-functioning body. Contentment is our lot if we are fortunate; intense satisfaction at achievement is entirely inappropriate.

Third, in the therapy world nothing is earned and what we receive comes to us through compassion, or through a desire to control us. Resentment is out of place. We can take credit for nothing but must always regard ourselves—if there are selves left to regard once actions disappear—as fortunate recipients of benefits or unfortunate carriers of disease who must be controlled. We know that within our own world human beings who have been so regarded and who come to accept this view of themselves come to look upon themselves as worthless. When what we do is met with resentment, we are indirectly paid something of a compliment.

Fourth, attention should also be drawn to a peculiar evil that may be attendant upon regarding a man's actions as symptoms of disease. The logic of cure will push us toward forms of therapy that inevitably involve changes in the person made against his will. The evil in this would be most apparent in those cases where the agent, whose action is determined to be a manifestation of some disease, does not regard his action in this way. He believes that what he has done is, in fact, 'right' but his conception of 'normality' is not the therapeutically accepted one. When we treat an illness we normally treat a condition that the person is not responsible for. He is 'suffering' from some disease and we treat the condition, relieving the person of something preventing his normal functioning. When we begin treating persons for actions that have been chosen, we do not lift from the person something that is interfering with his normal functioning but we change the person so that he functions in a way regarded as normal by the current therapeutic community. We have to change him and his judgments of value. In doing this we display a lack of respect for the moral status of individuals, that is, a lack of respect for the reasoning and choices of individuals. They are but animals who must be conditioned. I think we can understand and, indeed, sympathize with a man's preferring death to being forcibly turned into what he is not.

Finally, perhaps most frightening of all would be the derogation in status of all protests to treatment. If someone believes that he has done something right, and if he protests being treated and changed, the protest will itself be regarded as a sign of some pathological condition, for who would not wish to be cured of an affliction? What this leads to are questions of an important kind about the effect of this conception of man upon what we now understand by reasoning. Here what a person takes to be a reasoned defense of an act is treated, as the action was, on the model of a happening of a pathological kind. Not just a person's acts are taken from him but also his attempt at a reasoned justification for the acts. In a system of punishment a person who has committed a crime may argue that what he did was right. We make him pay the price and we respect his right to retain the judgment he has made. A conception of pathology precludes this form of respect.

It might be objected to the foregoing that all I have shown—if that—is that if the only alternatives open to us are a *just* system of punishment or the mad world of being treated like sick or healthy animals, we do in fact have a right to a system of punishment of this kind. But this hardly shows that we have a right *simpliciter* to punishment as we do, say, to be free. Indeed, it does not even show a right to a just system of punishment, for surely we can, without too much difficulty, imagine situations in which the alternatives to punishment are not this mad world but a world in which we are still treated as persons and there is, for example, not the pain and suffering attendant upon punishment. One such world is one in which there are rules but responses to their violation is not the deprivation of some good but forgiveness. Still another type of world would be one in which violation of the rules were responded to by merely comparing the conduct of the person to something commonly regarded as low or filthy, and thus, producing by this mode of moral criticism, feelings of shame rather than feelings of guilt.

I am prepared to allow that these objections have a point. While granting force to the above objections I want to offer a few additional comments with respect to each of them. First, any existent legal system permits the punishment of individuals under circumstances where the conditions I have set forth for a just system have not been satisfied. A glaring example of this would be criminal strict liability which is to be found in our own legal system. Nevertheless, I think it would be difficult to present any system we should regard as a system of punishment that would not still have a great advantage over our imagined therapy system. The system of punishment we imagine may more and more approximate a system of sheer terror in which human beings are treated as animals to be intimidated and prodded. To the degree that the system is of this character it is, in my judgment, not simply an unjust system but one that diverges from what we normally understand by a system of punishment. At least some deference to the choice of individuals is built into the idea of punishment. So there would be some truth in saying we have a right to any system of punishment if the only alternative to it was therapy.

Second, people may imagine systems in which there are rules and in which the response to their violation is not punishment but pardoning, the legal analogue of forgiveness. Surely this is a system to which we would claim a right as against one in which we are made to suffer for violating the rules. There are several comments that need to be made about this. It may be, of course, that a high incidence of pardoning would increase the incidence of rule violations. Further, the difficulty with suggesting pardoning as a general response is that pardoning presupposes the very responses that it is suggested it supplant. A system of deprivations, or a practice of deprivations on the happening of certain actions, underlies the practice of pardoning and forgiving, for it is only where we possess the idea of a wrong to be made up or of a debt owed to others, ideas we acquire within a world in which there have been deprivations for wrong acts, that we have the idea of pardoning for the wrong or forgiving the debt.

Finally, if we look at the responses I suggested would give rise to feelings of shame, we may rightly be troubled with the appropriateness of this response in any community in which each person assumes burdens so that each may derive benefits. In such situations might it not be that individuals have a right to a system of punishment so that each person could be assured that inequities in the distribution of benefits and burdens are unlikely to occur and if they do, procedures exist for correcting them? Further, it may well be that, everything considered, we should prefer the pain and suffering of a system of punishment to a world in which we only experience shame on the doing of wrong acts, for with guilt there are relatively simple ways of ridding ourselves of the feeling we have, that is, gaining forgiveness or taking the punishment, but with shame we have to bear it until we no longer are the person who has behaved in the shameful way. Thus, I suggest that we have, wherever there is a distribution of benefits and burdens of the kind I have described, a right to a system of punishment.

I want also to make clear in concluding this section that I have argued, though very indirectly, not just for a right to a system of punishment, but for a right to be punished once there is in existence such a system. Thus, a man has the right to be punished rather than treated if he is guilty of some offense. And, indeed, one can imagine a case in which, even in the face of an offer of a pardon, a man claims and ought to have acknowledged his right to be punished.

2. The primary reason for preferring the system of punishment as against the system of therapy might have been expressed in terms of the one system treating one as a person and the other not. In invoking the right to be punished, one justifies one's claim by reference to a more fundamental right. I want now to turn attention to this fundamental right and attempt to shed light—it will have to be little, for the topic is immense—on what is meant by 'treating an individual as a person'.

When we talk of not treating a human being as a person or 'showing no respect for one as a person' what we imply by our words is a contrast between the manner in which one acceptably responds to human beings and the manner in which one acceptably responds to animals and inanimate objects. When we treat a human being merely as an animal or some inanimate object our responses to the human being are determined, not by his choices, but ours in disregard of or with indifference to his. And when we 'look upon' a person as less than a person or not a person, we consider the person as incapable of rational choice. In cases of not treating a human being as a person we interfere with a person in such a way that what is done, even if the person is involved in the doing, is done not by the person but by the user of the person. In extreme cases there may even be an elision of a causal chain so that we might say that X killed Z even though Y's hand was the hand that held the weapon, for Y's hand may have been entirely in X's control. The one agent is in some way treating the other as a mere link in a causal chain. There is, of course, a wide range of cases in which a person is used to accomplish the aim of another and in which the person used is less than fully free. A person may be grabbed against his will and used as a shield. A person may be drugged or hypnotized and then employed for certain ends. A person may be deceived into doing other than he intends doing. A person may be ordered to do something and threatened with harm if he does not and coerced into doing what he does not want to. There is still another range of cases in which individuals are not used, but in which decisions by others are made that affect them in circumstances where they have the capacity for choice and where they are not being treated as persons.

But it is particularly important to look at coercion, for I have claimed that a just system of punishment treats human beings as persons; and it is not immediately apparent how ordering someone to do something and threatening harm differs essentially from having rules supported by threats of harm in case of noncompliance.

There are affinities between coercion and other cases of not treating someone as a person, for it is not the coerced person's choices but the coercer's that are responsible for what is done. But unlike other indisputable cases of not treating one as a person, for example using someone as a shield, there is some choice involved in coercion. And if this is so, why does the coercer stand in any different relation to the coerced person than the criminal law stands to individuals in society?

Suppose the person who is threatened disregards the order and gets the threatened harm. Now suppose he is told, "Well, you did after all bring it upon yourself." There is clearly something strange in this. It is the person doing the threatening and not the person threatened who is responsible. But our reaction to punishment, at least in a system that resembles the one I have described, is precisely that the person violating the rules brought it upon himself. What lies behind these different reactions?

There exist situations in the law, of course, which resemble coercion situations. There are occasions when in the law a person might justifiably say "I am not being treated as a person but being used" and where he might properly react to the punishment as something "he was hardly responsible for." But it is possible to have a system in which it would be misleading to say, over a wide range of cases of punishment for noncompliance, that we are using persons. The clearest case in which it would be inappropriate to so regard punishment would be one in which there were explicit agreement in advance that punishment should follow on the voluntary doing of certain acts. Even if one does not have such conditions satisfied, and obviously such explicit agreements are not characteristic, one can see significant differences between our system of just punishment and a coercion situation.

First, unlike the case with one person coercing another 'to do his will', the rules in our system apply to all, with the benefits and burdens equally distributed. About such a system it cannot be said that some are being subordinated to others or are being used by others or gotten to do things by others. To the extent that the rules are thought to be to the advantage of only some or to the extent there is a maldistribution of benefits and burdens, the difference between coercion and law disappears.

Second, it might be argued that at least any person inclined to act in a manner violative of the rules stands to all others as the person coerced stands to his coercer, and that he, at least, is a person disadvantaged as others are not. It is important here, I think, that he is part of a system in which it is commonly agreed that forbearance from the acts proscribed by the rules provides advantages for all. This system is the accepted setting; it is the norm. Thus, in any coercive situation, it is the coercer who deviates from the norm, with the responsibility of the person he is attempting to coerce, defeated. In a just punishment situation, it is the person deviating from the norm, indeed he might be a coercer, who is responsible, for it is the norm to restrain oneself from acts of that kind. A voluntary agent diverging in his conduct from what is expected or what the norm is, on general causal principles, regarded as the cause of what results from his conduct.

There is, then, some plausibility in the claim that, in a system of punishment of the kind I have sketched, a person chooses the punishment that is meted out to him. If, then, we can say in such a system that the rules provide none with advantages that others do not have, and further, that what happens to a person is conditioned by that person's choice and not that of others, then we can say that it is a system reponding to one as a person.

We treat a human being as a person provided: first, we permit the person to make the choices that will determine what happens to him and second, when our responses to the person are responses respecting the person's choices. When we respond to a person's illness by treating the illness, it is neither a case of treating or not treating the individual as a person. When we give a person a gift we are neither treating or not treating him as a person, unless, of course, he does not wish it, chooses not to have it, but we compel him to accept it.

3. This right to be treated as a person is a fundamental human right belonging to all human beings by virtue of their being human. It is also a natural, inalienable, and absolute right. I want now to defend these claims so reminiscent of an era of philosophical thinking about rights that many consider to have been seriously confused.

If the right is one that we possess by virtue of being human beings, we are immediately confronted with an apparent dilemma. If, to treat another as a person requires that we provide him with reasons for acting and avoid force or deception, how can we justify the force and deception we exercise with respect to children and the mentally ill? If they, too, have a right to be treated as persons are we not constantly infringing their rights? One way out of this is simply to restrict the right to those who satisfy the conditions of being a person. Infants and the insane, it might be argued, do not meet these conditions, and they would not then have the right. Another approach would be to describe the right they possess as a prima facie right to be treated as a person. This right might then be outweighed by other considerations. This approach generally seems to me, as I shall later argue, inadequate.

I prefer this tack. Children possess the right to be treated as persons but they possess this right as an individual might be said in the law of property to possess a future interest. There are advantages in talking of individuals as having a right though complete enjoyment of it is postponed. Brought to our attention, if we ascribe to them the right, is the legitimacy of their complaint if they are not provided with opportunities and conditions assuring their full enjoyment of the right when they acquire the characteristics of persons. More than this, all persons are charged with the sensitive task of not denying them the right to be a person and to be treated as a person by failing to provide the conditions for their becoming indi-

viduals who are able freely and in an informed way to choose and who are prepared themselves to assume responsibility for their choices. There is an obligation imposed upon us all, unlike that we have with respect to animals, to respond to children in such a way as to maximize the chances of their becoming persons. This may well impose upon us the obligation to treat them as persons from a very early age, that is, to respect their choices and to place upon them the responsibility for the choices to be made. There is no need to say that there is a close connection between how we respond to them and what they become. It also imposes upon us all the duty to display constantly the qualities of a person, for what they become they will largely become because of what they learn from us is acceptable behavior.

In claiming that the right is a right that human beings have by virtue of being human, there are several other features of the right, that should be noted, perhaps better conveyed by labelling them 'natural'. First, it is a right we have apart from any voluntary agreement into which we have entered. Second, it is not a right that derives from some defined position or status. Third, it is equally apparent that one has the right regardless of the society or community of which one is a member. Finally, it is a right linked to certain features of a class of beings. Were we fundamentally different than we now are, we would not have it. But it is more than that, for the right is linked to a feature of human beings which, were that feature absent—the capacity to reason and to choose on the basis of reasons—, profound conceptual changes would be involved in the thought about human beings. It is a right, then, connected with a feature of men that sets men apart from other natural phenomena.

The right to be treated as a person is inalienable. To say of a right that it is inalienable draws attention not to limitations placed on what others may do with respect to the possessor of the right but rather to limitations placed on the dispositive capacities of the possessor of the right. Something is to be gained in keeping the issues of alienability and absoluteness separate.

There are a variety of locutions qualifying what possessors of rights may and may not do. For example, on this issue of alienability, it would be worthwhile to look at, among other things, what is involved in abandoning, abdicating, conveying, giving up, granting, relinquishing, surrendering, transferring, and waiving one's rights. And with respect to each of these concepts we should also have to be sensitive to the variety of uses of the term 'rights'. What it is, for example, to waive a Hohfeldian 'right' in his strict sense will differ from what it is to waive a right in his 'privilege' sense.

Let us look at only two concepts very briefly, those of transferring and waiving rights. The clearest case of transferring rights is that of transferring rights with respect to specific objects. I own a watch and owning it I have a complicated relationship, captured in this area rather well I think by Hohfeld's four basic legal relationships, to all persons in the world with respect to the watch. We crudely capture these complex relationships by talking of my 'property rights' in or with respect to the watch. If I sell the watch, thus exercising a capacity provided by the rules of property, I have transferred rights in or with respect to the watch to someone else, the buyer, and the buyer now stands, as I formerly did, to all persons in the world in a series of complex relationships with respect to the watch.

While still the owner, I may have given to another permission to use it for several days. Had there not been the permission and had the person taken the watch, we should have spoken of interfering with or violating or, possibly, infringing my property rights. Or, to take a situation in which transferring rights is inappropriate, I may say to another "go ahead and slap me—you have my permission." In these types of situations philosophers and others have spoken of 'surrendering" rights or, alternatively and, I believe, less strangely, of 'waiving one's rights'. And recently, of course, the whole topic of 'waiving one's right to remain silent' in the context of police interrogation of suspects has been a subject of extensive litigation and discussion.

I confess to feeling that matters are not entirely perspicuous with respect to what is involved in 'waiving' or 'surrendering' rights. In conveying to another permission to take a watch or slap one, one makes legally permissible what otherwise would not have been. But in saying those words that constitute permission to take one's watch one is, of course, exercising precisely one of those capacities that leads us to say he has, while others have not, property rights with respect to the watch. Has one then waived his right in Hohfeld's strict sense in which the correlative is a duty to forebear on the part of others?

We may wish to distinguish here waiving the right to have others forbear to which there is a corresponding duty on their part to forbear, from placing oneself in a position where one has no legitimate right to complain. If I say the magic words "take the watch for a couple of days" or "go ahead and slap me," have I waived my right not to have my property taken or a right not to be struck or have I, rather, in saying what I have, simply stepped into a relation in which the rights no longer apply with respect to a specified other person? These observations find support in the following considerations. The right is that which gives rise, when infringed, to a legitimate claim against another person. What this suggests is that the right is that sphere interference with which entitles us to complain or gives us a right to complain. From this it seems to follow that a right to bodily security should be more precisely described as 'a right that others not interfere without permission'. And there is the corresponding duty not to interfere unless provided permission. Thus when we talk of waiving our rights or 'giving up our rights' in such cases we are not waiving or giving up our right to property nor our right to bodily security, for we still, of course, possess the right not to have our watch taken without permission. We have rather placed ourselves in a position where we do not possess the capacity, sometimes called a right, to complain if the person takes the watch or slaps us.

There is another type of situation in which we may speak of waiving our rights. If someone without permission slaps me, there is an infringement of my right to bodily security. If I now acquiesce or go further and say "forget it" or "you are forgiven," we might say that I had waived my right to complain. But here, too, I feel unconfortable about what is involved. For I do have the right to complain (a right without a corresponding duty) in the event I am slapped and I have that right whether I wish it or not. If I say to another after the slap, "you are forgiven" what I do is not waive the right to complain but rather make illegitimate my subsequent exercise of that right.

Now, if we turn to the right to be treated as a person, the claim that I made was that it was inalienable, and what I meant to convey by that word of respectable age is that (a) it is a right that cannot be transferred to another in the way one's right with respect to objects can be transferred and (b) that it cannot be waived in the ways in which people talk of waiving rights to property or waiving, within certain limitations, one's right to bodily security.

While the rules of the law of property are such that persons may, satisfying certain procedures, transfer rights, the right to be treated as a person logically cannot be transferred anymore than one person can transfer to another his right to life or privacy. What, indeed, would it be like for another to have our right to be treated as a person? We can understand transferring a right with respect to certain objects. The new owner stands where the old owner stood. But with a right to be treated as a person what could this mean? My having the right meant that my choices were respected. Now if I transfer it to another this will mean that he will posses the right that my choices be respected? This is nonsense. It is only each person himself that can have his choices respected. It is no more possible to transfer this right than it is to transfer one's right to life.

Nor can the right be waived. It cannot be waived because any agreement to being treated as an animal or an instrument does not provide others with the moral permission to so treat us. One can volunteer to be a shield, but then it is one's choice on a particular occasion to be a shield. If without our permission, without our choosing it, someone used us as a shield, we may, I should suppose, forgive the person for treating us as an object. But we do not thereby waive our right to be treated as a person, for that is a right that has been infringed and what we have at most done is put ourselves in a position where it is inappropriate any longer to exercise the right to complain.

This is the sort of right, then, such that the moral rules defining relationships among persons preclude anyone from morally giving others legitimate permissions or rights with respect to one by doing or saying certain things. One stands, then, with respect to one's person as the nonowner of goods stands to those goods. The nonowner cannot, given the rule-defined relationships, convey to others rights and privileges that only the owner possesses. Just as there are agreements nonenforceable because void is contrary to public policy, so there are permissions our moral outlook regards as without moral force. With respect to being treated as a person, one is 'disabled' from modifying relations of others to one.

The right is absolute. This claim is bound to raise eyebrows. I have an innocuous point in mind in making this claim.

In discussing alienability we focused on incapacities with respect to disposing of rights. Here what I want to bring out is a sense in which a right exists despite considerations for refusing to accord the person his rights. As with the topic of alienability there are a host of concepts that deserve a close look in this area. Among them are according, acknowledging, annulling, asserting, claiming, denying, destroying, exercising, infringing, insisting upon, interfering with, possessing, recognizing and violating.

The claim that rights are absolute has been construed to mean that 'assertions of rights cannot, for any reason under any circumstances be denied'. When there are considerations which warrant refusing to accord persons their rights, there are two prevalent views as to how this should be described: There is, first, the view that the person does not have the right, and second, the view that he has rights but of a prima facie kind and that these have been outweighed or overcome by the other considerations. "We can conceive times when such rights must give way, and, therefore, they are only prima facie and not absolute rights." (Brandt)

Perhaps there are cases in which a person claims a right to do a certain thing, say with his property, and argues that his property rights are absolute, meaning by this he has a right to do whatever he wishes with his property. Here, no doubt, it has to be explained to the person that the right he claims he has, he does not in fact possess. In such a case the person does not have and never did have, given a certain description of the right, a right that was prima facie or otherwise, to do what he claimed he had the right to do. If the assertion that a right is absolute implies that we have a right to do whatever we wish to do, it is an absurd claim and as such should not really ever have been attributed to political theorists arguing for absolute rights. But, of course, the claim that we have a prima facie right to do whatever we wish to do is equally absurd. The right is not prima facie either, for who would claim, thinking of the right to be free, that one has a prima facie right to kill others, if one wishes, unless there are moral considerations weighing against it?

There are, however, other situations in which it is accepted by all that a person possesses rights of a certain kind, and the difficulty we face is that of according the person the right he is claiming when this will promote more evil than good. The just act is to give the man his due and giving a man what it is his right to have is giving him his due. But it is a mistake to suppose that justice is the only dimension of morality. It may be justifiable not to accord to a man his rights. But it is no less a wrong to him, no less an infringement. It is seriously misleading to turn all justifiable infringements into noninfringements by saying that the right is only prima facie, as if we have, in concluding that we should not accord a man his rights, made out a case that he had none. To use the language of 'prima facie rights' misleads, for it suggests that a presumption of the existence of a right has been overcome in these cases where all that can be said is that the presumption in favor of according a man his rights has been overcome. If we begin to think the right itself is prima facie, we shall, in cases in which we are justified in not according it, fail sufficiently to bring out that we have interfered where justice says we should not. Our moral framework is unnecessarily and undesirably impoverished by the theory that there are such rights.

When I claim, then, that the right to be treated as a person is absolute what I claim is that given that one is a person, one always has the right so to be treated, and that while there may possibly be occasions morally requiring not according a person this right, this fact makes it no less true that the right exists and would be infringed if the person were not accorded it.

4. Having said something about the nature of this fundamental right I want now, in conclusion, to suggest that the denial of this right entails the denial of all moral rights and duties. This requires bringing out what is surely intuitively clear that any framework of rights and duties presupposes individuals that have the capacity to choose on the basis of reasons presented to them, and that what makes legitimate actions within such a system are the free choices of individuals. There is, in other words, a distribution of benefits and burdens in accord with a respect for the freedom of choice and freedom of action of all. I think that the best way to make this point may be to sketch some of the features of a world in which rights and duties are possessed.

First, rights exist only when there is some conception of some things valued and others not. Secondly, and implied in the first point, is the fact that there are dispositions to defend the valued commodities. Third, the valued commodities may be interfered with by others in this world. A group of animals might be said to satisfy these first three conditions. Fourth, rights exist when there are recognized rules establishing the legitimacy of some acts and ruling out others. Mistakes in the claim of right are possible. Rights imply the concepts of interference and infringement, concepts the elucidation of which requires the concept of a rule applying to the conduct of persons. Fifth, to possess a right is to possess something that constitutes a legitimate restraint on the freedom of action of others. It is clear, for

example, that if individuals were incapable of controlling their actions we would have no notion of a legitimate claim that they do so. If, for example, we were all disposed to object or disposed to complain, as the elephant seal is disposed to object when his territory is invaded, then the objection would operate in a causal way, or approximating a causal way, in getting the behavior of noninterference. In a system of rights, on the other hand, there is a point to appealing to the rules in legitimating one's complaint. Implied, then, in any conception of rights is the existence of individuals capable of choosing and capable of choosing on the basis of considerations with respect to rules. The distribution of freedom throughout such a system is determined by the free choice of individuals. Thus any denial of the right to be treated as a person would be a denial undercutting the whole system, for the system rests on the assumption that spheres of legitimate and illegitimate conduct are to be delimited with regard to the choices made by persons.

This conclusion stimulates one final reflection on the therapy world we imagined.

The denial of this fundamental right will also carry with it, ironically, the denial of the right to treatment to those who are ill. In the world as we now understand it, there are those who do wrong and who have a right to be responded to as persons who have done wrong. And there are those who have not done wrong but who are suffering from illnesses that in a variety of ways interfere with their capacity to live their lives as complete persons. These persons who are ill have a claim upon our compassion. But more than this they have, as animals do not, a right to be treated as persons. When an individual is ill he is entitled to that assistance which will make it possible for him to resume his functioning as a person. If it is an injustice to punish an innocent person, it is no less an injustice, and a far more significant one in our day, to fail to promote as best we can through adequate facilities and medical care the treatment of those who are ill. Those human beings who fill our mental institutions are entitled to more than they do in fact receive; they should be viewed as possessing the right to be treated as a person so that our responses to them may increase the likelihood that they will enjoy fully the right to be so treated. Like the child the mentally ill person has a future interest we cannot rightly deny him. Society is today sensitive to the infringement of justice in punishing the innocent; elaborate rules exist to avoid this evil. Society should be no less sensitive to the injustice of failing to bring back to the community of persons those whom it is possible to bring back.

NOTES

1. "When a man is suffering from an infectious disease, he is a danger to the community, and it is necessary to restrict his liberty of movement. But no one associates any idea of guilt with such a situation. On the contrary, he is an object of commiseration to his friends. Such steps as science recommends are taken to cure him of his disease, and he submits as a rule without reluctance to the curtailment of liberty involved meanwhile. The same method in spirit ought to be shown in the treatment of what is called 'crime.' "

Bertrand Russell, *Roads to Freedom* (London: George Allen and Unwin Ltd., 1918), p. 135.

"We do not hold people responsible for their reflexes—for example, for coughing in church. We hold them responsible for their operant behavior—for example, for whispering in church or remaining in church while coughing. But there are variables which are responsible for whispering as well as coughing, and these may be just as inexorable. When we recognize this, we are likely to drop the notion of responsibility altogether and with it the doctrine of free will as an inner causal agent."

B. F. Skinner, *Science and Human Behavior* (1953), pp. 115–6.

"Basically, criminality is but a symptom of insanity, using the term in its widest generic sense to express unacceptable social behavior based on unconscious motivation flowing from a disturbed instinctive and emotional life, whether this appears in frank psychoses, or in less obvious form in neuroses and unrecognized psychoses. . . . If criminals are products of early environmental influences in the same sense that psychotics and neurotics are, then it should be possible to reach them psychotherapeutically."

Benjamin Karpman, "Criminal Psychodynamics," *Journal of Criminal Law and Criminology*, 47 (1956), p. 9.

"We, the agents of society, must move to end the game of tit-for-tat and blow-for-blow in which the offender has foolishly and futilely engaged himself and us. We are not driven, as he is, to wild and impulsive actions. With knowledge comes power, and with power there is no need for the frightened vengeance of the old penology. In its place should go a quiet, dignified, therapeutic program for the rehabilitation of the disorganized one, if possible, the protection of society during the treatment period, and his guided return to useful citizenship, as soon as this can be effected."

Karl Menninger, "Therapy, Not Punishment," *Harper's Magazine* (August 1959), pp. 63–64.

DETAINING THE DANGEROUS OFFENDER
FERDINAND D. SCHOEMAN

On Incapacitating The Dangerous*

Given the extent and the intensity of public concern about violent crime, there is an ever increasing willingness to consider deterring and incapacitating potential offenders by means that until recently would have been summarily rejected as violative of respect for the rights and dignity of free and equal persons. Indeed, it is not just willingness to consider options that is expanding; it is actual practices, which include use of aversive conditioning, token economies, electrical, physical and chemical manipulation of the brain,[1] indeterminate sentencing, and criminal commitment of the legally innocent. What will be of concern in this paper is a variant of this last option. Specifically, the discussion will center on arguments both for and against civil preventive detention—the incapacitating of individuals thought to be dangerous—as a potentially legitimate means of promoting social protection.

Some opposition to the use of civil preventive detention to effect this end has focused on the inadequacy of available predictive techniques for determining carefully enough who is dangerous. Other attacks have been directed at the vagueness of what is meant by the label "dangerous," or have stressed how inadequate present protections are for those civilly committed, whatever the rationale.[2] On the face of it, such particular objections seem directed to circumstances which appear in principle remediable, leaving open the possibility that under some future circumstances civil preventive detention of those deemed dangerous might be legitimate. Part 1 of this paper is devoted to an investigation of what such conditions might be.

Still other attacks on civil preventive detention have stemmed from more philosophical worries having to do with implications such a practice, however perfected, would have on our understanding of a person as an autonomous being deserving respect as well as on our appreciation of the role of the power—restraint aspect of the criminal law. Part II of this paper is devoted to gauging the moral weight of these more Olympian worries. A motif of the whole paper is a comparison of civil preventive detention with the presently accepted practice of quarantine, arguing that once certain conditions are met, it would not be consistent to countenance the use of quarantine and associated public health measures and reject civil preventive detention of the dangerous. The point of the paper then will not be to argue that civil preventive detention is not problematic, or that given available technology it is to be recommended. Rather, it is that assuming certain developments in both technology and law, no more serious problems arise in defending civil preventive detention, suitably qualified, than arise from the practice of quarantine as a measure for protecting public health. Civil preventive detention represents an assault on our notion of autonomous moral being only to the degree that quarantine does.

It is an important feature of gauging the legitimacy of the practice being considered here to be clear that the persons whose rights are to be transgressed for social protection need not be judged guilty of anything, need not be judged blameworthy, morally or legally, for any act they have committed. Furthermore, the reason such persons need not be thought blameworthy does not stem from any kind of general skepticism about the notions of praise or blame. Advocates of this practice may believe that those who commit crimes are blameworthy and deserve punishment. The practice consists simply in incapacitating individuals predicted to be illegally violent, until such time as the potential for illegal violence diminishes to within tolerable levels. This practice of civil preventive detention involves restrictions on the liberty of persons who have not forfeited any rights by previous delinquent acts. For puposes of this paper, I shall include in the practice of civil preventive detention all interferences up to and including isolation of the dangerous person, with the presumption

*Reprinted from the *American Philosophical Quarterly*, Vol. 16, No. 1 (1979) by permission of the author and the publisher.

that the least restrictive means of accomplishing social protection is the maximum allowable under the practice.

I

As indicated, in this section I shall address the more practical and technical impediments to a morally legitimate system of preventive detention. Though, as I shall argue, some of the objections may prove decisive, I continue considering other objections and how a defender of civil preventive detention might be able to meet them. My justification for this procedure is first of all that we find out interesting things about our moral principles by continuing to address questions and press for answers. Second, since it could turn out that we are wrong in thinking that certain technical abilities are beyond human possibility, we should be prepared with contingency plans and contingency arguments just in case we find that we have been wrong. And third, as philosophers we might be interested in whether certain kinds of distinctions can be drawn, as well as whether theories can be defeated for certain kinds of reasons, even though we know that there may be practical objections which keep the issues from being pressing ones.

The first major source of opposition to civil preventive detention stems from skepticism about the adequacy of predictive techniques available or foreseeable on the basis of which mankind can be divided into two categories: the dangerous and the not-so-dangerous. The evidence on this predictability issue is reported to be as follows: There is no predictive technique available which does not include more false positives than true positives—which does not diagnose as future-guilty more persons who will not commit such crimes than persons who will. Furthermore, as one attempts to circumscribe a higher percentage of people who actually will commit crimes, the ratio of false positives to true positives increases.[3] (One does, after all, succeed in predicting all crimes that actually will be committed by claiming that everyone will commit every possible crime.)

It is worthwhile noting that some authorities on the issue of preventive detention treat this predictive problem as essentially the only problem with the practice, apparently conceding that if predictions improve sufficiently their opposition would vanish. No less an authority than Professor Alan Dershowitz expressed this view:

What difference is there between imprisoning a man for past crimes on the basis of "statistical likelihood" and detaining him to prevent future crimes on the same kind of less-than-certain information? The important difference may not be one of principle; it may be, as Justice Holmes said all legal issues are, one of degree. The available evidence suggests that our system of determining past guilt results in the erroneous conviction of relatively few innocent people ... But the indications are that any system of predicting future crimes would result in a vastly larger number of erroneous confinements—that is, confinements of persons predicted to engage in violent crimes who would not, in fact, do so.[4]

There are actually numerous problems which arise in working out solutions to this predictive problem. How accurate need the predictive techniques be before we can act on their basis? How invasive can the probing into the lives and thoughts of individuals be in order to achieve acceptable levels of accuracy? On what basis can an individual be required to submit to testing, the result of which might include civil confinement of that individual?

Perhaps the easiest question to deal with is the one relating to the standard of accuracy. If, following Dershowitz's suggestion, prediction of crime can be made as accurate as trials by juries, then we seem to have the problem of standards solved. In the legacy of the criminal law, the maxim that better that ten guilty men go free than that one innocent person be punished can be used to supply either qualitative or quantitative assistance here. Qualitatively what is asserted is the importance of not interfering with a person unless one is justifiably very confident that he did the wrong attributed to him. Quantitatively what is asserted is that the accuracy rate must be 90% or better. It cannot be interpreted as saying that the worst thing in the world is to find an innocent person guilty, for that interpretation would preclude all procedures for determining guilt we mortals know.

For our purposes, one can set the accuracy threshold as high as one desires, even at 100%, since the issues we want to address arise almost independently of the level of accuracy achievable. For the issue to be addressed is whether it would be legitimate to preventively detain someone when there is *moral certainty* that without such detention that person will perform some dangerous criminal act. In light of this requirement, it cannot be maintained that civil preventive detention must rest on "mere probabilities" while criminal conviction and quarantine are based on knowledge.

It is worth mentioning in passing that this moral certainty accuracy threshold is considerably higher than we would require in cases of serious danger from diseases. Suppose that someone has smallpox, and that the chance of being contagious at all is 50 percent and that the chance of dying from contagion is 50 percent. Under these conditions we would, I think, unhesitantly insist on the enforced isolation of the carrier, until such time as he no longer posed a threat to others.

With the level of accuracy set, we can now focus on the second question: how invasive can the information gathering process be? Given that accurate predictions of many natural phenomena involve acquiring as much information of details as possible, it would be rather startling if accurate predictions about people did not involve most extensive probing into every facet of persons' personalities and surroundings, both physical and social. Since so much of how a person responds to a situation depends on how he perceives or misperceives it, and since social situations will depend not only on how one perceives but how all involved do, the prospect of making accurate predictions seems negligible. The problems of interaction and interpretation seem to complicate the task of predicting what people will do beyond the point at which it can seem worthwhile even trying. It appears that we introduce problems of invasion of privacy as a result of our scruples about the minimization of false positives.

Granting this problem, it appears that we can and morally must dispense with civil preventive detention, not on grounds that isolating an individual for the protection of others is unjust, but on grounds that the process of finding out that someone is dangerous is itself so invasive of privacy that we are not entitled even to make the investigation into the threat potential of our citizenry. For purposes of this paper I am willing to grant the point that predictive techniques require such wholesale invasions of privacy that efforts at achieving this information might be prohibited on that score alone, depending on the stakes, without any reference to the fact that the practice involves the detention of the innocent for the wellbeing of others. But then I want to go on to ask: If the information necessary for adequate predictions could be gathered or were available without invasion of privacy, would preventive detention then be legitimate? In the event that psychics could be used to predict what people would do, without paraphernalia like bugs or binoculars, and without interviews, would government use of their abilities be invasive of privacy? Is privacy invaded as a result of the means used for acquiring information or as a result of the state of knowing what another rightfully regards as his to conceal?[5]

How invasive can investigations be into the personal characteristics of individuals, and on what basis can such investigations be initiated? Besides the obvious point just made that the adequacy of data upon which to make predictions is directly proportional to the invasiveness of the means used to acquire it, another equally obvious point can be made. The fewer the number of people that can be legitimately screened, the smaller the percentage of would-be crime that can be arrested.

Again drawing attention to an analogy from public health, suppose that there is a deadly disease which spreads easily from carriers, who cannot contract the disease, to those who are susceptible. Next suppose that treatment for being a carrier requires months of confinement—a fact which affords people with a strong incentive not to undergo diagnostic test to discover whether they are indeed carriers. Finally suppose that 50,000 persons a year die from this disease. What would it be legitimate for the state to do in order to find and treat carriers of this disease, and thereby save 50,000 lives each year? In this context, I suspect that we would tend to demote in importance our concern over invasion of privacy, thinking that saving that many lives is so important as to be the decisive consideration. I am suggesting that under this circumstance mass mandatory screening would not seem out of the question, provided that such measures were prerequisite to preventing such an epidemic. If we may consider such measures for saving that many lives that otherwise would be lost because of disease, why not consider such measures to save that many lives otherwise lost because of fear, greed, jealousy, anger, love, etc.?

Some might be tempted to respond to this question by saying that it just is legitimate to isolate a person who is sick, something over which one has no control, but not for impending crime. But here the point must be made that even under quarantine, persons are not isolated because they are sick. Most sick persons are not quarantined. Persons quarantined are isolated *because they are dangerous to others,* the sickness being the cause of the danger. We shall return to this point of contention in Part II.

We must now ask ourselves, who can be screened and on what account? Using the strategy that we should try to stay within the bounds set by other acceptable social practices when setting limits on civil prevention detention, we shall not step beyond what the law seems to allow in cases of protecting the public health.

What we find in the area of public health law is that " . . . there are legally sanctioned compulsory examinations in which the subject may not be a willing participant because the examination primarily furthers the aim of public protection."[6] But still, with the exception of impending disaster, compulsory examination of individuals for communicable diseases must be based on more than mere suspicion.[7]

Two obvious questions arise in extrapolating this description of screening policy in the area of public health to screening for prevention of crime: What will count as reasonable grounds for examination, and when are situations dire enough to warrant loosening restrictions on barriers to screening? As suggested above, there is a certain parallel between epidemics and certain classes of crime—deadly consequences; similarities in terms of predictability and preventability via isolation may also emerge. Provided mass screening is thought legitimate in one case, why should it not be similarly conceived in the other?

The practice of preventive detention, to be justified, would not only have to be based on tests which had a very low rate of false positives, but would have to be administered on such a basis as to allow some rather significant reduction in the crime rate. Whether this can be done without overextensive invasion of privacy is something one can have grave doubts about. But the question here is: If effective screening can be done without unconscionable invasion of privacy, and if it could be shown that measures up to and including preventive detention would prevent high percentages of projected crimes, would such a practice of detaining the innocent but dangerous be legitimate? Would civil preventive detention be allowable provided our anxiety over the accuracy of predictions and over the invasiveness of screening could be calmed?

The next major line of criticism of practices of preventive detention focuses on the vagueness implicit in talk about detaining the "dangerous." Who will define what it is to be dangerous, and on what basis? Evidence from the field of civil commitment for the insane suggests widely varying practices, depending on not much more than the political and ethical biases of the examining doctors.[8] Such disparity in the disposition of persons when based on individual value preferences rather than on clear standards represents the antithesis of a just system. On the other hand, there is no reason to think that the system of preventive detention which we have adumbrated thus far is differentially prey to this line of criticism. We can limit application of preventive measures to potential crimes which represent serious threat to life or bodily integrity, and we have specified already how accurate predictive devices must be before any interference is warranted, by indicating a moral certainty threshold.

There are, however, some related issues which must be addressed. Suppose that a person being tested for serious threat potential is found not to be dangerous, but is likely to violate a law of a less significant sort, like selling alcohol to minors. What should or can the government do with this information? Though it cannot detain the person to prevent such an act on the standards we have sketched, can it use this information to make eventual apprehension of the person inevitable by placing undercover officers in his bar? Can the government be asked, or expected and trusted not to give out information to businesses, which would have a great deal of interest in discovering whether potential employees are likely to embezzle, sell trade secrets, or do any of a large number of acts deleterious to the interests of the business?

In order to keep the practice of civil preventive detention a live option I shall distinguish between two types of tests. We shall distinguish between tests which indicate whether one specific crime type is likely and ones which give a read-out of a much more inclusive sort. Testing for dangerousness, we shall say, is only legitimate in case the tests devisable are of the specific sort and provide information only about behavior which is preventable according to the parameters already indicated.

The next major range of objections to systems of preventive detention, both civil and criminal, concentrates on issues falling under the heading of procedural safeguards. In this area of procedural safeguards, especially as it relates to civil commitment of the insane and the addicted, the fact that the infringements of liberties took place under a therapeutic rationale until recently blinded many people into thinking that talk of rights for such people interfered with acting on their behalf and in their interest.[9]

Recognizing the conflicts of interest involved in detention, we have not only demanded a very high level of predictive accuracy, but we here go on to recommend that the state supply those to be committed with resources to counteract state's expert testimony. Thus those in danger of being committed have a right to have the same accurate tests administered by non-state personnel, with differing results sufficient to preclude commitment.

There are other procedural safeguards which must be required. First of all, for those who are going to be committed, it has to be shown that nothing less invasive can be done feasibly. For instance, if a person "threatens" to seriously injure his child, supplying a guard or requiring counseling might do just as well as confining the parent. It is hard to conceive that for a high percentage of serious crimes such measures short of detention would not prove adequate.

What are the upper limits of confinement to prevent harm to others? Though it is not clear what the rationale would be for setting a limit, there is reason to require almost continual proof that the person confined is still dangerous. Here we find a similar situation to that of quarantine.

The nature of quarantine as a species of physical confinement is borne out by the fact that the legality of keeping a person in quarantined premises, like the legality of other forms of detention, is tested by a *writ of habeas corpus* . . .[10]

What it is that has to be shown is that the likelihood of committing a certain kind of crime is still above the threshold mark, whatever it is. Once again the model of public health serves us well. We should keep a person with a contagious and deadly disease confined for as long as it takes to eliminate or reduce significantly the possibility of contagion. Since this can involve potentially lifelong confinement in the case of some diseases, mere duration of confinement cannot serve to distinguish quarantine from preventive detention. Depending on how time-consuming and expensive retesting is, perhaps every day or every week those necessarily confined could be reexamined for signs of dangerousness. It would not be unreasonable to assume that for different kinds of crimes and for different kinds of persons schedules would eventually be available about minimum, maximum and average times required before detainees prove less likely to commit the acts feared. Such schedules could then serve as a basis for what counts as a reasonable interval between tests and what grounds would constitute a valid *habeas corpus* action.

What kind of compensation for losses should be available to those who are detained, their families and their business associates? How will it be possible for persons once detained not to have their reputations besmirched and their job prospects unaffected? I ask these questions not because the answers are readily available but because they focus on serious difficulties with the proposal here considered. The most consoling point that can be made is that since the action is civil and not criminal, there is no reason why almost all of one's normal activities could not be carried out, either in a place of safety or under some kind of supervision, or during hours or on occasions on which the predicted crime is unlikely to transpire. As Professor Lionel Frankel has said about civil commitment, requiring compensation for those detained would not only provide the state with an incentive to minimize the number of those committed as well as their period of detention, but it would "also serve to vindicate the compensated individual's dignity and status as a person" and "it would serve to affirm his continuing membership in a society as an individual before the law."[11]

II

Thus far in this paper we have considered three general problem areas for a system of preventive detention—problems with predicting, vagueness of standards of dangerousness, and inadequacy of procedural safeguards for persons civilly committed. We have shaped the practice when necessary to meet the major objections, elaborating a qualified version of civil preventive detention. On occasion the comparison has been made to the practices of quarantine and screening for contagious diseases to show the broad areas of similarity between measures designed to protect public health—measures which tend not to occasion much disagreement—and our practice of civil preventive detention.

But still someone might respond to the efforts so far made in favor of qualified preventive detention by saying: Besides the specific objections already mentioned, there is something more basic at stake in the issue of civil preventive detention. This more basic something has to do with our image of man as both autonomous and sacred, as entitled to a sphere of activity free from the interferences of others unless he intentionally interferes with another's sphere of freedom. To interfere preventively, this line of objection continues, even assuming the safeguards and provisions outlined, is to diminish the respect accorded to each individual's legitimate choices, to diminish one's sense of control over his own fate, and to impoverish the feeling for individual dignity protected by and encouraged through our present practices. The main issue that must be addressed is: does the very act of predicting and responding on the basis of a prediction to another person's behavior, when this response involves invoking nothing less than the police power of the state, violate something sacred in the human personality? Is it tantamount to denying that people are responsible? Does it involve seeing people as mere means to social ends? Does it presuppose a therapeutic and behavioristic, and not a moral and rights oriented, understanding of human activity? Is it an affront to human autonomy?[12]

Before responding to these challenges, it must be stressed that we are not saying about persons to be detained that they are as good as guilty and hence have no complaint against incapacitating efforts. Persons detained are detained not because they are guilty in any sense, but because they are dangerous—this danger being as real and as threatening if it results from free choice as if it results from involuntary spasm or microbe. But besides reiterating that the practice is to include numerous procedural safeguards, we emphasize that the practice in question involves no worse treatment of persons than does the practice of quarantine. In both practices persons are interfered with for the benefit of others.

Though civil preventive detention is not to be conceived as a cure for any disease—is not a therapeutic act—it does share with therapy several key features: both are imposed without any sense of moral outrage or resentment for those in its clutches, and the duration of detention is in both cases indeterminate. Perhaps it is thought that to deal with an individual's future conduct in this manner is tantamount to regarding his behavior in a medical-model and that such a perspective is what enervates our repeated claim that we are still looking on people as responsible. This allegation is made even more plausible by considering the perspective of a person about whom it is predicted that he will do some act unless detained in spite of his insistence that he won't, that he knows he won't, and that he is in the best position to know this, being the agent without whose intention the predicted behavior cannot take place. A person in this predicament will legitimately feel that his ability to control his conduct is questioned, if not denied outright. In the face of such a person's protests, our insistence that we are really still seeing him as free and responsible will surely seem disingenuous, if not self-deceptive.

So we have to show that we need not be denying a person's self-control just because we claim we have accurate predictive techniques which say he will do what he insists he won't. A number of alternatives present themselves. First of all, in disagreeing with a person about what he will do we might be saying that we know more about the circumstances than he does, our disagreement being attributed to his anticipation of circumstances different in significant ways from those he would actually confront. As an illustration of this, say we request of someone that he not use his telephone in the next few minutes to make a call. He responds saying that he will comply, at which point we know he is not going to adhere to his own decision. If we know that his wife will shortly run into the room and ask him to call the doctor quickly because their child stopped breathing, the person would have made a commitment he will not stick to. Here we shouldn't be tempted to think that the person couldn't control his behavior or that he wasn't acting as a responsible agent in acting in ways he just previously committed himself to avoiding.

Another way in which we might be successful in knowing more about what a person will do than the person himself knows is if we know more about how the agent will change than the agent himself does. If someone who just married maintained that he would never take an interest in pursuing extramarital relationships we might be skeptical, not on grounds that any such act is beyond the agent's control, but on the basis of our belief that the agent may not know very much about the natural history of human relationships, and hence is not in a favorable position to judge what he will eventually feel and what he will eventually find strong incentives for doing.

And finally, there are those cases in which we all act in ways we feel in cooler moments committed to avoiding. Though we usually do still want to regard ourselves as responsible for such behavior, it may well be predictable. And perhaps closely tied to such cases are those in which a person doesn't seem to lose control but still seems to be destined to act in ways he wants not to repeat. People who have bad eating, smoking, exercise or work habits fall into this category of persons who can be sincere in protesting that they will not do something which we have excellent inductive grounds for claiming that they will. Once again it would be probably too strong to say that they *cannot* act as they want, and hence are not responsible when they transgress their own resolutions. They just fail to muster the motivation at the crucial times or forget altogether that they are trying to do something different.

So without assuming compulsions or anything at all of a pathological nature, and without denying autonomy or choice to individuals, we can see how it is that we might come to discount people's own sincere assertions and resolutions about what they will do. Hence to make such predictions about people and deal with them on that basis does not necessarily involve us in changing our image of what it is to be a person, and does not force us to concede that we are implicitly using a medical model for interpreting people's behavior, for which issues of responsibility are inappropriate.

Of course some of the worries of those who oppose civil preventive detention are right on the mark: they worry that the basis of the preventive ideal involves denial of human dignity in the sense that it sanctions interfering with innocent people for the benefit of others. Though it is important for society not to coerce people for what they are, and we must all admit that, at times it *is* legitimate to coerce people though they have done nothing wrong. The issue cannot be over *whether* to coerce people in spite of no wrongdoing but over where to draw the line on thinking such coercion legitimate. We say this fully realizing that it involves considerably diminished capacity to avoid interferences of the state.[13] But it should be pointed out that, unlike quarantine, our practice of civil preventive detention is not invoked independent of a person's choices. It is after all, only because a person is likely to do what is proscribed or avoid what is required that confinement would be imposed. Still it is true in this case, as in the case of quarantine, that *given* a determination of future dangerousness to others there is little a person can then do to get himself reclassified.

One way of drawing this line as to when coercion prior to wrongdoing is justified is by distinguishing between controllable and uncontrollable harm, legitimizing preventive measures only in case the harm feared would be the product of some defective condition. Deference to autonomy and freedom from prior restraint would be accorded to those who can be thought responsible for their behavior—desirable or undesirable. Making civil preventive detention dependent upon the incapacity to make one's conduct conform to the law or to incapacities of any sort does enhance the scope of individual freedom and does underscore the significance of respecting people as ends in themselves. Recognizing a policy of restricting preventive detention to such conditions of incapacity would surely suffice to preclude restraint on the type of grounds being considered here. It *would* distinguish how we

could legitimately respond to the threat posed by the criminally insane on the one hand, and how we could respond to the threat posed by the ordinary person. Where responsible choices are possible, there would be no prior restraint. Such restraint would be legitimized only in case responsible choices were impossible.[14]

The problem with this criterion for distinguishing legitimate from illegitimate detention is that it will not distinguish quarantine from the practice of preventive detention we are considering. Responsible choices are not impossible for those who are either afflicted with, or mere carriers of, deadly contagious diseases. The person quarantined is dangerous, not just because he is ill, but because he might do something independent of his illness which would constitute a danger to others, like contaminate food at a restaurant or supermarket. Thus, such a person's disease is not sufficient to cause harm, except when conjoined with his choices and his actions. So, attractive as the present criterion is, it does not draw the distinction where most would like it drawn, between communicable diseases and ordinary kinds of dangerous conduct.

Someone might respond by saying that the line can still be drawn between quarantine and preventive detention in the way just now adumbrated if sufficient notice is taken of the following contrast: while the person quarantined is dangerous because of his illness—something over which he has no control—the person preventively detained is dangerous because of his choices, something over which a person does have control. So while carriers of a deadly contagious disease cannot lead a normal life without harming others, the criminally dangerous person apparently can but chooses not to. Consequently, if the government treated both of these cases in the same way, even though choice entered into one case in a way it did not enter into the other, it would represent an assault on respect for choice and a cheapening of the consideration paid to autonomy.[15]

Though this development of the criterion is powerful, it won't succeed. While it is true that the contagious person may not intend to endanger those with whom he comes into contact, it is clearly not true that the only things we can be said to control are those things we intend to do. The blind man who drives may not intend to kill pedestrians, or even to endanger them. But we would not call his dangerousness behind the wheel uncontrollable. Obviously, he can avoid getting behind the wheel in the first place. Though the person quarantined is restricted much further than is the case with the blind man, the situation is analogous. For though the sick man is dangerous because of a condition out of his control, the amount of actual harm that results is within his control. Hence it is just as significant an affront to autonomy and just as serious a limitation of choice to quarantine the sick as to detain the potential murderer.

Another tack one might take in trying to detach the practice of quarantine from that of civil preventive detention from a moral perspective might involve noting that while quarantine is clearly a response to an emergency, civil preventive detention would represent an everyday affair. And, after all, acts we tolerate during catastrophic episodes can hardly serve as a model for how we generally ought to behave. The fact that triage may be right in the midst of battle does not warrant its practice during less stressful periods.

Several points deserve mentioning in response to this distinction between emergency and non-emergency circumstances. First of all it is not clear that if plagues or other contagious diseases were with us most of the time, we would abandon belief in the legitimacy of quarantine and mandatory screening. It is not obvious that our concern for civil liberties overrides our concern with public health. The next point to be made in response to the distinction between emergency and non-emergency situations is that the rarity of an event can in itself hardly qualify as a legitimate moral basis for making distinctions. What excuses or legitimizes triage is not its rarity but its military necessity, its role in national defense. If it were not necessary for national defense, the rarity of the instance in which it would be practiced would hardly be a point in its favor.

Of course it is true that quarantine would be imposed in times of serious social threat, but so would preventive detention, each possibly being justified on the ground that tens of thousands of persons will otherwise die or suffer severely. I fail to see why if x number of people die from one cause it is an emergency, while if the same number die from some different cause, it is not an emergency situation, assuming everything else is left constant.

One could always try the response that making certain concessions in rare cases results in fewer abrogations of rights than does the same concession applied to frequently recurring situations. But this response is self-defeating since still fewer rights-abrogations would result if the concessions were never made.

If there is something worse about civil preventive detention, qualified in the ways indicated in Part I, than there is about quarantine, not only have we failed to locate it, but whatever it is that makes the distinction is nowhere to be found in the literature. Realizing this does not commit one to *actually* advocating civil preventive detention, for it must be remembered that there are grave practical and legal problems which keep our present world from being one in which the practice could be legitimized. In addition, the arguments throughout the paper relied on the reader's willingness to find quarantine morally acceptable. Those undisposed to think quarantine legitimate will find little in this paper to persuade them that preventive detention has virtues which outweigh its costs, even assuming the modifications in technology and law described above.[16]

NOTES

1. R. G. Spece, Jr., "Conditioning and Other Technologies Used to 'Treat?' 'Rehabilitate?' 'Demolish?' Prisoners and Mental Patients," *Southern California Law Review,* vol. 45 (1971), pp. 616-681, and *Individual Rights and the Federal Role in Behavior Modification* (Washington, 1974).

2. Andrew von Hirsch, "Prediction of Criminal Conduct and Preventive Confinement of Convicted Persons," *Buffalo Law Review,* vol. 21 (1972), pp. 717-758 at Section 11, and "Civil Commitment of the Mentally Ill: Theories and Procedures," *Harvard Law Review,* vol. 79 (1966), pp. 1288-1298 at 1291.

3. A. R. Angel, E. D. Green, H. R. Kaufman, E. E. VanLoon, "Preventive Detention: An Empirical Analysis," *Harvard Civil Rights - Civil Liberties Law Review,* vol. 6 (1971), pp. 300-396 at 342.

4. Alan Dershowitz, "The Law of Dangerousness: Some Fictions About Predictions," *Journal of Legal Education,* vol. 23 (1970), pp. 24-47 at 31-32.

5. See *Olmstead vs U.S.,* 277 U.S. 438-474 (1927), Brandeis, J. dissenting.

6. Frank Grad, *Public Health Law Manual* (New York, 1970), p. 42.

7. Frank Grad, pp. 42-43.

8. Joseph Goldstein and Jay Katz, "Dangerousness and Mental Illness: Some Observations on the Decision to Release Persons Acquitted by Reason of Insanity," *Yale Law Journal,* vol. 70, pp. 225-239 at 235, and Alan Dershowitz, pp. 40, 41, and 43, and J. M. Livermore, D. P. Malmquist and P. E. Meehl, "On the Justification for Civil Commitment," *University of Pennsylvania Law Review,* vol. 117 (1968), pp. 75-96 at 81-82.

9. "Civil Commitment of Narcotics Addicts," *Yale Law Journal,* vol. 76 (1967), pp. 1160-1189 at 1181.

10. Frank Grad, pp. 47-48.

11. Lionel Frankel, "Preventive Restraints and Just Compensation: Toward a Sanction Law of the Future" *Yale Law Journal,* vol. 78 (1968), pp. 229-267 at 257-258.

12. Herbert Packer, *The Limits of the Criminal Sanction* (Stanford, 1968), pp. 74-77.

13. Andrew von Hirsch, Sect. 11 and H. L. A. Hart, "Punishment and the Elimination of Responsibility," *Punishment and Responsibility* (Oxford, 1968) and Herbert Morris, "Persons and Punishment" *Monist,* vol. 52 (1968), pp. 475-501.

14. Lionel Frankel, pp. 247-250.

15. I am indebted to Professor Warner Wick for pressing this objection on my treatment of quarantine.

16. I wish to express my appreciation to Professors Joseph Goldstein, Alan Goldman, Kenneth Kipnis, Denis Nolan, Patrick Hubbard, Warner Wick, William McAninch, Herbert Fingarette and Barry Loewer for helpful comments on earlier versions of this paper.

FURMAN v. GEORGIA

United States Supreme Court, 1972*

Mr. Justice Douglas, concurring.

In these three cases the death penalty was imposed, one of them for murder, and two for rape. In each the determination of whether the penalty should be death or a lighter punishment was left by the State to the discretion of the judge or of the jury. In each of the three cases the trial was to a jury. They are here on petitions for certiorari which we granted limited to the question whether the imposition and execution of the death penalty constitutes "cruel and unusual punishment" within the meaning of the Eighth Amendment as applied to the States by the Fourteenth. I vote to vacate each judgment, believing that the exaction of the death penalty does violate the Eighth and Fourteenth Amendments.

... We cannot say from facts disclosed in these records that these defendants were sentenced to death because they were black. Yet our task is not restricted to an effort to divine what motives impelled these death penalties. Rather, we deal with a system of law and of justice that leaves to the uncontrolled discretion of judges or juries the determination whether defendants committing these crimes should die or be imprisoned. Under these laws no standards govern the selection of the penalty. People live or die, dependent on the whim of one man or of 12.

... In a Nation committed to equal protection of the laws there is no permissible "caste" aspect[18] of law enforcement. Yet we know that the discretion of judges and juries in imposing the death penalty enables the penalty to be selectively applied, feeding prejudices against the accused if he is poor and despised, and lacking political clout, or if he is a member of a suspect or unpopular minority, and saving those who by social position may be in a more protected position. In ancient Hindu law a Brahman was exempt from capital punishment,[19] and in those days, "[g]enerally, in the law books, punishment increased in severity as social status diminished."[20] We have, I fear, taken in practice the same position, partially as a result of making the death penalty discretionary and partially as a result of the ability of the rich to purchase the services of the most respected and most resourceful legal talent in the Nation.

The high service rendered by the "cruel and unusual" punishment clause of the Eighth Amendment is to require legislatures to write penal laws that are evenhanded, nonselective, and nonarbitrary, and to require judges to see to it that general laws are not applied sparsely, selectively, and spottily to unpopular groups.

A law that stated that anyone making more than $50,000 would be exempt from the death penalty would plainly fall, as would a law that in terms said that blacks, those who never went beyond the fifth grade in school, those who made less than $3,000 a year, or those who were unpopular or unstable should be the only people executed. A law which in the overall view reaches that result in practice[21] has no more sanctity than a law which in terms provides the same.

Thus, these discretionary statutes are unconstitutional in their operation. They are pregnant with discrimination and discrimination is an ingredient not compatible with the idea of equal protection of the laws that is implicit in the ban on "cruel and unusual" punishments.

Any law which is nondiscriminatory on its face may be applied in such a way as to violate the Equal Protection Clause of the Fourteenth Amendment. *Yick Wo* v. *Hopkins,* 118 U.S. 356. Such conceivably might be the fate of a mandatory death penalty, where equal or lesser sentences were imposed on the elite, a harsher one or the minorities or members of the lower castes. Whether a mandatory death penalty would otherwise be constitutional is a question I do not reach.

I concur in the judgments of the Court.

Mr. Justice Brennan, concurring.

... There are, then, four principles by which we may determine whether a particular punishment is "cruel and unusual." The primary principle, which I believe supplies the essential predicate for the application of the others, is that a punishment must not by its severity be degrading to human dignity. The paradigm violation of this principle would be the infliction of a tortur-

*408 U.S. 238 (1972). Excerpts only. Footnotes numbered as in the original. Two cases from Georgia and one from Texas were considered and decided together by the Supreme Court.

ous punishment of the type that the Clause has always prohibited. Yet "[i]t is unlikely that any State at this moment in history," *Robinson* v. *California,* 370 U.S., at 666, would pass a law providing for the infliction of such a punishment. Indeed, no such punishment has ever been before this Court. The same may be said of the other principles. It is unlikely that this Court will confront a severe punishment that is obviously inflicted in wholly arbitrary fashion; no State would engage in a reign of blind terror. Nor is it likely that this Court will be called upon to review a severe punishment that is clearly and totally rejected throughout society; no legislature would be able even to authorize the infliction of such a punishment. Nor, finally, is it likely that this Court will have to consider a severe punishment that is patently unnecessary; no State today would inflict a severe punishment knowing that there was no reason whatever for doing so. In short, we are unlikely to have occasion to determine that a punishment is fatally offensive under any one principle.

Since the Bill of Rights was adopted, this Court has adjudged only three punishments to be within the prohibition of the Clause. See *Weems* v. *United States,* 217 U.S. 349 (1910) (12 years in chains at hard and painful labor); *Trop* v. *Dulles,* 356 U.S. 86 (1958) (expatriation); *Robinson* v. *California,* 370 U.S. 660 (1962) (imprisonment for narcotics addiction). Each punishment, of course, was degrading to human dignity, but of none could it be said conclusively that it was fatally offensive under one or the other of the principles. Rather, these "cruel and unusual punishments" seriously implicated several of the principles, and it was the application of the principles in combination that supported the judgment. That, indeed, is not surprising. The function of these principles, after all, is simply to provide means by which a court can determine whether a challenged punishment comports with human dignity. They are, therefore, interrelated, and in most cases it will be their convergence that will justify the conclusion that a punishment is "cruel and unusual." The test, then, will ordinarily be a cumulative one: If a punishment is unusually severe, if there is a strong probability that it is inflicted arbitrarily, if it is substantially rejected by contemporary society, and if there is no reason to believe that it serves any penal purpose more effectively than some less severe punishment, then the continued infliction of that punishment violates the command of the Clause that the State may not inflict inhuman and uncivilized punishments upon those convicted of crimes.

. . . The question, then, is whether the deliberate infliction of death is today consistent with the command of the Clause that the State may not inflict punishments that do not comport with human dignity. I will analyze the punishment of death in terms of the principles set out above and the cumulative test to which they lead: It is a denial of human dignity for the State arbitrarily to subject a person to an unusually severe punishment that society has indicated it does not regard as acceptable, and that cannot be shown to serve any penal purpose more effectively than a significantly less drastic punishment. Under these principles and this test, death is today a "cruel and unusual" punishment.

Death is a unique punishment in the United States. In a society that so strongly affirms the sanctity of life, not surprisingly the common view is that death is the ultimate sanction. This natural human feeling appears all about us. There has been no national debate about punishment, in general or by imprisonment, comparable to the debate about the punishment of death. No other punishment has been so continuously restricted, see *infra,* at 296–298, nor has any State yet abolished prisons, as some have abolished this punishment. And those States that still inflict death reserve it for the most heinous crimes. Juries, of course, have always treated death cases differently, as have governors exercising their communication powers. Criminal defendants are of the same view. "As all practicing lawyers know, who have defended persons charged with capital offenses, often the only goal possible is to avoid the death penalty." *Griffin* v. *Illinois,* 351 U.S. 12, 28 (1956) (Burton and Minton, JJ., dissenting). Some legislatures have required particular procedures, such as two-stage trials and automatic appeals, applicable only in death cases. "It is the universal experience in the administration of criminal justice that those charged with capital offenses are granted special considerations." *Ibid.* See *Williams* v. *Florida,* 399 U.S. 78, 103 (1970) (all States require juries of 12 in death cases). This Court, too, almost always treats death cases as a class apart.[34] And the unfortunate effect of this punishment upon the functioning of the judicial process is well known; no other punishment has a similar effect.

The only explanation for the uniqueness of death is its extreme severity. Death is today an unusually severe punishment, unusual in its pain, in its finality, and in its enormity. No other existing punishment is comparable to death in terms of physical and mental suffering. Although our information is not conclusive, it appears that there is no method available that guarantees an immediate and painless death.[35] Since the discontinuance of flogging as a constitutionally permissible punishment, *Jackson* v. *Bishop,* 404 F. 2d 571 (CA8 1968), death remains as the only punishment that may involve the conscious infliction of physical pain. In addition, we know that mental pain is an inseparable part of our practice of punishing criminals by death for the prospect of pending execution exacts a frightful toll during the inevitable long wait between the imposition of sentence and the actual infliction of death. Cf *Ex parte Medley,* 134 U.S. 160, 172 (1890). As the California Supreme Court pointed out, "the process of carrying out a verdict of death is often so degrading and brutalizing to the human spirit as to constitute psychological torture." *People* v. *Anderson,* 6 Cal. 3d 628, 649, 493 P. 2d 880, 894 (1972).[36] Indeed, as Mr. Justice Frankfurter noted, "the onset of insanity while awaiting execution of a death sentence is not a rare phenomenon." *Solesbee* v. *Balkcom,* 339 U.S. 9, 14 (1950) (dissenting opinion). The "fate of ever-increasing fear and distress" to which the expatriate is subjected, *Trop* v. *Dulles,* 356 U.S., at 102, can only exist to a greater degree for a person confined in prison awaiting death.[37]

The unusual severity of death is manifested most clearly in its finality and enormity. Death, in these respects, is in a class by itself. Expatriation, for example, is a punishment that "destroys for the individual the political existence that was centuries in the development," that "strips the citizen of his status in the national and international political community," and that puts "[h]is very existence" in jeopardy. Expatriation thus inherently entails "the total destruction of the individual's status in organized society." *Id.,* at 101. "In short, the expatriate has lost the right to have rights." *Id.,* at 102. Yet, demonstrably, expatriation is not "a fate worse than death." *Id.,* at 125 (Frankfurther, J., dissenting).[38] Although death, like expatriation, destroys the individual's "political existence" and his "status in organized society," it does more, for, unlike expatriation, death also destroys "[h]is very existence." There is, too at least the possibility that the expatriate will in the future regain "the right to have rights." Death forecloses even that possibility.

Death is truly an awesome punishment. The calculated killing of a human being by the State involves, by its very nature, a denial of the executed person's humanity. The contrast with the plight of a person punished by imprisonment is evident. An individual in prison does not lose "the right to have rights." A prisoner retains, for example, the constitutional rights to the free exercise of religion, to be free of cruel and unusual punishments, and to treatment as a "person" for purposes of due process of law and the equal protection of the laws. A prisoner remains a member of the human family. Moreover, he retains the right of access to the courts. His punishment is not irrevocable. Apart from the common charge, grounded upon the recognition of human fallibility, that the punishment of death must inevitably be inflicted upon innocent men, we know that death has been the lot of men whose convictions were unconstitutionally secured in view of later, retroactively applied, holdings of this Court. The pun-

ishment itself may have been unconstitutionally inflicted, see *Witherspoon* v. *Illinois,* 391 U.S. 510 (1968), yet the finality of death precludes relief. An executed person has indeed 'lost the right to have rights." As one 19th century proponent of punishing criminals by death declared, "When a man is hung, there is an end of our relations with him. His execution is a way of saying, 'You are not fit for this world, take your chance elsewhere.' "[39]

In comparison to all other punishments today, then, the deliberate extinguishment of human life by the State is uniquely degrading to human dignity. I would not hesitate to hold, on that ground alone, that death is today a "cruel and unusual" punishment, were it not that death is a punishment of longstanding usage and acceptance in this country. I therefore turn to the second principle—that the State may not arbitrarily inflict an unusually severe punishment.

... When the punishment of death is inflicted in a trivial number of the cases in which it is legally available, the conclusion is virtually inescapable that it is being inflicted arbitrarily. Indeed, it smacks of little more than a lottery system. The States claim, however, that this rarity is evidence not of arbitrariness, but of informed selectivity: Death is inflicted, they say, only in "extreme" cases.

Informed selectivity, of course, is a value not to be denigrated. Yet presumably the States could make precisely the same claim if there were 10 executions per year, or five, or even if there were but one. That there may be as many as 50 per year does not strengthen the claim. When the rate of infliction is at this low level, it is highly implausible that only the worst criminals or the criminals who commit the worst crimes are selected for this punishment. No one has yet suggested a rational basis that could differentiate in those terms the few who die from the many who go to prison. Crimes and criminals simply do not admit of a distinction that can be drawn so finely as to explain, on that ground, the execution of such a tiny sample of those eligible. Certainly the laws that provide for this punishment do not attempt to draw that distinction; all cases to which the laws apply are necessarily "extreme." Nor is the distinction credible in fact. If, for example, petitioner Furman or his crime illustrates the "extreme," then nearly all murderers and their murders are also "extreme."[48] Furthermore, our procedures in death cases, rather than resulting in the selection of "extreme" cases for this punishment, actually sanction an arbitrary selection. For this Court has held that juries may, as they do, make the decision whether to impose a death sentence wholly unguided by standards governing that decision. *McGautha* v. *California,* 402 U.S. 183, 196–208 (1971). In other words, our procedures are not constructed to guard against the totally capricious selection of criminals for the punishment of death.

Although it is difficult to imagine what further facts would be necessary in order to prove that death is, as my Brother Stewart puts it, "wantonly and . . . freak-ishly" inflicted, I need not conclude that arbitrary in-fliction is patently obvious. I am not considering this punishment by the isolated light of one principle. The probability of arbitrariness is sufficiently substantial that it can be relied upon, in combination with the other principles, in reaching a judgment on the consti-tutionality of this punishment.

When there is a strong probability that an unusually severe and degrading punishment is being inflicted ar-bitrarily, we may well expect that society will disap-prove of its infliction. I turn, therefore, to the third principle. An examination of the history and present operation of the American practice of punishing crimi-nals by death reveals that this punishment has been almost totally rejected by contemporary society. . . . The progressive decline in, and the current rarity of, the infliction of death demonstrate that our society seriously questions the appropriateness of this punish-ment today. The States point out that many legisla-tures authorize death as the punishment for certain crimes and that substantial segments of the public, as reflected in opinion polls and referendum votes, con-tinue to support it. Yet the availability of this punish-ment through statutory authorization, as well as the polls and referenda, which amount simply to approval of that authorization, simply underscores the extent to which our society has in fact rejected this punishment. When an unusually severe punishment is authorized for wide-scale application but not, because of society's refusal, inflicted save in a few instances, the inference is compelling that there is a deep-seated reluctance to inflict it. Indeed, the likelihood is great that the punish-ment is tolerated only because of its disuse. The objec-tive indicator of society's view of an unusually severe punishment is what society does with it, and today society will inflict death upon only a small sample of the eligible criminals. Rejection could hardly be more complete without becoming absolute. At the very least, I must conclude that contemporary society views this punishment with substantial doubt.

The final principle to be considered is that an unusu-ally severe and degrading punishment may not be excessive in view of the purposes for which it is in-flicted. This principle, too, is related to the others. When there is a strong probability that the State is arbitrarily inflicting an unusually severe punishment that is subject to grave societal doubts, it is likely also that the punishment cannot be shown to be serving any penal purpose that could not be served equally well by some less severe punishment.

The States' primary claim is that death is a necessary punishment because it prevents the commission of cap-ital crimes more effectively than any less severe punish-ment. The first part of this claim is that the infliction of death is necessary to stop the individuals executed from committing further crimes. The sufficient answer to this is that if a criminal convicted of a capital crime poses a danger to society, effective administration of the State's pardon and parole laws can delay or deny his release from prison, and techniques of isolation can eliminate or minimize the danger while he remains confined.

The more significant argument is that the threat of death prevents the commission of capital crimes be-cause it deters potential criminals who would not be deterred by the threat of imprisonment. The argument is not based upon evidence that the threat of death is a superior deterrent. Indeed, as my Brother Marshall establishes, the available evidence uniformly indicates, although it does not conclusively prove, that the threat of death has no greater deterrent effect than the threat of imprisonment. The States argue, however, that they are entitled to rely upon common human experience, and that experience, they say, supports the conclusion that death must be a more effective deterrent than any less severe punishment. Because people fear death the most, the argument runs, the threat of death must be the greatest deterrent.

It is important to focus upon the precise import of this argument. It is not denied that many, and probably most, capital crimes cannot be deterred by the threat of punishment. Thus the argument can apply only to those who think rationally about the commission of capital crimes. Particularly is that true when the poten-tial criminal, under this argument, must not only con-sider the risk of punishment, but also distinguish between two possible punishments. The concern, then, is with a particular type of potential criminal, the ratio-nal person who will commit a capital crime knowing that the punishment is long-term imprisonment, which may well be for the rest of his life, but will not commit the crime knowing that the punishment is death. On the face of it, the assumption that such persons exist is implausible.

In any event, this argument cannot be appraised in the abstract. We are not presented with the theoretical question whether under any imaginable circumstances the threat of death might be a greater deterrent to the commission of capital crimes than the threat of impris-onment. We are concerned with the practice of punish-ming criminals by death as it exists in the United States today. Proponents of this argument necessarily admit that its validity depends upon the existence of a system in which the punishment of death is invariably and swiftly imposed. Our system, of course, satisfies neither condition. A rational person contemplating a murder or rape is confronted, not with the certainty of a speedy death, but with the slightest possibility that he will be executed in the distant future. The risk of death is remote and improbable; in contrast, the risk of long-term imprisonment is near and great. In short, whatever the speculative validity of the assumption that the threat of death is a superior deterrent, there is no reason to believe that as currently administered the punishment of death is necessary to deter the commission of capital crimes. Whatever might be the case were all or substantially all eligible criminals quickly put to death, unverifiable possibilities are an insufficient basis upon which to conclude that the threat of death today has any greater deterrent efficacy than the threat of imprisonment.[54]

There is, however, another aspect to the argument that the punishment of death is necessary for the protection of society. The infliction of death, the States urge, serves to manifest the community's outrage at the commission of the crime. It is, they say, a concrete public expression of moral indignation that inculcates respect for the law and helps assure a more peaceful community. Moreover, we are told, not only does the punishment of death exert this widespread moralizing influence upon community values, it also satisfies the popular demand for grievous condemnation of abhorrent crimes and thus prevents disorder, lynching, and attempts by private citizens to take the law into their own hands.

The question, however, is not whether death serves these supposed purposes of punishment, but whether death serves them more effectively than imprisonment. There is no evidence whatever that utilization of imprisonment rather than death encourages private blood feuds and other disorders. Surely if there were such a danger, the execution of a handful of criminals each year would not prevent it. The assertion that death alone is a sufficiently emphatic denunciation for capital crimes suffers from the same defect. If capital crimes require the punishment of death in order to provide moral reinforcement for the basic values of the community, those values can only be undermined when death is so rarely inflicted upon the criminals who commit the crimes. Furthermore, it is certainly doubtful that the infliction of death by the State does in fact strengthen the community's moral code; if the deliberate extinguishment of human life has any effect at all, it more likely tends to lower our respect for life and brutalize our values. That, after all, is why we no longer carry out public executions. In any event, this claim simply means that one purpose of punishment is to indicate social disapproval of crime. To serve that purpose our laws distribute punishments according to the gravity of crimes and punish more severely the crimes society regards as more serious. That purpose cannot justify any particular punishment as the upper limit of severity.

Mr. Justice White, concurring.

. . . Most important, a major goal of the criminal law —to deter others by punishing the convicted criminal —would not be substantially served where the penalty is so seldom invoked that it ceases to be the credible threat essential to influence the conduct of others. For present purposes I accept the morality and utility of punishing one person to influence another. I accept also the effectiveness of punishment generally and need not reject the death penalty as a more effective deterrent than a lesser punishment. But common sense and experience tell us that seldom-enforced laws become ineffective measures for controlling human conduct and that the death penalty, unless imposed with sufficient frequency, will make little contribution to deterring those crimes for which it may be exacted.

The imposition and execution of the death penalty are obviously cruel in the dictionary sense. But the penalty has not been considered cruel and unusual punishment in the constitutional sense because it was thought justified by the social ends it was deemed to serve. At the moment that it ceases realistically to further these purposes, however, the emerging question is whether its imposition in such circumstances would violate the Eighth Amendment. It is my view that it would, for its imposition would then be the pointless and needless extinction of life with only marginal contributions to any discernible social or public purposes. A penalty with such negligible returns to the State would be patently excessive and cruel and unusual punishment violative of the Eighth Amendment.

It is also my judgment that this point has been reached with respect to capital punishment as it is presently administered under the statutes involved in these cases. Concededly, it is difficult to prove as a general proposition that capital punishment, however administered, more effectively serves the ends of the criminal law than does imprisonment. But however that may be, I cannot avoid the conclusion that as the statutes before us are now administered, the penalty is so infrequently imposed that the threat of execution is too attenuated to be of substantial service to criminal justice.

I need not restate the facts and figures that appear in the opinions of my Brethren. Nor can I "prove" my conclusion from these data. But, like my Brethren, I must arrive at judgment; and I can do no more than state a conclusion based on 10 years of almost daily exposure to the facts and circumstances of hundreds and hundreds of federal and state criminal cases involving crimes for which death is the authorized penalty. That conclusion, as I have said, is that the death penalty is exacted with great infrequency even for the most atrocious crimes and that there is no meaningful basis for distinguishing the few cases in which it is imposed from the many cases in which it is not. The short of it is that the policy of vesting sentencing authority primarily in juries—a decision largely motivated by the desire to mitigate the harshness of the law and to bring community judgment to bear on the sentence as well as guilt or innocence—has so effectively achieved its aims that capital punishment within the confines of the statutes now before us has for all practical purposes run its course.

Mr. Chief Justice Burger, with whom Mr. Justice Blackmun, Mr. Justice Powell, and Mr. Justice Rehnquist join, dissenting.

... There are no obvious indications that capital punishment offends the conscience of society to such a degree that our traditional deference to the legislative judgment must be abandoned. It is not a punishment such as burning at the stake that everyone would ineffably find to be repugnant to all civilized standards. Nor is it a punishment so roundly condemned that only a few aberrant legislatures have retained it on the statute books. Capital punishment is authorized by statute in 40 States, the District of Columbia, and in the federal courts for the commission of certain crimes.[7] On four occasions in the last 11 years Congress has added to the list of federal crimes punishable by death.[8] In looking for reliable indicia of contemporary attitude, none more trustworthy has been advanced.

One conceivable source of evidence that legislatures have abdicated their essentially barometric role with respect to community values would be public opinion polls, of which there have been many in the past decade addressed to the question of capital punishment. Without assessing the reliability of such polls, or intimating that any judicial reliance could ever be placed on them, it need only be noted that the reported results have shown nothing approximating the universal condemnation of capital punishment that might lead us to suspect that the legislatures in general have lost touch with current social values.[9]

Counsel for petitioners rely on a different body of empirical evidence. They argue, in effect, that the number of cases in which the death penalty is imposed, as compared with the number of cases in which it is statutorily available, reflects a general revulsion toward the penalty that would lead to its repeal if only it were more generally and widely enforced. It cannot be gainsaid that by the choice of juries—and sometimes judges[10]—the death penalty is imposed in far fewer than half the cases in which it is available.[11] To go further and characterize the rate of imposition as "freakishly rare," as petitioners insist, is unwarranted hyperbole. And regardless of its characterization, the

rate of imposition does not impel the conclusion that capital punishment is now regarded as intolerably cruel or uncivilized.

It is argued that in those capital cases where juries have recommended mercy, they have given expression to civilized values and effectively renounced the legislative authorization for capital punishment. At the same time it is argued that where juries have made the awesome decision to send men to their deaths, they have acted arbitrarily and without sensitivity to prevailing standards of decency. This explanation for the infrequency of imposition of capital punishment is unsupported by known facts, and is inconsistent in principle with everything this Court has ever said about the functioning of juries in capital cases.

In *McGautha* v. *California,* decided only one year ago, the Court held that there was no mandate in the Due Process Clause of the Fourteenth Amendment that juries be given instructions as to when the death penalty should be imposed. After reviewing the autonomy that juries have traditionally exercised in capital cases and noting the practical difficulties of framing manageable instructions, this Court concluded that judicially articulated standards were not needed to insure a responsible decision as to penalty. Nothing in *McGautha* licenses capital juries to act arbitrarily or assumes that they have so acted in the past. On the contrary, the assumption underlying the *McGautha* ruling is that juries "will act with due regard for the consequences of their decision." 402 U.S., at 208.

The responsibility of juries deciding capital cases in our system of justice was nowhere better described than in *Witherspoon* v. *Illinois, supra:*

"[A] jury that must choose between life imprisonment and capital punishment can do little more—and must do nothing less—than express *the conscience of the community* on the ultimate question of life or death."

"And one of the most important functions any jury can perform in making such a selection is to maintain a link between contemporary community values and the penal system—a link without which the determination of punishment could hardly reflect 'the evolving standards of decency that mark the progress of a maturing society' " 391 U.S., at 519 and n. 15 (emphasis added).

The selectivity of juries in imposing the punishment of death is properly viewed as a refinement on rather than a repudiation of, the statutory authorization for that penalty. Legislatures prescribe the categories of crimes for which the death penalty should be available, and, acting as "the conscience of the community," juries are entrusted to determine in individual cases that the ultimate punishment is warranted. Juries are undoubtedly influenced in this judgment by myriad factors. The motive or lack of motive of the perpetrator, the degree of injury or suffering of the victim or victims, and the degree of brutality in the commission of the crime would seem to be prominent among these factors. Given the general awareness that death is no longer a routine punishment for the crimes for which it is made available, it is hardly surprising that juries have been increasingly meticulous in their imposition of the penalty. But to assume from the mere fact of relative infrequency that only a random assortment of pariahs are sentenced to death, is to cast grave doubt on the basic integrity of our jury system.

It would, of course, be unrealistic to assume that juries have been perfectly consistent in choosing the cases where the death penalty is to be imposed, for no human institution performs with perfect consistency. There are doubtless prisoners on death row who would not be there had they been tried before a different jury or in a different State. In this sense their fate has been controlled by a fortuitous circumstance. However, this element of fortuity does not stand as an indictment either of the general functioning of juries in capital cases or of the integrity of jury decisions in individual cases. There is no empirical basis for concluding that juries have generally failed to discharge in good faith the responsibility described in *Witherspoon*—that of choosing between life and death in individual cases according to the dictates of community values.[12]

. . . It seems remarkable to me that with our basic trust in lay jurors as the keystone in our system of criminal justice, it should now be suggested that we take the most sensitive and important of all decisions away from them. I could more easily be persuaded that mandatory sentences of death, without the intervening and ameliorating impact of lay jurors, are so arbitrary and doctrinaire that they violate the Constitution. The very infrequency of death penalties imposed by jurors attests their cautious and discriminating reservation of that penalty for the most extreme cases. I had thought that nothing was clearer in history, as we noted in *McGautha* one year ago, than the American abhorrence of "the common-law rule imposing a mandatory death sentence on all convicted murderers." 402 U.S., at 198. As the concurring opinion of Mr. Justice Marshall shows, *ante,* at 339, the 19th century movement away from mandatory death sentences marked an enlightened introduction of flexibility into the sentencing process. It recognized that individual culpability is not always measured by the category of the crime committed. This change in sentencing practice was greeted by the Court as a humanizing development. See *Winston v. United States,* 172 U.S. 303 (1899); cf. *Calton v. Utah,* 130 U.S. 83 (1889). See also *Andres v. United States,* 333 U.S. 740, 753 (1948) (Frankfurter, J., concurring). I do not see how this history can be ignored and how it can be suggested that the Eighth Amendment demands the elimination of the most sensitive feature of the sentencing system.

As a general matter, the evolution of penal concepts in this country has not been marked by great progress, nor have the results up to now been crowned with significant success. If anywhere in the whole spectrum of criminal justice fresh ideas deserve sober analysis, the sentencing and correctional area ranks high on the list. But it has been widely accepted that mandatory sentences for crimes do not best serve the ends of the criminal justice system. Now, after the long process of drawing away from the blind imposition of uniform sentences for every person convicted of a particular offense, we are confronted with an argument perhaps implying that only the legislatures may determine that a sentence of death is appropriate, without the intervening evaluation of jurors or judges. This approach threatens to turn back the progress of penal reform, which has moved until recently at too slow a rate to absorb significant setbacks.

NOTES

1. The opinion of the Supreme Court of Georgia affirming Furman's conviction of murder and sentence of death is reported in 225 Ga. 253, 167 S. E. 2d 628, and its opinion affirming Jackson's conviction of rape and sentence of death is reported in 225 Ga. 790, 171 S. E. 2d 501. The conviction of Branch of rape and the sentence of death were affirmed by the Court of Criminal Appeals of Texas and reported in 447 S. W. 2d 932.

18. See Johnson, The Negro and Crime, 217 Annals Amer. Acad. Pol. & Soc. Sci. 93 (1941).

19. See J. Spellman, Political Theory of Ancient India 112 (1964).

20. C. Drekmeier, Kingship and Community in Early India 233 (1962).

21. Cf. B. Prettyman, Jr., Death and The Supreme Court 296–297 (1961). "The disparity of representation in capital cases raises doubt about capital punishment itself, which has been abolished in only nine states. If a James Avery [345 U.S. 559] can be saved from electrocution because his attorney made timely objection to the selection of a jury by the use of yellow and white tickets, while an Aubry Williams [349 U.S. 375] can be sent to his death by a jury selected in precisely the same manner, we are imposing our most extreme penalty in an uneven fashion.

"The problem of proper representation is not a problem of money, as some have claimed, but of a lawyer's ability, and it is not true that only the rich have able lawyers. Both the rich and the poor usually are well represented—the poor because more often than not the best attorneys are appointed to defend them. It is the middle-class defendant, who can afford to hire an attorney but not a very good one, who is at a disadvantage. Certainly William Fikes [352 U.S. 191], despite the anomalous position in which he finds himself today, received as effective and intelligent a defense from his court-appointed attorneys as he would have received from an attorney his family had scraped together enough money to hire.

"And it is not only a matter of ability. An attorney must be found who is prepared to spend precious hours—the basic commodity he has to sell—on a case that seldom fully compensates him and often brings him no fee at all. The public has no conception of the time and effort devoted by attorneys to indigent cases. And in a first-degree case, the added responsibility of having a man's life depend upon the outcome exacts a heavy toll."

34.   "That life is at stake is of course another important factor in creating the extraordinary situation. The difference between capital and non-capital offenses is the basis of differentiation in law in diverse ways in which the distinction becomes relevant." *Williams* v. *Georiga,* 349 U.S. 375, 391 (1955) (Frankfurter, J.). "When the penalty is death, we, like state court judges, are tempted to strain the evidence and even, in close cases, the law in order to give a doubtfully condemned man another change." *Stein* v. *New York,* 346 U.S. 156, (1953) (Jackson, J.). "In death cases doubts such as those presented here should be resolved in favor of the accused." *Andres* v. *United States,* 333 U.S. 740, 752 (1948) (Reed, J.). Mr. Justice Harlan expressed the point strongly: "I do not concede that whatever process is 'due' an offender faced with a fine or a prison sentence necessarily satisfies the requirements of the Constitution in a capital case. The distinction is by no means novel, . . . nor is it negligible, being literally that between life and death." *Reid* v. *Covert,* 354 U.S. 1, 77 (1957) (concurring in result). And, of course, for many years this Court distinguished death cases from all others for purposes of the constitutional right to counsel. See *Powell* v. *Alabama,* 287 U.S. 45 (1932); *Betts* v. *Brady,* 316 U.S. 455 (1942); *Bute* v. *Illinois,* 333 U.S. 640 (1948).

35.   See Report of Royal Commission on Capital Punishment 1949–1953, ¶¶ 700–789, pp. 246–273 (1953); Hearings on S. 1760 before the Subcommittee on Criminal Laws and Procedures of the Senate Committee on the Judiciary, 90th Cong., 2d Sess., 19–21 (1968) (testimony of Clinton Duffy); H. Barnes & N. Teeters, New Horizons in Criminology 306–309 (3d ed. 1959); C. Chessman, Trial by Ordeal 195–202 (1955); M. DiSalle, The Power of Life and Death 84–85 (1965); C. Duffy, 88 Men and 2 Women 13–14 (1962); B. Eshelman, Death Row Chaplain 26–29, 101–104, 159–164 (1962); R. Hammer, Between Life and Death 208–212 (1969); K. Lamott, Chronicles of San Quentin 228–231 (1961); L. Lawes, Life and Death in Sing Sing 170–171 (1928); Rubin, The Supreme Court, Cruel and Unusual Punishment, and the Death Penalty, 15 Crime & Delin. 121, 128–129 (1969); Comment, The Death Penalty Cases, 56 Calif. L. Rev. 1268, 1338–1341 (1968); Brief *amici curiae* filed by James V. Bennett, Clinton T. Duffy, Robert G. Sarver, Harry C. Tinsley, and Lawrence E. Wilson 12–14.

36.   See H. Barnes & N. Teeters, New Horizons in Criminology 309–311 (2d ed. 1959); Camus, Reflections on the Guillotine, in A. Camus, Resistance, Rebellion, and Death 131, 151–156 (1960); C. Duffy, 88 Men and 2 Women 68–70, 254 (1962); R. Hammer, Between Life and Death 222–235, 244–250, 269–272 (1969); S. Rubin, The Law of Criminal Correction 340 (1963); Bluestone & McGahee, Reaction to Extreme Stress: Impending Death by Execution, 119 Amer. J. Psychiatry 393 (1962; Gottlieb, Capital Punishment, 15 Crime & Delin. 1, 8–10 (1969); West, Medicine and Capital Punishment, in Hearings on S. 1760 before the Subcommittee on Criminal Laws and Procedures of the Senate Committee on the Judiciary, 90th Cong., 2d Sess., 124 (1968); Ziferstein, Crime and Punishment, The Center Magazine 84 (Jan. 1968); Comment, The Death Penalty Cases, 56 Calif. L. Rev. 1268, 1342 (1968); Note, Mental Suffering under Sentence of Death: A Cruel and Unusual Punishment, 57 Iowa L. Rev. 814 (1972).

37.   The State, of course, does not purposely impose the lengthy waiting period in order to inflict further suffering. The impact upon the individual is not the less severe on that account. It is no answer to assert that long delays exist only because condemned criminals avail themselves of their full panoply of legal rights. The right not to be subjected to inhuman treatment cannot, of course, be played off against the right to pursue due process of law, but, apart from that, the plain truth is that it is society that demands, even against the wishes of the criminal, that all legal avenues be explored before the execution is finally carried out.

38.   It was recognized in *Trop* itself that expatriation is a "punishment short of death." 356 U.S., at 99. Death, however, was distinguished on the ground that it was "still widely accepted." *Ibid.*

39.   Stephen, Capital Punishments, 69 Fraser's Magazine 753 763 (1864).

48.   The victim surprised Furman in the act of burglarizing the victim's home in the middle of the night. While escaping, Furman killed the victim with one pistol shot fired through the closed kitchen door from the outside. At the trial, Furman gave his version of the killing:

"They got me charged with murder and I admit, I admit going to these folks' home and they did caught me in there and I was coming back out, backing up and there was a wire down there on the floor. I was coming out backwards and fell back and I didn't intend to kill nobody. I didn't know they was behind the door. The gun went off and I didn't know nothing about no murder until they arrested me, and when the gun went off I was down on the floor and I got up and ran. That's all to it." App. 54–55.

The Georgia Supreme Court accepted that version:
"The admission in open court by the accused . . . that during the period in which he was involved in the commission of a criminal act at the home of the deceased, he accidentally tripped over a wire in leaving the premises causing the gun to go off, together with other facts and circumstances surrounding the death of the deceased by violent means, was sufficient to support the verdict of guilty of murder. . . ." *Furman* v. *State,* 225 Ga. 253, 254, 167 S. E. 2d 628, 629 (1969).
About Furman himself, the jury knew only that he was black and that, according to his statement at trial, he was 26 years old and worked at "Superior Upholstery." App. 54. It took the jury one hour and 35 minutes to return a verdict of guilt and a sentence of death. *Id.,* at 64–65.

54.   There is also the more limited argument that death is a necessary punishment when criminals are already serving or subject to a sentence of life imprisonment. If the only punishment available is further imprisonment, it is said, those criminals will have nothing to lose by committing further crimes, and accordingly the threat of death is the sole deterrent. But "life" imprisonment is a misnomer today. Rarely, if ever, do crimes carry a mandatory life sentence without possibility of parole. That possibility ensures that criminals do not reach the point where further crimes are free of consequences. Moreover, if this argument is simply an assertion that the threat, of death is a more effective deterrent than the threat of increased imprisonment by denial of release on parole, then, as noted above, there is simply no evidence to support it.

7.   See Department of Justice, National Prisoner Statistics No. 46, Capital Punishment 1930–1970, p. 50 (Aug. 1971). Since the publication of the Department of Justice report, capital punishment has been judicially abolished in California, *People* v. *Anderson,* 6 Cal. 3d 628, 493 P. 2d 880, cert. denied, 406 U.S. 813 (1972). The States where capital punish-

ment is no longer authorized are Alaska, California, Hawaii, Iowa, Maine, Michigan, Minnesota, Oregon, West Virginia, and Wisconsin.

8. See Act of Jan. 2, 1971, Pub. L. 91–644, Tit. IV, § 15, 84 Stat. 1891, 18 U.S.C. § 351; see Act of Oct. 15, 1970, Pub. L. 91–452, Tit. XI, § 1102 (a), 84 Stat. 956, 18 U.S.C. § 844 (f) (i); Act of Aug. 28, 1965, 79 Stat. 580, 18 U.S.C. § 1751; Act of Sept. 5, 1961, § 1, 75 Stat. 466, 49 U.S.C. § 1472 (i). See also opinion of Mr. Justice Blackmun, *post,* at 412–413.

9. A 1966 poll indicated that 42% of those polled favored capital punishment while 47% opposed it, and 11% had no opinion. A 1969 poll found 51% in favor, 40% opposed, and 9% with no opinion. See Erskine, The Polls: Capital Punishment, 34 Public Opinion Quarterly 290 (1970).

10. The jury plays the predominant role in sentencing in capital cases in this country. Available evidence indicates that where the judge determines the sentence, the death penalty is imposed with a slightly greater frequency than where the jury makes the determination. H. Kalven & H. Zeisel, The American Jury 436 (1966).

11. In the decade from 1961–1970, an average of 106 persons per year received the death sentence in the United States, ranging from a low of 85 in 1967 to a high of 140 in 1961; 127 persons received the death sentence in 1970. Department of Justice, National Prisoner Statistics No. 46, Capital Punishment 1930–1970, p. 9. See also Bedau, The Death Penalty in America, 35 Fed. Prob., No. 2, p. 32 (1971). Although accurate figures are difficult to obtain, it is thought that from 15% to 20% of those convicted of murder are sentenced to death in States where it is authorized. See, for example, McGee, Capital Punishment as Seen by a Correc-

tional Administrator, 28 Fed. Prob., No. 2, pp. 11, 12 (1964); Bedau, Death Sentences in New Jersey 1907–1960, 19 Rutgers L. Rev. 1, 30 (1964); Florida Division of Corrections, Seventh Biennial Report (July 1 1968, to June 30, 1970) 82 and the few other crimes made punishable by death in certain States is considerably lower. See, for example, Florida Division of Corrections, Seventh Biennial Report, *supra,* at 83; Partington, The Incidence of the Death Penalty for Rape in Virginia, 22 Wash. & Lee L. Rev. 43–44, 71–73 (1965).

12. Counsel for petitioners make the conclusory statement that "[t]hose who are selected to die are the poor and powerless, personally ugly and socially unacceptable." Brief for Petitioner in No. 68–5027, p. 51. However, the sources cited contain no empirical findings to undermine the general premise that juries impose the death penalty in the most extreme cases. One study has discerned a statistically noticeable difference between the rate of imposition on blue collar and white collar defendants; the study otherwise concludes that juries do follow rational patterns in imposing the sentence of death. Note, A Study of the California Penalty Jury in First-Degree-Murder Cases, 21 Stan. L. Rev. 1297 (1969). See also H. Kalven & H. Zeisel, The American Jury 434–449 (1966).

Statistics are also cited to show that the death penalty has been imposed in a racially discriminatory manner. Such statistics suggest, at least as a historical matter, that Negroes have been sentenced to death with greater frequency than whites in several States, particularly for the crime of interracial rape. See, for example, Koeninger, Capital Punishment in Texas, 1924–1968, 15 Crime & Delin. 132 (1969).

GREGG V. GEORGIA

United States Supreme Court (1976)*

Judgment of the Court, and opinion of MR. JUSTICE STEWART, MR. JUSTICE POWELL, and MR. JUSTICE STEVENS, announced by MR. JUSTICE STEWART.

The issue in this case is whether the imposition of the sentence of death for the crime of murder under the law of Georgia violates the Eighth and Fourteenth Amendments.

I

The petitioner, Troy Gregg, was charged with committing armed robbery and murder. In accordance with Georgia procedure in capital cases, the trial was in two stages, a guilt stage and a sentencing stage. The evidence at the guilt trial established that on November 21, 1973, the petitioner and a traveling companion, Floyd Allen, while hitchhiking north in Florida were picked up by Fred Simmons and Bob Moore. Their car broke down, but they continued north after Simmons purchased another vehicle with some of the cash he was carrying. While still in Florida, they picked up another hitchhiker, Dennis Weaver, who rode with them to Atlanta, where he was let out about 11 p. m. A short time later the four men interrupted their journey for a rest stop along the highway. The next morning the bodies of Simmons and Moore were discovered in a ditch nearby.

On November 23, after reading about the shootings in an Atlanta newspaper, Weaver communicated with the Gwinnet County police and related information concerning the journey with the victims, including a description of the car. The next afternoon, the petitioner and Allen, while in Simmons' car, were arrested in Asheville, N.C. In the search incident to the arrest a .25-caliber pistol, later shown to be that used to kill Simmons and Moore, was found in the petitioner's pocket. After receiving the warnings required by *Miranda* v. *Arizona,* 384 U. S. 436 (1966), and signing a written waiver of his rights, the petitioner signed a statement in which he admitted shooting, then robbing Simmons and Moore. He justified the slayings

on grounds of self-defense. The next day, while being transferred to Lawrenceville, Ga., the petitioner and Allen were taken to the scene of the shootings. Upon arriving there, Allen recounted the events leading to the slayings. His version of these events was as follows: After Simmons and Moore left the car, the petitioner stated that he intended to rob them. The petitioner then took his pistol in hand and positioned himself on the car to improve his aim. As Simmons and Moore came up an embankment toward the car, the petitioner fired three shots and the two men fell near a ditch. The petitioner, at close range, then fired a shot into the head of each. He robbed them of valuables and drove away with Allen.

A medical examiner testified that Simmons died from a bullet wound in the eye and that Moore died from bullet wounds in the cheek and in the back of the head. He further testified that both men had several bruises and abrasions about the face and head which probably were sustained either from the fall into the ditch or from being dragged or pushed along the embankment. Although Allen did not testify, a police detective recounted the substance of Allen's statments about the slayings and indicated that directly after Allen had made these statements the petitioner had admitted that Allen's account was accurate. The petitioner testified in his own defense. He confirmed that Allen had made the statements described by the detective, but denied their truth or ever having admitted to their accuracy. He indicated that he had shot Simmons and Moore because of fear and in self-defense, testifying they had attacked Allen and him, one wielding a pipe and the other a knife.[1]

The trial judge submitted the murder charges to the jury on both felony-murder and nonfelony-murder theories. He also instructed on the issue of self-defense but declined to instruct on manslaughter. He submitted the robbery case to the jury on both an armed-robbery theory and on the lesser included offense of robbery by intimidation. The jury found the petitioner guilty of two counts of armed robbery and two counts of murder.

At the penalty stage, which took place before the same jury, neither the prosecutor nor the petitioner's

*428 U.S. 153. Excerpts only. Footnotes have been renumbered.

lawyer offered any additional evidence. Both counsel, however, made lengthy arguments dealing generally with the propriety of capital punishment under the circumstances and with the weight of the evidence of guilt. The trial judge instructed the jury that it could recommend either a death sentence or a life prison sentence on each count. The judge further charged the jury that in determining what sentence was appropriate the jury was free to consider the facts and circumstances, if any, presented by the parties in mitigation or aggravation.

Finally, the judge instructed the jury that it "would not be authorized to consider [imposing] the penalty of death" unless it first found beyond a reasonable doubt one of these aggravating circumstances:

"One—That the offense of murder was committed while the offender was engaged in the commission of two other capital felonies, to-wit the armed robbery of [Simmons and Moore].
"Two—That the offender committed the offense of murder for the purpose of receiving money and the automobile described in the indictment.
"Three—The offense of murder was outrageously and wantonly vile, horrible and inhuman, in that they [sic] involved the depravity of [the] mind of the defendant." Tr. 476–477.

Finding the first and second of these circumstances, the jury returned verdicts of death on each count.

The Supreme Court of Georgia affirmed the convictions and the imposition of the death sentences for murder. 233 Ga. 177, 210 S. E. 2d 659 (1974). After reviewing the trial transcript and the record, including the evidence, and comparing the evidence and sentence in similar cases in accordance with the requirements of Georgia law, the court concluded that, considering the nature of the crime and the defendant, the sentences of death had not resulted from prejudice or any other arbitrary factor and were not excessive or disproportionate to the penalty applied in similar cases.[2] The death sentences imposed for armed robbery, however, were vacated on the grounds that the death penalty had rarely been imposed in Georgia for that offense and that the jury improperly considered the murders as aggravating circumstances for the robberies after having considered the armed robberies as aggravating circumstances for the murders. Id., at 127, 210 S. E. 2d, at 667.

We granted the petitioner's application for a writ of certiorari limited to his challenge to the imposition of the death sentences in this case as "cruel and unusual" punishment in violation of the Eighth and the Fourteenth Amendments. . .

Four years ago, the petitioners in Furman and its companion cases predicated their argument primarily upon the asserted proposition that standards of decency had evolved to the point where capital punishment no longer could be tolerated. The petitioners in those cases said, in effect, that the evolutionary process had come to an end, and that standards of decency required that the Eighth Amendment be construed finally as prohibiting capital punishment for any crime regardless of its depravity and impact on society. This view was accepted by two Justices. Three other Justices were unwilling to go so far; focusing on the procedures by which convicted defendants were selected for the death penalty rather than on the actual punishment inflicted, they joined in the conclusion that the statutes before the Court were constitutionally invalid.

The petitioners in the capital cases before the Court today renew the "standards of decency" argument, but developments during the four years since Furman have undercut substantially the assumptions upon which their argument rested. Despite the continuing debate, dating back to the 19th century, over the morality and utility of capital punishment, it is now evident that a large proportion of American society continues to regard it as an appropriate and necessary criminal sanction.

The most marked indication of society's endorsement of the death penalty for murder is the legislative response to Furman. The legislatures of at least 35 States have enacted new statutes that provide for the death penalty for at least some crimes that result in the death of another person. And the Congress of the United States, in 1974, enacted a statute providing the death penalty for aircraft piracy that results in death. These recently adopted statutes have attempted to address the concerns expressed by the Court in Furman primarily (i) by specifying the factors to be weighed and the procedures to be followed in deciding when to impose a capital sentence, or (ii) by making the death penalty mandatory for specified crimes. But all of the post-Furman statutes make clear that capital punishment itself has not been rejected by the elected representatives of the people.

In the only statewide referendum occurring since Furman and brought to our attention, the people of California adopted a constitutional amendment that authorized capital punishment, in effect negating a prior ruling by the Supreme Court of California in People v. Anderson, 6 Cal. 3d 628, 493 P. 2d 880, cert. denied, 406 U.S. 958 (1972), that the death penalty violated the California Constitution.

The jury also is a significant and reliable objective index of contemporary values because it is so directly involved. See Furman v. Georgia, 408 U.S., at 439–440 (POWELL, J., dissenting). See generally Powell, Jury Trial of Crimes, 23 Wash. & Lee L. Rev. 1 (1966). The Court has said that "one of the most important functions any jury can perform in making ... a selection [between life imprisonment and death for a defendant convicted in a capital case] is to maintain a link between contemporary community values and the penal system." *Witherspoon* v. *Illinois,* 391 U.S. 510, 519 n. 15 (1968). It may be true that evolving standards have influenced juries in recent decades to be more discriminating in imposing the sentence of death. But the relative infrequency of jury verdicts imposing the death sentence does not indicate rejection of capital punishment *per se.* Rather, the reluctance of juries in many cases to impose the sentence may well reflect the humane feeling that this most irrevocable of sanctions should be reserved for a small number of extreme cases. See *Furman* v. *Georgia, supra,* at 388 (BURGER, C. J., dissenting). Indeed, the actions of juries in many States since *Furman* are fully compatible with the legislative judgments, reflected in the new statutes, as to the continued utility and necessity of capital punishment in appropriate cases. At the close of 1974 at least 254 persons had been sentenced to death since *Furman,* and by the end of March 1976, more than 460 persons were subject to death sentences.

As we have seen, however, the Eighth Amendment demands more than that a challenged punishment be acceptable to contemporary society. The Court also must ask whether it comports with the basic concept of human dignity at the core of the Amendment. *Trop* v. *Dulles,* 356 U. S., at 100 (plurality opinion). Although we cannot "invalidate a category of penalties because we deem less severe penalties adequate to serve the ends of penology," *Furman* v. *Georgia, supra,* at 451 (POWELL, J., dissenting), the sanction imposed cannot be so totally without penological justification that it results in the gratuitous infliction of suffering. *Cf. Wilkerson* v. *Utah,* 99 U.S., at 135–136; *In re Kemmler,* 136 U.S., at 447.

The death penalty is said to serve two principal social purposes: retribution and deterrence of capital crimes by prospective offenders.

In part, capital punishment is an expression of society's moral outrage at particularly offensive conduct. This function may be unappealing to many, but it is essential in an ordered society that asks its citizens to rely on legal processes rather than self-help to vindicate their wrongs.

"The instinct for retribution is part of the nature of man, and channeling that instinct in the administration of criminal justice serves an important purpose in promoting the stability of a society governed by law. When people begin to believe that organized society is unwilling or unable to impose upon criminal offenders the punishment they 'deserve' then there are sown the seeds of anarchy—of self-help, vigilante justice, and lynch law." *Furman* v. *Georgia, supra,* at 308 (STEWART, J., concurring).

"Retribution is no longer the dominant objective of the criminal law," *Williams* v. *New York,* 337 U.S. 241, 248 (1949), but neither is it a forbidden objective nor one inconsistent with our respect for the dignity of men. *Furman* v. *Georgia,* 408 U. S., at 394–395 (Burger, C. J., dissenting); id., at 452–454 (Powell, J., dissenting); *Powell* v. *Texas,* 392 U. S., at 531 535–536 (plurality opinion). Indeed, the decision that capital punishment may be the appropriate sanction in extreme cases is an expression of the community's belief that certain crimes are themselves so grievous an affront to humanity that the only adequate response may be the penalty of death: ...

We now turn to consideration of the constitutionality of Georgia's capital-sentencing procedures. In the wake of *Furman,* Georgia amended its capital punishment statute, but chose not to narrow the scope of its murder provisions. See Part II, *supra.* Thus, now as before *Furman,* in Georgia "[a] person commits murder when he unlawfully and with malice aforethought, either express or implied, causes the death of another human being." Ga. Code Ann., § 26-1101 (a) (1972). All persons convicted of murder "shall be punished by death or by imprisonment for life." § 26-1101 (c) (1972).

Georgia did act, however, to narrow the class of murderers subject to capital punishment by specifying 10 statutory aggravating circumstances, one of which must be found by the jury to exist beyond a reasonable doubt before a death sentence can ever be imposed. In addition, the jury is authorized to consider any other appropriate aggravating or mitigating circumstances. § 27-2534.1 (b) (Supp. 1975). The jury is not required to find any mitigating circumstance in order to make a recommendation of mercy that is binding on the trial court, see §27-2302 (Supp. 1975), but it must find a *statutory* aggravating circumstance before recommending a sentence of death.

These procedures require the jury to consider the circumstances of the crime and the criminal before it recommends sentence. No longer can a Georgia jury do as Furman's jury did: reach a finding of the defendant's guilt and then, without guidance or direction, decide whether he should live or die. Instead, the jury's attention is directed to the specific circumstances of the crime: Was it committed in the course of another capital felony? Was it committed for money? Was it committed upon a peace officer or judicial officer? Was it committed in a particularly heinous way or in a manner that endangered the lives of many persons? In addition, the jury's attention is focused on the characteristics of the person who committed the crime: Does he have a record of prior convictions for capital offenses? Are there any special facts about this defendant that mitigate against imposing capital punishment (*e. g.,* his youth, the extent of his cooperation with the police, his emotional state at the time of the crime)? As a result, while some jury discretion still exists, "the discretion to be exercised is controlled by clear and objective standards so as to produce non-discriminatory application." *Coley* v. *State,* 231 Ga. 829, 834, 204 S. E. 2d 612, 615 (1974).

As an important additional safeguard against arbitrariness and caprice, the Georgia statutory scheme provides for automatic appeal of all death sentences to the State's Supreme Court. That court is required by statute to review each sentence of death and determine whether it was imposed under the influence of passion or prejudice, whether the evidence supports the jury's finding of a statutory aggravating circumstance, and whether the sentence is disproportionate compared to those sentences imposed in similar cases. § 27-2537 (c) (Supp. 1975).

In short, Georgia's new sentencing procedures require as a prerequisite to the imposition of the death penalty, specific jury findings as to the circumstances of the crime or the character of the defendant. Moreover, to guard further against a situation comparable to that presented in *Furman,* the Supreme Court of Georgia compares each death sentence with the sentences imposed on similarly situated defendants to ensure that the sentence of death in a particular case is not disproportionate. On their face these procedures seem to satisfy the concerns of *Furman.* No longer should there be "no meaningful basis for distinguishing the few cases in which [the death penalty] is imposed from the many cases in which it is not." 408 U. S., at 313 (White, J., concurring).

The petitioner contends, however, that the changes in the Georgia sentencing procedures are only cosmetic, that the arbitrariness and capriciousness condemned by *Furman* continue to exist in Georgia—both in traditional practices that still remain and in the new sentencing procedures adopted in response to *Furman.*

1

First, the petitioner focuses on the opportunities for discretionary action that are inherent in the processing of any murder case under Georgia law. He notes that the state prosecutor has unfettered authority to select those persons whom he wishes to prosecute for a capital offense and to plea bargain with them. Further, at the trial the jury may choose to convict a defendant of a lesser included offense rather than find him guilty of a crime punishable by death, even if the evidence would support a capital verdict. And finally, a defendant who is convicted and sentenced to die may have

his sentence commuted by the Governor of the State and the Georgia Board of Pardons and Paroles.

The existence of these discretionary stages is not determinative of the issues before us. At each of these stages an actor in the criminal justice system makes a decision which may remove a defendant from consideration as a candidate for the death penalty. *Furman,* in contrast, dealt with the decision to impose the death sentence on a specific individual who had been convicted of a capital offense. Nothing in any of our cases suggests that the decision to afford an individual defendant mercy violates the Constitution. *Furman* held only that, in order to minimize the risk that the death penalty would be imposed on a capriciously selected group of offenders, the decision to impose it had to be guided by standards so that the sentencing authority would focus on the particularized circumstances of the crime and the defendant.[3]

2

The petitioner further contends that the capital-sentencing procedures adopted by Georgia in response to *Furman* do not eliminate the dangers of arbitrariness and caprice in jury sentencing that were held in *Furman* to be violative of the Eighth and Fourteenth Amendments. He claims that the statute is so broad and vague as to leave juries free to act as arbitrarily and capriciously as they wish in deciding whether to impose the death penalty. While there is no claim that the jury in this case relied upon a vague or overbroad provision to establish the existence of a statutory aggravating circumstance, the petitioner looks to the sentencing system as a whole (as the Court did in *Furman* and we do today) and argues that it fails to reduce sufficiently the risk of arbitrary infliction of death sentences. Specifically, Gregg urges that the statutory aggravating circumstances are too broad and too vague, that the sentencing procedure allows for arbitrary grants of mercy, and that the scope of the evidence and argument that can be considered at the presentence hearing is too wide.

The petitioner attacks the seventh statutory aggravating circumstance, which authorizes imposition of the death penalty if the murder was "outrageously or wantonly vile, horrible or inhuman in that it involved torture, depravity of mind, or an aggravated battery to the victim," contending that it is so broad that capital punishment could be imposed in any murder case. It is, of course, arguable that any murder involves depravity of mind or an aggravated battery. But this language need not be construed in this way, and there is no reason to assume that the Supreme Court of Georgia will adopt such an open-ended construction. In only one case has it upheld a jury's decision to sentence a defendant to death when the only statutory aggravating circumstance found was that of the seventh, see McCorquodale v. State, 233 Ga. 369, 211 S. E. 2d 577 (1974), and that homicide was a horrifying torture-murder.

The petitioner also argues that two of the statutory aggravating circumstances are vague and therefore susceptible of widely differing interpretations, thus creating a substantial risk that the death penalty will be arbitrarily inflicted by Georgia juries. In light of the decisions of the Supreme Court of Georgia we must disagree. First, the petitioner attacks that part of § 27-2534.1 (b)(1) that authorizes a jury to consider whether a defendant has a "substantial history of serious assaultive criminal convictions." The Supreme Court of Georgia, however, has demonstrated a concern that the new sentencing procedures provide guidance to juries. It held this provision to be impermissibly vague in *Arnold v. State,* 236 Ga. 534, 540, 224 S. E. 2d 386, 391 (1976), because it did not provide the jury with "sufficiently 'clear and objective standards.' " Second, the petitioner points to §27-2534.1 (b)(3) which speaks of creating a "great risk of death to more than one person." While such a phrase might be susceptible of an overly broad interpretation, the Supreme Court of Georgia has not so construed it. The only case in which the court upheld a conviction in reliance on this aggravating circumstance involved a man who stood up in a church and fired a gun indiscriminately into the audience. See *Chenault v. State,* 234 Ga. 216, 215 S. E. 2d 223 (1975). On the other hand, the court expressly reversed a finding of great risk when the victim was simply kidnaped in a parking lot. See *Jarrell v. State,* 234 Ga. 410, 424, 216 S. E. 2d 258, 269 (1975).

The petitioner next argues that the requirements of *Furman* are not met here because the jury has the power to decline to impose the death penalty even if it finds that one or more statutory aggravating circumstances are present in the case. This contention misinterprets *Furman.* See *supra,* at 198-199. Moreover, it ignores the role of the Supreme Court of Georgia which reviews each death sentence to determine whether it is proportional to other sentences imposed for similar crimes. Since the proportionality requirement on review is intended to prevent caprice in the decision to inflict the penalty, the isolated decision of a jury to afford mercy does not render unconstitutional death sentences imposed on defendants who were sentenced under a system that does not create a substantial risk of arbitrariness or caprice.

The petitioner objects, finally, to the wide scope of evidence and argument allowed at presentence hearings. We think that the Georgia court wisely has chosen not to impose unnecessary restrictions on the evidence that can be offered at such a hearing and to

approve open and far-ranging argument. See, *e. g.,* *Brown v. State,* 235 Ga. 644, 220 S. E. 2d 922 (1975). So long as the evidence introduced and the arguments made at the presentence hearing do not prejudice a defendant, it is preferable not to impose restrictions. We think it desirable for the jury to have as much information before it as possible when it makes the sentencing decision. See *supra, at* 189-190.

3

Finally, the Georgia statute has an additional provision designed to assure that the death penalty will not be imposed on a capriciously selected group of convicted defendants. The new sentencing procedures require that the State Supreme Court review every death sentence to determine whether it was imposed under the influence of passion, prejudice, or any other arbitrary factor, whether the evidence supports the findings of a statutory aggravating circumstance, and "[w]hether the sentence of death is excessive or disproportionate to the penalty imposed in similar cases, considering both the crime and the defendant." § 27-2537 (c)(3) (Supp. 1975). In performing its sentence-review function, the Georgia court has held that "if the death penalty is only rarely imposed for an act or it is substantially out of line with sentences imposed for other acts it will be set aside as excessive." *Coley v. State,* 231 Ga., at 834, 204 S. E. 2d, at 616. The court on another occasion stated that "we view it to be our duty under the similarity standard to assure that no death sentence is affirmed unless in similar cases throughout the state the death penalty has been imposed generally. . . ." *Moore v. State,* 233 Ga. 861, 864, 213 S. E. 2d 829, 832 (1975). See also *Jarrell v. State, supra,* at 425, 216 S. E. 2d, at 270 (standard is whether "juries generally throughout the state have imposed the death penalty"); *Smith v. State,* 236 Ga. 12, 24, 222 S. E. 2d 308, 318 (1976) (found "a clear pattern" of jury behavior).

It is apparent that the Supreme Court of Georgia has taken its review responsibilities seriously. In *Coley,* it held that "[t]he prior cases indicate that the past practice among juries faced with similar factual situations and like aggravating circumstances has been to impose only the sentence of life imprisonment for the offense of rape, rather than death." 231 Ga., at 835, 204 S. E. 2d, at 617. It thereupon reduced Coley's sentence from death to life imprisonment. Similarly, although armed robbery is a capital offense under Georgia law, § 26-1902 (1972), the Georgia court concluded that the death sentences imposed in this case for that crime were "unusual in that they are rarely imposed for [armed robbery]. Thus, under the test provided by statute, . . . they must be considered to be excessive or disproportionate to the penalties imposed in similar cases." 233 Ga., at 127, 210 S. E. 2d, at 667. The court therefore vacated Gregg's death sentences for armed robbery and has followed a similar course in every other armed robbery death penalty case to come before it. See *Floyd* v. *State,* 233 Ga. 280, 285, 210 S. E. 2d 810, 814 (1974); *Jarrell* v. *State,* 234 Ga., at 424-425, 216 S. E. 2d, at 270. See *Dorsey* v. *State,* 236 Ga. 591, 225 S. E. 2d 418 (1976).

The provision for appellate review in the Georgia capital-sentencing system serves as a check against the random or arbitrary imposition of the death penalty. In particular, the proportionality review substantially eliminates the possibility that a person will be sentenced to die by the action of an aberrant jury. If a time comes when juries generally do not impose the death sentence in a certain kind of murder case, the appellate review procedures assure that no defendant convicted under such circumstances will suffer a sentence of death.

V

The basic concern of *Furman* centered on those defendants who were being condemned to death capriciously and arbitrarily. Under the procedures before the Court in that case, sentencing authorities were not directed to give attention to the nature or circumstances of the crime committed or to the character or record of the defendant. Left unguided, juries imposed the death sentence in a way that could only be called freakish. The new Georgia sentencing procedures, by contrast, focus the jury's attention on the particularized nature of the crime and the particularized characteristics of the individual defendant. While the jury is permitted to consider any aggravating or mitigating circumstances, it must find and identify at least one statutory aggravating factor before it may impose a penalty of death. In this way the jury's discretion is channeled. No longer can a jury wantonly and freakishly impose the death sentence; it is always circumscribed by the legislative guidelines. In addition, the review function of the Supreme Court of Georgia affords additional assurance that the concerns that prompted our decision in *Furman* are not present to any significant degree in the Georgia procedure applied here.

For the reasons expressed in this opinion, we hold that the statutory system under which Gregg was sentenced to death does not violate the Constitution. Accordingly, the judgment of the Georgia Supreme Court is affirmed.

Mr. JUSTICE BRENNAN, dissenting.

. . . This Court inescapably has the duty, as the ultimate arbiter of the meaning of our Constitution, to say whether, when individuals condemned to death stand before our Bar, "moral concepts" require us to hold that the law has progressed to the point where we should declare that the punishment of death, like punishments on the rack, the screw, and the wheel, is no longer morally tolerable in our civilized society.[4] My opinion in *Furman* v. *Georgia* concluded that our civilization and the law had progressed to this point and that therefore the punishment of death, for whatever crime and under all circumstances, is "cruel and unusual" in violation of the Eighth and Fourteenth Amendments of the Constitution. I shall not again canvass the reasons that led to that conclusion. I emphasize only that foremost among the "moral concepts" recognized in our cases and inherent in the Clause is the primary moral principle that the State, even as it punishes, must treat its citizens in a manner consistent with their intrinsic worth as human beings —a punishment must not be so severe as to be degrading to human dignity. A judicial determination whether the punishment of death comports with human dignity is therefore not only permitted but compelled by the Clause. 408 U. S., at 270.

I do not understand that the Court disagrees that "[i]n comparison to all other punishments today . . . the deliberate extinguishment of human life by the State is uniquely degrading to humna dignity." Id., at 291. For three of my Brethren hold today mandatory infliction of the death penalty constitutes the penalty cruel and unusual punishment. I perceive no principled basis for this limitation. Death for whatever crime and under all circumstances "is truly an awesome punishment. The calculated killing of a human being by the State involves, by its very nature, a denial of the executed person's humanity. . . . An executed person has indeed 'lost the right to have rights.'" Id., at 290. Death is not only an unusually severe punishment, unusual in its pain, in its finality, and in its enormity, but it serves no penal purpose more effectively than a less severe punishment; therefore the principle inherent in the Clause that prohibits infliction of excessive punishment when less severe punishment can adequately achieve the same purposes invalidates the punishment. Id., at 279.

The fatal constitutional infirmity in the punishment of death is that it treats "members of the human race as nonhumans, as objects to be toyed with and discarded. [It is] thus inconsistent with the fundamental premise of the Clause that even the vilest criminal remains a human being possessed of common human dignity." Id. at 273. As such it is a penalty that "subjects the individual to a fate forbidden by the principle of civilized treatment guaranteed by the [Clause]." I therefore would hold, on that ground alone, that death is today a cruel and unusual punishment prohibited by the Clause. "Justice of this kind is obviously no less shocking than the crime itself, and the new 'official' murder, far from offering redress for the offense committed against society, adds instead a second defilement to the first."

NOTES

1. On cross-examination the State introduced a letter written by the petitioner to Allen entitled, "[a] statement for you," with the instructions that Allen memorize and then burn it. The statement was consistent with the petitioner's testimony at trial.

2. The court further held, in part, that the trial court did not err in refusing to instruct the jury with respect to voluntary manslaughter since there was no evidence to support that verdict.

3. The petitioner's argument is nothing more than a veiled contention that *Furman* indirectly outlawed capital punishment by placing totally unrealistic conditions on its use. In order to repair the alleged defects pointed to by the petitioner, it would be necessary to require that prosecuting authorities charge a capital offense whenever arguably there had been a capital murder and that they refuse to plea bargain with the defendant. If a jury refused to convict even though the evidence supported the charge, its verdict would have to be reversed and a verdict of guilty entered or a new trial ordered, since the discretionary act of jury nullification would not be permitted. Finally, acts of executive clemency would have to be prohibited. Such a system, of course, would be totally alien to our notions of criminal justice.

Moreover, it would be unconstitutional. Such a system in many respects would have the vices of the mandatory death penalty statutes we hold unconstitutional today in *Woodson* v. *North Carolina, post,* p. 280, and *Roberts* v. *Louisiana, post,* p. 325. The suggestion that a jury's verdict of acquittal could be overturned and a defendant retried would run afoul of the Sixth Amendment jury trial guarantee and the Double Jeopardy Clause of the Fifth Amendment. In the federal system it also would be unconstitutional to prohibit a President from deciding, as an act of executive clemency, to reprieve one sentenced to death. U. S. Cons., Art. II § 2.

COKER v. GEORGIA

United States Supreme Court (1977)*

SYLLABUS

While serving various sentences for murder, rape, kidnaping, and aggravated assault, petitioner escaped from a Georgia prison and, in the course of committing an armed robbery and other offenses, raped an adult woman. He was convicted of rape, armed robbery, and the other offenses and sentenced to death on the rape charge, when the jury found two of the aggravating circumstances present for imposing such a sentence, *viz.,* that the rape was committed (1) by a person with prior capital-felony convictions and (2) in the course of committing another capital felony, armed robbery. The Georgia Supreme Court affirmed both the conviction and sentence. *Held:* The judgment upholding the death sentence is reversed and the case is remanded.

Mr. Justice WHITE, joined by Mr. Justice STEWART, Mr. Justice BLACKMUN, and Mr. Justice STEVENS, concluded that the sentence of death for the crime of rape is grossly disproportionate and excessive punishment and is therefore forbidden by the Eighth Amendment as cruel and unusual punishment.

(a) The Eighth Amendment bars not only those punishments that are "barbaric" but also those that are "excessive" in relation to the crime committed, and a punishment is "excessive" and unconstitutional if it (1) makes no measurable contribution to acceptable goals of punishment and hence is nothing more than the purposeless and needless imposition of pain and suffering; or (2) is grossly out of proportion to the severity of the crime.

(b) That death is a disproportionate penalty for rape is strongly indicated by the objective evidence of present, public judgment, as represented by the attitude of state legislatures and sentencing juries, concerning the acceptability of such a penalty, it appearing that Georgia is currently the only State authorizing the death sentence for rape of an adult woman, that it is authorized for rape in only two other States but only when the victim is a child, and that in the vast majority (9 out of 10) of rape convictions in Georgia since 1973, juries have not imposed the death sentence.

(c) Although rape deserves serious punishment, the death penalty, which is unique in its severity and irrevocability, is an excessive penalty for the rapist who, as such and as opposed to the murderer, does not unjustifiably take human life.

(d) The conclusion that the death sentence imposed on petitioner is disproportionate punishment for rape is not affected by the fact that the jury found the aggravating circumstances of prior capital felony convictions and occurrence of the rape while committing armed robbery, a felony for which the death sentence is also authorized, since the prior convictions do not change the fact that the rape did not involve the taking of life, and since the jury did not deem the robbery itself deserving of the death penalty, even though accompanied by the aggravating circumstances of prior capital felony convictions.

(e) That under Georgia law a deliberate killer cannot be sentenced to death, absent aggravating circumstances, argues strongly against the notion that, with or without such circumstances, a rapist who does not take the life of his victim should be punished more severely than the deliberate killer.

Mr. Justice BRENNAN concluded that the death penalty is in all circumstances cruel and unusual punishment prohibited by the Eighth and Fourteenth Amendments.

Mr. Justice MARSHALL concluded that the death penalty is a cruel and unusual punishment prohibited by the Eighth and Fourteenth Amendments.

Mr. Justice POWELL concluded that death is disproportionate punishment for the crime of raping an adult woman where, as here, the crime was not committed with excessive brutality and the victim did not sustain serious or lasting injury.

DISSENTING OPINION

Mr. Chief Justice BURGER, with whom Mr. Justice REHNQUIST joins, dissenting.

In a case such as this, confusion often arises as to the Court's proper role in reaching a decision. Our task is

---

*975.Ct.2861 (1977).

The syllabus constitutes no part of the opinion of the Court but has been prepared by the Reporter of Decisions for the convenience of the reader.

not to give effect to our individual views on capital punishment; rather, we must determine what the Constitution permits a State to do under its reserved powers. In striking down the death penalty imposed upon the petitioner in this case, the Court has overstepped the bounds of proper constitutional adjudication by substituting its policy judgment for that of the state legislature. I accept that the Eighth Amendment's concept of disproportionality bars the death penalty for minor crimes. But rape is not a minor crime; hence the Cruel and Unusual Punishment Clause does not give the Members of this Court license to engraft their conceptions of proper public policy onto the considered legislative judgments of the States. Since I cannot agree that Georgia lacked the constitutional power to impose the penalty of death for rape, I dissent from the Court's judgment.

(1)

On December 5, 1971, the petitioner, Ehrlich Anthony Coker, raped and then stabbed to death a young woman. Less than eight months later Coker kidnapped and raped a second young woman. After twice raping this 16-year-old victim, he stripped her, severely beat her with a club, and dragged her into a wooded area where he left her for dead. He was apprehended and pleaded guilty to offenses stemming from these incidents. He was sentenced by three separate courts to three life terms, two 20-year terms, and one eight-year term of imprisonment.[1] Each judgment specified that the sentences it imposed were to run consecutively rather than concurrently. Approximately one and one-half years later, on September 2, 1974, petitioner escaped from the state prison where he was serving these sentences. He promptly raped another 16-year-old woman in the presence of her husband, abducted her from her home, and threatened her with death and serious bodily harm. It is this crime for which the sentence now under review was imposed.

The Court today holds that the State of Georgia may not impose the death penalty on Coker. In so doing, it prevents the State from imposing any effective punishment upon Coker for his latest rape. The Court's holding, moreover, bars Georgia from guaranteeing its citizens that they will suffer no further attacks by this habitual rapist. In fact, given the lengthy sentences Coker must serve for the crimes he has already committed, the Court's holding assures that petitioner—and others in his position—will henceforth feel no compunction whatsoever about committing further rapes as frequently as he may be able to escape from confinement and indeed even within the walls of the prison itself. To what extent we have left States "elbow room" to protect innocent persons from depraved human beings like Coker remains in doubt.

(2)

My first disagreement with the Court's holding is its unnecessary breadth. The narrow issue here presented is whether the State of Georgia may constitutionally execute this petitioner for the particular rape which he has committed, in light of all the facts and circumstances shown by this record. The plurality opinion goes to great lengths to consider societal mores and attitudes toward the generic crime of rape and the punishment for it; however, the opinion gives little attention on the special circumstances which bear directly on whether imposition of the death penalty is an appropriate societal response to Coker's criminal acts: (a) On account of his prior offenses, Coker is already serving such lengthy prison sentences that imposition of additional periods of imprisonment would have no incremental punitive effect; (b) by his life pattern Coker has shown that he presents a particular danger to the safety, welfare and chastity of women, and on his record the likelihood is therefore great that he will repeat his crime at first opportunity; (c) petitioner escaped from prison, only a year and a half after he commenced serving his latest sentences; he has nothing to lose by further escape attempts; and (d) should he again succeed in escaping from prison, it is reasonably predictable that he will repeat his pattern of attacks on women—and with impunity since the threat of added prison sentences will be no deterrent.

Unlike the Court, I would narrow the inquiry in this case to the question actually presented: Does the Eighth Amendment's ban against cruel and unusual punishment prohibit the State of Georgia from executing a person who has, within the space of three years, raped three separate women, killing one and attempting to kill another, who is serving prison terms exceeding his probable lifetime and who has not hesitated to escape confinement at the first available opportunity? Whatever one's view may be as to the State's constitutional power to impose the death penalty upon a rapist who stands before a court convicted for the first time, this case reveals a chronic rapist whose continuing danger to the community is abundantly clear.

Mr. Justice POWELL would hold the death sentence inappropriate in *this* case because "there is no indication that petitioner's offense was committed with excessive brutality or that the victim sustained serious or lasting injury."[2] Apart from the reality that rape is inherently one of the most egregiously brutal acts one human being can inflict upon another, there is nothing in the Eighth Amendment that so narrowly limits the factors which may be considered by a state legislature in determining whether a particular punishment is grossly excessive. Surely recidivism, especially the repeated commission of heinous crimes, is a factor which may properly be weighed as an aggravating circumstance, permitting the imposition of a punishment more severe than for one isolated offense. For example, as a matter of national policy, Congress has expressed its will that a person who has committed two felonies will suffer enhanced punishment for a third one, 18 U.S.C. § 3575(e)(1); Congress has also declared that a second conviction for assault on a mail carrier may be punished more seriously than a first such conviction, *id.,* § 2114. Many States provide an increased penalty for habitual criminality. See, *e. g.,* Wis. Stat. § 939.62; see also Annot., 58 A.L.R. 20, 82 A.L.R. 345, 79 A.L.R.2d 826.[3] As a factual matter, the plurality opinion is correct in stating that Coker's "prior convictions do not change the fact that the instant crime being punished is rape not involving the taking of life," *ante,* at 2869; however, it cannot be disputed that the existence of these prior convictions make Coker a substantially more serious menace to society than a first-time offender:[4]

"There is a widely held view that those who present the strongest case for severe measures of incapacitation are not murderers as a group (their offenses often are situational) *but rather those who have repeatedly engaged in violent, combative behavior.* A well-demonstrated propensity for life-endangering behavior is thought to provide a more solid basis for infliction of the most severe measures of incapacitation than does the fortuity of a single homicidal incident." Packer, Making the Punishment Fit the Crime, 77 Harv. L. Rev. 1071, 1080 (1964). (Emphasis added.)

In my view, the Eighth Amendment does not prevent the State from taking an individual's "well demonstrated propensity for life-endangering behavior" into account in devising punitive measures which will prevent inflicting further harm upon innocent victims. See *Gregg v. Georgia,* 428 U.S. 153, 183 n. 28, 96 S. Ct. 2909, 2930, 49 L. Ed. 2d 859 (1976). Only one year ago Mr. Justice White succinctly noted: "death finally forecloses the possibility that a prisoner will commit further crimes, whereas life imprisonment does not." *Roberts v. Louisiana,* 428 U.S. 325, 354, 96 S. Ct. 3001, 3016, 49 L. Ed. 2d 974 (1976) (White, J., dissenting); see also *Furman v. Georgia,* 408 U.S., at 310, 92 S. Ct., at 2763 (White, J., concurring).

In sum, once the Court has held that "the punishment of death does not invariably violate the Constitution," *Gregg v. Georgia,* 428 U.S., at 169, 96 S. Ct., at 2923, it seriously impinges upon the State's legislative judgment to hold that it may not impose such sentence upon an individual who has shown total and repeated disregard for the welfare, safety, personal integrity and human worth of others, and who seemingly cannot be deterred from continuing such conduct.[5] I therefore would hold that the death sentence here imposed is within the power reserved to the State and leave for another day the question of whether such sanction would be proper under other circumstances. The dangers which inhere whenever the Court casts its constitutional decisions in terms sweeping beyond the facts of the case presented, are magnified in the context of the Eighth Amendment. In *Furman v. Georgia,* 408 U.S., at 431, 92 S. Ct., at 2824, Mr. Justice POWELL, in dissent stated:

"where, as here, the language of the applicable [constitutional] provision provides great leeway and where the underlying social policies are felt to be of vital importance, the temptation to read personal preference into the Constitution is understandably great. *It is too easy to propound our subjective standards of wise policy under the rubric of more or less universally held standards of decency.*" (Emphasis added.)

Since the Court now invalidates the death penalty as a sanction for all rapes of adults at all times under all circumstances,[6] I reluctantly turn to what I see as the broader issues raised by this holding.

(3)

The plurality . . . acknowledges the gross nature of the crime of rape. A rapist not only violates a victim's privacy and personal integrity, but inevitably causes serious psychological harm as well as physical harm in the process. The long-range effect on the victim's life may be gravely affected, and this in turn may have a serious detrimental effect upon her husband and any children she may have. I therefore wholly agree with Mr. Justice WHITE'S conclusion as far as it goes— that "[s]hort of homicide, [rape] is the 'ultimate violation of the self.' " . . . Victims may recover from the physical damage of knife or bullet wounds, or a beating with fists or a club, but recovery from such a gross assault on the human personality is not healed by medicine or surgery. To speak blandly, as the plurality does, of rape victims which are "unharmed," or, as the concurrence, to classify the human outrage of rape in terms of "excessively brutal," . . . versus "moderately brutal," takes too little account of the profound suffering the crime imposes upon the victims and their loved ones.

Despite its strong condemnation of rape, the Court reaches the inexplicable conclusion that "the death penalty . . . is an excessive penalty" for the perpetrator of this heinous offense.[7] This, the Court holds, is true even though in Georgia the death penalty may be imposed only where the rape is coupled with one or more aggravating circumstances. The process by which this conclusion is reached is as startling as it is disquieting. It represents a clear departure from precedent by making this Court "under the aegis of the Cruel and Unusual Punishment Clause, the ultimate arbiter of the standards of criminal responsibility in diverse areas of the criminal law, throughout the country." *Powell v.*

Texas, 392 U.S. 514, 533, 88 S. Ct. 2145, 2154, 20 L. Ed. 2d 1254 (1968) (Opinion of Marshall, J.)[8] This seriously strains and distorts our federal system, removing much of the flexibility from which it has drawn strength for two centuries.

The analysis of the plurality opinion is divided into two parts: (a) an "objective" determination that most American Jurisdictions do not presently make rape a capital offense, and (b) a subjective judgment that death is an excessive punishment for rape because the crime does not, in and of itself, cause the death of the victim. I take issue with each of these points.

(a)

The plurality opinion bases its analysis, in part, on the fact that "Georgia is the sole jurisdiction in the United States at the present time that authorizes the sentence of death when the rape victim is an adult woman." . . . Surely, however, this statistic cannot be deemed determinative, or even particularly relevant. As the opinion concedes, . . . two other States—Louisiana and North Carolina—have enacted death penalty statutes for adult rape since this Court's 1972 decision in *Furman v. Georgia*, 408 U.S. 238, 92 S. Ct. 2726, 33 L. Ed. 2d 346. If the Court is to rely on some "public opinion" process, does this not suggest the beginning of a "trend?"

More to the point, however, it is myopic to base sweeping constitutional principles upon the narrow experience of the past five years. Considerable uncertainty was introduced into this area of the law by this Court's *Furman* decision. A large number of States found their death penalty statutes invalidated; legislatures were left in serious doubt by the expressions vacillating between discretionary and mandatory death penalties, as to whether this Court would sustain *any* statute imposing death as a criminal sanction.[9] Failure of more States to enact statutes imposing death for rape of an adult woman may thus reflect hasty legislative compromise occasioned by time pressures following *Furman*, a desire to wait on the experience of those States which did enact such statutes, or simply an accurate forecast of today's holding.

In any case, when considered in light of the experience since the turn of this century, where more than one-third of American jurisdictions have consistently provided the death penalty for rape, the plurality's focus on the experience of the immediate past must be viewed as truly disingenuous. Having in mind the swift changes in positions of some Members of this Court in the short span of five years, can it rationally be considered a relevant indicator of what our society deems "cruel and unusual" to look solely to what legislatures have *refrained* from doing under conditions of great

uncertainty arising from our less than lucid holdings on the Eighth Amendment? Far more representative of societal mores of the 20th Century is the accepted practice in a substantial number of jurisdictions preceding the *Furman* decision. "The problem . . . is the suddenness of the Court's perception of progress in the human attitude since decisions of only a short while ago." *Furman v. Georgia*, 408 U.S., at 410, 92 S. Ct., at 2814 (Blackmun, J., dissenting). Cf. *Rudolph v. Alabama*, 375 U.S. 889, 84 S. Ct. 155, 11 L. Ed. 2d 119 (1963).

However, even were one to give the most charitable acceptance to the plurality's statistical analysis, it still does not, to my mind support its conclusion. The most that can be claimed is that for the past year Georgia has been the only State whose adult rape death penalty statute has not otherwise been invalidated; two other state legislatures had enacted rape death penalty statutes in the last five years, but these were invalidated for reasons unrelated to rape under the Court's decisions last Term. *Woodson v. North Carolina*, 428 U.S. 280, 96 S.Ct. 2978, 49 L.Ed.2d 944 (1976); *Roberts v. Louisiana*, 428 U.S. 325, 96 S.Ct. 3001, 49 L.Ed.2d 974 (1976). Even if these figures could be read as indicating that no other States view the death penalty as an appropriate punishment for the rape of an adult woman, it would not necessarily follow that Georgia's imposition of such sanction violates the Eighth Amendment.

The Court has repeatedly pointed to the reserve strength of our federal system which allows state legislatures, within broad limits, to experiment with laws, both criminal and civil, in the effort to achieve socially desirable results. See, *e. g., Whalen v. Roe*,——U.S.——,——, and n. 22, 97 S.Ct. 869, 875–876, 51 L.Ed.2d 64 (1977); *Johnson v. Louisiana*, 406 U.S. 356, 376, 92 S.Ct. 1620, 1641, 32 L.Ed.2d 152 (1972) (opinion of Powell, J.); *California v. Green*, 399 U.S. 149, 184–185, 90 S.Ct. 1930, 1948–1949, 26 L.Ed.2d 489 (1970) (Harlan J., concurring); *Fay v. New York*, 332 U.S. 261, 296, 67 S.Ct. 1613, 1631, 91 L.Ed. 2043 (1947). Various provisions of the Constitution, including the Eighth Amendment and the Due Process Clause, of course place substantive limitations on the type of experimentation a State may undertake. However, as the plurality admits, the crime of rape is second perhaps only to murder in its gravity. It follows then that Georgia did not approach such substantive constraints by enacting the statute here in question. See also § (3)(b), *infra*.

Statutory provisions in criminal justice applied in one part of the country can be carefully watched by other state legislatures, so that the experience of one State becomes available to all. Although human lives are in the balance, it must be remembered that failure to allow flexibility may also jeopardize human lives—

those of the victims of undeterred criminal conduct.... Our concern for the accused ought not (to) foreclose legislative judgments showing a modicum of consideration for the potential victims.

Three state legislatures have, in the past five years, determined that the taking of human life and the devastating consequences of rape will be minimized if rapists may, in a limited class of cases, be executed for their offenses.[10] That these states are presently a minority does not, in my view, make their judgment less worthy of deference. Our concern for human life must not be confined to the guilty; a state legislature is not to be thought insensitive to human values because it acts firmly to protect the lives and related values of the innocent. In this area the choices for legislatures are at best painful and difficult and deserve a high degree of deference. Only last Term Mr. Justice White observed:

"It will not do to denigrate these legislative judgments as some form of vestigial savagery or as purely retributive in motivation; for they are solemn judgments, reasonably based, that imposition of the death penalty will save the lives of innocent persons. This concern for life and human values and sincere efforts of the States to pursue them are matters of the greatest moment *with which the judiciary should be most reluctant to interfere." Roberts v. Louisiana,* 428 U.S., at 355, 96 S.Ct., at 3017 (White, J., Dissenting). (Emphasis added.)

The question of whether the death penalty is an appropriate punishment for rape is surely an open one. It is arguable that many prospective rapists would be deterred by the possibility that they could suffer death for their offense; it is also arguable that the death penalty would have only minimal deterrent effect.[11] It may well be that rape victims would become more willing to report the crime and aid in the apprehension of the criminals if they knew that community disapproval of rapists was sufficiently strong to inflict the extreme penalty; or perhaps they would be reluctant to cooperate in the prosecution of rapists if they knew that a conviction might result in the imposition of the death penalty. Quite possibly, the occasional, well-publicized execution of egregious rapists may cause citizens to feel greater security in their daily lives,[12] or, on the contrary, it may be that members of a civilized community will suffer the pangs of a heavy conscience because such punishment will be perceived as excessive.[13] We cannot know which among this range of possibilities is correct, but today's holding forecloses the very exploration we have said federalism was intended to foster. It is difficult to believe that Georgia would long remain alone in punishing rape by death if the next decade demonstrated a drastic reduction in its incidence of rape, an increased cooperation by rape victims in the apprehension and prosecution of rapists, and a greater confidence in the rule of law on the part of the populace.

In order for Georgia's legislative program to develop it must be given time to take effect so that data may be evaluated for comparison with the experience of States which have not enacted death penalty statutes. Today, the Court repudiates the State's solemn judgment on how best to deal with the crime of rape before anyone can know whether the death penalty is an effective deterrent for one of the most horrible of all crimes. And this is done a few short years after Justice Powell's excellent statement:

"In a period in our country's history when the frequency of [rape] is increasing alarmingly, it is indeed a grave event for the Court to take from the States whatever deterrent and retributive weight the death penalty retains." *Furman v. Georgia,* 408 U.S., at 459, 92 S.Ct., at 2839 (Powell, J., dissenting) (footnote omitted).

To deprive States of this authority as the Court does, on the basis that "the current judgment with respect to the death penalty for rape ... weighs very heavily on the side of rejecting capital punishment as a suitable penalty for raping an adult woman," ... is impermissibly rash. The current judgment of some Members of this Court has undergone significant change in the short time since *Furman.*[14] Social change on great issues generally reveals itself in small increments, and the "current judgment" of many States could well be altered on the basis of Georgia's experience, were we to allow its statute to stand.[15]

(b)

The subjective judgment that the death penalty is simply disproportionate for the crime of rape is even more disturbing than the "objective" analysis discussed *supra.* The plurality's conclusion on this point is based upon the bare fact that murder necessarily results in the physical death of the victim, while rape does not.... However, no Member of the Court explains why this distinction has relevance, much less constitutional significance. It is, after all, not irrational —nor constitutionally impermissible—for a legislature to make the penalty more severe than the criminal act it punishes[16] in the hope it would deter wrongdoing:

"We may not require the legislature to select the least severe penalty possible so long as the penalty selected is not cruelly inhuman or disproportionate to the crime involved." *Gregg v. Georgia,* 428 U.S., at 175, 96 S.Ct., at 2926. Accord, *Furman v. Georgia,* 408 U.S., at 451, 92 S.Ct., at 2834 (Powell, J., dissenting).

It begs the question to state, as does the plurality opinion:

"Life is over for the victim of the murderers; for the rape victim, life may not be nearly so happy as it was, but is not over and normally is not beyond repair." ...

Until now, the issue under the Eighth Amendment has

not been the state of any particular victim after the crime, but rather whether the punishment imposed is grossly disproportionate to the evil committed by the perpetrator. See, *Gregg v. Georgia,* 428 U.S., at 173, 96 S.Ct., at 2925; *Furman v. Georgia,* 408 U.S., at 458, 92 S.Ct., at 2838 (Powell, J., dissenting). As a matter of constitutional principle, that test cannot have the primitive simplicity of "life for life, eye for eye, tooth for tooth." Rather States must be permitted to engage in a more sophisticated weighing of values in dealing with criminal activity which consistently poses serious danger of death or grave bodily harm. If innocent life and limb is to be preserved I see no constitutional barrier in punishing by death all who engage in such activity, regardless of whether the risk comes to fruition in any particular instance. See Packer, *supra,* 77 Harv.L.Rev., at 1077–1079.

Only one year ago the Court held it constitutionally permissible to impose the death penalty for the crime of murder, provided that certain procedural safeguards are followed. Compare *Gregg v. Georgia, supra; Profitt v. Florida,* 428 U.S. 242, 96 S.Ct. 2960, 19 L.Ed.2d 913 (1976), and *Jurek v. Texas,* 418 U.S. 262, 96, S.Ct. 2950, 49 L.Ed.2d 929 (1976), with *Roberts v. Louisiana, supra,* and *Woodson v. North Carolina, supra.* Today, the Court readily admits that "[s]hort of homicide, [rape] is the 'ultimate violation of self.' " Moreover, as stated by Mr. Justice Powell,

"[t]he threat of serious injury is implicit in the definition of rape; the victim is either forced into submission by physical violence or by the threat of violence." *Furman v. Georgia,* 408 U.S., at 460, 92 S.Ct., at 2839.

Rape thus is not a crime "light-years" removed from murder in the degree of its heinousness; it certainly poses a serious potential danger to the life and safety of innocent victims—apart from the devastating psychic consequences. It would seem to follow therefore that, affording the States proper leeway under the broad standard of the Eighth Amendment,[17] murder is properly punishable by death, rape should be also, if that is the considered judgment of the legislators.

The Court's conclusion to the contrary is very disturbing indeed. The clear implication of today's holding appears to be that the death penalty may be properly imposed only as to crimes resulting in death of the victim. This casts serious doubt upon the constitutional validity of statutes imposing the death penalty for a variety of conduct which, though dangerous, may not necessarily result in any immediate death, *e. g.,* treason, airplane hijacking, and kidnapping. In that respect, today's holding does even more harm than is initially apparent. We cannot avoid judicial notice that crimes such as airplane hijacking, kidnapping, and mass terrorist activity constitute a serious and increasing danger to the safety of the public. It would be unfortunate indeed if the effect of today's holding were to inhibit States and the Federal Government from experimenting with various remedies—including possibly imposition of the penalty of death—to prevent and deter such crimes.

Some sound observations, made only a few years ago, deserve repetition:

"Our task here, as must so frequently be emphasized and re-emphasized, is to pass upon the constitutionality of legislation that has been enacted and that is challenged. This is the sole task for judges. We should not allow our personal preferences as to the wisdom of legislative and congressional action, on our distaste for such action, to guide our judicial decision in cases such as these. The temptations to cross that policy line are very great. In fact, as today's decision reveals, they are almost irresistible." *Furman v. Georgia,* 408 U.S., at 411, 92 S.Ct., at 2815 (Blackmun, J., dissenting).

Whatever our individual views as to the wisdom of capital punishment, I cannot agree that it is constitutionally impermissible for a state legislature to make the "solemn judgment" to impose such penalty for the crime of rape. Accordingly, I would leave to the States the task of legislating in this area of the law.

NOTES

1. On March 12, 1973, the Superior Court of Richmond County, Ga., sentenced Coker to 20 years' imprisonment for the kidnapping of petitioner's second victim, and to life imprisonment for one act of rape upon her. On May 28, 1973, the Superior Court of Taliaferro County, Ga., sentenced Coker to eight years' imprisonment for aggravated assault upon the same victim, and to life imprisonment for the second rape upon her. On April 6, 1973, the Superior Court of Clayton County, Ga., sentenced Coker to 20 years' imprisonment for the rape of petitioner's first victim, and to life imprisonment for her murder. . . .

2. The position today adopted by Mr. Justice POWELL constitutes a disquieting shift from the view he embraced several Terms ago in *Furman v. Georgia,* 408 U.S. 238, 460–461, 92 S.Ct. 2725, 2839, 33 L.Ed.2d 346 (1972), where he stated:

"While I reject each of [petitioners'] attempts to establish specific categories of cases in which the death penalty may be deemed excessive, I view them as groping toward what is for me the appropriate application of the Eighth Amendment. While in my view *the disproportionality test may not be used either to strike down the death penalty for rape altogether or to install the Court as a tribunal for sentencing review, that test may find its application in the peculiar circumstances of specific cases. Its utilization should be limited to the rare case in which the death penalty is rendered for a crime technically falling within the legislatively defined class but factually falling outside the likely legislative intent in creating the category."* (Emphasis added.)

While Mr. Justice POWELL purports to dissent from the broadest sweep of the Court's holding, I cannot see that his view differs materially from that of the plurality. He suggests two situations where it might be proper to execute rapists: (1) where the "offense [is] committed with excessive brutality"; and (2) where "the victim sustained serious or lasting injury."

The second part of this test was rejected by Mr. Justice POW-ELL himself in *Furman,* and with good reason: "the emotional impact [upon the rape victim] may be impossible to gauge at any particular point in time. The extent and duration of psychological trauma may not be known or ascertainable prior to trial." *Id.,* at 460. 92 S.Ct., at 2839. Can any Member of the Court state with confidence that a 16-year-old woman who is raped in the presence of her husband three weeks after giving birth to a baby "sustained [no] serious or lasting injury?" This bifurcation of rape into categories of harmful and nonharmful eludes my comprehension.

The difficulty with the first part of Mr. Justice POWELL's test is that rape is inherently an aggravated offense; in Mr. Justice POWELL's own words, "the threat of both [physical and psychological] injury is always present." *Id.,* at 459, 92 S.Ct., at 2838. Therefore the "excessive brutality" requirement must refer to something more, I assume, than the force normally associated with physically coercing or overpowering the will of another. Rather, what must be meant is that the rapist has engaged in torture or has committed an aggravated battery upon the victim. See, *ante,* at 2863 and n. 1. However, torture and aggravated battery are offenses separate from rape, and ordinarily are punished separately. The clear negative inference of Mr. Justice POWELL's analysis therefore appears to be that where rape alone is committed, *i. e.,* rape unaccompanied by any other criminal conduct, the death penalty may never be imposed.

3.   This court has consistently upheld the constitutional validity of such punishment-enhancing statutes. See, *e. g., Spencer v. Texas,* 385 U.S. 554, 559–560, 87 S.Ct. 648, 651, 17 L.Ed.2d 606 (1967):

"No claim is made here that recidivist statutes are . . . unconstitutional, nor could there be under our cases. Such statutes and other enhanced-sentence laws, and procedures designed to implement their underlying policies, have been enacted in all the States, and by the Federal Government as well. . . . Such statutes . . . have been sustained in this Court on several occasions against contentions that they violate constitutional strictures dealing with double jeopardy *ex post facto* laws, *cruel and unusual punishment,* due process, equal protection, and privileges and immunities." (Footnote and citations omitted; emphasis added.) Accord, *Oyler v. Boles,* 368 U.S. 448, 451, 82 S.Ct. 501, 503, 7 L.Ed.2d 446 (1962).

4.   This special danger is demonstrated by the very record in this case. After tying and gagging the victim's husband, and raping the victim, petitioner sought to make his getaway in their automobile. Leaving the victim's husband tied and gagged in his bathroom, Coker took the victim with him. As he started to leave, he brandished the kitchen knife he was carrying and warned the husband that "if he would get pulled over or the police was following him in any way that he would kill—he would kill my wife. *He said he didn't have nothing to lose—that he was in prison for the rest of his life, anyway. . . .*" Testimony of the victim's husband, Appendix, at 121 (emphasis added).

5.   Professor Packer addressed this:

"What are we to do with those whom we cannot reform, and in particular, those who by our failure are thought to remain menaces to life? Current penal theories admit, indeed insist upon, the need for permanent incapacitation in such cases. Once this need is recognized, the death penalty as a means for incapacitation for the violent psychopath can hardly be objected to on grounds that will survive rational scrutiny, *if the use of the death penalty in any situation is to be permitted.* And its use in rape cases as a class, while inept, is no more so than its use for any other specific offense involving danger to life and limb." 77 Harv.L.Rev., at 1081. (Em-

phasis added.)

6.   I find a disturbing confusion as to this issue in the plurality opinion. The issue is whether Georgia can, under any circumstances and for any kind of rape—"mild" or "gross"—impose the death penalty. Yet the plurality opinion opens its discussion, apparently directed at demonstrating that this was not an "aggravated" rape, saying that following the rape and kidnapping, "Mrs. Carver was unharmed." . . . If the Court is holding that no rape can ever be punished by death, why is it relevant whether Mrs. Carver was "unharmed"?

7.   While only three Justices have joined Mr. Justice WHITE in this portion of his opinion, see separate opinion of Mr. Justice POWELL, *ante,* I take this to be the view of the Court in light of Mr. Justice BRENNAN's and Mr. Justice MARSHALL's statements joining the judgment.

8.   Only last term in *Gregg v. Georgia,* 428 U.S. 153, 96 S.Ct. 2909, 49 L.Ed.2d 859 (1976), Mr. Justice Stewart, Mr. Justice Powell, and Mr. Justice Stevens warned that "the requirement of the Eighth Amendment must be applied with an awareness of the limited role to be played by the courts," and noted that "we may not act as judges as we might as legislators." *Id.,* at 174–175, 96 S.Ct., at 295. Accord, *Roberts v. Louisiana,* 428 U.S., at 355–356, 96 S.Ct., at 3017. (White, J., dissenting). The plurality further noted that "[t]he deference we owe to decisions of the state legislatures under our federal system, [*Furman v. Georgia,* 407 U.S.] at 465–470, 92 S.Ct., at 2842–2844, (Rehnquist, J., Dissenting), is enhanced where the specification of punishments is concerned, for '*these are peculiarly questions of legislative policy.' Gore v. United States,* 357 U.S. 386, 393, 78 S.Ct. 1280, 1285, 2 L.Ed.2d 1405 (1958)." 428 U.S., at 176, 96 S.Ct., at 2926 (Emphasis added).

9.   I take no satisfaction in my predictive caveat in *Furman:*

"Since there is no majority of the Court on the ultimate issue presented in these cases, the future of capital punishment in this country has been left in an uncertain limbo. Rather than providing a final and unambiguous answer on the basic constitutional question, the collective impact of the majority's ruling is to demand an undetermined measure of change from the various state legislatures and the Congress." *Furman v. Georgia,* 408 U.S., at 403, 92 S.Ct., at 2811 (Burger, C. J., dissenting).

10.   The statute here in question does not provide the death penalty for any and all rapists. Rather, the jury must find that at least one statutorily defined aggravated circumstance is present. Ga.Code Ann. §§ 26–3102, 27–2534.-1(b)(1), (2) and (7).

11.   "The value of capital punishment as a deterrent of crime is a complex factual issue the resolution of which properly rests with the legislatures, which can evaluate the results of statistical studies in terms of their own local conditions and with a flexibility of approach that is not available to the courts. *Furman v. Georgia* [408 U.S.], at 403–405, 92 S.Ct., at 2810–2812 (Burger, C. J., dissenting)." *Gregg v. Georgia,* 428 U.S., at 186, 96 S.Ct., at 2931 (plurality opinion).

12.   "There are many cases in which the sordid, heinous nature of a particular [rape], demeaning, humiliating, and often physically or psychological traumatic, will call for public condemnation." *Furman v. Georgia,* 408 U.S. 459, 92 S.Ct. 2839 (Powell, J., dissenting).

13.   Obviously I have no special competence to make these judgments, but by the same token no other Member of the Court is competent to make a contrary judgment. This is why our system has, until now, left these difficult policy choices to the state legislatures, who may be no wiser, but surely are more attuned to the mores of their communities, than are we.

14. Indeed as recently as 1971—a year before *Furman*—a majority of this Court appeared to have no doubt about the constitutionality of the death penalty. See *McGautha v. California*, 402 U.S. 183, 91 S.Ct. 1454, 28 L.Ed.2d 711 (1971).

15. To paraphrase Mr. Justice Powell, "[w]hat]the Court is] saying, in effect, is that the evolutionary process has come suddenly to an end; that the ultimate wisdom as to the appropriateness of capital punishment [for adult rape] under all circumstances, and for all future generations, has somehow been revealed." *Furman v. Georgia*, 408 U.S., at 431, 92 S.Ct., at 2824 (Powell, J., dissenting).

16. For example, hardly any thief would be deterred from stealing if the only punishment upon being caught were return of the money stolen.

17. Mr. Justice Stewart, Mr. Justice Powell, and Mr. Justice Stevens in *Gregg v. Georgia* noted that "in assessing a punishment selected by a democratically elected legislature against the constitutional measure [of the Eighth Amendment], we presume its validity. . . . *A heavy burden rests on those who would attack the judgment of the representatives of the people.*" 428 U.S., at 175, 96 S.Ct., at 2926 (emphasis added). Accord, *Furman v. Georgia*, 408 U.S., at 451, 92 S.Ct., at 2834 (Powell, J., dissenting).

The reasons for this special deference to state legislative enactments was described:

"This is true in part because the constitutional test is intertwined with an assessment of contemporary standards and the legislative judgment weighs heavily in ascertaining such standards. '[I]n a democratic society legislatures, not courts, are constituted to respond to the will and consequently the moral values of the people.' *Furman v. Georgia*. [408 U.S.], at 383, 92 S.Ct., at 2800 (Burger, C. J., dissenting)." 428 U.S., at 175–176, 96 S.Ct., at 2926.

Suggestions for Further Reading

Acton, H. B., ed., *Philosophy of Punishment* (1969).

American Bar Association, Project on Minimum Standards for Criminal Justice: "Standards Relating to Appellate Review of Sentences," (Tent. Draft, 1967).

American Friends Service Committee, *Struggle for Justice: A Report on Crime and Punishment in America* (1971).

American Law Institute, *Model Penal Code*, Part III "Treatment and Correction," Proposed Official Draft (1962).

Andenaes, J., "General Prevention,." 43 *J. Crim. L.C. & P.S.* 176 (1952).

Bacon, Francis, "Of Revenge," *Essays* (1625).

Baier, K., "Is Punishment Retributive?" *Analysis*, Vol. 16, (1955) pp. 25–32.

Beccaria, Cesare, *On Crimes and Punishment*, trans. H. Paolucci, (1963).

Bedau, Hugo A., ed., *The Death Penalty in America* (1964).

Bedau, Hugo, "A Social Philosopher Looks at the Death Penalty," *American J. of Psychiatry*, Vol. 123 (1967).

Bedau, Hugo, "A Concluding Note [on Deterrence and the Death Penalty]." *Ethics*, Vol. 81 (1970). A reply to E. Van den Haag.

Bedau, Hugo, "Deterrence and the Death Penalty: A Reconsideration," *J. of Crim. L., Criminol., and Police Sci.*, Vol. 61 (1971).

Bedau, Hugo, and Pierce, Chester, eds., *Capital Punishment in the United States* (1976).

Bedau, Hugo, "Concessions to Retribution in Punishment," in Cederblom, J. B., and Blizek, W. L., eds., *Justice and Punishment* (1977).

Bedau, Hugo, *The Courts, the Constitution, and Capital Punishment* (1977).

Bedau, Hugo, "Retribution and the Theory of Punishment" *Journal of Philosophy*, Vol. 75 (1978), with commentaries by Andrew von Hirsch and Richard Wasserstrom. An A.P.A. symposium on "The New Retributivism."

Benn, Stanley, I., "An Approach to the Problems of Punishment," *Philosophy* Vol. 33 (1958).

Black, Charles L., Jr., *Capital Punishment: The Inevitability of Caprice and Mistake* (1974).

Bok, C., *Star Wormwood* (1959).

Butler, Samuel, *Erewhon* (1872).

Card, Claudia, "Retributive Penal Liability," *American Philosophical Quarterly Monographs*, no. 7, 1973.

Cederblom, J. B., and Blizek, W. L., eds., *Justice and Punishment* (1977).

Cohen, Bernard L., *Law Without Order: Capital Punishment and the Liberals* (1970).

Conway, David A., "Capital Punishment and Deterrence: Some Considerations in Dialogue Form," *Philosophy and Public Affairs*, Vol. 3 (1974).

Dershowitz, Alan M., "The Law of Dangerousness: Some Fictions About Predictions," 23 *J. Legal Ed.* 24, (1970).

Dershowitz, Alan M., *Fair and Certain Punishment* (1976).

DiSalle, Michael V., *The Power of Life or Death* (1965).

Ewing, A. C., *The Morality of Punishment* (1929).

Ezorsky, Gertrude, ed., *Philosophical Perspectives on Punishment* (1972).

Ezorsky, Gertrude, "Punishment and Excuses," in

Contemporary Moral Problems Series, Vol. 5, ed. by Peter French (1973).

Feinberg, Joel, "On Justifying Legal Punishment" in *Responsibility,* ed. Friedrich (*Nomos* III) 152 (1960).

Feinberg, Joel, "The Expressive Function of Punishment," reprinted In *Doing and Deserving* (1970), pp. 95–118.

Feinberg, Joel, "Justice and Personal Desert," in *Doing and Deserving* (1970), pp. 55–94.

Fingarette, Herbert, "Punishment and Suffering," Presidential address, *Proceedings and Addresses of the American Philosophical Association,* Vol. 50 (1977), University of Delaware.

Fitzgerald, P. H., *Criminal Law and Punishment* (1962).

Fletcher, George, *Rethinking Criminal Law* (1978).

Flew, A., "The Justification of Punishment," *Philosophy,* Vol. 24 (1954), pp. 291–307.

Frankel, Marvin E., *Criminal Sentences* (1973).

Gibbs, Jack R., *Crime, Punishment, and Deterrence* (1975).

Glenn, "The California Penalty Trial," 52 *Cal. L. Rev.* 368 (1964).

Green, T. H., "State's Rights to Punish," *Jour. of Crim. L. and Criminol.* vol. 1, (1910), pp. 19–43.

Gross, Hyman, *A Theory of Criminal Justice* (1978).

Hall, J., *General Principles of Criminal Law,* 2d ed. (1960).

Hall-Williams, J. E., "Publications on Sentencing," 10 *Brit. J. Delinq.* 145 (1959).

Hart, H. L. A., *Punishment and Responsibility* (1968).

Hart, H. M., "The Aims of the Criminal Law," *Law and Contemporary Problems* 23 401 (1958).

Hegel, G. F., *Philosophy of Right.* Trans. T. M. Knox. (1942).

Honderich, T., *Punishment, Its Supposed Justifications* (1970).

Kadish, S. H., "Some Observations on the Use of Criminal Sanctions in Enforcing Economic Regulations," 30 *U. Chi. L. Rev.* 423 (1963).

Kidder, Joel, "Requital and Criminal Justice," *International Philosophical Quarterly* Vol. 15 (1975).

Kleinig, John, *Punishment and Desert* (1973).

Kleinig, John, "Good Samaritanism," *Philosophy and Public Affairs* Vol 5 (1976).

Knowlton, R. E., "Problems of Jury Discretion in Capital Cases," 101 *U. Pa. L. Rev.* 1099, (1953).

Koestler, Arthur, *Reflections on Hanging* (1956).

Lewis, C. S., "Humanitarian Theory of Punishment," *Res Judicatae,* VI (1953), pp. 224–30, Reply by N. Morris & D. Bucke, VI, (1953), pp. 231–37. Comment by J. J. C. Smart, VI (1954), pp. 368–71. Reply by C. S. Lewis, VI (1954), pp. 519–23.

Lockett v. Ohio, 98 S. Ct. 2981 (1978).

Loftsgordon, D., "Present-Day British Philosophers on Punishment," *Journal of Philosophy,* Vol. 63 (1966) pp. 341 ff.

Longford, F. P., *The Idea of Punishment* (1961).

Mabbott, J. D., "Freewill and Punishment" in *Contemporary British Philosophy,* 3rd ser. ed. H. D. Lewis. (1956), pp. 287–370.

Mabbott, J. D., "Punishment," *Mind,* Vol. 48, (1939), pp. 152–67.

McCloskey, H. J., "Utilitarianism and Retributive Punishment," *Journal of Philosophy,* Vol. 64 (1967), pp. 91 ff.

McGautha v. California, 402 U.S. 207 (1970).

Menninger, Karl, *The Crime of Punishment* (1966).

Michael, J., and Wechsler, H., *Criminal Law and Its Administration* (1940).

Mitford, Jessica, *Kind and Usual Punishment* (1973).

Moberly, Walter, *The Ethics of Punishment* (1968).

Mundle, C. W. K., "Punishment and Desert," *Philos Q.,* Vol. 4 (1954), p. 216.

Murphy, Jeffrie G., "The Killing of the Innocent," *The Monist,* Vol. 57 (1973).

Murphy, Jeffrie G., *Retribution, Justice, and Therapy: Essays in the Philosophy of Law* (1979).

Neier, Aryeh, *Crime and Punishment: A Radical Solution* (1976).

Note, "Consecutive Sentences in Single Prosecutions: Judicial Multiplication of Statutory Penalties," 67 *Yale L.J.* 916 (1958).

Note, "Cruel and Unusual Punishment Clause and the Substantive Criminal Law" 79 *Harv. L. Rev.* 635 (1966).

Note, "Due Process and Legislative Standards in Sentencing," 101 *U. Pa. L. Rev.* 257 (1952).

Note, "The Effectiveness of the Eighth Amendment: An Appraisal of Cruel and Unusual Punishment," 36 *N.Y.U. L. Rev.* 846 (1961).

Note, "Revival of the Eighth Amendment: Development of Cruel-Punishment Doctrine by the Supreme Court," *Stan. L. Rev.* 996 (1964).

Note, "Statutory Multiple Punishment and Multiple Prosecution" 50 *Minn. L. Rev.* 1102 (1966).

Note, "Statutory Structures for Sentencing Felons to Prison," 60 *Colum. L. Rev.* 1134 (1960).

Note, "A Trial Judge's Freedom and Responsibility in Administering Probation," 71 *Yale L.J.* 551 (1962).

Packer, Herbert, *The Limits of the Criminal Sanction* (1968).

Packer, Herbert, "Making the Punishment Fit the Crime" 77 *Harv. L. Rev.* 1071 (1964).

Packer, Herbert, "Two Models of the Criminal Process," 113 *U.Pa. L. Rev.* (1964).

Pincoffs, Edmund, *The Rationale of Legal Punishment* (1966).

President's Commission on Law Enforcement and the

Administration of Justice, *Task Force Report: Corrections* (1967).

Radin, Margaret Jane, "The Jurisprudence of Death: Evolving Standards for the Cruel and Unusual Punishments Clause," 126 *U. Pa. L. Rev.* (1978).

Radzinowicz, L., *A History of English Law* Vol. 1 (1948).

Rashdall, H., *Theory of Good and Evil* Vol. I, (1924), Chap. 9.

Ross, W. D., *The Right and The Good* (1930), pp. 56–64.

Royal Commission on Capital Punishment, 1949–53, *Report* (London: Her Majesty's Stationery Office, 1953).

Sellin, J. T., "The Law and Some Aspects of Criminal Conduct" in *Aims and Methods of Legal Research,* ed. J. J. Conard. (1955).

Sharp, Frank C., *Ethics* (1928).

Shaw, G. B., *The Crime of Imprisonment* 1924.

Silberman, Charles E., *Criminal Violence, Criminal Justice* (1978).

Stanford, Phil, "A Model Clockwork-Orange Prison," *The New York Times Magazine,* Sept. 17, 1972.

Stephen, James F., *A History of the Criminal Law of England* (1883), Vol. II, Chap. 17.

Sterba, James P., "Retributive Justice," *Political Theory,* Vol. 5 (1977).

de Tarde, G., *Penal Philosophy* (1912).

Trop v. Dulles, 356 U.S. 86, (1958).

Van den Haag, E., "On Deterrence and the Death Penalty" *Ethics,* Vol. 78 (1968).

Van den Haag, *Punishing Criminals: Concerning a Very Old and Painful Question* (1975).

Von Hirsch, Andrew. "Prediction of Criminal Conduct and Preventive Confinement of Convicted Persons," 21 *Buffalo L. Rev.* (1972).

Von Hirsch, Andrew, *Doing Justice: The Choice of Punishments* (1976).

Walker, Nigel, *Sentencing in a Rational Society* (1969).

Wasserstrom, Richard, "Why Punish the Guilty?" *Princeton Univ. Mag.,* Vol. 20 (1964), pp. 14–19.

Wechsler, H., "Sentencing, Correction, and the Model Penal Code" 109 *U. Pa. L. Rev.* 465 (1961).

Weema v. United States 217 U.S. 357 (1909).

Zimring, F., *Perspectives on Deterrence* (1971).